BISK CPA REVIEW

ESSENTIALS FOR THE COMPUTER-BASED CPA EXAM

INSTRUCTOR-LED PROGRAMS

- Instructor-Led Online Reviews
- Live Review

SELF-DIRECTED MATERIALS

- Self-Directed Online Reviews
- Textbooks
- Video

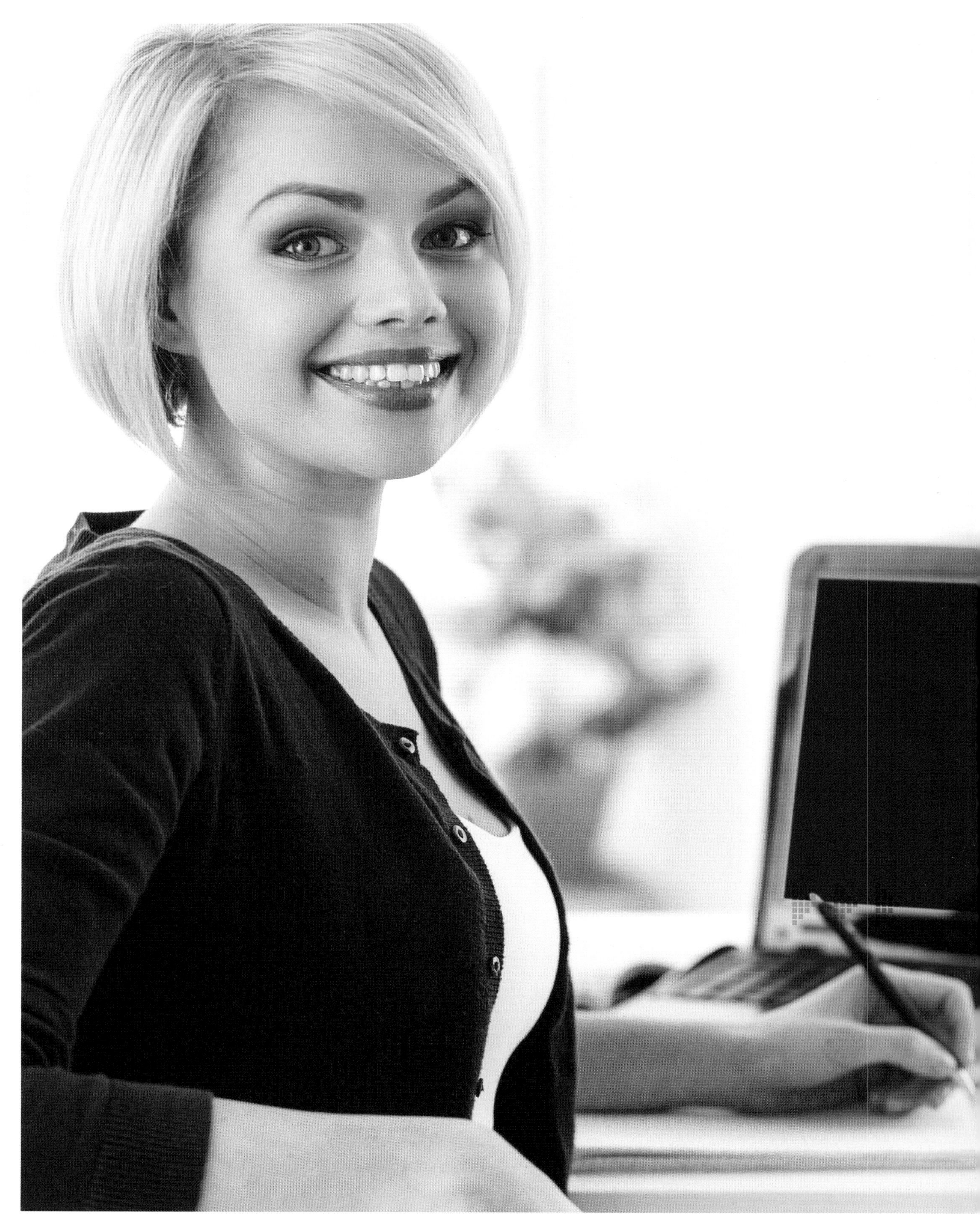

SIX CONVENIENT OPTIONS TO HELP YOU PASS

Bisk CPA Review has the materials you need to ensure you pass the computer-based exam. Let us customize a review package to meet your needs.

1 INSTRUCTOR-LED ONLINE CPA REVIEW

- Online CPA Review with guided assignment plan
- Professor communication (chat, message board, email)
- Electronic flashcards
- Video lectures (streamed or on CD)
- Classroom access for seven full months
- Textbooks available as iPad™-compatible e-books and embedded text in the online classroom (iPad compatible)
- Simulation Strategies DVDs

2 ADVANCED SELF-DIRECTED ONLINE CPA REVIEW

- Online self-study review with question bank and practice exams
- Electronic flashcards
- Textbooks available as iPad™-compatible e-books and embedded text in the online classroom (iPad compatible)
- Classroom access for 12 full months
- Video lecture CDs with viewer guide

3 SELF-DIRECTED ONLINE CPA REVIEW

- Online self-study review with question bank and practice exams
- Electronic flashcards
- Textbooks available as iPad™-compatible e-books and embedded text in the online classroom (iPad compatible)
- Classroom access for 12 full months

4 TEXTBOOKS

- Read complete, current, and comprehensive coverage of all exam topics
- Available in several formats including print and e-book

5 HOT-SPOT DVDS

- Cover every testable area on the computer-based test for firm-wide use
- Choose from topic-specific videos, each covering an important exam topic in detail
- Available by the topic, section or full set including viewer guides

6 SIMULATION STRATEGIES DVDS

- Comprehensive class overview of how to tackle difficult task-based simulations
- Available by the section or as a full set including viewer guides

SATISFY YOUR STATE'S 150-HOUR RULE

Bisk CPA Review's instructor-led or self-directed online reviews, when supplemented with the ACE program, allows you to earn up to 12 college credits without going to class! If your college or university doesn't offer enough accounting courses to fulfill your fifth-year requirement, why spend time and money on courses that will not benefit your career when CPA Review will teach you the relevant accounting information you need to succeed?

MONEY-BACK GUARANTEE

Bisk CPA Review has a remarkable record of helping CPA candidates pass the Uniform CPA Exam. In fact, since 1971, more than 150,000 candidates have used our products to pass the exam, including Elijah Watt Sells Award Gold Medal winners Michael Becker, Laura McClure, Paul Ito, Stephanie Seiberg and John McInnis, who achieved a PERFECT SCORE! We're so confident in our exam preparation materials that we back all of our packages with a money-back guarantee. (Certain restrictions and preparation requirements apply. Call 855-300-9392 for details.)

SELECT FROM THESE THREE GREAT FORMATS

FEATURES	INSTRUCTOR-LED	ADVANCED SELF-DIRECTED	SELF-DIRECTED
Default Online Access Length	Term Length: 7 months (Check online schedule)	Term Length: 12 months (Starts on student's first login)	Term Length: 12 months (Starts on student's first login)
Text in PDF Format	✓	✓	✓
Textbook	✓	Optional**	Optional**
Video Lectures Streamed	✓		
Video Lecture CDs	✓	✓	
Simulation Strategies DVDs	✓	Optional**	Optional**
Hot•Spot DVDs	Optional**	Optional**	Limited-time
Personal Trainer	✓	✓	✓
Help/Support	✓	✓	✓
Study Statistics	✓	✓	✓
Bookmarks	✓	✓	✓
Chapter Study	✓	✓	✓
Flag Questions for Review	✓	✓	✓
Flashcards	✓	✓	✓
Notes	✓	✓	✓
Study Online	✓	✓	✓
Discussion Board Post Alerts	✓		
Class Chat Room	✓		
Class Email	✓		
Class News and Discussion Boad	✓		
Live Access to Faculty Advisor or Professor	✓		
Social Media	✓		
Latest News	✓		
Tutorials	✓		
Weekly Class Syllabus	✓		
Weekly Progress Bar	✓		
Weekly Review Study	✓		
Weekly Statistics	✓		
Create Custom Study (flagged questions)		✓	✓
Create Custom Study (student selection)		✓	✓
Create Custom Exam		✓	✓
Final Exam Practice Questions	Unlimited	Unlimited	Unlimited
Retail Price **Payment Plans Available**	**$525** per section **$1,899** full set	**$475** per section **$1,700** full set	**$400** per section **$1,350** full set

*Call for Details. | **Can be purchased separately at retail price.

BISK CPA REVIEW
cpaexam.com/2015 | 855.300.9392
1211 N. Westshore Blvd., Suite 800, Tampa, FL 33607

UPDATED JULY 2014 | INSCPA-F 44-14

Bisk CPA Review

Auditing & Attestation

Thomson Reuters

We wish to thank the American Institute of Certified Public Accountants and other organizations for permission to reprint or adapt the following copyrighted materials:

1. Uniform CPA Examination Questions and Unofficial Answers, Copyright by American Institute of Certified Public Accountants, Inc. All rights reserved. Reprinted with permission.

2. Audit and Accounting Guides, Auditing Procedure Studies, Risk Alerts, Statements of Position, and Code of Professional Conduct, Copyright by American Institute of Certified Public Accountants, Inc. All rights reserved. Reprinted with permission.

3. *The FASB Accounting Standards Codification®* and Statements of Financial Accounting Concepts, Copyright by the Financial Accounting Standards Board, 401 Merritt 7, P.O. Box 5116, Norwalk, CT 06856, are reprinted with permission.

4. GASB Statements, Interpretations, and Technical Bulletins, Copyright by the Governmental Accounting Standards Board, 401 Merritt 7, P.O. Box 5116, Norwalk, CT 06856-5116.

5. Statements on Auditing Standards, Statements on Standards for Consulting Services, Statements on Responsibilities in Personal Financial Planning Practice, Statements on Standards for Accounting and Review Services, Statements on Quality Control Standards, Statements on Standards for Attestation Engagements, and Statements on Responsibilities in Tax Practice, Copyright by American Institute of Certified Public Accountants, Inc. All rights reserved. Reprinted with permission.

6. ISB Standards, Copyright by the Independence Standards Board, 6th Floor, 1211 Avenue of the Americas, New York, NY 10036-8775

7. International Standards on Auditing and Code of Ethics for Professional Accountants, Copyrights September 2013 and May 2013, respectively, by the International Federation of Accountants (IFAC). All rights reserved. Used with permission of IFAC, 545 Fifth Avenue, 14th Floor, New York, NY 10017 USA

FORTY-FOURTH EDITION

PREFACE

Our texts provide comprehensive coverage of all the topics repeatedly tested on all four sections of the CPA Examination: Financial Accounting and Reporting, Auditing and Attestation, Regulation, and Business Environment and Concepts. Used effectively, our materials will enable you to achieve maximum preparedness for the Uniform CPA Examination. Here is a brief summary of the features and benefits that our texts will provide for you:

1. **Thousands of Multiple-Choice Questions**...Including exclusive Bisk CPA Review questions and recent AICPA examination questions with unofficial answers. Solving these questions with immediate verification of results instills confidence.

2. **Other Question Formats**...We teach you to solve simulations and respond to written communications using our unique Solutions Approach™.

3. **Exclusive Explanations to Questions**...We explain *why* answer alternatives are either right or wrong.

4. **Research and Writing Skills**...Each volume contains a section to help you brush up on either your research or writing skills for the related exam section.

5. **Detailed Summaries**...We set forth the significant testable concepts in highly readable summaries to facilitate rapid and complete comprehension. The summaries emphasize topics repeatedly tested and explain all important AICPA, PCAOB, SEC, IAASB, FASB, GASB, and IASB pronouncements as well as relevant federal and state laws. We update our coverage to reflect current laws and authoritative pronouncements.

6. **Best Practices** and **Exam Preparation Tips**...Even the best students rarely have had to prepare for an exam of this breadth and depth. We discuss how to prepare for the exam from establishing a review plan to after the day you sit for your exam.

7. **Practice Examination to Test Your Preparedness**...We include a practice exam to test your exam preparedness to help you identify for further concentrated study any exam topic areas where you need further study after reviewing each of the chapters.

Our materials are designed for the candidate who previously has studied accounting in the United States. The rate at which a candidate studies and learns (not merely reads) our material will depend on a candidate's background and aptitude. For example, candidates who have been out of school for a period of years might need more time to prepare than recent graduates. The point to remember is that all the material you will need to know to pass the exam is here, except for the authoritative literature databases available for free to candidates with a *Notice to Schedule* from the examiners. All you need to do is apply yourself and learn this material at a rate that is appropriate to your situation. As a final thought, keep in mind that test confidence gained through disciplined preparation equals success.

CHANGE ALERTS

AU Identifier Used for Clarified US GAAS in This Textbook

We have not continued to use the temporary AU-C identifier for the clarified auditing standards issued by the American Institute of Certified Public Accountants (AICPA). In this textbook these standards have an AU identifier.

CSO Updated; issued 10/2013

In October 2013, the AICPA Board of Examiners approved changes to the CPA Examination Content Specification Outlines (CSO) for all exam sections except for Regulation. The new outlines are effective beginning with the January–February 2015 exam window. Please see the third section of appendix B of this textbook for the new AUD CSO—there were no substantive changes.

SAS 128 (AU 610), *Using the Work of Internal Auditors*; issued 2/2014

In February 2014 the Auditing Standards Board of the AICPA issued Statement on Auditing Standards (SAS) 128. It is effective for audits of financial statements for periods ending on or after December 15, 2014. (Chapter 4)

Title 2 of the Code of Federal Regulations (2 CFR)
Chapter I and Chapter II, Parts 200, 215, 220, 225, and 230
Uniform Administrative Requirements, Cost Principles, and Audit Requirements for Federal Awards
A Final Rule by the Office of Management and Budget

On December 26, 2013, the Office of Management and Budget published the above referenced document. This final guidance supersedes and streamlines requirements from OMB Circulars A-21, A-87, A-110, and A-122 (which have been placed in OMB guidances); Circulars A-89, A-102, and A-133; and the guidance in Circular A-50 on Single Audit Act follow-up. (Chapter 10)

PCAOB AS 17, *Auditing Supplemental Information Accompanying Audited Financial Statements*; issued 2/2014

On February 12, 2014, the Securities and Exchange Commission approved Public Company Accounting Oversight Board (PCAOB) Auditing Standard (AS) 17. It is effective for audit procedures and reports on supplemental information that accompany financial statements for fiscal years ending on or after June 1, 2014. (Chapter 11)

AICPA Code of Professional Conduct; issued electronically 5/14/14

On January 28, 2014, the Professional Ethics Executive Committee of the AICPA approved a revised Code of Professional Conduct. It was issued in electronic format on May 14, 2014, and will be effective December 15, 2014, with a delayed effective date of December 15, 2015 for the implementation of the two conceptual frameworks and related interpretations. The Revised Code applies to all professional services performed, with limited exceptions. (Chapter 15)

Editor Note: Please see the chapters indicated above for more information and when these new pronouncements are/were eligible to be tested. Accounting and auditing pronouncements are eligible to be tested on the CPA exam in the testing window beginning six months after a pronouncement's *effective* date, unless early application is permitted. When early application is permitted, a new pronouncement may be tested in the window beginning 6 months after the *issue* date. In this case, beginning with that exam window, *both* the extant [still existing] and the new pronouncement can be tested until the new pronouncement becomes effective. Regarding new US GAAS pronouncements, early application is permitted if the new or updated AU section does *not* expressly prohibit it.

AUDITING & ATTESTATION

VOLUME II of IV

TABLE OF CONTENTS

The editors strongly advise candidates to download *The Candidate Bulletin* from the AICPA's website (aicpa.org). (You will need to go to the "For Candidates" section within the exam area of their site to find the instructions to download it.) It is the official handbook for exam candidates—it covers exam requirements, candidate responsibilities, and other important information. Candidates should read the "Foreword: Best Practices" and "Appendix B: Exam Preparation Tips" of this volume for help with devising a study plan. It's also important to keep the extent of the exam's coverage of the various topics in mind while studying. The AICPA's content specification outline, which includes the approximate percentage of total exam questions associated with each area in the outline, is included in the "Appendix B: Exam Preparation Tips."

QUICK TEXT REFERENCE

The editors strongly recommend that candidates read the entire "Foreword: Best Practices," "Appendix B: Exam Preparation Tips," and "Appendix C: Research Skills" sections of this volume. The references on this page are provided to allow you to quickly locate selected parts of this volume. Add items to this list that you find yourself frequently revisiting.

FOREWORD: BEST PRACTICES

Step One: Read Sections One and Two of the Exam Preparation Tips Appendix

The first section of "Appendix B: Exam Preparation Tips" presents the AICPA's content and skill specification outline (CSO/SSO). Make sure you are aware of the areas covered by the exam. The CSO also includes the approximate percentage of total exam questions associated with each area.

The second section is designed to familiarize you with the exam. It includes an overview of the exam and other valuable information. You can avoid wasting time due to possible misconceptions by learning about the exam.

Step Two: View the Exam Tutorial and Sample Test on the AICPA's Website

AICPA.org/becomeacpa/cpaexam/forcandidates/tutorialandsampletest is the website address.

The tutorial is a guided tour of the exam. It demonstrates the functionality of question types, tools, resources, and navigation found in the Uniform CPA Examination. The tutorial does *not* contain actual exam content. Familiarize yourself with the exam functionality demonstrated in the tutorial *before* you review the sample tests.

The sample tests (one for each exam section) provide candidates with a preview of the exam experience. Each test is a functional replica of the exam and gives you the opportunity to become familiar with the exam's format in an interactive environment. The sample test software allows you to answer each type of question that appears on the exam.

The tutorial and sample tests are *not* available at the test centers—a thorough familiarity with the exam's functionality, format, and directions is required *before* you report to a test center.

Step Three: Estimate Your Strengths and Weaknesses

The typical exam candidate has recently or nearly completed a university's 5-year accounting program with above average grades in accounting and other business courses. Most candidates' first language is English. Consider your background and how it differs from this. You should also consider other factors. For example, if you work in a specialized area of accounting such as taxes, you may need to spend more time reviewing the auditing topics. Additionally, if you have already taken any exam section, analyze your performance to help determine how to refine your efforts for the remaining exam sections.

Step Four: Develop a Personalized Study Plan

Based on your analysis of your strengths and weaknesses, develop your personalized study plan. See our sample study plan for the AUD exam section at the end of this foreword. This plan entails a minimum of 20 hours of study per week. This level of intensity should increase during the final weeks of your review. If you cannot allot this many hours per week, you may need to start studying sooner. Use this plan as a benchmark—make any adjustments needed for your background and fine-tune it as you progress.

How to Find Time to Study

Most candidates have many other demands on their time. Consequently, your first reaction may be, "I don't have 20 hours a week to devote to studying for the CPA exam." We can show you how to find the time you need. Begin by preparing a chart with each column as a day of the week and each line as an hour of the day.

1. Keeping in mind what you would consider to be a typical week, first mark the time that you know you won't be able to study. For example, mark an "X" in each block which represents time you normally sleep or have a class, work, or some other commitment. Be realistic.

2. Next, put a "C" in each block that represents commuting time, an "M" (meal) in each block that represents when you normally eat, and an "E" in each block that represents when you exercise.

3. Now pick one hour each day to rest and relax and give yourself a break—write "R & R" in one block for each day. Do not skip this step. By taking a break, you will study more efficiently and effectively.

4. Write "S" (study) in the remaining blocks. Count the "S" blocks. Are there 20? If not, count your "C", "M", and "E" blocks; these blocks of time can be used to gain additional study time by using Bisk CPA Review video programs. For example, you may be able to watch video lectures a second time while eating or exercising to gain valuable study time.

5. If you do not have 20 "S" blocks, you may have several options: (a) try to reprioritize and make a block that has an "X" in it available for study time; (b) concentrate on fewer exam sections; or (c) start your regimen sooner—study for more weeks so you can decrease the number of hours per week. Many candidates find that the Bisk CPA Review video programs make their study time more effective, requiring fewer hours than without these valuable study aids.

How to Allocate Your Time

Develop your overall study plan. At the end of this foreword, we outline a sample study plan to prepare for just the AUD exam section. (On our website (www.cpaexam.com) on the support page, we also have plans for studying to sit for two exam sections concurrently—click on the link below "Sample Combination Review Plans.") The time allocated to each chapter is based on the amount and difficulty of the material and how heavily the content is tested on the exam (refer to the AUD AICPA content specification outline in the first section of this volume's "Appendix B: Exam Preparation Tips").

Keep in mind that this plan was developed for the typical candidate as previously defined in "Step Three" of this foreword. You should customize this plan based on your degree of comfort with the exam and the estimated level of your knowledge of each chapter's content.

These are the number of weeks needed to complete each of our sample study plans for candidates preparing for one exam section at a time. (Remember to customize these plans to your unique situation.)

Auditing & Attestation (AUD)	7	Regulation (REG)	6
Financial Accounting & Reporting (FAR)	8	Business Environment & Concepts (BEC)	4

Exam Scheduling Strategies

Most candidates spread taking the exam over two or more exam windows. Candidates who sit for all four sections during one window usually either want to pass the exam quickly or must travel to a test center from a great distance. Sitting for one exam section per window is the best means of ensuring a passing score; however, you must weigh this against a much more protracted commitment of your time.

Sitting for two exam sections per window obviously halves the number of windows. It also takes advantage of any synergy resulting from studying one exam section with or soon after another. You can arrange a separation of several weeks between sittings by scheduling one exam section near the beginning of a two-month testing window and the second near the end of the same window.

Bear in mind, the sample study plans are rigorous schedules that assume the candidate has recently graduated from a university with a strong accounting program. You may want to sit for only one section during your first window to get a realistic idea of the preparation involved for your particular circumstances. Once you have the experience of sitting for one exam section behind you, sitting for multiple exam sections in the next window will be facilitated by the study habits that you will have developed.

Online Review Recommendations

The editors strongly recommend that candidates working full time take no more than two sections of the online reviews concurrently. Information about integrating materials is available on the website for the online review.

The review plan incorporated within the online package generally works better for candidates with access to the site than the study plan in this foreword. In the unlikely event that you have questions after viewing this information, contact your faculty advisor once class starts.

Step Five: Read the Rest of the Exam Preparation Tips Appendix

The third section of this volume's "Appendix B: Exam Preparation Tips" covers test-taking strategies and the exam's scoring conventions. It explains our Solutions Approach™, an approach that will help you maximize your score.

Step Six: Integrate Your Review Materials

Optimize the effectiveness of your study plan. Use the resources available to you to the extent they help you pass the exam. Remember that question drill has a high positive correlation to exam scores. Many candidates inform the editors that, for them, a video presentation provides insights which the printed word simply does not.

Obviously, there is a full spectrum of strengths and review styles. Consider where you are on the strength spectrum and adapt the following guidelines to your situation.

In chapters where you are stronger:

1. Watch the related video.
2. Answer the multiple-choice questions for the chapter. Analyze your strong and weak areas.
3. Read the subsections of the chapter that correspond to your weak areas.
4. Answer at least one simulation.
5. Answer the multiple-choice questions that you previously answered incorrectly. If you answer 70% or more correctly, move on to the next chapter. (Your later weekly review should raise you to a passing score.) If you answer less than 70% correctly, this chapter counts as one of your weak areas.

In chapters where you are weaker:

1. Watch the related video.
2. Read the chapter in the book.
3. Watch the related video again.
4. Answer the multiple-choice questions for the chapter. Analyze your strong and weak areas.
5. For areas for which you remain weak, split the video, text material, and question into portions smaller than a chapter. Watch a few minutes of video and then concentrate on the related questions and text material.
6. Watch the related video again.
7. Answer at least one simulation (if there are any).
8. Answer the multiple-choice questions that you previously answered incorrectly. If you answer 70% or more correctly, move on to the next chapter. (Your later weekly review should raise you to a passing score.) If you answer less than 70% correctly, consider whether you need to allocate more time than you originally budgeted.

Step Seven: Use These Helpful Hints as You Study

1. Make notes while watching the lectures and highlight portions of the text and/or take notes as you read the chapters.

   You will find these notes very useful for weekly reviews and your final review.

2. Use the video lectures effectively.

   Watch the video lectures in an environment without distractions—especially the first time. Be prepared to take notes and answer questions just as if you were attending a live class.

   Frequently, the instructors will have you stop the program to work a question on your own. Be sure to do this rather than just watching the instructor work out the solution. (And in planning your study time, allow for this, i.e., a 20-minute lecture may take 30 minutes or more to view.)

   Consider playing select lectures or portions of lectures repeatedly when you are exercising or performing routine tasks. Repetition will help you to memorize and retain key concepts. It also will reinforce your reading and question drill. The more times that you listen to a lecture, the more familiar you will become with the material and the easier it will be for you to recall it during the exam.

3. Make flash cards.

   Make flash cards for topics that are tested heavily on the exam or are giving you trouble. By making your own flash cards, you learn during their creation plus you can tailor them to your individual learning style and problem areas.

   You will find these very useful for weekly reviews and your final review.

   Keep them handy so you can review them at opportune times, for example, while you are waiting in line, so you can turn nonproductive time into valuable study time.

   Put flash cards on information you know aside and replace them with new material as you progress through your study plan. Review your complete set during the last two weeks before the exam.

4. Do **not** mark question answers in the printed book.

   Do not circle your answers to multiple-choice questions or fill in the blanks on any simulations. You should work every multiple-choice question and simulation at least twice and you do not want to influence later answers by knowing how you previously answered.

   Record your answers separately. Retain these "answer sheets" to facilitate tracking your progress.

5. Flag questions that you answered incorrectly or merely guessed correctly.

   This will serve as a reminder to answer these questions again at a later time.

6. Spend your weekly review time effectively. During each weekly review:

   Answer the multiple-choice questions and simulations that you previously answered incorrectly or merely guessed correctly. This is particularly important if you moved on to the next chapter with a score at the minimum 70% suggested earlier ("Step Six") in this foreword. You need to increase that score to a *minimum* of 75% during your weekly review activities to expect to pass the exam. How high do you need to increase it? A cushion to assure that you pass the exam is preferable. The size of that cushion depends on your personal tolerance for risk.

   Go through your flash cards or notes.

   Answer at least one research simulation and one other type of simulation. Do *not* wait until the end of your review to attempt a research simulation or other types of simulations.

Supplement to Step Four: Sample Study Plan

The time allocated by the following plan to each chapter is based on the amount and difficulty of the material and how heavily the content is tested on the exam (refer to the AUD AICPA content specification outline in the first section of this volume's "Appendix B: Exam Preparation Tips").

The editors strongly recommend that candidates develop a personalized study plan. Modify this plan based on your study habits, available time, and level of knowledge of each chapter's content. There are also sample study plans on our website for candidates preparing to sit for two exam sections during the same testing window—go to cpaexam.com and click on the link under "Sample Combination Review Plans" on the support page.

AUD Sample Study Plan

		Hours
Week 1:	Read the "Foreword: Best Practices" and "Appendix B: Exam Preparation Tips"; review the AICPA exam tutorial and AUD sample test	3
	Chapter 1–An Audit Conducted in Accordance With US GAAS	4
	Chapter 2–Planning	10
	Chapter 3–Internal Control	3
Week 2:	Chapter 3–Internal Control	7
	Chapter 4–Evidence & Procedures	10
	Chapter 5–Audit Programs	3
Week 3:	Chapter 5–Audit Programs	4
	Weekly review: weeks 1–2	2
	Chapter 6–Audit Sampling	6
	Chapter 7–Auditing IT Systems	5
	Chapter 8–Reports on Audited Financial Statements	3
Week 4:	Chapter 8–Reports on Audited Financial Statements	4
	Chapter 9–Audits of Group Financial Statements	4
	Weekly review: weeks 1–3 and check for *updating supplement	2
	Chapter 10–Government Auditing	4
	Chapter 11–Other Auditing Standards	6
Week 5:	Weekly review: weeks 1–4 and check for *updating supplement	3
	Chapter 12–Other Types of Reports	6
	Chapter 13–Accounting & Review Services	8
	Chapter 14–Attestation Engagements	3
Week 6:	Chapter 14–Attestation Engagements	4
	Weekly review of weeks 1–5 and check for *updating supplement	3
	Chapter 15–Accountants' Professional Responsibilities	10
	Practice research skills (see appendix C)	3
Week 7:	Review areas in which you still feel weak & revisit the AICPA exam tutorial and AUD sample test	6
	Take practice exam under exam conditions (see page A-1)	4
	Do final review and check for *updating supplement	10

*UPDATING SUPPLEMENTS

Our updating supplements are small publications available from either customer service representatives or our CPA Review website (cpaexam.com/support/#.Ubd3meeOR8F). The editors recommend checking our website for new supplements at least once a month and again a week before your exam. Version 44 updating supplements are appropriate for candidates with the 44th edition. Information from supplements of earlier editions (through the version 43 series) has been incorporated into this edition. Supplements are issued only as appropriate information becomes available and is eligible to be tested.

CHANGE ALERT

AU Identifier Used for Clarified US GAAS in This Textbook

We have not continued to use the temporary AU-C identifier for the clarified auditing standards issued by the American Institute of Certified Public Accountants (AICPA). In this textbook these standards have an AU identifier.

CHAPTER 1

AN AUDIT CONDUCTED IN ACCORDANCE WITH US GAAS

AU Identifier Used for Clarified US GAAS in This Textbook

We have not continued to use the temporary AU-C identifier for the clarified auditing standards issued by the American Institute of Certified Public Accountants (AICPA). In this textbook these standards have an AU identifier.

CHAPTER 1

AN AUDIT CONDUCTED IN ACCORDANCE WITH US GAAS

I. Overview of an Audit of Financial Statements (AU 200 and AU Preface)

A. Purpose of an Audit of Financial Statements

1. **Opinion on Financial Statements** The purpose of an audit is to provide financial statement users with an opinion by the auditor on whether the financial statements are presented fairly, in all material respects, in accordance with the applicable financial reporting framework (AFRF)—such an opinion is common to all audits of financial statements.

   The auditor's opinion does *not* assure, for example, the future viability of the entity nor the efficiency or effectiveness with which management has conducted the affairs of the entity.

2. **US GAAS & Ethical Requirements** An audit conducted in accordance with US generally accepted auditing standards (GAAS) and relevant ethical requirements enables the auditor to form that opinion. An auditor's opinion enhances the degree of confidence that intended users can place in the financial statements.

   US GAAS are applicable to the preparation and issuance of audit reports for entities that are nonissuers. Nonissuers are nonpublic entities. (See the section on audit guidance in this chapter. Audit guidance for public companies is covered in chapter 11.)

Editor Note: GAAS is a universally accepted acronym; however, you may only see AFRF in this text.

3. **Determinants of Nature of Opinion on Financial Statements** The form of opinion expressed by the auditor on the financial statements will depend upon:

   a. **The Applicable Financial Reporting Framework**

   b. **Any Applicable Law or Regulation**

      Editor Note: US GAAS do *not* address the responsibilities of the auditor that may exist in legislation or regulations. Such responsibilities may differ from those established in US GAAS. Accordingly, it is the responsibility of the auditor to ensure compliance with all relevant legal, regulatory, or professional obligations.

4. **Opinions *Not* on Financial Statements** In some circumstances, applicable law or regulation may require auditors to provide opinions on other specific matters, such as the effectiveness of internal control. Although US GAAS include requirements and regarding such matters *to the extent that they are relevant to forming an opinion on the financial statements*, the auditor is required to undertake further work if the auditor has additional responsibilities to provide such other opinions.

B. Responsibilities

1. **Management** An audit in accordance with US GAAS is conducted on the premise that management and, when appropriate, those charged with governance, have acknowledged and understand that they have the following responsibilities.

   a. **Preparation & Fair Presentation of the Financial Statements in Accordance With the AFRF** The preparation and fair presentation of the financial statements in accordance with the AFRF includes:

      (1) **Identification of AFRF** The identification of the AFRF, in the context of any relevant laws or regulations

      (2) **Preparation of Financial Statement in Accordance with AFRF** The preparation and fair presentation of the financial statements in accordance with the AFRF which encompasses:

         (a) **Accounting Policies** Selecting and applying appropriate accounting policies

         (b) **Accounting Estimates** Making reasonable accounting estimates

      (3) **Description of AFRF** The inclusion of an adequate description of that framework in the financial statements

   Editor Note: Even though the auditor may make suggestions about the form or content of the financial statements, or assist management by drafting them, in whole or in part, based on information provided by management; the auditor's responsibility *for the financial statements* is confined to the expression an opinion on them.

   b. **Internal Control** The design, implementation, and maintenance of internal control relevant to the preparation and fair presentation of financial statements that are free from material misstatement, whether due to fraud or error

   c. **Support of Audit** To provide the auditor with:

      (1) **Financial Statement Information** Access to all information that is relevant to the preparation and fair presentation of the financial statements

      (2) **Additional Information** Additional information that the auditor may request for the purpose of the audit

      (3) **Unrestricted Access To Persons** Unrestricted access to persons within the entity from whom the auditor determines it necessary to obtain audit evidence

   Editor Note: US GAAS does *not* impose these or any responsibilities on management (neither does an audit relieve management nor those charged with governance of any of their responsibilities); however, an audit is *conducted on the premise* that management and those charged with governance have acknowledged certain responsibilities that are fundamental to the conduct of the audit.

2. **Auditor** Auditors have the following responsibilities.

   a. **Competence & Capabilities** Having appropriate competence and capabilities to perform the audit

   b. **Legal, Regulatory, or Ethical Requirements** Complying with relevant legal, regulatory, or professional (ethical) requirements

c. **Professional Skepticism & Professional Judgment** Maintaining professional skepticism and exercising professional judgment throughout the planning and performance of the audit

d. **Opinion** Expressing an opinion (or stating that an opinion cannot be expressed) on the financial statements in a written report based on an evaluation of the audit evidence

Editor Note: The auditor's responsibility to express an opinion on the financial statements based on the audit is stated explicitly in the first sentence of the auditor's responsibility section of the audit report (see chapter 8).

e. **Other Communication & Reporting Responsibilities** The auditor also may have certain other communication and reporting responsibilities to users, management, those charged with governance, or parties outside the entity, regarding matters arising from the audit. These responsibilities may be established by US GAAS or by applicable law or regulation.

C. Overall Objectives of the Auditor

1. **Obtain Reasonable Assurance About Whether the Financial Statements as a Whole Are Free From Material Misstatement** One of the overall objectives of the auditor is to obtain reasonable assurance about whether the financial statements as a whole are free from material misstatement, whether due to fraud or error—thereby enabling the auditor to express an opinion on whether the financial statements are presented fairly, in all material respects, in accordance with an AFRF.

a. **Reasonable Assurance** Most of the auditor's work in forming the auditor's opinion consists of obtaining and evaluating audit evidence. Reasonable assurance is obtained when the auditor has obtained sufficient appropriate audit evidence to reduce audit risk to an acceptably low level.

(1) **Not Absolute** Reasonable assurance is *not* an absolute level of assurance because there are inherent limitations of an audit that result in most of the audit evidence being persuasive rather than conclusive.

Editor Note: *Audit risk* is the risk that the auditor expresses an inappropriate opinion when the financial statements are materially misstated; see the definition of *reasonable assurance* in this chapter for information about inherent limitations.

(2) **Role of US GAAS** US GAAS contain objectives, requirements, and application and other explanatory material that are designed to support the auditor in obtaining reasonable assurance.

b. **Materiality** The concept of materiality is applied by the auditor when both planning and performing the audit; and in evaluating the effect of identified misstatements on the audit and uncorrected misstatements, if any, on the financial statements.

In general, misstatements, including omissions, are considered to be material if they could reasonably be expected to influence users' economic decisions based on the financial statements. Judgments about materiality are made in light of surrounding circumstances and involve both qualitative and quantitative considerations. These judgments are affected by the auditor's perception of the financial information needs of users of the financial statements and by the size and/or nature of a misstatement.

The auditor's opinion addresses the financial statements as a whole. Therefore, the auditor has *no* responsibility to plan and perform the audit to obtain reasonable assurance that misstatements that are not material to the financial statements as a whole are detected.

2. **Report & Communicate** The auditor's other overall objective is to report on the financial statements and communicate as required by US GAAS in accordance with the auditor's findings.

D. **Audit Process**
The auditor independently accumulates and evaluates audit evidence of an entity for the purpose of reporting on the degree of correspondence between the information produced and the established criteria of the AFRF, e.g., generally accepting accounting principles (GAAP).

Exhibit 1 ▸ Comparison of Financial Accounting & Auditing

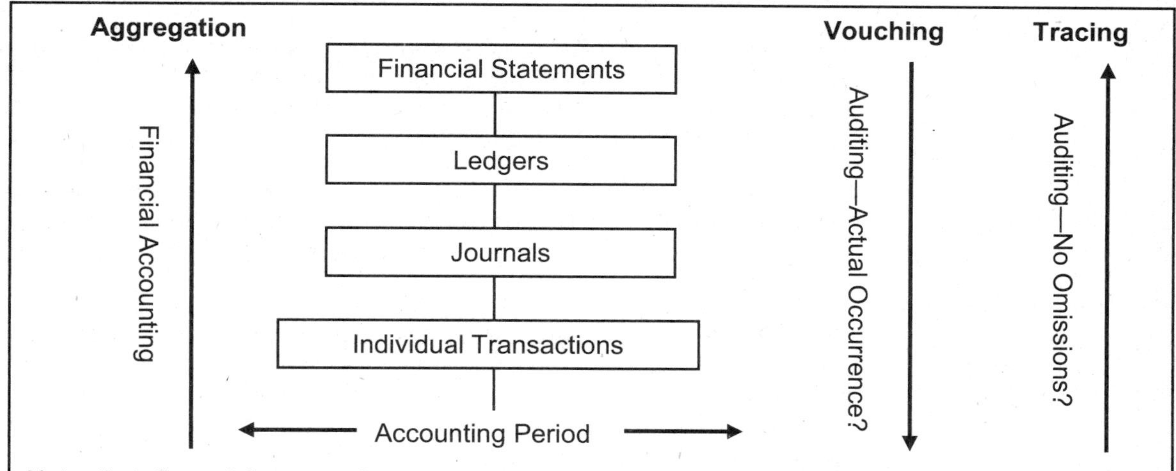

Note that financial accounting is a process of aggregation. Individual transactions are first recorded in journals; subsequently, the data in journals are classified in ledgers; and finally, the data in ledgers are summarized in the financial statements.

1. **Vouching** Did the transactions summarized in the financial statements actually occur? The auditor makes this determination by vouching items from the financial statements back to the accounts and ultimately to the original transaction documents. This is the downward process depicted on the right side of exhibit 1.

2. **Tracing** Have all transactions that occurred during the period been recorded properly in the accounts and summarized in the financial statements? (Are the financial statements complete?) The auditor makes this determination by tracing items from original transaction documents to the accounts and ultimately to the financial statements. This is the upward process depicted on the right side of exhibit 1.

   Editor Note: Although the AICPA examiners have not been 100% consistent in their use of the terms *vouching* and *tracing*, they can be valuable timesaving clues when answering questions which require distinguishing between whether an audit procedure is testing the assertion (see the definition of *assertion* in this chapter) of occurrence/existence vs. completion. *Generally*, if the described procedure involves vouching, an item found recorded in the financial statements is being tested to find the supporting proof that the recorded amount is valid; thus, the procedure is testing for occurrence or existence; if it involves tracing, an event or transaction evidenced by information in source documents is being traced to the financial statements to verify that it is included in the financial statements; thus, the procedure is testing the completeness of the financial statements.

3. **Audit Process Steps**

   a. **Establish Understanding With Client** The auditor should establish an understanding with the client regarding the engagement services, including the objectives, scope, and limitations of the engagement, as well as the auditor's and management's responsibilities.

The auditor should document the understanding in an engagement letter or other suitable form of *written* agreement.

b. **Obtain Understanding of the Entity & Its Environment, Including Internal Control** The auditor should perform risk assessment procedures to obtain this understanding. The nature, extent, and timing of these procedures depend on the size and complexity of the entity as well as the auditor's previous experience with the entity, if any.

   This process should include a discussion among the audit team concerning the susceptibility (risk) of the financial statements to material misstatements.

c. **Assess the Risk of Material Misstatement (RMM)** The auditor will identify and evaluate the RMM at the financial statement and relevant assertion levels. This will include identifying risks and potential misstatements, as well as considering the materiality and probability of potential misstatements.

   In representing that the financial statements are fairly presented in accordance with the AFRF, management implicitly or explicitly makes assertions regarding the recognition, measurement, presentation, and disclosure of information in the financial statements and related disclosures.

d. **Design & Perform Procedures to Address the RMM** The auditor uses the knowledge provided by the understanding of the entity and its environment and the assessed RMM in determining the nature, extent, and timing of further audit procedures. Further audit procedures include testing the operating effectiveness of controls [tests of controls] and substantive procedures.

   (1) **Tests of Controls** Tests of the operating effectiveness of controls in preventing, or detecting and correcting, material misstatements at the assertion level are required when either of the following circumstances exists.

      (a) **Auditor Relies on Effectiveness** The auditor intends to rely on the operating effectiveness of controls in determining the nature, extent, and timing of substantive procedures

      (b) **Substantive Procedures Alone Are Inadequate** Substantive procedures alone cannot provide sufficient appropriate audit evidence at the relevant assertion level

   (2) **Substantive Procedures** Irrespective of the assessed RMM, substantive procedures are required for all relevant assertions related to each material class of transactions, account balance, and disclosure.

e. **Evaluate Audit Evidence** Based on procedures performed, the auditor analyzes the accumulated audit evidence to determine whether the assessments of the RMM at the relevant assertion level are still appropriate. The auditor may need to reevaluate the planned audit procedures to obtain sufficient appropriate audit evidence to support the opinion on the financial statements.

f. **Form Opinion & Issue Audit Report** The audit report will describe the scope of the audit and state the auditor's conclusion regarding the fairness of the financial statements and related disclosures.

   Before issuing the audit report, the lead audit partner will perform a final review of the workpapers to ensure that the appropriate type of opinion will be expressed.

   Editor Note: For public companies (issuers), there must also be an engagement quality review and concurring approval of issuance. The objective of the engagement quality reviewer is to perform an evaluation of the significant judgments made by the engagement team and the related conclusions reached in forming the overall conclusion on the engagement and in preparing the engagement report to determine whether to provide concurring approval of issuance. (See chapter 15 for more information.)

E. Expanded Definitions of the Fundamental Concepts of an Audit

1. **Applicable Financial Reporting Framework (AFRF)** The financial reporting framework adopted by management and, when appropriate, those charged with governance in the preparation and fair presentation of the financial statements that is acceptable in view of the nature of the entity and the objective of the financial statements, or that is required by law or regulation

   a. **Sources** In some cases, the AFRF may encompass financial accounting standards promulgated by a standards-setting organization and/or legislative or regulatory requirements. The AFRF may encompass such other sources, or may even consist only of such sources. Such other sources may include:

      - The legal and ethical environment, including statutes, regulations, court decisions, and professional ethical obligations regarding accounting matters
      - Accounting interpretations of varying authority issued by standards-setting, professional, or regulatory organizations
      - Views of varying authority on emerging accounting issues issued by standards-setting, professional, or regulatory organizations
      - Prevalent general and industry practices
      - Accounting literature

   b. **Conflicts** Such other sources may provide direction on the application of the AFRF. When conflicts exist between the AFRF and the sources from which direction on its application may be obtained, or among the sources that encompass the financial reporting framework, the source with the highest authority prevails.

2. **Assertions** Representations by management, explicit or otherwise, that are embodied in the financial statements as used by the auditor to consider the different types of potential misstatements that may occur

   - **Relevant Assertion** A financial statement assertion that has a reasonable possibility of containing a misstatement or misstatements that would cause the financial statements to be materially misstated; the determination of whether an assertion is a *relevant assertion* is made without regard to the effect of internal controls

3. **Audit Evidence** Information used by the auditor in arriving at the conclusions on which the auditor's opinion is based; audit evidence includes both information contained in the accounting records underlying the financial statements and other information.

   a. **Sufficiency of Audit Evidence** The measure of the quantity of audit evidence

   b. **Appropriateness of Audit Evidence** The measure of the quality of audit evidence, i.e., its relevance and reliability in providing support for the conclusions on which the auditor's opinion is based

      Editor Note: The reliability of evidence is influenced by its source and by its nature, and is dependent on the individual circumstances under which it is obtained.

   Editor Note: The sufficiency and appropriateness of audit evidence are interrelated. Sufficiency is the measure of the quantity of audit evidence. The quantity of audit evidence needed is affected by the auditor's assessment of the RMM (the higher the assessed risks, the more audit evidence is likely to be required) and also by the quality of such audit evidence (the higher the quality, the less may be required). However, obtaining more audit evidence may not compensate for its poor quality.

4. **Audit Risk** The risk that the auditor expresses an inappropriate audit opinion when the financial statements are materially misstated; audit risk is a function of the RMM and detection risk.

The auditor is not expected to, and cannot, reduce audit risk to zero and cannot, therefore, obtain absolute assurance that the financial statements are free from material misstatement due to fraud or error. This is because of the inherent limitations of an audit (see the definition of *reasonable assurance* in this chapter for information on inherent limitations).

Editor Note:

- The assessment of risks is a matter of professional judgment, rather than a matter capable of precise measurement.
- The ordinarily insignificant risk that the auditor might express an opinion that the financial statements are materially misstated when they are not, is *not* an audit risk per US GAAS.

5. **Auditor** The term used to refer to the person or persons conducting the audit, usually the engagement partner or other members of the engagement team, or, as applicable, the firm.

6. **Detection Risk** The risk that the procedures performed by the auditor to reduce audit risk to an acceptably low level will not detect a misstatement that exists and that could be material, either individually or when aggregated with other misstatements.

Detection risk a function of the effectiveness of an audit procedure and of its application by the auditor.

The enhancement of the effectiveness of an audit procedure and of its application; and the reduction of the possibility that an auditor might select an inappropriate audit procedure, misapply an appropriate audit procedure, or misinterpret the audit results is assisted by:

- Adequate planning
- Proper assignment of personnel to the engagement team
- The application of professional skepticism
- Supervision and review of the audit work performed

However, detection risk can only be reduced, not eliminated, because of the inherent limitations of an audit (see the definition of *reasonable assurance* in this chapter for more information on inherent limitations).

Editor Note: The greater the RMM, the less the detection risk that can be accepted and the more persuasive the audit evidence required by the auditor. In other words, for a given level of audit risk, the acceptable level of detection risk bears an inverse relationship to the assessed RMM at the assertion level.

7. **Financial Reporting Framework** A set of criteria used to determine measurement, recognition, presentation, and disclosure of all material items appearing in the financial statements; e.g., US GAAP; International Financial Reporting Standards, issued by the International Accounting Standards Board; or a special purpose framework

   - **Fair Presentation Framework** A term used to refer to a financial reporting framework that requires compliance with the requirements of the framework and either of these acknowledgments.

     - **Possible Additional Disclosures** Explicit or implicit acknowledgment that, to achieve fair presentation of the financial statements, it may be necessary for management to provide disclosures beyond those specifically required by the framework

     - **Possible Rare Departure from Framework** Explicit acknowledgment that it may be necessary for management to depart from a requirement of the framework to achieve fair presentation of the financial statements—such departures are expected to be necessary only in extremely rare circumstances

   Editor Note: A financial reporting framework that requires compliance with the requirements of the framework, but does not contain one of the preceding acknowledgments is *not* a fair presentation framework.

8. **Financial Statements** A structured representation of historical financial information, including related notes, intended to communicate an entity's economic resources and obligations at a point in time or the changes therein for a period of time in accordance with a financial reporting framework; the related notes ordinarily comprise a summary of significant accounting policies and other explanatory information; the term *financial statements* ordinarily refers to a complete set of financial statements, but can also refer to a single financial statement

   a. **Requirements of AFRF**

      (1) **Determine Form & Content of Financial Statements** The requirements of the AFRF determine the form and content of the financial statements. Although the framework may not specify how to account for or disclose all transactions or events, it ordinarily embodies sufficiently broad principles that can serve as a basis for developing and applying accounting policies that are consistent with the concepts underlying the requirements of the framework.

      (2) **Determine Makeup of Complete Set of Financial Statements** The requirements of the AFRF also determine what constitutes a complete set of financial statements. (For example, a complete set of financial statements might include a balance sheet, an income statement, a statement of changes in equity, a cash flow statement, and related notes. For some other financial reporting frameworks, a single financial statement and the related notes might constitute a complete set of financial statements.

   b. **Financial Reporting Framework Categories** The financial statements may be prepared in accordance with either a general-purpose or special-purpose framework.

      (1) **General-Purpose Framework** A financial reporting framework designed to meet the common financial information needs of a wide range of users; the financial accounting standards promulgated by organizations that are authorized or recognized to promulgate standards to be used by entities for preparing financial statements in accordance with a general-purpose framework include:

         (a) **FASB *Accounting Standards Codification*™ (ASC)** Issued by the Financial Accounting Standards Board (FASB)

(b) **International Financial Reporting Standards (IFRS)** Issued by the International Accounting Standards Board (IASB)

(c) **Statements of Federal Financial Accounting Standards (SFFAS)** Issued by the Federal Accounting Standards Advisory Board (FASAB) for US federal government entities

(d) **Statements of Governmental Accounting Standards (GASB Statements)** Issued by the Governmental Accounting Standards Board (GASB) for US state and local government entities

(2) **Special-Purpose Framework** A financial reporting framework, other than GAAP, which is a cash, tax, regulatory, contractual, or an other basis of accounting (See chapter 12 for more information.)

9. **Historical Financial Information** Information expressed in financial terms regarding a particular entity, derived primarily from that entity's accounting system, about economic events occurring in past time periods or about economic conditions or circumstances at points in time in the past

10. **Interpretive Publications** Interpretive publications are **not** US GAAS. They *only* consist of:

- Auditing interpretations of US GAAS (included in the codification of US GAAS following the related AU section)
- Exhibits to US GAAS (included in the codification of US GAAS following the application & explanatory materials portion of AU sections)
- Audit guidance in:
    - AICPA Audit and Accounting Guides
    - AICPA Auditing Statements of Position

Editor Note: Auditing interpretations of US GAAS are included in the codification of US GAAS; each immediately follows the related AU section and has been assigned the same section number preceded by the number 9. (Not all AU sections have auditing interpretations of US GAAS.) Exhibits to US GAAS, if any, follow the application and other explanatory materials portion within an AU section (generally presented after the appendices, if any). AICPA Audit and Accounting Guides and AICPA Statements of Position are published separately.

11. **Management** The person(s) with executive responsibility for the conduct of the entity's operations; for some entities, management includes some or all of those charged with governance, e.g., executive members of a governance board or an owner-manager

12. **Misstatement** The difference between the amount, classification, presentation, or disclosure of a reported financial statement item and that which is required for the item to be presented fairly in accordance with the AFRF; misstatements can arise from fraud or error

13. **Other Auditing Publications** Publications other than *interpretive publications* (see the definition in this chapter); these include AICPA auditing publications not defined as interpretive publications; auditing articles in professional journals; continuing professional education programs and other instruction materials, textbooks, guide books, audit programs, and checklists; and other auditing publications from state CPA societies, other organizations, and individuals

14. **Premise, Relating to the Responsibilities of Management and, When Appropriate, Those Charged With Governance, on Which an Audit Is Conducted** Management and, when appropriate, those charged with governance have acknowledged and understand that

they have certain responsibilities that are fundamental to the conduct of an audit in accordance with US GAAS. (See the responsibilities topic is this chapter for more information.)

15. **Professional Judgment** The application of relevant training, knowledge, and experience, within the context provided by auditing, accounting, and ethical standards, in making informed decisions about the courses of action that are appropriate in the circumstances of the audit engagement

16. **Professional Responsibilities** US GAAS use the following two categories of professional requirements, identified by specific terms, to describe the degree of responsibility it imposes on auditors:

    a. **Unconditional Requirements** The auditor must comply with an unconditional requirement in all cases in which such requirement is relevant. US GAAS use the word *must* to indicate an unconditional requirement.

    b. **Presumptively Mandatory Requirements** The auditor must comply with a presumptively mandatory requirement in all cases in which such a requirement is relevant except in rare circumstances. US GAAS use the word *should* to indicate a presumptively mandatory requirement.

17. **Professional Skepticism** An attitude that includes a questioning mind; being alert to conditions that may indicate possible misstatement due to fraud or error; and a critical assessment of audit evidence

18. **Reasonable Assurance** In the context of an audit of financial statements, a high, but *not* absolute, level of assurance

    a. **Obtaining Reasonable Assurance** To express an opinion, the auditor obtains reasonable assurance about whether the financial statements as a whole are free from material misstatement, whether due to fraud or error. To obtain reasonable assurance, the auditor does the following and thereby is able to draw reasonable conclusions on which to base the opinion.

        (1) **Planning & Supervision** Plans the work and properly supervises any assistants

        (2) **Materiality** Determines and applies appropriate materiality level(s)s throughout the audit

        (3) **RMM** Identifies and assesses RMM, whether due to fraud or error, based on an understanding of the entity and its environment, including the entity's internal control

        (4) **Evidence** Obtains sufficient appropriate audit evidence about whether material misstatements exist, through designing and implementing appropriate responses to the assessed risks to reduce audit risk to an acceptably low level

b. **Inherent Limitations of an Audit** The auditor is unable to obtain absolute assurance that the financial statements as a whole are free from material misstatement because of inherent limitations of an audit.

Editor Note: However, the inherent limitations of an audit are *not* a justification for the auditor to be satisfied with less than persuasive audit evidence.

(1) **Sources of Inherent Limitations** The principal inherent limitations of an audit arise from the following.

(a) **Nature of Financial Reporting** The preparation and fair presentation of financial statements involve judgment by management in applying the requirements of the entity's AFRF to the facts and circumstances of the entity. In addition, many financial statement items involve subjective assessments or a degree of uncertainty; and a range exists of acceptable interpretations or judgments that may be made. Thus, some financial statement items are subject to an inherent level of variability that cannot be eliminated by the application of additional audit procedures, e.g., certain accounting estimates that are dependent on predictions of future events.

(b) **Nature of Audit Procedures** There are practical and legal limitations on the auditor's ability to obtain audit evidence, for example:

(i) **Incomplete Information Provided by Entity** There is the possibility that management or others may *not* provide, intentionally or unintentionally, complete information. Accordingly, the auditor cannot be certain of the completeness of information, even though the auditor has performed audit procedures to obtain assurance that all relevant information has been obtained.

(ii) **Fraud** Fraud may involve sophisticated and carefully organized schemes designed to conceal it. Therefore, audit procedures used to gather audit evidence may be ineffective for detecting an intentional misstatement that involves, e.g., collusion to falsify documentation that may cause the auditor to believe that audit evidence is valid when it is not. (The auditor is neither trained as nor expected to be an expert in the authentication of documents.)

(iii) **Auditor Has Limited Authority** An audit is not an official investigation into alleged wrongdoing. Accordingly, the auditor is not given specific legal powers, such as the power of search, which may be necessary for such an investigation.

(c) **Time Constraints** There is a need for the audit to be conducted within a reasonable period of time to achieve a balance between benefit and cost, recognizing that it is impracticable to address all information that may exist or to pursue every matter exhaustively on the assumption that information is fraudulent or erroneous until proven otherwise. Thus, it is necessary for the auditor to do the following.

(i) **Planning** Plan the audit so that it will be performed in an effective manner.

(ii) **Concentrate on High Risk Areas** Direct more audit effort to areas most expected to contain RMM.

- US GAAS requires the auditor have a basis for the identification and assessment of RMM at the financial statement and assertion levels by performing risk assessment procedures and related activities.

(iii) **Testing** Use testing and other means of examining populations for misstatements, e.g., sampling.

- US GAAS requires the auditor to use testing and other means of examining populations in a manner that provides a reasonable basis for the auditor to draw conclusions about the population.

Editor Note: The matter of difficulty, time, or cost involved is not in itself a valid basis for the auditor to omit an audit procedure for which there is no alternative or to be satisfied with audit evidence that is less than persuasive.

(2) **Significant Areas of Concern** In the case of certain assertions or subject matters, the potential effects of the inherent limitations on the auditor's ability to detect material misstatements are particularly significant. Such assertions or subject matters include the following.

(a) **Fraud** Fraud, particularly fraud involving senior management or collusion (see chapter 2)

(b) **Related Parties** The existence and completeness of related-party relationships and transactions (see chapter 4)

(c) **Noncompliance With Laws & Regulations** The occurrence of noncompliance with laws and regulations (see chapter 2)

(d) **Going Concern Issues** Future events or conditions that may cause an entity to cease to continue as a going concern (see chapter 8)

US GAAS relevant to these matters include procedures to assist in lessening the effect of an audit's inherent limitations.

19. **Risk of Material Misstatement (RMM)** The risk that the financial statements are materially misstated *prior* to the audit

Editor Note: The RMM is the *entity's* risk, i.e., it exists independently of the audit.

The risks of material misstatement exist at the following two levels.

a. **Overall Financial Statement Level** The RMM that relate pervasively to the financial statements as a whole and potentially affect many assertions

b. **Assertion Level for Classes of Transactions, Account Balances & Disclosures** The RMM at the assertion level are assessed in order to determine the nature, extent, and timing of further audit procedures necessary to obtain sufficient appropriate audit evidence. This evidence enables the auditor to express an opinion on the financial statements at an acceptably low level of audit risk.

At the assertion level, the RMM consists of two components: inherent risk and control risk.

US GAAS do not ordinarily refer to inherent risk and control risk separately, but rather to a combined assessment of the RMM; however, the auditor may make separate or combined assessments of inherent and control risk depending on preferred audit techniques or methodologies and practical considerations.

(1) **Inherent Risk** The susceptibility of an assertion about a class of transaction, account balance, or disclosure to a misstatement that could be material, either individually or when aggregated with other misstatements, *before* consideration of any related controls

(2) **Control Risk** The risk that a misstatement that could occur in an assertion about a class of transaction, account balance, or disclosure and that could be material, either individually or when aggregated with other misstatements, will not be prevented, or detected and corrected, on a timely basis by the entity's internal control

US GAAS provide the conditions, under which the auditor is required to, or may choose to, test the operating effectiveness of controls in determining the nature, extent, and timing of substantive procedures to be performed.

20. **Those Charged With Governance** The person(s) or organization(s), e.g., a corporate trustee, with responsibility for overseeing the strategic direction of the entity and the obligations related to the accountability of the entity; this includes overseeing the financial reporting process; those charged with governance may include management personnel, e.g., executive members of a governance board or an owner-manager

II. Audit Guidance (AU 200 continued)

A. US Generally Accepted Auditing Standards (GAAS)

An auditor is required to plan, conduct, and report the results of an audit in accordance with US GAAS for a nonissuer. The standards provide measures of quality of the auditor's performance and audit objectives.

1. **Codification & Applicability of US GAAS** US GAAS are developed and issued in the form of Statements on Auditing Standards (SAS) and are codified into AU sections. (SAS are issued by the Auditing Standards Board of the AICPA.) US GAAS are written in the context of an audit of financial statements by an auditor. They are to be adapted as necessary in the circumstances when applied to audits of other historical financial information. US GAAS do *not* address the responsibilities of the auditor that may exist in legislation, regulation, or otherwise, in connection with, for example, the offering of securities to the public.

a. **Applicability** Nonissuers are those entities not subject to the Sarbanes-Oxley Act of 2002 or the rules of the SEC. The AICPA Code of Professional Conduct requires adherence to US GAAS for audits of nonissuers. (See chapter 15 for coverage of this code.)

(1) **Association With Financial Statements Defined** An auditor is associated with financial information when the auditor has applied procedures sufficient to permit the auditor to report in accordance with US GAAS.

(2) **Unaudited Financial Statements** Statements on Standards for Accounting and Review Services (SSARS) address the accountant's considerations when preparing and presenting unaudited financial statements to an entity or to third parties. (See chapter 13.)

b. **Standards vs. Procedures** Audit standards are *not* the same as audit procedures.

(1) **Procedures Defined** Procedures relate to the acts to be performed, for example, the confirmation of a predetermined number of accounts receivable. Audit *procedures* are used to meet the requirements of generally accepted auditing *standards* and gather audit evidence. Audit procedures will vary from engagement to engagement.

(2) **Standards Defined** Standards provide the objectives that audit procedures are to attain and measures of the quality of procedures to be performed. Audit standards do *not* vary from engagement to engagement.

c. **US GAAS Personal Requirements**

(1) **Ethical Requirements** (See chapter 15 for more information.)

(a) **Independence** The auditor must be independent of the entity when performing an engagement in accordance with US GAAS unless US GAAS provides otherwise or the auditor is required by law or regulation to accept the engagement and report on the financial statements. When the auditor is not independent and neither of these exceptions is applicable, the auditor is precluded from issuing a report under US GAAS.

Editor Note: When the auditor is not independent but is required by law or regulation to report on the financial statements, the auditor should disclaim an opinion and should specifically state that the auditor is not independent. (See chapter 8 for more information.)

In the case of an audit engagement, it is in the public interest and, therefore, required that the auditor be independent of the entity subject to the audit. The concept of independence refers to both independence in fact and independence in appearance. The auditor's independence from the entity safeguards the auditor's ability to form an audit opinion without being affected by influences that might compromise that opinion. Independence enhances the auditor's ability to act with integrity; to be objective; and to maintain an attitude of professional skepticism. Independence implies an impartiality that recognizes an obligation to be fair not only to management and those charged with governance of an entity but also users of the financial statements who may rely upon the independent auditor's report.

(b) **Other Ethical Requirements** The auditor is subject to relevant ethical requirements relating to financial statement audit engagements. These consist of the AICPA Code of Professional Conduct together with rules of state boards of accountancy and applicable regulatory agencies that are more restrictive.

(2) **Professional Skepticism** The auditor should plan and perform an audit with professional skepticism, recognizing that circumstances may exist that cause the financial statements to be materially misstated.

Professional skepticism is necessary to the critical assessment of audit evidence. This includes questioning contradictory audit evidence and the reliability of documents and responses to inquiries and other information obtained from management and those charged with governance. (The auditor neither assumes that management is dishonest nor assumes unquestioned honesty.) The auditor may accept records and documents as genuine unless the auditor has reason to believe the contrary; however, the auditor is required to consider the reliability of information to be used as audit evidence. For example, if conditions identified during the audit cause the auditor to believe that a document may not be authentic or that terms in a document may have been falsified, US GAAS require that the auditor investigate further and determine what modifications or additions to audit procedures required by US GAAS are necessary to resolve the matter.

(3) **Professional Judgment** The exercise of professional judgment is essential throughout the audit. This is because interpretation of relevant ethical requirements and US GAAS and the informed decisions required throughout the audit cannot be made without the application of relevant knowledge and experience to the facts and circumstances.

(a) **Consultation** Consultation on difficult or contentious matters during the course of the audit, both within the engagement team and between the engagement team and others at the appropriate level within or outside the firm, assists the auditor in making informed and reasonable judgments.

(b) **Examples of Applicable Decisions** In particular, professional judgment is necessary regarding decisions about the following.

- Materiality and audit risk
- The nature, extent, and timing of audit procedures used to meet the requirements of US GAAS and gather audit evidence
- Evaluating whether sufficient appropriate audit evidence has been obtained, and whether more needs to be done to achieve the objectives of US GAAS and thereby, the overall objectives of the auditor
- The evaluation of management's judgments in applying the entity's AFRF
- The drawing of conclusions based on the audit evidence obtained; for example, assessing the reasonableness of the estimates made by management in preparing the financial statements

(c) **Documentation of Significant Judgments** When such judgment is exercised, it needs to be appropriately documented. The auditor should prepare audit documentation sufficient to enable an experienced auditor, having no previous connection with the audit, to understand the significant professional judgments made in reaching conclusions on significant findings or issues arising during the audit.

(d) **Basis of Evaluation** Professional judgment can be evaluated based on whether the judgment reached reflects a competent application of audit standards and accounting principles and is appropriate in light of, and consistent with, the facts and circumstances that were known to the auditor up to the date of the audit report.

Editor Note: Professional judgment is *not* to be used as the justification for decisions that are not otherwise supported by the facts and circumstances of the engagement or by sufficient appropriate audit evidence.

d. **Compliance With Individual AU Sections** The auditor should comply with all AU sections relevant to the audit.

(1) **Relevance** An AU section is relevant to the audit when it is in effect and the circumstances addressed by it exist.

(2) **Early Application** Unless otherwise stated in the AU section, an auditor is permitted to apply an AU section *before* the specified effective date.

(3) **Organization & Scope of Understanding** The auditor should have an understanding of the entire text of an AU section, including its application and other explanatory material, to understand its objectives and to apply its requirements properly.

The content of each AU section is organized as follows:

(a) **Introduction** This may include, e.g., the purpose and scope of the AU section; its context; and the respective responsibilities of the auditor and others. The effective date of the AU section is included here.

(b) **Objective(s)**

(c) **Definitions** A list of terms defined in the context of the section or an audit of financial statements may be included.

(d) **Requirements**

(e) **Application & Other Explanatory Material** The application and other explanatory material provides further explanation of the requirements and guidance for carrying them out.

(i) **Relevance** This material is relevant to the proper application of the requirements of an AU section.

(ii) **Language** The words *may*, *might*, and *could* are used.

(iii) **Understanding Required** The auditor is required to understand this material; but how it is applied is a matter of professional judgment.

(f) **Exhibits & Appendices** Exhibits and/or appendices, if any, are placed at the end of an AU section.

(4) **Relation to Audit Report** The auditor should *not* represent compliance with US GAAS in the audit report unless the auditor has complied with the requirements of AU 200, *Overall Objectives of the Independent Auditor and the Conduct of an Audit in Accordance With Generally Accepted Auditing Standards*, (the subject of this chapter) and all other relevant AU sections.

(5) **Objectives** Each AU section contains one or more objectives that provide a link between the requirements of that section and the overall objectives of the auditor (see this topic in this chapter).

(a) **Interrelationships Within US GAAS** The AU sections in some cases address general responsibilities and in others address the application of those responsibilities to specific topics. These general responsibilities apply throughout the audit and are not repeated in each AU section. Also, an AU section addressing specific aspects of the audit may expand on how the objectives and requirements of other AU sections are to be applied regarding the subject of that AU section, but does not repeat those objectives and requirements. Thus, in achieving the objective in one AU section, the auditor considers the objectives and requirements of other relevant AU sections.

To achieve the overall objectives, the auditor should use the objectives stated in individual AU sections in planning and performing the audit, considering the interrelationships within US GAAS to do the following.

(i) **Consider Additional Audit Procedures** The auditor should determine whether any audit procedures in addition to those required by individual AU sections are necessary.

Editor Note: The circumstances of audit engagements vary widely and all such circumstances cannot be anticipated in US GAAS—there may be particular matters that require the auditor to perform audit procedures in addition to those required by US GAAS to meet the objectives specified in US GAAS.

(ii) **Evaluate Audit Evidence** The auditor should evaluate whether sufficient appropriate audit evidence has been obtained.

(b) **When Objective Cannot Be Achieved** If an objective in a relevant AU section cannot be achieved, the auditor should evaluate whether this prevents the achievement of the overall audit objectives and thus, the modification of the auditor's opinion or withdrawal from the engagement (when withdrawal is possible under applicable law or regulation).

Editor Note: Failure to achieve an objective represents a significant finding or issue requiring documentation (see chapter 4). This record assists the auditor's evaluation of whether such a failure has prevented the auditor from achieving the overall objectives of the auditor.

(6) **Requirements**

(a) **Relevance** The auditor should comply with each requirement of an AU section unless either of the following circumstances exists.

(i) **Entire Section Irrelevant** The entire AU section is not relevant.

(ii) **Condition for Requirement Does *Not* Exist** The requirement is not relevant because it is conditional and the condition does not exist.

Editor Note: The conditionality of a requirement may either be explicit or implicit.

(b) **Professional Requirements/Responsibilities Defined** US GAAS use the following two categories of professional requirements, identified by specific terms, to describe the degree of responsibility imposed on auditors.

(i) **Unconditional Requirements** The auditor must comply with an unconditional requirement in all cases in which such requirement is relevant. US GAAS use the word *must* to indicate an unconditional requirement.

(ii) **Presumptively Mandatory Requirements** The auditor must comply with a presumptively mandatory requirement in all cases in which such a requirement is relevant except in rare circumstances. US GAAS use the word *should* to indicate a presumptively mandatory requirement.

If an AU section provides that a procedure or action is one that the auditor *should consider*, consideration of the procedure or action is presumptively required. Whether the auditor performs the procedure or action is based upon the outcome of the auditor's consideration and the auditor's professional judgment.

In rare circumstances, the auditor may judge it necessary to depart from a relevant presumptively mandatory requirement. In such circumstances, the auditor should perform alternative audit procedures. The need for the auditor to depart from a relevant presumptively mandatory requirement is expected to arise only when the requirement is for a specific procedure to be performed and, in the specific circumstances of the audit, that procedure would be *ineffective* in achieving the intent of the requirement.

Editor Note: The auditor must document the justification for the departure and how the alternative audit procedure(s) were sufficient.

Exhibit 2 ▸ *Requirements* vs. *Application & Other Explanatory Material* Guidance

	Requirements		Application & Other Explanatory Material
Professional requirement category	Unconditional	Presumptively Mandatory	NA
Nature of guidance	Required, if relevant; departure **not** allowed	Required, if relevant; departure allowed in *rare* circumstances	**Not** required to apply—required to understand; provides guidance for proper application of requirements
Language of guidance	Must	Should	May Might Could

2. **Other Than US GAAS Requirements** In certain audit engagements, the auditor also may be required to comply with other audit requirements in addition to US GAAS.

   a. **Laws & Regulations** US GAAS do *not* override laws or regulations that govern an audit of financial statements.

      In the event that such laws or regulations differ from US GAAS, an audit conducted only in accordance with such laws or regulations will *not*, of course, necessarily comply with US GAAS.

   b. **Other Audit Standards** The auditor may also conduct the audit in accordance with *both* US GAAS and:

      - PCAOB auditing standards
      - International Standards on Auditing
      - *Government Auditing Standards*
      - Auditing standards of a specific jurisdiction or country

      In such cases, in addition to complying with each of the AU sections relevant to the audit, it may be necessary for the auditor to perform additional audit procedures in order to comply with the other auditing standards.

B. Other Guidance Related to US GAAS Audits

1. **Interpretive Publications** Interpretive publications are recommendations on the application of US GAAS in specific circumstances; including engagements for entities in specialized industries. (See the definition of *interpretive publications* in this chapter for additional information.)

   The auditor should be aware of and *consider* applicable interpretive publications in planning and performing an audit.

   Even though their consideration is required and they are issued under the authority of the AICPA's Auditing Standards Board (ASB) after all ASB members have been provided an opportunity to consider and comment on whether the proposed interpretive publication is consistent with US GAAS, interpretive publications are **not** auditing standards.

2. **Other Auditing Publications** Other auditing publications have no authoritative status; however, they may help the auditor understand and apply US GAAS. The auditor is **not** expected to be aware of the full body of other auditing publications. (See the definition of *other auditing publications* in this chapter for additional information.)

   In applying the auditing guidance included in an other auditing publication, the auditor should, exercising professional judgment, assess the relevance and appropriateness of such guidance to the circumstances of the audit. The auditor may presume it is appropriate if published by the AICPA and reviewed by the AICPA Audit and Attest Standards staff. If this is *not* the case, the auditor may consider the degree to which it is recognized as being helpful in understanding and applying US GAAS and the degree to which the issuer or author is recognized as an authority on auditing matters.

Exhibit 3 ▸ Interpretive Publications vs. Other Auditing Publications

	Interpretive Publications	**Other Auditing Publications**
Definition	Recommendations on the application of US GAAS in specific circumstances; include only the list of publications below	Publications other than interpretive publications
Nature	**Not** auditing standards	**No** authoritative status
Requirement	Auditor should be: • aware of and • *consider* applicable interpretive publications in planning and performing an audit.	Auditor should assess the • relevance and • appropriateness to the circumstances of the audit. Auditor is **not** expected to be aware of the full body of other auditing publications.

Publications	*Only* include:
	• Auditing interpretations of US GAAS
	• Exhibits to US GAAS
	• Auditing guidance in:
	  • AICPA Audit & Accounting Guides
	  • AICPA Auditing Statements of Position
		Examples:
		• AICPA publications other than interpretive publications, e.g., Audit Risk Alerts
		• Auditing articles in professional journals
		• Continuing professional education programs and other instructional materials

---

CHAPTER 1—AN AUDIT CONDUCTED IN ACCORDANCE WITH US GAAS

Problem 1-1 MULTIPLE-CHOICE QUESTIONS

Purpose of an Audit

1. According to US GAAS, the auditor's opinion on the financial statements
   a. Assures the future viability of the entity
   b. Addresses whether the financial statements are presented fairly
   c. Evaluates the effectiveness with which management has conducted the affairs of the entity
   d. Evaluates the efficiency with which management has conducted the affairs of the entity (ID: 90057)

2. According to US GAAS, the purpose of an audit of financial statements is to
   a. Provide financial statement users with an opinion on whether the financial statements are presented fairly, in all material respects, in accordance with an applicable financial reporting framework
   b. Provide financial statement users with an opinion on as the effectiveness of the entity's internal control and provide financial statement users with an opinion on whether the financial statements are presented fairly, in all material respects, in accordance with an applicable financial reporting framework
   c. Enhance the degree of confidence that intended users can place in the financial statements
   d. Provide financial statement users with reasonable assurance of the entity's future viability (ID: 90369)

Audit Responsibilities

3. Which of the following statements is correct concerning an auditor's responsibilities regarding financial statements in an audit conducted in accordance with US GAAS?
   a. An auditor may not assist in drafting an entity's financial statements.
   b. The adoption of sound accounting policies is an implicit part of an auditor's responsibilities.
   c. An auditor's responsibility for audited financial statements is confined to the expression of the auditor's opinion.
   d. Making suggestions about an entity's internal control environment that are adopted impairs an auditor's independence. (ID: 7630)

4. An audit in accordance with US GAAS is conducted on the premise that
   a. Users of financial statements understand the inherent limitations of an audit.
   b. Estimated amounts in the financial statements are reasonable.
   c. Management and, when appropriate, those charged with governance have acknowledged certain responsibilities that are fundamental to the conduct of the audit.
   d. Those charged with governance understand their role according to US GAAS. (ID: 90046)

5. Management's acknowledgment of their responsibility for the preparation and fair presentation of the financial statements (part of the premise on which an audit in accordance with US GAAS is conducted), include all of the following **except**
   a. Knowledge of US GAAS related to the financial statements
   b. Inclusion of an adequate description of the applicable financial reporting framework in the financial statements
   c. Identification of the applicable financial reporting framework, in the context of any relevant laws or regulations
   d. The preparation and fair presentation of the financial statements in accordance with the applicable financial reporting framework (ID: 90055)

6. In addition to the opinion on the financial statements, the auditor's responsibilities in an audit in accordance with US GAAS, include all of the following **except**
   a. Having appropriate competence and capabilities to perform the audit and complying with relevant ethical requirements
   b. Other communication and reporting responsibilities regarding matters arising from the audit
   c. Maintaining professional skepticism and exercising professional judgment throughout the planning and performance of the audit
   d. Authentication of documents (ID: 90360)

7. An audit in accordance with US GAAS is conducted on the premise that management and, when appropriate, those charged with governance have certain responsibilities which they acknowledge and understand. Which of the following is the most accurate description of one of these areas of responsibility?
   a. The preparation of the financial statements
   b. The design, implementation, and maintenance of the entity's system of internal control
   c. To provide the auditor with access to all information that is relevant to the financial statements and any additional information that the auditor may request for the purpose of the audit
   d. To provide the auditor with access to persons within the entity that the entity has designated to support the audit (ID: 90362)

8. According to US GAAS, an auditor of an entity's financial statements
   a. May express an opinion either orally or in writing; however, if a written report is not issued, the auditor's findings should be documented
   b. States whether the financial statements are presented fairly, in all material respects, in accordance with US generally accepted accounting principles
   c. Bases the opinion on the financial statements on an evaluation of the evidence obtained and the effectiveness of the entity's internal control
   d. Expresses, in the form of a written report, an opinion or states that an opinion cannot be expressed (ID: 90365)

9. During an audit of financial statements conducted in accordance with US GAAS
   a. A shared responsibility for the financial statements is created between the auditor and the entity.
   b. Responsibilities are imposed by US GAAS on management and those charged with governance.
   c. Laws and regulations that normally govern the responsibilities of management or those charged with governance can be overridden by US GAAS.
   d. Management and, when appropriate, those charged with governance are required to acknowledge certain responsibilities that are fundamental to the conduct of the audit. (ID: 90370)

Overall Objectives

10. The overall objectives of the auditor, in conducting an audit of financial statements in accordance with US GAAS, include all of the following **except**
    a. To report on the financial statements
    b. To adequately plan the work and properly supervise any assistants
    c. To obtain reasonable assurance about whether the financial statements as a whole are free from material misstatement, whether due to fraud or error
    d. To communicate as required by GAAS, in accordance with the auditor's findings (ID: 89475)

11. As the basis for the auditor's opinion, GAAS require the auditor to obtain reasonable assurance about whether the financial statements as a whole are free from material misstatement, whether due to fraud or error. All of the following are true about the concept of reasonable assurance **except**
    a. It is obtained when the auditor has gathered sufficient appropriate audit evidence to reduce audit risk to an acceptably moderate level.
    b. It is obtained when the auditor has gathered sufficient appropriate audit evidence to reduce audit risk to an acceptably low level.
    c. It is the standard because there are inherent limitations of an audit that result in most of the audit evidence being persuasive rather than conclusive.
    d. It is a high, but not absolute, level of assurance. (ID: 90058)

12. According to US GAAS, in general, misstatements in the financial statements, including omissions, are considered to be material when, individually or in the aggregate,
    a. If uncorrected, would preclude a unmodified opinion on the financial statements.
    b. If uncorrected, would require an adverse opinion on the financial statements.
    c. They could reasonably be expected to influence the economic decisions of users that are taken based on the financial statements.
    d. They are inconsistent with the criteria of the applicable financial reporting framework. (ID: 90059)

13. US GAAS requires the auditor to obtain reasonable assurance that the financial statements as a whole are free from material misstatement. Reasonable assurance, which is a high, rather than absolute, level of assurance is acceptable because
    a. It is generally understood that conclusive evidence is rarely available.
    b. There are inherent limitations of an audit, some of which cannot be cured by further audit procedures.
    c. Auditors are human beings and accordingly, are fallible.
    d. The AICPA has established this as the standard for the profession. (ID: 90353)

Audit Process

14. Generally, when an audit procedure is described as *vouching*
    a. An item included in the financial statements is being tested for completeness by locating its source documentation.
    b. An item included in the financial statements is being tested for occurrence or existence by locating its source documentation.
    c. An event or transaction evidenced by information in source documents is located in the financial statements to verify its existence or occurrence.
    d. An event or transaction evidenced by information in source documents is located in the financial statements to verify their completeness. (ID: 90359)

Fundamental Concepts of an Audit

15. According to US GAAS, to express an opinion, the auditor obtains reasonable assurance about whether the financial statements are free from material misstatement. Obtaining reasonable assurance directly relates to all of the following **except**
    a. Planning the work and properly supervising any assistants
    b. Recognizing that circumstances may exist that cause the financial statements to be materially misstated
    c. Determining and applying appropriate materiality level(s) throughout the audit
    d. Identifying and assessing risks of material misstatement (RMM) (ID: 90363)

16. The auditor is unable to obtain absolute assurance that the financial statements as a whole are free from material misstatement because of the inherent limitations of an audit. According to US GAAS, the principal inherent limitations of an audit arise from all of the following **except**
    a. The nature of financial reporting
    b. The nature of audit procedures
    c. The depth of the auditor's understanding of the entity
    d. The need for the audit to be conducted within a reasonable period of time to achieve a balance between benefit and cost (ID: 90364)

17. According to US GAAS, an entity may prepare its financial statements in accordance with which of the following frameworks?

    I. General-purpose framework
    II. Special-purpose framework

    a. I. only
    b. II. only
    c. Both I. and II.
    d. Neither I. nor II. (ID: 90371)

18. The financial accounting standards (and the organizations that are authorized or recognized to promulgate them) to be used by nonissuers for preparing financial statements in accordance with a general-purpose framework include all of the following **except**
    a. FASB *Accounting Standards Codification*™ (ASC), issued by the Financial Accounting Standards Board (FASB)
    b. Generally Accepted Auditing Standards (GAAS), issued by the American Institute of Certified Public Accountants (AICPA)
    c. International Financial Reporting Standards (IFRS), issued by the International Accounting Standards Board (IASB)
    d. Statements of Federal Financial Accounting Standards (SFFAS), issued by the Federal Accounting Standards Advisory Board (FASAB) (ID: 90372)

19. According to US GAAS, the applicable financial reporting framework adopted by an entity may encompass financial accounting standards promulgated by a standards-setting organization; legislative or regulatory requirements; and/or other sources. These sources may also provide direction on the application of the applicable financial reporting framework. When conflicts in the guidance among these sources exist
    a. The source with the highest authority prevails.
    b. The auditor exercises professional judgment to determine the most appropriate guidance to advocate.
    c. The source that is the most prevalent in the entity's industry should be followed.
    d. Decisions about an entity's applicable financial reporting framework are the responsibility of management and, when appropriate, those charged with governance. (ID: 90373)

US GAAS

20. According to US GAAS, in an audit engagement, an auditor strives to achieve independence in appearance in order to
    a. Serve the public interest
    b. Become independent in fact
    c. Maintain an unbiased mental attitude
    d. Appear to be fair (ID: 20)

21. Because an audit in accordance with US GAAS is influenced by the possibility of materially misstated financial statements, the auditor should conduct the audit with

    a. Objective judgment
    b. Conservative advocacy
    c. Professional responsiveness
    d. Professional skepticism (ID: 213)

22. Which of the following best describes what is meant by the term *US generally accepted auditing standards*?

    a. Procedures to be used to gather evidence to support financial statements
    b. Measures of the audit quality and the objectives to be achieved in an audit
    c. Pronouncements issued by the Auditing Standards Board
    d. Rules acknowledged by the accounting profession because of their universal application (ID: 7485)

23. During an audit conducted in accordance with US GAAS, an auditor should depart from a relevant presumptively mandatory requirement only when

    a. A required specific procedure is conditional and the condition does not exist.
    b. The difficulty, time, or cost of a required specific procedure outweighs the benefit of applying it.
    c. The auditor documents the justification that an alternative procedure is sufficient to achieve the objectives of the required specific procedure.
    d. A required specific procedure would be ineffective in achieving the intent of the requirement. (ID: 89476)

24. Which of the following best describes the *Application and Other Explanatory Material* portion of a US GAAS section?

    a. Although such guidance does not in itself impose a requirement, it is relevant to the proper application of the requirements of a GAAS section. The auditor is required to understand it.
    b. It is explanatory material that provides further explanation and guidance for the professional requirements and is intended to be descriptive rather than imperative. It provides additional information for the auditor to consider.
    c. The auditor should consider applicable explanatory material in planning and performing the audit.
    d. It provides background information on matters addressed by a GAAS section and identifies and describes other procedures or actions relating to the activities of the auditor. (ID: 89477)

25. US GAAS require the auditor to include the justification for a departure from a relevant presumptively mandatory requirement in the audit documentation. What language indicates a presumptively mandatory requirement?

    a. Must
    b. Could
    c. May consider
    d. Should (ID: 90048)

26. According to US GAAS, an auditor is associated with financial information when

    a. The auditor submits to a client or others financial information that the auditor has prepared or assisted in preparing.
    b. The auditor has applied procedures sufficient to permit the auditor to report in accordance with US GAAS.
    c. The auditor has accepted an engagement to report on the financial information in accordance with US GAAS.
    d. The auditor has consented to the use of the auditor's name in a report, document, or written communication containing the financial information. (ID: 90056)

27. According to US GAAS, what is the distinguishing feature of the professional judgment expected of an auditor?
    a. It is exercised based on competencies necessary to achieve reasonable judgments, developed by the auditor through relevant training, knowledge, and experience.
    b. It is based on precedent established in prior audit engagements.
    c. It is achieved by the consensus of the lead auditor and the other auditors on the engagement.
    d. It adheres to the guidelines established by US GAAS; therefore, it does not vary according to the circumstances. (ID: 90060)

28. According to US GAAS, an auditor's professional judgment
    a. Should be documented so that it is sufficient to enable an experienced auditor, having no previous connection with the audit, to understand all professional judgments made
    b. Is not to be used as the justification for decisions that are not otherwise supported by the facts and circumstances of the engagement or by sufficient appropriate audit evidence
    c. Is exercised primarily during the planning and review stages of an audit
    d. Is not used regarding decisions about the nature, extent, and timing of audit procedures used to meet the requirements of GAAS and gather audit evidence, but is relevant to decisions regarding materiality and audit risk (ID: 90061)

29. US GAAS use two categories of professional requirements
    a. Identified as *conditional* and *presumptively mandatory*
    b. Identified as *mandatory* and *presumptively mandatory*
    c. Which, if relevant, require compliance without departure
    d. To describe the degree of responsibility it imposes on auditors (ID: 90361)

30. US GAAS
    a. Address the responsibilities of the auditor that may exist in legislation or regulations
    b. Override laws or regulations that govern an audit of financial statements
    c. Are developed and issued in the form of Statements on Auditing Standards
    d. Are codified into SAS sections (ID: 90366)

31. The auditor may also conduct an audit in accordance with both US GAAS and
    I. Public Company Accounting Oversight Board auditing standards
    II. International Standards on Auditing
    III. *Government Auditing Standards*
    IV. Auditing standards of a specific jurisdiction or country

    a. II. only
    b III. only
    c. II. though IV. only
    d. I. though IV. (ID: 90367)

32. US GAAS are written in the context of
    a. An audit of financial statements by an auditor
    b. An audit of historical financial information by an auditor
    c. An audit in accordance with applicable legislation or regulations by an auditor
    d. An audit in accordance with financial statements of an issuer by an auditor (ID: 90368)

Other Guidance Related to GAAS Audits

33. According to US GAAS, all of the following statements about interpretive publications are true, **except**
    a. Interpretive publications are not auditing standards; they are recommendations on the application of US GAAS in specific circumstances.
    b. An auditor is not required to consider applicable interpretive publications in planning and performing an audit.
    c. Interpretive publications are issued under the authority of the Auditing Standards Board (ASB).
    d. Auditing interpretations of US GAAS are included in the codification of US GAAS, following the related AU section. (ID: 90062)

34. According to US GAAS, interpretive publications include all of the following **except**
    a. Auditing interpretations of US GAAS
    b. Auditing guidance included in AICPA Audit and Accounting Guides
    c. Auditing guidance included in AICPA Statements of Position
    d. Auditing guidance included in AICPA Audit Risk Alerts (ID: 90063)

35. According to US GAAS, all of the following statements about other auditing publications are true, **except**
    a. The auditor is not expected to be aware of the full body of other auditing publications.
    b. In determining whether an other auditing publication is appropriate to the circumstances of the audit, the auditor should first consider the degree to which the issuer or author is recognized as an authority on auditing matters.
    c. In applying the auditing guidance, the auditor should, exercising professional judgment, assess its relevance and appropriateness to the circumstances of the audit.
    d. Other auditing publications have no authoritative status. (ID: 90064)

Problem 1-2 SIMULATION: Basic Concepts of a US GAAS Audit

The items in the table below are definitions of the basic concepts/terms related to a US GAAS audit. For each definition, select from the list provided the concept or term defined.

Definitions	Concept/Term
1. A financial statement assertion that has a reasonable possibility of containing a misstatement or misstatements that would cause the financial statements to be materially misstated.	
2. The degree of responsibility US GAAS imposes on auditors which includes two categories of professional requirements, identified by specific terms.	
3. Information used by the auditor in arriving at the conclusions on which the audit opinion is based.	
4. The risk that the auditor expresses an inappropriate audit opinion when the financial statements are materially misstated.	
5. The financial reporting framework adopted by management and, when appropriate, those charged with governance in the preparation and fair presentation of the financial statements that is acceptable in view of the nature of the entity and the objective of the financial statements, or that is required by law or regulation.	
6. The persons or organizations with responsibility for overseeing the strategic direction of the entity and the obligations related to the accountability of the entity.	
7. A financial reporting framework that requires compliance with its requirements and acknowledges either that (a) departures from these requirements may be necessary or (b) disclosures in addition to those required may be needed.	
8. The risk that the procedures performed by the auditor will not detect a misstatement that exists and that could be material, either individually or when aggregated with other misstatements.	
9. Except in rare circumstances, an auditor must comply with this category of requirement when it is relevant; such requirements use the word *should*.	
10. The measure of the quantity of audit evidence.	
11. Representations by management, explicit or otherwise, that are embodied in the financial statements as used by the auditor to consider the different types of potential misstatements that may occur.	
12. These consist of auditing interpretations of US GAAS, exhibits to US GAAS, auditing guidance included in AICPA Audit and Accounting Guides, and AICPA Auditing Statements of Position; they are *not* US GAAS.	
13. A difference between the amount, classification, presentation, or disclosure of a reported financial statement item and the amount, classification, presentation, or disclosure that is required for the item to be presented fairly in accordance with the applicable financial reporting framework.	
14. The risk that the financial statements are materially misstated prior to the audit.	
15. A structured representation of historical financial information, including related notes, intended to communicate an entity's economic resources and obligations at a point in time or the changes therein for a period of time in accordance with a financial reporting framework.	
16. The person(s) with executive responsibility for the conduct of the entity's operations.	

Problem 1-2 SIMULATION: Basic Concepts of a US GAAS Audit (contd.)

Definitions	Concept/Term
17. A financial reporting framework designed to meet the common financial information needs of a wide range of users.	
18. The acknowledgment by management and, when appropriate, those charged with governance that they understand they have certain responsibilities that are fundamental to the conduct of an audit in accordance with US GAAS.	
19. An attitude that includes a questioning mind, being alert to conditions that may indicate possible misstatement due to fraud or error, and a critical assessment of audit evidence.	
20. The measure of the quality of audit evidence, i.e., its relevance and reliability in providing support for the conclusions on which the auditor's opinion is based.	
21. The susceptibility of an assertion about a class of transaction, account balance, or disclosure to a misstatement that could be material, either individually or when aggregated with other misstatements, before consideration of any related controls.	
22. A set of criteria used to determine measurement, recognition, presentation, and disclosure of all material items appearing in the financial statements.	
23. In the context of an audit of financial statements, a high, but not absolute, level of assurance.	
24. Information expressed in financial terms regarding a particular entity, derived primarily from that entity's accounting system, about economic events occurring in past time periods or about economic conditions or circumstances at points in time in the past.	
25. Publications other than interpretive publications.	
26. An auditor must comply with this category of requirement when it is relevant; such requirements use the word *must*.	
27. The application of relevant training, knowledge, and experience, within the context provided by auditing, accounting, and ethical standards, in making informed decisions about the courses of action that are appropriate in the circumstances of the audit engagement.	
28. A financial reporting framework, other than US GAAP, which is a cash, tax, regulatory, contractual, or an other basis of accounting.	
29. The risk that a misstatement that could occur in an assertion about a class of transaction, account balance, or disclosure and that could be material, either individually or when aggregated with other misstatements, will not be prevented, or detected and corrected, on a timely basis by the entity's internal control.	
30. These prevent an auditor from obtaining absolute assurance that the financial statements as a whole are free from material misstatement.	

(ID: 90358)

Problem 1-2 SIMULATION: Basic Concepts of a US GAAS Audit (contd.)

Selection List of Concepts/Terms

A.	Applicable financial reporting framework	P.	Financial statements
B.	Financial reporting framework	Q.	Historical financial information
C.	Fair presentation framework	R.	Interpretive publications
D.	General-purpose framework	S.	Management
E.	Special-purpose framework	T.	Those charged with governance
F.	Assertions	U.	Other auditing publications
G.	Relevant assertion	V.	Premise on which an audit is conducted
H.	Audit evidence	W.	Professional judgment
I.	Sufficiency of audit evidence	X.	Professional responsibilities
J.	Appropriateness of audit evidence	Y	Unconditional requirements
K.	Audit risk	Z.	Presumptively mandatory requirements
L.	Detection risk	AA.	Professional skepticism
M.	Risk of material misstatement	BB.	Reasonable assurance
N.	Inherent risk	CC.	Inherent limitations of an audit
O.	Control risk	DD.	Misstatement

Problem 1-3 SIMULATION: Research

Which citation in the professional standards provides guidance regarding when an AU section is relevant to the audit?

Enter your response in the answer fields below.

Editor Note: See the link on the *For Candidates* page of the exam section of the AICPA's website (aicpa.org/BECOMEACPA/CPAEXAM/FORCANDIDATES/Pages/ForCandidates.aspx) to take the sample test which includes a research question in the simulation testlet that has guidance on correctly structuring your response.

[ ] § [ ] . [ ] (ID: 90045)

Editor Note:

- If you have your Notice to Schedule for the exam, you can visit the website (aicpa.org/becomeacpa/cpaexam/forcandidates/howtoprepare/pages/literature.aspx) of the American Institute of Certified Public Accountants (AICPA) to get a *free* six-month subscription to online access to the professional [authoritative] literature used on the AUD exam; however, they caution candidates that **the interface used by their online package is *not* exactly the same as that used in the exam**. Candidates must also review the tutorial and take the AUD sample test provided because the sample test reflects the functionality and interfaces used in the actual exam.
- **It is very important for you to utilize the AICPA's materials (tutorial, sample test, and authoritative literature subscription) to prepare for the exam's research questions. See appendix C in this textbook for more information on research questions.**
- If you are enrolled in one of our AUD online courses, please note that some of the questions included in our textbook are **not** included in our online course and vice versa. The authoritative literature provided for answering our online research questions may **not** include sections covered by the research questions that *only* appear in this textbook. (The authoritative literature provided in our AUD online courses is only a portion of the actual databases maintained by the standard-setting organizations. Our purpose in providing this was not to duplicate their databases (which would be cost prohibitive), but rather to provide a tool for candidates to use in answering research questions in our online courses.)

Solution 1-1 MULTIPLE-CHOICE ANSWERS

1. (b) The auditor's opinion on the financial statements addresses whether they are presented fairly, in all material respects, in accordance with the applicable financial reporting framework. Such an opinion is common to all audits of financial statements and enhances the degree of confidence that intended users can place on the financial statements. (The purpose of an audit is to provide financial statement users with an opinion.) Regarding incorrect answers a., c., and d., the auditor's opinion does *not* assure, for example, the future viability of the entity nor the efficiency or effectiveness with which management has conducted the affairs of the entity. (ID: 90057)

2. (a) According to US GAAS, the purpose of an audit of financial statements is to provide financial statement users with an opinion on whether the financial statements are presented fairly, in all material respects, in accordance with an applicable financial reporting framework. Regarding incorrect answer b., according to US GAAS, the purpose of an audit of financial statements is *not* to provide financial statement users with an opinion on as the effectiveness of the entity's internal control. (The audit includes consideration of internal control over financial reporting in order to design audit procedures that are appropriate in the circumstances, but not for the purpose of expressing an opinion on the effectiveness of internal control.) Regarding incorrect answer c., such an opinion on the financial statements does enhance the degree of confidence that intended users can place in the financial statements; however, providing an opinion is the purpose of an audit of financial statements. Regarding incorrect answer d., an audit and the resulting opinion does *not* assure the future viability of the entity nor the efficiency or effectiveness with which management has conducted the affairs of the entity. (ID: 90369)

3. (c) The auditor's responsibility for the financial statements audited is confined to the expression of an opinion on them. Regarding incorrect answer a., the auditor may make suggestions about the form or content of the financial statements or assist management by drafting them, in whole or in part, based on information from management during the performance of the audit; however, the financial statements are management's responsibility. Regarding incorrect answer b., management, not the auditor, is responsible for adopting sound accounting policies. (Management's responsibility for the preparation and fair presentation of the financial statements require management to select and apply appropriate accounting policies.) Regarding incorrect answer d., making suggestions about an entity's internal control environment that are adopted does *not* impair an auditor's independence. (ID: 7630)

4. (c) An audit in accordance with US GAAS is conducted on the premise that management and, when appropriate, those charged with governance have acknowledged [and understand] certain responsibilities that are fundamental to the conduct of the audit, i.e., responsibility (1) for the preparation and fair presentation of the financial statements in accordance with the applicable financial reporting framework; (2) for the design, implementation, and maintenance of internal control relevant to the preparation and fair presentation of financial statements that are free from material misstatement, whether due to fraud or error; and (3) to provide the auditor with access to all information of which management and, when appropriate, those charged with governance are aware that is relevant to the preparation and fair presentation of the financial statements, such as records, documentation, and other matters; additional information that the auditor may request from management and, when appropriate, those charged with governance for the purpose of the audit; and unrestricted access to persons within the entity from whom the auditor determines it necessary to obtain audit evidence. Editor Note: Because of the significance of the premise to the conduct of an audit, the auditor is required to obtain the agreement of management and, when appropriate, those charged with governance, that they acknowledge and understand that they have these responsibilities *as a precondition for accepting the audit engagement*. Regarding incorrect answer a., users of financial statements should be expected to understand some of the inherent limitations of an audit, but not all of the limitations; but more important, an audit is *not* conducted on any premise based on users' understanding. Regarding incorrect answer b., the acknowledgment by management of their responsibility for the fair presentation of the financial statements includes the responsibility for making accounting estimates that are reasonable, but the auditor does not accept that the estimates *are* reasonable as a premise for the audit. Regarding incorrect answer d., US GAAS does not impose responsibilities on management or those charged with governance nor does it override laws and regulations that govern their responsibilities; thus, their roles are not dictated by US GAAS. (ID: 90046)

5. (a) Management's knowledge of GAAS related to the financial statements is *not* part of the premise on which an audit conducted according to GAAS is based. The other answers cover the components of management's responsibility for the preparation and fair presentation of the financial statements. Answer d., the preparation and fair presentation of the financial statements in accordance with the applicable financial reporting framework, requires management to exercise judgment in making accounting estimates that are reasonable in the circumstances, as well as in selecting and applying appropriate accounting policies. These judgments are made in the context of the applicable financial reporting framework. Editor Note: Management's acknowledgment of their responsibility for the preparation and fair presentation of the financial statements is only part of the premise, relating to the responsibilities of management and, when appropriate, those charged with governance, on which an audit is conducted. The premise also includes their responsibilities related to internal control as well as their support of the audit by providing access to information and persons. (ID: 90055)

6. (d) The auditor is neither trained as nor expected to be an expert in the authentication of documents. All of the other answer alternatives are true. Regarding answer b., these other communication and reporting responsibilities may be to users, management, those charged with governance, or parties outside the entity. These responsibilities may be established by GAAS or by applicable law or regulation. (ID: 90360)

7. (c) Management and, when appropriate, those charged with governance, have the responsibility to provide the auditor with access to all information that is relevant to the preparation and fair presentation of the financial statements such as records, documentation, and other matters; and any additional information that the auditor may request for the purpose of the audit. Regarding incorrect answer a., it is not stringent enough to meet the requirements of the premise on which a GAAS audit is conducted. Management and, when appropriate, those charged with governance have the responsibility for the preparation *and fair presentation* of the financial statements *in accordance with the applicable financial reporting framework*. Regarding incorrect answer b., it is broader than required by the premise. The auditor is only concerned with the design, implementation, and maintenance of the entity's internal control that is relevant to the preparation and fair presentation of financial statements that are free from material misstatement, whether due to fraud or error. Regarding incorrect answer d., the premise requires that the auditor be provided with *unrestricted* access to persons within the entity from whom the auditor determines it necessary to obtain audit evidence; not just those designated by the entity to support the audit. (ID: 90362)

8. (d) According to GAAS, an auditor of an entity's financial statements expresses, in the form of a written report, an opinion or states that an opinion cannot be expressed (a disclaimer of opinion). Regarding incorrect answer a., the auditor's opinion or a statement that an opinion cannot be expressed is expressed in a *written* report. Regarding incorrect answer b., it is only true if the applicable financial reporting framework is US GAAP; thus, this is not the best answer. Regarding incorrect answer c., the auditor does base the opinion on an evaluation of the evidence obtained; however, the opinion on the financial statements is *not* based on the effectiveness of the entity's internal control. The auditor considers the entity's internal control over financial reporting in order to design audit procedures that are appropriate in the circumstances. (ID: 90365)

9. (d) During an audit of financial statements conducted in accordance with US GAAS, management and, when appropriate, those charged with governance are required to acknowledge certain responsibilities that are fundamental to the conduct of the audit. Regarding incorrect answer a., the audit of the financial statements does *not* relieve management or those charged with governance, in whole or in part, of their responsibilities for the financial statements. The financial statements are those of the entity, prepared and presented by management of the entity with oversight from those charged with governance. Regarding incorrect answers b. and c., US GAAS do *not* impose responsibilities on management or those charged with governance and do *not* override laws and regulations that govern their responsibilities. However, an audit in accordance with GAAS is conducted on the premise that management and, when appropriate, those charged with governance have acknowledged certain responsibilities that are fundamental to the conduct of the audit. (ID: 90370)

10. (b) To adequately plan the work and properly supervise any assistants is *not* part of the overall objectives of the auditor. The overall objectives of the auditor, in conducting an audit of financial statements, are to (1) obtain reasonable assurance about whether the financial statements as a whole are free from material misstatement, whether due to fraud or error, thereby enabling the auditor to express an opinion on whether the financial statements are presented fairly, in all material respects, in accordance with an applicable financial

reporting framework; and (2) report on the financial statements, and communicate as required by GAAS, in accordance with the auditor's findings. (ID: 89475)

11. (a) Answer a. is incorrect because reasonable assurance is obtained when the auditor has gathered sufficient appropriate audit evidence to reduce audit risk to an acceptably low (not moderate) level. (ID: 90058)

12. (c) In general, misstatements, including omissions, are considered to be material if, individually or in the aggregate, they could reasonably be expected to influence the economic decisions of users that are taken based on the financial statements. The concept of materiality is applied by the auditor when both planning and performing the audit; and in evaluating the effect of identified misstatements on the audit and uncorrected misstatements, if any, on the financial statements. Judgments about materiality are made in light of surrounding circumstances and involve both qualitative and quantitative considerations. These judgments are affected by the auditor's perception of the financial information needs of users of the financial statements and by the size and/or nature of a misstatement. Regarding incorrect answer d., it does not reflect the comprehensive nature of the considerations involved described in the preceding explanation of the correct answer. Regarding incorrect answers a. and b., they are not true because GAAS does not preclude nor require a type of opinion based solely on materiality—*all* modified opinions are due to matters that are judged by the auditor to be material. (ID: 90059)

13. (b) Reasonable assurance is acceptable because there are inherent limitations of an audit, some of which cannot be cured by further audit procedures. These inherent limitations result in most of the audit evidence, on which the auditor draws conclusions and bases the auditor's opinion, being persuasive rather than conclusive. Regarding incorrect answer a., although most of the audit evidence is persuasive rather than conclusive, it is *not* true that conclusive evidence is rarely available. Regarding incorrect answer c., the fallibility of humans [auditors] can increase detection risk and be considered part of the inherent limitations of an audit; however, it is not as complete an answer as answer c., i.e., it is not the best answer of the alternatives. Regarding answer d., although this is true, it is clearly not the best answer. It does not explain why reasonable assurance is acceptable. (ID: 90353)

14. (b) Generally, if an audit procedure is described as *vouching,* an item included in the financial statements is being tested to find the supporting proof [locating its source documentation] that the recorded amount is valid; thus, the procedure is testing for occurrence or existence. Regarding incorrect answer a., generally, *completeness* is tested by tracing an event or transaction from a source document to the financial statements to verify its inclusion in the financial statements. The starting point for the auditor is the source documentation, not the financial statements or a record in the accounting system. Regarding incorrect answer c., locating an event or transaction in the financial statements evidenced by source documents provides proof of the *completeness* of the financial statements—its existence is not in question per the source documents the auditor uses as a starting point. Regarding incorrect answer d., generally, locating an event or transaction evidenced by information in source documents in the financial statements to verify their completeness is described as *tracing*, not vouching. (ID: 90359)

15. (b) Answer b., recognizing that circumstances may exist that cause the financial statements to be materially misstated, is *not* one of the actions the auditor takes, according to GAAS, to obtain reasonable assurance; it is the reason that an auditor should plan and perform an audit with professional skepticism. The other answer alternatives are three of the four actions the auditor takes, according to GAAS, to obtain reasonable assurance about whether the financial statements as a whole are free from material misstatement, whether due to fraud or error. The remaining action the auditor takes to obtain reasonable assurance is obtaining sufficient appropriate audit evidence [about whether material misstatements exist, through designing and implementing appropriate responses to the assessed risks]. (ID: 90363)

16. (c) Answer c., the depth of the auditor's understanding of the entity, is *not* the source of an inherent limitation of an audit. This is controlled by the auditor—the auditor is required to exercise professional judgment to determine the extent of the required understanding of the entity. The principal inherent limitations of an audit arise from the other answer alternatives. Editor Note: See expanded explanations of the following in the text under the definition of *reasonable assurance* regarding the sources of the inherent limitations of an audit. Regarding answer a., the nature of financial reporting, some financial statement items are subject to an inherent level of variability that cannot be eliminated by the application of additional auditing procedures. For example,

this is often the case with respect to certain accounting estimates that are dependent on predictions of future events. Regarding answer b., the nature of audit procedures, there are practical and legal limitations on the auditor's ability to obtain audit evidence. For example, there is the possibility that management or others may not provide, intentionally or unintentionally, complete information. Regarding answer d., there is an expectation by users of financial statements that the auditor will achieve a balance between benefit and cost, recognizing that it is impracticable to address all information that may exist or to pursue every matter exhaustively on the assumption that information is fraudulent or erroneous until proven otherwise. (ID: 90364)

17. (c) Both—the financial statements may be prepared in accordance with either a general-purpose framework (a financial reporting framework designed to meet the common financial information needs of a wide range of users); or a special-purpose framework (a financial reporting framework, other than GAAP, which is a cash, tax, regulatory, contractual; or an other basis of accounting). The cash basis, tax basis, regulatory basis, and other basis of accounting (all of these, *except for* the contractual basis) are commonly referred to as *other comprehensive bases of accounting* (OCBOA). (ID: 90371)

18. (b) GAAS, issued by the AICPA are *auditing* standards; not accounting standards. The financial accounting standards (and the recognized organizations that issue them) used to prepare financial statements in accordance with a *general-purpose framework* (a financial reporting framework designed to meet the common financial information needs of a wide range of users) are: answer a., FASB *Accounting Standards Codification*™ (ASC), issued by the Financial Accounting Standards Board (FASB); answer c., International Financial Reporting Standards (IFRS), issued by the International Accounting Standards Board (IASB); answer d., Statements of Federal Financial Accounting Standards (SFFAS), issued by the Federal Accounting Standards Advisory Board (FASAB) for US federal government entities; and Statements of Governmental Accounting Standards (GASB Statements), issued by the Governmental Accounting Standards Board (GASB) for US state and local government entities (not included as an answer alternative in this question). (ID: 90372)

19. (a) When conflicts in the guidance among the sources of an entity's applicable financial reporting framework exist, the source with the highest authority prevails. Regarding incorrect answer b., it is a true statement, but it is not the best answer. Note that professional judgment is *not* to be used as the justification for decisions that are not otherwise supported by the facts and circumstances of the engagement or by sufficient appropriate audit evidence. Regarding incorrect answer c., prevalent general and industry practices may be considered, but they would only prevail in a conflict if they were the source with the highest authority available on a particular issue. Regarding incorrect answer d., it is a true statement, but it is not the best answer, i.e., it is not responsive to the question. As for the statement, management and, when appropriate, those charged with governance, have responsibility for the preparation and fair presentation of the financial statements in accordance with the applicable financial reporting framework. And the auditor evaluates management's judgments in applying the entity's applicable financial reporting framework. (ID: 90373)

20. (a) In an audit engagement, it is in the public interest and, therefore, required, that the auditor be independent of the entity subject to the audit. Regarding incorrect answer b., the concept of independence refers to both independence in fact and independence in appearance. Independence in appearance is needed to maintain public confidence in the profession. Incorrect answer b. is nonsensical, i.e., independence in appearance does not create independence in fact. Regarding incorrect answers c. and d., [objectivity] is related to independence, but neither is the best answer for the manner in which this question is worded. Editor Note: The auditor's independence from the entity safeguards the auditor's ability to form an audit opinion without being affected by influences that might compromise that opinion. It enhances the auditor's ability to act with integrity, to be objective, and to maintain an attitude of professional skepticism. Independence implies an impartiality that recognizes an obligation to be fair not only to management and those charged with governance of an entity, but also users of the financial statements who may rely upon the independent auditor's report. The auditor must be independent of the entity when performing an engagement in accordance with GAAS unless (1) GAAS provides otherwise or (2) the auditor is required by law or regulation to accept the engagement and report on the financial statements. When the auditor is not independent and neither (1) nor (2) are applicable, the auditor is precluded from issuing a report under GAAS. (ID: 20)

21. (d) Professional skepticism is an attitude that includes a questioning mind, being alert to conditions that may indicate possible misstatement due to fraud (the auditor neither assumes that management is dishonest nor assumes unquestioned honesty) or error, and a critical assessment of audit evidence. The other answer alternatives are *not* GAAS terms. Editor Note: The critical assessment of audit evidence includes questioning contradictory audit evidence and the reliability of documents and responses to inquiries and other information obtained from management and those charged with governance. It also includes consideration of the sufficiency and appropriateness of audit evidence obtained in light of the circumstances—circumstances may suggest the need for audit procedures in addition to those required by GAAS. Maintaining professional skepticism throughout the audit reduces the risks of, e.g., overlooking unusual circumstances; over-generalizing when drawing conclusions from audit observations; and using inappropriate assumptions in determining the nature, extent, and timing of the audit procedures and evaluating the results. (ID: 213)

22. (b) Generally accepted auditing standards provide a measure of audit quality and the objectives to be achieved in an audit. Regarding incorrect answer a., auditing *procedures* are the acts performed during an audit to meet the requirements of generally accepted auditing *standards* and gather audit evidence. Regarding incorrect answer c., GAAS are issued by the AICPA's Auditing Standards Board, but that does not describe what is meant by the term. Regarding incorrect answer d., GAAS must be followed by CPAs per the AICPA's Code of Professional Conduct, not because they are rules acknowledged by the accounting profession due to their universal application. (ID: 7485)

23. (d) The need for the auditor to depart from a relevant presumptively mandatory requirement is expected to arise only when the requirement is for a specific procedure to be performed and, in the specific circumstances of the audit, that procedure would be ineffective in achieving the intent of the requirement. In such rare circumstances, the auditor should perform alternative audit procedures to achieve the intent of that requirement. Regarding incorrect answer a., GAAS do not call for compliance with a requirement that is *not* relevant in the circumstances of the audit. The question states that the specific requirement is relevant, so a description of the criteria for an irrelevant requirement (incorrect answer a.) is not responsive to the question. Editor Note: The auditor should comply with each requirement of a section unless, in the circumstances of the audit, the entire section is not relevant; or the requirement is not relevant because it is conditional and the condition does not exist. Regarding incorrect answer b., the need for the audit to be conducted within a reasonable period of time so as to achieve a balance between benefit and cost is one of the factors that create inherent limitations in an audit. However, the matter of difficulty, time, or cost involved is not in itself a valid basis for the auditor to omit an audit procedure for which there is no alternative or to be satisfied with audit evidence that is less than persuasive. Regarding incorrect answer c., the auditor must document the justification for the departure and how the alternative audit procedure(s) performed were sufficient to achieve the intent of that requirement; however, this documentation requirement is *not* the criteria for a justified departure from a relevant presumptively mandatory requirement. (ID: 89476)

24. (a) Although the *Application and Other Explanatory Material* portion does not in itself impose a requirement, it is relevant to the proper application of the requirements of a GAAS section. Editor Note: The auditor is required to understand the entire text of a GAAS section, including its *Application and Other Explanatory Material* portion; how the auditor applies the guidance depends on the exercise of professional judgment in the circumstances consistent with the objective of the section. The *Application and Other Explanatory Material* portion provides further explanation of the requirements of a section and guidance for carrying them out, when needed. In particular, it may explain more precisely what a requirement means or is intended to cover. It may also include examples of procedures that may be appropriate in the circumstances. The words *may*, *might*, and *could* are used to describe these actions and procedures. Regarding incorrect answers b. and d., they are true statements, but neither is the best answer. Regarding incorrect answer c., it is the guidance on the use of interpretive publications; not the *Application and Other Explanatory Material* portion of a GAAS section. The auditor should consider applicable interpretive publications in planning and performing the audit. Interpretive publications are *not* auditing standards. They are recommendations on the application of GAAS in specific circumstances. (ID: 89477)

25. (d) GAAS use the word *should* to indicate a presumptively mandatory requirement. If GAAS include a procedure that the auditor *should consider*, the consideration of the procedure is a presumptively mandatory requirement, while carrying out the procedure is not. (Whether the auditor performs the procedure is based upon

the outcome of the auditor's consideration and the auditor's professional judgment.) Regarding incorrect answer a., GAAS use the word *must* to indicate an unconditional requirement; not a presumptively mandatory requirement. Regarding incorrect answers b. and c., the words *could, may*, and *might* are used to describe procedures included in the application and other explanatory material of a standard. Although such guidance does not in itself impose a requirement, it is relevant to the proper application of the requirements of that section. Editor Note: The auditor must comply with an unconditional requirement in all cases in which such requirement is relevant. The auditor must comply with a presumptively mandatory requirement in all cases in which such a requirement is relevant except in rare circumstances. *The need for the auditor to depart from a relevant presumptively mandatory requirement is expected to arise only when the requirement is for a specific procedure to be performed and, in the specific circumstances of the audit, that procedure would be* ***ineffective*** *in achieving the intent of the requirement.* If the auditor judges it necessary to make a departure, the auditor should perform alternative audit procedures. The auditor must document the justification for the departure and how the alternative audit procedure(s) were sufficient. (ID: 90048)

26. (b) According to GAAS, an auditor is associated with financial information when the auditor has applied procedures sufficient to permit the auditor to report in accordance with GAAS. Regarding incorrect answer a., Statements on Standards for Accounting and Review Services address the accountant's considerations when the accountant prepares and presents financial statements to the entity or third parties. Regarding incorrect answer c., the criteria is more stringent than accepting an engagement—the auditor is not associated with financial statements until the auditor has applied procedures sufficient to permit the auditor to report in accordance with GAAS. Regarding incorrect answer d., it is part of the superseded guidance for the determination of when an accountant was associated with financial statements. (ID: 90056)

27. (a) The distinguishing feature of professional judgment expected of an auditor is that such judgment is exercised based on competencies necessary to achieve reasonable judgments, developed by the auditor through relevant training, knowledge, and experience. Regarding incorrect answers b. and d., it is part of the nature of professional judgment to vary with the circumstances—its exercise in any particular case is based on the facts and circumstances of the current audit engagement. Regarding incorrect answer c., consultation on difficult or contentious matters during the course of the audit, both within the engagement team and between the engagement team and others at the appropriate level within or outside the firm, assists the auditor in making informed and reasonable judgments. However, a CPA's professional judgment should *not* be replaced by a consensus—quality control procedures should be followed to resolve differences of opinion. (ID: 90060)

28. (b) Professional judgment is *not* to be used as the justification for decisions that are not otherwise supported by the facts and circumstances of the engagement or by sufficient appropriate audit evidence. Regarding incorrect answer a., it would be true if it stated that the significant, not *all*, professional judgments made should be documented. Regarding incorrect answer c., professional judgment needs to be exercised throughout (in planning and performing) the audit; not just during the planning and review stages. Regarding incorrect answer d., all of the matters mentioned involve professional judgment. Other such decisions which, in particular, require the exercise of professional judgment include evaluating whether sufficient appropriate audit evidence has been obtained and whether more needs to be done to achieve the objectives of GAAS and thereby, the overall objectives of the auditor; the evaluation of management's judgments in applying the entity's applicable financial reporting framework; and the drawing of conclusions based on the audit evidence obtained, e.g., assessing the reasonableness of the estimates made by management in preparing the financial statements. (ID: 90061)

29. (d) GAAS use two categories of professional requirements, identified by specific terms (unconditional and presumptively mandatory), to describe the degree of responsibility it imposes on auditors. Regarding incorrect answers a. and b., the terms are *unconditional* (not conditional; not mandatory) and *presumptively mandatory.* Regarding incorrect answer c., the auditor must comply with an unconditional requirement in all cases in which such requirement is relevant and with a presumptively mandatory requirement in all cases in which such requirement is relevant **except** in rare circumstances in which the auditor may judge it necessary to depart. (ID: 90361)

30. (c) US GAAS are developed and issued in the form of Statements on Auditing Standards (SAS). The AICPA's Auditing Standards Board develops and issues standards in the form of SAS through a process that

includes deliberation in meetings open to the public, public exposure of proposed SAS, and a formal vote. Regarding incorrect answer a., they do *not* address the responsibilities of the auditor that may exist in legislation, regulation, or otherwise, in connection with, for example, the offering of securities to the public. Regarding incorrect answer b., US GAAS do *not* override laws or regulations that govern an audit of financial statements. (In certain audit engagements, the auditor also may be required to comply with other auditing requirements *in addition to* GAAS.) Regarding incorrect answer d., US GAAS are codified into AU sections; *not* SAS sections. (ID: 90366)

31. (d) The auditor may also conduct an audit in accordance with both US GAAS and all (I. through IV.) of the standards listed in the question. In such cases, in addition to complying with each of the AU sections relevant to the audit, it may be necessary for the auditor to perform additional audit procedures in order to comply with the other auditing standards. (ID: 90367)

32. (a) US GAAS are written in the context of an audit of financial statements by an auditor. Regarding incorrect answer b., US GAAS are to be adapted as necessary in the circumstances when applied to audits of other historical financial information; however, they are written in the context of an audit of financial statements. Regarding incorrect answer c., US GAAS do *not* address the responsibilities of the auditor that may exist in legislation or regulations. Such responsibilities may differ from those established in GAAS. (Accordingly, although the auditor may find aspects of GAAS helpful in such circumstances, it is the responsibility of the auditor to ensure that the audit is conducted in compliance with all relevant legal, regulatory, or professional obligations.) Regarding incorrect answer d., US GAAS are written in the context of an audit in accordance with financial statements of an entity that is a *non*issuer. Audits of issuers are conducted in accordance with auditing standards promulgated by the Public Company Accounting Oversight Board. (ID: 90368)

33. (b) An auditor *is* required to consider [should consider] applicable interpretive publications in planning and performing an audit. The other answer alternatives are all true statements. Editor Note: Regarding answer a., interpretive publications are not auditing standards. They are recommendations on the application of GAAS in specific circumstances, including engagements for entities in specialized industries. Regarding answer c., an interpretive publication is issued under the authority of the ASB after all ASB members have been provided an opportunity to consider and comment on whether it is consistent with GAAS. Regarding answer d., although interpretive publications are *not* auditing standards, auditing interpretations of GAAS, a type of interpretive publication, are included in the codification of GAAS. Auditing interpretations of GAAS immediately follow the related AU section and have been assigned the same section number preceded by the number 9. (Not all AU sections have auditing interpretations of GAAS.) Interpretive publications include: auditing interpretations of GAAS (included in the codification of GAAS following the related AU section); exhibits to GAAS (included in the codification of GAAS following the application and explanatory materials portion of AU sections); and auditing guidance in AICPA Audit and Accounting Guides and AICPA Auditing Statements of Position. (ID: 90062)

34. (d) An AICPA Audit Risk Alert is an example of an *other auditing publication*; not an *interpretive publication*. The other answer alternatives are three of the four types of interpretive publications. The only interpretive publication *not* included among the answer alternatives is exhibits to GAAS. (ID: 90063)

35. (b) Answer b. does **not** describe what is considered *first* when determining if a publication is appropriate. If the publication is relevant, the auditor may presume that it is appropriate if an other auditing publication is published by the AICPA and has been reviewed by the AICPA Audit and Attest Standards staff. The criteria in answer b. for determining whether a publication is appropriate is only applicable when a publication has *not* been reviewed by the AICPA. Only in this case would the auditor consider the degree to which a publication is recognized as being helpful in understanding and applying GAAS and the degree to which the issuer or author is recognized as an authority on auditing matters. All of the other answer alternatives are true statements. Editor Note: Other auditing publications are defined as publications other than interpretive publications. Examples include AICPA auditing publications not defined as interpretive publications; auditing articles in professional journals; textbooks; continuing professional education programs; and other instructional materials. (ID: 90064)

Solution 1-2: SIMULATION ANSWER: Basic Concepts of a US GAAS Audit

The items in the table below are definitions of the basic concepts/terms related to a US GAAS audit. For each definition, select from the list provided the concept or term defined.

Definitions	Concept/Term
1. A financial statement assertion that has a reasonable possibility of containing a misstatement that would cause the financial statements to be materially misstated.	G. Relevant assertion
2. The degree of responsibility US GAAS imposes on auditors which includes two categories of professional requirements, identified by specific terms.	X. Professional responsibilities
3. Information used by the auditor in arriving at the conclusions on which the audit opinion is based.	H. Audit evidence
4. The risk that the auditor expresses an inappropriate audit opinion when the financial statements are materially misstated.	K. Audit risk
5. The financial reporting framework adopted by management and, when appropriate, those charged with governance in the preparation and fair presentation of the financial statements that is acceptable in view of the nature of the entity and the objective of the financial statements, or that is required by law or regulation.	A. Applicable financial reporting framework
6. The persons or organizations with responsibility for overseeing the strategic direction of the entity and the obligations related to the accountability of the entity.	T. Those charged with governance
7. A financial reporting framework that requires compliance with its requirements and acknowledges either that (a) departures from these requirements may be necessary or (b) disclosures in addition to those required may be needed.	C. Fair presentation framework
8. The risk that the procedures performed by the auditor will not detect a misstatement that exists and that could be material, either individually or when aggregated with other misstatements.	L. Detection risk
9. Except in rare circumstances, an auditor must comply with this category of requirement when it is relevant; such requirements use the word *should*.	Z. Presumptively mandatory requirements
10. The measure of the quantity of audit evidence.	I. Sufficiency of audit evidence
11. Representations by management, explicit or otherwise, that are embodied in the financial statements as used by the auditor to consider the different types of potential misstatements that may occur.	F. Assertions
12. These consist of auditing interpretations of US GAAS, exhibits to US GAAS, auditing guidance included in AICPA Audit and Accounting Guides, and AICPA Auditing Statements of Position; they are *not* US GAAS.	R. Interpretive publications
13. A difference between the amount, classification, presentation, or disclosure of a reported financial statement item and the amount, classification, presentation, or disclosure that is required for the item to be presented fairly in accordance with the applicable financial reporting framework.	DD. Misstatement

Solution 1-2: SIMULATION ANSWER: Basic Concepts of a US GAAS Audit (contd.)

Definitions	Concept/Term
14. The risk that the financial statements are materially misstated prior to the audit.	M. Risk of material misstatement
15. A structured representation of historical financial information, including related notes, intended to communicate an entity's economic resources and obligations at a point in time or the changes therein for a period of time in accordance with a financial reporting framework.	P. Financial statements
16. The person(s) with executive responsibility for the conduct of the entity's operations.	S. Management
17. A financial reporting framework designed to meet the common financial information needs of a wide range of users.	D. General-purpose framework
18. The acknowledgment by management and, when appropriate, those charged with governance that they understand they have certain responsibilities that are fundamental to the conduct of an audit in accordance with US GAAS.	V. Premise on which an audit is conducted
19. An attitude that includes a questioning mind, being alert to conditions that may indicate possible misstatement due to fraud or error, and a critical assessment of audit evidence.	AA. Professional skepticism
20. The measure of the quality of audit evidence, i.e., its relevance and reliability in providing support for the conclusions on which the auditor's opinion is based.	J. Appropriateness of audit evidence
21. The susceptibility of an assertion about a class of transaction, account balance, or disclosure to a misstatement that could be material, either individually or when aggregated with other misstatements, before consideration of any related controls.	N. Inherent risk
22. A set of criteria used to determine measurement, recognition, presentation, and disclosure of all material items appearing in the financial statements.	B. Financial reporting framework
23. In the context of an audit of financial statements, a high, but not absolute, level of assurance.	BB. Reasonable assurance
24. Information expressed in financial terms regarding a particular entity, derived primarily from that entity's accounting system, about economic events occurring in past time periods or about economic conditions or circumstances at points in time in the past.	Q. Historical financial information
25. Publications other than interpretive publications.	U. Other auditing publications
26. An auditor must comply with this category of requirement when it is relevant; such requirements use the word *must*.	Y. Unconditional requirements
27. The application of relevant training, knowledge, and experience, within the context provided by auditing, accounting, and ethical standards, in making informed decisions about the courses of action that are appropriate in the circumstances of the audit engagement.	W. Professional judgment
28. A financial reporting framework, other than US GAAP, which is a cash, tax, regulatory, contractual, or an other basis of accounting.	E. Special-purpose framework

Solution 1-2: SIMULATION ANSWER: Basic Concepts of a US GAAS Audit (contd.)

29. The risk that a misstatement that could occur in an assertion about a class of transaction, account balance, or disclosure and that could be material, either individually or when aggregated with other misstatements, will not be prevented, or detected and corrected, on a timely basis by the entity's internal control.	O. Control risk
30. These prevent an auditor from obtaining absolute assurance that the financial statements as a whole are free from material misstatement.	CC. Inherent limitations of an audit

(ID: 90358)

Solution 1-3 SIMULATION ANSWER: Research

Which citation in the professional standards provides guidance regarding when an AU section is relevant to the audit?

AU	§	200	.	20	(ID: 90045)

.20

The auditor should comply with all AU sections relevant to the audit. An AU section is relevant to the audit when the AU section is in effect and the circumstances addressed by the AU section exist.

CHAPTER 2

PLANNING

AU Identifier Used for Clarified US GAAS in This Textbook

We have not continued to use the temporary AU-C identifier for the clarified auditing standards issued by the American Institute of Certified Public Accountants (AICPA). In this textbook these standards have an AU identifier.

CHAPTER 2

PLANNING

I. Terms of Audit Engagement (AU 210)

A. Objective

The objective of the auditor is to only accept an audit engagement for a new or existing audit client when certain preconditions are met by the client and there is a mutual understanding of the terms of the engagement.

1. **Preconditions Met** The auditor needs to establish whether certain preconditions (controlled by the client) for an audit are present. (See the definition of *preconditions for an audit* below.)

2. **Common Understanding of Terms** The auditor needs to confirm that a common understanding of the terms of the audit engagement exists between the auditor and management and, when appropriate, those charged with governance.

   Editor Note: The way in which the responsibilities for financial reporting are divided between management and those charged with governance varies; however, generally, management is responsible for execution and those charged with governance have oversight of management. In this text, references to *management* are to be read as *management and, when appropriate, those charged with governance* unless the context suggests otherwise.

B. Definitions

1. **Preconditions for an Audit** Preconditions include the following.

   a. **Acceptable Financial Reporting Framework** Management needs to use an acceptable financial reporting framework in the preparation and fair presentation of the financial statements.

   b. **Acknowledgment by Entity of Premise on Which Audit Conducted** Management needs to agree to the premise on which an audit is conducted.

   Editor Note: In regard to the financial statements:

   - Related to the *premise on which an audit is conducted*, management is responsible for the preparation and fair presentation of the financial statements in accordance with the *applicable* financial reporting framework.
   - Related to the *preconditions for an audit*, the auditor is responsible for determining if the financial reporting framework applied in the preparation of the financial statements is *acceptable*.

2. **Recurring Audit** An audit engagement for an existing audit client for whom the auditor performed the preceding audit

C. Audit Engagement Acceptance

1. Determine Presence of Preconditions for an Audit

a. **Acceptable Financial Reporting Framework** The auditor should determine whether the financial reporting framework is acceptable. Otherwise, management does not have an appropriate basis for the preparation of the financial statements and the auditor does not have suitable criteria for auditing the financial statements.

To make this determination, the auditor *may* consider the following factors.

- The nature of the entity, e.g., whether it is a business enterprise, a governmental entity, or a not-for-profit organization
- The purpose of the financial statements, e.g., whether they are prepared to meet the common financial information needs of a wide range of users, i.e., are general-purpose financial statements
- The nature of the financial statements, e.g., whether the financial statements are a complete set of financial statements or a single financial statement
- Whether law or regulation prescribes a financial reporting framework

b. **Entity's Acknowledgment & Understanding of Its Responsibilities** The auditor should obtain the agreement of management that it acknowledges and understands its responsibility for the following. This is the premise on which an audit is conducted.

(1) **Applicable Financial Reporting Framework (AFRF)** Management is responsible for the preparation and fair presentation of the financial statements in accordance with the AFRF.

Editor Note: An auditor may assist in drafting the financial statements, in whole or in part, based on information provided to the auditor by management during the performance of the audit. *However, the concept of an independent audit requires that the auditor's role does* **not** *involve assuming management's responsibility for the financial statements.*

(2) **Internal Control** Management is responsible for the design, implementation, and maintenance of internal control relevant to the preparation and fair presentation of financial statements that are free from material misstatement, whether due to fraud or error.

Editor Note: Obviously, management is also responsible for aspects of internal control other than those relevant to the preparation and fair presentation of financial statements; however, these are management's responsibilities relevant to the premise on which an audit is conducted.

(3) **Support for Audit** Management has the responsibility to provide the auditor with:

(a) **Financial Statement Information** Access to all information that is relevant to the preparation and fair presentation of the financial statements, such as records, documentation, and other matters

(b) **Additional Information** Additional information the auditor may request for the purpose of the audit

(c) **Unrestricted Access To Persons** Unrestricted access to persons within the entity from whom the auditor determines it necessary to obtain audit evidence

2. ***No* Acceptance If Preconditions *Not* Met** If the preconditions for an audit are not present, the auditor should discuss the matter with management. Unless the auditor is required by law or regulation to do so, the auditor should **not** accept the proposed audit engagement if the preconditions are not met.

3. **Other Factors Affecting Audit Engagement Acceptance**

   a. **If Management-Imposed Scope Limitation Would Result in a Disclaimer of Opinion** Prior to the auditor's acceptance of the engagement, management may impose a scope limitation that would result in a disclaimer of opinion. Whether acceptance of such an audit engagement is permitted depends on whether the entity is required by law or regulation to have an audit and if so, if a disclaimer is allowable.

   (1) **If Audit *Not* Required—Do *Not* Accept Engagement** If prior to the auditor's acceptance of the engagement, management of an entity that is *not* required by law or regulation to have an audit imposes a scope limitation that would result in a disclaimer of opinion, the auditor should **not** accept such a limited engagement as an audit engagement.

   Editor Note: If the scope limitation is imposed by circumstances beyond management's control, the auditor may accept the engagement—this restriction is only applicable when management imposes the scope limitation.

   (2) **If Audit Required & Disclaimer Is Allowed—OK to Accept Engagement** If management of an entity that *is* required by law or regulation to have an audit imposes such a scope limitation and a disclaimer of opinion is acceptable under the applicable law or regulation, the auditor is permitted, but *not* required, to accept the engagement.

   b. **If Audit Report Prescribed by Law or Regulation Would Be Misunderstood** If law or regulation prescribes a specific form (or layout or wording) for the audit report that significantly differs from US GAAS or would cause an auditor to make a statement that the auditor has no basis to make, and if users might misunderstand such a report, the auditor should determine if this can be remedied.

   (1) **OK to Accept Engagement If Allowed to Reword Report or Attach Separate Report** If it is permissible to reword the prescribed form to be in accordance with US GAAS or to attach an appropriately worded separate report and this provides a remedy, the auditor can accept such an engagement.

   (2) **Do *Not* Accept Engagement Unless Required to Do So If Remedy *Not* Possible** If rewording the prescribed form or attaching a separate report is not permitted or would not mitigate the risk of users misunderstanding the report, the auditor should **not** accept the audit engagement unless the auditor is required by law or regulation to do so. In this case, the auditor should not include any reference to the audit having been performed in accordance with US GAAS. Further, the auditor *may* consider including a statement in the audit report that the audit is not conducted in accordance with US GAAS. Even under these conditions, the auditor is nevertheless encouraged to apply US GAAS, including the reporting guidance, to the extent practicable.

c. **Inquiries of Predecessor Auditor About Matters Relevant to Acceptance** Before accepting an engagement for an initial audit, including a reaudit engagement, the auditor should make inquiries of the predecessor auditor about matters that will assist the auditor in deciding whether to accept the engagement. However, the auditor should *not* make such inquiries unless management has authorized it—the auditor should request that management do so.

Editor Note: An auditor may make a proposal for an audit engagement before being granted permission to make inquiries of a predecessor auditor. The auditor may advise management that the auditor's acceptance of the engagement cannot be final until the inquiries have been made and the responses evaluated.

(1) **Nature of Communication With Predecessor Auditor**

(a) **Oral or Written** The communication may be oral or written.

(b) **Possible Inquires** Matters covered by the auditor's inquiry *may* include:

(i) **Management Integrity** Information that might bear on the integrity of management

(ii) **Disagreements** Disagreements with management about accounting policies, auditing procedures, or other similarly significant matters

(iii) **Matters Related to Fraud & Noncompliance** Communications to those charged with governance regarding fraud and noncompliance with laws or regulations by the entity

(iv) **Internal Control Communications** Communications to management and those charged with governance regarding *significant deficiencies* and *material weaknesses* in internal control

(v) **Reason for Change in Auditors** The predecessor auditor's understanding about the reasons for the change of auditors

(c) **Professional Responsibilities**

(i) **Cooperation** The predecessor auditor is expected to respond to the auditor's inquiries promptly and, in the absence of unusual circumstances, fully. Unusual circumstances would include, e.g., pending, threatened, or potential litigation or disciplinary proceedings. If this is the case, the predecessor auditor is expected to clearly state that the response is limited.

(ii) **Confidentiality** Both the auditor and the predecessor auditor are required to hold in confidence information obtained from each other.

(2) **Evaluate Predecessor's Response** The auditor should evaluate the predecessor auditor's response, or consider the implications if the predecessor auditor provides no response or a limited response, in determining whether to accept the engagement.

(3) **If Management Refuses To Authorize Access to Predecessor Auditor** If management refuses to authorize the predecessor auditor to respond, or limits the response, the auditor should inquire about the reasons and consider the implications in deciding whether to accept the engagement.

D. Agreement on Audit Engagement Terms

1. **Parties to Agreement** The auditor should agree upon the terms of the audit engagement with management and/or those charged with governance, as appropriate.

   Editor Note: The roles of management and those charged with governance in agreeing upon the terms of the audit engagement for the entity depend on the governance structure of the entity and relevant law or regulation. *When the agreement on the terms of engagement is only with those charged with governance, the auditor is still required to obtain management's agreement that it acknowledges and understands its responsibilities. Similarly, when a third party has contracted for the audit of the entity's financial statements, agreeing the terms of the audit with management of the entity is necessary in order to establish that the preconditions for an audit are present.*

2. **Document Terms in a Written Agreement or Engagement Letter** The agreed-upon terms of the audit engagement should be documented in an audit engagement letter or other suitable form of written agreement. Both the auditor and the client have an interest in such documentation to help avoid misunderstandings.

   a. **Required Terms** The engagement letter/written agreement should cover:

      (1) **Objective & Scope of the Audit** See chapter 1 of this text or the example of an engagement letter that follows in this chapter.

      (2) **Responsibilities of the Auditor** See chapter 1 of this text or the example of an engagement letter that follows in this chapter.

      (3) **Responsibilities of Management** See chapter 1 of this text or the example of an engagement letter that follows in this chapter.

      (4) **Unavoidable Risk of Material Misstatements Due to Inherent Limitations** A statement should be included that, because of the inherent limitations of an audit together with the inherent limitations of internal control, an unavoidable risk exists that some material misstatements may not be detected, even though the audit is properly planned and performed in accordance with US GAAS.

      (5) **Identification of the AFRF** The AFRF used for the preparation of the financial statements should be identified.

      (6) **Form of Report(s)** Reference should be made to the expected form and content of any reports to be issued by the auditor and a statement that circumstances may arise in which a report may differ from its expected form and content.

      Editor Note: The auditor need *not* describe the type of opinion expected to be expressed.

   b. **Other Matters** In addition to the foregoing required matters, an audit engagement letter *may* make reference to, e.g., the following.

      - Elaboration of the scope of the audit, including reference to applicable legislation; regulations; US GAAS; and ethical and other relevant pronouncements of professional bodies
      - The form of any other communication of the results of the audit
      - Arrangements regarding the planning and performance of the audit, including the composition of the audit team

- The expectation that management will provide written representations
- The agreement of management to make available draft financial statements and any accompanying other information in time to allow the auditor to complete the audit in accordance with the proposed timetable
- The agreement of management to inform the auditor of events occurring or facts discovered subsequent to the date of the financial statements that may affect the financial statements
- The basis on which fees are computed and any billing arrangements
- A request for management to acknowledge receipt of the engagement letter and to agree to the terms of the engagement, as may be evidenced by their signature on the engagement letter

And when relevant, the following points *may* also be included:

- Arrangements concerning the involvement of other auditors and specialists
- Arrangements concerning the involvement of internal auditors and other staff of the entity
- Arrangements to be made with the predecessor auditor, if any, in the case of an initial audit
- Any restriction of the auditor's liability when not prohibited
- Any obligations of the auditor to provide audit documentation to other parties
- Additional services to be provided, such as those relating to regulatory requirements
- A reference to any further agreements between the auditor and the entity

Exhibit 1 ▸ Example of an Audit Engagement Letter for an Audit of General-Purpose Financial Statements Prepared in Accordance With US GAAP

To the appropriate representative of those charged with governance of ABC Company:

* [*The objective and scope of the audit:*]

You have requested that we audit the financial statements of ABC Company, which comprise the balance sheet as of December 31, 20XX, and the related statements of income, changes in stockholders' equity, and cash flows for the year then ended, and the related notes to the financial statements. We are pleased to confirm our acceptance and our understanding of this audit engagement by means of this letter. Our audit will be conducted with the objective of our expressing an opinion on the financial statements.

* [*The responsibilities of the auditor:*]

We will conduct our audit in accordance with auditing standards generally accepted in the United States of America (US GAAS). Those standards require that we plan and perform the audit to obtain reasonable assurance about whether the financial statements are free from material misstatement. An audit involves performing procedures to obtain audit evidence about the amounts and disclosures in the financial statements. The procedures selected depend on the auditor's judgment, including the assessment of the risk of material misstatement of the financial statements, whether due to fraud or error. An audit also includes evaluating the appropriateness of accounting policies used and the reasonableness of significant accounting estimates made by management, as well as evaluating the overall presentation of the financial statements.

Because of the inherent limitations of an audit, together with the inherent limitations of internal control, an unavoidable risk that some material misstatements may not be detected exists, even though the audit is properly planned and performed in accordance with US GAAS.

In making our risk assessments, we consider internal control relevant to the entity's preparation and fair presentation of the financial statements in order to design audit procedures that are appropriate in the circumstances but not for the purpose of expressing an opinion on the effectiveness of the entity's internal control. However, we will communicate to you in writing concerning any significant deficiencies or material weaknesses in internal control relevant to the audit of the financial statements that we have identified during the audit.

* [*The responsibilities of management and identification of the AFRF:*]

Our audit will be conducted on the basis that [*management and, when appropriate, those charged with governance*] acknowledge and understand that they have responsibility

a. for the preparation and fair presentation of the financial statements in accordance with accounting principles generally accepted in the United States of America;
b. for the design, implementation, and maintenance of internal control relevant to the preparation and fair presentation of financial statements that are free from material misstatement, whether due to fraud or error; and
c. to provide us with
    i. access to all information of which [*management*] is aware that is relevant to the preparation and fair presentation of the financial statements such as records, documentation, and other matters;
    ii. additional information that we may request from [*management*] for the purpose of the audit; and
    iii. unrestricted access to persons within the entity from whom we determine it necessary to obtain audit evidence.

As part of our audit process, we will request from [*management and, when appropriate, those charged with governance*], written confirmation concerning representations made to us in connection with the audit.

* [*Other relevant information:*]

[*Insert other information, such as fee arrangements, billings, and other specific terms, as appropriate.*]

Reporting

* [*Reference to the expected form and content of the audit report:*]

We will issue a written report upon completion of our audit of ABC Company's financial statements. Our report will be addressed to the board of directors of ABC Company. We cannot provide assurance that an unmodified opinion will be expressed. Circumstances may arise in which it is necessary for us to modify our opinion, add an emphasis-of-matter or other-matter paragraph(s), or withdraw from the engagement.

We also will issue a written report on [*Insert appropriate reference to other auditors' reports expected to be issued.*] upon completion of our audit.

Please sign and return the attached copy of this letter to indicate your acknowledgment of, and agreement with, the arrangements for our audit of the financial statements including our respective responsibilities.

XYZ & Co.

Acknowledged and agreed on behalf of ABC Company by

____

[*Signed*]

[*Name and Title*]

[*Date*]

* These are included to enhance this illustration by describing the information that follows; they do *not* represent headings or subtitles; or language that needs to be added for particular circumstances.

E. Changes in the Terms of an Audit Engagement

1. **Assessment of Terms of Engagement for Recurring Audits** For recurring audits, the auditor should assess whether circumstances require the terms of the audit engagement to be revised.

   a. **Document Annual Reminder to Client of Terms When No Revisions Are Needed** If the auditor concludes that the terms of the preceding engagement need *not* be revised for the current engagement, the auditor should remind management of the terms of the engagement (orally or in writing), and the reminder should be documented.

   b. **Revision Decision Factors** The following factors or changes *may* make it appropriate to revise the terms of a recurring audit engagement:

      - Any indication that management misunderstands the objective and scope of the audit
      - Any revised or special terms of the audit engagement
      - A change of senior management
      - A significant change in ownership
      - A significant change in the nature or size of the entity's business
      - A change in legal or regulatory requirements
      - A change in the financial reporting framework adopted in the preparation of the financial statements
      - A change in other reporting requirements

c. **Document New Terms in a Written Agreement or Engagement Letter** If the terms are changed, the auditor and management should agree on and document the new terms in an engagement letter or other suitable form of written agreement.

2. **Request for a Change in the Terms of Engagement or a Lower Level of Assurance**

a. **Reasonable Request**

(1) **Examples** A change in circumstances that affects management's requirements or a misunderstanding concerning the nature of the service originally requested may be considered a reasonable basis for requesting a change in the audit engagement.

(2) **Document New Terms in a Written Agreement or Engagement Letter** If the terms of the audit engagement are changed, the auditor and management should agree on and document the new terms in an engagement letter or other suitable form of written agreement.

b. **Unreasonable Request** The auditor should *not* agree to a change of the terms of an audit engagement or to change the audit engagement to a review or other service [lower level of assurance] when no reasonable justification for doing so exists. The auditor should be particularly careful when considering the implications of a scope limitation.

(1) **Example** A change may *not* be considered reasonable if the change appears to relate to information that is incorrect, incomplete, or otherwise unsatisfactory. An example might be when the auditor is unable to obtain sufficient appropriate audit evidence regarding receivables and management asks for the audit engagement to be changed to a review engagement to avoid a qualified opinion or a disclaimer of opinion.

(2) **Required Actions When Client Reneges on Original Engagement** When there is no reasonable justification for a change and the auditor is not permitted by management to continue the original audit engagement, the auditor should take the following actions.

(a) **Withdraw from the Engagement** The auditor should withdraw from the audit engagement when possible under applicable law or regulation.

(b) **Communicate With Those Charged With Governance** The auditor should communicate the circumstances to those charged with governance.

(c) **Determine If Obligation Exists to Communicate with Other Parties** The auditor should determine whether any obligation, legal, contractual, or otherwise, exists to report the circumstances to other parties, such as owners, or regulators.

II. Audit Risk (AU 200 continued)

To obtain reasonable assurance, the auditor should obtain sufficient appropriate audit evidence to reduce audit risk to an acceptably low level which enables the auditor to draw reasonable conclusions on which to base the opinion.

Audit risk is a function of the risk of material misstatement (RMM) and detection risk. The assessment of risks is based on audit procedures to obtain information necessary for that purpose [risk assessment procedures] and evidence obtained throughout the audit. The assessment of risks is a matter of professional judgment, rather than a matter of precise measurement.

A. Risk of Material Misstatement

The RMM is the risk that the financial statements are materially misstated *prior* to the audit.

1. **Levels of RMM** The RMM exist at two levels:

   a. **Overall Financial Statement Level** The RMM at the overall financial statement level refers to those risks that relate pervasively to the financial statements as a whole and potentially affect many assertions.

   b. **Assertion Level** The RMM at the assertion level for classes of transactions, account balances, and disclosures are assessed in order to determine the nature, extent, and timing of further audit procedures necessary to obtain sufficient appropriate audit evidence. This evidence enables the auditor to express an opinion on the financial statements at an acceptably low level of audit risk.

      (1) **Components of RMM at the Assertion Level** At the assertion level, the RMM consists of two components: inherent risk and control risk. Inherent risk and control risk are the entity's risks—they exist independently of the audit.

         (a) **Inherent Risk** Inherent risk is the susceptibility of an assertion about a class of transaction, account balance, or disclosure to a misstatement that could be material, either individually or when aggregated with other misstatements, before consideration of any related controls.

         Inherent risk is higher for some assertions and related classes of transactions, account balances, and disclosures than for others. For example, it may be higher for complex calculations or for accounts consisting of amounts derived from accounting estimates that are subject to significant estimation uncertainty. External circumstances giving rise to business risks may also influence inherent risk. For example, technological developments might make a particular product obsolete, thereby causing inventory to be more susceptible to overstatement. Factors in the entity and its environment that relate to several or all of the classes of transactions, account balances, or disclosures may also influence the inherent risk related to a specific assertion. Such factors may include, e.g., a lack of sufficient working capital to continue operations or a declining industry characterized by a large number of business failures.

         (b) **Control Risk** Control risk is the risk that a misstatement that could occur in an assertion about a class of transaction, account balance, or disclosure and that could be material, either individually or when aggregated with other misstatements, will not be prevented, or detected and corrected, on a timely basis by the entity's internal control.

         Control risk is a function of the effectiveness of the design, implementation, and maintenance of internal control by management to address identified risks relevant to preparation and fair presentation of the entity's financial statements. However, internal control, no matter how well designed and operated, can only reduce, but not eliminate, the RMM in the financial statements because of its inherent limitations. These include, e.g., the possibility of human errors or mistakes, or of controls being circumvented by collusion or inappropriate management override. Accordingly, some control risk will always exist.

(2) **Assessment of RMM at the Assertion Level**

(a) **Separate or Combined Assessment** US GAAS do not ordinarily refer to inherent risk and control risk separately, but rather to a combined assessment of the RMM. However, the auditor *may* make separate or combined assessments of inherent and control risk depending on preferred audit techniques or methodologies and practical considerations.

(b) **Express Assessment Quantitatively Or Nonquantitatively** The assessment of the RMM *may* be expressed in quantitative terms, such as in percentages, or in nonquantitative terms, such as low, medium, or high.

2. **RMM Is Directly Related to Substantive Testing Needed** If the auditor perceives an increase in the RMM, generally, the auditor will do more substantive testing.

B. Detection Risk

Detection risk is the risk that the procedures performed by the auditor to reduce audit risk to an acceptably low level will not detect a misstatement that exists and that could be material, either individually or when aggregated with other misstatements. Detection risk is a function of the effectiveness of an audit procedure and of its application by the auditor.

1. **Level of Detection Risk Accepted Is Auditor's Response to the RMM (Inversely Related to RMM)** Detection risk is managed by the auditor's response to the RMM. For a given level of audit risk, the acceptable level of detection risk bears an inverse relationship to the assessed RMM at the assertion level—the greater the RMM the auditor believes exists, the less the detection risk that can be accepted.

2. **Level of Detection Risk Accepted Is Inversely Related to Substantive Testing Needed** The level of detection risk also, generally, has an inverse relationship with the amount of substantive testing needed. If the auditor decreases the acceptable level of detection risk, more substantive testing *may* be in order. However, the auditor should perform substantive procedures for all relevant assertions related to all material account balances, classes of transactions, and disclosures *regardless of the assessed level of risk.*

Exhibit 2 ▶ Risk Relationships

RMM (Inherent Risk & Control Risk)	Acceptable Level of Detection Risk	Substantive Tests
Increase	Decrease	Increase
Decrease	Increase	Decrease

3. **How the RMM & Detection Risk Differ** Inherent risk and control risk (RMM) differ from detection risk in that they are the entity's risks and exist independently of the audit, whereas detection risk relates to the auditor's procedures and can be altered by adjusting the nature, extent, and timing of substantive procedures. Thus, the auditor assesses inherent risk and control risk (RMM).

III. Planning an Audit (AU 300)

A. Overview

1. **Objective** The objective of the auditor is to plan the audit so that it will be managed and performed in an effective and efficient manner.

2. **Audit Engagement Partner & Team Involvement** The engagement partner and other key members of the engagement team should be involved in planning the audit, including planning and participating in the discussion among team members.

    a. **Delegation** The engagement partner may delegate portions of the planning and supervision of the audit to other firm personnel.

    b. **Audit Team Discussions Required by US GAAS** US GAAS require a discussion among the audit team on the following. These discussions (covered later in this chapter) may be combined.

        (1) **Understanding the Entity & Its Environment and Assessing the RMM** A discussion is required about the susceptibility of the entity's financial statements to material misstatement.

        (2) **Consideration of Fraud** A discussion is required about the RMM due to fraud.

3. **Factors That Influence the Nature & Extent of Planning** The nature and extent of planning activities will vary according to the following.

    - The size and complexity of the entity
    - The auditor's previous experience with the entity
    - Changes in circumstances that occur during the audit

4. **The Role & Timing of Planning** Planning involves establishing the overall audit strategy and developing an audit plan.

    a. **Benefits of Planning** Adequate planning benefits the audit in several ways, including the following:

        - Helping the auditor identify and devote appropriate attention to important areas
        - Helping the auditor identify and resolve potential problems on a timely basis
        - Assisting in the selection of team members with appropriate capabilities and competence to respond to anticipated risks and allocating their responsibilities
        - Facilitating the direction and supervision of team members and the review of their work
        - Assisting, when applicable, in coordination of work done by auditors of components (group audits) and specialists

    b. **Timing**

        (1) **Planning Is Continual** Planning is not a discrete phase of an audit but rather a continual and iterative process that often begins in connection with the completion of the previous audit and continues until the completion of the current audit.

        (2) **First Things First** Planning includes consideration of the timing of certain activities and audit procedures that need to be completed prior to the performance

of others. For example, planning the nature, extent, and timing of specific further audit procedures depends on the outcome of risk assessment procedures for which planning occurs early in the audit process.

On the other hand, the auditor may begin the execution of further audit procedures for some classes of transactions, account balances, and disclosures before planning all remaining further audit procedures.

(3) **Planning Activities Prior to Risk Assessment** Planning includes the need to consider, prior to the auditor's identification and assessment of the RMM, such matters as the following:

- The analytical procedures to be applied as risk assessment procedures
- A general understanding of the legal and regulatory framework applicable to the entity and how the entity is complying with that framework
- The determination of materiality
- The involvement of specialists
- The performance of other risk assessment procedures

5. **Discussion of Planning With Management**

a. **Coordination** The auditor may decide to discuss certain elements of planning with the entity's management to facilitate the the audit, e.g., to coordinate some of the audit procedures with the work of the entity's personnel.

b. **Care Needed in Order Not to Compromise Audit** When discussing matters included in the overall audit strategy or audit plan, care is required in order not to compromise the effectiveness of the audit. For example, discussing the nature and timing of detailed audit procedures with management may compromise the effectiveness of the audit by making the audit procedures too predictable.

B. **Preliminary Engagement Activities**
Performing these preliminary activities assists the auditor in identifying and evaluating circumstances that may adversely affect the ability to plan and perform the audit. The auditor should undertake the following activities at the beginning of the current audit:

1. **Quality Control Procedures** Performing quality control procedures regarding the continuance of the client relationship and the specific audit engagement and, for an initial audit, any additional procedures required.

2. **Compliance With Ethical Requirements** Evaluating compliance with relevant ethical requirements

Editor Note: The auditor's consideration of client continuance and relevant ethical requirements, including independence, continues throughout the audit engagement as changes occur. These first two items are covered in chapter 15 of this text.

3. **Establishment of Terms of Engagement** Establishing an understanding of the terms of the engagement

C. **Planning Activities**
The auditor should establish an overall audit strategy that sets the scope, timing, and direction of the audit and guides the development of the audit plan.

1. **Overall Audit Strategy** In establishing the overall audit strategy, the auditor should:

a. **Characteristics That Define Scope of Audit** Identify the characteristics of the audit that define its scope, for example:

- Industry specific reporting requirements, such as reports mandated by industry regulators
- Whether the entity has an internal audit function and, if so, whether (in which areas and to what extent) the work of the internal audit function can be used in obtaining audit evidence or whether internal auditors can be used to provide direct assistance
- The entity's use of service organizations and how the auditor may obtain evidence concerning the design or operation of controls performed by them
- The effect of IT on audit procedures

b. **Reporting Objectives and Communication Required** Ascertain the reporting objectives in order to plan the timing of the audit and the nature of the communications required, for example:

- The entity's timetable for reporting, including interim periods
- The organization of meetings with management and those charged with governance to discuss the nature, extent and timing of the audit work
- Whether there are any other expected communications with third parties, including any statutory or contractual reporting responsibilities arising from the audit

c. **Significant Factors** Consider the factors that are significant in directing the team's efforts, for example:

- The determination of materiality
- Preliminary identification of areas in which there may be a higher RMM
- Significant business developments affecting the entity, including changes in IT and business processes; changes in key management; and acquisitions, mergers, and divestments
- Significant industry developments, such as changes in industry regulations and new reporting requirements

d. **Results From Preliminary Audit Activities & Past Engagements** Consider the results of preliminary activities and whether knowledge gained on other engagements performed for the entity is relevant, for example:

- Results of previous audits that involved evaluating the operating effectiveness of internal control, including the nature of identified deficiencies and action taken to address them

e. **Resources Needed** Ascertain the nature, extent, and timing of resources needed, for example:

- The resources to deploy for specific areas, such as the use of experienced team members for high risk areas or the involvement of specialists on complex matters
- The amount of resources to allocate to specific areas, such as the number of team members assigned to observe the inventory count at material locations or the audit budget to allocate to high risk areas
- When these resources are to be deployed, such as whether at an interim audit stage or at key cut-off dates
- How such resources are managed, directed, and supervised

2. **Audit Plan** Once the overall audit strategy has been established, the detailed audit plan can be developed to address the various matters identified in the overall audit strategy.

a. **Nature of Audit Plan** The audit plan is more detailed than the overall audit strategy in that it includes the nature, extent, and timing of audit procedures to be performed. Planning for these audit procedures takes place over the course of the audit as the audit plan for the engagement develops.

b. **Audit Plan & Overall Strategy Are Interrelated** The auditor should update and change the overall audit strategy and audit plan, as necessary, during the course of the audit. They are *not* the result of discrete or sequential processes, but are closely interrelated because changes in one may necessitate changes to the other.

c. **Audit Plan Elements** The auditor should develop an audit plan that includes a description of the following:

(1) **Risk Assessment Procedures** The nature and extent of planned risk assessment procedures

(2) **Further Audit Procedures** The nature, extent, and timing of planned further audit procedures at the relevant assertion level

(3) **Other Procedures to Comply With US GAAS** Other planned audit procedures that are required to be carried out so that the engagement complies with US GAAS

3. **Supervision** The auditor should plan the nature, extent, and timing of direction and supervision of engagement team members and the review of their work.

4. **Determining the Extent of Involvement of Specialists** The auditor should consider whether specialized skills are needed in performing the audit (using the work of an auditor's specialist is covered in chapter 4 of this text).

5. **Additional Planning Considerations in Initial Audits** The auditor's planning for an initial audit should incorporate the discussion with the predecessor auditor regarding acceptance of the engagement when there has been a change of auditors. It *may* also be necessary to plan opening balances procedures, including arrangements to review the predecessor auditor's working papers.

D. Audit Documentation

The auditor should include in the audit documentation the overall audit strategy; audit plan; and any significant changes made during the audit to the either and the reasons for such changes.

IV. Materiality in Planning & Performing an Audit (AU 320)

A. Overview

The concept of materiality is applied by the auditor both in planning and performing the audit (covered by this topic); evaluating the effect of identified misstatements on the audit and the effect of any uncorrected misstatements on the financial statements; and in forming the auditor's opinion.

1. **Materiality in the Context of an Audit** Financial reporting frameworks generally explain the following characteristics of the concept of materiality in the context of the preparation and fair presentation of the financial statements.

    - Misstatements, including omissions, are considered to be material if they, individually or in the aggregate, could reasonably be expected to influence the economic decisions of users made on the basis of the financial statements.
    - Judgments about materiality are made in light of surrounding circumstances and are affected by the size or nature of a misstatement, or a combination of both.
    - Judgments about matters that are material to users of the financial statements are based on a consideration of the common financial information needs of users as a group. The possible effect of misstatements on specific individual users, whose needs may vary widely, is *not* considered.

2. **Assumptions About Users** The auditor's determination of materiality is a matter of professional judgment and is affected by the auditor's perception of the financial information needs of users of the financial statements. In this context, it is reasonable for the auditor to assume that users:

    a. **Possess Reasonable Knowledge & Willingness to Study Financial Statements** Have a reasonable knowledge of business and economic activities and accounting and a willingness to study the information in the financial statements with reasonable diligence

    b. **Understand Concept of Materiality in Context of Financial Statements** Understand that financial statements are prepared, presented, and audited to levels of materiality

    c. **Recognize That Uncertainties Affect Measurement of Some Amounts** Recognize the uncertainties inherent in the measurement of amounts based on the use of estimates, judgment, and the consideration of future events

    d. **Make Reasonable Economic Decisions Based on Financial Statements** Make reasonable economic decisions on the basis of the information in the financial statements

3. **Purpose of Materiality Set During Planning an Audit** In planning the audit, the auditor makes judgments about the size of misstatements that will be considered material. These judgments provide a basis for:

    a. **Risk Assessment Procedures** Determining the nature and extent of risk assessment procedures

    b. **Risk of Material Misstatement (RMM)** Identifying and assessing the RMM

    c. **Further Audit Procedures** Determining the nature, extent, and timing of further audit procedures

4. **Auditor May Consider Amounts Below Materiality Set During Planning Due to Qualitative Considerations** The materiality determined when planning the audit does not necessarily establish an amount below which uncorrected misstatements, individually or in

the aggregate, will always be evaluated as immaterial. Although it is not practicable to design audit procedures to detect misstatements that could be material solely because of their nature, i.e., qualitative considerations, the auditor considers not only the size but also the nature of uncorrected misstatements, and the particular circumstances of their occurrence, when evaluating their effect on the financial statements.

B. Determining Materiality & Performance Materiality

1. **Determining Materiality for the Financial Statements as a Whole** When establishing the overall audit strategy, the auditor should determine materiality for the financial statements as a whole.

   a. **Use of Benchmarks** A percentage is often applied to a chosen benchmark as a starting point in determining materiality for the financial statements as a whole. However, the use of benchmarks is *not* required.

      Factors that *may* affect the identification of an appropriate benchmark include the following:

      - The elements of the financial statements, e.g., assets, liabilities, equity, revenue, or expenses
      - Whether items exist on which the attention of the users of the particular entity's financial statements tends to be focused, e.g., profit
      - The nature of the entity; where the entity is in its life cycle; and the industry and economic environment in which the entity operates
      - The entity's ownership structure and the way it is financed, e.g., if an entity is financed solely by debt rather than equity, users may put more emphasis on assets and claims on them rather than on the entity's earnings
      - The relative volatility of the benchmark

   b. **Relevant Financial Data** With regard to the chosen benchmark, relevant financial data ordinarily includes prior periods' financial results and financial positions; the period-to-date financial results and financial position, budgets, or forecasts for the current period, adjusted for significant changes in the circumstances of the entity, e.g., a significant business acquisition and relevant changes of conditions in the industry or economic environment in which the entity operates.

2. **Performance Materiality** The auditor should determine *performance materiality* for purposes of assessing the RMM; determining the nature, extent, and timing of further audit procedures; and, if warranted, for one or more particular classes of transactions, account balances, or disclosures.

   Planning the audit solely to detect individual material misstatements overlooks the fact that the aggregate of individually immaterial misstatements may cause the financial statements (or particular classes of transactions, account balances, or disclosures) to be materially misstated and leaves no margin for possible undetected misstatements. The determination of performance materiality addresses this issue.

   a. **Definition of Performance Materiality** Performance materiality is the amount or amounts set by the auditor at less than materiality for the financial statements as a whole to reduce to an appropriately low level the probability that the aggregate of uncorrected and undetected misstatements exceeds materiality for the financial statements as a whole. If applicable, performance materiality also refers to the amount or amounts set by the auditor at less than the materiality level or levels for particular classes of transactions, account balances, or disclosures.

b. **Determination of Performance Materiality** The determination of performance materiality is not a simple mechanical calculation and involves the exercise of professional judgment. It is affected by the auditor's understanding of the entity and the nature and extent of misstatements identified in previous audits, updated by the auditor's expectations regarding misstatements in the current period via the performance of risk assessment procedures.

C. **Revision of Materiality as the Audit Progresses**

1. **New Information That Would Have Resulted in a Different Initial Materiality Amount** If new information during the audit invalidates the initial materiality amount established for the financial statements as a whole, the auditor should, of course, revise it. For example, if the auditor determined materiality for planning purposes before the financial statements were prepared and it later appears as though the actual results are likely to be substantially different from the anticipated results. The revision could also be necessitated by a change of circumstances that occurred during the audit, e.g., the decision to dispose of a major part of the entity's business.

2. **When Materiality Is Lowered** If the auditor concludes that a lower materiality than that initially determined for the financial statements as a whole is appropriate, the auditor should also determine whether:

a. **Performance Materiality** It is necessary to revise performance materiality

b. **Further Audit Procedures** The nature, extent, and timing of the further audit procedures remain appropriate

D. **Audit Documentation**
The auditor should include in the audit documentation the following amounts and the factors considered in their determination:

1. **Materiality** Materiality for the financial statements as a whole

2. **Materiality Levels for Particular Classes** If applicable, the materiality level or levels for particular classes of transactions, account balances, or disclosures

3. **Performance Materiality** Performance materiality

4. **Revision of Any Materiality Levels** Any revision of the preceding amounts as the audit progressed

V. Understanding the Entity & Its Environment and Assessing the RMM (AU 315)

A. **Overview**
Obtaining an understanding of the entity and its environment, including the entity's internal control is a continuous, dynamic process of gathering, updating, and analyzing information. The understanding of the entity establishes a frame of reference within which the auditor plans the audit and exercises professional judgment throughout the audit.

Editor Note: Coverage of obtaining an understanding of the entity's internal control in accordance with AU 315 is included in the chapter 3 in this text.

B. **Objective**
The objective of the auditor is to identify and assess the risk of material misstatement (RMM), whether due to fraud or error, at the financial statement and relevant assertion levels through understanding the entity and its environment, including the entity's internal control, thereby providing a basis for designing and implementing responses to the assessed RMM.

C. Definitions

1. **Assertions** Representations by management, explicit or otherwise, that are embodied in the financial statements as used by the auditor to consider the different types of potential misstatements that may occur

2. **Business Risk** A risk resulting from significant conditions, events, circumstances, actions, or inactions that could adversely affect an entity's ability to achieve its objectives and execute its strategies or from the setting of inappropriate objectives and strategies

   Editor Note: Business risk is broader than the RMM of the financial statements; it includes the RMM of the financial statements.

3. **Internal Control** A process effected by those charged with governance, management, and other personnel that is designed to provide reasonable assurance about the achievement of the entity's objectives with regard to the reliability of financial reporting; effectiveness and efficiency of operations; and compliance with applicable laws and regulations—internal control over safeguarding of assets against unauthorized acquisition, use, or disposition may include controls relating to both financial reporting and operations objectives

4. **Relevant Assertion** A financial statement assertion that has a reasonable possibility of containing a misstatement or misstatements that would cause the financial statements to be materially misstated; the determination of whether an assertion is a relevant assertion is made without regard to the effect of internal controls

   Editor Note: Relevant assertions have a meaningful bearing on whether an account is fairly stated; thus, not all assertions pertaining to a particular account balance will always be relevant. For example, valuation may not be relevant to the cash account unless currency translation is involved; however, existence and completeness are always relevant. Similarly, valuation may not be relevant to the gross amount of the accounts receivable balance, but is relevant to the related allowance accounts.

5. **Risk Assessment Procedures** The audit procedures performed to obtain an understanding of the entity and its environment, including the entity's internal control, to identify and assess the RMM, whether due to fraud or error, at the financial statement and relevant assertion levels

6. **Significant Risk** An identified and assessed RMM that, in the auditor's professional judgment, requires special audit consideration

D. Risk Assessment Procedures & Related Activities

1. **Performed at Financial Statement & Relevant Assertion Levels** The auditor should perform risk assessment procedures to provide a basis for the identification and assessment of RMM at both the financial statement and relevant assertion levels.

2. **Can *Not* Provide Sufficient Appropriate Evidence By Themselves** Information obtained by performing risk assessment procedures and related activities may be used as audit evidence to support assessments of the RMM; however, they do **not**, by themselves, provide sufficient appropriate audit evidence on which to base the audit opinion.

3. **Used to Determine Further Audit Procedures** Risk assessment determines the nature, extent, and timing of further audit procedures.

4. **Can Be Performed Concurrently With Substantive Procedures or Tests of Controls** The auditor *may* choose to perform substantive procedures or tests of controls concurrently with risk assessment procedures when the auditor judges that it is efficient to do so.

5. **Types of Risk Assessment Procedures** The risk assessment procedures should include the following.

   a. **Inquiries** Inquiries of management, appropriate individuals within the internal audit function, and others within the entity

   b. **Analytical Procedures** Analytical procedures:

      (1) **May Include Financial & Nonfinancial Information** *May* include both financial and nonfinancial information, e.g., the relationship between sales and square footage of selling space or volume of goods sold

      (2) **Aid in Identification of Relationships and/or Trends** *May* help to identify unusual or unexpected relationships that *may* assist the auditor in identifying RMM, especially those due to fraud; or *may* identify trends that might indicate matters that have audit implications

      (3) **If High Level May Need to Be Considered With Other Information** When analytical procedures use data aggregated at a high level (which may be the situation with analytical procedures performed as risk assessment procedures), the results provide only a broad initial indication about whether a material misstatement may exist. Accordingly, consideration of other information may be needed to evaluate the results of such analytical procedures.

   c. **Observation & Inspection** Observation and inspection may either support inquiries of management and others or may provide additional information.

   Editor Note: Although the auditor is required to perform all the above risk assessment procedures in the course of obtaining the required understanding of the entity, the auditor is *not* required to perform all of them for each aspect of that understanding. And other procedures may be performed to the same end.

6. **Auditor's Client Acceptance or Continuance Process** The auditor should consider whether information obtained from the auditor's client acceptance or continuance process is relevant to identifying RMM.

7. **Prior Experience With Client** Work during previous audits may provide information about such matters as the following.

   - Past misstatements and whether they were corrected on a timely basis
   - The nature of the entity and its environment and the entity's internal control, including deficiencies
   - Significant changes that the entity may have undergone since the prior financial period

   a. **Relevance of Previously Obtained Information** The auditor should consider whether information previously obtained is relevant to identifying RMM.

   b. **Evaluate Whether Changes Since Previous Audit Affect Relevance** When the auditor intends to use information obtained during previous audits, the auditor should determine whether changes have occurred since the previous audit that may affect its relevance to the current audit.

8. **Fraud Assessment** During planning, the auditor should consider the results of the assessment of the RMM due to fraud along with other information gathered in the process of identifying the RMM.

9. **Audit Team Discussion** The engagement partner and other key engagement team members should discuss the susceptibility of the entity's financial statements to material misstatement and the application of the applicable financial reporting framework (AFRF) to the entity's facts and circumstances. The engagement partner should determine which matters are to be communicated to engagement team members not involved in the discussion.

   This discussion:

   - Provides an opportunity for more experienced engagement team members, including the engagement partner, to share their insights
   - Allows the engagement team members to exchange information about the entity's business risks and about how and where the financial statements might be susceptible to material misstatement due to fraud or error
   - Assists the engagement team members to gain a better understanding of the potential for material misstatement of the financial statements in the specific areas assigned to them and to understand how their audit procedures may affect other aspects of the audit, including the decisions about the nature, extent, and timing of further audit procedures
   - Provides a basis upon which engagement team members communicate and share new information obtained throughout the audit that may affect the assessment of RMM or the audit procedures performed to address these risks

   It *may* be held concurrently with the required team discussion regarding the susceptibility of the entity's financial statements to fraud.

E. Understanding the Entity & Its Environment

The auditor should obtain an understanding of the following aspects:

1. **External Factors, Including the AFRF** Relevant industry, regulatory, and other external factors, including the AFRF

2. **Nature of the Entity** The nature of the entity to enable the auditor to understand the classes of transactions, account balances, and disclosures to be expected in the financial statements. This should include an understanding of:

   a. **Operations** Its operations, such as products or services and markets; key customers; important suppliers of goods and services; research and development activities and expenditures; etc.

   b. **Ownership & Governance Structures** Its ownership and governance structures; this understanding helps the auditor to understand such matters as:

      (1) Whether the entity has a complex structure—complex structures often introduce issues that may give rise to RMM

      (2) The ownership and relations between owners and other people or entities; this understanding assists in determining whether related-party transactions and balances have been identified and accounted for appropriately

   c. **Types of Investments** The types of investments that the entity is making and plans to make, including investments in entities formed to accomplish specific objectives

   d. **Structure & How It Is Financed** The way that the entity is structured and how it is financed

3. **Accounting Policies** The entity's selection and application of accounting policies, including the reasons for changes to them; the auditor should evaluate whether the entity's accounting policies are appropriate for its business and consistent with the AFRF and accounting policies used in the relevant industry

4. **Objectives & Strategies And Related Business Risks** The entity's objectives and strategies and those related business risks that may result in RMM

5. **Financial Performance** The measurement and review of the entity's financial performance; an understanding of the entity's performance measures assists the auditor in considering whether pressures to achieve performance targets may result in management actions that increase the RMM, including those due to fraud.

Editor Note:

- Significant changes in the entity from prior periods may also give rise to, or change RMM.
- An understanding of the business risks facing the entity increases the likelihood of identifying RMM because most business risks will eventually have financial consequences and, therefore, an effect on the financial statements. However, the auditor does not have a responsibility to identify or assess all business risks because not all business risks give rise to RMM. Whether a business risk may result in a RMM is considered in light of the entity's circumstances. Usually, management identifies business risks and develops approaches to address them (the entity's risk assessment process is one of the components of the entity's internal control system).

F. Identifying & Assessing the RMM

1. **Levels** To provide a basis for designing and performing further audit procedures, the auditor should identify and assess the RMM at the:

   a. **Financial Statement Level** The RMM at the financial statement level refer to risks that relate pervasively to the financial statements as a whole and potentially affect many assertions. Risks of this nature are not necessarily risks identifiable with specific assertions at the class of transactions, account balance, or disclosure level. Rather, they represent circumstances that may increase the RMM at the assertion level, e.g., through management override of internal control. Financial statement level risks may be especially relevant to the auditor's consideration of the RMM arising from fraud.

   Risks at the financial statement level may derive, in particular, from a deficient control environment; although these risks also may relate to other factors such as declining economic conditions.

   b. **Relevant Assertion Level for Classes of Transactions, Account Balances & Disclosures (Relevant Assertion Level)** Consideration of RMM at the relevant assertion level directly assists in determining the nature, extent, and timing of further audit procedures at the assertion level.

   In representing that the financial statements are in accordance with the AFRF, management implicitly or explicitly makes assertions regarding the recognition, measurement, presentation, and disclosure of the various elements of financial statements and related disclosures.

(1) **Assertions** Assertions used by the auditor to consider the different types of potential misstatements that *may* occur fall into the following three categories and *may* take the following forms:

(a) **Classes of Transactions & Events** Assertions about classes of transactions and events for the period under audit, such as:

(i) **Occurrence** Transactions and events that have been recorded have occurred and pertain to the entity.

(ii) **Completeness** All transactions and events that should have been recorded have been recorded.

(iii) **Accuracy** Amounts and other data relating to recorded transactions and events have been recorded appropriately.

(iv) **Cutoff** Transactions and events have been recorded in the correct accounting period.

(v) **Classification** Transactions and events have been recorded in the proper accounts.

(b) **Account Balances** Assertions about ending account balances, such as:

(i) **Existence** Assets, liabilities, and equity interests exist.

(ii) **Rights & Obligations** The entity holds or controls the rights to assets, and liabilities are the obligations of the entity.

(iii) **Completeness** All assets, liabilities, and equity interests that should have been recorded have been recorded.

(iv) **Valuation & Allocation** Assets, liabilities, and equity interests are included in the financial statements at appropriate amounts, and any resulting valuation or allocation adjustments are appropriately recorded.

(c) **Presentation & Disclosure** Assertions about presentation and disclosure, such as:

(i) **Occurrence and Rights & Obligations** Disclosed events, transactions, and other matters have occurred and pertain to the entity.

(ii) **Completeness** All disclosures that should have been included in the financial statements have been included.

(iii) **Classification & Understandability** Financial information is appropriately presented and described, and disclosures are clearly expressed.

(iv) **Accuracy & Valuation** Financial and other information is disclosed fairly and in appropriate amounts.

(2) **Identifying *Relevant* Assertions** For each significant class of transactions, account balance, and disclosure, the auditor is required to determine the relevance (in part, by determining the source of likely potential misstatements) of each of the financial statement assertions.

Attributes indicating the potential relevance of an assertion include the:

(a) Nature of the assertion

(b) Volume of transactions or data related to the assertion

(c) Nature and complexity of the systems, including the use of IT, by which the entity processes and controls information supporting the assertion

2. Process of Identifying RMM For this purpose, the auditor should:

a. Identify Risks Identify risks throughout the process of obtaining an understanding of the entity and its environment, including relevant controls that relate to the risks, by considering the classes of transactions, account balances, and disclosures in the financial statements

b. Assess & Evaluate Identified Risks Assess the identified risks and evaluate whether they relate more pervasively to the financial statements as a whole and potentially affect many assertions

c. Consider Controls to Be Tested & Ask What Could Go Wrong Relate the identified risks to what can go wrong at the relevant assertion level, taking account of relevant controls that the auditor intends to test

d. Consider Likelihood & Materiality of Misstatement Consider the likelihood of misstatement, including the possibility of multiple misstatements, and whether the potential misstatement is of a magnitude that could result in a material misstatement

Examples of conditions and events that *may* indicate the existence of RMM include:

- Operations in regions that are economically unstable (e.g., countries with significant currency devaluation or highly inflationary economies)
- Operations exposed to volatile markets (e.g., futures trading)
- Operations that are subject to a high degree of complex regulation
- Going concern and liquidity issues, including loss of significant customers
- Constraints on the availability of capital and credit
- Changes in the industry in which the entity operates
- Changes in the supply chain
- Developing or offering new products or services or moving into new lines of business
- Expanding into new locations
- Changes in the entity, such as large acquisitions or reorganizations or other unusual events
- Entities or business segments likely to be sold
- The existence of complex alliances and joint ventures
- Use of off balance sheet finance, investments in entities formed to accomplish specific objectives, and other complex financing arrangements

- Significant transactions with related parties
- Lack of personnel with appropriate accounting and financial reporting skills
- Changes in key personnel, including departure of key executives
- Deficiencies in internal control, especially those not addressed by management
- Inconsistencies between the entity's IT strategy and its business strategies
- Changes in the IT environment
- Installation of significant new IT systems related to financial reporting
- Inquiries into the entity's operations or financial results by regulatory or government bodies
- Past misstatements, history of errors, or a significant amount of adjustments at period-end
- Significant amount of nonroutine or nonsystematic transactions, including intercompany transactions and large revenue transactions at period-end
- Transactions that are recorded based on management's intent, e.g., debt refinancing, assets to be sold, and classification of marketable securities
- Application of new accounting pronouncements
- Accounting measurements that involve complex processes
- Events or transactions that involve significant measurement uncertainty, including accounting estimates
- Pending litigation and contingent liabilities (e.g., sales warranties, financial guarantees, and environmental remediation)

3. **Special Risks** Significant risks and risks for which substantive procedures alone do *not* provide sufficient appropriate audit evidence require additional attention from the auditor.

   a. **Identification of Significant Risks, Excluding Effects of Controls** The auditor should determine whether any of the risks identified are significant risks and thus, require special audit consideration. In exercising this judgment, the auditor should exclude the effects of identified controls related to the risk.

      (1) **Considerations** In making the determination as to which risks are significant risks, the auditor should consider:

         (a) **Fraud Risks** Whether the risk is a risk of fraud

         (b) **Recent Developments** Whether the risk is related to recent significant economic, accounting, or other developments and, therefore, requires specific attention

         (c) **Complexity** The complexity of transactions

         (d) **Related Parties** Whether the risk involves significant transactions with related parties

         (e) **Degree of Subjectivity in Measurement** The degree of subjectivity in the measurement of financial information related to the risk, especially those measurements involving a wide range of measurement uncertainty and thus, require significant judgment

(f) **Nonroutine Transactions** Whether the risk involves significant transactions that are outside the normal course of business for the entity or that otherwise appear to be unusual; *nonroutine transactions* are transactions that are unusual, either due to size or nature, and that, therefore, occur infrequently—routine, noncomplex transactions that are subject to systematic processing are *less* likely to give rise to significant risks.

RMM *may* be greater for significant nonroutine transactions arising from matters such as:

- Greater management intervention to specify the accounting treatment
- Greater manual intervention for data collection and processing
- Complex calculations or accounting principles
- The nature of nonroutine transactions, which may make it difficult for the entity to implement effective controls over the risks
- Related-party transactions

(2) **Evaluate Relevant Controls** If the auditor has determined that a significant risk exists, the auditor should obtain an understanding of the entity's controls, including control activities, relevant to that risk and, based on that understanding, evaluate whether such controls have been suitably designed and implemented to mitigate such risks.

b. **Risks for Which Substantive Procedures Alone Do *Not* Provide Sufficient Appropriate Audit Evidence** In respect of some risks, the auditor may judge that it is not possible or practicable to obtain sufficient appropriate audit evidence only from substantive procedures. Such risks may relate to the inaccurate or incomplete recording of routine and significant classes of transactions or account balances (such as an entity's revenue; purchases; and cash receipts or cash payments), the characteristics of which often permit highly automated processing with little or no manual intervention. In such cases, the entity's controls over such risks are relevant to the audit, and the auditor should obtain an understanding of them.

4. **Revision of Risk Assessment** The auditor's assessment of the RMM at the assertion level may change during the course of the audit as additional audit evidence is obtained. In circumstances in which the auditor obtains audit evidence from performing further audit procedures or if new information is obtained, either of which is inconsistent with the audit evidence on which the auditor originally based the assessment, the auditor should revise the assessment and modify the further planned audit procedures accordingly.

Editor Note: For example, the risk assessment may be based on an expectation that controls are operating effectively. And in performing tests of controls, the auditor may obtain audit evidence that this is not the case. Similarly, substantive procedures may detect misstatements in amounts or frequency greater than is consistent with the auditor's risk assessment.

G. Audit Documentation

The auditor should include in the audit documentation the:

1. **Audit Team Discussion** Required discussion among the engagement team, including the significant decisions reached, how and when the discussion occurred, and the audit team members who participated

2. **Key Elements of Understanding** Key elements of the required understanding (see E. of this section) obtained regarding each of the aspects of the entity and its environment and each of the internal control components (see chapter 3); the sources of information from which the understanding was obtained; and the risk assessment procedures performed

3. **RMM** Identified and assessed RMM at the financial statement level and at the relevant assertion level for classes of transactions, account balances, and disclosures

4. **Special Risks & Relevant Controls** Risks for which substantive procedures alone do not provide sufficient appropriate audit evidence and significant risks identified and the related controls for each that were evaluated

VI. Service Organizations (AU 402)

A. Overview

This guidance addresses the user auditor's responsibility for obtaining sufficient appropriate audit evidence in an audit of the financial statements of a user entity that uses one or more service organizations.

1. **Factors That Affect Nature & Extent of Audit Work Performed** The nature and extent of work to be performed by the user auditor regarding the services provided by a service organization depend on the following.

   a. **Nature & Significance To User Entity** Nature and significance of those services to the user entity

   b. **Relevance to Audit—Depends on Whether Services & Related Controls Affect User Entity's IT System Related to Financial Reporting** Services provided by a service organization are relevant to the audit of a user entity's financial statements when those services and the controls over them affect the user entity's information system, including related business processes, relevant to financial reporting. Although most controls at the service organization are likely to relate to financial reporting, other controls may also be relevant to the audit, such as controls over the safeguarding of assets.

2. **Criteria for Services to Be Part of User Entity's IT System** A service organization's services are part of a user entity's information system, if they affect any of the following:

   - The classes of transactions in the user entity's operations that are significant to the user entity's financial statements
   - The procedures within both IT and manual systems by which the user entity's transactions are initiated; authorized; recorded; processed; corrected as necessary; transferred to the general ledger; and reported in the financial statements
   - The related accounting records, supporting information, and specific accounts in the user entity's financial statements that are used to initiate, authorize, record, process, and report the user entity's transactions; this includes the correction of incorrect information and how information is transferred to the general ledger; the records may be in either manual or in electronic form

- How the user entity's information system captures events and conditions, other than transactions, that are significant to the financial statements
- The financial reporting process used to prepare the user entity's financial statements, including significant accounting estimates and disclosures
- Controls surrounding journal entries, including nonstandard journal entries used to record nonrecurring, unusual transactions, or adjustments

Editor Note: This guidance does **not** apply to services that are limited to processing an entity's transactions that are specifically authorized by the entity, such as the processing of checking account transactions by a bank or the processing of securities transactions by a broker, i.e., when the user entity retains responsibility for authorizing the transactions and maintaining the related accountability. Nor does this section apply to the audit of transactions arising from an entity that holds a proprietary financial interest in another entity, such as a partnership, corporation, or joint venture, when it performs no processing on behalf of the entity.

B. **Objectives of the User Auditor**

1. **Obtain an Understanding Sufficient to Assess Risk Of Material Misstatement (RMM)** Obtain an understanding of the nature and significance of the services provided by the service organization and their effect on the user entity's internal control relevant to the audit, sufficient to identify and assess the RMM

2. **Perform Audit Procedures to Address RMM** Design and perform audit procedures responsive to those risks

C. **Definitions**

1. **Complementary User Entity Controls** Controls that management of the service organization assumes, in the design of its service, will be implemented by user entities, and which, if necessary to achieve the control objectives stated in management's description of the service organization's system, are identified as such in that description

2. **Type 1 Report; Report on Management's Description of a Service Organization's System & the Suitability of the Design of Controls** A report that comprises the following (language that is different from a type 2 report—see next definition—is underlined):

   a. **Description of System** Management's description of the service organization's system

   b. **Written Assertion** A written assertion by management of the service organization about whether, in all material respects, and based on suitable criteria

      (1) **Description of System Fairly Presented as of Specified Date** Management's description of the service organization's system fairly presents the service organization's system that was designed and implemented <u>as of a specified date</u>

      (2) **Controls Suitably Designed as of Specified Date** The controls related to the control objectives stated in management's description of the service organization's system were suitably designed to achieve those control objectives <u>as of the specified date</u>

   c. **Service Auditor's Opinion on Management's Assertion** A service auditor's report that expresses an opinion on management's written assertion described above

3. **Type 2 Report; Report on Management's Description of a Service Organization's System & the Suitability of the Design *& Operating Effectiveness of Controls*** A report that comprises the following (language that is different from a type 1 report—see previous definition—is underlined; content here that is not included in a type 1 report is italicized):

   a. **Description of System** Management's description of the service organization's system

   b. **Written Assertion** A written assertion by management of the service organization about whether in all material respects and, based on suitable criteria

      (1) **Description of System Fairly Presented for Specified Period** Management's description of the service organization's system fairly presents the service organization's system that was designed and implemented throughout the specified period

      (2) **Controls Suitably Designed for Specified Period** The controls related to the control objectives stated in management's description of the service organization's system were suitably designed throughout the specified period to achieve those control objectives

      (3) **Controls Operated Effectively for Specified Period** *The controls related to the control objectives stated in management's description of the service organization's system operated effectively throughout the specified period to achieve those control objectives*

   c. **Service Auditor's Report** A service auditor's report that:

      (1) **Opinion on Management's Assertion** Expresses an opinion on management's written assertion described above

      (2) **Description of Service Auditor's Tests of Controls** *Includes a description of the service auditor's tests of controls and the results*

   Editor Note: Type 1 or 2 reports may be issued in accordance with AT 801, *Reporting on Controls at a Service Organization* (see chapter 14).

4. **Service Auditor** A practitioner who reports on controls at a service organization

5. **Service Organization** An organization or segment of an organization that provides services to user entities that are relevant to those user entities' internal control over financial reporting

6. **Service Organization's System** The policies and procedures designed, implemented, and documented by management of the service organization to provide user entities with the services covered by the service auditor's report. Management's description of the service organization's system identifies the services covered; the period to which the description relates (or in the case of a type 1 report, the date to which the description relates); the control objectives specified by management or an outside party; the party specifying the control objectives (if not specified by management); and the related controls

7. **Subservice Organization** A service organization used by another service organization to perform some of the services provided to user entities that are relevant to those user entities' internal control over financial reporting

8. **User Auditor** An auditor who audits and reports on the financial statements of a user entity

9. **User Entity** An entity that uses a service organization and whose financial statements are being audited

D. **Understanding of the Services Provided by a Service Organization**
The user auditor should obtain an understanding of the services provided by a service organization, including internal control, to provide a basis for the identification and assessment of the RMM regarding the user's entity use of the service organization.

1. **How Services Are Used** When obtaining an understanding of the user entity, the user auditor should obtain an understanding of how the user entity uses the services of a service organization in the user entity's operations, including the following:

   a. **Nature & Significance of Services** The nature of the services provided by the service organization and the significance of those services to the user entity, including their effect on the user entity's internal control

   b. **User Entity Elements Affected** The nature and materiality of the transactions processed or accounts or financial reporting processes affected by the service organization

      Editor Note: A service organization may establish controls that affect the user entity's internal control. These controls are at least in part physically and operationally separate from the user entity. Their significance to the user entity's internal control depends on the nature of the services provided by the service organization, including the nature and materiality of the transactions it processes for the user entity. In certain situations, the transactions processed and the accounts affected by the service organization may not appear to be material to the user entity's financial statements, but the nature of the transactions processed may be significant and the user auditor *may* determine that an understanding of controls over the processing of those transactions is necessary in the circumstances.

   c. **Degree of Interaction** The degree of interaction between the activities of the service organization and those of the user entity; the *degree of interaction* refers to the extent to which a user entity is able to and elects to implement effective controls over the processing performed by the service organization.

      (1) **High Degree of Interaction—User Entity Likely to Implement Controls** When the user entity authorizes transactions and the service organization processes and accounts for those transactions, a high degree of interaction exists; thus, it may be practicable for the user entity to implement effective controls over those transactions.

      (2) **Lower Degree of Interaction—User Entity More Likely to Rely on Service Organization's Controls** On the other hand, when the service organization initiates or initially records, processes, and accounts for the user entity's transactions, a lower degree of interaction exists and the user entity may be unable to, or may elect not to, implement effective controls over these transactions at the user entity and may rely on controls at the service organization.

   d. **Relationship** The nature of the relationship between the user entity and the service organization, including the relevant contractual terms for the activities undertaken by the service organization

2. **Evaluation of User Controls Related to Services Provided** When obtaining an understanding of internal control relevant to the audit, the user auditor should evaluate the design and implementation of relevant controls at the user entity that relate to the services provided by the service organization, including those that are applied to the transactions processed by the service organization.

Editor Note: From the overall audit perspective, for some risks, the auditor *may* judge that it is not possible or practicable to obtain sufficient appropriate audit evidence only from substantive procedures. Such risks may relate to the inaccurate or incomplete recording of routine and significant classes of transactions and account balances that may involve highly automated processing with little or no manual intervention. *Risks related to such automated processing may be particularly present when the user entity uses a service organization.* In such cases, the user entity's controls over such risks are relevant to the audit and the user auditor is required to obtain an understanding of and to evaluate such controls.

3. **Determination of the Level of Understanding Attained** The user auditor should determine whether a sufficient understanding of the nature and significance of the services provided by the service organization and their effect on the user entity's internal control relevant to the audit has been obtained to provide a basis for the identification and assessment of RMM.

a. **When Understanding *Not* Attainable via User Entity** If the user auditor is unable to obtain a sufficient understanding from the user entity, the user auditor should obtain that understanding from *one or more* of the following procedures.

(1) **Obtain Type 1 or 2 Report** Obtaining and reading a type 1 or type 2 report

(a) **Determination of Sufficiency And Appropriateness Of The Audit Evidence Provided by Report** In determining the sufficiency and appropriateness of the audit evidence provided by a type 1 or type 2 report, the user auditor should be satisfied regarding the following:

(I) **Service Auditor's Competence & Independence From Service Organization** The service auditor's professional competence and independence from the *service organization*

Editor Note: A service auditor is **not** required to be independent of a *user entity*.

(ii) **Adequacy of Applicable Report Standards** The adequacy of the standards under which the type 1 or type 2 report was issued

(b) **Requirement If Report Used as Support for Understanding** If the user auditor plans to use a type 1 or type 2 report as audit evidence to support the user auditor's understanding about the design and implementation of controls at the service organization, the user auditor should:

(i) **Evaluate Appropriateness of Date of Report Coverage** Evaluate whether the type 1 report is as of a date, or in the case of a type 2 report, is for a period that is appropriate for the user auditor's purposes

Editor Note: If the report date or period is earlier than the reporting period of the user entity, the user auditor *may* perform procedures to update it.

(ii) **Evaluate Sufficiency & Appropriateness of Evidence Provided** Evaluate the sufficiency and appropriateness of the evidence provided by the report for the understanding of the user entity's internal control relevant to the audit

(iii) **Complementary User Entity Controls** Determine whether complementary user entity controls identified by the service organization are relevant in addressing the RMM relating to the relevant assertions in the user entity's financial statements and, if so, obtain an understanding of whether the user entity has designed and implemented such controls

(2) **Contact Service Organization for Information** Contacting the service organization, through the user entity, to obtain specific information

(3) **Perform Procedures at Service Organization** Visiting the service organization and performing procedures that will provide the necessary information about the relevant controls at the service organization

(4) **Use Another Auditor to Perform Procedures** Using another auditor to perform procedures that will provide the necessary information about the relevant controls at the service organization

b. **When Understanding Attainable via User Entity** On the other hand, the user entity may establish controls over the service organization's services that may be tested by the user auditor and that may enable the user auditor to conclude that the user entity's controls are operating effectively for some or all of the related assertions, regardless of the controls in place at the service organization.

E. **Responding to the Assessed RMM**

Whether the use of a service organization increases a user entity's RMM depends on the nature of the services provided and the controls over these services. (In some cases, the use of a service organization may decrease a user entity's RMM, particularly if the user entity itself does not possess the expertise necessary to undertake particular activities or does not have adequate resources.)

1. **Responding to Assessed Risks** In responding to assessed risks, the user auditor should:

a. **Determine If User Entity Records Provide Sufficient Appropriate Evidence** Determine whether sufficient appropriate audit evidence concerning the relevant financial statement assertions is available from records held at the user entity and, if not,

b. **If Evidence Unavailable at User Entity, Perform Procedures at Service Organization** Perform further audit procedures to obtain sufficient appropriate audit evidence or use another auditor to perform those procedures at the service organization on the user auditor's behalf

2. **Tests of Controls** The user auditor should obtain audit evidence about the operating effectiveness of relevant controls at the service organization when either:

- The user auditor's risk assessment includes an expectation that controls at the service organization are operating effectively (that is, the user auditor intends to rely on the operating effectiveness of controls at the service organization in determining the nature, extent, and timing of substantive procedures); or
- Substantive procedures alone or in combination with tests of the operating effectiveness of controls at the user entity, cannot provide sufficient appropriate audit evidence at the assertion level

In either case, the user auditor should obtain such evidence using *one or more* of the following procedures:

a. **Obtain Type 2 Report** Obtaining and reading a type 2 report; if the user auditor plans to use a type 2 report as audit evidence that controls at the service organization are operating effectively, the user auditor should determine whether the service auditor's report provides sufficient appropriate audit evidence about the effectiveness of the controls to support the user auditor's risk assessment by:

   (1) **Evaluate Appropriateness of Period of Report Coverage** Evaluating whether the type 2 report is for a period that is appropriate for the user auditor's purposes

   (2) **Complementary User Entity Controls** Determining whether complementary user entity controls identified by the service organization are relevant in addressing the RMM relating to the relevant assertions in the user entity's financial statements and, if so, obtaining an understanding of whether the user entity has designed and implemented such controls and, if so, testing their operating effectiveness

   Editor Note: For example, the service may be designed with the assumption that the user entity will have controls in place for authorizing transactions before they are sent to the service organization for processing.

   (3) **Evaluate Times Elapsed Since Controls Tested** Evaluating the adequacy of the time period covered by the tests of controls and the time elapsed since the controls were tested

   (4) **Evaluate Whether Tests of Control Provide Support for User's Risk Assessment** Evaluating whether the tests of controls performed by the service auditor and the results, as described in the service auditor's report, are relevant to the assertions in the user entity's financial statements and provide sufficient appropriate audit evidence to support the user auditor's risk assessment

b. **Perform Procedures at Service Organization** Performing appropriate tests of controls at the service organization

c. **Use Another Auditor to Perform Procedures** Using another auditor to perform tests of controls at the service organization on behalf of the user auditor

F. Other Considerations

1. Subservice Organizations

a. **When a Service Organization Uses a Subservice Organization** A user auditor *may* need to consider controls at the subservice organization. The degree of interaction between the user entity, the service organization, and the subservice organization as well as the nature and materiality of the transactions processed by the service organization and the subservice organization are the most important factors for the user auditor to consider in determining the significance of the service organization's and subservice organization's controls to the user entity's controls.

b. **Type 1 & Type 2 Reports That Exclude the Services of a Subservice Organization** If the user auditor plans to use a type 1 or a type 2 report that excludes the services provided by a subservice organization and those services are relevant to the audit of the user entity's financial statements, the user auditor should apply the requirements of this section with respect to the services provided by the subservice organization.

Editor Note: If a service organization uses a subservice organization, the service auditor's report may either include or exclude the subservice organization's relevant control objectives and related controls in the service organization's description of its system and in the scope of the service auditor's engagement. These two methods of reporting are known as the *inclusive method* and the *carve-out method*, respectively.

2. **Fraud, Noncompliance With Laws & Regulations, and Uncorrected Misstatements Related to Activities at the Service Organization** The user auditor should inquire of management of the user entity about whether it is aware of, any fraud, noncompliance with laws and regulations, or uncorrected misstatements affecting the financial statements of the user entity that are attributable to the service organization's management or employees. The user auditor should evaluate how such matters, if any, affect the nature, extent, and timing of the user auditor's further audit procedures, including the effect on the user auditor's conclusions and user auditor's report.

G. Reporting by the User Auditor

1. **Scope Limitation** The user auditor should modify the opinion in the user auditor's report, if the user auditor is unable to obtain sufficient appropriate audit evidence regarding the services provided by the service organization relevant to the audit of the user entity's financial statements.

2. **Reference to Service Auditor *Precluded* in User Auditor's Unmodified Opinion Report** The user auditor should **not** refer to the work of a service auditor in a user auditor's report containing an unmodified opinion.

3. **Reference to Service Auditor *Allowed* in User Auditor's Modified Opinion Report** However, when the user auditor expresses a modified opinion *because of a modified opinion in a service auditor's report*, the user auditor is allowed to make reference.

   a. **Condition Allowing Reference** Such reference should assist in explaining the reason for the user auditor's modified opinion. In such circumstances, the user auditor need not identify the service auditor by name and *may* need the consent of the service auditor before making such a reference.

   b. **Added Report Language Required If Reference Is Made** The user auditor's report should indicate that such reference does **not** diminish the user auditor's responsibility for that opinion.

VII. Consideration of Fraud in a Financial Statement Audit (AU 240)

A. Overview

The auditor is primarily concerned with fraud that causes a material misstatement in the financial statements.

1. **Characteristics of Fraud** Two types of intentional misstatements are relevant to the auditor—misstatements resulting from fraudulent financial reporting and misstatements resulting from misappropriation of assets.

   a. **Fraud vs. Error** Misstatements in the financial statements can arise from either fraud or error.

      (1) **Fraud Is Intentional** The distinguishing factor between fraud and error is whether the underlying action that results in the misstatement is intentional (fraud) or unintentional (error).

      (2) **Intent Can Be Difficult to Determine** Intent is often difficult to determine, particularly in matters involving accounting estimates and the application of

accounting principles, e.g., unreasonable accounting estimates may be unintentional or may be the result of an intentional attempt to misstate the financial statements. Thus, the auditor may be able to identify potential opportunities for fraud to be perpetrated, but not whether misstatements are caused by fraud vs. error.

b. **Fraudulent Financial Reporting** Fraudulent financial reporting involves intentional misstatements, including omissions of amounts or disclosures in financial statements, to deceive financial statement users.

(1) **Presumption of Risk of Material Misstatement (RMM) Due to Fraud Relating to Revenue Recognition** The auditor should ordinarily presume that there is a RMM due to fraud relating to revenue recognition. (If an auditor finds this not to be the case, the auditor should document the reasons supporting this conclusion.)

(a) **Fraudulent Reduction of Earnings** Management may be motivated to reduce earnings by a material amount to minimize taxes, e.g., through improperly shifting revenues to a later period.

(b) **Fraudulent Increase of Earnings** Management may also inflate earnings to secure bank financing, e.g., through premature revenue recognition or recording fictitious revenues.

(2) **Methods** Fraudulent financial reporting may be accomplished by:

(a) **Alteration of Accounting Records or Supporting Documents** Manipulation; falsification (including forgery); or alteration of accounting records or supporting documents from which financial statements are prepared

(b) **Financial Statement Misrepresentations or Intentional Omissions** Misrepresentation in, or intentional omission from, the financial statements of events, transactions, or other significant information

(c) **Intentional Misapplication of Accounting Principles** Intentional misapplication of accounting principles relating to amounts, classification, manner of presentation, or disclosure

(3) **Means—Inappropriate Management Override of Controls** Fraudulent financial reporting often involves management override of controls that otherwise may appear to be operating effectively. Fraud can be committed by management overriding controls using such techniques as the following:

- Recording fictitious journal entries, particularly close to the end of an accounting period, to manipulate operating results or achieve other objectives
- Inappropriately adjusting assumptions and changing judgments used to estimate account balances
- Omitting, advancing, or delaying recognition in the financial statements of events and transactions that have occurred during the reporting period
- Concealing, or not disclosing, facts that could affect the amounts recorded in the financial statements
- Engaging in complex transactions that are structured to misrepresent the financial position or financial performance of the entity
- Altering records and terms related to significant and unusual transactions

c. **Misappropriation of Assets** Misappropriation of assets involves the theft of an entity's assets. It is often accompanied by false or misleading records or documents in order to conceal the fact that the assets are missing or have been pledged without proper authorization. It can be accomplished in various ways, including:

- Embezzling receipts, e.g., misappropriating collections on accounts receivable or diverting receipts from written-off accounts to personal bank accounts
- Stealing physical assets or intellectual property, e.g., stealing inventory for personal use or for sale; stealing scrap for resale; or colluding with a competitor by disclosing technological data in return for payment
- Causing an entity to pay for goods and services not received, e.g., payments to fictitious vendors; kickbacks paid by vendors to the entity's purchasing agents in return for approving payment at inflated prices; or payments to fictitious employees
- Using an entity's assets for personal use, e.g., using the entity's assets as collateral for a personal loan or a loan to a related party

d. **Conditions Conducive to Fraud** Fraud, whether fraudulent financial reporting or misappropriation of assets, involves incentive or pressure to commit fraud; a perceived opportunity to do so; and some rationalization of the act, as follows.

(1) **Incentive/Pressure** Incentive or pressure to commit fraudulent financial reporting may exist when management is under pressure, from sources outside or inside the entity, to achieve an expected (and perhaps, unrealistic) earnings target or financial outcome—particularly because the consequences to management for failing to meet financial goals can be significant. Individuals may have an incentive to misappropriate assets, e.g., because the individuals are living beyond their means.

(2) **Opportunity** A perceived opportunity to commit fraud may exist when an individual believes internal control can be overridden, e.g., because the individual is in a position of trust or has knowledge of specific deficiencies in internal control.

(3) **Rationalization** Individuals may be able to rationalize committing a fraudulent act. Some individuals possess an attitude, character, or set of ethical values that allow them knowingly and intentionally to commit a dishonest act. However, even otherwise honest individuals can commit fraud in an environment that imposes sufficient pressure on them.

2. **Responsibilities Related to Prevention & Detection of Fraud**

a. **Management & Those Charged With Governance** The primary responsibility for the prevention and detection of fraud rests with both those charged with governance and management. It is important that management places a strong emphasis on fraud prevention, which may reduce opportunities for fraud to take place, and fraud deterrence, which could persuade individuals not to commit fraud because of the likelihood of detection and punishment. This involves a commitment to creating a culture of honesty and ethical behavior, which can be reinforced by active oversight by those charged with governance. Oversight by those charged with governance includes considering the potential for override of controls or other inappropriate influence over the financial reporting process.

b. **Auditor** An auditor conducting an audit in accordance with US GAAS is responsible for obtaining reasonable assurance that the financial statements as a whole are free from material misstatement, whether caused by fraud or error.

(1) **Detection of Fraud** The auditor's ability to detect a fraud depends on factors such as the skillfulness of the perpetrator; the frequency and extent of manipulation; the degree of collusion involved; the relative size of individual amounts manipulated; and the seniority of those individuals involved.

(a) **Risk of *Not* Detecting Fraud Higher Than Not Detecting Error** The risk of the auditor not detecting a material misstatement resulting from fraud is higher than the risk of the auditor not detecting one resulting from error. This is because fraud may involve sophisticated and carefully organized schemes designed to conceal it, such as forgery; deliberate failure to record transactions; or intentional misrepresentations being made to the auditor. Such attempts at concealment may be even more difficult to detect when accompanied by collusion. Collusion may cause the auditor to believe that audit evidence is persuasive when it is, in fact, false.

(b) **Risk of *Not* Detecting Management Fraud Higher Than Not Detecting Employee Fraud** The risk of the auditor not detecting a material misstatement resulting from management fraud is greater than for employee fraud because management is frequently in a position to directly or indirectly manipulate accounting records; present fraudulent financial information; or override control procedures designed to prevent similar frauds by other employees.

(c) **Inherent Limitations of an Audit** Due to the inherent limitations of an audit, an unavoidable risk exists that some material misstatements may not be detected, even though the audit is properly planned and performed in accordance with US GAAS. The potential effects of the inherent limitations of an audit are particularly significant in the case of misstatement resulting from fraud.

(2) **Auditor Does *Not* Make Legal Determination of Fraud** Although the auditor may suspect or, in rare cases, identify the occurrence of fraud, the auditor does *not* make legal determinations of whether fraud has actually occurred—the auditor is interested in acts that result in a material misstatement of the financial statements.

B. Objectives

The objectives of the auditor are to:

1. **Identify & Assess RMM Due To Fraud** Identify and assess the RMM of the financial statements due to fraud

2. **Obtain Sufficient Appropriate Audit Evidence by Responding Appropriately to RMM** Obtain sufficient appropriate audit evidence regarding the assessed RMM due to fraud, through designing and implementing appropriate responses

3. **Respond Appropriately to Fraud or Suspected Fraud** Respond appropriately to fraud or suspected fraud identified during the audit

C. **Definitions**

1. **Fraud** An intentional act by one or more individuals among management, those charged with governance, employees, or third parties, involving the use of deception that results in a misstatement in financial statements that are the subject of an audit

2. **Fraud Risk Factors** Events or conditions that indicate an incentive or pressure to perpetrate fraud, provide an opportunity to commit fraud, or indicate attitudes or rationalizations to justify a fraudulent action

D. **Professional Skepticism**
The auditor should maintain professional skepticism throughout the audit, recognizing the possibility that a material misstatement due to fraud could exist, notwithstanding the auditor's past experience of the honesty and integrity of the entity's management and those charged with governance.

1. **Documents** If conditions identified during the audit cause the auditor to believe that a document may not be authentic or that terms in a document have been modified but not disclosed to the auditor, the auditor should investigate further. (Unless the auditor has reason to believe the contrary, the auditor may accept records and documents as genuine.)

2. **Inconsistencies or Unsatisfactory Responses** When responses to inquiries of management, those charged with governance, or others are inconsistent or otherwise unsatisfactory, e.g., vague or implausible, the auditor should further investigate the inconsistencies or unsatisfactory responses.

E. **Discussion Among the Engagement Team**
Communication among the engagement team members about the RMM due to fraud should continue throughout the audit, particularly upon discovery of new facts during the audit.

1. **Overview** The engagement partner and other key engagement team members are required by US GAAS to discuss the susceptibility of the entity's financial statements to material misstatement and the application of the applicable financial reporting framework to the entity's facts and circumstances.

   This discussion (relevant to this topic—fraud) should include an exchange of ideas or brainstorming among the engagement team members about how:

   - And where the financial statements might be susceptible to material misstatement due to fraud
   - Management could perpetrate and conceal fraudulent financial reporting
   - Assets of the entity could be misappropriated

2. **Matters for Discussion** The discussion should occur setting aside beliefs that the engagement team members may have that management and those charged with governance are honest and have integrity. and should, in particular, also address:

   a. **Factors That Create Incentives/Pressures** Known external and internal factors that may create an incentive or pressure for management or others to:

      - Commit fraud
      - Provide the opportunity for fraud to be perpetrated
      - Indicate a culture or environment that enables management or others to rationalize committing fraud

   b. **Management Override** The risk of management override of controls

c. **Manipulation of Revenue Recognition or Other Financial Measures** Consideration of circumstances that might be indicative of earnings management or manipulation of other financial measures and the practices that might be followed by management to manage earnings or other financial measures that could lead to fraudulent financial reporting

d. **Maintaining Professional Skepticism** The importance of maintaining professional skepticism throughout the audit regarding the potential for material misstatement due to fraud

e. **Auditor Response to Fraud** How the auditor might respond to the susceptibility of the entity's financial statements to material misstatement due to fraud

F. **Risk Assessment Procedures & Related Activities**

When performing risk assessment procedures and related activities to obtain an understanding of the entity and its environment, including the entity's internal control required by US GAAS, the auditor should perform the following procedures to obtain information for use in identifying the RMM due to fraud.

1. **Inquiries About Management's Risk Assessment Process** The auditor should make inquiries of management regarding its:

a. **Entity's Assessment of Risk to Misstatement of Financial Statements Due to Fraud** Assessment of the risk that the financial statements may be materially misstated due to fraud, including the nature, extent, and frequency of such assessments

b. **Entity's Process for Identifying, Responding to, and Monitoring Risks Of Fraud** Process for identifying, responding to, and monitoring the risks of fraud in the entity, including any specific risks of fraud that management has identified or that have been brought to its attention, or classes of transactions, account balances, or disclosures for which a risk of fraud is likely to exist

c. **Related Communication to Those Charged With Governance** Communication, if any, to those charged with governance regarding its processes for identifying and responding to the risks of fraud in the entity

2. **Inquiries About Management's & Others' Knowledge of Fraud** The auditor should make inquiries of management, and others within the entity as appropriate, to determine whether they have knowledge of any actual, suspected, or alleged fraud.

Editor Note: The auditor's inquiries of management may provide useful information concerning the RMM resulting from employee fraud; however, such inquiries are unlikely to provide useful information regarding the RMM resulting from *management* fraud. Making inquiries of others within the entity, in addition to management, may provide individuals with an opportunity to convey information to the auditor that may not otherwise be communicated.

a. **Corroboration of Management's Responses May Be Appropriate** Management is often in the best position to perpetrate fraud. Accordingly, when evaluating management's responses to inquiries with professional skepticism, the auditor *may* judge it necessary to corroborate responses to inquiries with other information.

b. **Internal Audit** For those entities that have an internal audit function, the auditor should make inquiries of internal audit to learn:

- Its views about the risks of fraud
- Whether it has knowledge of any actual, suspected, or alleged fraud

- Whether it has performed any procedures to identify or detect fraud during the year
- Whether management has satisfactorily responded to any findings resulting from these procedures

3. **Discussions With Those Charged With Governance** Unless all of those charged with governance are involved in managing the entity, the auditor should:

   a. **Obtain Understanding of Oversight Exercised** Obtain an understanding of how those charged with governance exercise oversight of management's processes for identifying and responding to the risks of fraud and relevant internal controls

   b. **Inquire About Views on Fraud Risk & Knowledge of Fraud** Make inquiries of those charged with governance to determine their views about the risks of fraud and whether they have knowledge of any actual, suspected, or alleged fraud. These inquiries are made, in part, to corroborate the responses received from the inquiries of management.

4. **Unusual or Unexpected Relationships Revealed by Analytical Procedures, Particularly Those Involving Revenue Accounts** Based on analytical procedures performed as part of the risk assessment procedures, the auditor should evaluate whether unusual or unexpected relationships identified indicate RMM due to fraud, particularly those involving revenue accounts.

   a. **Analytical Procedures Related to Revenue** Examples of such analytical procedures relating to revenue *may* include:

      - A comparison of sales volume, as determined from recorded revenue amounts, with production capacity; an excess of sales volume over production capacity may be indicative of recording fictitious sales
      - A trend analysis of revenues by month and sales returns by month, during and shortly after the reporting period; this may indicate the existence of undisclosed side agreements with customers involving the return of goods, which, if known, would preclude revenue recognition
      - A trend analysis of sales by month compared with units shipped; this may identify a material misstatement of recorded revenues

   b. **Determine If Results of Analytical Procedures Need to Be Considered With Other Information** Analytical procedures performed during planning ordinarily use data aggregated at a high level; thus, the results *may* provide only a broad initial indication about whether a material misstatement exists. Accordingly, such results would probably need to be considered along with other information gathered by the auditor in identifying the RMM due to fraud.

5. **Other Information** The auditor should consider whether other information obtained by the auditor about its entity and its environment indicates RMM due to fraud.

6. **Evaluation of Fraud Risk Factors** The auditor should evaluate whether the information obtained from the risk assessment procedures and related activities performed indicates that one or more fraud risk factors are present. (The auditor should consider evidence that indicates the existence of the three conditions that are conducive to fraud covered earlier in this topic—incentive or pressure to commit fraud; a perceived opportunity to commit fraud; and an attitude that permits rationalization to justify a fraudulent act. The inability to observe one or more of these conditions does not necessarily mean that no RMM due to fraud exists.)

The determination of whether a fraud risk factor is present and whether it is to be considered in assessing the RMM due to fraud requires the exercise of professional judgment.

Editor Note:

- Fraud risk factors cannot easily be ranked in order of importance.
- The significance of fraud risk factors varies widely. The size, complexity, and ownership characteristics of the entity have a significant influence on the consideration of relevant fraud risk factors. For example, in the case of a large entity, there may be factors that generally constrain improper conduct by management, such as:
    - Effective oversight by those charged with governance
    - An effective internal audit function
    - The existence and enforcement of a written code of conduct
- Risk factors reflective of an attitude that permits rationalization of the fraudulent action may not be susceptible to observation by the auditor; nevertheless, the auditor may become aware of the existence of such information.

a. **Examples of Risk Factors Arising From Misstatements Due to Fraudulent Financial Reporting**

(1) Incentives & Pressures

(a) Financial stability or profitability is threatened by economic, industry, or entity operating conditions, such as or as indicated by:

(i) A high degree of competition or market saturation, accompanied by declining margins

(ii) A high vulnerability to rapid changes, such as changes in technology, product obsolescence, or interest rates

(iii) Significant declines in customer demand and increasing business failures in either the industry or overall economy

(iv) Operating losses making the threat of bankruptcy, foreclosure, or hostile takeover imminent

(v) Recurring negative cash flows from operations and an inability to generate cash flows from operations while reporting earnings and earnings growth

(vi) Rapid growth or unusual profitability, especially compared to that of other companies in the same industry

(vii) New accounting, statutory, or regulatory requirements

(b) Excessive pressure exists for management to meet the requirements or expectations of third parties due to:

(i) Profitability or trend level expectations of investment analysts, institutional investors, significant creditors, or other external parties (particularly expectations that are unduly aggressive or unrealistic), including expectations created by management in, e.g., overly optimistic press releases or annual report messages

(ii) The need to obtain additional debt or equity financing to stay competitive—including financing of major research and development or capital expenditures

(iii) A marginal ability to meet exchange listing requirements or debt repayment or other debt covenant requirements

(iv) Perceived or real adverse effects of reporting poor financial results on significant pending transactions, such as business combinations or contract awards

(v) A need to achieve financial targets required in bond covenants

(vi) Pressure for management to meet the expectations of legislative or oversight bodies or to achieve political outcomes, or both

(c) Information available indicates that the personal financial situation of management or those charged with governance is threatened by the entity's financial performance arising from:

(i) Significant financial interests in the entity

(ii) Significant portions of their compensation, e.g., bonuses, stock options, and earn-out arrangements, being contingent upon achieving aggressive targets for stock price, operating results, financial position, or cash flow

(iii) Personal guarantees of debts of the entity

(d) Management or operating personnel are under excessive pressure to meet financial targets established by those charged with governance, including sales or profitability incentive goals

(2) **Opportunities**

(a) The nature of the industry or the entity's operations provides opportunities to engage in fraudulent financial reporting that can arise from:

(i) Significant related-party transactions not in the ordinary course of business or with related entities not audited or audited by another firm

(ii) A strong financial presence or ability to dominate a certain industry sector that allows the entity to dictate terms or conditions to suppliers or customers that may result in inappropriate or nonarm's-length transactions

(iii) Assets, liabilities, revenues, or expenses based on significant estimates that involve subjective judgments or uncertainties that are difficult to corroborate

(iv) Significant, unusual, or highly complex transactions, especially those close to period end that pose difficult "substance over form" questions

(v) Significant operations located or conducted across jurisdictional borders where differing business environments and regulations exist

(vi) Use of business intermediaries for which there appears to be no clear business justification

(vii) Significant bank accounts or subsidiary or branch operations in tax-haven jurisdictions for which there appears to be no clear business justification

(b) The monitoring of management is not effective as a result of:

(i) Domination of management by a single person or small group (in a nonowner-managed business) without compensating controls

(ii) Oversight by those charged with governance over the financial reporting process and internal control is not effective

(c) The organizational structure is complex or unstable, as evidenced by:

(i) Difficulty in determining the organization or individuals that have controlling interest in the entity

(ii) Overly complex organizational structure involving unusual legal entities or managerial lines of authority

(iii) High turnover of senior management, legal counsel, or those charged with governance

(d) Internal control components are deficient as a result of

(i) Inadequate monitoring of controls, including automated controls and controls over interim financial reporting (when external reporting is required)

(ii) High turnover rates or employment of staff in accounting, IT, or the internal audit function who are not effective

(iii) Accounting and information systems that are not effective, including situations involving significant deficiencies or material weaknesses in internal control

(iv) Weak controls over budget preparation and development and compliance with law or regulation

(3) **Attitudes & Rationalizations**

(a) Communication, implementation, support, or enforcement of the entity's values or ethical standards by management, or the communication of inappropriate values or ethical standards that are not effective

(b) Nonfinancial management's excessive participation in or preoccupation with the selection of accounting policies or the determination of significant estimates

(c) Known history of violations of securities law or other law or regulation, or claims against the entity, its senior management, or those charged with governance alleging fraud or violations of law or regulation

(d) Excessive interest by management in maintaining or increasing the entity's stock price or earnings trend

(e) The practice by management of committing to analysts, creditors, and other third parties to achieve aggressive or unrealistic forecasts

(f) Management failing to remedy known significant deficiencies or material weaknesses in internal control on a timely basis

(g) An interest by management in employing inappropriate means to minimize reported earnings for tax-motivated reasons

(h) Low morale among senior management

(i) The owner-manager makes no distinction between personal and business transactions

(j) Dispute between shareholders in a closely held entity

(k) Recurring attempts by management to justify marginal or inappropriate accounting on the basis of materiality

(l) A strained relationship between management and the current or predecessor auditor, as exhibited by:

(i) Frequent disputes with the current or predecessor auditor on accounting, auditing, or reporting matters

(ii) Unreasonable demands on the auditor, such as unrealistic time constraints regarding the completion of the audit or the issuance of the audit report

(iii) Restrictions on the auditor that inappropriately limit access to people or information or the ability to communicate effectively with those charged with governance

(iv) Domineering management behavior in dealing with the auditor, especially involving attempts to influence the scope of the auditor's work or the selection or continuance of personnel assigned to or consulted on the audit

b. Examples of Risk Factors Arising From Misstatements Due to Misappropriation of Assets Some of the risk factors related to misstatements arising from fraudulent financial reporting also may be present when misstatements arising from misappropriation of assets occur. For example, ineffective monitoring of management and other deficiencies in internal control that are not effective may be present when misstatements due to either fraudulent financial reporting or misappropriation of assets exist.

(1) Incentives & Pressures

(a) Personal financial obligations may create pressure on management or employees with access to cash or other assets susceptible to theft to misappropriate those assets

(b) Adverse relationships between the entity and employees with access to cash or other assets susceptible to theft may motivate those employees to misappropriate those assets, e.g., adverse relationships may be created by:

(i) Known or anticipated future employee layoffs

(ii) Recent or anticipated changes to employee compensation or benefit plans

(iii) Promotions, compensation, or other rewards inconsistent with expectations

(2) **Opportunities**

(a) Certain characteristics or circumstances may increase the susceptibility of assets to misappropriation, e.g., opportunities to misappropriate assets increase when there are:

(i) Large amounts of cash on hand or processed

(ii) Inventory items that are small in size, of high value, or in high demand

(iii) Easily convertible assets, such as bearer bonds, diamonds, or computer chips

(iv) Fixed assets that are small in size, marketable, or lacking observable identification of ownership

(b) Inadequate internal control over assets may increase the susceptibility of misappropriation of those assets, e.g., misappropriation of assets may occur because there is / are:

(i) Inadequate segregation of duties or independent checks

(ii) Inadequate oversight of senior management expenditures, such as travel and other reimbursements

(iii) Inadequate management oversight of employees responsible for assets, e.g., inadequate supervision or monitoring of remote locations

(iv) Inadequate job applicant screening of employees with access to assets

(v) Inadequate record keeping with respect to assets

(vi) An inadequate system of authorization and approval of transactions, e.g., in purchasing

(vii) Inadequate physical safeguards over cash, investments, inventory, or fixed assets

(viii) A lack of complete and timely reconciliations of assets

(ix) A lack of timely and appropriate documentation of transactions, e.g., credits for merchandise returns

(x) A lack of mandatory vacations for employees performing key control functions

(xi) Inadequate management understanding of IT, which enables IT employees to perpetrate a misappropriation

(xii) Inadequate access controls over automated records, including controls over and review of computer systems event logs

(3) **Attitudes & Rationalizations**

(a) Disregard for the need for monitoring or reducing risks related to misappropriation of assets

(b) Disregard for internal control over misappropriation of assets by overriding existing controls or by failing to take appropriate remedial action on known deficiencies in internal control

(c) Behavior indicating displeasure or dissatisfaction with the company or its treatment of the employee

(d) Changes in behavior or lifestyle that may indicate assets have been misappropriated

(e) The belief by some government or other officials that their level of authority justifies a certain level of compensation and personal privileges

(f) Tolerance of petty theft

G. Identification & Assessment of the RMM Due to Fraud

The auditor should identify and assess the RMM due to fraud at the financial statement level, and at the assertion level for classes of transactions, account balances, and disclosures. The auditor's risk assessment should be ongoing throughout the audit, following the initial assessment.

1. **Revenue Recognition** The auditor should, based on a presumption that risks of fraud exist in revenue recognition, evaluate which types of revenue, revenue transactions, or assertions give rise to such risks.

2. **Treat Fraud Risks as Significant Risks & Obtain Understanding of Related Controls** The auditor should treat those assessed RMM due to fraud as significant risks and, accordingly, the auditor should obtain an understanding of the entity's related controls, including control activities, relevant to such risks. The related controls should be evaluated to determine if they have been suitably designed and implemented to mitigate such fraud risks.

H. Responses to the Assessed RMM Due to Fraud

1. **Overall Responses (Financial Statement Level)** The auditor should determine overall responses to address the assessed RMM due to fraud at the financial statement level. (Determining overall responses to address the assessed RMM due to fraud generally includes the consideration of how the overall conduct of the audit can reflect increased professional skepticism.)

   In determining such overall responses, the auditor should:

   a. **Assignment of Personnel & Supervision** Assign and supervise personnel, taking into account the knowledge, skill, and ability of the individuals to be given significant engagement responsibilities and the auditor's assessment of the RMM due to fraud for the engagement.

   b. **Evaluate Management's Selection & Application of Accounting Principles** Evaluate whether management's selection and application of accounting principles, particularly those related to subjective measurements and complex transactions, may be indicative of fraudulent financial reporting resulting from management's effort to manage earnings, or a bias that may create a material misstatement.

c. **Ensure the Unpredictability of Auditing Procedures** Incorporate an element of unpredictability in the selection of the nature, extent, and timing of audit procedures.

2. **Audit Procedures Responsive to Assessed RMM Due to Fraud at the Assertion Level** The auditor should design and perform further audit procedures whose nature, extent, and timing are responsive to the assessed RMM due to fraud at the assertion level.

   The auditor's responses to address the assessed RMM due to fraud at the assertion level *may* include changing the nature, extent, and timing of audit procedures in the following ways:

   a. **More Reliable & Relevant Evidence** The nature of audit procedures to be performed *may* need to be changed to obtain audit evidence that is more reliable and relevant. This *may* affect both the type of audit procedures to be performed and their combination. For example:

      - Physical observation or inspection of certain assets may become more important
      - The auditor may design procedures to obtain additional corroborative information

   b. **Increase Extent Of Substantive Procedures** The extent of substantive procedures may need to be increased, e.g., increasing sample sizes or performing analytical procedures at a more detailed level may be appropriate.

   c. **Performing Substantive Procedures at or Near Period-End** The timing of substantive procedures may need to be modified, e.g., performing substantive testing at or near the period end may be appropriate.

3. **Audit Procedures Responsive to Risks Related to Management Override of Controls** Although the level of risk of management override of controls will vary from entity to entity, it is, nevertheless, present in all entities. The auditor should address this risk apart from any conclusions regarding the existence of more specifically identifiable risks by designing and performing audit procedures to:

   a. **Journal Entries** Test the appropriateness of journal entries recorded in the general ledger and other adjustments made in the preparation of the financial statements, including entries posted directly to financial statement drafts. In designing and performing audit procedures for such tests, the auditor should:

      (1) **Financial Reporting Process & Controls Over Entries** Obtain an understanding of the entity's financial reporting process and controls over journal entries and other adjustments, and the suitability of design and implementation of such controls.

      (2) **Unusual Entries** Make inquiries of individuals involved in the financial reporting process about inappropriate or unusual activity relating to the processing of journal entries and other adjustments.

      (3) **Fraud Risk Indicators** Consider fraud risk indicators; the nature and complexity of accounts; and entries processed outside the normal course of business.

      (4) **End of Period Entries** Select journal entries and other adjustments made at the end of a reporting period.

      (5) **Consider Testing Throughout the Period** Consider the need to test journal entries and other adjustments throughout the period.

b. **Accounting Estimates** Review accounting estimates included in the financial statements for biases and evaluate whether the circumstances producing the bias, if any, represent a RMM due to fraud. In performing this review, the auditor should:

(1) **Management Bias** Evaluate whether the judgments made by management in making the accounting estimates, even if they are individually reasonable, indicate a possible bias on the part of the management that may represent a RMM due to fraud; and, if so, re-evaluate the accounting estimates taken as a whole.

(2) **Retrospective Review of Management Judgments & Assumptions Related to Significant Accounting Estimates** Perform a retrospective review of management judgments and assumptions related to significant accounting estimates of the prior year. Estimates selected for review should include those that are based on highly sensitive assumptions or are otherwise significantly affected by judgments made by management.

Editor Note: As a practical matter, the auditor's review of management judgments and assumptions for biases that could represent a RMM due to fraud may be carried out in conjunction with the review required by AU 540, *Auditing Accounting Estimates, Including Fair Value Accounting Estimates, and Related Disclosures* (see chapter 5).

c. **Significant Unusual Transactions** Evaluate, for significant transactions that are outside the normal course of business for the entity or that otherwise appear to be unusual, whether the business rationale (or the lack thereof) of the transactions suggests that they may have been entered into to engage in fraudulent financial reporting or to conceal misappropriation of assets.

d. **Other Audit Procedures** The auditor should determine whether, in order to respond to the identified risks of management override of controls, the auditor needs to perform further audit procedures in addition to these, i.e., when specific additional risks of management override exist that are not addressed by the preceding required procedures.

Editor Note: RMM, including misstatements due to fraud, cannot be reduced to an appropriately low level by performing only tests of controls.

I. Evaluation of Audit Evidence

1. **Accumulated Results** The auditor should evaluate, at or near the end of the audit, whether the accumulated results of auditing procedures (including analytical procedures that were performed as substantive tests or when forming an overall conclusion) affect the assessment of the RMM due to fraud made earlier in the audit or indicate a previously unrecognized RMM due to fraud.

When forming an overall conclusion, the analytical procedures relating to revenue should be performed through the end of the reporting period.

2. **Misstatements**

a. **Misstatements Indicative of Fraud** If the auditor identifies a misstatement, the auditor should evaluate whether such a misstatement is indicative of fraud. If such an indication exists, the auditor should evaluate the implications of the misstatement with regard to other aspects of the audit, particularly the auditor's evaluation of materiality; management and employee integrity; and the reliability of management representations—recognizing that an instance of fraud is unlikely to be an isolated occurrence.

b. **Management Involvement in Fraud** If the auditor identifies a misstatement, *whether material or not*, and the auditor has reason to believe that it is, or may be, the result of fraud and that management (in particular, senior management) is involved, the auditor should re-evaluate the assessment of the RMM due to fraud and its resulting effect on the nature, extent, and timing of audit procedures to respond to the assessed risks. The auditor should also consider whether circumstances or conditions indicate possible collusion involving employees, management, or third parties when reconsidering the reliability of evidence previously obtained.

c. **Financial Statements** If the auditor concludes that, or is unable to conclude whether, the financial statements are materially misstated as a result of fraud, the auditor should evaluate the implications for the audit.

J. **Auditor Unable to Continue the Engagement**
If, as a result of identified fraud or suspected fraud, the auditor encounters circumstances that bring into question the auditor's ability to continue performing the audit, the auditor should:

1. **Determine Professional & Legal Responsibilities to Report Fraud to Others** Determine the professional and legal responsibilities applicable in the circumstances, including whether a requirement exists for the auditor to report to the person or persons who engaged the auditor or, in some cases, to regulatory authorities.

2. **Consider Withdrawal From Engagement** Consider whether it is appropriate to withdraw from the engagement, when withdrawal is possible under applicable law or regulation.

3. **Withdrawal From Engagement** If the auditor withdraws:

   a. **Discuss With Appropriate Level of Management & Those Charged With Governance** Discuss with the appropriate level of management and those charged with governance the auditor's withdrawal from the engagement and the reasons for the withdrawal.

   b. **Determine Professional & Legal Reporting of Withdrawal Requirements to Others** Determine whether a professional or legal requirement exists to report to the person or persons who engaged the auditor or, in some cases, to regulatory authorities, the auditor's withdrawal from the engagement and the reasons for the withdrawal.

4. Examples of circumstances that *may* arise and bring into question the auditor's ability to continue performing the audit include:

   - The entity does not take the appropriate action regarding fraud that the auditor considers necessary in the circumstances, even when the fraud is not material to the financial statements.
   - The auditor's consideration of the RMM due to fraud and the results of audit tests indicate a significant risk of material and pervasive fraud.
   - The auditor has significant concern about the competence or integrity of management or those charged with governance.

K. **Communications**

1. **Within the Entity** Communications with management and those charged with governance:

   a. **Management** If the auditor has identified a fraud or has obtained information that indicates that a fraud may exist, the auditor should communicate these matters on a timely basis to the appropriate level of management in order to inform those with primary responsibility for the prevention and detection of fraud of matters relevant to their responsibilities. (Ordinarily, the appropriate level of management is at least one level above the persons who appear to be involved with the suspected fraud.)

b. **Those Charged With Governance**

(1) **Parties** Unless all of those charged with governance are involved in managing the entity, if the auditor has identified or suspects fraud involving:

- Management
- Employees who have significant roles in internal control
- Others, when the fraud results in a material misstatement in the financial statements

(2) **Communicate on a Timely Basis** The auditor should communicate these matters on a timely basis. If the auditor suspects fraud involving management, the auditor should communicate these suspicions to those charged with governance and discuss with them the nature, extent, and timing of audit procedures necessary to complete the audit.

(3) **Communicate Matters That Are Relevant to Their Responsibilities** The auditor should communicate with those charged with governance any other matters related to fraud that are relevant to their responsibilities.

(4) **Communication May Be Oral or Written** The auditor's communication may be made orally or in writing; however, due to the nature and sensitivity of fraud involving senior management, or fraud that results in a material misstatement in the financial statements, the auditor communicates such matters on a timely basis and *may* consider it necessary to also communicate such matters in writing.

Editor Note: When the auditor has doubts about the integrity or honesty of management or those charged with governance, the auditor *may* consider it appropriate to obtain legal advice to assist in determining the appropriate course of action.

2. **Communications to Regulatory & Enforcement Authorities** If the auditor has identified or suspects a fraud, the auditor should determine whether the auditor has a responsibility to report the occurrence or suspicion to a party outside the entity. Although the auditor's professional duty to maintain the confidentiality of client information may preclude such reporting, the auditor's legal responsibilities may override the duty of confidentiality in some circumstances.

The duty of confidentiality *may* be overridden by statute, regulation, courts of law, specific requirements of audits of entities that receive government financial assistance, or waived by agreement. In *some* circumstances, the auditor has a statutory duty to report the occurrence of fraud to supervisory authorities. Also, in *some* circumstances, the auditor has a duty to report misstatements to authorities in those cases when management and those charged with governance fail to take corrective action.

Editor Note: The auditor may consider it appropriate to obtain legal advice to ascertain the steps necessary in considering the public interest aspects of identified fraud.

L. **Audit Documentation**

1. **Understanding of the Entity & Its Environment and the Assessment of RMM** The auditor should include in the audit documentation of the auditor's understanding of the entity and its environment and the assessment of the RMM the following:

    a. **Audit Team Discussion** The significant decisions reached during the discussion among the engagement team regarding the susceptibility of the entity's financial statements to material misstatement due to fraud, and how and when the discussion occurred and the audit team members who participated

    b. **Identified & Assessed RMM** The identified and assessed RMM due to fraud at the financial statement level and at the assertion level

2. **Auditor's Responses to the Assessed RMM** The auditor should include in the audit documentation of the auditor's responses to the assessed RMM:

    a. **Overall Responses** The overall responses to the assessed RMM due to fraud at the financial statement level and the nature, extent, and timing of audit procedures; and the linkage of those procedures with the assessed RMM due to fraud at the assertion level

    b. **Results of the Audit Procedures** The results of the audit procedures, including those designed to address the risk of management override of controls

3. **Communications** The auditor should include communications about fraud made to management, those charged with governance, regulators, and others.

4. **Revenue Recognition** If the auditor has concluded that the presumption that there is a RMM due to fraud related to revenue recognition is overcome in the circumstances of the engagement, the auditor should include in the audit documentation the reasons for that conclusion.

VIII. Consideration of Laws & Regulations in an Audit of Financial Statements (AU 250)

A. **Effect of Laws & Regulations**
Given the extent and variation of laws and regulations that can affect an entity, maintaining professional skepticism throughout the audit is important in this context.

1. **Direct Effect** The provisions of some laws and regulations have a direct effect on the determination of material amounts and disclosures in the financial statements, such as tax and pension laws and regulations.

2. **Indirect Effect** The provisions of other laws and regulations do *not* have a direct effect on the determination of the amounts and disclosures in the financial statements; however, compliance with them may be:

    a. Fundamental to the operating aspects of the business;

    b. Fundamental to an entity's ability to continue its business; or

    c. Necessary for the entity to avoid material penalties

    Noncompliance with such laws and regulations can have a material effect on the financial statements.

3. **Definition of Noncompliance** Noncompliance is defined as acts of omission or commission by the entity, either intentional or unintentional, which are contrary to the prevailing laws or

regulations. Such acts include transactions entered into by, or in the name of, the entity or on its behalf by those charged with governance, management, or employees. Noncompliance does **not** include personal misconduct (unrelated to the business activities of the entity) by these individuals.

4. **Potential Effects of Inherent Limitations of an Audit** In the context of laws and regulations, the potential effects of the inherent limitations on the auditor's ability to detect material misstatements are greater for the following reasons:

   a. Many laws and regulations relating principally to the operating aspects of an entity typically do not affect the financial statements and are not captured by the entity's information systems relevant to financial reporting.

      Editor Note: Ordinarily, the further removed noncompliance is from the events and transactions reflected in the financial statements, the *less* likely the auditor is to become aware of, or recognize, the noncompliance.

   b. Noncompliance may involve conduct designed to conceal it, such as collusion; forgery; deliberate failure to record transactions; management override of controls; or intentional misrepresentations made to the auditor.

   c. Whether an act constitutes noncompliance is ultimately a matter for legal determination, such as by a court of law.

B. Responsibility for Compliance With Laws & Regulations

1. **Management** It is the responsibility of management, with the oversight of those charged with governance, to ensure that the entity's operations are conducted in accordance with the provisions of laws and regulations, including compliance with the provisions of laws and regulations that determine the reported amounts and disclosures in an entity's financial statements.

2. **Auditor** The requirements in this section are designed to assist the auditor in identifying material misstatement of the financial statements due to noncompliance with laws and regulations. However, the auditor is **not** responsible for preventing noncompliance and cannot be expected to detect noncompliance with all laws and regulations, i.e., an audit performed in accordance with US GAAS provides *no* assurance that *all* noncompliance with laws and regulations will be detected or that any contingent liabilities that result will be disclosed.

   The responsibilities imposed on the auditor by US GAAS differ as follows (based on the effect of laws and regulations on the financial statements):

   a. **Direct Effect** The auditor's responsibility regarding misstatements resulting from noncompliance with laws and regulations having a direct effect on the determination of material amounts and disclosures in the financial statements is the same as that for misstatements caused by fraud or error.

      The auditor's responsibility is to obtain sufficient appropriate audit evidence regarding material amounts and disclosures in the financial statements that are determined by the provisions of those laws and regulations.

   b. **Indirect Effect** The auditor's responsibility is limited to performing specified audit procedures that may identify noncompliance with those laws and regulations that may have a material effect on the financial statements.

   The auditor then responds appropriately to noncompliance or suspected noncompliance with laws and regulations identified during the audit.

C. The Auditor's Consideration of Compliance With Laws & Regulations

In the absence of identified or suspected noncompliance, the auditor is **not** required to perform audit procedures regarding the entity's compliance, other than those set out below and obtaining written representations—along with the other written representations required—from management regarding the entity's compliance with laws and regulations. (However, written representations do not provide sufficient appropriate audit evidence on their own and, accordingly, do not affect the nature and extent of other audit evidence that is to be obtained by the auditor.)

1. **Obtain Understanding of & Degree of Compliance With Framework** The auditor should obtain a general understanding of the following:

   a. The legal and regulatory framework applicable to the entity and the industry or sector in which the entity operates

   b. How the entity is complying with that framework

2. **Direct Effect: Obtain Evidence to Support Related Financial Statement Items** The auditor should obtain sufficient appropriate audit evidence regarding material amounts and disclosures in the financial statements that are determined by the provisions of those laws and regulations generally recognized to have a direct effect on their determination.

3. **Indirect Effect: Perform Procedures That May Identify Noncompliance** The auditor should perform the following audit procedures that may identify instances of noncompliance with other laws and regulations that may have a material effect on the financial statements:

   a. Inquiring of management about whether the entity is in compliance with such laws and regulations

   b. Inspecting correspondence, if any, with the relevant licensing or regulatory authorities

      Editor Note: If the amount of an entity's correspondence with licensing or regulatory authorities is voluminous, the auditor *may consider* the nature of the entity as well as the nature and type of correspondence in determining the extent of the inspection.

   Even when these procedures are performed, the auditor may not become aware of the existence of noncompliance unless there is evidence in the records, documents, or other information normally inspected in an audit of financial statements.

4. **Other Procedures** During the audit, the auditor should remain alert to the possibility that other audit procedures applied for other purposes may bring instances of noncompliance or suspected noncompliance with laws and regulations to the auditor's attention.

   Examples of such other audit procedures include:

   - Reading minutes
   - Inquiring of the entity's management and in-house or external legal counsel concerning litigation, claims, and assessments
   - Performing substantive tests of details of classes of transactions, account balances, or disclosures

D. Audit Procedures When Noncompliance Is Identified or Suspected

1. **Possible Indicators of Noncompliance (Red Flags)** If the auditor becomes aware of the existence of, or information about, the following matters, it may be an indication of noncompliance with laws and regulations:

   - Investigations by regulatory organizations and government departments or payment of fines or penalties
   - Payments for unspecified services or loans to consultants, related parties, employees, or government officials or government employees
   - Sales commissions or agent's fees that appear excessive in relation to those ordinarily paid by the entity or in its industry or to the services actually received
   - Purchases made at prices significantly above or below market price
   - Unusual payments in cash, purchases in the form of cashiers' checks payable to bearer, or transfers to numbered bank accounts
   - Unusual transactions with companies registered in tax havens
   - Payments for goods or services made other than to the country from which the goods or services originated
   - Existence of an information system that fails, whether by design or accident, to provide an adequate audit trail or sufficient evidence
   - Unauthorized transactions or improperly recorded transactions
   - Adverse media comment
   - Noncompliance with laws or regulations cited in reports of examinations by regulatory agencies that have been made available to the auditor
   - Failure to file tax returns or pay government duties or similar fees that are common to the entity's industry or the nature of its business

2. **Procedures** If the auditor becomes aware of information concerning an instance of noncompliance or suspected noncompliance with laws and regulations, the auditor should obtain an understanding of the nature of the act and the circumstances in which it has occurred. Next, the auditor should obtain further information to evaluate the possible effect on the financial statements.

   Procedures the auditor *may* perform include:

   - Examining supporting documents, such as invoices, cancelled checks, and agreements, and comparing with accounting records
   - Confirming significant information concerning the matter with the other party to the transaction or intermediaries, such as banks or lawyers
   - Determining whether the transaction has been properly authorized
   - Considering whether other similar transactions or events may have occurred and applying procedures to identify them

   Matters relevant to the auditor's evaluation of the possible effect on the financial statements include the following:

   - The quantitative effect of noncompliance: the potential financial consequences of noncompliance with laws and regulations on the financial statements may include the imposition of fines, penalties, or damages; the threat of expropriation of assets; enforced discontinuation of operations; and litigation

- The qualitative materiality of the effect of noncompliance: for example, an illegal payment of an otherwise immaterial amount could be material if a reasonable possibility exists that it could lead to a material contingent liability or a material loss of revenue
- Whether the potential financial consequences require accrual or disclosure under the AFRF; e.g., if material revenue or earnings are derived from transactions involving noncompliance, or if noncompliance creates significant risks associated with material revenue or earnings, such as loss of a significant business relationship, that information may require disclosure; loss contingencies resulting from noncompliance that may require disclosure may be evaluated in the same manner as other loss contingencies under the AFRF
- Whether the potential financial consequences are so serious as to call into question the fair presentation of the financial statements or otherwise make the financial statements misleading

3. **Hold Discussion With Client** If the auditor suspects noncompliance, the auditor should discuss it with management (at a level above those involved, if possible)..

4. **Consider Legal Consult If Discussion With Client Doesn't Resolve Matter** If sufficient information that supports that the entity is in compliance is not provided and the effect of the suspected noncompliance may be material to the financial statements, the auditor should consider consultation with the entity's in-house legal counsel, if appropriate, or external legal counsel about the application of the laws and regulations to the circumstances, including the possibility of fraud, and the possible effects on the financial statements.

   Editor Note: Even if the discussion with those charged with governance does not result in additional information, the auditor may at least be able to confirm that those charged with governance have the same understanding of the facts and circumstances relevant to the possibility of the noncompliance.

5. **Consider Impact of Insufficient Information**

   a. **On Audit Opinion** When sufficient information about suspected noncompliance cannot be obtained, the auditor should evaluate the effect of the lack of sufficient appropriate audit evidence on the auditor's opinion.

   b. **On Other Aspects of Audit** The auditor should evaluate the implications of noncompliance in relation to other aspects of the audit, including the auditor's risk assessment and the reliability of written representations, and take appropriate action.

      The implications of particular instances of noncompliance identified by the auditor will depend on the relationship of the perpetration and concealment, if any, of the act to specific control activities and the level of management or employees involved, especially implications arising from the involvement of the highest authority within the entity.

   The auditor *may consider* whether withdrawal from the engagement, when withdrawal is possible under applicable law or regulation, is necessary when management or those charged with governance do not take the remedial action that the auditor considers appropriate in the circumstances, *even when the noncompliance is **not** material to the financial statements*. Factors that may affect the auditor's decision may include the implications of the failure to take remedial action, which may affect the auditor's ability to rely on management representations, and the effects of continuing association with the entity. When deciding whether withdrawal from the engagement is necessary, the auditor may consider seeking legal advice.

   If withdrawal from the engagement is not possible under applicable law or regulation, the auditor may consider alternative actions, including describing the noncompliance in an other-matter paragraph in the audit report.

E. Reporting of Identified or Suspected Noncompliance

1. Reporting Noncompliance to Those Charged With Governance

a. **Communicate All Noncompliance Except Inconsequential Matters** Unless all of those charged with governance are involved in management of the entity and aware of matters involving identified or suspected noncompliance already communicated by the auditor, the auditor should communicate with those charged with governance such matters, other than those that are clearly inconsequential. (The auditor *may* reach agreement in advance with those charged with governance on the nature of matters that would be considered clearly inconsequential and, thus, need not be communicated.)

   The communication of matters involving identified or suspected noncompliance *may* describe the act, the circumstances of its occurrence, and the effect on the financial statements.

b. **Timely Notice If Noncompliance Is Intentional & Material** If such noncompliance is believed to be intentional and material, the auditor should communicate it as soon as practicable.

c. **Consider Legal Consult When Management or Those Charged With Governance May Be Involved** If the auditor suspects that management or those charged with governance are involved in the noncompliance, the auditor should communicate the matter to the next higher level of authority at the entity, if it exists. When no higher authority exists, or if the auditor believes that the communication may not be acted upon or is unsure about the person to whom to report, the auditor *should consider* the need to obtain legal advice.

2. Reporting Noncompliance in the Audit Report

a. **Financial Statements Materially Misstated** If the auditor concludes that the noncompliance has a material effect on the financial statements and has not been adequately reflected in the financial statements, the auditor should express a qualified or adverse opinion on the financial statements.

b. **Scope Limitation**

   (1) **Imposed by Entity** If the auditor is precluded by management or those charged with governance from obtaining sufficient appropriate audit evidence to evaluate whether noncompliance that may be material to the financial statements has, or is likely to have, occurred, the auditor should express a qualified opinion or disclaim an opinion on the financial statements on the basis of a limitation on the scope of the audit.

   (2) **Imposed by Circumstances** If the auditor is unable to determine whether noncompliance has occurred because of limitations imposed by the circumstances rather than by management or those charged with governance, the auditor should evaluate the effect on the auditor's opinion.

Editor Note: If the client refuses to accept a modified opinion on the financial statements, the auditor may withdraw from the engagement, when withdrawal is possible under applicable law or regulation, and indicate the reasons for withdrawal in writing to those charged with governance.

3. Reporting Noncompliance to Regulatory & Enforcement Authorities
If the auditor has identified or suspects noncompliance with laws and regulations, the auditor should determine

whether the auditor has a responsibility to report the identified or suspected noncompliance to parties outside the entity.

The auditor's professional duty to maintain the confidentiality of client information may preclude reporting identified or suspected noncompliance with laws and regulations to a party outside the entity. However, the auditor's legal responsibilities vary by jurisdiction, and in certain circumstances, the duty of confidentiality may be overridden by statute, the law, or courts of law. Because these potential conflicts may be complex, the auditor *may* consult with legal counsel before discussing noncompliance with parties outside the entity.

In the following circumstances, a duty to notify parties outside the entity *may* exist:

- In response to inquiries from an auditor to a predecessor auditor
- In response to a court order
- In compliance with requirements for the audits of entities that receive financial assistance from a government agency

F. Audit Documentation

The auditor should include in the audit documentation a description of the identified or suspected noncompliance with laws and regulations and the results of the discussion with management and, when applicable, those charged with governance and other parties inside or outside the entity. Such documentation *may* include copies of records or documents and minutes of discussions held.

IX. Responding to Assessed Risks (AU 330)

A. Objective

The objective of the auditor is to obtain sufficient appropriate audit evidence regarding the assessed risk of material misstatement (RMM) through designing and implementing appropriate responses to those risks.

B. Definitions

1. **Substantive Procedure** An audit procedure designed to detect material misstatements at the assertion level. Substantive procedures comprise:

    a. **Tests of Details** Tests of details (classes of transactions, account balances, and disclosures)

    b. **Analytical Procedures** Substantive analytical procedures

2. **Tests of Controls** An audit procedure designed to evaluate the operating effectiveness of controls in preventing, or detecting and correcting, material misstatements at the assertion level.

Editor Note: Coverage (in accordance with AU 330) in this text of tests of controls is included in chapter on internal control; coverage of substantive procedures is included in chapter on audit programs; and coverage of evaluating the sufficiency and appropriateness of audit evidence is included in chapter on evidence and procedures.

C. Financial Statement Level

The auditor should design and implement overall responses to address the assessed RMM at the financial statement level. Overall responses *may* include:

1. Examples of Overall Responses

a. **Professional Skepticism** Emphasizing to the audit team the need to maintain professional skepticism

b. **Assignments** Assigning more experienced staff or those with specialized skills or using specialists

c. **Supervision** Providing more supervision

d. **Unpredictability** Incorporating more unpredictable elements in the selection of further audit procedures

e. **General Changes** Making general changes to the nature, extent, and timing of audit procedures (for example, performing substantive procedures at period-end instead of at an interim date or modifying the nature of audit procedures to obtain more persuasive audit evidence)

2. Impact of Control Environment

Impact of Control Environment The assessment of the RMM at the financial statement level and, thereby, the auditor's overall responses are affected by the auditor's understanding of the control environment.

a. **Effective Control Environment** An effective control environment *may* allow the auditor to have more confidence in internal control and the reliability of audit evidence generated internally by the entity and, thus, for example, allow the auditor to conduct some audit procedures at an interim date rather than at the period-end. The auditor can take a combined approach, i.e., one that uses tests of controls as well as substantive procedures.

b. **Deficient Control Environment** Deficiencies in the control environment, however, have the opposite effect, for example, the auditor may respond to an ineffective control environment by:

- Conducting more audit procedures as of the period-end rather than at an interim date
- Obtaining more extensive audit evidence from substantive procedures
- Increasing the number of locations to be included in the audit scope

D. Audit Procedures at the Relevant Assertion Level

1. **Responsive to the Assessed RMM** The auditor should design further audit procedures whose nature, extent, and timing are based on, and are responsive to, the assessed RMM at the relevant assertion level. *This provides a clear linkage between the auditor's further audit procedures and the risk assessment.*

    a. **Audit Approach** The auditor's assessment of the identified risks at the relevant assertion level provides a basis for considering the appropriate audit approach for designing and performing further audit procedures. The auditor may determine that the effective response *for a particular assertion*:

    (1) **Tests of Controls** *May* be achieved only by performing tests of controls (in addition to the substantive procedures that are required for all relevant assertions)

    (2) **Substantive Procedures** *May* be to perform only substantive procedures; thus, the auditor excludes the effect of controls from the relevant risk assessment

    Editor Note: This may be because the auditor's risk assessment procedures have not identified any effective controls relevant to the assertion or because testing controls would be inefficient, and therefore, the auditor does *not* intend to rely on the operating effectiveness of controls in determining the nature, extent, and timing of substantive procedures.

    (3) **Combined Approach** *May* be achieved by a combined approach using both tests of controls and substantive procedures

    Editor Note: Because effective internal controls generally reduce but do not eliminate the RMM, tests of controls reduce but do not eliminate the need for substantive procedures. In addition, analytical [substantive] procedures alone may not be sufficient in some cases. For example, when auditing certain estimation processes, such as the allowance for doubtful accounts, the auditor may perform substantive procedures beyond analytical procedures (for example, examining cash collections subsequent to the period-end) due to the risk of management override of controls or the subjectivity of the account balance.

    b. **Nature** The nature of an audit procedure refers to its purpose (test of controls or substantive procedure) and its type (inspection, observation, inquiry, confirmation, recalculation, reperformance, or analytical procedure). The nature of the audit procedures is most important in responding to the assessed risks.

    The auditor's assessed risks may affect both the types of audit procedures to be performed and their combination.

    (1) **Type** For example, when an assessed risk is high, the auditor may confirm the completeness [assertion] of the terms of a contract with the counterparty, in addition to inspecting the document.

    (2) **Purpose** Further, certain audit procedures may be more appropriate for some assertions than others. For example, regarding revenue, tests of controls may be most responsive to the assessed risk of misstatement of the completeness assertion, whereas substantive procedures may be most responsive to the assessed risk of misstatement of the occurrence assertion.

c. **Extent** The extent of an audit procedure refers to the quantity to be performed, for example, a sample size or the number of observations of a control activity. The extent of an audit procedure is determined after considering the:

(1) Materiality

(2) Assessed risk

(3) Degree of assurance the auditor plans to obtain

In general, the extent of audit procedures increases as the RMM increase; however, increasing the extent of an audit procedure is effective only if the audit procedure itself is relevant to the specific risk.

d. **Timing** The timing of an audit procedure refers to when it is performed or the period or date to which the audit evidence applies.

(1) **Interim Date** Performing audit procedures before the period-end may assist the auditor in identifying significant issues at an early stage of the audit and consequently resolving them with the assistance of management or developing an effective audit approach to address such issues.

(2) **Period-End** The higher the RMM, the more likely it is that the auditor may decide it is more effective to perform substantive procedures nearer to or at the period-end.

Also, certain audit procedures can only be performed at or after the period-end, such as:

- Agreeing the financial statements to the accounting records
- Examining adjustments made during the course of preparing the financial statements
- Procedures to respond to a risk that, at the period-end, the entity may have entered into improper sales contracts; or transactions may not have been finalized

(3) **Unpredictable Times** The higher the RMM, the more likely it is that the auditor may decide it is more effective to perform audit procedures unannounced or at unpredictable times.

This is particularly relevant when considering the response to the risks of fraud—the auditor *may* conclude that, when the risks of intentional misstatement or manipulation have been identified, audit procedures to extend audit conclusions from the interim date to the period-end would **not** be effective.

(4) **Other Timing Factors** Further relevant factors that influence the auditor's consideration of when to perform audit procedures include:

- The effectiveness of the control environment
- When relevant information is available (for example, electronic files may subsequently be overwritten; or procedures to be observed may occur only at certain times)
- The nature of the risk (for example, if there is a risk of inflated revenues to meet earnings expectations by subsequent creation of false sales agreements, the auditor may examine contracts available on the date of the period-end)

- The period or date to which the audit evidence relates

2. **Other Important Design Considerations** In designing the further audit procedures, the auditor should:

   a. Consider the reasons for the assessed RMM at the relevant assertion level for each class of transactions, account balance, and disclosure, including:

      (1) **Inherent Risk** The likelihood of material misstatement due to the particular characteristics of the relevant class of transactions, account balance, or disclosure

      For example, if an assessed risk is lower because of the particular characteristics of a class of transactions without consideration of the related controls (lower inherent risk), then the auditor may determine that substantive analytical procedures alone provide sufficient appropriate audit evidence.

      (2) **Control Risk** Whether the risk assessment takes account of relevant controls (the control risk), thereby requiring the auditor to obtain audit evidence to determine whether the controls are operating effectively, i.e., the auditor intends to rely on the operating effectiveness of controls in determining the nature, extent, and timing of substantive procedures

      If the assessed risk is lower because of internal controls and the auditor intends to base the substantive procedures on that low assessment, then the auditor performs tests of those controls. This may be the case, for example, for a class of transactions of reasonably uniform, noncomplex characteristics that are routinely processed and controlled by the entity's information system.

   b. Obtain more persuasive audit evidence the higher the auditor's assessment of risk—the auditor may increase the quantity of the evidence; or obtain evidence that is more relevant or reliable.

E. Adequacy of Presentation & Disclosure

The auditor should perform audit procedures to evaluate whether the overall presentation of the financial statements, including the related disclosures, is in accordance with the AFRF.

Evaluating the overall presentation of the financial statements, including the related disclosures, relates to whether the individual financial statements are presented in a manner that reflects the appropriate classification and description of financial information and the form, arrangement, and content of the financial statements, including the related notes. This includes, for example, the terminology used, the amount of detail given, the classification of items in the financial statements, and the basis of amounts set forth.

F. Audit Documentation

The following should be included in the audit documentation:

1. Overall responses to address the assessed RMM at the financial statement level and the nature, extent, and timing of the further audit procedures performed

2. Linkage of those procedures with the assessed risks at the relevant assertion level

3. Results of the audit procedures, including the conclusions when such conclusions are not otherwise clear

4. If the auditor plans to use audit evidence about the operating effectiveness of controls obtained in previous audits, the conclusions reached about relying on such controls that were tested in a previous audit

5. Basis for any determination *not* to use external confirmation procedures for accounts receivable when the account balance is material

6. Demonstration that the financial statements agree or reconcile with the underlying accounting records

X. Evaluation of Misstatements Identified During the Audit (AU 450)

A. Objective

The objective of the auditor is to evaluate the effect of:

1. Identified misstatements on the audit

2. Uncorrected misstatements, if any, on the financial statements

B. Definitions

1. **Misstatement** A difference between the amount, classification, presentation, or disclosure of a reported financial statement item and the same aspects that are required for the item to be presented fairly in accordance with the AFRF; misstatements can arise from fraud or error

   Misstatements *may* result from fraud or error; examples resulting from error include:

   a. An inaccuracy in gathering or processing data from which the financial statements are prepared

   b. An omission of an amount or disclosure

   c. A financial statement disclosure that is not presented in accordance with the AFRF

   d. An incorrect accounting estimate arising from overlooking or clear misinterpretation of facts

   e. Judgments of management concerning accounting estimates that the auditor considers unreasonable or the selection or application of accounting policies that the auditor considers inappropriate

   Editor Note: See the topic on fraud in this chapter for examples of misstatements resulting from fraud.

2. **Uncorrected Misstatements** Misstatements that the auditor has accumulated during the audit and that have not been corrected

C. Accumulation of Identified Misstatements

1. **Accumulation** The auditor should accumulate misstatements identified during the audit, other than those that are clearly trivial.

   Editor Note: *Clearly trivial* is **not** another expression for *not material*. Matters that are clearly trivial will be of a wholly different (smaller) order of magnitude than the determined level of materiality and will be matters that are clearly inconsequential, whether taken individually or in the aggregate and whether judged by any criteria of size, nature, or circumstances. When there is *any* uncertainty about whether one or more items are clearly trivial, the matter is considered *not* to be clearly trivial.

2. **Categories of Misstatements** To assist the auditor in evaluating the effect of misstatements accumulated during the audit and in communicating misstatements to management and those charged with governance, the auditor *may* find it useful to distinguish between the following categories of misstatements:

   a. **Factual Misstatements** Factual misstatements are misstatements about which there is no doubt.

   b. **Judgmental Misstatements** Judgmental misstatements are differences arising from the judgments of management concerning accounting estimates that the auditor considers unreasonable or the selection or application of accounting policies that the auditor considers inappropriate.

      Editor Note: When the auditor has identified a judgmental misstatement involving differences in estimates, such as a difference in a fair value estimate, the auditor *may* request management to review the assumptions and methods used in developing management's estimate.

   c. **Projected Misstatements** Projected misstatements are the auditor's best estimate of misstatements in populations, involving the projection of misstatements identified in audit samples to the entire population from which the samples were drawn.

D. **Consideration of Identified Misstatements as the Audit Progresses**
The auditor should determine whether the overall audit strategy and audit plan need to be revised if *either* the:

1. Nature of identified misstatements and the circumstances of their occurrence indicate that other misstatements may exist that, when aggregated with misstatements accumulated during the audit, could be material

   Editor Note: A misstatement may not be an isolated occurrence. Evidence that other misstatements *may* exist include, for example, when the auditor identifies that a misstatement arose from a breakdown in internal control or from inappropriate assumptions or valuation methods that have been widely applied by the entity.

2. Aggregate of misstatements accumulated during the audit approaches the determined materiality

   Editor Note: If the aggregate of misstatements accumulated during the audit approaches materiality, a greater than acceptably low level of risk may exist that possible undetected misstatements, when taken with the aggregate of uncorrected misstatements accumulated during the audit, could exceed materiality. (Undetected misstatements could exist because of the presence of sampling risk and nonsampling risk; see the chapter on audit sampling in this text.)

E. **Communication & Correction of Misstatements**

1. **Communication** The auditor should communicate on a timely basis with the appropriate level of management all misstatements accumulated during the audit.

2. **Request Correction of Misstatements** The auditor should request management to correct those misstatements.

   a. **Additional Audit Procedures** If, at the auditor's request, management has examined a class of transactions, account balance, or disclosure and corrected misstatements that were detected, the auditor should perform additional audit procedures to determine whether misstatements remain.

b. **When Management Refuses to Make Corrections** If management refuses to correct some or all of the misstatements communicated by the auditor, the auditor should obtain an understanding of management's reasons for not making the corrections and should take that understanding into account when evaluating whether the financial statements as a whole are free from material misstatement.

Editor Note: One of the written representations which US GAAS requires the auditor to request is about whether management believes the effects of uncorrected misstatements are immaterial, individually and in the aggregate, to the financial statements as a whole. A summary of such items should be included in, or attached to, the written representation.

F. Evaluating the Effect of Uncorrected Misstatements

1. **Reassess Materiality** Prior to evaluating the effect of uncorrected misstatements, the auditor should reassess materiality to confirm whether it remains appropriate in the context of the entity's *actual* financial results—often the auditor's initial determination of materiality is based on *estimates* of the entity's financial results because the actual financial results may not yet be known. (However, as the auditor became aware of more information during the audit, any significant revision of materiality is likely to have already been made before the auditor evaluates the effect of uncorrected misstatements.)

2. **Determine Whether Uncorrected Misstatements Are Material** The auditor should determine whether uncorrected misstatements are material, individually or in the aggregate. In making this determination, the auditor should consider:

a. **Effect of Uncorrected Misstatements Related to Prior Periods** The effect of uncorrected misstatements related to prior periods on the relevant classes of transactions, account balances, or disclosures and the financial statements as a whole

b. **Size & Nature of the Misstatements** The size and nature of the misstatements, both in relation to particular classes of transactions, account balances, or disclosures and the financial statements as a whole, and the particular circumstances of their occurrence

(1) **Offsetting Misstatements** If an individual misstatement is judged to be material, it is *un*likely that it can be offset by other misstatements. For example, if revenue has been materially overstated, the financial statements as a whole will be materially misstated, even if the effect of the misstatement on earnings is completely offset by an equivalent overstatement of expenses. On the other hand, it may be appropriate to offset misstatements within the same account balance or class of transactions; however, the risk that further undetected misstatements may exist is considered before concluding that offsetting even immaterial misstatements is appropriate. The auditor may need to reassess the risk of material misstatement (RMM) for a specific account balance or class of transactions upon identification of a number of immaterial misstatements within it.

(2) **Circumstances That *May* Cause a Misstatement to Be Judged as Material** The circumstances related to some misstatements *may* cause the auditor to evaluate them as material, individually or when considered together with other misstatements accumulated during the audit, even if they are lower than materiality for the financial statements as a whole.

Circumstances that *may* affect the evaluation include the extent to which the misstatement:

- Affects compliance with regulatory requirements

- Affects compliance with debt covenants or other contractual requirements
- Relates to the incorrect selection or application of an accounting policy that has an immaterial effect on the current period's financial statements but is likely to have a material effect on future periods' financial statements
- Masks a change in earnings or other trends, especially in the context of general economic and industry conditions
- Affects ratios used to evaluate the entity's financial position, results of operations, or cash flows
- Affects segment information presented in the financial statements, for example, the significance of the matter to a segment or other portion of the entity's business that has been identified as playing a significant role in the entity's operations or profitability
- Has the effect of increasing management compensation, for example, by ensuring that the requirements for the award of bonuses or other incentives are satisfied
- Is significant with regard to the auditor's understanding of known previous communications to users, for example, regarding forecast earnings
- Relates to items involving particular parties, for example, whether external parties to the transaction are related to members of the entity's management
- Is an omission of information not specifically required by the AFRF but that, in the professional judgment of the auditor, is important to the users' understanding of the financial position, financial performance, or cash flows of the entity
- Affects other information that will be communicated in documents containing the audited financial statements, for example, information to be included in a "Management Discussion and Analysis" or an "Operating and Financial Review", that may reasonably be expected to influence the economic decisions of the users of the financial statements
- Is a misclassification between certain account balances affecting items disclosed separately in the financial statements, for example, misclassification between operating and nonoperating income; recurring and nonrecurring income items; or a misclassification between restricted and unrestricted resources in a not-for-profit entity
- Offsets effects of individually significant but different misstatements
- Is currently immaterial and likely to have a material effect in future periods because of a cumulative effect, for example, that builds over several periods
- Is too costly to correct; it may not be cost beneficial for the client to develop a system to calculate a basis to record the effect of an immaterial misstatement; on the other hand, if management appears to have developed a system to calculate an amount that represents an immaterial misstatement, it may reflect a motivation of management
- Represents a risk that possible additional undetected misstatements would affect the auditor's evaluation
- Changes a loss into income or vice versa
- Heightens the sensitivity of the circumstances surrounding the misstatement, for example, the implications of misstatements involving fraud and

possible instances of noncompliance with laws or regulations; violations of contractual provisions; and conflicts of interest

- Has a significant effect relative to reasonable user needs, for example,
  - Earnings to investors and the equity amounts to creditors
  - The magnifying effects of a misstatement on the calculation of purchase price in a transfer of interests (buy-sell agreement)
  - The effect of misstatements of earnings when contrasted with expectations
- Relates to the definitive character of the misstatement, for example, the precision of an error that is objectively determinable as contrasted with a misstatement that unavoidably involves a degree of subjectivity through estimation, allocation, or uncertainty
- Indicates the motivation of management, for example, an indication of a possible pattern of bias by management when developing and accumulating accounting estimates; a misstatement precipitated by management's continued unwillingness to correct weaknesses in the financial reporting process; or an intentional decision not to follow the AFRF

G. Audit Documentation
The auditor should include in the audit documentation:

1. The amount below which misstatements would be regarded as clearly trivial
2. All misstatements accumulated during the audit and whether they have been corrected
3. The auditor's conclusion about whether uncorrected misstatements are material, individually

XI. Communication With Those Charged With Governance (AU 260)
AU 260, *The Auditor's Communication With Those Charged With Governance*, provides an overarching framework for the auditor's communication with those charged with governance and identifies *some* of the specific matters to be communicated. Additional matters to be communicated are identified in other AU sections covered in this text.

Editor Note: Nothing precludes the auditor from communicating any other matters not covered by US GAAS to those charged with governance.

A. Objectives
The objectives of the auditor are to:

1. Communicate clearly the responsibilities of the auditor regarding the financial statement audit and an overview of the planned scope and timing of the audit
2. Obtain from those charged with governance information relevant to the audit
3. Provide those charged with governance with timely observations arising from the audit that are significant and relevant to their responsibility to oversee the financial reporting process
4. Promote effective two-way communication between the auditor and those charged with governance

   Effective two-way communication is important in assisting:

   a. Both in understanding matters related to the audit in context and in developing a constructive working relationship—this relationship is developed while maintaining the auditor's independence and objectivity

b. The auditor in obtaining information relevant to the audit, e.g., those charged with governance may assist the auditor in understanding the entity and its environment, in identifying appropriate sources of audit evidence, and in providing information about specific transactions or events

c. Those charged with governance in fulfilling their responsibility to oversee the financial reporting process, thereby reducing the risk of material misstatement (RMM) of the financial statements

Editor Note:

- Communication by the auditor does not relieve management of its responsibility to communicate matters of governance interest to those charged with governance. Similarly, management's communication of such matters to those charged with governance does not relieve the auditor of the responsibility to also communicate them; however, it may affect the form or timing of the auditor's communication.
- US GAAS do not require the auditor to perform procedures specifically to identify other matters (not required by US GAAS) to communicate with those charged with governance.

B. Definitions

1. **Management** The person(s) with executive responsibility for the conduct of the entity's operations; for some entities, management includes some or all of those charged with governance, e.g., executive members of a governance board or an owner-manager

2. **Those Charged With Governance** The person(s) or organization(s), e.g., a corporate trustee, with responsibility for overseeing the strategic direction of the entity and the obligations related to the accountability of the entity; this includes overseeing the financial reporting process; those charged with governance may include management personnel, e.g., executive members of a governance board or an owner-manager

C. Determination of Persons With Whom the Auditor Should Communicate
The auditor should determine the appropriate person(s) within the entity's governance structure with whom to communicate. Government structures vary so it is not possible to specify this for all audits. When the appropriate person(s) with whom to communicate is not clearly identifiable, the auditor and the engaging party *may* need to agree on the relevant person(s). And the appropriate person(s) may vary depending on the matter to be communicated.

1. **Communication With an Audit Committee or Other Subgroup** When governance is a collective responsibility, a subgroup, such as an audit committee (or an individual), may be charged with specific tasks to assist the governing body in meeting its responsibilities. Communication with such a subgroup is a key element in the auditor's communication with those charged with governance.

a. The auditor should determine whether the auditor also needs to communicate with the governing body. This decision will, of course, be influenced by the auditor's assessment of how effectively and appropriately the subgroup communicates relevant information with the governing body. The auditor *may* make explicit in the terms of the engagement that the auditor retains the right to communicate directly with the governing body.

b. Good governance principles *suggest* that:

(1) The auditor has access to the audit committee as necessary

(2) The chair of the audit committee and, when relevant, the other members of the audit committee meet with the auditor periodically

(3) The audit committee meets with the auditor without management present at least annually, unless prohibited by law or regulation

2. **When All of Those Charged With Governance Are Involved in Managing the Entity** When all of those charged with governance are involved in managing the entity, e.g., a small business, if matters required by this section are communicated with a person with management responsibilities, the matters need not be communicated again with the same person in their governance role. The auditor should, nonetheless, be satisfied that communication with persons with management responsibilities adequately informs all of those with whom the auditor would otherwise communicate in their governance capacity.

D. Matters to Be Communicated

1. **The Auditor's Responsibilities With Regard to the Financial Statement Audit** The auditor should communicate the auditor's responsibilities with regard to the financial statement audit, including that:

   a. **Opinion** The auditor is responsible for forming and expressing an opinion about whether the financial statements that have been prepared by management, with the oversight of those charged with governance, are prepared, in all material respects, in accordance with the AFRF.

   b. **Responsibilities** The audit of the financial statements does **not** relieve management or those charged with governance of their responsibilities.

   Editor Note: Although the audit report affirms the auditor's independence, the auditor *may* determine that it is appropriate to communicate circumstances or relationships, e.g., financial interests, business or family relationships, or nonaudit services provided or expected to be provided, to which the auditor gave significant consideration in reaching the conclusion that independence has *not* been impaired. This *may* be particularly appropriate in audits of public interest entities, i.e., employee benefit and health and welfare plans; entities or programs subject to specific government program oversight; and financial institutions, credit unions, and insurance companies.

   Unlike the AICPA (US GAAS), the PCAOB has requirements (rules) for communication with audit committees concerning independence. A registered public accounting firm must:

   - Prior to accepting an initial engagement:
     - Describe, in writing, to the audit committee of the issuer, all relationships between the firm or any affiliates of the firm and the potential audit client or persons in financial reporting oversight roles at the potential audit client that, as of the date of the communication, may reasonably be thought to bear on independence
     - Discuss with the audit committee of the issuer the potential effects of the relationships described above on the independence of the registered public accounting firm, should it be appointed the issuer's auditor
     - Document the substance of its discussion with the audit committee of the issuer
   - At least annually with respect to each of its issuer audit clients:
     - Describe, in writing, to the audit committee of the issuer, all relationships between the registered public accounting firm or any affiliates of the firm and the audit client or persons in financial reporting oversight roles at the audit client that, as of the date of the communication, may reasonably be thought to bear on independence

- Discuss with the audit committee of the issuer the potential effects of the relationships described above on the independence of the registered public accounting firm
- Affirm to the audit committee of the issuer, in writing, that, as of the date of the communication, the registered public accounting firm is independent in compliance with rules of the PCAOB and federal securities laws
- Document the substance of its discussion with the audit committee of the issuer

2. **Planned Scope & Timing of the Audit** The auditor should communicate an *overview* of the planned scope and timing of the audit. (Although communication with those charged with governance may assist the auditor with planning the scope and timing of the audit, it does *not* change the auditor's *sole* responsibility to establish the overall audit strategy and the audit plan, including the nature, extent, and timing of procedures necessary to obtain sufficient appropriate audit evidence.)

Matters communicated *may* include the following:

- How the auditor proposes to address the significant RMM
- The auditor's approach to internal control relevant to the audit including, whether the auditor will express an opinion on the effectiveness of internal control over financial reporting (see this topic in chapter 14)
- The application of materiality in the context of an audit
- How the auditor and the internal auditors can work together, including any planned use of the work of the internal audit function in obtaining audit evidence and the nature and extent of any planned use of internal auditors to provide direct assistance
- The attitudes, awareness, and actions of those charged with governance concerning (a) the entity's internal control and its importance in the entity, including how those charged with governance oversee the effectiveness of internal control, and (b) the detection or the possibility of fraud
- The actions of those charged with governance in response to developments in law, accounting standards, corporate governance practices, and other related matters
- The actions of those charged with governance in response to previous communications with the auditor
- The views of those charged with governance about:
    - The appropriate person(s) in the entity's governance structure with whom to communicate
    - The allocation of responsibilities between those charged with governance and management
    - The entity's objectives and strategies and the related business risks that may result in material misstatements
    - Matters those charged with governance consider as warranting particular attention during the audit and any areas for which they request additional procedures to be undertaken
    - Significant communications with regulators

Editor Note: Care is required when communicating with those charged with governance about the planned scope and timing of the audit so as not to compromise the effectiveness of the audit, particularly when some or all of those charged with governance are involved in managing the entity. (Communicating the nature and timing of detailed audit procedures may reduce the effectiveness of those procedures by making them too predictable.)

3. **Significant Findings or Issues From the Audit** The communication of significant findings from the audit may include requesting further information from those charged with governance in order to complete the audit evidence already obtained.

   The auditor should communicate in writing significant findings or issues from the audit, *if* oral communication would not be adequate—this communication need *not* include matters that arose during the course of the audit that were communicated and satisfactorily resolved.

   The auditor should communicate:

   a. **The Entity's Significant Accounting Practices** The auditor's views about qualitative aspects of the entity's significant accounting practices, including accounting policies, accounting estimates, and financial statement disclosures. When applicable, the auditor should:

      (1) **Inappropriate Accounting Practices** Explain why the auditor considers a significant accounting practice that is acceptable under the AFRF *not* to be the most appropriate for the particular circumstances of the entity

      (2) **Sensitive Accounting Estimates** Determine that those charged with governance are informed about the process used by management in formulating particularly sensitive accounting estimates, including fair value estimates, and about the basis for the auditor's conclusions regarding the reasonableness of those estimates

   b. **Significant Difficulties Encountered During the Audit** Examples include: significant delays in management providing required information; an unnecessarily brief time within which to complete the audit; extensive unexpected effort required to obtain sufficient appropriate audit evidence; the unavailability of expected information; restrictions imposed on the auditor by management; and management's unwillingness to provide information about management's plans for dealing with the adverse effects of the conditions or events that lead the auditor to believe there is substantial doubt about the entity's ability to continue as a going concern.

      Editor Note: Such difficulties may constitute a scope limitation that leads to a modification of the audit opinion.

   c. **Disagreements With Management** Discussions with those charged with governance should include any disagreements with management that arose during the audit, *regardless of whether they were satisfactorily resolved*, about matters that, individually or in the aggregate, could be significant to the entity's financial statements or the audit report. (Disagreements do **not** include differences of opinion based on incomplete facts or preliminary information that are later resolved.)

   d. ***Un*corrected Misstatements** Uncorrected misstatements accumulated by the auditor and the effect that they, individually or in the aggregate, may have on the opinion in the audit report

      (1) The auditor's communication should identify *material* uncorrected misstatements *individually*.

      (2) The auditor should request that uncorrected misstatements be corrected.

e. **Other** Other findings or issues, if any, arising from the audit that are significant and relevant to those charged with governance regarding their responsibility to oversee the financial reporting process

And, unless all of those charged with governance are involved in managing the entity, the auditor should *also* communicate the *written representations from management the auditor is requesting* plus:

f. **Material Corrected Misstatements** Material, corrected misstatements that were brought to the attention of management as a result of audit procedures

- The auditor *may* also communicate corrected *im*material misstatements, such as frequently recurring immaterial misstatements that may indicate a particular bias

g. **Significant Findings or Issues Discussed With Management** Significant findings or issues, if any, arising from the audit that were discussed, or the subject of correspondence, with management

h. **Management's Consultations With Other Accountants** The auditor's views about significant accounting or auditing matters that were the subject of management's consultations with other accountants

E. The Communication Process

1. **Establishing the Communication Process** The auditor should communicate the form, timing, and expected general content of communications.

2. **Forms of Communication** Effective communication can be formal or informal; in writing or oral. As mentioned previously, the auditor should communicate in writing significant findings or issues from the audit if, in the auditor's professional judgment, oral communication would not be adequate.

3. **Restricted Use** When the auditor communicates matters in accordance with this section in writing, the communication is considered a by-product report. Accordingly, the auditor should indicate in the communication that it is intended solely for the information and use of those charged with governance and, if appropriate, management, and is not intended to be, and should not be, used by anyone other than these specified parties.

4. **Timing of Communications** The auditor should communicate on a timely basis.

5. **Evaluation of the Adequacy of the Communication Process** The auditor should evaluate whether the two-way communication between the auditor and those charged with governance has been adequate for the purpose of the audit. If it has not, the auditor should evaluate the effect, if any, on the auditor's assessment of the RMM and the ability to obtain sufficient appropriate audit evidence and should take appropriate action.

F. Audit Documentation

The auditor should document matters communicated orally, including when and to whom they were communicated, and retain those in writing.

G. Legal or Regulatory Restrictions on Communications

1. **Restrictions** Law or regulation may restrict the auditor's communication of certain matters with those charged with governance. For example, law or regulation may specifically prohibit a communication or other action that might prejudice an investigation by an appropriate authority into an actual or suspected illegal act. In some circumstances, potential conflicts

between the auditor's obligations of confidentiality and obligations to communicate may be complex. In such cases, the auditor *may consider* obtaining legal advice.

2. **Other Reporting Requirements** In certain circumstances, the auditor *may* be required to report to a regulatory or enforcement body certain matters that have been communicated with those charged with governance.

CHAPTER 2—PLANNING

Problem 2-1 MULTIPLE-CHOICE QUESTIONS

Terms of Audit Engagement

1. A recurring audit is an audit engagement

   a. For an audit client that has had an audit for the preceding period
   b. For an audit client that has had an audit for at least the two preceding periods
   c. For an existing audit client for whom the auditor performed the preceding audit
   d For an existing audit client for whom the auditor previously performed an audit (ID: 90065)

2. Which of the following best describes the preconditions for an audit?

   a. The use by management of an acceptable financial reporting framework in the preparation and fair presentation of the financial statements and the agreement of management and, when appropriate, those charged with governance, to the premise on which an audit is conducted
   b. The acknowledgement by management and, when appropriate, those charged with governance that they understand they have certain responsibilities that are fundamental to the conduct of an audit in accordance with US GAAS
   c. The acknowledgement by management and, when appropriate, those charged with governance that they understand they have the responsibility for design, implementation, and maintenance of internal control relevant to the preparation and fair presentation of financial statements that are free from material misstatement, whether due to fraud or error
   d The acknowledgement by management and, when appropriate, those charged with governance that they understand they have the responsibility to provide the auditor with access to all information that is relevant to the preparation and fair presentation of the financial statements (ID: 90066)

3. Before accepting an engagement for an initial audit, the auditor should request management to authorize the predecessor auditor to respond fully to the auditor's inquiries. Which of the following matters would be the most likely to be the subject of the auditor's inquiry?

   a. Knowledge of any subsequent events occurring since the predecessor's audit report was issued
   b. Communications to those charged with governance regarding fraud and noncompliance with laws or regulations by the entity
   c. Opening balances
   d Consistency of accounting policies (ID: 4666)

4. Before accepting an engagement to audit a new client, a CPA is required to

   a. Obtain an understanding of the prospective client's industry and business
   b. Obtain written representations from management and, when appropriate, those charged with governance
   c. Obtain a preliminary understanding of the prospective client's control environment
   d Request the client to authorize the predecessor auditor to respond fully to inquiries that will assist the auditor in determining whether to accept the engagement (ID: 6391)

5. Which of the following statements is true regarding an auditor's communications with a predecessor auditor prior to engagement acceptance?

   a. Inquiries addressing specific matters are required, for example, the predecessor's understanding about the reasons for the change in auditors.
   b. US GAAS provides a list of matters that may be subject to the auditor's inquiry of the predecessor auditor.
   c. If management refuses to authorize the predecessor auditor to respond, or limits the response, the auditor should not accept the engagement.
   d. If the predecessor auditor provides no response or a limited response, the auditor should not accept the engagement. (ID: 89480)

6. Part of an auditor's process of establishing whether the preconditions for an audit are present, involves obtaining management's acknowledgement of its responsibility for all of the following **except**

   a. The preparation and fair presentation of the financial statements in accordance with the applicable financial reporting framework
   b. Providing the auditor with access to key persons within the entity who have been authorized by management or those charged with governance to be involved in the audit
   c. The design, implementation, and maintenance of internal control relevant to the preparation and fair presentation of financial statements
   d. Providing the auditor with access to all information that is relevant to the preparation and fair presentation of the financial statements (ID: 89500)

7. All of the following describe conditions which require the auditor to refuse a proposed audit engagement (that is not required by law or regulation) **except**

   a. A scope limitation is imposed by management or those charged with governance that would result in a disclaimer of opinion.
   b. The preconditions for the audit are not present.
   c. The auditor is not permitted to attach a separate audit report or reword a prescribed audit report form that is misleading.
   d In an initial audit, management does not authorize contact with the predecessor auditor. (ID: 90068)

8. A document in an auditor's working papers includes the following statement:

   "Because of the inherent limitations of an audit, together with the inherent limitations of internal control, an unavoidable risk that some material misstatements may not be detected exists, even though the audit is properly planned and performed in accordance with US GAAS."

   The above passage is most likely from a(an)?

   a. Comfort letter
   b. Engagement letter
   c. Letter of audit inquiry
   d Representation letter (ID: 7634)

9. Which of the following would **least** likely appear in an auditor's engagement letter?

   a. The basis on which fees are computed and any billing arrangements
   b. A request for management to acknowledge receipt of the letter and to agree to its terms, as may be evidenced by their signature on the letter and its return to the auditor
   c. Reference to the expected form and content of any reports to be issued by the auditor
   d A statement that, after performing preliminary procedures, the auditor will discuss the other procedures considered necessary to complete the engagement (ID: 90067)

10. For recurring audits, when the auditor concludes that the terms of the preceding engagement need **not** be revised for the current engagement, the auditor

    a. Should send a written reminder to management confirming that the terms of the terms of the preceding engagement will govern the current audit
    b. Should remind management of the terms orally or in writing, but if done orally, the reminder should be documented
    c. Is not required to take any action with respect to management, but should document the reason for the conclusion
    d. Should resend the same engagement letter without changing the date of the letter, but it should be resigned with the current date next to the signatures (ID: 90070)

11. For recurring audits, the auditor should assess whether circumstances require the terms of the audit engagement to be revised. Factors that may make this appropriate include all of the following **except**
    a. A change in senior management
    b. A change in the financial reporting framework
    c. A change in the composition of the audit team
    d. A change in legal or regulatory requirements (ID: 90071)

12. When a client requests a change in the terms of an audit engagement prior to the completion of the engagement,
    a. If the auditor agrees to a change to a lower level of assurance, the report should include an other-matter paragraph that refers to the original audit engagement and explains the reason for the change
    b. If the auditor does not consider the request to be reasonable, the auditor should disclaim an opinion
    c. A misunderstanding concerning the nature of the service originally requested may be considered a reasonable basis for the request
    d. The auditor must comply with the client's request under any circumstances, but should consider the implications of an unreasonable request regarding the continuance of the relationship with the client (ID: 90072)

13. All of the following are likely to be examples of an unreasonable justification for a request to change the terms of an audit engagement to a lower level of assurance prior to the completion of an audit **except**
    a. The auditor is unable to obtain sufficient appropriate audit evidence regarding receivables.
    b. An audit is no longer needed to meet the requirements of membership in a trade organization the entity plans to join.
    c. Management refuses to give the auditor permission to communicate with the entity's external legal counsel.
    d. Management does not want to provide requested written representations. (ID: 90073)

Audit Risk

14. An auditor assesses the risk of material misstatement at the assertion level to
    a. Obtain an understanding of the entity's environment
    b. Determine the auditor's materiality levels
    c. Determine further risk assessment procedures
    d. Determine further audit procedures (ID: 5968)

15. The risk of material misstatement at the assertion level consists of which of the following sets of two components?
    a. Audit risk and detection risk
    b. Inherent risk and control risk
    c. Detection risk and control risk
    d. Audit risk and control risk (ID: 90074)

16. When the auditor believes the risk of material misstatement is high, generally, the auditor will do ________ substantive testing.
    a. More
    b. Less
    c. Equal
    d. No (ID: 90078)

17. The acceptable level of detection risk is inversely related to the
    a. Assurance provided by substantive tests
    b. Risk of misapplying auditing procedures
    c. Preliminary judgment about materiality levels
    d. Risk of failing to discover material misstatements (ID: 44)

18. The risk that an auditor will conclude, based on substantive tests, that a material error does **not** exist in an account balance when, in fact, such error does exist is referred to as
    a. Sampling risk
    b. Detection risk
    c. Nonsampling risk
    d. Inherent risk (ID: 2275)

19. Inherent risk and control risk differ from detection risk in that inherent risk and control risk are
    a. Functions of the client and its environment, while detection risk is not
    b. Changed at the auditor's discretion, while detection risk is not
    c. Considered at the individual account-balance level, while detection risk is not
    d. Elements of audit risk, while detection risk is not (ID: 2810)

20. On the basis of audit evidence gathered and evaluated, an auditor decides to increase the assessed level of control risk from that originally planned. To achieve an overall audit risk level that is substantially the same as the planned audit risk level, the auditor would
    a. Decrease substantive testing
    b. Decrease detection risk
    c. Increase inherent risk
    d. Increase materiality levels (ID: 5083)

21. Which of the following audit risk components may be assessed in nonquantitative terms?

	Control risk	Detection risk	Inherent risk
a.	Yes	Yes	No
b.	Yes	No	Yes
c.	Yes	Yes	Yes
d.	No	Yes	Yes

(ID: 5628)

22. As the acceptable level of detection risk decreases, an auditor may
    a. Reduce substantive testing by relying on the assessments of inherent risk and control risk
    b. Postpone the planned timing of substantive tests from interim dates to the year-end
    c. Eliminate the assessed level of inherent risk from consideration as a planning factor
    d. Lower the assessed level of control risk from high to low (ID: 5630)

23. When an auditor increases the assessed level of control risk because certain control activities were determined to be ineffective, the auditor most likely would increase the
    a. Level of detection risk
    b. Extent of tests of details
    c. Level of inherent risk
    d. Extent of tests of controls (ID: 7799)

24. Which of the following is a definition of control risk?
    a. The risk that a material misstatement will not be prevented or detected on a timely basis by the client's internal controls.
    b. The risk that the auditor will not detect a material misstatement.
    c. The risk that the auditor's assessment of internal controls will be at less than the maximum level.
    d. The susceptibility of material misstatement assuming there are no related internal controls, policies, or procedures. (ID: 9917)

25. Which of the following statements is correct regarding internal control?
    a. A well-designed internal control environment ensures the achievement of an entity's control objectives.
    b. An inherent limitation to internal control is the fact that controls can be circumvented by management override.
    c. A well-designed and operated internal control environment should detect collusion perpetrated by two people.
    d. Internal control is a necessary business function and should be designed and operated to detect all errors and fraud. (ID: 9931)

26. Audit risk is a function of
    a. The risk of material misstatement and inherent risk
    b. Control risk and detection risk
    c. Inherent risk and control risk
    d. The risk of material misstatement and detection risk (ID: 90075)

27. When the risk of material misstatement is high, the auditor should accept ______ detection risk.
    a. More
    b. Less
    c. Equal
    d. No (ID: 90076)

28. If the auditor sets the acceptable level of detection risk low, the auditor will do _________ substantive testing.
    a. More
    b. Less
    c. Equal
    d. No (ID: 90077)

Planning an Audit

29. The element of the audit planning process most likely to be agreed upon with the client before implementation of the audit strategy is the determination of the
    a. Evidence to be gathered to provide a sufficient basis for the auditor's opinion
    b. Procedures to be undertaken to discover litigation, claims, and assessments
    c. Pending legal matters to be included in the inquiry of the client's attorney
    d. Timing of inventory observation procedures to be performed (ID: 5619)

30. During the initial planning phase of an audit, a CPA most likely would
    a. Identify specific internal control activities that are likely to prevent fraud
    b. Evaluate the reasonableness of the client's accounting estimates
    c. Discuss the timing of an audit procedure with the client's management
    d. Inquire of the client's attorney as to whether any unrecorded claims are probable of assertion (ID: 7798)

31. Prior to the auditor's identification and assessment of the risks of material misstatement, the auditor should consider all of the following **except**
    a. The determination of materiality
    b. The involvement of specialists
    c. A general understanding of the legal and regulatory framework applicable to the entity and how the entity is complying with that framework
    d. Results of analytical procedures (ID: 90079)

32. Required preliminary engagement activities include all of the following **except**

    a. Performing quality control procedures related to the continuance of the client relationship and the specific audit engagement
    b. Evaluating compliance with relevant ethical requirements
    c. Establishing an understanding of the terms of the engagement
    d. Consideration of factors that are significant in directing the engagement team's efforts (ID: 90084)

33. Which of the following procedures would an auditor most likely include in developing the overall audit strategy of a financial statement audit?

    a. Obtaining a representation letter from the client
    b. Examining documents to detect noncompliance with laws and regulations having a material effect on the financial statements
    c. Considering whether the client's accounting estimates are reasonable in the circumstances
    d. Determining the extent of involvement of the client's internal auditors (ID: 5074)

34. Audit programs should be designed so that

    a. Most of the required procedures can be performed as interim work.
    b. Inherent risk is assessed at a sufficiently low level.
    c. The auditor can make constructive suggestions to management.
    d. The audit evidence gathered supports the auditor's conclusions. (ID: 5089)

35. An auditor should design the written audit plan (or program) so that

    a. All material transactions will be selected for substantive testing.
    b. Substantive tests prior to the balance sheet date will be minimized.
    c. The audit procedures selected will achieve specific audit objectives.
    d. Each account balance will be tested under either tests of controls or tests of details. (ID: 5634)

36. Which of the following procedures would an auditor most likely include in establishing the overall audit strategy of a financial statement audit?

    a. Obtain an understanding of the entity's risk assessment process
    b. Identify specific internal control activities designed to prevent fraud
    c. Evaluate the reasonableness of the entity's accounting estimates
    d. Perform cutoff tests of the entity's sales and purchases (ID: 6709)

37. Which of the following factors would a CPA ordinarily consider in the planning stage of an audit engagement?

    I. Financial statement accounts likely to contain a misstatement
    II. Conditions that require extension of audit tests

    a. I only
    b. II only
    c. Both I and II
    d. Neither I nor II (ID: 7102)

38. Regarding the planning of an audit engagement,

    a. The auditor's primary objective in planning is to provide a common understanding of the terms of the engagement.
    b. The detailed audit plan provides a basis for the overall audit strategy.
    c. Planning for further audit procedures should be completed before beginning the performance of any further audit procedures to ensure an effective audit.
    d. Planning the nature, extent, and timing of specific further audit procedures depends on the outcome of risk assessment procedures. (ID: 90085)

39. During the planning phase of an audit the auditor should
    a. Consider whether specialized skills are needed in performing the audit
    b. Obtain written representations from the client
    c. Make inquiries of the client's in-house legal counsel
    d. Confirm that the financial statements can be reconciled to the accounting records (ID: 90086)

40. The establishment of the overall audit strategy, includes all of the following activities **except**
    a. Identification of the characteristics of the engagement that define its scope
    b. Determination of the reporting objectives of the engagement in order to plan the timing of the audit and the nature of the communications required
    c. Determination of the nature, timing, and extent of resources necessary to perform the engagement
    d. The nature, timing, and extent of planned further audit procedures at the relevant assertion level (ID: 90087)

41. The auditor should develop an audit plan that includes a description of all of the following **except**
    a. The nature and extent of planned risk assessment procedures
    b. The nature, timing, and extent of planned further audit procedures at the relevant assertion level
    c. The terms of the engagement
    d. Other planned audit procedures that are required to be carried out so that the engagement complies with generally accepted auditing standards (ID: 90088)

42. The overall audit strategy
    a. Sets the scope, timing, and direction of the audit and guides the development of the audit plan
    b. Includes a description of nature and extent of planned risk assessment procedures
    c. Although the detailed audit plan will ordinarily be updated during the course of the audit, the overall strategy should remain largely unchanged
    d. Is based on the detailed audit plan (ID: 90089)

43. Related to the planning of an audit, the auditor should include in the audit documentation all of the following, **except**
    a. The overall audit strategy
    b. The audit plan
    c. Records of discussions with management related to planning activities, including the agreed upon dates for their delivery of requested data
    d. Any significant changes made during the audit engagement to the overall audit strategy or the audit plan and the reasons for such changes (ID: 90082)

Materiality in Planning & Performing an Audit

44. The concept of materiality is applied by the auditor in all of the following instances **except**
    a. In planning and performing the audit
    b. In evaluating the effect of identified misstatements on the audit
    c. In evaluating the effect of fraud by senior management
    d. In forming the opinion in the audit report (ID: 90090)

45. Although financial reporting frameworks may discuss materiality in different terms, they generally explain all of the following **except**

   a. Misstatements, including omissions, are considered to be material if they, individually or in the aggregate, could reasonably be expected to influence the economic decisions of users made on the basis of the financial statements.
   b. Judgments about materiality are made in light of surrounding circumstances and are affected by the size or nature of a misstatement, or a combination of both.
   c. Judgments about matters that are material to users of the financial statements are based on a consideration of the common financial information needs of users as a group.
   d. The possible effect of misstatements on specific individual users is also considered. (ID: 90091)

46. Regarding materiality considerations

   a. It is not practicable to design audit procedures to detect misstatements that could be material solely because of their nature; thus, the auditor does not make qualitative considerations.
   b. Auditors are aware that most users of financial statements have limited backgrounds in accounting.
   c. The materiality determined when planning the audit does not necessarily establish an amount below which uncorrected misstatements, individually or in the aggregate, will always be evaluated as immaterial.
   d. Risk and materiality are mainly considered during the planning phase of an audit. (ID: 90092)

47. In planning the audit, the auditor makes judgments about the size of misstatements that will be considered material. It is **least** likely that these judgments provide a basis for

   a. Determining the nature and extent of risk assessment procedures
   b. Identifying and assessing the risk of material misstatement
   c. Determining whether to accept an engagement and the related fees
   d. Determining the nature, timing, and extent of further audit procedures (ID: 90093)

48. Which of the following would an auditor most likely use in determining materiality for the financial statements as a whole?

   a. The anticipated sample size of the planned substantive tests
   b. The entity's annualized interim financial statements
   c. The results of the internal control questionnaire
   d. The contents of the representation letter (ID: 5629)

49. Regarding materiality,

   a. When establishing the overall audit strategy, the auditor should determine materiality for each relevant class of transactions, account balance, or disclosure.
   b. When determining materiality, one factor that may affect the identification of an appropriate benchmark is its relative volatility.
   c. Auditors are aware that most financial statement users are more likely to rely on financial advisors to help them make decisions on the basis of the information in the financial statements rather than studying the information themselves.
   d. Exercising professional judgment, the auditor should set materiality based on a percentage applied to a benchmark appropriate to the entity. (ID: 90094)

50. Performance materiality

   a. Is set higher than materiality for the financial statements as a whole
   b. Is the auditor's acknowledgment that the aggregate of uncorrected and undetected misstatements may exceed set materiality levels
   c. Is defined as one amount
   d. Is determined solely for the purpose of assessing the risks of material misstatement (ID: 90095)

51. If during the audit, the auditor concludes that the materiality for the financial statements as a whole (and, if applicable, materiality level or levels for particular classes of transactions, account balances, or disclosures) is inappropriate and thus revises materiality levels, the auditor is required to

    a. Determine whether it is also necessary to revise performance materiality and whether the nature, timing, and extent of the further audit procedures remain appropriate, but only when the materiality for the financial statements as a whole is lowered
    b. Determine whether it is also necessary to revise performance materiality, but only when the materiality for the financial statements as a whole is lowered
    c. Determine whether it is also necessary to revise performance materiality and whether the nature, timing, and extent of the further audit procedures remain appropriate if the materiality for the financial statements as whole is revised in either direction
    d. Determine whether it is also necessary to revise performance materiality if the materiality for the financial statements as whole is revised in either direction (ID: 90096)

52. The auditor should include in the audit documentation related to materiality considerations

    a. Materiality for the financial statements as a whole, performance materiality, and, if applicable, the materiality level or levels for particular classes of transactions, account balances, or disclosures
    b. If the materiality level or levels for particular classes of transactions, account balances, or disclosures are not determined, the reason why this was not considered necessary
    c. Significant revisions to materiality as the audit progressed
    d. The factors considered in the determination of all amounts if a methodology other than benchmarking was used (ID: 90097)

Understanding the Entity & Its Environment and Assessing the RMM

53. The primary objective of procedures performed to obtain an understanding of the entity and its environment, including its internal control, is to provide an auditor with

    a. Knowledge necessary to assess the risk of material misstatement and design further audit procedures
    b. An evaluation of the consistency of application of management's policies
    c. A basis for modifying tests of controls
    d. Audit evidence to use in assessing inherent risk (ID: 5642)

54. Which of the following procedures would an auditor most likely perform in planning a financial statement audit?

    a. Inquiring of the client's legal counsel concerning pending litigation
    b. Comparing the financial statements to anticipated results
    c. Searching for unauthorized transactions that may aid in detecting unrecorded liabilities
    d. Examining computer generated exception reports to verify the effectiveness of internal controls (ID: 5622)

55. Which of the following statements is correct concerning analytical procedures used in planning an audit engagement?

    a. They often replace the tests of controls.
    b. They may use financial and nonfinancial data aggregated at a high level.
    c. They often involve the comparison of assertions developed by management to ratios calculated by an auditor.
    d. They are often used to develop an auditor's preliminary judgment about materiality. (ID: 9929)

56. Which procedures, by themselves, do **not** provide sufficient appropriate audit evidence on which to base an audit opinion?
    a. Risk assessment procedures
    b. Substantive analytical procedures
    c. Tests of details
    d. Tests of controls (ID: 90080)

57. In addition to risk assessment procedures, when the auditor is obtaining an understanding of the entity and its environment, which of the following is a related activity the auditor should perform?
    a. The auditor should consider whether information obtained from the auditor's client acceptance or continuance process is relevant to identifying risks of material misstatement.
    b. If the engagement partner has performed other engagements for the entity, the engagement partner should consider whether there is a need to redetermine materiality for the current audit.
    c. When the auditor intends to use information from procedures performed in previous audits, the auditor should confirm that the previous audit's workpapers include such procedures.
    d. The engagement partner should hold a discussion with all members of the engagement team about the susceptibility of the entity's financial statements to material misstatement and the application of the applicable financial reporting framework to the entity's facts and circumstances. (ID: 90294)

58. When obtaining an understanding of the entity and its environment, the auditor should obtain an understanding of the relevant industry, regulatory, and other external factors, including the applicable financial reporting framework. In relation to this, the matter **least** likely to be considered is
    a. Cyclical or seasonal activity
    b. Environmental requirements affecting the industry and the entity's business
    c. Whether the entity has a complex structure
    d. Government policies currently affecting the conduct of the entity's business (ID: 90286)

59. It is primarily important for the auditor to obtain an understanding of the nature of an entity in order to be able to
    a. Understand the classes of transactions, account balances, and disclosures to be expected in the financial statements
    b. Assess the risk of material misstatement
    c. Plan further audit procedures
    d. Plan risk assessment procedures (ID: 90287)

60. The auditor is required to obtain an understanding of the components of the nature of entity which include all of the following **except**
    a. Its operations
    b. The entity's selection and application of accounting policies
    c. Its ownership and governance structures
    d. The way that the entity is structured and how it is financed (ID: 90288)

61. When obtaining an understanding of the entity and its environment, the auditor should obtain an understanding of the nature of the entity. In relation to this, the matter **least** likely to be considered is
    a. The location of production facilities, warehouses, and offices and the location and quantities of inventories
    b. Planned or recently executed acquisitions or divestitures
    c. Beneficial owners and related parties
    d. Taxation (ID: 90289)

62. When obtaining an understanding of the entity and its environment, the auditor should obtain an understanding of the entity's selection and application of accounting policies. In relation to this, the matter **least** likely to be considered is

    a. The methods the entity uses to account for significant and unusual transactions
    b. The financial reporting competencies of personnel involved in selecting and applying significant new or complex accounting standards
    c. Current and prospective financing requirements
    d. Financial reporting standards, and laws and regulations that are new to the entity and when and how the entity will adopt such requirements (ID: 90290)

63. Business risk

    a. Is broader than the risk of material misstatement of the financial statements
    b. Does not include the risk of material misstatement of the financial statements
    c. Is management's concern, not the auditor's
    d. Gives rise to risks of material misstatement in all cases (ID: 90291)

64. When obtaining an understanding of the entity and its environment, the auditor should obtain an understanding of the entity's objectives and strategies and those related business risks that may result in risks of material misstatement. In relation to this, the matter **least** likely to be considered is

    a. New products and services
    b. Expansion of the business
    c. Capital investment activities
    d. Use of IT (ID: 90292)

65. When obtaining an understanding of the entity and its environment, the auditor should obtain an understanding of the measurement and review of the entity's financial performance. In relation to this, the matter **least** likely to be considered is

    a. Forecasts, budgets, and variance analyses
    b. Trends
    c. Competitor analysis
    d. Risk appetite of mangers and stakeholders (ID: 90293)

66. In auditing intangible assets, an auditor most likely would review or recompute amortization and determine whether the amortization period is reasonable in support of management's financial statement assertion of

    a. Valuation and allocation
    b. Existence
    c. Completeness
    d. Rights and obligations (ID: 5659)

67. An auditor scans a client's investment records for the period just before and just after the year-end to determine that any transfers between categories of investments have been properly recorded. The primary purpose of this procedure is to obtain evidence about management's financial statement assertions of

    a. Rights and obligations; and existence or occurrence
    b. Valuation and allocation; and rights and obligations
    c. Existence or occurrence; and classification
    d. Classification; and valuation and allocation (ID: 7824)

68. The auditor's inventory observation test counts are traced to the client's inventory listing to test for which of the following financial statement assertions?

a. Completeness
b. Rights & obligations
c. Valuation & allocation
d. Classification & understandability (ID: 8396)

69. After making inquiries about credit granting policies, an auditor selects a sample of sales transactions and examines evidence of credit approval. This test of controls most likely supports management's financial statement assertion(s) of

	Rights and obligations	Valuation and allocation
a.	Yes	Yes
b.	Yes	No
c.	No	Yes
d.	No	No

(ID: 8403)

70. Risks of material misstatement should be identified and assessed at

I. The financial statement level
II. The relevant assertion level for classes of transactions, account balances, and disclosures

a. I only
b. II only
c. Both I and II
d. Neither I nor II (ID: 90295)

71. Why do the risks of material misstatement need to identified and assessed at the financial statement level in addition to the relevant assertion level for classes of transactions, account balances, and disclosures?

a. Risks at the financial statement level require an overall response by the auditor.
b. The audit opinion is based on the financial statement as a whole.
c. When establishing the overall audit strategy, the auditor should determine materiality for the financial statements as a whole.
d. Misstatements in the financial statements can arise from either fraud or error. (ID: 90296)

72. Risks of material misstatement at the financial statement level

a. Should be linked with specific assertions at the class of transactions, account balance, or disclosure level
b. Are rarely relevant to the consideration of the risks of material misstatement arising from fraud due to its nature
c. Refer to risks that relate pervasively to the financial statements as a whole and potentially affect many assertions
d. Are not related to the entity's control environment (ID: 90297)

73. A significant risk

a. Should be communicated to those charged with governance
b. Requires special audit consideration
c. Should be identified by considering the related controls that mitigate its potential effects
d. Is related to fraud (ID: 90298)

74. What makes a financial statement assertion relevant to an audit conducted in accordance with US GAAS?
    a. It has a reasonable possibility of containing a misstatement that would cause the financial statements to be materially misstated.
    b. US GAAS defines it as relevant to an audit of financial statements.
    c. A regulatory agency requires proof of it.
    d. It is an unconditional requirement rather than a presumptively mandatory requirement. (ID: 90299)

75. Which explanation best describes how an auditor determines (as required by US GAAS) if a financial statement assertion is relevant for each significant class of transactions, account balance, and disclosure?
    a. By exercising professional judgment for the particular nature and characteristics of the entity
    b. By exercising professional skepticism, recognizing that circumstances may exist that cause the financial statements to be materially misstated
    c. By determining the source of likely potential misstatements in each significant class of transactions, account balance, and disclosure
    d. By performing walk-throughs of the related systems (ID: 90300)

Service Organizations

76. Services provided by a service organization are relevant to the audit of a user entity's financial statements when those services and the controls over them affect the user entity's information system, including related business processes, relevant to financial reporting. A user auditor should consider a service organization's services a part of an entity's information system if they affect any of the following **except**
    a. The classes of transactions in the user entity's operations that are significant to the entity's financial statements
    b. The procedures within both IT and manual systems by which the user entity's transactions are initiated, authorized, recorded, processed, corrected as necessary, transferred to the general ledger, and reported in the financial statements
    c. The financial reporting process used to prepare the user entity's financial statements, including significant accounting estimates and disclosures
    d. Transactions that are specifically authorized by the entity, such as the processing of checking account transactions by a bank or the processing of securities transactions by a broker (ID: 9293)

77. When are services provided by a service organization relevant to the audit of a user entity's financial statements?
    a. The service organization's information systems are integrated with those of the user entity.
    b. Services and the controls over them affect the user entity's information system, including related business processes, relevant to financial reporting.
    c. The service organization and the user entity have a written service level agreement.
    d. The user entity has outsourced aspects of their business activities to a service organization that are integral to the entity's business operations. (ID: 90301)

78. Which of the following describes a difference between a service auditor's type 1 report and a type 2 report?
    a. A type 2 report includes written assertions by management of the service organization as of a specified date while those in the type 1 report cover a specified period.
    b. Only the type 1 report includes a description of the service organization's system by management of the service organization.
    c. Only the type 2 report includes an assertion by management of the service organization related to the operating effectiveness of the service organization's controls.
    d. Only the type 1 report includes an assertion by management of the service organization related to the suitability of the design of the service organization's controls. (ID: 90302)

79. The user auditor should apply the same procedures with respect to the services provided by a subservice organization as a service organization when the user auditor plans to use a type 1 or type 2 report that
    a. Was for an engagement for a subservice organization that did not require complementary controls
    b. Was prepared using the carve-out method
    c. Contains a system description that is as of a date or for a period that precedes the beginning of the audit of the user entity
    d. Was prepared by a service auditor who was not independent of the user entity (ID: 90047)

80. When the user entity uses the services of a service organization
    a. The user auditor does not make reference to the service auditor's report as a basis, in part, for the user auditor's opinion on the user entity's financial statements.
    b. If the user auditor makes reference to the service auditor, the service auditor's name and signature should be included in the user auditor's report.
    c. The user auditor should not refer to the work of a service auditor in the user auditor's report containing a modified opinion.
    d. If the user auditor makes reference to the service auditor, the user auditor's report should indicate that the portion of the audit and opinion related to the services of the service organization are the responsibility of the service auditor. (ID: 90303)

Consideration of Fraud in a Financial Statement Audit

81. Which of the following statements best describes an auditor's responsibility for detecting errors and fraud?
    a. An auditor is responsible for detecting employee errors and simple fraud, but not for discovering fraud involving employee collusion or management override.
    b. An auditor should plan the audit to detect errors and fraud that are caused by departures from the applicable financial reporting framework.
    c. An auditor is not responsible for detecting errors and fraud unless the application of US GAAS would result in such detection.
    d. An auditor should design the audit to provide reasonable assurance of detecting errors and fraud that would cause the financial statements to be materially misstated. (ID: 5633)

82. Misstatements in the financial statements can arise from either fraud or error. What is the distinguishing factor between fraud and error?
    a. Whether the underlying action that results in the misstatement of the financial statements involves noncompliance with laws or regulations
    b. Whether the underlying action that results in the misstatement of the financial statements is intentional or unintentional
    c. Whether the underlying action that results in the misstatement of the financial statements is acknowledged and corrected by management
    d. Whether the underlying action that results in the misstatement of the financial statements is discovered by the entity in the normal course of operations, i.e., by its internal control system, or by the auditor's procedures (ID: 90304)

83. Regarding fraud, the auditor is primarily concerned with
    a. Fraudulent financial reporting
    b. Fraud resulting from misappropriation of assets
    c. Making a legal determination of whether fraud has actually occurred
    d. Fraud that causes a material misstatement in the financial statements (ID: 90305)

84. The primary responsibility for the prevention and detection of fraud rests with
    a. The auditor
    b. Management and those charged with governance
    c. The audit committee
    d. Governmental agencies such as the Securities and Exchange Commission (ID: 90306)

85. Why is it that, even though an audit is properly planned and performed in accordance with US GAAS, some material misstatements of the financial statements may **not** be detected?
    a. Due to the nature of fraud, an auditor may not detect some material misstatements of the financial statements.
    b. Due to the inherent limitations of an audit, an unavoidable risk exists that some material misstatements of the financial statements may not be detected.
    c. Collusion or management override of controls may prevent an auditor from detecting some material misstatements of the financial statements.
    d. Fraud may involve sophisticated and carefully organized schemes designed to conceal it; thus, some material misstatements of the financial statements may not be detected. (ID: 90307)

86. The risk of not detecting a material misstatement resulting from fraud
    a. Is higher when employees collude than when management is involved in fraud
    b. Is higher than the risk of not detecting one resulting from the misappropriation of assets
    c. Is higher than the risk of not detecting one resulting from error
    d. Is higher than the risk of not detecting one resulting from error, excluding omissions (ID: 90308)

87. In recognition of the possibility that a material misstatement due to fraud could exist, the auditor should maintain professional skepticism
    a. Investigating further to corroborate responses to inquiries of management and those charged with governance
    b. Investigating further if conditions identified during the audit cause the auditor to believe that a document may not be authentic or that terms in a document have been modified but not disclosed to the auditor
    c. Unless the auditor's past experience places the honesty and integrity of the entity's management and those charged with governance above reproach
    d. More so in the response to assessed risks of material misstatement due to fraud at the assertion level rather than at the financial statement level (ID: 90309)

88. The auditor's consideration of circumstances that might be indicative of the manipulation of earnings or other financial measures and how management could accomplish this should
    a. Be part of the required informative session with new member(s) of the audit committee
    b. Be part of the engagement team discussion about how and where the entity's financial statements might be susceptible to material misstatement due to fraud
    c. Be limited to key members of the audit team to lower the risk of compromising the effectiveness of detection procedures
    d. Be part of the final review of the adequacy of the conclusions reached as a result of the audit evidence obtained (ID: 90039)

89. Regarding fraud, the required discussion among the key engagement team members, including the engagement partner, should include
    a. An exchange of ideas or brainstorming among the engagement team members about how and where the entity's financial statements might be susceptible to material misstatement due to fraud
    b. How employees could perpetrate and conceal fraudulent financial reporting
    c. How assets of the entity could be misappropriated by management
    d. The importance of exercising professional judgment throughout the audit (ID: 90310)

90. Which of the following factors most likely would heighten an auditor's concern about the risk of fraudulent financial reporting?
    a. Large amounts of assets that are easily convertible into cash
    b. Low growth and profitability as compared to other entities in the same industry
    c. Financial management's participation in the initial selection of accounting principles
    d. An overly complex organizational structure involving unusual lines of authority (ID: 7018)

91. Which of the following circumstances would an auditor most likely consider a risk factor relating to misstatements arising from fraudulent financial reporting?
    a. Several members of management have recently purchased additional shares of the entity's stock.
    b. Several members of the board of directors have recently sold shares of the entity's stock.
    c. The entity distributes financial forecasts to financial analysts that predict conservative operating results.
    d. Management is interested in maintaining the entity's earnings trend by using aggressive accounting practices. (ID: 8155)

92. Which of the following characteristics most likely would heighten an auditor's concern about the risk of material misstatement arising from fraudulent financial reporting?
    a. There is a lack of interest by management in maintaining an earnings trend.
    b. Computer hardware is usually sold at a loss before being fully depreciated.
    c. Management had frequent disputes with the auditor on accounting matters.
    d. Monthly bank reconciliations usually include several large checks outstanding. (ID: 8420)

93. Which of the following situations represents a risk factor that relates to misstatements arising from misappropriation of assets?
    a. A high turnover of senior management
    b. A lack of independent checks
    c. A strained relationship between management and the current or predecessor auditor
    d. An inability to generate cash flows from operations while reporting earnings and earnings growth (ID: 8646)

94. Which of the following analytical procedures most likely would be used during the planning stage of an audit?
    a. Comparing current year to prior year sales volumes
    b. Reading the financial statements and notes and considering the adequacy of evidence
    c. Comparing the current year ratio of aggregate salaries paid to the number of employees to the prior year's ratio
    d. Reading the letter from the client's attorney and considering the threat of litigation (ID: 9942)

95. Which of the following situations most likely represents the highest risk of a misstatement arising from the misappropriation of assets?
    a. A large number of bearer bonds on hand
    b. A large number of inventory items with low sales prices
    c. A large number of transactions processed in a short period of time
    d. A large number of fixed assets with easily identifiable serial numbers (ID: 89762)

96. Regarding risk assessment procedures related to fraud

    a. Inquiries should be made of management and, when appropriate, those charged with governance.
    b. Analytical procedures should include procedures related to revenue accounts.
    c. If fraud risk factors are present, the auditor should rank them in order of importance and investigate accordingly.
    d. Due to the sensitivity of the subject matter, auditors should only inquire of management and, when appropriate, those charged with governance whether they have knowledge of any actual, suspected, or alleged fraud. (ID: 90311)

97. Which statement regarding the auditor's risk assessment of material misstatement due to fraud is **not** true?

    a. It should be ongoing throughout the audit
    b. It should be based on the presumption that risks of fraud exist in revenue recognition
    c. Assessed risks due to fraud should all be treated by the auditor as significant risks
    d. The auditor should evaluate whether each assessed risk due to fraud is a significant risk (ID: 90312)

98. Which of the following is most likely to be a response to the assessed risk of material misstatement at the assertion level?

    a. Assigning more experienced individuals or additional individuals with specialized skill and knowledge to the engagement
    b. Evaluating whether the selection and application of accounting policies by the entity is indicative of management bias
    c. Incorporating an element of unpredictability in the selection of the nature, timing, and extent of audit procedures
    d. Inspecting certain assets (ID: 90313)

99. Management is in a unique position to perpetrate fraud because of management's ability to manipulate accounting records and prepare fraudulent financial statements by overriding controls that otherwise appear to be operating effectively. Management override

    a. Is presumed to be present in all entities
    b. Should be considered by the auditor to determine if it is present
    c. Is considered a fraud risk due to its predictability
    d. Risk responses should include a review of journal entries near year-end as opposed to throughout the reporting period (ID: 90314)

100. Which of the following procedures would an auditor most likely perform during the overall review stage of an audit of an entity's financial statements?

    a. Obtain assurance from the entity's attorney that all material litigation has been disclosed in the financial statements
    b. Verify the clerical accuracy of the entity's proof of cash and its bank cutoff statement
    c. Determine whether controls for the safeguarding of assets are effective
    d. Consider whether the results of audit procedures affect the assessment of the risk of material misstatement due to fraud (ID: 7027)

101. The auditor should re-evaluate the assessment of the risks of material misstatement due to fraud and its resulting effect on the nature, extent, and timing of audit procedures to respond to the assessed risks when

    a. The auditor identifies a misstatement that is indicative of fraud
    b. The auditor identifies a misstatement, whether material or not, that is, or may be, the result of fraud that involves management
    c. The auditor concludes that, or is unable to conclude whether, the financial statements are materially misstated as a result of fraud
    d. The auditor discovers a specific instance of management override of controls (ID: 90315)

102. As a result of identified fraud or suspected fraud, the auditor may encounter circumstances that bring into question the auditor's ability to continue performing the audit. Examples of such circumstances include all of the following **except**

   a. The entity does not take the appropriate action regarding fraud that the auditor considers necessary in the circumstances, but only when the fraud is material to the financial statements.
   b. The entity does not take the appropriate action regarding fraud that the auditor considers necessary in the circumstances, even when the fraud is not material to the financial statements.
   c. The auditor's consideration of the risks of material misstatement due to fraud and the results of audit tests indicate a significant risk of material and pervasive fraud.
   d. The auditor has significant concern about the competence or integrity of management or those charged with governance. (ID: 90316)

103. If, as a result of identified fraud or suspected fraud, the auditor encounters circumstances that bring into question the auditor's ability to continue performing the audit, the auditor should consider whether it is appropriate to withdraw from the engagement, when withdrawal is possible under applicable law or regulation. If the auditor withdraws, the auditor should

   a. Issue an audit report with an adverse opinion
   b. Issue an audit report with a disclaimer of opinion
   c. Determine whether a professional or legal requirement exists to report to those who engaged the auditor the auditor's withdrawal from the engagement and the reasons for the withdrawal
   d. Only discuss with those charged with governance the auditor's withdrawal from the engagement and the reasons for the withdrawal (ID: 90317)

104. Regarding the auditor's communication responsibilities related to fraud or suspected fraud,

   a. The auditor should communicate these matters on a timely basis to the appropriate level of management unless the matter is considered inconsequential.
   b. Only when senior management or employees who have significant roles in internal control are involved in the fraud or suspected fraud should the auditor communicate these matters on a timely basis to those charged with governance.
   c. When management is involved in the fraud or suspected fraud the auditor should communicate these matters to those charged with governance and discuss with them the nature, timing, and extent of audit procedures necessary to complete the audit.
   d. The auditor should communicate the occurrence or suspicion of fraud to stakeholders outside the entity. (ID: 90318)

105. The audit documentation related to fraud should include

   a. Communications about fraud made to management, those charged with governance, regulators, and others
   b. The reasons for a conclusion not to consider the risk of material misstatement due to fraud related to revenue recognition, unless the audit report expresses substantial doubt about the entity's ability to continue as a going concern that is related to revenue
   c. The assessed risks of material misstatements due to fraud and the related audit procedures to address such risks, but the auditor need not include the responses to such assessed risks
   d. The information that was communicated by the engagement partner to those engagement team members not involved in the team discussion about fraud (ID: 90319)

Consideration of Laws & Regulations in an Audit of Financial Statements

106. US GAAS distinguishes the auditor's responsibilities related to compliance with laws and regulations by using the following two categories:
   a. Those that are likely vs. those that are unlikely to result in fines, litigation, or other consequences for the entity
   b. Those that have a direct effect on the determination of material amounts and disclosures in the financial statements vs. those that do not have such a direct effect, but noncompliance with them may have a material effect on the financial statements
   c. Those that involve the assessment of fees by regulatory agencies vs. punitive damages imposed by judicial authority
   d. Those that represent ongoing obligations, i.e., the price of doing business, vs. payments resulting from the entity's misconduct (ID: 90320)

107. Noncompliance with laws and regulations
   a. Encompasses either intentional or unintentional acts by the entity that are contrary to prevailing laws or regulations
   b. Encompasses only intentional acts by the entity that are contrary to prevailing laws or regulations
   c. Does not encompass transactions that are contrary to the prevailing laws or regulations entered into by, or in the name of, the entity or on its behalf by those charged with governance, management, or employees
   d. Encompasses personal misconduct (even when unrelated to the entity's interests) by those charged with governance, management, or employees of the entity if the individual was engaged in a business activity of the entity at the time (ID: 90321)

108. In the context of the entity's applicable legal and regulatory framework,
   a. Due to the inherent limitations of an audit, an audit performed in accordance with US GAAS provides only limited assurance that all noncompliance with laws and regulations will be detected or that any contingent liabilities that result will be disclosed
   b. Due to the inherent limitations of an audit, an audit performed in accordance with US GAAS provides no assurance that all noncompliance with laws and regulations will be detected or that any contingent liabilities that result will be disclosed
   c. Due to the inherent limitations of an audit an audit performed in accordance with US GAAS provides only reasonable assurance that all noncompliance with laws and regulations will be detected or that any contingent liabilities that result will be disclosed
   d. Ordinarily, the further removed noncompliance is from the events and transactions reflected in the financial statements, the more likely the auditor is to become aware of, or recognize, the noncompliance. (ID: 90322)

109. Why does US GAAS establish two categories of laws and regulations?
   a. US GAAS requires a different auditing approach for each category because the auditor has different responsibilities for each.
   b. One category affects the determination of amounts in the financial statements while the other may only affect the financial statement disclosures.
   c. The auditor is required to have the professional competence to determine whether an act constitutes noncompliance in one of the categories, but is not expected to be able to make such a legal determination with regard to the other.
   d. Different materiality considerations are applied to one category vs. the other. (ID: 90323)

110. Regarding the auditor's consideration of compliance with laws and regulations, the auditor

a. Is required to obtain a general understanding of the legal and regulatory framework applicable to the entity and the industry in which the entity operates and how the entity is complying with that framework
b. Is required to inspect correspondence, if any, with the licensing or regulatory authorities that enforce laws and regulations generally recognized to have a direct effect on the determination of material amounts and disclosures in the financial statements
c. Is required to consult with the entity's external legal counsel
d. Is required, even when no instances of noncompliance are identified or suspected, to presume that the risk of noncompliance is at least moderate (ID: 90324)

111. When the auditor identifies or suspects noncompliance with laws and regulations, the auditor should

a. Consider withdrawing from the engagement.
b. Discuss the matter with those charged with governance to obtain their guidance as to which level of management should be notified.
c. Discuss the matter with the auditor's legal counsel prior to notifying either management or those charged with governance.
d. Obtain an understanding of the nature of the act; the circumstances in which it has occurred; and evaluate the possible effect on the financial statements. (ID: 90325)

112. If the auditor is precluded by the client from obtaining sufficient appropriate audit evidence to evaluate whether noncompliance with laws and regulations that may be material to the financial statements has, or is likely to have, occurred, the auditor should

a. Disclaim an opinion on the financial statements
b. Withdraw from the engagement and indicate the reasons for withdrawal in writing to those charged with governance
c. Express a qualified opinion or disclaim an opinion on the financial statements
d. Express a qualified or adverse opinion on the financial statements (ID: 89499)

113. When is timely, i. e., as soon as practicable, communication of matters involving noncompliance with laws and regulations to those charged with governance required?

a. When the noncompliance is believed to be intentional and its effect on the financial statements is material
b. If the effect of the noncompliance on the financial statements is material, whether intentional or unintentional
c. When the effect of the noncompliance on the financial statements is believed to be both material and pervasive
d. When the appropriate response by the entity includes reporting the noncompliance to parties outside the entity (ID: 90326)

114. Regarding identified or suspected noncompliance with laws and regulations, the auditor should include in the audit documentation all of the following **except**

a. A description of the identified or suspected noncompliance
b. A copy of the applicable law or regulation or portion thereof violated when noncompliance is identified
c. The results of the discussion with management and, when applicable, those charged with governance about any identified or suspected noncompliance
d. The results of the discussion with other parties inside or outside the entity about any identified or suspected noncompliance (ID: 90327)

Responding to Assessed Risks

115. An auditor may decide to perform only substantive procedures for specific assertions because the auditor believes

  a. Control policies and procedures are unlikely to pertain to the assertions.
  b. The entity's control environment, monitoring, and control activities are interrelated.
  c. Sufficient audit evidence to support the assertions is likely to be available.
  d. More emphasis on tests of controls than substantive tests is warranted. (ID: 4258)

116. Regardless of the assessed risks of material misstatement, an auditor would perform some

  a. Tests of controls to determine the effectiveness of internal control policies
  b. Analytical procedures to verify the design of internal control procedures
  c. Substantive tests to restrict detection risk for material transaction classes
  d. Dual-purpose tests to evaluate both the risk of monetary misstatement and preliminary control risk (ID: 4260)

117. An auditor uses the assessed risk of material misstatement to

  a. Evaluate the effectiveness of the entity's internal control policies and procedures
  b. Identify transactions and account balances where inherent risk is at the maximum
  c. Indicate whether materiality thresholds for planning and evaluation purposes are sufficiently high
  d. Determine the acceptable level of detection risk for financial statement assertions (ID: 4689)

118. After obtaining an understanding of the entity and its environment and assessing the risk of material misstatement, an auditor decided to perform tests of controls. The auditor most likely decided that

  a. It would be efficient to perform tests of controls that would result in a reduction in planned substantive tests.
  b. Additional evidence to support a further reduction in control risk is not available.
  c. An increase in the assessed level of control risk is justified for certain financial statement assertions.
  d. There were many internal control weaknesses that could allow errors to enter the accounting system. (ID: 5651)

119. Which of the following statements best describes why an auditor would use only substantive procedures to evaluate specific relevant assertions and risks?

  a. The relevant internal control components are not well documented.
  b. The internal auditor already has tested the relevant controls and found them effective.
  c. Testing the operating effectiveness of the relevant controls would not be efficient.
  d. The cost of substantive procedures will exceed the cost of testing the relevant controls. (ID: 89792)

120. Which of the following courses of action is the most appropriate if an auditor concludes that there is a high risk of material misstatement?

  a. Use smaller, rather than larger, sample sizes
  b. Perform substantive tests as of an interim date
  c. Select more effective substantive tests
  d. Increase of tests of controls (ID: 89793)

121. When responding to the assessed risk of material misstatement (RMM), an auditor is required to document:

  I. Overall responses to address the assessed RMM at the financial statement level and further audit procedures performed
  II. Linkage of those procedures with the assessed RMM at the relevant assertion level

  a. I only
  b. II only
  c. Both I and II
  d. Neither I nor II (ID: 8265)

Evaluation of Misstatements Identified During the Audit

122. Regarding the evaluation of misstatements, the overall objective of the auditor is to evaluate the effect of

   a. Corrected misstatements on the financial statements
   b. Uncorrected misstatements on the audit
   c. Identified misstatements on the financial statements
   d. Identified misstatements on the audit (ID: 30330)

123. Prior to evaluating the effect of uncorrected misstatements, the auditor should

   a. Reassess materiality to confirm whether it remains appropriate in the context of the entity's projected financial results
   b. Reassess materiality to confirm whether it remains appropriate in the context of the entity's actual financial results
   c. Reassess materiality to confirm whether it remains appropriate in the context of the entity's latest available interim financial results
   d. Reassess materiality to confirm whether it remains appropriate in the context of the entity's actual financial results adjusted for uncorrected misstatements (ID: 90331)

124. The auditor should determine whether uncorrected misstatements are material, individually or in the aggregate. In making this determination, one of the aspects the auditor should consider is the size and nature of the misstatements, in relation to all **except** which of the following?

   a. Particular classes of transactions, account balances, or disclosure
   b. The financial statements as a whole
   c. The particular circumstances of their occurrence
   d. Prior period uncorrected misstatements (ID: 90332)

125. If an individual uncorrected misstatement is judged to be material, other offsetting misstatements

   a. Should not be considered by the auditor
   b. May be considered by the auditor as appropriate if, for example, an overstatement of revenue is completely offset by an overstatement of expense
   c. May be considered by the auditor as appropriate if the offsetting misstatements are within the same account balance or class of transactions
   d. May be considered by the auditor as appropriate if the offsetting misstatements are within the same account balance or class of transactions if the risk that further undetected misstatements may exist is considered (ID: 90333)

126. The auditor should

   a. Accumulate misstatements identified during the audit, other than those that are clearly trivial
   b. Accumulate uncorrected misstatements identified during the audit, other than those that are clearly trivial
   c. Communicate on a timely basis with the appropriate level of management all uncorrected misstatements accumulated during the audit
   d. Include in the audit documentation all uncorrected misstatements accumulated during the audit (ID: 90329)

Communication With Those Charged With Governance

127. Regarding communication with the client,
    a. The auditor takes into account that management and those charged with government, by definition, constitute two exclusive groups.
    b. If the auditor is directed by the client to communicate with a client's audit committee, the auditor need not repeat the communications made to them to the entire governing body of the entity.
    c. The auditor may presume that if a company has an audit committee, communications required by US GAAS to be made to those charged with governance should be made to such a subgroup of their members appointed by them for this purpose.
    d. If matters required by US GAAS are communicated with a person with management responsibilities who also has governance responsibilities, the matters need not be communicated twice. (ID: 90334)

128. Should an auditor communicate the following matters to those charged with governance in an audit of financial statements?

	Significant difficulties encountered during the audit	Disagreements with management
a.	Yes	Yes
b.	Yes	No
c.	No	Yes
d.	No	No

(ID: 2768)

129. Which of the following matters is an auditor required to communicate to those charged with governance?
    I. The auditor is responsible for forming and expressing an opinion about whether the financial statements that have been prepared by management, with the oversight of those charged with governance, are prepared, in all material respects, in accordance with the applicable financial reporting framework
    II. The audit of the financial statements does not relieve management or those charged with governance of their responsibilities.

    a. I only
    b. II only
    c. Both I and II
    d. Neither I nor II

(ID: 2994)

Problem 2-2 SIMULATION: Risk of Material Misstatement

Company

The year under audit is year 2. Scott, Inc. is a manufacturer of handmade glycerin soap and candles. The company has been in business for 15 years and has its headquarters in Yorba Linda, California.

Marketing

Scott, Inc. is divided into two divisions, which serve the major markets for the company's products. One division focuses on sales to department stores. The other division focuses on placing company products in small specialty shops. Currently, each division generates about half of Scott, Inc.'s revenues and net income.

Management

Management realized it must strictly control all costs to make its overall operations more efficient. As a result, Scott, Inc. announced that it would make a series of restructuring changes as of the end of year 2 as part of its overall business plan. During year 2, the company issued long-term debt with complex financial covenants. The debt was incurred to purchase property, plant and equipment. The company also issued additional common stock during year 2.

Senior management at the company experienced significant turnover in recent years. The CEO has been with the company for only one year. The CEO was hired from a major competitor after the previous CEO left to take a position with a large manufacturing company in the Northeast. In another management change, the company's CFO retired, and the current CFO was hired only six months ago. The new CFO was an audit manager from the predecessor audit firm.

Engagement

For year 2, Scott, Inc. switched audit firms. There have been no internal disagreements over accounting issues in any of the prior three years.

Based on the information in Scott, Inc.'s profile, determine whether each of the factors below would be likely to increase audit risk or have no impact on the risk of material misstatement (RMM).

Factors	Impact on RMM	
	Increases	**No Impact**
1. The company has begun to focus on a strategic advertising plan so it may expand its market into other states.		
2. During year 2, management issued additional long-term debt with complex financial covenants.		
3. Scott, Inc. is divided into two divisions, which serve the major markets of the company's products.		
4. The new CFO was an audit manager from the predecessor audit firm.		

(ID: 9201)

Problem 2-3 SIMULATION: Risk of Material Misstatement

Green, CPA, is considering the risk of material misstatement (RMM) at the financial statement level in planning the audit of National Federal Bank (NFB) Company's financial statements for the year ended December 31, year 1. The RMM at the financial statement level may be indicated by a combination of factors related to management, the industry, and the entity. In assessing such factors, Green has gathered the following information concerning NFB's environment.

NFB is a federally insured bank that has been consistently more profitable than the industry average by marketing mortgages on properties in a prosperous rural area, which has experienced considerable growth in recent years. NFB packages its mortgages and sells them to large mortgage investment trusts. Despite recent volatility of interest rates, NFB has been able to continue selling its mortgages as a source of new lendable funds.

Based only on the information given, determine whether each of the factors below *increases* or *decreases* the risk of material misstatement.

Factors	Effect on Risk of Material Misstatement
1. Governmental regulation over the banking industry is extensive.	
2. NFB operates profitably in growing prosperous area.	
3. Overall demand for the industry's product is high.	
4. Interest rates have been volatile recently.	
5. The availability of funds for additional mortgages is promising.	

(ID: 9202)

Problem 2-4 SIMULATION: Risk of Material Misstatement

Edwards, CPA, is considering the risk of material misstatement (RMM) at the financial statement level in planning the audit of Middleton Bank financial statements for the year ended December 31, year 1. The RMM at the financial statement level may be indicated by a combination of factors related to management, the industry, and the entity. In assessing such factors, Edwards has gathered the following information concerning Middleton Bank's environment.

Middleton Bank's board of directors is controlled by Smith, the majority stockholder, who also acts as the chief executive officer. Management at the bank's branch offices has authority for directing and controlling Middleton Bank's operations and is compensated based on branch profitability. The internal auditor reports directly to the chairman of the board's audit committee. The Accounting Department has experienced little turnover in personnel during the five years Edwards has audited Middleton Bank.

Based only on the information given, determine whether each of the factors below *increases* or *decreases* the risk of material misstatement.

Factors	Effect on Risk of Material Misstatement
1. The principal shareholder is also the chief executive officer and controls the board of directors.	
2. Branch management is compensated based on branch profitability.	
3. The internal auditor reports directly to the chairman of the board's audit committee.	
4. The Accounting Department has experienced little turnover in personnel recently.	

(ID: 9203)

Problem 2-5 SIMULATION: Risk of Material Misstatement

Howard, CPA, is considering the risk of material misstatement (RMM) at the financial statement level in planning the audit of Oak Bank financial statements for the year ended December 31, year 1. The RMM at the financial statement level may be indicated by a combination of factors related to management, the industry, and the entity. In assessing such factors, Howard has gathered the following information concerning Oak Bank's environment.

Oak Bank's formula consistently underestimates the allowance for loan losses, but its controller has always been receptive to Howard's suggestions to increase the allowance during each engagement.

During year 1, Oak Bank opened a branch office in a suburban town thirty miles from its principal place of business. Although this branch is not yet profitable due to competition from several well-established local banks, management believes that the branch will be profitable by year 3.

Also, during year 1, Oak Bank increased the efficiency of its accounting operations by installing a new, sophisticated computer system.

Based only on the information given, determine whether each of the factors below *increases* or *decreases* the risk of material misstatement.

Factors	Effect on Risk of Material Misstatement
1. Management fails to establish proper procedures to provide reasonable assurance of reliable accounting estimates.	
2. Management has been receptive to Howard's suggestions relating to accounting adjustments.	
3. Oak Bank recently opened a new branch office that is not yet profitable.	
4. Oak Bank recently installed a new sophisticated computer system.	

(ID: 9204)

Problem 2-6 SIMULATION: Research

Which citation in the professional standards addresses that although fraudulent journal entries often are made at the end of a reporting period, the auditor should consider whether there is a need to test journal entries throughout the reporting period under audit?

[ ] § [ ] . [ ] (ID: 9205)

Problem 2-7 SIMULATION: Research

Which citation in the professional standards states that the discussion among the audit team about the susceptibility of the entity's financial statements to material misstatement can be held concurrently with the discussion about the susceptibility of the financial statements to fraud?

[ ] § [ ] . [ ] (ID: 9217)

Solution 2-1 MULTIPLE-CHOICE ANSWERS

1. (c) A recurring audit is an audit engagement for an existing audit client for whom the auditor performed the preceding audit. (ID: 90065)

2. (a) The preconditions for an audit are the use by management of an acceptable financial reporting framework in the preparation and fair presentation of the financial statements and the agreement of management and, when appropriate, those charged with governance, to the premise on which an audit is conducted. Incorrect answer b. is the overview of the premise on which an audit is conducted; the acceptance of this premise by management and, when appropriate, those charged with governance is *one* of the preconditions for an audit. Incorrect answers c. and d. are two of the responsibilities included in that premise on which an audit is conducted. Editor Note: The other management responsibilities included in that premise are responsibility for (1) the preparation and fair presentation of the financial statements in accordance with the applicable financial reporting framework; (2) to provide the auditor with (in addition to answer d.) additional information that the auditor may request from management and, when appropriate, those charged with governance for the purpose of the audit; and (3) unrestricted access to persons within the entity from whom the auditor determines it necessary to obtain audit evidence. (ID: 90066)

3. (b) Such inquiries should relate to *matters that will assist the auditor in determining whether to accept the engagement*. Inquiries about communications to those charged with governance regarding fraud and noncompliance with laws or regulations by the entity would be the most likely matter of those given to be subject to the auditor's inquiry for this purpose. Regarding incorrect answer b., subsequent events that occurred after the predecessor's audit report was issued would be covered in the current audit period. Regarding incorrect answers c. and d., opening balances and consistency of accounting policies are, of course, matters of interest to the auditor; however, the timing of such procedures is more flexible, i.e., they may, but are much less likely to occur prior to acceptance of the engagement. Editor Note: Matters subject to the auditor's inquiry of the predecessor auditor related to engagement acceptance may also include the following: (1) information that might bear on the integrity of management; (2) disagreements with management about accounting policies, auditing procedures, or other similarly significant matters; (3) communications to management and those charged with governance regarding significant deficiencies and material weaknesses in internal control; and (4) the predecessor auditor's understanding about the reasons for the change of auditors. (ID: 4666)

4. (d) Before accepting an engagement for an initial audit, including a reaudit engagement, the auditor should request management to authorize the predecessor auditor to respond fully to the auditor's inquiries regarding matters that will assist the auditor in determining whether to accept the engagement. The other answers describe activities that are not required prior to the acceptance of an engagement. Regarding incorrect answer a., the Code of Professional Conduct of the AICPA requires an auditor who does not possess an understanding of the client's industry and business prior to the acceptance of the engagement to have the ability to gain it. (ID: 6391)

5. (b) Matters subject to the auditor's inquiry of the predecessor auditor prior to engagement acceptance *may* include (specific inquiries are *not* required—see incorrect answer a.): (1) information that might bear on the integrity of management; (2) disagreements with management about accounting policies, auditing procedures, or other similarly significant matters; (3) communications to those charged with governance regarding fraud and noncompliance with laws or regulations by the entity; (4) communications to management and those charged with governance regarding significant deficiencies and material weaknesses in internal control; (5) the predecessor auditor's understanding about the reasons for the change of auditors. Regarding incorrect answer c., if management refuses to authorize the predecessor auditor to respond, or limits the response, the auditor should inquire about the reasons and consider the implications of that refusal in deciding whether to accept the engagement. The auditor is *not* automatically precluded from accepting the engagement. Regarding incorrect answer d., if the predecessor auditor provides no response or a limited response, the auditor should evaluate the predecessor auditor's response, or consider the implications, in determining whether to accept the engagement. Again, the auditor is *not* automatically precluded from accepting the engagement. (ID: 89480)

6. (b) To establish whether the preconditions for an audit are present, the auditor should obtain the agreement of management that it acknowledges and understands its responsibility to provide the auditor with

unrestricted access to persons within the entity from whom the auditor determines it necessary to obtain audit evidence; the auditor should *not* be limited to a list of employees authorized by the client. (ID: 89500)

7. (d) If management refuses to authorize the predecessor auditor to respond, or limits the response, the auditor should inquire about the reasons and consider the implications of that refusal in deciding whether to accept the engagement. However, the auditor is not precluded by this circumstance from accepting the engagement. (Editor Note: Before accepting an engagement for an initial audit, including a reaudit engagement, the auditor should request management to authorize the predecessor auditor to respond fully to the auditor's inquiries *regarding matters that will assist the auditor in determining whether to accept the engagement.*) All of the other answer alternatives describe situations which would preclude the auditor from accepting the engagement. Regarding answer a., a client-imposed scope limitation that would result in a disclaimer of opinion, the auditor should not accept such a limited engagement. If management or those charged with governance of an entity that is required by law or regulation to have an audit imposes such a scope limitation and a disclaimer of opinion is acceptable under the applicable law or to the regulator, the auditor is permitted, but not required, to accept the engagement. (Editor Note: The auditor is *not* precluded from accepting the engagement if the restriction is imposed by circumstances beyond the control of management.) Regarding answer c., a misleading prescribed audit report form, if the auditor is required by law or regulation to accept the engagement, such an audit does not comply with US GAAS. Accordingly, the auditor should *not* include any reference to the audit having been performed in accordance with US GAAS within the audit report—the auditor *may* consider including a statement in the audit report that the audit is not conducted in accordance with US GAAS. However, even under these conditions, the auditor is encouraged to apply US GAAS, including the standards that address the audit report, to the extent practicable. (ID: 90068)

8. (b) The agreed-upon terms of the audit engagement should be documented in an audit engagement letter (or other suitable form of written agreement) and should include a statement that because of the inherent limitations of an audit, together with the inherent limitations of internal control, an unavoidable risk exists that some material misstatements may not be detected, even though the audit is properly planned and performed in accordance with US GAAS. The required elements of the terms of the engagement are: (1) the objective and scope of the audit; (2) the responsibilities of the auditor; (3) the responsibilities of management; (4) a statement regarding the inherent limitations of an audit (see this question's quote); (4) identification of the applicable financial reporting framework for the preparation of the financial statements; (6) reference to the expected form and content of any reports to be issued by the auditor and a statement that circumstances may arise in which a report may differ from its expected form and content. (ID: 7634)

9. (d) Answer d., the auditor would *no*t promise to discuss the specific procedures to be performed during the audit. (However, the auditor is required to include the objective and scope of the audit in the written agreement to the terms of the engagement.) Answers a. and b., fees/billing arrangements and the request for management's acknowledgment of the agreement, respectively, are examples of matters that are not required to be included, but may be included. Answer c. is the only answer alternative that is required to be included in the written agreement as to the terms of an audit engagement. Such reference may include a description of the types of reports to be issued; of course, the auditor need not describe the type of opinion expected to be expressed. A related statement that circumstances may arise in which a report may differ from its expected form and content is also required. Other items, in addition to answers a. and b., that are not required, but may be referenced in an engagement letter include: (1) elaboration of the scope of the audit, including reference to applicable legislation, regulations, US GAAS, and ethical and other pronouncements of professional bodies to which the auditor adheres; (2) the form of any other communication of results of the audit engagement; (3) arrangements regarding the planning and performance of the audit, including the composition of the audit team; (4) the expectation that management will provide written representations; (5) the agreement of management to make available to the auditor draft financial statements and any accompanying other information in a timely fashion; (6) the agreement of management to inform the auditor of events occurring or facts discovered subsequent to the date of the financial statements that may affect the financial statements; (7) arrangements concerning the involvement of other auditors or specialists; (8) arrangements concerning the involvement of internal auditors and other staff of the entity; (9) arrangements to be made with the predecessor auditor, if any, in the case of an initial audit; (10) any restriction of the auditor's liability when not prohibited; (11) any obligations of the auditor to provide audit documentation to other parties; (12) additional services to be provided; and (13) a reference to any further agreements between the auditor and the entity. (ID: 90067)

10. (b) The auditor may remind management of the terms of the engagement in writing or orally. A written reminder might be a letter confirming that the terms of the preceding engagement will govern the current engagement. If the reminder is oral, audit documentation may include with whom the discussion took place, when, and the significant points discussed. (ID: 90070)

11. (c) In and of itself, a change in personnel of the audit team should not affect the terms of an audit engagement. Additional factors that may make it appropriate to revise the terms of the audit engagement include any indication that management misunderstands the objective and scope of the audit; any revised or special terms of the audit engagement; a significant change in ownership; a significant change in the nature or size of the entity's business; and a change in other reporting requirements. If the terms of the audit engagement are changed, the auditor and management should agree on and document the new terms of the engagement in an engagement letter or other suitable form of written agreement. (ID: 90071)

12. (c) A change in circumstances that affects management's requirements or a misunderstanding concerning the nature of the service originally requested may be considered a reasonable basis for requesting a change in the audit engagement. Regarding incorrect answer a., in order to avoid confusing the reader, the report on the lower level of service would *not* include reference to the original audit engagement nor any procedures that may have been performed in the original audit engagement, except when the audit engagement is changed to an engagement to undertake agreed-upon procedures and, thus, reference to the procedures performed is a normal part of the report. Regarding incorrect answer b., if the auditor concludes that no reasonable justification for a change of the terms of the audit engagement exists and is not permitted by management to continue the original audit engagement, the auditor should withdraw from the engagement (when possible under applicable law or regulation), *not* disclaim an opinion. The auditor should also communicate the circumstances to those charged with governance; and determine whether any obligation, either legal, contractual, or otherwise, exists to report the circumstances to other parties, such as owners, or regulators. Regarding incorrect answer, d., the auditor should not agree to a change in the terms of the audit engagement when no reasonable justification for doing so exists—the auditor is *not* required to comply with all requests. (ID: 90072)

13. (b) When an audit is no longer needed to meet the membership requirements of a trade organization is an example of a change in circumstances that affects management's requirements and may be considered a reasonable basis for requesting a change in the audit engagement. The auditor is required to consider the justification given for the request, particularly the implications of a restriction on the scope of the audit engagement. A change request may not be considered reasonable if the change appears to relate to information that is incorrect, incomplete, or otherwise unsatisfactory. Under these circumstances, if management asks for the audit engagement to be changed to a lower level of assurance to avoid a qualified opinion or a disclaimer of opinion, such a request for a change in engagement may not be considered reasonable. (ID: 90073)

14. (d) The risk of material misstatement (RMM) at the assertion level is assessed in order to determine the nature, timing, and extent of further audit procedures necessary to obtain sufficient appropriate audit evidence. This evidence enables the auditor to express an opinion on the financial statements at an acceptably low level of audit risk. Regarding incorrect answer a., the audit performs risk assessment procedures to obtain an understanding of the entity and its environment, including its internal control. This understanding aids the identification and assessment of the RMM; gaining an understanding of the entity's environment is not the result of the assessment of the RMM. Regarding incorrect answer b., judgments about materiality levels provide a basis for the assessment of the RMM as well as the determination of the nature and extent of risk assessment procedures and the nature, extent, and timing of further audit procedures. They are not a result of the assessment of the RMM. Regarding incorrect answer c., risk assessment procedures are also performed (in addition to obtain an understanding of the entity), to identify and assess the RMM; not vice versa. (ID: 5968)

15. (b) At the assertion level, the risk of material misstatement consists of (1) inherent risk:, the susceptibility of an assertion about a class of transaction, account balance, or disclosure to a misstatement that could be material, either individually or when aggregated with other misstatements, before consideration of any related controls, and (2) control risk, the risk that a misstatement that could occur in an assertion about a class of transaction, account balance, or disclosure and that could be material, either individually or when aggregated with other misstatements, will not be prevented, or detected and corrected, on a timely basis by the entity's internal control. Editor Note: The RMM is the risk that the financial statements are materially misstated prior to

the audit. It exists at both the overall financial statement level and the assertion level. (RMM at the overall financial statement level refers to those risks that relate pervasively to the financial statements as a whole and potentially could affect many assertions.) (ID: 90074)

16. (a) The higher the risk of material misstatement (RMM), generally, the more substantive testing will be needed to provide more persuasive audit evidence. The RMM and the amount of substantive testing are generally directly (rather than inversely) related. (ID: 90078)

17. (a) Detection risk relates to substantive audit procedures and is managed by the auditor's response to the risk of material misstatement (RMM). For a given level of audit risk, detection risk should bear an inverse relationship to the RMM at the relevant assertion level. As the RMM increases, the level of detection risk that can be accepted by the auditor decreases (and the need for the assurance provided by substantive tests increases). Likewise, as the RMM decreases, the level of detection risk that can be accepted by the auditor increases. (However, the auditor should perform substantive procedures for all relevant assertions related to material classes of transactions, account balances, and disclosures regardless of the assessed level of risk.) Regarding incorrect answer b., the risk of misapplying audit procedures is a part of detection risk. Regarding incorrect answer c., the preliminary judgment about materiality levels provides a basis for, i.e., is made prior to, the auditor's identification and assessment of the RMM. Thus, as detection risk is set by the auditor in response to the RMM, the setting of the preliminary materiality levels is unrelated to detection risk. Moreover, the judgment about what constitutes a material misstatement is not related to the determination of the degree of risk the auditor is willing to accept that a material misstatement will be undetected. Regarding incorrect answer d., the risk of failing to discover material misstatements during an audit is detection risk. (ID: 44)

18. (b) Detection risk is the risk that the auditor will not detect a material misstatement that exists in an assertion. Inherent risk is the susceptibility of an assertion to a material misstatement assuming that there are no related controls. Sampling risk arises from the possibility that, when a test of controls or a substantive test is restricted to a sample, the auditor's conclusions may be different from the conclusions the auditor would reach if the test were applied in the same way to all items in the account balance or class of transactions. Nonsampling risk includes all the aspects of audit risk that are not due to sampling. (ID: 2275)

19. (a) Inherent risk is the susceptibility of an assertion to a material misstatement, assuming that there are no related controls. Control risk is the risk that a material misstatement that could occur in an assertion will not be prevented, or detected and corrected, on a timely basis by the entity's internal control. Detection risk is the risk that the auditor will not detect a material misstatement that exists in an assertion. Thus, inherent risk and control risk are functions of the client and its environment while detection risk is not. Inherent risk, control risk, and detection risk are all a part of audit risk. Inherent risk and control risk differ from detection risk in that they exist independently of the audit of financial statements, whereas detection risk relates to the auditor's procedures and can be changed at the auditor's discretion. All of the elements of audit risk should be considered in relation to individual account balances, classes of transactions and disclosures; and at the overall financial statement level. (ID: 2810)

20. (b) Detection risk has an inverse relationship to control risk. Therefore, if an auditor decides to increase the assessed level of control risk from the originally planned level, in order to achieve an equivalent overall level of risk, detection risk must be decreased. (ID: 5083)

21. (c) All three components of audit risk (control risk, detection risk, and inherent risk) may be assessed in quantitative terms, such as percentages, or nonquantitative terms, such as high, medium, or low risk. (ID: 5628)

22. (b) Performing principal substantive tests at an interim date rather than as of the balance sheet date potentially increases the risk that misstatements that may exist at the balance sheet date will not be detected. Therefore, postponing the planned timing of substantive tests from interim dates to the year-end decreases detection risk. (ID: 5630)

23. (b) As the assessed level of control risk increases, the acceptable level of detection risk decreases. To decrease detection risk, an auditor changes the nature, extent, or timing of tests of details. To decrease detection risk, an auditor increases the extent of test of details. The level of inherent risk doesn't change, although an

auditor may change the assessment of the level of inherent risk. As inherent risk is the susceptibility of an assertion to misstatement, assuming no related internal controls, the assessment of inherent risk level rarely changes due to a change in control risk. Increased testing of controls that the auditor already has determined to be ineffective provides no benefit. (ID: 7799)

24. (a) Control risk is the risk that a misstatement that could occur in an assertion about a class of transaction, account balance, or disclosure and that could be material, either individually or when aggregated with other misstatements, will not be prevented, or detected and corrected, on a timely basis by the entity's internal control. The risk that the auditor will not detect a material misstatement refers to detection risk, not control risk. The risk that the auditor's assessment of internal controls will be at less than the maximum level is not a risk—the use of risk assessment procedures and tests of controls may appropriately result in such a conclusion. The susceptibility of material misstatement assuming there are no related internal controls, policies, or procedures refers to inherent risk, not control risk. (ID: 9917)

25. (b) An inherent limitation to internal control is the fact that controls can be circumvented by management override. Other limitations inherent to internal control include human failures such a faulty decision making and simple errors or mistakes. Additionally, controls can be circumvented by the collusion of two or more people. A well-designed internal control system does not ensure the achievement of an entity's control objectives nor can it be designed and operated to detect all errors and fraud; it only provides the entity with reasonable, not absolute, assurance due to these inherent limitations. (ID: 9931)

26. (d) Audit risk is the risk that the auditor expresses an inappropriate audit opinion when the financial statements are materially misstated. Audit risk is a function of the risk of material misstatement (RMM) and detection risk. The RMM is the risk that the financial statements are materially misstated prior to the audit. This consists of two components at the assertion level: (1) inherent risk, which is the susceptibility of an assertion about a class of transaction, account balance, or disclosure to a misstatement that could be material, either individually or when aggregated with other misstatements, before consideration of any related controls; and (2) control risk, which is the risk that a misstatement that could occur in an assertion about a class of transaction, account balance, or disclosure and that could be material, either individually or when aggregated with other misstatements, will not be prevented, or detected and corrected, on a timely basis by the entity's internal control. Detection risk is the risk that the procedures performed by the auditor to reduce audit risk to an acceptably low level will not detect a misstatement that exists and that could be material, either individually or when aggregated with other misstatements. It is a function of the effectiveness of an audit procedure and of its application by the auditor, i.e., an auditor might select an inappropriate audit procedure, misapply an appropriate audit procedure, or misinterpret the audit results. (ID: 90075)

27. (b) When the auditor believes the risk of material misstatement (RMM) is high, the auditor responds by accepting less detection risk; accordingly, the auditor requires more persuasive audit evidence. Audit risk is a function of the RMM and detection risk. RMM is the entity's risk; it exists independently of the audit. Detection risk is the auditor's risk. They are inversely related. (ID: 90076)

28. (a) The level of detection risk, generally, has an inverse relationship with the amount of substantive testing needed. If the auditor decreases the acceptable level of detection risk, more substantive testing may be in order and vice versa. However, the auditor should perform substantive procedures for all relevant assertions related to all material account balances, classes of transactions, and disclosures regardless of the assessed level of risk. (ID: 90077)

29. (d) The element of the audit planning process most likely to be agreed upon with the client before implementation of the audit strategy is the timing of inventory observation procedures to be performed. Evidence to be gathered to provide a sufficient basis for the auditor's opinion is solely a matter of auditor judgment. The procedures to be undertaken to discover litigation, claims, and assessments are determined by the auditor. Pending legal matters to be included in the inquiry of the client's attorney are more likely to be discussed after implementation of the audit strategy. (ID: 5619)

30. (c) The auditor may decide to discuss elements of planning with the entity's management to facilitate the conduct and management of the audit engagement, for example, to coordinate some of the planned audit procedures with the work of the entity's personnel such as the physical count of the inventory. (Although these

discussions often occur, the overall audit strategy and the audit plan remain the auditor's responsibility.) When discussing matters included in the overall audit strategy or audit plan, care is required in order not to compromise the effectiveness of the audit. For example, discussing the nature and timing of detailed audit procedures with management may compromise the effectiveness of the audit by making the audit procedures too predictable. An auditor would identify specific internal control activities that are likely to prevent fraud during the review of internal control or when fraud factors are discovered. An auditor would evaluate the reasonableness of a client's accounting estimates and inquire of a client's attorney regarding unrecorded claims when collecting evidence. (ID: 7798)

31. (d) Which analytical procedures to be applied as risk assessment procedures, not the results of analytical procedures, should be considered prior to the identification and assessment of the risk of material misstatement (RMM). Prior to the auditor's identification and assessment of the RMM, planning includes the need to also consider, of course, the performance of risk assessment procedures other than analytical procedures. (ID: 90079)

32. (d) The auditor should consider the factors that, in the auditor's professional judgment, are significant in directing the engagement team's efforts when establishing the overall audit strategy, rather than during the earlier preliminary stage. The other answer alternatives comprise all of the required preliminary engagement activities. Performing them at the beginning of the current audit engagement assists the auditor in identifying and evaluating events or circumstances that may adversely affect the auditor's ability to plan and perform the audit engagement. Their performance should enable the auditor to plan an engagement for which the auditor maintains the necessary independence and ability to perform the engagement; has no issues with management integrity; or has no misunderstanding with the entity about the terms of the engagement. (ID: 90084)

33. (d) Of the procedures listed, an auditor is most likely to determine the extent of involvement of the client's internal auditors in developing the overall audit strategy of a financial statement audit. A representation letter from the client's management (and, when appropriate, those charged with governance) is obtained at the end of an audit, not the beginning—it should be as of the date of the audit report on the financial statements. Examining documents and considering the reasonableness of estimates are procedures performed during the audit. (ID: 5074)

34. (d) The primary purpose of the audit is to provide users of the financial statements with an opinion. The objective of the auditor is to design and perform audit procedures that enable the auditor to obtain sufficient appropriate audit evidence to be able to draw reasonable conclusions on which to base the auditor's opinion. The design of the audit program has no effect on inherent risk. Procedures may be performed prior to the balance sheet date only if the effectiveness of interim work is not likely to be impaired. Suggestions to management are secondary considerations in an audit. (ID: 5089)

35. (c) The auditor should prepare a written audit plan (or program). The audit plan should detail the nature, extent, and timing of the audit procedures that are necessary to accomplish the objectives of the audit. All material transactions* and all account balances are not required to be tested in all circumstances. Minimizing substantive tests prior to the balance sheet date is not required. *Editor Note: Irrespective of the assessed risks of material misstatement, the auditor should design and perform substantive procedures for all relevant assertions related to each material *class* of transactions, account balance, and disclosure. (ID: 5634)

36. (a) The entity's risk assessment process is part of its internal control. Gaining an understanding of the entity's internal control is the first of these four procedures to be performed in an audit and is an example of a matter considered in establishing the overall audit strategy. The auditor identifies specific activities designed to prevent fraud when considering relying on internal control. The other two options are substantive procedures performed during the audit. (ID: 6709)

37. (c) Planning involves the development of an overall strategy for the expected conduct, organization, and staffing of the audit. The auditor must plan the audit to be responsive to the assessment of the risk of material misstatement. In establishing the overall audit strategy, the auditor should consider the important factors that will determine the focus of the audit team's efforts, such as the determination of appropriate materiality levels; preliminary identification of areas where there may be higher risks of material misstatement; preliminary

identification of material locations and account balances; evaluation of whether the auditor plans to perform tests of controls; and identification of recent significant entity-specific, industry, financial reporting, or other relevant developments. (ID: 7102)

38. (d) Planning the nature, extent, and timing of specific further audit procedures depends on the outcome of risk assessment procedures. This is why planning risk assessment procedures occurs early in the audit process. Confirming that a common understanding of the terms of the audit engagement exists between the auditor and the client—a preliminary engagement activity—is an objective of the appropriate acceptance of an engagement; not the objective of planning the audit. The primary objective of the auditor is to plan the audit so that it will be performed in an effective manner. The overall audit strategy provides a basis for the detailed audit plan; not vice versa. Once the overall audit strategy has been established, an audit plan can be developed to address the various matters identified in the overall audit strategy, taking into account the need to achieve the audit objectives through the efficient use of the auditor's resources. That said, the establishment of the overall audit strategy and the detailed audit plan are not necessarily discrete or sequential processes but are closely interrelated because changes in one may result in consequential changes to the other. (The audit plan is more detailed than the overall audit strategy in that it includes the nature, timing, and extent of audit procedures to be performed by engagement team members.) Planning for audit procedures takes place over the course of the audit as the audit plan for the engagement develops. The auditor may begin the execution of further audit procedures for some classes of transactions, account balances, and disclosures before planning all remaining further audit procedures. (ID: 90085)

39. (a) During the planning phase the auditor should consider whether specialized skills are needed in performing the audit. If so, the auditor should seek assistance. Someone possessing these skills may either be on the auditor's staff or an outside professional. The auditor should have sufficient knowledge to communicate the objectives of the other professional's work; evaluate whether the specified audit procedures will meet the auditor's objectives; and evaluate the results of the audit procedures applied as they relate to the nature, timing, and extent of further planned audit procedures. The other answer alternatives are procedures that are performed during the audit. (ID: 90086)

40. (d) The detailed audit plan, not the overall audit strategy, includes a description of the nature, timing, and extent of planned further audit procedures at the relevant assertion level. In addition to the other answer alternatives, in establishing the overall audit strategy, the auditor should consider the factors that, in the auditor's professional judgment, are significant in directing the engagement team's efforts; consider the results of preliminary engagement activities; and, when applicable, consider whether knowledge gained on other engagements performed by the engagement partner for the entity is relevant. (ID: 90087)

41. (c) The terms of the engagement should be documented in an audit engagement letter or other suitable form of written agreement; not described in the audit plan. Moreover, reaching this understanding is a preliminary engagement activity. The detailed audit plan focuses on the audit procedures. The other answer alternatives comprise all the required elements of an audit plan. (ID: 90088)

42. (a) The auditor should establish an overall audit strategy that sets the scope, timing, and direction of the audit and that guides the development of the audit plan. The detailed audit plan, not the overall audit strategy, includes a description of the nature and extent of planned risk assessment procedures. The auditor should update and change the overall audit strategy and audit plan, as necessary, during the course of the audit. As a result of unexpected events, changes in conditions, or the audit evidence obtained from the results of audit procedures, the auditor may need to modify the overall audit strategy and audit plan and, thereby, the resulting planned nature, timing, and extent of further audit procedures, based on the revised consideration of assessed risks. The overall audit strategy provides a basis for the detailed audit plan; not vice versa. Once the overall audit strategy has been established, an audit plan can be developed to address the various matters identified in the overall audit strategy, taking into account the need to achieve the audit objectives through the efficient use of the auditor's resources. That said, the establishment of the overall audit strategy and the detailed audit plan are not necessarily discrete or sequential processes but are closely interrelated because changes in one may result in consequential changes to the other. (ID: 90089)

43. (c) The auditor is not required to document the discussions with management related to planning activities, including the agreed upon dates for their delivery of requested data. The other answer alternatives include all the required documentation related to planning. (ID: 90082)

44. (c) If the auditor identifies a misstatement, whether material or not, and the auditor has reason to believe that it is, or may be, the result of fraud and that management (in particular, senior management) is involved, the auditor should reevaluate the assessment of the risks of material misstatement due to fraud and its resulting effect on the nature, timing, and extent of audit procedures to respond to the assessed risks. For example, an otherwise insignificant fraud may be significant if it involves senior management. In such circumstances, the reliability of evidence previously obtained may be called into question because there may be doubts about the completeness and truthfulness of representations made and the genuineness of accounting records and documentation. There may also be a possibility of collusion involving employees, management, or third parties. In addition to the alternative answers, the concept of materiality is applied by the auditor in evaluating the effect of uncorrected misstatements, if any, on the financial statements. (ID: 90090)

45. (d) The possible effect of misstatements on specific individual users, whose needs may vary widely, is not considered. (ID: 90091)

46. (c) The materiality determined when planning the audit does not necessarily establish an amount below which uncorrected misstatements, individually or in the aggregate, will always be evaluated as immaterial. The circumstances related to some misstatements may cause the auditor to evaluate them as material even if they are below materiality. Although it is not practicable to design audit procedures to detect misstatements that could be material solely because of their nature (that is, qualitative considerations), the auditor considers not only the size but also the nature of uncorrected misstatements, and the particular circumstances of their occurrence, when evaluating their effect on the financial statements. One of the assumptions auditors make about financial statement users is that they have a reasonable knowledge of business and economic activities and accounting and a willingness to study the information in the financial statements with reasonable diligence. Materiality and audit risk are considered throughout the audit. (ID: 90092)

47. (c) Judgments about materiality provide a basis for all of the answer alternatives except determining whether to accept an engagement and the related fees. (ID: 90093)

48. (b) The auditor would most likely use the entity's annualized interim financial statements. Although applying a percentage to a chosen benchmark, such as a category of reported income, as a starting point to determine materiality for the financial statements as a whole is not required, it is a method that is often used. With regard to the chosen benchmark, relevant financial data ordinarily includes prior periods' financial results and financial positions; the period-to-date financial results and financial position; and budgets or forecasts for the current period. The auditor should take into account any significant changes in the entity's circumstances and relevant changes in the economy or the industry in which the entity operates. The anticipated sample size of the planned substantive tests and the internal control questionnaire are, if anything, dependent on materiality, not vice versa. The representation letter is dated as the date of the audit report and thus its content would not be available during the planning stage of the audit. (ID: 5629)

49. (b) When determining materiality, one factor that may affect the identification of an appropriate benchmark is its relative volatility. When establishing the overall audit strategy, the auditor should determine materiality for the financial statements as a whole. Only if, in the specific circumstances of the entity, one or more particular classes of transactions, account balances, or disclosures exist for which misstatements of lesser amounts than materiality for the financial statements as a whole could reasonably be expected to influence the economic decisions of users, then, taken on the basis of the financial statements, the auditor also should determine the materiality level or levels to be applied to those particular classes of transactions, account balances, or disclosures. One of the assumptions auditors make about financial statement users is that users make reasonable economic decisions on the basis of the information in the financial statements. US GAAS does not assume that is it is more likely that a financial advisor will be consulted. Determining materiality does involve the exercise of professional judgment. A percentage is often applied to a chosen benchmark as a starting point in determining materiality for the financial statements as a whole; however, this methodology is not required. (ID: 90094)

50. (b) Planning the audit solely to detect individual material misstatements overlooks the fact that the aggregate of individually immaterial misstatements may cause the financial statements to be materially misstated and leaves no margin for possible undetected misstatements. Performance materiality is set to reduce to an appropriately low level the probability that the aggregate of uncorrected and undetected misstatements in the financial statements exceeds materiality for the financial statements as a whole. Similarly, performance materiality relating to a materiality level determined for a particular class of transactions, account balance, or disclosure is set to reduce to an appropriately low level the probability that the aggregate of uncorrected and undetected misstatements in that particular class of transactions, account balance, or disclosure exceeds the materiality level for that particular class of transactions, account balance, or disclosure. Performance materiality is defined as the amount or amounts (not one amount) set by the auditor at less than (not higher) materiality for the financial statements as a whole. The auditor should determine performance materiality for purposes of assessing the risks of material misstatement and determining the nature, timing, and extent of further audit procedures. (ID: 90095)

51. (a) If the auditor concludes that a lower materiality than that initially determined for the financial statements as a whole (and, if applicable, materiality level or levels for particular classes of transactions, account balances, or disclosures) is appropriate, the auditor should determine whether it is necessary to revise performance materiality and whether the nature, timing, and extent of the further audit procedures remain appropriate. (ID: 90096)

52. (a) The auditor should include in the audit documentation the following amounts and the factors considered in their determination (1) materiality for the financial statements as a whole; (2) if applicable, the materiality level or levels for particular classes of transactions, account balances, or disclosures; (3) performance materiality; and (4) any revision of 1–3 as the audit progressed. Documentation of the reason why materiality was not determined for any classes of transactions, account balances, or disclosures is not required. Any revision to a materiality amount should be documented; not just significant revisions. The factors considered in their determination should be documented regardless of the methodology used. (ID: 90097)

53. (a) The objective of the auditor is to identify and assess the risks of material misstatement [perform risk assessment procedures], whether due to fraud or error, at the financial statement and relevant assertion levels through understanding the entity and its environment, including the entity's internal control, thereby providing a basis for designing and implementing responses [determining the nature, extent, and timing of further audit procedures] to the assessed risks of material misstatement. (ID: 5642)

54. (b) Analytical procedures, such as comparing the financial statements to anticipated results, are used as risk assessment procedures during the planning phase of an audit to provide the basis for planning further audit procedures. Inquiry of the client's legal counsel about pending litigation is an audit procedure that would be performed near the end of the engagement. (It is preferable that the legal counsel's response be as close to the date of the audit report as is practicable to avoid the need to obtain updated information.) Even if the inquiry (as opposed to the date of the response) occurs earlier in the audit, it is unlikely to be made during the planning (risk assessment) phase. A related activity, i.e., obtaining a general understanding of the legal and regulatory framework applicable to the entity and how the entity is complying with that framework, is actually best performed very early in the planning phase (prior to the auditor's identification and assessment of the risks of material misstatement), but this is different than the substantive audit procedure known as the letter of inquiry. Answer c. is a substantive audit procedure that would be performed during the audit engagement to support management's assertion of completeness. When performing risk assessment procedures to obtain an understanding of controls that are relevant to the audit, the auditor evaluates the design of those controls and determines whether they have been implemented. This is different than answer d. which is an example of testing the operating effectiveness of a control. Testing the operating effectiveness of a control is a substantive procedure (tests of controls) performed during the audit as a response to the auditor's assessment of the risks of material misstatement. Editor Note: Analytical procedures are also used as substantive procedures during the audit to detect material misstatements at the assertion level and near the end of the audit to assist the auditor when forming an overall conclusion on the financial statements. (ID: 5622)

55. (b) Analytical procedures performed as risk assessment procedures, i.e., analytical procedures used to plan the audit, often use data aggregated at a high level. The objective is to identify the existence of unusual

transactions or events and amounts, ratios, and trends that might indicate matters that have financial statement and audit planning ramifications. Analytical procedures are not used to replace tests of controls. Analytical procedures can be used as substantive tests to obtain audit evidence about particular assertions (which is not part of the planning stage). Substantive analytical procedures often involve the comparison of expectations developed by the auditor (not assertions developed by management) to recorded amounts (or ratios developed from recorded amounts) to achieve an audit objective related to a particular assertion made by management. The determination of materiality is made early in the planning process. A percentage is often applied to a chosen benchmark as a starting point in determining materiality for the financial statements as a whole. However, this type of analysis is not the same as performing analytical procedures in the context of an audit. (Analytical procedures are defined by US GAAS as evaluations of financial information through analysis of plausible relationships among both financial and nonfinancial data. Analytical procedures also encompass such investigation, as is necessary, of identified fluctuations or relationships that are inconsistent with other relevant information or that differ from expected values by a significant amount.) (ID: 9929)

56. (a) The auditor should perform risk assessment procedures to provide a basis for the identification and assessment of risks of material misstatement at the financial statement and relevant assertion levels. Risk assessment procedures by themselves; however, do not provide sufficient appropriate audit evidence on which to base the audit opinion. (ID: 90080)

57. (a) The auditor should consider whether information obtained from the auditor's client acceptance or continuance process is relevant to identifying risks of material misstatement. If the engagement partner has performed other engagements for the entity, the engagement partner should consider whether information obtained is relevant to identifying risks of material misstatement. The determination of materiality for a previous audit is not carried forward to the current audit. When the auditor intends to use information obtained from the auditor's previous experience with the entity and from audit procedures performed in previous audits, the auditor should determine whether changes have occurred since the previous audit that may affect its relevance to the current audit. Confirmation of the inclusion of the procedures in the previous engagement's documentation is not required. The engagement partner is only required to include key members of the engagement team. The engagement partner should determine which matters are to be communicated to engagement team members not involved in the discussion. Editor Note: Another related activity that should be performed is the consideration of the results of the assessment of the risk of material misstatement due to fraud along with other information gathered in the process of identifying the risks of material misstatements (performance of risk assessment procedures). (ID: 90294)

58. (c) Whether the entity has a complex structure is an example of a matter the auditor may consider when obtaining an understanding about the nature of the entity; rather than a matter related to relevant industry, regulatory, or other external factors, including the applicable financial reporting framework. (ID: 90286)

59. (a) It is primarily important for the auditor to obtain an understanding of the nature of an entity to enable the auditor to understand the classes of transactions, account balances, and disclosures to be expected in the financial statements. (ID: 90287)

60. (b) The entity's selection and application of accounting policies, including the reasons for changes (the auditor should evaluate whether the entity's accounting policies are appropriate for its business and consistent with the applicable financial reporting framework and accounting policies used in the relevant industry) is another aspect of the entity the auditor is required to understand—distinct from the components of the nature of the entity. In addition to the other answer alternatives, the components of the nature of an entity that the auditor is required to understand include the types of investments that the entity is making and plans to make, including investments in entities formed to accomplish specific objectives. Editor Note: The understanding of the nature of an entity enables the auditor to understand the classes of transactions, account balances, and disclosures to be expected in the financial statements. (ID: 90288)

61. (d) Taxation is an example of a matter the auditor may consider when obtaining an understanding about external factors; rather than a matter related to the nature of the entity. (ID: 90289)

62. (c) Current and prospective financing requirements is an example of a matter the auditor may consider when obtaining an understanding about the entity's objectives and strategies and those related business risks that may result in risks of material misstatement; rather than a matter related to the entity's selection and application of accounting policies, including the reasons for any changes (the auditor should evaluate whether the entity's accounting policies are appropriate for its business and consistent with the applicable financial reporting framework and accounting policies used in the relevant industry). (ID: 90290)

63. (a) Business risk is broader than the risk of material misstatement of the financial statements, though it includes the latter. Usually, management identifies business risks and develops approaches to address them. (Such a risk assessment process is part of internal control.) The auditor should also consider business risk because an understanding of the business risks facing the entity increases the likelihood of identifying risks of material misstatement. This is because most business risks will eventually have financial consequences and, therefore, an effect on the financial statements. Not all business risks give rise to risks of material misstatement; thus, the auditor does not have a responsibility to identify or assess all business risks. (Whether a business risk may result in a risk of material misstatement is considered in light of the entity's circumstances.) Editor Note: Business risk is defined by US GAAS as the risk resulting from significant conditions, events, circumstances, actions, or inactions that could adversely affect an entity's ability to achieve its objectives and execute its strategies or from the setting of inappropriate objectives and strategies. (ID: 90291)

64. (c) Capital investment activities is an example of a matter the auditor may consider when obtaining an understanding about the nature of the entity; rather than a matter related to the entity's objectives and strategies and those related business risks that may result in risks of material misstatement. (ID: 90292)

65. (d) The risk appetite of mangers and stakeholders is an example of a matter the auditor may consider when obtaining an understanding about the entity's objectives and strategies and those related business risks that may result in risks of material misstatement; rather than a matter related to the measurement and review of the entity's financial performance. An understanding of the entity's performance measures assists the auditor in considering whether pressures to achieve performance targets may result in management actions that increase the risks of material misstatement, including those due to fraud. (ID: 90293)

66. (a) Amortization allocates the cost of the intangible to the periods in which the benefit is received and yields an appropriate valuation of the intangible in those periods. (ID: 5659)

67. (d) Classification concerns whether financial information is appropriately presented in the proper accounts within the financial statements. Valuation and allocation deals with whether assets, liabilities, and equity interests are valued properly and any resulting valuation or allocation adjustments are appropriately recorded. When accounting for investments, the classification has an impact on the appropriate method of valuation in the financial statements. Rights and obligations concern whether, at a given date, recorded assets indeed represent rights of the entity and liabilities represent obligations. Reviewing investment records regarding transfers between categories (internal documents) provides little evidence that ownership rights in the investments still exists at the balance sheet date, that the investment is not pledged as loan collateral, that the investments exist at the balance sheet date, or that an external transaction involving the investment occurred during the period. (ID: 7824)

68. (a) Tracing the auditor's inventory observations test counts to the client's inventory listings is testing to see if all assets that should have been recorded have been recorded, i.e., completeness. Rights and obligations would be concerned with, for example, whether the inventory was pledged as collateral or under contract to be sold for other than market value. Valuation or allocation would be concerned with, for example, the value assigned to the inventory and whether its historical cost is under market value as of the balance sheet date. Classification and understandability would be concerned with, for example, whether the inventory was appropriately in short-term assets. (ID: 8396)

69. (c) If credit is granted in accordance with policies, there is a greater chance that accounts receivable are correctly valued as allowance account amounts are based on the assumption that those policies are followed. Confirming that credit is granted in accordance with policies provides little evidence as to the rights and obligations connected with those sales. (ID: 8403)

70. (c) To provide a basis for designing and performing further audit procedures, the auditor should identify and assess the risks of material misstatement at both the financial statement level and the relevant assertion level for classes of transactions, account balances, and disclosures. Risks at the financial statement level require an overall response by the auditor. (ID: 90295)

71. (a) The nature of risks at the financial statement level requires an overall response by the auditor. All of the other answer alternatives are true, but they are not responsive to the question. (ID: 90296)

72. (c) Risks of material misstatement at the financial statement level refers to risks that relate pervasively to the financial statements as a whole and potentially affect many assertions. Risks of this nature are not necessarily risks identifiable with (linked to) specific assertions at the class of transactions, account balance, or disclosure level. Rather, they represent circumstances that may increase the risks of material misstatement at the assertion level (for example, through management override of internal control). Financial statement level risks may be especially (not rarely) relevant to the auditor's consideration of the risks of material misstatement arising from fraud. The assessment of the risks of material misstatement at the financial statement level and, thereby, the auditor's overall responses are affected by (related to) the auditor's understanding of the control environment. An effective control environment may allow the auditor to have more confidence in internal control and the reliability of audit evidence generated internally within the entity and, thus, for example, allow the auditor to conduct some audit procedures at an interim date rather than at the period-end. Deficiencies in the control environment, however, have the opposite effect. Risks at the financial statement level may derive, in particular, from a deficient control environment (although these risks also may relate to factors such as declining economic conditions). For example, deficiencies such as management's lack of competence may have a more pervasive effect on the financial statements and may require an overall response by the auditor. (ID: 90297)

73. (b) A significant risk is an identified and assessed risk of material misstatement that, in the auditor's professional judgment, requires special audit consideration. The auditor is required to communicate with those charged with governance an overview of the planned scope and timing of the audit and this may include how the auditor proposes to address the significant risks, but it is not required. In exercising judgment as to whether a risk is significant, the auditor should exclude the effects of identified controls related to the risk. One of the factors the auditor considers in identifying significant risks is whether the risk is a risk of fraud, but not all significant risks are fraud risks. (ID: 90298)

74. (a) A relevant assertion has a reasonable possibility of containing a misstatement that would cause the financial statements to be materially misstated, i.e., it has a meaningful bearing on whether the subject of the assertion, for example, an account, is fairly stated. (ID: 90299)

75. (c) Identifying relevant assertions includes determining the source of likely potential misstatements in each significant class of transactions, account balance, and disclosure. Attributes indicating the potential relevance of an assertion include the nature of the assertion; volume of transactions or data related to the assertion; and the nature and complexity of the systems, including the use of information technology (IT), by which the entity processes and controls information supporting the assertion. (ID: 90300)

76. (d) US GAAS regarding service organizations do *not* apply to services that are limited to processing an entity's transactions that are specifically authorized by the entity, such as the processing of checking account transactions by a bank or the processing of securities transactions by a broker. Nor do they apply to the audit of transactions arising from an entity that holds a proprietary financial interest in another entity, such as a partnership, corporation, or joint venture, when the partnership, corporation, or joint venture performs no processing on behalf of the entity. In addition to the other answer alternatives, a service organization's services are part of a user entity's information system, including related business processes, relevant to financial reporting if these services affect any of the following: (1) the related accounting records, supporting information, and specific accounts in the user entity's financial statements that are used to initiate, authorize, record, process, and report the user entity's transactions; this includes the correction of incorrect information and how information is transferred to the general ledger; the records may be in either manual or electronic form; (2) How the user entity's information system captures events and conditions, other than transactions, that are significant to the financial statements; and (3) controls surrounding journal entries, including nonstandard journal entries used to record nonrecurring, unusual transactions, or adjustments. (ID: 9293)

77. (b) Services provided by a service organization are relevant to the audit of a user entity's financial statements when those services and the controls over them affect the user entity's information system, including related business processes, relevant to financial reporting and thus to the audit. Although it is likely that services and the controls over them affect the user entity's information system when the service organization's information systems are integrated with those of the user entity, this is not the best answer. A written agreement does not mean that the services provided are relevant to the audit. Even when services provided are integral to an entity's business operations, they may not be relevant to the audit. (ID: 90301)

78. (c) Only the type 2 report includes an assertion by management of the service organization related to the operating effectiveness of the service organization's controls. A type 1 report includes written assertions by management of the service organization as of a specified date while those in the type 2 report cover a specified period; not vice versa. Both types of reports, not just the type 1 per answers b. and d., include a description of the service organization's system (which includes control objectives) and assertions related to the suitability of the design of the service organization's controls related to the control objectives. Editor Note: All of the assertions in a type 1 report are as of a specified date. All assertions in a type 2 report are as of a specified period. The assertions by management of the service organization in both reports are prefaced by a statement that indicates they are true in all material respects and are based on suitable criteria. The reports include, per management of the service organization: (1) both include a description of the service organization's system; (2) both include an assertion that the description of the system provided fairly presents that the service organization's system was designed and implemented as of a specified date (type 1) or throughout a specified period (type 2); (3) both include an assertion that the controls related to the control objectives included in the system description were suitably designed and implemented as of a specified date (type 1) or throughout a specified period (type 2); and (4) the type 2 report also includes an assertion that the controls related to the control objectives included in the system description operated effectively throughout the specified period to achieve those control objectives. The reports include, per the service auditor: (1) both include an opinion on the assertions included in the respective reports and (2) the type 2 report also includes a description of the service auditor's tests of controls and the results. (ID: 90302)

79. (b) If the user auditor plans to use a type 1 or a type 2 report that excludes the services provided by a subservice organization, i.e., was prepared using the carve-out method instead of the inclusive method, and those services are relevant to the audit of the user entity's financial statements, the same US GAAS requirements imposed on the user auditor that are applicable to the service organization are applicable to the subservice organization. None of the other answers describe situations that require this response by the user auditor. Regarding incorrect answer a., the absence of complementary controls does not; as such controls may not be applicable. Regarding incorrect answer c., the user auditor may use a service auditor's report to support the user auditor's understanding of the service organization or, in the case of a type 2 report, as audit evidence that controls at the service organization are operating effectively. When a type 1 or 2 report is used to support the user auditor's understanding and the description of the service organization's system is as of a date or for a period that precedes the beginning of the period under audit, the user auditor may perform procedures to update the information in a type 1 or type 2 report to remedy this matter. Regarding incorrect answer d., a service auditor should be independent of the service organization, but the service auditor need not be independent of the user entity. (ID: 90047)

80. (a) The user auditor does **not** make reference to the service auditor's report as a basis, in part, for the user auditor's opinion on the user entity's financial statements. The fact that a user entity uses a service organization does not alter the user auditor's responsibility to obtain sufficient appropriate audit evidence to afford a reasonable basis to support the user auditor's opinion. However, when the user auditor expresses a modified opinion because of a modified opinion in a service auditor's report, the user auditor is not precluded from referring to the service auditor's report if such reference assists in explaining the reason for the user auditor's modified opinion. The user auditor's report should indicate that such reference to the service auditor does not diminish the user auditor's responsibility for that opinion. In such circumstances, the user auditor need not identify the service auditor by name and may need the consent of the service auditor before making such a reference. Regarding incorrect answer b., the service auditor does not sign the user's auditor's report under any circumstances. Regarding incorrect answer c., the user auditor should not refer to the work of a service auditor if the user auditor's report contains an *un*modified opinion. The only reason a reference should be made to the work of a service auditor is explained above in the explanation for the correct answer a.—a reason that does not

apply if the user audit report contains an unmodified opinion. Regarding incorrect answer d., the user auditor's report should not indicate shared responsibility with the service auditor under any circumstances. (ID: 90303)

81. (d) An auditor conducting an audit in accordance with US GAAS has a responsibility to plan and perform the audit to obtain reasonable assurance that the financial statements as a whole are free of material misstatement, whether caused by fraud or error. (ID: 5633)

82. (b) The distinguishing factor between fraud and error is whether the underlying action that results in the misstatement of the financial statements is intentional (fraud) or unintentional (error). Editor Note: However, intent is sometimes difficult to determine; moreover, an audit is not designed to do so—the auditor's objective (primary responsibility) is to obtain reasonable assurance about whether the financial statements as a whole are free from material misstatement, whether due to fraud or error. (ID: 90304)

83. (d) The auditor is primarily concerned with fraud that causes a material misstatement in the financial statements. Two types of intentional (fraudulent) misstatements are relevant to the auditor—misstatements resulting from fraudulent financial reporting and misstatements resulting from misappropriation of assets. Obviously, the auditor is concerned with both answers a. and b., but neither, by itself, is the best answer to the question. Although the auditor may suspect or, in rare cases, identify the occurrence of fraud, the auditor does not make legal determinations of whether fraud has actually occurred. (ID: 90305)

84. (b) The primary responsibility for the prevention and detection of fraud rests with both those charged with governance and management. It is important that management places a strong emphasis on fraud prevention, which may reduce opportunities for fraud to take place, and fraud deterrence, which could persuade individuals not to commit fraud because of the likelihood of detection and punishment. This involves a commitment to creating a culture of honesty and ethical behavior, which can be reinforced by active oversight by those charged with governance. (ID: 90306)

85. (b) Due to the inherent limitations of an audit, an unavoidable risk exists that some material misstatements of the financial statements may not be detected, even though the audit is properly planned and performed in accordance with US GAAS. The potential effects of such inherent limitations are particularly significant in the case of misstatements resulting from fraud. The other answers may be true, but answer b. is the best description of why, even when an audit is properly planned and performed in accordance with US GAAS, some material misstatements of the financial statements may not be detected. (ID: 90307)

86. (c) The risk of not detecting a material misstatement resulting from fraud is higher than the risk of not detecting one resulting from error. This is because fraud may involve sophisticated and carefully organized schemes designed to conceal it, such as forgery, deliberate failure to record transactions, or intentional misrepresentations being made to the auditor. Regarding incorrect answer a., the risk of the auditor not detecting a material misstatement resulting from management fraud is greater than for employee fraud (even when employees collude) because management is frequently in a position to directly or indirectly manipulate accounting records, present fraudulent financial information, or override control procedures designed to prevent similar frauds by other employees. Regarding incorrect answer b., it is nonsensical. Misappropriation (theft) of assets is a type of fraud. Regarding incorrect answer d., the risk of not detecting a material misstatement resulting from fraud is higher than the risk of not detecting one resulting from error whether or not the error involves an omission. (ID: 90308)

87. (b) If conditions identified during the audit cause the auditor to believe that a document may not be authentic or that terms in a document have been modified but not disclosed to the auditor, the auditor should investigate further. (Unless the auditor has reason to believe the contrary, the auditor may accept records and documents as genuine.) Regarding incorrect answer a., management is often in the best position to perpetrate fraud. Accordingly, when evaluating management's responses to inquiries with professional skepticism, the auditor *may* judge it necessary to corroborate responses to inquiries with other information, but it is not required. However, when responses to inquiries of management, those charged with governance, or others are inconsistent or otherwise unsatisfactory (for example, vague or implausible), the auditor is, of course, required to further investigate the inconsistencies or unsatisfactory responses. Regarding incorrect answer c., the auditor neither assumes that management is dishonest nor assumes unquestioned honesty. The auditor should maintain

professional skepticism throughout the audit, recognizing the possibility that a material misstatement due to fraud could exist, notwithstanding the auditor's past experience of the honesty and integrity of the entity's management and those charged with governance. The auditor cannot be expected to disregard positive past experience; nevertheless, such a belief does not relieve the auditor of the need to maintain professional skepticism or allow the auditor to be satisfied with less than persuasive audit evidence when obtaining reasonable assurance. Regarding incorrect answer d., the exercise of professional skepticism is more directly related to determining overall responses to address the assessed risks of material misstatement due to fraud required at the financial statement level than to responses at the assertion level. The responses at the financial statement level generally include the consideration of how the overall conduct of the audit can reflect increased professional skepticism through, for example, increased sensitivity in the selection of the nature and extent of documentation to be examined in support of material transactions; or recognition of the need to corroborate management explanations or representations concerning material matters. (ID: 90309)

88. (b) The brainstorming session among key engagement team members about how and where the entity's financial statements might be susceptible to material misstatement due to fraud should address consideration of circumstances that might be indicative of earnings management or manipulation of other financial measures and the practices that might be followed by management to manage earnings or other financial measures that could lead to fraudulent financial reporting. Regarding incorrect answer a., the auditor is not required to conduct a training session for audit committee members. Regarding incorrect answer c., although this discussion may be limited to key members of the audit team, this is done for practical reasons, not due to concern about a lack of discretion on the part of auditors. Regarding incorrect answer d., this discussion occurs during the early part of the audit and should continue throughout the audit. (ID: 90039)

89. (a) Regarding fraud, the discussion should include an exchange of ideas or brainstorming among the engagement team members about how and where the entity's financial statements might be susceptible to material misstatement due to fraud; how management could perpetrate and conceal fraudulent financial reporting; and how assets of the entity could be misappropriated. The discussion should occur setting aside beliefs that the engagement team members may have that management and those charged with governance are honest and have integrity. Regarding incorrect answer b, the discussion should include how management (not employees) could perpetrate and conceal fraudulent financial reporting. Regarding correct answer c., the discussion should not be limited to how management could misappropriate assets; but rather how the assets could be stolen by anyone. Regarding incorrect answer d., the discussion should include the importance of maintaining professional skepticism throughout the audit regarding the potential for material misstatement due to fraud. Although exercising professional judgment throughout the planning and performance of the audit is also required, it is not a required topic for the discussion. Editor Note: US GAAS requires the engagement partner and other key engagement team members to engage in discussions for two different purposes. The purpose of one is to discuss the susceptibility of the entity's financial statements to material misstatement and the application of the applicable financial reporting framework to the entity's facts and circumstances. This requirement is included in the guidance on obtaining an understanding of the entity and its environment and assessing the risks of material misstatement. The other discussion, which may be held concurrently with this discussion, is to discuss the susceptibility of the entity's financial statements to fraud. ID: 90310)

90. (d) Answer d., an example of a risk factor related to misstatements arising from fraudulent financial reporting is an organizational structure that is complex or unstable, as evidenced by: (1) difficulty in determining the organization or individuals that have controlling interest in the entity; (2) overly complex organizational structure involving unusual legal entities or managerial lines of authority; and/or (3) high turnover of senior management, legal counsel, or those charged with governance. Regarding incorrect answer a., large amounts of liquid assets is an example of a risk factor related to misstatements arising from misappropriation of assets (not fraudulent financial reporting). Editor Note: There are two types of fraud relevant to the auditor's consideration—fraudulent financial reporting and misappropriation of assets. Regarding incorrect answer b., it is more likely that rapid growth or unusual profitability (rather than low growth and profitability) especially compared to that of other companies in the same industry, would heighten an auditor's concern. Regarding incorrect answer c., financial management should participate in the initial selection of accounting principles. The recognized risk factor is when nonfinancial management excessively participates in or is preoccupied with the selection of accounting policies or the determination of significant estimates. (ID: 7018)

91. (d) The fact that management is interested in maintaining the entity's earnings trend by using aggressive accounting practices indicates that management may have an incentive to engage in fraudulent financial reporting also. Stock transactions of management or the board of directors are not ordinarily considered fraud risk factors. Aggressive financial forecasts as opposed to conservative financial forecasts would be considered a fraud risk factor. (ID: 8155)

92. (c) A strained relationship between management and the current or predecessor auditor is one of the risk factors related to fraudulent financial reporting, categorized as an attitude or rationalization. Regarding incorrect answer a., a lack of interest in maintaining an earnings trend tends to reduce the risk of fraud related to fraudulent financial reporting. Regarding incorrect answer b., it may be in an entity's best interest to sell computer hardware before it is fully depreciated. Regarding incorrect answer d., the existence of outstanding checks in any amount in a monthly bank reconciliation is a normal occurrence. (ID: 8420)

93. (b) Answer b., a lack of independent checks (or inadequate segregation of duties) is one of the risk factors related to misstatements arising from the misappropriation of assets. The other answer alternatives are risk factors related to misstatements arising from fraudulent financial reporting rather than the misappropriation of assets. Editor Note: There are two types of fraud relevant to the auditor's consideration—fraudulent financial reporting and misappropriation of assets. (ID: 8646)

94. (a) Answer a., comparing current year to prior year sales volumes, is the analytical procedure most likely to be used during the planning stage of the audit. Incorrect answer c., comparing the current year ratio of aggregate salaries paid to the number of employees to the prior year's ratio is the next best answer. Analytical procedures used in planning (risk assessment procedures) often use data aggregated at a high level which is true of both of these answers. However, in planning the audit, the auditor should perform analytical procedures relating to revenue with the objective of identifying unusual or unexpected relationships that may indicate a material misstatement due to fraudulent financial reporting. Thus, answer a. (comparing sales volumes) is the more likely of the two procedures. The other two answer alternatives (reading the financial statements and notes and considering the adequacy of evidence; and consideration of the letter of inquiry to the entity's external legal counsel) do not describe analytical procedures; further, they are usually performed near the end of the audit rather than during the planning stage. (ID: 9942)

95. (a) A large number of bearer bonds on hand most likely represents the highest risk of a misstatement arising from the misappropriation of assets. This is a risk factor categorized as an opportunity. Certain characteristics or circumstances may increase the susceptibility of assets to misappropriation, for example, large amounts of cash on hand or processed; inventory items that are small in size, of high value, or in high demand; easily convertible assets, such as bearer bonds, diamonds, or computer chips; or fixed assets that are small in size, marketable, or lacking observable identification of ownership. Answer b., a large number of inventory items with low sales prices or answer d., a large number of fixed assets with easily identifiable serial numbers (as just explained in the explanation for the correct answer) would not be as attractive to a thief as bearer bonds. Answer c., a large number of transactions processed in a short period of time is not a fraud risk factor.

96. (b) Analytical procedures related to revenue accounts are required to be performed with the objective of identifying unusual or unexpected relationships that may indicate a material misstatement due to fraudulent financial reporting. (Editor Note: These procedures should be also performed through the end of the reporting period when forming an overall audit conclusion and to evaluate whether the accumulated results of all auditing procedures affect the assessment of the risks of material misstatement (RMM) due to fraud made earlier in the audit or indicate a previously unrecognized RMM due to fraud.) Regarding incorrect answer a., inquiries should be made of both management and those charged with governance. The only circumstance allowed by US GAAS that does not require specific inquires (regarding oversight of management's processes for identifying and responding to the risks of fraud and the related controls) to be made of those charged with governance is when they are all involved in managing the entity and thus no oversight exists separate from management. Regarding incorrect answer c., fraud risk factors cannot easily be ranked in order of importance and may not necessarily indicate the existence of fraud; however, they have often been present in circumstances in which fraud has occurred and, therefore, may indicate risks of material misstatement (RMM) due to fraud. Their significance varies widely. Accordingly, the determination of whether a fraud risk factor is present and whether it is to be considered in assessing the RMM due to fraud requires the exercise of professional judgment. That

said, the auditor is required to evaluate whether the information obtained from the risk assessment procedures and related activities performed indicates that one or more fraud risk factors are present. Regarding incorrect answer d., both management and those charged with governance; and others within the entity as appropriate should be asked whether they have knowledge of any actual, suspected, or alleged fraud. (ID: 90311)

97. (d) There is no need for the auditor to evaluate whether each assessed risk due to fraud is a significant risk; thus, answer d. is the correct answer, i.e., the only statement that is *not* true. The auditor should treat all of them as significant risks (answer c.) and, accordingly, obtain an understanding of the entity's related controls, including the evaluation of whether such controls have been suitably designed and implemented to mitigate such fraud risks. Answers a., and b. are also true statements. Regarding answer a., the auditor's risk assessment of material misstatement due to fraud should be ongoing throughout the audit, following the initial assessment. Regarding answer b., when identifying and assessing the risks of material misstatement (RMM) due to fraud, the auditor should, based on a presumption that risks of fraud exist in revenue recognition, evaluate which types of revenue, revenue transactions, or assertions give rise to such risks. (If the auditor has concluded that this presumption is overcome in the circumstances of the engagement, the auditor should include in the audit documentation the reasons for that conclusion.) (ID: 90312)

98. (d) The physical observation and/or inspection of assets are examples of procedures performed in response to the assessed risk of material misstatement at the assertion level, i.e., the assertion of existence. The other answer alternatives are overall responses to address the assessed risks of material misstatement due to fraud at the financial statement level rather than the assertion level. (ID: 90313)

99. (a) Although the level of risk of management override of controls (override risk) will vary from entity to entity, the risk is, nevertheless, present in all entities. (Thus, answer a. is correct and answer b. is not.) Even if specific risks of material misstatement (RMM) due to fraud are not identified by the auditor, a possibility exists that management override could occur. Accordingly, the auditor should address this risk apart from any conclusions regarding the existence of more specifically identifiable risks by designing and performing audit procedures as discussed in the editor note below. Regarding incorrect answer c., due to the *un*predictable way in which override could occur, it is a RMM due to fraud and thus a significant risk. Regarding incorrect answer d., one of the procedures required by US GAAS as a response to override risk is to select journal entries (and other adjustments) made at the end of a reporting period *and* to (not as opposed to) consider the need to test both throughout the period. (ID: 90314)

100. (d) Considering whether audit results affect the assessment of fraud risk is an overall review stage procedure. Auditors obtain assurance from the entity's attorney, verify clerical accuracy, and test the operating effectiveness of controls during the evidence gathering stage of the audit. (ID: 7027)

101. (b) If the auditor identifies a misstatement, whether material or not, that is, or may be, the result of fraud that involves management (in particular, senior management), the auditor should re-evaluate the assessment of the risks of material misstatement due to fraud and its resulting effect on the nature, timing, and extent of audit procedures to respond to the assessed risks. The auditor should also consider whether circumstances indicate possible collusion involving employees, management, or third parties when reconsidering the reliability of evidence previously obtained. Regarding incorrect answer a., if a misstatement is indicative of fraud and there is no indication that management is involved, the auditor is required to evaluate the implications of the misstatement with regard to other aspects of the audit, particularly the auditor's evaluation of materiality, management and employee integrity, and the reliability of management representations—recognizing that an instance of fraud is unlikely to be an isolated occurrence. Regarding incorrect answer c., if the auditor concludes that, or is unable to conclude whether, the financial statements are materially misstated as a result of fraud, the auditor should evaluate the implications for the audit. Regarding incorrect answer d., if the auditor discovers a specific instance of management override of controls, the auditor should investigate it; however, as an audit according to US GAAS presumes that the risk of management override of controls exists in all entities; the audit should already include responses to it. (ID: 90315)

102. (a) When the entity does not take the appropriate action regarding fraud, the identified or suspected fraud does **not** need to be material to the financial statements for the auditor's ability to continue performing the

audit to be brought into question; thus, answer a. is the only statement that is *not* an example of the question's circumstances. (ID: 90316)

103. (c) If the auditor withdraws, the auditor should determine whether a professional or legal requirement exists to report to the person or persons who engaged the auditor or, in some cases, to regulatory authorities, the auditor's withdrawal from the engagement and the reasons for the withdrawal. Regarding incorrect answers a. and b., if the auditor withdraws from the engagement, the auditor would not issue an audit report. Regarding incorrect answer d., if the auditor withdraws, the auditor should discuss with the appropriate level of management and those charged with governance (not just those charged with governance) the auditor's withdrawal from the engagement and the reasons for the withdrawal. (This corrected version of answer d. and the correct answer c. explanation are the only required actions when the auditor withdraws under the question's circumstances.) (ID: 90317)

104. (c) If the auditor identifies or suspects fraud involving management, the auditor should communicate these matters to those charged with governance and discuss with them the nature, timing, and extent of audit procedures necessary to complete the audit. The auditor should also communicate with those charged with governance any other matters related to fraud that are, in the auditor's professional judgment, relevant to their responsibilities. Regarding incorrect answer a., when the auditor has obtained evidence that fraud exists or may exist, it is important that the matter be brought to the attention of the appropriate level of management as soon as practicable. This is true even if the matter might be considered inconsequential. The determination of which level of management is the appropriate one is a matter of professional judgment and is affected by such factors as the likelihood of collusion and the nature and magnitude of the suspected fraud. Ordinarily, the appropriate level of management is at least one level above the persons who appear to be involved with the suspected fraud. Regarding incorrect answer b., unless all of those charged with governance are involved in managing the entity, if the auditor has identified or suspects fraud involving, (1) management (not just senior management); (2) employees who have significant roles internal control; or (3) others, when the fraud results in a material misstatement in the financial statements, the auditor should communicate these matters to those charged with governance on a timely basis. Regarding incorrect answer d., reporting fraud to parties outside the entity is not automatic. If the auditor has identified or suspects a fraud, the auditor should determine whether the auditor has a responsibility to report the occurrence or suspicion to a party outside the entity. Although the auditor's professional duty to maintain the confidentiality of client information may preclude such reporting, the auditor's legal responsibilities may override the duty of confidentiality in some circumstances, i.e., via statute; regulation; courts of law; specific requirements of audits of entities that receive government financial assistance; or it may be waived by agreement. Such requirements to report to others may come into play when fraud occurs or is suspected and/or if the entity fails to take appropriate corrective action. Editor Note: The auditor's communication with those charged with governance may be made orally or in writing; however, due to the nature and sensitivity of fraud involving senior management or fraud that results in a material misstatement in the financial statements, the auditor may consider it necessary to do both—orally in order to make it as timely as practicable, followed up with a written statement. (ID: 90318)

105. (a) The auditor should include in the audit documentation communications about fraud made to management, those charged with governance, regulators, and others. Regarding incorrect answer b., if the auditor has concluded that the presumption that there is a risk of material misstatement due to fraud related to revenue recognition is overcome in the circumstances of the engagement, the auditor should include in the audit documentation the reasons for that conclusion regardless of whether the audit report includes an emphasis-of-matter paragraph expressing doubt about the entity's ability to continue as a going concern (even if the paragraph references revenue). Incorrect answer c. is nonsensical—the related audit procedures are the auditor's response to the assessed risk of material misstatement due to fraud. Regarding incorrect answer d., the information that was communicated by the engagement partner to those engagement team members not involved in the discussion about fraud is not required to be included in the audit documentation. The audit documentation should include the significant decisions reached during the discussion regarding the susceptibility of the entity's financial statements to material misstatement due to fraud; how and when the discussion occurred; and the audit team members who participated. (Editor Note: US GAAS requires that the discussion include the engagement partner and only the key team members; the engagement partner determines the matters to be communicated to those not in attendance.) See the text for other audit documentation requirements related to fraud. (ID: 90319)

106. (b) US GAAS distinguishes the auditor's responsibilities regarding compliance with the following two categories of laws and regulations: (1) the provisions of those laws and regulations generally recognized to have a direct effect on the determination of material amounts and disclosures in the financial statements, such as tax and pension laws and regulations; and (2) the provisions of other laws and regulations that do not have a direct effect on the determination of the amounts and disclosures in the financial statements, for example, environmental regulations, but compliance with which may be fundamental to the operating aspects of the business; fundamental to an entity's ability to continue its business; or necessary for the entity to avoid material penalties. Thus, noncompliance with this 2nd category of laws and regulations may have a material effect on the financial statements. In other words, the 2nd category of laws and regulations may result in fines, litigation, or other consequences for the entity, the costs of which may need to be provided for or disclosed in the financial statements but are not considered to have a direct effect on the financial statements as described for the 1st category. (ID: 90320)

107. (a) US GAAS defines noncompliance as acts of omission or commission by the entity, either intentional or unintentional, which are contrary to the prevailing laws or regulations. Regarding incorrect answer b., unintentional acts are also included. Regarding incorrect answer c., such acts include transactions entered into by, or in the name of, the entity or on its behalf by those charged with governance, management, or employees. Regarding incorrect answer d., noncompliance does not include personal misconduct (unrelated to the business activities of the entity) by those charged with governance, management, or employees of the entity. (If the personal misconduct is unrelated to the business activities of the entity it is not considered noncompliance even if the misconduct occurred when the individual was engaged in a business activity of the entity.) (ID: 90321)

108. (b) Due to the inherent limitations of an audit, an audit performed in accordance with US GAAS provides no assurance that all noncompliance with laws and regulations will be detected or that any contingent liabilities that result will be disclosed. Ordinarily, the further removed noncompliance is from the events and transactions reflected in the financial statements, the less (not more) likely the auditor is to become aware of, or recognize, the noncompliance. (ID: 90322)

109. (a) US GAAS requires a different auditing approach for each category because the auditor has different responsibilities for each, as follows. (1) For the provisions of those laws and regulations generally recognized to have a direct effect on the determination of material amounts and disclosures in the financial statements, the auditor's responsibility is the same as that for misstatements caused by fraud or error—to obtain sufficient appropriate audit evidence regarding material amounts and disclosures in the financial statements that are determined by the provisions of those laws and regulations. (2) For the other category, that does not have such a direct effect; the auditor's responsibility is limited to performing specified audit procedures that may identify noncompliance with those laws and regulations that may have a material effect on the financial statements. The other answer alternatives are false statements. In regard to answer c., whether an act assignable to either US GAAS category constitutes noncompliance with laws and regulations is a matter for legal determination, which ordinarily is beyond the auditor's professional competence to determine. Nevertheless, the auditor's training, experience, and understanding of the entity and its industry or sector may provide a basis to recognize that some acts coming to the auditor's attention may constitute noncompliance with laws and regulations. (ID: 90323)

110. (a) As part of obtaining an understanding of the entity and its environment, the auditor should obtain a general understanding of the legal and regulatory framework applicable to the entity and the industry or sector in which the entity operates and how the entity is complying with that framework. Incorrect answer b. is not a requirement for "direct effect" (on the determination of financial statement amounts and disclosures) laws and regulations. The audit procedure to inspect correspondence, if any, with relevant licensing or regulatory authorities is required to help identify instances of noncompliance with other laws and regulations that may have a material effect on the financial statements. The auditor is also required to make inquiries of management and, when appropriate, those charged with governance about whether the entity is in compliance with such laws and regulations. Editor Note: Although neither of these specific procedures just described are required for "direct effect" laws and regulations, they *may* be performed—the auditor should obtain sufficient appropriate audit evidence regarding material amounts and disclosures in the financial statements that are determined by the provisions of those laws and regulations generally recognized to have a direct effect on their determination. Regarding incorrect answer c., when the auditor identifies or suspects noncompliance, the auditor may consider, but is not required, to consult with the entity's external legal counsel. Under these circumstances, the auditor

should discuss the matter with management and, when appropriate, those charged with governance. If they do not provide sufficient information to the auditor that the entity is in fact in compliance with laws and regulations, the auditor may consider it appropriate to consult with the entity's in-house legal counsel or external legal counsel about the application of the laws and regulations to the circumstances, including the possibility of fraud, and the possible effects on the financial statements. The auditor may request management to arrange for such consultation with the entity's legal counsel. If it is not considered appropriate to consult with the entity's legal counsel or if the auditor is not satisfied with the legal counsel's opinion, the auditor may consider it appropriate to consult the auditor's own legal counsel. Regarding incorrect answer d., the auditor is not required to presume a level of risk associated with noncompliance. In the absence of identified or suspected noncompliance, the auditor is not required to perform audit procedures regarding the entity's compliance with laws and regulations, except for those covered in this answer explanation and requesting written representations from management regarding the entity's compliance with laws and regulations. And, of course, during the audit, the auditor should remain alert to the possibility that other audit procedures applied may bring instances of noncompliance or suspected noncompliance to the auditor's attention. (ID: 90324)

111. (d) When the auditor identifies or suspects noncompliance with laws and regulations, the auditor should obtain an understanding of the nature of the act; the circumstances in which it has occurred; and obtain further information to evaluate the possible effect on the financial statements. Regarding incorrect answer a., at this stage, the consideration of withdrawal would be premature. The auditor may consider whether withdrawal from the engagement is necessary when management or those charged with governance (1) do not take the remedial action that the auditor considers appropriate, even when the noncompliance is not material to the financial statements; or (2) refuse to accept a modified opinion on the financial statements; either when the noncompliance has a material effect on the financial statements and it has not been adequately reflected in the financial statements; or management or those charged with governance have limited the scope of the audit such that the auditor cannot make a determination about noncompliance. Under these circumstances, the auditor may withdraw from the engagement and indicate the reasons in writing to those charged with governance. Incorrect answers b. and c. are false statements. If the auditor suspects noncompliance may exist, the auditor should discuss the matter with management (at a level above those involved with the suspected noncompliance, if possible) and, when appropriate, those charged with governance. If management or, as appropriate, those charged with governance do not provide sufficient information that supports that the entity is in compliance with laws and regulations and the effect of the suspected noncompliance may be material to the financial statements, the auditor should consider the need to obtain legal advice. (ID: 90325)

112. (c) The auditor should express a qualified opinion *or* disclaim an opinion on the financial statements on the basis of a limitation on the scope of the audit if the auditor is precluded by management or those charged with governance from obtaining sufficient appropriate audit evidence to evaluate whether noncompliance that may be material to the financial statements has, or is likely to have, occurred. Regarding incorrect answer a., the auditor is not required to disclaim an opinion. Regarding incorrect answer b., if management or those charged with governance refuse to accept a modified opinion on the financial statements under these circumstances, the auditor *may* withdraw from the engagement, when withdrawal is possible under applicable law or regulation, and indicate the reasons for withdrawal in writing to those charged with governance. Regarding incorrect answer d., a qualified or adverse opinion should be expressed when the auditor concludes that the noncompliance has a material effect on the financial statements, and it has not been adequately reflected in the financial statements. (ID: 89499)

113. (a) The auditor should, of course, communicate with those charged with governance matters involving noncompliance with laws and regulations that come to the auditor's attention during the course of the audit, other than when the matters are clearly inconsequential; however, US GAAS only requires that the communication take place as soon as practicable when the noncompliance is believed to be intentional and material. None of the other answer alternatives reflect the US GAAS requirement regarding timely communication with those charged with governance. Although the circumstance in incorrect answer d. is not a factor in determining if the communication to those charged with governance is required to be timely, if the auditor has identified or suspects noncompliance with laws and regulations, the auditor is required to determine whether the auditor has a responsibility to report the identified or suspected noncompliance to parties outside the entity. (ID: 90326)

114. (b) US GAAS does not require the inclusion of a copy of the law or regulation related to the noncompliance. Examples of documentation of findings may include copies of records or documents and minutes of discussions held. (ID: 90327)

115. (a) In some cases, the auditor may determine that performing only substantive procedures is appropriate for specific relevant assertions and risks. In those circumstances, the auditor may exclude the effect of controls from the relevant risk assessment. This may be because the auditor's risk assessment procedures have not identified any effective controls relevant to the assertion or because testing the operating effectiveness of controls would be inefficient. (ID: 4258)

116. (c) Regardless of the assessed risk of material misstatement, the auditor should design and perform substantive procedures for all relevant assertions related to each material class of transactions, account balance, and disclosure. The auditor should perform tests of controls when the auditor's risk assessment includes an expectation of the operating effectiveness of controls or when it is not possible or practicable to reduce detection risk at the relevant assertion level to an acceptably low level with audit evidence obtained from substantive procedures alone. Analytical procedures are required to be used in the planning stage of the audit (and the final review stage); however, they would not be performed to verify the design of internal control procedures. A dual-purpose test is a procedure that is designed to test both the operating effectiveness of the controls and details of the same transaction; this is efficient, but not required. (ID: 4260)

117. (d) The auditor should design and perform further audit procedures whose nature, timing, and extent are responsive to the assessed risks of material misstatement at the relevant assertion level. Detection risk is a function of the effectiveness of an auditing procedure and its application by the auditor; therefore, the assessed risk of material misstatement will determine the acceptable level of detection risk and hence the appropriate audit procedures to be performed. The effectiveness of internal control, inherent risk, and materiality thresholds are all factors that help the auditor assess the risk of material misstatement. (ID: 4689)

118. (a) The auditor's assessment of the identified risks at the relevant assertion level provides a basis for considering the appropriate audit approach for designing and performing further audit procedures. In some cases, the auditor may determine that performing only substantive procedures is appropriate for specific relevant assertions and risks. In those circumstances, the auditor may exclude the effect of controls from the relevant risk assessment. This may be because the auditor's risk assessment procedures have not identified any effective controls relevant to the assertion or because testing the operating effectiveness of controls would be inefficient. Regarding incorrect answer b., if evidence is not available, tests of controls are not performed. Regarding incorrect answer c., as the assessed level of control risk increases, the auditor is less likely to test controls. Regarding incorrect answer d., if the auditor is aware of many internal control weaknesses, the assessed level of control risk will be high, and controls will not be tested. (ID: 5651)

119. (c) In some cases, the auditor may determine that performing only substantive procedures is appropriate to evaluate specific relevant assertions and risks. In those circumstances, the auditor may exclude the effect of controls from the relevant risk assessment. This may be because the auditor's risk assessment procedures have not identified any effective controls relevant to the assertion or because testing the operating effectiveness of controls would be not be efficient. However, the auditor needs to be satisfied that performing only substantive procedures for the relevant assertions would be effective in reducing detection risk to an acceptably low level. (A combined audit approach using both tests of the operating effectiveness of controls and substantive procedures is often most effective.) Regarding incorrect answer a., the quality of the documentation of the internal control components would not be a factor in the auditor's determination to use only substantive procedures. Regarding incorrect answer b., because the auditor has the ultimate responsibility to express an opinion on the financial statements, judgments about assessments of inherent and control risks, the materiality of misstatements, the sufficiency of tests performed, the evaluation of significant accounting estimates, and other matters affecting the auditor's report should always be those of the auditor. Regarding incorrect answer d., the auditor may consider cost/benefit in the determination of an appropriate audit procedure; however, in this case, there is no information about a benefit, the answer only states that the proposed action is more expensive. (ID: 89792)

120. (c) When an auditor concludes that there is a high risk of material misstatement (RMM) the most appropriate course of action is to select more effective substantive tests. The auditor's selection of audit procedures is based on the RMM. The higher the auditor's assessment of risk, the more reliable and relevant is the audit evidence sought by the auditor from substantive procedures. Regarding incorrect answer a., when there is a high RMM, the auditor is more likely to use larger, rather than smaller, sample sizes. Regarding incorrect answer b., the higher the RMM, the more likely it is that the auditor may decide it is more effective to perform substantive procedures nearer to, or at, the period end rather than at an earlier date, or to perform audit procedures unannounced or at unpredictable times. Regarding incorrect answer d., the auditor should increase the extent of tests of controls the more the auditor relies on the operating effectiveness of controls in the assessment of risk. This reliance on controls by the auditor is due to an expectation of a low, not high, RMM because the auditor believes the entity has effective controls. (ID: 89793)

121. (c) The auditor should document both I. and II. as follows, with more detail provided for I. than included in the question: (I.) Overall responses to address the assessed RMM at the financial statement level and the nature, extent, and timing of the further audit procedures performed and (II.) Linkage of those procedures with the assessed RMM at the relevant assertion level. The auditor should also include in the audit documentation: (1) results of the audit procedures, including the conclusions when such conclusions are not otherwise clear; (2) if the auditor plans to use audit evidence about the operating effectiveness of controls obtained in previous audits, the conclusions reached about relying on such controls that were tested in a previous audit; (3) the basis for any determination not to use external confirmation procedures for accounts receivable when the account balance is material; and (4) demonstration that the financial statements agree or reconcile with the underlying accounting records. (ID: 8265)

122. (d) The auditor evaluates the effect of identified misstatements *on the audit* because the auditor should determine whether the overall audit strategy and audit plan need to be revised if: (1) the nature of identified misstatements and the circumstances of their occurrence indicate that other misstatements may exist that, when aggregated with misstatements accumulated during the audit, could be material or (2) the aggregate of misstatements accumulated during the audit approaches materiality. Regarding incorrect answer a., misstatements that are corrected, of course, do not have an effect on the financial statements. Regarding incorrect answer b., the auditor is concerned with the effect of all identified misstatements on the *audit* per the explanation for the correct answer; not just uncorrected misstatements. Regarding incorrect answer c., only uncorrected misstatements, if any, affect the financial statements. (ID: 30330)

123. (b) The auditor's determination of materiality is often is based on estimates of the entity's financial results because the actual financial results may not yet be known. Therefore, prior to the auditor's evaluation of the effect of uncorrected misstatements, it may be necessary to revise materiality based on the actual financial results. That said, any significant revision is likely to have been made (based on information the auditor became aware of during the audit) before the auditor evaluates the effect of uncorrected misstatements. Regarding incorrect answers a. and c., the reassessment should be based on the actual, not the projected or interim, financial results. Regarding incorrect answer d., the auditor would not adjust the financial statements for the uncorrected misstatements. The auditor's objective is to reassess materiality based on the actual financial statements without the corrections. (ID: 90331)

124. (d) The size and nature of misstatements in relation to prior period uncorrected misstatements is **not** relevant. The size and nature of the misstatements are considered in relation to all of the other answer alternatives. Regarding answer a., each individual misstatement is considered to evaluate its effect on the relevant classes of transactions, account balances, or disclosures, including whether the particular materiality level for that particular class of transactions, account balance, or disclosure, if any, has been exceeded. Editor Note: When determining whether uncorrected misstatements are material, individually or in the aggregate, the auditor should also consider the effect of uncorrected misstatements related to prior periods on the relevant classes of transactions, account balances, or disclosures and the financial statements as a whole. The cumulative effect of immaterial uncorrected misstatements related to prior periods may have a material effect on the current period's financial statements. (ID: 90332)

125. (d) It may be appropriate to offset misstatements within the same account balance or class of transactions; however, the risk that further undetected misstatements may exist should be considered before

concluding that offsetting even immaterial misstatements is appropriate. (The auditor may need to reassess the risks of material misstatement for a specific account balance or class of transactions upon identification of a number of immaterial misstatements within that account balance or class of transactions.) Regarding incorrect answer b., if revenue has been materially overstated, the financial statements as a whole will be materially misstated, even if the effect of the misstatement on earnings is completely offset by an equivalent overstatement of expenses. (ID: 90333)

126. (a) The auditor should accumulate all (not just uncorrected, per incorrect answer b.) misstatements identified during the audit, other than those that are clearly trivial. Regarding incorrect answer c., the auditor should communicate on a timely basis with the appropriate level of management all (not just uncorrected) misstatements accumulated during the audit. The auditor should request management to correct those misstatements. Regarding incorrect answer d., the auditor should include in the audit documentation all (not just uncorrected) misstatements accumulated during the audit and whether they have been corrected. The auditor should also include in the audit documentation related to evaluation of misstatements identified: (1) the amount below which misstatements would be regarded as clearly trivial; and (2) the auditor's conclusion about whether uncorrected misstatements are material, individually or in the aggregate, and the basis for that conclusion. (ID: 90329)

127. (d) In some cases, all of those charged with governance are involved in managing the entity; for example, a small business in which a single owner manages the entity and no one else has a governance role. In these cases, if matters required by US GAAS are communicated with a person(s) with management responsibilities and that person(s) also has governance responsibilities, the matters need not be communicated again with the same person(s) in that person's governance role. Regarding incorrect answer a., the two groups are not mutually exclusive. For some entities, management includes some or all of those charged with governance; for example, executive members of a governance board or an owner-manager. And those charged with governance may include management personnel; for example, executive members of a governance board or an owner-manager. This can affect how the auditor communicates with a client. Regarding incorrect answer b., this may or may not be the case; if the auditor communicates with a subgroup of those charged with governance, such as the audit committee or an individual, the auditor should determine whether the auditor also needs to communicate with the governing body. Regarding incorrect answer c., the auditor should determine the appropriate person(s) within the entity's governance structure with whom to communicate. (ID: 90334)

128. (a) Answer a., both matters should be communicated. The auditor should communicate with those charged with governance significant findings or issues from the audit. These include (but, of course, are not limited to) significant difficulties, if any, encountered during the audit and disagreements with management, if any. (ID: 2768)

129. (c) The auditor should communicate with those charged with governance the auditor's responsibilities with regard to the financial statement audit which include both of these matters. (ID: 2994)

Solution 2-2 SIMULATION ANSWER: Risk of Material Misstatement

Based on the information in Scott, Inc.'s profile, determine whether each of the factors below would be likely to increase audit risk or have no impact on audit risk.

Factors	Impact on RMM	
	Increases	No Impact
1. The company has begun to focus on a strategic advertising plan so it may expand its market into other states.		✓
2. During year 2, management issued additional long-term debt with complex financial covenants.	✓	
3. Scott, Inc. is divided into two divisions, which serve the major markets of the company's products.		✓
4. The new CFO was an audit manager from the predecessor audit firm.	✓	

(ID: 9201)

Explanations

1. It is not likely that an advertising plan will increase the RMM.

2. The RMM is increased. The auditor will need to focus more attention on the complex financial covenants to determine whether there have been any violations and whether they need to be disclosed in the financial statements.

3. It is not likely that having two divisions that serve different markets will increase the RMM. This is an example of a customary business practice.

4. The RMM is increased. When a company hires its prior audit firm's audit manager as its CFO the current auditors must consider whether the audit manager exercised an appropriate level of skepticism during the audit process prior to leaving the audit firm.

Solution 2-3 SIMULATION ANSWER: Risk of Material Misstatement

Based only on the information given, determine whether each of the factors below *increases* or *decreases* the risk of material misstatement.

Factors	Effect on Risk of Material Misstatement
1. Governmental regulation over the banking industry is extensive.	Decreases
2. NFB operates profitably in growing prosperous area.	Decreases
3. Overall demand for the industry's product is high.	Decreases
4. Interest rates have been volatile recently.	Increases
5. The availability of funds for additional mortgages is promising.	Decreases

(ID: 9202)

Explanations

Decreases

1. Regulation over the industry creates more accountability, thus risk is decreased.

Decreases

2. Profitability reduces the pressures that can increase risks, for example, the risk of fraudulent financial reporting by management tasked with achieving profitable results, so risk is decreased.

Decreases

3. High demand for the industry's product, like profitability, reduces the pressures that can increase risks, so risk is decreased.

Increases

4. Having to constantly react to volatile interest rates increases risk because more judgment is needed and error rates usually increase under these conditions.

Decreases

5. The availability of funds allows the industry to meet the high demand for its products, thereby increasing stability, so risk is decreased.

Solution 2-4 SIMULATION ANSWER: Risk of Material Misstatement

Based only on the information given, determine whether each of the factors below *increases* or *decreases* the risk of material misstatement.

Factors	Effect on Risk of Material Misstatement
1. The principal shareholder is also the chief executive officer and controls the board of directors.	Increases
2. Branch management is compensated based on branch profitability.	Increases
3. The internal auditor reports directly to the chairman of the board's audit committee.	Decreases
4. The Accounting Department has experienced little turnover in personnel recently.	Decreases

(ID: 9203)

Explanations

Increases

1. Risk is increased if management's or those charged with governance's personal financial situation is tied to that of the entity. Risk is also increased when too much control rests with one individual.

Increases

2. Risk is increased when management's compensation is based on profitability goals due to increased pressure to falsify results.

Decreases

3. Risk is decreased when the internal auditor reports to such an officer with the status to ensure broad audit coverage and adequate consideration of, and action on, findings and recommendations of the internal auditor.

Decreases

4. Risk is decreased when the accounting department has low turnover because error rates are usually lower.

Solution 2-5 SIMULATION ANSWER: Risk of Material Misstatement

Based only on the information given, determine whether each of the factors below *increases* or *decreases* the risk of material misstatement.

Factors	Effect on Risk of Material Misstatement
1. Management fails to establish proper procedures to provide reasonable assurance of reliable accounting estimates.	Increases
2. Management has been receptive to Howard's suggestions relating to accounting adjustments.	Decreases
3. Oak Bank recently opened a new branch office that is not yet profitable.	Increases
4. Oak Bank recently installed a new sophisticated computer system.	Increases

(ID: 9204)

Explanations

Increases

1. Risk is increased if management doesn't have proper procedures in place to provide reasonable assurance of reliable accounting estimates because results will usually be more inconsistent and less accurate.

Decreases

2. Risk is decreased when management is receptive to the auditor's recommendations.

Increases

3. Risk is increased when a company expands and particularly so if the new venture is unprofitable. This creates pressures which increase risk.

Increases

4. Risk is increased when a new computer system is installed because until it is fully tested under actual conditions the degree of its reliability is unknown.

Solution 2-6 SIMULATION ANSWER: Research

Which citation in the professional standards explains that although fraudulent journal entries often are made at the end of a reporting period, the auditor should consider whether there is a need to test journal entries throughout the reporting period under audit?

AU § 240 . A50 (ID: 9205)

.A50 The auditor exercises professional judgment in determining the nature, timing, and extent of testing of journal entries and other adjustments. However, because fraudulent journal entries and other adjustments are often made at the end of a reporting period, paragraph .32*a*(iv) requires the auditor to select the journal entries and other adjustments made at that time. Further, because material misstatements in financial statements due to fraud can occur throughout the period and may involve extensive efforts to conceal how the fraud is accomplished, paragraph .32*a*(v) requires the auditor to consider whether a need also exists to test journal entries and other adjustments throughout the period.

Solution 2-7 SIMULATION ANSWER: Research

Which citation in the professional standards states that the discussion among the audit team about the susceptibility of the entity's financial statements to material misstatement can be held concurrently with the discussion about the susceptibility of the financial statements to fraud?

*Editor Note: Statement on Auditing Standards 128 (effective for audits of financial statements for periods ending on or after December 15, 2014) revised AU 610, *Using the Work of Internal Auditors*, and amended AU 315 and various other sections. The content of the paragraph cited below did *not* change due to these amendments; however, the paragraph number changed from A14 to A21.

AU	§	315	.	*A21	(ID: 9217)

*.A21 The discussion among the engagement team about the susceptibility of the entity's financial statements to material misstatement:

- Provides an opportunity for more experienced engagement team members, including the engagement partner, to share their insights based on their knowledge of the entity.
- Allows the engagement team members to exchange information about the business risks to which the entity is subject and about how and where the financial statements might be susceptible to material misstatement due to fraud or error.
- Assists the engagement team members to gain a better understanding of the potential for material misstatement of the financial statements in the specific areas assigned to them and to understand how the results of the audit procedures that they perform may affect other aspects of the audit, including the decisions about the nature, timing, and extent of further audit procedures.
- Provides a basis upon which engagement team members communicate and share new information obtained throughout the audit that may affect the assessment of risks of material misstatement or the audit procedures performed to address these risks.

This discussion may be held concurrently with the discussion among the engagement team that is required by section 240 to discuss the susceptibility of the entity's financial statements to fraud. Section 240 further addresses the discussion among the engagement team about the risks of fraud.

CHAPTER 3

INTERNAL CONTROL

AU Identifier Used for Clarified US GAAS in This Textbook

We have not continued to use the temporary AU-C identifier for the clarified auditing standards issued by the American Institute of Certified Public Accountants (AICPA). In this textbook these standards have an AU identifier.

CHAPTER 3

INTERNAL CONTROL

I. Understanding of the Entity's Internal Control (AU 315 continued)

The objective of the auditor is to identify and assess the risks of material misstatement (RMM), whether due to fraud or error, at the financial statement and relevant assertion levels through understanding the entity and its environment, *including the entity's internal control*, thereby providing a basis for designing and implementing responses to the assessed RMM.

A. Overview

An understanding of internal control assists the auditor in identifying types of potential misstatements and factors that affect the RMM and in designing the nature, extent, and timing of further audit procedures.

1. **Definitions**

   a. **Internal Control** Internal control is a process effected by those charged with governance, management and other personnel designed to provide reasonable assurance about the achievement of the entity's objectives with regard to reliability of financial reporting, effectiveness and efficiency of operations, and compliance with applicable laws and regulations. Internal control over safeguarding of assets against unauthorized acquisition, use, or disposition may include controls relating to financial reporting and operations objectives.

   b. **Risk Assessment Procedures** The audit procedures performed to obtain an understanding of the entity and its environment, *including the entity's internal control*, to identify and assess the RMM, whether due to fraud or error, at the financial statement and relevant assertion levels

2. **Inherent Limitations of Internal Control** Internal control, no matter how effective, can provide an entity with only reasonable assurance about achieving the entity's financial reporting objectives. The likelihood of their achievement is affected by the inherent limitations of internal control. These include:

   a. Faulty human judgment in decision making

   b. Human errors that cause breakdowns in internal control

   c. Controls circumvented by the collusion of two or more people

   d. Inappropriate management override of controls

   Editor Note: Another limitation (*not* inherent) is that in designing and implementing controls, management may make judgments on the nature and extent of the controls it chooses to implement and the nature and extent of the risks it chooses to assume.

3. **Relevance of Controls to the Audit** The auditor should obtain an understanding of internal control activities relevant to the audit, which are those control activities the auditor needs to understand to assess the RMM at the assertion level and design further audit procedures responsive to assessed risks. Although most such controls are likely to relate to financial reporting, not all controls that relate to financial reporting are relevant to the audit. It is a matter of the auditor's professional judgment whether a control, individually or in combination with others, is relevant.

Factors relevant to the auditor's professional judgment about whether a control, individually or in combination with others, is relevant to the audit *may* include:

- Materiality
- The significance of the related risk
- The size of the entity
- The nature of the entity's business, including its organization and ownership characteristics
- The diversity and complexity of the entity's operations
- Applicable legal and regulatory requirements
- The circumstances and the applicable component of internal control
- The nature and complexity of the systems that are part of the entity's internal control, including the use of service organizations
- Whether and how a specific control, individually or in combination with other controls, prevents, or detects and corrects, material misstatements

4. **Characteristics of Manual & Automated Elements of Internal Control Relevant to the Auditor's Risk Assessment** An entity's system of internal control contains both manual and automated elements. The characteristics of each are relevant to the auditor's risk assessment and further audit procedures based on that risk assessment. An entity's use of IT may affect any of the five components of internal control relevant to the achievement of the entity's financial reporting, operations, or compliance objectives and its operating units or business functions. (The effect of an entity's use of IT on an audit is covered in chapter 7 of this text.)

B. Nature & Extent of the Understanding of Relevant Controls

When obtaining an understanding of controls that are relevant to the audit, the auditor should evaluate the design of those controls and determine whether they have been implemented by performing procedures *in addition to* inquiry of the entity's personnel.

1. **Evaluating the Design of a Control** Evaluating the design of a control involves considering whether the control, individually or in combination with other controls, is capable of effectively preventing, or detecting and correcting, material misstatements. Implementation of a control means that the control exists and that the entity is using it. Assessing the implementation of a control that is not effectively designed is of little use, and so the design of a control is considered first. An improperly designed control may represent a significant deficiency or material weakness in the entity's internal control.

2. **Risk Assessment Procedures Related to the Design & Implementation of Relevant Controls** Risk assessment procedures to obtain audit evidence about the design and implementation of relevant controls *may* include:

- Inquiring of entity personnel; however, inquiry alone is not sufficient for such purposes
- Observing the application of specific controls
- Inspecting documents and reports
- Tracing transactions through the information system relevant to financial reporting

C. Obtaining an Understanding of the Components of Internal Control

Internal control consists of five interrelated components. The division of internal control into these components, for purposes of US GAAS, provides a useful framework for auditors when considering how different aspects of an entity's internal control may affect the audit.

Exhibit 1 ▸ Components of Internal Control Mnemonic

C	**C**ontrol Activities
R	**R**isk Assessment
I	**I**nformation & Communication Systems
M	**M**onitoring of Controls
E	Control **E**nvironment

Editor Note: Auditors may use different terminology or frameworks to describe the various aspects of internal control and their effect on the audit other than these used in US GAAS, provided that all the components described in US GAAS are addressed.

1. **Control Activities** The auditor should obtain an understanding of control activities relevant to the audit, which are those control activities the auditor judges it necessary to understand in order to assess the RMM at the assertion level and design further audit procedures responsive to assessed risks.

   An audit does **not** require an understanding of all the control activities related to each significant class of transactions, account balance, and disclosure in the financial statements or to every assertion relevant to them. And when multiple control activities each achieve the same objective, it is unnecessary to obtain an understanding of each of the control activities related to such an objective.

   However, the auditor should obtain an understanding of:

   - The process of reconciling detailed records to the general ledger for material account balances
   - How the entity has responded to risks arising from IT

     Editor Note: From the auditor's perspective, controls over IT systems are effective when they maintain the integrity of information and the security of the data such systems process and when they include effective general IT controls and application controls. Internal control related to IT systems is covered in chapter 7 of this text.

   a. **Definition of Control Activities** Control activities are the policies and procedures that help ensure that management directives are carried out. Control activities, whether within IT or manual systems, have various objectives and are applied at various organizational and functional levels.

   b. **Control Activities Relevant to the Audit** Control activities that are relevant to the audit are those that are:

      - Required to be treated as such, being control activities that relate to significant risks and those that relate to risks for which substantive procedures alone do not provide sufficient appropriate audit evidence; or
      - Considered to be relevant in the professional judgment of the auditor

The auditor's professional judgment about whether a control activity is relevant to the audit is influenced by the risk that the auditor has identified that may give rise to a material misstatement and whether the auditor thinks it is likely to be appropriate to test the operating effectiveness of the control in determining the extent of substantive testing.

c. **Identification of Relevant Control Activities** The auditor's emphasis *may* be on identifying and obtaining an understanding of control activities that address the areas in which the auditor considers that RMM are likely to be higher.

2. **The Entity's Risk Assessment Process** An entity's risk assessment process for financial reporting purposes is its identification, analysis, and management of risks relevant to the preparation and fair presentation of financial statements. If that process is appropriate to the circumstances, including the nature, size, and complexity of the entity, it assists the auditor in identifying RMM.

Risks relevant to financial reporting include external and internal events and circumstances that may occur and adversely affect an entity's ability to initiate, authorize, record, process, and report financial data consistent with the assertions of management in the financial statements. Risks can arise or change due to circumstances such as:

- Changes in operating environment
- New personnel
- New or revamped information systems
- Rapid growth
- New technology
- New business models, products, or activities
- Corporate restructurings
- Expanded foreign operations
- New accounting pronouncements
- Changes in economic conditions

a. **Determine If the Entity Has a Risk Assessment Process** The auditor should obtain an understanding of whether the entity has a process for:

   (1) Identifying business risks relevant to financial reporting objectives

   (2) Estimating the significance of the risks

   (3) Assessing the likelihood of their occurrence

   (4) Deciding about actions to address those risks

b. **If Entity Has Risk Assessment Process** If the entity has established a risk assessment process:

   (1) The auditor should obtain an understanding of it and its results.

   (2) If the auditor identifies RMM that management failed to identify, the auditor should evaluate whether an underlying risk existed that the auditor expects would have been identified by the entity's risk assessment process.

(3) If such a risk exists, the auditor should obtain an understanding of why that process failed to identify it and evaluate whether the process is appropriate to its circumstances or determine if a significant deficiency or material weakness exists in internal control regarding the entity's risk assessment process.

c. **If Entity Has *Not* Established a Risk Assessment Process** If the entity has not established such a process or has an ad hoc process, the auditor should:

(1) Discuss with management whether business risks relevant to financial reporting objectives have been identified and how they have been addressed

(2) Evaluate whether the absence of a documented risk assessment process is appropriate in the circumstances or determine whether it represents a significant deficiency or material weakness in the entity's internal control

3. **The Information System, Including the Related Business Processes Relevant to Financial Reporting & Communication**

a. **Information System Relevant to Financial Reporting** The auditor should obtain an understanding of the information system, including the related business processes relevant to financial reporting, including the following areas:

(1) The classes of transactions in the entity's operations that are significant to the financial statements

(2) The procedures within both IT and manual systems by which those transactions are initiated, authorized, recorded, processed, corrected as necessary, transferred to the general ledger, and reported in the financial statements

(3) The related accounting records supporting information and specific accounts in the financial statements that are used to initiate, authorize, record, process, and report transactions; this includes the correction of incorrect information and how information is transferred to the general ledger; the records may be in either manual or electronic form

(4) How the information system captures events and conditions, other than transactions, that are significant to the financial statements

(5) The financial reporting process used to prepare the entity's financial statements, including significant accounting estimates and disclosures

(6) Controls surrounding journal entries, including nonstandard journal entries used to record nonrecurring, unusual transactions, or adjustments

Editor Note: An entity's business processes result in the transactions that are recorded, processed, and reported by the information system. Business processes are the activities designed to:

- Develop, purchase, produce, sell, and distribute an entity's products and services
- Ensure compliance with laws and regulations
- Record information, including accounting and financial reporting information

b. **Information System Relevant to Communication of Financial Reporting Matters** The auditor should obtain an understanding of how the entity communicates financial reporting roles and responsibilities and significant matters relating to financial reporting, including:

(1) Communications between management and those charged with governance

(2) External communications, such as those with regulatory authorities

4. **Monitoring of Controls** Monitoring of controls is a process to assess the effectiveness of internal control performance over time. Management accomplishes monitoring of controls through ongoing activities, separate evaluations, or a combination of the two.

a. **Monitoring Controls Over Financial Reporting** The auditor should obtain an understanding of:

(1) **Major Activities** The major activities that the entity uses to monitor internal control over financial reporting, including those related to those control activities relevant to the audit

(2) **Remedial Actions** How the entity initiates remedial actions to deficiencies in its controls.

b. **Internal Audit** If the entity has an internal audit function, the auditor should obtain an understanding of the following in order to determine whether the internal audit function is likely to be relevant to the audit:

(1) The nature of the internal audit function's responsibilities and how the internal audit function fits in the entity's organizational structure

(2) The activities performed or to be performed by the internal audit function

Editor Note: The entity's internal audit function is likely to be relevant to the audit if the nature of the internal audit function's responsibilities and activities are related to the entity's financial reporting and the auditor expects to use the work of the internal auditors to modify the nature or timing or reduce the extent of audit procedures to be performed. (The responsibilities of the internal audit function may be limited to the review of the economy, efficiency, and effectiveness of operations, for example, and, accordingly, may *not* relate to the entity's financial reporting.) The auditor's consideration of the internal audit function is covered in chapter 4 of this text.

c. **Sources of & Reliability of Information** Much of the information used in monitoring may be produced by the entity's information system. If management assumes that data used for monitoring are accurate without having a basis for that assumption, errors that may exist in the information could potentially lead management to incorrect conclusions from its monitoring activities.

Accordingly, an understanding of the following is required as part of the auditor's understanding of the entity's monitoring activities component of internal control:

(1) **Sources** The sources of the information related to the entity's monitoring activities

(2) **Reliability** The basis upon which management considers the information to be sufficiently reliable for the purpose

5. **Control Environment** The control environment includes the governance and management functions and the attitudes, awareness, and actions of those charged with governance and

management concerning the entity's internal control and its importance in the entity. The control environment sets the tone of an organization, influencing the control consciousness of its people. It is the foundation for all other components of internal control, providing discipline and structure.

The auditor should obtain an understanding of the control environment. As part of obtaining this understanding, the auditor should evaluate whether:

a. **Culture of Honesty & Ethical Behavior** Management, with the oversight of those charged with governance, has created and maintained a culture of honesty and ethical behavior

b. **Foundation for Other Components** The strengths in the control environment elements collectively provide an appropriate foundation for the other components of internal control and whether those other components are undermined by deficiencies in the control environment

c. **Possible Relevant Elements of Control Environment** Elements that *may* be relevant to obtaining an understanding of the control environment include:

   (1) **Communication & Enforcement of Integrity and Ethical Values** Essential elements that influence the effectiveness of the design, administration, and monitoring of controls

   (2) **Commitment to Competence** Matters such as management's consideration of the competence levels for particular jobs and how those levels translate into requisite skills and knowledge

   (3) **Participation of Those Charged With Governance** Attributes of those charged with governance, such as:

      (a) Their independence from management

      (b) Their experience and stature

      (c) The extent of their involvement and the information they receive and the scrutiny of activities

      (d) The appropriateness of their actions, including the degree to which difficult questions are raised and pursued with management

      (e) Their interaction with internal and external auditors

   (4) **Management's Philosophy & Operating Style** Characteristics such as management's:

      (a) Approach to taking and managing business risks

      (b) Attitudes and actions toward financial reporting

      (c) Attitudes toward information processing and accounting functions and personnel

   (5) **Organizational Structure** The framework within which an entity's activities for achieving its objectives are planned, executed, controlled, and reviewed

(6) **Assignment of Authority & Responsibility** Matters such as how authority and responsibility for operating activities are assigned and how reporting relationships and authorization hierarchies are established

(7) **Human Resource Policies & Practices** Policies and practices that relate to, for example, recruitment, orientation, training, evaluation, counseling, promotion, compensation, and remedial actions

d. **Audit Evidence of Elements of the Control Environment** Relevant audit evidence may be obtained through a combination of inquiries and other risk assessment procedures, such as corroborating inquiries through observation or inspection of documents. For example, whether management has a written code of conduct and whether it acts in a manner that supports the code.

e. **Effect of the Control Environment on the Assessment of RMM** The control environment in itself does not prevent, or detect and correct, a material misstatement. It *may*, however, influence the auditor's evaluation of the effectiveness of other controls, for example, the monitoring of controls and the operation of specific control activities and, thereby, the auditor's assessment of the RMM.

Some elements of an entity's control environment have a pervasive effect on assessing the RMM. For example, an active and independent board of directors may influence the philosophy and operating style of senior management. On the other hand, other elements may be more limited in their effect. For example, although human resource policies and practices directed toward hiring competent financial, accounting, and IT personnel may reduce the risk of errors in processing financial information, they may not mitigate a strong bias by top management to overstate earnings.

D. **Role of Relevant Controls in Identifying & Assessing the RMM**

See chapter 2 in this text for complete coverage of identifying and assessing the RMM in accordance with AU 315.

1. **Controls Related to Identified Risks** Throughout the process of obtaining an understanding of the entity, the auditor identifies risks and the controls that relate to those risks.

2. **Identification of Controls to Be Tested** The auditor relates the identified risks to what can go wrong at the relevant assertion level, taking into account the relevant controls that the auditor intends to test.

3. **Significant Risks** If the auditor has determined that a significant risk exists, the auditor should obtain an understanding of the entity's controls, including control activities, relevant to that risk and, based on that understanding, evaluate whether such controls have been suitably designed and implemented to mitigate such risks.

4. **Risks for Which Substantive Procedures Alone Do Not Provide Sufficient Appropriate Audit Evidence** In respect of some risks, the auditor may judge that it is not possible or practicable to obtain sufficient appropriate audit evidence only from substantive procedures. In such cases, the entity's controls over such risks are relevant to the audit, and the auditor should obtain an understanding of them.

E. **Audit Documentation**

1. **Components of Internal Control** Key elements of the understanding obtained regarding each of the internal control components; the sources of information from which the understanding was obtained; and the risk assessment procedures performed should be documented.

2. **Risks & Related Controls** Risks identified and related controls about which the auditor has obtained an understanding should be documented.

3. **Tools That *May* Be Used to Document the Understanding of Internal Control**

   a. **Flowchart Approach** An internal control flowchart is a sequential, graphic representation of a portion of a company's internal control system. It shows the segregation of functions, document flows, controls, etc.

Exhibit 2 ▶ Common Flowchart Symbols

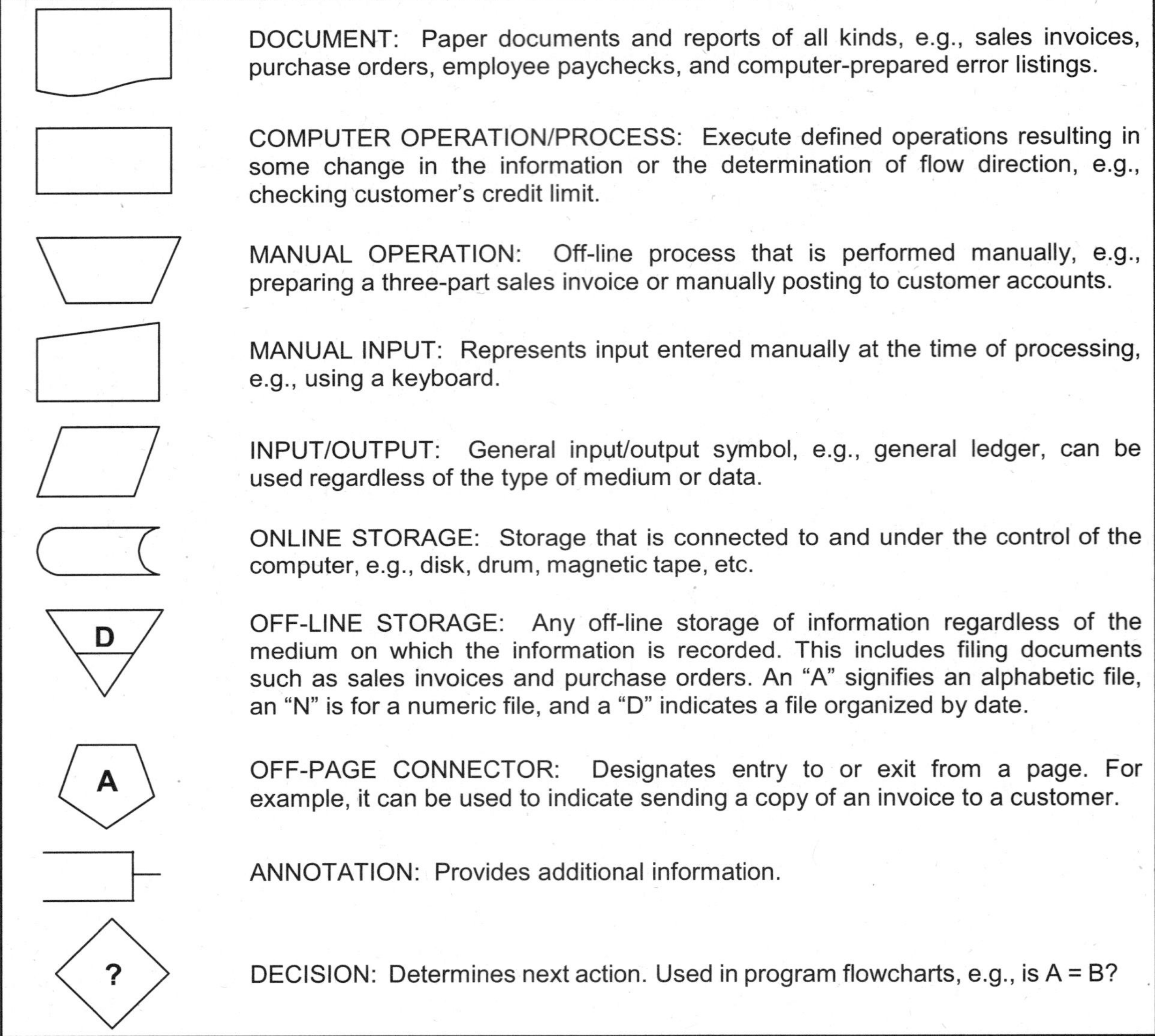

(1) **Advantages** The internal control flowchart shows the steps required and the flow of documents from person to person in carrying out the functions depicted. Therefore, overlooking controls existing between functions or departments is less likely to occur. Another advantage is that the flowchart clearly communicates the structure. The use of a flowchart is especially useful in the evaluation of electronic IT systems because it avoids much of the terminology that would be present in a narrative. Finally, its construction by the auditor requires a complete understanding of the structure.

(2) **Disadvantage** It may be more time consuming to construct a flowchart rather than to fill out an internal control questionnaire.

b. **Questionnaire Approach** An internal control questionnaire is simply an enumeration of the matters to be investigated in the auditor's consideration of internal control. It should be designed by persons who are fully conversant with the problems of internal control and who have experience in the kind of structure being reviewed.

(1) **Sample Questions** While the size and scope of internal control questionnaires will vary, some possible questions for an accounts receivable system are as follows.

(a) Are the following functions performed by employees other than accounts receivable bookkeepers?

(i) Handling cash and maintaining cash records

(ii) Opening incoming mail

(iii) Credit and collection

(iv) Review and mailing of statements to customers

(b) Are the accounts receivable ledgers unavailable to the cashier?

(c) Are the subsidiary ledgers regularly balanced with the control accounts?

(d) Are the subsidiary ledgers occasionally balanced with the control accounts by someone other than the accounts receivable bookkeepers?

(e) Are aged trial balances of accounts receivable regularly prepared and submitted for executive approval?

(f) Are statements sent at regular intervals to all customers?

(2) **Advantages** One advantage of the internal control questionnaire is that it is easy to complete. Another advantage is that the comprehensive list of questions provides assurance that relevant points will be covered. Also, weaknesses are obvious because they are usually the "no" answers.

(3) **Disadvantage** A possible problem is that if the questionnaire is too general, it may not be adequate to evaluate an entity's internal control.

c. **Narrative (Memorandum) Approach** The auditor determines what the prescribed system of internal control is, and then writes it out in the auditor's own words.

(1) **Advantages** The narrative is tailor-made for each engagement. Another advantage is that it requires a detailed analysis of the client's internal control because the auditor must thoroughly understand the structure in order to describe it.

(2) **Disadvantages** The narrative approach is very time consuming. It does not have built-in safeguards to prevent the auditor from overlooking some aspect of internal control—weaknesses are not always obvious and might not be detected by this approach.

II. Tests of Controls (AU 330 continued)

A. Overview

1. **Definition of Tests of Controls** An audit procedure designed to evaluate the operating effectiveness of controls in preventing, or detecting and correcting, material misstatements at the assertion level

   a. **Operating Effectiveness vs. Design & Implementation** Testing the operating effectiveness of controls is different from the risk assessment procedure of obtaining an understanding of and evaluating the design and implementation of controls; however, the same types of audit procedures are used. The auditor may, therefore, decide it is efficient to test the operating effectiveness of controls at the same time the auditor is evaluating their design and determining that they have been implemented.

   b. **Dual-Purpose Test** Performing a test of controls and a test of details on the same transaction is a dual-purpose test. Although their purposes are different, both may be accomplished concurrently. For example, the auditor may design and evaluate the results of a test to examine an invoice to determine whether it has been approved and to provide substantive audit evidence of a transaction. A dual-purpose test is designed and evaluated by considering each purpose of the test separately.

2. **Applicability** The auditor should design and perform tests of controls to obtain sufficient appropriate audit evidence about the operating effectiveness of relevant controls for *either* of the following circumstances.

   a. The auditor's assessment of the risk of material misstatement (RMM) at the relevant assertion level includes an expectation that the controls are operating effectively, i.e., the auditor intends to rely on the operating effectiveness of controls in determining the nature, extent, and timing of substantive procedures; or

   b. Substantive procedures alone cannot provide sufficient appropriate audit evidence at the relevant assertion level, for example, this may occur when an entity conducts its business using IT and no documentation of transactions is produced or maintained, other than through the IT system. In such cases, the auditor should perform tests of the relevant controls.

3. **Reliance** In designing and performing tests of controls, the auditor should obtain more persuasive audit evidence the greater the reliance the auditor places on the effectiveness of a control. This may be particularly true when it is not possible or practicable to obtain sufficient appropriate audit evidence only from substantive procedures.

B. Nature & Extent of Tests of Controls

1. **Overview**

   a. **Nature** The nature of the particular control influences the type of audit procedure necessary to obtain audit evidence about whether the control was operating effectively. For example, if operating effectiveness is evidenced by documentation, the auditor may decide to inspect such documentation to obtain audit evidence about operating effectiveness. For other controls, however, documentation may not be available or relevant.

   b. **Extent** When more persuasive audit evidence is needed regarding the effectiveness of a control, it *may* be appropriate to increase the extent of testing of the control.

In addition to the degree of reliance on controls, matters the auditor *may* consider in determining the extent of tests of controls include:

- The frequency of the performance of the control by the entity during the period
- The length of time during the audit period that the auditor is relying on the operating effectiveness of the control
- The expected rate of deviation from a control
- The relevance and reliability of the audit evidence to be obtained regarding the operating effectiveness of the control at the relevant assertion level
- The extent to which audit evidence is obtained from tests of other controls related to the relevant assertion

2. **Inquiry Alone Is *Not* Sufficient to Test the Operating Effectiveness of Controls** In designing and performing tests of controls, the auditor should perform other audit procedures in combination with inquiry to obtain audit evidence about the operating effectiveness of the controls, including:

   a. How the controls were applied at relevant times during the period under audit

   b. The consistency with which they were applied

   c. By whom or by what means they were applied, including, when applicable, whether the person performing the control possesses the necessary authority and competence to perform the control effectively

   Editor Note: Inquiry combined with inspection, recalculation, or reperformance may provide more assurance than inquiry and observation because an observation is pertinent only at the point in time at which it is made.

3. **Indirect Controls** The auditor should determine whether the controls to be tested depend upon other controls (indirect controls) and, if so, whether it is necessary to obtain audit evidence supporting the operating effectiveness of those indirect controls.

C. **Timing of Tests of Controls**

The auditor should test controls for the particular time or throughout the period for which the auditor intends to rely on those controls in order to provide an appropriate basis for the auditor's intended reliance, subject to special circumstances described below regarding using audit evidence obtained during an interim period or controls over significant risks.

Editor Note: Audit evidence pertaining only to a point in time may be sufficient for the auditor's purpose, for example, when testing controls over the entity's physical inventory counting at the period-end. If, on the other hand, the auditor intends to rely on a control over a period, tests that are capable of providing audit evidence that the control operated effectively at relevant times during that period are appropriate. Such tests may include tests of the entity's monitoring of controls.

1. **Using Audit Evidence Obtained During an Interim Period** If the auditor obtains audit evidence about the operating effectiveness of controls during an interim period, the auditor should:

   a. Obtain audit evidence about significant changes to those controls subsequent to the interim period

   b. Determine the additional audit evidence to be obtained for the remaining period

Editor Note: Additional audit evidence may be obtained, for example, by extending the testing of the operating effectiveness of controls over the remaining period or testing the entity's monitoring of controls.

2. **Using Audit Evidence Obtained in Previous Audits**

a. **Considerations** In determining whether it is appropriate to use audit evidence about the operating effectiveness of controls obtained in previous audits and, if so, the length of the time period that may elapse before retesting a control, the auditor should consider:

(1) The effectiveness of other elements of internal control, including the control environment; the entity's monitoring of controls; and the entity's risk assessment process

(2) The risks arising from the characteristics of the control, including whether the control is manual or automated

(3) The effectiveness of general IT controls

(4) The effectiveness of the control and its application by the entity, including the nature and extent of deviations in the application of the control noted in previous audits and whether there have been personnel changes that significantly affect the application of the control

(5) Whether the lack of a change in a particular control poses a risk due to changing circumstances

(6) The RMM and the extent of reliance on the control

Editor Note: In general, the higher the RMM or the greater the reliance on controls, the shorter the acceptable time period elapsed, if any, is likely to be and the less viable it will be to use evidence from a previous audit.

b. **Establish Relevance to Current Audit** If the auditor plans to use audit evidence from a previous audit about the operating effectiveness of specific controls, the auditor should perform audit procedures to establish the continuing relevance of that information to the current audit. The auditor should obtain this evidence by performing inquiry, combined with observation or inspection, to confirm the understanding of those specific controls, and:

(1) **Test in Current Audit If There Have Been Relevant Changes** If there have been changes *that affect the continuing relevance of the audit evidence* from the previous audit, the auditor should test the controls in the current audit.

Editor Note: For example, changes in a system that enable an entity to receive a new report from the system probably do not affect the relevance of audit evidence from a previous audit; however, a change that causes data to be accumulated or calculated differently does affect it.

(2) **If No Relevant Changes Test Every *Third* Audit *But Not All in Same Audit*** If there have not been such changes, the auditor should test the controls *at least* once in every third audit and should test some controls during each audit to avoid the possibility of testing all the controls on which the auditor intends to rely in a single audit period with no testing of controls in the subsequent two audit periods. Testing some of the controls in each audit also provides corroborating information about the continuing effectiveness of the control environment.

3. **Test Controls Over Significant Risks in Current Audit** If the auditor plans to rely on controls over a risk the auditor has determined to be a significant risk, the auditor should test the operating effectiveness of those controls in the current period.

4. **Evaluating the Operating Effectiveness of Controls**

   a. When evaluating the operating effectiveness of relevant controls, the auditor should evaluate whether misstatements that have been detected by substantive procedures indicate that controls are not operating effectively. *The absence of misstatements detected by substantive procedures, however, does* ***not*** *provide audit evidence that controls related to the relevant assertion being tested are effective.*

      Editor Note: The identification by the auditor of a material misstatement of the financial statements in circumstances that indicate that the misstatement would not have been detected by the entity's internal control is an indicator of a material weakness.

   b. If deviations from controls upon which the auditor intends to rely are detected, the auditor should make specific inquiries to understand these matters and their potential consequences and should determine whether:

      (1) The tests of controls that have been performed provide an appropriate basis for reliance on the controls; or

      (2) Additional tests of controls are necessary; or

      (3) The potential risks of misstatement need to be addressed using substantive procedures

D. Selecting Items for Testing to Obtain Audit Evidence
When designing tests of controls and tests of details, the auditor should determine the means of selecting items for testing that are effective in meeting the purpose of the audit procedure.

That is, in selecting the items, US GAAS requires the auditor to determine the relevance and reliability (appropriateness) of information to be used as audit evidence. Sufficiency, the other aspect of effectiveness, is also an important consideration in selecting items to test.

The following are the means available to the auditor for selecting items for testing. The application of any one or combination of these means *may* be appropriate depending on the particular circumstances—the RMM related to the assertion being tested and the practicality and efficiency of the different means.

1. **Selecting All Items** A 100 percent examination is unlikely in the case of tests of controls; however, it may be more common for tests of details. It *may* be appropriate when, for example:

   - The population constitutes a small number of large value items; or
   - A significant risk exists and other means do not provide sufficient appropriate audit evidence, or
   - The repetitive nature of a calculation or other process performed automatically by an information system makes a 100 percent examination cost effective

2. **Selecting Specific Items** The auditor *may* decide to select specific items from a population. In making this decision, factors that may be relevant include the auditor's understanding of the entity, the assessed RMM, and the characteristics of the population being tested. The judgmental selection of specific items is subject to nonsampling risk.

Specific items selected *may* include:

a. **High Value or Key Items** The auditor may decide to select specific items within a population because they are of high value or exhibit some other characteristic, for example, items that are suspicious, unusual, particularly risk prone, or have a history of error.

b. **All Items Over a Certain Amount** The auditor may decide to examine items whose recorded values exceed a certain amount in order to verify a large proportion of the total amount of a class of transactions or account balance.

c. **Items to Obtain Information** The auditor may examine items to obtain information about matters such as the nature of the entity or the nature of transactions.

Editor Note: Although selective examination of specific items from a class of transactions or account balance often will be an efficient means of obtaining audit evidence, it does **not** constitute audit sampling. Consequently, the results of audit procedures applied to items selected in this way cannot be projected to the entire population; furthermore, selective examination of specific items does *not*, by itself, provide sufficient appropriate audit evidence concerning the remainder of the population.

3. **Audit Sampling** Audit sampling is designed to enable conclusions to be drawn about an entire population on the basis of testing a sample drawn from the population. Audit sampling is covered in this text in chapter 6.

E. **Audit Documentation**
If the auditor plans to use audit evidence about the operating effectiveness of controls obtained in previous audits, the auditor should include in the audit documentation the conclusions reached about relying on such controls that were tested in a previous audit.

III. Communicating Internal Control Related Matters Identified in an Audit (AU 265)

A. **Overview**
During an audit the auditor may identify deficiencies in internal control. US GAAS specifies which such deficiencies the auditor is required to communicate to those charged with governance and management; however, nothing precludes the auditor from communicating other identified internal control matters.

The objective of the auditor is to appropriately communicate identified internal control deficiencies that are of sufficient importance to merit the attention of those charged with governance and management.

B. **Definitions**

1. **Deficiency in Internal Control** A deficiency in internal control exists when the design or operation of a control does not allow management or employees, in the normal course of performing their assigned functions, to prevent, or detect and correct, misstatements on a timely basis.

a. **Deficiency in Design** A deficiency in design exists when *either*:

(1) A control necessary to meet the control objective is missing; or

(2) An existing control is not properly designed so that, even if the control operates as designed, the control objective would not be met

b. **Deficiency in Operation** A deficiency in operation exists when *either:*

(1) A properly designed control does not operate as designed; or

(2) When the person performing the control does not possess the necessary authority or competence to perform the control effectively

2. **Material Weakness** A material weakness is a deficiency, or a combination of deficiencies, in internal control, such that there is a reasonable possibility that a material misstatement of the entity's financial statements will not be prevented, or detected and corrected, on a timely basis.

3. **Significant Deficiency** A significant deficiency is a deficiency, or a combination of deficiencies, in internal control that is less severe than a material weakness yet important enough to merit attention by those charged with governance.

C. **Identification & Evaluation Procedures**

1. **Determination of Whether Deficiencies in Internal Control Have Been Identified** The auditor should determine whether, on the basis of the audit work performed, the auditor has identified one or more deficiencies in internal control.

In making this determination, the auditor *may* discuss the relevant facts and circumstances with the appropriate level of management. The appropriate level of management with whom to discuss the findings is one that is both familiar with the internal control area concerned and has the authority to take remedial action.

2. **Evaluating Identified Deficiencies in Internal Control**

a. **Significant Deficiency vs. Material Weakness** If the auditor has identified one or more deficiencies in internal control, the auditor should evaluate each deficiency to determine, on the basis of the audit work performed, whether, individually or in combination, they constitute significant deficiencies or material weaknesses.

Editor Note: A deficiency in internal control on its own may not be sufficiently important to constitute a significant deficiency or a material weakness. However, a combination of deficiencies affecting the *same* significant account or disclosure, relevant assertion, or component of internal control may increase the RMM to such an extent to give rise to a significant deficiency or material weakness.

(1) **Severity** The severity of a deficiency, or a combination of deficiencies, depends not only on whether a misstatement has actually occurred but also on:

(a) **Magnitude** The magnitude of the potential misstatement; the maximum amount by which an account balance or total of transactions can be overstated generally is the recorded amount, whereas understatements could be larger

Examples of factors that affect magnitude include:

(i) The financial statement amounts or total of transactions exposed to the deficiency

(ii) The volume of activity (in the current period or expected in future periods) in the account or class of transactions exposed to the deficiency

(b) **Likelihood** Whether there is a reasonable possibility that the entity's controls will fail to prevent, or detect and correct, a misstatement of an account balance or disclosure; a reasonable possibility exists when the chance of the future event or events occurring is *more than remote*

(i) The evaluation of whether a deficiency presents a reasonable possibility of misstatement may be made *without* quantifying the probability of occurrence as a specific percentage or range.

(ii) In many cases, the probability of a small misstatement will be greater than the probability of a large misstatement.

(iii) Risk factors that affect whether there is a reasonable possibility that a deficiency, or a combination of deficiencies, in internal control will result in a misstatement of an account balance or disclosure include the:

- Nature of the financial statement accounts, classes of transactions, disclosures, and assertions involved
- Cause and frequency of the exceptions detected as a result of the deficiency, or deficiencies, in internal control
- Susceptibility of the related asset or liability to loss or fraud
- Subjectivity, complexity, or extent of judgment required to determine the amount involved
- Interaction or relationship of the control(s) with other controls
- Interaction with other deficiencies in internal control
- Possible future consequences of the deficiency, or deficiencies, in internal control
- Importance of the controls to the financial reporting process, for example, general monitoring controls (such as oversight of management) and controls over
  - Prevention and detection of fraud
  - Selection and application of significant accounting policies
  - Significant transactions with related parties
  - Significant transactions outside the entity's normal course of business
  - Period-end financial reporting process (such as controls over nonrecurring journal entries)

(2) **Identification of Resultant Misstatements Is *Not* Required** Significant deficiencies and material weaknesses may exist even though the auditor has not identified misstatements during the audit.

b. **Prudent Official Standard for a Material Weakness** If the auditor determines that a deficiency, or a combination of deficiencies, in internal control is *not* a material weakness, the auditor should consider whether prudent officials, having knowledge of the same facts and circumstances, would likely reach the same conclusion.

c. **Indicators of Material Weaknesses** Indicators of material weaknesses in internal control include:

- Identification of fraud, whether or not material, on the part of senior management
- Restatement of previously issued financial statements to reflect the correction of a material misstatement due to fraud or error
- Identification by the auditor of a material misstatement of the financial statements under audit in circumstances that indicate that the misstatement would not have been detected by the entity's internal control
- Ineffective oversight of the entity's financial reporting and internal control by those charged with governance

D. Communication of Deficiencies in Internal Control

1. **Those Charged With Governance** The auditor should communicate *in writing* to those charged with governance the significant deficiencies and material weaknesses identified during the audit, including those that were remediated during the audit, *no later than 60 days following the report release date*.

2. **Management** The auditor also should communicate to management at an appropriate level of responsibility, *no later than 60 days following the report release date*:

   a. **Significant Deficiencies & Material Weaknesses** *In writing*, significant deficiencies and material weaknesses that the auditor has communicated or intends to communicate to those charged with governance, unless it would be inappropriate to communicate directly to management in the circumstances

   b. **Other Deficiencies** In writing or orally, other deficiencies in internal control identified during the audit that have not been communicated to management by other parties and that are of sufficient importance to merit management's attention.

   If other deficiencies in internal control are communicated orally, the auditor should document the communication.

   Editor Note: If the auditor or other parties, such as internal auditors or regulators, have communicated deficiencies in internal control, other than significant deficiencies or material weaknesses, to management in a prior period and management has chosen not to remedy them, the auditor need not repeat the communication in the current period. (Nevertheless, the failure of management to remedy other deficiencies in internal control that were previously communicated may become a significant deficiency requiring communication with those charged with governance.)

   c. **Level of Management** The appropriate level of management for significant deficiencies and material weaknesses identified is likely to be the CEO or CFO. For other deficiencies in internal control, the appropriate level *may* be operational management with more direct involvement in the control areas affected and with the authority to take appropriate remedial action.

3. **Timeliness of Communication** Although the auditor is required to make these communications no later than 60 days following the report release date, the communication is best made by the report release date because receipt of such communication may be an important factor in enabling those charged with governance to discharge their oversight responsibilities.

4. **Previous Communications** The fact that the auditor communicated a significant deficiency or material weakness to those charged with governance and management in a previous audit

does not eliminate the need for the auditor to repeat the communication if remedial action has not yet been taken. (The current year's communication may repeat the description or simply reference the previous communication and its date.)

a. A failure to act, in the absence of a rational explanation, *may* in itself represent a significant deficiency or material weakness.

b. The requirements to communicate significant deficiencies and material weaknesses apply, regardless of cost or other considerations that management and those charged with governance may consider relevant in determining whether to remedy such deficiencies.

5. **Oral Communications** Early communication may be important for some matters because of their relative significance and the urgency for corrective follow-up action. The auditor *may* communicate these orally to assist the client in taking timely remedial action to minimize the RMM. However, oral communication does **not** relieve the auditor of the responsibility to repeat these matters in the required written communication of significant deficiencies and material weaknesses.

6. **Elements of the Written Communication of Significant Deficiencies & Material Weaknesses**

a. The definition of the term *material weakness* and, when relevant, the definition of the term *significant deficiency*

b. A description of the significant deficiencies and material weaknesses and an explanation of their potential effects

(1) In explaining the potential effects of the significant deficiencies and material weaknesses, the auditor need not quantify those effects. The potential effects may be described in terms of the control objectives and types of errors the control was designed to prevent, or detect and correct; or in terms of the RMM that the control was designed to address. The potential effects may be evident from the description of the significant deficiencies or material weaknesses.

(2) The significant deficiencies or material weaknesses may be grouped together for reporting purposes when it is appropriate to do so.

(3) The auditor *may* also include in the written communication:

(a) Suggestions for remedial action on the deficiencies

(b) Management's actual or proposed responses

(c) A statement about whether the auditor has undertaken any steps to verify whether management's responses have been implemented

c. Sufficient information to enable those charged with governance and management to understand the context of the communication; in particular, the auditor should include in the communication the following elements that explain that the:

(1) Purpose of the audit was for the auditor to express an opinion on the financial statements

(2) Audit included consideration of internal control over financial reporting in order to design audit procedures that are appropriate in the circumstances, but not for the purpose of expressing an opinion on the effectiveness of internal control

(3) Auditor is not expressing an opinion on the effectiveness of internal control

(4) Auditor's consideration of internal control was not designed to identify all deficiencies in internal control that might be material weaknesses or significant deficiencies, and therefore, material weaknesses or significant deficiencies may exist that were not identified

Editor Note: The auditor *may* consider it appropriate to include the following information as additional context for the communication:

- The general inherent limitations of internal control, including the possibility of management override of controls
- The specific nature and extent of the auditor's consideration of internal control during the audit

d. An appropriate alert that restricts the use of the auditor's written communication

e. The illustration of the communication in the standard includes this instruction: If the auditor is communicating significant deficiencies and did not identify any material weaknesses, the auditor may state that none of the identified significant deficiencies are considered to be material weaknesses.

Exhibit 3 ▸ Illustrative Auditor's Written Communication

To Management and [*identify the body or individuals charged with governance, such as the entity's Board of Directors*] of ABC Company

In planning and performing our audit of the financial statements of ABC Company (the "Company") as of and for the year ended December 31, 20XX, in accordance with auditing standards generally accepted in the United States of America, we considered the Company's internal control over financial reporting (internal control) as a basis for designing audit procedures that are appropriate in the circumstances for the purpose of expressing our opinion on the financial statements, but not for the purpose of expressing an opinion on the effectiveness of the Company's internal control. Accordingly, we do not express an opinion on the effectiveness of the Company's internal control.

Our consideration of internal control was for the limited purpose described in the preceding paragraph and was not designed to identify all deficiencies in internal control that might be [*material weaknesses* or *material weaknesses or significant deficiencies*] and therefore, [*material weaknesses* or *material weaknesses or significant deficiencies*] may exist that were not identified. However, as discussed below, we identified certain deficiencies in internal control that we consider to be [*material weaknesses* or *significant deficiencies* or *material weaknesses and significant deficiencies*].

A deficiency in internal control exists when the design or operation of a control does not allow management or employees, in the normal course of performing their assigned functions, to prevent, or detect and correct, misstatements on a timely basis. A material weakness is a deficiency, or a combination of deficiencies, in internal control, such that there is a reasonable possibility that a material misstatement of the entity's financial statements will not be prevented, or detected and corrected, on a timely basis. [*We consider the following deficiencies in the Company's internal control to be material weaknesses:*]

[*Describe the material weaknesses that were identified and an explanation of their potential effects.*]

[*A significant deficiency is a deficiency, or a combination of deficiencies, in internal control that is less severe than a material weakness, yet important enough to merit attention by those charged with governance. We consider the following deficiencies in the Company's internal control to be significant deficiencies:*]

[*Describe the significant deficiencies that were identified and an explanation of their potential effects.*]

[*If the auditor is communicating significant deficiencies and did not identify any material weaknesses, the auditor may state that none of the identified significant deficiencies are considered to be material weaknesses.*]

This communication is intended solely for the information and use of management, [*identify the body or individuals charged with governance*], others within the organization, and [*identify any governmental authorities to which the auditor is required to report*] and is not intended to be, and should not be, used by anyone other than these specified parties.

[*Auditor's signature*]

[*Auditor's city and state*]

[*Date*]

7. **Elements of a Written Communication of *No* Material Weaknesses** When the auditor issues a written communication stating that no material weaknesses were identified during the audit, the communication should include all of the elements just described **except** a description of the significant deficiencies and material weaknesses and an explanation of their potential effects.

Editor Note: A written communication indicating that no material weaknesses were identified during the audit does **not** provide any assurance about the effectiveness of an entity's internal control over financial reporting.

Exhibit 4 ▸ Illustrative Auditor's No Material Weakness Written Communication

To Management and [*identify the body or individuals charged with governance, such as the entity's Board of Directors*] of NPO Organization

In planning and performing our audit of the financial statements of NPO Organization (the "Organization") as of and for the year ended December 31, 20XX, in accordance with auditing standards generally accepted in the United States of America, we considered the Organization's internal control over financial reporting (internal control) as a basis for designing audit procedures that are appropriate in the circumstances for the purpose of expressing our opinion on the financial statements, but not for the purpose of expressing an opinion on the effectiveness of the Organization's internal control. Accordingly, we do not express an opinion on the effectiveness of the Organization's internal control.

A deficiency in internal control exists when the design or operation of a control does not allow management or employees, in the normal course of performing their assigned functions, to prevent, or detect and correct, misstatements on a timely basis. A material weakness is a deficiency, or a combination of deficiencies, in internal control, such that there is a reasonable possibility that a material misstatement of the entity's financial statements will not be prevented, or detected and corrected, on a timely basis.

Our consideration of internal control was for the limited purpose described in the first paragraph and was not designed to identify all deficiencies in internal control that might be material weaknesses. Given these limitations, during our audit we did not identify any deficiencies in internal control that we consider to be material weaknesses. However, material weaknesses may exist that have not been identified.

[*If one or more significant deficiencies have been identified, the auditor may add the following: Our audit was also not designed to identify deficiencies in internal control that might be significant deficiencies. A significant deficiency is a deficiency, or a combination of deficiencies, in internal control that is less severe than a material weakness, yet important enough to merit attention by those charged with governance. We communicated the significant deficiencies identified during our audit in a separate communication dated [date].*]

This communication is intended solely for the information and use of management, [*identify the body or individuals charged with governance*], others within the organization, and [*identify any governmental authorities to which the auditor is required to report*] and is not intended to be, and should not be, used by anyone other than these specified parties.

[*Auditor's signature*]

[*Auditor's city and state*]

[*Date*]

8. ***No* Written Communication for *No* Significant Deficiencies** However, the auditor should **not** issue a written communication stating that no significant deficiencies were identified during the audit. Such a communication has the potential to be misunderstood or misused.

9. **Management's Response** Management may wish to or may be required by a regulator to prepare a written response to the auditor's communication regarding significant deficiencies or material weaknesses identified during the audit.

If such a written response is included in a document containing the auditor's written communication, the auditor *may* add a paragraph to the written communication disclaiming an opinion on such information. The following is an example of such a paragraph:

> ABC Company's written response to the significant deficiencies [*and material weaknesses*] identified in our audit was not subjected to the auditing procedures applied in the audit of the financial statements and, accordingly, we express no opinion on it.

IV. Internal Control Objectives & Procedures for Specific Transaction Cycles

A. Objectives of Internal Control

A well-designed internal control should ensure five objectives.

1. **Authorization** The starting point for establishing accounting control of transactions is appropriate authorization. Obtaining reasonable assurance of appropriate general or specific authorization requires independent evidence that authorizations are issued by persons acting within the scope of their authority and that transactions conform with the terms of the authorizations.

2. **Validity** Controls should provide reasonable assurance relative to the validity or existence of assets and liabilities at a given date and whether recorded transactions have occurred during a given period.

3. **Proper Recording** The objective of internal control with respect to the proper recording of transactions encompasses several sub-objectives. These include the following.

   a. **Completeness** Transactions are not omitted from the accounting records.

   b. **Valuation** Transactions are recorded at the actual amounts at which they transpired.

   c. **Classification** Transactions are classified in the appropriate accounts.

   d. **Timing** Transactions are recorded in the accounting period in which they occurred. Additionally, they are recorded as promptly as practicable when recording is necessary to maintain accountability.

4. **Accountability & Comparison** The accountability objective of internal control is to assure the availability of information necessary to follow assets from the time of their acquisition until their disposition. This requires maintaining records for accountability of assets and periodic comparison of these records with the related assets. The purpose of comparing recorded accountability with assets is to determine whether the actual assets agree with the recorded accountability. Consequently, it is related closely to the above discussion of proper recording of transactions.

5. **Protection & Limited Access** Controls should provide adequate protection of assets. Such protection is facilitated through segregation of incompatible functions and requires that access to assets be limited to authorized personnel. Access to assets includes both direct physical access and indirect access through documents that authorize use or disposition of assets.

B. Source Documents & Accounting Records

To determine the correct test of an internal control or to identify an internal control weakness, you must understand how source documents and accounting records relate to each other and what type of internal controls should exist.

1. **Segregation** Remember that authorization of a transaction, recording of the transaction, and custody of the related asset should all be separated. If any person or department was responsible for more than one of these functions, an internal control weakness would exist. For example, in the payroll function:

a. The Personnel Department should authorize pay rates (authorization).

b. The Timekeeping Department should prepare attendance and timekeeping data (record keeping).

c. The Payroll Department prepares the payroll (record keeping).

d. The Treasurer's Department prepares the payroll checks and distributes them to employees (custody).

2. **Tracking** Source documents should be prenumbered and controlled so that they all can be accounted for.

3. **Reconciliation** Subsidiary ledgers should be reconciled to general ledgers.

4. **Perspective** When considering a question about testing an internal control, first determine what is being asked.

   a. Tracing from a source document to the recorded entry tests the completeness assertion by looking for understatements.

   b. Vouching from a recorded entry to the source document tests the existence assertion by looking for overstatements.

C. **Policies & Procedures Within Transaction Cycles**
This section examines the five transaction cycles more closely by relating specific internal control policies and procedures within the cycles to the objectives of internal control. Additionally, for each control, an audit test of controls is suggested to evaluate the effectiveness of the policies and procedures.

1. **Transaction Cycles** Internal control objectives can be analyzed based on specific business activities or logical groups of transactions. Groupings of similar transactions or functions of an entity are known as transaction cycles. Dividing the audit into transaction cycles is known as the cycle approach. The cycle approach combines similar transactions with the ledger balances that result from those transactions. This is more efficient than treating each account balance as a separate segment. Although classification is somewhat arbitrary, the following is representative of the cycles of most businesses.

   a. Sales, Receivables & Cash Receipts Cycle

   b. Purchases, Payables & Cash Disbursements Cycle

   c. Inventory & Production Cycle

   d. Personnel & Payroll Cycle

   e. Property, Plant & Equipment Cycle

2. **Universal Procedures** Several internal control policies and procedures are common to most, if not all, transaction cycles. Listed in the last section of this chapter are general internal control questions that can be asked for most of the transaction cycles indicated. These questions are presented in this format to help you become familiar with the general questions. Specific internal control questions applicable to the individual transaction cycles are included under the transaction cycle titles. Questions generally should be worded to require a yes or no answer.

3. Sales, Receivables & Cash Receipts Cycle

Objective	*Internal Control*	*Test of Controls*
Authorization	Credit approval occurs before shipment is authorized.	Examine appropriate document for approval.
	Existence of a cash discount policy.	Discuss policy with management. Review sales orders for evidence of compliance.
	Approval of cash discounts and adjustments.	Examine remittance advices for proper approval.
	Sales prices are from authorized price list or executed contract.	Compare sales invoice prices to appropriate price list or contract.
Validity	Prenumbered sales invoices.	Account for numerical sequence of sales invoices.
	Sales are supported by authorized shipping documents and approved customer orders.	Examine supporting bills of lading and customer orders.
	Monthly statements are mailed to customers.	Observe mailing of statements.
	Independent follow-up of customer complaints.	Examine customer correspondence files.
	Separation of the functions of cash handling and record keeping.	Observation. Discuss with management and review employee job descriptions.
	Shipment is acknowledged by Shipping Department.	Examine acknowledgment on sales order copy.
Proper Recording	Shipping documents are prenumbered (Completeness).	Accounting for numerical sequence of shipping documents. Trace documents to recording of sales and accounts receivable subsidiary ledger.
	A chart of accounts is used and is adequate (Classification).	Review adequacy and use of proper accounts. Examine sales documents to determine if sales transactions are properly classified.
	Cash receipts are recorded immediately and deposited on a daily basis (Timing).	Observation. Trace totals to duplicate deposit slips.
	Sales invoices and credit memoranda are prenumbered (Completeness).	Account for numerical sequence of sales invoices and credit memoranda.
	Internal verification of invoice preparation and posting (Valuation, Completeness, Classification).	Observation. Discuss policy with management.

Objective	*Internal Control*	*Test of Controls*
Accountability and Comparison	Independent reconciliation of bank statements.	Observation. Review bank reconciliation.
	Cash register totals are verified by persons not having access to cash or cash records.	Examine documentation of verification.
	Cash receipts are recorded immediately to establish accountability.	Observe the cash receiving process.
	A list of checks is prepared as the mail is opened.	Observation. Compare check listing total to duplicate deposit slip.
Protection and Limited Access	Persons receiving or otherwise handling cash are bonded.	Discuss with management. Review appropriate documentation of bonding.
	Checks are immediately endorsed.	Observation.
	Separation of cash handling and record keeping functions.	Observation. Discuss with management and review employee job descriptions.

4. Purchases, Payables & Cash Disbursements Cycle

Objective	*Internal Control*	*Test of Controls*
Authorization	Appropriate approval is required for all purchases.	Examine supporting documentation for indication of approval (purchase requisition and order).
	Payment approval required before check signing.	Observation. Examine documentation for indication of approval.
	Authorized signatures on checks. Two signatures on large checks.	Select a sample of large disbursements from the cash disbursements journal and examine the correlating canceled checks for two signatures.
Validity	Purchases are supported by purchase requisition, purchase order, receiving report, and vendor invoice.	Examine supporting documentation of vouchers.
	Documentation is canceled to prevent reuse.	Examine documentation for indication of cancellation.
	Receiving reports are prenumbered.	Account for numerical sequence of receiving reports.
	Receiving reports are required before approval of invoice for payment.	Discuss policy with management. Observation. Compare payment approval and receiving report dates.
Proper Recording	Vouchers are prenumbered (Completeness).	Account for numerical sequence of vouchers.
	Internal verification of vendor invoice amounts and calculations. (Valuation).	Examine invoice copy for indication of clerical accuracy verification.
	Transactions are recorded as soon as possible after receiving goods. (Timing).	Compare purchases journal dates to receiving report and invoice dates. (Observation).

Objective	*Internal Control*	*Test of Controls*
Proper Recording (cont'd)	Purchase orders are prenumbered (Completeness).	Account for numerical sequence of purchase orders.
	A chart of accounts is used and is adequate (Classification).	Review adequacy and use of proper accounts. Examine sales documents to determine if sales transactions are properly classified.
Accountability and Comparison	Independent reconciliation of bank statement.	Observation. Review bank reconciliation.
	Checks are signed only with appropriate support, by the treasurer, and the treasurer mails the checks.	Observation. Examine canceled check signatures.
	Monthly suppliers' statements are compared to accounts payable.	Examine statements for indication of agreement.
	Receiving Department examines quantity and quality of merchandise upon receipt.	Examine copies of receiving reports and purchase orders for indication of goods received.
	Accountability is established for unused and voided checks.	Discuss policy with management.
Protection and Limited Access	Separation of functions between accounts payable and custody of signed checks.	Observation. Review employee job descriptions.
	Checks are prenumbered.	Account for numerical sequence of checks.
	Mechanical check protector is used.	Examine check copies for evidence of check protector use.
	Separation of Purchasing Department functions from receiving and record keeping.	Observation. Review employee job descriptions.
	Physical control of unused checks is properly and securely maintained.	Observation. Discuss policy with management.

5. Inventory & Production Cycle

Objective	*Internal Control*	*Test of Controls*
Authorization	Movement of inventory items is authorized by requisitions.	Examine requisitions for indication of approval. Inquire of client personnel.
	Inventory purchases are appropriately authorized.	Select a sample of recorded purchases and vouch to documents authorizing purchase.
	Write-offs and write-downs of obsolete inventory are appropriately authorized.	Examine appropriate documentation for indication of authorization.
Validity	Receiving prepares prenumbered receiving reports.	Account for numerical sequence of receiving reports.
	Payment for inventory is approved only after verification of quantity and prices of vendor invoice.	Examine documentation for indication of verification.
Proper Recording	Merchandise receiving reports are matched with vendor invoices (Valuation, Completeness).	Examine vendor invoice copy for indication of agreement with receiving report.
	Purchase orders are prenumbered (Completeness).	Account for numerical sequence of purchase orders.
	Shipping or transfer reports are prenumbered (Completeness).	Account for numerical sequence of reports.
	Movement of inventory items is accounted for on a timely basis by authorized requisitions (Timing, Completeness, Classification).	Compare dates recorded for shipping reports of transferor with receiving report and requisition data of Receiving Department.
	Clerical accuracy of vendor invoices is checked prior to payment (Valuation).	Examine invoice for indication of accuracy check.
Accountability and Comparison	Receiving Department indicates description and quantity of inventory received on prenumbered receiving reports.	Examine receiving reports.
	Perpetual inventory records maintained for large dollar value items.	Review inventory records. Discuss policy with management.
	Periodic comparison made between inventory records and physical inventory.	Review inventory records for indication of agreement with physical count.
Protection and Limited Access	Inventory is stored under the control of a custodian. Access is limited.	Observation. Discuss procedures with management and custodian.
	Inventory purchasers and handlers are bonded.	Review appropriate documentation of bonding.
	Inventory records are maintained separate from the functions of shipping, receiving, and custody.	Observation.

Objective	Internal Control	Test of Controls
Protection and Limited Access (cont'd)	Physical safeguards against theft and fire exist.	Examine physical safeguards.
	Insurance coverage on inventory is adequate.	Review insurance policies.

6. Personnel & Payroll Cycle

Objective	Internal Control	Test of Controls
Authorization	Employment is authorized before hiring.	Review hiring policies and verify the hiring authorization of a sample of employees.
	Payment rates (including commissions and bonuses) and hours to be worked are authorized at the appropriate levels.	Examine approval for rates or union contracts and approval for hours to be worked.
	Deduction authorizations are obtained for each payroll deduction.	Review personnel file for authorizations.
	Personnel Department authorizes all changes to payroll master file.	Review change authorizations for sample of changes made during the year.
	Authorized signature(s) required on payroll checks.	Examine payroll checks for evidence of appropriate signature(s).
Validity	Time clock is used to record time worked by employees.	Observation.
	Department head or foreman approves and signs time cards.	Examine time cards for indication of approval.
	A paymaster (with no other payroll responsibilities) distributes payroll checks.	Observation. Discuss policy with management.
	Personnel Department keeps personnel files on each employee.	Review personnel files.
	Terminations are properly documented.	Review personnel files.
Proper Recording	Accounting procedures require recording payroll transactions as timely as possible (Timing).	Compare time card dates with recording date and paycheck dates for proper timing.
	Job time tickets are reconciled to time clock cards.	Examine job time tickets for indication of reconciliation and/or approval.
	An adequate chart of accounts is maintained including appropriate payroll accounts (Classification).	Review adequacy and use of proper accounts.
	Calculation and amounts of payroll are internally verified. (Completeness, Valuation).	Examine indication of internal verification.

Objective	*Internal Control*	*Test of Controls*
Proper Recording (cont'd)	Account classification of payroll-related transactions is internally verified (Classification).	Review reconciliation of monthly payroll with labor distribution.
Accountability and Comparison	Independent reconciliation of bank statement for imprest payroll account.	Observation. Review reconciliation of bank statement.
	Unclaimed payroll checks are returned to a person responsible for their custody (e.g., internal audit).	Discuss policy with management. Observe distribution of paychecks. Inquire of client personnel.
	Accountability is established for unused and voided payroll account checks.	Discuss policy with management and personnel responsible for check accountability (Observation).
Protection and Limited Access	Separation of personnel, payroll, and timekeeping functions.	Observation. Discuss functions with management.
	Use of a separate imprest payroll account.	Review separate documentation such as bank statements.
	Payroll checks are prenumbered.	Account for numerical sequence of payroll checks.
	Treasurer signs payroll checks.	Observation. Examine canceled payroll checks.

7. Property, Plant & Equipment Cycle

Objective	*Internal Control*	*Test of Controls*
Authorization	Authorization is required for all purchases over a certain amount.	Discuss policy with management. Review documentation of a sample of large purchases for indication of approval.
Validity	Major purchases require authorization by the board of directors.	Examine documentation of major purchases for approval by board. Review minutes of board meetings.
	Movements or sales of equipment have prior approval.	Examine appropriate documentation for existence of approval.
	Abandonments are reported to Accounting Department by operations supervisors.	Discuss abandonment policy with management and operations supervisors.
	Purchases are supported by appropriate authorizations, purchase order, receiving report, and vendor invoice.	Examine acquisition files for supporting documentation.
	Policies exist for classification of fixed assets, including a policy for expensing or capitalizing items (Classification).	Examine written policies. Vouch a selected sample of capitalized and expensed disbursements for compliance with policies.
	Policies exist for asset life estimations and depreciation tables used (Valuation, Timing).	Review written policies. Discuss with management. Vouch a sample of items for compliance with policies.

Objective	*Internal Control*	*Test of Controls*
Validity (cont'd)	Depreciation charges are recorded in subsidiary ledgers and amounts are internally verified periodically (Valuation, Completeness).	Examine subsidiary ledgers for appropriate depreciation charges and evidence of internal verification.
	Accounting procedures require timely recording of purchases and associated depreciation (Timing).	Compare receiving report dates, invoice dates, and recording dates for appropriate timing.
Accountability and Comparison	Subsidiary ledgers exist and are used.	Verify the existence of subsidiary ledgers and review entry detail for appropriateness.
	The responsibility for small tools is assigned to operations supervisors.	Review tool responsibility with management and operations supervisors. Examine the internal verification of the existence of tools.
	Internal verification is performed to examine existence and condition of fixed assets on a periodic basis.	Discuss policy with internal audit. Examine records for indication of verification.
Protection and Limited Access	Equipment has identification numbers to protect against loss.	Examine assets for existence of identification numbers.
	Insurance coverage on property, plant, and equipment is adequate.	Review insurance policies for adequacy of coverage.
	Physical safeguards are available for protection of assets from fire and theft (e.g., fire extinguishers, burglar alarms, etc.).	Examine physical safeguards for adequacy.

V. General Internal Control Questionnaires

A. Control Environment

This questionnaire's objective is to determine if responsibilities are defined and authority is assigned to specific individuals to permit identification of whether persons are acting within the scope of their authority.

Management Philosophy and Operating Style

1. Does management have clear objectives in terms of budget, profit, and other financial and operating goals?
2. Are policies
   a. Clearly written?
   b. Communicated throughout the entity?
   c. Actively monitored?
3. Does management adequately consider the effects of taking business risks?

Organizational Structure

1. Is the organization of the entity clearly defined in terms of lines of authority and responsibility?
2. Does the entity have a current organization chart?
3. Are policies and procedures for authorization of transactions established at adequately high levels?

Audit Committee

1. Does the board of directors have an audit committee?
2. Does the audit committee take an active role in overseeing the entity's accounting and financial reporting policies and practices?
3. Does the audit committee
   a. Hold regular meetings?
   b. Appoint members with adequate qualifications?
   c. Adequately assist the board in meeting its fiduciary responsibilities?
   d. Assist the board in maintaining a direct line of communication with the internal and external auditors?

Methods of Assigning Authority and Responsibility

1. Does the entity have code of conduct and conflict of interest requirements?
2. Are employees given job descriptions which delineate specific duties, reporting relationships, and constraints?
3. Has the entity developed computer systems documentation which indicates procedures for authorizing transactions and approving systems changes?

Management Control Methods

1. Are there regular meetings of the board of directors and are minutes of such meetings prepared on a timely basis?

2. Does the entity have in place planning and reporting systems that

    a. Identify variances from planned performance?

    b. Communicate variances to the appropriate management level?

    c. Adequately investigate variances?

    d. Allow management to take appropriate and timely corrective action?

3. Has the company established a records retention policy and made arrangements for the storage of the information?

Internal Audit Function

1. Does the entity have an internal audit function?

2. If the entity has an internal audit function

    a. Are internal auditors independent of the activities they audit?

    b. Is the internal audit function adequately staffed?

    c. Do internal auditors document internal control and perform tests of controls?

    d. Do internal auditors perform substantive tests of the details of transactions and account balances?

    e. Do internal auditors document the planning and execution of their work?

    f. Do the internal auditors render written reports on their findings and conclusions?

    g. Are internal auditors' reports submitted to the board or to a similar committee?

3. Does management take timely action to correct conditions reported by internal auditors?

Personnel Policies and Procedures

1. Are employees adequately trained?

2. Is performance systematically evaluated?

3. Does the entity dismiss employees on a timely basis for critical violations of control policies?

4. Are employees in positions of trust bonded?

5. Are employees required to take mandatory vacations?

6. Is access to records limited to authorized persons?

B. **Accounting System**
This questionnaire's objective is to determine if accounting policies and procedures are determined in accordance with management's authorization.

- Access to the accounting and financial records is limited to minimize opportunity for errors and fraud, and to provide reasonable protection from physical hazards.
- Accounting entries are initiated and approved in accordance with management's authorization.
- Accounting entries are appropriately accumulated, classified, and summarized.
- The general ledger and related records permit preparation of financial statements in conformity with the applicable financial reporting framework.
- Financial statements with related disclosures are prepared and released in accordance with management's authorization.
- Individuals at appropriate levels consider reliable information in making estimates and judgments required for preparation of the financial statements and related disclosures.

General Accounting

1. Does the entity have adequate written statements and explanations of its accounting policies and procedures, such as

  a. Chart of accounts?

  b. Assignment of responsibilities and delegation of authority?

  c. Explanations of documentation and approval requirements for various types of transactions and journal entries?

2. Is access to the general ledger and related records restricted to those who are assigned general ledger responsibilities?

3. Is appropriate insurance coverage maintained (such as loss of records coverage and fidelity bonding of employees in positions of trust) in accordance with management's authorization?

4. Are all journal entries reviewed and approved?

5. Are all journal entries explained and supported?

6. Are individuals who review and approve journal entries independent of initiation of the entries they are authorized to approve?

Preparation of Financial Statements

1. Are the general ledger accounts arranged in orderly groupings which are conducive to efficient statement preparation?

2. Are there adequate instructions and procedures for:

  a. Assignment of specific preparation and review responsibilities?

  b. Accumulation of information on intercompany transactions?

  c. Accumulation of information for footnote disclosure?

3. Are estimates and adjustments to provide valuation allowances reviewed and approved by appropriate levels in the organization independent of the persons originating the estimates and adjustments?

4. Are procedures adequate for the review and comparison of working papers to source data, and comparison of elimination and reclassification entries to those made in prior periods?

5. Are financial statements subjected to overall review and comparisons with the prior period and with budgeted amounts by appropriate levels of management?

VI. Transaction Cycle Internal Control Questionnaires

A. Revenue & Receivables

This questionnaire's objectives are to determine if the types of goods and services provided, the manner in which they will be provided, and the customers to which they will be provided are in accordance with management's authorization.

- The prices and other terms of sales are established in accordance with management's authorization.
- Credit terms and limits are established.
- Goods delivered and services provided are based on orders which have been approved.
- Deliveries of goods and services result in preparation of accurate and timely billings.
- Sales related deductions and adjustments are made in accordance with management's authorization.

1. Are sales orders approved before shipment?
2. Do approved sales orders record the terms of sales in detail?
3. Are unfilled sales commitments periodically reviewed?
4. Is current information on prices, discounts, sales taxes, freight, warranties, and returned goods clearly communicated to the sales and billing personnel (i.e., approved sales catalogs, manuals, and price lists)?
5. Is the credit of prospective customers investigated before it is extended to them?
6. Is there a periodic review of credit limits?
7. Are shipping documents prepared for all shipments?
8. Are goods shipped based on documented sales orders which have been approved?
9. Are shipping documents subjected to
   a. Timely communication to persons who physically perform the shipping function?
   b. Timely communication to persons who perform the billing function?
10. Are quantities of goods shipped verified by double counting or comparison with counts by common carriers?
11. Are shipping documents compared with billings to determine that all goods shipped are billed and accounted for?
12. Are sales invoices prepared for all shipments of goods?
13. Are sales invoices
    a. Matched with approved sales orders?
    b. Matched with shipping documents?
14. Are credit memos

   a. Prenumbered and accounted for?

   b. Matched with applicable receiving reports for returns?

   c. Approved by a responsible employee independent of the person preparing the credit memo?

15. Are monthly statements reviewed and mailed by a responsible employee who is independent of the accounts receivable and cash functions?

16. Is an aging schedule of past due accounts prepared monthly?

17. Is there documentation of review and analysis of accounts receivable balances for determining valuation allowances and any specific balances to be written off?

18. Are valuation allowances and write-offs approved?

B. Cash Receipts

This questionnaire's objectives are to determine if access to cash receipts records, accounts receivable records, and billing and shipping records is controlled to prevent the interception and theft of unrecorded cash receipts or theft of recorded cash receipts.

- Detailed transaction and account balance records are reconciled with control accounts and bank statements at least monthly for the timely detection and correction of errors.
- All cash receipts are recorded at the correct amounts in the period in which received and are classified and summarized properly.

1. Does the person who opens the mail

   a. Place restrictive endorsements on all checks received so they are for deposit only?

   b. List all remittances and prepare totals daily?

   c. Forward all remittances to the person who prepares and makes a daily bank deposit?

2. Are currency receipts forwarded daily to the person who prepares the daily bank deposit?

3. Is a summary listing of daily currency receipts forwarded to a person independent of physical handling of remittances and accounts receivable?

4. Are each day's receipts deposited intact daily?

5. Are all employees who handle receipts adequately bonded?

6. Does company policy prohibit the cashing of any accommodation checks (payroll, personal) out of collections?

7. Are bank charge-backs received directly from the bank and investigated by a person independent of the physical handling of collections and posting of accounts receivable subsidiary ledgers?

8. Are entries to the cash receipts journal compared with

   a. Duplicate deposit slips authenticated by the bank?

   b. Deposits per the bank statement?

   c. Listings prepared when the mail is opened?

9. Is information from remittance documentation adequate for the accurate posting of credits to individual accounts receivable subsidiary records or accounts such as investment income, rents, and sales of property?

10. Are details of collections posted to subsidiary accounts receivable records by a person independent of the general ledger functions, physical handling of collections, and receipt and investigation of bank charge-backs?

C. **Purchases & Accounts Payable**

This questionnaire's objectives are to determine if the types of goods and services to be obtained, the manner in which they are obtained, the vendors from which they are obtained, the quantities to be obtained, and the prices and terms initiated and executed are in accordance with management's authorization.

- Adjustments to vendor accounts and account distributions are made in accordance with management's authorization.
- All goods and services received are accounted for accurately and on a timely basis.
- Only authorized goods and services are accepted and paid for.
- Amounts payable for goods and services received are recorded at the correct amounts in the appropriate period and classified properly.
- Access to purchasing, receiving, and accounts payable records is controlled to prevent or detect duplicate or improper payments.

1. Are written purchase orders used for all commitments and do those orders include the vendor description, quantity, quality, price, terms, and delivery requirements for the goods or services ordered?

2. Is there a record of open purchase commitments?

3. Are open purchase orders periodically reviewed and investigated?

4. Are goods received inspected for condition and independently counted for comparison with the applicable purchase order?

5. Are receiving reports prepared promptly for all goods received?

6. Do receiving reports provide for recording of

   a. Description, quantity, and acceptability of goods?

   b. Date on which the goods or services are received?

   c. Signature of the individual approving the receipt?

7. Are receiving reports subjected to

   a. Accounting for all receiving reports used?

   b. Distribution for timely matching of copies with purchase orders and vendor invoices?

8. Is control established over all invoices received?

9. Are duplicate invoices stamped or destroyed as a precaution against duplicate payment?

10. Are vendors' invoices, prior to payment, compared in detail to purchase orders and receiving reports?

11. Are all available discounts taken?

12. Are there procedures for periodic review and investigation of unprocessed invoices, unmatched purchase orders, and receiving reports to provide for follow-up and proper accruals, and to result in a proper cutoff for financial reporting purposes?

13. Are vendors' statements reviewed for, and proper follow-up made of, overdue items?

D. Payroll

This questionnaire's objectives are to determine if employees are hired and retained only at rates and benefits determined by management's authorization.

- Payroll withholdings and deductions are based on evidence of appropriate authorization.
- Compensation is made only to company employees at authorized rates and for services rendered.
- Gross pay, withholdings, deductions, and net pay are computed correctly using authorized rates and properly authorized withholding exemptions and deductions.
- Payroll costs and related liabilities are accumulated, classified, and summarized correctly in the accounts in the proper period.
- Comparisons are made of personnel, payroll, and work records at reasonable intervals for timely detection and correction of errors.
- Net pay and related withholdings and deductions are remitted to the appropriate employees when due.
- Functions are assigned so that no single individual is in a position to both perpetrate and conceal errors and fraud in the normal course of their duties.
- Access to personnel and payroll records is limited.

1. Are all new hires, rates of pay and changes thereto, changes in position, and terminations based on written authorizations by management's criteria?

2. Are appropriate written authorizations obtained from employees for all payroll deductions and withholding exemptions?

3. Are personnel files maintained on individual employees which include appropriate written authorizations for rates of pay, payroll deductions, and withholding exemptions?

4. Are methods for determining premium pay rates for matters such as overtime, night shift work, and employee benefits determined in accordance with management's authorizations?

5. Do employees who perform the payroll processing function receive timely notification of wage and salary rate changes, new hires, changes in position, terminations, and changes in authorized deductions and withholding exemptions?

6. Is there an adequate chart of accounts for determining account distributions for wages and related taxes and controlling liabilities for payroll deductions and taxes withheld?

7. Are clerical operations in the preparation of payrolls verified by re-performance or reconciliation with independent controls over source data?

8. Are piece rate records reconciled with production records, or salary commission records reconciled with recorded sales, or total production hours reconciled with production statistics?

9. Are payroll checks drawn on a separate imprest account, and are deposits equal to the amount of net pay?

10. Is responsibility for custody and follow-up of unclaimed wages assigned to a responsible person independent of personnel, payroll processing, and cash disbursement functions?

11. Are procedures adequate to result in timely and accurate preparation and filing of payroll tax returns and payment of accumulated withholdings and related accrued taxes?

12. Are personnel and payroll records reasonably safeguarded (locked file cabinets, work areas with limited access)?

E. **Cash Disbursements**

This questionnaire's objectives are to determine if functions are assigned so that no single individual is in a position to both perpetrate and conceal errors or fraud in the normal course of their duties.

- Disbursements are made only for expenditures incurred in accordance with management's authorization.
- Adjustments to cash accounts are made only in accordance with management's authorizations.
- Disbursements are recorded at correct amounts in the appropriate period and are classified properly in the accounts.
- Access to cash and disbursement records is restricted to minimize opportunities for irregular or erroneous disbursements.
- Comparison of detail records, control accounts, and bank statements are made at reasonable intervals for detection and appropriate disposition of errors or fraud.

1. Are bank accounts and check signers authorized by the board of directors?

2. Are approved supporting documents presented with the checks to the check signer?

3. Is a mechanical check protector used to inscribe amounts on checks to protect against alteration?

4. Are supporting documents for checks canceled to avoid reuse?

5. Are signed checks independently mailed directly after signing without being returned to persons involved in the invoice processing, check preparation, and recording functions?

6. Are all voided checks retained and mutilated?

7. Are there written policies that prohibit making checks payable to cash or bearer, and signing blank checks?

8. Are dual signatures required for large disbursements, and are the signers independent of one another?

9. If a check-signing machine is used, are the keys, signature plate, and operation of the signing machine under control at all times of the official whose signature is on the plate? Are employees who have custody of them independent of voucher and check preparation functions, and are they denied access to blank checks?

10. If cash funds are maintained on the premises, they should be kept on an imprest basis; and

    a. Are they kept in a safe place?

    b. Are they reasonable in amount?

    c. Are they controlled by one custodian?

d. Are disbursements supported by vouchers?

e. Are vouchers approved with management's authorization?

f. Are cash funds on a surprise basis counted by someone other than the custodian?

g. Is the custodian independent of cash receipts?

h. Does the custodian have no access to accounting records?

i. Are reimbursements of the cash fund remitted by checks made payable to the order of the custodian?

11. Are old outstanding checks investigated, controlled, and their proper disposition arranged?

F. Inventory & Cost of Sales

This questionnaire's objectives are to determine if all production activity and accounting therefore is determined in accordance with management's general or specific authorizations.

- Resources obtained and used in the production process and completed results are recorded accurately on a timely basis.
- Transfer of finished products to customers and other dispositions such as sales of scrap are recorded accurately.
- Inventory, production costs, and costs of sales are accumulated and classified in the accounts to maintain accountability for costs and permit preparation of statements in conformity with the applicable financial reporting framework.
- Inventory is protected from unauthorized use or removal.
- Recorded balances of inventory are substantiated and evaluated at reasonable intervals by comparison with quantities on hand.

1. Are production goals and schedules based on accompanying sales forecasts?

2. Are methods and materials to be used based upon product engineering plans and specifications?

3. Does the company have budgeted inventory levels and predetermined reorder points authorized by management?

4. Does the company have policies for identification and disposition of excess or obsolete inventory?

5. Are all adjustments to inventory and cost of sales made in accordance with management's authorizations?

6. Are all dispositions of obsolete or excess inventory approved?

7. Does the chart of accounts provide adequate general ledger control accounts and subsidiary detail for the accumulation and classification of costs of materials, direct labor, and overhead?

8. Is access to the detailed inventory records and control accounts limited to persons responsible for their maintenance, oversight, and internal audit?

9. Are there physical safeguards against theft, fire, and flooding?

10. Is insurance coverage of the inventory maintained and reviewed periodically for adequacy?

11. Do detailed written inventory procedures and instructions exist that have been approved and are they adequately communicated to the persons who perform the physical counts?

12. Are inventory physical counts performed by persons whose duties do not include the physical custody and detailed record keeping of inventory or maintenance of control accounts?

13. Are differences in physical counts and detailed records investigated?

14. Are adjustments of the inventory detail records and control accounts given prior approval by management?

15. Are dispositions of obsolete or excess inventories made in accordance with criteria authorized by management?

G. Property, Plant & Equipment

This questionnaire's objectives are to determine if additions and related accumulation of depreciation, retirements, and dispositions of property, plant, and equipment (PPE) are made in accordance with management's authorization.

- Transactions involving PPE and depreciation are recorded, accumulated, and classified accurately in detail and in control accounts to maintain accountability for the assets.
- PPE are reasonably safeguarded from loss.

1. Are work order forms approved by management for property additions?

2. Are contracts and agreements signed by individuals in accordance with appropriately documented designation by the board of directors?

3. Are detailed records maintained for PPE indicating a description of the assets; their location, cost, acquisition date, date of service, depreciable life, and method of depreciation used?

4. Are PPE insured and coverage reviewed periodically for additions, disposals, and adequacy?

5. Is there a written capitalization/expense policy for PPE purchases?

H. Stockholders' Equity & Capital Accounts

This questionnaire's objectives are to determine if capital transactions are authorized and approved in conformity with the entity's governing document (corporate charter, partnership agreement).

- Transactions and obligations are recorded promptly and accurately.
- Access to records, agreements, and negotiable documents is permitted only in accordance with management's authorization.
- Records, agreements, and documents are subjected to adequate physical safeguards and custodial procedures.
- Dividends are disbursed accurately and in conformity with decisions of the board of directors.

1. Are authorizations and approvals for specific capital transactions appropriately recorded?

2. Are two officials authorized by the board required to sign and countersign stock certificates?

3. Are all stock certificates prepared and approved before issuance within management's authorization?

4. Are appropriate control records maintained for each class of stock on information such as number of shares authorized, issued and outstanding, and the number of shares subject to options, warrants, and conversion privileges?

5. Are timely detailed records maintained on specific stock certificates issued and outstanding for each class of capital stock and the identity of holders of record and the number of shares for each certificate?

6. Are detailed stock certificate records reconciled at reasonable intervals with the control records and the general ledger?

7. Are reconciliations of detailed records with the control records and general ledger performed by persons independent of custody of unissued stock certificates, maintenance of the detailed records, and cash functions?

8. Are unissued stock certificates, reacquired certificates, and detailed stockholder records subject to reasonable physical safeguards?

9. Are stock certificates prenumbered so that all certificates (unissued, issued, and retired) may be accounted for?

10. Are retired stock certificates examined for proper endorsement and effectively canceled by a person whose duties do not include maintenance of the detailed stockholder records?

11. Are treasury stock certificates registered in the name of the company and recorded to be readily distinguished from other outstanding shares?

12. Are dividends declared recorded in the minutes of the board of directors meetings?

13. Do procedures result in an accurate cutoff and accurate listing of stockholders as of the record date?

14. Are total dividends disbursed reconciled to total outstanding shares as of the record date?

VII. General Internal Control Questions

General Control Questions	Cash Receipts	Cash Disbursements	Payroll
1. Are forms used that are prenumbered?	Prenumbered Receipts, Cash Register tapes by date	Prenumbered Checks	Prenumbered Payroll Checks
2. Is adequate control maintained of unissued forms to prevent misuse?	Unused Blank Receipts controlled	Unused Blank Checks controlled	Unused Blank Payroll Checks controlled
3. Are policies and procedures in place for the authorization of transactions?	Remittance listing prepared by designated mail opener.	Check signers authorized by board of directors. Authorization for bank accounts to be maintained.	Payroll approved in writing by responsible employee prior to issuance of paychecks.
4. Is approval of transaction obtained prior to processing?	Comparison of remittance listing and validated deposit slip before processing.	Invoice matched to approved receiving report and approved purchase order. Disbursements and bank transfers approved.	Supervisor reviews and approves time cards.
5. Is a proper segregation of duties maintained to reduce potential errors and fraud?	Employee responsible for preparing remittance lists independent of billing, cash disbursement, and general ledger functions. Employee making deposit independent of cash disbursement, billing, and general ledger functions.	Employee performing bank reconciliation independent of invoice processing, cash disbursements, cash receipts, petty cash, and general ledger functions.	Payroll checks signed by treasurer. Payroll checks distributed by person independent of personnel, payroll preparation, time—keeping, and check preparation.
6. Are all prenumbered forms accounted for?	Detail Cash Receipts Journal	Outstanding check list maintained.	Payroll Journal, Outstanding check list maintained.
7. Is a detailed record of transactions maintained?	Cash Receipts Journal	Check Register, Cash Disbursements Journal	Payroll Journal
8. Are periodic (monthly, annual) reconciliations made between source documents, quantities on hand, subsidiary ledgers, and the general ledger?	Trace cash receipts journal total to bank statement and/or validated deposit slips.	Bank reconciliations, Cash Disbursements Journal reconciled to general ledger.	Time card hours reconciled to job time tickets.
9. Is access to assets and/or accounting records limited?	Mail received by same person daily who is independent of cash, billings, general ledger and shipping functions.	Bank statement received directly by person who will reconcile.	Payroll records and Personnel files kept in locked file cabinets.
10. Are transactions and source documents checked for clerical accuracy?	Remittance list footed and agreed to validated deposit slip.	Checks compared to approved invoice and supporting documents before signing. Discounts, if available, have been taken.	Time card totals checked by supervisor.
11. Is there a proper cutoff of transactions for accurate reporting?	Bank reconciliations are prepared and approved on a timely basis.	Bank reconciliations are pre-pared and approved on a timely basis.	Bank reconciliations are pre-pared and approved on a timely basis.

Inventory	Cost of Sales	Fixed Assets	Accounts Receivable	Accounts Payable
Prenumbered: Shipping Documents, Purchase Orders, Receiving Reports	Prenumbered Inventory Requisitions	Prenumbered Purchase Orders	Prenumbered Invoices	Prenumbered Vouchers
Unused Purchase Orders, Receiving Reports, Shipping Documents controlled.	Unused Inventory Requisitions controlled.	Unused Purchased Orders controlled	Unused Invoices controlled	Unused Vouchers controlled
Purchases made in accordance with vendor acceptability. Customer Acceptance/Terms of Sale, credit clearance all preestablished.	Pre-established overhead rates, requisition processing controls	Additions/Retirements have authorization in Board of Directors meeting minutes.	Invoices prepared from approved shipping reports and matching vendor purchase orders.	Authorization by Board of Directors for large purchases (contracts).
Approved purchase order, Approved inventory requisitions, sales orders approved before shipment	Inventory requisitions, overhead rate changes and personnel rate changes are properly approved.	Approval of additions and retirements in writing; Board minutes, manager approval.	Approval noted on invoice.	Invoices and supporting documents approved before payment.
Credit, Sales, Shipping, Billing, Collections, receiving, and general accounting all independent of one another.	Authority to approve inventory requisitions assigned to employees independent of physical custody, and maintenance of inventory records and inventory control accounts.	Responsibility for physical custody assigned to employees independent of maintaining detailed property records and general ledger functions.	Individual responsible for accounts receivable function is independent of cash and general ledger functions.	Vendors' invoices processed by employee independent of purchasing, receiving, shipping, and cash functions.
Purchase Orders, Shipping Documents, Receiving Reports	Work Orders, Inventory Requisitions	Physical asset identi-fication plates numbered consecutively	Numbered sales invoices properly filed.	Numbered vouchers and Purchase Orders maintained in open, pending, or paid files.
Shipment Log, Receiving Log, Purchases Journal	Work-in-Process and Finished Goods journals	Detailed listing of fixed assets maintained	Sales Invoice Register	Purchases Journal and Accounts Payable Subsidiary Ledger maintained
Inventory physically counted annually. Inventory detail records and control accounts reconciled to physical count. Perpetual records reconciled to general ledger and physical counts.	Cost accounting system reconciled to general ledger.	Detailed records of assets compared to actual PPE on hand, and reconciled to general ledger.	Accounts receivable subsidiary ledger reconciled to general ledger control account.	Accounts payable sub-sidiary ledger reconciled with general ledger control account.
Finished goods and merchandise are restricted so that withdrawals are based on approved sales orders.	Releases from storage of raw materials and supplies based upon approved requisitions.	Physical controls such as fences, burglar alarms, fire alarms, security guards, and requisitioning procedures for the use of portable equipment.	Passwords used on computer system limiting data entry to designated individuals.	Passwords used on computer system limiting data entry to designated individuals.
Receiving Reports, Shipping Documents, Purchase Orders	Inventory Requisitions checked	Invoices compared to approved purchase order and totals including taxes and freight are checked for reasonableness.	Sales Invoices	Vendors' Invoices
Inventory received included, goods on consignment included, goods sold but not shipped excluded from inventory totals.	See Inventory	Cash receipts and dis-bursements checked and compared to bank reconciliation for cutoff.	Shipping documents and related billings compared for proper cutoff.	Receiving reports or service dates and vendor invoices compared prior to recording.

The CPA Exam

The exam is one component of the CPA licensing requirements—it is designed to measure the technical competence of candidates.

It is to your advantage to take the exam as soon as possible after completing the formal education requirements because it is essentially an academic exam that tests the breadth of material covered by a good accounting curriculum. The exam emphasizes the body of knowledge and entry-level skills required for the practice of public accounting.

Although licensing occurs at the state or territory level (usually by a board of accountancy), the exam is uniform at all sites and has national acceptance. Passing the exam in one jurisdiction generally allows you to obtain a reciprocal certificate or license in another jurisdiction if you meet that jurisdiction's other requirements.

Each jurisdiction sets its own requirements for education, examination, and experience. Boards of accountancy rely upon other means to ensure that candidates possess the necessary attributes, including background checks, interviews, letters of reference, affidavits of employment, ethics exams, and educational requirements. The NASBA website (nasba.org) has links to all of the board sites.

More helpful exam information is included in "Appendix B: Exam Preparation Tips."

CHAPTER 3—INTERNAL CONTROL

Problem 3-1 MULTIPLE-CHOICE QUESTIONS

Understanding of the Entity's Internal Control

1. Proper segregation of duties reduces the opportunities to allow persons to be in positions to both
   a. Journalize entries and prepare financial statements
   b. Record cash receipts and cash disbursements
   c. Establish internal controls and authorize transactions
   d. Perpetrate and conceal errors and fraud (ID: 5099)

2. Which of the following is **not** a component of an entity's internal control?
   a. Control risk
   b. Control activities
   c. The information system
   d. The control environment (ID: 86)

3. Which of the following are considered control environment factors?

	Detection risk	Personnel policies and practices
a.	Yes	Yes
b.	Yes	No
c.	No	Yes
d.	No	No

(ID: 5102)

4. Which of the following is a management control method that most likely could improve management's ability to supervise company activities effectively?
   a. Monitoring compliance with internal control requirements imposed by regulatory bodies
   b. Limiting direct access to assets by physical segregation and protective devices
   c. Establishing budgets and forecasts to identify variances from expectations
   d. Supporting employees with the resources necessary to discharge their responsibilities (ID: 5955)

5. Which of the following events most likely would indicate the existence of related parties?
   a. Granting stock options to key executives at favorable prices
   b. High turnover of senior management and members of the board of directors
   c. Failure to correct internal control weaknesses on a timely basis
   d. Selling real estate at a price significantly different from appraised value (ID: 8159)

6. The overall attitude and awareness of an entity's board of directors concerning the importance of internal control usually is reflected in its
   a. Computer-based controls
   b. System of segregation of duties
   c. Control environment
   d. Safeguards over access to assets (ID: 5643)

7. In an audit of financial statements, an auditor's primary consideration regarding an internal control policy or procedure is whether the policy or procedure
   a. Reflects management's philosophy and operating style
   b. Affects management's financial statement assertions
   c. Provides adequate safeguards over access to assets
   d. Enhances management's decision-making processes (ID: 5101)

8. Proper segregation of functional responsibilities in an effective internal control structure calls for separation of the functions of

   a. Authorization, payment, and recording
   b. Authorization, recording, and custody
   c. Custody, execution, and reporting
   d. Authorization, execution, and payment (ID: 92)

9. Which of the following situations most likely could lead to an embezzlement scheme?

   a. The accounts receivable bookkeeper receives a list of payments prepared by the cashier and personally makes entries in the customers' accounts receivable subsidiary ledger.
   b. Each vendor invoice is matched with the related purchase order and receiving report by the vouchers payable bookkeeper who personally approves the voucher for payment.
   c. Access to blank checks and signature plates is restricted to the cash disbursements bookkeeper who personally reconciles the monthly bank statement.
   d. Vouchers and supporting documentation are examined and then canceled by the treasurer who personally mails the checks to vendors. (ID: 8818)

10. Which of the following factors is most relevant when an auditor considers the client's organizational structure in the context of control risk?

    a. Management's attitude toward information processing and accounting departments
    b. The organization's recruiting and hiring practices
    c. Physical proximity of the accounting function to upper management
    d. The suitability of the client's lines of reporting (ID: 8845)

11. Which of the following is **not** a component of internal control?

    a. Control environment
    b. Control activities
    c. Inherent risk
    d. Monitoring (ID: 9918)

12. Which of the following most likely would **not** be considered an inherent limitation of the potential effectiveness of an entity's internal control?

    a. Incompatible duties
    b. Management override
    c. Mistakes in judgment
    d. Collusion among employees (ID: 4687)

13. Which of the following auditor concerns most likely could be so serious that the auditor concludes that a financial statement audit cannot be conducted?

    a. The entity has no formal written code of conduct.
    b. The integrity of the entity's management is suspect.
    c. Procedures requiring segregation of duties are subject to management override.
    d. Management fails to modify prescribed controls for changes in conditions. (ID: 5953)

14. Which of the following factors would most likely be considered an inherent limitation to an entity's internal control?

    a. The complexity of the information processing system
    b. Human judgment in the decision making process
    c. The ineffectiveness of the board of directors
    d. The lack of management incentives to improve the control environment (ID: 8136)

15. Which of the following factors would **least** likely affect the extent of the auditor's consideration of the client's internal controls?

 a. The amount of time budgeted to complete the engagement
 b. The size and complexity of the client
 c. The nature of specific relevant controls
 d. The auditor's prior experience with client operations (ID: 8138)

16. An auditor would most likely be concerned with internal control policies and procedures that provide reasonable assurance about the

 a. Methods of assigning production tasks to employees
 b. Appropriate prices the entity should charge for its products
 c. Efficiency of management's decision-making process
 d. Entity's ability to process and summarize financial data (ID: 2303)

17. In obtaining an understanding of an entity's internal control in a financial statement audit, an auditor is **not** obligated to

 a. Determine whether the control procedures have been implemented
 b. Perform procedures to understand the design of the internal control policies
 c. Document the understanding of the entity's internal control
 d. Search for significant deficiencies in the operation of the entity's internal control (ID: 4256)

18. In obtaining an understanding of an entity's internal control, an auditor is required to obtain knowledge about the

	Operating effectiveness of policies and procedures	Design of policies and procedures	
a.	Yes	Yes	
b.	No	Yes	
c.	Yes	No	
d.	No	No	(ID: 3908)

19. When obtaining an understanding of an entity's internal control, an auditor should concentrate on the implementation of the procedures because

 a. The procedures may be operating effectively but may not be documented.
 b. Management may implement procedures whose costs exceed their benefits.
 c. The procedures may be so inappropriate that no reliance is contemplated by the auditor.
 d. Management may establish appropriate procedures but not enforce compliance with them. (ID: 4686)

20. An auditor should obtain sufficient knowledge of an entity's accounting system to understand the

 a. Safeguards used to limit access to computer facilities
 b. Process used to prepare significant accounting estimates
 c. Procedures used to assure proper authorization of transactions
 d. Policies used to detect the concealment of fraud (ID: 4685)

21. When considering internal control, an auditor should be aware of the concept of reasonable assurance, which recognizes that

 a. Internal control policies and procedures may be ineffective due to mistakes in judgment and personal carelessness.
 b. Adequate safeguards over access to assets and records should permit an entity to maintain proper accountability.
 c. Establishing and maintaining internal control is an important responsibility of management.
 d. The cost of an entity's internal control should not exceed the benefits expected to be derived. (ID: 5644)

22. Which of the following auditor concerns most likely could be so serious that the auditor concludes that a financial statement audit cannot be performed?
    a. Management fails to modify prescribed internal controls for changes in information technology.
    b. Internal control activities requiring segregation of duties are rarely monitored by management.
    c. Management is dominated by one person who is also the majority stockholder.
    d. There is a substantial risk of intentional misapplication of accounting principles. (ID: 7099)

23. Which of the following procedures most likely would provide an auditor with evidence about whether an entity's internal control activities are suitably designed to prevent or detect material misstatements?
    a. Reperforming the activities for a sample of transactions
    b. Performing analytical procedures using data aggregated at a high level
    c. Vouching a sample of transactions directly related to the activities
    d. Observing the entity's personnel applying the activities (ID: 6393)

24. Which of the following is an inherent limitation in internal control?
    a. Incompatible duties
    b. Lack of segregation of duties
    c. Faulty human judgment
    d. Lack of an audit committee (ID: 8377)

25. Which of the following factors most likely would cause a CPA to decide **not** to accept a new audit engagement?
    a. The CPA's lack of understanding of the prospective client's internal auditor's computer-assisted audit techniques
    b. Management's disregard of its responsibility to maintain an adequate internal control environment
    c. The CPA's inability to determine whether related party transactions were consummated on terms equivalent to arm's-length transactions
    d. Management's refusal to permit the CPA to perform substantive tests before the year-end (ID: 6928)

26. Which of the following is an inherent limitation of internal controls?
    a. Judgmental sampling
    b. Collusion
    c. Segregation of duties
    d. Employee peer review (ID: 8621)

27. Which of the following represents an inherent limitation of internal controls?
    a. Bank reconciliations are not performed on a timely basis.
    b. The CEO can request a check with no purchase order.
    c. Customer credit checks are not performed.
    d. Shipping documents are not matched to sales invoices. (ID: 8836)

28. An audit client failed to maintain copies of its procedures manuals and organizational flowcharts. What should the auditor do in an audit of financial statements?
    a. Issue a qualified opinion on the basis of a scope limitation.
    b. Document the auditor's understanding of internal controls.
    c. Assess control risk at the maximum level.
    d. Restrict the auditor's responsibility to assess the effectiveness of controls in the audit engagement letter. (ID: 8639)

29. Which of the following factors is most likely to affect the extent of the documentation of the auditor's understanding of a client's system of internal controls?
    a. The industry and the business and regulatory environments in which the client operates
    b. The degree to which information technology is used in the accounting function
    c. The relationship between management, the board of directors, and external stakeholders
    d. The degree to which the auditor intends to use internal audit personnel to perform substantive tests (ID: 9358)

30. An auditor is concerned about a policy of management override as a limitation of internal control. Which of the following tests would best assess the validity of the auditor's concern?
    a. Matching purchase orders to accounts payable
    b. Verifying that approved spending limits are **not** exceeded
    c. Tracing sales orders to the revenue account
    d. Reviewing minutes of board meetings (ID: 9383)

31. Which of the following should an auditor do when control risk is assessed at the maximum level?
    a. Perform fewer substantive tests of details.
    b. Perform more tests of controls.
    c. Document the assessment.
    d. Document the control structure more extensively. (ID: 9943)

Tests of Controls

32. The objective of tests of details of transactions performed as tests of controls is to
    a. Monitor the design and use of entity documents such as prenumbered shipping forms
    b. Determine whether internal controls have been implemented
    c. Detect material misstatements in the account balances of the financial statements
    d. Evaluate whether internal control procedures operated effectively (ID: 5115)

33. Which of the following types of evidence would an auditor most likely examine to determine whether internal control policies and procedures are operating as designed?
    a. Gross margin information regarding the client's industry
    b. Confirmations of receivables verifying account balances
    c. Client records documenting the use of computer programs
    d. Anticipated results documented in budgets or forecasts (ID: 5958)

34. Audit evidence concerning segregation of duties ordinarily is best obtained by
    a. Performing tests of transactions that corroborate management's financial statement assertions
    b. Observing the employees as they apply control procedures
    c. Obtaining a flowchart of activities performed by available personnel
    d. Developing audit objectives that reduce control risk (ID: 3906)

35. Which of the following statements is correct concerning the use of prior audit evidence regarding the operating effectiveness of controls?
    a. If the auditor plans to rely on controls that have changed since they were last tested, the auditor should test those controls at least once every three years.
    b. If the auditor plans to rely on controls that have not changed since they were last tested, the auditor should test the controls at least once in every third audit and should test some controls during each audit.
    c. If the auditor plans to rely on controls that have not changed since they were last tested, the auditor should test those controls at least every other year.
    d. If the auditor plans to rely on controls that mitigate a significant risk, those controls should be tested at least every other year. (ID: 8267)

36. Which of the following audit techniques ordinarily would provide an auditor with the **least** assurance about the operating effectiveness of an internal control activity?

    a. Inquiry of client personnel
    b. Inspection of documents and reports
    c. Observation of client personnel
    d. Preparation of system flowcharts (ID: 7810)

37. After testing a client's internal control activities, an auditor discovers a material weakness in the operation of a client's internal controls. Under these circumstances the auditor most likely would

    a. Issue a disclaimer of opinion about the internal controls as part of the auditor's report
    b. Increase the assessment of control risk and increase the extent of substantive tests
    c. Issue a qualified opinion of this finding as part of the auditor's report
    d. Withdraw from the audit because the internal controls are ineffective (ID: 8375)

38. The ultimate purpose of assessing control risk is to contribute to the auditor's evaluation of the risk that

    a. Specific internal control activities are not operating as designed.
    b. The collective effect of the control environment may not achieve the control objectives.
    c. Tests of controls may fail to identify activities relevant to assertions.
    d. Material misstatements may exist in the financial statements. (ID: 8402)

39. A client maintains a large data center where access is limited to authorized employees. How may an auditor best determine the effectiveness of this control activity?

    a. Inspect the policy manual establishing this control activity.
    b. Ask the chief technology officer about known problems.
    c. Observe whether the data center is monitored.
    d. Obtain a list of current data center employees. (ID: 8616)

40. When an auditor plans to rely on controls that have changed since they were last tested, which of the following courses of action would be most appropriate?

    a. Test the operating effectiveness of such controls in the current audit
    b. Document that reliance and proceed with the original audit strategy
    c. Inquire of management as to the effectiveness of the controls
    d. Report the reliance in the report on internal controls (ID: 9384)

41. An auditor has identified the controller's review of the bank reconciliation as a control to test. In connection with this test, the auditor interviews the controller to understand the specific data reviewed on the reconciliation. In addition, the auditor verifies that the bank reconciliation is properly prepared by the accountant and reviewed by the controller as evidenced by their respective sign-offs. Which of the following types of audit procedures do these actions illustrate?

    a. Observation and inspection of records
    b. Confirmation and reperformance
    c. Inquiry and inspection of records
    d. Analytical procedures and reperformance (ID: 9916)

Communicating Internal Control Related Matters Identified in an Audit

42. Which of the following is true regarding significant deficiencies and material weaknesses in an audit of financial statements?

    a. Auditors must search for them.
    b. Auditors must communicate them to management and those charged with governance.
    c. Auditors must communicate them to those charged with governance.
    d. They must be disclosed in the notes to the financial statements. (ID: 8142)

43. Which of the following is **least** likely to indicate the existence of a material weakness in internal control?
    a. Fraud on the part of senior management
    b. Previously issued financial statements were restated to reflect the correction of a material misstatement due to error or fraud
    c. Those charged with governance exercise ineffective oversight of the entity's financial reporting and internal control
    d. There is substantial doubt about the entity's ability to continue as a going concern. (ID: 9037)

44. Which of the following statements is correct concerning an auditor's required communication of significant deficiencies and material weaknesses identified during an audit of financial statements?
    a. A significant deficiency previously communicated during the prior year's audit that remains uncorrected causes a scope limitation.
    b. An auditor should perform tests of controls on significant deficiencies before communicating them to the client.
    c. An auditor's written communication on deficiencies in internal control should include a restriction on the use of the communication.
    d. An auditor should communicate significant deficiencies after tests of controls, but before commencing substantive tests. (ID: 5118)

45. Which of the following statements should **not** be included in a written communication regarding significant deficiencies and material weaknesses identified in an audit of financial statements?
    a. The auditor's consideration of internal control was not designed to identify all deficiencies in internal control that might be significant deficiencies or material weaknesses.
    b. There were no significant deficiencies identified during the audit.
    c. A material weakness is a deficiency, or combination of deficiencies, in internal control, such that there is a reasonable possibility that a material misstatement of the entity's financial statements will not be prevented, or detected and corrected on a timely basis.
    d. The purpose of the auditor's consideration of internal control was to express an opinion on the financial statements, but not to express an opinion on the effectiveness of the entity's internal control. (ID: 2957)

46. A deficiency in internal control exists when misstatements of the financial statements may occur and not be prevented, detected, or corrected on a timely basis by
    a. Outside consultants who issue a special-purpose report on internal control
    b. Management or employees in the normal course of performing their assigned functions
    c. Management when reviewing interim financial statements and reconciling account balances
    d. An independent auditor during the testing of controls phase of the consideration of internal control (ID: 7489)

47. Which of the following factors should an auditor consider in evaluating the severity a deficiency in internal control to determine if it should be communicated to management and those charged with governance, i.e., that it is a significant deficiency or a material weakness?

    I. Magnitude of the potential misstatement
    II. Likelihood of the misstatement

    a. I only
    b. II only
    c. Both I and II
    d. Neither I nor II (7105)

48. An auditor's written communication regarding significant deficiencies and material weaknesses identified during a financial statement audit should
    a. Include a brief description of the tests of controls performed in searching for significant deficiencies and material weaknesses
    b. Indicate that the purpose of the auditor's consideration of internal control was to express an opinion on the financial statements but not to express an opinion on the effectiveness of the entity's internal control
    c. Include a paragraph describing management's assertion concerning the effectiveness of internal control
    d. Indicate that the deficiencies should be disclosed in the annual report to the entity's shareholders (ID: 5982)

49. Which of the following actions should the auditor take in response to discovering a deviation from the prescribed control procedure?
    a. Make inquiries to understand the potential consequence of the deviation
    b. Assume that the deviation is an isolated occurrence without audit significance
    c. Report the matter to the next higher level of authority within the entity
    d. Increase sample size of tests of controls (ID: 8821)

50. Regarding internal control related matters identified in an audit of financial statements, the auditor should include in the written communication of significant deficiencies and material weaknesses
    a. A description of the significant deficiencies and material weaknesses and an analysis of their effects, including the magnitude expressed as a percentage of the applicable accounts
    b. A description of the significant deficiencies and material weaknesses and an explanation of their effect on the auditor's overall risk assessment
    c. Not include suggestions for remedial action on the deficiencies as this may tend to overshadow the reporting of the deficiencies
    d. A description of the significant deficiencies and material weaknesses and an explanation of their potential effects (ID: 90040)

Source Documents & Accounting Records

51. Which of the following documents are examples of audit evidence generated by the client?
    a. Customer purchase orders and bank statements
    b. Shipping documents and receiving reports
    c. Vendor invoices and packing slips
    d. Bills of lading and accounts receivable confirmations (ID: 8610)

52. Which of the following describes a weakness in accounts payable procedures?
    a. The accounts payable clerk files invoices and supporting documentation after payment.
    b. The accounts payable clerk manually verifies arithmetic on the vendor invoice.
    c. The accounts payable system compares the receiving report to the vendor invoice.
    d. The accounts payable manager issues purchase orders. (ID: 8807)

53. An auditor's tests of controls for completeness for the revenue cycle usually include determining whether
    a. Each receivable is collected subsequent to the year-end.
    b. An invoice is prepared for each shipping document.
    c. Each invoice is supported by a customer purchase order.
    d. Each credit memo is properly approved. (ID: 8837)

Cash Receipts

54. Evidence concerning the proper segregation of duties for receiving and depositing cash receipts ordinarily is obtained by

    a. Completing an internal control questionnaire that describes the control activities
    b. Observing the employees who are performing the control activities
    c. Performing substantive tests to verify the details of the bank balance
    d. Preparing a flowchart of the duties performed and the entity's available personnel (ID: 8609)

55. Which of the following procedures would an auditor most likely perform to test controls relating to management's assertion about the completeness of cash receipts for cash sales at a retail outlet?

    a. Observe the consistency of the employees' use of cash registers and tapes
    b. Inquire about employees' access to recorded but undeposited cash
    c. Trace the deposits in the cash receipts journal to the cash balance in the general ledger
    d. Compare the cash balance in the general ledger with the bank confirmation request (ID: 6578)

Revenue & Receivables

56. Which of the following procedures most likely would **not** be an internal control procedure designed to reduce the risk of errors in the billing process?

    a. Comparing control totals for shipping documents with corresponding totals for sales invoices
    b. Using computer programmed controls on the pricing and mathematical accuracy of sales invoices
    c. Matching shipping documents with approved sales orders before invoice preparation
    d. Reconciling the control totals for sales invoices with the accounts receivable subsidiary ledger (ID: 5109)

57. Tracing shipping documents to prenumbered sales invoices provides evidence that

    a. No duplicate shipments or billings occurred.
    b. Shipments to customers were properly invoiced.
    c. All goods ordered by customers were shipped.
    d. All prenumbered sales invoices were accounted for. (ID: 5650)

58. Proper authorization of write-offs of uncollectible accounts should be approved in which of the following departments?

    a. Accounts receivable
    b. Credit
    c. Accounts payable
    d. Treasurer (ID: 5108)

59. Which of the following controls most likely would be effective in offsetting the tendency of sales personnel to maximize sales volume at the expense of high bad debt write-offs?

    a. Employees responsible for authorizing sales and bad debt write-offs are denied access to cash.
    b. Shipping documents and sales invoices are matched by an employee who does not have authority to write off bad debts.
    c. Employees involved in the credit-granting function are separated from the sales function.
    d. Subsidiary accounts receivable records are reconciled to the control account by an employee independent of the authorization of credit. (ID: 2798)

60. Which of the following internal controls most likely would reduce the risk of diversion of customer receipts by an entity's employees?

    a. A bank lockbox system
    b. Prenumbered remittance advices
    c. Monthly bank reconciliations
    d. Daily deposit of cash receipts (ID: 5959)

61. An auditor who uses a transaction cycle approach to assessing control risk most likely would test control activities related to transactions involving the sale of goods to customers with the

    a. Collection of receivables
    b. Purchase of merchandise inventory
    c. Payment of accounts payable
    d. Sale of long-term debt (ID: 8144)

62. Management's emphasis on meeting projected profit goals most likely would significantly influence an entity's control environment when

    a. Internal auditors have direct access to the entity's board of directors.
    b. A significant portion of management compensation is represented by stock options.
    c. External policies established by parties outside the entity affect accounting policies.
    d. The audit committee is active in overseeing the entity's financial reporting policies. (ID: 8160)

63. Which of the following fraudulent activities most likely could be perpetrated due to the lack of effective internal controls in the revenue cycle?

    a. Merchandise received is not promptly reconciled to the outstanding purchase order file.
    b. Obsolete items included in inventory balances are rarely reduced to the lower of cost or market value.
    c. The write-off of receivables by personnel who receive cash permits the misappropriation of cash.
    d. Fictitious transactions are recorded that cause an understatement of revenue and overstatement of receivables. (ID: 8162)

64. Sound internal control procedures dictate that immediately upon receiving checks from customers by mail, a responsible employee should

    a. Add the checks to the daily cash summary
    b. Verify that each check is supported by a prenumbered sales invoice
    c. Prepare a duplicate listing of checks received
    d. Record the checks in the cash receipts journal (ID: 5648)

65. Which of the following procedures concerning accounts receivable would an auditor most likely perform to obtain audit evidence to support the operating effectiveness of a control?

    a. Observing an entity's employee prepare the schedule of past due accounts receivable
    b. Sending confirmation requests to an entity's principal customers to verify the existence of accounts receivable
    c. Inspecting an entity's analysis of accounts receivable for unusual balances
    d. Comparing an entity's uncollectible accounts expense to actual uncollectible accounts receivable (ID: 6234)

66. To determine whether internal control relative to the revenue cycle of a wholesaling entity is operating effectively in minimizing the failure to prepare sales invoices, an auditor most likely would select a sample of transactions from the population represented by the

    a. Sales order file
    b. Customer order file
    c. Shipping document file
    d. Sales invoice file (ID: 7815)

67. Employers bond employees who handle cash receipts because fidelity bonds reduce the possibility of employing dishonest individuals and

    a. Protect employees who make unintentional errors from possible monetary damages resulting from their errors.
    b. Deter dishonesty by making employees aware that insurance companies may investigate and prosecute dishonest acts.
    c. Facilitate an independent monitoring of the receiving and depositing of cash receipts.
    d. Force employees in positions of trust to take periodic vacations and rotate their assigned duties.

    (ID: 73)

68. Which of the following fraudulent activities most likely could be perpetrated due to the lack of effective internal controls in the revenue cycle?

    a. Fictitious transactions may be recorded that cause an understatement of revenues and an overstatement of receivables.
    b. Claims received from customers for goods returned may be intentionally recorded in other customers' accounts.
    c. Authorization of credit memos by personnel who receive cash may permit the misappropriation of cash.
    d. The failure to prepare shipping documents may cause an overstatement of inventory balances.

    (ID: 6577)

69. For the most effective internal control, monthly bank statements should be received directly from the banks and reviewed by the

    a. Cash disbursements accountant
    b. Cash receipts accountant
    c. Controller
    d. Internal auditor (ID: 111)

70. Which of the following best represents a key control for ensuring sales are properly authorized when assessing control risks for sales?

    a. The separation of duties between the billing department and the cash receipts approval department
    b. The use of an approved price list to determine unit selling price
    c. Copies of approved sales orders sent to the shipping, billing, and accounting departments
    d. Sales orders are sent to the credit department for approval (ID: 8612)

71. An auditor is determining if internal control relative to the revenue cycle of a wholesaling entity is operating effectively in minimizing the failure to prepare sales invoices. The auditor most likely would select a sample of transactions from the population represented by the

    a. Cash receipts file
    b. Shipping document file
    c. Customer order file
    d. Sales invoice file (ID: 8636)

Disbursements

72. Which of the following internal control procedures is **not** usually performed in the vouchers payable department?

    a. Matching the vendor's invoice with the related receiving report
    b. Approving vouchers for payment by having an authorized employee sign the vouchers
    c. Indicating the asset and expense accounts to be debited
    d. Accounting for unused prenumbered purchase orders and receiving reports (ID: 5113)

73. For effective internal control, the Accounts Payable Department generally should
    a. Stamp, perforate, or otherwise cancel supporting documentation after payment is mailed
    b. Ascertain that each requisition is approved as to price, quantity, and quality by an authorized employee
    c. Obliterate the quantity ordered on the Receiving Department copy of the purchase order
    d. Establish the agreement of the vendor's invoice with the receiving report and purchase order

(ID: 5977)

74. When the shipping department returns nonconforming goods to a vendor, the purchasing department should send to the accounting department the
    a. Unpaid voucher
    b. Debit memo
    c. Vendor invoice
    d. Credit memo

(ID: 2950)

75. To provide assurance that each voucher is submitted and paid only once, an auditor most likely would examine a sample of paid vouchers and determine whether each voucher is
    a. Supported by a vendor's invoice
    b. Stamped "paid" by the check signer
    c. Prenumbered and accounted for
    d. Approved for authorized purchases

(ID: 5652)

76. The authority to accept incoming goods in receiving should be based on a(an)
    a. Vendor's invoice
    b. Materials requisition
    c. Bill of lading
    d. Approved purchase order

(ID: 3913)

77. In testing controls over cash disbursements, an auditor most likely would determine that the person who signs checks also
    a. Reviews the monthly bank reconciliation
    b. Returns the checks to accounts payable
    c. Is denied access to the supporting documents
    d. Is responsible for mailing the checks

(ID: 5976)

78. Which of the following questions would most likely be included in an internal control questionnaire concerning the completeness assertion for purchases?
    a. Is an authorized purchase order required before the receiving department can accept a shipment or the vouchers payable department can record a voucher?
    b. Are purchase requisitions prenumbered and independently matched with vendor invoices?
    c. Is the unpaid voucher file periodically reconciled with inventory records by an employee who does not have access to purchase requisitions?
    d. Are purchase orders, receiving reports, and vouchers prenumbered and periodically accounted for?

(ID: 2799)

79. Which of the following questions would an auditor most likely include on an internal control questionnaire for notes payable?
    a. Are assets that collateralize notes payable critically needed for the entity's continued existence?
    b. Are two or more authorized signatures required on checks that repay notes payable?
    c. Are the proceeds from notes payable used for the purchase of noncurrent assets?
    d. Are direct borrowings on notes payable authorized by the board of directors?

(ID: 4269)

80. Mailing disbursement checks and remittance advices should be controlled by the employee who
    a. Matches the receiving reports, purchase orders, and vendors' invoices
    b. Signs the checks last
    c. Prepares the daily voucher summary
    d. Agrees the check register to the daily check summary (ID: 3914)

81. Which of the following internal control procedures is **not** usually performed in the treasurer's department?
    a. Verifying the accuracy of checks and vouchers
    b. Controlling the mailing of checks to vendors
    c. Approving vendors' invoices for payment
    d. Canceling payment vouchers when paid (ID: 4264)

82. Which of the following controls would be most effective in assuring that recorded purchases are free of material errors?
    a. The Receiving Department compares the quantity ordered on purchase orders with the quantity received on receiving reports.
    b. Vendors' invoices are compared with purchase orders by an employee who is independent of the Receiving Department.
    c. Receiving reports require the signature of the individual who authorized the purchase.
    d. Purchase orders, receiving reports, and vendors' invoices are independently matched in preparing vouchers. (ID: 7491)

83. Which of the following events occurring in the year under audit would most likely indicate that internal controls utilized in previous years may be inadequate in the year under audit?
    a. The entity announced that the internal audit function would be eliminated after the balance sheet date.
    b. The audit committee chairperson unexpectedly resigned during the year under audit.
    c. The chief financial officer waived approvals on all checks to one vendor to expedite payment.
    d. The frequency of accounts payable check runs was changed from biweekly to weekly. (ID: 7843)

84. To provide assurance that each voucher is submitted and paid only once, an auditor most likely would examine a sample of paid vouchers and determine whether each voucher is
    a. Stamped *paid* by the check signer
    b. Returned to the vouchers payable department
    c. Supported by a vendor's invoice and purchase order
    d. Prenumbered and accounted for (ID: 8618)

Inventory & Production

85. An auditor generally tests the segregation of duties related to inventory by
    a. Personal inquiry and observation
    b. Test counts and cutoff procedures
    c. Analytical procedures and invoice recomputation
    d. Document inspection and reconciliation (ID: 5649)

86. Sound internal control procedures dictate that defective merchandise returned by customers should be presented initially to the
    a. Accounts receivable supervisor
    b. Receiving clerk
    c. Shipping department supervisor
    d. Sales clerk (ID: 3916)

87. Which of the following internal control procedures most likely would prevent direct labor hours from being charged to manufacturing overhead?
    a. Periodic independent counts of work in process for comparison to recorded amounts
    b. Comparison of daily journal entries with approved production orders
    c. Use of time tickets to record actual labor worked on production orders
    d. Reconciliation of work-in-process inventory with periodic cost budgets (ID: 4697)

88. Which of the following internal control procedures most likely would be used to maintain accurate inventory records?
    a. Perpetual inventory records are periodically compared with the current cost of individual inventory items
    b. A just-in-time inventory ordering system keeps inventory levels to a desired minimum
    c. Requisitions, receiving reports, and purchase orders are independently matched before payment is approved
    d. Periodic inventory counts are used to adjust the perpetual inventory records (ID: 4698)

89. The objectives of the internal control for a production cycle are to provide assurance that transactions are properly executed and recorded, and that
    a. Production orders are prenumbered and signed by a supervisor.
    b. Custody of work in process and of finished goods is properly maintained.
    c. Independent internal verification of activity reports is established.
    d. Transfers to finished goods are documented by a completed production report and a quality control report. (ID: 4265)

90. In obtaining an understanding of a manufacturing entity's internal control concerning inventory balances, an auditor most likely would
    a. Analyze the liquidity and turnover ratios of the inventory
    b. Perform analytical procedures designed to identify cost variances
    c. Review the entity's descriptions of inventory policies and procedures
    d. Perform test counts of inventory during the entity's physical count (ID: 5979)

91. Which of the following most likely would be an internal control procedure designed to detect errors and fraud concerning the custody of inventory?
    a. Periodic reconciliation of work in process with job cost sheets
    b. Segregation of functions between general accounting and cost accounting
    c. Independent comparisons of finished goods records with counts of goods on hand
    d. Approval of inventory journal entries by the storekeeper (ID: 7492)

92. What is the most likely course of action that an auditor would take after determining that performing substantive tests on inventory will take less time than performing tests of controls?
    a. Assess control risk at the minimum level
    b. Perform both tests of controls and substantive tests on inventory
    c. Perform only substantive tests on inventory
    d. Perform only tests of controls on inventory (ID: 8419)

Payroll

93. An auditor most likely would **not** rely on controls if the payroll department supervisor is responsible for
    a. Examining authorization forms for new employees
    b. Comparing payroll registers with original batch transmittal data
    c. Authorizing payroll rate changes for all employees
    d. Hiring all subordinate payroll department employees (ID: 4694)

94. The purpose of segregating the duties of hiring personnel and distributing payroll checks is to separate the
    a. Human resources function from the controllership function
    b. Administrative controls from the internal accounting controls
    c. Authorization of transactions from the custody of related assets
    d. Operational responsibility from the record keeping responsibility (ID: 4267)

95. In determining the effectiveness of an entity's policies and procedures relating to the existence or occurrence assertion for payroll transactions, an auditor most likely would inquire about and
    a. Observe the segregation of duties concerning personnel responsibilities and payroll disbursement
    b. Inspect evidence of accounting for prenumbered payroll checks
    c. Recompute the payroll deductions for employee fringe benefits
    d. Verify the preparation of the monthly payroll account bank reconciliation (ID: 5978)

96. Which of the following is a control procedure that most likely could help prevent employee payroll fraud?
    a. The personnel department promptly sends employee termination notices to the payroll supervisor.
    b. Employees who distribute payroll checks forward unclaimed payroll checks to the absent employees' supervisors.
    c. Salary rates resulting from new hires are approved by the payroll supervisor.
    d. Total hours used for determination of gross pay are calculated by the payroll supervisor. ID: 5962)

97. Which of the following circumstances most likely would cause an auditor to suspect an employee payroll fraud scheme?
    a. There are significant unexplained variances between standard and actual labor cost.
    b. Payroll checks are disbursed by the same employee each payday.
    c. Employee time cards are approved by individual departmental supervisors.
    d. A separate payroll bank account is maintained on an impress basis. (ID: 5997)

98. Which of the following departments most likely would approve changes in pay rates and deductions from employee salaries?
    a. Personnel
    b. Treasurer
    c. Controller
    d. Payroll (ID: 4268)

99. Which of the following procedures represents a weakness in internal controls for payroll?
    a. The payroll clerk distributes signed payroll checks. Undistributed checks are returned to the payroll department.
    b. The accounting department wires transfers funds to the payroll bank account. The transfer is based on totals from the payroll department summary.
    c. The payroll department prepares checks using a signature plate. The treasurer supervises the process before payroll checks are distributed.
    d. The payroll department prepares checks. The chief financial officer signs the payroll checks. (ID: 7831)

100. Which of the following activities performed by a department supervisor most likely would help in the prevention or detection of a payroll fraud?
    a. Distributing paychecks directly to department employees
    b. Setting the pay rate for department employees
    c. Hiring employees and authorizing them to be added to payroll
    d. Approving a summary of hours each employee worked during the pay period (ID: 9382)

Property, Plant & Equipment

101. Equipment acquisitions that are misclassified as maintenance expense most likely would be detected by an internal control procedure that provides for

   a. Segregation of duties of employees in the accounts payable department
   b. Authorization by the board of directors of significant equipment acquisitions
   c. Investigation of variances within a formal budgeting system
   d. Independent verification of invoices for disbursements recorded as equipment acquisitions (ID: 4271)

102. Which of the following internal control procedures most likely would justify a reduced assessed level of control risk concerning property, plant and equipment acquisitions?

   a. Periodic physical inspection of property, plant and equipment by the internal audit staff
   b. Comparison of current year property, plant and equipment account balances with prior year actual balances
   c. The review of prenumbered purchase orders to detect unrecorded trade-ins
   d. Approval of periodic depreciation entries by a supervisor independent of the accounting department (ID: 3917)

103. Which of the following questions would an auditor **least** likely include on an internal control questionnaire concerning the initiation and execution of equipment transactions?

   a. Are requests for major repairs approved at a higher level than the department initiating the request?
   b. Are prenumbered purchase orders used for equipment and periodically accounted for?
   c. Are requests for purchases of equipment reviewed for consideration of soliciting competitive bids?
   d. Are procedures in place to monitor and properly restrict access to equipment? (ID: 5114)

Investing

104. Which of the following controls would an entity most likely use in safeguarding against the loss of marketable securities?

   a. An independent trust company that has no direct contact with the employees who have record keeping responsibilities has possession of the securities.
   b. The internal auditor verifies the marketable securities in the entity's safe each year on the balance sheet date.
   c. The independent auditor traces all purchases and sales of marketable securities through the subsidiary ledgers to the general ledger.
   d. A designated member of the board of directors controls the securities in a bank safe-deposit box. (ID: 2956)

105. When an entity uses a trust company as custodian of its marketable securities, the possibility of concealing fraud most likely would be reduced if the

   a. Trust company has no direct contact with the entity employees responsible for maintaining investment accounting records.
   b. Securities are registered in the name of the trust company, rather than the entity itself.
   c. Interest and dividend checks are mailed directly to an entity employee who is authorized to sell securities.
   d. Trust company places the securities in a bank safe-deposit vault under the custodian's exclusive control. (ID: 4699)

106. Which of the following controls would a company most likely use to safeguard marketable securities when an independent trust agent is **not** employed?

   a. The investment committee of the board of directors periodically reviews the investment decisions delegated to the treasurer.
   b. Two company officials have joint control of marketable securities, which are kept in a bank safe-deposit box.
   c. The internal auditor and the controller independently trace all purchases and sales of marketable securities from the subsidiary ledgers to the general ledger.
   d. The chairman of the board verifies the marketable securities which are kept in a bank safe-deposit box, each year on the balance sheet date. (ID: 5963)

107. Which of the following procedures most likely would give the greatest assurance that securities held as investments are safeguarded?

   a. There is no access to securities between the year-end and the date of the auditor's security count.
   b. Proceeds from the sale of investments are received by an employee who does not have access to securities.
   c. Investment acquisitions are authorized by a member of the Board of Directors before execution.
   d. Custody of investment securities is assigned to an outside agent such as a brokerage house, and access to securities requires the signatures and presence of two designated officials. (ID: 3918)

Problem 3-2 SIMULATION: Research

Which citation in the professional standards provides guidance about determining whether it is appropriate to use audit evidence about the operating effectiveness of controls obtained in previous audits and, if so, the length of the time period that may elapse before retesting a control?

[   ] § [   ] . [   ] (ID: 90391)

Problem 3-3 SIMULATION: Revenue & Accounts Receivable Internal Control Procedures

Field, CPA, is auditing the financial statements of Miller Mailorder, Inc. (MMI) for the year ended January 31, year 1. Field has compiled a list of possible errors and fraud that may result in the misstatement of MMI's financial statements.

For each possible error and fraud listed, select one internal control procedure from the list that, if properly designed and implemented, most likely could assist MMI in preventing or detecting the errors and fraud.

Each response in the list of internal control procedures may be selected once, more than once, or not at all.

Possible Errors & Fraud	Internal Control Procedure
1. Invoices for goods sold are posted to incorrect customer accounts.	
2. Goods ordered by customers are shipped, but are not billed to anyone.	
3. Invoices are sent for shipped goods, but are not recorded in the sales journal.	
4. Invoices are sent for shipped goods and are recorded in the sales journal, but are not posted to any customer account.	
5. Credit sales are made to individuals with unsatisfactory credit ratings.	
6. Goods are removed from inventory for unauthorized orders.	
7. Goods shipped to customers do not agree with goods ordered by customers.	
8. Invoices are sent to allies in a fraudulent scheme and sales are recorded for fictitious transactions.	

(ID: 9215)

Internal Control Procedures

A. Shipping clerks compare goods received from the warehouse with the details on the shipping documents.
B. Approved sales orders are required for goods to be released from the warehouse.
C. Monthly statements are mailed to all customers with outstanding balances.
D. Shipping clerks compare goods received from the warehouse with approved sales orders.
E. Customer orders are compared with the inventory master file to determine whether items ordered are in stock.
F. Daily sales summaries are compared with control totals of invoices.
G. Shipping documents are compared with sales invoices when goods are shipped.
H. Sales invoices are compared with the master price file.
I. Customer orders are compared with an approved customer list.
J. Sales orders are prepared for each customer order.
K. Control amounts posted to the accounts receivable ledger are compared with control totals of invoices.
L. Sales invoices are compared with shipping documents and approved customer orders before invoices are mailed.
M. Prenumbered credit memos are used for granting credit for goods returned.
N. Goods returned for credit are approved by the supervisor of the Sales Department.
O. Remittance advices are separated from the checks in the mailroom and forwarded to the Accounting Department.
P. Total amounts posted to the accounts receivable ledger from remittance advices are compared with the validated bank deposit slip.
Q. The cashier examines each check for proper endorsement.
R. Validated deposit slips are compared with the cashier's daily cash summaries.
S. An employee, other than the bookkeeper, periodically prepares a bank reconciliation.
T. Sales returns are approved by the same employee who issues receiving reports evidencing actual return of goods.

Problem 3-4 SIMULATION: Revenue Cycle Internal Controls Flowchart

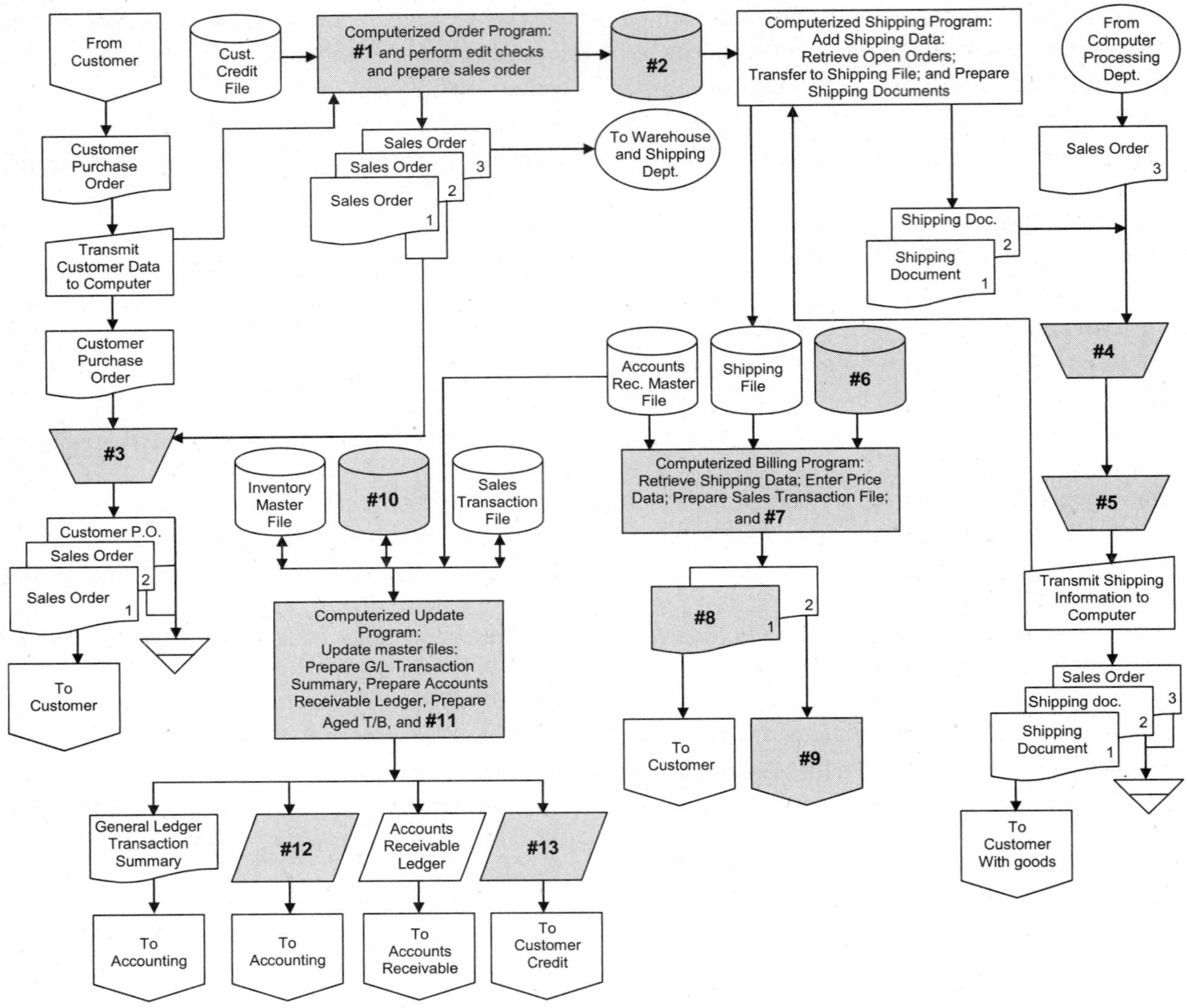

From Customer
Cust. Credit File
Computerized Order Program: **#1** and perform edit checks and prepare sales order
#2
Computerized Shipping Program: Add Shipping Data: Retrieve Open Orders; Transfer to Shipping File; and Prepare Shipping Documents
From Computer Processing Dept.
Customer Purchase Order
Sales Order 3
Sales Order 2
Sales Order 1
To Warehouse and Shipping Dept.
Sales Order 3
Shipping Doc. 2
Shipping Document 1
Transmit Customer Data to Computer
Customer Purchase Order
Accounts Rec. Master File
Shipping File
#6
#4
#3
Computerized Billing Program: Retrieve Shipping Data; Enter Price Data; Prepare Sales Transaction File; and **#7**
Inventory Master File
#10
Sales Transaction File
#5
Customer P.O.
Sales Order 2
Sales Order 1
Computerized Update Program: Update master files: Prepare G/L Transaction Summary, Prepare Accounts Receivable Ledger, Prepare Aged T/B, and **#11**
#8 1
2
Transmit Shipping Information to Computer
To Customer
Sales Order 3
Shipping doc. 2
Shipping Document 1
To Customer
#9
To Customer With goods
General Ledger Transaction Summary
#12
Accounts Receivable Ledger
#13
To Accounting
To Accounting
To Accounts Receivable
To Customer Credit

The accompanying flowchart depicts part of a client's revenue cycle. Some of the flowchart symbols are labeled to indicate control procedures and/or records. For each symbol labeled 1 through 13, select from the answer list the procedure or record it represents.

Flowchart Symbol No.	Procedure or Record Letter	Flowchart Symbol No.	Procedure or Record Letter
#1		#8	
#2		#9	
#3		#10	
#4		#11	
#5		#12	
#6		#13	
#7			

(ID: 9216)

Answer List

Operations and control procedures

A. Enter shipping data
B. Verify agreement of sales order and shipping document
C. Write off accounts receivable
D. To warehouse and Shipping Department
E. Authorize account receivable write-off
F. Prepare aged trial balance
G. To Sales Department
H. Release goods for shipment
I. To Accounts Receivable Department
J. Enter price data
K. Determine that customer exists
L. Match customer purchase order with sales order
M. Perform customer credit check
N. Prepare sales journal
O. Prepare sales invoice

Documents, journals, ledgers, and files

P. Shipping document
Q. General ledger master file
R. General journal
S. Master price file
T. Sales journal
U. Sales invoice
V. Cash receipts journal
W. Uncollectible accounts file
X. Shipping file
Y. Aged trial balance
Z. Open order file

Solution 3-1 MULTIPLE-CHOICE ANSWERS

1. (d) Assigning different people the responsibilities of authorizing transactions, recording transactions, and maintaining custody of assets is intended to reduce the opportunities to allow any person to be in a position to both perpetrate and conceal errors or fraud in the normal course of their duties. Answers a. and b. list tasks that are record keeping. Answer c. lists tasks that are both authorization. (ID: 5099)

2. (a) Control risk is not one of the components of an entity's internal control. At the assertion level, control risk along with inherent risk make up the risk of material misstatement. Internal control consists of five inter-related components: the control environment; the entity's risk assessment process; the information system, including the related business processes relevant to financial reporting and communication; control activities relevant to the audit, and monitoring of controls. (ID: 86)

3. (c) The control environment sets the tone of an organization, influencing the control consciousness of its people. Factors include management's philosophy and operating style, personnel policies and practices, etc. Detection risk is an element of audit risk, not a factor of the control environment. (ID: 5102)

4. (c) Performance reviews is a category of control activities that includes reviewing and analyzing actual performance versus budgets, forecasts, and prior-period performance. (ID: 5955)

5. (d) Selling real estate at a price considerably different from its appraised value may indicate the existence of related parties. Granting stock options to key executives at favorable prices is a common method of compensation. While high turnover of senior management and members of the board of directors may be a cause for concern, it usually does not provide indications of related parties. Failure to correct internal control weaknesses is often due to cost/benefit considerations. (ID: 8159)

6. (c) The auditor should obtain sufficient knowledge of the control environment to understand the attitudes, awareness, and actions of those charged with governance concerning the entity's internal control and its importance in achieving reliable financial reporting. Computer-based controls, the system of segregation of duties, and safeguards over access to assets are day-to-day details with which board members are unlikely to have as much influence (unless they are also officers). (ID: 5643)

7. (b) In an audit of financial statements, an auditor's primary consideration is whether, and how, a specific control prevents, or detects and corrects, material misstatements in relevant assertions related to classes of transactions, account balances, or disclosures. Management's philosophy and operating style are elements of the control environment that would influence policies and procedures, but are not the auditor's primary consideration. Whether controls provide adequate safeguards over access to assets is not relevant to *all* controls (as is answer b.) nor is it the auditor's primary consideration. The enhancement of management's decision-making processes is not an auditor's primary consideration. (ID: 5101)

8. (b) Incompatible functions are those that place any person in a position to both perpetrate and conceal errors or fraud in the normal course of their duties. Therefore, a well-designed plan of organization separates the duties of authorization, record keeping, and custody of assets. (ID: 92)

9. (c) Access to blank checks and signature plates is restricted to the cash disbursements bookkeeper who personally reconciles the monthly bank statement is the situation that most likely could lead to an embezzlement scheme. Bank reconciliations should not be prepared by persons who sign checks or keep the records for receipts or disbursements. This is an example of incompatible functions which place a person in the position to both perpetrate and conceal errors or fraud in the normal course of their duties. The duties of authorization, record keeping, and custody of assets should be separated. Additionally, bank reconciliations should not be done by persons with responsibility for handling cash receipts. The other answer alternatives are examples of appropriate duties/control practices. (ID: 8818)

10. (d) Control risk is a function of the effectiveness of the design and operation of internal control in achieving a company's objectives relevant to the preparation of the financial statements. One of the five components of internal control is the control environment. One of the elements of the control environment is a company's

organizational structure. As it provides the framework for accomplishing the company's objectives, a relevant organizational structure includes considering key areas of authority and responsibility and appropriate (suitable) lines of reporting. The key to selecting the best answer was to determine which was most related to a company's organizational structure. Management's attitude and recruiting and hiring practices are not directly related to organizational structure, as is the case with lines of reporting. The physical proximity of the accounting function to upper management could be completely unrelated to organizational structure. (ID: 8845)

11. (c) Inherent risk is not one of the components of internal control; rather, along with control risk it is a component of the risk of material misstatement. Internal control consists of five interrelated components: (1) control environment; (2) risk assessment; (3) information and communication systems; (4) control activities; and (5) monitoring. (ID: 9918)

12. (a) While incompatible duties can be segregated and therefore controlled, the possibility of management override and collusion among employees to circumvent controls will still exist. Mistakes in judgment also cannot be controlled. (ID: 4687)

13. (b) Concerns about the integrity of the entity's management may be so serious as to cause the auditor to conclude that the risk of management misrepresentations in the financial statements is such that an audit cannot be conducted. Answers a., c., and d. should be considered by the auditor but are not necessarily serious enough to raise an auditability question. (ID: 5953)

14. (b) Human judgment in the decision making process is usually considered an inherent limitation because mistakes may occur in the application of certain policies and procedures due to misunderstanding of instructions or personal carelessness. The complexity of the information processing system is not in itself an inherent limitation; it is the incorrect use of the complex system by humans that causes the majority of errors. The ineffectiveness of the board of directors and the lack of management incentives to improve the control environment are correctible weaknesses in internal control; they are not inherent. (ID: 8136)

15. (a) The nature, extent, and timing of procedures the auditor chooses to perform in the consideration of internal control will vary depending on the size and complexity of the entity, previous experience with the entity, the nature of the specific controls used by the entity including the entity's use of IT, the nature and extent of changes in systems and operations, and the nature of the entity's documentation of specific controls. (ID: 8138)

16. (d) Ordinarily, controls that are relevant to an audit pertain to the entity's objective of preparing financial statements that are fairly presented in conformity with generally accepted accounting principles, including the management of risk that may give rise to a risk of material misstatement in those financial statements. (ID: 2303)

17. (d) While the auditor should be alert to significant deficiencies, the auditor is not obligated to search for them. Obtaining an understanding of internal control involves evaluating the design of a control and determining whether it has been implemented. This understanding should be documented. (ID: 4256)

18. (b) Obtaining an understanding of internal control consists of evaluating the design and implementation of controls. This is not the same as testing the operating effectiveness of controls. The auditor only tests the operating effectiveness of controls when: (1) the auditor's risk assessment includes an expectation of the operating effectiveness of controls or (2) when it is not possible or practicable to reduce detection risk at the relevant assertion level to an acceptably low level with audit evidence obtained from substantive procedures alone. (ID: 3908)

19. (d) When obtaining an understanding of an entity's internal control, an auditor should concentrate on the implementation of procedures because management may establish appropriate procedures but not enforce compliance with them. Depending on the size of the entity, written policies may not be necessary. The implementation of procedures whose costs exceed their benefits would not affect the auditor's assessment of the performance of control procedures. An auditor should consider the design (appropriateness) of a control in determining whether to consider its implementation, thus as the question asks the reason for the auditor's concentration on the implementation of controls, an inappropriate control is not directly related to the question. (ID: 4686)

20. (b) The information system relevant to financial reporting objectives, which includes the accounting system, consists of the procedures and records established to authorize, process, and report an entity's transactions. The auditor should obtain sufficient knowledge of the information system, including the related business processes relevant to financial reporting, to understand the financial reporting process used to prepare the entity's financial statements, including significant accounting estimates and disclosures. Safeguards used to limit access to computer facilities, procedures used to assure proper authorization of transactions, and policies used to detect the concealment of fraud are all examples of control policies and procedures. (ID: 4685)

21. (a) Internal control, no matter how well designed and operated, can provide an entity with reasonable, but not absolute, assurance about achieving an entity's objectives. The likelihood of achievement is affected by limitations inherent to internal control. These include the realities that human judgment in decision making can be faulty and that breakdowns in internal control can occur because of human failures such as simple errors or mistakes. While answers b., c., and d. are generally true statements, they are not included in the concept of reasonable assurance. (ID: 5644)

22. (d) Concerns about the integrity of the entity's management may be so serious as to cause the auditor to conclude that the risk of management misrepresentations in the financial statements is such that an audit cannot be conducted. Answers a., b., and c. may be considerations, but are not necessarily so serious as to cause an auditor to question whether the entity can be audited. (ID: 7099)

23. (d) Observing the entity's personnel applying the activities provides evidence about the design and implementation of internal control activities. Entity personnel may have trouble implementing poorly designed activities. Reperformance alone would not provide evidence about whether and how the activities are actually performed. The procedures in answers b. and c. might detect misstatements, but would not provide much information about internal controls. (ID: 6393)

24. (c) Internal control, no matter how well designed and operated, can provide an entity with reasonable, but not absolute, assurance about achieving an entity's objectives. The likelihood of achievement is affected by limitations inherent to internal control. These include the realities that human judgment in decision making can be faulty. An inherent quality is part of the very nature of something and thus is not considered alterable as are incompatible duties, lack of segregation of duties or the lack of an audit committee. (ID: 8377)

25. (b) Management's carelessness regarding an adequate internal control environment may make it improbable that an auditor will be able to collect sufficient appropriate audit evidence to form an opinion. An auditor need not understand the internal auditor's techniques, particularly before accepting an engagement. The auditor merely needs to determine if related party transactions are properly disclosed, not whether they occur similarly to arm's-length transactions. Performing substantive tests at year-end is adequate if all records are available. (ID: 6928)

26. (b) Collusion is an inherent limitation of any system of internal control. An internal control system, no matter how well designed and operated, cannot give an entity absolute assurance that its objectives will be met because any system has inherent limitations. Other inherent limitations of internal control are faulty human judgment, human failures that lead to errors or mistakes, and inappropriate management override of controls. Judgmental sampling is part of the application of an auditing procedure; not an inherent limitation of internal control. Segregation of duties and employee peer reviews are examples of controls; not inherent limitations. (ID: 8621)

27. (b) One of the inherent limitations of internal control is inappropriate management override of internal control. An example of this would be if the CEO can request a check with no purchase order. The other answer alternatives describe weaknesses in internal control, but they are not inherent limitations. Inherent limitations are intrinsic—no matter how well designed and operated, internal control can only provide an entity with reasonable, not absolute, assurance. (ID: 8836)

28. (b) The auditor should document key elements of the auditor's understanding of internal control regardless of the client's records. The client's failure to do so does not constitute a scope limitation; necessitate that the auditor assess control risk at the maximum level; nor restrict the auditor's responsibility to assess the effectiveness of controls. (ID: 8639)

29. (b) The degree to which information technology (IT) is used in the accounting function is most likely to affect the extent of the documentation of the auditor's understanding of a client's system of internal control. The form and extent of documentation are influenced by the nature, size, and complexity of the entity and its environment, including its internal control, and the availability of information from the entity and the specific audit methodology and technology used in the course of the audit. An entity's use of IT may affect any of the five components of internal control relevant to the achievement of the entity's financial reporting, operations, or compliance objectives, and its operating units or business functions. The use of IT also affects the fundamental manner in which transactions are initiated, authorized, recorded, processed, and reported. And an entity's mix of manual and automated controls varies with the nature and complexity of the entity's use of IT. Documentation of the understanding of a complex information system in which a large volume of transactions are electronically initiated, authorized, recorded, processed, or reported may include flowcharts, questionnaires, or decision tables. For an information system making limited or no use of IT or for which few transactions are processed, documentation in the form of a memorandum may be sufficient. The effect on the internal control system of an entity of the other answer alternatives is not as pervasive, thus their impact on the extent of the documentation of the auditor's understanding of it is less. (ID: 9358)

30. (b) Verifying that approved spending limits are not exceeded would best assess the validity of the auditor's concern about a policy of management override because It is management's responsibility to authorize expenditures. Irregularities which might be discovered by matching purchase orders to accounts payable or tracing sales orders to revenue accounts might not involve management. Undetected management override of controls would not be described in minutes of board meetings. (ID: 9383)

31. (c) Assessed risks and the basis for those assessments should be documented whether or not control risk is assessed at the maximum level. There is a direct relationship between control risk and substantive testing, thus if control risk is high the auditor should perform more, not fewer, substantive tests of details. If the auditor assesses control risk at the maximum level there is no point in performing more tests of controls. Documenting a control structure more extensively because it is not functioning well is nonsensical. (ID: 9943)

32. (d) The auditor may design a test of controls to be performed concurrently with a test of details on the same transaction. The objective of tests of controls is to evaluate whether a control operated effectively. Answer a. would be a substantive test rather than a test of controls. Answer b. is an objective of obtaining an understanding of an entity's internal control. Answer c. is the objective of substantive procedures. (ID: 5115)

33. (c) When a client has documentation regarding the use of computer programs, it is an effective internal control. Answer b. is a substantive procedure. Answers a. and d. are analytical procedures. (ID: 5958)

34. (b) Audit evidence is more reliable when it is obtained directly by the auditor rather than evidence obtained indirectly or by inference. Performing tests of transactions tests segregation of duties from the past which may not be operating currently. A flowchart reflects the ideal operating conditions of the company, established at a point in time, which may not be representative of the actual processing procedures being performed. Audit objectives cannot in themselves reduce control risk. (ID: 3906)

35. (b) If there have been no changes that affect the continuing relevance of the audit evidence from the previous audit, the auditor should test the controls at least once in every third audit and should test some controls during each audit to avoid the possibility of testing all the controls on which the auditor intends to rely in a single audit period with no testing of controls in the subsequent two audit periods. Editor Note: If the auditor plans to use audit evidence from a previous audit about the operating effectiveness of specific controls, the auditor should first perform audit procedures to establish the continuing relevance of that information to the current audit. The auditor should obtain this evidence by performing inquiry, combined with observation or inspection, to confirm the understanding of those specific controls. Regarding incorrect answer a., if there have been changes that affect the continuing relevance of the audit evidence from the previous audit, the auditor should test the controls in the current audit; not at least once every three years. Regarding incorrect answer c., if there have been no such changes, the auditor should test the controls at least once in every third audit as described above in the explanation of the correct answer b.; not at least every other year. Incorrect answer d., regards controls over a significant risk—the requirements for the use of prior audit evidence is not relevant to controls over a significant risk. If the auditor plans to rely on controls over a risk the auditor has determined to be a

significant risk, the auditor should test the operating effectiveness of those controls in the current period; not at least every other year. (ID: 8267)

36. (d) The CPA examiners generally recognize four types of tests of internal controls to determine the degree of operating effectiveness: inquiries of appropriate entity personnel, inspection of documents and reports, observation of the application of specific internal control policies and procedures, and re-performance of the application of the policy or procedures by the auditor. System flowcharts may document the auditor's understanding of internal control, but flowchart preparation provides little assurance about the documented activity's operating effectiveness. (ID: 7810)

37. (b) An audit is a cumulative and iterative process. As the auditor performs planned audit procedures, the audit evidence obtained may cause the auditor to modify the nature, extent, or timing of other planned audit procedures. In particular, the risk assessment may be based on an expectation that controls are operating effectively. If, after testing a client's internal control activities, the auditor discovers a material weakness in the operation of a client's internal controls, the auditor most likely would increase the assessment of control risk and increase the extent of substantive procedures in order to obtain more audit evidence rather than withdraw from the audit. In an audit of financial statements, the auditor is not required to perform procedures to identify deficiencies in internal control or to express an opinion on the effectiveness of the entity's internal control. (ID: 8375)

38. (d) The purpose of an audit is to express an opinion on the financial statements; an auditor assesses control risk as part of an evaluation of the likelihood that material misstatements exist in the financial statements. (ID: 8402)

39. (c) Observation of the application of the control, i.e., whether the data center is monitored to limit access, yields the most reliable audit evidence about the effectiveness of this control. The control may not be practiced as it is described in the policy manual. Inquiry of the chief technology officer does not provide as reliable evidence as the auditor's observation of the control's application. Obtaining a list of current data center employees by itself does not provide evidence of the effectiveness of the control's application. (ID: 8616)

40. (a) When an auditor plans to rely on controls that have changed since they were last tested, the auditor should test the operating effectiveness of such controls in the current audit. Changes may affect the relevance of the audit evidence obtained in prior periods, thus it may no longer be a basis for continued reliance. (ID: 9384)

41. (c) The question describes inquiries and inspection of records. It describes the auditor interviewing the controller (making inquiries) and inspecting the records (the verification that the reconciliation was properly prepared and included appropriate sign-offs) after the procedure had taken place, so it was not observation. A confirmation, which is a specific type of inquiry, is the process of obtaining and evaluating a direct communication from a third party in response to a request for information about a particular item—this was not described. The auditor did not perform the control procedure (the reconciliation) so it wasn't reperformance. And no analytical procedures are described. (ID: 9916)

42. (b) If the auditor finds significant deficiencies or material weaknesses as a consequence of performing audit procedures in an audit of financial statements, the auditor is required to communicate them *in writing* to those charged with governance *and* management, including those that were remediated during the audit, no later than 60 days following the report release date. The auditor is also required to communicate to management at an appropriate level of responsibility, in writing or orally, other deficiencies in internal control identified during the audit that have not been communicated to management by other parties and that are of sufficient importance to merit management's attention. If such other deficiencies in internal control are communicated orally, the auditor should document the communication. It is not the auditor's duty to search for them or to express an opinion on the effectiveness of internal control. They are not required to be disclosed in the notes to the financial statements. (ID: 8142)

43. (d) Answers a. – c. are listed as indicators of material weaknesses by the standard setters. Their list also includes the identification by the auditor of a material misstatement of the financial statements in circumstances that indicate that the misstatement would not have been detected by the entity's internal control. Sub-

stantial doubt about the entity's ability to continue as a going concern does not indicate the existence of a material weakness in internal control. (ID: 9037)

44. (c) The written communication regarding significant deficiencies and material weaknesses identified during an audit of financial statements should include a restriction on its use (an appropriate alert). Significant deficiencies, previously communicated and uncorrected or not, do not create scope limitations unless when aggregated with other internal control deficiencies they are so pervasive that an entity cannot be audited which was not indicated by this question. The auditor is not required to perform tests of controls on significant deficiencies; however, performing tests of controls in an audit may reveal significant deficiencies. For a nonissuer, the required written communication is best made by the audit report release date, but should be made no later than 60 days after this date. For an issuer, it must be made prior to the issuance of the audit report. In some circumstances, the auditor may decide to communicate certain identified significant deficiencies and material weaknesses during the audit; however these should ultimately be included in the formal final written communication even if remediated during the audit. (ID: 5118)

45. (b) The auditor should not issue an written communication stating that no significant deficiencies were identified during an audit. The other answer alternatives are all examples of items that should be included in the written communication regarding significant deficiencies and material weaknesses identified during an audit of financial statements. (ID: 2957)

46. (b) A deficiency in internal control exists when the design or operation of a control does not allow management or employees, in the normal course of performing their assigned functions, to prevent, or detect and correct, misstatements on a timely basis. (ID: 7489)

47. (c) The severity of a deficiency in internal control is dependent on the magnitude of the potential misstatement that could result from the deficiency or deficiencies and whether there is a reasonable possibility (the likelihood) that the entity's controls will fail to prevent, or detect and correct, a misstatement of an account balance or disclosure. It's also important to note that whether a misstatement actually occurred is not relevant to the determination of a control deficiency's severity. (ID: 7105)

48. (b) The written communication regarding significant deficiencies and material weaknesses identified during a financial statement audit should include sufficient information to enable those charged with governance and management to understand the context of the communication. The communication should: (1) include a statement that indicates that the purpose of the audit was for the auditor to express an opinion on the financial statements; (2) state that the audit included consideration of internal control over financial reporting in order to design audit procedures that are appropriate in the circumstances but not for the purpose of expressing an opinion on the effectiveness of internal control; (3) state that the auditor is not expressing an opinion on the effectiveness of internal control; (4) state that the auditor's consideration of internal control was not designed to identify all deficiencies in internal control that might be material weaknesses or significant deficiencies, and therefore, material weaknesses or significant deficiencies may exist that were not identified; (5) include the definition of the term *material weakness* and, when relevant, the definition of the term *significant deficiency*; (6) include a description of the significant deficiencies and material weaknesses and an explanation of their potential effects; and (7) include an appropriate alert that restricts its use. (If an entity is required to furnish the auditor's written communication to a governmental authority, a specific reference to the governmental authority may be included in the paragraph that restricts its use.) (ID: 5982)

49. (a) When deviations from prescribed controls are discovered the auditor should make inquiries to understand the potential consequences of the deviation, i.e., the auditor should determine whether, on the basis of the audit work performed, the auditor has identified one or more deficiencies in internal control. And if the auditor has identified one or more deficiencies in internal control, the auditor should evaluate each deficiency to determine, on the basis of the audit work performed, whether, individually or in combination, they constitute significant deficiencies or material weaknesses. (If the auditor determines that a deficiency, or a combination of deficiencies, in internal control is *not* a material weakness, the auditor should consider whether prudent officials, having knowledge of the same facts and circumstances, would likely reach the same conclusion.) The auditor should never assume that a deviation is an isolated occurrence without audit significance. Answers c. and d. may or may not be determined to be appropriate actions after the auditor has gained an understanding of the potential

consequences; however, in determining whether the auditor has identified one or more deficiencies in internal control, the auditor may discuss the relevant facts and circumstances of the auditor's findings with the appropriate level of management. The level of management with whom it is appropriate to discuss the findings is one that is familiar with the internal control area concerned and that has the authority to take remedial action on any identified deficiencies in internal control; in many cases this may *not* be answer c., the next higher level of authority within the entity. (ID: 8821)

50. (d) The auditor should include in the auditor's written communication of significant deficiencies and material weaknesses a description of the significant deficiencies and material weaknesses and an explanation of their potential effects. In explaining the potential effects of the significant deficiencies and material weaknesses, the auditor need not quantify those effects. The potential effects may be described in terms of the control objectives and types of errors the control was designed to prevent, or detect and correct; or in terms of the risk of misstatement that the control was designed to address. The purpose of the communication is to report matters to management and those charged with governance that merit their attention in meeting their responsibilities; not how it relates to the audit. Thus, the auditor should not communicate their effect on the auditor's overall risk assessment. The auditor may also include in the written communication suggestions for remedial action on the deficiencies, management's actual or proposed responses, and a statement about whether the auditor has undertaken any steps to verify whether management's responses have been implemented. (ID: 90040)

51. (b) Shipping documents (records of goods shipped by the client) and receiving reports (records of goods received by the client) are generated by the client. Customer purchase orders and bank statements are generated externally by the client's customers and the client's financial institutions, respectively. Vendor invoices and packing slips (records of goods shipped to the client) are generated externally by the client's vendors. Bills of lading (records of receipt of goods by a shipper) are generated externally usually by common carriers used by the client. Accounts receivable confirmation requests are sent out by the auditor or the client; the confirmations are completed (generated) by the client's customers and returned directly to the auditor by the client's customers. (ID: 8610)

52. (d) If the accounts payable manager issues purchase orders, incompatible functions of authorization and record keeping are combined creating a weakness in internal control. A person should not be in the position to both perpetrate and conceal errors or fraud in the normal course of their duties, thus the duties of authorization, record keeping, and custody of assets should be separated. The other answer alternatives describe appropriate internal controls. (ID: 8807)

53. (b) When testing for completeness for the revenue cycle, the auditor is checking to see that all sales have been recorded. Tracing ("up the house") from a shipping document to an invoice tests that goods that were shipped were also invoiced. The auditor would also need to confirm that the invoice was recorded. Testing receivables to see if they were collected subsequent to the year-end is done to determine if there was proper cutoff. Checking to see that each invoice is supported by a customer purchase order and that credit memos are properly authorized is testing for occurrence (validity). (ID: 8837)

54. (b) The best way to obtain evidence about the proper segregation of duties is by observing the employees who are performing the control activities. Procedures to verify the details of the bank balance, if they included examining signatures on deposit slips, could indicate which employees prepared the deposits, but this would not provide conclusive evidence as to which employees actually collected (physically handled) the receipts. Flowcharts and internal control questionnaires speak more to the effectiveness of the design rather than the operation of this control, but even if they are based on inquiries about the operation of the control, they do not provide as high a degree of evidence as simply actually observing who does what. (ID: 8609)

55. (a) Assertions about completeness are tested by testing whether or not all cash is recorded. If employees consistently use cash registers and tapes, it is likely that all cash is recorded. Inquiry about employees' access to undeposited recorded cash, comparing the cash receipts journal to the general ledger, and comparing the cash balance in the general ledger with the bank confirmation request, only test assertions about *recorded* cash. (ID: 6578)

56. (d) Answers a. – c. are all controls applicable to the billing process. Answer d. is a control used *after* the billing process. (ID: 5109)

57. (b) Tracing from shipping documents to the sales invoice provides evidence that shipments to customers were properly invoiced. (ID: 5650)

58. (d) The treasury department is independent of record keeping and custodial functions for accounts receivable. Incompatible functions are those that place any person in a position to both perpetrate and conceal errors or fraud in the normal course of their duties. Therefore, a well-designed plan of organization separates the duties of authorization, record keeping, and custody of assets. Answer a. would not separate the authorization and record keeping functions. Credit authorization and write-off of accounts by the same department could allow for an employee defalcation scheme. The A/P department would not have adequate information to make such a recommendation which could result in error or fraud concealment. (ID: 5108)

59. (c) The most effective control in offsetting the tendency of sales personnel to maximize sales volume at the expense of high bad debt write-offs would be the segregation of duties of those employees involved in credit-granting and sales functions. If this segregation exists, credit-granting employees should help to screen out those potential customers likely to result in high bad-debt write-offs. (ID: 2798)

60. (a) A bank lockbox system assures accountability control as cash enters the client's cash receipts system. Answers b. – d. are controls imposed after cash is captured in the system. (ID: 5959)

61. (a) The cycle approach combines similar transactions with the ledger balances that result from those transactions. Receivables result from the sale of goods; therefore, it is logical and more efficient to test these items together. (ID: 8144)

62. (b) Management's emphasis on meeting projected profit goals most likely would significantly influence the control environment when a significant portion of management compensation is represented by stock options because it provides an incentive to commit fraud. Answers a., c., and d. would mitigate this risk factor. (ID: 8160)

63. (c) Segregation of duties prevents an employee from committing fraud and subsequently concealing it. Proper segregation of duties separates the functions of record keeping, custody and authorization. Answers a. and b. are not necessarily fraudulent activities. Fictitious transactions that overstate receivables also tend to overstate revenue, not understate it. (ID: 8162)

64. (c) By immediately recording the receipt of the checks, the employee provides evidence of the existence of cash. While the procedures in answers a., b., and d. are appropriate, preparing a duplicate listing of the checks is of immediate concern. (ID: 5648)

65. (a) Observation of an entity's preparation of a schedule is a test of a control. Confirmation requests, inspection of an analysis of accounts receivables, and comparison of an entity's uncollectible accounts expense to actual uncollectible accounts receivables are all substantive procedures. (ID: 6234)

66. (c) For each shipment, there should be a sales invoice. If the auditor selects a sample of transactions from the shipping document file and does not find corresponding sales invoices, the auditor knows the controls are ineffective. For each sales order and customer order, there may or may not be a sales invoice, depending on whether the product was shipped. When testing to see if there is a failure to produce sales invoices, by selecting a sample from the sales invoice file, an auditor would guarantee to get only transactions where this failure did not occur. (ID: 7815)

67. (b) In addition to indemnification in case of loss, fidelity bonds provide a psychological deterrent to employees considering defalcations. The insurance company's investigation before an employee is bonded tends to discourage those with intentions of committing defalcations from accepting jobs requiring bonds. A further deterrent is the employee's knowledge that the insurance company will prosecute in an effort to recover a loss, whereas an employer might forego prosecution. (ID: 73)

68. (c) One of the most effective means of detecting or preventing fraud is the segregation of duties involving authorization, custody, and record keeping. Authorization of credit memos by personnel who receive cash (custody) is not segregation of these duties. The recording of fictitious transactions and failure to prepare shipping documents resulting in an overstatement of inventory likely would be discovered during reconciliations. Return claims applied to inappropriate accounts likely would be discovered by customers when monthly statements are issued. (ID: 6577)

69. (d) Internal verifications of cash balances generally should be made monthly. Recorded cash on hand and petty cash balances should be compared with cash counts and recorded bank balances should be reconciled to balances shown on bank statements. These verifications should be made by personnel who are not otherwise involved in executing or recording cash transactions to maintain a segregation of functions. The cash receipts accountant, the cash disbursements accountant, and the controller should not reconcile the monthly statements as they are involved in the executing or recording of cash transactions. (ID: 111)

70. (d) Sending sales orders to the credit department for approval is a key control for ensuring that sales are properly authorized. Although the billing and cash receipts departments should be separate (to reduce the opportunity for any one person to both perpetrate and conceal fraud or errors in the normal course of their duties), their separation does not impact whether sales are properly authorized. Use of an approved price list is a control to ensure the accuracy of sales transactions rather than proper authorization. The receipt of approved sales orders by the shipping, billing, and accounting departments occurs after the fact. (ID: 8612)

71. (b) The auditor should make the selection from the shipping document file. Attempting to match shipping documents to invoices would reveal goods shipped that were not invoiced. The cash receipts file contains evidence of payments, so it would be highly unlikely to discover payments received from customers who weren't billed. The customer order file would be a workable but inefficient choice by the auditor because normally goods are not invoiced until they are shipped, so it would involve checking shipping documents as well to confirm the sale. The sales invoice file would not be used because the auditor is looking for sales that were not invoiced. (ID: 8636)

72. (d) Accounting for unused purchase orders and receiving reports by the same department does not provide sufficient segregation of duties for the authorization, custody, and reporting functions of an effective internal control system. The lack of segregation of these items could result in an employee defalcation scheme. Answers a. – c. each represent a procedure that is usually performed in the vouchers payable department. (ID: 5113)

73. (d) The agreement of the documents will verify that the goods were ordered (purchase order), received (receiving report), and the company has been billed (vendor's invoice). The individual signing the checks, not accounts payable, should stamp, perforate, or otherwise cancel the supporting documentation. The purchasing department, not accounting, is involved with the approval of purchase requisitions and blanking out the quantity ordered on the receiving department copy of the purchase order. (ID: 5977)

74. (b) When the shipping department returns nonconforming goods to a vendor, the purchasing department should send a debit memo to the accounting department. This enables the accounting department to make the appropriate adjustment to the vendor's account. Answers a. and c. are incorrect because the accounting department would have no use for the unpaid voucher and the vendor invoice. A credit memo would be provided by the vendor, not by the purchasing department. (ID: 2950)

75. (b) By immediately stamping "paid" on the paid voucher, the check signer prevents the voucher from being paid again. While each of the items in answers a., c., and d. is a recommended practice, none prevent the voucher from being paid again. (ID: 5652)

76. (d) A good internal control system will include the segregation of duties, such as the comparison of an approved purchase order to items received. Answers a. and c. represent documentation included with the order as it is received, without any indication of authorization. Answer b. represents a form used when goods and materials are taken from inventory to be used or shipped. (ID: 3913)

77. (d) A control for cash disbursements is for the person who signs the checks to compare them to supporting documents, cancel the documents, and to mail the checks. The person who signs checks should have access to the supporting documents in order to validate their legitimacy. Reconciliation of the monthly bank statement is a control that should be done by a person independent of cash transactions. Checks should not be returned or given to anyone with cash disbursement responsibilities. (ID: 5976)

78. (d) Assertions about completeness deal with whether all transactions and accounts that should be presented in the financial statements are so included. One step in assuring this is the periodic reconciliation of prenumbered purchase orders, receiving reports, and vouchers. (ID: 2799)

79. (d) Approved borrowings by the board of directors indicate that transactions must be approved before the recording and custody functions can take place. This is also performed by a party independent of the recording and custody functions. (ID: 4269)

80. (b) Good internal controls require that the person who last signs the checks keep control of them until they are mailed. Answers a., c., and d. do not provide sufficient segregation of duties for the authorization, custodial, and reporting functions of an effective internal control system. (ID: 3914)

81. (c) Incompatible functions are those that place any person in a position to both perpetrate and conceal errors or fraud in the normal course of their duties. Therefore, a well-designed plan of organization separates the duties of authorization, record keeping, and custody of assets. The treasurer generally would perform the other procedures. (ID: 4264)

82. (d) The most effective controls over recorded purchases occur when supporting forms such as purchase orders, receiving reports, and vendor invoices are compared independently for agreement. For good control, the Receiving Department should not know the quantity ordered. Answer b. is a step in the right direction, but does not encompass as many independent comparisons as does answer d. Answer c. is an example of incompatible functions. Assets should not be checked in and recorded by the person who authorized their purchase. (ID: 7491)

83. (c) The chief financial officer's willingness to override the internal controls reveals a management philosophy that values meeting goals higher than working within established procedures. Little time would be saved by adhering to approval procedures at most entities, indicating, at best, poor organization regarding the transactions. Elimination of the internal audit function, in itself, doesn't indicate that controls are now inadequate, although this is a second-best answer. As the audit committee chair is unlikely to have been in a position to commit a disreputable act with regard to the entity under audit, the chair's resignation probably doesn't indicate personal misconduct. If an audit committee chair resigned in protest of entity misconduct, the chair likely would have informed the auditor directly of the reasons for the resignation. Check-run frequency rarely effects the quality of internal controls. (ID: 7843)

84. (a) The voucher and all supporting documents should be canceled (stamped paid) by the check signer to avoid duplicate payments. The return of the voucher to the vouchers payable department provides no control to prevent it from being paid more than once. Confirmation that each voucher is supported by a vendor's invoice and purchase order provides evidence that the payment is based on a valid purchase, but would not stop a duplicate payment. Prenumbering and accounting for vouchers allows confirmation that all vouchers were recorded and should allow the discovery of a duplicate payment, but it would not prevent it. (ID: 8618)

85. (a) To test for appropriate segregation of duties, the auditor observes and makes inquiries. The procedures in answers b – d. are not applicable to testing for segregation of duties. (ID: 5649)

86. (b) For sound internal controls, all receipts for goods, including returned goods or materials, should be handled by the receiving clerk. Receiving reports should be prepared for all items received. Employees who have recording responsibilities should not also have custody of the related assets. (ID: 3916)

87. (c) Use of time tickets indicates the amount of actual labor employed during the day on a given job. An internal control procedure requiring the use of charging the actual time to the job in progress would help prevent

mistakes in the recording of direct and indirect labor. Answers a. and d. would indicate variances after improperly charging direct labor to factory overhead, but would be poor preventative measures. Answer b. would have no effect on identifying misposted direct labor. (ID: 4697)

88. (d) Assertions about existence or occurrence deal with whether assets or liabilities of the entity exist at a given date and whether recorded transactions have occurred during a given period. Periodically comparing goods on hand with perpetual inventory records would assist in identifying potential errors. Answer a. addresses the valuation of the inventory. Answer b. would not identify variances in actual inventory compared to recorded amounts. Answer c. represents examples of controls necessary for the proper segregation of duties in purchasing inventory. (ID: 4698)

89. (b) Controlling the access to assets is an important objective of proper inventory control. The other answer alternatives are procedures for satisfying inventory control objectives—not actual internal control objectives. (ID: 4265)

90. (c) To obtain an understanding of a manufacturer's internal control concerning inventory balances, an auditor would review the entity's descriptions of inventory policies and procedures. Analyzing inventory ratios, performing cost variance analytical procedures, and performing inventory test counts are substantive procedures. (ID: 5979)

91. (c) An independent comparison of finished goods records with counts of goods on hand is designed to detect errors and fraud concerning inventory custody as it provides an independent reconciliation of the two amounts. Answers a. and b. do not consider the inventory itself nor inventory custody. The storekeeper should not be able to approve inventory journal entries because he or she has custody of the assets. (ID: 7492)

92. (c) An auditor need consider only the objectives and related controls relevant to the audit. An auditor performs tests of the design and operation of internal controls to determine if the auditor may rely upon them. If the auditor has determined that it will take less time to perform substantive tests than it will to perform tests of controls, there is no reason to assess control risk or perform any tests of controls on inventory. Control risk may be assessed at a minimum level only after testing controls and finding them strong. (ID: 8419)

93. (c) Incompatible functions are those that place any person in a position to both perpetrate and conceal errors or fraud in the normal course of their duties. Therefore, a well-designed plan of organization separates the duties of authorization, record keeping, and asset custody. Authorizing payroll rate changes for all employees would be incompatible with record keeping. Examining authorization forms for new employees is not the same as authorization; therefore, the payroll department supervisor would only be in control of record keeping. While hiring all subordinate payroll department employees would not be a compatible function with record keeping, it is not as serious as authorizing pay rate changes for all employees. (ID: 4694)

94. (c) Incompatible functions are those that place any person in a position to both perpetrate and conceal errors or fraud in the normal course of their duties. A well-designed organization plan separates authorization, record keeping, and asset custody. (ID: 4267)

95. (a) Observing the segregation of duties concerning personnel responsibilities and payroll disbursement is a common audit procedure relating to the existence or occurrence assertion for payroll transactions. Inspecting evidence of accounting for prenumbered payroll checks would provide evidence related to the completeness assertion. Recomputing the payroll deductions for employee fringe benefits would provide evidence related to the valuation and the rights and obligations assertions. An auditor would likely review payroll checks and bank reconciliations to determine that all checks were cashed as part of obtaining evidence for the existence or occurrence assertion and not just verify the preparation of the monthly payroll account bank reconciliation. (ID: 5978)

96. (a) By promptly notifying the payroll supervisor of employee terminations, the personnel department would avoid a terminated employee from continuing to be paid. Unclaimed payroll checks should be forwarded to the Treasurer's office. Salary rates should be controlled in the personnel office. Total hours should be determined and approved prior to getting to the payroll department. Although answers c. and d. are good controls, they would not prevent employee payroll fraud. (ID: 5962)

97. (a) Significant unexplained variances between standard and actual labor cost could cause an auditor to suspect a payroll fraud scheme. Payroll checks disbursed by the same employee each payday (as long as that person has no other payroll responsibilities), employee time cards being approved by individual departmental supervisors, and a separate payroll bank account maintained on an imprest basis are proper internal control procedures. (ID: 5997)

98. (a) The authorization of a transaction, its record keeping, and the custody of the related asset should all be separated. In a payroll function, the treasurer's department prepares and distributes payroll checks to employees (custody), the controller reviews the payroll, and the payroll department prepares the payroll (record keeping). (ID: 4268)

99. (a) An important internal control is the separation of the duties of authorization, record keeping, and custody. As the payroll department prepares the payroll (record keeping) and has custody of the related assets, a payroll clerk is in a position to both perpetrate and conceal misappropriation of assets. Having the accounting department wire transfer funds (authorization) based on total from a payroll summary (record keeping) may be unusual, but the two mentioned types of duties are separated. With the treasurer supervises the use of a signature plate (custody) by the payroll department to prepare checks (record keeping), segregation of duties is maintained. With the chief financial officer signing checks (custody) prepared by the payroll department (record keeping), segregation of duties is maintained. (ID: 7831)

100. (d) Having the department supervisor approve a summary of hours each employee worked during the pay period would be most likely to help in the prevention or detection of a payroll fraud. The other answer alternatives are examples of improper segregation of duties. (ID: 9382)

101. (c) The investigation of variances within a formal budgeting system would identify any unusual and unanticipated fluctuations in the repair and maintenance accounts when asset acquisitions are recorded there incorrectly. The segregation of duties is a good control; however, answer a. would not ensure that equipment acquisitions were not misclassified. Answer b. would not prevent the recording of an acquisition to the repair and maintenance accounts, nor would it serve to identify misclassifications. Answer d. would not ensure that equipment purchases were recorded properly because these invoices only represent those acquisitions which are already properly recorded as fixed assets. (ID: 4271)

102. (a) The periodic inspection of physical equipment and comparison to the accounting records by the internal auditor (who does not participate in the acquisition or disposal process) may allow for a reduction in the scope of the auditor's tests of asset acquisitions. The comparison of account balances and entries is an analytical procedure that would highlight unusual and unanticipated fluctuations; however, it would not indicate acquisitions that were not approved. The review of prenumbered purchase orders would indicate trade-ins or retirements of fixed assets in exchange for new assets; thus, there would be no change in the quantity of fixed assets on hand. (ID: 3917)

103. (d) The procedures in place to monitor and properly restrict access to equipment would more likely be observed by the auditor than be part of a questionnaire, as this is very important. Answer a. represents the authorization function of the control structure, which would be included on the internal control questionnaire. Answer b. represents a procedure to test the accounting and recording function of the control structure, which the auditor would include in an internal control questionnaire. Requests for competitive bids reduce the possibility of an individual's personal gain at the expense of the business in unusual and material transactions. (ID: 5114)

104. (a) Of the choices given, the strongest internal control in safeguarding against the loss of marketable securities would be the use of an independent trust company that has no direct contact with the employees who have record keeping responsibilities. The fact that only the trust company has access to the securities should prevent unauthorized entity personnel with record keeping responsibility from conspiring or colluding to misappropriate securities. In determining appropriate controls in safeguarding an asset against loss, the auditor would start with those controls involving access to the asset in question. Neither verifying the securities in the safe nor tracing all purchases and sales provides evidence as to who has access to, or custody of, the marketable secu-

rities. Allowing just one person access to an asset enables the individual to take the asset without being discovered. (ID: 2956)

105. (a) The fact that only the trust company has access to the securities should prevent unauthorized entity personnel with record keeping responsibility from conspiring or colluding to misappropriate the securities. Trust company employees or management potentially could sell or otherwise mismanage the assets. Answers c. and d. put custody and record keeping functions in the hands of one party which could result in unauthorized transactions. (ID: 4699)

106. (b) A bank safe-deposit box with two company officials in control of the assets provides strong physical control over the securities. Answers a. and c. would not safeguard the physical marketable security. Answer d. does not provide for dual control throughout the year, as is preferred. (ID: 5963)

107. (d) Custody of investment securities usually is maintained on company premises or assigned to an outside agent such as a brokerage house. Good controls dictate that at least two officers should sign for, and be present to access, these investments to prevent unauthorized sales. Having no access to securities between the year-end and the date of the auditor's security count provides no guarantee that unauthorized access to the investments during the time period indicated did not occur. Having proceeds from the sale of investments received by an employee who does not have access to securities and investment acquisitions authorized by a member of the Board of Directors before execution are good controls, but do not address the physical control of the assets. (ID: 3918)

Solution 3-2 SIMULATION ANSWER: Research

Which citation in the professional standards provides guidance about determining whether it is appropriate to use audit evidence about the operating effectiveness of controls obtained in previous audits and, if so, the length of the time period that may elapse before retesting a control?

AU § 330 . 13 (ID: 90391)

.13 In determining whether it is appropriate to use audit evidence about the operating effectiveness of controls obtained in previous audits and, if so, the length of the time period that may elapse before retesting a control, the auditor should consider:

a. The effectiveness of other elements of internal control, including the control environment, the entity's monitoring of controls, and the entity's risk assessment process

b. The risks arising from the characteristics of the control, including whether the control is manual or automated

c. The effectiveness of general IT controls

d. The effectiveness of the control and its application by the entity, including the nature and extent of deviations in the application of the control noted in previous audits and whether there have been personnel changes that significantly affect the application of the control

e. Whether the lack of a change in a particular control poses a risk due to changing circumstances

f. The risks of material misstatement and the extent of reliance on the control

---

Solution 3-3 SIMULATION ANSWER: Revenue & Accounts Receivable Internal Control Procedures

Possible Errors & Fraud	Internal Control Procedure
1. Invoices for goods sold are posted to incorrect customer accounts.	C
2. Goods ordered by customers are shipped, but are not billed to anyone.	G
3. Invoices are sent for shipped goods, but are not recorded in the sales journal.	F
4. Invoices are sent for shipped goods and are recorded in the sales journal, but are not posted to any customer account.	K
5. Credit sales are made to individuals with unsatisfactory credit ratings.	I
6. Goods are removed from inventory for unauthorized orders.	B
7. Goods shipped to customers do not agree with goods ordered by customers.	D
8. Invoices are sent to allies in a fraudulent scheme and sales are recorded for fictitious transactions.	L

(ID: 9215)

1. C The error of posting a customer's invoice to the wrong account would be detected when a monthly statement was received, indicating a balance due, when no payment is owed.

2. G Before goods are shipped from the warehouse, an employee should determine that a valid sales invoice exists that matches the shipping documents and actual shipment being made. This would prevent shipments being made that have not been invoiced.

3. F To prevent having unrecorded sales, the company should make a comparison each day of the total sales invoices with the daily sales summaries. This comparison would detect differences between the total sales made vs. recorded.

4. K Unrecorded accounts receivable would be prevented by comparing the control total of sales invoices to the control total amount posted to the accounts receivable ledger. Any differences would indicate possible errors in the recording function and require a reconciliation, which would detect unposted customer sales.

5. I Requiring employees to use an approved customer list before making credit sales to customers would prevent the company from allowing sales to be made to uncreditworthy customers.

6. B An internal control procedure that would prevent goods being removed from the warehouse when a *bona fide* sale does not exist would be the requirement that an approved sales order be received in the warehouse before the goods could be released from the warehouse.

7. D If shipping clerks compare the order received from the warehouse to the approved customer sales order before shipment, this would prevent the error of shipping the wrong goods to customers.

8. L The company would be able to prevent a fraudulent sales scheme where sales were recorded for fictitious transactions if certain control procedures were in place. For example, requiring an employee not in the Sales Department to compare customer sales invoices to shipping documents and approved customer orders before invoices were recorded and sent would prevent other than *bona fide* sales transactions from being recorded.

Solution 3-4 SIMULATION ANSWER: Revenue Cycle Internal Controls Flowchart

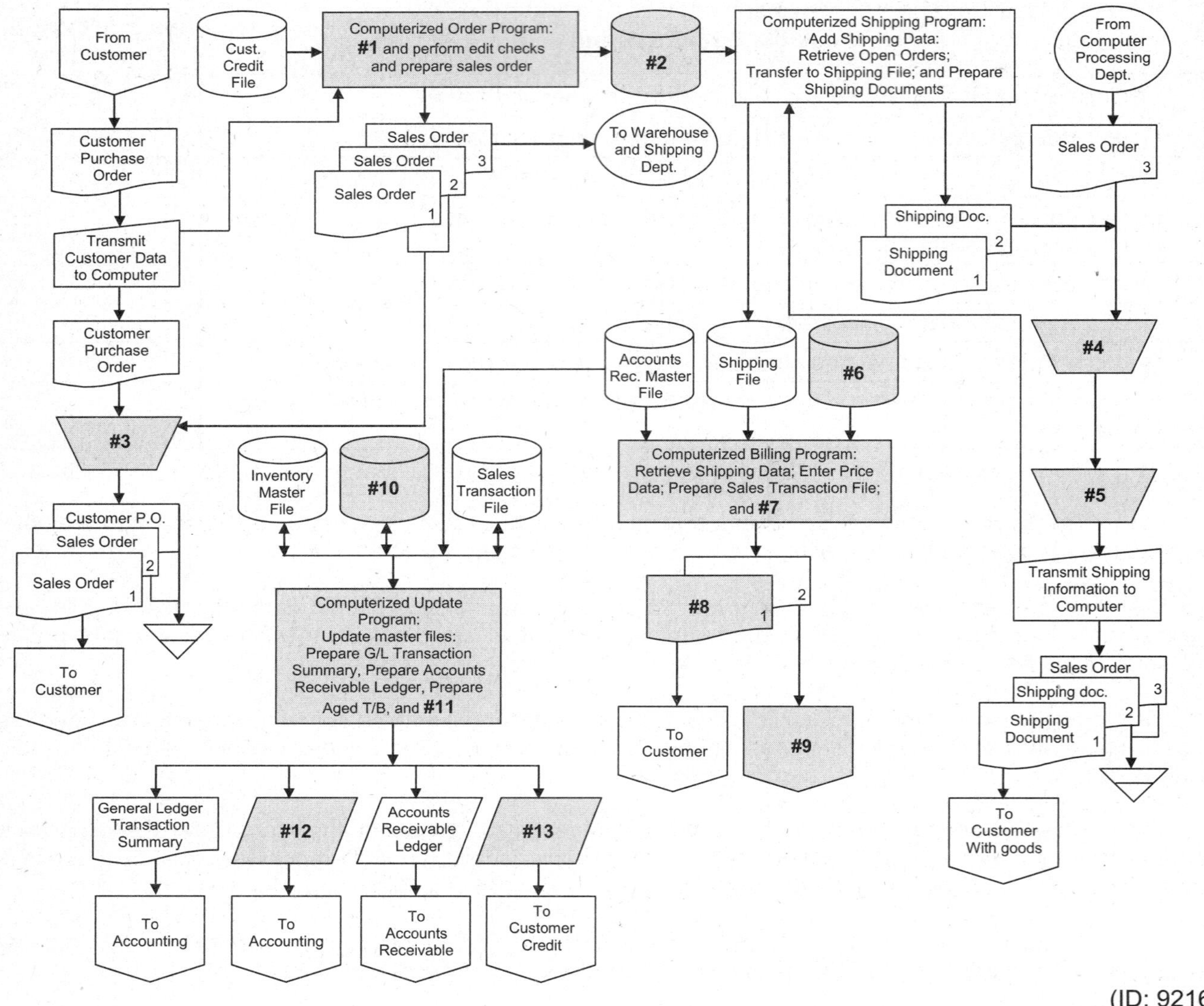

(ID: 9216)

1. M Before preparing a sales order, the Computer Processing Department should perform a credit check to determine that the sale will be made to a creditworthy customer. This information may be obtained from the customer credit file or from outside sources.

2. Z Once the sales order has been prepared, it will be recorded and placed in the open order file.

3. L This manual operation represents the process of matching customer purchase orders with sales orders for agreement.

4. B This manual operation represents matching the shipping document with the sales order for agreement.

5. H Once the shipping document and sales order have been matched, the goods will be released for shipment.

6. S In order to prepare the customer bill, the computerized billing program will retrieve the shipping data from the shipping file and enter the price data from the master price file.

7. O Once the shipping data and price data have been retrieved and the sale to the customer generated, the sales invoice will be prepared.

8. U This document represents the duplicate copy of the sales invoice generated by the computerized billing program.

9. I One copy of the sales invoice will be sent to the customer, and another copy will be sent to the Accounts Receivable Department as support for the entry to the accounts receivable ledger—to be held until remittance is made by the customer.

10. Q The Computer Processing Department will (daily, weekly, or monthly) update the master files, such as the accounts receivable ledger, the inventory master file, the sales transaction file, and the general ledger master file.

11. N The computer processing department will prepare, based upon the update program, an accounts receivable ledger, an aged trial balance, a general ledger transaction summary, and a sales journal.

12. T This output function represents the sales journal which was generated by the computerized update program for the day, week, or month, depending upon the frequency of report generation established by management.

13. Y This output report represents the aged trial balance generated by the computerized update program, which combined information from the general ledger master file, the sales transaction file, and the inventory master file.

CHANGE ALERT

SAS 128 (AU 610), *Using the Work of Internal Auditors*; issued 2/2014

In February 2014, the Auditing Standards Board of the American Institute of Certified Public Accountants (AICPA) issued Statement on Auditing Standards (SAS) 128, *Using the Work of Internal Auditors*, codified in AU 610 of the same title. It is effective for audits of financial statements for periods ending on or after December 15, 2014. Early application is permitted because it is not expressly prohibited.

The extant [still existing when this volume went to press] guidance (superseded by the issuance of this SAS) has been recodified via the addition of the suffix "A" to the same section number. AU 610A, *The Auditor's Consideration of the Internal Audit Function in an Audit of Financial Statements*, will be retained by the AICPA until the new guidance becomes effective—for audits of financial statements for periods ending on or after December 15, 2014.

If you are testing in the October–November 2014 exam window, both the extant and new guidance are eligible to be tested.

Beginning with the January–February 2015 exam window, only the new guidance is eligible to be tested.

This was the only remaining standard that was not revised by the AICPA's previous clarifying pronouncements. It was recodified along with the rest, i.e., given a new AU section number (610); however, until this SAS (128) was issued, AU 610 had been updated only for cross-references to the other redrafted (clarified) standards. SAS 128 redrafts AU 610 according to the conforming directives of the AICPA's Clarity Project. If you would like more information about the Clarity Project, please download our version 42 series updating supplement from our CPA Review website (cpaexam.com/support/#.Ubd3meeOR8F).

The new guidance is covered in topic V. of this chapter. For our coverage of the differences between the extant and new guidance, please see our version 43 series updating supplement, also available for download our CPA Review website (cpaexam.com/support/#.Ubd3meeOR8F).

AU Identifier Used for Clarified US GAAS in This Textbook

We have not continued to use the temporary AU-C identifier for the clarified auditing standards issued by the AICPA. In this textbook these standards have an AU identifier.

CHAPTER 4

EVIDENCE & PROCEDURES

AU Identifier Used for Clarified US GAAS in This Textbook

We have not continued to use the temporary AU-C identifier for the clarified auditing standards issued by the American Institute of Certified Public Accountants (AICPA). In this textbook these standards have an AU identifier.

CHAPTER 4

EVIDENCE & PROCEDURES

I. Audit Evidence (AU 500)

The objective of the auditor is to design and perform audit procedures that enable the auditor to obtain sufficient appropriate audit evidence to be able to draw reasonable conclusions on which to base the auditor's opinion.

Most of the auditor's work in forming the auditor's opinion consists of obtaining and evaluating audit evidence.

A. Definitions

1. **Accounting Records** The records of initial accounting entries and supporting records, such as checks and records of electronic fund transfers; invoices; contracts; the general and subsidiary ledgers; journal entries and other adjustments to the financial statements that are not reflected in journal entries; and records, such as work sheets and spreadsheets, supporting cost allocations, computations, reconciliations, and disclosures

2. **Appropriateness of Audit Evidence** The measure of the quality of audit evidence, i.e., its relevance and reliability in providing support for the conclusions on which the auditor's opinion is based

3. **Audit Evidence** Information used by the auditor in arriving at the conclusions on which the auditor's opinion is based; audit evidence includes both information contained in the accounting records underlying the financial statements and other information

4. **Management's Specialist** An individual or organization possessing expertise in a field other than accounting or auditing, whose work in that field is used by the entity to assist the entity in preparing the financial statements

   Editor Note: If the specialist is engaged directly by the auditor instead of the entity, the specialist is known as an *auditor's specialist* and the related US GAAS (AU 620) is covered in another section of this chapter.

5. **Sufficiency of Audit Evidence** The measure of the quantity of audit evidence; the quantity of the audit evidence needed is affected by the auditor's assessment of the risks of material misstatement (RMM) and also by the quality of such audit evidence

B. Sufficient Appropriate Audit Evidence

The auditor should design and perform audit procedures that are appropriate in the circumstances for the purpose of obtaining sufficient appropriate audit evidence.

1. **Reasonable Assurance Is the Goal** Reasonable assurance is obtained when the auditor has obtained sufficient appropriate audit evidence to reduce audit risk, i.e., the risk that the auditor expresses an inappropriate opinion when the financial statements are materially misstated, to an acceptably low level.

2. **Nature & Timing of Audit Evidence** Audit evidence is cumulative in nature and comprises both information that supports and corroborates management's assertions and any information that contradicts such assertions. In addition, in some cases, the absence of information (for example, management's refusal to provide a requested representation) constitutes evidence.

The nature and timing of the audit procedures may be affected by the fact that some of the accounting data and other information may be available only in electronic form and/or only at certain points or periods in time.

3. **Sources of Audit Evidence** Audit evidence is primarily obtained from audit procedures performed during the course of the audit, often through testing the entity's accounting records, but also from other sources both inside and outside the entity. It may also include information obtained from previous audits (provided that the auditor has determined whether changes have occurred since the previous audits that may affect its relevance to the current audit) or a firm's quality control procedures for client acceptance and continuance.

   a. **Limitations of Accounting Records as a Source of Audit Evidence** Through the performance of audit procedures that test the accounting records, the auditor may determine that the records are internally consistent and agree to the financial statements. However, accounting records alone do **not** provide sufficient appropriate audit evidence on which to base an audit opinion.

   b. **Sources of Evidence That Provide More Assurance** More assurance is ordinarily obtained from:

      (1) Consistent audit evidence obtained from different sources or of a different nature (corroborating information) than from items of audit evidence considered individually

      (2) Information obtained from a source independent of the entity, such as:

         (a) Confirmations from third parties

         (b) Analysts' reports

         (c) Comparable data about competitors (benchmarking data)

4. **Categories of Audit Procedures for Obtaining Audit Evidence** Audit evidence is obtained by performing:

   a. Risk assessment procedures

   b. Further audit procedures, which comprise:

      (1) Tests of controls, when required by US GAAS or when the auditor has chosen to do so

      (2) Substantive procedures, which include:

         (a) Tests of details

         (b) Substantive analytical procedures

5. **Types of Procedures** The following audit procedures, often in some combination, may be used as risk assessment procedures, tests of controls, or substantive procedures, depending on the context in which they are applied by the auditor.

   a. **Inspection** Inspection involves examining records or documents, whether internal or external, in paper form, electronic form, or other media; or a physical examination of an asset. Inspection of records and documents provides audit evidence of varying degrees of reliability, depending on their nature and source and, in the case of internal records and documents, the effectiveness of the controls over their production.

Examples and aspects of the nature of inspection to consider include:

(1) An example of inspection used as a test of controls is the inspection of records for evidence of authorization.

(2) Some documents represent direct audit evidence of the existence of an asset, for example, a document constituting a financial instrument such as a stock or bond; however, inspection of such documents may *not* necessarily provide audit evidence about ownership or value. Similarly, inspection of tangible assets may provide reliable audit evidence with respect to their existence, but not necessarily about the entity's rights and obligations or the valuation of the assets.

(3) Inspecting an executed contract may provide audit evidence relevant to the entity's application of accounting policies, such as revenue recognition.

(4) Inspection of individual inventory items may accompany the observation of inventory counting. For example, when observing an inventory count, the auditor may inspect individual inventory items (such as opening containers included in the inventory count to determine whether they are full or empty) to verify their existence.

b. **Observation** Observation consists of looking at a process or procedure being performed by others.

(1) **Limitations** Observation is limited:

(a) To the point in time at which the observation takes place

(b) By the fact that the act of being observed may affect how the process or procedure is performed

(2) **Examples** The auditor's observation of

- Inventory counting by the entity's personnel
- Performance of control activities

c. **External Confirmation** An external confirmation is a direct written response to the auditor from a third party (the confirming party) in paper form or by electronic or other medium.

External confirmation procedures frequently are relevant when addressing assertions associated with certain account balances and their elements; however, external confirmations need not be restricted to account balances. For example, the auditor may request confirmation of the terms of agreements or transactions an entity has with third parties. (US GAAS related to external confirmations is covered in chapter 5 of this text.)

d. **Recalculation** Recalculation consists of checking the mathematical accuracy of documents or records; it may be performed manually or electronically.

e. **Reperformance** Reperformance involves the independent execution of procedures or controls that were originally performed as part of the entity's internal control.

f. **Analytical Procedures** Analytical procedures consist of evaluations of financial information through analysis of plausible relationships among both financial and nonfinancial data.

Analytical procedures also encompass such investigation as is necessary of identified fluctuations and relationships that are inconsistent with other relevant information or that differ from expected values by a significant amount. (US GAAS related to analytical procedures is covered in another section of this chapter.)

g. **Inquiry**

(1) **Nature** Inquiry consists of seeking information of knowledgeable persons, both financial and nonfinancial, within the entity or outside the entity. It is used extensively throughout the audit, in addition to other audit procedures.

Inquiries may range from formal written inquiries to informal oral inquiries. Regarding some matters, the auditor may consider it necessary to obtain written representations from management and, when appropriate, those charged with governance, to confirm responses to oral inquiries. (US GAAS related to written representations is covered in another section of this chapter.)

(2) **Limitations of Inquiries by an Auditor** Although inquiry may provide important audit evidence and may even produce evidence of a misstatement, inquiry *alone* ordinarily:

(a) Does **not** provide sufficient audit evidence of the absence of a material misstatement at the assertion level

(b) Is **not** sufficient to test the operating effectiveness of controls

(3) **Evaluating Responses to Inquiries** Evaluating responses to inquiries is an integral part of the inquiry process. Responses to inquiries may provide the auditor with information not previously possessed or with corroborative audit evidence. Alternatively, responses might provide information that differs significantly from other information that the auditor has obtained. In some cases, responses to inquiries provide a basis for the auditor to modify or perform additional audit procedures.

(4) **Corroboration of Inquiries About Management Intent** Although corroboration of evidence obtained through inquiry is often of particular importance, in the case of inquiries about management intent, the information available to support management's intent may be limited.

Relevant information to corroborate evidence about management intent may include:

(a) Understanding management's past history of carrying out its stated intentions

(b) Management's stated reasons for choosing a particular course of action

(c) Management's ability to pursue a specific course of action

C. Information to Be Used as Audit Evidence

1. **Consideration of Relevance & Reliability of Evidence** When designing and performing audit procedures, the auditor should consider the relevance and reliability (the quality) of the information to be used as audit evidence.

    a. **Relevance** Relevance relates to the logical connection with, or bearing upon, the purpose of the audit procedure and, when appropriate, the assertion under consideration.

    (1) **Direction of Testing** The relevance of information to be used as audit evidence may be affected by the direction of testing. For example:

    (a) **Overstatement of Accounts Payable / Existence or Valuation Assertion** If the purpose of an audit procedure is to test for overstatement in the existence or valuation of accounts payable, testing the recorded accounts payable may be a relevant audit procedure.

    (b) **Understatement of Accounts Payable / Existence or Valuation Assertion** On the other hand, when testing for understatement in the existence or valuation of accounts payable, testing the recorded accounts payable would **not** be relevant (because the auditor is looking for items that are *not* recorded that should have been recorded), but testing such information as subsequent disbursements, unpaid invoices, suppliers' statements, and unmatched receiving reports may be relevant.

    (2) **Nature of the Assertion** A given set of audit procedures may provide audit evidence that is relevant to certain assertions but not others. For example, inspection of documents related to the collection of receivables after the period-end may provide audit evidence regarding existence and valuation but not necessarily cutoff. Similarly, obtaining audit evidence regarding a particular assertion (for example, the existence of inventory) is not a substitute for obtaining audit evidence regarding another assertion (for example, the valuation of that inventory). On the other hand, audit evidence from different sources or of a different nature may often be relevant to the same assertion.

    (3) **Tests of Controls** Designing tests of controls to obtain *relevant* audit evidence includes identifying conditions (characteristics or attributes) that indicate performance of a control and identifying deviation conditions that indicate departures from adequate performance. The presence or absence of those conditions can then be tested by the auditor.

    (4) **Substantive Procedures** Designing substantive procedures includes identifying conditions *relevant* to the purpose of the test that constitute a misstatement in the *relevant* assertion.

    b. **Reliability** The reliability of information to be used as audit evidence is influenced by its source and nature and the circumstances under which it is obtained, including the controls over its preparation and maintenance, when relevant.

    (1) **Generalizations About the Reliability of Audit Evidence** The following generalizations about the reliability of audit evidence may be useful:

    (a) **Independent Sources Outside the Entity** The reliability of audit evidence is increased when it is obtained from independent sources outside the entity.

(b) **Effective Controls** The reliability of audit evidence that is generated internally is increased when the related controls, including those over its preparation and maintenance, imposed by the entity are effective.

(c) **Audit Evidence Obtained Directly** Audit evidence obtained directly by the auditor (for example, observation of the application of a control) is more reliable than audit evidence obtained indirectly or by inference (for example, inquiry about the application of a control).

(d) **Written vs. Oral** Audit evidence in documentary form, whether paper, electronic, or other medium, is more reliable than evidence obtained orally (for example, a contemporaneously written record of a meeting is more reliable than a subsequent oral representation of the matters discussed).

(e) **Original Documents** Audit evidence provided by original documents is more reliable than audit evidence provided by photocopies, facsimiles, or documents that have been filmed, digitized, or otherwise transformed into electronic form, the reliability of which may depend on the controls over their preparation and maintenance.

(2) **Exceptions to the Generalizations About the Reliability of Audit Evidence** Generalizations about the reliability of various kinds of audit evidence are subject to important exceptions. For example, information obtained from an independent external source may not be reliable if the source is not knowledgeable or lacks objectivity.

2. **Audit Evidence Prepared Using the Work of a Management's Specialist** If information to be used as audit evidence has been prepared using the work of a management's specialist, the auditor should, to the extent necessary, taking into account the significance of that specialist's work for the auditor's purposes:

- Evaluate the competence, capabilities, and objectivity of that specialist
- Obtain an understanding of the work of that specialist
- Evaluate the appropriateness of that specialist's work as audit evidence for the relevant assertion

The above requirements only apply when information to be used as audit evidence has been prepared using the *work* of a management's specialist; however, for example, if the entity uses data supplied by a specialist, but uses its own estimation methods, these requirements do **not** apply.

a. **Overview** The preparation of an entity's financial statements may require expertise in a field other than accounting or auditing, such as actuarial calculations, valuations, or engineering data. The entity uses a management's specialist in these fields to obtain the needed expertise to prepare the financial statements. (Failure to do so when such expertise is necessary increases the RMM and may be a significant deficiency or material weakness.)

b. **Nature, Extent & Timing of Related Procedures** The nature, extent, and timing of audit procedures with regard to the requirements regarding the management's specialist *may* be affected by such matters as:

- The nature and complexity of the matter to which the management's specialist relates
- The RMM of the matter

- The availability of alternative sources of audit evidence
- The nature, scope, and objectives of the work of the management's specialist
- Whether the management's specialist is employed by the entity or is a party engaged by it to provide relevant services
- The extent to which management can exercise control or influence over the work of the management's specialist
- Whether the management's specialist is subject to technical performance standards or other professional or industry requirements
- The nature and extent of any controls within the entity over the work of the management's specialist
- The auditor's knowledge and experience of the field of expertise management's specialist
- The auditor's previous experience of the work of that specialist

c. **Evaluation of the Specialist's Competence, Capabilities & Objectivity**

(1) **Reliability** The competence, capabilities, and objectivity of a management's specialist, and any controls within the entity over that specialist's work, are important factors with regard to the reliability of any information produced by a management's specialist.

(2) **Competence vs. Capability** Competence relates to the nature and level of expertise of the management's specialist. Capability relates to the ability of the management's specialist to exercise that competence in the circumstances. Factors that influence capability may include, for example, geographic location and the availability of time and resources.

(3) **Objectivity** Objectivity relates to the possible effects that bias, conflict of interest, or the influence of others may have on the professional or business judgment of the management's specialist.

When evaluating the objectivity of a specialist engaged by the entity, it may be relevant to discuss with management and that specialist any interests and relationships that may create threats to the specialist's objectivity and any applicable safeguards, including any professional requirements that apply to the specialist, and to evaluate whether the safeguards are adequate.

(4) **Matters Relevant to the Evaluation** Matters relevant to the evaluation *may* include:

- Whether that specialist's work is subject to technical performance standards or other professional or industry requirements; accreditation standards of a licensing body; or requirements imposed by law or regulation
- The competence of the management's specialist with respect to relevant accounting requirements

d. **Obtain an Understanding of the Work of the Specialist** An understanding of the work of the management's specialist includes an understanding of the relevant field of expertise.

(1) **Determine If an Auditor's Specialist Is Needed** An understanding of the relevant field of expertise *may* be obtained in conjunction with the auditor's determination of whether the auditor has the expertise to evaluate the work of

the management's specialist, or whether the auditor needs an auditor's specialist for this purpose.

(2) **Review Specialist's Agreement With Entity** In the case of a management's specialist engaged by the entity, there will ordinarily be an engagement letter or other written form of agreement between the entity and that specialist. A review of this agreement *may* assist the auditor in determining for the auditor's purposes the appropriateness of:

- The nature, scope, and objectives of that specialist's work
- The respective roles and responsibilities of management and that specialist
- The nature, extent, and timing of communication between management and that specialist, including the form of any report to be provided by that specialist

Editor Note: In the case of a management's specialist employed by the entity, it is less likely that there will be a written agreement of this kind; thus, inquiry of the specialist and other members of management may be the most appropriate way for the auditor to obtain the necessary understanding.

e. **Evaluate the Appropriateness of the Specialist's Work as Audit Evidence for the Relevant Assertion** Considerations when evaluating the appropriateness of the work of the management's specialist as audit evidence for the relevant assertion *may* include:

- The relevance and reasonableness of that specialist's findings or conclusions; their consistency with other audit evidence; and whether they have been appropriately reflected in the financial statements
- If that specialist's work involves use of significant assumptions and methods, the relevance and reasonableness of those assumptions and methods
- If that specialist's work involves significant use of source data, the relevance, completeness, and accuracy of that source data

3. **Audit Evidence Produced by the Entity** When using information produced by the entity, including any by the management's specialist, the auditor should evaluate whether the information is sufficiently reliable for the auditor's purposes, including, as necessary, in the following circumstances:

a. **Obtaining Audit Evidence About the Accuracy & Completeness of the Information** Obtaining audit evidence about the accuracy and completeness of such information may be accomplished concurrently with the actual audit procedure applied to the information when obtaining such audit evidence is an integral part of the audit procedure itself. In other situations, the auditor may have obtained audit evidence of the accuracy and completeness of such information by testing controls over the preparation and maintenance of the information. In some situations; however, the auditor may determine that additional audit procedures are needed.

b. **Evaluating Whether the Information Is Sufficiently Precise & Detailed for the Auditor's Purposes** The appropriateness of the audit evidence obtained is affected by whether the information is sufficiently precise or detailed for the auditor's purposes.

D. Inconsistency in, or Doubts Over Reliability of, Audit Evidence

1. **Additional Audit Procedures** When audit evidence obtained from one source is inconsistent with that obtained from another or the auditor has doubts about the reliability of information, the auditor should determine what modifications or additions to audit procedures are necessary to resolve the matter and should consider the effect of the matter, if any, on other aspects of the audit.

2. **Documentation If Significant Finding Affected** In accordance with the standard on documentation (covered in another section of this chapter), if the auditor identified information that is inconsistent with the auditor's final conclusion regarding a significant finding or issue, the auditor should document how the auditor addressed the inconsistency.

E. Evaluating the Sufficiency & Appropriateness of Audit Evidence (AU 330)

1. **Evaluation of RMM at the Relevant Assertion Level** Based on the audit procedures performed and the audit evidence obtained, the auditor should evaluate, before the conclusion of the audit, whether the assessments of the RMM at the relevant assertion level remain appropriate.

   An audit of financial statements is a cumulative and iterative process. As the auditor performs planned audit procedures, the audit evidence obtained *may* cause the auditor to modify the nature, extent, or timing of other planned audit procedures. Additionally, information may come to the auditor's attention that differs significantly from the information on which the risk assessments were based. For example:

   - The extent of misstatements that the auditor detects by performing substantive procedures may alter the auditor's professional judgment about the risk assessments and indicate a significant deficiency or material weakness in internal control.
   - The auditor may become aware of discrepancies in accounting records or conflicting or missing evidence.
   - Analytical procedures performed at the overall review stage of the audit may indicate a previously unrecognized RMM.

2. **Determine If Sufficient Appropriate Audit Evidence Has Been Obtained** The auditor should conclude whether sufficient appropriate audit evidence has been obtained. In forming a conclusion, the auditor should consider all relevant audit evidence, regardless of whether it appears to corroborate or contradict the assertions in the financial statements.

   The auditor's professional judgment about what constitutes sufficient appropriate audit evidence *may* be influenced by such factors as the:

   - Significance of the potential misstatement in the relevant assertion and the likelihood of its having a material effect, individually or aggregated with other potential misstatements, on the financial statements (evaluation of misstatements identified during the audit is covered in chapter 2 of this text.)
   - Effectiveness of management's responses and controls to address the risks
   - Experience gained during previous audits with respect to similar potential misstatements
   - Results of audit procedures performed, including whether such audit procedures identified specific instances of fraud or error
   - Source and reliability of the available information
   - Persuasiveness of the audit evidence
   - Understanding of the entity and its environment, including its internal control

3. **Audit Evidence Is Lacking** If the auditor has **not** obtained sufficient appropriate audit evidence about a relevant assertion:

   a. The auditor should attempt to obtain further audit evidence.

   b. If the auditor is unable to obtain sufficient appropriate audit evidence, the auditor should express a qualified opinion or disclaim an opinion on the financial statements.

II. Analytical Procedures (AU 520)

A. Overview

1. Objectives

a. Obtain relevant and reliable audit evidence when using substantive analytical procedures

b. Design and perform analytical procedures near the end of the audit that assist the auditor (corroborate audit evidence obtained during the audit) when forming an overall conclusion about whether the financial statements are consistent with the auditor's understanding of the entity

Editor Note: The use of *substantive* analytical procedures during the audit is left to the auditor's professional judgment; however, US GAAS requires the use of analytical procedures at the start of the audit and near its end. Analytical procedures used as risk assessment procedures to plan the audit are required, as are analytical procedures during the overall review phase of the audit to help the auditor form a conclusion about the financial statements. US GAAS defines *analytical procedures* (see the following definition) in the same manner regardless of their purpose in an audit.

2. **Definition of Analytical Procedures** Evaluations of financial information through analysis of plausible relationships among both financial and nonfinancial data; analytical procedures also encompass such investigation, as is necessary, of identified fluctuations or relationships that are inconsistent with other relevant information or that differ from expected values by a significant amount

3. **Nature of Analytical Procedures** Various methods may be used to perform analytical procedures. These methods range from performing simple comparisons to performing complex analyses using advanced statistical techniques. Analytical procedures may be applied to consolidated financial statements, components, and individual elements of information.

   a. **Comparisons** Analytical procedures include the consideration of comparisons of the entity's financial information with:

      - Comparable information for prior periods
      - Anticipated results of the entity, such as budgets or forecasts, or expectations of the auditor, such as an estimation of depreciation
      - Similar industry information, such as a comparison of the entity's ratio of sales to accounts receivable and gross margin percentages with industry averages or other entities of comparable size in the same industry

   b. **Relationships** Analytical procedures also include consideration of relationships:

      - Among elements of financial information, such as gross margin percentages, that would be expected to conform to a predictable pattern based on recent history of the entity and industry

- Between financial information and relevant nonfinancial information, such as payroll costs to number of employees

c. **Scanning**

(1) **Definition** A type of analytical procedure involving the auditor's exercise of professional judgment to review accounting data to identify significant or unusual items to test

(2) **Use in Obtaining Audit Evidence** This may include the identification of unusual individual items within account balances or other data through the reading or analysis of, for example, entries in transaction listings, subsidiary ledgers, general ledger control accounts, adjusting entries, suspense accounts, reconciliations, and other detailed reports. Scanning may include searching for large or unusual items in the accounting records (for example, nonstandard journal entries), as well as in transaction data (for example, suspense accounts and adjusting journal entries) for indications of misstatements that have occurred. Electronic audit procedures may assist the auditor in identifying unusual items. When the auditor selects items for testing by scanning and those items are tested, the auditor obtains audit evidence about those items. The auditor's scanning also may provide some audit evidence about the items not selected for testing because the auditor has exercised professional judgment to determine that the items not selected are less likely to be misstated.

4. **Addressing the Assessed RMM** The auditor's substantive procedures to address the assessed risk of material misstatement (RMM) for relevant assertions may be tests of details, substantive analytical procedures, or a combination of both.

The decision about which audit procedures to perform, including whether to use substantive analytical procedures, is based on the auditor's professional judgment about the expected effectiveness and efficiency of the available audit procedures to reduce the assessed RMM to an acceptably low level.

The expected effectiveness and efficiency of a substantive analytical procedure in addressing RMM depends on, among other things, the:

- Nature of the assertion
- Plausibility and predictability of the relationship
- Availability and reliability of the data used to develop the expectation
- Precision of the expectation

B. Substantive Analytical Procedures

When designing and performing analytical procedures, either alone or in combination with tests of details, the auditor should:

- Determine the suitability of particular substantive analytical procedures for given assertions, taking into account the assessed RMM and tests of details, if any, for these assertions
- Evaluate the reliability of data from which the auditor's expectation of recorded amounts or ratios is developed, taking into account the source, comparability, and nature and relevance of information available and controls over preparation
- Develop an expectation of recorded amounts or ratios and evaluate whether the expectation is sufficiently precise (taking into account whether substantive analytical procedures are to be performed alone or in combination with tests of details) to identify a misstatement that, individually or when aggregated with other misstatements, may cause the financial statements to be materially misstated

- Determine the amount of any difference of recorded amounts from expected values that is acceptable without further investigation and compare the recorded amounts, or ratios developed from recorded amounts, with the expectations

1. **Determine Suitability of Procedures for Given Assertions** The determination of the suitability of particular substantive analytical procedures is influenced by the nature of the assertion; the auditor's assessment of the RMM; and tests of details, if any, for these assertions

   a. **More Persuasive Audit Evidence Requires More Predictable Relationships** When more persuasive audit evidence is desired from substantive analytical procedures, more predictable relationships are necessary to develop the expectation, such as:

   - Relationships in a stable environment are usually more predictable than relationships in a dynamic or unstable environment.
   - Relationships involving income statement accounts tend to be more predictable than relationships involving only balance sheet accounts because income statement accounts represent transactions over a period of time, whereas balance sheet accounts represent amounts as of a point in time.
   - Relationships involving transactions subject to management discretion may be less predictable. For example, management may elect to incur maintenance expense rather than replace plant and equipment, or they may delay advertising expenditures.

   b. **Analytical Procedures Are Suited to Large Volumes of Transactions That Are Predictable Over Time** Substantive analytical procedures are generally more effective for large volumes of transactions that tend to be predictable over time. (The application of planned analytical procedures is based on the expectation that relationships among data exist and continue in the absence of known conditions to the contrary.)

   In addition to misstatements, particular conditions that can cause variations in these relationships include:

   - Specific unusual transactions or events
   - Accounting changes
   - Business changes
   - Random fluctuations

   The suitability of a particular analytical procedure will depend upon the auditor's assessment of how effective it will be in detecting a misstatement that, individually or when aggregated with other misstatements, may cause the financial statements to be materially misstated.

   c. **Different Types of Analytical Procedures Provide Different Levels of Assurance** Analytical procedures may be used to predict with a high degree of accuracy, for example, total rental income on a building divided into apartments or payroll costs for a known number of employees at fixed rates of pay, providing persuasive evidence for significant items and perhaps eliminating the need for further verification by tests of details. On the other hand, calculation and comparison of gross margin percentages as a means of confirming a revenue figure may provide less persuasive evidence, but may provide useful corroboration if used in combination with other audit procedures.

   d. **When Tests of Details & Analytical Procedures Are Performed on the Same Assertion** Particular substantive analytical procedures may also be considered suitable when tests of details are performed on the same assertion. For example, when obtaining audit evidence regarding the valuation assertion for accounts receivable balances, the auditor may apply analytical procedures to an aging of customers' accounts, in addition to performing tests of details on subsequent cash receipts, to determine the collectability of the receivables.

2. **Evaluate the Reliability of the Data From Which the Auditor's Expectation of Recorded Amounts or Ratios Is Developed**

   a. **Influences on the Reliability of the Data** The reliability of data is influenced by its source and nature and is dependent on the circumstances under which it is obtained. Accordingly, the following are relevant when determining whether data is reliable for purposes of designing substantive analytical procedures:

      (1) **Source** The source of the information available, for example, information may be more reliable when it is obtained from independent sources outside the entity

      (2) **Comparability** The comparability of the information available, for example, broad industry data may need to be supplemented to be comparable to that of an entity that produces and sells specialized products

      (3) **Nature & Relevance** The nature and relevance of the information available, for example, whether budgets have been established as results to be expected rather than as goals to be achieved

      (4) **Controls Over Preparation** Controls over the preparation of the information that are designed to ensure its completeness, accuracy, and validity, for example, controls over the preparation, review, and maintenance of budgets

   b. **Use of Tests of Controls to Obtain More Confidence in the Reliability of the Data** The auditor may consider testing the operating effectiveness of controls, if any, over the entity's preparation of information used by the auditor in performing substantive analytical procedures. When such controls are effective, the auditor may have greater confidence in the reliability of the information and, therefore, in the results of analytical procedures.

3. **Develop Expectation Precise Enough to Identify a Material Misstatement** Develop an expectation of recorded amounts or ratios and evaluate whether the expectation is sufficiently precise (taking into account whether substantive analytical procedures are to be performed alone or in combination with tests of details) to identify a misstatement that, individually or when aggregated with other misstatements, may cause the financial statements to be materially misstated

   a. **A More Precise Expectation Is Needed If Substantive Analytical Procedures Are to Be Performed Alone** A more precise expectation is necessary when the substantive analytical procedure is the only procedure planned to address a particular risk of misstatement for a relevant assertion.

   b. **The Range of Expected Differences Narrows As Expectations Become More Precise** As expectations become more precise, the range of expected differences becomes narrower, and accordingly, the likelihood increases that significant differences from the expectations are due to misstatements.

Matters relevant to the auditor's evaluation of whether the expectation can be developed with sufficient precision to identify a misstatement that, when aggregated with other misstatements, may cause the financial statements to be materially misstated, include the following:

- The accuracy with which the expected results of substantive analytical procedures can be predicted, for example, the auditor may expect greater consistency in comparing gross profit margins from one period to another than in comparing discretionary expenses, such as research or advertising
- The degree to which information can be disaggregated, for example, substantive analytical procedures may be more effective when applied to financial information on individual sections of an operation or to financial statements of components of a diversified entity than when applied to the financial statements of the entity as a whole

c. **Expectations Developed at a More Detailed Level Are More Likely to Be Effective** When expectations are developed at a more detailed level, it is more likely that the analytical procedure will more effectively address the assessed RMM to which it is directed.

The appropriate level of detail may be influenced by the nature of the entity, its size, and its complexity. The risk that material misstatements may be obscured by offsetting factors increases as an entity's operations become more complex and diversified. Disaggregation of the information helps reduce this risk.

4. **Determine Acceptable Difference & Compare** Determine the amount of any difference of recorded amounts from expected values that is acceptable without further investigation and compare the recorded amounts, or ratios developed from recorded amounts, with the expectations

The auditor's determination of the amount of difference from the expectation that can be accepted without further investigation is influenced by materiality and the desired level of assurance, while taking into account the possibility that a misstatement, individually or when aggregated with other misstatements, may cause the financial statements to be materially misstated. US GAAS requires the auditor to obtain more persuasive audit evidence the higher the auditor's assessment of risk. Accordingly, as the assessed risk increases, the amount of difference considered acceptable without further investigation decreases in order to achieve the desired level of persuasive evidence.

C. Analytical Procedures That Assist When Forming an Overall Conclusion

1. **Analytical Procedures for Overall Review** The auditor should design and perform analytical procedures near the end of the audit that assist the auditor when forming an overall conclusion about whether the financial statements are consistent with the auditor's understanding of the entity.

The analytical procedures performed for the overall review *may* be similar to those that would be used as risk assessment procedures.

These procedures *may* include reading the financial statements and considering:

- The adequacy of the evidence gathered in response to unusual or unexpected balances identified during the course of the audit
- Unusual or unexpected balances or relationships that were not previously identified

Results of these analytical procedures may indicate that additional evidence is needed.

2. **When a Previously Unrecognized RMM Is Revealed** The results of analytical procedures designed and performed for the overall review may identify a previously unrecognized RMM. In such circumstances, US GAAS requires the auditor to revise the auditor's assessment of the RMM and modify the further planned audit procedures accordingly.

D. **Investigating Results of Analytical Procedures**
If analytical procedures performed identify fluctuations or relationships that are inconsistent with other relevant information or that differ from expected values by a significant amount, the auditor should investigate such differences by:

1. Inquiring of management and obtaining appropriate audit evidence relevant to management's responses

   Audit evidence relevant to management's responses *may* be obtained by evaluating those responses, taking into account the auditor's understanding of the entity and its environment and other audit evidence obtained during the course of the audit.

2. Performing other audit procedures as necessary in the circumstances

   The need to perform other audit procedures *may* arise when, for example, management is unable to provide an explanation, or the explanation, together with the audit evidence obtained relevant to management's response, is not considered adequate.

E. **Audit Documentation**
When substantive analytical procedures have been performed, the auditor should include in the audit documentation:

1. The expectation of recorded amounts or ratios developed and the factors considered in its development when that expectation or those factors are not otherwise readily determinable from the audit documentation

2. Results of the comparison of the recorded amounts, or ratios developed from recorded amounts, with the expectations

3. Any additional auditing procedures performed relating to the investigation of fluctuations or relationships that are inconsistent with other relevant information or that differ from expected values by a significant amount and the results of such additional procedures

III. Opening Balances in an Initial Audit Engagement (AU 510)

This guidance*, with respect to predecessor auditors*, does **not** apply if the most recent audited financial statements are more than one year prior to the beginning of the earliest period to be audited.

A. Overview

1. **Objective** The objective of the auditor, in conducting an initial audit engagement, including a reaudit engagement, is to obtain sufficient appropriate audit evidence regarding opening balances about whether:

   a. **Accuracy of Opening Balances** Opening balances contain misstatements that materially affect the current period's financial statements

   b. **Consistency of Accounting Principles** Appropriate accounting policies reflected in the opening balances have been consistently applied in the current period's financial statements or changes are appropriately accounted for and adequately presented and disclosed in accordance with the AFRF

2. **Definitions**

   a. **Initial Audit Engagement** An engagement in which the financial statements for the prior period were *either*:

      (1) Not audited; or

      (2) Audited by a predecessor auditor

   b. **Opening Balances** Those account balances that exist at the beginning of the period

      (1) Opening balances are based upon the closing balances of the prior period and reflect the effects of transactions and events of prior periods and accounting policies applied in the prior period.

      (2) Opening balances also include matters requiring disclosure that existed at the beginning of the period, such as contingencies and commitments.

   c. **Predecessor Auditor** The auditor from a different audit firm who has reported on the most recent audited financial statements or was engaged to perform but did not complete an audit of the financial statements

   d. **Reaudit** An initial audit engagement to audit financial statements that have been previously audited by a predecessor auditor

B. **Audit Procedures**

1. **Read the Most Recent Financial Statements & Related Audit Report** The auditor should read the most recent financial statements, if any, and the predecessor auditor's related report, if any, for information relevant to opening balances, including disclosures, and consistency in the application of accounting policies.

2. **Review the Predecessor's Audit Documentation & Make Inquiries** In instances in which the prior period financial statements were audited by a predecessor auditor, the auditor should request management to authorize the predecessor auditor to allow a review of the predecessor auditor's audit documentation and for the predecessor auditor to respond fully to inquiries by the auditor, thereby providing the auditor with information to assist in planning and performing the engagement.

   a. **Timing** The auditor *may* initiate communications with management to authorize this review either before or after accepting the engagement.

   b. **Predecessor *May* Request Acknowledgement Letters**

      (1) **From the Entity** The predecessor auditor *may* request a consent and acknowledgment letter from the entity to document this authorization in an effort to reduce misunderstandings about the scope of the communications being authorized.

      (2) **From the Auditor** Before permitting access to the audit documentation, the predecessor auditor may request written confirmation of the auditor's agreement regarding the use of the audit documentation.

   c. **Level of Cooperation Is Determined by the Predecessor** The extent, if any, to which a predecessor auditor permits access to the audit documentation or responds to inquiries from the auditor is a matter of the predecessor auditor's professional judgment. The predecessor auditor determines which audit documentation is to be made available for review and which may be copied; however, it is customary for the predecessor auditor to make himself or herself available to the auditor and to make available for review certain audit documentation.

(1) **Types of Audit Documentation Normally Made Available** The predecessor auditor ordinarily permits the auditor to review audit documentation of planning; risk assessment procedures; further audit procedures; audit results; and other matters of continuing accounting and auditing significance, such as the schedule of uncorrected misstatements, working paper analysis of balance sheet accounts, and those relating to contingencies.

(2) **If Predecessor Denies or Restricts Access** The predecessor auditor's denial or limitation of access may affect the auditor's assessment of risk regarding the opening balances or the nature, extent, and timing of the auditor's procedures with respect to the opening balances and consistency of accounting principles.

d. **Auditor's Assessment of the Professional Competence & Independence of the Predecessor Auditor** The auditor's determination of whether to use information resulting from such review as part of the auditor's risk assessment procedures or as evidence regarding the opening balances is influenced by the auditor's assessment of the professional competence and independence of the predecessor auditor. The auditor *may* make inquiries about these attributes of the predecessor auditor.

e. **Audit Work & Conclusions Are Solely Those of the Auditor** The auditor's review of the predecessor auditor's audit documentation may provide audit evidence about the opening balances and consistency of accounting principles; however, the nature, extent, and timing of audit work performed and the conclusions reached are solely the responsibility of the auditor.

3. **Opening Balances** The auditor should obtain sufficient appropriate audit evidence about whether the opening balances contain misstatements that materially affect the current period's financial statements by:

a. **Closing Balances Correctly Brought Forward** Determining whether the prior period's closing balances have been correctly brought forward to the current period or, when appropriate, have been restated

b. **Appropriate Accounting Policies** Determining whether the opening balances reflect the application of appropriate accounting policies

c. **Evidence** Evaluating whether audit procedures performed in the current period provide evidence relevant to the opening balances and performing one or both of the following:

(1) When the prior year financial statements were audited, reviewing the predecessor auditor's audit documentation to obtain evidence regarding the opening balances

(2) Performing specific audit procedures to obtain evidence regarding the opening balances

(a) The nature and extent of audit procedures are influenced by:

- The accounting policies followed by the entity
- The nature of the account balances, classes of transactions and disclosures, and the risk of material misstatement (RMM) in the current period's financial statements

- The significance of the opening balances relative to the current period's financial statements
- Whether the prior period's financial statements were audited and, if so, whether the predecessor auditor's opinion was modified

(b) **Current Assets & Liabilities** For current assets and liabilities, some audit evidence about opening balances *may* be obtained as part of the current period's audit procedures. For example, the collection (payment) of opening accounts receivable (accounts payable) during the current period will provide some audit evidence of their existence, rights and obligations, completeness, and valuation at the beginning of the period.

In the case of inventories, however, the current period's audit procedures on the closing inventory balance provide little audit evidence regarding inventory on hand at the beginning of the period. Therefore, additional audit procedures, such as one or more of the following, *may* be necessary to obtain sufficient appropriate audit evidence:

- Observing a current physical inventory count and reconciling it to the opening inventory quantities
- Performing audit procedures on the valuation of the opening inventory items
- Performing audit procedures on gross profit and cutoff

(c) **Noncurrent Assets & Liabilities** For noncurrent assets and liabilities, such as property, plant, and equipment; investments; and long-term debt, some audit evidence *may* be obtained by examining the accounting records and other information underlying the opening balances. In certain cases, the auditor may be able to obtain some audit evidence regarding opening balances through confirmation with third parties (for example, for long-term debt and investments). In other cases, the auditor *may* need to carry out additional audit procedures.

(d) **Examples of Evidence** Audit evidence regarding opening balances and the consistency of accounting principles *may* include the most recent audited financial statements; the predecessor's related audit report; the results of inquiry of the predecessor auditor; the results of the auditor's review of the predecessor auditor's audit documentation relating to the most recently completed audit; and audit procedures performed on the current period's transactions that may provide evidence about the opening balances or consistency.

4. **When Opening Balances Contain Material Misstatements** If the auditor obtains audit evidence that the opening balances contain misstatements that could materially affect the current period's financial statements, the auditor should:

   a. **Determine Effect on the Current Period's Financial Statements** Perform such additional audit procedures as are appropriate in the circumstances to determine the effect on the current period's financial statements

   b. **Communicate Such Misstatements** If the auditor concludes that such misstatements exist in the current period's financial statements, the auditor should communicate the misstatements to the appropriate level of management and those charged with governance.

c. **Possible Material Misstatements in Financial Statements Reported on by a Predecessor Auditor** If the prior period financial statements were audited by a predecessor auditor:

(1) **Attempt to Resolve the Matter by Meeting With Management & the Predecessor Auditor** In this situation (opening balances contain misstatements) or if the auditor becomes aware of information during the audit that leads the auditor to believe that financial statements reported on by the predecessor auditor may require revision, the auditor should request management to inform the predecessor auditor of the situation and arrange for the three parties to discuss this information and attempt to resolve the matter.

The auditor should communicate to the predecessor auditor information that the auditor believes the predecessor auditor may need to consider, in accordance with AU 560, *Subsequent Events and Subsequently Discovered Facts*, which addresses the auditor's responsibilities when facts become known to the auditor after the date of the audit report that, had they been known to the auditor at that date, may have caused the auditor to amend the audit report.

(2) **When the Matter Is *Not* Resolved** If management refuses to inform the predecessor auditor that the prior period financial statements may need revision or if the auditor is not satisfied with the resolution of the matter, the auditor should evaluate:

(a) The implications on the current engagement

(b) Whether to withdraw from the engagement or, when withdrawal is not possible under applicable law or regulation, disclaim an opinion on the financial statements; the auditor *may* seek legal advice in determining an appropriate course of action

5. **Consistency of Accounting Policies** The auditor should obtain sufficient appropriate audit evidence about whether the accounting policies reflected in the opening balances have been consistently applied in the current period's financial statements and whether changes in the accounting policies have been appropriately accounted for and adequately presented and disclosed in accordance with the AFRF.

6. **If Predecessor Auditor's Opinion Was Modified Address Impact on RMM** If the prior period's financial statements were audited by a predecessor auditor, and a modification was made to the opinion, the auditor should evaluate the effect of the matter giving rise to the modification in assessing the RMM in the current period's financial statements.

C. **Audit Conclusions & Reporting**

1. **Audit Report Should *Not* Reference Predecessor Auditor's Work or Report** The auditor should **not** make reference to the report or work of the predecessor auditor as the basis, in part, for the auditor's own opinion.

2. **Opening Balances**

a. **Scope Limitation** If the auditor is unable to obtain sufficient appropriate audit evidence regarding the opening balances, the auditor should express a qualified opinion or disclaim an opinion on the financial statements, as appropriate.

b. **Material Misstatement** If the auditor concludes that the opening balances contain a misstatement that materially affects the current period's financial statements, and the effect of the misstatement is not appropriately accounted for or adequately presented or disclosed, the auditor should express a qualified opinion or an adverse opinion, as appropriate.

3. **Consistency of Accounting Policies** The auditor should express a qualified opinion or an adverse opinion, as appropriate, if the auditor concludes that *either*:

   a. **Accounting Policies *Not* Consistently Applied** The current period's accounting policies are not consistently applied regarding opening balances, in accordance with the AFRF; or

   b. **Change in Accounting Policies *Not* Handled Correctly** A change in accounting policies is not appropriately accounted for or adequately presented or disclosed, in accordance with the AFRF

4. **Prior Year Modified Opinion *May* Result in Current Year Modified Opinion** If the predecessor auditor's opinion on the prior period's financial statements was modified and the reason for the modification remains relevant and material to the current period's financial statements, the auditor should modify the auditor's opinion on the current period's financial statements.

   Editor Note: An example of when a modification to the predecessor auditor's opinion that would *not* be relevant and material to the opinion on the current period's financial statements would be when the matter giving rise to a scope limitation in the prior period has been resolved in the current period.

IV. Using the Work of an Auditor's Specialist (AU 620)

A. Overview

1. **Objectives** The objectives of the auditor are:

   a. To determine whether to use the work of an auditor's specialist

   b. If using the work of an auditor's specialist, to determine whether that work is adequate for the auditor's purposes

2. **Definitions**

   a. **Auditor's Specialist** An individual or organization possessing expertise in a field other than accounting or auditing, whose work in that field is used by the auditor to assist the auditor in obtaining sufficient appropriate audit evidence; an auditor's specialist may be either an auditor's internal specialist (who is a partner or staff, including temporary staff, of the auditor's firm or a network firm) or an auditor's external specialist

   b. **Expertise** Skills, knowledge, and experience in a particular field

      Expertise in a field other than accounting or auditing *may* include expertise regarding such matters as:

      - The valuation of complex financial instruments and nonfinancial assets and liabilities measured at fair value such as land and buildings, plant and machinery, jewelry, works of art, antiques, intangible assets, assets acquired and liabilities assumed in business combinations, and assets that may have been impaired
      - The actuarial calculation of liabilities associated with insurance contracts or employee benefit plans
      - The estimation of oil and other mineral reserves

- The valuation of environmental liabilities and site cleanup costs
- The interpretation of contracts, laws, and regulations
- The analysis of complex or unusual tax compliance issues
- The determination of physical characteristics relating to quantity on hand or condition (for example, quantity or condition of minerals, or materials stored in stockpiles)

c. **Management's Specialist** An individual or organization possessing expertise in a field other than accounting or auditing, whose work in that field is used by the entity to assist the entity in preparing the financial statements

Editor Note: US GAAS (AU 500) related to a management's specialist is covered in another section of this chapter.

B. Determining the Need for an Auditor's Specialist
If expertise in a field other than accounting or auditing is necessary to obtain sufficient appropriate audit evidence, the auditor should determine whether to use the work of an auditor's specialist.

1. **Areas of Possible Assistance** An auditor's specialist *may* be needed to assist the auditor in one or more of the following:

   - Obtaining an understanding of the entity and its environment, including its internal control
   - Identifying and assessing the risk of material misstatement (RMM)
   - Determining and implementing overall responses to assessed risks at the financial statement level
   - Designing and performing additional audit procedures to respond to assessed risks at the relevant assertion level, which may comprise tests of controls or substantive procedures
   - Evaluating the sufficiency and appropriateness of audit evidence obtained in forming an opinion on the financial statements

2. **The Auditor *May* Gain an Understanding Instead of Using a Specialist** An auditor who is not a specialist in a relevant field may nevertheless be able to obtain a sufficient understanding of that field to perform the audit without an auditor's specialist. This understanding may be obtained through, for example:

   - Experience in auditing entities that require such expertise in the preparation of their financial statements
   - Education or professional development in the particular field

3. **Considerations When Making the Determination Whether to Use an Auditor's Specialist** Considerations when deciding whether to use an auditor's specialist *may* include:

   - The nature and significance of the matter, including its complexity
   - The RMM of the matter
   - The expected nature of procedures to respond to identified risks, including the auditor's knowledge of, and experience with, the work of specialists regarding such matters and the availability of alternative sources of audit evidence

- Whether management has used a management's specialist in preparing the financial statements; in this situation, the auditor's decision whether to use an auditor's specialist *may* also be influenced by such factors as:
  - The nature, scope, and objectives of the work of the management's specialist
  - Whether the management's specialist is employed by the entity or is a party engaged by it to provide relevant services
  - The extent to which management can exercise control or influence over the work of the management's specialist
  - The competence and capabilities of the management's specialist
  - Whether the management's specialist is subject to technical performance standards or other professional or industry requirements
  - Any controls within the entity over the work of the management's specialist
  - The auditor's ability to evaluate the work and findings of the management's specialist without the assistance of an auditor's specialist

C. Audit Procedures

1. **Determination of the Nature, Extent & Timing of the Audit Procedures** In determining the nature, extent, and timing of the auditor's procedures (which will vary depending on the circumstances), the auditor should consider:

   a. The nature of the matter to which the work of the auditor's specialist relates

   b. The RMM in the matter to which the work of the auditor's specialist relates

   c. The significance of the work of the auditor's specialist in the context of the audit

   d. The auditor's knowledge of, and experience with, previous work performed by the auditor's specialist

   e. Whether the auditor's specialist is subject to the auditor's firm's quality control policies and procedures

   The following factors *may* suggest the need for different or more extensive procedures than would otherwise be the case:

   - The work of the auditor's specialist relates to a significant finding or issue that involves subjective and complex judgments.
   - The auditor has not previously used the work of the auditor's specialist and has no prior knowledge of that specialist's competence, capabilities, and objectivity.
   - The auditor's specialist is performing procedures that are integral to the audit rather than being consulted to provide advice on an individual matter.
   - The specialist is an auditor's external specialist and is not, therefore, subject to the firm's quality control policies and procedures.

2. **Evaluating the Competence, Capabilities & Objectivity of the Auditor's Specialist**

   a. The auditor should evaluate whether the auditor's specialist has the necessary competence, capabilities, and objectivity for the auditor's purposes.

b. In the case of an auditor's external specialist, the evaluation of objectivity should include inquiry regarding interests and relationships that may create a threat to the objectivity of the auditor's specialist.

Editor Note: The guidance for this evaluation is similar to that covered for a management's specialist in this chapter per AU 500.

3. **Obtaining an Understanding of the Field of Expertise of the Auditor's Specialist** The auditor should obtain a sufficient understanding of the field of expertise of the auditor's specialist to enable the auditor to:

   a. Determine the nature, scope, and objectives of the work of the auditor's specialist for the auditor's purposes

   b. Evaluate the adequacy of that work for the auditor's purposes

Editor Note: The guidance for obtaining this understanding is similar to that covered for a management's specialist in this chapter per AU 500.

4. **Agreement With the Auditor's Specialist**

   a. **Required Matters of Agreement With Both an Auditor's External or Internal Specialist** The following matters may vary considerably with the circumstances; thus, it is required that the following matters are agreed between the auditor and the auditor's specialist regardless of whether the specialist is an auditor's external specialist or internal specialist.

      (1) **Nature, Scope & Objectives** Nature, scope, and objectives of the work of the auditor's specialist

      (2) **Respective Roles & Responsibilities** Respective roles and responsibilities of the auditor and the auditor's specialist

      (3) **Communication & the Specialist's Report** Nature, extent, and timing of communication between the auditor and the auditor's specialist, including the form of any report to be provided by the auditor's specialist

   b. **Agreement on Confidentiality Requirements** *In addition to the preceding requirements*, the agreement between the auditor and an auditor's specialist should include the need for the auditor's specialist to observe confidentiality requirements. It is necessary for the confidentiality provisions of relevant ethical requirements that apply to the auditor also to apply to the auditor's specialist. Additional requirements may be imposed by law or regulation.

      The entity *may* also have requested that specific confidentiality provisions be agreed with the auditor's external specialists.

   c. **External Auditor's Specialist Agreement** The agreement between the auditor and an auditor's external specialist is generally in the form of an engagement letter.

   d. **Considerations for the Agreement Related to the Nature, Scope & Objectives of the Work of the Auditor's Specialist** It often *may* be relevant when agreeing on the nature, scope, and objectives of the work of the auditor's specialist to include discussion of any relevant technical performance standards or other professional or industry requirements that the auditor's specialist will follow.

   e. **Considerations for the Agreement Related to the Respective Roles & Responsibilities of the Auditor & the Auditor's Specialist** Agreement on the respective roles and responsibilities of the auditor and the auditor's specialist *may* include the following:

- Whether the auditor or the auditor's specialist will perform detailed testing of source data
- Consent for the auditor to discuss the findings or conclusions of the auditor's specialist with the entity and others and to include details of the findings or conclusions of the auditor's specialist in the basis for a modified opinion in the audit report, if necessary
- Any agreement to inform the auditor's specialist of the auditor's conclusions concerning the work of the auditor's specialist
- Access to, and retention of, each other's working papers
    - When the auditor uses the work of an internal specialist, the working papers of the auditor's specialist form part of the audit documentation.
    - Subject to any agreement to the contrary, the auditor's external specialist's working papers are its own and do **not** form part of the audit documentation.

f. **Oral vs. Written Agreement**

(1) **Oral** When no written agreement exists between the auditor and the auditor's specialist, evidence of the agreement may be included in, for example:

- Planning memoranda or related working papers, such as the audit program
- The policies and procedures of the auditor's firm

(2) **Written** The agreement should be in writing when appropriate. The following factors *may* suggest the need for a more detailed agreement than would otherwise be the case or for the agreement to be in writing.

- The auditor's specialist will have access to sensitive or confidential entity information.
- The respective roles or responsibilities of the auditor and the auditor's specialist are different from those normally expected.
- Multijurisdictional legal or regulatory requirements apply.
- The matter to which the work of the auditor's specialist relates is highly complex.
- The auditor has not previously used work performed by the auditor's specialist.
- The auditor's use of the work of the auditor's specialist and its significance in the context of the audit is extensive.

g. **When the Work of the Auditor's Specialist Is Subject to Restrictions** In establishing the agreement with the auditor's specialist, an important consideration is whether the work of the auditor's specialist is subject to any reservation, limitation, or restriction and whether this has implications for the auditor.

5. **Evaluating the Adequacy of the Work of the Auditor's Specialist**

a. **Relevance & Reasonableness of the Findings and Consistency With Other Evidence** The auditor should evaluate the adequacy of the work of the auditor's specialist for the auditor's purposes, including the relevance and reasonableness of the findings and conclusions of the auditor's specialist and their consistency with other audit evidence.

(1) **Examples of Procedures** Specific procedures to evaluate the adequacy of the work of the auditor's specialist for the auditor's purposes *may* include the following:

- Making inquiries of the auditor's specialist
- Reviewing the working papers and reports of the auditor's specialist
- Performing corroborative procedures, such as:
    - Observing the work of the auditor's specialist
    - Examining published data, such as statistical reports from reputable, authoritative sources
    - Confirming relevant matters with third parties
    - Performing detailed analytical procedures
    - Reperforming calculations
- Engaging in discussion with another specialist with relevant expertise when, for example, the findings or conclusions of the auditor's specialist are not consistent with other audit evidence
- Discussing the report of the auditor's specialist with management

(2) **Factors for Evaluating the Relevance & Reasonableness of Findings** Factors when evaluating the relevance and reasonableness of the findings or conclusions of the auditor's specialist, whether in a report or other form, *may* include whether they are:

- Presented in a manner that is consistent with any standards of the profession or industry of the auditor's specialist
- Clearly expressed, including reference to the objectives agreed with the auditor, the scope of the work performed, and standards applied
- Based on an appropriate period and take into account subsequent events, when relevant
- Based on appropriate consideration of errors or deviations encountered by the auditor's specialist

b. **When the Work of the Auditor's Specialist Involves the Use of Significant Assumptions** The auditor should evaluate the adequacy of the work of the auditor's specialist for the auditor's purposes, if the work of the auditor's specialist involves the use of significant assumptions and methods, by:

(1) **Obtaining an Understanding** Obtaining an understanding of those assumptions and methods

(2) **Evaluating Their Relevance & Reasonableness** Evaluating the relevance and reasonableness of those assumptions and methods in the circumstances, giving consideration to the rationale and support provided by the specialist, and in relation to the auditor's other findings and conclusions

Factors relevant to the auditor's evaluation of those assumptions and methods *may* include whether they are:

- Generally accepted within the field of the auditor's specialist
- Consistent with the requirements of the AFRF
- Dependent on the use of specialized models
- Consistent with those of management and, if not, the reason for, and effects of, the differences

c. **Relevance, Completeness & Accuracy of the Source Data** The auditor should evaluate the relevance, completeness, and accuracy of the source data if the work of the auditor's specialist involves the use of source data that is significant to the work of the auditor's specialist.

(1) **Examples of Procedures** The following procedures *may* be used to test such data:

- Verifying the origin of the data, including obtaining an understanding of and, when applicable, testing the internal controls over the data and, when relevant, its transmission to the auditor's specialist
- Reviewing the data for completeness and internal consistency

(2) **Testing Source Data** In many cases, the auditor *may* test source data; however, when the nature of the source data used by an auditor's specialist is highly technical in relation to the field of the auditor's specialist, that specialist *may* test the source data. If the auditor's specialist has tested the source data, inquiry of the auditor's specialist by the auditor or supervision or review of the test of the auditor's specialist *may* be an appropriate way for the auditor to evaluate that data's relevance, completeness, and accuracy.

d. **If the Work of the Auditor's Specialist Is *Not* Adequate** If the auditor determines that the work of the auditor's specialist is **not** adequate for the auditor's purposes, the auditor should:

(1) **Agree on Further Work to Be Performed by the Auditor's Specialist** Agree with the auditor's specialist on the nature and extent of further work to be performed by the auditor's specialist

(2) **Perform Additional Audit Procedures** Perform additional audit procedures appropriate to the circumstances

(3) **When Additional Procedures Do Not Resolve Problems** If the auditor concludes that the work of the auditor's specialist is not adequate for the auditor's purposes and the auditor cannot resolve the matter through additional audit procedures, which may involve additional work being performed by both the auditor's specialist and the auditor or include employing or engaging another specialist, it *may* be necessary to express a modified opinion in the audit report.

D. Reference to the Auditor's Specialist in the Audit Report

1. ***No* Reference Is Allowed If the Opinion Is Unmodified** The auditor should **not** refer to the work of an auditor's specialist in an audit report containing an unmodified opinion.

2. **Reference Allowed If Opinion Modified & Relevant to the Understanding of the Modification** If the auditor makes reference to the work of an auditor's external specialist in the audit report because it is relevant to an understanding of a modification to the opinion:

   a. **Add Language to Audit Report That Auditor's Responsibility Is *Not* Reduced** The auditor should indicate in the audit report that such reference does **not** reduce the auditor's responsibility for that opinion.

   b. ***May* Need Permission** In such circumstances, the auditor *may* need the permission of the auditor's specialist before making such a reference.

V. Internal Audit Function (AU 610)

A. Overview

1. **Scope** The use of the internal auditors' work in obtaining audit evidence modifies the nature or timing, or reduces the extent, of audit procedures to be performed directly by the external auditor. This guidance defines the conditions that are necessary for the external auditor to be able to use the work of internal auditors. It also addresses the external auditor's responsibilities if using their work, i.e., it defines what should be done to obtain sufficient appropriate evidence that the work of internal auditors is adequate and provides guidance to prevent the over or undue [excessive or inappropriate] use of their work.

   This guidance does not apply if the entity does not have an internal audit function. If the entity does have an internal audit function, it does not apply if the responsibilities and activities of the internal audit function are not relevant to the audit or the external auditor does not expect to use its work (based on the external auditor's required preliminary understanding of the internal audit function).

2. **Relationship Between This Guidance and the Guidance on Understanding the Entity & Risk Assessment** The guidance on understanding the entity and risk assessment explains that the internal audit function can inform the external auditor's understanding of the entity and its environment and the identification and assessment of the risks of material misstatement (RMM). Thus, the auditor is required to obtain an understanding of the internal audit function sufficient to identify such internal audit activities *regardless* of whether the external auditor expects to use the work of the internal auditors. Then, if based on this preliminary understanding, the external auditors expect to use their work, this guidance is applicable.

3. **Objectives** When the external auditor expects to use the work of internal auditors, the objectives are as follows.

   a. **Determine Nature of Internal Auditors' Assistance** The external auditor needs to determine whether to use the work of the internal audit function as follows.

      (1) **Obtaining Audit Evidence** Obtaining audit evidence and/or

      (2) **Providing Direct Assistance** Providing direct assistance

   b. **Determine Areas & Extent of Internal Auditors' Assistance** Having made this determination, the external auditor needs to decide in which areas and to what extent to use their work.

   c. **Internal Audit Used to Obtain Audit Evidence—Determine Adequacy of Their Work** If they are to be used to obtain audit evidence, the external auditor needs to determine whether their work is adequate for the purposes of the audit.

d. **Internal Audit Provides Direct Assistance—Determine Coordination** If they are to provide direct assistance, the external auditor needs to appropriately direct, supervise, and review their work.

4. **Definitions**

a. **Internal Audit Function** The internal audit function is a function of an entity that performs assurance and consulting activities designed to evaluate and improve the effectiveness of the entity's governance, risk management, and internal control processes.

b. **Direct Assistance** Direct assistance is the use of internal auditors to perform audit procedures under the direction, supervision, and review of the external auditor. (These are procedures that otherwise would be performed by the external auditors themselves.)

c. **Objectivity** Objectivity refers to the ability to perform tasks without allowing bias, conflict of interest, or undue influence of others to override professional judgments.

d. **Competence** Competence refers to the attainment and maintenance of knowledge and skills at the level required to enable assigned tasks to be performed diligently and with the appropriate level of quality.

5. **Use of Internal Audit Function Is *Not* Required** The external auditors are not required to use the work of internal auditors—it remains the external auditor's decision to establish the overall audit strategy.

6. **External Auditor's Sole Responsibility for the Audit** The external auditor has sole responsibility for the audit opinion expressed, and that responsibility is not reduced by the external auditor's use of the work of the internal auditors—they are not independent of the entity as is required of the external auditor.

B. **Planning the Use of the Internal Audit Function to Obtain Audit Evidence**

1. **Evaluating the Internal Audit Function/Prerequisites for Their Use in Obtaining Audit Evidence** The external auditor should determine whether the work of the internal audit function can be used in obtaining audit evidence by evaluating the following. The adequacy of all three—objectivity, competence, and overall approach—are prerequisites for using the work of the internal auditors to obtain audit evidence.

a. **Objectivity** The extent to which their organizational status and relevant policies and procedures supports their objectivity

b. **Competence** The sufficiency of their level of competence

c. **Systematic & Disciplined Approach** Whether the internal audit function applies a systematic and disciplined approach, including quality control

Editor Note: The determination that a systematic and disciplined approach exists is intended to address the risk that the external auditor inappropriately uses internal audit-like work performed in an informal, unstructured, or ad hoc manner.

2. **Determining the Nature & Extent of Internal Auditors' Work That Can Be Used in Obtaining Audit Evidence**

a. **Basis** The external auditor should consider the nature, timing, and extent of the work that has been performed, or is planned to be performed, by the internal audit function and its relevance to the external auditor's overall audit strategy and audit plan.

b. **Significant Judgments Are Those of the External Auditor** The external auditor has sole responsibility for the audit opinion; thus, the external auditor should make all significant judgments in the audit engagement.

Editor Note: Significant judgments include, but are not limited to, the following.

- Assessing the RMM
- Evaluating the sufficiency of tests performed
- Evaluating the appropriateness of management's use of the going concern assumption and whether substantial doubt exists about the entity's ability to continue as a going concern for a reasonable period of time
- Evaluating significant accounting estimates
- Evaluating the adequacy of disclosures in the financial statements and other matters affecting the audit report

c. **Prevention of Undue Use of Internal Audit Function**

(1) **Factors** To prevent undue use of the internal audit function in obtaining audit evidence, the external auditor should plan to use less of the work of the internal audit function and perform more of the work directly in the following situations.

(a) **Amount of Judgment Involved** The more judgment that is involved in planning and performing audit procedures or evaluating the evidence obtained

(b) **RMM/Significant Risks** The higher the assessed RMM at the assertion level, with special consideration given to significant risks

(c) **Objectivity** The less the internal audit function's organizational status and relevant policies and procedures adequately support the objectivity of the internal auditors

(d) **Competence** The lower the level of competence of the internal audit function

(2) **Evaluate Whether External Auditor Had Sufficient Involvement in Audit** The external auditor should also evaluate whether the planned use of the internal audit function both in obtaining audit evidence and in providing direct assistance allows sufficient involvement in the audit by the external auditor, given the external auditor's sole responsibility for the audit opinion.

3. **Communicating With Those Charged With Governance** The external auditor should include how the work of the internal audit function will be used in obtaining audit evidence in the required communication of the overview of the planned scope and timing of the audit to those charged with governance. Editor Note: The guidance emphasizes that the use of the work of internal auditors in obtaining audit evidence is an integral part of the overall audit strategy and, therefore, is relevant to those charged with governance for their understanding of the proposed audit approach.

4. **Using the Work of the Internal Audit Function in Obtaining Audit Evidence**

a. **Coordination** The external auditor should discuss the planned use of the work with the internal auditors as a basis for coordinating their respective activities.

b. **Reading Internal Audit Function's Reports** The external auditor should read the reports of the internal audit function relevant to their planned use to obtain an understanding of the nature and extent of audit procedures the internal audit function performed and the related findings.

c. **Evaluate Internal Audit Function's Work by Performing Audit Procedures** The external auditor should perform sufficient audit procedures on the body of work of the internal audit function as a whole that the external auditor plans to use to determine its adequacy for the purposes of the audit. The nature and extent of the procedures performed by the external auditor should reflect the external auditor's evaluation of the internal auditors' objectivity and competence as well as the amount of judgment involved in the work and the assessed RMM. Such procedures should include evaluating whether:

(1) **Quality of Work** The internal auditors' work was properly planned, performed, supervised, reviewed, and documented.

(2) **Sufficient Appropriate Evidence** The internal auditors obtained sufficient appropriate evidence to enable them to draw reasonable conclusions.

(3) **Appropriate Conclusions/Reports** Their conclusions were appropriate in the circumstances and their reports were consistent with the results of the work performed.

d. **Reperform Some of the Work of Internal Auditors** The external auditor should also reperform some of the body of work of the internal audit function that the external auditor intends to use in obtaining audit evidence.

e. **Revisit Evaluations/Decisions About Use of Internal Audit Function** Before the conclusion of the audit the external auditor should revisit the following to determine if the conclusions are still appropriate.

(1) The evaluation of the internal audit function

(2) The decisions about the nature and extent of the use of its work

(3) The evaluation of the sufficiency of the external auditor's involvement in the audit

C. Planning to Have the Internal Audit Function Provide Direct Assistance

1. Determining Whether Internal Auditors Can Provide Direct Assistance

a. **Threats to Objectivity & Related Safeguards** The external auditor should evaluate the existence and significance of threats to the objectivity of the internal auditors as well as any safeguards applied to reduce or eliminate the threats. They should not provide direct assistance if they lack the necessary objectivity.

b. **Competence** If their level of competence is not sufficient; they should not provide direct assistance.

2. Determining the Nature & Extent of Work That Can Be Assigned to Internal Auditors Providing Direct Assistance

a. **Factors** In determining the nature and extent of work that may be assigned to internal auditors providing direct assistance and the nature, timing, and extent of direction, supervision, and review that is appropriate in the circumstances, the external auditor should consider the following.

(1) **Results of External Auditor's Evaluation of Internal Auditors** The external auditor's evaluation of the existence and significance of threats to the internal

auditors' objectivity; the effectiveness of the safeguards applied to reduce or eliminate such threats; and their level of competence

(2) **RMM** The assessed level of the RMM

(3) **Amount of Judgment Involved** The amount of judgment involved in planning and performing the audit procedures and evaluating the evidence obtained

3. **Communicating With Those Charged With Governance** The external auditor should include how internal auditors will provide direct assistance in the required communication of the overview of the planned scope and timing of the audit to those charged with governance.

4. **Using Internal Auditors to Provide Direct Assistance**

a. **Written Acknowledgement From Entity Regarding Direct Assistance** Prior to using internal auditors to provide direct assistance, the external auditor should obtain written acknowledgment from management or those charged with governance, as appropriate, that:

(1) Internal auditors will be allowed to follow the external auditor's instructions

(2) The entity will not intervene in such work

b. **Supervision** The external auditor should direct, supervise, and review the work performed by internal auditors in accordance with US GAAS guidance on quality control to ensure the following.

(1) **Results of External Auditor's Evaluation of Internal Auditors Reflected in Supervision** The nature, timing, and extent of direction, supervision, and review should be responsive to the outcome of the evaluation of the internal auditors by the external auditor.

(2) **Surfacing of Issues** The external auditor should instruct the internal auditors to bring accounting and auditing issues identified during the audit to the attention of the external auditor.

(3) **Review Procedures** The review procedures should include the external auditor testing some of the work performed by the internal auditors.

c. **Evaluate Whether External Auditor Had Sufficient Involvement in Audit** The external auditor should also evaluate whether the planned use of the internal audit function both in obtaining audit evidence and in providing direct assistance allows sufficient involvement in the audit by the external auditor, given the external auditor's sole responsibility for the audit opinion.

d. **Revisit Evaluation of Internal Auditors** When supervising and reviewing the work of the internal auditors, the external auditor should be alert for signs that the evaluation of the internal auditors is no longer appropriate.

D. **Audit Documentation**

1. **Evaluation of Whether External Auditor Had Sufficient Involvement in Audit** The external auditor should include the evaluation of whether the use of the internal audit function in obtaining audit evidence and/or in providing direct assistance allowed sufficient involvement in the audit by the external auditor, given the external auditor's sole responsibility for the audit opinion.

2. **When Internal Audit Function Is Used to Obtain Audit Evidence** If the external auditor uses the work of the internal audit function in obtaining audit evidence, the audit documentation should include the following.

   a. **Results of Evaluation of Internal Auditors** All three components, i.e., objectivity, competence, and the application by the internal audit function of a systematic and disciplined approach, including quality control

   b. **How the Internal Audit Function Was Used** The nature and extent of the work used (including the period covered by, and the results of, such work) and the basis for that decision

   c. **Evaluation Procedures** The audit procedures performed by the external auditor to evaluate the adequacy of the work used, including the procedures performed by the external auditor to reperform some of the body of work of the internal audit function in obtaining audit evidence

3. **When Internal Auditors Provide Direct Assistance** If the internal auditors provide direct assistance, the audit documentation should include the following.

   a. **Evaluation of Threats to Objectivity & Related Safeguards and Competence of Internal Auditors** The evaluation of the existence and significance of threats to the objectivity of the internal auditors, including any safeguards applied to reduce or eliminate the threats, and the level of competence of the internal auditors

   b. **How the Internal Audit Function Was Used** The basis for the decision regarding the nature and extent of the work performed by the internal auditors

   c. **Review of Internal Auditors' Work** The nature and extent of the external auditor's review of the internal auditors' work, including the testing, by the external auditor, of some of the work performed by the internal auditors

   d. **Internal Auditors' Workpapers** The workpapers prepared by the internal auditors who provided direct assistance

VI. Related Parties (AU 550)

A. Overview

1. **Nature of Related-Party Relationships & Transactions** Many related-party transactions are in the normal course of business. In such circumstances, they may carry no higher risk of material misstatement (RMM) of the financial statements than similar transactions with unrelated parties. However, the nature of related-party relationships and transactions may, in some circumstances, give rise to higher RMM than transactions with unrelated parties.

   For example:

   - Related parties may operate through an extensive and complex range of relationships and structures, with a corresponding increase in the complexity of related-party transactions.
   - Information systems may be ineffective at identifying or summarizing transactions and outstanding balances between an entity and its related parties.
   - Related-party transactions may not be conducted under normal market terms and conditions (for example, some related-party transactions may be conducted with no exchange of consideration).

- Related-party transactions may be motivated solely or in large measure to engage in fraudulent financial reporting or conceal misappropriation of assets.

Transactions that because of their nature *may* be indicative of the existence of related parties include:

- Borrowing or lending on an interest free basis or at a rate of interest significantly above or below market rates prevailing at the time of the transaction
- Selling real estate at a price that differs significantly from its appraised value
- Exchanging property for similar property in a nonmonetary transaction
- Making loans with no scheduled terms for when or how the funds will be repaid

2. **Responsibilities of the Auditor**

Because related parties are not independent of each other, financial reporting frameworks establish specific accounting and disclosure requirements for related-party relationships, transactions, and balances to enable users of the financial statements to understand their nature and actual or potential effects on the financial statements. Therefore, the auditor has a responsibility to perform audit procedures to identify, assess, and respond to the RMM arising from the entity's failure to appropriately account for or disclose related-party relationships, transactions, or balances.

In addition, an understanding of the entity's related-party relationships and transactions is relevant to the auditor's evaluation of whether one or more fraud risk factors are present, because fraud may be more easily committed through related parties.

Editor Note: *Fraud risk factors* are events or conditions that indicate an incentive or pressure to perpetrate fraud, provide an opportunity to commit fraud, or indicate attitudes or rationalizations to justify a fraudulent action. Fraud is covered in chapter 2 of this text.

Owing to the inherent limitations of an audit, an unavoidable risk exists that some material misstatements may not be detected, even though the audit is properly planned and performed in accordance with US GAAS. In the context of related parties, the potential effects of inherent limitations on the auditor's ability to detect material misstatements are greater because of reasons such as:

- Management may be unaware of the existence of all related-party relationships and transactions.
- Related-party relationships may present a greater opportunity for collusion, concealment, or manipulation by management.

Planning and performing the audit with professional skepticism is particularly important in this context, given the potential for undisclosed related-party relationships and transactions.

3. **Objectives** The objectives of the auditor are to:

   a. Obtain an understanding of related-party relationships and transactions sufficient to be able to:

      (1) Recognize fraud risk factors arising from related-party relationships and transactions that are relevant to the identification and assessment of the RMM due to fraud

      (2) Conclude whether the financial statements, insofar as they are affected by those relationships and transactions, achieve fair presentation

b. Obtain sufficient appropriate audit evidence about whether related-party relationships and transactions have been appropriately identified, accounted for, and disclosed in the financial statements

4. **Definitions**

a. **Arm's-Length Transaction** A transaction conducted on such terms and conditions between a willing buyer and a willing seller who are unrelated and are acting independently of each other and pursuing their own best interests.

b. **Related Party** A party defined as a *related party* in GAAP.

Per GAAP, related parties include:

(1) Affiliates of the entity

(2) Entities for which investments in their equity securities would be required, absent the election of the fair value option, to be accounted for by the equity method by the investing entity

(3) Trusts for the benefit of employees, such as pension and profit-sharing trusts that are managed by or under the trusteeship of management

(4) Principal owners of the entity and members of their immediate families

(5) Management of the entity and members of their immediate families

(6) Other parties with which the entity may deal if one party controls or can significantly influence the management or operating policies of the other to an extent that one of the transacting parties might be prevented from fully pursuing its own separate interests

(7) Other parties that can significantly influence the management or operating policies of the transacting parties or that have an ownership interest in one of the transacting parties and can significantly influence the other to an extent that one or more of the transacting parties might be prevented from fully pursuing its own separate interests

Editor Note: According to the AICPA, GAAP frameworks include or refer to specific disclosure requirements for related-party relationships and transactions. If the AFRF does *not* have specific disclosure requirements, the auditor, nonetheless, evaluates whether related-party information is disclosed in a manner comparable to GAAP in order for the financial statements to achieve fair presentation.

B. **Risk Assessment Procedures & Related Activities**
The auditor should perform the following audit procedures and related activities to obtain information relevant to identifying the RMM associated with related-party relationships and transactions.

1. **Understanding the Entity's Related-Party Relationships & Transactions**

a. **Engagement Team Discussion** The auditor should include specific consideration of the susceptibility of the financial statements to material misstatement due to fraud or error that could result from the entity's related-party relationships and transactions.

Editor Note: The risk of management override of controls is higher if management has relationships that involve control or significant influence with parties with which the entity does business because these relationships may present management with greater incentives and opportunities to perpetrate fraud. For example, management's financial interests in certain related parties may provide incentives for management to override controls by (1) directing the entity, against its interests, to conclude transactions for the benefit of these parties, or (2) colluding with such parties or controlling their actions.

b. **Inquiries** The auditor should inquire of management regarding:

(1) The identity of the entity's related parties, including changes from the prior period

- In a group audit, the group engagement team is required to provide each component auditor with a list of related parties prepared by group management and any other related parties of which the group engagement team is aware. When the entity is a component within a group, this information provides a useful basis for the auditor's inquiries of management regarding the identity of the entity's related parties.

(2) The nature of the relationships between the entity and these related parties

(3) Whether the entity entered into any transactions with these related parties during the period and, if so, the type and purpose of the transactions

Editor Note: The auditor is required to obtain written representations that management and, when appropriate, those charged with governance, have (a) disclosed to the auditor the identity of the entity's related parties and all the related-party relationships of which they are aware; and (b) appropriately accounted for and disclosed such relationships and transactions. Written representations are covered in another section of this chapter.

c. **Entity's Controls** The auditor should inquire of management and others within the entity and perform other risk assessment procedures to obtain an understanding of the controls that management has established to:

(1) Identify, account for, and disclose related-party relationships and transactions

(2) Authorize and approve significant transactions and arrangements with related parties

(3) Authorize and approve significant transactions and arrangements outside the normal course of business

(4) Examples of such entity controls *may* include:

- Internal ethical codes, appropriately communicated to the entity's personnel and enforced, governing the circumstances in which the entity may enter into specific types of related-party transactions
- Policies and procedures for open and timely disclosure of the interests that management and those charged with governance have in related-party transactions
- The assignment of responsibilities within the entity for identifying, recording, summarizing, and disclosing related-party transactions
- Timely disclosure and discussion between management and those charged with governance of significant related-party transactions outside the entity's normal course of business, including whether those charged with governance have appropriately challenged the business rationale of such transactions (for example, by seeking advice from external professional advisors)

- Clear guidelines for the approval of related-party transactions involving actual or perceived conflicts of interest, such as approval by a subcommittee of those charged with governance comprising individuals independent of management
- Periodic reviews by internal auditors, when applicable
- Proactive action taken by management to resolve related-party disclosure issues, such as by seeking advice from the auditor or external legal counsel
- The existence of whistle-blowing policies and procedures, when applicable

Editor Note: When such controls are ineffective or nonexistent, the auditor may be unable to obtain sufficient appropriate audit evidence about related-party relationships and transactions. When this is the case, the auditor should consider the implications for the audit, including the opinion in the audit report.

2. Maintaining Alertness for Related-Party Information When Reviewing Records or Documents

a. **Undisclosed Relationships** During the audit, the auditor should remain alert when inspecting records or documents for arrangements or other information that may indicate the existence of related-party relationships or transactions that management has *not* previously identified or disclosed to the auditor. Examples of arrangements that *may* indicate the existence of such related-party relationships or transactions include: participation in unincorporated partnerships with other parties; agreements for the provision of services to certain parties under terms and conditions that are outside the entity's normal course of business; and guarantees and guarantor relationships.

In particular, the auditor should inspect the following for indications of the existence of related-party relationships or transactions that management has not previously identified or disclosed to the auditor:

(1) Bank and legal confirmations

(2) Minutes of meetings of shareholders and of those charged with governance

(3) Such other records or documents as the auditor considers necessary in the circumstances of the entity

b. **Transactions Outside the Normal Course of Business** If the auditor identifies significant transactions outside the entity's normal course of business, the auditor should inquire of management about the following:

(1) The nature of these transactions

(2) Whether related parties could be involved

Editor Note: Inquiring into the nature of the significant transactions outside the entity's normal course of business involves obtaining an understanding of the business rationale of the transactions and their terms and conditions. If a related party is involved, it *may* indicate the presence of a fraud risk factor.

(3) Examples of transactions outside the entity's normal course of business *may* include:

- Complex equity transactions, such as corporate restructurings or acquisitions

- Transactions with offshore entities in jurisdictions with less rigorous corporate governance structures, laws, or regulations
- The leasing of premises or the rendering of management services by the entity to another party if no consideration is exchanged
- Sales transactions with unusually large discounts or returns
- Transactions with circular arrangements (for example, sales with a commitment to repurchase)
- Transactions under contracts whose terms are changed before expiration

3. **Sharing Related-Party Information With the Engagement Team** The auditor should share with the other members of the engagement team the identity of the entity's related parties and other relevant information obtained about the related parties.

   - In group audits, to achieve uniformity and comparability of financial information, group management ordinarily issues instructions to components. The instructions ordinarily include coverage of related-party relationships and transactions, providing information regarding the disclosures that are sufficient to comply with the requirements of the AFRF.

C. RMM Associated With Related-Party Relationships & Transactions

1. **Significant Risks** The auditor should identify and assess the RMM associated with related-party relationships and transactions and determine whether any of those risks are significant risks. In making this determination, the auditor should treat identified significant related-party transactions outside the entity's normal course of business as giving rise to significant risks.

   Editor Note: A *significant risk* is an identified and assessed RMM that requires special audit consideration.

2. **Fraud Risk Factors** If the auditor identifies fraud risk factors (including circumstances relating to the existence of a related party with dominant influence), the auditor should consider such information when identifying and assessing the RMM due to fraud.

   Indicators of dominant influence exerted by a related party *may* include:

   - The related party has vetoed significant business decisions taken by management or those charged with governance.
   - Significant transactions are referred to the related party for final approval.
   - Little or no debate occurs among management and those charged with governance regarding business proposals initiated by the related party.
   - Transactions involving the related party (or a close family member of the related party) are rarely independently reviewed and approved.
   - Evidence of the related party's excessive participation in, or preoccupation with, the selection of accounting policies or the determination of significant estimates *may* suggest the possibility of fraudulent financial reporting.

D. Responses to the RMM Associated With Related-Party Relationships & Transactions

The auditor should design and perform further audit procedures to obtain sufficient appropriate audit evidence about the assessed RMM associated with related-party relationships and transactions.

1. Identification of Previously Unidentified or Undisclosed Related Parties or Significant Related-Party Transactions

a. **Confirm Their Existence** If the auditor identifies arrangements or information that suggests the existence of related-party relationships or transactions that management has not previously identified or disclosed to the auditor, the auditor should determine whether the underlying circumstances confirm the existence of those relationships or transactions.

b. **Procedures If Existence Confirmed** If the auditor identifies related parties or significant related-party transactions that management has not previously identified or disclosed to the auditor, the auditor should:

(1) Promptly communicate the relevant information to the other members of the engagement team

(2) Request management to identify all transactions with the newly identified related parties for the auditor's further evaluation

(3) Inquire why the entity's controls over related-party relationships and transactions failed to enable the identification or disclosure of the related-party relationships or transactions

(4) Perform appropriate substantive audit procedures relating to such newly identified related parties or significant related-party transactions

(5) Reconsider the risk that other related parties or significant related-party transactions may exist that management has not previously identified or disclosed to the auditor and perform additional audit procedures as necessary

(6) Evaluate the implications for the audit if the nondisclosure by management appears intentional and, therefore, indicative of a RMM due to fraud

Examples of substantive audit procedures that the auditor *may* perform relating to newly identified related parties or significant related-party transactions include:

- Making inquiries regarding the nature of the entity's relationships with the newly identified related parties, including inquiring of parties outside the entity who are presumed to have significant knowledge of the entity and its business, such as legal counsel, principal agents, major representatives, consultants, guarantors, or other close business partners.
- Conducting an analysis of accounting records for transactions with the newly identified related parties.
- Verifying the terms and conditions of the newly identified related-party transactions and evaluating whether the transactions have been appropriately accounted for and disclosed.

2. **Procedures for Identified Significant Related-Party Transactions Outside the Entity's Normal Course of Business** For identified significant related-party transactions outside the entity's normal course of business, the auditor should:

   a. Inspect the underlying contracts or agreements and evaluate whether:

      (1) The business rationale (or lack thereof) of the transactions suggests that they may have been entered into to engage in fraudulent financial reporting or to conceal misappropriation of assets

      (2) The terms of the transactions are consistent with management's explanations

      (3) The transactions have been appropriately accounted for and disclosed

   b. Obtain audit evidence that the transactions have been appropriately authorized and approved.

3. **Assertions That Related-Party Transactions Were Conducted on Terms Equivalent to Those Prevailing in an Arm's-Length Transaction** If management has made an assertion in the financial statements to the effect that a related-party transaction was conducted on terms equivalent to those prevailing in an arm's-length transaction, the auditor should obtain sufficient appropriate audit evidence about the assertion.

   Editor Note: It is difficult to substantiate representations that a transaction was consummated on terms equivalent to those that prevail in arm's-length transactions. Management should provide support for their assertion that this was the case. The auditor should evaluate this support. If the auditor believes that management's assertion is unsubstantiated or the auditor cannot obtain sufficient appropriate audit evidence to support the assertion, the auditor should consider the implications for the audit, including the opinion in the audit report.

E. Accounting for, and Disclosure of, Related-Party Relationships & Transactions
In forming an opinion on the financial statements the auditor should evaluate whether the:

1. Identified related-party relationships and transactions have been appropriately accounted for and disclosed

2. Effects of the related-party relationships and transactions prevent the financial statements from achieving fair presentation

Editor Note: Evaluating the related-party disclosures means considering whether the disclosures are understandable. Disclosures may *not* be understandable if:

- The business rationale and the effects of the transactions on the financial statements are unclear or misstated
- Key terms, conditions, or other important elements of the transactions necessary for understanding them are not appropriately disclosed

F. Communication With Those Charged With Governance
Unless all of those charged with governance are involved in managing the entity, the auditor should communicate with those charged with governance significant findings and issues arising during the audit in connection with the entity's related parties.

Examples of significant related-party findings and issues include:

- Nondisclosure (whether or not intentional) by management to the auditor of related parties or significant related-party transactions, which may alert those charged with governance to significant related-party relationships and transactions of which they may not have been previously aware

- The identification of significant related-party transactions that have not been appropriately authorized and approved, which may give rise to suspected fraud
- Disagreement with management regarding the accounting for, and disclosure of, significant related-party transactions
- Noncompliance with applicable laws or regulations prohibiting or restricting specific types of related-party transactions
- Difficulties in identifying the party that ultimately controls the entity

G. Audit Documentation
The auditor should include in the audit documentation the:

1. Names of the identified related parties

2. Nature of the related-party relationships

VII. Litigation, Claims & Assessments (AU 501)

Litigation, claims, and assessments involving the entity may have a material effect on the financial statements and, thus, may be required to be recognized, measured, or disclosed in the financial statements. The objective of the auditor is to obtain sufficient appropriate audit evidence regarding their completeness.

A. Audit Procedures

1. Identification of Litigation, Claims & Assessments Giving Rise to RMM The auditor should design and perform audit procedures to identify litigation, claims, and assessments involving the entity that may give rise to a RMM, including:

a. Inquiries Inquiring of management and, when applicable, others within the entity, including in-house legal counsel

Editor Note: The auditor should request management to provide written representations that all known actual or possible litigation and claims whose effects should be considered by management when preparing the financial statements have been disclosed to the auditor and accounted for and disclosed in accordance with the AFRF. Written representations are covered in another section of this chapter.

b. Obtain Description & Evaluation of Litigation, Claims, and Assessments Obtaining from management a description and evaluation of litigation, claims, and assessments that:

(1) Existed at the date of the financial statements

(2) Existed during the period from the date of the financial statements to the date the information is furnished

Management should also include an identification of those matters referred to legal counsel.

c. Review of Minutes, Documents & Correspondence Reviewing:

(1) Minutes of meetings of those charged with governance

(2) Documents obtained from management concerning litigation, claims, and assessments

(3) Correspondence between the entity and its external legal counsel

d. **Review of Legal Expense Accounts** Reviewing legal expense accounts and invoices from external legal counsel

Editor Note: The auditor is not required to obtain evidence about matters which may not have a material effect on the financial statements, i.e., would not give rise to the risk of material misstatement (RMM), for example, matters in which the entity's insurance coverage exceeds the amount of the actual or potential litigation, claim, or assessment sought against the entity.

2. **Procedures for Litigation, Claims & Assessments Identified** For actual or potential litigation, claims, and assessments identified (via the preceding required audit procedures), the auditor should obtain audit evidence relevant to the following factors:

   a. The period in which the underlying cause for legal action occurred

   b. The degree of probability of an unfavorable outcome

   c. The amount or range of potential loss

3. **Communication With the Entity's Legal Counsel**

   a. **Purpose** Direct communication with the entity's legal counsel assists the auditor in obtaining sufficient appropriate audit evidence about whether potentially material litigation, claims, and assessments are known and management's estimates of the financial implications, including costs, are reasonable—corroboration. (An auditor ordinarily does *not* possess legal skills and, therefore, cannot make legal judgments concerning information coming to the auditor's attention.)

   b. **When *No* Actual or Potential Litigation, Claims, or Assessments Are Identified** If no actual or potential litigation, claims, or assessments that may give rise to RMM are identified, the auditor is **not** required to seek direct communication with the entity's legal counsel; however, the auditor should document the basis for any determination not to do so.

   c. **Considerations When the Entity Has *Not* Consulted Legal Counsel** Also, if management has *not* consulted legal counsel, the auditor should rely on the preceding procedures required to identify litigation, claims, and assessments which may give rise to a RMM and the written representation of management regarding litigation, claims, and assessments. However, under these circumstances, if the auditor believes that there may be actual or potential material litigation, claims, or assessments, the auditor *may* discuss with the client the possible need to consult legal counsel to assist the client in determining the appropriate measurement, recognition, or disclosure of related liabilities or loss contingencies. Depending on the significance of the matter(s), refusal by management to consult legal counsel may result in a scope limitation sufficient to preclude an unmodified opinion.

   d. **Letter of Inquiry to Entity's External Legal Counsel** When actual or potential litigation, claims, and assessments are identified that may give rise to RMM, the auditor should inquire of legal counsel through a letter that:

      (1) Is prepared by management

      (2) Is sent by the auditor

      (3) Requests the entity's external legal counsel to communicate directly with the auditor

The auditor should request management to authorize the entity's legal counsel to discuss applicable matters with the auditor.

e. **Letter of Inquiry to Entity's In-House Legal Counsel** In cases when the entity's in-house legal counsel has the responsibility for the entity's litigation, claims, and assessments, the auditor should also send a letter of inquiry similar to the letter sent to the entity's external legal counsel.

However, audit evidence obtained from in-house legal counsel is **not** a substitute for the auditor seeking direct communication with the entity's *external* legal counsel.

f. **Elements of the Letters of Inquiry** The auditor should request, via the letters of inquiry, the entity's legal counsel to inform the auditor of any litigation, claims, assessments, and unasserted claims that the counsel is aware of, together with an assessment of the outcome of the litigation, claims, and assessments, and an estimate of the financial implications, including costs involved.

Each letter of inquiry should include, but not be limited to, the following matters:

(1) **Entity & Date of the Audit** Identification of the entity, including subsidiaries, and the date of the audit

(2) **Pending or Threatened Litigation, Claims & Assessments** A list prepared by management (or a request by management that the legal counsel prepare a list) that describes and evaluates pending or threatened litigation, claims, and assessments with respect to which the legal counsel has been engaged and to which the legal counsel has devoted substantive attention on behalf of the company in the form of legal consultation or representation

(3) **Unasserted Claims & Assessments** A list prepared by management that describes and evaluates unasserted claims and assessments that management considers to be probable of assertion and that, if asserted, would have at least a reasonable possibility of an unfavorable outcome with respect to which the legal counsel has been engaged and to which the legal counsel has devoted substantive attention on behalf of the entity in the form of legal consultation or representation

(4) **Pending or Threatened Litigation, Claims & Assessments** Regarding each matter listed in item (2), a request that the legal counsel either provide the following information or comment on those matters on which the legal counsel's views may differ from those stated by management, as appropriate:

(a) **Nature, Progress & Planned Action** A description of the nature of the matter, the progress of the case to date, and the action that the entity intends to take (for example, to contest the matter vigorously or to seek an out-of-court settlement)

(b) **Likelihood & Estimate of Potential Loss** An evaluation of the likelihood of an unfavorable outcome and an estimate, if one can be made, of the amount or range of potential loss

(c) **Completeness of List** With respect to a list prepared by management (or by the legal counsel at management's request), an identification of the omission of any pending or threatened litigation, claims, and assessments or a statement that the list of such matters is complete

(5) **Different Views Regarding Unasserted Claims & Assessments** Regarding each matter listed in item (3), a request that the legal counsel comment on those

matters on which the legal counsel's views concerning the description or evaluation of the matter may differ from those stated by management

(6) **Financial Statement Disclosure Advice** A statement that management understands that whenever, in the course of performing legal services for the entity with respect to a matter recognized to involve an unasserted possible claim or assessment that may call for financial statement disclosure, the legal counsel has formed a professional conclusion that the entity should disclose or consider disclosure concerning such possible claim or assessment, the legal counsel, as a matter of professional responsibility to the entity, will so advise the entity and will consult with the entity concerning the question of such disclosure and the requirements of the AFRF

(7) **Confirmation That Financial Statement Disclosure Advice Will Be Offered** A request that the legal counsel confirm whether the understanding described in item (6) is correct

(8) **When Response Is Limited** A request that the legal counsel specifically identify the nature of, and reasons for, any limitation on the response

(9) **Effective Date of the Response** A request that the legal counsel specify the effective date of the response

Editor Note: The auditor is required to date the audit report no earlier than the date on which the auditor has obtained sufficient appropriate audit evidence on which to base the auditor's opinion on the financial statements. Accordingly, it is preferable that the entity's legal counsel's response be as close to the date of the audit report as is practicable in the circumstances. Specifying the effective date of the entity's legal counsel's response to reasonably approximate the expected date of the audit report may prevent the need to obtain updated information from the entity's legal counsel.

g. **Clarity of Legal Counsel's Evaluation of the Outcome of Litigation, Claims, or Assessments** Legal counsel is **not** required to use the terms *probable*; *reasonably possible;* or *remote* (per the FASB) to evaluate the likelihood of unfavorable outcomes. Other terms may be used, as long as the other wording is sufficiently clear to allow the auditor to classify the outcome under one of these three probability classifications established by the FASB.

If the auditor is uncertain about the meaning of the legal counsel's evaluation, clarification either in a follow-up letter or conference with the legal counsel and entity, appropriately documented, *may* be appropriate. If the legal counsel is still unable to give an unequivocal evaluation of the likelihood of an unfavorable outcome in writing or orally, the auditor is required to determine the effect, if any, of the legal counsel's response on the audit report.

(1) **Examples of Clear Evaluations for Outcomes** Some examples of evaluations concerning litigation that may be considered to provide sufficient clarity that the likelihood of an unfavorable outcome is remote, even though they do not use that term, include:

- We are of the opinion that this action will not result in any liability to the company.
- It is our opinion that the possible liability to the company in this proceeding is nominal in amount.
- We believe the company will be able to defend this action successfully.

- We believe that the plaintiff's case against the company is without merit.
- Based on the facts known to us, after a full investigation, it is our opinion that no liability will be established against the company in these suits.

(2) **Examples of Evaluations of Outcomes That Are *Not* Clear** The following are examples of the legal counsel's evaluations that are *un*clear about the likelihood of an unfavorable outcome:

- This action involves unique characteristics wherein authoritative legal precedents do not seem to exist. We believe that the plaintiff will have serious problems establishing the company's liability under the act; nevertheless, if the plaintiff is successful, the award may be substantial.
- It is our opinion that the company will be able to assert meritorious defenses to this action. (The term *meritorious defenses* indicates that the entity's defenses will not be summarily dismissed by the court; it does not necessarily indicate the legal counsel's opinion that the entity will prevail.)
- We believe the action can be settled for less than the damages claimed.
- We are unable to express an opinion as to the merits of the litigation at this time. The company believes there is absolutely no merit to the litigation. (If the entity's legal counsel, with the benefit of all relevant information, is unable to conclude that the likelihood of an unfavorable outcome is remote, it is unlikely that management would be able to form a judgment to that effect.)
- In our opinion, the company has a substantial chance of prevailing in this action. (A substantial chance, a reasonable opportunity, and similar terms indicate more uncertainty than an evaluation that the company will prevail.)

h. **Change in Legal Counsel** When the auditor is aware that an entity has changed legal counsel or that the legal counsel previously engaged by the entity has resigned, the auditor should consider making inquiries of management or others about the reasons such legal counsel is no longer associated with the entity.

i. **Scope Limitations Related to the Communication With Legal Counsel** The auditor should modify the opinion in the audit report if *either*:

(1) **Management Refusal** Management refuses to give the auditor permission to communicate or meet with the entity's external legal counsel; or

(2) **Legal Counsel Refusal** The entity's legal counsel refuses to respond appropriately to the letter of inquiry *and* the auditor is unable to obtain sufficient appropriate audit evidence by performing alternative audit procedures

B. Audit Documentation

The auditor should document the basis for any determination *not* to seek direct communication with either the entity's external or in-house legal counsel.

VIII. Written Representations (AU 580)

A. Overview

1. Evidentiary Value of Written Representations

a. **Written Representations Are Complementary Evidence** Although written representations provide necessary audit evidence, they complement other auditing procedures and do **not** provide sufficient appropriate audit evidence on their own (similar to responses to inquiries) about any of the matters with which they deal.

b. **Written Representations Do *Not* Affect the Nature or Extent of Other Audit Procedures** Furthermore, obtaining reliable written representations does **not** affect the nature or extent of other audit procedures that the auditor applies to obtain audit evidence about the fulfillment of management's responsibilities or about specific assertions.

2. **Objectives** The objectives of the auditor are to:

a. Obtain written representations from management and, when appropriate, those charged with governance (the term *management* will represent the phrase *management and, when appropriate, those charged with governance* for the remainder of this section) that they believe that they have fulfilled their responsibility for the preparation and fair presentation of the financial statements and for the completeness of the information provided to the auditor

b. Support other audit evidence relevant to the financial statements or specific assertions in the financial statements by means of written representations if determined necessary by the auditor or required by other AU sections

c. Respond appropriately to written representations provided by management or if management does *not* provide the written representations requested by the auditor

3. **Definition of Written Representation** A written representation is a written statement by management provided to the auditor to confirm certain matters or to support other audit evidence. Written representations in this context do **not** include financial statements, the assertions therein, or supporting books and records.

4. **Form of Written Representations** The written representations should be in the form of a representation letter addressed to the auditor.

5. **A Materiality Threshold for Written Representations *May* Be Established With Some Important Exceptions** Management's representations *may* be limited to matters that are considered either individually or collectively material to the financial statements, provided management and the auditor have reached an understanding on materiality for this purpose. Materiality may be different for different representations. A discussion of materiality may be included explicitly in the representation letter in either qualitative or quantitative terms.

There are some *exceptions*:

a. **Materiality Considerations Do *Not* Apply to Representations Related to Fraud** Because of the possible effects of fraud on other aspects of the audit, materiality would **not** apply to management's acknowledgment regarding its responsibility for the design, implementation, and maintenance of internal control to prevent and detect fraud.

b. **Materiality Considerations Do *Not* Apply to Representations That Are Not Directly Related to Financial Statement Amounts** Materiality considerations do **not** apply to those representations that are not directly related to amounts included in the financial statements, for example, management's representations about the premise underlying the audit.

6. **Management From Whom Written Representations Are Requested** The auditor should request written representations from management with appropriate responsibilities for the financial statements and knowledge of the matters concerned.

   In some cases, management may include in the written representations qualifying language to the effect that representations are made to the best of its knowledge and belief. It is reasonable for the auditor to accept such wording if, in the auditor's professional judgment, the representations are being made by those with appropriate responsibilities and knowledge of the matters included in the representations.

7. **Date of, & Period(s) Covered by, Written Representations** The date of the written representations should be as of the date of the audit report on the financial statements. The written representations should be for all financial statements and period(s) referred to in the audit report—even when current management was not present during all periods referred to in the audit report.

   The auditor should have possession of the signed management representation letter prior to releasing the audit report.

8. **Communication With Those Charged With Governance** US GAAS require the auditor to communicate with those charged with governance the written representations that the auditor has requested from management.

B. Written Representations About Management's Responsibilities

These written representations draw on the agreed acknowledgment and understanding of management of its responsibilities in the terms of the audit engagement by requesting confirmation that it has fulfilled them.

In addition to requesting management to confirm that it has fulfilled its responsibilities, the auditor also *may* ask management to *unconditionally* reconfirm its acknowledgment and understanding of those responsibilities in written representations. This is common but, in any event, *may* be particularly appropriate in any of the following situations.

- Those who signed the terms of the audit engagement on behalf of the entity no longer have the relevant responsibilities
- The terms of the audit engagement were prepared in a previous year
- Any indication exists that management misunderstands those responsibilities
- Other changes in circumstances make it appropriate to do so

1. **Preparation & Fair Presentation of the Financial Statements** The auditor should request management to provide a written representation that it has fulfilled its responsibility, as set out in the terms of the audit engagement for the:

   a. Preparation and fair presentation of the financial statements in accordance with the AFRF

   b. Design, implementation, and maintenance of internal control relevant to the preparation and fair presentation of financial statements that are free from material misstatement, whether due to fraud or error

2. **Information Provided & Completeness of Transactions** The auditor should request management to provide written representations that:

    a. It has provided the auditor with all relevant information and access, as agreed upon in the terms of the audit engagement

    b. All transactions have been recorded and are reflected in the financial statements

    Editor Note: In addition to these written representation about the information provided and completeness of transactions, the auditor *may* consider it necessary to request management to provide a written representation that it has communicated to the auditor all deficiencies in internal control of which management is aware.

C. Other Required Written Representations

1. **Fraud** The auditor should request management to provide written representations that it:

    a. Acknowledges its responsibility for the design, implementation, and maintenance of internal controls to prevent and detect fraud

    b. Has disclosed to the auditor the results of its assessment of the risk that the financial statements may be materially misstated as a result of fraud

    c. Has disclosed to the auditor its knowledge of fraud or suspected fraud affecting the entity involving:

        (1) Management

        (2) Employees who have significant roles in internal control

        (3) Others when the fraud could have a material effect on the financial statements

    d. Has disclosed to the auditor its knowledge of any allegations of fraud or suspected fraud affecting the entity's financial statements communicated by employees, former employees, regulators, or others

2. **Laws & Regulations** The auditor should request management to provide written representations that all instances of identified or suspected noncompliance with laws and regulations whose effects should be considered by management when preparing financial statements have been disclosed to the auditor.

3. **Uncorrected Misstatements** The auditor should request management to provide written representations about whether it believes the effects of uncorrected misstatements are immaterial, individually and in the aggregate, to the financial statements as a whole.

    A summary of such items should be included in, or attached to, the written representation.

4. **Litigation & Claims** The auditor should request management to provide written representations that all known actual or possible litigation and claims whose effects should be considered by management when preparing the financial statements have been disclosed to the auditor and accounted for and disclosed in accordance with the AFRF.

5. **Estimates** The auditor should request management to provide written representations about whether it believes significant assumptions used by it in making accounting estimates are reasonable.

6. **Related-Party Transactions** The auditor should request management to provide written representations that:

   a. It has disclosed to the auditor the identity of the entity's related parties and all the related-party relationships and transactions of which it is aware

   b. It has appropriately accounted for and disclosed such relationships and transactions

7. **Subsequent Events** The auditor should request management to provide written representations that all events occurring subsequent to the date of the financial statements and for which the AFRF requires adjustment or disclosure have been adjusted or disclosed.

   Editor Note: If the auditor dual-dates the audit report for a revision relating to a subsequent event, the auditor *may* determine that obtaining additional representations relating to the subsequent event is appropriate.

8. **Additional Written Representations**

   a. Other AU sections require the auditor to request the following written representations.

      (1) **AU 560, *Subsequent Events and Subsequently Discovered Facts*** One of the procedures the predecessor auditor should perform before reissuing a previously issued audit report on financial statements that are to be presented on a comparative basis with audited financial statements of a subsequent period, is to inquire of, and request written representations from, management of the former client, at or near the date of reissuance, about whether:

         (a) Any information has come to management's attention that would cause management to believe that any of the previous representations should be modified

         (b) Any events have occurred subsequent to the date of the latest prior period financial statements reported on by the predecessor auditor that would require adjustment to, or disclosure in, those financial statements

      (2) **AU 700, *Forming an Opinion and Reporting on Financial Statements*** Regarding comparative financial statements and comparative information, the auditor should obtain a specific written representation regarding any restatement made to correct a material misstatement in a prior period that affects the comparative financial statements.

      (3) **AU 725, *Supplementary Information in Relation to the Financial Statements as a Whole*** One of the procedures the auditor should perform (using the same materiality level used in the audit of the financial statements) in order to opine on whether supplementary information is fairly stated, in all material respects, in relation to the financial statements as a whole is to obtain written representations from management:

         (a) That it acknowledges its responsibility for the presentation of the supplementary information in accordance with the applicable criteria

         (b) That it believes the supplementary information, including its form and content, is fairly presented in accordance with the applicable criteria

         (c) That the methods of measurement or presentation have not changed from those used in the prior period or, if the methods of measurement or presentation have changed, the reasons for such changes

(d) About any significant assumptions or interpretations underlying the measurement or presentation of the supplementary information

(e) That when the supplementary information is not presented with the audited financial statements, management will make the audited financial statements readily available to the intended users of the supplementary information no later than the date of issuance by the entity of the supplementary information and the related audit report

(4) **AU 935, *Compliance Audits*** The auditor should request from management written representations that are tailored to the entity and the governmental audit requirement:

(a) Acknowledging management's responsibility for understanding and complying with the compliance requirements

(b) Acknowledging management's responsibility for establishing and maintaining controls that provide reasonable assurance that the entity administers government programs in accordance with the compliance requirements

(c) Stating that management has identified and disclosed to the auditor all of its government programs and related activities subject to the governmental audit requirement

(d) Stating that management has made available to the auditor all contracts and grant agreements, including amendments, if any, and any other correspondence relevant to the programs and related activities subject to the governmental audit requirement

(e) Stating that management has disclosed to the auditor all known noncompliance with the applicable compliance requirements or stating that there was no such noncompliance

(f) Stating whether management believes that the entity has complied with the applicable compliance requirements (except for noncompliance it has disclosed to the auditor)

(g) Stating that management has made available to the auditor all documentation related to compliance with the applicable compliance requirements

(h) Identifying management's interpretation of any applicable compliance requirements that are subject to varying interpretations

(i) Stating that management has disclosed to the auditor any communications from grantors and pass-through entities concerning possible noncompliance with the applicable compliance requirements, including communications received from the end of the period covered by the compliance audit to the date of the audit report

(j) Stating that management has disclosed to the auditor the findings received and related corrective actions taken for previous audits, attestation engagements, and internal or external monitoring that directly relate to the objectives of the compliance audit, including findings received and corrective actions taken from the end of the period covered by the compliance audit to the date of the audit report

(k) Stating that management has disclosed to the auditor all known noncompliance with the applicable compliance requirements subsequent to the period covered by the audit report or stating that there were no such known instances

(l) Stating that management is responsible for taking corrective action on audit findings of the compliance audit.

b. If, in addition to such required representations, the auditor determines that it is necessary to obtain one or more written representations to support other audit evidence relevant to the financial statements or one or more specific assertions in the financial statements, the auditor should request such other written representations.

Exhibit 1 ▸ Representation Letter (With GAAP as the Applicable Financial Reporting Framework)

[Entity Letterhead]

[*Date*]

To [*Auditor*]

This representation letter is provided in connection with your audit of the financial statements of ABC Company, which comprise the balance sheet as of December 31, 20XX, and the related statements of income, changes in stockholders' equity, and cash flows for the year then ended, and the related notes to the financial statements, for the purpose of expressing an opinion on whether the financial statements are presented fairly, in all material respects, in accordance with accounting principles generally accepted in the United States (US GAAP).

Certain representations in this letter are described as being limited to matters that are material. Items are considered material, regardless of size, if they involve an omission or misstatement of accounting information that, in the light of surrounding circumstances, makes it probable that the judgment of a reasonable person relying on the information would be changed or influenced by the omission or misstatement.

Except where otherwise stated below, immaterial matters less than $[*insert amount*] collectively are not considered to be exceptions that require disclosure for the purpose of the following representations. This amount is not necessarily indicative of amounts that would require adjustment to or disclosure in the financial statements.

We confirm that [, *to the best of our knowledge and belief, having made such inquiries as we considered necessary for the purpose of appropriately informing ourselves*] [*as of (date of audit report)*,]:

Financial Statements

- We have fulfilled our responsibilities, as set out in the terms of the audit engagement dated [*insert date*], for the preparation and fair presentation of the financial statements in accordance with US GAAP.
- We acknowledge our responsibility for the design, implementation, and maintenance of internal control relevant to the preparation and fair presentation of financial statements that are free from material misstatement, whether due to fraud or error.
- We acknowledge our responsibility for the design, implementation, and maintenance of internal control to prevent and detect fraud.
- Significant assumptions used by us in making accounting estimates, including those measured at fair value, are reasonable.
- Related-party relationships and transactions have been appropriately accounted for and disclosed in accordance with the requirements of US GAAP.

- All events subsequent to the date of the financial statements and for which US GAAP requires adjustment or disclosure have been adjusted or disclosed.
- The effects of uncorrected misstatements are immaterial, both individually and in the aggregate, to the financial statements as a whole. A list of the uncorrected misstatements is attached to this representation letter.
- The effects of all known actual or possible litigation and claims have been accounted for and disclosed in accordance with US GAAP.

[*Any other matters that the auditor may consider appropriate*]

Information Provided

- We have provided you with:
    - Access to all information, of which we are aware that is relevant to the preparation and fair presentation of the financial statements such as records, documentation and other matters;
    - Additional information that you have requested from us for the purpose of the audit; and
    - Unrestricted access to persons within the entity from whom you determined it necessary to obtain audit evidence.
- All transactions have been recorded in the accounting records and are reflected in the financial statements.
- We have disclosed to you the results of our assessment of the risk that the financial statements may be materially misstated as a result of fraud.
- We have [*no knowledge of any*] [*disclosed to you all information that we are aware of regarding*] fraud or suspected fraud that affects the entity and involves:
    - Management;
    - Employees who have significant roles in internal control; or
    - Others when the fraud could have a material effect on the financial statements
- We have [*no knowledge of any*] [*disclosed to you all information that we are aware of regarding*] allegations of fraud, or suspected fraud, affecting the entity's financial statements communicated by employees, former employees, analysts, regulators or others.
- We have disclosed to you all known instances of noncompliance or suspected noncompliance with laws and regulations whose effects should be considered when preparing financial statements.
- We [*have disclosed to you all known actual or possible*] [*are not aware of any pending or threatened*] litigation, claims, and assessments whose effects should be considered when preparing the financial statements [*and we have not consulted legal counsel concerning litigation, claims, or assessments*].
- We have disclosed to you the identity of the entity's related parties and all the related-party relationships and transactions of which we are aware.

[*Any other matters that the auditor may consider necessary.*]

____

[*Name of Chief Executive Officer and Title*]

____

[*Name of Chief Financial Officer and Title*]

D. **When the Reliability of Representations Is Doubtful or Representations Are *Not* Provided**

1. **When the Reliability of Representations Is Doubtful**

   a. **Concerns About Management's Character** If the auditor has concerns about the competence, integrity, ethical values, or diligence of management or about management's commitment to, or enforcement of, these, the auditor should determine the effect that such concerns may have on the reliability of representations (oral or written) and audit evidence in general.

   Such concerns *may* cause the auditor to conclude that the risk of management misrepresentation in the financial statements is such that an audit cannot be conducted. In such a case, the auditor *may* consider withdrawing from the engagement, when withdrawal is possible under applicable law or regulation, unless those charged with governance put in place appropriate corrective measures. Such measures, however, may not be sufficient to enable the auditor to issue an unmodified audit opinion.

   b. **When Written Representations Are Inconsistent With Other Evidence**

      (1) **Perform Audit Procedures to Resolve Inconsistency** If written representations are inconsistent with other audit evidence, the auditor should perform audit procedures to attempt to resolve the matter.

      The auditor *may* consider whether the risk assessment remains appropriate and, if not, *may* revise it, and determine the nature, extent, and timing of further audit procedures to respond to the assessed risks.

      (2) **When Inconsistency Remains Unresolved** If the matter remains unresolved, the auditor should reconsider the assessment of the competence, integrity, ethical values, or diligence of management or of management's commitment to, or enforcement of, these and should determine the effect that this may have on the reliability of representations (oral or written) and audit evidence in general.

2. **Auditor Concludes Written Representations About Management's Responsibilities Are Unreliable or Representations Are *Not* Provided** The auditor should disclaim an opinion on the financial statements or withdraw from the engagement if:

   a. The auditor concludes that sufficient doubt exists about the integrity of management such that the required written representations about management's responsibilities are **not** reliable, or

   b. Management does **not** provide the required written representations about management's responsibilities

   Editor Note:

   - The auditor is not able to judge solely on other audit evidence whether management has fulfilled its responsibilities; thus, without obtaining confirmation from management that it believes that it has fulfilled those responsibilities the auditor does not have sufficient appropriate evidence.

     The possible effects on the financial statements of such an inability to obtain sufficient appropriate evidence are not confined to specific elements, accounts, or items of the financial statements and are, hence, pervasive. US GAAS requires the auditor to disclaim an opinion on the financial statements in such circumstances (when the auditor does not withdraw).

   - As stated earlier in this section, the required written representations about management's responsibilities are:

Preparation & Fair Presentation of the Financial Statements

- The auditor should request management to provide a written representation that it has fulfilled its responsibility, as set out in the terms of the audit engagement for the:
    - Preparation and fair presentation of the financial statements in accordance with the AFRF
    - Design, implementation, and maintenance of internal control relevant to the preparation and fair presentation of financial statements that are free from material misstatement, whether due to fraud or error

Information Provided & Completeness of Transactions

- The auditor should request management to provide written representations that:
    - It has provided the auditor with all relevant information and access, as agreed upon in the terms of the audit engagement
    - All transactions have been recorded and are reflected in the financial statements

The following guidance is applicable to all requested representations ***except*** *those about management's responsibilities for financial statement preparation and presentation; information and access provided to the auditor; and completeness of records. See the preceding item for the more stringent requirements, i.e., disclaimer or opinion or withdrawal from the engagement, when representations about management's responsibilities are unreliable or are not provided.*

3. **Auditor Concludes Other Written Representations Are Unreliable** If the auditor concludes that the other written representations are not reliable, the auditor should take appropriate action, including determining the possible effect on the opinion in the audit report.

4. **Other Written Representations *Not* Provided**

   If management does **not** provide one or more of the other requested written representations, the auditor should:

   a. Discuss the matter with management

   b. Re-evaluate the integrity of management and evaluate the effect that this may have on the reliability of representations (oral or written) and audit evidence in general

   c. Take appropriate actions, including determining the possible effect on the opinion in the audit report

   Management's refusal to furnish other requested written representations constitutes a limitation on the scope of the audit. Such refusal is often sufficient to preclude an unmodified opinion and, in particular with respect to the other required representations, *may* cause an auditor to disclaim an opinion or withdraw from the engagement when withdrawal is possible under applicable law or regulation. However, based on the nature of the representations not obtained or the circumstances of the refusal, the auditor *may* conclude that a qualified opinion is appropriate.

   Editor Note: A written representation that has been modified from that requested by the auditor does not necessarily mean that management did not provide the written representation. However, the underlying reason for such modification *may* affect the opinion in the audit report.

IX. Audit Documentation (AU 230)

Audit documentation is the property of the auditor. The auditor may make available to the entity at the auditor's discretion copies of the audit documentation, provided such disclosure does not undermine the effectiveness and integrity of the audit process.

Many other AU sections include specific audit documentation requirements. Such requirements are included with our coverage of those sections and are not repeated here.

A. Overview

1. **Nature & Purposes of Audit Documentation** Audit documentation that meets the requirements of this section and the specific documentation requirements of other relevant AU sections provides:

   a. Evidence of the auditor's basis for a conclusion about the achievement of the overall objectives of the auditor

   b. Evidence that the audit was planned and performed in accordance with US GAAS and applicable legal and regulatory requirements

   It also serves additional purposes, including:

   - Assisting the engagement team to plan and perform the audit
   - Assisting members of the engagement team responsible for supervision to direct and supervise the audit work and to discharge their review responsibilities
   - Enabling the engagement team to demonstrate that it is accountable for its work by documenting the procedures performed; the audit evidence examined; and the conclusions reached
   - Retaining a record of matters of continuing significance to future audits of the same entity
   - Enabling the conduct of quality control reviews and inspections
   - Enabling the conduct of external inspections or peer reviews in accordance with applicable legal, regulatory, or other requirements
   - Assisting an auditor who reviews a predecessor auditor's audit documentation
   - Assisting auditors to understand the work performed in the prior year as an aid in planning and performing the current engagement

2. **Objective** The objective of the auditor is to prepare documentation that provides:

   a. A sufficient and appropriate record of the basis for the audit report

   b. Evidence that the audit was planned and performed in accordance with US GAAS and applicable legal and regulatory requirements

3. **Definitions**

   a. **Audit Documentation** The record of audit procedures performed, relevant audit evidence obtained, and conclusions the auditor reached (terms such as *working papers* or *workpapers* are also sometimes used)

      Examples of audit documentation include:

      - Audit plans
      - Analyses

- Issues memorandums
- Summaries of significant findings or issues
- Letters of confirmation and representation
- Checklists
- Minutes of meetings (audit documentation is not limited to documents prepared by the auditor)
- Correspondence (including e-mail) concerning significant findings or issues

b. **Audit File** One or more folders or other storage media, in physical or electronic form, containing the records that constitute the audit documentation for a specific engagement

c. **Documentation Completion Date** The date, no later than 60 days following the report release date, on which the auditor has assembled for retention a complete and final set of documentation in an audit file

d. **Experienced Auditor** An individual (whether internal or external to the firm) who has practical audit experience, and a reasonable understanding of:

(1) Audit processes

(2) US GAAS and applicable legal and regulatory requirements

(3) The business environment in which the entity operates

(4) Auditing and financial reporting issues relevant to the entity's industry

e. **Report Release Date** The date the auditor grants the entity permission to use the audit report in connection with the financial statements

4. **Timely Preparation of Audit Documentation** The auditor should prepare audit documentation on a timely basis.

Preparing sufficient and appropriate audit documentation on a timely basis throughout the audit helps to enhance the quality of the audit and facilitates the effective review and evaluation of the audit evidence obtained and conclusions reached before the audit report is finalized.

Documentation prepared at the time such work is performed or shortly thereafter is likely to be more accurate than documentation prepared at a much later time.

B. Documentation of Audit Procedures Performed & Audit Evidence Obtained

1. Content & Extent of Audit Documentation

a. Content

(1) **Report Release Date** The auditor should document the report release date in the audit documentation.

(2) **Requirements for All Procedures** In documenting the nature, timing, and extent of the audit procedures performed, the auditor should record:

(a) **Characteristics** The identifying characteristics of the specific items or matters tested, for example, for a detailed test of purchase orders, the auditor may identify the documents selected for testing by their dates and unique purchase order numbers

(b) **Performer & Date of Completion** Who performed the audit work and the date such work was completed

(c) **Reviewer and Date & Extent of Review** Who reviewed the audit work performed and the date and extent of such review

(3) **Requirements for Specific Procedures**

(a) **Inspection of Contracts** For audit procedures related to the inspection of significant contracts or agreements, the auditor should include abstracts or copies of those contracts or agreements in the audit documentation.

(b) **Discussions of Significant Findings**

(i) **Nature, Date & Participants** The auditor should document discussions of significant findings or issues with management, those charged with governance, and others, including the nature of the significant findings or issues discussed, and when and with whom the discussions took place.

(ii) **How Inconsistencies With Final Conclusion Were Addressed** If the auditor identified information that is inconsistent with the auditor's final conclusion regarding a significant finding or issue, the auditor should document how the auditor addressed the inconsistency.

(4) **Role of Oral Explanations** On their own, oral explanations by the auditor do **not** represent adequate support for the work the auditor performed or conclusions the auditor reached, but may be used to explain or clarify information contained in the audit documentation.

b. **Sufficiency of the Documentation—Experienced Auditor Standard** The auditor should prepare audit documentation that is sufficient to enable an experienced auditor, having no previous connection with the audit, to understand:

(1) **Nature, Extent & Timing of Procedures** The nature, timing, and extent of the audit procedures performed to comply with US GAAS and applicable legal and regulatory requirements

(2) **Results of Audit Procedures & Evidence Obtained** The results of the audit procedures performed and the audit evidence obtained

(3) **Significant Findings, Judgments & Conclusions** Significant findings or issues arising during the audit, the conclusions reached, and significant professional judgments made in reaching those conclusions

Editor Note: The auditor *may* consider it helpful to prepare and retain as part of the audit documentation a summary (sometimes known as a completion memorandum) that describes the significant findings or issues identified during the audit and how they were addressed, or that includes cross-references to other relevant supporting audit documentation that provides such information. Such a summary may facilitate effective and efficient reviews and inspections of the audit documentation, particularly for large and complex audits.

Examples of significant findings *may* include:

- Matters involving the selection, application, and consistency of significant accounting practices, including related disclosures. Such matters include, but are not limited to (a) accounting for complex or unusual transactions or (b) accounting estimates and uncertainties and, if applicable, the related management assumptions
- Matters that give rise to significant risks
- Results of audit procedures (including identification of corrected and uncorrected misstatements) indicating (a) that the financial statements could be materially misstated or (b) a need to revise the auditor's previous assessment of the risks of material misstatement (RMM) and the auditor's responses to those risks
- Circumstances that cause the auditor significant difficulty in applying necessary audit procedures
- Findings that could result in a modification to the audit opinion or the inclusion of an emphasis-of-matter paragraph in the audit report

Editor Note: Audit documentation provides evidence that the audit complies with US GAAS; however, it is neither necessary nor practicable for the auditor to document every matter considered, or professional judgment made, in an audit.

c. **Factors That *May* Affect the Form, Content & Extent of the Audit Documentation** The form, content, and extent of audit documentation depend on factors such as the:

- Size and complexity of the entity
- Nature of the audit procedures to be performed
- Identified RMM
- Significance of the audit evidence obtained
- Nature and extent of exceptions identified
- Need to document a conclusion or the basis for a conclusion not readily determinable from the documentation of the work performed or audit evidence obtained
- Audit methodology and tools used
- Extent of judgment involved in performing the work and evaluating the results

2. **Departure From a Relevant Requirement** If, in rare circumstances, the auditor judges it necessary to depart from a relevant presumptively mandatory requirement, the auditor must document the justification for the departure and how the alternative audit procedure(s) were sufficient to achieve the intent of that requirement.

3. **Matters Arising After the Date of the Audit Report** If, in rare circumstances, the auditor performs new or additional audit procedures or draws new conclusions after the date of the audit report, the auditor should document:

a. **Circumstances** The circumstances encountered

b. **Procedures, Evidence Obtained, Conclusions & Effect on Audit Report** The new or additional audit procedures performed, audit evidence obtained, and conclusions reached, and their effect on the audit report

c. **Performer & Reviewer and Respective Dates** When and by whom the resulting changes to audit documentation were made and reviewed

Editor Note: Examples of rare circumstances in which the auditor performs new or additional audit procedures or draws new conclusions after the date of the audit report include:

- When, after the date of the audit report, the auditor becomes aware of facts that existed at that date and which, if known at that date, might have caused the financial statements to be revised or the auditor to modify the opinion in the audit report
- When the auditor concludes that procedures necessary at the time of the audit, in the circumstances then existing, were omitted from the audit of the financial information

C. **Assembly & Retention of the Final Audit File**

1. **Timeliness** The auditor should assemble the audit documentation in an audit file and complete the administrative process of assembling the final audit file on a timely basis, **no later than 60 days following the report release date**.

The completion of the assembly of the final audit file after the date of the audit report is an administrative process that does *not* involve the performance of new audit procedures or the drawing of new conclusions. Changes *may*, however, be made to the audit documentation during the final assembly process if they are administrative in nature

2. **Retention Period**

a. **Preservation of the Contents of the Audit File** After the documentation completion date, the auditor should not delete or discard audit documentation of any nature before the end of the specified retention period.

b. **Span of Retention Period** The retention period should not be shorter than five years from the report release date.

Statutes, regulations, or the audit firm's quality control policies *may* specify a retention period longer than five years.

c. **Changes to the File** In circumstances *other than* when the auditor finds it necessary to modify existing audit documentation or add new audit documentation after the documentation completion date, i.e., when matters arise after the date of the audit report as discussed above, the auditor should, regardless of the nature of the modifications or additions, document:

(1) **Reasons for the Changes** The specific reasons for making the changes

(2) **Performer & Reviewer and Respective Dates** When and by whom they were made and reviewed

Editor Note: An example of a circumstance in which the auditor *may* find it necessary to modify existing audit documentation or add new audit documentation after the documentation completion date is the need to clarify existing audit documentation arising from comments received during monitoring inspections performed by internal or external parties.

3. **Procedures to Maintain Confidentiality of Client Information** The auditor should adopt reasonable procedures to maintain the confidentiality of client information.

CHAPTER 4—EVIDENCE & PROCEDURES

Problem 4-1 MULTIPLE-CHOICE QUESTIONS

Audit Evidence

1. The best primary audit evidence regarding year-end bank balances is documented in the
   a. Standard bank confirmations
   b. Interbank transfer schedule
   c. Bank reconciliations
   d. Bank deposit lead schedule (ID: 146)

2. Which of the following procedures would provide the most reliable audit evidence?
   a. Inquiries of the client's internal audit staff held in private
   b. Inspection of prenumbered client purchase orders filed in the Vouchers Payable Department
   c. Analytical procedures performed by the auditor on the entity's trial balance
   d. Inspection of bank statements obtained directly from the client's financial institution (ID: 3922)

3. Which of the following presumptions is correct about the reliability of audit evidence?
   a. Information obtained indirectly from outside sources is the most reliable audit evidence.
   b. To be reliable, audit evidence should be convincing rather than persuasive.
   c. Reliability of audit evidence refers to the amount of corroborative evidence obtained.
   d. An effective internal control structure provides more assurance about the reliability of audit evidence. (ID: 5120)

4. The most reliable procedure for an auditor to use to test the existence of a client's inventory at an outside location would be to
   a. Observe physical counts of the inventory items
   b. Trace the total on the inventory listing to the general ledger inventory account
   c. Obtain a confirmation from the client indicating inventory ownership
   d. Analytically compare the current-year inventory balance to the prior-year balance (ID: 8139)

5. A client uses a suspense account for unresolved questions whose final accounting has not been determined. If a balance remains in the suspense account at year-end, the auditor would be most concerned about
   a. Suspense debits that management believes will benefit future operations
   b. Suspense debits that the auditor verifies will have realizable value to the client
   c. Suspense credits that management believes should be classified as "Current liability"
   d. Suspense credits that the auditor determines to be customer deposits (ID: 6365)

6. An entity's income statements were misstated due to the recording of journal entries that involved debits and credits to an unusual combination of expense and revenue accounts. The auditor most likely could have detected this misstatement by
   a. Tracing a sample of journal entries to the general ledger
   b. Evaluating the effectiveness of internal control policies and procedures
   c. Investigating the reconciliations between controlling accounts and subsidiary records
   d. Performing analytical procedures designed to disclose differences from expectations (ID: 5087)

7. An auditor may achieve audit objectives related to particular assertions by
   a. Performing analytical procedures
   b. Adhering to a system of quality control
   c. Preparing auditor working papers
   d. Increasing the level of detection risk (ID: 5985)

8. In addition to evaluating the frequency of deviations in tests of controls, an auditor should also consider certain qualitative aspects of the deviations. The auditor most likely would give broader consideration to the implications of a deviation if it was

   a. The only deviation discovered in the sample
   b. Identical to a deviation discovered during the prior year's audit
   c. Caused by an employee's misunderstanding of instructions
   d. Initially concealed by a forged document (ID: 5973)

9. Which of the following circumstances most likely would cause an auditor to suspect that material misstatements exist in a client's financial statements?

   a. The assumptions used in developing the prior year's accounting estimates have changed.
   b. Differences between reconciliations of control accounts and subsidiary records are not investigated.
   c. Negative confirmation requests yield fewer responses than in the prior year's audit.
   d. Management consults with another CPA firm about complex accounting matters. (ID: 7097)

10. Which of the following types of audit evidence is the most persuasive?

    a. Prenumbered client purchase order forms
    b. Client work sheets supporting cost allocations
    c. Bank statements obtained from the client
    d. Representation letter (ID: 5657)

11. Which of the following circumstances most likely would cause an auditor to consider whether material misstatements exist in an entity's financial statements?

    a. Management places little emphasis on meeting earnings projections.
    b. The board of directors makes all major financing decisions.
    c. Significant deficiencies previously communicated to management are not corrected.
    d. Transactions selected for testing are not supported by proper documentation. (ID: 5086)

12. Which of the following procedures would yield the most appropriate evidence?

    a. A scanning of trial balances
    b. An inquiry of client personnel
    c. A comparison of beginning and ending retained earnings
    d. A recalculation of bad debt expense (ID: 8143)

13. An auditor observes the mailing of monthly statements to a client's customers and reviews evidence of follow-up on errors reported by the customers. This test of controls most likely is performed to support management's financial statement assertions of

	Classification and understandability	Existence or occurrence	
a.	Yes	Yes	
b.	Yes	No	
c.	No	Yes	
d.	No	No	(ID: 8119)

14. At the conclusion of an audit, an auditor is reviewing the evidence gathered in support of the financial statements. With regard to the valuation of inventory, the auditor concludes that the evidence obtained is not sufficient to support management's representations. Which of the following actions is the auditor most likely to take?

    a. Consult with the audit committee and issue a disclaimer of opinion
    b. Consult with the audit committee and issue a qualified opinion
    c. Obtain additional evidence regarding the valuation of inventory
    d. Obtain a statement from management supporting their inventory valuation (ID: 8394)

15. Which of the following procedures would an auditor most likely perform in auditing the statement of cash flows?
    a. Reconcile the amounts included in the statement of cash flows to the other financial statements' amounts
    b. Vouch a sample of cash receipts and disbursements for the last few days of the current year
    c. Reconcile the cutoff bank statement to the proof of cash to verify the accuracy of the year-end cash balance
    d. Confirm the amounts included in the statement of cash flows with the entity's financial institution

    (ID: 8408)

16. Which of the following procedures is considered a test of controls?
    a. An auditor reviews the entity's check register for unrecorded liabilities.
    b. An auditor evaluates whether a general journal entry was recorded at the proper amount.
    c. An auditor interviews and observes appropriate personnel to determine segregation of duties.
    d. An auditor reviews the audit workpapers to ensure proper sign-off. (ID: 9360)

17. Which of the following factors most likely would lead a CPA to conclude that a potential audit engagement should not be accepted?
    a. There are significant related-party transactions that management claims occurred in the ordinary course of business.
    b. Internal control activities requiring the segregation of duties are subject to management override.
    c. Management continues to employ an inefficient system of information technology to record financial transactions.
    d. It is unlikely that sufficient appropriate evidence is available to support an opinion on the financial statements. (ID: 8161)

Internal Auditors

18. The work of internal auditors may be used by the external auditor to

    I. Obtain audit evidence
    II. Provide direct assistance

    a. I. only
    b. II. only
    c. Neither I. nor II.
    d. Both I. and II. (ID: 6000)

19. In assessing the competence and objectivity of an entity's internal audit function, an external auditor would be **least** likely to consider information obtained from
    a. Discussions with management personnel
    b. External quality reviews of the internal auditor's activities
    c. Previous experience with the internal auditor
    d. The results of analytical procedures (ID: 5141)

20. In assessing the competence of an internal auditor, an external auditor most likely would obtain information about the
    a. Quality of the internal auditor's working paper documentation
    b. Organization's commitment to integrity and ethical values
    c. Influence of management on the scope of the internal auditor's duties
    d. Organizational level to which the internal auditor reports (ID: 6832)

21. The external auditor should determine whether the work of the internal audit function can be used in obtaining audit evidence by evaluating all of the following **except**

    a. The amount of judgment involved in performing the planned audit procedures
    b. The extent to which the internal audit function's organizational status and relevant policies and procedures support the objectivity of the internal auditors
    c. The level of competence of the internal audit function
    d. The application by the internal audit function of a systematic and disciplined approach, including quality control (ID: 8127)

22. For which of the following judgments may an external auditor share responsibility with an entity's internal auditor who is assessed to be both competent and objective?

	Assessment of risk of material misstatement	Evaluating Going Concern Issues
a.	Yes	Yes
b.	Yes	No
c.	No	Yes
d.	No	No

(ID: 6235)

23. During an audit an internal auditor may provide direct assistance to an external auditor in

	Obtaining an understanding of internal control	Performing tests of controls	Performing substantive tests
a.	No	No	No
b.	Yes	No	No
c.	Yes	Yes	No
d.	Yes	Yes	Yes

(ID: 5678)

24. Miller Retailing, Inc. maintains a staff of three full-time internal auditors who report directly to the controller. In planning to use the work of internal auditors, the external auditor most likely will

    a. Place limited reliance on the work performed by the internal auditors
    b. Decrease the extent of the tests of controls needed to support the assessed level of detection risk
    c. Increase the extent of the procedures needed to reduce control risk to an acceptable level
    d. Avoid using the work performed by the internal auditors (ID: 157)

25. In assessing the objectivity of internal auditors, the external auditor would be most likely to consider the

    a. Internal auditing standards developed by The Institute of Internal Auditors
    b. Tests of internal control activities that could detect errors and fraud
    c. Materiality of the accounts recently inspected by the internal auditors
    d. Results of the tests of transactions recently performed by the internal auditors (ID: 7108)

26. In assessing the competence of internal auditors, an external auditor would be most likely to obtain information about the

    a. Influence of management on the scope of the internal auditors' duties
    b. Policies limiting internal auditors from communicating with the audit committee
    c. Quality of the internal auditors' working paper documentation
    d. Entity's ability to continue as a going concern for a reasonable period of time

(ID: 8614)

27. Which of the following factors most likely would assist an independent auditor in assessing the objectivity of the internal auditor?

    a. The organizational status of the director of internal audit
    b. The professional certifications of the internal audit staff
    c. The consistency of the internal audit reports with the results of work performed
    d. The appropriateness of internal audit conclusions in the circumstances (ID: 8640)

28. Prior to using internal auditors to provide direct assistance, the external auditor should perform all of the following procedures **except**
    a. Evaluate the existence and significance of threats to the objectivity of the internal auditors, as well as any safeguards applied to reduce or eliminate the threats
    b. Obtain written acknowledgment from the entity that the internal auditors will be allowed to follow the external auditor's instructions
    c. Obtain written acknowledgment from the entity that the internal auditors will complete the work assigned to them by the external auditor by the agreed upon dates
    d. Obtain written acknowledgment from the entity that the entity will not intervene in the work the internal auditors perform for the external auditor (ID: 8841)

29. In communicating an overview of the planned scope and timing of the audit to those charged with governance, the external auditor should communicate how the external auditor has planned to use internal auditors
    a. In obtaining audit evidence and providing direct assistance
    b. As a liaison between the controller of the entity and the external auditor
    c. To evaluate the sufficiency of the tests of controls
    d. To assess the risks of material misstatement (ID: 9933)

30. Given the external auditor's sole responsibility for the audit opinion expressed, when using the work of the internal audit function, the external auditor should
    a. Limit the use of internal auditors to the testing of controls
    b. Evaluate whether the use of internal auditors will result in the external auditor still being sufficiently involved in the audit
    c. Put all instructions to internal auditors in writing
    d. Limit the use of internal auditors to working on accounting estimates because these are not, by definition, exact measurements (ID: 9934)

31. If the external auditor uses internal auditors to provide direct assistance on the audit, the external auditor should include in the audit documentation
    a. The working papers prepared by the internal auditors
    b. Evidence that the internal auditors are bonded
    c. Copies of internal auditor's credentials, such as the proof of their membership in relevant professional bodies
    d. Records of their past employment (ID: 9944)

Written Representations

32. When considering the use of written representations as audit evidence about the completeness assertion, an auditor should understand that such representations
    a. Complement, but do not replace, substantive tests designed to support the assertion
    b. Constitute sufficient evidence to support the assertion when considered in combination with the assessment of control risk
    c. Replace the assessment of control risk as evidence to support the assertion
    d. Are not part of the audit evidence considered to support the assertion (ID: 218)

33. Key Co. plans to present comparative financial statements for the years ended December 31, year 7, and year 8, respectively. Smith, CPA, audited Key's financial statements for both years and plans to report on the comparative financial statements on May 1, year 9. Key's current management team was not present until January 1, year 8. What period of time should be covered by Key's representation letter?
    a. January 1, year 7, through December 31, year 8.
    b. January 1, year 7, through May 1, year 9.
    c. January 1, year 8, through December 31, year 8.
    d. January 1, year 8, through May 1, year 9. (ID: 6842)

34. For which of the following matters should an auditor obtain written representations?
    a. Management's cost-benefit justifications for not correcting internal control weaknesses
    b. Management's knowledge of future plans that may affect the price of the entity's stock
    c. Management's compliance with contractual agreements that may affect the financial statements
    d. Management's acknowledgment of its responsibility for employees' violations of laws (ID: 6841)

35. Which of the following matters most likely would be included in a representation letter?
    a. An assessment of the risk factors concerning the misappropriation of assets
    b. An evaluation of the litigation that has been filed against the entity
    c. A confirmation that the entity has complied with contractual agreements
    d. A statement that all material internal control weaknesses have been corrected (ID: 8164)

36. To which of the following matters would materiality limits **not** apply in obtaining written representations?
    a. The availability of minutes of stockholders' and directors' meetings
    b. Losses from purchase commitments at prices in excess of market value
    c. The disclosure of compensating balance arrangements involving related parties
    d. Reductions of obsolete inventory to net realizable value (ID: 5684)

37. To which of the following matters would materiality limits **not** apply when obtaining written client representations?
    a. Violations of state labor regulations
    b. Disclosure of line-of-credit arrangements
    c. Information about related-party transactions
    d. Instances of fraud involving management (ID: 8124)

38. In obtaining written representations from management, materiality limits ordinarily would apply to representations related to
    a. Amounts concerning related-party transactions
    b. Irregularities involving members of management
    c. The availability of financial records
    d. The completeness of minutes of directors' meetings (ID: 8826)

Analytics

39. Which of the following would **not** be considered an analytical procedure?
    a. Estimating payroll expense by multiplying the number of employees by the average hourly wage rate and the total hours worked
    b. Projecting an error rate by comparing the results of a statistical sample with the actual population characteristics
    c. Computing accounts receivable turnover by dividing credit sales by the average net receivables
    d. Developing the expected current year sales based on the sales trend of the prior five years (ID: 5666)

40. Analytical procedures used in planning an audit should focus on
    a. Reducing the scope of tests of controls and substantive tests
    b. Providing assurance that potential material misstatements will be identified
    c. Enhancing the auditor's understanding of the client's business
    d. Assessing the adequacy of the available audit evidence (ID: 5626)

41. An auditor compares annual revenues and expenses with similar amounts from the prior year and investigates all changes exceeding 10%. This procedure most likely could indicate that

    a. Fourth quarter payroll taxes were properly accrued and recorded, but were not paid until early in the subsequent year.
    b. Unrealized gains from increases in the value of available-for-sale securities were recorded in the income account for trading securities.
    c. The annual provision for uncollectible accounts expense was inadequate because of worsening economic conditions.
    d. Notice of an increase in property tax rates was received by management, but was not recorded until early in the subsequent year. (ID: 8146)

42. An auditor discovered that a client's accounts receivable turnover is substantially lower for the current year than for the prior year. This may indicate that

    a. Obsolete inventory has not yet been reduced to fair market value.
    b. There was an improper cutoff of sales at the end of the year.
    c. An unusually large receivable was written off near the end of the year.
    d. The aging of accounts receivable was improperly performed in both years. (ID: 8163)

43. Which of the following ratios would an engagement partner most likely calculate when reviewing the balance sheet in the overall review stage of an audit?

    a. Quick assets/current assets
    b. Accounts receivable/inventory
    c. Interest payable/interest receivable
    d. Total debt/total assets (ID: 6366)

44. An auditor most likely would apply analytical procedures in the overall review stage of an audit to

    a. Enhance the auditor's understanding of subsequent events
    b. Identify auditing procedures omitted by the staff accountants
    c. Determine whether additional audit evidence may be needed
    d. Evaluate the effectiveness of the internal control activities (ID: 8157)

45. Which of the following nonfinancial information would an auditor most likely consider in performing analytical procedures during the planning phase of an audit?

    a. Turnover of personnel in the Accounting Department
    b. Objectivity of audit committee members
    c. Square footage of selling space
    d. Management's plans to repurchase stock (ID: 6392)

46. An auditor's analytical procedures most likely would be facilitated if the entity

    a. Segregates obsolete inventory before the physical inventory count
    b. Uses a standard cost system that produces variance reports
    c. Corrects material weaknesses in internal control before the beginning of the audit
    d. Develops its data from sources solely within the entity (ID: 5988)

47. An auditor's analytical procedures performed during the overall review stage indicated that the client's accounts receivable had doubled since the end of the prior year. However, the allowance for doubtful accounts as a percentage of accounts receivable remained about the same. Which of the following client explanations most likely would satisfy the auditor?

    a. The client liberalized its credit standards in the current year and sold much more merchandise to customers with poor credit ratings.
    b. Twice as many accounts receivable were written off in the prior year than in the current year.
    c. A greater percentage of accounts receivable were currently listed in the "more than 90 days overdue" category than in the prior year.
    d. The client opened a second retail outlet in the current year and its credit sales approximately equaled the older, established outlet. (ID: 7623)

48. Analytical procedures performed during an audit indicate that accounts receivable doubled since the end of the prior year. However, the allowance for doubtful accounts as a percentage of accounts receivable remained about the same. Which of the following client explanations would satisfy the auditor?

    a. A greater percentage of accounts receivable are listed in the "more than 120 days overdue" category than in the prior year.
    b. Internal control activities over the recording of cash receipts have been improved since the end of the prior year.
    c. The client opened a second retail outlet during the current year and its credit sales approximately equaled the older outlet.
    d. The client tightened its credit policy during the current year and sold considerably less merchandise to customers with poor credit ratings. (ID: 8133)

49. For all audits of financial statements made in accordance with generally accepted auditing standards, the use of analytical procedures is required to some extent

	In the planning stage	As a substantive test	In the review stage
a.	Yes	No	Yes
b.	No	Yes	No
c.	No	Yes	Yes
d.	Yes	No	No

(ID: 141)

50. An auditor's decision either to apply analytical procedures as substantive tests or to perform tests of transactions and account balances usually is determined by the

    a. Availability of data aggregated at a high level
    b. Auditor's familiarity with industry trends
    c. Timing of tests performed after the balance sheet date
    d. Relative effectiveness and efficiency of the tests (ID: 2965)

51. To be effective, analytical procedures in the overall review stage of an audit engagement should be performed by

    a. The staff accountant who performed the substantive auditing procedures
    b. The managing partner who has responsibility for all audit engagements at that practice office
    c. A manager or partner who has a comprehensive knowledge of the client's business and industry
    d. The CPA firm's quality control manager or partner who has responsibility for the firm's peer review program (ID: 7025)

52. Analytical procedures performed in the overall review stage of an audit suggest that several accounts have unexpected relationships. The results of these procedures most likely would indicate that

    a. Fraud exists among the relevant account balances.
    b. Internal control activities are not operating effectively.
    c. Additional tests of details are required.
    d. The communication with the audit committee should be revised. (ID: 6398)

53. The accounts receivable turnover ratio increased significantly over a two-year period. This trend could indicate that

    a. The accounts receivable aging has deteriorated.
    b. The company has eliminated its discount policy.
    c. The company is more aggressively collecting customer accounts.
    d. Customer sales have substantially decreased. (ID: 7842)

54. Analytical procedures performed in the final review stage of an audit generally would include

    a. Reassessing the factors that assisted the auditor in deciding on preliminary materiality levels and audit risk
    b. Considering the adequacy of the evidence gathered in response to unexpected balances identified in planning
    c. Summarizing uncorrected misstatements specifically identified through tests of details of transactions and balances
    d. Calculating projected uncorrected misstatements estimated through audit sampling techniques (ID: 7813)

55. Which one of the following tend to be most predictable for purposes of analytical procedures applied as substantive tests?

    a. Data subject to audit testing in the prior year
    b. Transactions subject to management discretion
    c. Relationships involving income statement accounts
    d. Relationships involving balance sheet accounts (ID: 2773)

56. An auditor compares current annual revenues and expenses with those of the prior year and investigates all changes exceeding 10%. By this procedure the auditor would be most likely to learn that

    a. An increase in property tax rates has not been recognized in the client's accrual.
    b. The client changed its capitalization policy for small tools in the current year.
    c. Fourth quarter payroll taxes were not paid.
    d. The current provision for uncollectible accounts is inadequate because of worsening economic conditions. (ID: 7493)

57. Which of the following factors would most likely influence an auditor's consideration of the reliability of data when performing analytical procedures?

    a. Whether the data were developed in a computerized or a manual accounting system
    b. Whether the data were prepared on the cash basis or in conformity with GAAP
    c. Whether the data were developed under a system with adequate controls
    d. Whether the data were processed in an online system or a batch entry system (ID: 8388)

58. Which of the following procedures would a CPA most likely perform in the planning stage of a financial statement audit?

    a. Obtain representations from management regarding the availability of all financial records
    b. Communicate with the audit committee concerning the prior year's audit adjustments
    c. Make inquiries of the client's attorney regarding pending and threatened litigation and assessments
    d. Compare recorded financial information with anticipated results from budgets and forecasts (ID: 8414)

59. When performing analytical procedures in the planning stage, the auditor most likely would develop expectations by reviewing which of the following sources of information?

    a. Unaudited information from internal quarterly reports
    b. Various account assertions in the planning memorandum
    c. Comments in the prior year's management letter
    d. The control risk assessment relating to specific financial assertions (ID: 8831)

60. Analytical procedures used in the planning phase of an audit should focus on
    a. Documenting the risk factors relating to the susceptibility of assets to misappropriation
    b. Identifying the internal control activities that could reduce the assessed level of control risk
    c. Discovering uncorrected misstatements that should be communicated to the audit committee
    d. Enhancing the auditor's understanding of the transactions and events that have occurred since the last audit (ID: 8843)

61. Which of the following is an analytical procedure that an auditor most likely would perform during the final review stage of an audit?
    a. Comparing each individual expense account balance with the relevant budgeted amounts and investigating any significant variations
    b. Testing the effectiveness of internal control procedures that appear to be suitably designed to prevent or detect material misstatements
    c. Reading the financial statements and considering whether there are any unusual or unexpected balances that were not previously identified
    d. Calculating each individual expense account balance as a percentage of total entity expenses and comparing the results with industry averages (ID: 8801)

62. Which of the following ratios would an engagement partner most likely consider in the overall review stage of an audit?
    a. Total liabilities/net sales
    b. Accounts receivable/inventory
    c. Cost of goods sold/average inventory
    d. Current assets/quick assets (ID: 8847)

63. Which of the following most likely would cause an auditor to consider whether a client's financial statements contain material misstatements?
    a. Management did not disclose to the auditor that it consulted with other accountants about significant accounting matters.
    b. The chief financial officer will not sign the representation letter until the last day of the auditor's fieldwork.
    c. Audit trails of computer-generated transactions exist only for a short time.
    d. The results of an analytical procedure disclose unexpected differences. (ID: 8809)

64. An auditor's decision whether to apply analytical procedures as substantive tests usually is determined by the
    a. Availability of documentary evidence that should be verified
    b. Extent of accounting estimates used in preparing the financial statements
    c. Precision and reliability of the data used to develop expectations
    d. Number of transactions recorded just before and just after the year-end (ID: 8832)

65. Auditors try to identify predictable relationships when applying analytical procedures. Relationships involving transactions from which of the following accounts most likely would yield the highest level of evidence?
    a. Interest expense
    b. Allowance for doubtful accounts
    c. Accounts receivable
    d. Accounts payable (ID: 8641)

66. An auditor's analytical procedures indicate a lower than expected return on an equity method investment. This situation most likely could have been caused by
    a. An error in recording amortization of the excess of the investor's cost over the investment's underlying book value
    b. The investee's decision to reduce cash dividends declared per share of its common stock
    c. An error in recording the unrealized gain from an increase in the fair value of available-for-sale securities in the income account for trading securities
    d. A substantial fluctuation in the price of the investee's common stock on a national stock exchange (ID: 9362)

67. Analytical procedures are most appropriate when testing which of the following types of transactions?
    a. Payroll and benefit liabilities
    b. Acquisitions and disposals of fixed assets
    c. Operating expense transactions
    d. Long-term debt transactions (ID: 9379)

68. Which of the following activities is an analytical procedure an auditor would perform in the final overall review stage of an audit to ensure that the financial statements are free from material misstatement?
    a. Reading the minutes of the board of directors' meetings for the year under audit
    b. Obtaining a letter concerning potential liabilities from the client's attorney
    c. Comparing the current year's financial statements with those of the prior year
    d. Ensuring that a representation letter signed by management is in the file (ID: 9912)

Using a Specialist's Work

69. In using the work of a specialist, an auditor may refer to the specialist in the auditor's report if, as a result of the specialist's findings, the auditor
    a. Becomes aware of conditions causing substantial doubt about the entity's ability to continue as a going concern.
    b. Desires to disclose the specialist's findings, which imply that a more thorough audit was performed.
    c. Is able to corroborate another specialist's earlier findings that were consistent with management's written representations.
    d. Discovers significant deficiencies in the design of the entity's internal control that management does not correct. (ID: 5680)

70. An auditor intends to use the work of an actuary who has a relationship with the client. Under these circumstances, the auditor
    a. Is required to disclose the contractual relationship in the auditor's report
    b. Should assess the risk that the actuary's objectivity might be impaired
    c. Is not permitted to rely on the actuary because of a lack of independence
    d. May communicate this matter to management as a control deficiency (ID: 8412)

71. An auditor who uses the work of a specialist may refer to the specialist in the auditor's report if the
    a. Auditor believes that the specialist's findings are reasonable in the circumstances.
    b. Specialist's findings support the related assertions in the financial statements.
    c. Auditor modifies the report because of the difference between the client's and the specialist's valuations of an asset.
    d. Specialist's findings provide the auditor with greater assurance of reliability about written representations. (ID: 8846)

Inquiry of Client's Lawyer

72. The scope of an audit is **not** restricted when an attorney's response to an auditor as a result of a client's letter of audit inquiry limits the response to

    a. Matters to which the attorney has given substantive attention in the form of legal representation
    b. An evaluation of the likelihood of an unfavorable outcome of the matters disclosed by the entity
    c. The attorney's opinion of the entity's historical experience in recent similar litigation
    d. The probable outcome of asserted claims and pending or threatened litigation (ID: 138)

73. The primary source of information to be reported about litigation, claims, and assessments is the

    a. Client's lawyer
    b. Court records
    c. Client's management
    d. Independent auditor (ID: 4276)

74. A lawyer's response to an auditor's inquiry concerning litigation, claims, and assessments may be limited to matters that are considered individually or collectively material to the client's financial statements. Which parties should reach an understanding on the limits of materiality for this purpose?

    a. The auditor and the client's management
    b. The client's audit committee and the lawyer
    c. The client's management and the lawyer
    d. The lawyer and the auditor (ID: 6840)

75. "In connection with an audit of our financial statements, management has prepared, and furnished to our auditors a description and evaluation of certain contingencies." The foregoing passage most likely is from a(an)

    a. Audit inquiry letter to legal counsel
    b. Representation letter
    c. Audit committee's communication to the auditor
    d. Financial statement footnote disclosure (ID: 7817)

76. The primary reason an auditor requests letters of inquiry be sent to a client's attorneys is to provide the auditor with

    a. The probable outcome of asserted claims and pending or threatened litigation
    b. Corroboration of the information furnished by management about litigation, claims, and assessments
    c. The attorneys' opinions of the client's historical experiences in recent similar litigation
    d. A description and evaluation of litigation, claims, and assessments that existed at the balance sheet date (ID: 5139)

77. Which of the following is an audit procedure that an auditor most likely would perform concerning litigation, claims, and assessments?

    a. Request the client's lawyer to evaluate whether the client's pending litigation, claims, and assessments indicate a going concern problem
    b. Examine the legal documents in the client's lawyer's possession concerning litigation, claims, and assessments to which the lawyer has devoted substantive attention
    c. Discuss with management its policies and procedures adopted for evaluating and accounting for litigation, claims, and assessments
    d. Confirm directly with the client's lawyer that all litigation, claims, and assessments have been recorded or disclosed in the financial statements (ID: 6002)

78. Which of the following statements extracted from a client's lawyer's letter concerning litigation, claims, and assessments most likely would cause the auditor to request clarification?

    a. "I believe that the plaintiff will have problems establishing any liability."
    b. "I believe that this action has only a remote chance in establishing any liability."
    c. "I believe that the plaintiff's case against the company is without merit."
    d. "I believe that the company will be able to defend this action successfully." (ID: 8156)

79. A client's lawyer is unable to form a conclusion about the likelihood of an unfavorable outcome of pending litigation because of inherent uncertainties. If the litigation's effect on the client's financial statements could be material, the auditor most likely would

    a. Issue a qualified opinion in the auditor's report because of the lawyer's scope limitation
    b. Withdraw from the engagement because of the lack of information furnished by the lawyer
    c. Disclaim an opinion on the financial statements because of the materiality of the litigation's effect
    d. Add an explanatory paragraph to the auditor's report because of the uncertainty (ID: 5682)

80. Which of the following factors most likely would cause a CPA to decline to accept a new audit engagement?

    a. The CPA does not understand the entity's operations and industry.
    b. Management acknowledges that the entity has had recurring operating losses.
    c. The CPA is unable to review the predecessor auditor's working papers.
    d. Management is unwilling to permit inquiry of its legal counsel. (ID: 8384)

81. Which of the following procedures would an auditor most likely perform regarding litigation?

    a. Confirm directly with the clerk of the court that the client's litigation is properly disclosed.
    b. Discuss with management its policies and procedures for identifying and evaluating litigation.
    c. Inspect the legal documents in the client's lawyer's possession regarding pending litigation.
    d. Confirm the details of pending litigation with the client's adversaries' legal representatives. (ID: 8643)

82. Which of the following procedures would an auditor most likely perform to assist in the evaluation of loss contingencies?

    a. Checking arithmetic accuracy of the accounting records
    b. Performing appropriate analytical procedures
    c. Obtaining a letter of audit inquiry from the client's lawyer
    d. Reading the financial statements, including footnotes (ID: 8615)

83. An auditor requests a client to send letters of audit inquiry to attorneys who have been consulted concerning litigation, claims, and assessments. The primary reason for this request is to obtain

    a. The attorneys' assurance that litigation, claims, and assessments that are probable of assertion are properly accounted for
    b. Corroboration of the information furnished by management concerning litigation, claims, and assessments
    c. A description of litigation, claims, and assessments that have a reasonable possibility of unfavorable outcomes
    d. The opinion of an expert whether any loss contingencies are possible, probable, or remote (ID: 8620)

84. A client is a defendant in a patent infringement lawsuit against a major competitor. Which of the following items would **least** likely be included in the attorney's response to the auditor's letter of inquiry?
    a. A description of potential litigation in other matters or related to an unfavorable verdict in the patent infringement lawsuit
    b. A discussion of case progress and the strategy currently in place by client management to resolve the lawsuit
    c. An evaluation of the probability of loss and a statement of the amount or range of loss if an unfavorable outcome is reasonably possible
    d. An evaluation of the ability of the client to continue as a going concern if the verdict is unfavorable and maximum damages are awarded (ID: 8651)

85. Which of the following procedures most likely would assist an auditor to identify litigation, claims, and assessments?
    a. Inspect checks included with the client's cutoff bank statement
    b. Obtain a letter of representations from the client's underwriter of securities
    c. Apply ratio analysis on the current year's liability accounts
    d. Read the file of correspondence from taxing authorities (ID: 8839)

86. What is an auditor's primary method to corroborate information on litigation, claims, and assessments?
    a. Examining legal invoices sent by the client's attorney
    b. Verifying attorney-client privilege through interviews
    c. Reviewing the response from the client's lawyer to a letter of audit inquiry
    d. Reviewing the representation letter obtained from management (ID: 9365)

87. Which of the following statements extracted from a client's lawyer's letter concerning litigation, claims, and assessments most likely would cause the auditor to request clarification?
    a. "We believe that the possible liability to the company is nominal in amount."
    b. "We believe that the action can be settled for less than the damages claimed."
    c. "We believe that the plaintiff's case against the company is without merit."
    d. "We believe that the company will be able to defend this action successfully." (ID: 9904)

Audit Documentation

88. Which of the following sets of information does an auditor usually confirm on one form?
    a. Accounts payable and purchase commitments
    b. Cash in bank and collateral for loans
    c. Inventory on consignment and contingent liabilities
    d. Accounts receivable and accrued interest receivable (ID: 5987)

89. In creating lead schedules for an audit engagement, a CPA often uses automated workpaper software. What client information is needed to begin this process?
    a. Interim financial information such as third quarter sales, net income, and inventory and receivables balances
    b. Specialized journal information such as the invoice and purchase order numbers of the last few sales and purchases of the year
    c. General ledger information such as account numbers, prior-year account balances, and current-year unadjusted information
    d. Adjusting entry information such as deferrals and accruals, and reclassification journal entries (ID: 6628)

90. In performing a count of negotiable securities, an auditor records the details of the count on a security count worksheet. What other information is usually included on this worksheet?

    a. An acknowledgment by a client representative that the securities were returned intact
    b. An analysis of realized gains and losses from the sale of securities during the year
    c. An evaluation of the client's internal control concerning physical access to the securities
    d. A description of the client's procedures that prevent the negotiation of securities by just one person

    (ID: 6937)

91. Which of the following factors would **least** likely affect the quantity and content of an auditor's working papers?

    a. The condition of the client's records
    b. The assessed risk of material misstatement
    c. The nature of the auditor's report
    d. The content of the representation letter (ID: 5146)

92. The permanent (continuing) file of an auditor's working papers most likely would include copies of the

    a. Lead schedules
    b. Attorney's letters
    c. Bank statements
    d. Debt agreements (ID: 6007)

93. The audit working paper that reflects the major components of an amount reported in the financial statements is the

    a. Interbank transfer schedule
    b. Carryforward schedule
    c. Supporting schedule
    d. Lead schedule (ID: 2320)

94. An auditor ordinarily uses a working trial balance resembling the financial statements without footnotes, but containing columns for

    a. Cash flow increases and decreases
    b. Audit objectives and assertions
    c. Reclassifications and adjustments
    d. Reconciliations and tick marks (ID: 5145)

95. "There are no violations or possible violations of laws or regulations whose effects should be considered for disclosure in the financial statements or as a basis for recording a loss contingency." The foregoing passage most likely is from a (an)

    a. Client engagement letter
    b. Report on compliance with laws and regulations
    c. Representation letter
    d. Attestation report on an entity's internal control (ID: 5137)

96. Which of the following statements is most accurate regarding sufficient and appropriate documentation?

    a. Accounting estimates are **not** considered sufficient and appropriate documentation.
    b. Sufficient and appropriate documentation should include evidence that the audit working papers have been reviewed.
    c. If additional evidence is required to document significant findings or issues, the original evidence is **not** considered sufficient and appropriate and therefore should be deleted from the working papers.
    d. Audit documentation is the property of the client, and sufficient and appropriate copies should be retained by the auditor for at least five years. (ID: 9395)

Related Parties

97. Which of the following procedures most likely could assist an auditor in identifying related-party transactions?

    a. Performing tests of controls concerning the segregation of duties
    b. Evaluating the reasonableness of management's accounting estimates
    c. Reviewing confirmations of compensating balance arrangements
    d. Scanning the accounting records for recurring transactions (ID: 7811)

98. An auditor searching for related-party transactions should obtain an understanding of each subsidiary's relationship to the total entity because

    a. The business structure may be deliberately designed to obscure related-party transactions.
    b. Intercompany transactions may have been consummated on terms equivalent to arm's-length transactions.
    c. This may reveal whether particular transactions would have taken place if the parties had not been related.
    d. This may permit the audit of intercompany account balances to be performed as of concurrent dates. (ID: 185)

99. After determining that a related-party transaction has, in fact, occurred, an auditor should

    a. Add a separate paragraph to the auditor's standard report to explain the transaction
    b. Perform analytical procedures to verify whether similar transactions occurred, but were not recorded
    c. Obtain an understanding of the business purpose of the transaction
    d. Substantiate that the transaction was consummated on terms equivalent to an arm's-length transaction (ID: 5142)

100. Which of the following most likely would indicate the existence of related parties?

    a. Writing down obsolete inventory just before year-end
    b. Failing to correct previously identified internal control structure deficiencies
    c. Depending on a single product for the success of the entity
    d. Borrowing money at an interest rate significantly below the market rate (ID: 2974)

101. When determining whether related-party transactions have been properly accounted for in the financial statements, the auditor should be most concerned that

    a. The transactions represent the appropriate legal form
    b. The method of accounting for the transactions reflects that related parties are involved
    c. The financial statements recognize the substance of the transactions
    d. All related parties have been identified (ID: 9269)

102. Which of the following steps should an auditor perform first to determine the existence of related parties?

    a. Examine invoices, contracts, and purchasing orders
    b. Request a list of related parties from management
    c. Review the company's business structure
    d. Review proxy and other materials filed with the SEC (ID: 9356)

Problem 4-2 SIMULATION: Type and Classification of Audit Procedures

For each of the descriptions of procedures in column A of the table below, select the type of audit procedure performed from the selection list for column B and then indicate in column C whether it was a substantive procedure or a test of controls. Selections may be used once, more than once, or not at all.

A	B	C
Description of Procedure	**Type of Audit Procedure**	**Classification of Audit Procedure**
1. Examined sales invoices to see if they were initialed by the credit manager indicating credit approval.		
2. Compared this year's expenses with last year's expenses and investigated unusual fluctuations.		
3. Requested responses directly from customers.		
4. Questioned management about subsequent events.		
5. Observed the accounting clerk record the daily deposit of cash receipts.		
6. Examined invoices to support additions to the fixed asset account during the year.		
7. Agreed sales invoices to credit files to determine whether the customer had a credit file and had been approved for credit.		
8. Asked the accounting manager how often cash is deposited and by whom.		

(ID: 9833)

Selection List of Types of Audit Procedures

A. Analytical procedure	F. Monitoring
B. Confirmation	G. Observation
C. Disclosure	H. Recalculation
D. Inquiry	I. Reperformance
E. Inspection	

Selection List of Classifications of Audit Procedures

A. Substantive procedures	B. Tests of controls

Problem 4-3 SIMULATION: Documentation

For each of the following unrelated statements, questions, excerpts, and comments taken from various parts of an auditor's working paper file, select the most likely source from the list of sources. A source may be used once, more than once, or not at all.

Excerpts From Working Papers	Source
1. During our audit we discovered evidence of the company's failure to safeguard inventory from loss, damage, and misappropriation.	
2. The company considers the decline in value of equity securities classified as available-for-sale to be temporary.	
3. Was the difference of opinion on the accrued pension liabilities that existed between the engagement personnel and the actuarial specialist resolved in accordance with firm policy and appropriately documented?	
4. Our audit is designed to provide reasonable assurance of detecting misstatements that, in our judgment, could have a material effect on the financial statements taken as a whole. Consequently, our audit will not necessarily detect all misstatements that exist due to error, fraudulent financial reporting, or misappropriation of assets.	
5. There have been no communications from regulatory agencies concerning noncompliance with or deficiencies in financial reporting practices.	
6. Nothing came to our attention that caused us to believe that at October 31, year 1, there was any change in the capital stock, increase in long-term debt, or decrease in consolidated net current assets or stockholders' equity as compared with the amounts shown in the September 30, year 1 unaudited condensed consolidated balance sheet.	
7. It is our opinion that the possible liability to the company in this proceeding is nominal in amount.	
8. As discussed in Note 4 to the financial statements, the company experienced a net loss for the year ended July 31, year 1, and is currently in default under substantially all of its debt agreements. In addition, on September 25, year 1, the company filed a prenegotiated voluntary petition for relief under Chapter 11 of the U.S. Bankruptcy Code. These matters raise substantial doubt about the company's ability to continue as a going concern.	
9. During the year under audit, we were advised that management consulted with Better & Best, CPAs. The purpose of this consultation was to obtain another CPA firm's opinion concerning the company's recognition of certain revenue that we believe should be deferred to future periods. Better & Best's opinion was consistent with our opinion, so management did not recognize the revenue in the current year.	
10. The company believes that all material expenditures that have been deferred to future periods will be recoverable.	

(ID: 9218)

List of Sources

A. Practitioner's report on management's assertion about an entity's compliance with specified requirements

B. Auditor's communications on significant deficiencies

C. Audit inquiry letter to legal counsel

D. Lawyer's response to audit inquiry letter

E. Audit committee's communication to the auditor

F. Auditor's communication to the audit committee (other than with respect to significant deficiencies)

G. Report on the application of accounting principles

H. Auditor's engagement letter

I. Letter for underwriters

J. Accounts receivable confirmation request

K. Request for bank cutoff statement

L. Explanatory paragraph of an auditor's report on financial statements

M. Partner's engagement review notes

N. Representation letter

O. Successor auditor's communication with predecessor auditor

P. Predecessor auditor's communication with successor auditor

---

Problem 4-4 SIMULATION: Documentation

For each of the following unrelated statements, questions, excerpts, and comments taken from various parts of an auditor's working paper file, select the most likely source from the list of sources. A source may be used once, more than once, or not at all.

Excerpts From Working Papers	Source
1. Our use of professional judgment and the assessment of audit risk and materiality for the purpose of our audit mean that matters may have existed that would have been assessed differently by you. We make no representation as to the sufficiency or appropriateness of the information in our working papers for your purposes.	
2. Indicate in the space provided below whether this information agrees with your records. If there are exceptions, please provide any information that will assist the auditor in reconciling the difference.	
3. Blank checks are maintained in an unlocked cabinet along with the check-signing machine. Blank checks and the check-signing machine should be locked in separate locations to prevent the embezzlement of funds.	
4. Our audit cannot be relied upon to disclose significant deficiencies in the design or operation of internal control. Nevertheless, we will communicate to you all significant deficiencies and potential areas for improvement that we become aware of during the course of our audit.	
5. The timetable set by management to complete our audit was unreasonable considering the failure of the company's personnel to complete schedules on a timely basis and delays in providing necessary information.	
6. Several employees have disabled the anti-virus detection software on their PCs because the software slows the processing of data and occasionally rings false alarms. The company should obtain anti-virus software that runs continuously at all system entry points and that cannot be disabled by unauthorized personnel.	
7. In connection with an audit of our financial statements, management has prepared, and furnished to our auditors, a description and evaluation of certain contingencies.	
8. The company has no plans or intentions that may materially affect the carrying value or classification of assets and liabilities.	
9. In planning the sampling application, was appropriate consideration given to the relationship of the sample to the audit objective and to preliminary judgments about materiality levels?	

(ID: 9220)

List of Sources

A. Practitioner's report on management's assertion about an entity's compliance with specified requirements

B. Auditor's communications on significant deficiencies

C. Audit inquiry letter to legal counsel

D. Lawyer's response to audit inquiry letter

E. Audit committee's communication to the auditor

F. Auditor's communication to the audit committee (other than with respect to significant deficiencies)

G. Report on the application of accounting principles

H. Auditor's engagement letter

I. Letter for underwriters

J. Accounts receivable confirmation request

K. Request for bank cutoff statement

L. Explanatory paragraph of an auditor's report on financial statements

M. Partner's engagement review notes

N. Representation letter

O. Successor auditor's communication with predecessor auditor

P. Predecessor auditor's communication with successor auditor

---

Problem 4-5 SIMULATION: Ratios

Analytical procedures are evaluations of financial information made by a study of plausible relationships among financial and nonfinancial data. Understanding and evaluating such relationships is essential to the audit process. The following financial statements were prepared by Holiday Manufacturing Co. for the year ended December 31, year 2. Also presented are various financial statement ratios for Holiday as calculated from the prior year's financial statements. Sales represent net credit sales. The total assets, receivables, and inventory balances at December 31, year 2, were the same as at December 31, year 1.

Holiday Manufacturing Co.
Balance Sheet
December 31, Year 2

Assets		Liabilities and Capital	
Cash	$ 240,000	Accounts payable	$ 160,000
Receivables	400,000	Notes payable	100,000
Inventory	600,000	Other current liabilities	140,000
Total current assets	$1,240,000	Total current liabilities	$ 400,000
Plant and equipment—net	760,000	Long-term debt	350,000
		Common stock	750,000
		Retained earnings	500,000
Total assets	$2,000,000	Total liabilities and capital	$2,000,000

Holiday Manufacturing Co.
Income Statement
Year Ended December 31, Year 2

Sales		$3,000,000
Cost of goods sold		
Material	$800,000	
Labor	700,000	
Overhead	300,000	1,800,000
Gross margin		$1,200,000
Selling expenses	$240,000	
General and administrative expenses	300,000	540,000
Operating income		$ 660,000
Less interest expense		40,000
Income before taxes		$ 620,000
Less federal income taxes		220,000
Net income		$ 400,000

Each of the following represents a financial ratio that the auditor calculated during the prior year's audit. For each ratio, calculate the current year's ratio from the financial statements presented and select the answer from the list. Calculations should be rounded, if necessary, to the same number of places as the prior year's ratios.

Ratio	Year 2	Year 1
1. Current ratio		2.5
2. Quick ratio		1.3
3. Accounts receivable turnover		5.5
4. Inventory turnover		2.5
5. Total asset turnover		1.2
6. Gross margin percentage		35%
7. Net operating margin percentage		25%
8. Times interest earned		10.3
9. Total debt to equity percentage		50%

(ID: 9221)

List of Ratio Calculations			
A. 0.6	H. 3.1	O. 13%	V. 67%
B. 0.7	I. 4.5	P. 22%	
C. 1.0	J. 5.0	Q. 28%	
D. 1.5	K. 7.5	R. 33%	
E. 1.6	L. 10.0	S. 38%	
F. 2.0	M. 15.5	T. 40%	
G. 3.0	N. 16.5	U. 60%	

Problem 4-6 SIMULATION: Financial Statement Analysis

Each of the following items represent an auditor's observed changes, independent of each other, in certain financial statement ratios or amounts from the prior year's ratios or amounts. For each observed change, select the most likely explanation or explanations from the accompanying list. An explanation may be used once, more than once, or not at all.

Auditor's Observed Changes	Explanations
1. Allowance for doubtful accounts increased from the prior year, but allowance for doubtful accounts as a percentage of accounts receivable decreased from the prior year. (3 explanations)	
2. Long-term debt increased from the prior year, but interest expense increased a larger-than-proportionate amount than long-term debt. (1 explanation)	
3. Operating income increased from the prior year although the entity was less profitable than in the prior year. (2 explanations)	
4. Gross margin percentage was unchanged from the prior year although gross margin increased from the prior year. (1 explanation)	

(ID: 9222)

Explanations

A. Items shipped on consignment during the last month of the year were recorded as sales.

B. A significant number of credit memos for returned merchandise that were issued during the last month of the year were not recorded.

C. Year-end purchases of inventory were overstated by incorrectly including items received in the first month of the subsequent year.

D. Year-end purchases of inventory were understated by incorrectly excluding items received before the year-end.

E. A larger percentage of sales occurred during the last month of the year, as compared to the prior year.

F. A smaller percentage of sales occurred during the last month of the year, as compared to the prior year.

G. The same percentage of sales occurred during the last month of the year, as compared to the prior year.

H. Sales increased at the same percentage as cost of goods sold, as compared to the prior year.

I. Sales increased at a greater percentage than cost of goods sold increased, as compared to the prior year.

J. Sales increased at a lower percentage than cost of goods sold increased, as compared to the prior year.

K. Interest expense decreased, as compared to the prior year.

L. The effective income tax rate increased, as compared to the prior year.

M. The effective income tax rate decreased, as compared to the prior year.

N. Short-term borrowing was refinanced on a long-term basis at the same interest rate.

O. Short-term borrowing was refinanced on a long-term basis at lower interest rates.

P. Short-term borrowing was refinanced on a long-term basis at higher interest rates.

Problem 4-7 SIMULATION: Substantive Tests

For each of the following audit objectives, select the substantive test that would most likely provide support for the objective. A substantive test may be used once, more than once, or not at all.

Part a:

Objective	Substantive Tests
1. Verify existence of accounts receivable.	
2. Determine that inventory balance is accurately stated.	

(ID: 9224)

Selection List

A. Perform tests of subsequent cash receipts after the balance sheet date.
B. Review and assess an aging schedule of accounts receivable.
C. Compare recognized revenue to related industry statistics.
D. Tour the storage facility for inventory to determine adequacy of security controls.
E. Perform shipping cutoff procedures.
F. Review payments to vendors subsequent to year-end.

Part b:

An auditor has chosen to increase attention on the financial statement assertion of valuation. Procedures that might be used in an audit are listed below. From the following list, choose the two procedures that would be most appropriate to perform in an audit that is giving increased attention to the valuation assertion. Only **two** procedures may be chosen.

Selection List

A. Observing the client count the physical inventory
B. Testing shipping and receiving cutoff procedures
C. Obtaining confirmation from lenders regarding inventories pledged under loan agreements
D. Examining paid vendors' invoices
E. Obtaining confirmation of inventories at locations outside the entity
F. Examining an analysis of inventory turnover
G. Tracing test counts recorded during the physical inventory observation to the inventory listing

---

Problem 4-8 SIMULATION: Analytics

Pacific Gourmet, Inc. and Subsidiary
Consolidated Balance Sheets
December 31, Year 2 and Year 1

	Year 2	Year 1
Assets		
Current assets		
Cash and cash equivalents	$ 54,280,000	$ 42,500,000
Receivables - net	12,000,000	10,000,000
Inventory	12,000,000	10,000,000
Other current assets	7,000,000	5,000,000
Total current assets	85,280,000	67,500,000
Property, plant and equipment - net	23,000,000	25,000,000
Other assets	30,000,000	30,000,000
Total assets	$138,280,000	$122,500,000
Liabilities and Stockholders' Equity		
Current liabilities		
Accounts payable	$ 23,000,000	$ 20,000,000
Current portion of long-term debt	1,000,000	1,000,000
Other current liabilities	965,000	1,000,000
Total current liabilities	24,965,000	22,000,000
Long-term debt	13,000,000	14,000,000
Total liabilities	37,965,000	36,000,000
Stockholders' equity		
Common stock	100,000	100,000
Additional paid-in capital	9,900,000	9,900,000
Retained earnings	90,315,000	76,500,000
Total Stockholders' equity	100,315,000	86,500,000
Total liabilities and stockholders' equity	$138,280,000	$122,500,000

Pacific Gourmet, Inc. and Subsidiary
Consolidated Income Statements
For the Years Ended December 31, Year 2 and Year 1

	Year 2	Year 1
Sales	$100,850,000	$ 95,600,000
Cost of goods sold	55,000,000	42,500,000
Gross profit on sales	45,850,000	53,100,000
Expenses		
Selling expenses	17,600,000	15,000,000
General and administrative	6,015,000	5,000,000
Interest expense	1,120,000	1,200,000
Total expense	24,735,000	21,200,000
Income before taxes	21,115,000	31,900,000
Provision for income taxes	7,300,000	7,500,000
Net income	$ 13,815,000	$ 24,400,000

Pacific Gourmet, Inc. and Subsidiary
Consolidated Statement of Cash Flows
For the Year Ended December 31, Year 2

Cash flows from operating activities:	$13,815,000
Net income (loss)	
Adjustments to reconcile net income (loss) to cash provided by (used for) operating activities	
Depreciation	1,500,000
Changes in certain assets and liabilities:	
Decrease (increase) in receivables	(2,000,000)
Decrease (increase) in inventory	(2,000,000)
Decrease (increase) in other current assets	(2,000,000)
Increase (decrease) in accounts payable	3,000,000
Increase (decrease) in other current liabilities	(35,000)
Net Cash provided by (used for) operating activities	12,280,000
Cash flows from investing activities:	
Proceeds from sales of property, plant and equipment	500,000
Net cash provided by (used for) investing activities	500,000
Cash flows from financing activities:	
Principal payments on long-term debt	(1,000,000)
Net cash provided by (used for) financing activities	(1,000,000)
Net increase (decrease) in cash and cash equivalents	11,780,000
Cash and cash equivalents at beginning of year	42,500,000
Cash and cash equivalents at end of year	$54,280,000

Part a:

Use the data in Pacific Gourmet's financial statements to calculate for year 2 the analytical ratios indicated in the table below to 2 decimal places. (For turnover ratios, year-end balances should be used. All calculations are based on a 365-day year.)

Ratio	Year 2	Year 1
1. Current ratio		3.07
2. Return on equity		28.21%

Part b:

The table below presents several ratios that were considered significant in the current and prior year's audits of Pacific Gourmet. Compare the values for each ratio. Then select the most likely explanation for the analytical results. An explanation may be used once, more than once, or not at all. (You should not recalculate ratios. Turnover ratios are based on average balances.)

Ratio	Year 2	Year 1	Explanations
1. Days sales in accounts receivable	40	39	
2. Operating profit margin	22.05%	34.62%	

(ID: 9223)

Explanations

A. Credit terms were restricted on several large accounts during the current year.

B. Operating expenses increased at a higher rate than sales revenue.

C. Sales revenue increased at a higher rate than operating expenses.

D. A smaller percentage of sales occurred during the last month of the year, as compared to the prior year.

E. A larger percentage of sales occurred during the last month of the year, as compared to the prior year.

F. Sales increased as compared to the prior year.

Problem 4-9 SIMULATION: Ratios

The following financial statements were prepared by Feiler Hardware for the year ended December 31, year 2. Sales represent net credit sales. The total assets, the receivables, and inventory balances at December 31, year 2, were the same as at December 31, year 1.

Feiler Hardware
Balance Sheet
December 31, Year 2

Assets		Liabilities and Capital	
Cash	$ 60,000	Accounts payable	$ 40,000
Receivables	100,000	Notes payable	25,000
Inventory	150,000	Other current liabilities	35,000
Total current assets	$310,000	Total current liabilities	$100,000
Plant and equipment—net	190,000	Long-term debt	87,500
		Feiler, Capital	312,500
Total assets	$500,000	Total liabilities and capital	$500,000

Feiler Hardware
Income Statement
Year Ended December 31, Year 2

Sales		$750,000
Less Cost of goods sold		450,000
Gross margin		$300,000
Selling expenses	$60,000	
General and administrative expenses	75,000	135,000
Operating income		$165,000
Less interest expense		10,000
Income before taxes		$155,000
Less federal income taxes		55,000
Net income		$100,000

Each of the following represent financial ratios calculated from the prior year's financial statements. For each ratio, calculate the current year's ratio from the financial statements presented. Calculations should be rounded, if necessary, to the same number of places as the prior year's ratios.

Ratio	Year 2	Year 1
1. Current ratio		2.5
2. Quick ratio		1.3
3. Accounts receivable turnover		9.0
4. Inventory turnover		1.5

(ID: 9225)

Problem 4-10 SIMULATION: Analytics

Analytical procedures are evaluations of financial information made by a study of plausible relationships among financial and nonfinancial data. Understanding and evaluating such relationships are essential to the audit process. For each observed change, select the most likely explanations from the accompanying list.

Observed Changes	Explanations
1. Inventory turnover increased substantially from the prior year. (3 explanations)	
2. Accounts receivable turnover decreased substantially from the prior year. (3 explanations)	

(ID: 9226)

Explanations

A. Items shipped on consignment during the last month of the year were recorded as sales.
B. A significant number of credit memos for returned merchandise that were issued during the last month of the year were not recorded.
C. Year-end purchases of inventory were overstated by incorrectly including items received in the first month of the subsequent year.
D. Year-end purchases of inventory were understated by incorrectly excluding items received before the year-end.
E. A larger percentage of sales occurred during the last month of the year, as compared to the prior year.
F. A smaller percentage of sales occurred during the last month of the year, as compared to the prior year.
G. The same percentage of sales occurred during the last month of the year, as compared to the prior year.
H. Sales increased at the same percentage as cost of goods sold, as compared to the prior year.
I. Sales increased at a greater percentage than cost of goods sold increased, as compared to the prior year.
J. Sales increased at a lower percentage than cost of goods sold increased, as compared to the prior year.

Problem 4-11 SIMULATION: Research

Which citation in the professional standards provides guidance when the auditor finds it necessary to modify existing audit documentation or add new audit documentation after the documentation completion date in circumstances other than when new audit procedures are performed or the auditor draws new conclusions after the date of the audit report?

[ ] § [ ] [ ] (ID: 90392)

Problem 4-12 SIMULATION: Analytics

You are the audit manager assigned to Joe's Office Supply. Based on substantive test work, the staff auditor has proposed the journal entries below to be presented to the client. Assume all proposed journal entries are valid and material.

For each journal entry, indicate its effect (*increased*, *decreased,* or had *no impact*) on the calculations in columns D, E, and F.

A	B	C	D	E	F
Proposed Journal Entry	**Debit**	**Credit**	**Earnings per Share**	**Days Sales in Accounts Receivable**	**Gross Profit**
1. Sales reported after year-end that should have been reported before year-end: Cost of sales Accounts receivable Sales Inventory	 90 100	 100 90			
2. Error in adjusting entry: Cost of sales PP&E Utilities expense Cash Sales Accrued expenses Inventory Interest expense	 45 45 12 10	 45 12 45 10			
3. To record current and deferred income taxes: Income tax expense-current Deferred tax asset Income tax expense-deferred Deferred tax liability Income tax payable	 50 15	 10 5 50			

(ID: 89451)

Problem 4-13 SIMULATION: Analytics

The year under audit is year 2. Duke, Inc. (Duke) is a manufacturing company. Duke experienced record profitability in year 1 and management anticipated that year 2 would be another banner year. However, sales declined in year 2 because of regional economic conditions related to a recent recession, and the financial results for year 2 did not meet management's expectations. Sales for year 2 decreased 5% compared to year 1 and gross profit also declined due to increases in manufacturing costs. Management, after reviewing its operations for year 2, recognized that its sales growth had slowed in the past several years and its manufacturing costs had increased.

Duke, Inc.
Consolidated Balance Sheets
December 31, Year 2 and Year 1

	Year 2	Year 1
Assets		
Current assets		
Cash and cash equivalents	$ 3,385,000	$ 6,620,000
Receivables—net	2,964,000	3,124,000
Inventory	3,158,000	3,016,000
Other current assets	639,000	1,379,000
Total current assets	10,146,000	14,139,000
Property, plant and equipment—net	25,900,000	22,000,000
Other assets	800,000	800,000
Total assets	$36,846,000	$36,939,000
Liabilities and Stockholders' Equity	Year 2	Year 1
Current liabilities		
Current portion of long-term debt	$ 1,200,000	$ 1,200,000
Accounts payable	3,300,000	11,200,000
Other current liabilities	516,000	1,459,000
Total current liabilities	5,016,000	13,859,000
Long-term debt	19,500,000	16,500,000
Total liabilities	24,516,000	30,359,000
Stockholders' equity		
Common stock	7,280,000	3,280,000
Retained earnings	5,050,000	3,300,000
Total stockholders' equity	12,330,000	6,580,000
Total liabilities and stockholders' equity	$36,846,000	$36,939,000

Duke, Inc.
Consolidated Income Statements
For the Years Ended December 31, Year 2 and Year 1

	Year 2	Year 1
Sales	$19,672,000	$20,730,000
Cost of goods sold	12,197,000	12,231,000
Gross profit on sales	7,475,000	8,499,000
Other operating expenses		
Selling expenses	1,978,000	2,151,000
General administrative	1,377,000	1,248,000
Total other operating expenses	3,355,000	3,399,000
Income from operations before interest expense	4,120,000	5,100,000
Interest expense	1,250,000	1,300,000
Income before taxes	2,870,000	3,800,000
Provision for income taxes	1,120,000	1,520,000
Net income	$ 1,750,000	$ 2,280,000

Duke, Inc.
Consolidated Statements of Cash Flows
For the Years Ended December 31, Year 2 and Year 1

	Year 2	Year 1
Cash flows from operating activities:		
Net income (loss)	$ 1,750,000	$ 2,280,000
Adjustments to reconcile net income (loss) to cash provided by (used for) operating activities:		
Depreciation and amortization	2,000,000	1,900,000
Changes in certain assets and liabilities:		
Decrease (increase) in receivables	160,000	76,000
Decrease (increase) in inventory	(142,000)	(116,000)
Decrease (increase) in other current assets	740,000	
Decrease (increase) in other assets		
Increase (decrease) in accounts payable	(7,900,000)	760,000
Increase (decrease) in other current liabilities	(943,000)	500,000
Net cash provided by (used for) operating activities	(4,335,000)	5,400,000
Cash flows from investing activities:		
Purchase of property, plant and equipment	(5,900,000)	(2,900,000)
Net cash provided by (used for) investing activities	(5,900,000)	(2,900,000)
Cash flows from financing activities:		
Proceeds from issuance of long-term debt	4,200,000	
Principal payments on long-term debt	(1,200,000)	(1,100,000)
Proceeds from issuance of common stock	4,000,000	
Net cash provided by (used for) financing activities	7,000,000	(1,100,000)
Net increase (decrease) in cash and cash equivalents	(3,235,000)	1,400,000
Cash and cash equivalents at beginning of year	6,620,000	5,220,000
Cash and cash equivalents at end of year	$ 3,385,000	$ 6,620,000

The table below presents some ratios that were considered significant in the current and prior year's audit of Duke. Compare the values for each ratio. Then select the most likely explanation for the analytical results. An explanation may be used once, more than once, or not at all. (You should **not** recalculate ratios.)

Ratio	Year 2	Year 1	Explanations
1. Debt to equity	1.99	4.61	
2. Gross profit percentage	38.00%	41.00%	

(ID: 9227)

Selection List

A. Sales decreased as compared to the prior year.

B. Manufacturing costs increased during the year at a greater rate than sales increased.

C. Proceeds from the sale of stock and issuance of debt were used to pay payables on a more current basis.

D. Capital stock was issued during the year.

E. The company may have accumulated excess and obsolete inventory.

F. Manufacturing cost decreased less than sales decreased during the year.

Problem 4-14 SIMULATION: Types of Audit Procedures

During the year 1 audit of Numbaro Co., the auditor performed various procedures.

For each of the descriptions of audit procedures listed below, select the type of audit procedure that the auditor performed. A type of audit procedure may be selected once, more than once, or not at all.

Description of Procedure	Type of Audit Procedure
1. During the physical inventory count, the auditor requested that certain material containers be opened to ensure they were not empty.	
2. During a site visit to a branch warehouse, the auditor noted unauthorized personnel have access to the inventory.	
3. The auditor obtained a copy of the company's accounting manual and read the section on inventory to prepare for the physical inventory observation.	
4. The auditor sent a letter to the company's outside attorney accompanied by management's request for information concerning pending or threatened litigation, claims, and assessments.	
5. The auditing firm's computer assisted audit specialist obtained an electronic billing file from the company and checked the accuracy of the summarized billings file.	
6. The auditor obtained the company's aging of accounts receivable and independently created the aging of certain accounts.	
7. The auditor scanned the repairs and maintenance account for unusually large amounts.	

(ID: 89452)

Selection List for Types of Audit Procedures	
A. Analytical procedure	G. Inspection
B. Certification	H. Monetization
C. Compliance	I. Observation
D. Confirmation	J. Recalculation
E. Guarantee	K. Reperformance
F. Inquiry	L. Valuation

Problem 4-15 SIMULATION: Attorney Letters

The following situations represent excerpts from the responses to audit inquiries of external legal counsel of XYZ Co. during the annual audit of year 1. Each excerpt is independent.

- The client's year-end is December 31, year 1.
- The anticipated audit report date is February 15, year 2.
- All amounts are material to the financial statements.

For each excerpt, select the most appropriate audit response related to the financial statements in the audit response (financial statements) column. Then, in the audit response (attorney letter or audit report) column, select whether the attorney's legal response letter or the audit report needs to be updated; or if it is appropriately dated. Responses may be used once, more than once, or not at all.

Situations	Audit Response	
	Financial Statements	**Attorney Letter or Audit Report**
1. Letter dated February 14, year 2: "I advise you that at and since December 31, year 1, I have not been engaged to give substantive attention to, or represent XYZ Co. in connection with any pending or threatened litigation, claims, or assessments, nor am I aware of any loss contingencies. No amounts were due to this office for services provided at December 31, year 1."		
2. Letter dated January 21, year 2: "I advise you that at and since December 31, year 1, I have not been engaged to give substantive attention to, or represent XYZ Co. in connection with any pending or threatened litigation, claims, or assessments, nor am I aware of any loss contingencies. There were fees outstanding of $3,675 due to this office for services provided at December 31, year 1."		
3. Letter dated February 26, year 2: "I advise you that at and since December 31, year 1, I have not been engaged to give substantive attention to, or represent XYZ Co. in connection with any pending or threatened litigation, claims, or assessments, except as follows: K. Bowt v. XYZ Co.: This matter commenced in December, year 1. The plaintiff alleges discrimination relating to his termination on November 17, year 1. The company intends to defend this case vigorously. At this time, we are unable to evaluate the likelihood of an unfavorable outcome or estimate the amount or range of potential loss.		
4. Letter dated March 16, year 2: "I advise you that at and since December 31, year 1, I have not been engaged to give substantive attention to, or represent XYZ Co. in connection with any pending or threatened litigation, claims, or assessments, except as follows: J. Myers v. XYZ Co.: This matter commenced in March, year 2. The plaintiff alleges discrimination relating to his termination on November 17, year 1. The company intends to defend this case vigorously. At this time, we are unable to evaluate the likelihood of an unfavorable outcome. The plaintiff is demanding $50,000.		

Situations	Audit Response	
	Financial Statements	**Attorney Letter or Audit Report**
5. Letter dated January 10, year 2: "I advise you that at and since December 31, year 1, I have not been engaged to give substantive attention to, or represent XYZ Co. in connection with any pending or threatened litigation, claims, or assessments, except as follows: R. Brown v. XYZ Co.: This matter commenced in November, year 1. The plaintiff alleges discrimination relating to his termination on March 17, year 1. The case was tentatively settled for $35,000, which will be covered by XYZ's insurance carrier.		
6. Letter dated January 20, year 2: "I advise you that at and since December 31, year 1, I have not been engaged to give substantive attention to, or represent XYZ Co. in connection with any pending or threatened litigation, claims, or assessments, except as follows: L. Peep v. XYZ Co.: This matter commenced in November, year 1. The plaintiff alleges discrimination relating to his termination on March 17, year 1. The case was tentatively settled for $35,000.		

(ID: 89453)

Selection List for Audit Responses (Financials)	
A. Disclosure in the notes to the financial statements relating to nature of litigation, but no amount disclosed	D. Potential litigation settlement accrued in financial statements
B. Disclosure in the notes to the financial statements relating to nature of litigation, including loss amount	E. Potential litigation settlement not accrued in financial statements, amount disclosed in the notes to the financial statements
C. No impact on financial statements or the notes to the financial statements	F. Verify amount due attorney is recorded in financial statements

Selection List for Audit Responses (Audit Report or Attorney Letter)
A. Legal response is appropriately dated
B. Update report date
C. Update legal response

Solution 4-1 MULTIPLE-CHOICE ANSWERS

1. (a) The bank confirmations provide the best primary evidence of the year-end bank balance. In an audit engagement, the best evidence is from an independent third party. If no confirmation is present, a bank reconciliation would provide primary evidence. Neither a bank deposit lead schedule nor an interbank transfer schedule is primary evidence by itself. (ID: 146)

2. (d) Audit evidence is more reliable when it is obtained from independent sources outside the entity. Answers a., b., and c. are examples of auditing procedures performed on information obtained from within the entity. (ID: 3922)

3. (d) Audit evidence that is generated internally is more reliable when the related controls imposed by the entity are effective. Information obtained directly, not indirectly, from outside sources would provide the most reliable evidence. The auditor may find it necessary to rely on audit evidence that is persuasive rather than conclusive. The reliability of audit evidence refers to its source and nature and is dependent on the individual circumstances under which it is obtained. (ID: 5120)

4. (a) The independent auditor's direct personal knowledge, obtained through physical examination, observation, computation, and inspection, is more persuasive than information obtained indirectly. (ID: 8139)

5. (a) Suspense debits that management believes will benefit future operations are assets. The auditor is most concerned that assets are not overstated and that liabilities are not understated. Suspense debits that the auditor verifies will have realizable value to the client are, insofar as the auditor knows, correct. Thus, for these items, there would be no overstatement. The other two answer options contain items that, if incorrect, would overstate liabilities. (ID: 6365)

6. (d) Performing analytical procedures designed to disclose differences from expectations would be the most likely way to detect unusual entries. The other answers are not as likely to detect journal entries with unusual combinations of accounts. (ID: 5087)

7. (a) One of the uses of analytics is as a substantive test to obtain audit evidence about particular assertions. In the process of achieving objectives, auditors adhere to a system of quality control, prepare working papers, and may possibly increase the level of detection risk; however, none of these actually cause the auditor to achieve audit objectives. (ID: 5985)

8. (d) Evidence that a deviation was covered up in a fraudulent manner would require the auditor to consider the implications of the deviation more closely. Answers a., b., and c. give no causes for added concern. (ID: 5973)

9. (b) Unreconciled differences between control and subsidiary accounts indicate a disregard for common accounting safeguards. Assumptions used in developing estimates should change with changing circumstances. A lower response rate for negative confirmation requests indicates fewer customer account misstatements. Consultation with a CPA firm about complex accounting matters often indicates conscientious accounting and reporting. (ID: 7097)

10. (c) Despite being handled by the client, bank statements originate outside the entity and, therefore, are the most persuasive of the choices. Both purchase orders and work sheets originate within the client. The representation letter only documents the client's oral representations. (ID: 5657)

11. (d) The auditor most likely would consider whether material misstatements exist when transactions selected for testing are not supported by proper documentation. Reduced emphasis on meeting earnings projections would be a factor decreasing the likelihood of earnings overstatements and assets (the most frequent misstatement). Having the board of directors make major financing decisions would decrease the incentive for management to use questionable reporting by reducing the amount of management's responsibility. Significant deficiencies previously communicated to management may not have been corrected because of an unfavorable cost-benefit relationship. (ID: 5086)

12. (d) Appropriate evidence is both valid and relevant. The validity of audit evidence is highly dependent upon the circumstances under which it is obtained. The independent auditor's direct personal knowledge, obtained through physical examination, observation, computation, and inspection, is more persuasive than information obtained indirectly. (ID: 8143)

13. (c) The existence or occurrence assertions concern whether assets or liabilities exist as of the financial statement date and whether recorded transactions actually occurred during a reporting period. Even though this is a test of controls, this procedure also provides evidence that customers' balances actually exist. The presentation and disclosure assertions concern proper classification, description, and disclosure in the financial statements. (ID: 8119)

14. (c) Evidence obtained during an audit may cause the auditor to change the nature, extent, or timing of other planned audit procedures. A disclaimer of opinion or a qualified opinion would be issued if the auditor could not obtain sufficient evidence; there is no indication that that is the case in this situation. A statement from management supporting their inventory valuation is merely another written representation and likely would be an insufficient substitute for additional audit procedures. (ID: 8394)

15. (a) Reconciling the amount included in the statement of cash flows to other statements is a basic procedure. Relationships among elements of financial information within the period are one source of expectations regarding relationships that reasonably are expect to exist. The other procedures generally are involved in auditing the balance in the cash accounts, not necessarily the statement of cash flows. (ID: 8408)

16. (c) An auditor interviewing and observing appropriate personnel to determine segregation of duties is considered a test of controls. Reviewing the check register for unrecorded liabilities and evaluating a journal entry are examples of tests of details of classes of transactions, account balances—substantive procedures. Reviewing the audit workpapers is an example of a quality control procedure performed by an audit firm to ensure the quality of its engagement performance—tests of controls refer to tests of the client's internal control system. (ID: 9360)

17. (d) If sufficient appropriate evidence is not available to support an opinion on the financial statements, then an audit cannot be performed. In the absence of evidence to the contrary, transactions with related parties should not be assumed to be outside the ordinary course of business. Further, established accounting principles ordinarily do not require them to be accounted for on a different basis because related parties are involved; however, the auditor must be satisfied that disclosure is adequate. Their existence, in and of itself, would not preclude the performance of an audit. Many internal control activities are subject to management override. The cost of a new efficient information system may outweigh its benefits. (ID: 8161)

18. (d) The external auditor may use the work of internal auditors to (1) obtain audit evidence and/or (2) provide direct assistance under the direction, supervision, and review of the external auditor. Editor Note: However, US GAAS does *not* require the external auditor to use the work of the internal audit function to modify the nature or timing, or reduce the extent, of audit procedures to be performed directly by the external auditor; it remains the external auditor's decision to establish the overall audit strategy. (ID: 6000)

19. (d) Answers a., b., and c. are all items the external auditor may consider in assessing the internal auditor's competence and objectivity. (ID: 5141)

20. (a) The quality of internal auditors' documentation reflects on their competence. The other answers are concerned with objectivity. (ID: 6832)

21. (a) The more judgment involved in planning and performing relevant audit procedures or evaluating the audit evidence obtained is a factor in the external auditor's decision to perform more of the audit work directly, i.e., to use the work of the internal audit function less, rather than in the determination of whether to use the internal audit function at all to obtain evidence. (ID: 8127)

22. (d) Because the external auditor has sole responsibility for the audit opinion expressed, the external auditor is required to make the significant judgments in the audit engagement. Significant judgments include, but

are not limited to, the following: (1) assessing the risks of material misstatement; (2) evaluating the appropriateness of management's use of the going concern assumption and whether substantial doubt exists about the entity's ability to continue as a going concern for a reasonable period of time; (3) evaluating the sufficiency of tests performed; (4) evaluating significant accounting estimates; and (5) evaluating the adequacy of disclosures in the financial statements and other matters affecting the external auditor's report. (ID: 6235)

23. (d) In performing an audit, the auditor may request direct assistance from the internal auditors including assistance in obtaining an understanding of internal control or in performing tests of controls or substantive tests. (ID: 5678)

24. (a) If the external auditor expects to use the work of the internal auditors, the external auditor should assess their competence and objectivity and evaluate whether their work is adequate for the purposes of the audit. When assessing the internal auditor's objectivity, the external auditor should consider whether the organizational status of the internal audit function, including the function's authority and accountability, supports the ability of the function to be free from bias, conflict of interest, or undue influence of others to override professional judgments (for example, whether the internal audit function reports to those charged with governance or an officer with appropriate authority, or if the function reports to management, whether it has direct access to those charged with governance). In this case, the external auditor would place limited reliance on the work performed by the internal auditors because they report to the controller and, thus, may be reluctant to report weaknesses in the controller's activities. (ID: 157)

25. (a) Considering professional standards and whether internal auditors meet them provides an indication regarding their objectivity. Neither the tests of activities that could detect errors and fraud, materiality of recently inspected accounts, nor the results of tests performed by internal auditors influence an internal auditor's objectivity. An internal auditor may concentrate appropriately on compliance testing, rather than tests of errors and fraud. The accounts to be audited may be selected by people other than the auditors. A biased internal auditor conceivably might be unusually careful in work performed just before the external audit. (ID: 7108)

26. (c) The assessment of the competence of internal auditors by the external auditor should include obtaining information about the quality of working paper documentation, reports, and recommendations. Information about the influence of management on the scope of the internal auditor's duties and the policies limiting their communication with the audit committee bear on the assessment of their objectivity rather than their competence. Information about the entity's ability to continue as a going concern would not reflect on the competence of the internal auditors. (ID: 8614)

27. (a) When assessing the internal auditors' objectivity, the external auditor may obtain information about such factors as the organizational status of the director of the internal audit function. The professional certifications of the internal audit staff is a factor to consider when assessing their competence; not their objectivity. Answers c. and d. are factors to consider when developing evaluation procedures for testing the effectiveness of internal auditors' work rather than their objectivity. (ID: 8640)

28. (c) The external auditor is *not* required to obtain written acknowledgment from the entity that the internal auditors will complete the work assigned to them by the external auditor by the agreed upon dates. (ID: 8841)

29. (a) In communicating an overview of the planned scope and timing of the audit to those charged with governance, the external auditor should communicate how the external auditor has planned to use the work of the internal audit function in obtaining audit evidence and providing direct assistance. According to US GAAS, the planned use of the work of the internal audit function in obtaining audit evidence is an integral part of the external auditor's overall audit strategy and, therefore, is relevant to those charged with governance for their understanding of the proposed audit approach. An external auditor is not likely to use an internal auditor as a liaison rather than working directly with the controller of an entity and, at any rate, this is not a required communication. Evaluating the sufficiency of tests performed and assessing the risks of material misstatement are examples of significant judgments that are required to be made by the external auditor. (ID: 9933)

30. (b) The external auditor should evaluate whether, in the aggregate, using the work of the internal audit function in obtaining audit evidence to the extent planned, together with any planned use of internal auditors to provide direct assistance, would result in the external auditor still being sufficiently involved in the audit, given the external auditor's sole responsibility for the audit opinion expressed. (ID: 9934)

31. (a) The working papers prepared by the internal auditors who provided direct assistance on the audit engagement are required to be included in the audit documentation. Although the evaluation of their competence and significant threats to their objectivity and related safeguards is required to be included in the audit documentation when internal auditors provide direct assistance, the items described in the remaining answer alternatives are not required to support this evaluation.. (ID: 9944)

32. (a) During an audit, management makes many representations to the auditor in response to specific inquiries or through the financial statements. Such representations from management are part of the audit evidence the independent auditor obtains, but they are not a substitute for the application of those auditing procedures necessary to afford a reasonable basis for an opinion regarding the financial statements under audit. Written representations from management ordinarily confirm representations given to the auditor, indicate and document the continuing appropriateness of such representations, and reduce the possibility of misunderstanding concerning the matters that are the subject of the representations. (ID: 218)

33. (b) If comparative financial statements are reported on, the written representations obtained at the completion of the most recent audit should address all periods being reported on. The representations should be made as of the date of the auditor's report. If current management was not present during all periods covered by the auditor's report, the auditor should nevertheless obtain written representations from current management on all such periods. (ID: 6842)

34. (c) Compliance with aspects of contractual agreements that may affect the financial statements is a matter ordinarily included in written representations. Management's justifications for not correcting control weaknesses are primarily of concern to the audit committee, not the auditor. Generally, the auditor is not concerned with forecasts of the entity's stock price. Management is unlikely to acknowledge any responsibility for employees' violations of laws—merely responsibility for having reasonable controls in place. (ID: 6841)

35. (c) Compliance with contractual agreements that may affect the financial statements is a matter ordinarily included in written representations. It is the auditor's responsibility to assess the risk factors concerning the misappropriation of assets. An evaluation of the litigation that has been filed against the entity is a matter to be covered in a lawyer's response to a letter of audit inquiry. Management is not required to correct all material internal control weaknesses. (ID: 8164)

36. (a) Written representations may be limited to matters that are considered material. Materiality limitations would not apply to those representations that are not directly related to amounts included in the financial statements, such as the availability of minutes of stockholders' and directors' meetings. Answers b., c., and d. relate directly to amounts in the financial statements and, thus, materiality limits would apply. (ID: 5684)

37. (d) Because of the possible effects of fraud and the importance of management integrity on other aspects of the audit, materiality limits do not apply with respect to fraud involving management. This means that no incident involving management fraud may be ignored no matter how minor it may seem. Some instances of answers a., b., and c. may not be significant enough to matter. (ID: 8124)

38. (a) Materiality limits ordinarily would apply to written representations related to amounts concerning related-party transactions. Materiality considerations would not apply to those representations that are not directly related to amounts included in the financial statements such as the availability of financial records or the completeness of minutes of directors' meetings. Other items of this nature are management's acknowledgement of its responsibility for the fair presentation of financial statements in conformity with the applicable financial reporting framework and communications from regulatory agencies concerning noncompliance with or deficiencies in financial reporting practices. Nor would materiality apply to irregularities involving members of management because of the possible effects of fraud on other aspects of the audit. (ID: 8826)

39. (b) Analytical procedures consist of evaluations of financial information made by a study of plausible relationships among both financial and nonfinancial data. Projecting an error rate is not such an evaluation. (ID: 5666)

40. (c) The purpose of applying analytical procedures in planning the audit is to assist in planning the nature, timing, and extent of auditing procedures that will be used to obtain audit evidence for specific account balances or classes of transactions. To accomplish this, the analytical procedures used in planning the audit should focus on enhancing the auditor's understanding of the client's business and the transactions and events that have occurred since the last audit date. Consideration of reductions in the scope of test of controls and substantive tests occurs after the auditor understands the client's business. The audit as a whole provides reasonable assurance that potential material misstatements will be identified. Assessing the adequacy of available audit evidence can occur only after examination of audit evidence, not in the planning stage. (ID: 5626)

41. (b) This procedure would most likely provide indications of any material improper entries in the revenue and expense accounts. This procedure would not indicate when something was paid. The auditor did not expect much change as the question states that similar amounts from the prior year were used as the expectation to compare. That is, if the auditor did not consider increased property taxes or a change in uncollectible accounts in his or her expectation, then those changes that should have been recorded, but weren't, would not be detected. (ID: 8146)

42. (b) If the client did not properly cutoff sales at the end of the year, then A/R would be overstated as well as sales. A/R turnover equals net credit sales divided by average net accounts receivable. Therefore, if net credit sales is overstated and average net receivables is overstated disproportionately, the turnover would be lower than expected when compared to the prior year. Answers a. and d. would not affect A/R turnover. A/R turnover would increase if a large receivable were written off near the end of the year. (ID: 8163)

43. (d) The overall review of the audit is concerned with the big picture. The other answer options are analytical procedures that likely are performed during earlier stages, or not at all. (ID: 6366)

44. (c) Analytics are used in the overall review stage to assist the auditor in assessing conclusions reached and in evaluating the overall financial statement presentation. The overall review generally would include reading the financial statements and notes and considering the adequacy of evidence gathered in response to unusual or unexpected balances. The results of these procedures may indicate that additional evidence may be needed. Procedures to achieve the objectives in answers a. and d. would be performed before the overall review stage. The auditor would examine the workpapers to determine if any procedures were omitted. (ID: 8157)

45. (c) Analytics are concerned with plausible relationships. The square footage of selling space might be used to compared retail revenues and expenses to industry figures and prior year performance. Personnel turnover and objectivity of audit committee members are concerned with the control environment. Management plans are considered when evaluating the control environment, valuation, and disclosure. (ID: 6392)

46. (b) The use of a standard cost system that produces variance reports allows the auditor an opportunity to compare the output from the standard cost system with the financial information presented by management. Segregating obsolete inventory before the physical inventory count would likely facilitate inventory procedures, but not necessarily the analytical procedures. The auditor should assess the reliability of the data by considering the source of the data and the conditions under which it was gathered. Stronger internal controls and independent sources enhance the reliability of data used in analytics, but b. is the best answer. (ID: 5988)

47. (d) Increased sales to comparable customers would double accounts receivable (A/R) without a change in the allowance for doubtful accounts as a percentage of A/R. The client should increase this percentage if it has more customers with poor credit ratings. With no other changes, if twice as many A/R were written off previously or if more A/R are old, it suggests the current write-offs are inadequate. (ID: 7623)

48. (c) Increased sales to comparable customers would double accounts receivable (A/R) without a change in the allowance for doubtful accounts as a percentage of A/R. The allowance for doubtful accounts as a percentage should increase if a greater percentage of A/R is overdue this year. Improved internal control over

cash receipts would tend to decrease accounts receivable balances. The allowance for doubtful accounts as a percentage should decrease if the client has less customers with poor credit ratings. (ID: 8133)

49. (a) US GAAS require that analytics are to be used to some extent in all audits in the planning of the audit and in the final review stages. The use of analytics as a substantive test is not mandated, but it should be noted that analytics can be more effective or efficient than tests of details for achieving certain substantive testing objectives. (ID: 141)

50. (d) The auditor's reliance on substantive tests to achieve an audit objective related to a particular assertion may be derived from tests of details, from analytical procedures, or from a combination of both. The decision about which procedure or procedures to use to achieve a particular audit objective is based on the auditor's judgment on the expected effectiveness and efficiency of the available procedures. An auditor's decision whether to apply analytics or to perform tests of transactions and account balances is not determined solely by the availability of data aggregated at a high level, the auditor's familiarity with industry trends, or the timing of tests performed after the balance sheet date. (ID: 2965)

51. (c) Understanding financial relationships is essential to evaluating the results of analytics and usually requires knowledge of the client and the industry. The staff accountant may not be objective regarding his or her own work and may have limited industry knowledge. It would not be practicable for the managing partner who has responsibility for all audit engagements at that practice office to perform this procedure for all audits. A firm's quality control manager is not a member of the engagement team and, thus, may not participate in this manner in the engagement. (ID: 7025)

52. (c) Unexpected relationships discovered through analytics indicate additional investigation is appropriate. To assume that fraud exists in the relevant accounts or to revise communications with the audit committee without further investigation would be an over-reaction. Analytics are a substantive test, not a test of internal control. (ID: 6398)

53. (c) A basic premise underlying the application of analytics is that plausible relationships among data reasonably may be expected to exist and continue in the absence of known conditions to the contrary. The accounts receivable (A/R) turnover formula is net credit sales divided by average net A/R. A/R turnover is a measure of how many times in a year an entity collects its A/R. If the ratio increased, either average net A/R decreased or net credit sales increased. An increase in collections results in decreased average net A/R. The A/R aging is said to have deteriorated when collection times lengthen, an unusual circumstance if average net A/R decreased in proportion to sales. The elimination of a discount policy might decrease sales, but its relative impact on net credit sales and average net A/R is not known; in the absence of information to the contrary, assume that this did not have a significant impact on the ratio. A decrease in net credit sales would decrease the ratio. (ID: 7842)

54. (b) The final review stage of the audit provides an overall review of financial information in light of the audit opinion expressed. A final consideration of the adequacy of evidence is appropriate for this stage. Factors that determined the preliminary materially and audit risk levels would have been reassessed before arriving at final materially and audit risk levels. Summarizing specified uncorrected misstatements and calculating projected uncorrected misstatements estimated through sampling techniques is done before deciding on an audit opinion. (ID: 7813)

55. (c) As higher levels of assurance are desired from analytical procedures, more predictable relationships are required to develop the expectation. Relationships involving income statement accounts tend to be more predictable than relationships involving only balance sheet accounts because income statement accounts represent transactions over a period of time, whereas balance sheet accounts represent amounts as of a point in time. Relationships involving transactions subject to management discretion are sometimes less predictable. (ID: 2773)

56. (b) A comparison of revenues and expenses with those of the prior year is likely to reveal a change in the capitalization policy for small tools. For instance, if tools costing less than $25 formerly were expensed and the policy is changed to $100, this is likely to show a substantial increase in the amount of tools expensed during

the period. Answer c. concerns a liability account (payroll taxes payable), not a revenue or expense account. Failure to recognize the property tax increase would make the account balances comparable and so the auditor would not investigate. (ID: 7493)

57. (c) The following factors influence the auditor's consideration of the reliability of data for purposes of achieving audit objectives: whether the data was obtained from independent sources outside the entity or from sources within the entity; whether sources within the entity were independent of those who are responsible for the amount being audited; whether the data was developed under a reliable system with adequate controls; whether the data was subjected to audit testing in the current or prior year; and whether the expectations were developed using data from a variety of sources. Whether the data was processed in an IT system or in a manual accounting system, whether the data was prepared on the cash basis or in conformity with GAAP, and whether the data was processed in an online system or a batch entry system generally would not influence the auditor's consideration of the reliability of data for purposes of analytics. (ID: 8388)

58. (d) The auditor is required to perform analytics in the planning stage of the audit. These procedures assist the auditor in planning the nature, extent, and timing of substantive tests; thus, they should focus on enhancing the auditor's understanding of the client's business and the transactions and events that have occurred since the last audit and identifying areas that may represent specific risks relevant to the audit. Analytics involve comparisons of recorded amounts or ratios developed from recorded amounts to expectations developed by the auditor. Comparison of recorded financial information with anticipated results from budgets and forecasts is appropriate for this planning stage. Representations from management are dated the same date as the auditor's report. Communication regarding the prior year's audit adjustments typically occurs near the end of the audit for that year. Inquiry of the client's attorney tends to occur after the planning stage, as part of the substantive tests. (ID: 8414)

59. (a) The purpose of analytics in the planning stage of the audit is to assist in planning the audit procedures that will be used to obtain audit evidence for specific account balances or classes of transactions. To accomplish this one of the things the auditor should focus on is the transactions and events that have occurred since the last audit date. The unaudited information from internal quarterly reports would be the best source of information for developing expectations. Expectations, in this context, are the auditor's predictions of recorded accounts or ratios. The effectiveness of analytical procedures depends on developing expectations that can reasonably be expected to identify unexpected relationships. Account assertions in the planning memorandum would not provide the needed data to develop such expectations. The auditor is interested in transactions and events that have occurred since the last audit date, so comments in the prior year's management letter would have limited usefulness and, again, would probably not include data needed to derive expectations. Control risk affects the reliability of data and, thus, the precision of the expectation, but it would not be considered a source for developing expectations. (ID: 8831)

60. (d) Analytical procedures used in the planning phase of an audit should focus on enhancing the auditor's understanding of the client's business and the auditor's understanding of the transactions and events that have occurred since the last audit, and identifying areas that may represent specific risks relevant to the audit. The other answers do not describe activities that would occur during the planning phase of an audit. (ID: 8843)

61. (c) The objective of analytical procedures used in the final review stage of the audit is to assess the conclusions reached and evaluate the overall financial statement presentation. It would generally include reading the financial statements and notes and considering the adequacy of the evidence gathered in response to unusual or unexpected balances identified and any unusual or unexpected balances or relationships that were not previously identified. Comparing each individual expense account balance with the relevant budgeted amounts and investigating any significant variations; and calculating each individual expense account balance as a percentage of total entity expenses and comparing the results with industry averages are analytical procedures that would be performed during the course of the audit (used as substantive procedures), not during the final review stage. Analytical procedures are not applicable to tests of controls. (ID: 8801)

62. (c) An engagement partner would most likely consider cost of goods sold/average inventory in the overall review stage of an audit. Known as inventory turnover, it measures the number of times inventory is acquired

and sold during a period and is thus used as an indicator of the efficiency of the operations of a company. The other answers are not meaningful financial statement analysis calculations. (ID: 8847)

63. (d) An auditor would most likely consider the possibility that a client's financial statements contained material misstatements if the results of an analytical procedure disclosed unexpected differences. An auditor should evaluate significant unexpected differences. If an explanation for the difference cannot be obtained, the auditor should design further audit procedures to determine whether the difference is a likely misstatement. Whenever an auditor becomes aware that management has consulted with other accountants about significant accounting matters (whether or not this was disclosed to the auditor by management) the auditor should discuss with those charged with governance the auditor's views about those same matters. Whether this would cause the auditor to consider that the financial statements might be materially misstated would depend on the circumstances. The delivery of the representation letter is an issue that should be explained to the client during the initial stage of the planning stage of the audit and documented in an engagement letter along with other understandings with the client. The representations should be dated as of the date of the auditor's report. (The reference to completion of fieldwork is based on superseded guidance.) At any rate, the CFO is not refusing to sign and although such representations are part of the audit evidence, they complement, rather than serve as a substitute for, other audit procedures; thus, any issue with them would be less of a concern regarding material misstatements than an unexpected difference disclosed by analytical procedures. Audit trails of computer-generated transactions existing for a short time are not an indication of a material misstatement. The auditor should be aware of the client's record retention policies and either arrange to test the transactions during their existence or develop alternative auditing procedures. (ID: 8809)

64. (c) The decision about which procedure to use (analytics or tests of details, or a combination) is based on the auditor's judgment of their effectiveness and efficiency in identifying potential misstatements in the given situation. The effectiveness and efficiency of analytical procedures is based on the nature of the assertion; the plausibility and predictability of the relationship; the availability and reliability of the data used to develop expectations; and the precision of the expectation. The other answers are not relevant considerations. (ID: 8832)

65. (a) Relationships involving income statement accounts, such as interest expense, tend to be more predictable than relationships involving only balance sheet accounts because income statement accounts represent transactions over a period of time, whereas balance sheet accounts represent amounts as of a point in time. (ID: 8641)

66. (a) A lower than expected return on an equity method investment most likely could have been caused by an error in recording amortization of the excess of the investor's cost over the investment's underlying book value. The investee's decision to reduce cash dividends would increase the expected carrying amount of the investment under the equity method. Marketable securities (available-for-sale or trading securities) are not accounted for using the equity method. A fluctuation in the market price of the investee's common stock would not affect investments accounted for using the equity method. (ID: 9362)

67. (c) Analytical procedures are most appropriate when testing operating expense transactions. Relationships involving income statement accounts tend to be more predictable than relationships involving only balance sheet accounts because income statement accounts represent transactions over a period of time, whereas balance sheet accounts represent amounts as of a point in time. (ID: 9379)

68. (c) Only comparing the current year's financial statements with those of the prior year is a description of an analytical procedure. Although analytics involve evaluations of financial information made by a study of plausible relationships among both financial and nonfinancial data, the other answers which refer to nonfinancial information do not describe a review of relationships of financial information with relevant nonfinancial information. Additionally, obtaining a letter from the client's attorney and reading the minutes of the board of director's meetings should be done prior to the final review stage. (ID: 9912)

69. (a) Reference to and identification of the specialist may be made in the auditor's report if such reference will facilitate an understanding of the reason for the departure from the unmodified opinion. If, as a result of the use of a specialist, the auditor concludes that conditions exist that cause substantial doubt about the entity's ability to continue as a going concern and the auditor believes a reference to the specialist will facilitate

an understanding of the reason for the reference to this conclusion, the auditor may refer to the specialist in the auditor's report. Disclosure of the specialist's findings, implying that a more thorough audit was performed, is not appropriate. If a specialist's findings are consistent with written representations and corroborate another specialist's earlier findings, there would be no need to disclose the findings of the specialist for the reasons above. Internal control is generally not a matter that would require the use of a specialist. (ID: 5680)

70. (b) An auditor may use the work of a specialist who has a relationship with the client, but must assess the risk that the specialist might not be objective. If the relationship might impair the specialist's objectivity, the auditor should perform additional procedures or engage another specialist. Normally, an auditor should not refer to the work or findings of the specialist. In expressing a modified opinion, the auditor may refer to the specialist only if doing so will help clarify the reason for the modified opinion. If there is a material departure from the applicable financial reporting framework, the auditor may refer to the specialist only if doing so will help clarify the reason for the qualified or adverse opinion. Control deficiencies result from the client's actions or inactions, not the auditor's actions. (ID: 8412)

71. (c) An auditor who uses the work of a specialist may refer to the specialist in the auditor's report if the auditor modifies the report because of the difference between the client's and the specialist's valuations of an asset and the auditor believes such reference will facilitate the understanding of the reason for the modification. If the auditor believes that the specialist's findings are reasonable in the circumstances, ordinarily the auditor would use the findings, but this does not speak to whether a reference in the auditor's report is appropriate because there is no indication of whether the findings support the related assertions in the financial statements and, thus, do or do not require modification of the auditor's report. If the specialist's findings support the related assertions in the financial statements or provide the auditor with greater assurance of reliability about written representations, it follows that the auditor will be able to conclude that sufficient appropriate audit evidence has been obtained. As no modification of the auditor's report is needed as a result of the specialist's findings, no reference should be made to the specialist because it could be misinterpreted as either a qualification or a division of responsibility. (Editor Note: This question is an example of when candidates must choose the best answer. The other answers are clearly wrong and answer c. is at least partially correct.) (ID: 8846)

72. (a) A lawyer may limit the response to matters to which the lawyer has given substantive attention in the form of legal consultation or representation. Answers b., c., and d. are sufficient to cause a scope limitation. (ID: 138)

73. (c) As the events or conditions that should be considered in accounting for and reporting litigation, claims, and assessments are matters within the direct knowledge, and often control of, an entity's management, that management is the primary source of information about such matters. Although a letter of audit inquiry to the client's lawyer is the auditor's primary means of obtaining corroboration of the information furnished by management concerning litigation, claims, and assessments, it is not the primary means of obtaining that information. (ID: 4276)

74. (d) A lawyer's response may be limited to matters that are considered individually or collectively material to the financial statements provided the lawyer and auditor have reached an understanding on the limits of materiality for this purpose. (ID: 6840)

75. (a) The passage is a quote from a sample inquiry letter to legal counsel. It is rare to refer to "our auditors" in a letter to that auditor; it is more likely that a third party is being addressed using this language. The representation letter states that the financial statements are presented fairly in conformity with GAAP and that, "there are no...other liabilities or gain or loss contingencies that are required to be accrued or disclosed...." That information was furnished to auditors generally is inappropriate for footnotes to financial statement. (ID: 7817)

76. (b) The letter of inquiry to the client's attorney is the primary means the auditor has to obtain corroboration of information furnished by management concerning litigation, claims, and assessments. The terms mentioned in answers a. and c. might be covered by the attorney, but are not the primary reasons the auditor makes the request. The items in answer d. normally are furnished by management (or management may request that the attorney prepare the description and evaluation); they are not the primary reason that the auditor sends a letter of inquiry. (ID: 5139)

77. (c) As the events that should be considered in the financial accounting for and reporting of litigation, claims, and assessments are matters within the direct knowledge and, often, control of management of an entity, management is the primary source of information about such matters. Accordingly, the independent auditor's procedures should include inquiry and discussion with management concerning the policies and procedures adopted for identifying, evaluating, and accounting for litigation, claims, and assessments. A letter of audit inquiry to the client's lawyer is the auditor's primary means of obtaining corroboration of the information furnished by management concerning litigation, claims, and assessments. However, the lawyer does not evaluate the client's ability to continue as a going concern or whether all litigation, claims, and assessments have been recorded or disclosed in the financial statements. Examination of documents in the client's lawyer's possession is an atypical procedure. (ID: 6002)

78. (a) Only the statement in answer a. would require further clarification. The statements in answers b., c., and d. clearly indicate the probability of an unfavorable outcome. (ID: 8156)

79. (d) When a client's lawyer is unable to form a conclusion about the likelihood of an unfavorable outcome of pending litigation because of inherent uncertainties and the effect on the financial statements could be material, the auditor ordinarily will conclude that an explanatory paragraph should be added to the report. (ID: 5682)

80. (d) The refusal of a client to allow necessary communications with a lawyer is a scope limitation that usually results in a disclaimer of opinion; knowing that an audit could not be performed, a CPA could not accept the engagement. A CPA need not understand a client's operations and industry when accepting an engagement if the CPA reasonably can expect to gain an appropriate understanding. Recurring operating losses do not prohibit audit completion. An inquiry of the predecessor auditor is a necessary procedure because the predecessor auditor may be able to provide information that will assist the successor auditor in determining whether to accept the engagement. However, the review of the predecessor auditor's working papers assists the successor auditor in the planning of the engagement. The successor auditor may initiate this after accepting the engagement. Furthermore, although the predecessor auditor should ordinarily permit the successor auditor to review the working papers, the extent, if any, to which a predecessor auditor permits access to working papers, is a matter of judgment. (ID: 8384)

81. (b) The auditor's procedures should include a discussion with management about the policies and procedures adopted for identifying, evaluating, and accounting for litigation, claims, and assessments. The events or conditions that should be considered in the financial accounting for and reporting of litigation, claims, and assessments are matters within the direct knowledge and, often, control of management of an entity. Accordingly, management is the primary source of information about such matters. It is the auditor's responsibility to conclude whether the client's litigation is properly disclosed. The auditor requests the client's attorney's opinion on this, not the clerk of the court. The clerk of the court would not have the information needed. The auditor would examine documents in the client's possession; not the lawyer's possession. The auditor would not likely inspect documents in the client's lawyer's possession due to confidentiality considerations. If the attorney's response does not provide enough information, the auditor would arrange a conference with the attorney rather than request documentation. It would not be appropriate for the auditor to contact the client's adversaries' legal representatives. (ID: 8643)

82. (c) Loss contingencies include those arising from litigation, claims and assessments. A letter of inquiry to the client's lawyer is the auditor's primary means of corroboration of the information furnished by management about such matters. The financial statements (including footnotes), which may include accrual or disclosure of loss contingencies, are part of the information furnished by management. Performing appropriate analytical procedures and checking the arithmetic accuracy of the accounting records are not likely to provide information about the evaluation of loss contingencies. (ID: 8615)

83. (b) The primary reason for a letter of audit inquiry to the client's attorneys is to obtain corroboration of the information furnished by management concerning litigation, claims, and assessments. The attorney's legal expertise is sought by the auditor, not the assurance that matters are properly accounted for. The letter of inquiry should address two lists; one comprised of pending or threatened litigation, claims, and assessments; and the other, unasserted claims and assessments that would, if asserted, have a reasonable possibility of an unfavorable outcome. The pending matters list is not limited to those that management believes have a reasonable

possibility of an unfavorable outcome. And although an attorney's response does include addressing the description of matters and the evaluation of their likely outcome, the primary reason for the auditor's request is to corroborate management's information. The attorney is asked to evaluate the likelihood of an unfavorable outcome, not give an opinion using the terms *possible*, *probable* or *remote*. (ID: 8620)

84. (d) An auditor would not seek an evaluation of the client's ability to continue as a going concern from an attorney regardless of the cause of the client's financial difficulties; that is the auditor's responsibility and does not involve legal expertise. Answers a., b., and c. would be likely to be covered in the client's attorney's response to a letter of audit inquiry. (ID: 8651)

85. (d) Management is the primary source of information about litigation, claims and assessments, however, most audits include other procedures (usually for other purposes) that may also assist the auditor in identifying such matters. These include reading minutes of meetings of stockholders, directors, and appropriate committees held during and subsequent to the period being audited; reading contracts, loan agreements, leases, and correspondence from taxing or other governmental authorities, and similar documents; obtaining information concerning guarantees from bank confirmation forms, and inspecting other documents for possible guarantees by the client. Answers a. and b. could possibly reveal evidence of litigation, claims, and assessments, but correspondence from taxing authorities is a more likely source. Applying ratio analysis on the current year's liability accounts is the least likely procedure of the answers to disclose such information. (ID: 8839)

86. (c) An auditor's primary method to corroborate information on litigation, claims, and assessments is to review the response from the client's lawyer to a letter of audit inquiry. Verifying attorney-client privilege would not provide information about litigation, claims, and assessments. Examining legal invoices does not provide as much evidence about the substance (nature) of the litigation, claims, and assessments as the attorney's letter. Reviewing written representations is an incorrect response because management cannot corroborate its own information. (ID: 9365)

87. (b) The letter requests the attorney to provide an evaluation of the likelihood of an unfavorable outcome and an estimate, if one can be made, of the amount or range of potential loss concerning litigation, claims, and assessments. The statement that it is the attorney's belief that the action can be settled for less than the damages claimed begs for a follow-up question (clarification) as to whether an estimate of how much less can be made; the other answers are definitive responses. (ID: 9904)

88. (b) A standard confirmation request sent to a financial institution at which the client has both a checking or savings account and a loan would include requests on one form regarding the cash balance and the loan balance and, in addition, a description of the loan collateral. While confirmation of accounts receivable is a generally accepted auditing procedure, confirmation of accounts payable is not. It generally is used only in cases of suspected fraud, sloppy or missing records, or suspected understatements. An entity holding inventory on consignment generally would not have information related to contingent liabilities. Accrued interest receivable most likely would be related to notes receivable rather than accounts receivable. (ID: 5987)

89. (c) Lead schedules generally summarize information, such as a summary of all cash accounts with debits and credits summarized into major categories and information about beginning and ending balances. (ID: 6628)

90. (a) A physical count of assets that could be stolen readily (negotiable securities or gems, for instance) should include acknowledgement that the assets are again in the client's custody, if they are handled by the auditor. Sold securities would not be counted, so an analysis of realized gains and losses is not related closely to a count. An evaluation of control policies concerning physical access or negotiation generally would be documented with other control evaluations, not with substantive tests. (ID: 6937)

91. (d) The matters noted in answers a., b., and c. would all have a significant impact on the quantity and content of the auditor's working papers. While the content of the representation letter may affect the quantity and content of the auditor's workpapers, the effect is minimal. (ID: 5146)

92. (d) Permanent files contain items of continuing interest, such as debt agreements, internal control flowcharts, and articles of incorporation. The other items are of temporary interest only. (ID: 6007)

93. (d) Workpapers for each asset, liability, and equity account begin with a lead schedule summarizing the account's balance per the general ledger, and then showing adjusting and reclassification entries, and the final balance per audit. The lead schedule also includes the auditor's conclusion about whether the account is stated fairly. (ID: 2320)

94. (c) Working trial balances contain reclassification and adjustments columns. The items in answers a., b., and d. are included in the audit workpapers, but are not included in the working trial balance. (ID: 5145)

95. (c) The representation letter should address that there are no violations or possible violations of laws or regulations whose effects should be considered for disclosure in the financial statements or as a basis for recording a loss contingency. (ID: 5137)

96. (b) Sufficient and appropriate documentation should include evidence that the audit working papers have been reviewed. It should be clear who reviewed specified elements of the audit work performed and when. Accounting estimates are an example of the significant findings or issues that should be documented along with the actions taken to address them and the basis for the final conclusions reached. If additional evidence is required to document significant findings or issues, the original evidence should not be deleted. Audit documentation is the property of the auditor, not the client. Note: The retention period of at least five years from the report release date is correct for nonissuers—it is seven years for issuers. After the documentation completion date, the auditor must not delete or discard audit documentation before the end of the specified retention period; any time prior to this date, the auditor may make changes to delete superseded or incorrect material. (ID: 9395)

97. (c) Business structure and operating style occasionally are designed deliberately to obscure relationships. Because compensating balance arrangements and nonmonetary transactions obscure the form of transactions, they are suspect. Compensating balance arrangements involve related parties more often than the other answer options. Segregation of duties applies whether the parties to a transaction are related or not. Reasonable and unreasonable accounting estimates both exist with and without related parties present. Entities frequently have recurring transactions with independent entities. (ID: 7811)

98. (a) When searching for related-party transactions, the auditor should obtain an understanding of each subsidiary's relationship to the total entity because business structure and operating style are occasionally deliberately designed to obscure related-party transactions. Answers b., c., and d. are not reasons for an auditor to obtain an understanding of each subsidiary's relationship to the total entity. (ID: 185)

99. (c) After identifying related-party transactions, the auditor should obtain an understanding of the business purpose of the transactions. The other answers are all procedures that may be performed later. (ID: 5142)

100. (d) Transactions that because of their nature may be indicative of the existence of related parties include borrowing or lending on an interest-free basis or at a rate of interest significantly above or below market rates prevailing at the time of the transaction; selling real estate at a price that differs significantly from its appraised value; exchanging property for similar property in a nonmonetary transaction; and making loans with no scheduled terms for when or how the funds will be repaid. (ID: 2974)

101. (c) The auditor should be aware that the substance of a particular transaction could be significantly different from its form and that financial statements should recognize the substance of particular transactions rather than merely their legal form. Established accounting principles ordinarily do not require transactions with related parties to be accounted for on a basis different from that which would be appropriate if the parties were not related—generally, the auditor should view related-party transactions within the framework of existing pronouncements. The identification of related parties relates more to the disclosure concern rather than the auditor's review for their proper accounting. (ID: 9269)

102. (b) One of the first steps an auditor should perform to determine the existence of related parties is to request a list of related parties from management. Reviewing proxy and other material filed with the SEC is a close second choice, but it is usually best to start with inquiries to management and then corroborate those results with the SEC and other regulatory agencies. Reviewing the company's business structure should be done to determine the scope of work to be performed with respect to possible transactions with related parties rather than determining their existence. Examining invoices, contracts, and purchase orders would be done after related-party transactions have been identified rather than to determine their existence. It would be done to obtain satisfaction or evidence concerning the purpose, nature, and extent of related-party transactions and their effect on the financial statements. (ID: 9356)

Solution 4-2 SIMULATION ANSWER: Type and Classification of Audit Procedures

For each of the descriptions of procedures in column A of the table below, select the type of audit procedure performed from the selection list for column B and then indicate in column C whether it was a substantive procedure or a test of controls. Selections may be used once, more than once, or not at all.

A	B	C
Description of Procedure	**Type of Audit Procedure**	**Classification of Audit Procedure**
1. Examined sales invoices to see if they were initialed by the credit manager indicating credit approval.	E. Inspection	B. Test of controls
2. Compared this year's expenses with last year's expenses and investigated unusual fluctuations.	A. Analytical procedure	A. Substantive procedures
3. Requested responses directly from customers.	B. Confirmation	A. Substantive procedures
4. Questioned management about subsequent events.	D. Inquiry	A. Substantive procedures
5. Observed the accounting clerk record the daily deposit of cash receipts.	G. Observation	B. Test of controls
6. Examined invoices to support additions to the fixed asset account during the year.	E. Inspection	A. Substantive procedures
7. Agreed sales invoices to credit files to determine whether the customer had a credit file and had been approved for credit.	I. Reperformance	B. Test of controls
8. Asked the accounting manager how often cash is deposited and by whom.	D. Inquiry	B. Test of controls

(ID: 9833)

1. E. Inspection; B. Test of controls

Inspection consists of examining records or documents, whether internal or external, in paper form, electronic form or other media. In this case, the auditor inspected the sales invoices for evidence of authorization by the credit manager. Approval of sales by the credit manager is a control to prevent credit sales to customers who have not been approved for credit. This procedure tested that control.

2. A. Analytical procedure; A. Substantive procedures

Analytical procedures consist of evaluations of financial information made by a study of plausible relationships among both financial and nonfinancial data. Analytical procedures also encompass the investigation of identified fluctuations and relationships that are inconsistent with other relevant information or deviate significantly from predicted amounts. They range from simple comparisons, like this example, to the use of complex models. The comparison of expenses between years and the investigation of unusual fluctuations was a substantive procedure performed to detect material misstatements in expenses for the assertions of completeness and accuracy.

3. B. Confirmation; A. Substantive procedures

A confirmation, which is a specific type of inquiry, is the process of obtaining and evaluating a direct communication from a third party in response to a request for information about a particular item affecting financial statement assertions. It was a substantive test of details of the assertions of completeness, existence, and accuracy of the customers' accounts.

4. D. Inquiry; A. Substantive procedures

Inquiry consists of seeking information of knowledgeable persons, both financial and nonfinancial, inside or outside of the entity. Inquiries can be formal written inquiries or informal oral inquiries. The auditor should consider the reasonableness and consistency of the responses in light of the results of other procedures and the auditor's knowledge of the entity and its industry—evaluating responses to inquiries is an integral part of the inquiry process. Inquiry by itself does not provide sufficient appropriate audit evidence to detect misstatements or to test the operating effectiveness of controls; thus, auditors complement inquiries with other procedures to corroborate the responses received. This inquiry was a substantive procedure to test the assertion of the completeness of disclosures regarding type two subsequent events and other assertions, depending on the nature of the event, regarding type one events.

5. G. Observation; B. Test of controls

Observation consists of looking at a process or procedure being performed by others. Observation provides audit evidence about the performance of a process or procedure, but is limited to the point in time at which the observation takes place and by the fact that the act of being observed may affect how the process or procedure is performed. Depositing cash receipts on a daily basis is a control. This procedure tested that control.

6. E. Inspection; A. Substantive procedures

Inspection consists of examining records or documents, whether internal or external, in paper form, electronic form or other media. In this case, the auditor inspected the invoices to see if they provided evidence for the additions to the fixed asset account. This procedure was a substantive test of details of the assertions of completeness, existence, and accuracy of the fixed asset additions.

7. I. Reperformance; B. Test of controls

Reperformance is the auditor's independent execution of procedures or controls that were originally performed as part of the entity's internal control, either manually or through the use of computer-assisted audit techniques (CAAT). Investigating a customer's credit worthiness and approving a credit sale by reference to the customer's resulting credit file is a control to prevent credit sales to customers who have not been approved for credit. This procedure tested that control.

8. D. Inquiry; B. Test of controls

Inquiry consists of seeking information of knowledgeable persons, both financial and nonfinancial, inside or outside of the entity. Inquiries can be formal written inquiries or informal oral inquiries. The auditor should consider the reasonableness and consistency of the responses in light of the results of other procedures and the auditor's knowledge of the entity and its industry—evaluating responses to inquiries is an integral part of the inquiry process. Inquiry by itself does not provide sufficient appropriate audit evidence to detect misstatements or to test the operating effectiveness of controls; thus, auditors complement inquiries with other procedures to corroborate the responses received. This inquiry was a test of the controls over the deposit of cash receipts.

Solution 4-3 SIMULATION ANSWER: Documentation

For each of the following unrelated statements, questions, excerpts, and comments taken from various parts of an auditor's working paper file, select the most likely source from the list of sources. A source may be used once, more than once, or not at all.

Excerpts From Working Papers	Source
1. During our audit we discovered evidence of the company's failure to safeguard inventory from loss, damage, and misappropriation.	B
2. The company considers the decline in value of equity securities classified as available-for-sale to be temporary.	N
3. Was the difference of opinion on the accrued pension liabilities that existed between the engagement personnel and the actuarial specialist resolved in accordance with firm policy and appropriately documented?	M
4. Our audit is designed to provide reasonable assurance of detecting misstatements that, in our judgment, could have a material effect on the financial statements taken as a whole. Consequently, our audit will not necessarily detect all misstatements that exist due to error, fraudulent financial reporting, or misappropriation of assets.	H
5. There have been no communications from regulatory agencies concerning noncompliance with or deficiencies in financial reporting practices.	N
6. Nothing came to our attention that caused us to believe that at October 31, year 1, there was any change in the capital stock, increase in long-term debt, or decrease in consolidated net current assets or stockholders' equity as compared with the amounts shown in the September 30, year 1 unaudited condensed consolidated balance sheet.	I
7. It is our opinion that the possible liability to the company in this proceeding is nominal in amount.	D
8. As discussed in Note 4 to the financial statements, the company experienced a net loss for the year ended July 31, year 1, and is currently in default under substantially all of its debt agreements. In addition, on September 25, year 1, the company filed a prenegotiated voluntary petition for relief under Chapter 11 of the U.S. Bankruptcy Code. These matters raise substantial doubt about the company's ability to continue as a going concern.	L
9. During the year under audit, we were advised that management consulted with Better & Best, CPAs. The purpose of this consultation was to obtain another CPA firm's opinion concerning the company's recognition of certain revenue that we believe should be deferred to future periods. Better & Best's opinion was consistent with our opinion, so management did not recognize the revenue in the current year.	F
10. The company believes that all material expenditures that have been deferred to future periods will be recoverable.	N

(ID: 9218)

1. B

The auditor's communication to the audit committee regarding significant deficiencies includes a description of the conditions noted.

2. N

Management is a knowledgeable source of the company's viewpoint, beliefs, intentions, and occurrence of events.

3. M

An auditor's review notes include reminders of select conditions to allow a double check to ensure that all matters are resolved appropriately.

4. H

Appropriate places for disclaimers are the engagement letter and post-engagement reports. The statement speaks of the audit in the future ("Consequently, our audit will not...") from the perspective of the auditor.

5. N

Management is a knowledgeable source of the company's viewpoint, beliefs, intentions, and occurrence of events.

6. I

Letters to underwriters may contain negative assurance, which is used in few instances, certainly not in a report on significant deficiencies. A practitioner's report on a management assertion would not be discussing stockholder's equity in relation to previous unaudited financial statements; it would discuss the practitioner's work in relation to management's assertion.

7. D

An opinion regarding liability related to a proceeding is usually from a lawyer in response to an audit inquiry letter. The representation letter usually has a less specific statement of all possible liabilities being included in the financial statements as appropriate. These are the two parties most likely to be knowledgeable about proceedings related to the client.

8. L

The phrases *substantial doubt* and *ability to continue as a going concern* are required in the auditor's report when there is a going concern uncertainty.

9. F

The auditor's communication to the audit committee should include any disagreements, whether or not resolved, with management about matters that, individually or in the aggregate, could have a significant impact on the financial statements.

10. N

Management is a knowledgeable source of the company's viewpoint, beliefs, intentions, and occurrence of events.

Solution 4-4 SIMULATION ANSWER: Documentation

For each of the following unrelated statements, questions, excerpts, and comments taken from various parts of an auditor's working paper file, select the most likely source from the list of sources. A source may be used once, more than once, or not at all.

Excerpts From Working Papers	Source
1. Our use of professional judgment and the assessment of audit risk and materiality for the purpose of our audit mean that matters may have existed that would have been assessed differently by you. We make no representation as to the sufficiency or appropriateness of the information in our working papers for your purposes.	P
2. Indicate in the space provided below whether this information agrees with your records. If there are exceptions, please provide any information that will assist the auditor in reconciling the difference.	J
3. Blank checks are maintained in an unlocked cabinet along with the check-signing machine. Blank checks and the check-signing machine should be locked in separate locations to prevent the embezzlement of funds.	B
4. Our audit cannot be relied upon to disclose significant deficiencies in the design or operation of internal control. Nevertheless, we will communicate to you all significant deficiencies and potential areas for improvement that we become aware of during the course of our audit.	H
5. The timetable set by management to complete our audit was unreasonable considering the failure of the company's personnel to complete schedules on a timely basis and delays in providing necessary information.	F
6. Several employees have disabled the anti-virus detection software on their PCs because the software slows the processing of data and occasionally rings false alarms. The company should obtain anti-virus software that runs continuously at all system entry points and that cannot be disabled by unauthorized personnel.	B
7. In connection with an audit of our financial statements, management has prepared, and furnished to our auditors, a description and evaluation of certain contingencies.	C
8. The company has no plans or intentions that may materially affect the carrying value or classification of assets and liabilities.	N
9. In planning the sampling application, was appropriate consideration given to the relationship of the sample to the audit objective and to preliminary judgments about materiality levels?	M

(ID: 9220)

1. P

The client, a CPA performing a review, and a successor auditor are most likely to be the external viewers of workpapers. Typically, each successor will try to view a predecessor's workpapers, but the opposite will be rare. A client is the most atypical user of the three. Further, there is no answer option with a communication regarding the client or reviewer viewing the workpapers.

2. J

A confirmation request seeks an indication of agreement between provided information with another's records. The language in this statement is more suitable to an accounts receivable confirmation (a relatively straightforward matter of matching amounts) than an inquiry of legal counsel (a relatively complex matter requiring the judgment by counsel, and, thus, a more complex letter of inquiry).

3. B

The auditor's communication to the audit committee regarding significant deficiencies includes a description of the conditions noted.

4. H

The statement speaks of the future ("...we will communicate to you....") from the perspective of the auditor. It is most likely that an auditor would send this message to management. The appropriate place for this disclaimer is in the engagement letter.

5. F

The auditor's communication to the audit committee should include any serious difficulties encountered in dealing with management related to the performance of the audit.

6. B

The auditor's communication to the audit committee regarding significant deficiencies includes a description of the conditions noted.

7. C

This statement is from the entity's management ("our financial statements") to a party (other than the auditor) who is knowledgeable about the company's contingent liabilities. In connection with audits, lawyers frequently are asked to provide their opinion of contingent liabilities related to the services that they provide to clients.

8. N

Management is a knowledgeable source of the company's viewpoint, beliefs, intentions, and occurrence of events.

9. M

An auditor's review notes include reminders to check on issues where mistakes have a relatively high probability of being made.

Solution 4-5 SIMULATION ANSWER: Ratios

Each of the following represents a financial ratio that the auditor calculated during the prior year's audit. For each ratio, calculate the current year's ratio from the financial statements presented and select the answer from the list. Calculations should be rounded, if necessary, to the same number of places as the prior year's ratios.

Ratio	Year 2	Year 1
1. Current ratio	H. 3.1	2.5
2. Quick ratio	E. 1.6	1.3
3. Accounts receivable turnover	K. 7.5	5.5
4. Inventory turnover	G. 3.0	2.5
5. Total asset turnover	D. 1.5	1.2
6. Gross margin percentage	T. 40%	35%
7. Net operating margin percentage	P. 22%	25%
8. Times interest earned	N. 16.5	10.3
9. Total debt to equity percentage	U. 60%	50%

(ID: 9221)

1. H

The current ratio is total current assets divided by total current liabilities. ($1,240,000 / $400,000 = 3.1)

2. E

The quick (or acid-test) ratio is cash plus marketable securities plus net receivables divided by current liabilities. [($240,000 + $400,000) / $400,000 = 1.6]

3. K

Accounts receivable turnover is net credit sales divided by average net receivables. {$3,000,000 / [($400,000 + $400,000) / 2] = 7.5}

4. G

Inventory turnover is cost of goods sold divided by average inventory. {$1,800,000 / [($600,000 + $600,000) / 2] = 3.0}

5. D

Total asset turnover is sales divided by total assets. ($3,000,000 / $2,000.000 = 1.5)

6. T

Gross margin percentage is the gross margin divided by sales, expressed as a percentage. ($1,200,000 / $3,000,000 = 0.4 = 40%)

7. P

Net operating margin percentage is operating income divided by sales, expressed as a percentage. [($660,000 / $3,000,000 = .22 = 22%)]

8. N

Times interest earned is income before income taxes and interest charges divided by interest charges. ($660,000 / $40,000 = 16.5)

9. U

Total debt to equity percentage is total liabilities divided by owners' equity, expressed as a percentage. [($400,000 + $350,000) / ($750,000 + $500,000) = 0.6 = 60%]

Solution 4-6 SIMULATION ANSWER: Financial Statement Analysis

Each of the following items represent an auditor's observed changes, independent of each other, in certain financial statement ratios or amounts from the prior year's ratios or amounts. For each observed change, select the most likely explanation or explanations from the accompanying list. An explanation may be used once, more than once, or not at all.

Auditor's Observed Changes	Explanations
1. Allowance for doubtful accounts increased from the prior year, but allowance for doubtful accounts as a percentage of accounts receivable decreased from the prior year. (3 explanations)	A, B, E
2. Long-term debt increased from the prior year, but interest expense increased a larger-than-proportionate amount than long-term debt. (1 explanation)	P
3. Operating income increased from the prior year although the entity was less profitable than in the prior year. (2 explanations)	L, P
4. Gross margin percentage was unchanged from the prior year although gross margin increased from the prior year. (1 explanation)	H

(ID: 9222)

1. A, B, E

The allowance for doubtful accounts as a percentage of accounts receivable will decrease when the allowance for doubtful accounts decreases proportionately less than the accounts receivable does or when accounts receivable increases. Due to recording consignment items shipped during the last month as sales, accounts receivable is overstated. Due to not recording a significant number of credit memos for returned merchandise, accounts receivable is overstated. However, these occurrences do not impact the allowance for doubtful accounts. A larger percentage of sales occurring during the last month of the year, as compared to the prior year, increases the amount in accounts receivable. This increases average accounts receivable, as compared to last year, without increasing the allowance for doubtful accounts, as compared to last year.

2. P

An increase in the interest rate is the only explanation for the larger-than-proportionate increase in interest expense.

3. L, P

Income tax expense and interest expense appear in the income statement below operating income, i.e., neither are part of the calculation to arrive at operating income. This understanding is the first step in identifying the reasons that could cause such a change. If operating income increased from the prior year (year 1), but the entity was less profitable in year 2 (net income was lower in year 2), then expenses that appear in the income statement between operating income and net income, i.e., expenses that are deducted from operating income, must have been greater in year 2 than in year 1. An increase in income tax expense or interest expense could explain how even though operating income in year 2 was higher than in year 1, if income taxes or interest expense were also higher, this could have resulted in a lower net income for year 2 if the increase in either of these expenses was greater than the increase in operating income.

4. H

Percentages measure proportional changes. The items being compared must have changed proportionately if the percentage did not change.

Solution 4-7 SIMULATION ANSWER: Substantive Tests

Part a:

Objective	Substantive Tests
1. Verify existence of accounts receivable.	A
2. Determine that inventory balance is accurately stated.	E

(ID: 9224)

1. A

Performing tests of subsequent cash receipts after the balance sheet date would help verify the existence of accounts receivable since they should have been paid by then if they were valid balances. False accounts receivable would not be paid.

2. E

Performing shipping cut-off procedures would help determine that the inventory balance is accurately stated because to include inventory that was shipped before the end of the year would overstate the inventory balance.

Part b:

Answers: D, F

Examining paid vendors' invoices would allow the auditor to determine whether liabilities are valued accurately in the financial statements. Also, examining an analysis of inventory turnover would allow the auditor to determine whether there may be slow moving or obsolete inventory.

Solution 4-8 SIMULATION ANSWER: Analytics

Part a:

Use the data in Pacific Gourmet's financial statements to calculate for year 2 the analytical ratios indicated in the table below to 2 decimal places. (For turnover ratios, year-end balances should be used. All calculations are based on a 365-day year.)

Ratio	Year 2	Year 1
1. Current ratio	3.42	3.07
2. Return on equity	13.77%	28.21%

1. 3.42

The current ratio equals current assets divided by current liabilities (85,280,000/24,965,000).

2. 13.77%

Return on equity equals net income divided by average stockholder's equity. Editor Note: Be careful to follow directions. This problem specifies that for turnover ratios, year-end balances should be used (13,815,000 / 100,315,000).

Part b:

The table below presents several ratios that were considered significant in the current and prior year's audits of Pacific Gourmet. Compare the values for each ratio. Then select the most likely explanation for the analytical results. An explanation may be used once, more than once, or not at all. (You should not recalculate ratios. Turnover ratios are based on average balances.)

Ratio	Year 2	Year 1	Explanations
1. Days sales in accounts receivable	40	39	E
2. Operating profit margin	22.05%	34.62%	B

(ID: 9223)

1. E

Days sales in accounts receivable equals 360 days divided by receivables turnover. Receivables turnover equals net credit sales divided by average net receivables. If a larger percentage of sales occurred during the last month of the year, average receivables would increase which would then decrease receivables turnover, thereby increasing days sales in accounts receivable.

2. B

Operating profit margin equals operating profit divided by total sales revenue. Operating profit equals gross profit minus operating expenses. Therefore, if operating expenses increase at a higher rate than sales revenue, then operating profit would decrease more than sales revenue would increase, thereby decreasing operating profit margin.

Solution 4-9 SIMULATION ANSWER: Ratios

Each of the following represent financial ratios calculated from the prior year's financial statements. For each ratio, calculate the current year's ratio from the financial statements presented. Calculations should be rounded, if necessary, to the same number of places as the prior year's ratios.

Ratio	Year 2	Year 1
1. Current ratio	3.1	2.5
2. Quick ratio	1.6	1.3
3. Accounts receivable turnover	7.5	9.0
4. Inventory turnover	3.0	1.5

(ID: 9225)

1. 3.1

The current ratio is total current assets divided by total current liabilities. ($310,000 / $100,000 = 3.1)

2. 1.6

The quick (or acid-test) ratio is cash plus marketable securities plus net receivables divided by current liabilities. [($60,000 + $100,000) / $100,000 = 1.6]

3. 7.5

Accounts receivable turnover is net credit sales divided by average net receivables. {$750,000 / [($100,000 + $100,000) / 2] = 7.5}

4. 3.0

Inventory turnover is cost of goods sold divided by average inventory. {$450,000 / [($150,000 + $150,000) / 2] = 3.0}

Solution 4-10 SIMULATION ANSWER: Analytics

For each observed change, select the most likely explanations from the accompanying list.

Observed Changes	Explanations
1. Inventory turnover increased substantially from the prior year. (3 explanations)	A, B, D
2. Accounts receivable turnover decreased substantially from the prior year. (3 explanations)	A, B, E

(ID: 9226)

1. A, B, D

Inventory turnover is cost of goods sold divided by average inventory. When cost of goods sold is overstated, this ratio will increase. Due to recording consignment items shipped during the last month as sales, the cost of goods sold is overstated. Due to not recording a significant number of credit memos for returned merchandise, the cost of goods sold is overstated. When average inventory is understated, this ratio will increase. The incorrect exclusion of inventory received before year-end, caused average inventory to be understated.

2. A, B, E

Accounts receivable turnover is net credit sales divided by average net receivables. This ratio will decrease when net credit sales decreases or average net receivables increases. Due to recording consignment items shipped during the last month as sales, sales and accounts receivable are both overstated by the same amount.

However, proportionately, accounts receivable increases more than net credit sales, decreasing the ratio. Due to not recording a significant number of credit memos for returned merchandise, sales and accounts receivable are disproportionately overstated. A larger percentage of sales occurring during the last month of the year, as compared to the prior year, increases the amount in accounts receivable. This increases average accounts receivable, as compared to last year, without increasing sales, as compared to last year.

Solution 4-11 SIMULATION ANSWER: Research

Which citation in the professional standards provides guidance when the auditor finds it necessary to modify existing audit documentation or add new audit documentation after the documentation completion date in circumstances other than when new audit procedures are performed or the auditor draws new conclusions after the date of the audit report?

AU	§	230	18	(ID: 90392)

18. In circumstances other than those addressed in paragraph .14 in which the auditor finds it necessary to modify existing audit documentation or add new audit documentation after the documentation completion date, the auditor should, regardless of the nature of the modifications or additions, document
    a. the specific reasons for making the changes; and
    b. when and by whom they were made and reviewed.

Solution 4-12 SIMULATION ANSWER: Analytics

You are the audit manager assigned to Joe's Office Supply. Based on substantive test work, the staff auditor has proposed the journal entries below to be presented to the client. Assume all proposed journal entries are valid and material.

For each journal entry, indicate its effect (*increased*, *decreased*, or had *no impact*) on the calculations in columns D, E, and F.

A	B	C	D	E	F
Proposed Journal Entry	**Debit**	**Credit**	**Earnings per Share**	**Days Sales in Accounts Receivable**	**Gross Profit**
1. Sales reported after year-end that should have been reported before year-end: Cost of sales Accounts receivable Sales Inventory	 90 100	 100 90	Increased	Increased	Increased
2. Error in adjusting entry: Cost of sales PP&E Utilities expense Cash Sales Accrued expenses Inventory Interest expense	 45 45 12 10	 45 12 45 10	Decreased	Decreased	No Impact
3. To record current and deferred income taxes: Income tax expense-current Deferred tax asset Income tax expense-deferred Deferred tax liability Income tax payable	 50 15	 10 5 50	Decreased	No Impact	No Impact

(ID: 89451)

Ratios:

Earnings per Share: $\frac{\text{Net Income – Preferred Dividends}}{\text{Average Number of Common Shares Outstanding}}$

Days Sales in Accounts Receivable: $\frac{\text{Net Accounts Receivable}}{\text{Net Credit Sales / 360}}$

Gross Profit: Sales-Cost of Goods Sold

1. Earnings per Share: Increased

   The increase in sales increased net income so the earnings per share ratio would increase.

   Days Sales in Accounts Receivable: Increased

   Accounts receivable increased proportionately more than credit sales per day increased so the days sales in accounts receivable ratio would increase.

   Gross Profit: Increased

   Sales increased more than the cost of sales so gross profit would increase.

2. Earnings per Share: Decreased

   The increase in expense decreased net income so the earnings per share ratio would decrease.

   Days Sales in Accounts Receivable: Decreased

   Accounts receivable did not change and credit sales per day increased so the days sales in accounts receivable ratio would decrease.

   Gross Profit: No impact

   Sales and cost of sales increased by the same amount so there was no change in gross profit.

3. Earnings per Share: Decreased

   The increase in taxes decreased net income so the earnings per share ratio would decrease.

   Days Sales in Accounts Receivable: No impact

   The accounts that changed are not used in the calculation of this ratio.

   Gross Profit: No impact

   The accounts that changed are not used in the calculation of gross profit.

Solution 4-13 SIMULATION ANSWER: Analytics

The table below presents some ratios that were considered significant in the current and prior year's audit of Duke. Compare the values for each ratio. Then select the most likely explanation for the analytical results. An explanation may be used once, more than once, or not at all. (You should **not** recalculate ratios.)

Ratio	Year 2	Year 1	Explanations
1. Debt to equity	1.99	4.61	D
2. Gross profit percentage	38.00%	41.00%	F

(ID: 9227)

1. D

The debt to equity ratio equals total liabilities divided by shareholder's equity. Therefore, if capital stock was issued during the year, equity would increase, thereby decreasing the ratio.

2. F

Gross profit percentage equals sales less the cost of goods sold divided by sales. If manufacturing cost decreased less than sales decreased during the year, then the numerator would decrease more in proportion to the denominator, thereby decreasing the percentage.

Solution 4-14 SIMULATION ANSWER: Types of Audit Procedures

During the year 1 audit of Numbaro Co., the auditor performed various procedures.

For each of the descriptions of audit procedures listed below, select the type of audit procedure that the auditor performed. A type of audit procedure may be selected once, more than once, or not at all.

Description of Procedure	Type of Audit Procedure
1. During the physical inventory count, the auditor requested that certain material containers be opened to ensure they were not empty.	Inspection
2. During a site visit to a branch warehouse, the auditor noted unauthorized personnel have access to the inventory.	Observation
3. The auditor obtained a copy of the company's accounting manual and read the section on inventory to prepare for the physical inventory observation.	Inspection
4. The auditor sent a letter to the company's outside attorney accompanied by management's request for information concerning pending or threatened litigation, claims, and assessments.	Inquiry
5. The auditing firm's computer assisted audit specialist obtained an electronic billing file from the company and checked the accuracy of the summarized billings file.	Recalculation
6. The auditor obtained the company's aging of accounts receivable and independently created the aging of certain accounts.	Reperformance
7. The auditor scanned the repairs and maintenance account for unusually large amounts.	Analytical

(ID: 89452)

1. G. Inspection

   Inspection consists of examining records, documents, or tangible assets. Inspection of individual inventory items ordinarily accompanies the observation of inventory counting. Note: Inspection of tangible assets may provide appropriate audit evidence with respect to their existence, but not necessarily about the entity's rights and obligations or the valuation of the assets.

2. I. Observation

   Observation consists of looking at a process or procedure being performed by others. Observation provides audit evidence about the performance of a process or procedure, but is limited to the point in time at which the observation takes place and by the fact that the act of being observed may affect how the process or procedure is performed.

3. G. Inspection

   Inspection consists of examining records, documents, or tangible assets. Note: Inspection of records or documents consists of examining records or documents, whether internal or external, in paper form, electronic form or other media.

4. F. Inquiry

   Inquiry consists of seeking information of knowledgeable persons, both financial and nonfinancial, inside or outside of the entity. Inquiries can be formal written inquiries or informal oral inquiries. The auditor should consider the reasonableness and consistency of the responses in light of the results of other procedures and the auditor's knowledge of the entity and its industry—evaluating responses to inquiries is an integral part of the inquiry process. Inquiry by itself does not provide sufficient appropriate audit evidence to detect misstatements or to test the operating effectiveness of controls; thus, auditors complement inquiries with other procedures to corroborate the responses received.

5. J. Recalculation

   Recalculation involves checking the mathematical accuracy of documents or records.

6. K. Reperformance

   Reperformance is the auditor's independent execution of procedures or controls that were originally performed as part of the entity's internal control, either manually or through the use of computer-assisted audit techniques (CAAT).

7. A. Analytical procedure

   Analytical procedures consist of evaluations of financial information made by a study of plausible relationships among both financial and nonfinancial data. Analytical procedures also encompass the investigation of identified fluctuations and relationships that are inconsistent with other relevant information or deviate significantly from predicted amounts. They range from simple comparisons, like this example, to the use of complex models.

Solution 4-15 SIMULATION ANSWER: Attorney Letters

The following situations represent excerpts from the responses to audit inquiries of external legal counsel of XYZ Co. during the annual audit of year 1. Each excerpt is independent.

- The client's year-end is December 31, year 1.
- The anticipated audit report date is February 15, year 2.
- All amounts are material to the financial statements.

For each excerpt, select the most appropriate audit response related to the financial statements in the audit response (financial statements) column. Then, in the audit response (attorney letter or audit report) column, select whether the attorney's legal response letter or the audit report needs to be updated; or if it is appropriately dated. Responses may be used once, more than once, or not at all.

Situations	Audit response	
	Financial Statements	**Attorney Letter or Audit Report**
1. Letter dated February 14, year 2: "I advise you that at and since December 31, year 1, I have not been engaged to give substantive attention to, or represent XYZ Co. in connection with any pending or threatened litigation, claims, or assessments, nor am I aware of any loss contingencies. No amounts were due to this office for services provided at December 31, year 1."	C. No impact on financial statements or the notes to the financial statements	A. Legal response is appropriately dated
2. Letter dated January 21, year 2: "I advise you that at and since December 31, year 1, I have not been engaged to give substantive attention to, or represent XYZ Co. in connection with any pending or threatened litigation, claims, or assessments, nor am I aware of any loss contingencies. There were fees outstanding of $3,675 due to this office for services provided at December 31, year 1."	F. Verify amount due attorney is recorded in financial statements	C. Update legal response
3. Letter dated February 26, year 2: "I advise you that at and since December 31, year 1, I have not been engaged to give substantive attention to, or represent XYZ Co. in connection with any pending or threatened litigation, claims, or assessments, except as follows: K. Bowt v. XYZ Co.: This matter commenced in December, year 1. The plaintiff alleges discrimination relating to his termination on November 17, year 1. The company intends to defend this case vigorously. At this time, we are unable to evaluate the likelihood of an unfavorable outcome or estimate the amount or range of potential loss.	A. Disclosure in the notes to the financial statements relating to nature of litigation, but no amount disclosed	B. Update report date

Solution 4-15 SIMULATION ANSWER: Attorney Letters (contd.)

Situations	Audit response	
	Financial Statements	**Attorney Letter or Audit Report**
4. Letter dated March 16, year 2: "I advise you that at and since December 31, year 1, I have not been engaged to give substantive attention to, or represent XYZ Co. in connection with any pending or threatened litigation, claims, or assessments, except as follows: J. Myers v. XYZ Co.: This matter commenced in March, year 2. The plaintiff alleges discrimination relating to his termination on November 17, year 1. The company intends to defend this case vigorously. At this time, we are unable to evaluate the likelihood of an unfavorable outcome. The plaintiff is demanding $50,000.	A. Disclosure in the notes to the financial statements relating to nature of litigation, but no amount disclosed	B. Update report date
5. Letter dated January 10, year 2: "I advise you that at and since December 31, year 1, I have not been engaged to give substantive attention to, or represent XYZ Co. in connection with any pending or threatened litigation, claims, or assessments, except as follows: R. Brown v. XYZ Co.: This matter commenced in November, year 1. The plaintiff alleges discrimination relating to his termination on March 17, year 1. The case was tentatively settled for $35,000, which will be covered by XYZ's insurance carrier.	E. Potential litigation settlement not accrued in financial statements, amount disclosed in the notes to the financial statements	C. Update legal response
6. Letter dated January 20, year 2: "I advise you that at and since December 31, year 1, I have not been engaged to give substantive attention to, or represent XYZ Co. in connection with any pending or threatened litigation, claims, or assessments, except as follows: L. Peep v. XYZ Co.: This matter commenced in November, year 1. The plaintiff alleges discrimination relating to his termination on March 17, year 1. The case was tentatively settled for $35,000.	D. Potential litigation settlement accrued in financial statements	C. Update legal response

(ID: 89453)

1. Financial Statements

C. No impact on financial statements or the notes to the financial statements

The attorney reported no activity.

2. Letter / Report

A. Legal response is appropriately dated

The date of the attorney's response and the anticipated release date of the audit report are only one day apart.

3. Financial Statements

F. Verify amount due attorney is recorded in financial statements

The attorney's response included the balance of fees outstanding, but no pending litigation, claims, or assessments.

4.	Letter / Report	C. Update legal response The date of the attorney's response (January 21, year 2) is not close enough to the anticipated release date of the audit report (February 15, year 2).
5.	Financial Statements	A. Disclosure in the notes to financial statements relating to nature of litigation, but no amount disclosed The attorney described pending litigation whose underlying cause was an event that existed at the date of the financial statements, but is unable to evaluate the likelihood of an unfavorable outcome or estimate the amount or range of the potential loss.
6.	Letter / Report	B. Update report date The attorney's response is dated after the anticipated release date of the audit report, thus the report would need to be updated.
7.	Financial Statements	A. Disclosure in notes to financial statements relating to nature of litigation, but no amount disclosed The attorney described pending litigation whose underlying cause was an event that existed at the date of the financial statements, but is unable to evaluate the likelihood of an unfavorable outcome.
8.	Letter / Report	B. Update report date The attorney's response is dated after the anticipated release date of the audit report, thus the report would need to be updated.
9.	Financial Statements	E. Potential litigation settlement not accrued in financial statements; amount disclosed in notes to financial statements The attorney's response described a tentative settlement of a claim (covered by the XYZ Company's insurance carrier) whose underlying cause was an event that existed at the date of the financial statements.
10.	Letter / Report	C. Update legal response The date of the attorney's response (January 10, year 2) is not close enough to the anticipated release date of the audit report (February 15, year 2).
11.	Financial Statements	D. Potential litigation settlement accrued in financial statements The attorney's response described a tentative settlement of a claim whose underlying cause was an event that existed at the date of the financial statements.
12.	Letter / Report	C. Update legal response The date of the attorney's response (January 20, year 2) is not close enough to the anticipated release date of the audit report (February 15, year 2).

CHAPTER 5

AUDIT PROGRAMS

AU Identifier Used for Clarified US GAAS in This Textbook

We have not continued to use the temporary AU-C identifier for the clarified auditing standards issued by the American Institute of Certified Public Accountants (AICPA). In this textbook these standards have an AU identifier.

CHAPTER 5

AUDIT PROGRAMS

I. Substantive Procedures (AU 330 continued)

A. Overview

The objective of the auditor is to obtain sufficient appropriate audit evidence regarding the assessed risk of material misstatement (RMM) through designing and implementing appropriate responses to those risks. Substantive procedures performed at the relevant assertion level are part of that response.

1. **Definition of Substantive Procedure** A substantive procedure is an audit procedure designed to detect material misstatements at the assertion level. Substantive procedures comprise:

   a. **Tests Of Details** Tests of details of classes of transactions, account balances, and disclosures

   b. **Substantive Analytical Procedures** Analytical procedures used as substantive procedures (as opposed to the use of analytical procedures as risk assessment procedures)

      Editor Note: The use of *substantive* analytical procedures during the audit is left to the auditor's professional judgment; however, US GAAS requires the use of analytical procedures at the start of the audit and near its end. Analytical procedures used as risk assessment procedures to plan the audit are required, as are analytical procedures during the overall review phase of the audit to help the auditor form a conclusion about the financial statements.

      US GAAS defines *analytical procedures* in the same manner regardless of their purpose in an audit: as evaluations of financial information through analysis of plausible relationships among both financial and nonfinancial data. Analytical procedures also encompass such investigation, as is necessary, of identified fluctuations or relationships that are inconsistent with other relevant information or that differ from expected values by a significant amount.

Exhibit 1 ▸ Substantive Procedures Mnemonic

C	Confirm
O	Observe
R	Retrace (Trace)
V	Vouch
A	Analytics
I	Inquire
R	Recompute

2. **Context: Further Audit Procedures Responsive to the Assessed RMM at the Relevant Assertion Level** The auditor should design and perform further audit procedures whose nature, extent, and timing are based on, and are responsive to, the assessed RMM at the relevant assertion level. In designing the further audit procedures to be performed, the auditor should:

   a. Consider the reasons for the assessed RMM at the relevant assertion level for each class of transactions, account balance, and disclosure, including:

      (1) The likelihood of material misstatement due to the particular characteristics of the relevant class of transactions, account balance, or disclosure (the inherent risk)

      (2) Whether the risk assessment takes account of relevant controls (the control risk), thereby requiring the auditor to obtain audit evidence to determine whether the controls are operating effectively (that is, the auditor intends to rely on the operating effectiveness of controls *in determining the nature, extent, and timing of substantive procedures*)

   b. Obtain more persuasive audit evidence the higher the auditor's assessment of risk

   Editor Note: Our comprehensive coverage of responding to assessed risks is covered in chapter 2; tests of controls are covered in chapter 3 and evaluating the audit evidence obtained from responding to assessed risks is covered in the first section of chapter 4.

B. Nature & Extent of Substantive Procedures
Depending on the circumstances, the auditor *may* determine:

- Performing only substantive analytical procedures will be sufficient to reduce audit risk to an acceptably low level, such as, for example, when the auditor's assessment of risk is supported by audit evidence from tests of controls
- Only tests of details are appropriate
- A combination of substantive analytical procedures and tests of details are most responsive to the assessed risks

1. **Nature**

   a. **The Nature of Both the Risk & the Assertion Is Relevant to the Design of Tests Of Details** For example, tests of details related to the existence or occurrence assertion *may* involve selecting from items contained in a financial statement amount and obtaining the relevant audit evidence (vouching). On the other hand, tests of details related to the completeness assertion may involve selecting from items that are expected to be included in the relevant financial statement amount and investigating whether they are included (tracing). For example, the auditor might inspect subsequent cash disbursements and compare them with the recorded accounts payable to determine whether any purchases had been omitted from accounts payable.

   b. **Applicability of Substantive Analytical Procedures** Substantive analytical procedures are *generally* more applicable to large volumes of transactions that tend to be predictable over time.

2. **Extent**

   a. **Substantive Procedures Are *Required* for All Relevant Assertions Related To Each Material Class** *Irrespective of the assessed RMM*, the auditor should design and perform substantive procedures for all relevant assertions related to each material class of transactions, account balance, and disclosure. This requirement reflects the facts that (a) the auditor's assessment of risk is judgmental and may not identify all RMM and (b) inherent limitations to internal control exist, including management override.

b. **Substantive Procedures *May* Need to Be Increased When Tests of Controls Indicate Weaknesses** Because the assessment of the RMM takes account of internal control, the extent of substantive procedures may need to be increased when the results from tests of controls are unsatisfactory. However, increasing the extent of an audit procedure is appropriate only if the audit procedure itself is relevant to the specific risk.

C. Timing of Substantive Procedures / Testing at an Interim Date

1. **Coverage of Remaining Period** If substantive procedures are performed at an interim date, the auditor should cover the remaining period by performing *either*:

   a. Substantive procedures, combined with tests of controls, or

   b. Further substantive procedures only

   —whichever provides a reasonable basis for extending the audit conclusions from the interim date to the period-end.

   In some circumstances, the auditor *may* determine that it is effective to perform substantive procedures at an interim date and compare and reconcile information concerning the balance at the period-end with the comparable information at the interim date to:

   - Identify amounts that appear unusual
   - Investigate any such amounts
   - Perform substantive analytical procedures or tests of details to test the intervening period

   Performing substantive procedures at an interim date without undertaking additional procedures at a later date increases the risk that the auditor will not detect misstatements that may exist at the period-end. This risk increases as the remaining period is lengthened. Factors such as the following *may* influence whether to perform substantive procedures at an interim date:

   - Effectiveness of the control environment and other relevant controls
   - Availability at a later date of information necessary for the auditor's procedures
   - Purpose of the substantive procedure
   - Assessed RMM
   - Nature of the class of transactions or account balance and relevant assertions
   - Ability of the auditor to perform appropriate substantive procedures or substantive procedures combined with tests of controls to cover the remaining period in order to reduce the risk that misstatements that may exist at the period-end will not be detected

   In circumstances in which the auditor has identified RMM due to fraud, the auditor *might* conclude that substantive procedures performed at or near the end of the reporting period best address such a risk because audit procedures to extend audit conclusions from an interim date to the period-end reporting date would not be effective.

Factors such as the following *may* influence whether to perform substantive *analytical* procedures with respect to the period between the interim date and the period-end:

- Whether the period-end balances of the particular classes of transactions or account balances are reasonably predictable with respect to amount, relative significance, and composition
- Whether the entity's procedures for analyzing and adjusting such classes of transactions or account balances at interim dates and establishing proper accounting cutoffs are appropriate
- Whether the information system relevant to financial reporting will provide information concerning the balances at the period-end and the transactions in the remaining period that is sufficient to permit investigation of the following:
    - Significant unusual transactions or entries (including those at or near the period-end)
    - Other causes of significant fluctuations or expected fluctuations that did not occur
    - Changes in the composition of the classes of transactions or account balances

2. **Re-evaluate Risk & the Need for Further Procedures for Remaining Period If Unexpected Misstatements Are Discovered at Interim Date** If misstatements that the auditor did not expect when assessing the RMM are detected at an interim date, the auditor should evaluate whether the related assessment of risk and the planned nature, extent, and timing of substantive procedures covering the remaining period need to be modified. Such modification *may* include extending or repeating, at the period-end, the procedures performed at the interim date.

D. Conditions That Require Substantive Procedures or Their Consideration

1. External Confirmations

a. **Determination of Whether to Use External Confirmations** The auditor should consider whether external confirmation procedures are to be performed as substantive audit procedures.

Editor Note: External confirmation procedures frequently *may* be relevant when addressing assertions associated with account balances and their elements but need not be restricted to these items. For example, the auditor *may* request external confirmation of the terms of agreements, contracts, or transactions between an entity and other parties. External confirmation procedures also *may* be performed to obtain audit evidence about the absence of certain conditions. For example, a request may specifically seek confirmation that no "side agreement" exists that may be relevant to an entity's revenue cut-off assertion.

Other situations in which external confirmation procedures *may* provide relevant audit evidence in responding to assessed RMM include the following:

- Bank balances and other information relevant to banking relationships
- Inventories held by third parties at bonded warehouses for processing or on consignment
- Property title deeds held by lawyers or financiers for safe custody or as security
- Investments held for safekeeping by third parties or purchased from stockbrokers but not delivered at the balance sheet date

- Amounts due to lenders, including relevant terms of repayment and restrictive covenants
- Accounts payable balances and terms

The auditor *may* determine that external confirmation procedures performed for one purpose provide an opportunity to obtain audit evidence about other matters. For example, confirmation requests for bank balances often include requests for information relevant to other financial statement assertions. Such considerations *may* influence the auditor's decision about whether to perform external confirmation procedures.

Factors that *may* assist the auditor in determining whether external confirmation procedures are to be performed as substantive audit procedures include the following:

- The confirming party's knowledge of the subject matter; responses may be more reliable if provided by a person at the confirming party who has the requisite knowledge about the information being confirmed
- The ability or willingness of the intended confirming party to respond (in such situations, confirming parties may not respond, may respond in a casual manner, or may attempt to restrict the reliance placed on the response); for example, the confirming party:
  - May not accept responsibility for responding to a confirmation request
  - May consider responding too costly or time consuming
  - May have concerns about the potential legal liability resulting from responding
  - May account for transactions in different currencies
  - May operate in an environment in which responding to confirmation requests is not a significant aspect of day-to-day operations
- The objectivity of the intended confirming party; if the confirming party is a related party of the entity, responses to confirmation requests may be less reliable

b. Accounts Receivable Confirmations Are Required With Three Exceptions The auditor should use external confirmation procedures for accounts receivable, **except** when one or more of the following is applicable:

(1) Immaterial Balance The overall account balance is immaterial.

(2) Ineffective External confirmation procedures for accounts receivable would be ineffective.

Editor Note: External confirmation procedures may be ineffective when, based on prior years' audit experience or experience with similar entities, response rates to properly designed confirmation requests will be inadequate; or responses are known or expected to be unreliable.

(3) Low Assessed RMM at Relevant Assertion Level & Other Procedures Address Same Risk The auditor's assessed level of RMM at the relevant assertion level is low, and the other planned substantive procedures address the assessed risk. However, in many situations, the use of external confirmation procedures for accounts receivable *and* the performance of other substantive procedures are necessary to reduce the assessed RMM to an acceptably low level.

In this context, *accounts receivable* means the entity's claims against customers that have arisen from the sale of goods or services in the normal course of business; and a financial institution's loans.

Editor Note: Although external confirmations may provide relevant audit evidence relating to certain assertions, some assertions exist for which external confirmations provide less relevant audit evidence. For example, external confirmations provide less relevant audit evidence relating to the recoverability of accounts receivable balances than they do of their existence.

2. **Substantive Procedures Related to the Financial Statement Closing Process** The auditor's substantive procedures should include audit procedures related to the financial statement closing process, such as:

   a. **Reconciling the Financial Statements With the Accounting Records** Agreeing or reconciling the financial statements with the underlying accounting records

   b. **Examining Material Journal Entries** Examining material journal entries and other adjustments made during the course of preparing the financial statements

      The nature and also the extent of the auditor's examination of journal entries and other adjustments depend on the nature and complexity of the entity's financial reporting process and the related RMM.

3. **Substantive Procedures Responsive to Significant Risks**

   a. If the auditor has determined that an assessed RMM at the relevant assertion level is a significant risk, the auditor should perform substantive procedures that are specifically responsive to that risk.

      Editor Note: For example, if the auditor identifies that management is under pressure to meet earnings expectations, a risk may exist that management is inflating sales by improperly recognizing revenue related to sales agreements with terms that preclude revenue recognition or by invoicing sales before shipment. In these circumstances, the auditor may, for example, design external confirmation procedures not only to confirm outstanding amounts but also to confirm the details of the sales agreements, including date, any rights of return, and delivery terms. In addition, the auditor may find it effective to supplement such external confirmation procedures with inquiries of nonfinancial personnel in the entity regarding any changes in sales agreements and delivery terms.

   b. When the approach to a significant risk consists only of substantive procedures, those procedures should include tests of details.

4. **Audit Documentation Related to Substantive Procedures**

   a. The auditor should include in the audit documentation the basis for any determination not to use external confirmation procedures for accounts receivable when the account balance is material.

   b. The auditor's documentation should demonstrate that the financial statements agree or reconcile with the underlying accounting records.

II. External Confirmations (AU 505)

A. Overview

Audit evidence in the form of external confirmations received directly by the auditor from confirming parties may be more reliable than evidence generated internally by the entity.

US GAAS (covered in the preceding section of this chapter) requires the auditor to (1) consider whether external confirmation procedures are to be performed as substantive audit procedures and (2) to use external confirmation procedures for accounts receivable unless:

- The overall account balance is immaterial
- External confirmation procedures would be ineffective, or
- The auditor's assessed level of the risk of material misstatement (RMM) at the relevant assertion level is low, and the other planned substantive procedures address the assessed risk

1. **Objective** The objective of the auditor, when using external confirmation procedures, is to design and perform such procedures to obtain relevant and reliable audit evidence.

2. **Definitions**

   a. **Exception** An exception is a response that indicates a difference between information requested to be confirmed, or contained in the entity's records, and the information provided by the confirming party.

   b. **External Confirmation** An external confirmation is audit evidence obtained as a direct *written* response to the auditor from a third party (the confirming party), either in paper form or by electronic or other medium, for example, through the auditor's direct access to information held by a third party. However, the auditor's access to a secure website (where data that addresses the subject matter of the confirmation is held) must be provided by the confirming party or a third-party service provider. Access codes or information necessary to access the confirming party's data that is provided to the auditor by management, does **not** meet the definition of an external confirmation.

   c. **Negative Confirmation Request** A negative confirmation request is a request that the confirming party respond directly to the auditor only if the confirming party disagrees with the information provided in the request.

   d. **Nonresponse** A nonresponse is a failure of the confirming party to respond, or fully respond, to a positive confirmation request or a confirmation request returned undelivered.

   e. **Positive Confirmation Request** A positive confirmation request is a request that the confirming party respond directly to the auditor by providing the requested information (known as a "blank" confirmation request) or indicating whether the confirming party agrees or disagrees with the information in the request.

   Editor Note: A response to a properly designed positive confirmation request ordinarily is expected to provide reliable audit evidence. A risk exists, however, that a confirming party may reply to the confirmation request without verifying that the information is correct. The auditor may reduce this risk by using positive confirmation requests that do not state the amount (or other information) on the confirmation request and that ask the confirming party to fill in the amount or furnish other information. On the other hand, use of this type of "blank" confirmation request may result in lower response rates because additional effort is required from the confirming parties to provide the requested information.

B. **External Confirmation Procedures**

1. **Maintain Control Over the Process** When using external confirmation procedures, the auditor should maintain control over external confirmation requests, including:

   a. **Determination of the Information Requested** Determining the information to be confirmed or requested

   b. **Selection of the Confirming Party** Selecting the appropriate confirming party

   c. **Design** Designing the confirmation requests, including determining that requests are properly directed to the appropriate confirming party and provide for being responded to directly to the auditor

   Determining that requests are properly addressed includes verifying the accuracy of the addresses, including testing the validity of some or all of the addresses on the confirmation requests before they are sent out, regardless of the confirmation method used. The nature and extent of the necessary procedures is dependent on the risks associated with the particular type of confirmation or address.

   d. **Sending the Requests** Sending the requests, including follow-up requests, when applicable, to the confirming party; the auditor *may* send an additional confirmation request when a reply to a previous request has not been received within a reasonable time

   Editor Note: The design of a confirmation request may directly affect the confirmation response rate and the reliability and nature of the audit evidence obtained from responses. Factors to consider when designing confirmation requests include:

   - The assertions being addressed
   - Specific identified RMM, including fraud risks
   - The layout and presentation of the confirmation request
   - Prior experience on the audit or similar engagements
   - The method of communication, for example, in paper form or by electronic or other medium
   - Management's authorization or encouragement to the confirming parties to respond to the auditor—confirming parties may only be willing to respond to a confirmation request containing management's authorization
   - The ability of the intended confirming party to confirm or provide the requested information, for example, individual invoice amount versus total balance

2. **Management's Refusal to Allow the Auditor to Perform External Confirmation Procedures** If management refuses to allow the auditor to perform external confirmation procedures, the auditor should:

   a. **Inquire About Management's Reasons & Determine Their Validity** Inquire about management's reasons for the refusal and seek audit evidence about their validity and reasonableness

   b. **Evaluate Effect on RMM & the Need for Further Audit Procedures** Evaluate the implications of management's refusal on the auditor's assessment of the relevant RMM, including the risk of fraud, and on the nature, extent, and timing of other audit procedures

c. **Perform Alternative Audit Procedures** Perform alternative audit procedures designed to obtain relevant and reliable audit evidence

Editor Note: The alternative audit procedures performed may be similar to those appropriate for a nonresponse covered in an editor note later in this section.

d. **When Refusal is Unreasonable or No Evidence Can Be Obtained by Other Means** If the auditor concludes that management's refusal to allow the auditor to perform external confirmation procedures is unreasonable or the auditor is unable to obtain relevant and reliable audit evidence from alternative audit procedures, the auditor should:

(1) Communicate with those charged with governance

(2) Determine the implications for the audit and the auditor's opinion

3. **Negative Confirmations** Negative confirmations provide less persuasive audit evidence than positive confirmations. Accordingly, the auditor should *not* use negative confirmation requests as the sole substantive audit procedure to address an assessed RMM at the assertion level, *unless* **all** of the following conditions are present:

a. The auditor has assessed the RMM as low and has obtained sufficient appropriate audit evidence regarding the operating effectiveness of controls relevant to the assertion.

b. The population of items subject to negative confirmation procedures comprises a large number of small, homogeneous account balances, transactions, or conditions.

c. A very low exception rate is expected.

d. The auditor is not aware of circumstances or conditions that would cause recipients of negative confirmation requests to disregard such requests.

Editor Note: The failure to receive a response to a negative confirmation request does not indicate either receipt by the intended confirming party of the confirmation request or verification of the accuracy of the information contained in the request. Accordingly, a failure of a confirming party to respond to a negative confirmation request provides significantly less persuasive audit evidence than does a response to a positive confirmation request.

Confirming parties also may be more likely to respond indicating their disagreement with a confirmation request when the information in the request is not in their favor but less likely to respond otherwise. For example, holders of bank deposit accounts may be more likely to respond if they believe that the balance in their account is understated in the confirmation request, but less likely to respond when they believe the balance is overstated. Therefore, sending negative confirmation requests to holders of bank deposit accounts *may* be a useful procedure in considering whether such balances may be understated, but is unlikely to be effective if the auditor is seeking evidence regarding overstatement.

4. Results of the External Confirmation Procedures

a. **Obtain Further Evidence When the Reliability of Responses Is Doubtful** Even when audit evidence is obtained from sources external to the entity, circumstances may exist that affect its reliability. If the auditor identifies factors that give rise to doubts about the reliability of the response to a confirmation request, the auditor should obtain further audit evidence to resolve those doubts. (All responses carry some risk of interception, alteration, or fraud—such risk exists regardless of whether a response is obtained in paper form or by electronic or other medium.)

(1) **Reliability Risks** The auditor's consideration of the reliability of the information obtained through the confirmation process to be used as audit evidence includes consideration of the risks that:

(a) The information obtained may not be from an authentic source.

(b) A respondent may not be knowledgeable about the information to be confirmed.

(c) The integrity of the information may have been compromised.

(2) **Consider Security Risks of System When Electronic Processes Are Used** When an electronic confirmation process or system is used, the auditor's consideration of the preceding risks includes the consideration of risks that the electronic confirmation process is not secure or is improperly controlled.

Responses received electronically (for example, by fax or e-mail) involve risks relating to reliability because proof of origin or identity of the confirming party may be difficult to establish, and alterations may be difficult to detect. The auditor *may* determine that it is appropriate to address such risks by utilizing a system or process that validates the respondent or by directly contacting the purported sender (for example, by telephone) to validate the identity of the sender of the response and to validate that the information received by the auditor corresponds to what was transmitted by the sender.

An electronic confirmation system or process that creates a secure confirmation environment *may* mitigate the risks of interception or alteration. If the auditor is satisfied that such a system or process is secure and properly controlled, evidence provided by responses received using the system or process *may* be considered reliable.

(3) **Evaluation of Disclaimers or Restrictions Included in Responses** A response to a confirmation request may contain restrictive language regarding its use. Such restrictions do not necessarily invalidate the reliability of the response as audit evidence. Whether the auditor may rely on the information confirmed and the degree of such reliance will depend on the nature and substance of the restrictive language. For example, boilerplate disclaimers of liability may not affect the reliability of the information; nor will restrictive language that does not relate to the assertion being tested.

When the auditor has doubts about the reliability of the response as a result of restrictive language, the auditor should obtain further audit evidence to resolve those doubts.

(4) **Unreliable Responses** If the auditor determines that a response to a confirmation request is *not* reliable, the auditor should evaluate the implications on the assessment of the relevant RMM, including the risk of fraud, and on the related nature, extent, and timing of other audit procedures.

b. **Perform Alternative Audit Procedures for Nonresponses** In the case of each nonresponse, the auditor should perform alternative audit procedures to obtain relevant and reliable audit evidence *unless* a determination (based on an evaluation of the confirmation results) can be made that it is not necessary to do so because relevant and reliable audit evidence has already been obtained. This may be the case if (1) even when all the nonresponses are assumed to be misstatements this would still not affect the auditor's decision about whether the financial statements are materially misstated; and (2) the auditor has not identified unusual qualitative factors or systematic characteristics related to the nonresponses, such as that all nonresponses pertain to year-end transactions.

Editor Note: The nature and extent of alternative procedures are affected by the account and assertion in question. Examples of alternative audit procedures the auditor *may* perform include:

- For accounts receivable balances, examining specific subsequent cash receipts (including matching such receipts with the actual items being paid), shipping documentation, or other client documentation providing evidence for the existence assertion

- For accounts payable balances, examining subsequent cash disbursements or correspondence from third parties and other records, such as receiving reports and statements that the client receives from vendors providing evidence for the completeness assertion

c. **An Oral Response Is a Nonresponse** An oral response to a confirmation request does **not** meet the definition of an *external confirmation* because it is not a direct written response to the auditor. However, provided that the auditor has not concluded that a direct written response to a positive confirmation is necessary to obtain sufficient appropriate audit evidence, the auditor may take the receipt of an oral response to a confirmation request into consideration *when determining the nature and extent of alternative audit procedures* required to be performed for nonresponses.

d. **When a Written Response to a Positive Confirmation Request Is Necessary to Obtain Sufficient Appropriate Audit Evidence** If the auditor has determined that a written response to a positive confirmation request is necessary to obtain sufficient appropriate audit evidence, alternative audit procedures will **not** provide the audit evidence the auditor requires. If the auditor does not obtain such confirmation, the auditor should determine the implications for the audit and the auditor's opinion.

e. **Investigate Exceptions to Determine If They Indicate a Misstatement** The auditor should investigate exceptions to determine whether they are indicative of misstatements. When a misstatement is identified, the auditor is required by US GAAS to evaluate whether such misstatement is indicative of fraud.

Editor Note: Exceptions also *may* indicate a deficiency, or deficiencies, in the entity's internal control over financial reporting.

f. **Evaluating the Evidence Obtained** The auditor should evaluate whether the results of the external confirmation procedures provide relevant and reliable audit evidence or whether further audit evidence is necessary.

III. Valuation of Investments in Securities & Derivative Instruments (AU 501 continued)

The objective of the auditor is to obtain sufficient appropriate audit evidence regarding the valuation of investments in securities and derivative instruments.

A. Audit Procedures Based on the Valuation Method

1. **Audit Procedures for Investments in Securities When Valuations Are Based on the Investee's Financial Results** When investments in securities are valued based on an investee's financial results, excluding investments accounted for using the equity method of accounting (investments accounted for using the equity method of accounting are considered a component of group financial statements), the auditor should obtain sufficient appropriate audit evidence in support of the investee's financial results, as follows:

   a. Obtain and read available financial statements of the investee and the accompanying audit report, if any, including determining whether the report of the other auditor is satisfactory for this purpose.

      (1) After obtaining and reading the audited financial statements of an investee, the auditor *may* conclude that additional audit procedures are necessary to obtain sufficient appropriate audit evidence. For example, the auditor may conclude that additional audit evidence is needed because of significant differences in fiscal year-ends, significant differences in accounting principles, changes in ownership, or the significance of the investment to the investor's financial position or results of operations.

      The auditor *may* need to obtain evidence relating to transactions between the entity and investee to evaluate the:

      (a) Propriety of the elimination of unrealized profits and losses on transactions between the entity and investee, if applicable

      (b) Adequacy of disclosures about material related party transactions or relationships

      (2) In determining whether the report of another auditor is satisfactory, the auditor *may* perform procedures such as making inquiries regarding the professional reputation and standing of the other auditor, visiting the other auditor, discussing the audit procedures followed and the results, and reviewing the audit plan and audit documentation of the other auditor.

   b. If the investee's financial statements are not audited, or if the audit report on such financial statements is not satisfactory, apply, or request that the investor entity arrange with the investee to have another auditor apply, appropriate auditing procedures to such financial statements, considering the materiality of the investment in relation to the financial statements of the investor entity.

   c. If the carrying amount of the investment reflects factors that are not recognized in the investee's financial statements or fair values of assets that are materially different from the investee's carrying amounts, obtain sufficient appropriate audit evidence in support of such amounts.

   d. If the difference between the financial statement period of the entity and the investee has or could have a material effect on the entity's financial statements, determine whether the entity's management has properly considered the lack of comparability and determine the effect, if any, on the audit report.

   e. With respect to subsequent events and transactions of the investee occurring after the date of the investee's financial statements but before the date of the audit report, the auditor should obtain and read available interim financial statements of the investee and make appropriate inquiries of management of the investor to identify such events and transactions that may be material to the investor's financial statements and that may need to be recognized or disclosed in the investor's financial statements.

f. If the auditor is not able to obtain sufficient appropriate audit evidence because of an inability to perform one or more of these procedures, the auditor should determine the effect on the auditor's opinion.

2. **Audit Procedures for Investments in Derivative Instruments & Securities Measured or Disclosed at Fair Value** With respect to investments in derivative instruments and securities measured or disclosed at fair value, the auditor should:

a. Determine whether the applicable financial reporting framework (AFRF) specifies the method to be used to determine the fair value of the entity's derivative instruments and investments in securities.

b. Evaluate whether the determination of fair value is consistent with the specified valuation method.

c. If estimates of fair value of derivative instruments or securities are based on valuation models:

(1) Used by broker-dealers or other third-party sources, the auditor should understand the method used in developing the estimate and consider if the guidance regarding the specialist's work is applicable, i.e., the auditor should, to the extent necessary, taking into account the significance of that specialist's work for the auditor's purposes, (in other words, if the specialist is a *management's specialist* per the definition in AU 500):

(a) Evaluate the competence, capabilities, and objectivity of that specialist.

(b) Obtain an understanding of the work of that specialist.

(c) Evaluate the appropriateness of that specialist's work as audit evidence for the relevant assertion.

(2) Used by the entity, the auditor should obtain sufficient appropriate audit evidence supporting management's assertions about fair value determined using the model.

3. **Audit Procedures for Investments in Securities Based on Cost** Procedures to obtain evidence about the valuation of securities that are recorded at cost *may* include inspection of documentation of the purchase price, confirmation with the issuer or holder, and testing discount or premium amortization either by recomputation or through the use of analytical procedures.

B. **Audit Procedures for Impairment Losses**
Regardless of the valuation method used, the AFRF *might* require recognizing, in earnings or other comprehensive income, an impairment loss for a decline in fair value that is other than temporary.

The auditor should:

1. Evaluate management's conclusion (including the relevance of the information considered) about the need to recognize an impairment loss for a decline in a security's fair value below its cost or carrying amount.

2. Obtain sufficient appropriate audit evidence supporting the amount of any impairment adjustment recorded, including an evaluation of compliance with the requirements of the AFRF.

Editor Note: Determinations of whether losses are other than temporary *may* involve estimating the outcome of future events and making judgments in determining whether factors exist that indicate that an impairment loss has been incurred at the end of the reporting period. These judgments are based on subjective as well as objective factors, including knowledge and experience about past and current events and assumptions about future events. The following are examples of such factors:

- Fair value is significantly below cost or carrying value and
  - The decline is attributable to adverse conditions specifically related to the security or specific conditions in an industry or a geographic area
  - The decline has existed for an extended period of time
  - For an equity security, management has the intent to sell the security or it is more likely than not that it will be required to sell the security before recovery
  - For a debt security, management has the intent to sell the security or it is more likely than not it will be required to sell the security before the security's anticipated recovery of its amortized cost basis (for example, if the entity's cash or working capital requirements or contractual or regulatory obligations indicate that the debt security will be required to be sold before the forecasted recovery occurs)
- The security has been downgraded by a rating agency.
- The financial condition of the issuer has deteriorated.
- Dividends have been reduced or eliminated or scheduled interest payments have not been made.
- The entity recorded losses from the security subsequent to the end of the reporting period.

C. Audit Procedures for Unrealized Appreciation or Depreciation

The auditor should obtain sufficient appropriate audit evidence about the amount of unrealized appreciation or depreciation in the fair value of a derivative that is recognized or that is disclosed because of the ineffectiveness of a hedge, including an evaluation of compliance with the requirements of the AFRF.

IV. Existence & Condition of Inventory (AU 501 continued)

A. Objective

The objective of the auditor is to obtain sufficient appropriate audit evidence regarding the existence and condition of inventory.

B. Audit Procedures

1. **When Inventory Is Material to the Financial Statements** If inventory is material to the financial statements, the auditor should:

   a. **Attend Counting of Physical Inventory** Attend the physical inventory counting, unless impracticable (general inconvenience is *not* a sufficient excuse), to:

      (1) Evaluate management's instructions and procedures for recording and controlling the results of the entity's physical inventory counting

      Matters relevant in evaluating management's instructions and procedures for recording and controlling the physical inventory counting *may* include whether they address:

      - The application of appropriate control activities (for example, the collection of used physical inventory count records, accounting for unused physical inventory count records, and count and recount procedures)
      - The accurate identification of the stage of completion of work in progress; slow moving, obsolete, or damaged items; and inventory owned by a third party (for example, on consignment)
      - The procedures used to estimate physical quantities, when applicable, such as may be needed in estimating the physical quantity of a coal pile
      - Control over the movement of inventory between areas and the shipping and receipt of inventory before and after the cutoff date

      (2) Observe the performance of management's count procedures

      (3) Inspect the inventory

      Editor Note: Inspecting inventory when attending physical inventory counting assists the auditor in ascertaining the existence of the inventory (though not necessarily its ownership) and in identifying obsolete, damaged, or aging inventory.

      (4) Perform test counts

      Editor Note: Performing test counts (for example, by tracing items selected from management's count records to the physical inventory and tracing items selected from the physical inventory to management's count records) provides audit evidence about the completeness and accuracy of those records.

   b. **Perform Audit Procedures Over the Entity's Final Inventory Records** Perform audit procedures over the entity's final inventory records to determine whether they accurately reflect actual inventory count results

   c. **When a Management's Specialist Takes the Inventory** When management engages specialists who take the physical inventory:

      (1) An inventory count performed by an external inventory firm engaged as a management specialist does not, by itself, provide the auditor with sufficient appropriate audit evidence. The auditor is required by US GAAS to perform certain procedures if information to be used as audit evidence has been prepared using the work of a management's specialist (see the first section of chapter 4).

(2) Although the auditor may adjust the extent of the work on the physical count of inventory because of the work of management's specialist, any restriction imposed on the auditor such that the auditor is unable to perform the procedures that the auditor considers necessary is a scope limitation. In such cases, US GAAS requires the auditor to modify the opinion in the audit report as a result of the scope limitation.

2. **When Physical Inventory Counting Is *Not* Conducted on the Date of the Financial Statements** If physical inventory counting is conducted at a date other than the date of the financial statements, the auditor should, in addition to the preceding procedures, perform audit procedures to obtain audit evidence about whether changes in inventory between the count date and the date of the financial statements are recorded properly.

Relevant matters for consideration when designing audit procedures to obtain audit evidence about whether changes in inventory amounts between the count date, or dates, and the final inventory records are recorded properly *may* include:

- Whether the perpetual inventory records are properly adjusted
- Reliability of the entity's perpetual inventory records
- Reasons for significant differences between the information obtained during the physical count and the perpetual inventory records

3. **When the Auditor Is Unable to Attend Physical Inventory Counting** If attendance at physical inventory counting is impracticable, the auditor should perform alternative audit procedures. If it is not possible to do so, the auditor should modify the opinion in the audit report.

a. **Alternate Audit Procedures *May* Provide Sufficient Appropriate Evidence** In some cases, when attendance is impracticable, alternative audit procedures (for example, observing a current physical inventory count and reconciling it to the opening inventory quantities or inspection of documentation of the subsequent sale of specific inventory items acquired or purchased prior to the physical inventory counting) may provide sufficient appropriate audit evidence. If the audit covers the current period and one or more periods for which the auditor had not observed or made some physical counts of prior inventories, alternative audit procedures, such as tests of prior transactions or reviews of the records of prior counts, may provide sufficient appropriate audit evidence about the prior inventories. The effectiveness of the alternative procedures that an auditor may perform is affected by the length of the period that the alternative procedures cover.

b. **When Alternate Audit Procedures Do *Not* Provide Sufficient Appropriate Evidence** In other cases, however, it may not be possible to obtain sufficient appropriate audit evidence by performing alternative audit procedures. In such cases, US GAAS requires the auditor to modify the opinion in the audit report as a result of the scope limitation.

4. **When the Inventory Is Material and Under the Custody & Control of a Third Party** If inventory under the custody and control of a third party is material to the financial statements, the auditor should perform one or both of the following:

   a. Request confirmation from the third party regarding the quantities and condition of inventory held on behalf of the entity

   b. Perform inspection or other audit procedures appropriate in the circumstances

      Depending on the circumstances (for example, when information is obtained that raises doubt about the integrity and objectivity of the third party), the auditor *may* consider it appropriate to perform other audit procedures instead of, or in addition to, confirmation with the third party. Examples of other audit procedures include:

      - Attending, or arranging for another auditor to attend, the third party's physical counting of inventory, if practicable
      - Obtaining another auditor's report on the adequacy of the third party's internal control for ensuring that inventory is properly counted and adequately safeguarded
      - Inspecting documentation regarding inventory held by third parties (for example, warehouse receipts)
      - Requesting confirmation from other parties when inventory has been pledged as collateral

V. Auditing Accounting Estimates & Related Disclosures (AU 540)

A. Overview

Some financial statement items cannot be measured precisely, but can only be estimated. US GAAS refers to such items as *accounting estimates*. The nature and reliability of information available to management to support the making of an accounting estimate varies widely, which affects the degree of estimation uncertainty associated with accounting estimates. The degree of estimation uncertainty varies based on the nature of the accounting estimate, the extent to which there is a generally accepted method or model used to make the accounting estimate, and the subjectivity of the assumptions used to make the accounting estimate. The degree of estimation uncertainty affects, in turn, the risks of material misstatement (RMM) of accounting estimates, including their susceptibility to unintentional or intentional management bias.

Some accounting estimates involve relatively low estimation uncertainty and may give rise to lower RMM. For example:

- Accounting estimates arising in entities that engage in business activities that are not complex
- Accounting estimates that are frequently made and updated because they relate to routine transactions
- Accounting estimates derived from data that is readily available, such as published interest rate data or exchange-traded prices of securities—such data may be referred to as observable in the context of a fair value accounting estimate
- Fair value accounting estimates in which the method of measurement prescribed by the applicable financial reporting framework (AFRF) is simple and applied easily to the asset or liability requiring measurement at fair value
- Fair value accounting estimates in which the model used to measure the accounting estimate is well-known or generally accepted, provided that the assumptions or inputs to the model are observable

However, for some accounting estimates, relatively high estimation uncertainty may exist, particularly when they are based on significant assumptions. For example:

- Accounting estimates relating to the outcome of litigation
- Fair value accounting estimates for derivative financial instruments not publicly traded
- Fair value accounting estimates for which a highly specialized entity-developed model is used or for which there are assumptions or inputs that cannot be observed in the marketplace

The measurement objective of accounting estimates can vary, depending on the AFRF and the financial item being reported. The measurement objective for some accounting estimates is to forecast the outcome of one or more transactions, events, or conditions giving rise to the need for the accounting estimate. For other accounting estimates, including many fair value accounting estimates, the measurement objective is different and is expressed in terms of the value of a current transaction or financial statement item based on conditions prevalent at the measurement date, such as estimated market price for a particular type of asset or liability. For example, the AFRF may require fair value measurement based on an assumed hypothetical current transaction between knowledgeable, willing parties (sometimes referred to as market participants) in an arm's length transaction, rather than the settlement of a transaction at some past or future date.

A difference between the outcome of an accounting estimate and the amount originally recognized or disclosed in the financial statements does *not* necessarily represent a misstatement of the financial statements; rather, it could be an outcome of estimation uncertainty. This is particularly the case for fair value accounting estimates because any observed outcome may be affected by events or conditions subsequent to the date at which the measurement is estimated for purposes of the financial statements.

1. **Objectives** The objective of the auditor is to obtain sufficient appropriate audit evidence about whether, in the context of the AFRF:

   a. Accounting estimates, including fair value accounting estimates, in the financial statements, whether recognized or disclosed, are reasonable

   b. Related disclosures in the financial statements are adequate

2. **Definitions**

   a. **Accounting Estimate** An accounting estimate is an approximation of a monetary amount in the absence of a precise means of measurement. This term is used for an amount measured at fair value when there is estimation uncertainty, as well as for other amounts that require estimation.

   b. **Auditor's Point Estimate or Auditor's Range** The amount or range of amounts, respectively, derived from audit evidence for use in evaluating the recorded or disclosed amount(s)

   c. **Estimation Uncertainty** The susceptibility of an accounting estimate and related disclosures to an inherent lack of precision in its measurement

   d. **Management Bias** A lack of neutrality by management in the preparation and fair presentation of information

      The susceptibility of an accounting estimate to management bias increases with the subjectivity involved in making it. Management bias may be unintentional or intentional. (When intention to mislead exists, management bias is fraudulent in nature.)

      Management bias can be difficult to detect at an account level. It may only be identified when considered in the aggregate of groups of accounting estimates or all accounting estimates or when observed over a number of accounting periods.

   e. **Management's Point Estimate** The amount selected by management for recognition or disclosure in the financial statements as an accounting estimate

   f. **Outcome of an Accounting Estimate** The actual monetary amount that results from the resolution of the underlying transaction(s), event(s), or condition(s) addressed by the accounting estimate

3. **Examples of Situations When Accounting Estimates May Be Required**

   a. **Examples of Other Than Fair Value Accounting Estimates**

      - Allowance for doubtful accounts
      - Inventory obsolescence
      - Warranty obligations
      - Depreciation method or asset useful life
      - Provision against the carrying amount of an investment when uncertainty regarding its recoverability exists
      - Outcome of long-term contracts
      - Costs arising from litigation settlements and judgments

b. Examples of Fair Value Accounting Estimates

- Complex financial instruments, which are not traded in an active and open market
- Share-based payments
- Property or equipment held for disposal
- Certain assets or liabilities acquired in a business combination, including goodwill and intangible assets
- Transactions involving the exchange of assets or liabilities between independent parties without monetary consideration (for example, a nonmonetary exchange of plant facilities in different lines of business)

B. Risk Assessment Procedures & Related Activities
The auditor should obtain an understanding of the following to provide a basis for the identification and assessment of the RMM for accounting estimates and to plan the nature, extent, and timing of further audit procedures:

1. **AFRF Requirements** The requirements of the AFRF relevant to accounting estimates, including related disclosures

2. **How Management Identifies Items to Estimate**

 a. How management identifies those transactions, events, and conditions that may give rise to the need for accounting estimates to be recognized or disclosed in the financial statements

 b. In obtaining this understanding, the auditor should make inquiries of management about changes in circumstances that may give rise to new, or the need to revise existing, accounting estimates

 Inquiries of management about changes in circumstances *may* include, for example, inquiries about whether:

 - The entity has engaged in new types of transactions that may give rise to accounting estimates
 - Terms of transactions that gave rise to accounting estimates have changed
 - Accounting policies relating to accounting estimates have changed as a result of changes to the requirements of the AFRF or otherwise
 - Regulatory or other changes outside the control of management have occurred that may require management to revise, or make new, accounting estimates

 In some cases, the auditor *may* obtain an understanding of how management identifies the need for accounting estimates and when to revise them primarily through inquiry of management. In other cases, when management's process is more structured, the auditor *may* perform risk assessment procedures directed at management's system for periodically reviewing the circumstances that give rise to the accounting estimates and re-estimating the accounting estimates as necessary. (The completeness of accounting estimates is often an important consideration of the auditor, particularly accounting estimates relating to liabilities.)

3. **Management's Methods** How management makes the accounting estimates and the data on which they are based, including:

 a. **Methods** Method(s), including, when applicable, the model, used in making the accounting estimate.

In some cases, the AFRF may prescribe the method, but often it does not. When it does not, there *may* be greater RMM.

b. **Relevant Controls** The preparation and fair presentation of the financial statements also requires management to establish financial reporting processes for making accounting estimates, *including adequate internal control.*

The auditor *may* consider the experience and competence of those who make the accounting estimates; and controls related to, for example, the review and approval of accounting estimates; or if a model is used, controls to prevent unauthorized changes to the model.

c. **Use of a Specialist** Whether management has used a specialist.

d. **Assumptions** The assumptions underlying the accounting estimates.

Assumptions may be characterized by predictions of future conditions, transactions, or events used in making an estimate and are integral components of accounting estimates. Their relevance and reliability vary.

In the case of fair value accounting estimates, assumptions are consistent with what knowledgeable, willing arm's-length parties would use in determining fair value when exchanging an asset or settling a liability.

e. **Changes** Whether there has been or ought to have been a change from the prior period in the method(s) or assumption(s) for making the accounting estimates and, if so, the reasons

If management has changed the method or assumption for making an accounting estimate, it is important that management can demonstrate that the new method or assumption is more appropriate; or is in response to changes in the environment or circumstances affecting the entity; or in the requirements of the AFRF.

f. **Estimation Uncertainty** Whether and, if so, how management has assessed the effect of estimation uncertainty

Matters the auditor *may* consider, to obtain this understanding include:

- Whether and, if so, how management has considered alternative assumptions or outcomes
- How management determines the accounting estimate when analysis indicates a number of outcome scenarios
- Whether management monitors the outcome of accounting estimates made in the prior period and has appropriately responded to the results of the monitoring process

4. **Review the Outcome of Accounting Estimates** The auditor should review the outcome of selected accounting estimates included in the prior period financial statements or, when applicable, their subsequent re-estimation for the current period.

The nature and extent of the auditor's review takes account of the nature of the accounting estimates and whether the information obtained from the review would be relevant to identifying and assessing RMM of accounting estimates made in the current period financial statements. However, the review is *not* intended to call into question the auditor's professional judgments made in the prior periods that were based on information available at the time.

As a practical matter, this risk assessment review *may* be done in conjunction with the review required by US GAAS related to fraud; see chapter 2 of this text. (That review of management judgments and assumptions related to significant accounting estimates is conducted as part of the requirement for the auditor to design and perform procedures to review accounting estimates for biases that could represent a RMM due to fraud, in response to the risks of management override of controls.)

The outcome of an accounting estimate will often differ from the accounting estimate recognized in the prior period financial statements. By performing risk assessment procedures to identify and understand the reasons for such differences, the auditor *may* obtain:

- Information regarding the effectiveness of management's prior period estimation process, from which the auditor can judge the likely effectiveness of management's current process
- Audit evidence that is pertinent to the re-estimation, in the current period, of prior period accounting estimates
- Audit evidence of matters that may be required to be disclosed in the financial statements, such as estimation uncertainty

Editor Note:

- A difference between the outcome of an accounting estimate and the amount recognized in the prior period financial statements does not necessarily represent a misstatement of the prior period financial statements. However, it may do so if the difference arises from information that was available to management when the prior period's financial statements were finalized or that could reasonably be expected to have been obtained and taken into account in the preparation of those financial statements; see chapter 8 of this text regarding subsequently discovered facts.
- When the RMM related to an accounting estimate has been significantly reduced by audit evidence relating to events occurring after management has made the estimate (for example, if litigation has been settled; the entity has sold an impaired asset; or receivables have been collected), the nature and extent of the activities and procedures just described in 3 and 4 may be significantly reduced or may not be necessary at all.

C. Identifying & Assessing the RMM

1. **Evaluate the Estimation Uncertainty** The auditor should evaluate the degree of estimation uncertainty associated with an accounting estimate. (This may influence the estimate's susceptibility to bias.)

   The degree of estimation uncertainty associated with an accounting estimate *may* be influenced by factors such as the:

   - Extent to which the accounting estimate depends on judgment
   - Sensitivity of the accounting estimate to changes in assumptions
   - Existence of recognized measurement techniques that may mitigate the estimation uncertainty (though the subjectivity of the assumptions used as inputs may, nevertheless, give rise to estimation uncertainty)
   - Length of the forecast period and the relevance of data drawn from past events to forecast future events
   - Availability of reliable data from external sources

- Extent to which the accounting estimate is based on observable or unobservable inputs
    - Observable inputs are developed based on market data obtained from sources independent of the reporting entity and are readily available, such as published interest rate data or exchange-traded prices of securities
    - Unobservable inputs reflect the entity's own judgments about what assumptions market participants would use in pricing the asset or liability, developed based on the best information available in the circumstances

Editor Note: In practice, the distinction between the two is not always apparent.

2. **Identify Significant Risks** The auditor should determine whether any of those accounting estimates that have been identified as having high estimation uncertainty give rise to significant risks.

D. **Responding to the Assessed RMM**
The auditor should consider whether specialized skills or knowledge with regard to one or more aspects of the accounting estimates is required to perform the following procedures.

However, for the majority of accounting estimates, even when estimation uncertainty exists, it is unlikely that specialized skills or knowledge will be required.

Matters that *may* affect the auditor's consideration of whether specialized skills or knowledge is required include:

- The nature of the underlying asset, liability, or component of equity in a particular business or industry (for example, mineral deposits, agricultural assets, or complex financial instruments)
- A high degree of estimation uncertainty
- Complex calculations or specialized models are involved (for example, when estimating fair value when no observable market exists)
- The complexity of the requirements of the AFRF relevant to accounting estimates, including whether there are areas known to be subject to differing interpretation or practice is inconsistent or developing
- The procedures that the auditor intends to undertake in responding to assessed risks

1. **Determinations Based on RMM** Based on the assessed RMM, the auditor should determine:

a. **Determine If AFRF Requirements Met** Whether management has appropriately applied the requirements of the AFRF relevant to the accounting estimate

Based on the understanding obtained in performing risk assessment procedures, the requirements of the AFRF that may be susceptible to misapplication or differing interpretations become the focus of the auditor's attention.

(1) In some situations, additional audit procedures, such as the inspection by the auditor of the current physical condition of an asset, *may* be necessary to determine whether management has appropriately applied the requirements of the AFRF.

(2) Collateral often is assigned for certain types of investments in debt instruments that either are required to be measured at fair value or are evaluated for possible impairment. If the collateral is an important factor in measuring the fair value of the investment or evaluating its carrying amount, it *may* be necessary for the auditor—in determining whether management has appropriately applied the requirements of the AFRF—to obtain audit evidence regarding the existence; value; rights; and access to, or transferability of, such collateral (including consideration of whether all appropriate liens have been filed and appropriate disclosures have been made).

b. **Determine If Methods Are Appropriate & Consistent** Whether the methods for making the accounting estimates are appropriate and have been applied consistently and whether any changes from the prior period in accounting estimates or the method for making them are appropriate in the circumstances

Editor Note: The auditor's consideration of a change in an accounting estimate or in the method for making it from the prior period is important because a change that is not based on a change in circumstances or new information is considered arbitrary. Arbitrary changes in an accounting estimate result in inconsistent financial statements over time and may give rise to a financial statement misstatement or be an indicator of possible management bias.

2. **Audit Procedures in Response to RMM** In responding to the assessed RMM, the auditor should undertake *one or more* of the following, *taking into account the nature of the accounting estimate*:

a. Determine whether events occurring up to the date of the audit report provide audit evidence regarding the accounting estimate

Obviously, this procedure *may* be an appropriate response when such events are both expected to occur and provide audit evidence that confirms or contradicts the accounting estimate.

For some accounting estimates, however, events occurring up to the date of the audit report are unlikely to provide audit evidence regarding the accounting estimate—the conditions or events relating to some accounting estimates develop only over an extended period.

b. Test how management made the accounting estimate and the data on which it is based; in doing so, the auditor should evaluate whether the:

(1) Method of measurement used is appropriate in the circumstances

For this purpose, matters that the auditor *may* consider include, for example, whether:

- Management's rationale for the method selected is reasonable
- Management sufficiently and appropriately has evaluated and applied the criteria, if any, provided in the AFRF to support the selected method
- The method is appropriate and sufficient data is available in the circumstances, given the nature of the asset or liability being estimated and the requirements of the AFRF relevant to accounting estimates
- The method is appropriate with regard to the business, industry, and environment in which the entity operates

In some cases, particularly when making fair value accounting estimates, management may use a model. Depending on the circumstances, matters that the auditor *may* also consider in testing the model include, for example, whether:

- The model is validated prior to usage, with periodic reviews to ensure it is still suitable for its intended use; the entity's validation process may include evaluation of:
  - The model's theoretical soundness and mathematical integrity, including the appropriateness of model parameters
  - The consistency and completeness of the model's inputs with market practices
  - The model's output compared with actual transactions
- Appropriate change control policies and procedures exist
- The model is periodically calibrated and tested for validity, particularly when inputs are subjective
- Adjustments are made to the output of the model, including in the case of fair value accounting estimates whether such adjustments reflect the assumptions that market participants would use in similar circumstances
- The model is adequately documented, including the model's intended applications and limitations and its key parameters, required inputs, and results of any validation analysis performed

(2) Assumptions used by management are reasonable in light of the measurement objectives of the AFRF

In evaluating the reasonableness of the assumptions supporting an accounting estimate, the auditor may identify one or more significant assumptions. If so, the existence of one or more significant assumptions *may* be an indicator that the accounting estimate has high estimation uncertainty and may, therefore, give rise to a significant risk related to recognition, measurement, or disclosure.

Matters that the auditor may consider in evaluating the reasonableness of the assumptions used by management *may* include:

- Whether individual assumptions appear reasonable
- Whether the assumptions are interdependent and internally consistent
- Whether the assumptions appear reasonable when considered collectively or in conjunction with other assumptions, either for that accounting estimate or for other accounting estimates
- In the case of fair value accounting estimates, whether the assumptions appropriately reflect observable market assumptions

The assumptions on which accounting estimates are based may reflect what management expects will be the outcome of specific objectives and strategies. In such cases, the auditor *may* perform audit procedures to evaluate the reasonableness of such assumptions by considering, for example, whether the assumptions are consistent with:

- The general economic environment and the entity's economic circumstances
- The plans of the entity

- Assumptions made in prior periods, if relevant
- The experience of, or previous conditions experienced by, the entity to the extent this historical information may be considered representative of future conditions or events
- Other assumptions used by management relating to the financial statements

The reasonableness of the assumptions used may depend on management's intent and ability to carry out certain courses of action and the auditor *may* use professional judgment to evaluate this; however, certain financial reporting frameworks may not permit management's intentions or plans to be taken into account when making an accounting estimate. This is often the case for fair value accounting estimates because their measurement objective requires that assumptions reflect those used by market participants.

Additional matters that the auditor *may* consider in evaluating the reasonableness of assumptions used by management underlying fair value accounting estimates include:

- When relevant, whether and, if so, how management has incorporated market-specific inputs into the development of assumptions
- Whether the assumptions are consistent with observable market conditions and the characteristics of the asset or liability being measured at fair value
- Whether the sources of market-participant assumptions are relevant and reliable and how management has selected the assumptions to use when a number of different market participant assumptions exist
- When appropriate, whether and, if so, how management considered assumptions used in, or information about, comparable transactions, assets, or liabilities

Further, fair value accounting estimates may comprise observable inputs, as well as unobservable inputs. When fair value accounting estimates are based on unobservable inputs, matters that the auditor *may* consider include, for example, how management supports:

- The identification of the characteristics of market participants relevant to the accounting estimate
- Modifications it has made to its own assumptions to reflect its view of assumptions market participants would use
- Whether it has incorporated appropriate information
- When applicable, how its assumptions take account of comparable transactions, assets, or liabilities

(3) Data on which the estimate is based is sufficiently reliable for the auditor's purposes

This procedure (testing how management made the accounting estimate and the data on which it is based) *may* be an appropriate response when the:

- Accounting estimate is a fair value accounting estimate developed on a model that uses observable and unobservable inputs

- Accounting estimate is derived from the routine processing of data by the entity's accounting system
- Auditor's review of similar accounting estimates made in the prior period financial statements suggests that management's current period process is likely to be effective
- Accounting estimate is based on a large population of items of a similar nature that individually are not significant

Testing how management made the accounting estimate and the data on which it is based *may* involve:

- Testing the extent to which data on which the accounting estimate is based is accurate, complete, and relevant; and whether the accounting estimate has been properly determined using such data and management assumptions
- Considering the source, relevance, and reliability of external data or information, including that received from management's specialists, to assist in making an accounting estimate
- Determining how management has taken into account the effect of events, transactions, and changes in circumstances occurring between the date that the estimate or inputs to the estimate were determined and the reporting date, if the estimate was not made as of a date that coincides with the reporting date (for example, a valuation by an independent appraiser may be as of a different date)
- Recalculating the accounting estimate and reviewing, for internal consistency, information used to determine the estimate
- Considering management's review and approval processes

c. Test the operating effectiveness of the controls over how management made the accounting estimate, together with appropriate substantive procedures.

This procedure *may* be an appropriate response when management's process has been well-designed, implemented, and maintained. For example:

- When controls exist for the review and approval of the accounting estimates by appropriate levels of management and, when appropriate, those charged with governance
- When the accounting estimate is derived from the routine processing of data by the entity's accounting system

d. Develop a point estimate or range to evaluate management's point estimate; for this purpose:

(1) If the auditor uses assumptions or methods that differ from management's, the auditor should obtain an understanding of management's assumptions or methods sufficient to establish that the auditor's point estimate or range takes into account relevant variables and to evaluate any significant differences from management's point estimate.

(2) If the auditor concludes that it is appropriate to use a range, the auditor should narrow the range, based on audit evidence available, until all outcomes within the range are considered reasonable.

Ordinarily, a range that has been narrowed to be equal to or less than performance materiality (see the section on materiality in chapter 2 of this text) is adequate for the purposes of evaluating the reasonableness of management's point estimate.

Developing a point estimate or range to evaluate management's point estimate *may* be an appropriate response when:

- An accounting estimate is not derived from the routine processing of data by the accounting system
- The auditor's review of similar accounting estimates made in the prior period financial statements suggests that management's current period process is unlikely to be effective
- The entity's controls within and over management's processes for determining accounting estimates are not well-designed or properly implemented
- Events or transactions between the period-end and the date of the audit report contradict management's point estimate
- There are alternative sources of relevant data available to the auditor that can be used in developing a point estimate or range

3. **Further Substantive Procedures to Respond to Significant Risks** In auditing accounting estimates that give rise to significant risks, the auditor's further substantive procedures are focused on the evaluation of:

- How management has assessed the effect of estimation uncertainty on the accounting estimate and the effect that such uncertainty may have on the appropriateness of the recognition of the accounting estimate in the financial statements
- The adequacy of related disclosures

a. **Estimation Uncertainty**

(1) **Perform Additional Procedures** For accounting estimates that give rise to significant risks, in addition to other required substantive procedures performed, the auditor should evaluate the following:

(a) How management has considered alternative assumptions or outcomes and why it has rejected them or how management has otherwise addressed estimation uncertainty in making the accounting estimate

When management has *not* considered alternative assumptions or outcomes, it may be necessary for the auditor to discuss with management, and request support for how it has addressed, the effects of estimation uncertainty on the accounting estimate.

(b) Whether the significant assumptions used by management are reasonable

An assumption used in making an accounting estimate may be deemed to be significant if a reasonable variation in the assumption would materially affect the measurement of the accounting estimate.

Support for significant assumptions derived from management's knowledge may be obtained from management's continuing processes of strategic analysis and risk management. Even without formal established processes, such as may be the case in smaller entities, the auditor *may* be able to evaluate the assumptions through inquiries of, and discussions with, management, along with other audit procedures, in order to obtain sufficient appropriate audit evidence. The auditor's considerations in evaluating management's assumptions have already been described in this section.

(c) When relevant to the reasonableness of the significant assumptions used by management or the appropriate application of the AFRF, management's intent to carry out specific courses of action and its ability to do so

(2) **Develop Auditor's Range** If management has not adequately addressed the effects of estimation uncertainty on the accounting estimates that give rise to significant risks, the auditor should, if considered necessary, develop a range with which to evaluate the reasonableness of the accounting estimate.

In preparing the financial statements, management may be satisfied that it has adequately addressed the effects of estimation uncertainty on the accounting estimates that give rise to significant risks. In some circumstances, however, the auditor *may* view the efforts of management as inadequate. This *may* be the case, for example, when, in the auditor's professional judgment:

- Sufficient appropriate audit evidence could not be obtained through the auditor's evaluation of how management has addressed the effects of estimation uncertainty
- It is necessary to explore further the degree of estimation uncertainty associated with an accounting estimate (for example, when the auditor is aware of wide variation in outcomes for similar accounting estimates in similar circumstances)
- It is unlikely that other audit evidence can be obtained (for example, through the review of events occurring up to the date of the audit report)
- Indicators of management bias in the making of accounting estimates may exist

The auditor's considerations in determining a range for this purpose have already been described in this section.

b. **Determine If Recognition & Measurement Criteria Comply With AFRF** For accounting estimates that give rise to significant risks, the auditor should obtain sufficient appropriate audit evidence about whether the following are in accordance with the requirements of the AFRF:

(1) Management's decision to recognize or not recognize the accounting estimates in the financial statements

When management has recognized an accounting estimate in the financial statements, the focus of the auditor's evaluation is on whether the measurement of the accounting estimate is *sufficiently reliable* to meet the recognition criteria of the AFRF.

With respect to accounting estimates that have *not* been recognized, the focus of the auditor's evaluation is on whether the recognition criteria of the AFRF have, in fact, been met. Even when an accounting estimate has appropriately not been recognized, there may be a need for disclosure of the circumstances in the notes to the financial statements. The auditor may also determine that there is a need to draw the reader's attention to a significant uncertainty by adding an emphasis-of-matter paragraph to the audit report.

(2) The selected measurement basis for the accounting estimates

With respect to fair value accounting estimates, some financial reporting frameworks presume that fair value can be measured reliably as a prerequisite to either requiring or permitting fair value measurements and disclosures. In some cases, this presumption may be overcome when, for example, no appropriate method or basis for measurement exists. In such cases, the focus of the auditor's evaluation is on whether management's basis for overcoming the presumption relating to the use of fair value set forth under the AFRF is appropriate.

4. **Evaluating the Reasonableness of the Accounting Estimates & Determining Misstatements** The auditor should evaluate, *based on the audit evidence*, whether the accounting estimates in the financial statements are either reasonable in the context of the AFRF or are misstated.

a. **Nature of Misstatements Related to Accounting Estimates** With regard to accounting estimates, a misstatement, whether caused by fraud or error, may arise as a result of one or some combination of the following circumstances.

(1) **Factual Misstatements** Misstatements about which no doubt exists

(2) **Judgmental Misstatements** Differences arising from management's judgments concerning accounting estimates that the auditor considers unreasonable; or the selection or application of accounting policies that the auditor considers inappropriate

(3) **Projected Misstatements** The auditor's best estimate of misstatements in populations involving the projection of misstatements identified in audit samples to the entire population from which the samples were drawn

b. **Misstatement Due to a Difference Between Management's & the Auditor's Point Estimate** When the audit evidence supports the development of a point estimate by the auditor, the difference between the auditor's and management's point estimate constitutes a misstatement. The misstatement is no less than the difference between management's point estimate and the nearest point of the auditor's range.

c. **Misstatement Due to an Arbitrary Change in Accounting Principle or Method of Applying It** When management has changed an accounting estimate, or the method in making it, from the prior period based on a subjective assessment that there has been a change in circumstances, the auditor may conclude that the accounting estimate is misstated as a result of an arbitrary change by management or may regard it as an indicator of possible management bias.

d. **Accounting Estimates Included in Notes to the Financial Statements Are Evaluated Similarly to Those in the Financial Statements** Evaluating the reasonableness of accounting estimates and related disclosures included in the notes to the financial statements, whether required by the AFRF or disclosed voluntarily, involves essentially the same types of considerations applied when auditing an accounting estimate recognized in the financial statements.

e. **Written Representations About the Reasonableness of Accounting Estimates** Part of the auditor's audit evidence includes written representations from management about whether management believes significant assumptions used in making accounting estimates are reasonable.

f. **Communication With Those Charged With Governance Related to Accounting Estimates** The auditor is required to communicate the auditor's views about the qualitative aspects of the entity's significant accounting practices, including accounting estimates, and, when applicable, is required to determine that those charged with governance are informed about the process used by management in formulating particularly sensitive accounting estimates and about the basis for the auditor's conclusions regarding the reasonableness of those estimates.

5. **Indicators of Possible Management Bias** The auditor should review the judgments and decisions made by management in the making of accounting estimates to identify whether indicators of possible management bias exist. Indicators of possible management bias do not, themselves, constitute misstatements for the purposes of drawing conclusions on the reasonableness of individual accounting estimates.

   Examples of indicators of possible management bias with respect to accounting estimates *may* include:

   - Changes in an accounting estimate, or the method for making it, when management has made a subjective assessment that there has been a change in circumstances
   - The use of an entity's own assumptions for fair value accounting estimates when they are inconsistent with observable market assumptions
   - The selection or construction of significant assumptions that yield a point estimate favorable for management objectives
   - The selection of a point estimate that may indicate a pattern of optimism or pessimism

   Such indicators *may* affect the auditor's conclusion about whether the auditor's risk assessment and related responses remain appropriate, and the auditor *may* need to consider the implications for the rest of the audit and the auditor's opinion.

E. Disclosures Related to Accounting Estimates

1. **AFRF Requirements** The auditor should obtain sufficient appropriate audit evidence about whether the disclosures in the financial statements related to accounting estimates are in accordance with the requirements of the AFRF.

   Disclosures *may* include the:

   - Assumptions used
   - Method of estimation used, including any applicable model(s)
   - Basis for the selection of the method of estimation
   - Effect of any changes to the method of estimation from the prior period
   - Sources and implications of estimation uncertainty

   Some financial reporting frameworks *may* require specific disclosures regarding uncertainties:

   - The disclosure of key assumptions and other sources of estimation uncertainty that have a significant risk of causing a material adjustment to the carrying amounts of assets and liabilities; such requirements may be described using terms such as *key sources of estimation uncertainty* or *critical accounting estimates*
   - The disclosure of the range of possible outcomes and the assumptions used in determining the range
   - The disclosure of information regarding the significance of fair value accounting estimates to the entity's financial position and performance
   - Qualitative disclosures, such as the exposures to risk and how they arise; the entity's objectives, policies, and procedures for managing the risk; and the methods used to

measure the risk, and any changes from the previous period of these qualitative concepts

- Quantitative disclosures, such as the extent to which the entity is exposed to risk, based on information provided internally to the entity's key management personnel, including credit risk, liquidity risk, and market risk

2. **Significant Risks / Estimation Uncertainty** For accounting estimates that give rise to significant risks, the auditor should also evaluate the adequacy of the disclosure of estimation uncertainty in the financial statements even when the disclosures are in accordance with the AFRF.

   The auditor's evaluation of the adequacy of disclosure of estimation uncertainty increases in importance the greater the range of possible outcomes of the accounting estimate in relation to materiality.

F. **Audit Documentation**
The auditor should include in the audit documentation:

1. **Significant Risks** For those accounting estimates that give rise to significant risks, the basis for the auditor's conclusions about the reasonableness of accounting estimates and their disclosure

2. **Management Bias** Any indicators of possible management bias

G. **Examples of Accounting Estimates Included in Financial Statements**
The following are examples of accounting estimates that are included in financial statements. The list is not all-inclusive.

- Receivables
  - Uncollectible receivables
  - Allowance for loan losses
  - Valuation of long-term unconditional promises to give
- Inventories
  - Obsolete inventory
  - Net realizable value of inventories when future selling prices and future costs are involved
  - Losses on purchase commitments
- Financial instruments
  - Valuation of securities
  - Probability of high correlation of a hedge
  - Sales of securities with puts and calls
- Productive facilities, natural resources, and intangibles
  - Useful lives and residual values
  - Depreciation and amortization methods
  - Impairment analysis
  - Recoverability of costs
  - Recoverable reserves

- Accruals
  - Property and casualty insurance company loss reserves
  - Compensation in stock option plans and deferred plans
  - Warranty claims
  - Taxes on real and personal property
  - Renegotiation refunds
  - Actuarial assumptions in benefit costs
- Revenues
  - Airline passenger revenue
  - Subscription income
  - Freight and cargo revenue
  - Dues income
  - Losses on sales contracts
- Contracts
  - Revenue to be earned
  - Costs to be incurred
  - Percent of completion
- Leases
  - Initial direct costs
  - Executory costs
- Litigation
  - Probability of loss
  - Amount of loss
- Rates
  - Annual effective tax rate in interim reporting
  - Imputed interest rates on receivables and payables
  - Gross profit rates under program method of accounting
- Other
  - Losses and net realizable value on disposal of segment or restructuring of a business
  - Fair values in nonmonetary exchanges
  - Interim period costs in interim reporting
  - Current values in personal financial statements

VI. Audit Programs

The exhibits of sample audit programs and their related objectives, examples, and descriptions in this section are **not** US GAAS; they are provided as illustrations to enhance the understanding of audit procedures (and assertions) for specific types of accounts.

A. Cash

The audit procedures in exhibit 2 generally are performed during the audit of cash accounts to obtain supporting evidence of the objectives.

1. **Audit Objectives' Focus** To ensure (a) there are adequate internal control policies and procedures over cash, (b) all cash that should be in the custody of the client is (existence), (c) all of the cash in custody of the client is recorded properly (completeness), and (d) the cash in the custody of the client is disclosed properly in the financial statements.

2. **Subfunctions** Subfunctions for cash include (a) accounts receivable, (b) accounts payable, (c) cash sales, and (d) general ledger accounting.

3. **Kiting** This is the practice whereby an employee who is embezzling funds makes a transfer of funds from a bank account in one bank to a bank account in another bank near the end of the period. The transfer is effected through the use of a check and, therefore, does not show up as a withdrawal from the first bank until the check clears. It is listed as a deposit in transit on the receiving bank's books but not as an outstanding check on the disbursing bank's books. As a result, the overall cash balance is temporarily overstated at the balance sheet date and the embezzlement is not detected.

Example 1 ▸ Kiting

Allen Richards is the bookkeeper for Diversified Inc. Diversified has two bank accounts—one in the First Federal Bank and another in the Fourth National Bank. On a hot tip from Allen's investment broker, Allen writes himself a $5,000 check on the First Federal account, makes no entry, and purchases stock in STCG Inc. Shortly thereafter, STCG Inc. is subjected to SEC investigation and all trading in its stock is frozen. As the end of the year nears, Allen's predicament remains unchanged. To cover the defalcation, Allen writes a $5,000 check on the Fourth National account on December 31 and deposits it in the First Federal account on the same day. Furthermore, he makes no entry in the cash disbursements journal and fails to list the check as outstanding on the year-end bank reconciliation. The check will not show up as a decrease in the Fourth National account until it clears, so that account will still reflect the same account balance without the check deduction, and the First Bank will reflect the $5,000 deposited as of December 31. The money "appears" to be in both accounts, when in reality, only due to the delay in transaction posting, it is not.

Exhibit 2 ▶ Sample Program for Cash

Procedures	Assertions*
1. Prepare proof of cash—to ascertain that all recorded receipts have been deposited in the bank	Existence
2. Account for all check numbers—to determine whether there are any missing or outstanding checks that might cause the cash balance to be overstated	Completeness
3. Obtain and review or prepare a year-end bank reconciliation—to accurately determine the client's actual cash position at the close of the period	Completeness
4. Obtain a bank cutoff statement directly from the bank—to ascertain whether the items on the year-end reconciliation have cleared the bank and, therefore, were valid. Bank cutoff statements generally are requested for one to two weeks after year-end. After finishing this procedure, the cutoff bank statement is given to the client. This procedure is useful for detecting kiting between account balances.	Completeness Cutoff
5. Investigate any checks made to cash or bearer—to determine the propriety of the disbursement	Rights & Obligations
6. Trace a sample of entries in the cash receipts journal to the A/R subsidiary ledger, duplicate deposit ticket, and general ledger—to determine whether the cash is stated accurately	Valuation & Allocation Completeness
7. Simultaneously count all cash on hand—to ensure that no cash is counted more than once (coordinate with count of marketable securities on hand)	Existence
8 Investigate NSF checks and other debit memos—because these may be an indication of the covering up of a cash shortage	Existence
9. Prepare a schedule of bank transfers around year-end—to help detect kiting	Existence
10. Confirm the existence of year-end bank balances of the following: a. Amounts on deposit b. Direct liabilities c. Contingent liabilities on notes discounted d. Other direct or contingent liabilities e. Other security agreements	Existence Rights & Obligations
11. Determine If any cash is restricted—so that the restricted balance is classified properly on the balance sheet, and requirements of compensating balance agreements are disclosed properly	All Presentation & Disclosure Assertions

* Note that many procedures may test multiple assertions. This program is not intended to be a complete presentation. See chapter 2 in section V.F.1.b. for details on assertions.

B. Accounts Receivable & Sales

The procedures (and the purpose behind each procedure) in exhibit 3 generally are performed during the audit of accounts receivable and sales to obtain supporting evidence of the objectives.

1. **Audit Objectives' Focus** To ascertain: (a) adequate internal control policies and procedures exist; (b) all sales and receivables that should be recorded are properly recorded (completeness); (c) only sales and receivables that should be recorded are recorded (existence); and (d) accounts receivable are presented at approximate realizable value

2. **Subfunctions** After the audit objectives for an audit area are specified, they should be broken into subfunctions. For accounts receivable and sales, possible subfunctions include (a) credit granting, (b) billing, (c) shipping, (d) cash receipts, (e) detailed ledger bookkeeping, and (f) general ledger accounting

3. **Broad Outline of Audit Program for Accounts Receivable & Sales**

   a. **Interim Work** Possibilities include (1) obtaining an understanding of the internal control (may include walking through a transaction, inquiry, and observation), and (2) performing tests of controls as to operating effectiveness

   b. **Year-End Work: Sales** (1) Analytics (including ratio and trend analysis), (2) review sales cutoff and consignment sales, and (3) review sales returns and allowances and sales discounts

   c. **Year-End Work: Accounts Receivable** (1) Review aged trial balance, (2) confirm accounts receivable by positive and/or negative confirmations, and (3) review the bad debts allowance and expense

4. **Lapping** One of the most common types of fraud in connection with accounts receivable is lapping. Lapping occurs when a cashier conceals the theft of cash by stealing one customer's payment and then covering the theft by applying the next customer's payment received to the first customer's account and so on. The cashier may replace the stolen cash—ending the need to lap accounts—before the theft is discovered. In other cases, if inadequate segregation of duties allows the cashier to do so, the cashier may instead write off a customer's account equal to the amount of the cash stolen. This also ends the thief's need to lap accounts.

   Lapping is made possible through either bad internal control (i.e., having the same employee handle both the cash and the accounts receivable records) or collusion. In order to detect a lapping scheme, the auditor must compare the name, amounts, and dates shown on the customers' remittance advices with entries in the cash receipts journal and the related deposit slips.

Example 2 ▸ Lapping

Georgia Thomas is the bookkeeper for Farley Fabrics (a retail cloth distributor), and her duties consist of receiving the checks from the customers and recording the payments in the A/R subsidiary ledger. On January 8th, Georgia hears the president talk about a one-time purchase of a unique fabric by Colin's Casuals. She also hears that Colin's is going to make a $640 purchase. The next day, Colin's Casuals submits its order for that $640 of fabric. With all of this in mind, Georgia embezzles $640 of that day's payments received from Mama's Moo Moos and Jabba's Jammies (both of whom are regular customers of Farley). Georgia makes no entries in the accounts. Five days later, Colin's Casuals pays its bill, and Georgia credits the payments to Mama's and Jabba's accounts. Colin does no more business with Farley and, at the end of the year, Georgia writes off Colin's receivable as uncollectible.

Exhibit 3 ▸ Sample Program for A/R & Sales

Procedures	Assertions*
1. Compare a sample of shipping documents to the related sales invoices—to discover orders that have been shipped, but not billed	Completeness
2. Reconcile a sample of cash register tapes and sales tickets with the sales journals—so that evidence is gathered that shows that all sales have been recorded, and recorded accurately	Completeness Accuracy
3. Perform analytics—for example, a gross profit test, to determine that all sales have been recorded and classified correctly; investigate any unexpected fluctuations	Completeness Classification
4. Review sales discount procedures and documentation—to determine that discounts were granted only for payments received within the discount period	Accuracy
5. Vouch debits in individual A/R accounts to sales invoices—to determine whether the sales actually occurred	Occurrence Rights & Obligations
6. Review sales and receipts occurring near year-end—to ascertain that such transactions were recorded in the proper time period and were valid transactions	Cutoff Occurrence
7. Test foot the sales journal and reconcile with postings to the general ledger—to find out if the sales figures are accurate	Accuracy
8. Vouch debit entries in the allowance for doubtful accounts to individual accounts and original write-off authorizations—so that it can be determined that such write-offs were reflected properly in the accounts and were authorized	Valuation & Allocation
9. Prepare or obtain an aged A/R schedule—to (a) help identify accounts that should be written off, (b) determine the reasonableness of the bad-debt expense and allowance for doubtful accounts, and (c) aid the confirmation of A/R	Valuation & Allocation
10. Recalculate and review bad-debt expense and allowance—for reasonableness of expense and adequacy of the allowance	Valuation & Allocation
11. Examine cash receipts after the balance sheet date—to provide evidence of collectability at the balance sheet date	Valuation & Allocation
12. Confirm A/R on a test basis—to verify the existence and accuracy of the account balances and that the receivables are the rights of the company	Existence Accuracy Rights & Obligations
13. Examine all aspects of a sample of sales transactions—to determine whether the internal control procedures are being applied properly (i.e., perform tests of controls directed toward operating effectiveness); this procedure includes the following: a. Comparing the sales invoice with the customer's purchase order b. Checking for proper credit approval c. Comparing prices on sales invoice with those on price list; ascertaining the propriety of discounts granted to purchasers d. Recomputing extensions and footings e. Checking the recording in the sales journal and the posting of the sale in the A/R subsidiary ledger	Occurrence Accuracy
14. Review loan agreements—for pledging of accounts and agreements, for any factoring of accounts, and for disclosure purposes	All Presentation & Disclosure Assertions

* Note that many procedures may test multiple assertions. This program is not intended to be a complete presentation. See chapter 2 in section V.F.1.b. for details on assertions.

C. Inventory

The audit procedures in exhibit 4 typically are performed during the audit of the inventory account to obtain supporting evidence of the objectives.

1. **Audit Objectives' Focus** To ascertain (a) the inventory exists and the client owns it (existence and rights), (b) it is priced correctly, (c) the quantities shown are reasonable (rights), (d) the computations used to arrive at the inventory dollar amounts are accurate (valuation), and (e) there is adequate disclosure in the financial statements

2. **Subfunctions** Subfunctions for inventory include (a) purchasing, (b) receiving, (c) storing, (d) processing, (e) shipping, (f) detailed bookkeeping, and (g) general ledger accounting

Exhibit 4 ▸ Sample Program for Inventory

	Procedures	Assertions*
1.	Account for the numerical sequence of inventory purchase requisitions—to ascertain that none are missing, thereby helping to assure that no unauthorized purchases were made	Completeness
2.	Trace a sample of receiving reports for inventory to the perpetual inventory records—to determine that all shipments were reflected properly in the accounts; (this cutoff test must be performed at the inventory observation date and at the balance sheet date, if different)	Completeness Cutoff
3.	Perform analytics on cost of goods sold—to determine if significant fluctuations exist that would necessitate an audit investigation; perform procedures to test turnover and compare gross margin of current year with that of prior year to test for overstatement or understatement	Completeness
4.	Account for inventory tags and count sheets—to verify the inventory has been accounted for completely	Completeness
5.	Trace test counts of inventory items from the floor to the client's inventory listing—to ensure all items of inventory have been counted and included	Completeness
6.	Vouch a sample of inventory requisitions to customer or department order—so that evidence is obtained that all requisitions are valid	Rights & Obligations
7.	Review purchase and sales cutoffs—to ascertain that ending inventory is valued properly and that the inventory transactions are recorded in the proper time period	Cutoff Rights & Obligations
8.	Review inventory on consignment (as both consignee and consignor)—to determine the inventory actually owned by the client	Rights & Obligations
9.	Confirm inventory held at public warehouses and with third parties—to identify other inventory actually owned by the client	Rights & Obligations Existence
10.	Test pricing method used by the client—so that the proper inventory value is attained	Valuation & Allocation
11.	Apply lower-of-cost-or-market rule—so that the proper inventory value and any losses are recognized and disclosed	Valuation & Allocation
12.	Perform analytics—such as, gross profit percentage calculations, inventory turnover ratios, and number of days sales in inventory ratio analysis	Valuation & Allocation

In addition, inventory audit procedures for a manufacturing client could include the following:	
13. Test cost accumulation process—so that the ending inventory and cost-of-goods-sold are valued properly	Valuation & Allocation
14. Review the overhead allocations and rates—for accuracy when compared with actual experience	Valuation & Allocation
15. Vouch a sample of additions to perpetual inventory to supporting receiving reports—to assure that the recorded inventory actually was received	Existence
16. Physical inventory: observe the physical count—to become satisfied that the counting methods are effective and the client's representations are reliable	Existence
17. Physical inventory: trace client's physical counts to perpetual records and inventory sheets—to test the completeness of perpetual records	Completeness
18. Physical inventory: vouch the validity of the perpetual records and inventory sheets against the physical count—to determine that items in perpetual records exist and quantities are correct	Existence
19. Physical inventory: test inventory sheet and perpetual record computation for clerical accuracy—thereby helping to ascertain that the inventory is valued properly and quantities are correct	Valuation & Allocation
20. Physical inventory: make random test counts—to assure that the counts made by the client are accurate; test counts of inventory items also should be traced to client's inventory sheets and to client's final inventory compilation report	Existence
21. Review purchase and sales commitments—to determine whether there is a need to accrue a loss and disclose its relevant facts	Completeness of Disclosures
22. Determine whether any inventory has been pledged—to assure that such facts are disclosed properly in the financial statements	All Presentation & Disclosure Assertions

* Note that many procedures may test multiple assertions. This program is not intended to be a complete presentation. See chapter 2 in section V.F.1.b. for details on assertions.

D. Fixed Assets

The procedures in exhibit 5 normally are performed during the audit of fixed assets to obtain supporting evidence of the objectives.

1. **Audit Objectives' Focus** To (a) ascertain the adequacy of internal control policies and procedures over fixed assets, (b) verify the existence and ownership of the fixed assets, and (c) ascertain the adequacy of valuation and disclosure of the fixed assets in the financial statements

2. **Subfunctions** Subfunctions for fixed assets include (a) depreciation, (b) financing, (c) detailed ledger bookkeeping, and (d) general ledger accounting

Exhibit 5 ▸ Sample Program for Fixed Assets

Procedures	Assertions*
1. Trace from fixed assets to the property, plant and equipment subsidiary ledger—to determine that the assets are recorded	Completeness
2. Obtain or prepare an analysis of the repair and maintenance expense account—to consider if any items should be classified as capital expenditures	Classification
3. Review rental revenue and property tax expense—by obtaining a map of rented and leased property; this procedure will help determine the accuracy of the rental revenue and tax expense accounts by exposing all the client's real property, thereby enabling a thorough evaluation	Accuracy
4. Verify the client's ownership of the assets—by examining titles to the fixed assets	Rights & Obligations
5. Review lease agreements—for determining whether assets should be capitalized	Classification
6. Reconcile the property, plant and equipment subsidiary ledger with the general ledger—to determine that the accounting for property, plant and equipment transactions was consistent	Valuation & Allocation
7. Recalculate the accounting for retirements of fixed assets	Valuation & Allocation
8. Review depreciation methods—for consistency with prior periods	Valuation & Allocation
9. Review useful lives—for appropriateness and consistency with prior periods	Valuation & Allocation
10. Recalculate depreciation computations	Valuation & Allocation
11. Vouch from the property, plant and equipment subsidiary ledger to the fixed assets—to determine that the assets actually exist	Existence
12. Vouch acquisitions to purchase orders or contracts approved by appropriate personnel	Existence
13. Review loan agreements—to verify any loans collateralized by property or equipment for proper disclosure	All Presentation & Disclosure Assertions

* Note that many procedures may test multiple assertions. This program is not intended to be a complete presentation. See chapter 2 in section V.F.1.b. for details on assertions.

E. Investments

The procedures in exhibit 6 normally are performed during the audit of investments (derivatives and securities) to obtain supporting evidence of the objectives.

1. **Audit Objectives** Audit objectives include: (a) to ascertain the adequacy of internal control policies and procedures; (b) to ascertain whether investments are accounted for in conformity with the applicable financial reporting framework; (c) to ascertain the adequacy of financial statement disclosure; (d) to determine whether a loss in value of such investments should be considered as temporary or permanent; and (e) to obtain evidence as to their existence by inspection and/or confirmation.

2. **Subfunctions** Subfunctions for long-term investments include (a) financing, (b) cash, (c) detailed ledger bookkeeping, and (d) general ledger accounting.

Exhibit 6 ▸ Sample Program for Investments

	Procedures	Assertions*
1.	Confirmation with the issuer of the security	Existence or Occurrence Valuation (cost method)
2.	Confirmation with the holder of the security, including securities in electronic form, or with the counterparty to the derivative	Existence or Occurrence
3.	Confirmation of both settled and unsettled transactions with the broker-dealer or counterparty	Existence or Occurrence
4.	Physical inspection of the security or derivative contract; inspect securities on hand and compare serial numbers with those shown in previous year's working papers—will help identify any undisclosed sales or purchases of investments; coordinate with cash count to prevent substitution	Existence or Occurrence
5.	Read executed partnership or similar agreements	Existence or Occurrence
6.	Inspect underlying agreements and other forms of supporting documentation, in paper or electronic form, for the following: amounts reported; evidence that would preclude the sales treatment of a transfer; and unrecorded repurchase agreements	Existence or Occurrence Rights & Obligations Valuation (cost method)
7.	Inspect supporting documentation for subsequent realization or settlement (or any activity) after the end of the reporting period	Existence or Occurrence Completeness
8.	Perform analytics—by comparing dividends, interest and other investment income with those of prior years to ascertain the reasonableness of the completeness of recorded investment income, calculate the percentage of accrued investment income to total investments, and estimate total accrued income based on current investments	Completeness Existence or Occurrence
9.	Request the counterparty to a derivative or the holder of a security to provide information about it (confirm significant terms), such as whether there are any side agreements or agreements to repurchase securities sold	Completeness Rights & Obligations
10.	Obtain or prepare an account analysis for the long-term investment and related revenue or loss accounts to establish the accuracy of the individual debits and credits occurring during the year and prove the validity of the year-end balance in the accounts	Completeness

	Procedure	Assertion
11.	Request counterparties or holders who are frequently used, but with whom the accounting records indicate there are presently no derivatives or securities, to state whether they are counterparties to derivatives with the entity or holders of its securities	Completeness
12.	Inspect financial instruments and other agreements to identify embedded derivatives	Completeness
13.	Compare previous and current account detail to identify assets that have been removed from the accounts and test those items further to determine that the criteria for sales treatment have been met	Completeness
14.	Read other information, such as minutes of meetings of the board of directors or finance, asset/liability, investment, or other committees to obtain evidence about completeness or about rights and obligations, such as pledging of securities as collateral or selling securities with a commitment to repurchase them	Completeness Rights & Obligations
15.	Test calculations of premium and discount amortization	Valuation (cost method)
16.	Read financial statements/audit report of investee companies and read their interim financial information and make inquiries to identify subsequent events and transactions that are material to the entity's financial statements	Valuation (equity method)
17.	Evaluate management's conclusion about the need to recognize an impairment loss for a decline in the security's fair value below its carrying amount that is other than temporary	Valuation (equity method)
18.	Investigate material transactions between entity and the investee	Valuation (equity method)
19.	Determine fair value of securities on the balance sheet date	Valuation (fair value method)
20.	Inquire of management and review loan documents as to possible pledging of securities for appropriate disclosure purposes; if the collateral is an important factor in evaluating the fair value and collectability of the security, the auditor should obtain evidence regarding the existence, fair value, and transferability of such collateral as well as the investor's rights to the collateral	Valuation (fair value method)
21.	Examine financial presentation of long-term investments to determine whether the applicable financial reporting framework is followed	Presentation & Disclosure
22.	Evaluate whether management's stated intent to buy and hold an investment is supported by actual activities and the entity's ability to do so	Classification

* Note that many procedures may test multiple assertions. This program is not intended to be a complete presentation. See chapter 2 in section V.F.1.b. for details on assertions.

F. Accounts Payable, Purchases & Other Liabilities

The audit procedures in exhibit 7 commonly are performed during the audit of the A/P, purchasing, and other liability accounts to obtain supporting evidence of the objectives.

1. **Audit Objectives' Focus** To ensure: (a) there are adequate internal control policies and procedures over payables and purchases; (b) all transactions that should be recorded are recorded (completeness); (c) those transactions that are recorded are recorded properly (valuation); and (d) the financial statement presentation is adequate (disclosure and obligation)

2. **Subfunctions** Subfunctions for payables and purchases include (a) purchasing, (b) receiving, (c) payment, (d) detailed ledger bookkeeping, and (e) general ledger accounting

Exhibit 7 ▸ Sample Program for Short-Term Liabilities

Procedures	Assertions*
1. Perform search for unrecorded liabilities—to ascertain that all payables have been recorded in the proper period; performed, at the balance sheet date, in the following areas: a. Unmatched invoices and unbilled receiving reports b. Significant payments subsequent to the end of the period may indicate liabilities that existed at the end of the period c. Invoices received after the end of the period may have been for goods received at, or before, the end of the period d. Customer deposits recorded as credits to A/R e. Unbilled professional fees at the end of the period under audit f. Perform inventory receiving cutoff test	Completeness Cutoff Classification
2. Perform analytics—to assess the reasonableness of balances; compare the average number of days purchases in accounts payable at the end of the current year to prior years; compare purchases divided by payables to payables divided by total current liabilities for the current and prior years; compare payables and purchases to budgeted or forecasted amounts	Completeness
3. Vouch the paid check and invoice from the vendor to the receiving report—to determine if any payments were made for goods that were not received	Existence
4. Review the cutoff of purchases, returns, and disbursements—to determine that transactions are recorded in the proper periods	Cutoff
5. Recalculate the extensions and footings on customer invoices—to determine whether such invoices were priced and computed accurately	Accuracy Valuation & Allocation
6. Trace vendor invoices to voucher register and checks to check register—to determine that all payables and related disbursements were recorded properly	Valuation & Allocation
7. Foot voucher register and trace to general ledger—to substantiate the entries in the general ledger	Valuation & Allocation
8. Reclassify debit balances as receivables and review for collectability	Valuation & Allocation
9. Recalculate other (accrued) liabilities—to test computations for reasonableness and consistent treatment when compared to prior years; examples include property and income taxes, commissions, profit-sharing and pension plans, and warranties	Valuation & Allocation
10. Vouch purchase requisitions of a sample of purchase orders—to determine if any unrequested purchases were made	Existence
11. Confirm A/P balances with vendors—although not a generally accepted audit procedure, confirm in cases of suspected fraud, sloppy or missing records, or suspected understatements	Completeness
12. Inspect copies of notes and other agreements	Existence
13. Review purchase commitments—to determine whether there are any losses to be accrued and/or disclosed	Completeness

* Note that many procedures may test multiple assertions. This program is not intended to be a complete presentation. See chapter 2 in section V.F.1.b. for details on assertions.

G. Payroll

The audit procedures in exhibit 8 usually are performed during the audit of the payroll accounts to obtain supporting evidence of the objectives.

1. **Audit Objectives' Focus** To (a) ascertain the adequacy of internal control over payroll, (b) verify that all employees included in the payroll actually exist and work for the client (existence), (c) verify the accuracy of the payroll computations (valuation), and (d) ascertain the adequacy of disclosure in the financial statements.

2. **Subfunctions** Subfunctions for payroll include (a) personnel, (b) production, (c) detailed ledger bookkeeping, and (d) general ledger accounting.

Exhibit 8 ▸ Sample Program for Payroll

	Procedures	Assertions*
1.	Review time reports & piecework or commission records to determine that such reports and records agree with production records	Completeness
2.	Examine payroll cutoff to determine that wages were reported in the proper time period	Cutoff
3.	Review accounting for unclaimed wages to ascertain that they are being classified properly	Classification Rights & Obligations
4.	Verify payroll deductions to ascertain that they are computed appropriately and that they agree with withholding authorizations	Valuation & Allocation
5.	Analyze officers' compensation to determine if authorization is proper	Rights & Obligations
6.	Recompute payroll register to determine its accuracy	Accuracy Valuation & Allocation
7.	Vouch items from the payroll register to employee time cards to verify employees worked the number of hours for which pay was computed	Occurrence
8.	Observe the use of time clocks by employees to be assured that each employee punches only one time card	Valuation & Allocation Occurrence
9.	Review the results of audits of related pension and profit-sharing plans	Valuation & Allocation
10.	Perform analytics to determine reasonableness of balances; calculate ratios to determine whether accounts relate to each other in the manner expected; if relationships vary significantly from expected results, additional substantive tests of account balances may be necessary; compare payroll expenses with prior periods and investigate differences to determine the accuracy and validity of the expense	Valuation & Allocation Accuracy
11.	Review payroll checks and bank reconciliations to determine that all checks were cashed	Existence
12.	Review the payroll register to determine if all payroll transactions were recorded	Completeness
13.	Examine personnel records to determine that a name, salary rate, and job position all exist for each employee on the payroll	Existence
14.	On a surprise basis, observe the distribution of paychecks to determine that every name on the company payroll is an employee	Existence
15.	Review related tax expense and liability, unemployment insurance, and other payroll deduction accounts to determine accuracy and proper classification in the financial statements	Accuracy & Valuation Classification

* Note that many procedures may test multiple assertions. This program is not intended to be a complete presentation. See chapter 2 in section V.F.1.b. for details on assertions.

H. Long-Term Liabilities

The audit procedures in exhibit 9 normally are performed during the audit of long-term liabilities to obtain supporting evidence of the objectives.

1. **Audit Objectives' Focus** To (a) ascertain the adequacy of internal control policies and procedures over long-term liabilities; (b) verify that all long-term liabilities are recorded properly (existence and obligation); (c) verify that interest expense is computed correctly and that other contractual obligations are satisfied (valuation); and (d) ascertain the adequacy of disclosure of long-term liabilities in the financial statements

2. **Subfunctions** Subfunctions for long-term liabilities include (a) financing, (b) fixed assets, (c) cash, (d) detailed ledger bookkeeping, and (e) general ledger accounting.

Exhibit 9 ▸ Sample Program for Long-Term Liabilities

Procedures	Assertions*
1. Obtain or prepare an account analysis for the long-term debt, discount, premium, and related interest accounts—allows the auditor to: a. Verify the payment or other disposition of the debt listed as outstanding at the beginning of the period b. Establish the accuracy of the individual debits and credits occurring during the year c. Prove the validity of the year-end balance in the accounts	Accuracy Completeness
2. Perform analytics—compare current amortization amounts to prior actual and current budget amounts; compare current interest costs to prior actual and current budget amounts; compare current and non-current debt obligations to prior actual and current budget amounts	Completeness
3. Review bank confirmation—for indication of loans and other commitments, including any unrecorded debt	Completeness Rights & Obligations
4. Review cutoff—to determine that transactions recorded at the end of the year are recorded in the proper period	Cutoff
5. Verify interest computations and amortization of premiums and/or discounts—to determine whether such amounts were disclosed properly and accurately; also aids in the discovery of undisclosed liabilities	Valuation & Allocation Accuracy Completeness
6. Confirm with creditor the transactions of the period and compliance with the contractual provisions—provides evidence that the transactions actually occurred and that the transactions were carried out properly (e.g., deposits into a sinking fund)	Occurrence Rights & Obligations
7. Review contractual provisions and supporting documents of long-term debt—to determine that details of the debt instruments correspond to those in the account analysis and that such details are disclosed accurately in the financial statements; supporting documents include note and loan agreements, bond indentures, and lease agreements	All Presentation & Disclosure Assertions

* Note that many procedures may test multiple assertions. This program is not intended to be a complete presentation. See chapter 2 in section V.F.1.b. for details on assertions.

I. **Stockholders' Equity**

The audit procedures in exhibit 10 normally are performed during the audit of stockholders' equity to obtain supporting evidence of the objectives.

1. **Audit Objectives' Focus** To (a) ascertain the adequacy of internal control over stock transactions, stock certificates, receipts and payments; (b) verify that the transactions are authorized properly and comply with applicable regulations; (c) verify that the transactions are recorded in conformity with the applicable financial reporting framework; and (d) ascertain the adequacy of disclosure of stockholders' equity in the financial statements

2. **Subfunctions** Subfunctions for stockholders' equity include (a) financing, (b) cash, (c) detailed ledger bookkeeping, and (d) general ledger accounting.

Exhibit 10 ▸ Sample Program for Stockholders' Equity

Procedures	Assertions*
1. Obtain or prepare an account analysis for all accounts—to outline the historical picture of corporate capital and any changes to corporate capital	Completeness
2. Account for all certificate numbers—to determine that no unauthorized securities were issued during the period	Completeness
3. Perform analytics—by computing the return on stockholders' equity, the book value per share, and the dividend payout ratio and comparing them to those of prior years; compare current year dividend amounts and balances for common and preferred stock and additional paid-in capital to those of prior years	Completeness
4. Vouch all retirements of securities—to ascertain that no certificates were reissued fraudulently	Rights & Obligations
5. Review compliance with stock option plans and other restrictions on capital stocks—allows the auditor to do the following:	All Presentations & Disclosure Assertions
a. Determine the adequacy of disclosure with respect to these arrangements	
b. Verify the number of shares issued during the year through conversion or exercise of convertible stocks and bonds, stock options, and stock warrants	
c. Ascertain whether the shares held in reserve exceed the shares authorized, but unissued	
d. Determine that the call provisions of preferred stock are carried out accurately	
6. Review minutes of board of directors' meetings—to verify that stock and dividend transactions have been authorized properly	Rights & Obligations
7. Account for all proceeds from security issues—to determine whether the transactions were accounted for in accordance with underwriting contracts, state stock issuance permits, and SEC registration statements	Valuation & Allocation
8. Analyze treasury stock transactions—to determine that such transactions were authorized properly and recorded in conformity with the applicable financial reporting framework	Accuracy Valuation & Allocation

	Procedure	Assertion
9.	Reconcile subsidiary ledger with general ledger control account—to establish the amount of outstanding stock and to rule out the possibility of an over-issuance of shares	Valuation & Allocation
10.	Reconcile dividend distributions and verify dividend calculations—to ascertain the accurate dividend amount and to discover any declared, but yet unpaid, dividends	Accuracy Completeness
11.	Confirm shares outstanding with registrar—to ascertain whether the corporate records are accurate and that stock is issued in accordance with the authorization of the board of directors and the articles of incorporation	Accuracy Existence
12.	Analyze the retained earnings account—to determine whether it is disclosed accurately in the financial statements, and determine the amount of any restrictions on retained earnings that result from loans, other agreements, or state law	All Presentation & Disclosure Assertions
13.	Analyze prior-period adjustments—to ascertain whether they are valid and are treated properly in the financial statements and determine the amount of any restrictions on retained earnings that result from loans, other agreements, or state law	All Presentation & Disclosure Assertions

* Note that many procedures may test multiple assertions. This program is not intended to be a complete presentation. See chapter 2 in section V.F.1.b. for details on assertions.

CHAPTER 5—AUDIT PROGRAMS

Problem 5-1 MULTIPLE-CHOICE QUESTIONS

Substantive Procedures

1. In testing the existence assertion for an asset, an auditor ordinarily works from the
   a. Financial statements to the potentially unrecorded items
   b. Potentially unrecorded items to the financial statements
   c. Accounting records to the supporting evidence
   d. Supporting evidence to the accounting records (ID: 136)

2. Which of the following procedures would an auditor most likely perform in auditing the statement of cash flows?
   a. Compare the amounts included in the statement of cash flows to similar amounts in the prior year's statement of cash flows
   b. Reconcile the cutoff bank statements to verify the accuracy of the year-end bank balances
   c. Vouch all bank transfers for the last week of the year and first week of the subsequent year
   d. Reconcile the amounts included in the statement of cash flows to the other financial statements' balances and amounts (ID: 5674)

3. In determining whether transactions have been recorded, the direction of the audit testing should be from the
   a. General ledger balances
   b. Adjusted trial balance
   c. Original source documents
   d. General journal entries (ID: 5675)

4. The objective of tests of details of transactions performed as substantive tests is to
   a. Comply with generally accepted auditing standards
   b. Attain assurance about the reliability of the accounting system
   c. Detect material misstatements in the financial statements
   d. Evaluate whether management's policies and procedures operated effectively (ID: 5998)

5. Which of the following procedures would an auditor **least** likely perform before the balance sheet date?
   a. Confirmation of accounts payable
   b. Observation of merchandise inventory
   c. Assessment of control risk
   d. Identification of related parties (ID: 5691)

6. An auditor confirmed accounts receivable as of an interim date, and all confirmations were returned and appeared reasonable. Which of the following additional procedures most likely should be performed at year-end?
   a. Send confirmations for all new customer balances incurred from the interim date to year-end
   b. Resend confirmations for any significant customer balances remaining at year-end
   c. Review supporting documents for new large balances occurring after the interim date, and evaluate any significant changes in balances at year-end
   d. Review cash collections subsequent to the interim date and the year-end (ID: 7840)

7. An auditor plans to apply substantive tests to the details of asset and liability accounts as of an interim date rather than as of the balance sheet date. The auditor should be aware that this practice
   a. Eliminates the use of certain statistical sampling methods that would otherwise be available
   b. Presumes that the auditor will reperform the tests as of the balance sheet date
   c. Should be especially considered when there are rapidly changing economic conditions
   d. Potentially increases the risk that errors that exist at the balance sheet date will not be detected (ID: 8126)

8. In which of the following circumstances is substantive testing of accounts receivable before the balance sheet date most appropriate?
   a. The client has a new sales incentive program in place.
   b. Internal controls during the remaining period are effective.
   c. There is a high turnover of senior management.
   d. It is a first engagement of a new client. (ID: 8398)

9. Before applying principal substantive tests to an entity's accounts receivable at an interim date, an auditor should
   a. Consider the likelihood of assessing the risk of incorrect rejection too low
   b. Project sampling risk at the maximum for tests covering the remaining period
   c. Ascertain that accounts receivable are immaterial to the financial statements
   d. Assess the difficulty in controlling the incremental audit risk (ID: 8413)

10. Which of the following procedures would an auditor most likely perform prior to the balance sheet date?
    a. Review subsequent events
    b. Perform search for unrecorded liabilities
    c. Send inquiry letter to client's legal counsel
    d. Review detail and test significant travel and entertainment expenses (ID: 8638)

11. Which of the following procedures would an auditor most likely perform in obtaining evidence about subsequent events?
    a. Determine that changes in employee pay rates after year-end were properly authorized
    b. Recompute depreciation charges for plant assets sold after year-end
    c. Investigate changes in long-term debt occurring after year-end
    d. Inquire about payroll checks that were recorded before year-end but cashed after year-end (ID: 5683)

12. An auditor compared the current year gross margin with the prior year gross margin to determine if cost of sales is reasonable. What type of audit procedure was performed?
    a. Test of transactions
    b. Analytical procedures
    c. Test of controls
    d. Test of details (ID: 8140)

External Confirmations

13. Hemp, CPA, is auditing the financial statements of a small rural municipality. The receivable balances represent residents' delinquent real estate taxes. Internal control at the municipality is weak. To determine the existence of the accounts receivable balances at the balance sheet date, Hemp would most likely
    a. Send positive confirmation requests
    b. Send negative confirmation requests
    c. Inspect the internal records such as copies of the tax invoices that were mailed to the residents
    d. Examine evidence of subsequent cash receipts (ID: 178)

14. Which of the following statements is correct concerning the use of negative confirmation requests?
    a. Unreturned negative confirmation requests rarely provide significant explicit evidence.
    b. Negative confirmation requests are effective when detection risk is low.
    c. Unreturned negative confirmation requests indicate that alternative procedures are necessary.
    d. Negative confirmation requests are effective when understatements of account balances are suspected. (ID: 5663)

15. The confirmation of customers' accounts receivable rarely provides reliable evidence about the completeness assertion because
    a. Many customers merely sign and return the confirmation without verifying its details.
    b. Recipients usually respond only if they disagree with the information on the request.
    c. Customers may not be inclined to report understatement errors in their accounts.
    d. Auditors typically select many accounts with low recorded balances to be confirmed. (ID: 5986)

16. In auditing accounts receivable, the negative form of confirmation request most likely would be used when
    a. The total recorded amount of accounts receivable is immaterial to the financial statements taken as a whole.
    b. Response rates in prior years to properly designed positive confirmation requests were inadequate.
    c. Recipients are likely to return positive confirmation requests without verifying the accuracy of the information.
    d. The combined assessed level of inherent risk and control risk relative to accounts receivable is low. (ID: 6582)

17. Under which of the following circumstances would the use of the blank form of confirmations of accounts receivable most likely be preferable to positive confirmations?
    a. The recipients are likely to sign the confirmations without devoting proper attention to them.
    b. Subsequent cash receipts are unusually difficult to verify.
    c. Analytical procedures indicate that few exceptions are expected.
    d. The combined assessed level of inherent risk and control risk is low. (ID: 6714)

18. In confirming accounts receivable, an auditor decided to confirm customers' account balances rather than individual invoices. Which of the following most likely would be included with the client's confirmation letter?
    a. An auditor-prepared letter explaining that a nonresponse may cause an inference that the account balance is correct
    b. A client-prepared letter reminding the customer that a nonresponse will cause a second request to be sent
    c. An auditor-prepared letter requesting the customer to supply missing and incorrect information directly to the auditor
    d. A client-prepared statement of account showing the details of the customer's account balance (ID: 6834)

19. Which of the following statements would an auditor most likely add to the negative form of confirmation of accounts receivable to encourage timely consideration by the recipients?
    a. "This is not a request for payment; remittances should not be sent to our auditors in the enclosed envelope."
    b. "Report any differences on the enclosed statement directly to our auditors; no reply is necessary if this amount agrees with your records."
    c. "If you do not report any differences within 15 days, it will be assumed that this statement is correct."
    d. "The following invoices have been selected for confirmation and represent amounts that are overdue." (ID: 6835)

20. An auditor decides to use the blank form of accounts receivable confirmation rather than the positive form. The auditor should be aware that the blank form may be less efficient because

    a. Subsequent cash receipts need to be verified.
    b. Statistical sampling may not be used.
    c. A higher assessed level of detection risk is required.
    d. More nonresponses are likely to occur. (ID: 7640)

21. An independent auditor asked a client's internal auditor to assist in preparing a standard financial institution confirmation request for a payroll account that had been closed during the year under audit. After the internal auditor prepared the form, the controller signed it and mailed it to the bank. What was the major flaw in this procedure?

    a. The internal auditor did not sign the form.
    b. The form was mailed by the controller.
    c. The form was prepared by the internal auditor.
    d. The account was closed, so the balance was zero. (ID: 7800)

22. Which of the following strategies most likely could improve the response rate of the confirmations of accounts receivable?

    a. Restrict the selection of accounts to be confirmed to those customers with large balances
    b. Include a list of items or invoices that constitute the customers' account balances
    c. Explain to customers that discrepancies will be investigated by an independent third party
    d. Ask customers to respond to the confirmation requests directly to the auditor by fax (ID: 8407)

23. When an auditor decides to confirm accounts receivable balances rather than individual invoices, it most likely would be beneficial to include with the confirmations

    a. Copies of the client's shipping documents that support the account balances
    b. Lists of the customers' recent payments that the client has already recorded
    c. Client-prepared statements of account that show the details of the account balances
    d. Copies of the customers' purchase orders that support the account balances (ID: 9907)

24. An auditor is required to confirm accounts receivable if the accounts receivable balances are

    a. Older than the prior year
    b. Material to the financial statements
    c. Smaller than expected
    d. Subject to valuation estimates (ID: 89764)

25. Under which of the following circumstances should an auditor consider confirming the terms of a large complex sale?

    a. When the assessed level of control risk over the sale is low
    b. When the assessed level of detection risk over the sale is high
    c. When the combined assessed level of inherent and control risk over the sale is moderate
    d. When the combined assessed level of inherent and control risk over the sale is high (ID: 89765)

Accounting Estimates

26. Which of the following procedures most likely would assist an auditor in determining whether management has identified all accounting estimates that could be material to the financial statements?

    a. Inquire about the existence of related-party transactions
    b. Determine whether accounting estimates deviate from historical patterns
    c. Confirm inventories at locations outside the entity
    d. Review the lawyer's letter for information about litigation (ID: 7094)

27. In evaluating an entity's accounting estimates, one of the auditor's objectives is to determine whether the estimates are
    a. Prepared in a satisfactory control environment
    b. Consistent with industry guidelines
    c. Based on verifiable objective assumptions
    d. Reasonable in the circumstances (ID: 8166)

28. In evaluating the reasonableness of an entity's accounting estimates, an auditor most likely concentrates on key factors and assumptions that are
    a. Stable and not sensitive to variation
    b. Objective and not susceptible to bias
    c. Deviations from historical patterns
    d. Similar to industry guidelines (ID: 8649)

29. In evaluating the reasonableness of an entity's accounting estimates, an auditor normally would be concerned about assumptions that are
    a. Susceptible to bias
    b. Consistent with prior periods
    c. Insensitive to variations
    d. Similar to industry guidelines (ID: 6395)

30. Which of the following statements is correct regarding accounting estimates?
    a. The auditor's objective is to evaluate whether accounting estimates are reasonable in the circumstances.
    b. Accounting estimates should be used when data concerning past events can be accumulated in a timely, cost-effective manner.
    c. An important accounting estimate is management's listing of accounts receivable greater than 90 days past due.
    d. Accounting estimates should not be used when the outcome of future events related to the estimated item is unknown. (ID: 8810)

Cash

31. The primary purpose of sending a standard confirmation request to financial institutions with which the client has done business during the year is to
    a. Detect kiting activities that may otherwise not be discovered
    b. Corroborate information regarding deposit and loan balances
    c. Provide the data necessary to prepare a proof of cash
    d. Request information about contingent liabilities and secured transactions (ID: 3930)

32. An auditor suspects that a client's cashier is misappropriating cash receipts for personal use by lapping customer checks received in the mail. In attempting to uncover this embezzlement scheme, the auditor most likely would compare the
    a. Dates checks are deposited per bank statements with the dates remittance credits are recorded.
    b. Daily cash summaries with the sums of the cash receipts journal entries.
    c. Individual bank deposit slips with the details of the monthly bank statements.
    d. Dates uncollectible accounts are authorized to be written off with the dates the write-offs are actually recorded. (ID: 5975)

33. The usefulness of the standard bank confirmation request may be limited because the bank employee who completes the form may

    a. Not believe that the bank is obligated to verify confidential information to a third party
    b. Sign and return the form without inspecting the accuracy of the client's bank reconciliation
    c. Not have access to the client's cutoff bank statement
    d. Be unaware of all the financial relationships that the bank has with the client (ID: 5992)

34. On receiving a client's bank cutoff statement, an auditor most likely would trace

    a. Prior year checks listed in the cutoff statement to the year-end outstanding checks
    b. Deposits in transit listed in the cutoff statement to the year-end bank reconciliation
    c. Checks dated after year-end listed in the cutoff statement to the year-end outstanding checks
    d. Deposits recorded in the cash receipts journal after year-end to the cutoff statement (ID: 7098)

35. Which of the following characteristics most likely would be indicative of check kiting?

    a. High turnover of employees who have access to cash
    b. Many large checks that are recorded on Mondays
    c. Low average balance compared to high level of deposits
    d. Frequent ATM checking account withdrawals (ID: 7107)

36. Which of the following cash transfers results in a misstatement of cash at December 31, 20X1?

	Bank Transfer Schedule			
	Disbursement Date		Receipt Date	
	per books	per bank	per books	per bank
a.	12/31/X1	01/05/X2	12/31/X1	01/04/X2
b.	01/04/X2	01/11/X2	01/04/X2	01/04/X2
c.	12/31/X1	01/04/X2	12/31/X1	12/31/X1
d.	01/04/X2	01/05/X2	12/31/X1	01/04/X2

(ID: 8380)

Accounts Receivable & Sales

37. Which of the following most likely would be detected by an auditor's review of a client's sales cutoff?

    a. Shipments lacking sales invoices and shipping documents
    b. Excessive write-offs of accounts receivable
    c. Unrecorded sales at year-end
    d. Lapping of year-end accounts receivable (ID: 2778)

38. Which of the following internal control procedures most likely would deter lapping of collections from customers?

    a. Independent internal verification of dates of entry in the cash receipts journal with dates of daily cash summaries
    b. Authorization of write-offs of uncollectible accounts by a supervisor independent of credit approval
    c. Segregation of duties between receiving cash and posting the accounts receivable ledger
    d. Supervisory comparison of the daily cash summary with the sum of the cash receipts journal entries (ID: 3910)

39. An auditor most likely would review an entity's periodic accounting for the numerical sequence of shipping documents and invoices to support management's financial statement assertion of

    a. Occurrence
    b. Rights and obligations
    c. Valuation and allocation
    d. Completeness (ID: 3923)

40. In evaluating the adequacy of the allowance for doubtful accounts, an auditor most likely reviews the entity's aging of receivables to support management's financial statement assertion of

    a. Existence
    b. Valuation and allocation
    c. Completeness
    d. Rights and obligations (ID: 3925)

41. Which of the following audit procedures would an auditor most likely perform to test controls relating to management's assertion concerning the completeness of sales transactions?

    a. Verify that extensions and footings on the entity's sales invoices and monthly customer statements have been recomputed
    b. Inspect the entity's reports of prenumbered shipping documents that have not been recorded in the sales journal
    c. Compare the invoiced prices on prenumbered sales invoices to the entity's authorized price list
    d. Inquire about the entity's credit granting policies and the consistent application of credit checks (ID: 4692)

42. An auditor's purpose in reviewing credit ratings of customers with delinquent accounts receivable most likely is to obtain evidence concerning management's assertions about

    a. Valuation and allocation
    b. Classification and understandability
    c. Existence
    d. Rights and obligations (ID: 5123)

43. An auditor most likely would limit substantive audit tests of sales transactions when control risk is assessed as low for the occurrence assertion concerning sales transactions and the auditor has already gathered evidence supporting

    a. Opening and closing inventory balances
    b. Cash receipts and accounts receivable
    c. Shipping and receiving activities
    d. Cutoffs of sales and purchases (ID: 5993)

44. An auditor observed that a client mails monthly statements to customers. Subsequently, the auditor reviewed evidence of follow-up on the errors reported by the customers. This test of controls most likely was performed to support management's financial statement assertion(s) of

	Classification and understandability	Rights and obligations
a.	Yes	Yes
b.	Yes	No
c.	No	Yes
d.	No	No

(ID: 7101)

45. An auditor discovered that a client's accounts receivable turnover is substantially lower for the current year than for the prior year. This may indicate that

    a. Fictitious credit sales have been recorded during the year.
    b. Employees have stolen inventory just before the year-end.
    c. The client recently tightened its credit-granting policies.
    d. An employee has been lapping receivables in both years. (ID: 7109)

46. An auditor selects a sample from the file of shipping documents to determine whether invoices were prepared. This test is performed to satisfy the audit objective of

    a. Accuracy
    b. Completeness
    c. Existence
    d. Control (ID: 7494)

47. If the objective of an auditor's test of details is to detect a possible understatement of sales, the auditor most likely would trace transactions from the

    a. Sales invoices to the shipping documents
    b. Cash receipts journal to the sales journal
    c. Shipping documents to the sales invoices
    d. Sales journal to the cash receipts journal (ID: 8622)

Inventory

48. Which of the following audit procedures probably would provide the most reliable evidence concerning the entity's assertion of rights and obligations related to inventories?

    a. Inspect the open purchase order file for significant commitments that should be considered for disclosure
    b. Inspect agreements to determine whether any inventory is pledged as collateral or subject to any liens
    c. Select the last few shipping advices used before the physical count and determine whether the shipments were recorded as sales
    d. Trace test counts noted during the entity's physical count to the entity's summarization of quantities (ID: 2770)

49. An auditor selected items for test counts while observing a client's physical inventory. The auditor then traced the test counts to the client's inventory listing. This procedure most likely obtained evidence concerning management's assertion of

    a. Rights and obligations
    b. Completeness
    c. Existence
    d. Valuation (ID: 4706)

50. Which of the following auditing procedures most likely would provide assurance about a manufacturing entity's inventory valuation?

    a. Testing the entity's computation of standard overhead rates
    b. Obtaining confirmation of inventories pledged under loan agreements
    c. Reviewing shipping and receiving cutoff procedures for inventories
    d. Tracing test counts to the entity's inventory listing (ID: 5121)

51. A client maintains perpetual inventory records in both quantities and dollars. If the assessed level of control risk is high, an auditor would probably

    a. Increase the extent of tests of controls of the inventory cycle
    b. Request the client to schedule the physical inventory count at the end of the year
    c. Insist that the client perform physical counts of inventory items several times during the year
    d. Apply gross profit tests to ascertain the reasonableness of the physical counts (ID: 5131)

52. An auditor most likely would inspect loan agreements under which an entity's inventories are pledged to support management's financial statement assertion of

    a. Completeness of disclosures
    b. Valuation of inventory
    c. Existence of inventory
    d. Completeness of inventory (ID: 5658)

53. An auditor most likely would make inquiries of production and sales personnel concerning possible obsolete or slow-moving inventory to support management's financial statement assertion of

    a. Valuation and allocation
    b. Rights and obligations
    c. Existence
    d. Classification and understandability (ID: 5661)

54 While observing a client's annual physical inventory, an auditor recorded test counts for several items and noticed that certain test counts were higher than the recorded quantities in the client's perpetual records. This situation could be the result of the client's failure to record

    a. Purchase discounts
    b. Purchase returns
    c. Sales
    d. Sales returns (ID: 5670)

55. To gain assurance that all inventory items in a client's inventory listing schedule are valid, an auditor most likely would trace

    a. Inventory tags noted during the auditor's observation to items listed in the inventory listing schedule
    b. Inventory tags noted during the auditor's observation to items listed in receiving reports and vendors' invoices
    c. Items listed in the inventory listing schedule to inventory tags and the auditor's recorded count sheets
    d. Items listed in receiving reports and vendors' invoices to the inventory listing schedule (ID: 5671)

56. To measure how effectively an entity employs its resources, an auditor calculates inventory turnover by dividing average inventory into

    a. Net sales
    b. Cost of goods sold
    c. Operating income
    d. Gross sales (ID: 5989)

57. When auditing inventories, an auditor would **least** likely verify that

    a. The financial statement presentation of inventories is appropriate.
    b. Damaged goods and obsolete items have been properly accounted for.
    c. All inventory owned by the client is on hand at the time of the count.
    d. The client has used proper inventory pricing. (ID: 7495)

58. Which of the following procedures would an auditor most likely perform to obtain assurance that slow-moving and obsolete items included in inventories are properly identified?

    a. Testing shipping and receiving cutoff procedures
    b. Confirming inventories at locations outside the entity's premises
    c. Examining an analysis of inventory turnover
    d. Tracing inventory observation test counts to perpetual listings (ID: 7804)

59. In auditing a manufacturing entity, which of the following procedures would an auditor **least** likely perform to determine whether slow-moving, defective, and obsolete items included in inventory are properly identified?

    a. Test the computation of standard overhead rates
    b. Tour the manufacturing plant or production facility
    c. Compare inventory balances to anticipated sales volume
    d. Review inventory experience and trends (ID: 8152)

60. To obtain assurance that all inventory items in a client's inventory listing are valid, an auditor most likely would trace

    a. Inventory tags noted during the auditor's observation to items listed in receiving reports and vendors' invoices
    b. Items listed in receiving reports and vendors' invoices to the inventory listing
    c. Inventory tags noted during the auditor's observation to items in the inventory listing
    d. Items in the inventory listing to inventory tags and the auditor's recorded count sheets (ID: 8418)

61. The purpose of tracing a sample of inventory tags to a client's computerized listing of inventory items is to determine whether the inventory items

    a. Represented by tags were included on the listing
    b. Included on the listing were properly counted
    c. Represented by tags were reduced to the lower of cost or market
    d. Included in the listing were properly valued (ID: 9911)

62. A portion of a client's inventory is in public warehouses. Evidence of the existence of this merchandise can most efficiently be acquired through which of the following methods?

    a. Observation
    b. Confirmation
    c. Calculation
    d. Inspection (ID: 9939)

63. Which of the following management assertions is an auditor most likely testing if the audit objective states that all inventory on hand is reflected in the ending inventory balance?

    a. The entity has rights to the inventory.
    b. Inventory is properly valued.
    c. Inventory is properly presented in the financial statements.
    d. Inventory is complete. (ID: 89789)

64. As part of the process of observing a client's physical inventories, an auditor should be alert to

    a. The inclusion of any obsolete or damaged goods
    b. Any change in the method of pricing from prior years
    c. The existence of outstanding purchase commitments
    d. The verification of inventory values assigned to goods in process (ID: 8823)

65. Under which of the following conditions may an auditor's observation procedure for inventory be performed during or after the end of the period under audit?

    a. When the client maintains periodic inventory records
    b. When the auditor finds minimal variations in client records and test counts in prior periods
    c. When total inventory has **not** varied more than 5% in the last five years
    d. When well-kept perpetual inventory records are checked by the client periodically by comparisons with physical counts (ID: 9363)

66. Which of the following procedures would be most appropriate for testing the completeness assertion as it applies to inventory?

    a. Scanning perpetual inventory, production, and purchasing records
    b. Examining paid vendor invoices
    c. Tracing inventory items from the tag listing back to the physical inventory quantities
    d. Performing cutoff procedures for shipping and receiving (ID: 9381)

Fixed Assets

67. An auditor analyzes repairs and maintenance accounts primarily to obtain evidence in support of the audit assertion that all

    a. Noncapitalizable expenditures for repairs and maintenance have been recorded in the proper period.
    b. Expenditures for property and equipment have been recorded in the proper period.
    c. Noncapitalizable expenditures for repairs and maintenance have been properly charged to expense.
    d. Expenditures for property and equipment have not been charged to expense. (ID: 5135)

68. When there are numerous property and equipment transactions during the year, an auditor who plans to assess control risk at a low level usually performs

    a. Analytical procedures for property and equipment balances at the end of the year
    b. Analytical procedures for current year property and equipment transactions
    c. Tests of controls and limited tests of current year property and equipment transactions
    d. Tests of controls and extensive tests of property and equipment balances at the end of the year (ID: 5974)

69. A weakness of internal control over recording retirements of equipment may cause an auditor to

    a. Inspect certain items of equipment in the plant and trace those items to the accounting records
    b. Review the subsidiary ledger to ascertain whether depreciation was taken on each item of equipment during the year
    c. Trace additions to the "other assets" account to search for equipment that is still on hand but no longer being used
    d. Select certain items of equipment from the accounting records and locate them in the plant (ID: 5981)

70. Which of the following explanations most likely would satisfy an auditor who questions management about significant debits to the accumulated depreciation accounts?

    a. The estimated remaining useful lives of plant assets were revised upward.
    b. Plant assets were retired during the year.
    c. The prior year's depreciation expense was erroneously understated.
    d. Overhead allocations were revised at year-end. (ID: 5996)

71. An auditor's principal objective in analyzing repairs and maintenance expense accounts is to

    a. Determine that all obsolete property, plant, and equipment assets were written off before the year-end
    b. Verify that all recorded property, plant, and equipment assets actually exist
    c. Discover expenditures that were expensed but should have been capitalized
    d. Identify property, plant, and equipment assets that cannot be repaired and should be written off (ID: 8391)

72. An analysis of which of the following accounts would best aid in verifying that all fixed assets have been capitalized?

    a. Cash
    b. Depreciation expense
    c. Property tax expense
    d. Repairs and maintenance (ID: 8400)

Investments

73. To satisfy the valuation assertion when auditing an investment accounted for by the equity method, an auditor most likely would
    a. Inspect the stock certificates evidencing the investment
    b. Examine the audited financial statements of the investee company
    c. Review the broker's advice or canceled check for the investment's acquisition
    d. Obtain market quotations from financial newspapers or periodicals (ID: 2312)

74. In testing long-term investments, an auditor ordinarily would use analytical procedures to ascertain the reasonableness of the
    a. Completeness of recorded investment income
    b. Classification between current and noncurrent portfolios
    c. Valuation of marketable equity securities
    d. Existence of unrealized gains or losses in the portfolio (ID: 3927)

75. In establishing the existence and ownership of a long-term investment in the form of publicly-traded stock, an auditor should inspect the securities or
    a. Correspond with the investee company to verify the number of shares owned
    b. Inspect the audited financial statements of the investee company
    c. Confirm the number of shares owned that are held by an independent custodian
    d. Determine that the investment is carried at the fair market value (ID: 5122)

76. In confirming with an outside agent, such as a financial institution, that the agent is holding investment securities in the client's name, an auditor most likely gathers evidence in support of management's financial statement assertions of existence and
    a. Valuation and allocation
    b. Rights and obligations
    c. Completeness
    d. Classification and understandability (ID: 5662)

77. An auditor usually tests the reasonableness of dividend income from investments in publicly-held companies by computing the amounts that should have been received by referring to
    a. Dividend record books produced by investment advisory services
    b. Stock indentures published by corporate transfer agents
    c. Stock ledgers maintained by independent registrars
    d. Annual audited financial statements issued by the investee companies (ID: 6363)

78. When a client engages in transactions involving derivatives, the auditor should
    a. Develop an understanding of the economic substance of each derivative
    b. Confirm with the client's broker whether the derivatives are for trading purposes
    c. Notify the audit committee about the risks involved in derivative transactions
    d. Add an explanatory paragraph to the auditor's report describing the risks associated with each derivative (ID: 8131)

79. An auditor usually determines whether dividend income from publicly-held investments is reasonable by computing the amounts that should have been received by referring to
    a. Stock ledgers maintained by independent registrars
    b. Dividend records on file with the SEC
    c. Records produced by investment services
    d. Minutes of the investee's board of directors (ID: 8135)

80. An auditor's inquiries of management disclosed that the entity recently invested in a series of energy derivatives to hedge against the risks associated with fluctuating oil prices. Under these circumstances, the auditor should

    a. Perform analytical procedures to determine if the derivatives are properly valued
    b. Examine the contracts for possible risk exposure and the need to recognize losses
    c. Confirm the marketability of the derivatives with a commodity specialist
    d. Document the derivatives in the auditor's communication with the audit committee (ID: 8148)

81. In establishing the existence and ownership of long-term investments in the form of publicly-traded stock, an auditor most likely would inspect the securities or

    a. Correspond with the investee company to verify the number of shares owned
    b. Confirm the number of shares owned that are held by an independent custodian
    c. Apply analytical procedures to the dividend income and investments accounts
    d. Inspect the cash receipts journal for amounts that could represent the sale of securities (ID: 8409)

82. An auditor is testing the reasonableness of dividend income from investments in publicly-held companies. The auditor most likely would compute the amount that should have been received and recorded by the client by

    a. Reading the details of the board of directors' meetings
    b. Confirming the details with the investee companies' registrars
    c. Electronically accessing the details of dividend records on the Internet
    d. Examining the details of the client's most recent cutoff bank statement (ID: 8842)

Accounts Payable, Purchases, & Other Liabilities

83. Cooper, CPA, performs a test to determine whether all merchandise for which the client was billed was received. The population for this test consists of all

    a. Merchandise received
    b. Vendors' invoices
    c. Receiving reports
    d. Canceled checks (ID: 195)

84. Which of the following is a substantive test that an auditor most likely would perform to verify the existence and valuation of recorded accounts payable?

    a. Investigating the open purchase order file to ascertain that prenumbered purchase orders are used and accounted for
    b. Receiving the client's mail, unopened, for a reasonable period of time after the year-end to search for unrecorded vendor's invoices
    c. Vouching selected entries in the accounts payable subsidiary ledger to purchase orders and receiving reports
    d. Confirming accounts payable balances with known suppliers who have zero balances (ID: 3932)

85. To determine whether accounts payable are complete, an auditor performs a test to verify that all merchandise received is recorded. The population of documents for this test consists of all

    a. Payment vouchers
    b. Receiving reports
    c. Purchase requisitions
    d. Vendor's invoices (ID: 4263)

86. In auditing accounts payable, an auditor's procedures most likely would focus primarily on management's assertion of
    a. Existence
    b. Classification and understandability
    c. Completeness
    d. Valuation and allocation (ID: 4274)

87. Which of the following procedures would an auditor most likely perform in searching for unrecorded liabilities?
    a. Trace a sample of accounts payable entries recorded just before year-end to the unmatched receiving report file
    b. Compare a sample of purchase orders issued just after year-end with the year-end accounts payable trial balance
    c. Vouch a sample of cash disbursements recorded just after year-end to receiving reports and vendor invoices
    d. Scan the cash disbursements entries recorded just before year-end for indications of unusual transactions (ID: 5994)

88. An auditor traced a sample of purchase orders and the related receiving reports to the purchases journal and the cash disbursements journal. The purpose of this substantive audit procedure most likely was to
    a. Identify unusually large purchases that should be investigated further
    b. Verify that cash disbursements were for goods actually received
    c. Determine that purchases were properly recorded
    d. Test whether payments were for goods actually ordered (ID: 5995)

89. An auditor suspects that certain client employees are ordering merchandise for themselves over the Internet without recording the purchase or receipt of the merchandise. When vendors' invoices arrive, one of the employees approves the invoices for payment. After the invoices are paid, the employee destroys the invoices and the related vouchers. In gathering evidence regarding the fraud, the auditor most likely would select items for testing from the file of all
    a. Cash disbursements
    b. Approved vouchers
    c. Receiving reports
    d. Vendors' invoices (ID: 7019)

90. Which of the following procedures would best detect a liability omission by management?
    a. Inquiry of senior support staff and recently departed employees
    b. Review and check mathematical accuracy of financial statements
    c. Review articles of incorporation and corporate bylaws
    d. Review purchase contracts and other legal documents (ID: 8608)

91. Which of the following tests of details most likely would help an auditor determine whether accounts payable have been misstated?
    a. Examining reported purchase returns that appear too low
    b. Examining vendor statements for amounts **not** reported as purchases
    c. Searching for customer-returned goods that were **not** reported as returns
    d. Reviewing bank transfers recorded as cash received from customers (ID: 9388)

Payroll

92. An auditor most likely would extend substantive tests of payroll when

    a. Payroll is extensively audited by the state government.
    b. Payroll expense is substantially higher than in the prior year.
    c. Overpayments are discovered in performing tests of details.
    d. Employees complain to management about too much overtime. (ID: 4714)

93. An auditor vouched data for a sample of employees in a payroll register to approved clock card data to provide assurance that

    a. Payments to employees are computed at authorized rates.
    b. Employees work the number of hours for which they are paid.
    c. Segregation of duties exists between the preparation and distribution of the payroll.
    d. Internal controls relating to unclaimed payroll checks are operating effectively. (ID: 5655)

94. When control risk is assessed as low for assertions related to payroll, substantive tests of payroll balances most likely would be limited to applying analytical procedures and

    a. Observing the distribution of paychecks
    b. Footing and cross-footing the payroll register
    c. Inspecting payroll tax returns
    d. Recalculating payroll accruals (ID: 5672)

95. An auditor reviews the reconciliation of payroll tax forms that a client is responsible for filing in order to

    a. Verify that payroll taxes are deducted from employees' gross pay
    b. Determine whether internal control activities are operating effectively
    c. Uncover fictitious employees who are receiving payroll checks
    d. Identify potential liabilities for unpaid payroll taxes (ID: 7104)

96. Which of the following payroll control activities would most effectively ensure that payment is made only for work performed?

    a. Require all employees to record arrival and departure by using the time clock
    b. Have a payroll clerk recalculate all time cards
    c. Require all employees to sign their time cards
    d. Require employees to have their direct supervisors approve their time cards (ID: 9357)

Long-Term Liabilities

97. An auditor's program to examine long-term debt most likely would include steps that require

    a. Comparing the carrying amount of the debt to its year-end market value
    b. Correlating interest expense recorded for the period with outstanding debt
    c. Verifying the existence of the holders of the debt by direct confirmation
    d. Inspecting the accounts payable subsidiary ledger for unrecorded long-term debt (ID: 127)

98. In auditing long-term bonds payable, an auditor most likely would

    a. Perform analytical procedures on the bond premium and discount accounts
    b. Examine documentation of assets purchased with bond proceeds for liens
    c. Compare interest expense with the bonds payable amount for reasonableness
    d. Confirm the existence of individual bondholders at year-end (ID: 5133)

Stockholders' Equity

99. The primary responsibility of a bank acting as registrar of capital stock is to
    a. Ascertain that dividends declared do not exceed the statutory amount allowable in the state of incorporation
    b. Account for stock certificates by comparing the total shares outstanding to the total in the shareholders subsidiary ledger
    c. Act as an independent third party between the board of directors and outside investors concerning mergers, acquisitions, and the sale of treasury stock
    d. Verify that stock is issued in accordance with the authorization of the board of directors and the articles of incorporation (ID: 133)

100. In performing tests concerning the granting of stock options, an auditor should
    a. Confirm the transaction with the Secretary of State in the state of incorporation
    b. Verify the existence of option holders in the entity's payroll records or stock ledgers
    c. Determine that sufficient treasury stock is available to cover any new stock issued
    d. Trace the authorization for the transaction to a vote of the board of directors (ID: 5134)

101. In auditing a client's retained earnings account, an auditor should determine whether there are any restrictions on retained earnings that result from loans, agreements, or state law. This procedure is designed to corroborate management's financial statement assertion of
    a. Valuation and allocation
    b. Occurrence
    c. Completeness of disclosures
    d. Rights and obligations (ID: 6713)

102. An auditor usually obtains evidence of stockholders' equity transactions by reviewing the entity's
    a. Minutes of board of directors meetings
    b. Transfer agent's records
    c. Canceled stock certificates
    d. Treasury stock certificate book (ID: 6837)

103. When a company's stock record books are maintained by an outside registrar or transfer agent, the auditor should obtain confirmation from the registrar or transfer agent concerning the
    a. Amount of dividends paid to related parties
    b. Expected proceeds from stock subscriptions receivable
    c. Number of shares issued and outstanding
    d. Proper authorization of stock rights and warrants (ID: 8120)

SIMULATIONS

Problem 5-2 SIMULATION: Kiting

The information below was taken from the bank transfer schedule prepared during the audit of Fox Co.'s financial statements for the year ended December 31, year 1. All checks are dated and issued on December 30, year 1.

Check	Bank Accounts		Disbursement Date		Receipt Date	
No.	From	To	Per Books	Per Bank	Per Books	Per Bank
1	National	Federal	Dec. 30	Jan. 4	Dec. 30	Jan. 3
2	County	State	Jan. 3	Jan. 2	Dec. 30	Dec. 31
3	Federal	American	Dec. 31	Jan. 3	Jan. 2	Jan. 2
4	State	Republic	Jan. 2	Jan. 2	Jan. 2	Dec. 31

A. Which two checks might indicate kiting?

B. Which two checks illustrate deposits/transfers in transit at December 31, year 1? (ID: 9229)

Problem 5-3 SIMULATION: Audit Procedures for Errors & Fraud

The following items represent possible errors and fraud that an auditor suspects are present. The accompanying list of audit procedures represents procedures that the auditor would consider performing to gather evidence concerning possible errors and fraud. For each item, select one or two procedures, as indicated, that the auditor most likely would perform to gather evidence in support of that item.

Possible Errors and Fraud	Audit Procedures
1. The auditor suspects that a kiting scheme exists because an Accounting Department employee who can issue and record checks seems to be leading an unusually luxurious lifestyle. (Select only 1 procedure)	
2. The auditor suspects that the controller wrote several checks and recorded the cash disbursements just before the year-end but did not mail the checks until after the first week of the subsequent year. (Select only 1 procedure)	
3. The entity borrowed funds from a financial institution. Although the transaction was properly recorded, the auditor suspects that the loan created a lien on the entity's real estate that is not disclosed in its financial statements. (Select only 1 procedure)	
4. The auditor discovered an unusually large receivable from one of the entity's new customers. The auditor suspects that the receivable may be fictitious because the auditor has never heard of the customer and because the auditor's initial attempt to confirm the receivable has been ignored by the customer. (Select only 2 procedures)	
5. The auditor suspects that fictitious employees have been placed on the payroll by the entity's payroll supervisor, who has access to payroll records and to the paychecks. (Select only 1 procedure)	
6. The auditor suspects that selected employees of the entity received unauthorized raises from the entity's payroll supervisor, who has access to payroll records. (Select only 1 procedure)	

(ID: 9230)

List of Audit Procedures

A. Compare the details of the cash receipts journal entries with the details of the corresponding daily deposit slips.

B. Scan the debits to the fixed asset accounts and vouch selected amounts to vendors' invoices and management authorization.

C. Perform analytical procedures that compare documented authorized pay rates to the entity's budget and forecast.

D. Obtain the cutoff bank statement and compare the cleared checks to the year-end bank reconciliation.

E. Prepare a bank transfer schedule.

F. Inspect the entity's deeds to its real estate.

G. Make inquiries of the entity's attorney concerning the details of real estate transactions.

H. Confirm the terms of borrowing arrangements with the lender.

I. Examine selected equipment repair orders and supporting documentation to determine the propriety of the charges.

J. Send requests to confirm the entity's accounts receivable on a surprise basis at an interim date.

K. Send a second request for confirmation of the receivable to the customer and make inquiries of a reputable credit agency concerning the customer's creditworthiness.

L. Examine the entity's shipping documents to verify that the merchandise that produced the receivable was actually sent to the customer.

M. Inspect the entity's correspondence files for indications of customer disputes or for evidence that certain shipments were on consignment.

N. Perform edit checks of data on the payroll transaction tapes.

O. Inspect payroll check endorsements for similar handwriting.

P. Observe payroll check distribution on a surprise basis.

Q. Vouch data in the payroll register to documented authorized pay rates in the Human Resources Department's files.

R. Reconcile the payroll checking account and determine if there were unusual time lags between the issuance and payment of payroll checks.

S. Inspect the file of prenumbered vouchers for consecutive numbering and proper approval by an appropriate employee.

T. Determine that the details of selected prenumbered vouchers match the related vendor's invoices.

U. Examine the supporting purchase orders and receiving reports for selected paid vouchers.

Problem 5-4 SIMULATION: Audit Procedures for Long-Term Debt

American Manufacturers, Inc.
Long-Term Debt
October 31, Year 20X1

Lender	Interest rate	Payment terms	Collateral	Balance 10/31/X0	Current year borrowings	Current year reductions	Balance 10/31/X1	Interest paid to	Accrued interest payable 10/31/X1	Comments
▲ First National Bank	10%	Interest only on last day of each quarter; principal due in full on 9/30/X3	Manufacturing equipment	$ 500,000 ■	$200,000 ◆ 3/31/X1	$(100,000) ✪ 6/30/X1	$ 600,000 √	9/30/X1	$5,000 ✖	[1]
▲ Second State Bank	9%	$10,000 principal plus interest due on the 1st of each month; due in full on 1/1/X4	First mortgage on production facilities	380,000 ■	0	(110,000) ✚	270,000 √★	9/30/X1	2,025 ✖	[2]
▲ Third Savings & Loan	12%	$5,000 principal plus interest due on the 15th of each month; due in full on 10/15/X3	Second mortgage on production facilities	180,000 ■	0	(60,000)	120,000 ∗★	10/15/X1	600	[3]
▲ A. Clark, majority stockholder	0%	Due in full 10/31/X3	Unsecured	700,000 ■	0	(200,000) 10/28/X1	500,000 √		0	[4]
				$1,760,000	$200,000	$(470,000)	$1,490,000 ●		$7,625 ●	

[1] First National confirms that interest payments are current and agrees with account balance.

[2] Monthly payment for $12,025 was mailed on 11/3/X1; Second State agrees with account balance.

[3] Third Savings & Loan claims 10/15/X1 payment wasn't received as of 11/5/X1; adjusting entry proposed to increase accrued interest payable.

[4] Borrowed additional $200,000 from Clark on 11/5/X1; need to investigate reborrowing just after year-end and consider imputed interest on 0% stockholder loan.

(ID: 9231)

The items to be answered represent tick marks (symbols) that indicate procedures performed or comments documented in auditing the long-term debt account of American Manufacturers, Inc.

Select, from the accompanying lists of procedures/comments, the procedure/comment that the auditor most likely performed/documented at each point of the audit where a tick mark was made on the working papers. Select only one procedure/comment for each item. Assume that the working papers foot and cross-foot.

Tick Marks	Procedure/Comment
1. ▲	
2. ■	
3. ♦	
4. ✪	
5. ✚	
6. √	
7. ★	
8. ✱	
9. •	
10. ×	

List of Procedures/Comments

A. Confirmed, without exception.

B. Confirmed, with exception.

C. Traced amount to prior year's working papers.

D. Traced amount to current year's trial balance and general ledger.

E. Does not recompute correctly.

F. Tested reasonableness of calculations.

G. Agreed to canceled checks and lender's monthly statements.

H. Agreed to canceled check and board of directors' authorization.

I. Agreed interest rate, terms, and collateral to note & loan agreement.

J. Agreed to loan agreement, validated bank deposit ticket, and board of directors' authorization.

K. Reclassification entry proposed for current portion of long-term debt.

Problem 5-5 SIMULATION: Audit Procedures for Property, Plant & Equipment

American Manufacturers, Inc.
Property, Plant & Equipment and Accumulated Depreciation
October 31, Year 20X1

Property, Plant & Equipment

Account	Balance 10/31/X0		Additions		Disposals		Other		Balance 10/31/X1	
Land	650,000	➢	70,000	↨	0		0		720,000	→
Buildings	3,270,000	➢	230,000	✓	0		(30,000)	⊗	3,470,000	→
Equipment	1,750,000	➢	90,000	<	(12,000)	↔	0		1,828,000	→
Fixtures	850,000	➢	200,000	✓	0		30,000	⊗	1,080,000	→
	6,520,000		590,000		(12,000)		0		7,098,000	

Accumulated Depreciation

Account	Depreciation Rate	Depreciation Method	Balance 10/31/X0		Provision		Disposal	Balance 10/31/X1	
Buildings	5%	SL	1,144,500	➢	168,500	↲	0	1,313,000	→
Equipment	10%	SL	700,000	➢	179,500	↲	(12,000)	867,500	→
Fixtures	15%	SL	510,000	➢	144,750	↲	0	654,750	→
			2,354,500		492,750		(12,000)	2,835,250	

The items to be answered represent tick marks (symbols) that indicate procedures performed or comments documented in auditing the Property, Plant & Equipment and Accumulated Depreciation accounts of American Manufacturers, Inc. During the year under audit, American Manufacturers purchased new computers directly from wholesalers and constructed an addition to one of its buildings. The company's employees also refurbished the fixtures of several older buildings.

Select, from the accompanying lists of procedures/comments, the procedure/comment that the auditor most likely performed/documented at each point of the audit where a tick mark was made on the working papers. Select only one procedure/comment for each item. Assume that the working papers foot and cross-foot.

Tick Marks	Procedure/Comment
1. ➢	
2. ↨	
3. ✓	
4. <	
5. ↔	
6. ⊗	
7. →	
8. ↲	

(ID: 9232)

List of Procedures/Comments

A. Does not recompute correctly.

B. Tested reasonableness of calculation.

C. Traced amount to current year's trial balance and general ledger.

D. Reclassification entry for fixtures erroneously recorded as buildings.

E. Reclassification entry for buildings erroneously recorded as fixtures.

F. Traced amount to prior year's working papers.

G. Sold six fully-depreciated computers to employees; no audit procedures necessary.

H. Confirmed, with exception.

I. Confirmed, without exception.

J. Examined supporting vendors' invoices, canceled checks, asset subsidiary ledger and board of directors' minutes of meetings authorizing transactions.

K. Examined supporting work orders and engineers' reports, canceled checks, asset subsidiary ledger, and board of directors' minutes of meetings authorizing transactions.

L. Examined supporting deed and purchase contract, canceled checks, asset subsidiary ledger, and board of directors' minutes of meeting authorizing transactions.

Problem 5-6 SIMULATION: Accounts Receivable (AR) Confirmations

The auditor requested the company's aged accounts receivable schedule listing the total amount owed by each customer as of December 31, year 2. The audit team sent the following positive confirmation requests to a sample of the company's customers.

Confirmation Letters

February 15, year 3

Chip Technology
500 E. Fifth Street
Cincinnati, OH 45202

Re: Balance at December 31, year 2 - $95,000

Dear Sirs:

As of December 31, year 2, our records indicate that you have a balance due to our company in the amount listed above. Please complete and sign the bottom portion of this letter, and return the entire letter to our auditors, Whisp, LLP, P.O. Box 100, Cleveland, Ohio 44115.

A stamped, self-addressed envelope is enclosed for your convenience.

Sincerely,

Jim Johnston
Company Controller

The above balance is [ ] Correct

[X] Incorrect (show amount) $92,000

If incorrect, please provide information that could help to reconcile your account.

Recipient's Comment: Our records indicate that check #45998 for $3,000 was mailed on December 24, year 2.

Sue Smith	AP Supervisor	3/2/year 3
Signature	Title	Date

Auditor's note to file:

Per discussion with the controller, this customer's payment was received on December 28, but was not processed until January 4.

February 15, year 3

BiCon Semiconductor
8700 West Ave.
Rockland, KY 46009

Re: Balance at December 31, year 2 - $66,700

Dear Sirs:

As of December 31, year 2, our records indicate that you have a balance due to our company in the amount listed above. Please complete and sign the bottom portion of this letter, and return the entire letter to our auditors, Whisp, LLP, P.O. Box 100, Cleveland, Ohio 44115.

A stamped, self-addressed envelope is enclosed for your convenience.

Sincerely,

Jim Johnston
Company Controller

The above balance is [ ] Correct

[ ] Incorrect (show amount) ______

If incorrect, please provide information that could help to reconcile your account.

Recipient's Comment: *Blank*

Signature	Title	Date

Auditor's note to file:

This confirmation was returned by the postal service as "return to sender—no such addressee at this location." This was the second attempt to reach the customer.

February 15, year 3

Whistler's Computer Warehouse
700 – 800 Adams St.
Newport, CT 11223

Re: Balance at December 31, year 2 - $120,050

Dear Sirs:

As of December 31, year 2, our records indicate that you have a balance due to our company in the amount listed above. Please complete and sign the bottom portion of this letter, and return the entire letter to our auditors, Whisp, LLP, P.O. Box 100, Cleveland, Ohio 44115.

A stamped, self-addressed envelope is enclosed for your convenience.

Sincerely,

Jim Johnston
Company Controller

The above balance is ☐ Correct

☒ Incorrect (show amount) $118,050

If incorrect, please provide information that could help to reconcile your account.

Recipient's Comment: The materials from invoice #145 were returned on December 12, year 2.

Warren C. Worth	AP Supervisor	2/25/year 3
Signature	Title	Date

Auditor's note to file:

Firm confirmed this with the A/R supervisor.

February 15, year 3

Digital Digits
15 8th Ave.
Washington, OR 78899

Re: Balance at December 31, year 2 - $2,000,000

Dear Sirs:

As of December 31, year 2, our records indicate that you have a balance due to our company in the amount listed above. Please complete and sign the bottom portion of this letter, and return the entire letter to our auditors, Whisp, LLP, P.O. Box 100, Cleveland, Ohio 44115.

A stamped, self-addressed envelope is enclosed for your convenience.

Sincerely,

Jim Johnston
Company Controller

The above balance is ☐ Correct

☒ Incorrect (show amount) $2,760,000

If incorrect, please provide information that could help to reconcile your account.

Recipient's Comment: In addition, we have invoices #A1768 ($360,000) & A1769 ($400,000), but I'm not sure when they are from.

Darlene Dunham	AP Supervisor	3/5/year 3
Signature	Title	Date

Auditor's note to file:

Blank.

February 15, year 3

Rockford's
37 73rd Street
Leder, VA 39281

Re: Balance at December 31, year 2 - $1,288,698

Dear Sirs:

As of December 31, year 2, our records indicate that you have a balance due to our company in the amount listed above. Please complete and sign the bottom portion of this letter, and return the entire letter to our auditors, Whisp, LLP, P.O. Box 100, Cleveland, Ohio 44115.

A stamped, self-addressed envelope is enclosed for your convenience.

Sincerely,

Jim Johnston
Company Controller.

The above balance is [X] Correct

[ ] Incorrect (show amount) $______

If incorrect, please provide information that could help to reconcile your account.

Recipient's Comment: Please be aware that as of March 1, we are changing our name to Richards' Service and Support.

Signature	Title	Date

Auditor's note to file:

Blank

February 15, year 3

Jungle Applications
1200 East End Drive
Richelieu, KY 18998

Re: Balance at December 31, year 2 - $40,000

Dear Sirs:

As of December 31, year 2, our records indicate that you have a balance due to our company in the amount listed above. Please complete and sign the bottom portion of this letter, and return the entire letter to our auditors, Whisp, LLP, P.O. Box 100, Cleveland, Ohio 44115.

A stamped, self-addressed envelope is enclosed for your convenience.

Sincerely,

Jim Johnston
Company Controller

The above balance is [ ] Correct

[ ] Incorrect (show amount) $______

If incorrect, please provide information that could help to reconcile your account.

Recipient's Comment: Sorry for the inconvenience, but our A/P system is unable to confirm balances unless we have purchase order numbers.

Julie Ashton	AP Supervisor	2/26/year 3
Signature	Title	Date

Auditor's note to file:

Blank

Review the confirmations and subsequent comments at the bottom of each confirmation and determine the action required for each one. Select the best action to follow from the selection list below. Choose only one action per confirmation. An action may be used once, more than once, or not at all.

Customer	Action Required
1. Chip Technology	
2. BiCon Semiconductor	
3. Whistler's Computer Warehouse	
4. Digital Digits	
5. Rockford's	
6. Jungle Applications	

(ID: 9832)

Selection List

A. Exception noted; propose adjustment and request that the controller post it to the accounting records.	D. Verify by examining shipping documents and subsequent cash collections.
B. Send a second request for confirmation to the customer.	E. Verify that additional invoices noted on confirmation pertain to the subsequent year.
C. Trace to open sales order detail as of December 31, year 2.	F. Not an exception, no further audit work deemed necessary.

Problem 5-7 SIMULATION: Audit Procedures for Errors & Fraud

The following items represent possible errors and fraud that an auditor suspects are present. The accompanying list of audit procedures represents procedures that the auditor would consider performing to gather evidence concerning possible errors and fraud. For each item, select one or two procedures, as indicated, that the auditor most likely would perform to gather evidence in support of that item.

Possible Errors and Fraud	Audit Procedures
1. The entity's cash receipts of the first few days of the subsequent year were properly deposited in its general operating account after the year-end. However, the auditor suspects that the entity recorded the cash receipts in its books during the last week of the year under audit. (Select only 1 procedure)	
2. The auditor suspects that vouchers were prepared and processed by an Accounting Department employee for merchandise that was neither ordered nor received by the entity. (Select only 1 procedure)	
3. The details of invoices for equipment repairs were not clearly identified or explained to the Accounting Department employees. The auditor suspects that the bookkeeper incorrectly recorded the repairs as fixed assets. (Select only 1 procedure)	
4. The auditor suspects that a lapping scheme exists because an Accounting Department employee who has access to cash receipts also maintains the accounts receivable ledger and refuses to take any vacation or sick days. (Select only 2 procedures)	
5. The auditor suspects that the entity is inappropriately increasing the cash reported on its balance sheet by drawing a check on one account and not recording it as an outstanding check on that account, and simultaneously recording it as a deposit in a second account. (Select only 1 procedure)	
6. The auditor suspects that the entity's controller has overstated sales and accounts receivable by recording fictitious sales to regular customers in the entity's books. (Select only 2 procedures)	

(ID: 9233)

List of Audit Procedures

A. Compare the details of the cash receipts journal entries with the details of the corresponding daily deposit slips.

B. Scan the debits to the fixed asset accounts and vouch selected amounts to vendors' invoices and management authorization.

C. Perform analytical procedures that compare documented authorized pay rates to the entity's budget and forecast.

D. Obtain the cutoff bank statement and compare the cleared checks to the year-end bank reconciliation.

E. Prepare a bank transfer schedule.

F. Inspect the entity's deeds to its real estate.

G. Make inquiries of the entity's attorney concerning the details of real estate transactions.

H. Confirm the terms of borrowing arrangements with the lender.

I. Examine selected equipment repair orders and supporting documentation to determine the propriety of the charges.

J. Send requests to confirm the entity's accounts receivable on a surprise basis at an interim date.

K. Send a second request for confirmation of the receivable to the customer and make inquiries of a reputable credit agency concerning the customer's creditworthiness.

L. Examine the entity's shipping documents to verify that the merchandise that produced the receivable was actually sent to the customer.

M. Inspect the entity's correspondence files for indications of customer disputes or for evidence that certain shipments were on consignment.

N. Perform edit checks of data on the payroll transaction tapes.

O. Inspect payroll check endorsements for similar handwriting.

P. Observe payroll check distribution on a surprise basis.

Q. Vouch data in the payroll register to documented authorized pay rates in the Human Resources Department's files.

R. Reconcile the payroll checking account and determine if there were unusual time lags between the issuance and payment of payroll checks.

S. Inspect the file of prenumbered vouchers for consecutive numbering and proper approval by an appropriate employee.

T. Determine that the details of selected prenumbered vouchers match the related vendor's invoices.

U. Examine the supporting purchase orders and receiving reports for selected paid vouchers.

Problem 5-8 SIMULATION: Financial Statement Assertions for Investments

Larkin, CPA, has been engaged to audit the financial statements of Vernon Distributors, Inc., a continuing audit client, for the year ended September 30, year 1. After obtaining an understanding of Vernon's internal control, Larkin assessed the risk of material misstatement as high for all financial statement assertions concerning investments.

Larkin prepared a partial audit program of substantive procedures listed in the table below.

Identify the primary financial statement assertion relative to investments that would be addressed by each of the procedures. An assertion may be used once, more than once, or not at all.

Audit Procedures	Primary Assertion
1. Obtain positive confirmation as of the balance sheet date of the investments held by any independent custodian.	
2. Determine that income from investments has been properly recorded as accrued or collected by reference to published sources, by computation, and by tracing to recorded amounts.	
3. For investments in nonpublic entities, compare carrying value to information in the most recently available audited financial statements.	
4. Determine that all transfers between trading and available-for-sale portfolios have been properly authorized and recorded.	
5. Determine that any other-than-temporary decline in the price of an investment has been properly recorded.	

(ID: 9234)

Financial Statement Assertions

A. Presentation & disclosure

B. Existence

C. Contingency disclosure

D. Monetary adjustments

E. Occurrence & rights & obligations

F. Completeness

G. Classes of transactions

H. Valuation & accuracy & allocation

I. Account balances

J. Classification & understandability

Problem 5-9 SIMULATION: Research

With regard to substantive procedures performed at an interim date, which citation in the professional standards provides guidance on covering the remaining period?

[ ] § [ ] [ ] (ID: 90380)

Problem 5-10 SIMULATION: Research

Which citation in the professional standards provides guidance regarding the conditions that should be present to allow an auditor to use negative confirmation requests as the sole substantive audit procedure to address an assessed risk of material misstatement at the assertion level?

[ ] § [ ] [ ] (ID: 90381)

Solution 5-1 MULTIPLE-CHOICE ANSWERS

1. (c) In testing the existence assertion for an asset, the auditor would start with the accounting records themselves to determine that the assets recorded on the client's books do exist. Further evidence of the asset existence would then be found in the supporting evidence. (ID: 136)

2. (d) A reconciliation between the amounts included in the cash flow statement and other financial statements would be a procedure the auditor would perform because the cash flow statement amounts are a result of the transactions reflected in and the changes in balances on the other financial statements. Relationships between current year and prior year amounts due do not necessarily exist as can be expected on the balance sheet and income statement. This procedure would provide more audit evidence in the overall review stage of the audit for the balance sheet and income statement. Answer b. is a procedure an auditor would perform in auditing the cash balance on the balance sheet. Answer c. is a procedure the auditor would perform in auditing the cash balance on the balance sheet. (ID: 5674)

3. (c) To determine whether transactions have been recorded (completeness), procedures include tracing from supporting documentation (original source documents) to accounting records. Testing from general ledger balances, the adjusted trial balance, and general journal entries (vouching) would provide evidence of existence or occurrence. (ID: 5675)

4. (c) In selecting particular substantive procedures to achieve audit objectives, an auditor considers, among other things, the risk of material misstatement of the financial statements. Omitting a test of details of transactions in some situations would not be a violation of auditing standards. Attaining assurance about the reliability of the accounting system and evaluating whether management's policies and procedures operated effectively are objectives of tests of controls. (ID: 5998)

5. (a) While the confirmation of accounts receivable and the other answers are common audit procedures, confirmation of accounts payable is an extended procedure and usually occurs under unusual conditions. The greater the combined level of risk, the greater the assurance that the auditor needs from substantive tests related to a financial statement assertion. In these situations, the auditor might use confirmation procedures rather than or in conjunction with tests directed toward documents or parties within the entity. In a low risk situation, review of post balance sheet date payments to vendors may adequately substantiate the accounts payable balance. (ID: 5691)

6. (c) The lack of misstatements at the interim date would not cause the auditor to increase the assessment of control risk. The auditor most likely would review supporting documents for new large balances and evaluate significant changes in year-end balances. Without an increase in the assessment of control risk, additional extensive procedures, such as sending confirmations to new customers and reviewing subsequent cash collections are unlikely. If the auditor planned to resend confirmations for any customer balances remaining at year-end when interim confirmations returned from these same customers appeared reasonable, it is unlikely that the auditor would plan to confirm accounts receivable as of an interim date. (ID: 7840)

7. (d) Applying principal substantive tests to the details of an asset or liability account as of an interim date rather than as of the balance sheet date potentially increases the risk that misstatements that may exist at the balance sheet date will not be detected by the auditor. Performing substantive tests at an interim date does not eliminate the use of any sampling techniques. The auditor would only need to consider reperforming substantive tests, as of the balance sheet date, if misstatements are detected at the interim date. Asset and liability accounts should be examined as of the balance sheet date if there are rapidly changing economic conditions. (ID: 8126)

8. (b) The higher the risk of material misstatement, the more effective it may be to perform substantive procedures nearer to, or at, the period end. If the auditor performs test of controls or substantive procedures at an interim date, the auditor needs to consider the additional evidence for the reminder of the period, including the control environment. Effective internal controls allow the auditor greater confidence in such evidence than ineffective controls. A new sales incentive program may provide increased motivation for employees to inflate sales numbers, and hence, accounts receivable; any new program provides increased potential for errors or

fraud. A high turnover of senior management is a risk factor of fraud due to fraudulent financial reporting. A first engagement of a new client tends to increase the risk that something will be overlooked due to the unfamiliarity with the client's operations. Editor Note: While one could argue that interim testing of A/R would be appropriate for a new client, in order that audit staff have additional time to investigate unusual items and, if significant issues are found, more time for management and the auditor to address such issues; however, the examiners instruct candidates to select the best answer. (ID: 8398)

9. (d) When substantive procedures are performed at an interim date, the auditor should perform further substantive procedures or a combination of substantive procedures and tests of controls covering the remaining period to provide a reasonable basis for extending the audit conclusions to the end of the period. Interim testing increases the risk that misstatements existing at the period end will not be detected. Evaluations of inappropriate assessments of risk would not be a factor in deciding whether interim testing would be appropriate. Sampling risk need not necessarily be projected at the maximum for tests covering the remaining period. Whether or not substantive tests of accounts receivable may be performed at an interim date does not hinge on whether the balance is material to the financial statements. (ID: 8413)

10. (d) The review of travel and entertainment expenses can be done prior to the balance sheet date; however, when substantive procedures are performed at an interim date, the auditor should perform further audit procedures to cover the remaining period that provide a reasonable basis for extending the audit conclusion from the interim date to the balance sheet date. Various phases of an audit are completed during the subsequent period that extends from after the balance sheet date to the date of the audit report. These include the other answers: review of subsequent events (self-explanatory), the search for unrecorded liabilities, and inquiry of the client's legal counsel. Certain procedures are applied to transactions occurring after the balance sheet date such as the examination of data to assure that proper cutoffs have been made and the examination of data that would provide information to aid the auditor in the evaluation of the assets and liabilities as of the balance sheet date. These procedures would include the search through these post balance sheet transactions for evidence of liabilities that existed at the balance sheet date, but were not recorded. The attorney's response should include coverage of as much of this subsequent period as possible, i.e., have an effective date (the latest date of the period covered by the response) as close to the date of the auditor's report as practicable. Editor Note: As a practical matter, an auditor may choose to send an initial request to the attorney earlier in the audit, so that the completion of the audit is not delayed, with the understanding that an update will be needed close to the report date. (ID: 8638)

11. (c) The auditor should perform other auditing procedures with respect to the period after the balance sheet date for the purpose of ascertaining the occurrence of subsequent events that may require adjustment or disclosure including investigating changes in long-term debt after year-end. Other procedures are applied to transactions occurring after the balance sheet date for the purpose of assurance that proper cutoffs have been made, and for the purpose of obtaining information to aid in the evaluation of the assets and liabilities as of the balance sheet date. Answers a., b., and d. would not provide evidence about subsequent events as a. is a test of controls and b. and d. are not common procedures. (ID: 5683)

12. (b) Analytics involve comparisons of recorded amounts, or ratios developed from recorded amounts, to expectations developed by the auditor. The auditor develops expectations by identifying relationships that reasonably are expected to exist from understanding the client and the industry in which the client operates. In this case, the auditor expected the current year's gross margin to be comparable to the prior year's gross margin. Tests of transactions are test of details that involves other types of procedures such as tracing and vouching to determine whether transactions were recorded correctly. Tests of controls evaluate the effectiveness of the design and operation of policies and procedures in preventing or detecting material misstatements. (ID: 8140)

13. (a) The positive (confirmation) form is preferable when individual account balances are relatively large or when there is reason to believe that there may be a substantial number of accounts in dispute or with errors or fraud. In this case, errors or fraud are likely since internal controls are weak. Negative confirmations are used when the assessed level of control risk is low. With weak internal controls, the auditor needs to obtain third party verification. (ID: 178)

14. (a) Unreturned negative confirmations do not provide explicit evidence. Negative confirmations may be effective when the combined assessed level of inherent and control risk is low. Alternative procedures are used for unreturned positive confirmations. The auditor would be more likely to use positive confirmations, which provide more persuasive evidence, if understatements are suspected. (ID: 5663)

15. (c) The A/R and sales audit objective related to the completeness assertion is to ascertain that all sales and receivables that should be recorded are properly recorded. Customers may not be inclined to report understatement errors in their accounts, and thus not all the sales and receivables that should be recorded are necessarily recorded. It is not as likely that customers will merely sign and return the confirmation without verifying its details; the accounts they are verifying represent liabilities to them. It is more likely that the customers will not return forms. A nonresponse could mean that the intended recipient did not receive the request, has misplaced or not processed the request, or has returned the request but it was delayed or lost in transit. Auditors typically confirm few accounts with low recorded balances and a high percentage of accounts with large balances. (ID: 5986)

16. (d) Negative confirmations are used when the auditor can tolerate a high level of detection risk, i.e., when the combined assessed level of inherent risk and control risk relative to accounts receivable is low. Negative confirmations provide less persuasive evidence than positive confirmations because the auditor is unable to determine if a lack of response is due to customer agreement or lack of delivery of the request for confirmation, etc. If the total recorded amount of accounts receivable is immaterial to the financial statement taken as a whole, confirmations of any kind would be unlikely. If response rates in prior years were inadequate, the auditor is more likely to consider other procedures rather than a type of confirmation for which response rates cannot be determined. If recipients are likely to return positive confirmations requests without verifying the accuracy of the information, it is unlikely they would have greater inclination to verify the accuracy of the information for negative confirmations. (ID: 6582)

17. (a) Blank A/R confirmations request that the customers supply the amount owed, if any. By having the customers provide the information, the auditor increases the likelihood that customers did examine their records. Positive confirmations have the amount that the customers owe provided by the client, typically invoice-by-invoice. The invoice-by-invoice form simplifies verifying subsequent cash receipts as compared to a single sum owed. Negative confirmations request the customer to return the confirmation, with corrections, only if their records differ. They usually are used if the combined assessed level of inherent risk and control risk is low, i.e., if few exceptions are expected. (ID: 6714)

18. (d) The client prepares account confirmation requests. To maintain customer goodwill, an indication that a nonresponse will cause a second request should be avoided. A nonresponse to a positive confirmation request generates further inquiries, not an assumption that a balance is correct. (ID: 6834)

19. (c) Answer c. clearly states the consequences of the client's customer's actions and informs the customer of the deadline. Answer b. omits any indication of a deadline. While informing the client's customers that the confirmation request is not a payment request may be included in the letter, it only informs the client's customers what not to do—rather than the desired action. Amounts on A/R confirmation requests represent all owed amounts, not just those that are overdue. (ID: 6835)

20. (d) Blank confirmations merely ask for a balance owed, whereas regular positive confirmations include the amount that the customer owes provided by the client, either listed by invoice or as a single sum. Providing additional information may make the task of confirming debts appear easier to the client's customers' employees, resulting in a response getting prepared and approved, rather than indefinitely waiting in stacks for a supervisor to assign, examine, and then approve. (ID: 7640)

21. (b) Confirmation requests always should be mailed by the auditor and be returned directly to the auditor's place of business. This is to diminish the possibility that the confirmation request could be altered by the client, either during the mailing process or upon receipt. The internal auditor need not sign the form. It is not inappropriate to get confirmations for closed accounts. The internal auditor may prepare confirmation requests. (ID: 7800)

22. (b) By including a list of items or invoices that constitute the customers' account balances, the auditor makes it easier for the customers to respond, irrespective of how the customers' records are organized; this tends to increase the response rate. Neither restricting the selection of accounts to be confirmed to those customers with large balances nor explaining to customers that discrepancies will be investigated by an independent third party will likely have much impact on the response rate. (Furthermore; most customers understand that an auditor is independent and is the one investigating discrepancies.) If anything, asking customers to respond to the request by fax may slow or decrease the response rate, as this may be cumbersome for some customers. (ID: 8407)

23. (c) The inclusion of client-prepared statements (that show the details of the account balance) with the confirmation requests would most likely prove beneficial, i.e., improve the response rate. Copies of shipping documents or purchase orders would not be as beneficial as a detailed statement tied to the actual account balance. Shipping documents often do not include the cost of the goods shipped. Lists of the customer's recent payments that the client has already recorded would not be included in the account balance and thus, are irrelevant—the purpose of the confirmation process is to confirm unpaid amounts. Prices included on purchase orders are generated by the client's customers rather than the client and thus may not be current or include applicable or correct discounts. Also, individual purchase orders may include items that were back-ordered by your client and thus not yet billed, i.e., not part of the current account balance. (ID: 9907)

24. (b) An auditor is required to confirm accounts receivable if the accounts receivable balances are material to the financial statements. Confirmation of accounts receivable is a generally accepted auditing procedure. It is generally presumed that evidence obtained from third parties will provide the auditor with higher-quality audit evidence than is typically available from within the entity. Thus, there is a presumption that the auditor will request the confirmation of accounts receivable during an audit unless one of the following is true: accounts receivable are immaterial to the financial statements; the use of confirmations would be ineffective; or the auditor's combined assessed level of inherent and control risk is low, and the assessed level, in conjunction with the evidence expected to be provided by analytical procedures or other substantive tests of details, is sufficient to reduce audit risk to an acceptably low level for the applicable financial statement assertions. (In many situations, both confirmation of accounts receivable and other substantive tests of details are necessary to reduce audit risk to an acceptably low level for the applicable financial statement assertions.) An auditor who has not requested confirmations in the examination of accounts receivable should document how he or she overcame this presumption. (ID: 89764)

25. (d) Unusual or complex transactions may be associated with high levels of inherent risk and control risk. If the combined assessed level of inherent and control risk over the occurrence of revenue related to a large complex sale is high, the auditor should consider confirming the terms of that sale. (ID: 89765)

26. (d) Inquiries about related-party transactions and inventories at external locations are not focused on accounting estimates. Accounting estimates appropriately change with changes in circumstances; further, determining deviation from historical patterns doesn't indicate that all accounting estimates are identified. Unresolved litigation is a frequent reason for accounting estimates, due to the uncertainty in the litigation outcome. (ID: 7094)

27. (d) The auditor's objectives in evaluating an entity's accounting estimates are to ensure (1) all accounting estimates that could be material to the financial statements have been developed, (2) the estimates are reasonable, and (3) the estimates are in conformity with the applicable financial reporting framework and are disclosed properly. (ID: 8166)

28. (c) In evaluating the reasonableness of an estimate, the auditor normally concentrates on key factors and assumptions that are deviations from historical patterns; sensitive to variations (not stable and insensitive to variations); subjective and susceptible to misstatement and bias (not the opposite); and, of course, significant to the accounting estimate. The auditor would expect the estimates to be consistent with industry guidelines, so estimates that did not conform would bear more scrutiny to obtain evidence that the variation was reasonable under the circumstances. (ID: 8649)

29. (a) Assumptions that are susceptible to bias provide an opportunity for the overstatement of assets and income and understatement of liabilities. Assumptions that meet the criteria of the other answers offer less scope for creative accounting. (ID: 6395)

30. (a) The auditor's objective when evaluating accounting estimates is to determine if all accounting estimates that could be material to the financial statements have been developed; are reasonable in the circumstances; and are presented in conformity with the applicable financial reporting framework and are properly disclosed. The opposite is true of alternatives "b" and "d", i.e., accounting estimates should be used when data concerning past events can**not** be accumulated in a timely, cost-effective manner; and accounting estimates **should** be used when the measurement of some amounts or the valuation of some accounts is uncertain, pending the outcome of future events. Obviously, there is no need to use an estimate for accounts receivable greater than 90 days past due or any other account / amount that can be readily calculated using actual data. (ID: 8810)

31. (b) Confirmation is undertaken to obtain evidence about financial assertions made by management. When audit evidence can be obtained from knowledgeable independent sources outside an entity, it provides greater assurance of reliability. Answers a., c., and d. represent audit procedures that may be performed and evidence that can be obtained as a by-product of receiving the standard confirmation; however, they do not represent the primary purpose for obtaining the confirmation. (ID: 3930)

32. (a) Lapping involves the theft of one customer's payment and subsequently crediting the customer with payment made by another customer. Future remittances may be deposited but would be credited to the account from which funds were stolen, thus comparison of remittance dates would detect the scheme. Answers b., c., and d. occur after the theft and would not show differences to pursue. (ID: 5975)

33. (d) The AICPA Standard Form to Confirm Account Balance Information With Financial Institutions is designed to substantiate information that is stated on the confirmation request; the form is not designed to provide assurance that information about accounts not listed on the form will be reported. The bank employee completing the form may be unaware of all the financial relationships that the client has with the bank and the request may not ask specifically about all the financial relationships, thus the usefulness of the confirmation in providing evidence for financial statement assertions may be limited. Responding to bank confirmation requests is a normal activity for a bank. It would be unlikely that a bank employee would not believe that the bank is obligated to verify confidential information to the third party, especially as the confirmation request is signed by the client authorizing the bank to release the information to the auditor. The bank would not have access to the client's bank reconciliation and thus would not inspect its accuracy. The bank does have access to the client's cutoff bank statements, but that information is not used by the bank to confirm year-end balances. (ID: 5992)

34. (a) An auditor compares prior year checks listed in the cutoff statement compared to the year-end outstanding checks to make sure that all year-end outstanding checks were handled correctly on the bank reconciliation. Deposits in transit are listed on the bank reconciliation, not on the cutoff statements; once on the cutoff statement, they cease to be in transit. Checks dated after year-end in the cutoff statement should not be listed as outstanding at year-end. Checks and deposits dated after year-end merely provide information about liabilities or assets available at year-end. (ID: 7098)

35. (c) One would expect a high account balance with a high deposit level. A kiting scheme involves drawing a check on one account to inflate the balance in another; it usually requires careful attention by a trusted perpetrator who is familiar with the operation, and especially, knows the time for checks to clear. This would tend not to be the situation with high turnover. An ATM withdrawal is posted quickly, reducing the time lag necessary for kiting. Kiting would not tend to produce large checks on any one particular day of the week, unless the perpetrator had an unusual work pattern. (ID: 7107)

36. (d) This bank transfer results in an overstatement of cash at December 31. The receipt of the transfer was recorded in the books on December 31, thus increasing that bank account's cash balance on that date. However, the disbursement of the transfer was not recorded in the books until January 4; thus, that bank account's cash balance was not decreased until after the financial statement date. The bank transfers indicated

in answers a., b., and c. do not result in a misstatement of cash. The books recorded the disbursement and receipt of each of these bank transfers in the same fiscal year. (ID: 8380)

37. (c) In general, cutoff tests are used to detect unrecorded transactions at the end of the period. In this question, the auditor would most likely detect unrecorded sales for the year by reviewing a sales cutoff to determine that sales were recorded in the period in which title to the goods passed to the customer. Such a review would not reveal shipments lacking invoices, excessive write-offs of accounts receivable, or lapping of year-end accounts receivable. (ID: 2778)

38. (c) The segregation of custody and reporting is an important internal control that is most likely to deter a lapping scheme. Authorization of write-offs by a supervisor is a good control but would not in itself prevent an employee from misappropriating accounts receivable collections because the supervisor is unfamiliar with the accounts, as indicated in the question, and would, therefore, not be aware of customers who are delinquent in their payments. Answers a. and d. are examples of good internal controls but would not by themselves uncover a lapping scheme. (ID: 3910)

39. (d) Assertions about completeness deal with whether all transactions, accounts, and disclosures that should be presented in the financial statements are included. Periodically accounting for the numerical sequence of documents and invoices helps ensure that all entries affecting those accounts have been recognized and posted. Answer a. deals with whether recorded transactions have actually occurred and pertain to the entity. Answer b. deals with whether assets are the rights of the entity and liabilities are the obligations of the entity. Answer c. deals with whether assets, liabilities, and equity interests have been included in the financial statements at appropriate amounts. (ID: 3923)

40. (b) Valuation and allocation is the assertion that assets, liabilities, and equity interests are included in the financial statements at appropriate amounts and any resulting valuation or allocation adjustments are appropriately recorded. Answer a. deals with whether assets, liabilities, or equity interests exist at a given date. Answer c. deals with whether all transactions, accounts, and disclosures that should be presented in the financial statements are so included. Answer d. deals with whether assets are the rights of the entity and liabilities are the obligations of the entity. (ID: 3925)

41. (b) Assertions about completeness deal with whether all transactions, assets, liabilities, equity interests and disclosures that should be presented in the financial statements are included. Inspecting the entity's reports of prenumbered shipping documents that have not been recorded in the sales journal will help the auditor determine whether all transactions have been accounted for. Answer a. is a clerical test for accuracy. Answer c. relates to management's assertion of accuracy and valuation. Answer d. is a test of controls for authorization of credit prior to the sale being approved. (ID: 4692)

42. (a) Valuation and allocation deal with whether assets, liabilities, and equity interests are included in financial statements at appropriate amounts. If the bad debt allowance account is too low, net accounts receivable would be too high, and the assets would, therefore, be overstated. (ID: 5123)

43. (b) When the auditor has already gathered evidence supporting cash receipts and accounts receivable, the same evidence would support sales. Thus, having already gathered this evidence and having assessed control risk as low for the existence or occurrence assertion regarding sales transactions, the auditor most likely would conclude that he or she has substantial evidence for sales and would limit substantive tests of sales transactions. Evidence supporting opening and closing inventory balances, shipping and receiving activities, and cutoffs of sales and purchases would give only limited information regarding sales. (ID: 5993)

44. (c) This procedure helps ensure that the accounts receivable (a right to payment) amount is correct, but not that it is reported or disclosed appropriately and clearly. Classification and understandability is an assertion about presentation and disclosure. (ID: 7101)

45. (a) A/R turnover is the number of times that the A/R balance is collected during the year. Fictitious sales increase A/R, but leave collections the same, so A/R turnover decreases. A/R turnover would be unaffected by current inventory levels. Tightening credit-granting policies would tend to increase A/R turnover. Lap-

ping receivables in two years would result in both years' receivables being misstated, but unless the volume of lapped amounts changed, turnover would not be affected. (ID: 7109)

46. (b) This test is performed to satisfy the audit objective of completeness. The primary purpose of this objective is to establish whether all transactions that should have been recorded by the client are included in the accounts. (ID: 7494)

47. (c) To discover understated (unrecorded) sales, the auditor would most likely trace transactions from shipping documents to sales invoices. This would reveal orders that have been shipped, but not billed and is an example of testing for completeness. Vouching from sales invoices to shipping documents (the opposite direction) is a test to substantiate that sales are not overstated (verify their occurrence or existence). Comparing entries between the cash receipts journal and the sales journal would verify that the entries were posted correctly, but it would not locate an unrecorded sale. Editor Note: The sales and cash receipts journals are often combined in one journal. (ID: 8622)

48. (b) Inspecting agreements to determine whether any inventory is pledged as collateral or subject to any liens would provide the accountant with evidence concerning the assertions about rights and obligations which deal with whether assets are the rights of the entity and liabilities are the obligations of the entity. (ID: 2770)

49. (b) Assertions about completeness deal with whether all transactions, accounts, and disclosures that should be presented in the financial statements are so included. By tracing from the inventory floor to the records, the auditor is checking for completeness. Answer a. would deal with the rights to the inventory which would be evidenced by vendor invoices. Answer c. would be tested by vouching or going from the inventory list to the floor to identify the assets are in existence. Answer d. would be tested by multiplying the inventory count of an item by its cost based on a vendor's invoice. (ID: 4706)

50. (a) The procedure in answer a. helps provide assurance about valuation of inventory. The procedures in answers b., c., and d. provide assurance regarding existence. (ID: 5121)

51. (b) Normally, when perpetual inventory records are well-kept and physical count comparisons are made on a regular basis, an auditor may perform inventory observation during or after the end of the period being audited. An auditor would probably request that the physical inventory count be done at year-end if the auditor does not have much confidence in the ability of the internal controls to detect errors when control risk is high. (ID: 5131)

52. (a) The valuation, existence, and completeness of the inventory are not in question. The inventory is collateral for a loan; disclosure is the issue. (ID: 5658)

53. (a) The cost of obsolete or slow-moving inventory may have to be written down; this affects the valuation assertion. Rights, obligations, existence, classification, and understandability are not affected by obsolete or slow-moving items. (ID: 5661)

54. (d) Physical counts of inventory items higher than the recorded quantities in perpetual inventory records could be the result of the failure to record sales returns in the books when sales return items were returned to inventory. Failure to record purchase discounts would have nothing to do with the recorded quantities in the records. Failure to record purchase returns and sales would result in the physical counts being lower than the quantities in the perpetual records. (ID: 5670)

55. (c) To gain assurance that all items in a client's inventory listing schedule are valid, an auditor most likely would trace items listed in the listing schedule to inventory tags and the auditor's recorded count sheets. To trace the inventory tags to the listing schedule and to trace items listed in receiving reports and vendors' invoices to the listing schedule would provide assurance that all the inventory items are on the schedule, but would not give assurance that all of the items on the schedule are valid; some items on the schedule may not exist. Tracing tags to receiving reports and vendors' invoices does not involve the inventory listing schedule and thus does not provide any assurances related to the listing schedule. (ID: 5671)

56. (b) The formula for inventory turnover is cost of goods sold divided by average inventory. Cost of goods sold includes only inventory related expenses and thus is the best value to use to compare to average inventory to calculate inventory turnover. Net sales, operating income, and gross sales are all based on the prices charged the customers, not the actual costs to the company for the goods that were sold, and thus are not as closely related to the costs associated with inventory. (ID: 5989)

57. (c) When auditing inventory, the auditor needs to obtain evidence supporting management's assertions about presentation and disclosure, answer a., and valuation, answers b. and d. It would not be unusual for the client to have inventory out on consignment or held in a warehouse beyond the client's premises. Also, some of the inventory items could be in transit at the inventory date. The auditor needs to obtain confirmation or perform other auditing procedures to support management's assertions as to the existence and valuation of these assets, but the assets would not necessarily need to be on hand. (ID: 7495)

58. (c) Inventory turnover ratios measure the speed with which inventory is purchased or made and subsequently sold. Slow-moving and obsolete items have low turnover ratios. Slow-moving and obsolete items are unlikely to be shipped or received. Existence at locations outside the entity's premises occurs with slow-moving, obsolete, and current items. Slow-moving, obsolete, and current items may all be traced easily to inventory observation test counts to perpetual listings. (ID: 7804)

59. (a) Testing the computation of standard overhead rates would not help identify any slow-moving, defective, or obsolete inventory. While touring the plant or production facility, the auditor may actually see these types of items. In comparing inventory balances to anticipated sales volume and reviewing inventory experience and trends, the auditor may become aware of an excessive inventory balance that may indicate that these types of items have not been properly accounted for. (ID: 8152)

60. (d) To test that all items in the inventory listing are valid, the auditor would work from the inventory listing to the tags. An auditor would be unlikely to work directly from inventory tags to receiving reports and vendor invoices, or vice versa, without an intermediate step—as these documents don't reference each other, this process would be awkward; moreover, neither of these procedures would test the items in the inventory listing. Working from inventory tags to the inventory listing tests that all items on tags are included in the inventory listing (completeness). (ID: 8418)

61. (a) The purpose of tracing a sample of inventory tags to a client's computerized listing of inventory items is to determine whether the inventory items represented by the tags were included on the listing. It is a way of testing the assertion of completeness. The other answers are objectives that would not be accomplished by the procedure as described in the question. (ID: 9911)

62. (b) If inventories are in the hands of public warehouses or other outside custodians, the auditor ordinarily would obtain direct confirmation in writing from the custodian. If such inventories represent a significant proportion of current or total assets (which this question did not indicate was the case), to obtain reasonable assurance with respect to their existence, the auditor should apply one or more of the following procedures that the auditor considers necessary in the circumstances: (1) test the owner's procedures for investigating the warehouse and evaluating the warehouse's performance; (2) obtain an independent accountant's report on the warehouse's control procedures relevant to custody of goods and, if applicable, pledging of receipts, or apply alternative procedures at the warehouse to gain reasonable assurance that information received from the warehouse is reliable; (3) observe physical counts of the goods, if practicable and reasonable; and/or (4) if warehouse receipts have been pledged as collateral, confirm with lenders pertinent details of the pledged receipts (on a test basis, if appropriate). (ID: 9939)

63. (d) If the audit objective states that all inventory on hand is reflected in the ending inventory balance, an auditor is most likely testing the management assertion of completeness (inventory is complete): all assets, liabilities, and equity interests that should have been recorded have been recorded. Two of the other answers also are included in the category of assertions for account balances. The entity has rights to the inventory relates to the assertion of rights and obligations: the entity holds or controls the rights to assets, and liabilities are the obligations of the entity. The inventory is properly valued relates to the assertion of valuation and allocation: assets, liabilities, and equity interests are included in the financial statements at appropriate amounts and any

resulting valuation or allocation adjustments are recorded appropriately. The inventory is properly presented in the financial statements relates to the assertion of classification and understandability: financial information is appropriately presented and described and disclosures are clearly expressed. This assertion is included in the category of presentation and disclosure. (ID: 89789)

64. (a) As part of the process of observing a client's physical inventories, an auditor should be alert to the inclusion of any obsolete or damaged goods. The other answers are auditing considerations for inventories, but they do not directly relate to the observation of the client's physical count of inventory quantities. (ID: 8823)

65. (d) When well-kept perpetual inventory records are checked by the client periodically by comparisons with physical counts, an auditor's observation procedures for inventory may be performed either during or after the end of the period under audit. When a client maintains periodic inventory records, the physical count required is normally made at the balance sheet date or very close to it. Minimal variation in client records and test counts in prior periods or lack of significant variation in the last five years are not sufficient justification for leaving the observation of inventories to after the end of the period under audit. (ID: 9363)

66. (d) Performing cutoff procedures for shipping and receiving would be the best test for the completeness assertion as it applies to inventory. The completeness assertion means that all transactions that should have been recorded have been recorded. Many procedures test multiple assertions, so candidates must select the best answer—some of the other answers are better tests of other assertions. Scanning perpetual inventory, production, and purchasing records test accuracy. Examining paid vendor invoices tests accuracy and occurrence. Tracing inventory items from the tag listing back to the physical inventory quantities tests accuracy and existence. (ID: 9381)

67. (d) The repairs and maintenance expense accounts are analyzed by an auditor in obtaining evidence regarding the completeness of fixed assets, since there is the possibility that items were expensed that should have been capitalized. (ID: 5135)

68. (c) The auditor should perform tests of controls when the auditor's risk assessment includes an expectation of the operating effectiveness of controls (control risk is low) or when substantive procedures alone do not provide sufficient appropriate audit evidence. Regardless of the audit approach selected, the auditor should design and perform substantive procedures for all relevant assertions related to each material class of transactions, account balance, and disclosure because effective internal controls generally reduce, but do not eliminate, risk of material misstatement, tests of controls reduce, but do not eliminate, the need for substantive procedures. (ID: 5974)

69. (d) A weakness in internal control over recording retirements of equipment most likely would result in assets that have been retired continuing to be carried in the accounting records. Vouching from the records to the actual assets would be an audit procedure designed to detect such errors. Tracing equipment in the plant to the accounting records would only provide evidence about equipment not yet retired. Depreciation is applied to assets carried on the books and thus depreciation would continue to be taken on retired equipment erroneously still on the books. A review of depreciation would not by itself indicate that certain equipment had been retired. Additions to the "other assets" account would be newly acquired other assets rather than retired equipment and would not likely give any evidence about retired equipment. (ID: 5981)

70. (b) When plant assets are retired, the accumulated depreciation account is debited for the amount of depreciation that has been recorded for those assets, which could be a satisfactory explanation for significant debits to this account. When the estimated remaining useful life of a plant asset is revised upward, the calculation for current and future depreciation is revised to reflect the new estimate of remaining useful life; accumulated depreciation is not affected. If the prior year's depreciation expense was erroneously understated, a correction would require a credit, not a debit, to accumulated depreciation. Revisions in overhead allocations would not affect the accumulated depreciation accounts. (ID: 5996)

71. (c) By reviewing the repairs and maintenance expense accounts, an auditor may uncover transactions that involve assets that should be capitalized rather than expensed. The repairs and maintenance expense accounts are not involved in the write-off of obsolete assets. Property, plant and equipment (PP&E) that cannot

be repaired would not tend to involve transactions in the repairs and maintenance expense accounts either. To verify that all recorded PP&E assets exist, an auditor would tend to inspect the assets themselves against the listings in the PP&E accounts, rather than review expense accounts. (ID: 8391)

72. (d) By reviewing the repairs and maintenance expense accounts, an auditor may uncover transactions that involve assets that should be capitalized rather than expensed. Analysis of depreciation expense accounts would not reveal the existence of assets that should be capitalized, but are not; all entries to these accounts are due to assets being capitalized already. It is less likely that an asset would be involved in the calculation of property tax and yet not be capitalized than it is that an asset would be expensed in the repair and maintenance account; if the entity prepares a property tax report, it probably would be prepared based on the listing of capital assets. (ID: 8400)

73. (b) The valuation assertion for an investment accounted for by the equity method can generally be satisfied by referring to the audited financial statements of the investee company. (ID: 2312)

74. (a) Analytical tests as a source of information for developing expectations include analysis of the relationships among elements of financial information within the period. The reasonableness of answers b., c., and d. cannot be analytically determined due to the nature of the assertions. (ID: 3927)

75. (c) In the case of investments in the form of securities (such as stocks, bonds, and notes), existence and ownership can be corroborated by inspection of the securities, or by written confirmation from an independent custodian of securities on deposit, pledged, or in safekeeping. Shares owned and signed over to new owners or purchased from other investors would not always be made known to the issuing company on a timely basis. Inspecting the financial statements of the investee company would not indicate the number of shares owned and who the owners are. Answer d. would provide evidence about the valuation assertion. (ID: 5122)

76. (b) An auditor confirms with an outside agent that the agent is holding investment securities in the client's name to support the existence and rights and obligations assertions. The auditor would check valuation with a listing of market values. Completeness would not be confirmed, as an entity might have more than one agent or have some securities in transit. Classification and understandability is an assertion about presentation and disclosure and would depend, in part, on the nature of the securities, not that they are being held. (ID: 5662)

77. (a) Investment advisory services have an interest in having accurate records of dividends and are ordinarily independent of the audit client. Stock indentures and stock ledgers may not have dividend records. Annual audited investee financial statements may not be timely available. (ID: 6363)

78. (a) The auditor will need to understand the economic substance of each derivative in order to evaluate the application of financial reporting framework. The client's broker would not be knowledgeable about management's classification of derivatives. The audit committee should already be aware of the risks involved in derivative transactions. The risks associated with each derivative would not be appropriate to include in the auditor's report. (ID: 8131)

79. (c) Published dividend records provide the strongest evidence supporting dividends earned on publicly-held investments. Answers a., b., and d. are not common procedures. (ID: 8135)

80. (b) The auditor is required to design procedures to obtain reasonable assurance of detecting misstatements of assertions about derivatives and securities. When designing such procedures, the auditor should consider the inherent risk and control risk for these assertions. Analytical procedures would not provide sufficient evidence to determine the valuation of any investment. The auditor does not need to confirm the marketability of a derivative nor inform the audit committee of them. (ID: 8148)

81. (b) Confirmation from a third-party custodian provides evidence as to the existence and ownership of securities. In the event of a sale close to the period end, an investee company might not yet be aware of a sale unrecorded in the audit client books; further, if the investment is held by a custodian, the investee company might not realize the audit client has an ownership interest. In the event of a sale close to the period end,

analytics applied to the dividend income and investment accounts would not necessarily detect an unrecorded sale. A sale of stolen securities most likely would not appear in the cash receipts journal. (ID: 8409)

82. (c) Published dividend records provide the strongest evidence supporting dividends earned on marketable equity securities. (ID: 8842)

83. (b) The objective of the auditor's test is to determine whether all merchandise for which the client was billed was received. The population for this test consists of all vendor's invoices (bills for merchandise). The auditor would select a sample of vendor's invoices and then trace them to supporting receiving reports to assure that the merchandise for which the client was billed was received. (ID: 195)

84. (c) In order to verify the existence and valuation of the accounts payable account, the auditor should go to the source documents. These would include purchase orders and receiving reports. Answer a. pertains to the completeness assertion and whether or not management has included all obligations in the account. Answer b. is not a standard auditing procedure but deals with determining whether management has included all obligations for the rights and obligations assertion for the account. Answer d. also pertains to determining whether or not there are any unrecorded obligations of the company not recorded in the account. (ID: 3932)

85. (b) To verify that all merchandise received is recorded, the auditor would trace from the receiving reports to the related records. Payment vouchers, purchase requisitions, and vendor's invoices would not provide evidence that the related merchandise was actually received. (ID: 4263)

86. (c) Completeness deals with whether all transactions, assets, liabilities, and equity interests that should have been recorded have been recorded. Completeness also pertains to whether all disclosures that should have been included in the financial statements have been included. Because liabilities have the inherent risk of being understated, substantive tests and tests of controls are directed towards determining that all liabilities of the company as of the balance sheet date are properly included. (ID: 4274)

87. (c) In searching for unrecorded liabilities, the auditor would most likely vouch a sample of cash disbursements recorded just after year-end to receiving reports and vendor invoices to ascertain that payables had been recorded in the proper period. Tracing a sample of accounts payable entries recorded just after (not just before) year-end to the year-end unmatched receiving report file, comparing a sample of purchase orders issued just before (not just after) year-end with the year-end accounts payable, and scanning the cash disbursements entries recorded just after (not just before) year-end for indications of unusual transactions may also aid in the detection of unrecorded liabilities. (ID: 5994)

88. (c) Tracing a sample of purchase orders and the related receiving reports to the purchases journal and the cash disbursements journal provides evidence to determine that purchases were properly recorded. Although during this audit procedure the auditor might identify unusually large purchases that should be investigated further, this would not be the prevailing purpose of this substantive audit procedure. To verify that cash disbursements were for goods actually received would require vouching from the cash disbursements journal to the receiving reports. To test whether payments were for goods actually ordered would require vouching from the cash disbursements journal to the purchase orders. (ID: 5995)

89. (a) When internal control dictates that each cash disbursement be accompanied by an approved voucher and supported by a prenumbered purchase order and a prenumbered receiving report, the auditor would select items for testing from the population of all cash disbursements (canceled checks). If the auditor were to consider populations made up of all approved vouchers, receiving reports, or invoices, the canceled checks that did not have supporting documentation would not be discovered. (ID: 7019)

90. (d) This is an instance of testing for completeness, i.e., that all transactions and events that should have been recorded have been recorded. The best test for this would be to trace (review) information contained in source documents (purchase contracts and other legal documents) to the financial statements. Inquiry is not as effective as this tracing procedure. Reviewing the financial statements for mathematical accuracy would not detect an unrecorded liability; this would only provide evidence about recorded liabilities. A company's articles of

incorporation and corporate bylaws generally do not contain liability information and they would prove an even less likely source of evidence of recent omissions. (ID: 8608)

91. (b) Examining vendor statements for amounts not reported as purchases is the test of details that would most likely help an auditor determine whether accounts payable have been misstated. The vendor statements are directly related to amounts that should be recorded as accounts payable. Cash received from customers and customer-returned goods are related to sales and accounts receivable, not accounts payable. The examination of reported purchase returns would not reveal evidence of unrecorded purchase returns. (ID: 9388)

92. (c) Finding overpayments while performing tests of details may cause the auditor to increase the assessed risk of material misstatement. Generally, as the risk of material misstatement increases, the acceptable level of detection risk decreases; this means, the extent of substantive procedures must increase. Answer a., b., and d. do not necessarily increase the risk of material misstatement. (ID: 4714)

93. (b) To test for the appropriate number of hours worked, the auditor examines clock card data. To test for answer a., the auditor checks personnel records. To test for answers c. and d., the auditor uses inquiries and observation. (ID: 5655)

94. (d) Substantive tests of payroll balances when control risk is assessed as low most likely would be limited to applying analytical procedures and recalculating payroll accruals to assure the accuracy of the payroll liabilities. Observing the distribution of paychecks, recomputing the payroll register and inspecting payroll tax returns would be of greater importance if control risk related to payroll was assessed as high. In such a case, these procedures would be required to assure the accuracy and other assertions related to payroll accounts. (ID: 5672)

95. (d) When reviewing payroll tax form reconciliations, an auditor is concerned with unrecorded liabilities. Analytics or review of the calculation process would be better to determine accuracy in the deductions calculation. The effective operation of internal control is determined by tests of controls. Observing check distribution, rather than reconciling tax forms, would bring fictitious employees to light. (ID: 7104)

96. (d) Requiring employees to have their direct supervisors approve their time cards would most effectively ensure that payment is made only for work performed. The other answers are good controls, but they are not as effective for this purpose. In most cases, the direct supervisor witnesses the actual work performed. Requiring employees to use a time clock improves accuracy and validity of amounts recorded. Having a payroll clerk recalculate the time cards also improves accuracy. Requiring employees to sign their time cards allows verification of employee existence and improves accuracy. (ID: 9357)

97. (b) An auditor's program to examine long-term debt should include a step where the auditor reconciles interest expense with debt outstanding during the year (period). This step would provide information as to the completeness and valuation of the account balance. The auditor is not concerned with the year-end market value of the debt. The auditor would not verify the existence of the holders of the debt by direct confirmation. Outstanding balances, terms, and conditions are confirmed with the credit grantor or independent trustee. The search for unrecorded liabilities would generally be made by scanning cash disbursements made in the period following the balance sheet date. Also, the accounts payable subsidiary ledger would not likely provide evidence as to long-term liabilities. (ID: 127)

98. (c) One of the audit objectives of long-term liabilities is to verify that interest expense is correctly computed and that other contractual obligations are satisfied. The auditor would most likely compare interest expense with the bonds payable amount to see if it is reasonable, and thereby test valuation. This could also aid discovery of undisclosed liabilities. (ID: 5133)

99. (d) The primary responsibility of a registrar of capital stock is to verify that securities are properly issued, recorded, and transferred. (ID: 133)

100. (d) One of the primary objectives in testing related to Stockholders' Equity and Capital accounts is to verify that capital transactions are appropriately authorized and approved. The granting of stock options would require board of director approval because it could affect the number of shares outstanding. (ID: 5134)

101. (c) Restrictions on retained earnings should be disclosed in the financial statements. Restrictions would not impact the valuation, allocation, or occurrence of retained earnings. Rights and obligations pertain to assets and liabilities, not retained earnings. (ID: 6713)

102. (a) One of the auditor's objectives in the examination of owners' equity is to determine that all transactions during the year affecting owners' equity accounts were properly authorized and recorded. In the case of a corporation, changes in capital stock accounts should receive formal advance approval by the board of directors. A transfer agent's records show detail about the owners of the stock, and do not focus on the total outstanding. Canceled stock certificates and a treasury stock certificate book are less reliable than the minutes, as they would be updated only after the transaction is complete. (ID: 6837)

103. (c) The auditor will need to confirm the shares issued and outstanding with the registrar to ascertain whether the corporate records are accurate and that stock is issued in accordance with the authorization of the board of directors and the articles of incorporation. Confirming the amount of dividends paid to related parties is not a common procedure. The auditor would obtain confirmations from subscribers to determine the expected proceeds from stock subscriptions receivable. Proper authorization of stock rights and warrants would be verified through reading the minutes of the board of directors' meetings. (ID: 8120)

Solution 5-2 SIMULATION ANSWER: Kiting

A. 2, 4

The term kiting refers to the practice of transferring cash between or among various bank accounts, with recording of the cash receipt (deposit) being made on a timely basis, while the recording of the disbursement (withdrawal) is delayed. Thus, for a period of time, the amount of the check could appear in two different accounts simultaneously. In this question, note that the receipt of check #2 was recorded (per the books) at 12/30, while the disbursement was not recorded (per the books) until 1/3. Also, note that check #4 (written from State Bank) was received by the bank on 12/31 but was not recorded on the Fox Co.'s books until 1/2.

B. 1, 3

Deposits/transfers in transit refer to checks which have been recorded on the entity's books but have not yet cleared the bank. In this question, note that checks #1 and #3 were disbursed (per books) at the end of December, but were not received by the bank until early January. (ID: 9229)

Solution 5-3 SIMULATION ANSWER: Audit Procedures for Errors & Fraud

1. E

Preparing a bank transfer schedule would permit the auditor to determine whether a kiting scheme exists.

2. D

Obtaining a cutoff bank statement and comparing the cleared checks to the year-end bank reconciliation would provide some evidence that checks were not mailed until after the first week of the subsequent year.

3. H

Confirming loan terms with a lender would reveal that lender's lien on the real estate.

4. K, L

Sending a second confirmation request and making inquiries of a reputable credit agency would provide evidence of the customer's existence and credit worthiness. Examining the shipping documents assists the auditor to determine whether merchandise was actually shipped to the customer.

5. P

A surprise observation of the distribution of payroll checks would provide evidence that the new employees exist and are currently working.

6. Q

Vouching data in the payroll register to authorized pay rates in the human resource files would permit the auditor to determine whether rate increases are properly authorized. (ID: 9230)

Solution 5-4 SIMULATION ANSWER: Audit Procedures for Long-Term Debt

1. I

A mark next to the lenders' names is most likely to indicate that the information in the next 3 columns is accurate. This mark is unlikely to relate to a dollar balance as it is not positioned closely to any numbers.

2. C

Material beginning balances are generally traced to the prior year's working papers.

3. J

Increased borrowings should be processed with the board of directors' authorization, should correspond to the loan agreement, and their disposition should be traceable. These are all items of interest to an auditor.

4. H

As the loan to First National Bank has the principal due in 20X3, any payment before that date should have specific authorization by the board of directors. The auditor would also likely examine the canceled check(s) associated with this transfer.

5. G

The repayments did not agree to the board of directors (BOD) authorization. [Assume the BOD authorized payment of the full $120,000 ($10,000 × 12 months), based on the terms of the loan.] Confirmation of receipt of the $110,000 is obtained from the monthly statement that the bank issues. The auditor also would likely examine the canceled check(s) associated with this transfer.

6. A

The comments column shows that two of the three lenders with this mark in the ending balance column agrees with the account balance. The third doesn't show a dispute about the amount. The lender without this mark does have a comment about a dispute.

7. K

This mark is next to the two loans that have required payments due in the next year.

8. B

This mark is next to the one loan that has a dispute between the lender and the audit client.

9. D

The total long-term debt and the total accrued interest payable are likely to be entire, separate accounts in the trial balance and general ledger. It is reasonable to trace accounts to the current year financial statements (via the trial balance etc.) after examining them.

10. F

It is normal for the auditor to recompute interest accruals and check the reasonableness of the client's interest accrual. (ID: 9231)

Solution 5-5 SIMULATION ANSWER: Audit Procedures for Property, Plant & Equipment

1. F

Material beginning balances are generally traced to the prior year's working papers.

2. L

Documentation for additions to PP&E generally is examined in an audit. Deeds and purchase contracts would be appropriate documents to examine for a land purchase.

3. K

Documentation for additions to PP&E generally is examined in an audit. Work orders and engineers' reports would be appropriate documents to examine for constructed assets.

4. J

Documentation for additions to PP&E generally is examined in an audit. Vendors' invoices would be appropriate documents to examine for purchased assets.

5. G

As the disposals are fully depreciated and of relatively small amount, procedures may not be necessary.

6. D

An amount is removed from buildings and added to fixtures, but the net for PP&E is zero.

7. C

The individual categories of PP&E and accumulated depreciation are likely to be entire, separate accounts in the trial balance and general ledger. It is reasonable to trace accounts to the current year financial statements (via the trial balance etc.) after auditing them.

8. B

The provision for accumulated depreciation can be easily checked against the PP&E accounts, as the rate and method for each category is known. (ID: 9232)

Solution 5-6 SIMULATION ANSWER: Accounts Receivable (AR) Confirmations

1. A

The client should adjust the accounting records to reflect the receipt of the payment during year 2.

2. D

The auditor should perform the additional audit procedures described, i.e., examining shipping documents and subsequent cash receipts to confirm the accounting records are correct because two attempts to reach the customer failed.

3. A

The client should adjust the accounting records to reflect the return of the materials.

4. E

The auditor should perform the additional audit procedures described, i.e., examining the invoices noted on the confirmation to confirm they pertain to the subsequent year and thus, the accounting records are correct.

5. F

There is no exception so no action is required.

6. D

The auditor should perform the additional audit procedures described, i.e., examining shipping documents and subsequent cash receipts to confirm the accounting records are correct. Editor Note: The simulation did not offer supplying the purchase order numbers to the customer on a second request as an option. (ID: 9832)

Solution 5-7 SIMULATION ANSWER: Audit Procedures for Errors & Fraud

1. A

Comparing the details of the cash receipts journal entries with the corresponding daily deposit slips would permit the auditor to determine whether the receipts were properly recorded.

2. U

Examining the purchase orders and receiving reports for selected vouchers would permit the auditor to determine whether the merchandise was ordered and received by the entity.

3. B

Vouching fixed asset accounts debits to the vendors' invoices would permit the auditor to determine whether equipment repairs had been misclassified as fixed assets.

4. A, J

Comparing the details of cash receipts journal entries with the corresponding daily deposit slips and confirming the entity's accounts receivable on a surprise basis would permit the auditor to determine whether a lapping scheme exists.

5. E

Preparing a bank transfer schedule would permit the auditor to determine whether cash is being inappropriately increased by drawing an unrecorded check on one account and simultaneously recording a deposit in a second account.

6. J, L

Confirming the entity's accounts receivable on a surprise basis would permit the auditor to determine whether sales to those customers were genuine. Examining the shipping documents would permit the auditor to determine whether merchandise was actually shipped to those customers. (ID: 9233)

Solution 5-8 SIMULATION ANSWER: Financial Statement Assertions for Investments

Primary Assertion	Explanation
1. B. Existence	To determine that the custodian holds the securities as identified in the confirmation.
2. F. Completeness	To determine that all income and related collections from the investments are properly recorded.
3. H. Valuation & accuracy & allocation	To determine that the market or other value of the investments is fairly stated.
4. J. Classification & understandability	To determine that the financial statement presentation and disclosure of investments is in conformity with generally accepted accounting principles consistently applied.
5. H. Valuation & accuracy & allocation	To determine that the market or other value of the investments is fairly stated and the loss is properly recognized and recorded. (ID: 9234)

Solution 5-9 SIMULATION ANSWER: Research

With regard to substantive procedures performed at an interim date, which citation in the professional standards provides guidance on covering the remaining period?

AU § 330 23 (ID: 90380)

.23 If substantive procedures are performed at an interim date, the auditor should cover the remaining period by performing

a. substantive procedures, combined with tests of controls for the intervening period, or

b. if the auditor determines that it is sufficient, further substantive procedures only,

that provide a reasonable basis for extending the audit conclusions from the interim date to the period-end.

Solution 5-10 SIMULATION ANSWER: Research

Which citation in the professional standards provides guidance regarding the conditions that should be present to allow an auditor to use negative confirmation requests as the sole substantive audit procedure to address an assessed risk of material misstatement at the assertion level?

AU § 505 15 (ID: 90381)

.15 Negative confirmations provide less persuasive audit evidence than positive confirmations. Accordingly, the auditor should not use negative confirmation requests as the sole substantive audit procedure to address an assessed risk of material misstatement at the assertion level, unless all of the following are present:

a. The auditor has assessed the risk of material misstatement as low and has obtained sufficient appropriate audit evidence regarding the operating effectiveness of controls relevant to the assertion

b. The population of items subject to negative confirmation procedures comprises a large number of small, homogeneous account balances, transactions, or conditions

c. A very low exception rate is expected.

d. The auditor is not aware of circumstances or conditions that would cause recipients of negative confirmation requests to disregard such requests

---

CHAPTER 6

AUDIT SAMPLING

AU Identifier Used for Clarified GAAS in This Textbook

We have not continued to use the temporary AU-C identifier for the clarified auditing standards issued by the American Institute of Certified Public Accountants (AICPA). In this textbook these standards have an AU identifier.

CHAPTER 6

AUDIT SAMPLING

I. Overview

A. Definition

Audit sampling is defined to be the application of an audit procedure to less than 100 percent of the items within an account balance or class of transactions (the population) with the intent of drawing conclusions about the population based on the results of the sample. The underlying principle of sampling is that the results of a sample yield information about the population from which the sample was taken. Sampling, therefore, can be looked upon as an effective and efficient method of gathering audit evidence.

1. **Efficient** Without sampling procedures, an auditor would examine every item comprising an account balance or every transaction occurring within a class of transactions. The cost would (a) be prohibitive due to the amount of time required to perform the examination and (b) far outweigh the benefit obtained. Sampling provides the auditor with a means of obtaining information, but at a much lower cost.

2. **Approaches** The two general approaches to audit sampling are: statistical and nonstatistical. Both require the auditor to use professional judgment.

3. **Appropriate** The appropriateness of audit evidence is determined by auditor judgment—not the design and evaluation of an audit sample. The auditor exercises professional judgment in a variety of ways:

   - Define the population and sampling unit
   - Select the appropriate sampling method
   - Evaluate the appropriateness of audit evidence
   - Evaluate the nature of deviations and/or errors
   - Consider sampling risk
   - Evaluate the results and project those results to the population

B. Types of Sampling

1. **Attributes Sampling** In the auditor's consideration of internal control, tests are performed on the client's internal control policies and procedures in order to determine the degree to which the client's employees have complied (i.e., tests of controls). These tests involve the determination of the rate of occurrence of some characteristic (i.e., attribute), in a population. The attribute of interest is frequently a deviation from the particular control procedure. Thus, the auditor takes a sample from the population, computes the deviation rate in the sample, and draws conclusions about the true population deviation rate.

2. **Variables Sampling** In performing the tests of details of transactions and account balances (i.e., substantive tests), the auditor is concerned with the dollar amounts reported in the financial statements. Thus, the auditor draws a sample from the population of interest, determines the proper dollar value of the items sampled, and makes inferences, based upon projection of the sample results to the population, about the fairness of the amounts reported in the financial statements.

3. **Dual-Purpose Sampling** In some circumstances, the auditor may design a test that will be used for dual purposes—tests of controls and substantive testing. A dual-purpose sample is a sample that is designed to both test the operating effectiveness of an identified control and test whether the recorded monetary amounts of a transaction are correct.

    a. **Low Risk Factor** Generally, the auditor who plans to use this type of sample believes that there is an acceptably low risk that the rate of deviations from prescribed internal controls in the population is greater than the tolerable rate.

    b. **Size** The size of the sample should be the larger of the samples that would have been designed for the two separate purposes.

C. **Uncertainty**
The concept of a *reasonable basis for an opinion* suggests some degree of uncertainty or audit risk. The theory of sampling is well established in auditing practice because it is unusual to find instances where 100 percent of the items need to be examined for each account balance and class of transactions.

1. **Circumstances** There are some situations in which the surrounding factors do not justify the acceptance of any amount of sampling risk, and, therefore, *all* related data is examined.

2. **Audit Risk** The uncertainty inherent in applying audit procedures is referred to as audit risk. Audit risk involves uncertainties due to both sampling and nonsampling risks.

    a. **Sampling Risk** Sampling risk results from the possibility that if a test is restricted to a sample, the conclusions reached may be different than the conclusions that would have resulted if the entire population was examined. The smaller the sample size is, the greater the sampling risk becomes; thus sampling risk varies inversely with sample size.

    b. **Nonsampling Risk** Nonsampling risk includes all aspects of audit risk not due to sampling. Nonsampling risk can be reduced by adequate planning and supervision of audit work and adherence to quality control standards. Examples of nonsampling risks include: failure to select appropriate audit procedures for a given objective; and failure to recognize misstatements, thus making a procedure ineffective.

D. **Assessing Sampling Risk**
The judgment of the auditor should be used to assess sampling risk.

1. **Audit Risk Model** Because the acceptable level of audit risk is a matter of professional judgment, the audit risk model is not intended to be a mathematical formula including all factors that may influence the determination of audit risk. However, the model may be useful for planning appropriate risk levels for audit procedures to achieve the desired audit risk.

2. **Subjective Assessments** The auditor can compute TD mathematically, by assigning an acceptable audit risk (AR); subjectively quantifying the risk of material misstatement (RMM); and the risk that analytical procedures will not detect misstatements (AP). To compute TD, the model must be restated as TD = AR/(RMM × AP).

Exhibit 1 ▸ Audit Risk Model

AR = RMM × DR or AR = (IR × CR) × (AP × TD)

AR	=	The allowable audit risk that monetary misstatements equal to tolerable misstatements might remain undetected for the account balances, class of transactions, or disclosures for the related relevant assertions after the auditor has completed all audit procedures deemed necessary.
RMM	=	The risk (consisting of inherent risk and control risk) that the relevant assertions related to account balances, classes of transactions, or disclosures contain misstatements that could be material to the financial statements when aggregated with other misstatements.
IR	=	Inherent risk is the susceptibility of a relevant assertion to a material misstatement, assuming there are no related internal control policies or procedures.
CR	=	Control risk is the risk that a material misstatement that could occur in a relevant assertion will not be prevented or detected on a timely basis by the entity's controls.
DR	=	Detection risk is the risk that the auditor will not detect a material misstatement that exists in a relevant assertion.
AP	=	The auditor's assessment of the risk that analytical procedures and other relevant substantive tests will not detect misstatements that could occur in an assertion equal to tolerable misstatement, given that such misstatements are not detected by internal controls.
TD	=	The allowable risk of incorrect acceptance that tests of details will not detect misstatements equal to tolerable misstatement, given that such misstatements are not detected by internal controls or analytical procedures and other relevant substantive procedures.

Example 1 ▸ Audit Risk Model Use

Assume the auditor is planning a sampling application to test a client's accounts receivable voucher register. If AR = .05 and the auditor has subjectively assessed RMM and AP equal to 50% and 30%, respectively, then the auditor can use the model to compute an appropriate level of risk of incorrect acceptance (sampling risk).

TD = AR/(RMM × AP)
TD = 0.05/(0.5 × 0.3)
TD = 0.33 (or 33%)

3. **Tests of Internal Control** The auditor is concerned with two aspects of sampling risk while performing tests of controls.

   a. **Risk of Assessing Control Risk Too Low** The risk that the assessed level of control risk based on the sample is less than the true operating effectiveness of the internal control policy or procedure.

   b. **Risk of Assessing Control Risk Too High** The risk that the assessed level of control risk based on the sample is greater than the true operating effectiveness of the internal control policy or procedure.

Exhibit 2 ▸ Risk for Tests of Control Procedures

Auditor's Assessment of Control Risk Is	Client's Control Risk Is: Less Than Maximum	Client's Control Risk Is: Maximum
Less than Maximum Level	Correct Decision (1)	Incorrect Decision (2)
Maximum Level	Incorrect Decision (3)	Correct Decision (4)

(2) Assessing Control Risk Too Low (effectiveness)
(3) Assessing Control Risk Too High (efficiency)

4. **Substantive Tests of Details** The auditor is concerned with two aspects of sampling risk while performing substantive tests.

   a. **Risk of Incorrect Acceptance (Beta Risk)** The risk that the sample supports the conclusion that the recorded account balance is not misstated materially, when in fact, it is misstated materially.

   b. **Risk of Incorrect Rejection (Alpha Risk)** The risk that the sample supports the conclusion that the recorded account balance is misstated materially, when in fact, it is not misstated materially.

Exhibit 3 ▸ Risk for Substantive Tests

Indication of Sample Results	Client's Book Value Is: Fairly Stated	Client's Book Value Is: Not Fairly Stated
Accept Book Value	Correct Decision (5)	Incorrect Decision (6)
Reject Book Value	Incorrect Decision (7)	Correct Decision (8)

(6) Incorrect Acceptance (effectiveness)
(7) Incorrect Rejection (efficiency)

5. **Efficiency and Effectiveness** The risk of incorrect rejection and the risk of assessing control risk too high relate to the efficiency of the audit. Thus, if the auditor assesses control risk too high, additional substantive tests will be performed beyond what is necessary. The risk of incorrect acceptance and the risk of assessing control risk too low relate to the effectiveness of the audit in the detection of existing material misstatements. This potentially could result in materially misstated financial statements from not expanding substantive audit tests to a necessary level.

E. Sample Selection

Items for sampling should be chosen in such a way that the sample can be representative of the population. The auditor should ensure that all items have an opportunity to be selected. Commonly used selection procedures include: haphazard sampling, random sampling, systematic sampling, stratified sampling, block sampling, and probability-proportional-to-size sampling. Note that block sampling does not meet the requirements for a representative sample.

F. Tests of Internal Controls

Sampling applies to tests of controls when the auditor needs to decide whether a rate of deviation is equal to or less than a tolerable rate. However, sampling does not apply to risk assessment procedures performed to obtain an understanding of internal control. Furthermore, sampling concepts may not apply to some tests of controls such as the following: (1) tests of automated application controls (generally these are tested only once or a few times when effective IT general controls are present); (2) analyses of controls for determining appropriate segregation of duties or other analyses that do not examine documentary evidence of performance; (3) tests of certain documented controls or analyses of the effectiveness of security and access controls; or (4) tests directed toward obtaining audit evidence about the operation of the control environment or accounting system.

1. **Planning Sample** The auditor should take the following judgmental factors into consideration when planning samples for tests of controls:

   a. **Relationship** The relationship of the sample to the objective of the test of controls.

   b. **Tolerable Rate of Deviations** The maximum, or tolerable, rate of deviations from prescribed internal control policies and procedures that would support the auditor's assessed level of control risk. The tolerable rate is assessed by considering the relationship of procedural deviations to (1) the assessed level of control risk and (2) the degree of assurance desired by the auditor related to the audit evidence in the sample.

   c. **Allowable Risk** The auditor's allowable risk of assessing control risk too low. When the degree of assurance desired by the sample is high, the auditor should allow for a low level of sampling risk (that is, the risk of assessing control risk too low).

   d. **Characteristics** Characteristics of the population, that is, the items comprising the account balance or class of transactions of interest

   e. **Size** The auditor uses professional judgment to relate the following factors in determining a sample size for a test of controls: (1) the tolerable rate of deviation from the tested control, (2) the likely rate of deviations, and (3) the allowable risk of assessing control risk too low.

2. **Performance and Evaluation** If the auditor is unable to perform all tests on a selected item, it is considered a deviation. If the auditor concludes that the sample results do not support the assessed level of control risk for an assertion, the auditor should reevaluate the nature, timing, and extent of substantive procedures based on a revised consideration of the assessed level of control risk.

G. Substantive Tests of Details

1. **Planning Sample** The auditor should consider the audit objectives to be achieved and decide on the procedure(s) to be applied that will achieve those objectives. The auditor should consider the following factors in planning a sample for a substantive test of details:

   a. **Relationship** The relationship of the sample to the relevant audit objectives, i.e., the population being sampled should be appropriate for the audit objective.

   b. **Materiality** Preliminary judgments of materiality levels

   c. **Allowable Risk** Auditor's allowable risk of incorrect acceptance

   d. **Characteristics** The auditor may be able to reduce the needed sample size by separating the population into relatively homogenous groups on the basis of some characteristic related to the specific audit objective. (For example, dividing accounts receivable into several groups based on the size of the individual account balances.)

   e. **Tolerable Misstatement** How much monetary misstatement in the related account balance may exist when combined with misstatements that may be found in other tests without causing the financial statements to be misstated materially. This is called the tolerable misstatement or tolerable error for the sample. Tolerable misstatement should usually be set for a particular audit procedure at less than financial statement materiality so that when the results of all audit procedures are aggregated, the required overall assurance will be attained.

   f. **Size** The required sample size for a test of details is influenced by (1) the tolerable misstatement and expected misstatement, (2) the audit risk, (3) the characteristics of the population, (4) the assessed risk of material misstatement (RMM), and (5) the assessed risk for other substantive procedures related to the same assertion.

2. **Performance** If certain selected sample items cannot be examined, the auditor's treatment of these unexpected items will depend upon their effect on the auditor's evaluation of the sample. If the auditor's evaluation of the sample results would not be altered by considering those unexamined items to be misstated, it is not necessary to examine the items. However, if considering those unexamined items to be misstated would lead to a conclusion that the balance or class contains material misstatements, the auditor should consider alternative procedures, and should consider whether the inability to examine the items has implications in relation to (a) assessing the risks of material misstatement due to fraud, (b) the assessed level of control risk the auditor expects to be supported, or (c) the degree of reliance on management representations.

3. **Evaluation** The auditor compares total projected misstatement with the tolerable misstatement.

   a. **Judgment** The auditor's judgment is a necessary factor in this evaluation for both statistical and nonstatistical sampling.

   b. **Quality** In addition to the evaluation of the frequency and amounts of monetary misstatements, consideration should be given to the qualitative aspects of the misstatements. Specifically, the auditor considers the nature and cause of the misstatement and the possible relationship of the misstatement to other phases of the audit.

   c. **Aggregate** When the auditor evaluates whether the financial statements taken as a whole may be misstated materially, projected misstatement results for all audit sampling applications and all known misstatements from nonsampling applications should be considered in the aggregate along with other relevant audit evidence.

H. **Statistical vs. Nonstatistical Sampling**
The auditor must choose between statistical and nonstatistical sampling to gather audit evidence. For either nonstatistical or statistical sampling, some sampling risk is always present. The choice between the two methods is primarily a cost/benefit consideration.

1. **Similarities** Both statistical and nonstatistical sampling involve examining less than the whole body of data to express a conclusion about the total body of data. Both methods involve audit judgment in planning and performing a sampling procedure and evaluating the results of the sample. Both provide sufficient appropriate audit evidence. Also, the audit procedures involved in examining the selected items in a sample generally do not depend on the sampling approach used.

2. **Distinguishing Feature** A properly designed nonstatistical sampling application can provide results that are as effective as those from a properly designed statistical sampling application. The distinguishing feature of statistical sampling methods as opposed to nonstatistical methods is that the user is able to provide a mathematical measurement of the degree of uncertainty (i.e., sampling risk) that results from examining only part of a population.

3. **Sample Sizes** Another benefit of statistical sampling is that it provides a model for determining sample size while explicitly recognizing relevant factors such as the risk of assessing control risk too low, tolerable misstatement, and the expected population deviation rate. With nonstatistical sampling, on the other hand, the auditor implicitly recognizes the relevant factors while determining the sample size based on her/his own judgment and experience.

4. **Costs** Statistical sampling might involve additional costs for (a) training auditors, (b) designing individual samples to meet the statistical requirements, and (c) selecting the items to be examined. For example, if the individual balances comprising an account balance to be tested are not maintained in an organized pattern, it might not be cost effective for an auditor to select items in a way that would satisfy the requirements of a properly designed statistical sample.

II. Classical Sample Selection Methods

A. **Judgmental (Haphazard) Sampling**
The auditor uses professional judgment to decide how many and which items should be included in the sample (i.e., the items included in the sample are selected without any conscious bias and without any special reason for including or omitting items from the sample). While haphazard sampling is useful for nonstatistical sampling, it is not used for statistical sampling because it does not allow measurement of the probability of selecting the combination of sampling units.

B. **Random Number Sampling**
The auditor may select a random sample by matching random numbers generated by a computer or selected from a random number table with, for example, document numbers. With this method, every item in the population has the same probability of being selected as every other item in the population, and every sample has the same probability of being selected as every other sample of the same size. This approach is useful for both statistical and nonstatistical sampling.

C. **Systematic Sampling**
For this method, the auditor determines a uniform interval by dividing the number of physical units in the population by the sample size. A random number is selected as a starting point for the first interval, and one item is selected throughout the population at each of the uniform intervals from the starting point (every nth item). This method is useful for both statistical and nonstatistical sampling.

D. Stratified Sampling

The population is divided into groups, called strata, according to some common characteristic, and then random sampling is applied to each stratum. For example, the auditor may divide the client's accounts receivable into three strata—those with balances of $2,000 and above, those with balances between $500 and $2,000, and those with balances of $500 and below. The auditor might positively confirm the whole population of accounts with balances of $2,000 and above, positively confirm a random sample of the accounts with balances between $500 and $2,000, and negatively confirm a random sample of those accounts with balances of $500 and below. The primary objective of stratified sampling is to decrease the effect of variance in the total population thereby reducing sample size.

E. Mean-Per-Unit

The mean-per-unit (MPU) method is a classical variables sampling technique that uses the sample average to project the total population dollar value by multiplying the sample average by the number of items in the population. A smaller sample size can be obtained by stratifying a highly variable population into segments. These segments then will have a minimum of variability within segments and variability between segments will be eliminated. As a result, the total sample size of all combined segments will be less. This is accomplished without a loss of reliability or precision. Therefore, stratified MPU sampling may be more efficient than unstratified MPU because it usually produces an estimate having the desired level of precision, with a smaller sample size.

F. Block Sampling

A block sample consists of selecting contiguous transactions. For example, a block sample from a population of all vouchers processed for the year 20X8 might be all vouchers processed on February 3, May 17, and July 19, 20X8. This sample includes only three sampling units out of 250 business days because the sampling unit, in this case, is a period of time rather than an individual transaction. A sample with so few blocks generally is not adequate to reach a reasonable audit conclusion. Although a block sample might be designed with enough blocks to minimize this limitation, using such samples might be inefficient. If an auditor decides to use a block sample, special care should be exercised to control sampling risk in designing that sample. Block sampling should not be used with statistical sampling approaches. Block sampling is often used to evaluate changes in control procedures by examining all transactions at that time.

III. Attributes Sampling

A. Operating Effectiveness of Internal Control Policies and Procedures

The attribute of interest normally is a control procedure. For example, the auditor may be concerned with estimating the percentage of purchase orders that do not have proper authorization.

1. **Deviation Rate** In performing tests of controls, the auditor frequently is interested in determining the rate of deviation from prescribed internal control policies and procedures. The sampling plan generally used in this situation is attribute sampling.

   Tests of Controls → Attribute Sampling → Deviation Rate

2. **Impact** A weakness in internal control does not necessarily mean that there will be a misstatement in the financial statements. If a material misstatement occurs and is not detected by internal controls or substantive tests, only then will the financial statements be misstated.

3. **Tolerable Rate** The auditor should determine the maximum rate of deviations from the prescribed internal control policy and procedure that s/he would be willing to accept without altering the planned assessed level of control risk. This is referred to as the tolerable rate.

B. Methods

1. **Sequential Sampling** The sample is selected in several steps, with each step conditional on the results of previous steps.

2. **Attribute Estimation Method** A sample is selected and its attribute error rate is determined. This rate serves as an estimate of the error rate in the population and allows the auditor to make statistical statements about the population attribute error rate.

3. **Acceptance Sampling Method** A special case of estimation of attributes. An acceptance sampling table, which utilizes the population size, sample size, and number of errors found in the sample, is used to make a statistical statement that the error rate in the population is not greater than a specified error rate. For example, based on sample results, an auditor may obtain 95-percent confidence that the actual error rate in the population does not exceed 8 percent.

4. **Discovery Sampling Method** Discovery sampling frequently is used when the auditor expects an extremely low error rate, usually zero. It often is used in testing for critical problems such as forgery. If a forgery is found, the auditor would discontinue sampling and investigate further. The objective is to attain a specified level of confidence that if the error rate in the population is at least a certain percentage the sample will include at least one instance of failure to comply with the control procedure being audited. For example, discovery sampling can determine how large a sample needs to be for the auditor to have 95-percent confidence that, if the error rate in the population is 1 percent or higher, the auditor's sample will include at least one example of an error.

C. Steps

The following general steps are appropriate for attributes sampling in tests of compliance with prescribed internal control procedures:

1. **Determine Objective** In a compliance test of control procedures, the objective is to compare the actual deviation rate to the tolerable rate. It should be remembered that the purpose of the test is to provide reasonable assurance that internal controls are operating in an effective manner.

2. **Determine Tolerable Rate** This is the maximum rate of deviations from the prescribed internal control procedure (i.e., maximum misstatement rate) that the auditor is willing to accept without altering the assessment of control risk on the particular internal control procedure and is a judgmental decision. Therefore, the tolerable rate is a function of both the expected level of control risk and the degree of assurance desired. Thus, an increase in the tolerable rate would allow a reduction in sample size. If, after performing the sampling application, the auditor finds that the rate of deviations from the prescribed control procedure is close to or exceeds the tolerable rate, the auditor normally would decide that there is an unacceptably high risk that the deviation rate for the population exceeds the tolerable rate. In such cases, the auditor should consider modifying the assessed level of control risk.

3. **Determine Confidence (Reliability) Level** This is a judgmental decision that quantifies the level of sampling risk that the auditor is willing to accept. The auditor's willingness to accept sampling risk is determined, to a large extent, by the nature of the other tests that the auditor intends to perform that would complement the test of controls.

4. **Determine Expected Population Deviation Rate** This is the expected rate of occurrence of deviations from the prescribed internal control procedure (i.e., the expected error rate). The expected population deviation rate should not exceed the tolerable rate. If prior to testing, the auditor believes that the actual deviation rate is higher than the tolerable rate, the auditor generally omits testing of that control procedure and either seeks to obtain assurance by testing other relevant internal controls, or assesses control risk at the maximum level for the related financial statement assertion.

5. **Consider Effect of Population Size** When a sample is small in relation to the population, the population size has little or no effect on the determination of an appropriate sample size. If the sample size is greater than 10 percent of the population size, which rarely is the case, a finite population correction factor may be used. However, the finite population correction factor tends to decrease the sample size. Therefore, most auditors ignore the factor because any error in sample size that results will be on the conservative side.

6. **Determine Method of Selecting Sample** The sample should be representative of the population, and all items should have a chance of being selected. The various methods for selecting samples are discussed in Section III.B.

7. **Compute Sample Size** Sample sizes can be computed by the use of formulas, computer software, and sample size tables. Consideration should be given to the following when determining sample size:

    a. **Assessing Control Risk Too Low** As discussed earlier, there is an inverse relationship between the risk of assessing control risk too low and sample size.

    b. **Tolerable Deviation Rate** The maximum rate of deviation from a prescribed control policy or procedure that the auditor is willing to accept without modifying the planned level of control risk.

Table 1 ▸ Tolerable Rate

5% Risk of Assessing Control Risk Too Low
(with number of expected errors in parentheses)

Expected Population Deviation Rate	2%	3%	4%	5%	6%	7%	8%	9%	10%	15%	20%
0.00%	149(0)	99(0)	74(0)	59(0)	49(0)	42(0)	36(0)	32(0)	29(0)	19(0)	14(0)
.25	236(1)	157(1)	117(1)	93(1)	78(1)	66(1)	58(1)	51(1)	46(1)	30(1)	22(1)
.50	*	157(1)	117(1)	93(1)	78(1)	66(1)	58(1)	51(1)	46(1)	30(1)	22(1)
.75	*	208(2)	117(1)	93(1)	78(1)	66(1)	58(1)	51(1)	46(1)	30(1)	22(1)
1.00	*	*	156(2)	93(1)	78(1)	66(1)	58(1)	51(1)	46(1)	30(1)	22(1)
1.25	*	*	156(2)	124(2)	78(1)	66(1)	58(1)	51(1)	46(1)	30(1)	22(1)
1.50	*	*	192(3)	124(2)	103(2)	66(1)	58(1)	51(1)	46(1)	30(1)	22(1)
1.75	*	*	227(4)	153(3)	103(2)	88(2)	77(2)	51(1)	46(1)	30(1)	22(1)
2.00	*	*	*	181(4)	127(3)	88(2)	77(2)	68(2)	46(1)	30(1)	22(1)
2.25	*	*	*	208(5)	127(3)	88(2)	77(2)	68(2)	61(2)	30(1)	22(1)
2.50	*	*	*	*	150(4)	109(3)	77(2)	68(2)	61(2)	30(1)	22(1)
2.75	*	*	*	*	173(5)	109(3)	95(3)	68(2)	61(2)	30(1)	22(1)
3.00	*	*	*	*	195(6)	129(4)	95(3)	84(3)	61(2)	30(1)	22(1)
3.25	*	*	*	*	*	148(5)	112(4)	84(3)	61(2)	30(1)	22(1)
3.50	*	*	*	*	*	167(6)	112(4)	84(3)	76(3)	40(2)	22(1)
3.75	*	*	*	*	*	185(7)	129(5)	100(4)	76(3)	40(2)	22(1)
4.00	*	*	*	*	*	*	146(6)	100(4)	89(4)	40(2)	22(1)
5.00	*	*	*	*	*	*	*	158(8)	116(6)	40(2)	30(2)
6.00	*	*	*	*	*	*	*	*	179(11)	50(3)	30(2)
7.00	*	*	*	*	*	*	*	*	*	68(5)	37(3)

* Sample size is too large to be cost-effective for most audit applications.

NOTE: This table assumes a large population.

Example 2 ▸ Use of Table 1 to Determine Sample Size

> The auditor would like to assess control risk at below the maximum level. In this case, in order to do this, the auditor must have 95% confidence that the actual population deviation rate (i.e., the percentage of vouchers that are paid without being approved) is not greater than 6%. Therefore, the tolerable rate is 6%; i.e., the auditor will be able to assess control risk at below the maximum level as long as the auditor can conclude with 95% confidence that not more than 6% of the unpaid vouchers lack approval. Based on the error rate observed in last year's sample, the auditor expects a population deviation rate of only 1.50% this year. Using Table 1, 103 vouchers should be examined to yield the desired confidence about the population error rate.

8. **Select and Audit Sample Items** Audit procedures should be applied to the items in the sample to determine deviations from the prescribed control procedures previously identified. Deviations should be grouped according to whether they are occurring with some regularity or are isolated events. In cases where selected items cannot be examined, they should be counted as deviations from control procedures. This occurs, for example, when documentation used to test for the procedures has been misplaced, lost, or destroyed. A voided item generally would be replaced by another randomly selected item, if it was voided properly.

9. **Evaluate Sample Results** The results of the sample must be analyzed in order to make an inference about the population error rate. This can be done by formula, but most often is accomplished by tables or computer programs based on the appropriate formula.

Table 2 ▸ Actual Number of Deviations Found

Statistical Sample Results Evaluation
Upper Limit at 5% of Assessing Control Risk Too Low

Sample Size	0	1	2	3	4	5	6	7	8	9	10
25	11.3	17.6	*	*	*	*	*	*	*	*	*
30	9.5	14.9	19.6	*	*	*	*	*	*	*	*
35	8.3	12.9	17.0	*	*	*	*	*	*	*	*
40	7.3	11.4	15.0	18.3	*	*	*	*	*	*	*
45	6.5	10.2	13.4	16.4	19.2	*	*	*	*	*	*
50	5.9	9.2	12.1	14.8	17.4	19.9	*	*	*	*	*
55	5.4	8.4	11.1	13.5	15.9	18.2	*	*	*	*	*
60	4.9	7.7	10.2	12.5	14.7	16.8	18.8	*	*	*	*
65	4.6	7.1	9.4	11.5	13.6	15.5	17.4	19.3	*	*	*
70	4.2	6.6	8.8	10.8	12.6	14.5	16.3	18.0	19.7	*	*
75	4.0	6.2	8.2	10.1	11.8	13.6	15.2	16.9	18.5	20.0	*
80	3.7	5.8	7.7	9.5	11.1	12.7	14.3	15.9	17.4	18.9	*
90	3.3	5.2	6.9	8.4	9.9	11.4	12.8	14.2	15.5	16.8	18.2
100	3.0	4.7	6.2	7.6	9.0	10.3	11.5	12.8	14.0	15.2	16.4
125	2.4	3.8	5.0	6.1	7.2	8.3	9.3	10.3	11.3	12.3	13.2
150	2.0	3.2	4.2	5.1	6.0	6.9	7.8	8.6	9.5	10.3	11.1
200	1.5	2.4	3.2	3.9	4.6	5.2	5.9	6.5	7.2	7.8	8.4

* Over 20 percent

NOTE: This table presents upper limits as percentages. This table assumes a large population.

a. The first step in the evaluation of the results is tabulating the number of deviations found and comparing this to the number of deviations expected to occur using the sample size determined from the above table. The expected number of deviations is the parenthetical number found next to each sample size. In cases where the deviations found are less than the number that would be expected (the parenthetical number), it can be assumed that the risk of assessing control risk too low and the allowance for sampling risk is not more than the tolerable rate.

b. When the actual deviations are more than those that would be expected according to the parenthetical number in Table 1, the auditor can calculate the maximum deviation rate in the population using a table similar to Table 2. Table 2 is for evaluating sample results for a 5-percent risk of assessing control risk too low or a 95-percent confidence level.

c. No one table can accommodate an evaluation of every possible size and number of deviations, and the auditor often will need to use other references to find appropriate tables. In cases where a particular sample size does not appear in a table, it is a good idea to be conservative by using the next smaller sample size shown.

Example 3 ▸ Table 2 Use

Only one error is discovered from the 103 sample items selected in Example 2. Use of Table 2, reveals that there is no corresponding sample size for 103 items, so the next lowest (100 sample size) is used. The intersection of the sample size and the number of deviations found reveals the maximum population deviation rate in this case is 4.7%. This maximum population deviation rate is less than the tolerable rate of 6%, so it can be concluded that within a 95% reliability level, the control is functioning as required.

10. **Reach Overall Conclusion** The auditor uses professional judgment to reach an overall conclusion about the effect of the evaluation of the test of controls on the nature, timing, and extent of planned substantive tests. If the sample results, along with other relevant audit evidence, support the assessed level of control risk, the auditor generally does not need to modify planned substantive tests. If the sample results do not support the assessed level of control risk, the auditor ordinarily either would perform tests of controls on other relevant internal controls for which control risk can be assessed at below the maximum level, or assess control risk at a higher, or the maximum, level and modify the nature, timing, and/or extent of substantive testing. In addition to the evaluation of the frequency and amounts of monetary misstatements, consideration should be given to the qualitative aspects of the misstatements. These would include the nature and cause of the misstatements. For example, were there differences in principle or applications or differences due to misunderstanding of instructions or carelessness? Also, consideration should be given to the possible relationship of the misstatements to other phases of the audit.

11. **Document Sampling Procedure** Documentation might include such items as follows: (a) a description of the prescribed control procedure being tested; (b) the objectives of the test, including the relationship to planned substantive testing; (c) the definition of the population and sampling unit; (d) the definition of the deviation condition (i.e., what is considered a deviation from prescribed internal control policies and procedures); (e) the rationale for the confidence level, the tolerable rate, and the expected population deviation rate used in the application; (f) the method of sample size determination; (g) the method of sample selection; (h) a description of the sampling procedure performed and a listing of compliance deviations identified in the sample; and (i) the evaluation of the sample and a summary of the overall conclusion.

IV. Variables Sampling

A. Substantive Tests of Details

The auditor performs substantive tests either to detect misstatements or to obtain evidence about the validity and propriety of the accounting treatment of transactions and balances. In substantive testing, the auditor is interested primarily in dollar amounts. An example of a substantive test is the use of a sample from the accounts receivable subsidiary ledger to estimate the balance in the control account. The traditional method of performing substantive tests of details is by variables sampling.

Substantive Tests → Variables Sampling → Dollar Amount

B. Methods

1. **Simple Extension (Mean-Per-Unit Approach)** A method of estimating variables in which the auditor finds the average audited value for the items in the sample and then estimates the population value by multiplying the average sample value by the size of the population. For example, if the mean of a sample of 50 accounts is calculated to be $100 and there are 1,000 accounts in the population, the total value of the 1,000 accounts would be estimated at $100,000 [i.e., ($100 per account) × (1,000 accounts)] plus or minus an allowance for sampling error that is determined statistically. Note that the auditor needs to know the audited values of the items in the sample but does not need to know their book values.

2. **Difference Estimation** The auditor first finds the average difference between the audited value and the book value of the items in the sample. This average difference is then multiplied by the size of the population in order to estimate the difference between the book value of the population and its actual value. The interval is then compared against the precision required (i.e., against the amount of acceptable difference) in order to decide if the account appears to be stated reasonably.

3. **Ratio Method** The auditor uses sample results to estimate the ratio of audited value to book value. This ratio then is applied to the population to estimate the actual value. Ratio estimation should be used when each population item has a book value, an audited value may be ascertained for each sample item, and differences occur frequently. For example, if the auditor finds that the average ratio of audited value to book value for the sample is 1.05 and if the book value for the population is $100,000, the actual value for the population can be estimated to be $105,000 (i.e., 1.05 × $100,000) plus or minus an allowance for sampling risk.

C. Steps

The following general steps are appropriate in substantive tests of details:

1. **Determine Objectives** It is important for the auditor to specify the purpose of the test because this will determine the population of the test. For example, the purpose may be to prove the existence of an account balance or to show that the account is complete.

2. **Define Population** The auditor must match the objectives of the test to the appropriate population. The population is made up of the account balances or class of transactions of interest to the auditor. Defining the population involves consideration of the individual sampling units of the entire population, whether the entire population is available to be picked, and the identification of those items that are individually significant. Those items that are individually significant may be accounts that are large enough to exceed the level of tolerable deviation by themselves. These would not be included in the population available for sampling, but should be tested separately.

3. **Determine Confidence Level** The confidence level for the auditor's substantive tests generally will vary inversely with the assessed level of control risk (i.e., the stronger the internal control is judged to be, the lower the assessed level of control risk, thereby affecting the extent of substantive tests). The confidence level for a particular substantive test is a matter of judgment, but the auditor should consider the overall confidence level in making the determination. This confidence level is related to the auditor's assessment of sampling risk.

4. **Determine Expected Standard Deviation of Population or Expected Amount of Misstatement Directly in Dollar Value** This also is a matter of judgment, frequently based on the prior year's audit or on the results of a small pilot sample. As expected misstatement increases, a larger sample size is required.

5. **Determine Tolerable Misstatement** The tolerable misstatement is the maximum monetary misstatement that may exist when combined with misstatements that may be found in other tests without causing the financial statements to be misstated materially. This is a judgmental value which should relate closely to the auditor's preliminary estimates of materiality levels. As tolerable misstatement increases, sample size decreases.

6. **Select Method of Audit Sampling** These can be either statistical or nonstatistical. If statistical sampling is used, either PPS or classical variables techniques would be used.

7. **Determine Sample Size** Compute the sample size by using a sample size table, formula, or software. The sample size formula for substantive testing is illustrated in Exhibit 4.

Exhibit 4 ▸ Substantive Testing Sample Size Formula

$$n = \frac{c^2 \times s^2 \times N^2}{A^2} = \frac{c^2 \times s^2}{a^2}$$

Where:

n = Size of the sample

c = Confidence (reliability) coefficient; this is the number of standard deviations that corresponds to the selected confidence level.

s = Standard deviation of the population (usually the standard deviation of a small pilot sample or the standard deviation found in previous years)

N = Size of the population

A = Population allowance for sampling error (tolerable misstatement less expected amount of misstatement)

a = Allowance for sampling error per population item

Exhibit 5 ▸ Summary of Sampling Factor Relationships

Decrease in	Effect on Sample Size
Confidence (reliability) coefficient	Decrease
Tolerable misstatement	Increase
Expected standard deviation of the population	Decrease

Sample Size	Decrease in
Increase	Risk-Incorrect Acceptance
Increase	Risk-Incorrect Rejection

8. **Inspection** Select and audit the sample items.

Example 4 ▸ Sample Size

An auditor wishes to apply statistical sampling as part of substantive testing of the accounts receivable control account. The account has a book value of $500,000 and is composed of 5,000 individual accounts. The auditor determines that 90% confidence is necessary in the results of substantive testing for this account. The auditor sets total allowance for sampling error (precision) at $40,000. Next, the auditor takes a small pilot sample in order to estimate the standard deviation of the population. The pilot sample has a standard deviation of $40. The number of standard deviations corresponding to 90% for a normal distribution is 1.64.

N	=	5,000	A	=	$40,000
c	=	1.64	s	=	$40
a	=	$40,000/5,000 = $8			

Required: Calculate the sample size.

Solution: Substituting the information into the sample size formula and solving the equation gives the following:

$$n = \frac{(1.64)^2\ (\$40)^2}{(\$8)^2} = 67.24 \approx 68 \text{ accounts}$$

The auditor should take a random sample of 68 accounts from the population of 5,000 accounts receivable in order to have 90% confidence that the inference based on the sample results will be within $40,000 of the true (actual) value of accounts receivable. That is, if a population of 5,000 accounts actually has a standard deviation of $40, 90% of the possible samples of 68 accounts will yield estimates that are within $40,000 of the actual value of accounts receivable.

9. **Evaluate Sample Results** The auditor computes the actual sampling error (precision) and confidence level attained by the sample.

   a. Compute the actual sampling error by solving for A

   b. Compute the actual confidence level by solving for c

Example 5 ▸ Computation of Sampling Error

The auditor selects a sample of 68 accounts as described in Example 4. The auditor would audit these accounts to determine the actual value of each account, then compute the average audited balance. Assume that the average audited balance is $95 per account. The estimated population value is $475,000 ($95 × 5,000 accounts). If the standard deviation of the sample is assumed to be $40, we can compute the actual sampling error (precision) as follows:

$$A = \frac{c \times s \times N}{\sqrt{n}} = \frac{(1.64)\ (\$40)\ (5{,}000)}{\sqrt{68}} = \$39{,}775 \approx \$40{,}000$$

And the confidence level coefficient as follows:

$$c = \frac{A \times \sqrt{n}}{s \times N} = \frac{\$40{,}000 \times \sqrt{68}}{(\$40)\ (5{,}000)} = 1.649 \approx 1.65$$

The auditor can rely on the results of the test, with 90% confidence, yielding an estimated value for accounts receivable that differs from the true value by no more than $40,000.

10. **Reach Overall Conclusion** The auditor should project the results of the sample to the population from which the sample was taken before evaluating the results of the sample. The client may adjust the book value of the account to correct the misstatements actually found in the sample and any misstatements discovered in any 100 percent-examined items. The total projected misstatement after the book value has been adjusted should be compared with the tolerable misstatement. If the auditor considers the projected misstatement unacceptable, the auditor should take appropriate action (for example, performing other substantive tests on the account).

11. **Document Sampling Procedure** Documentation might include the following: (a) the objectives of the test and a description of other audit procedures related to those objectives; (b) the definition of the population and the sampling unit, including how the auditor considered completeness of the population; (c) the definition of a misstatement; (d) the rationale for the risk of incorrect acceptance, the risk of incorrect rejection, the tolerable misstatement, and the expected population deviation amount used in the application; (e) the audit sampling technique used; (f) the method of sample selection; (g) a description of the performance of the sampling procedure and a listing of misstatements identified in the sample; and (h) the evaluation of the sample and a summary of the overall conclusion.

V. Probability-Proportional-to-Size Sampling

A. Distinguishing Features

Probability-proportional-to-size sampling (PPS) is a form of variables sampling that uses attribute sampling theory for substantive testing. The sampling unit is not an individual account or transaction, but an individual dollar in an account balance (or another logical unit). PPS sampling has two unique properties.

1. **Stratification** The audit population is stratified automatically by monetary value.

2. **Overstatements** Larger dollar amounts have a higher probability of being selected. Therefore, overstatements are more likely to be detected than understatements. Hence, PPS sampling is most appropriate when an auditor desires testing for material overstatements. PPS sampling is ineffective in searching for unrecorded items. (The probability of an item being selected is directly proportional to its recorded dollar value.)

Example 6 ▸ PPS Sampling

X Co.'s account receivable balance is \$2,000,000 Customer Y has a balance of \$120,000	The population is 2,000,000 The sampling unit is 1

Required: Figure the probability that Customer Y has of being selected.

Solution: Customer Y has a 6% chance of being selected (120,000 / 2,000,000 = 6%).

3. **Select Sample Items** Systematic sampling selection is used most often. Audit procedures then are employed to determine the value of each sample item.

4. **Sample Size** Sample sizes in low-error environments tend to be relatively small because their approach does not use standard deviations (which tend to be large in most credit environments) in determining sample size.

5. **Other Advantages** This method also reduces audit work because several dollars selected will appear in the same sample item (for example, a customer's account balance) and, therefore, the same audit procedures often determine the audited value of more than one sample item. Also, this approach does not require a high number of errors to be observed in the sample for the results to be statistically valid, as is the case with Difference Estimation and Ratio Estimation.

B. Disadvantages

An understatement is less likely to be discovered than an overstatement because those accounts with higher dollar values have a greater chance of being selected. Therefore, PPS sampling generally is considered inappropriate for liability accounts. Also, special consideration must be given to zero and negative balance accounts which usually are excluded from the PPS sample. A third disadvantage occurs when the population has a high expected misstatement rate; the auditor then must obtain sample sizes larger than those required by classical variables sampling.

C. Determining Sample Size

Requires that the auditor determine a reliability factor for overstatement errors, a tolerable rate, and an expected error rate.

1. **Reliability Factor for Overstatement Errors** Can be determined from tables after specifying the expected number of overstatement errors and the risk of incorrect acceptance. The auditor controls the risk of incorrect acceptance by specifying the risk level for the sampling plan. As PPS sampling is most appropriate when no errors are expected, zero is the appropriate estimate for the number of overstatement errors. The risk of incorrect acceptance is a matter of professional judgment; with PPS sampling, it represents an auditor's risk that book value is not overstated materially when material monetary overstatements exist.

Table 3 ▶ Reliability Factors for Errors of Overstatement

Number of Over-statement Errors	Risk of Incorrect Acceptance								
	1%	5%	10%	15%	20%	25%	30%	37%	50%
0	4.61	3.00	2.31	1.90	1.61	1.39	1.21	1.00	.70
1	6.64	4.75	3.89	3.38	3.00	2.70	2.44	2.14	1.68
2	8.41	6.30	5.33	4.72	4.28	3.93	3.62	3.25	2.68
3	10.05	7.76	6.69	6.02	5.52	5.11	4.77	4.34	3.68
4	11.61	9.16	8.00	7.27	6.73	6.28	5.90	5.43	4.68
5	13.11	10.52	9.28	8.50	7.91	7.43	7.01	6.49	5.68
6	14.57	11.85	10.54	9.71	9.08	8.56	8.12	7.56	6.67
7	16.00	13.15	11.78	10.90	10.24	9.69	9.21	8.63	7.67
8	17.41	14.44	13.00	12.08	11.38	10.81	10.31	9.68	8.67
9	18.79	15.71	14.21	13.25	12.52	11.92	11.39	10.74	9.67
10	20.15	16.97	15.41	14.42	13.66	13.02	12.47	11.79	10.67
11	21.49	18.21	16.60	15.57	14.78	14.13	13.55	12.84	11.67
12	22.83	19.45	17.79	16.72	15.90	15.22	14.63	13.89	12.67
13	24.14	20.67	18.96	17.86	17.02	16.32	15.70	14.93	13.67
14	25.45	21.89	20.13	19.00	18.13	17.40	16.77	15.97	14.67
15	26.75	23.10	21.30	20.13	19.24	18.49	17.84	17.02	15.67
16	28.03	24.31	22.46	21.26	20.34	19.58	18.90	18.06	16.67
17	29.31	25.50	23.61	22.39	21.44	20.66	19.97	19.10	17.67
18	30.59	26.70	24.76	23.51	22.54	21.74	21.03	20.14	18.67
19	31.85	27.88	25.91	24.63	23.64	22.81	22.09	21.18	19.67
20	33.11	29.07	27.05	25.74	24.73	23.89	23.15	22.22	20.67

Example 7 ▶ Table 3 Use

The auditor's risk of incorrect acceptance for Co. X is 5% and the number of overstatement errors is 0. The reliability factor for errors of overstatement is 3.00.

2. **Tolerable Rate** The tolerable rate (or tolerable error) is the maximum monetary error that may exist in an account balance without causing the financial statements to be misstated materially. Thus, tolerable error in PPS sampling is related closely to the auditor's planned level of materiality. The sampling interval and the sample size can be determined using the formulas in Exhibit 6.

Exhibit 6 ▸ PPS Sampling Interval and Sample Size

$$n = \frac{c^2 \times s^2 \times N^2}{A^2} = \frac{c^2 \times s^2}{a^2}$$

$$\textit{Sampling Interval} = \frac{\textit{Tolerable Misstatement}}{\textit{Reliability Factor for the Error of Overstatement}}$$

$$\textit{Sample Size} = \frac{\textit{Population}}{\textit{Sampling Interval}}$$

Example 8 ▸ Sampling Interval and Sample Size

Using the same assumptions as Example 7, the population is 2,000,000 and the tolerable misstatement is $60,000.

Required: Figure the sampling interval and the sample size.

Solution: The sampling interval is $20,000. (60,000 / 3.00 = 20,000)

The sample size is 100. (2,000,000 / 20,000 = 100)

3. **Expected Error Rate** If some errors are expected, the sample interval can be computed by determining the expected error rate. In cases where the expected error rate is not shown on the table, the auditor would use the sample size for the next higher percentage. If the tolerable rate percentage is not found it would be appropriate to select the sample size for the next smaller percentage shown. This follows the accounting convention of conservatism.

Exhibit 7 ▸ PPS Expected Error Rate

$$n = \frac{c^2 \times s^2 \times N^2}{A^2} = \frac{c^2 \times s^2}{a^2}$$

$$\textit{Expected Error Rate} = \frac{\textit{Expected Misstatements}}{\textit{Population}}$$

Example 9 ▸ Sampling Interval and Sample Size

Using the same assumptions as Example 7, we determine that the expected misstatement for Co. X is $10,000 based on our prior experience with the client. The population is 2,000,000. Our expected error rate is .005 (10,000 / 2,000,000 = .005). The tolerable rate has been determined to be 3%. (This example is unrelated to Example 8.)

Required: Figure the sampling interval and the sample size.

Solution: Using Table 1, our sample size is 157.

The sampling interval is then computed by dividing the population by the sample size. (2,000,000 / 157 = 12,739)

D. Evaluate Sample Results

Misstatements from the sample should be projected to the population to calculate an allowance for sampling risk. This allowance for sampling risk is a calculation with an incremental allowance for projected errors (misstatements). If the sample contains less than 100-percent errors, the formula for determining the upper limit is as in Exhibit 8.

Exhibit 8 ▸ PPS Upper Limit for Misstatements

Upper limit for errors (misstatements)	=	*Projected errors (misstatements)*	+	*Basic precision*	+	*Incremental allowance for projected errors (misstatements)*

1. **Upper Limit for Misstatements** The upper limit on misstatement is calculated by adding the projected misstatement, the basic precision, and the incremental allowance for projected errors.

   a. Projected misstatements are calculated for each sample item depending on whether the recorded book value is less than or greater than the sampling interval. If less than, the difference between the recorded value and the audited value is divided by the recorded value to arrive at a percentage error known as tainting. The projected misstatement is the tainting percentage multiplied by the sampling interval.

   b. Basic precision is calculated by multiplying the reliability factor by the sampling interval.

   c. An incremental allowance for projected misstatement is calculated using only those errors in logical units less than the sampling interval. These are ranked from highest to lowest (in terms of tainting percentage), considering the incremental changes in reliability factors for the actual number of errors found.

2. **Comparison** Compare the upper limit on errors to the previously estimated tolerable error. If the upper limit on misstatements is less than the tolerable misstatement, it can be concluded that the total population is not misstated by an amount greater than the originally estimated tolerable misstatement, at the specified risk of incorrect acceptance.

   a. If the upper limit on misstatements is greater than the tolerable misstatement, then the sample results do not support the conclusion that the population is not misstated by more than the tolerable misstatement. This may occur if the population was not represented by the sample, the sample was too small due to an excessively low expectation of misstatement, or if the population itself was misstated.

   b. In cases where the recorded book value is greater than the sampling interval, the projected misstatement is equal to the actual error.

   c. If no errors are found, both the projected errors and the incremental allowance for projected errors would be zero. Therefore, the auditor could conclude that the recorded amount of accounts is not overstated by more than the tolerable error estimated earlier because the only factor with a value other than zero would be the basic precision.

Example 10 ▸ Evaluating Sample Results

Audit procedures reveal four errors. The projected misstatement total is calculated first, followed by the other two components of the upper limits, precision, and the incremental allowance for projected misstatement.

a. Projected Misstatement:

(1) Book value	(2) Audited value	(3) Tainting % (1) – (2) / (1)	(4) Sampling interval	(5) Projected error (3) × (4)
$ 500	$ 450	0.10	$12,739	$1,274
11,000	10,340	0.06	12,739	764
5,700	5,625	0.013	12,739	166
25,350	23,350	—	—	2,000
				$4,204

b. Basic precision: 3 × $12,739 = $38,217

c. Incremental allowance:

(1) Projected error	(2) Reliability factor (from table)	(3) Incremental change in reliability factor (from table) (increment–1)	(4) Incremental allowance (3) × (1)
$1,274	4.75	0.75 [1]	$ 956
764	6.30	0.55 [2]	420
166	7.76	0.46 [3]	76
			$1,452

[1] 4.75 – 3.00 – 1.00 = 0.75 [2] 6.30 – 4.75 – 1.00 = 0.55 [3] 7.76 – 6.30 – 1.00 = 0.46

d. Overall conclusion:

Projected misstatement	$ 4,204
Precision	38,217
Incremental allowance	1,452
Upper limit	$43,873

In this example, it can be concluded that the audited sample supports the conclusion that the population is not misstated by more than the tolerable misstatement.

VI. Appendix: Sampling Terms

allowance for sampling error (precision; sampling error) A measure of the closeness of a sample estimate to the corresponding population characteristic for a specified sampling risk.

attribute Any characteristic that is either present or absent. In tests of controls directed toward operating effectiveness, the presence or absence of evidence of the application of a specified internal control policy or procedure is sometimes referred to as an attribute.

attributes sampling A statistical procedure based on estimating whether the rate of occurrence of a particular attribute in a population exceeds a tolerable rate.

audit sampling The application of an audit procedure to less than 100 percent of the items within an account balance or class of transactions.

classical variables sampling A sampling approach that measures sampling risk using the variation of the underlying characteristic of interest. This approach includes methods such as mean-per-unit, ratio estimation, and difference estimation.

confidence level (reliability level) The complement of the applicable sampling risk (see risk of incorrect acceptance, risk of assessing control risk too low, risk of incorrect rejection, and risk of assessing control risk too high). In practice, the confidence level is often set equal to the complement of the risk of incorrect rejection (i.e., to the complement of the alpha risk).

difference estimation A classical variables sampling technique that uses the total difference between audited values and individual book values to estimate the total dollar error in a population and an allowance for sampling error.

expected population deviation rate An anticipation of the deviation rate in the entire population. It is used in determining an appropriate sample size for an attributes sample.

population (field; universe) The items comprising the account balance or class of transactions, or a portion of that balance or class of interest. The population excludes individually significant items of which the auditor has decided to examine 100 percent or other items that will be tested separately.

probability-proportional-to-size (PPS) sampling (Dollar-unit sampling; CMA sampling) A variables sampling procedure that uses attributes theory to express a projection of the error in a population in dollar amounts.

ratio estimation A classical variables sampling technique that uses the ratio of audited values to book values in the sample to estimate the total dollar value of the population and an allowance for sampling error.

sampling risk The risk that the auditor's conclusion based on a sample may be different from the conclusion the auditor would reach if the test were applied in the same way to the entire population. For tests of controls, sampling risk is the risk of assessing control risk too high or too low. For substantive testing, sampling risk is the risk of incorrect acceptance or rejection.

standard deviation A measure of the dispersion among the respective values of a particular characteristic as measured for all items in the population for which a sample estimate is developed.

tolerable misstatement An estimate of the maximum monetary misstatement that may exist in an account balance or class of transactions when combined with misstatements that may be found in other tests without causing the financial statements to be materially misstated.

tolerable rate The maximum population rate of deviations from a prescribed control procedure that the auditor will tolerate without modifying the nature, timing, or extent of substantive testing.

CHAPTER 6—AUDIT SAMPLING

Problem 6-1 MULTIPLE-CHOICE QUESTIONS

Types of Sampling

1. Which of the following sampling methods would be used to estimate a numerical measurement of a population, such as a dollar value?
   a. Attributes sampling
   b. Stop-or-go sampling
   c. Variables sampling
   d. Random-number sampling (ID: 5127)

2. For which of the following audit tests would an auditor most likely use attribute sampling?
   a. Inspecting purchase orders for proper approval by supervisors
   b. Making an independent estimate of recorded payroll expense
   c. Determining that all payables are recorded at year end
   d. Selecting accounts receivable for confirmation of account balances (ID: 89783)

3. For which of the following audit tests would a CPA most likely use attribute sampling?
   a. Identifying entries posted to incorrect accounts
   b. Estimating the amount in an expense account
   c. Evaluating the reasonableness of depreciation expense
   d. Selecting receivables for confirmation of account balances (ID: 8406)

4. An auditor examining inventory most likely would use variables sampling rather than attributes sampling to
   a. Identify whether inventory items are properly priced
   b. Estimate whether the dollar amount of inventory is reasonable
   c. Discover whether misstatements exist in inventory records
   d. Determine whether discounts for inventory are properly recorded (ID: 7816)

Audit Risk

5. Which of the following statements about audit sampling risks is correct for a nonissue?
   a. Nonsampling risk arises from the possibility that, when a substantive test is restricted to a sample, conclusions might be different than if the auditor had tested each item in the population.
   b. Nonsampling risk can arise because an auditor failed to recognize misstatements.
   c. Sampling risk is derived from the uncertainty in applying audit procedures to specific risks.
   d. Sampling risk includes the possibility of selecting audit procedures that are not appropriate to achieve the specific objective. (ID: 90192)

6. While performing a test of details during an audit, an auditor determined that the sample results supported the conclusion that the recorded account balance was materially misstated. It was, in fact, not materially misstated. This situation illustrates the risk of
   a. Assessing control risk too high
   b. Assessing control risk too low
   c. Incorrect rejection
   d. Incorrect acceptance (ID: 4708)

7. As a result of sampling procedures applied as tests of controls, an auditor incorrectly assesses control risk higher than appropriate. The most likely explanation for this situation is that
   a. The deviation rate in the auditor's sample is less than the tolerable rate, but the deviation rate in the population exceeds the tolerable rate.
   b. The deviation rate in the auditor's sample exceeds the tolerable rate, but the deviation rate in the population is less than the tolerable rate.
   c. The deviation rates of both the auditor's sample and the population exceed the tolerable rate.
   d. The deviation rates of both the auditor's sample and the population are less than the tolerable rate. (ID: 8827)

8. An auditor discovers that an account balance believed not to be materially misstated based on an audit sample was materially misstated based on the total population of the account balance. This is an example of which of the following sampling types of risks?
   a. Incorrect rejection
   b. Incorrect acceptance
   c. Assessing control risk too low
   d. Assessing control risk too high (ID: 9945)

9. As a result of tests of controls, an auditor assesses control risk too high. This incorrect assessment most likely occurred because
   a. Control risk based on the auditor's sample is less than the true operating effectiveness of the client's control activity.
   b. The auditor believes that the control activity relates to the client's assertions when, in fact, it does not.
   c. The auditor believes that the control activity will reduce the extent of substantive testing when, in fact, it will not.
   d. Control risk based on the auditor's sample is greater than the true operating effectiveness of the client's control activity. (ID: 8393)

10. In confirming a client's accounts receivable in prior years, an auditor discovered many differences between recorded account balances and confirmation replies. These differences were resolved and were not misstatements. In defining the sampling unit for the current year's audit, the auditor most likely would choose
    a. Customers with credit balances
    b. Small account balances
    c. Individual overdue balances
    d. Individual invoices (ID: 89781)

11. Which of the following would be a consideration in planning an auditor's sample for a test of controls?
    a. Preliminary judgments about materiality levels.
    b. The auditor's allowable risk of assessing control risk too high
    c. The level of detection risk for the account
    d. The auditor's allowable risk of assessing control risk too low (ID: 8632)

Statistical Sampling

12. As a result of tests of controls, an auditor assessed control risk too low and decreased substantive testing. This assessment occurred because the true deviation rate in the population was
    a. Less than the risk of assessing control risk too low, based on the auditor's sample
    b. Less than the deviation rate in the auditor's sample
    c. More than the risk of assessing control risk too low, based on the auditor's sample
    d. More than the deviation rate in the auditor's sample (ID: 5646)

13. A principal advantage of statistical methods of attribute sampling over nonstatistical methods is that they provide a scientific basis for planning the

    a. Risk of assessing control risk too low
    b. Expected population deviation rate
    c. Tolerable rate
    d. Sample size (ID: 0260)

14. Which of the following would be a consideration in planning a sample for a test of subsequent cash receipts?

    a. Preliminary judgments about materiality levels
    b. The amount of bad debt write-offs in the prior year
    c. The size of the intercompany receivable balance
    d. The auditor's allowable risk of assessing control risk is too low (ID: 9361)

15. When performing a substantive test of a random sample of cash disbursements, an auditor is supplied with a photocopy of vendor invoices supporting the disbursements for one particular vendor rather than the original invoices. The auditor is told that the vendor's original invoices have been misplaced. What should the auditor do in response to this situation?

    a. Increase randomly the number of items in the substantive test to increase the reliance that may be placed on the overall test
    b. Reevaluate the risk of fraud, and design alternate tests for the related transactions
    c. Increase testing by agreeing more of the payments to this particular vendor to the photocopies of its invoices
    d. Count the missing original documents as misstatements, and project the total amount of the error based on the size of the population and the dollar amount of the errors (ID: 9370)

16. An advantage of statistical sampling over nonstatistical sampling is that statistical sampling helps an auditor to

    a. Eliminate the risk of nonsampling errors
    b. Reduce the level of audit risk and materiality to a relatively low amount
    c. Measure the sufficiency of the audit evidence obtained
    d. Minimize the failure to detect errors and fraud (ID: 5991)

17. Which of the following statements is ordinarily correct about the sample size in statistical sampling when testing controls?

    a. The expected population deviation rate has little effect on determining the sample size.
    b. As the population size doubles, the sample size should also double.
    c. As the tolerable deviation rate increases, the sample size should also increase.
    d. The population size has little effect on the sample size. (ID: 9930)

18. Which of the following factors is (are) considered in determining the sample size for a test of controls?

	Expected deviation rate	Tolerable deviation rate
a.	Yes	Yes
b.	No	No
c.	No	Yes
d.	Yes	No

(ID: 5980)

Classical Sampling

19. An auditor is determining the sample size for an inventory observation using mean-per-unit estimation, which is a variables sampling plan. To calculate the required sample size, the auditor usually determines the

	Variability in the dollar amounts of inventory items	Risk of incorrect acceptance
a.	Yes	Yes
b.	Yes	No
c.	No	Yes
d.	No	No

(ID: 6836)

20. Given random selection, the same sample size, and the same precision requirement for the testing of two unequal populations, the risk of assessing control risk too low on the smaller population is

    a. Higher than assessing control risk too low for the larger population
    b. Indeterminate relative to assessing control risk too low for the larger population
    c. Lower than assessing control risk too low for the larger population
    d. The same as assessing control risk too low for the larger population (ID: 7498)

21. An auditor may use a systematic sampling technique with a start at any randomly selected item when performing a test of controls with respect to control over cash receipts. The biggest disadvantage of this type of sampling is that the items in the population

    a. Must be systematically replaced in the population after sampling
    b. May occur in a systematic pattern, thus destroying the sample randomness
    c. Must be recorded in a systematic pattern before the sample can be drawn
    d. May systematically occur more than once in the sample (ID: 0267)

22. In statistical sampling methods used in substantive testing, an auditor most likely would stratify a population into meaningful groups if

    a. Probability-proportional-to-size (PPS) sampling is used.
    b. The population has highly variable recorded amounts.
    c. The auditor's estimated tolerable misstatement is extremely small.
    d. The standard deviation of recorded amounts is relatively small. (ID: 5668)

Attributes Sampling

23. An auditor should consider the tolerable rate of deviation when determining the number of check requests to select for a test to obtain assurance that all check requests have been properly authorized. The auditor should also consider

	The average dollar value of the check requests	The allowable risk of assessing control risk too low
a.	Yes	Yes
b.	Yes	No
c.	No	Yes
d.	No	No

(ID: 6833)

24. Which of the following statements is generally correct about the sample size in statistical sampling when testing internal controls?

    a. As the population size doubles, the sample size should increase by about 67%.
    b. The sample size is inversely proportional to the expected error rate.
    c. There is **no** relationship between the tolerable error rate and the sample size.
    d. The population size has little or **no** effect on the sample size. (ID: 89800)

Items 25 and 26 are based on the following:

An auditor desired to test credit approval on 10,000 sales invoices processed during the year. The auditor designed a statistical sample that would provide 1% risk of assessing control risk too low (99% confidence) that not more than 7% of the sales invoices lacked approval. The auditor estimated from previous experience that about 2½% of the sales invoices lacked approval. A sample of 200 invoices was examined and 7 of them were lacking approval. The auditor then determined the achieved upper precision limit to be 8%.

25. In the evaluation of this sample, the auditor decided to increase the level of the preliminary assessment of control risk because the

    a. Tolerable rate (7%) was less than the achieved upper precision limit (8%)
    b. Expected deviation rate (7%) was more than the percentage of errors in the sample (3½%)
    c. Expected deviation rate (2½%) was less than the tolerable rate (7%)
    d. Achieved upper precision limit (8%) was more than the percentage of errors in the sample (3½%)

    (ID: 0250)

26. The allowance for sampling risk was

    a. 5½%
    b. 4½%
    c. 3½%
    d. 1% (ID: 0251)

27. What is an auditor's evaluation of a statistical sample for attributes when a test of 50 documents results in 3 deviations if tolerable rate is 7%, the expected population deviation rate is 5%, and the allowance for sampling risk is 2%?

    a. Modify the planned assessed level of control risk because the tolerable rate plus the allowance for sampling risk exceeds the expected population deviation rate
    b. Accept the sample results as support for the planned assessed level of control risk because the sample deviation rate plus the allowance for sampling risk exceeds the tolerable rate
    c. Accept the sample results as support for the planned assessed level of control risk because the tolerable rate less the allowance for sampling risk equals the expected population deviation rate
    d. Modify the planned assessed level of control risk because the sample deviation rate plus the allowance for sampling risk exceeds the tolerable rate (ID: 2807)

28. Which of the following statements is correct about the sample size in statistical sampling when testing internal controls?

    a. The auditor should consider the tolerable rate of deviation from the controls being tested in determining sample size.
    b. As the likely rate of deviation decreases, the auditor should increase the planned sample size.
    c. The allowable risk of assessing control risk too low has no effect on the planned sample size.
    d. Of all the factors to be considered, the population size has the greatest effect on the sample size.

    (ID: 8134)

29. An auditor is selecting vouchers for testing an entity's internal control activities related to the proper approval of vouchers before checks are prepared. The auditor is matching random numbers with voucher numbers to determine which vouchers to inspect. If a random number matches a voided voucher, that voucher ordinarily would be replaced by another voucher in the random sample if the voided voucher

    a. Cannot be located in the voucher file
    b. Represents a dollar amount that is material
    c. Indicates a deviation from the prescribed activity
    d. Has been properly voided (ID: 7636)

30. In attribute sampling, a 25% change in which of the following factors will have the smallest effect on the size of the sample?

    a. Tolerable rate of deviation
    b. Number of items in the population
    c. Degree of assurance desired
    d. Planned assessed level of control risk (ID: 8848)

Variables Sampling

31. Using statistical sampling to assist in verifying the year-end accounts payable balance, an auditor has accumulated the following data:

	Number of accounts	Book balance	Balance determined by the auditor
Population	4,100	$5,000,000	?
Sample	200	$ 125,000	$150,000

Using the ratio estimation technique, the auditor's estimate of year-end accounts payable balance would be

    a. $6,150,000
    b. $6,000,000
    c. $5,125,000
    d. $5,050,000 (ID: 7496)

32. Which of the following statements is correct concerning the auditor's use of statistical sampling?

    a. An auditor needs to estimate the dollar amount of the standard deviation of the population to use classical variables sampling.
    b. The selection of zero balances usually does not require special sample design considerations when using PPS sampling.
    c. A classical variables sample needs to be designed with special considerations to include negative balances in the sample.
    d. An assumption of PPS sampling is that the underlying accounting population is normally distributed. (ID: 0265)

33. An auditor established a $60,000 tolerable misstatement for an asset with an account balance of $1,000,000. The auditor selected a sample of every twentieth item from the population that represented the asset account balance and discovered overstatements of $3,700 and understatements of $200. Under these circumstances, the auditor most likely would conclude that

    a. There is an unacceptably high risk that the actual misstatements in the population exceed the tolerable misstatement because the total projected misstatement is more than the tolerable misstatement.
    b. There is an unacceptably high risk that the tolerable misstatement exceeds the sum of actual overstatements and understatements.
    c. The asset account is fairly stated because the total projected misstatement is less than the tolerable misstatement.
    d. The asset account is fairly stated because the tolerable misstatement exceeds the net of projected actual overstatements and understatements. (ID: 6938)

34. Which of the following statements is correct concerning probability-proportional-to-size (PPS) sampling, also known as dollar-unit sampling?

    a. The sampling distribution should approximate the normal distribution.
    b. Overstated units have a lower probability of sample selection than units that are understated.
    c. The auditor controls the risk of incorrect acceptance by specifying that risk level for the sampling plan.
    d. The sampling interval is calculated by dividing the number of physical units in the population by the sample size. (ID: 0243)

35. Which of the following characteristics most likely would be an advantage of using classical variables sampling rather than probability-proportional-to-size (PPS) sampling?
    a. The selection of negative balances requires no special design considerations.
    b. The sampling process can begin before the complete population is available.
    c. The auditor need not consider the preliminary judgments about materiality.
    d. The sample will result in a smaller sample size if few errors are expected. (ID: 8404)

36. Which of the following is the primary objective of probability-proportional-to-size (PPS) sample?
    a. To identify overstatement errors
    b. To increase the proportion of smaller-value items in the sample
    c. To identify items where controls were not properly applied
    d. To identify zero and negative balances (ID: 8840)

Problem 6-2 SIMULATION: Probability to Proportional to Size Sampling

An auditor has decided to use probability-proportional-to-size (PPS) sampling, sometimes called dollar-unit sampling, in the audit of a client's accounts receivable balance. Few, if any, misstatements of account balance overstatement are expected. The auditor plans to use the following PPS sampling table.

TABLE
Reliability Factors for Errors of Overstatement

Number of overstatements misstatements	Risk of incorrect acceptance				
	1%	5%	10%	15%	20%
0	4.61	3.00	2.31	1.90	1.61
1	6.64	4.75	3.89	3.38	3.00
2	8.41	6.30	5.33	4.72	4.28
3	10.05	7.76	6.69	6.02	5.52
4	11.61	9.16	8.00	7.27	6.73

1. Calculate the sampling interval and the sample size Edwards should use given the following information:

Tolerable misstatement	$ 15,000
Risk of incorrect acceptance	5%
Number of misstatements allowed	0
Recorded amount of accounts receivable	$300,000

2. Calculate the total projected misstatement if the following three misstatements were discovered in a different PPS sample:

	Recorded amount	Audit amount	Sampling interval
1st misstatement	$ 400	$ 320	$1,000
2nd misstatement	500	0	1,000
3rd misstatement	3,000	2,500	1,000

(ID: 9209)

Problem 6-3 SIMULATION: Research

What authoritative reference provides guidance to an auditor on choosing between statistical and nonstatistical sampling?

Reminder: On the actual exam, you will use an electronic database of authoritative literature to find and select the reference (appropriate section and paragraph of the relevant guidance). Please see the AICPA's tutorial and sample test on the exam section of their website.

[ ] § [ ] [ ]

(ID: 9211)

Solution 6-1 MULTIPLE-CHOICE ANSWERS

1. (c) Substantive tests of details are performed by the auditor to either detect misstatements or obtain evidence about the validity and propriety of the accounting treatment of transactions and balances. In substantive testing, the auditor is primarily interested in dollar amounts, and the traditional method of performing substantive tests is by variables sampling. (ID: 5127)

2. (a) Attribute sampling is used to test the effectiveness of internal control procedures. For example, the auditor may be concerned with estimating the percentage of purchase orders that do not have proper authorization. Variable sampling is utilized when testing details of transactions and account balances. (ID: 89783)

3. (a) Attributes sampling involves the determination of the rate of occurrence of some characteristic (attribute) in a population. In an audit, the attribute of interest is frequently a deviation from a particular control procedure. Identifying entries posted to incorrect accounts is an example of testing compliance with the use of correct accounts. In estimating the amount in an expense account, evaluating the reasonableness of depreciation expense, and selecting receivables for confirmation of balances, a CPA is testing for dollar amounts which would involve variables sampling. (ID: 8406)

4. (b) Generally, variables sampling involves the determining of proper dollar value of the sampled items and makes inferences about the fairness of the amounts reported in the financial statements. Variables sampling typically involves deciding whether the dollar value of an account is reasonable. Generally, attributes sampling involves the determination of the rate of occurrence of some characteristic in a population. Proper prices, the number of misstatements, or proper recording are attributes. (ID: 7816)

5. (b) Nonsampling risk arises from issues unconnected with sampling, such as failing to recognize misstatements. Sampling risk arises from the possibility that, when a substantive test is restricted to a sample, conclusions might be different than if the auditor had tested each item in the population. The risk derived from the uncertainty in applying audit procedures to specific risks and the possibility of selecting audit procedures that are not appropriate to achieve the specific objective are unconnected with sampling. (ID: 90192)

6. (c) The risk of incorrect rejection is the risk that the sample supports the conclusion that the recorded account balance is materially misstated when it is not materially misstated. The risk of assessing control risk too high is the risk that the assessed level of control risk based on the sample is greater than the true operating effectiveness of the control. The risk of assessing control risk too low is just the opposite. The risk of incorrect acceptance is the risk that the sample supports the conclusion that the recorded account balance is not materially misstated when it is materially misstated. (ID: 4708)

7. (b) The tolerable rate is the maximum rate of deviation from the prescribed internal control policies and procedures that would support the auditor's assessed level of control risk. In this case, the auditor has assessed control risk too high. The risk of assessing control risk too high is the risk that the assessed level of control risk based on the sample is greater (the deviation rate in the auditor's sample exceeds the tolerable rate...) than the true operating effectiveness of the control (...but the deviation rate in the population is less than the tolerable rate). The situation described in answer a. would result in assessing control risk too low. Answers c. and d. would support the auditor's assessment of control risk. (ID: 8827)

8. (b) The risk of incorrect acceptance is the risk that the sample supports the conclusion that the recorded account balance is not materially misstated when it is materially misstated. The risk of incorrect rejection is the risk that the sample supports the conclusion that the recorded account balance is materially misstated when it is not materially misstated. These are sampling risks related to substantive tests of details. The risk of assessing control risk too low is the risk that the assessed level of control risk based on the sample is less than the true operating effectiveness of the control. The risk of assessing control risk too high is the risk that the assessed level of control risk based on the sample is greater than the true operating effectiveness of the control. (ID: 9945)

9. (d) The risk of assessing control risk too high is the risk that the assessed level of control risk based on the sample is greater than the true operating effectiveness of the control. If a control activity is unrelated to the client's assertions, the assessment could have been either too low or too high. The auditor's decisions reduce the extent of substantive testing, not the control activity itself. (ID: 8393)

10. (d) When planning samples for tests of controls, the auditor will consider the relationship of the sample to the objective of the test of controls as well as the characteristics of the population. Confirmation replies relate directly to items appearing on individual invoices. (ID: 89781)

11. (d) When planning an audit sample for a test of controls, the auditor should consider the auditor's allowable risk of assessing control risk too low; not too high. The auditor should also consider the relationship of the sample to the objective of the test of controls; the maximum rate of deviations from prescribed controls that would support the planned assessed level of control risk; and characteristics of the population, i.e., the items comprising the account balance or class of transactions of interest. Preliminary judgments about material levels and the level of detection risk are considerations for planning a sample for a substantive test of detail. (ID: 8632)

12. (d) If the sample deviation rate is lower than the true deviation rate in the population, the auditor mistakenly assesses control risk too low. The result is that detection risk is allowed to rise too high and substantive testing is decreased. (ID: 5646)

13. (d) The principal advantage of statistical over nonstatistical sampling methods is that statistical methods provide a model for determining sample size while explicitly recognizing relevant factors (e.g. risk of assessing control risk too low, tolerable rate, and expected deviation rate). In nonstatistical sampling, the auditor implicitly recognizes the relevant factors while determining the sample size based on his or her own judgment and experience. (ID: 0260)

14. (a) When planning a particular sample for a substantive test of details, such as subsequent cash receipts, the auditor should consider (1) the relationship of the sample to the relevant audit objective; (2) preliminary judgments about materiality levels; (3) the auditor's allowable risk of incorrect acceptance; and (4) characteristics of the population, i.e., the items comprising the account balance or class of transactions of interest. The amount of bad debt write-offs from the prior year would not be appropriate to consider to detect information about subsequent cash receipts. The size of the intercompany receivable balance is not related to subsequent cash receipts. The risk of assessing control risk too low (the risk that the assessed level of control risk based on the sample is less than the true operating effectiveness of the control) relates to sampling risk in performing tests of controls rather than a substantive test of details as described in this question. (ID: 9361)

15. (b) When an auditor is supplied with copies of vendor invoices instead of originals and told the originals have been misplaced, the auditor should reevaluate the risk of fraud and design alternate tests for the related transactions. Audit procedures that are appropriate to the particular audit objective should be applied to each sample item. If considering those unexamined items (the originals) to be misstated would lead to a conclusion that the balance or class contains material misstatement, the auditor should consider alternative audit procedures that would provide sufficient appropriate audit evidence to form a conclusion. The auditor should also consider whether the reasons for the lack of availability of the items have implications in relation to assessing risks of material misstatement due to fraud, the assessed level of control risk that the auditor expects to be supported, or the degree of reliance on management representations. (ID: 9370)

16. (c) Both statistical and nonstatistical sampling plans can provide sufficient audit evidence if properly applied. The distinguishing feature of statistical sampling methods as opposed to nonstatistical methods is that the user is able to provide a mathematical measurement of the degree of uncertainty that results from examining only part of a population. Statistical sampling, as well as nonstatistical sampling, is subject to nonsampling errors (procedural mistakes or human error). Both methods of sampling may be used to reduce audit risk, but neither would affect the level of materiality. Both can be used to reduce the risk of failing to detect errors and fraud, which is the risk of incorrect acceptance. (ID: 5991)

17. (d) The population size has little effect on the sample size. To determine the number of items to be selected for a particular sample for a test of controls, the auditor should consider the tolerable rate of deviation from the controls being tested, the likely rate of deviations, and the allowable risk of assessing control risk too low. An auditor applies professional judgment to relate these factors in determining the appropriate sample size. As the tolerable deviation rate increases, the sample size can be decreased, not increased. (ID: 9930)

18. (a) Both the expected (likely) deviation rate and the tolerable deviation rate are considerations in determining the sample size for a test of controls. (ID: 5980)

19. (a) With the mean-per-unit method, stratification of a highly variable population into segments allows an auditor to use a smaller sample size. Thus, variability in the dollar amounts of inventory items is considered. The risk of incorrect assessment has an inverse relationship with sample size. (ID: 6836)

20. (c) The risk of assessing control risk too low is the risk that the assessed level of control risk based on the sample is less than the true operating effectiveness of the control. All things being equal, a sample taken from a smaller population will be more representative of the population than a sample of the same size taken from a larger population. Thus, the risk that the sample taken from the smaller population will yield a result different from the result obtained had the entire population been examined, is lower than such a risk inherent in sampling from a larger population. (ID: 7498)

21. (b) When using the systematic sampling technique, the auditor determines a uniform interval by dividing the number of physical units in the population by the sample size. A random number is selected as a starting point for the first interval, and one item is selected throughout the population at each of the uniform intervals from the starting point. The randomness of the sample can be destroyed if the items in the population occur in a systematic pattern. For example, a population of employees on a payroll for a construction company might be organized by teams; each team consists of a crew leader and nine other workers. A selection of every tenth employee will list either every crew leader or no crew leaders, depending on the random start. No combination would include both crew leaders and other employees. (ID: 0267)

22. (b) Stratified sampling can be particularly useful in reducing the overall sample size on populations that have a wide range of dollar values (or highly variable recorded amounts). The primary objective is to decrease the effect of variance in the total population, thereby reducing sample size. PPS sampling insures items with large amounts all make it into the sample, but not by stratifying the population. The estimated tolerable misstatement and standard deviation are irrelevant to a decision to stratify. (ID: 5668)

23. (c) Check authorization is an internal control. In tests of internal controls, the auditor is determining the rate of occurrence of a deviation from the control procedure, not testing the dollar amounts reported in the financial statements. The allowable risk of assessing control risk too low affects the degree of assurance desired by the auditor. If a high degree of assurance is sought, sampling risk must be low. Sample size and risk are inversely related. (ID: 6833)

24. (d) When a sample is small in relation to the population, the population size has little or no effect on the determination of an appropriate sample size. (ID: 89800)

25. (a) The auditor would increase the preliminary assessment of control risk because the achieved upper precision limit of 8% (sample error rate plus an allowance for sampling risk) exceeded the tolerable error rate of 7% (determined by professional judgment). Therefore, the results of the test did not allow the auditor to conclude with 99% confidence that the error rate in the population did not exceed 7%. All other answers describe comparisons that are meaningless. (ID: 0250)

26. (b) The allowance for sampling risk is the difference between the observed sample rate and the achieved upper precision limit. The observed sample rate was 3.5% (7/200). Therefore, the allowance for sampling risk would be 4.5% (8% – 3.5%). (ID: 0251)

27. (d) The auditor should modify her/his planned assessed level of control risk when the sample deviation rate plus the allowance for sampling risk exceeds the tolerable rate. In this question, the deviation rate of 6% (3 deviations among 50 documents) plus the allowance for sampling risk of 2% is greater than the given tolerable rate of 7%. (ID: 2807)

28. (a) An increase in the tolerable rate of deviation would allow a reduction in sample size. As the likely deviation rate decreases, the auditor may decrease the planned sample size. The allowable risk of assessing control risk too low has an inverse effect on the sample size. Of all the factors to be considered, the population size has the *least* effect on the sample size. (ID: 8134)

29. (d) In an auditor's test of transactions, if a random number matches the number of a voided voucher, that voucher ordinarily should be replaced by another voucher in the random sample if the voucher has been properly voided. The voucher would be counted as an error and would not be replaced if it could not be located or constituted a deviation. The materiality of the dollar amount is irrelevant because the focus in a test of controls is whether or not procedures are properly performed, not the dollar value of the transaction being tested. (ID: 7636)

30. (b) The number of items in the population has virtually no effect on the sample size unless the population is very small. (ID: 8848)

31. (b) Under the ratio estimation technique, the auditor uses sample results to estimate the ratio of audited value to book value. The ratio is then applied to the population book value to estimate the audited value of the population. The sample "audited value/book value" ratio equals 1.2:1 ($150,000 ÷ $125,000). When this ratio is applied to the population book balance of $5,000,000, an estimated $6,000,000 audited value results. (ID: 7496)

32. (a) The factors affecting sample size when using classical variables sampling are (1) desired precision, (2) desired sample reliability, (3) variability among item values in the population (the estimate of the population's standard deviation) and (4) population size. PPS is a non-parametric method that does not assume a normal distribution. PPS plans require special design to deal with negative balances and zero balances because sample selection is based on the cumulative sum of dollars of the population. Negative figures distort the cumulative sum and zero balances would not be considered without special adjustments in a PPS plan. Classical variables techniques are unaffected by either zero balances or negative balances. (ID: 0265)

33. (a) The net of projected actual misstatements [($3,700 – $200) × 20 =] is $70,000, which is larger than the tolerable misstatement of $60,000. If the tolerable misstatement exceeds the sum of actual overstatements and understatements, the auditor may consider the account fairly stated. (ID: 6938)

34. (c) In PPS sampling, the auditor achieves control over the risk of incorrect acceptance by specifying the level of risk the auditor is willing to assume. PPS sampling does not require direct consideration of the standard deviation of dollar amounts to determine the appropriate sample. The book value of the unit determines how probable it is that it will be included in the sample, not whether it is over or understated. The sampling interval is calculated by dividing the book value of the population by the sample size. (ID: 0243)

35. (a) Special consideration must be given to zero and negative balance accounts which usually are excluded from a probability-proportional-to-size (PPS) sample. For both classical variables sampling and PPS sampling, the sampling process may begin before the complete population is available and the auditor must consider the preliminary judgments about materiality. If few errors are expected, the sample will result in a smaller sample size using PPS sampling than if classical variables sampling is used. (ID: 8404)

36. (a) In PPS sampling, because the sample is selected proportional to size, larger dollar amounts have a higher probability of being selected, thus overstatements (errors) are more likely to be selected than understatements. An auditor will normally use PPS sampling when testing for material overstatements. For the reason just stated, PPS sampling is unlikely to select smaller-value items and these amounts may be significantly understated in the sample, not increased. PPS sampling is a form of variables sampling which is normally used in substantive testing where the auditor is usually interested in the selection of dollar amounts, not attributes as is usually the case in tests of controls. Additionally, samples taken to test the operating effectiveness of controls (to provide a basis for the auditor to conclude whether the controls are being properly applied) should be selected in a manner such that the sample is representative of the population, thus all items in the population should have an opportunity to be selected which is not the case with PPS sampling. Zero balances are not subject to PPS selection and negative balances would have to be segregated into a separate population for testing. (ID: 8840)

Solution 6-2 SIMULATION ANSWER: Probability to Proportional to Size Sampling

1. PPS Sampling Interval and Sample Size

$$\text{Sampling Interval} = \frac{\text{Tolerable Misstatement}}{\text{Reliability Factor for Misstatement of Overstatement}}$$

$$= \frac{\$15{,}000}{3.00} = \$5{,}000$$

$$\text{Sample Size} = \frac{\text{Recorded Amount}}{\text{Sample Interval}}$$

$$= \frac{\$300{,}000}{\$5{,}000} = \$60$$

2. Projected Misstatement in a PPS Sample

	Recorded amount	Audit amount	Tainting	Sampling Interval	Projected misstatement
1st misstatement	$ 400	$ 320	20%	$1,000	$ 200
2nd misstatement	500	0	100%	1,000	1,000
3rd misstatement	3,000	2,500	*	1,000	500
Total projected misstatement					$1,700

* The recorded amount is greater than the sampling interval; therefore, the projected misstatement equals the actual misstatement. (ID: 9209)

Solution 6-3 SIMULATION ANSWER: Research

AU	§	530		A14

.A14 The decision whether to use a statistical or nonstatistical sampling approach is a matter for the auditor's professional judgment; however, sample size is not a valid criterion to use in deciding between statistical and nonstatistical approaches. An auditor who applies statistical sampling may use tables or formulas to compute sample size. An auditor who applies nonstatistical sampling exercises professional judgment to relate the same factors used in statistical sampling in determining the appropriate sample size. Ordinarily, this would result in a sample size comparable with the sample size resulting from an efficient and effectively designed statistical sample, considering the same sampling parameters. This guidance does not suggest that the auditor using nonstatistical sampling also compute a corresponding sample size using an appropriate statistical technique. (ID: 9211)

CHAPTER 7

AUDITING IT SYSTEMS

AU Identifier Used for Clarified GAAS in This Textbook

We have not continued to use the temporary AU-C identifier for the clarified auditing standards issued by the American Institute of Certified Public Accountants (AICPA). In this textbook these standards have an AU identifier.

CHAPTER 7

AUDITING IT SYSTEMS

I. Introduction

A. Engagement Planning

The use of information technology (IT) systems to initiate, process, record, and communicate financial information has exploded over the past decade. As a result, an auditor must now consider how IT affects the client's system of internal control, the types of IT controls that are important to the client's financial reporting process, and to the audit itself.

1. **Effect on Planning** An auditor must obtain a sufficient understanding of internal controls to plan an audit. An entity's IT system(s) affects: its control environment; risk assessment; control activities, information, communication and monitoring; and transaction processing. The auditor will need to decide whether to design and perform tests of controls or to perform only substantive tests.

2. **IT Benefits** An IT environment provides benefits to the auditor related to effectiveness and efficiency because it enables the entity to perform the following:

   - Consistently apply predefined business rules and perform complex calculations in processing large volumes of transactions or data
   - Enhance the timeliness, availability, and accuracy of information
   - Facilitate the additional analysis of information
   - Enhance the ability to monitor the performance of the entity's activities and its policies and procedures
   - Reduce the risk that controls will be circumvented, especially if controls over changes to the IT system are effective

3. **IT Risks** Some of the risks that an auditor faces when working within an IT environment include the following:

   - Overreliance on information provided by the IT system that could be incorrectly processing data or consistently processing inaccurate data
   - Unauthorized access to data that may result in destruction of data or improper changes to data including the recording of unauthorized or nonexistent transactions or inaccurate recording of transactions
   - Unauthorized changes to computer programs
   - Failure to make necessary changes to computer programs
   - Inappropriate manual intervention
   - Potential loss of data

4. **Control Considerations** An auditor's objectives do not change when auditing the financial statements of a company using an IT system. An auditor must still decide whether the controls are operating effectively to provide reasonable assurance that the related assertions (for example, that the transactions actually occurred and were properly recorded and valued) are not materially misstated. The ultimate objective is still to express an opinion on the fairness of presentation of the financial statements. While the audit objectives do not change, the audit procedures used to accomplish them may change. The auditor should consider the following matters:

   a. **Extent** The extent to which the computer is used in each significant accounting application.

   b. **Complexity** The complexity of the entity's computer operations, including the use of an outside service center.

   c. **Organization** The organizational structure of the computer processing activities.

   d. **Audit Trail** Some data may only be available for a limited time.

   e. **CAAT** Computer-Assisted Audit Techniques (CAAT) can increase the efficiency of performing audit procedures. If specific skills are needed, and a specialist is used, the auditor should have sufficient computer-related knowledge to (1) communicate the objectives of the other professional's work; (2) evaluate whether the specified procedures will meet the auditor's objectives; and (3) evaluate the results of the procedures applied as they relate to the nature, timing, and extent of other planned audit procedures.

B. Electronic Data Processing

An IT-based, or EDP-based, system includes (1) hardware, (2) software, (3) documentation, (4) personnel, (5) data, and (6) controls. There can be significant differences between IT-based activities and non-IT activities.

1. Considerations

   a. **Documentation** Many control procedures in IT systems do not leave documentary evidence of performance.

   b. **Electronic Information** Files and records are usually in machine-readable form and cannot be read without using a computer.

   c. **Reduced Human Involvement** Computers may obscure errors that a human would notice while handling the transaction.

   d. **Reliability** IT systems are more reliable than manual systems because all of the data are subjected to the same controls. Manual systems are subject to human error on a random basis. Computer processing virtually eliminates computational errors associated with manual processing.

   e. **Knowledge** An auditor may need specialized IT knowledge to perform an audit.

   f. **Difficulty of Change** It is harder to change an IT system once it is implemented than it is to change a manual system. Therefore, the auditor will want to become familiar with a new IT system at an early stage of the development process so that the auditor can anticipate possible future audit problems.

2. **Internal Processing** Transactions may be processed in a variety of ways:

   a. **Batch Processing** Transactions to be processed are accumulated in groups (batches) and are then processed as a batch. Batch processing frequently involves sequential access to the data files. For example, a company may accumulate a day's charge sales before processing them against the master file during the night. Before they are processed, the transactions would be sorted into the order of the records on the master file. One disadvantage of batch processing is that, because of the time delays, errors may not be detected immediately.

   b. **Online Processing** Transactions are processed and the file is updated as the transactions occur. Online processing usually involves files that can be accessed directly. For example, a cash register terminal may update the inventory file automatically when a sale is made.

   c. **Real-Time Processing** An online system is operating in real time if the data is processed fast enough to get the response back in time to influence the process. For example, an airline reservation system is an online, real-time (OLRT) system because the customer receives reservations after waiting only a few moments.

   d. **Integrated System** All files affected by a transaction are updated in one transaction-processing run, rather than having a separate run for each file. For example, in an integrated system, a sales transaction may update the sales summary file, the accounts receivable master file, and the inventory file during one processing run.

3. **External Processing** While many companies have their own equipment to do their processing internally, others utilize outside processors. Several common arrangements are:

   a. **Block Time** Client rents a certain block of computer time from an outside party. For example, a company may rent time from a bank that does not utilize its computer system 24 hours per day.

   b. **Time-Sharing** A number of users share a computer system. Each may have a terminal that it can use to access a CPU located outside of the client. Each user can access the system whenever it wishes.

   c. **Service Bureau** An outside organization that provides a wide range of data processing services for a fee (discussed later in the chapter).

   d. **Cloud Computing** The delivery of computing as a service rather than a product. Shared resources, software, and information are provided to computers as a metered service over the Internet. Computing clouds provide computation, software, data access, and storage resources without requiring cloud users to know the location and other details of the computing infrastructure.

C. **Client Documentation**
Documentation is an important aspect of control and communication. It generally provides (1) an understanding of the system's objectives, concepts, and output, (2) a source of information for systems analysts and programmers when involved in program maintenance and revision, (3) information that is needed for a supervisory review, (4) a basis for training new personnel, (5) a means of communicating common information, (6) a source of information about accounting controls, and (7) a source of information that will aid in providing continuity in the event experienced personnel leave. If reliable documentation is not available, the auditor must find other sources of information. There are several types of documentation.

Exhibit 1 ▸ IT System Documentation Mnemonic

O	Operations documentation
P	Problem definition documentation
S	Systems documentation
O	Operator documentation
U	User documentation
P	Program documentation

1. **Operator Documentation** Documentation should be prepared that will indicate the jobs run and any operator interaction. This usually includes: a daily computer log (jobs run, the time required, who ran them, etc.) and a console log (listing of all interactions between the console and the CPU).

2. **Problem Definition Documentation** Permits the auditor to gain a general understanding of the system without having to become involved in the details of the programs. Contents include: a description of the reasons for implementing the system; a description of the operations performed by the system; and evidence of approval of the system and subsequent changes.

3. **Systems Documentation** Provides sufficient information to trace accounting data from its original entry to system output. Contents include: a description of the system, including flowcharts; input, output, and file descriptions; descriptions of controls; and copies of authorizations and their effective dates for systems changes.

4. **Operations Documentation** Information provided to the computer operator; it can be used by the auditor to obtain an understanding of the functions performed by the operator and to determine how data is processed; contents include the following:

5. **User Documentation** A description of the input required for processing and an output listing. The auditor may use it to gain an understanding of the functions performed by a user and the general flow of information. Contents include a description of the system, description of the input and output, list of control procedures and an indication of the position of the person performing the procedures, error correction procedures, cutoff procedures for submitting the data to the IT Department, and a description of how a user department should check reports for accuracy.

6. **Program Documentation** Primarily used by systems analysts and programmers to provide a control over program corrections and revisions. However, it may be useful to the auditor to determine the current status of a program.

D. Control Environments

The characteristics that distinguish manual processing from computer processing include:

1. **Audit Trails** Some computer systems are designed so that a complete transaction trail that is useful for audit purposes might exist for only a short period of time or only in computer-readable form. This trail is used to monitor the system, answer queries, and deter fraud.

2. **Uniform Processing of Transactions** Computer processing uniformly subjects like transactions to the same processing instructions. Consequently, computer processing virtually eliminates the occurrence of clerical error normally associated with manual processing. Conversely, errors will result in all like transactions being processed incorrectly.

3. **Segregation of Functions** Many internal control procedures once performed by separate individuals in manual systems may be concentrated in systems that use computer processing. Therefore, an individual who has access to the computer may be in a position to perform incompatible functions. As a result, other control procedures may be necessary in computer systems to achieve the control objectives ordinarily accomplished by segregation of functions in manual systems.

4. **Potential for Errors and Fraud** Decreased human involvement in handling transactions processed by computers can reduce the potential for observing errors and fraud. Errors or fraud occurring during the design or changing of application programs can remain undetected for long periods of time.

5. **Potential for Increased Supervision** Computer systems offer management a wide variety of analytical tools that may be used to review and supervise the operations of the company. The availability of these additional controls may serve to enhance the entire internal control structure on which the auditor may wish to assess control risk at below the maximum level. For example, comparisons by management of budget to actual results and the response by management to unusual fluctuations indicate management's monitoring of the ongoing operations as a prevention of unfavorable crisis situations.

6. **Computer-Initiation of Transactions** The authorization of "automatic" transactions or procedures might not be documented in the same way as those initiated in a manual accounting system, and management's authorization of those transactions may be implicit in its acceptance of the design of the computer system.

7. **Dependence General Controls** Computer processing may produce reports and other output that are used in performing manual control procedures. The effectiveness of these manual control procedures can be dependent on the effectiveness of controls over the completeness and accuracy of computer processing.

E. **Types of Controls**

Internal accounting control procedures sometimes are defined by classifying control procedures into two types: general and application control procedures.

1. **General Controls** Those controls that relate to all or many computerized accounting applications and often include control over the development, modification, and maintenance of computer programs and control over the use of and changes to data maintained on computer files. When an auditor anticipates assessing control risk at a low level, the auditor would focus initially on these general controls.

2. **Application Controls** Those controls that relate to specific computerized accounting applications, i.e., input, processing, and output controls for an accounts payable application.

3. **Manual Controls** Controls in a traditional system are manual, and may include procedures such as approvals and reviews of activities, and reconciliations and follow-up of reconciling items. Manual controls may be less reliable than automated controls because they can be more easily bypassed, ignored, or overridden; they are also more prone to errors and mistakes. However, manual controls may be more appropriate when judgment is required, such as in the following circumstances:

   a. Large, unusual, or nonrecurring transactions

   b. Circumstances where misstatements are difficult to define, anticipate, or predict

   c. In changing circumstances that require a control response outside the scope of an existing automated control

   d. In monitoring the effectiveness of automated controls

4. **Automated Controls** Controls in systems that use IT consist of a combination of automated controls (e.g., controls embedded in computer programs) and manual controls. Further, manual controls may be independent of the IT system and may use information produced by the IT system, or may be limited to monitoring the effective functioning of the system and the automated controls and handling exceptions. An entity's mix of manual and automated controls varies with the nature and complexity of the entity's use of IT.

II. General Auditing Approaches

A. Around (Without) the Computer

The computer is treated as a "black box" that is ignored for all practical purposes. The auditor concentrates on input and output; i.e., if the inputs are correct and the outputs are correct, what went on within the computer also must be correct. The auditor does not test or directly examine the computer program, nor use the computer to perform the tests. Auditing around the computer is appropriate for simple systems that provide extensive printouts of processing, i.e., systems that provide a good audit trail.

1. **Testing of Controls** Extensive use is made of the error listing (error log) to verify the existence and functioning of the control procedures. For example, if the error listing shows that a payroll transaction was not processed because the "hours-worked" field exceeded the limit allowed, the auditor has evidence that the limit test exists and is functioning. The auditor also will trace transactions from the source documents (for example, a sales slip) through processing to their final place in the accounts and reports. Note that while computer-generated output is being used, the computer is not being used as an audit tool.

2. **Substantive Testing** The computer-prepared output is used as a basis for substantive testing. For example, the auditor may select a sample of accounts receivable to be confirmed from a computer-prepared listing of all the individual accounts receivable.

B. Through (With) the Computer

The computer is used to perform tests of controls and substantive testing. The auditor places emphasis on the input data and the processing of the data. While output is not ignored, the auditor reasons that if the input is correct and the processing is correct, then the output must be correct. As a system becomes more complex, more processing is done within the computer and more data files are kept only in machine-readable form. This causes the audit trail to disappear. When this happens, auditing through the computer is really the only alternative open to the auditor. The following techniques are available to the auditor:

Exhibit 2 ▸ Auditing Through the Computer Mnemonic

W	Writing own program
E	Embedded audit modules
T	Tagging
C	Client-prepared program
U	Utility programs (utility routines)
P	Program comparison
T	Test data (test deck)
R	Review of program logic
I	Integrated test facility (ITF, minicompany approach)
P	Parallel simulation
P	Program tracing

1. **Writing Own Program** The auditor writes a program for the specific substantive test to be performed. The major drawback is the time and effort required to get the program operational.

2. **Embedded Audit Modules** Sections of program code are included in the client's application program to collect audit data for the auditor. This monitors the client's system as transactions are actually processed. It can be hard to install once the application program is operational. Thus, it may be most efficiently included during system design.

3. **Tagging** Selected transactions are "tagged" (i.e., specially marked) at the auditor's direction. Then, as they are processed, additional documentation is generated so that the auditor can see how the transactions are handled as they are processed, i.e., it allows the auditor to examine the transactions at the intermediate steps in processing that normally are done within the computer but not displayed.

4. **Client-Prepared Program** Often the internal audit staff has programs to do the same things the auditor would like to do. Therefore, the auditor may be able to use the programs. However, first the auditor must test them to make sure that they do what they are supposed to do and that their integrity can be relied on.

5. **Utility Programs (Utility Routines)** Standard programs are furnished by the computer manufacturer for performing common data processing functions such: modifying data by changing or deleting records within a file; creating or destroying a file; changing the name or password of a file; etc. The auditor may have to be more technically proficient with IT to use utility programs. efficiently. The auditor must be sure the utility program has not been altered.

6. **Program Comparison** The auditor-controlled copy of the program is compared with the program the client is using currently (usually done on a surprise basis). The idea behind this technique is that the comparison will disclose unauthorized changes made in the program. While the auditor may do this manually, there is software available to do it. A major drawback is the problem of the auditor maintaining a current copy of the program. Routine maintenance (updating) by programmers may mean that the auditor's copy does not agree with the copy being used, and it is the auditor's copy that is wrong.

7. **Test Data (Test Deck)** The auditor prepares a series of fictitious transactions (test data), some of which are valid and some of which contain errors that should be detected by the controls the auditor wants to test. The auditor uses the client's programs to process the test data and then examines the output to check processing, including the computer-prepared error listing. There are at least three potential problems with using test data:

   a. Care must be exercised to prevent the fictitious data from becoming part of the client's real data files.

   b. Time and care are required to prepare the test data so that it will test for the things that could go wrong and that are of interest to the auditor.

   c. The auditor must take steps to make sure that the program being tested (i.e., the program testing the fictitious data) is the one that actually is used in routine processing.

8. **Review of Program Logic** The auditor reviews the application program's documentation, including the flowcharts and possibly the program listing, to obtain a sufficient understanding of the logic of the program in order to evaluate it. This may be time consuming. Unless the auditor specifically believes there is a logic error in the program, other audit techniques probably will be more efficient.

9. **Integrated Test Facility (ITF), Minicompany Approach** The auditor creates a fictitious entity within the client's actual data files. The fictitious data then is processed for the entity as part of the client's regular data processing. These transactions would be processed as part of the client's normal processing. The auditor knows what effect the various transactions should have on the account balance, so the auditor can check the status of the account at any time to verify that transactions are being processed correctly, i.e., that the application programs are working as they should.

10. **Parallel Simulation** Once the auditor has checked a program, the auditor must determine that the client continues to use it. Parallel simulation involves processing actual client data through an auditor's software program, possibly using the client's computer. After processing the data, the auditor compares the output with output obtained from the client. Two techniques that can be used to help the auditor verify that the program being used for routine processing is the one that has been checked are as follows:

    a. **Controlled Processing** The auditor observes (i.e., controls) an actual processing run and compares the results against those expected.

    b. **Controlled Reprocessing** The auditor tests a program and keeps a copy of the program. At some future point in time, the auditor has the client use the auditor's control copy of the program to process some actual transactions. The results are compared with those from the client's routine processing run. For example, the auditor may have a control copy of the payroll program. The auditor would select the time cards and payroll data for several employees and have them processed using the control copy. The auditor would then compare the results of gross pay, net pay, withholding, etc., from the program with those that were attained by the payroll program the client had just used. A major problem is for the auditor to keep the control copy of the program current.

11. **Program Tracing** This prints a listing of the program instructions (steps) that were executed in processing a transaction. The auditor must be familiar with the programming language in which the client's application program is written. Even then, it may be time consuming to follow through the program listing.

12. **Generalized Audit Software** Also known as General Purpose Audit Software or General Purpose Computer Audit Software. This is a set of programs or routines (i.e., a software package) specifically designed to perform certain data processing functions that are useful to the auditor. The auditor can use generalized audit software (GAS) on the data files of a variety of clients.

    a. **Benefits** The auditor only need describe the organization of each client's files to GAS briefly, rather than write computer programs. Benefits of GAS include:

        - Much of a client's data is retained only in machine-readable form. GAS makes it possible for the auditor to access the data, analyze it, and present the results in a meaningful and convenient form.
        - GAS lets the auditor examine more data in more detail; GAS produces economies in the audit while increasing audit quality without having to rely as much on client personnel.
        - GAS enables the auditor to gain access and test information stored in the client's files without having to acquire a complete understanding of the client's IT system.

b. **Audit Tasks Performed by GAS** While the exact procedures performed will vary among software packages, audit software is used to accomplish six basic types of audit tasks.

- Examining Records for Quality, Completeness, Consistency and Correctness.
- Testing Calculations and Making Computations
- Comparing Data on Separate Files
- Selecting, Printing and Analyzing Audit Samples
- Summarizing or Resequencing Data and Performing Analyses
- Comparing Data Obtained Through Other Audit Procedures With Company Records

c. **Facilitate Statistical Sampling** Computer programs have been developed to assist the auditor in planning and evaluating sampling procedures. These programs overcome the limitations of tables and perform calculations, such as a standard deviation computation, that are difficult and time consuming to perform manually.

III. Information Technology Controls

A. Overview

IT controls are policies and procedures that relate to the confidentiality, integrity, and availability of data and the overall management of the IT function within the business entity. Passage of the Sarbanes-Oxley Act (SOX) resulted in an increased focus on IT controls, as these support financial processing and therefore fall into the scope of management's assessment of internal control under SOX. SOX compliance focuses on those IT controls that are associated with a material account or are related to business process. IT controls that are part of SOX compliance include:

1. **Specific Application Controls** Transaction processing procedures that directly mitigate identified financial reporting risks. The focus is on "key" controls (those that specifically address risks), not on the entire application.

2. **IT General Controls** These controls support the assertions that programs function as intended and that key financial reports are reliable, primarily change control and security controls.

3. **IT Operations Controls** These controls ensure that problems with processing are identified and corrected.

B. General Controls (GC)

IT general controls are policies and procedures that relate to software applications. GC apply to mainframe, server, and end-user environments, and help ensure: the reliability of data generated by IT systems; that systems operate as intended; and that output is reliable. GC also relate to the general control environment—they're reflect the corporate culture, or the "tone at the top."

1. **Organization and Operation Controls**

a. **Data Integrity** Data must be safeguarded for maximum control. Users are given passwords or IDs to ensure that only authorized persons can access selected data. These passwords and IDs are changed frequently to further ensure the integrity of the system and its data. Passwords can be used to limit access to the entire system and to limit what the individual can access and/or change once in the system.

b. **Database Administrator** The database administrator is responsible for maintaining the database and restricting its access to authorized personnel.

c. **Segregation of Functions** Part of proper internal control is the segregation of functions within the IT Department Among the various functions that should be segregated are the following:

Exhibit 3 ▸ IT Department Functions Segregation Mnemonic

C	Control group	Responsible for internal control within IT Department
O	Operators	Convert data into machine readable form
P	Programmer	Develops and writes the computer programs; responsible for debugging of programs; writes the run manual
A	Analyst	Designs the overall system and prepares the system flowchart
L	Librarian	Keeps track of program and file use; maintains storage of all data and backups; controls access to programs

2. **Systems Development and Documentation Controls** A weakness in systems development and documentation controls means that an auditor usually will have to spend more time in order to understand the system and evaluate the controls. Because application controls often are dependent on the quality of general controls, the absence of effective system development controls may weaken the accounting application controls.

3. **Hardware and Systems Software Controls** Hardware controls are controls that are built into the computer. A weakness in hardware and systems software controls may affect the auditor's assessed level of control risk.

   a. **Parity Bit (Redundant Character Check)** In odd parity, the computer verifies that an odd number of magnetized dots (on tape, disk, etc.) represents each character. In even parity, an even number of magnetized dots is used to represent each character. Parity bits can detect transmission errors.

   b. **Echo Check** A CPU sends a signal to activate an input or output device in a certain manner. The device then sends a signal back to verify activation. The CPU then compares the signals.

   c. **Hardware Check** Computer checks to make sure the equipment is functioning properly (e.g. periodically the computer may search for circuits that are going bad).

   d. **Boundary Protection** Keeps several files or programs separate when they share a common storage. For example, in time-sharing, several users may share primary storage. Boundary protection would prevent their data and/or programs from becoming mixed and the different users from accessing each other's data.

4. **Access Controls** Physical access controls ensure that only authorized personnel can access the facilities housing IT equipment, files and documentation. Electronic access controls limit access to control software. A weakness in access controls increases the opportunity for unauthorized modifications of files and programs and misuse of the system; thereby decreasing the integrity of the system.

5. **Data and Procedural Controls** Serious weaknesses in data and procedural controls can affect the auditor's assessment of control risk when establishing the scope of the substantive testing.

   a. **File Labels** Include external (i.e. human-readable) and internal (i.e. machine-readable) labels. Internal labels can be either a header or trailer label.

   b. **File Protection Ring** A plastic ring attached to a reel of magnetic tape before the tape drive will write on the tape. Writing on magnetic tape automatically erases the data already there, so the file protection ring guards against the inadvertent erasure of the information on the tape.

   c. **File Protection Plans** Examples include: creating duplicate/backup files, stored offsite; disk reconstruction plans; and retention concepts. One such concept is a Grandparent-Parent-Child Retention Concept, also known as Grandfather-Father-Son Retention. The master file is updated at the end of each day by the day's transaction file,. After updating on Thursday, the Thursday updated master file (TUMF) is the child, the Wednesday updated master file (WUMF) is the parent, and the Tuesday updated master file (TSUMF) is the grandparent. These three files plus Wednesday's and Thursday's transaction files (WTF and TTF, respectively) are retained. If there is a problem during Friday's update run, the TUMF can be regenerated by running the copy of the WUMF with Thursday's transaction file. If necessary the WUMF could be reconstructed by processing TSUMF with Wednesday's transaction file.

   Once updating is completed on Friday, Friday's updated master file (FUMF) becomes the child, TUMF becomes the parent and WUMF becomes the grandparent. Therefore, at that time, TSUMF and Wednesday's transaction file can be erased.

Exhibit 4 ▸ Grandparent-Parent-Child Retention Concept

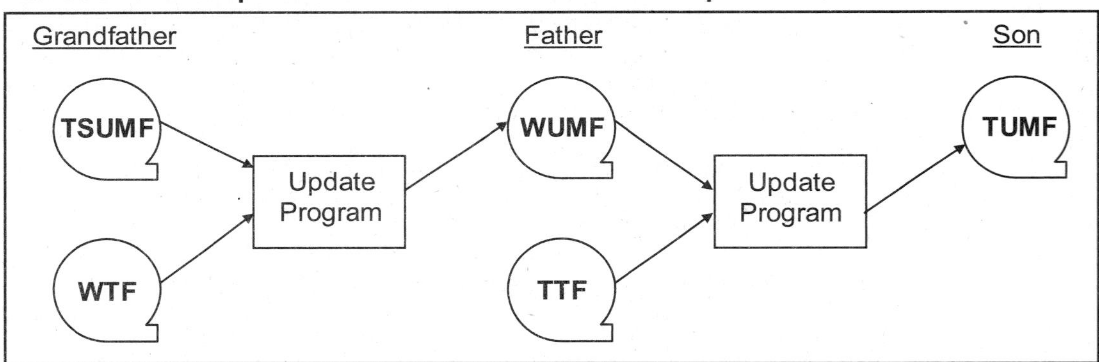

   d. **Physical Safeguards** Include: environmental issues, such as extreme temperature, humidity, dust; disaster issues, such as proper fireproofing and locating the computer in a safe place; backup facility issues, such as making arrangements to use other equipment in the case of disasters or other serious problems (backup arrangements are frequently made with service bureaus or with computer installations of subsidiaries. Backup facilities are referred to as "hot" or "cold" sites, depending on their state of readiness.); and control access issues.

C. Application Controls (AC)

These controls relate to specific computer software applications and the individual transactions processed by the system (e.g. payroll system, inventory system, integrated ERP system). AC are fully automated (i.e., performed automatically by the systems) and are designed to ensure the complete and accurate processing of data, from input through output. They may also help ensure the privacy and security of data transmitted between applications.

1. **Input Controls** Input controls are designed to provide reasonable assurance that transactions have been properly authorized, captured, and accurately recorded. They assure that data has not been lost, suppressed, added, duplicated, or otherwise changed improperly. Input controls include:

   a. **Control Totals** A total is computed and then recomputed at a later time. The totals are compared and should be the same. Control totals can be used as input, processing, and output controls. Examples include: financial totals; hash totals; and record count totals.

   b. **Computer Edit Tests** Computers can be programmed to perform a wide range of edit tests (i.e., edit checks) on records as they are being entered into the system. If a particular record does not meet the test, it is not processed. Edit tests include: limit/reasonableness tests; valid field/character tests; valid number/code tests; sequence checks; missing data tests; valid transmission tests; valid combination of fields; check digits; valid sign tests; and error logs.

2. **Processing Controls** These controls are designed to provide assurance that transaction processing has been performed as intended. Processing can be discrete, batch or continuous. Many input controls are also valid processing controls.

3. **Output Controls** These controls concern the accuracy of processing results, and include primarily balancing, visual scanning or verification, and distribution.

IV. Special Systems

A. Service Center (Service Bureau)

A service center provides IT services to its clients for a fee. Processing of client data occurs at the service center and the client's computerized master files are usually maintained at the center. Certain controls are particularly important because of the nature of the client-service center relationship.

Exhibit 5 ▸ IT Service Center Controls Mnemonic

T	Transmission
E	Error correction
A	Audit trail
M	Master file changes
O	Output
S	Security

1. **Transmission** Document counts, hash totals, financial totals, etc., may be used to control the transmission of data to and from the client's office.

2. **Error Correction** Client should receive an error listing that identifies all of the errors that occurred in the system. Correction, review, and approval procedures should be established and used.

3. **Audit Trail** An audit trail must be maintained. This may be done through proper filing and sequencing of original transaction documents, and also through periodic printouts of journal and ledger balances.

4. **Master File Changes** Printout of all master file changes should be sent to the client. Control counts of master file records and control totals of items within master file records may be used.

5. **Output** Output must be restricted to the client. An output distribution list (indicating who should receive the output) and control tests on samples of output may be used.

6. **Security** Service centers must have adequate controls to protect the client's data (while being stored and during processing). There must also be adequate reconstruction procedures if all or part of the client's records are destroyed.

B. **Online, Real-Time (OLRT) Systems**
These also are called quick response systems. Transactions are processed and files updated as transactions occur. The data is processed fast enough to get the response back in time to influence the process. Common examples include airline reservations systems in which the customer receives the reservations after waiting only a few moments and point-of-sale (POS) terminals in retail stores. Because of the technical complexity of OLRT systems, the auditor will need more expertise to consider internal control. Techniques such as test data (integrated test facility) and tagging may be used.

C. **Personal Computer Systems**
The basic control and audit considerations in a small computer environment are the same as those in a larger and more complex IT system. The number of records that can be stored in a minicomputer system is limited, so audit trails often are retained for a limited period of time; therefore, the auditor must plan the audit steps to take place when sufficient supporting information is available.

D. **Distributed Systems**
Distributed systems are a network of remote computer sites where small computers are connected to the main computer system. A reduced work load on the main computer results, since edit and processing functions can be performed at the small computer station, as well as increased efficiency from faster turnaround of information. Access at each location should be well controlled and audited separately to verify the integrity of the data processed. Also, because users may have both authorization and recording duties, compensating controls should exist for this lack of segregation of duties.

E. **Time-Sharing Systems**
A time-sharing center rents time on its central computer to a number of users, with each user having one or more remote input and output devices. The user usually accesses the central computer over telephone lines. User files and programs are maintained at the time-sharing center. Audit considerations are primarily the same as discussed for online, real-time systems.

V. Appendix: IT Terms

***Ad Hoc* Report** Nonstandardized report composed when the need arises. Frequently developed by users, rather than programmers with extensive training, for limited use.

Application Program Designed to perform the processing of a specific application. For example, an accounts receivable update program is an application program that processes accounts receivable data to update the accounts receivable master file.

Collaborative Computing Applications (Groupware, Shareware) A program that allows several people to have access to the same information and attempts to track the authors of changes. It is designed to allow several people to work on a single project. While this allows for greater flexibility, there is a loss of accountability.

Database Management System (DBMS) A set of programs (software) that manages a database (i.e., creates, accesses, and maintains a database).

Enterprise Resource Planning (ERP) Software Complex, highly integrated, multi-module applications that manage a business' different aspects, from traditional accounting to inventory management and advanced planning and forecasting. These systems are used to support all aspects of the entity's financial reporting, operations, and compliance objectives. Responsiveness and flexibility are increased in an ERP system since all modules are intricately connected and share data simultaneously. This can greatly aid the decisionmaking process.

Heuristic In computing, the adjective heuristic signifies able to change; it is used to describe a computer program that can modify itself in response to the user, for example, a spell check program that allows the user to add words or voice recognition software that adapts to an individual user's speech.

Management Information System (MIS) An information system within an organization that provides management with the information needed for planning and control. This involves an integration of the functions of gathering and analyzing data, and reporting (i.e., communicating) the results to management in a meaningful form. It frequently involves several subsidiary systems; for instance, an inventory control system tracks the quantity of inventory bought and sold.

Pass (Run) A complete cycle of input, processing, and output in the execution of a program, typically an application program.

Relational Database Model A flexible database approach supporting the information needs of multiple users from a common set of integrated database tables or files. Each file contains common data on a particular group, for instance, a master customer file. The file is comprised of rows, or records, containing common data for each particular customer. Each record is comprised of fields containing different data elements of each customer. Examples of fields would be customer number, customer name, address, phone number, etc. Each field element is made up of characters (letters, numbers, special characters). These characters are referred to as bytes and are in program language that is directly readable by the computer.

Bit A binary digit (0 or 1, on or off, etc.), representing the smallest unit of data possible.

Byte A group of bits that represents a single character, whether alphabetic or numeric.

Central Processing Unit (CPU, Mainframe) Primary hardware component. The actual processing of data occurs in the CPU. It contains primary storage, a control unit, and an arithmetic/logic unit.

Arithmetic/Logic Unit Portion of the CPU that has special circuitry for performing arithmetic calculations and logical operations. This may be combined with the control unit.

Bus Circuitry connecting the CPU to primary memory or to peripheral devices, transmitting a byte or more in one action.

Control Unit Portion of the CPU that controls and directs the operations of the computer. It interprets the instructions from the program and directs the computer system to carry them out.

Primary Storage (Main Memory) Portion of the CPU that holds the program, data, and results (intermediate and final) during processing; therefore, this includes only temporary storage. The primary storage contains the data and program steps that are being processed by the CPU and is divided into RAM (random-access memory) and ROM (read-only memory).

Characters Letters, numbers, and special symbols (e.g., periods, commas, and hyphens).

Cloud Computing The delivery of computing resources as a metered service over the Internet.

Cold Site Location where equipment and power is available in the event of disaster at the primary location, but requiring considerable effort to get an operational system functioning. (Compare to hot site.)

Concentrator A device that combines multiple communication channels into one. A concentrator differs from a multiplexer in that the total bandwidth of a concentrators' inputs doesn't necessarily equal the total bandwidth of its outputs. A concentrator temporarily stores data to compensate for this imbalance.

CPA SysTrust An attestation service developed in part by the AICPA, that is designed to provide assurance on whether a system's controls are operating effectively and allow the system to function reliably.

CPA WebTrust A symbol appearing on a Web site that indicates that the organization meets joint Canadian Institute of Chartered Accountants and AICPA business practice disclosures, transaction integrity, and information protection criteria.

Data Information that is transmitted, processed, maintained, and/or accessed by electronic means (e.g., using a computer, scanner, sensor, and/or magnetic media).

Data Transmission Transmission protocols are sets of rules used by the transmitting and receiving devices so that they both interpret the transmitted data identically. File Transfer Protocol (FTP) is one set of rules establishing how files are transferred. Switching mechanisms route messages through available communication paths.

Database A structured set of interrelated files combined to eliminate redundancy of data items within the files and to establish logical connections between data items. For example, within personnel and payroll files, some of the data in the two records will be the same; in a database system, these files would be combined to eliminate the redundant data.

Decision Tables Decision tables emphasize the relationships among conditions and actions, and present decision choices. Decision tables often supplement systems flowcharts.

Decode Convert data from an encoded state to its original form.

Digital Signature A digital signature is a guarantee that information has not been modified. Digital signatures are used for establishing secure website connections and verifying the validity, but not the privacy, of transmitted files. A digital signature does not verify the receiving person or address.

Disaster Recovery Restoration of data and business function after loss.

Document Management Electronic document storage and retrieval.

Downtime Time when the computer is not functioning. This may be scheduled or unscheduled.

Edit Refers to the addition, deletion, and/or rearrangement of data. **Input editing** refers to editing before processing and **output editing** refers to editing after processing.

Electronic Commerce (E-Commerce) Business via the Internet, including EDI. Electronic commerce involves the electronic initiation, processing, and conclusion of the sales cycle (from order entry to payment) by electronic means.

Electronic Data Interchange (EDI) Electronic communication among entities such as financial institutions and customer-vendor partners (typically involving order placement, invoicing, and payment and may involve inventory monitoring and automatic restocking). ANSI X12 is a domestic EDI format. EDIFACT is an international EDI format. Typically, a standing agreement (usually business-to-business) for electronic data interchange (EDI) transactions also is considered electronic commerce. EDI typically involves automatic monitoring of inventory levels and sales orders (by the business customer's system), purchase order placement and fulfillment, and payment. While there is not necessarily a website, the back-end transaction processing is similar.

Electronic Document Submission Submission of documents such as federal tax returns and securities reports in electronic form, usually over the Internet.

E-Mail Electronic messages, typically delivered through the Internet. The messages may have attached files, including documents and programs.

Encode Scrambling data to prevent unauthorized use.

Encryption Encryption is a mathematical process of coding data so that it cannot be read by unauthorized people. Decryption is transforming an encrypted file into the file that existed before the encryption process. A key is used to lock and unlock the data.

Enterprise Resource Planning Software Large multimodule applications that manage a business' different aspects, from traditional accounting to inventory management and advanced planning and forecasting.

Field Group of related characters. For example, a customer name.

File Group of related records. For example, a customer file. (Also see master file and transaction file.)

Firewall Software designed to prevent unauthorized access to data by separating one segment from another.

Gateway Software or hardware that links two or more computer networks.

Graphical User Interface (GUI) A GUI allows user access to software functions depicted through use of icons, scroll bars, frames, and other pictorial means, rather than line-by-line commands or requests.

Groupware A program designed to allow several people to work on a single project. While this allows for greater flexibility, there is a loss of accountability. (Also see collaborative computing applications.)

Hackers A classic hacker is a computer enthusiast, someone who's interested in learning the nitty-gritty of how computers and computer networks work, simply for the joy of it or for peer recognition.

Crackers (criminal + hackers) are hackers that are intentionally involved in unethical activity. Crackers break into systems to violate laws, to steal information, or otherwise to use computers inappropriately.

Script Kiddies Script kiddies use tools (oftentimes, in an automated fashion) and cause damage without understanding what they're doing.

Hardware Physical computer equipment

Hardware Maintenance Involves equipment service. Routine service is scheduled. Unscheduled maintenance arises when there are unanticipated problems.

Hot Site Location where a functioning system is planned for use with minimal preparation in the event of a disaster at the primary work location. (Compare to cold site.)

Input/Output Devices Devices for transferring data in and out of the CPU. Examples include:

Bar Code Reader An input device to scan bar codes, such as universal product codes on merchandise.

Keyboard Typewriter-like device to allow the user to type information into the computer.

Magnetic Ink Character Recognition (MICR) Sensing information recorded in special magnetized ink. MICR is commonly used by the banking industry for check processing.

Magnetic Tape Reader A device to sense information recorded as magnetized spots on magnetic tape (e.g., the magnetic strips used on credit cards and ATM cards).

Modem A device to allow users to transfer files over telephone lines to distant computers.

Monitor, Screen A television-like screen to display information, providing feedback to the user.

Mouse, Trackball A pointing device to manipulate representations displayed on a screen.

Optical Character Recognition (OCR) Scanner A device to sense printed information through the use of light-sensitive devices.

Printer A device to produce output on paper, including invoices and checks.

IP Number or Address An Internet Protocol number (IP number) is a unique number assigned to a computer in a network. A registered IP number is registered with a central database to eliminate duplication on the Web. Since IP numbers are not easy to remember, unique domain names may be assigned to these numbers. A Uniform Resource Locator (URL) is another name for a Web address

Library Program (Library Routine) Programs that are frequently used by other programs. They are kept within the system and "called up" whenever necessary. One example is generating random numbers.

Mapping Converting data between application format and a standard format, such as EDI.

Master File Contains relatively permanent data. For example, an accounts receivable master file would contain a record for each customer and each record would include fields for customer number, name, address, credit limit, amount owed, etc. (Compare to transaction file.)

Multiplexer A device that converts several low-speed transmissions into one high-speed transmission and back again for communication purposes.

Network A network is an arrangement of computers to allow users access to common data, hardware, and/or software.

Extranet A password-protected internet, usually for established vendors and customers. LANs are typically intranets.

Internet A network of networks. The Internet is a public network of many networks, also called the Web.

Intranet A network generally restricted to employee access.

Local Area Network (LAN) A network of computers within a small area (i.e., a building) to transmit information electronically and share files and peripheral equipment among members (compare to wide area network).

Value-Added Network (VAN) A network service that provides additional services beyond mere connections to the Internet, particularly increased security services enabling EDI.

Virtual Private Network (VPN) A combination of public and private resources that appears as if a remote user is accessing a private network directly, rather than through public lines.

Wide Area Network (WAN) A computer network encompassing a large area (i.e., city-wide or globally) to transmit information electronically and share files among members (typically company-wide only).

Operating System (OS) Manages the coordinating and scheduling of various application programs and computer functions. The operating system is like a traffic controller for data between peripheral equipment and application programs. Operating systems generally provide a user interface and allocate memory. Examples include the following:

Job Control Language (JCL) A command language that launches applications, specifying priorities, program sizes, running sequences, databases used, and files used.

Multiprocessing Allows the execution of two or more programs at the same time and requires the utilization of more than one CPU.

Multiprogramming A program is processed until some type of input or output is needed. The OS then delegates the process to a piece of peripheral equipment, and the CPU begins executing other programs. Processing speed is enhanced considerably, making it appear as if more than one program is being processed concurrently, while utilizing only one CPU.

Virtual Storage The OS divides a program into segments (called pages) and brings only sections of the program into memory as needed to execute the instructions. This saves memory and processing cost because the majority of the program remains in less expensive secondary storage.

Patch Addition of a new part to a program. It may be added to correct or update a program. For example, if a new government regulation affecting withholding tax becomes effective, a patch may be added to the payroll program to provide for this. A patch may also be added for a fraudulent purpose. For example, an employee might insert a patch into a payroll program to print an extra check.

Peripheral Equipment Equipment that is not part of the CPU but that may be placed under the control of the CPU, i.e., which may be accessed directly by the CPU. Input/output devices and secondary storage devices are peripheral equipment.

Point-Of-Sale (POS) System A system that records goods sold and figures the amount due at the cash register, frequently also verifying credit cards or checks.

Program Set of instructions that the computer follows to accomplish a specified task (e.g., accounts receivable update program, inventory management program, and payroll program).

Program Language Programs may be written in one of several different languages. A compiler translates from a high-level language into machine language.

Assembly Language Assembly language is a machine-dependent language that has short commands for repetitive functions, simplifying the programmer's task as opposed to working with machine language. An assembler is a program that translates assembly language into machine language. Assembly language is called second-generation language.

Fourth-Generation Language (4GL) Fourth-generation languages have many routine procedures preprogrammed; the programmer states what is to be done, but not necessarily how to do it. 4GLs often are related to DBMS that allow programmers to create database structures and manipulate data quickly and relatively easily. Many programs written in 4GL make inefficient use of computer resources, especially memory.

Machine Language Machine language is a machine-dependent binary language that computer hardware can interpret (on-off signals). Each group of computers sharing the same features has a particular language that fits the specific hardware. In other words, machine language is machine dependent. Writing programs in machine language is time-consuming and prone to error; further, such programs could not be transferred readily to another type of computer. Machine language is called first-generation language.

Object-Oriented Programming (OOP) OOP uses a modular approach, increasing development efficiency and maintenance ease. Routine operations are kept with the data to be processed. The focus is not on the procedure to accomplish a task, but on the object involved in accomplishing that task. OOP languages include C++ and Java.

Procedural Language Procedural, or problem-oriented, languages are largely machine independent, allowing programmers to focus on the program procedures and function. They are significantly more like English than assembly language. A programmer writes a program in source code in a procedural language; a program translates the source code into object code (machine language for a specific machine). FORTRAN, COBOL, and BASIC are examples of procedural languages. FORTRAN (FORmula TRANslation) was designed for scientific purposes. COBOL (COmmon Business-Oriented Language) was designed for business purposes. BASIC (Beginners All-purpose Symbolic Instruction Code) was designed for educational purposes. Traditionally, data and operations to manipulate that data are kept separately from each other. Procedural languages are called third-generation languages.

Program Maintenance Refers to making changes in the program in order to keep it current and functioning properly. For example, maintenance of the payroll program may involve modifying it because of changes in the social security law or to provide for a greater number of employees.

Proxy Server An application or device that manages requests from Web browsers. A proxy server caches (saves) a copy of pages retrieved from a Web server. Future requests for the same page are supplied from the cache, rather than another access of the Web server, resulting in shorter response time.

Record Group of related fields. For example, a customer record would include ID number, name, address, etc.

Router Switches that transfer incoming messages to outgoing links via the most efficient route possible, for example, over the Internet.

Secondary Storage Devices external to the CPU that store data.

Disk, Diskette Randomly accessible data is represented in concentric circles called "tracks." A magnetic disk is a platter coated on both sides with a material on which data can be represented as magnetized dots according to a predetermined code. Diskettes are more common than disks, as they hold more data. Still more data can be stored on CDs (also called laser disks). A disk drive is used to read data from the disk into the CPU and to write data from the CPU onto the disk. A hard drive is more permanently fixed than a disk or diskette, with faster retrieval. Disks are usually more easily moved than a hard drive.

Magnetic Tape Plastic tape that is coated with a material on which data can be represented as magnetized dots according to a predetermined code. It resembles audio tape.

Off-Line Storage Not in direct communication with the CPU. Human intervention is needed for the data to be processed. For example, a disk must be inserted in a disk drive before it can be accessed.

Online Storage In direct communication with the CPU without human intervention. For example, a hard drive ordinarily is accessed by the CPU without human intervention.

Randomly Accessible (Direct Access) Data records can be accessed directly. Disks are an example. For example, if the customer records are stored in a file on a disk, the disk drive could go directly to a specific customer's record without having to read any of the other customer records.

Redundant Array Of Independent Disks (RAID) An arrangement whereby data is written to multiple disks. If one disk is damaged, data most likely can be retrieved from another (typically seamlessly).

Sequentially Accessible Requires the reading of all data between the starting point and the information sought. Magnetic tape is sequentially accessible. For example, if alphabetized records are on magnetic tape and none are read, most of the tape must be read to get to a specific customer's data.

Self-Service Applications Software that allows customers to provide much of their own customer service.

Software Programs, routines, documentation, manuals, etc., that make it possible for the computer system to operate and process data. (Compare to hardware.)

Systems Programs (Supervisory Programs) Perform the functions of coordinating and controlling the overall operation of the computer system.

Telecommuting Working outside of a traditional office, remaining connected by the Internet, phone, etc. Usually implies a office in the employee's home, although a sales agent or insurance adjuster might also work from a vehicle and/or customer sites.

Transaction (Detail) File Contains current, temporary data. A transaction file is used to update a master file. For example, the day's charge sales would be accumulated on a transaction file that would be used to update the accounts receivable master file during an update run.

Topology The physical layout of a network. Typically, only small networks use a single topology. Many networks use a combination of topologies.

> **Bus** A topology with each device connected to a line with disconnected ends. While devices are added to the network easily, communication between devices on either side of a failed device is impossible.
>
> **Ring** A topology with each device connected to two other devices such that a schematic drawing of the network resembles a circle; all messages pass through all intermediate devices from sender to recipient. If one failed device is on the ring, the other devices still may communicate. A device between two failed devices cannot communicate. Devices are added to the network easily, but communication may be slow as messages often pass through many devices.
>
> **Star** A topology with all subsidiary devices are connected to a central device; all messages pass through the central device. While star communications may be quick, this generally is an expensive topology.
>
> **Tree** A topology with each device connected to other devices in a hierarchical manner such that a schematic drawing of the network resembles the trunk and branches of a tree. Some devices have many connections and some have few.

Trojan Horse A seemingly legitimate program that operates in an unauthorized manner, usually causing damage.

Universal In-Box A system to collect email and voice mail in one "place," accessible by either regular phone or computer.

Utility Program (Utility Routine) Standard program for performing routine functions, e.g., sorting and merging.

Video Conference Real-time meeting over the Internet.

Virus A program that replicates and attaches itself to other programs. The effects of a virus can be a merely annoying message or malicious activity, such as reformatting a hard drive or flooding an e-mail system.

Virus Hoax An e-mail message with a false warning. Its originator tries to get it circulated as widely as possible.

Voice Mail A system that records, directs, stores, and replays telephone messages.

Web Browser A program used to find and display World Wide Web files meeting user criteria.

Web Crawler A program used to search the World Wide Web for files meeting user criteria.

CHAPTER 7—AUDITING IT SYSTEMS

Problem 7-1 MULTIPLE-CHOICE QUESTIONS

Assessing Audit Risk

1. Which of the following computer documentations would an auditor most likely utilize in obtaining an understanding of internal control?

   a. Systems flowcharts
   b. Record counts
   c. Program listings
   d. Record layouts (ID: 0278)

2. An auditor anticipates assessing control risk at a low level in a computerized environment. Under these circumstances, on which of the following procedures would the auditor initially focus?

   a. Programmed control procedures
   b. Application control procedures
   c. Output control procedures
   d. General control procedures (ID: 2789)

3. A retailing entity uses the Internet to execute and record its purchase transactions. The entity's auditor recognizes that the documentation of details of transactions will be retained for only a short period of time. To compensate for this limitation, the auditor most likely would

   a. Compare a sample of paid vendors' invoices to the receiving records at year-end
   b. Plan for a large measure of tolerable misstatement in substantive tests
   c. Perform tests several times during the year, rather than only at year-end
   d. Increase the sample of transactions to be selected for cutoff tests (ID: 8374)

4. Which of the following is an example of how specific internal controls in a database environment may differ from controls in a nondatabase environment?

   a. Controls should exist to ensure that users have access to and can update only the data elements that they have been authorized to access.
   b. Controls over data sharing by diverse users within an entity should be the same for every user.
   c. The employee who manages the computer hardware should also develop and debug the computer programs.
   d. Controls can provide assurance that all processed transactions are authorized, but cannot verify that all authorized transactions are processed. (ID: 6933)

5. Misstatements in a batch computer system caused by incorrect programs or data may not be detected immediately because

   a. Errors in some transactions may cause rejection of other transactions in the batch.
   b. The identification of errors in input data typically is not part of the program.
   c. There are time delays in processing transactions in a batch system.
   d. The processing of transactions in a batch system is not uniform. (ID: 5110)

6. Which of the following statements is correct concerning internal control in an electronic data interchange (EDI) system?

   a. Preventive controls generally are more important than detective controls in EDI systems.
   b. Control objectives for EDI systems generally are different from the objectives for other information systems.
   c. Internal controls in EDI systems rarely permit control risk to be assessed at below the maximum.
   d. Internal controls related to the segregation of duties generally are the most important controls in EDI systems. (ID: 6827)

7. Which of the following would most likely be a weakness in internal control of a client that utilizes microcomputers rather than a larger computer system?
   a. Employee collusion possibilities are increased because microcomputers from one vendor can process the programs of a system from a different vendor.
   b. The microcomputer operators may be able to remove hardware and software components and modify them at home.
   c. Programming errors result in all similar transactions being processed incorrectly when those transactions are processed under the same conditions.
   d. Certain transactions may be automatically initiated by the microcomputers and management's authorization of these transactions may be implicit in its acceptance of the system design. (ID: 7500)

8. Which of the following control procedures most likely could prevent IT personnel from modifying programs to bypass programmed controls?
   a. Periodic management review of computer utilization reports and systems documentation
   b. Segregation of duties within IT for computer programming and computer operations
   c. Participation of user department personnel in designing and approving new systems
   d. Physical security of IT facilities in limiting access to IT equipment (ID: 5961)

9. Which of the following outcomes is a likely benefit of information technology used for internal control?
   a. Processing of unusual or nonrecurring transactions
   b. Enhanced timeliness of information
   c. Potential loss of data
   d. Recording of unauthorized transactions (ID: 9378)

10. In which of the following circumstances would an auditor expect to find that an entity implemented automated controls to reduce risks of misstatement?
    a. When errors are difficult to predict
    b. When misstatements are difficult to define
    c. When large, unusual, or nonrecurring transactions require judgment
    d. When transactions are high-volume and recurring (ID: 9385)

11. In an environment that is highly automated, an auditor determines that it is not possible to reduce detection risk solely by substantive tests of transactions. Under these circumstances, the auditor most likely would
    a. Perform tests of controls to support a lower level of assessed control risk
    b. Increase the sample size to reduce sampling risk and detection risk
    c. Adjust the materiality level and consider the effect on inherent risk
    d. Apply analytical procedures and consider the effect on control risk (ID: 7839)

12. Which of the following is an essential element of the audit trail in an electronic data interchange (EDI) system?
    a. Disaster recovery plans that ensure proper back-up of files
    b. Encrypted hash totals that authenticate messages
    c. Activity logs that indicate failed transactions
    d. Hardware security modules that store sensitive data (ID: 6829)

13. An auditor would most likely be concerned with which of the following controls in a distributed data processing system?
    a. Hardware controls
    b. Systems documentation controls
    c. Access controls
    d. Disaster recovery controls (ID: 0273)

14. Which of the following is usually a benefit of using electronic funds transfer for international cash transactions?
    a. Improvement of the audit trail for cash receipts and disbursements
    b. Creation of self-monitoring access controls
    c. Reduction of the frequency of data entry errors
    d. Off-site storage of source documents for cash transactions (ID: 6824)

15. Which of the following statements is correct concerning the security of messages in an electronic data interchange (EDI) system?
    a. When the confidentiality of data is the primary risk, message authentication is the preferred control rather than encryption.
    b. Encryption performed by physically secure hardware devices is more secure than encryption performed by software.
    c. Message authentication in EDI systems performs the same function as segregation of duties in other information systems.
    d. Security at the transaction phase in EDI systems is not necessary because problems at that level will usually be identified by the service provider. (ID: 6828)

General and Application Controls

16. Which of the following characteristics distinguishes computer processing from manual processing?
    a. Computer processing virtually eliminates the occurrence of computational error normally associated with manual processing.
    b. The potential for systematic error is ordinarily greater in manual processing than in computerized processing.
    c. Errors or fraud in computer processing will be detected soon after their occurrences.
    d. Most computer systems are designed so that transaction trails useful for audit purposes do not exist. (ID: 0289)

17. To obtain evidence that online access controls are properly functioning, an auditor most likely would
    a. Create checkpoints at periodic intervals after live data processing to test for unauthorized use of the system
    b. Examine the transaction log to discover whether any transactions were lost or entered twice due to a system malfunction
    c. Enter invalid identification numbers or passwords to ascertain whether the system rejects them
    d. Vouch a random sample of processed transactions to assure proper authorization (ID: 3937)

18. Which of the following controls is a processing control designed to ensure the reliability and accuracy of data processing?

	Limit test	Validity check test
a.	Yes	Yes
b.	No	No
c.	No	Yes
d.	Yes	No

(ID: 5111)

Items 19 and 20 are based on the following:

Invoice #	Product	Quantity	Unit price
201	F10	150	$ 5.00
202	G15	200	$10.00
203	H20	250	$25.00
204	K35	300	$30.00

19. Which of the following numbers represents the record count?
    a. 1
    b. 4
    c. 810
    d. 900 (ID: 6620)

20. Which of the following most likely represents a hash total?
    a. FGHK80
    b. 4
    c. 204
    d. 810 (ID: 6621)

21. An IT input control is designed to ensure that
    a. Only authorized personnel have access to the computer area.
    b. Machine processing is accurate.
    c. Data received for processing are properly authorized and converted to machine readable form.
    d. Electronic data processing has been performed as intended for the particular application. (ID: 0306)

22. A customer intended to order 100 units of product Z96014, but incorrectly ordered nonexistent product Z96015. Which of the following controls most likely would detect this error?
    a. Check digit verification
    b. Record count
    c. Hash total
    d. Redundant data check (ID: 6622)

23. Which of the following input controls is a numeric value computed to provide assurance that the original value has not been altered in construction or transmission?
    a. Hash total
    b. Parity check
    c. Encryption
    d. Check digit (ID: 6625)

Auditing Approaches

24. Which of the following activities most likely would detect whether payroll data were altered during processing?
    a. Monitor authorized distribution of data control sheets
    b. Use test data to verify the performance of edit routines
    c. Examine source documents for approval by supervisors
    d. Segregate duties between approval of hardware and software specifications (ID: 6939)

25. Which of the following could be difficult to determine because electronic evidence may not be retrievable after a specific period?
    a. The acceptance level of detection risk
    b. The timing of control and substantive tests
    c. Whether to adopt substantive or reliance test strategies
    d. The assessed level of inherent risk (ID: 8816)

26. When an auditor tests a computerized accounting system, which of the following is true of the test data approach?
    a. Several transactions of each type must be tested.
    b. Test data are processed by the client's computer programs under the auditor's control.
    c. Test data must consist of all possible valid and invalid conditions.
    d. The program tested is different from the program used throughout the year by the client. (ID: 5690)

27. Which of the following is the primary reason that many auditors hesitate to use embedded audit modules?
    a. Embedded audit modules cannot be protected from computer viruses.
    b. Auditors are required to monitor embedded audit modules continuously to obtain valid results.
    c. Embedded audit modules can easily be modified through management tampering.
    d. Auditors are required to be involved in the system design of the application to be monitored. (ID: 7110)

28. An auditor most likely would test for the presence of unauthorized IT program changes by running
    a. A program with test data
    b. A check digit verification program
    c. A source code comparison program
    d. A program that computes control totals (ID: 2971)

29. Which of the following computer-assisted auditing techniques allows fictitious and real transactions to be processed together without client operating personnel being aware of the testing process?
    a. Integrated test facility
    b. Input controls matrix
    c. Parallel simulation
    d. Data entry monitor (ID: 5143)

30. An auditor would least likely use computer software to
    a. Construct parallel simulations
    b. Access client data files
    c. Prepare spreadsheets
    d. Assess IT control risk (ID: 3936)

31. An auditor who wishes to capture an entity's data as transactions are processed and continuously test the entity's computerized information system most likely would use which of the following techniques?
    a. Snapshot application
    b. Embedded audit module
    c. Integrated data check
    d. Test data generator (ID: 7030)

32. In parallel simulation, actual client data are reprocessed using an auditor software program. An advantage of using parallel simulation, instead of performing tests of controls without a computer, is that
    a. The test includes all types of transaction errors and exceptions that may be encountered.
    b. The client's computer personnel do not know when the data are being tested.
    c. There is no risk of creating potentially material errors in the client's data.
    d. The size of the sample can be greatly expanded at relatively little additional cost. (ID: 7812)

33. When an auditor tests the internal controls of a computerized accounting system, which of the following is true of the test data approach?

    a. Test data are coded to a dummy subsidiary so they can be extracted from the system under actual operating conditions.
    b. Test data programs need not be tailor-made by the auditor for each client's computer applications.
    c. Test data programs usually consist of all possible valid and invalid conditions regarding compliance with internal controls.
    d. Test data are processed with the client's computer and the results are compared with the auditor's pre-determined results. (ID: 8389)

34. In auditing an entity's computerized payroll transactions, an auditor would be least likely to use test data to test controls concerning

    a. Overpayment of employees for hours not worked
    b. Control and distribution of unclaimed checks
    c. Withholding of taxes and Social Security contributions
    d. Missing employee identification numbers (ID: 8844)

35. Which of the following is a computer-assisted audit technique that permits an auditor to insert the auditor's version of a client's program to process data and compare the output with the client's output?

    a. Test data module
    b. Frame relay protocol
    c. Remote node router
    d. Parallel simulation (ID: 9364)

36. A primary advantage of using generalized audit software packages to audit the financial statements of a client is that the auditor may

    a. Access information stored on computer files while having a limited understanding of the client's hardware and software features
    b. Consider increasing the use of substantive tests of transactions in place of analytical procedures
    c. Substantiate the accuracy of data through self-checking digits and hash totals
    d. Reduce the level of required tests of controls to a relatively small amount (ID: 5999)

37. When companies use information technology (IT) extensively, evidence may be available only in electronic form. What is an auditor's best course of action in such situations?

    a. Assess the control risk as high
    b. Use audit software to perform analytical procedures
    c. Use generalized audit software to extract evidence from client databases
    d. Perform limited tests of controls over electronic data (ID: 8401)

Problem 7-2 SIMULATION: Flowchart

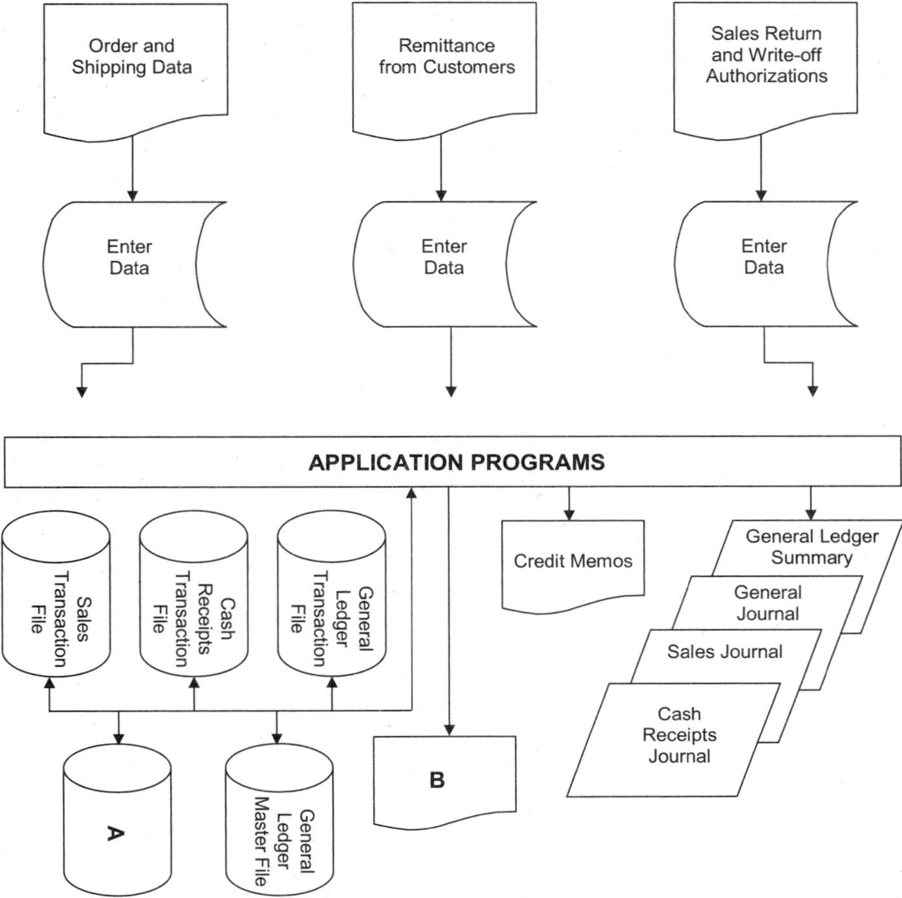

Based on the accompanying flowchart of a client's revenue cycle, what do the symbols marked A and B most likely represent?

<u>Answer List</u>

1. Accounts receivable master file
2. Cash disbursements transaction file
3. Customer checks
4. Customer orders
5. Receiving reports
6. Receiving report file
7. Remittance advice file
8. Sales invoices

(ID: 9207)

Problem 7-3 SIMULATION: Research

IT poses specific risks to an entity's internal control. What section of the professional literature lists some of these risks?

[ ] § [ ] [ ] (ID: 9208)

Solution 7-1 MULTIPLE-CHOICE ANSWERS

1. (a) An auditor is likely to use systems flowcharts in obtaining an understanding of internal control. Systems flowcharts show the flow of data through the system and the interrelationships between the processing steps and computer runs. A record count is an input control technique. Program listings are the source statements or language of the client's programs. Record layouts are the input and output formats. (ID: 0278)

2. (d) When an auditor anticipates assessing control risk at a low level in a computerized environment, generally, the auditor would initially focus on general control procedures, which are those controls that relate to all or many computerized accounting activities and often include control over the development, modification, and maintenance of computer programs and control over the use of and changes to data maintained on computer files. (ID: 2789)

3. (c) When documentation is only retained for a short period of time, the auditor most likely would compensate for this limitation by performing tests several times during the year, rather than only at year-end. (ID: 8374)

4. (a) Controls in a database environment can be very specific as to which elements of a record can be accessed or changed, resulting in a more detailed set of authorizations. [Note: The examiners say to select the best answer.] Controls over data sharing should be appropriate for each user, usually resulting in diverse controls. Preferably, hardware management and software development are segregated. The relationship between authorization and processing usually is the same within a database and a non-database environment. (ID: 6933)

5. (c) There are time delays when data is processed in batches, so errors may not be detected immediately. The identification of errors in input data would be identified through various means such as the use of batch totals and normally would be part of the program. The processing of transactions in a batch system is uniform. (ID: 5110)

6. (a) Preventive controls are generally more important than detective controls in EDI systems because of the speed with which goods and services are delivered. Objectives remain the same as for other information systems. Internal controls in EDI systems must be strong to minimize losses. Segregation of duties is not as important as protection of assets in an EDI system. (ID: 6827)

7. (b) Both large computer systems and microcomputers are vulnerable to employee collusion and programming errors. Microcomputer hardware and software could more readily be removed from a place of business than large computer systems. (ID: 7500)

8. (b) A control procedure for preventing employees from modifying programs to bypass programmed controls is to segregate the functions of programming and computer operations. Answers (a), (c), and (d) are all appropriate IT controls but by themselves would not prevent IT employees from modifying programs. (ID: 5961)

9. (b) A likely benefit of IT used for internal control is enhanced timeliness, availability, and accuracy of information. Processing of large, unusual, or nonrecurring transactions is an example of a circumstance where manual controls of systems may be more suitable. Potential loss of data or inability to access data as required as well as recording of unauthorized or nonexistent transactions or inaccurate recording of transactions are examples of specific risks that IT poses to an entity's internal control. (ID: 9378)

10. (d) An auditor would expect to find that an entity implemented automated controls to reduce risks of misstatement when transactions are high-volume and recurring; in situations where errors can be anticipated or predicted; or for control activities where the specific ways to perform the control can be adequately designed and automated. The other answer alternatives describe circumstances where judgment and discretion are required and thus manual controls of systems may be more suitable. (ID: 9385)

11. (a) When the auditor has determined that it is not possible or practicable to reduce the detection risks at the relevant assertion level to an acceptably low level with audit evidence obtained only from substantive procedures, s/he should perform tests of controls to obtain audit evidence about their operating effectiveness. The auditor may find it impossible to design effective substantive procedures that by themselves provide sufficient appropriate audit evidence at the relevant assertion level when an entity conducts its business using information technology (IT) and no documentation of transactions is produced or maintained, other than through the IT system. Increasing the sample size for substantive tests in this circumstance would be ineffective as the question states that it is not possible to reduce detection risk solely by substantive tests of transactions. Changing the materiality level would be inappropriate. Further, changing the materiality level does not have an effect on inherent risk, which is the susceptibility of an assertion to misstatement without any internal controls. Analytics performed by the auditor do not have an effect on control risk, which is the risk that the entity's internal controls will not detect material misstatements in the financial statements. (ID: 7839)

12. (c) Logs with failed transactions are examined to determine whether the corrected transactions were eventually executed and to detect attempts of unauthorized system use. Proper file backup is a recovery issue. Message authentication and hardware security modules are security issues. (ID: 6829)

13. (c) A distributed data processing system is one in which many different users have access to the main computer through various computer locations. Thus, access controls, which restrict access to the main computer, are necessary to maintain a strong internal control structure, because those with access to the computer are in a position to perform incompatible functions. Hardware controls, systems documentation controls, and disaster recovery controls would not be as important in assessing control risk and would not likely present unusual problems in a distributed system. (ID: 0273)

14. (c) With EDI, information is entered into a system once and transmitted to other parties. These other parties do not have to re-enter the information into their systems, eliminating an opportunity for errors to occur. Using EDI, audit trails typically are less clear, if anything. Creation of self-monitoring access controls and off-site storage of source documents for cash transactions could occur with or without EDI. (ID: 6824)

15. (b) Physically secure hardware devices are less likely to be compromised than software. Message authentication provides assurance about messages' sources. Encryption provides assurance about privacy. Message authentication performs similarly to control duties in non-IT systems, but not the segregation of duties aspect. Service providers usually do not provide security at the transaction level. (ID: 6828)

16. (a) An advantage of computer processing is that it virtually eliminates computational errors. Errors or fraud are not detected more quickly when computer processing is used. The potential for systematic errors is greater in computer processing than in manual processing. Transaction trails useful for audit purposes are created but the data may be available for only a short period of time. (ID: 0289)

17. (c) Password controls, used in restricting access to computers, are designed to preclude access capabilities of those employees whose regular functions are incompatible with computer use. To obtain evidence that user identification and password controls are functioning as designed, an auditor would most likely examine a sample of invalid passwords or numbers to determine whether the computer is recognizing the invalid passwords and rejecting access. Answer (a) checks the level of authorization an employee has once within the system rather than access to the online system. Answer (b) is a procedure for determining the completeness of transaction processing. Answer (d) does not address whether the online access is being limited or circumvented. (ID: 3937)

18. (a) Computers can be programmed to perform a wide range of edit tasks on records as they are being inputted into the system. If a particular record does not meet the test, it would not be processed. Edit tests include limit tests, validity check tests, check digit tests, etc. (ID: 5111)

19. (b) A record count is a count of the number of records in a batch or file or similar group. (ID: 6620)

20. (d) A hash total is a numeric total with meaning only as a control. Because of the alpha characters in the product codes, a hash total cannot be derived from product codes without a conversion of letters into numeric amounts. Totals of quantities have meaning beyond a control. (ID: 6621)

21. (c) Input controls are designed to provide reasonable assurance that data received by IT have been properly authorized, converted into machine readable form and identified as well as that data has not been lost, added, duplicated, or otherwise improperly changed. Answer (a) describes an access control. Answer (b) describes an output control. Answer (d) describes a processing control. (ID: 0306)

22. (a) A check digit is a digit that is appended to a piece of numeric data following a pre-specified routine. A record count is a count of the number of records in a batch or file or similar group. A hash total is a numeric total with meaning only as a control. A redundant data check would check one piece of data against another, not the elements of a product code label against each other. (ID: 6622)

23. (d) A check digit is a digit that is appended to a piece of numeric data following a pre-specified routine. A hash total is a numeric total with meaning only as a control. A parity check is an extra bit attached to the end of a string of bits to detect errors resulting from electronic interference when transmitting the string. Encryption is the conversion of a message into a coded message. (ID: 6625)

24. (b) With test data, the auditor can readily compare actual results to anticipated results. Monitoring distribution wouldn't detect data alteration. Source documents could be correctly approved and data could be later altered in processing without impact on the source documents. Segregation of duties discourages fraud, but not unintentional mistakes. Further, approval of hardware and software specifications are not necessarily the most critical functions to segregate in the IT area. (ID: 6939)

25. (b) The timing of control and substantive tests could be difficult to determine because electronic evidence may not be retrievable after a specific period if files are changed and if backup files do not exist. The auditor must consider the entity's data retention policies when determining the timing of some procedures. The determination of the other answer alternatives is not made more difficult because electronic evidence may not be retrievable after a specific period. (ID: 8816)

26. (b) In the test data approach to testing a computerized accounting system, test data are processed by the client's computer programs under the auditor's control. The auditor will determine how many transactions and what types of transactions to test which may or may not include several transactions of each type. The auditor need not include test data for all possible valid and invalid conditions. The object is to test the client's program that is used throughout the year and the auditor must take steps to make sure that the program being tested is the one that is actually used in routine processing; thus, a different program would not be tested. (ID: 5690)

27. (d) Embedded audit modules can be difficult to install once the application program is operational, but efficiently included during system design. Embedded audit modules can be protected from viruses as well as other applications. Sporadic or occasional monitoring of embedded audit modules can produce valid results. Management tampering can modify other applications as easily as embedded audit modules. (ID: 7110)

28. (c) A source code comparison program could be used to compare the original code written for a specific program to the current code in use for that program. Thus, it would make note of any differences in the program from the time it was originally written. Test data would generally be used to test the output of the program but would provide no evidence as to whether the program code had been changed. A check digit program involves the use of a digit that is added to the end of a piece of numeric data to permit the data to be checked for accuracy during input, processing, or output. Control totals are totals computed at different times in the computer process and are used as input, processing, and output controls. They would not provide evidence as to whether any changes were made to the original program code. (ID: 2971)

29. (a) An integrated test facility (ITF) processes fictitious data with real data in order to test computer controls; client personnel are unaware of the testing. An input control matrix documents controls and their presence. Parallel simulation processes client input data on an auditor-controlled program to test controls; test data is not utilized. The term "data entry monitor" is not commonly used. (ID: 5143)

30. (d) After obtaining an understanding of the client's IT controls, the auditor must assess control risk for the IT portion of the client's internal control. Assessing control risk is the process of evaluating the effectiveness of an entity's internal control policies and procedures in preventing or detecting material misstatements in the financial statements. Procedures to judge the effectiveness of internal control design would include inquiries, observations, and inspections. One would not need computer software to accomplish this task. Gaining access to client data files, preparing spreadsheets, and constructing parallel simulations would all make use of computer software. (ID: 3936)

31. (b) Embedded audit modules are coded into a client's application to collect data for the auditor. Integrated data checks and test data generators involve auditor-controlled fictitious data. Snapshot applications capture screen images. (ID: 7030)

32. (d) Compared to auditing without a computer, the size of the sample can be greatly expanded at little cost using a computer. Parallel simulation might not include all types of transaction errors and exceptions that may be encountered. Using parallel simulation is no guarantee that the client's personnel are unaware that the data is being tested. As there is little risk of creating material errors in the client's data with a non-computer audit procedure, this hardly can be said to be an advantage of parallel simulation using a computer over not using a computer at all. (ID: 7812)

33. (d) In the test data approach to testing a computerized accounting system, test data are processed by the client's computer programs under the auditor's control. No dummy subsidiary is involved. Test data must be customized to each audit. The auditor need not include test data for all possible valid and invalid conditions. (ID: 8389)

34. (b) In auditing an entity's computerized payroll transactions, an auditor would be least likely to use test data to test controls concerning control and distribution of unclaimed checks. The other answer alternatives are examples of data that can be accessed and tested via computer applications while controls over unclaimed checks are more likely to be manual. (ID: 8844)

35. (d) A parallel simulation is a computer-assisted audit technique that permits an auditor to insert the auditor's version of a client's program to process data and compare the output with the client's output. (ID: 9364)

36. (a) One of the reasons for using generalized audit software (GAS) is that it enables the auditor to gain access and test information stored in the client's files without having to acquire a complete understanding of the client's IT system. Although the use of GAS enables the auditor to deal more effectively with large quantities of data and produces economies in the audit while increasing the quality of the audit, it cannot replace analytical procedures. Self-checking digits and hash totals are controls in the client system. Reducing the level of required tests of controls to a relatively small amount is the result of assessing control risk and applying preliminary tests of controls, not a result of using a GAS package. (ID: 5999)

37. (c) Generalized audit software (GAS) makes it possible for an auditor to access data in electronic form; typical GAS will analyze data and present results in a meaningful and convenient form. Assessing control risk as high may result in unnecessary additional audit procedures; an IT system may have strong internal control, and consequently, low control risk. Analytics cannot be performed if the information is available only in electronic form and there is no means to access it. If data is available only in electronic form, tests of controls over that data likely should be extensive, rather than limited. (ID: 8401)

Solution 7-2 SIMULATION ANSWER: Flowchart

A. 1

This symbol represents a file. In the revenue cycle application process, the most likely output among the choices given is an accounts receivable master file, especially since there is a cash receipts transaction file. A remittance file (G) is not typically a separately constructed file. Answers F and B are not part of the revenue cycle.

B. 8

This symbol represents some sort of printed output. Sales invoices are the most likely output from the system at this point. The customer orders would most likely be at the beginning of the revenue cycle. Receiving reports are not part of the revenue cycle. Customer checks are not created by the system but are received from the customer. (ID: 9207)

Solution 7-3 SIMULATION ANSWER: Research

AU	§ 314	60	(ID: 9208)

.60 IT also poses specific risks to an entity's internal control, including:

- Reliance on systems or programs that are processing data inaccurately, processing inaccurate data, or both.
- Unauthorized access to data that may result in destruction of data or improper changes to data, including the recording of unauthorized or nonexistent transactions or inaccurate recording of transactions.
- Unauthorized changes to data in master files.
- Unauthorized changes to systems or programs.
- Failure to make necessary changes to systems or programs.
- Inappropriate manual intervention.
- Potential loss of data or inability to access data as required.

CHAPTER 8

REPORTS ON AUDITED FINANCIAL STATEMENTS

AU Identifier Used for Clarified US GAAS in This Textbook

We have not continued to use the temporary AU-C identifier for the clarified auditing standards issued by the American Institute of Certified Public Accountants (AICPA). In this textbook these standards have an AU identifier.

CHAPTER 8

REPORTS ON AUDITED FINANCIAL STATEMENTS

I. Forming an Opinion on the Financial Statements (AU 700)

A. Objectives

The objectives of the auditor are to:

1. Form an opinion on the financial statements based on an evaluation of the audit evidence obtained, including evidence obtained about comparative financial statements or comparative financial information

2. Clearly express that opinion on the financial statements through a written report that also describes the basis for that opinion

B. Definitions

1. **Applicable Financial Reporting Framework (AFRF)** The financial reporting framework adopted by management and, when appropriate, those charged with governance in the preparation and fair presentation of the financial statements that is acceptable in view of the nature of the entity and the objective of the financial statements, or that is required by law or regulation; the term also means the financial reporting framework that applies to the group financial statements

2. **Fair Presentation Framework** The term fair presentation framework is used to refer to a financial reporting framework that requires compliance with the requirements of the framework and *either* acknowledges:

   a. Explicitly or implicitly that, to achieve fair presentation of the financial statements, it may be necessary for management to provide disclosures beyond those specifically required by the framework

   or

   b. Explicitly that it may be necessary for management to depart from a requirement of the framework to achieve fair presentation of the financial statements; such departures are expected to be necessary only in extremely rare circumstances

   Editor Note: A financial reporting framework that requires compliance with the requirements of the framework, but does not contain one of the preceding two acknowledgments is *not* a fair presentation framework.

3. **Financial Reporting Framework** A set of criteria used to determine measurement, recognition, presentation, and disclosure of all material items in the financial statements; for example, US GAAP, International Financial Reporting Standards, or a special-purpose framework

4. **Financial Statements** A structured representation of historical financial information, including related notes, intended to communicate an entity's economic resources and obligations at a point in time or the changes therein for a period of time in accordance with a financial reporting framework; the related notes ordinarily comprise a summary of significant accounting policies and other explanatory information; the term *financial statements* ordinarily refers to a complete set of financial statements as determined by the requirements of the AFRF, but can also refer to a single financial statement

5. **General-Purpose Financial Statements** Financial statements prepared in accordance with a general-purpose framework

6. **General-Purpose Framework** A financial reporting framework designed to meet the common financial information needs of a wide range of users

7. **Group Financial Statements** Financial statements that include the financial information of more than one component; the term *group financial statements* also refers to combined financial statements aggregating the financial information prepared by components that are under common control

8. **Special-Purpose Financial Statements** Financial statements prepared in accordance with a special-purpose framework

9. **Special-Purpose Framework** A financial reporting framework other than GAAP that is one of the following bases of accounting: cash, tax, regulatory, other, or contractual. The cash, tax, regulatory, and other bases of accounting are commonly referred to as *other comprehensive bases of accounting*. (See the coverage of audits of financial statements prepared in accordance with a special-purpose framework in chapter 12.)

   Editor Note: Unless noted otherwise, the term *financial statements* refers to a complete set of general-purpose financial statements. The requirements of the AFRF determine the form and content of the financial statements and what constitutes a complete set.

C. **Basis for Reasonable Assurance**

The auditor should form an opinion based on an evaluation of the audit evidence obtained on whether the financial statements are presented fairly, in all material respects, in accordance with the AFRF. In order to form that opinion, the auditor should conclude whether the auditor has obtained reasonable assurance about whether the financial statements as a whole are free from material misstatement, whether due to fraud or error.

1. **Sufficient Appropriate Audit Evidence** The auditor should conclude whether sufficient appropriate audit evidence has been obtained. All relevant audit evidence, regardless of whether it appears to corroborate or contradict the assertions in the financial statements, should be considered.

2. **Material Uncorrected Misstatements** The auditor should determine whether uncorrected misstatements are material, individually or in the aggregate, by consideration of the following.

   a. **Size & Nature** The size and nature of the misstatements, both in relation to particular classes of transactions, account balances, or disclosures and the financial statements as a whole, and the particular circumstances of their occurrence

   b. **Effect Related to Prior Periods** The effect of uncorrected misstatements related to prior periods; the cumulative effect of immaterial uncorrected misstatements related to prior periods may have a material effect on the current period financial statements

3. **Evaluation of Conformity of Financial Statements With Requirements of AFRF** The auditor should evaluate whether the financial statements are prepared, in all material respects, in accordance with the requirements of the AFRF. This evaluation should include consideration of the qualitative aspects of the entity's accounting practices, including indicators of possible bias in management's judgments.

   In particular, the auditor should evaluate whether:

   a. The financial statements adequately refer to or describe the AFRF

Editor Note: The preparation and fair presentation of the financial statements by management and, when appropriate, those charged with governance require:

- The identification of the AFRF, in the context of any relevant laws or regulations
- The preparation and fair presentation of the financial statements in accordance with that framework
- The inclusion of an adequate description of that framework in the financial statements

b. The financial statements achieve fair presentation within the context of the AFRF, including consideration of

(1) The overall presentation, structure, and content of the financial statements

(2) Whether the financial statements, including the related notes, represent the underlying transactions and events in a manner that achieves fair presentation

c. The financial statements adequately disclose the significant accounting policies selected and applied

d. The accounting policies selected and applied are consistent with the AFRF and are appropriate

e. The accounting estimates made by management are reasonable

f. The information presented in the financial statements is relevant, reliable, comparable, and understandable

g. The financial statements provide adequate disclosures to enable the intended users to understand the effect of material transactions and events on the information conveyed in the financial statements

h. The terminology used in the financial statements, including the title of each financial statement, is appropriate

D. Form of Opinion

1. Unmodified Opinion The auditor should express an unmodified opinion when the financial statements are presented fairly, in all material respects, in accordance with the AFRF.

2. Modified Opinion The auditor should modify the opinion for *either* of these conditions:

a. Financial Statements Are Materially Misstated The auditor concludes that, based on the audit evidence obtained, the financial statements as a whole are materially misstated

- This includes fair presentation—if the auditor concludes that the financial statements do not achieve fair presentation, the auditor should discuss the matter with management and, depending on how the matter is resolved, should determine whether it is necessary to modify the opinion (the topic on modified opinions in this chapter covers the nature of material misstatements)

b. Scope Limitation The auditor is unable to obtain sufficient appropriate audit evidence to conclude that the financial statements as a whole are free from material misstatement.

3. **Opinion Coverage of Information in Financial Statements *Not* Required by AFRF** In some circumstances, the entity may be required by law, regulation, or standards, or may voluntarily choose, to include in the basic financial statements information that is not required by the AFRF.

   a. **When Information Can *Not* Be Clearly Differentiated From Financial Statements** Information that is *not* required by the AFRF, but is nevertheless presented as part of the basic financial statements, should be covered by the auditor's opinion if it cannot be clearly differentiated from the financial statements.

   b. **When Information Can Be Clearly Differentiated From Financial Statements** If the information included in the basic financial statements is *not* required by the AFRF and is *not* necessary for fair presentation, but is clearly differentiated, then such information may be identified as *unaudited* or as *not covered by the audit report*.

II. Audit Report With an Unmodified Opinion (AU 700 continued)

A. Overview

The auditor should clearly express an opinion on the financial statements through a *written* report that also describes the basis for that opinion. A written report encompasses reports issued in hard copy format and those using an electronic medium.

B. Elements of an Audit Report With an Unmodified Opinion

Much of the following is applicable to audit reports containing other types of opinions and/or additional paragraphs. (The coverage of these types of audit reports that follows in this chapter will indicate how those reports differ from one containing an unmodified opinion, i.e., a "standard" report.)

1. ***Independent* in Title** A title that includes the word *independent* to clearly indicate that it is the report of an independent auditor

2. **Addressee** An addressee as required by the circumstances of the engagement; normally, to those for whom the report is prepared, i.e., either the entity whose financial statements are being audited or to those charged with governance of that entity

   Editor Note: Occasionally, an auditor may be retained to audit the financial statements of an entity that is not a client; the report may then be addressed to the client and *not* to those charged with governance of the entity whose financial statements are being audited.

3. **Introductory Paragraph** The introductory paragraph in the audit report should:

   a. Identify the entity whose financial statements have been audited

   b. State that the financial statements have been audited

   c. Identify the title of each of the financial statements

      Editor Note: The titles of the financial statements identified in the introductory paragraph describe the information that is the subject of the auditor's opinion. In the case of many general-purpose frameworks, this includes the notes to the financial statements.

   d. Specify the date or period covered by each of the financial statements

4. **Management's Responsibility Section**

   a. **Heading With Specific Language Is Required** The auditor's report should include a section with the heading *Management's Responsibility for the Financial Statements*.

b. **Identification of AFRF & Its Origin**

c. **Description of Management's Responsibilities** The audit is conducted on the premise that management is responsible for the preparation and fair presentation of the financial statements, in accordance with the AFRF, that are free from material misstatement, whether due to fraud or error, as well as related internal controls. This paragraph should describe these responsibilities and identify the AFRF. (See the illustrated report included in this section of this chapter to read the complete description that is required.)

(1) **Financial Statements**

(2) **Relevant Internal Controls**

d. **Description of Responsibilities Should Be Included in Audit Report—*Not* Referenced** The description about management's responsibility for the financial statements in the audit report should **not** be referenced to a separate statement by management about such responsibilities if such a statement is included in a document containing the audit report. Further, the description should be limited to the breadth illustrated in the sample audit report in this section of this chapter. Any reference to a statement by management or elaboration in the audit report may lead users to erroneously believe that the auditor is providing assurances about representations made by management.

5. **Auditor's Responsibility Section**

a. **Heading With Specific Language Is Required** The audit report should include a section with the heading *Auditor's Responsibility*.

b. **Responsibility to Express an Opinion** The audit report should state that the responsibility of the auditor is to express an opinion on the financial statements based on the audit; this statement contrasts the auditor's responsibility with that of management's for the preparation of the financial statements.

c. **Conduct of Audit**

(1) **In Accordance With US GAAS** The auditor's report should state that the audit was conducted in accordance with generally accepted auditing standards and should identify the United States of America as the country of origin of those standards.

Editor Note: The auditor should not represent compliance with US GAAS in the report, unless the auditor has complied with the requirements of AU 200, *Overall Objectives of the Independent Auditor and the Conduct of an Audit in Accordance With Generally Accepted Auditing Standards*, and all other AU sections relevant to the audit.

(2) **To Obtain Reasonable Assurance About Whether Financial Statements Are Free From Material Misstatement** The auditor's report should also explain that those standards require that the auditor plan and perform the audit to obtain reasonable assurance about whether the financial statements are free from material misstatement.

Editor Note: An audit may also be conducted in accordance with another set of auditing standards in addition to US GAAS, for example, International Standards on Auditing (ISA), the standards of the Public Company Accounting Oversight Board, or *Government Auditing Standards*. The auditor should *not* refer to having conducted an audit in accordance with another set of auditing standards in addition to US GAAS,

except when the audit was conducted in accordance with *both* sets of standards in their *entirety*. If so, the audit report should identify the other set of auditing standards, as well as their origin. (There is no country of origin for ISA.)

d. **Description of Audit** The auditor's report should describe an audit by stating that:

(1) An audit involves performing procedures to obtain audit evidence about the amounts and disclosures in the financial statements.

(2) The procedures selected depend on the auditor's judgment, including the assessment of the risks of material misstatement of the financial statements, whether due to fraud or error. In making those risk assessments, the auditor considers internal control relevant to the entity's preparation and fair presentation of the financial statements in order to design audit procedures that are appropriate in the circumstances but not for the purpose of expressing an opinion on the effectiveness of the entity's internal control, and accordingly, no such opinion is expressed.

Editor Note: Of course, when the auditor also has a responsibility to express an opinion on the effectiveness of internal control in conjunction with an audit of the financial statements, the statements that the auditor's consideration of internal control is not for the purpose of expressing an opinion on the effectiveness of internal control, and accordingly, no such opinion is expressed should be omitted.

(3) An audit also includes evaluating the appropriateness of the accounting policies used and the reasonableness of significant accounting estimates made by management, as well as the overall presentation of the financial statements.

e. **Evidence Is Sufficient & Appropriate to Support Opinion** The audit report should state whether the auditor believes that the audit evidence the auditor has obtained is sufficient and appropriate to provide a basis for the auditor's opinion.

6. **Opinion Section**

a. **Heading With Specific Language Is Required** The auditor's report should include a section with the heading *Opinion*.

b. **Unmodified Opinion** When expressing an unmodified opinion on financial statements, the auditor's opinion should state that the financial statements present fairly, in all material respects, the financial position of the entity as of the balance sheet date and the results of its operations and its cash flows for the period then ended, in accordance with the applicable financial reporting framework.

c. **Identification of AFRF & Its Origin** The auditor's opinion should identify the AFRF and its origin. The identification of the AFRF is intended to advise users of the audit report of the context in which the opinion is expressed.

See the illustrated report included in this section of this chapter to read the unmodified opinion statement.

7. **Subtitles Required If Audit Report Includes Other Reporting Responsibilities** If other reporting responsibilities are addressed in the audit report in addition to the auditor's responsibility under US GAAS to report on the financial statements, they should be addressed in a separate section of the report subtitled, *Report on Other Legal and Regulatory Requirements* or otherwise, as appropriate to the content. When relevant, this section may contain headings that describe the content of the other reporting responsibility paragraphs, but headings are

not required. (The required headings described previously only apply to the section of the report on the financial statements.)

The other reporting responsibilities section should *follow* the section on the financial statements.

If other reporting responsibilities are *not* included, there is no need for a subtitle for the section on the financial statements. (The only purpose of the subtitles is to differentiate the two sections.)

8. **Auditor's Signature** The audit report should include the manual or printed signature of the auditor's firm.

9. **Auditor's City & State (Address)** The audit report should name the city and state where the auditor practices. In the United States, the location of the issuing office is the city and state. In another country, it may be the city and country.

10. **Date of Audit Report** The date informs the user that the auditor has considered the effect of events and transactions of which the auditor became aware and that occurred up to that date.

    The audit report should be dated no earlier than the date on which sufficient appropriate audit evidence has been obtained on which to base an opinion on the financial statements, including evidence that:

    a. The audit documentation has been reviewed

    b. All the statements that the financial statements comprise, including the related notes, have been prepared

    c. Management has asserted that they have taken responsibility for those financial statements

Editor Note: As explained previously, the first subtitle included in this illustration, *Report on the Financial Statements*, is only included when the last subtitle for other reporting responsibilities, shown as, for example, *Report on Other Legal and Regulatory Requirements*, is included in an audit report. Then, both subtitles are needed to differentiate the two sections of the report. We have chosen to only include them in this illustration, but they can be used when needed in all other US GAAS audit reports.

Exhibit 1 ▸ Report on Financial Statements for a Single Year With an Unmodified Opinion

Independent Auditor's Report

[*Appropriate Addressee*]

Report on the Financial Statements

We have audited the accompanying financial statements of ABC Company, which comprise the balance sheet as of December 31, 20X1, and the related statements of income, changes in stockholders' equity, and cash flows for the year then ended, and the related notes to the financial statements.

Management's Responsibility for the Financial Statements

Management is responsible for the preparation and fair presentation of these financial statements in accordance with accounting principles generally accepted in the United States of America; this includes the design, implementation, and maintenance of internal control relevant to the preparation and fair presentation of financial statements that are free from material misstatement, whether due to fraud or error.

Auditor's Responsibility

Our responsibility is to express an opinion on these financial statements based on our audit. We conducted our audit in accordance with auditing standards generally accepted in the United States of America. Those standards require that we plan and perform the audit to obtain reasonable assurance about whether the financial statements are free from material misstatement.

An audit involves performing procedures to obtain audit evidence about the amounts and disclosures in the financial statements. The procedures selected depend on the auditor's judgment, including the assessment of the risks of material misstatement of the financial statements, whether due to fraud or error. In making those risk assessments, the auditor considers internal control relevant to the entity's preparation and fair presentation of the financial statements in order to design audit procedures that are appropriate in the circumstances, but not for the purpose of expressing an opinion on the effectiveness of the entity's internal control. Accordingly, we express no such opinion. An audit also includes evaluating the appropriateness of accounting policies used and the reasonableness of significant accounting estimates made by management, as well as evaluating the overall presentation of the financial statements.

We believe that the audit evidence we have obtained is sufficient and appropriate to provide a basis for our audit opinion.

Opinion

In our opinion, the financial statements referred to above present fairly, in all material respects, the financial position of ABC Company as of December 31, 20X1, and the results of its operations and its cash flows for the year then ended in accordance with accounting principles generally accepted in the United States of America.

Report on Other Legal and Regulatory Requirements

[*Form and content of this section of the audit report will vary depending on the nature of the auditor's other reporting responsibilities.*]

[*Auditor's signature*]

[*Auditor's city and state*]

[*Date of the audit report*]

III. Emphasis-of-Matter & Other-Matter Paragraphs (AU 706)

These paragraphs address situations when the auditor considers it necessary, or is required, to include additional communications in the audit report that are **not** modifications to the auditor's opinion.

A. Definitions

Under the following circumstances, an auditor adds these paragraphs to the audit report (*after* the opinion section) to draw users' attention to a matter.

1. **Emphasis-of-Matter [Presented or Disclosed in Financial Statements] Paragraph** A paragraph included in the audit report that is required by US GAAS, or is included at the auditor's discretion, and that refers to a matter appropriately presented or disclosed in the financial statements that, in the auditor's professional judgment, is of such importance that it is fundamental to users' understanding of the financial statements; an emphasis-of-matter paragraph is **not** a substitute for either (a) the auditor expressing a modified opinion, or (b) required disclosures in the financial statements

2. **Other-Matter [Related to Audit; *Not* in Financial Statements] Paragraph** A paragraph included in the audit report that is required by US GAAS, or is included at the auditor's discretion, and that refers to a matter other than those presented or disclosed in the financial statements that, in the auditor's professional judgment, is relevant to users' understanding of the audit, the auditor's responsibilities, or the audit report

B. Communication With Those Charged With Governance

The auditor should communicate with those charged with governance the expectation of the inclusion of either of these paragraphs and the proposed wording. However, when the inclusion of an other-matter paragraph on the same matter recurs on each successive engagement, it may be unnecessary to repeat the communication for each engagement.

C. Emphasis-of-Matter Paragraphs

Such a paragraph should refer only to information appropriately presented or disclosed in the financial statements and should be fundamental to the users' understanding of the financial statements.

The auditor should have also obtained sufficient appropriate audit evidence that the matter is not materially misstated in the financial statements.

1. **Presentation** The requirements for the form and placement of the paragraph apply whether or not the paragraph is required to be included in the audit report. When the auditor includes an emphasis-of-matter paragraph in the audit report, the auditor should:

   a. **Place After Opinion** Include it immediately *after* the opinion paragraph in the audit report

   b. **Use Heading** Use the heading *Emphasis of Matter* or other appropriate heading if it adequately describes the nature of the matter

   c. **Make Clear Reference**

      (1) **Include Brief Description** Include a clear reference to the matter being emphasized

      (2) **State Where Described in Financial Statements** State where relevant disclosures that fully describe the matter can be found in the financial statements

d. **State That It Does *Not* Modify Opinion** Indicate that the auditor's opinion is **not** modified with respect to the matter emphasized

Editor Note: Although other-matter paragraphs do not affect the opinion either, this statement is only required to be included in emphasis-of-matter paragraphs because an emphasis-of-matter paragraph and the opinion both regard the financial statements while the subject matter of an other-matter paragraph does not.

2. **Circumstances That Require Emphasis-of-Matter Paragraphs** The following matters should be brought to the attention of users by the inclusion of an emphasis-of-matter paragraph in the audit report in *all* instances rather than at the discretion of the auditor.

a. **Consistency of Financial Statements—Change in Accounting Principle (AU 708)** If certain conditions are met and the change in accounting principle has a material effect on the comparability of the financial statements (See the coverage of consistency in this chapter.)

b. **Consistency of Financial Statements—Correction of a Misstatement in Previously Issued Financial Statements (AU 708)** When there has been a material effect on the comparability of the financial statements due to adjustments to correct a material misstatement in previously issued financial statements (See the coverage of consistency in this chapter.)

c. **Comparative Financial Statements—Change From Opinion Previously Expressed on Prior Period Financial Statements (AU 700)** When reporting on prior period financial statements in connection with the current period audit, if the auditor's opinion differs from the opinion previously expressed due to a matter disclosed in the financial statements (See the coverage of comparative financial statements and comparative information in this chapter.)

d. **Subsequently Discovered Facts That Become Known to Auditor After Audit Report Release Date (AU 560)** If management revises the financial statements and if the auditor's opinion on the revised financial statements differs from the opinion the auditor previously expressed due to a matter disclosed in the financial statements (See the coverage of subsequently discovered facts in this chapter.)

e. **Substantial Doubt About Entity's Ability to Continue as a Going Concern (AU 570)** If there is substantial doubt about the entity's ability to continue as a going concern for a reasonable period of time (See the coverage of going concern issues in this chapter.)

f. **When Financial Statements Prepared in Accordance With a Financial Reporting Framework Generally Accepted in Another Country Also Are Intended for Use in United States (AU 910)** When financial statements prepared in accordance with a financial reporting framework generally accepted in another country also are intended for use in the United States, the auditor should include an emphasis-of-matter paragraph that identifies the AFRF and indicates that such framework differs from US GAAP. (See the coverage of financial statements prepared in accordance with a financial reporting framework generally accepted in another country in chapter 12.)

g. **Special-Purpose Financial Statements** (See the coverage of audits of financial statements prepared in accordance with a special-purpose framework in chapter 12.)

(1) **General Rule (AU 800)** The audit report on special-purpose financial statements should include an emphasis-of-matter paragraph that alerts users of the report that the financial statements are prepared in accordance with a special-purpose framework and that the basis of accounting is a basis of accounting other than GAAP.

(2) **Exception (AU 800)** If the special-purpose financial statements are prepared in accordance with a regulatory basis of accounting, and the special-purpose financial statements together with the audit report are intended for general use, the auditor should **not** include the emphasis-of-matter paragraph. Instead, the auditor should express an opinion about whether the special-purpose financial statements are presented fairly, in all material respects, in accordance with GAAP. The auditor should also, in a separate paragraph, express an opinion about whether the financial statements are prepared in accordance with the special-purpose framework.

h. **Audits of Single Financial Statements & Specific Elements, Accounts, or Items of a Financial Statement (AU 805)** When the auditor reports on an incomplete presentation that is otherwise in accordance with GAAP, the auditor should include an emphasis-of-matter paragraph. (See coverage of this topic in chapter 12.)

3. The following are examples of circumstances when the auditor *may* consider it necessary to include an emphasis-of-matter paragraph.

- An uncertainty relating to the future outcome of unusually important litigation or regulatory action
- A major catastrophe that has had, or continues to have, a significant effect on the entity's financial position
- Significant transactions with related parties
- Unusually important subsequent events

Exhibit 2 ▶ Changes to Audit Report for Emphasis-of-Matter Paragraphs—Opinion Is *Not* Modified; Emphasis-of-Matter Paragraph Is Added *After* Opinion Paragraph

Reasons for Change	Paragraph Required?	Specific *Additional** Elements of Paragraph Required Under Each Circumstance
A lack of consistency has materially affected the comparability of the financial statements between periods:		
A change in accounting principle or method in applying it, including a: Change inseparable from a change in estimate; Change by equity-method investee; Change in reporting entity not resulting from a transaction or event	Yes	
Adjustments to correct a material misstatement in previously issued financial statements	Yes	A statement that the previously issued F/S have been restated for the correction of a material misstatement in the respective period
Comparative F/S: change from opinion previously expressed (when reporting on prior period F/S in connection with the current period audit) due to a matter disclosed in F/S	Yes	• Date of previous report • Type of opinion previously expressed • Substantive reasons for the different opinion • That the opinion on the amended F/S is different from the previous opinion
Subsequently discovered facts after audit report released result in change of opinion on revised F/S due to a matter disclosed in F/S	Yes	Same as previous item
Going concern doubt**	Yes	Describe conclusion using the terms *substantial doubt* and *going concern*
F/S prepared in accordance with a financial reporting framework generally accepted in another country intended for use outside & inside the USA	Yes	Statements that identify the AFRF & indicate that such framework differs from US GAAP
Special-purpose financial statements:		
Cash basis Tax basis Regulatory basis, if restricted use Other basis Contractual basis	Yes	• Statement that the F/S are prepared in accordance with the applicable special-purpose framework • Statement that the special-purpose framework is a basis of accounting other than GAAP
Regulatory basis, general use	NA	NA Instead, the auditor should express an opinion about whether the F/S are presented fairly in accordance with GAAP. And, in a separate paragraph, express an opinion about whether the F/S are prepared in accordance with the regulatory basis of accounting.
Incomplete presentation otherwise in accordance with GAAP	Yes	• Statement on the purpose of presentation • Statement that indicates presentation is not intended to be a complete presentation
Examples of when it *may* be necessary to include an emphasis-of-matter paragraph		
An uncertainty relating to the future outcome of unusually important litigation or regulatory action	**No**	
Unusually important subsequent events	**No**	

* This is content related to the specific circumstances given, i.e., not listed are the elements common to all emphasis-of-matter paragraphs (heading: *Emphasis of Matter* or other appropriate heading; description of the matter being emphasized; reference to where it is disclosed in the F/S; and an indication that the opinion is *not* modified with respect to the matter of emphasis).

** The auditor is not precluded from disclaiming an opinion.

D. Other-Matter Paragraphs

The content of an other-matter paragraph should clearly reflect the matter is **not** required to be presented and disclosed in the financial statements. The matter described should be relevant to users' understanding of the audit, the auditor's responsibilities, or the audit report.

Editor Note: An other-matter paragraph does **not** address circumstances when the auditor has other reporting responsibilities that are in addition to the auditor's responsibility under US GAAS to report on the financial statements or when the auditor has been asked to perform and report on additional specified procedures or to express an opinion on specific matters. Nor does it include information that is required to be provided by management.

1. **Presentation** The requirements for the form and placement of the paragraph apply whether or not the paragraph is required to be included in the audit report. When the auditor includes an other-matter paragraph in the audit report, the auditor should:

   a. Generally, include it *after* the opinion paragraph and *after* any emphasis-of-matter paragraph in the audit report

      It can be placed elsewhere in the report if its content is relevant to the "Other Reporting Responsibilities" section instead of the audit of the financial statements.

      Editor Note: The placement of an other-matter paragraph depends on the nature of the information to be communicated. When relevant to all the auditor's responsibilities or users' understanding of the audit report, the other-matter paragraph may be included as a separate section following the "Report on the Financial Statements" and the "Report on Other Legal and Regulatory Requirements."

   b. Use the heading *Other Matter* or an other appropriate heading

2. **Circumstances That Require Other-Matter Paragraphs** The following matters should be brought to the attention of users by the inclusion of an other-matter paragraph in the audit report in *all* instances rather than at the discretion of the auditor.

   a. **Comparative Financial Statements—Change From Opinion Previously Expressed on Prior Period Financial Statements (AU 700)** When reporting on prior period financial statements in connection with the current period audit, if the auditor's opinion differs from the opinion previously expressed due to a matter related to the audit, appropriately not presented or disclosed in the financial statements (See the coverage of comparative financial statements and comparative information in this chapter.)

   b. **Comparative Financial Statements—Prior Period Financial Statements Audited by a Predecessor Auditor (AU 700)** If the financial statements of the prior period were audited by a predecessor auditor, and the predecessor audit report is *not* reissued (See the coverage of comparative financial statements and comparative information in this chapter.)

   c. **Comparative Financial Statements—Prior Period Financial Statements Were *Not* Audited [but Were Reviewed or Compiled] (AU 700)** When current period financial statements are audited and presented in comparative form with compiled or reviewed financial statements for the prior period, and the report on the prior period is *not* reissued (See the coverage of comparative financial statements and comparative information in this chapter.)

   d. **Comparative Financial Statements—Prior Period Financial Statements *Not* Audited, Reviewed, or Compiled (AU 700)** If the prior period financial statements were not audited, reviewed, or compiled (See the coverage of comparative financial statements and comparative information in this chapter.)

e. **Subsequently Discovered Facts That Become Known to Auditor *After* Audit Report Release Date (AU 560)** If management revises the financial statements and if the auditor's opinion on the revised financial statements differs from the opinion the auditor previously expressed due to a matter related to the audit, appropriately not presented or disclosed in the financial statements (See the coverage of subsequently discovered facts in this chapter.)

f. **Other Information Included With Financial Statements Requires Revision But Management Refuses to Change It (AU 720)** When the auditor identifies a material inconsistency prior to the audit report release date that requires revision of the other information and management refuses to make the revision, the auditor should communicate this matter to those charged with governance. The auditor must then take one of three courses of action: include in the audit report an other-matter paragraph describing the material inconsistency; withhold the audit report; or withdraw from the engagement if possible under applicable law or regulation. (See the coverage of other information in documents containing audited financial statements in this chapter.)

g. **Engagement to Report on Supplementary Information Presented With Financial Statements (AU 725)** When the entity presents the supplementary information with the financial statements, the auditor should report on the supplementary information in either an other-matter paragraph in the audit report or in a separate report. (See the coverage of engagements to report on supplementary information in chapter 12.)

h. **Required Supplementary Information (AU 730)** The auditor should include an other-matter paragraph in the audit report on the financial statements to refer to the required supplementary information. (See the coverage of required supplementary information in this chapter.)

i. **Special-Purpose Financial Statements** (See the coverage of audits of financial statements prepared in accordance with a special-purpose framework in chapter 12.)

   (1) **General Rule (AU 800)** The audit report on special-purpose financial statements should include an other-matter paragraph that restricts the use of the audit report when the special-purpose financial statements are prepared in accordance with:

      (a) A contractual basis of accounting

      (b) A regulatory basis of accounting (see exception that follows)

      (c) An other basis of accounting when the subject matter is based on measurement or disclosure criteria that are either:

         (i) Suitable only for a limited number of users who can be presumed to have an adequate understanding, or

         (ii) Available only to the specified parties

   (2) **Exception (AU 800)** If the special-purpose financial statements are prepared in accordance with a regulatory basis of accounting, and the special-purpose financial statements together with the audit report are intended for general use, the auditor should, of course, **not** include the other-matter paragraph (or emphasis-of-matter paragraph covered previously).

j. **Report on Compliance With Aspects of Contractual Agreements or Regulatory Requirements Included in Audit Report (AU 806)** When a report on compliance is included in the audit report on the financial statements (See the coverage of reporting on an entity's compliance with aspects of contractual agreements or regulatory requirements in connection with an audit of financial statements in chapter 12.)

k. **Restricted Use Audit Report (AU 905)** The audit report should include an other-matter paragraph that restricts its use when the subject matter of the report is based on:

   (1) Measurement or disclosure criteria that are suitable only for a limited number of users who can be presumed to have an adequate understanding of the criteria

   (2) Measurement or disclosure criteria that are available only to the specified parties

   (3) Matters identified by the auditor during the course of the audit engagement when the identification of such matters is *not* the primary objective of the audit engagement (commonly referred to as a by-product report)

   (See the coverage of restricting the use of an audit report in chapter 12.)

l. **Interim Financial Information Accompanying Audited Financial Statements (AU 930)** The auditor should include an other-matter paragraph in the audit report on the audited financial statements when interim financial information accompanies audited financial statements and when certain conditions exist. (See the coverage on interim financial information in this chapter.)

3. The following are examples of circumstances when the auditor *may* consider it necessary to include an other-matter paragraph.

a. **Relevant to Users' Understanding of Audit**

   - The auditor may consider it necessary to include an other-matter paragraph in the audit report to explain why it is not possible to withdraw from an engagement—generally due to a law or regulation—even though the possible effect of a scope limitation imposed by management is pervasive (this is rare).

b. **Relevant to Users' Understanding of Auditor's Responsibilities or Audit Report**

   - Law, regulation, or generally accepted practice may require or permit the auditor to elaborate on matters that provide further explanation of the auditor's responsibilities in the audit of the financial statements or the audit report.

c. **Reporting on More Than One Set of Financial Statements**

   - An entity may prepare one set of financial statements in accordance with a general-purpose framework (for example, US GAAP) and another set of financial statements in accordance with another general-purpose framework (for example, IFRS) and engage the auditor to report on both sets of financial statements. If the auditor has determined that the frameworks are acceptable in the respective circumstances, the auditor may include an other-matter paragraph in the audit report referring to the fact that another set of financial statements has been prepared by the same entity in accordance with another general-purpose framework and that the auditor has issued a report on those financial statements.

Exhibit 3 ▸ Changes to Audit Report for Other-Matter Paragraphs—Opinion Is *Not* Modified; Other-Matter Paragraph Is Added *After* Opinion Paragraph & Any Emphasis-of-Matter Paragraphs

Reasons for Change	Paragraph Required?	Specific *Additional** Elements of Paragraph Required Under Each Circumstance
Comparative F/S:		
Change from opinion previously expressed (when reporting on prior period F/S in connection with the current period audit) due to a matter related to the audit	Yes	• Date of previous report • Type of opinion previously expressed • Substantive reasons for the different opinion • That the opinion on the amended F/S is different from the previous opinion
Prior period F/S audited by predecessor auditor (predecessor's report *not* reissued)	Yes	• Statement that the F/S of the prior period were audited by a predecessor auditor • Type of opinion expressed and, if the opinion was modified, the reasons • The nature of any emphasis-of-matter or other-matter paragraphs included in the predecessor's report • Date of predecessor's report
Predecessor's report *not* reissued when prior period F/S *restated* (if the successor has audited the adjustments to the prior period F/S)	**No**	An other-matter paragraph *may* be included by the successor indicating that a predecessor reported on the F/S of the prior period before restatement. **
Current period F/S audited, prior period F/S only reviewed or compiled (report on prior period *not* reissued)	Yes	• Service performed in the prior period • Date of that report • Description of any material modifications noted in that report • Statement that the service was less in scope than an audit and does not provide the basis for the expression of an opinion on the F/S
Current period F/S audited, but prior period F/S *not* audited, reviewed, or compiled (F/S should be clearly marked to indicate their status)	Yes	• Indication that the auditor has not audited, reviewed, or compiled the prior period F/S • Statement that the auditor assumes no responsibility for them
Subsequently discovered facts after audit report released result in change of opinion on revised F/S due to a matter related to the audit	Yes	Same as first item in this table
Other information included with F/S requires revision but management refuses to change it ***	Yes	
Engagement to report on supplementary information presented with the F/S ****	Yes	See coverage in chapter 12.
Required Supplementary Information (RSI)	Yes	See coverage of RSI in this chapter for the requirements depending on the various scenarios.
Special-purpose F/S:		
Regulatory basis, if restricted use Contractual basis Other basis, if restricted use	Yes	Statement that restricts the use of the audit report; see list associated with this item in this table: "When the audit report is restricted as to use" US GAAS illustrated reports use heading *Restricted on Use*, but another appropriate heading may be used
Cash basis Tax basis	**No**	The auditor *may* consider it necessary in the circumstances of the engagement to include an other-matter paragraph that restricts the use of the report.
Regulatory basis, general use	NA	NA
Report on compliance with contracts or regulations included in the audit report	Yes	See coverage in chapter 12.

Reasons for Change	Paragraph Required?	Specific *Additional** Elements of Paragraph Required Under Each Circumstance
When the audit report is restricted as to use	Yes	Generally, the following should be included: • Statement that the report is intended solely for the information and use of the specified parties • Identification of the specified parties • Statement that the report is not intended to be and should not be used by anyone other than the specified parties
When interim financial information accompanies audited financial statements and certain conditions exist	Yes	See coverage in this chapter.
Examples of when it *may* be necessary to include an other-matter paragraph		
Auditor wishes to explain why withdrawal from engagement is not possible even though the possible effect of a scope limitation imposed by management is pervasive (rare)	**No**	
Law, regulation, or accepted practice requires or permits auditor to provide further explanation about the auditor's responsibilities	**No**	
Auditor has issued a report on another set of F/S prepared by the same entity in accordance with a different general-purpose framework	**No**	

* This is content related to the specific circumstances given, i.e., not given are the content requirements for all other-matter paragraphs (heading: *Other Matter* or other appropriate heading; a clear reflection that such other matter is **not** required to be presented and disclosed in the F/S).

** More information can be included if the successor is engaged to audit (and is satisfied with) the restatement.

*** If auditor deems it inappropriate to withhold report or withdraw from the engagement (if withdrawal is possible).

**** Auditor can report on supplementary information in a separate report instead of an other-matter paragraph.

IV. Modified Opinions (AU 705)

A. Overview

The auditor should modify the opinion in the audit report under the following circumstances.

1. **Financial Statements Are Materially Misstated** The auditor concludes that, based on the audit evidence obtained, the financial statements as a whole are materially misstated.

2. **Scope Limitation** The auditor is unable to obtain sufficient appropriate audit evidence to conclude that the financial statements as a whole are free from material misstatement.

B. Definitions

1. **Modified Opinion** There are three types of modified opinions: qualified, adverse, and a disclaimer of opinion.

2 **Misstatement** A difference between the amount, classification, presentation, or disclosure of a reported financial statement item and the same that is required for the item to be presented fairly in accordance with the applicable financial reporting framework (AFRF). Misstatements can arise from fraud or error.

3. **Pervasive** A term used in the context of misstatements to describe the effects (or possible effects, in the case of a scope limitation) on the financial statements of misstatements. Pervasive effects are those that:

   - Are not confined to specific elements, accounts, or items of the financial statements
   - Or *if* so confined, represent or could represent a substantial proportion of the financial statements; or
   - With regard to disclosures, are fundamental to users' understanding of the financial statements

C. Nature of Material Misstatements

A misstatement exists when these facets of financial statement items are *not* presented fairly in accordance with the AFRF.

- Amount
- Classification
- Presentation
- Disclosure

Accordingly, a material misstatement of the financial statements may arise in relation to the following.

- Selected accounting policies
  - Appropriateness
  - Application
- Financial statement presentation
  - Appropriateness
- Disclosures in the financial statements
  - Appropriateness
  - Adequacy

1. **Appropriateness of Selected Accounting Policies** With regard to the appropriateness of the accounting policies management has selected, material misstatements may arise when:

   a. The accounting policies are *not* in accordance with the AFRF

   b. The financial statements, including the related notes, do *not* fairly represent the underlying transactions and events

   Editor Note: Financial reporting frameworks often contain requirements for the accounting for, and disclosure of, changes in accounting policies. A material misstatement may arise when the entity has not complied with these requirements related to the consistency of financial statements between periods. (See the coverage of consistency in this chapter.)

2. **Application of Selected Accounting Policies** With regard to the application of accounting policies, material misstatements may arise:

   a. When management has *not* applied the accounting policies in accordance with the AFRF, including when management has *not* applied them consistently between periods or to similar transactions and events

b. Due to the method of application of the accounting policies, such as an unintentional error in application

3. **Appropriateness of Financial Statement Presentation or Appropriateness or Adequacy of Disclosures in Financial Statements** With regard to the appropriateness of the financial statement presentation or the appropriateness or adequacy of disclosures, material misstatements may arise when:

   a. The financial statements do not include all of the disclosures required by the AFRF

   b. The disclosures are not presented in accordance with the AFRF

   c. The financial statements do not provide the disclosures necessary to achieve fair presentation

   d. Information required to be presented in accordance with the AFRF is omitted either because a required statement, for example, a statement of cash flows, has not been included or the information has not otherwise been disclosed in the financial statements

   Editor Note: Adequate disclosures relate to the form, arrangement, and content of the financial statements and their related notes, including, for example, the terminology used, the amount of detail given, the classification of items in the statements, and the bases of amounts set forth. Whether a particular disclosure is adequate depends on the facts and circumstances.

D. Nature of Scope Limitations

A scope limitation of the audit may arise from the following.

- Circumstances beyond the control of the entity
- Circumstances relating to the nature or timing of the auditor's work
- Limitations imposed by management

Editor Note: If the auditor is able to obtain sufficient appropriate audit evidence by performing alternative procedures, an inability to perform a *specific* procedure does **not** constitute a scope limitation.

1. **Circumstances Beyond Control of Entity** Examples of scope limitations beyond the control of the entity include the following.

   - The entity's accounting records have been destroyed.
   - The accounting records of a significant component have been seized indefinitely by governmental authorities.

2. **Circumstances Relating to Nature or Timing of Auditor's Work** Examples of scope limitations relating to the nature or timing of the auditor's work include the following.

   - The entity is required to use the equity method of accounting for an associated entity, and the auditor is unable to obtain sufficient appropriate audit evidence about the latter's financial information to evaluate whether the equity method has been appropriately applied.
   - The timing of the auditor's engagement is such that the auditor is unable to observe the counting of the physical inventories, and is unable to perform a rollback of the inventory or other appropriate procedures.

- The auditor determines that performing substantive procedures alone is not sufficient, but the entity's controls are not effective.
- When accounting for long-term investments, the auditor is unable to obtain audited financial statements of an investee.

3. **Limitations Imposed by Management** Examples of scope limitations imposed by management include the following.

   - Management prevents the auditor from observing the counting of the physical inventory.
   - Management prevents the auditor from requesting external confirmation of specific account balances

E. Factors That Determine the Type of Modified Opinion

1. **Nature of Cause** The nature of the matter giving rise to the modification, i.e., whether the financial statements are materially misstated or, in the case of scope limitation, *may* be materially misstated
2. **Pervasiveness of Effect** The auditor's professional judgment about the pervasiveness of the effects or possible effects of the matter on the financial statements

Exhibit 4 ▸ Determination of Type of Modified Opinion

Cause for Modification of Opinion	Opinion Type	
	Matter Is Material but *Not* Pervasive	**Matter Is Material *and* Pervasive**
Financial statements are materially misstated	Qualified opinion	Adverse opinion
Scope limitation (Inability to obtain sufficient appropriate audit evidence)	Qualified opinion	Disclaimer of opinion

F. Conditions for Modified Opinions

1. **Qualified Opinion** The auditor should express a qualified opinion when:

   a. The auditor, having obtained sufficient appropriate audit evidence, concludes that misstatements, individually or in the aggregate, are material but **not** pervasive to the financial statements

   b. The auditor is unable to obtain sufficient appropriate audit evidence (scope limitation) on which to base the opinion, but concludes that the possible effects on the financial statements of undetected misstatements, if any, could be material but **not** pervasive

2. **Adverse Opinion** The auditor should express an adverse opinion when, having obtained sufficient appropriate audit evidence, concludes that misstatements, individually or in the aggregate, are *both material and pervasive* to the financial statements.

3. **Disclaimer of Opinion**

   a. **Scope Limitation** The auditor should disclaim an opinion when unable to obtain sufficient appropriate audit evidence on which to base the opinion, and the auditor concludes that the possible effects on the financial statements of undetected misstatements, if any, could be *both material and pervasive*.

b. **Auditor Lacks Independence But Required to Report** When the auditor is not independent but is required by law or regulation to report on the financial statements, the auditor should disclaim an opinion and should specifically state that the auditor is not independent. The auditor is neither required to provide, nor precluded from providing, the reasons for the lack of independence; however, if the auditor chooses to provide the reasons, the auditor should include all of them.

4. **Adverse Opinion or Disclaimer of Opinion Limitations** If an adverse opinion or disclaimer of opinion on the financial statements *as a whole* is expressed, the audit report should **not** also include an unmodified opinion on a single financial statement or one or more specific elements of a financial statement. To include such an unmodified opinion in the same report in these circumstances would contradict the auditor's adverse opinion or disclaimer of opinion on the financial statements as a whole. (See coverage of audits of a single financial statement or a specific element of a financial statement in chapter 12.)

   Editor Note: In an initial audit, it is acceptable for the auditor to express an unmodified opinion regarding the financial position and disclaim an opinion regarding the results of operations and cash flows, when relevant. For example, when an auditor of a new client cannot become satisfied with the accuracy of opening inventory balances, this scope limitation affects the income, changes in stockholders' equity, and cash flow statements, but not the balance sheet. (This is because cost of goods sold cannot be verified.) Thus, an unmodified opinion could be issued on the balance sheet and a disclaimer of opinion should be issued on the other financial statements. In this case, the auditor has *not* disclaimed an opinion on the financial statements *as a whole*.

G. Effect of Uncertainties

1. **Overview of Uncertainties** Uncertainties include, but are not limited to, contingencies and matters related to estimates.

   Conclusive audit evidence concerning the ultimate outcome of uncertainties cannot be expected to exist at the time of the audit because the outcome and related audit evidence are prospective. (A matter involving an uncertainty is one that is expected to be resolved at a future date, at which time conclusive audit evidence concerning its outcome would be expected to become available.)

2. **Management's Responsibility Regarding Uncertainties** In these circumstances, management is responsible for analyzing existing conditions and estimating the effect of future events on the financial statements, or determining that a reasonable estimate cannot be made and making the required disclosures. An audit includes an assessment of whether the audit evidence is sufficient to support management's analysis and estimate.

3. **Basis for an *Un*modified Opinion When There Is an Uncertainty** Absence of the existence of information related to the outcome of an uncertainty does not necessarily lead to a conclusion that the audit evidence supporting management's assertion is not sufficient. Rather, the auditor's judgment regarding the sufficiency of the audit evidence is based on the audit evidence that is, or should be, available.

   An unmodified opinion is ordinarily appropriate if, after considering the existing conditions and available evidence, the auditor concludes that sufficient appropriate audit evidence supports management's assertions about the nature of a matter involving an uncertainty and its presentation or disclosure in the financial statements.

4. **Basis for a Modified Opinion When There Is an Uncertainty** If the auditor is unable to obtain sufficient audit evidence to support management's assertions, the auditor should consider the need to express a qualified opinion or to disclaim an opinion because of a scope limitation.

   A qualification or disclaimer of opinion because of a scope limitation is ordinarily appropriate if sufficient audit evidence related to an uncertainty does or did exist but was *not* available to the auditor for reasons such as management's record retention policies or a restriction imposed by management.

   In cases involving multiple uncertainties, the auditor *may* conclude that it is not possible to form an opinion on the financial statements as a whole due to the interaction and possible cumulative effect of the uncertainties.

H. Procedures When Management Imposes a Scope Limitation

1. **Request Removal** If, after accepting the engagement, management imposes a scope limitation that is likely to result in the expression of a qualified opinion or disclaimer of opinion, the auditor should request that management remove the limitation.

2. **When Management Refuses to Remove Scope Limitation** If management refuses to remove the limitation, the auditor should:

   a. Communicate the matter to those charged with governance

   b. Determine whether it is possible to perform alternative procedures to obtain sufficient appropriate audit evidence

3. **When Alternative Procedures Are *Not* Sufficient** If the auditor is unable to obtain sufficient appropriate audit evidence due to a management-imposed scope limitation, and concludes that the possible effects on the financial statements of undetected misstatements, if any, could be both material and pervasive, the auditor should either

   a. Disclaim an opinion on the financial statements

   b. Or, when practicable and possible, withdraw from the audit

      Editor Note: Withdrawal may not be practicable if the audit is near completion when the scope limitation is imposed. (If the auditor has substantially completed the audit, the auditor may decide to complete the audit to the extent possible, disclaim an opinion, and explain the scope limitation in the basis for disclaimer of opinion paragraph.) Withdrawal may not be possible if the auditor is required by law or regulation to continue the audit engagement. In this rare circumstance, the auditor *may* also consider it necessary to include an other-matter paragraph in the audit report to explain why withdrawal is not possible.

4. **Communicate Misstatements to Those Charged With Governance Before Withdrawing** If the auditor decides to withdraw, before doing so, the auditor should communicate to those charged with governance any matters regarding misstatements identified during the audit that would have given rise to a modified opinion.

I. Audit Report With a Modified Opinion

1. **Introductory Paragraph Is Amended for a Disclaimer of Opinion** When the auditor disclaims an opinion due to a scope limitation, the auditor should amend the introductory paragraph to state that the auditor was *engaged to* audit the financial statements. This is the opening phrase for a report with an *un*modified, qualified, or adverse opinion: "We *have audited* the accompanying financial statements..." When an opinion is disclaimed the opening phrase is changed to "We *were engaged to audit* the accompanying financial statements..."

2. **Management's Responsibility Section Is Unchanged** The management's responsibility section is **not** changed when the auditor expresses a qualified or adverse opinion or disclaims an opinion.

3. **Auditor's Responsibility Section**

   a. **Indicate the Type of Opinion for a Qualified or an Adverse Opinion in Last Paragraph of Auditor's Responsibility Section** This is the last paragraph of the auditor's responsibility section for an *un*modified opinion: "We believe that the audit evidence we have obtained is sufficient and appropriate to provide a basis for our audit opinion." When the auditor expresses a qualified or adverse opinion the type of opinion is added to this statement as shown below.

      (1) **Change Required for a Qualified Opinion Shown in Boldface** "We believe that the audit evidence we have obtained is sufficient and appropriate to provide a basis for our **qualified** audit opinion."

      (2) **Change Required for a Adverse Opinion Shown in Boldface** "We believe that the audit evidence we have obtained is sufficient and appropriate to provide a basis for our **adverse** audit opinion."

   b. **Auditor's Responsibility Section Is Reduced to 1 Paragraph for a Disclaimer of Opinion** The description of the auditor's responsibility and the description of the scope of the audit should state only the following:

      > Our responsibility is to express an opinion on these financial statements based on conducting the audit in accordance with auditing standards generally accepted in the United States of America. Because of the matter(s) described in the Basis for Disclaimer of Opinion paragraph, however, we were not able to obtain sufficient appropriate audit evidence to provide a basis for an audit opinion.

4. **A Basis for Modification Paragraph Is Added** In addition to the elements of an audit report with an unmodified opinion, a paragraph should be added that provides a description of the matter giving rise to the modification of the opinion.

   a. **Placement** The auditor should place this paragraph immediately *before* the opinion paragraph.

   b. **Appropriate Heading** The auditor should use a heading that includes *Basis for Qualified Opinion*, *Basis for Adverse Opinion*, or *Basis for Disclaimer of Opinion*, as applicable.

   c. **Content**

      (1) **Specific Amounts** If there is a material misstatement that relates to specific amounts in the financial statements (including quantitative disclosures), a

description and quantification of the financial effects should be included, unless impracticable. If it is not practicable, the auditor should state that is the case.

Editor Note: If such disclosures are made in a note to the financial statements, the basis for modification paragraph may be shortened by referring to it.

(2) **Narrative Disclosures** If there is a material misstatement that relates to narrative disclosures, an explanation of how the disclosures are misstated should be included.

(3) **Omission of Information** If there is a material misstatement that relates to the omission of information required to be presented or disclosed, the auditor should

(a) Discuss the omission with those charged with governance

(b) Describe in the basis for modification paragraph the nature of the omitted information

(c) Include the omitted information, provided that it is practicable to do so and sufficient appropriate audit evidence about it has been obtained

Editor Note: *Practicable*, in this context, means that the information is reasonably obtainable from management's accounts and records and that providing it in the report does not require the auditor to assume the position of a preparer of financial information. For example, the auditor would not be expected to prepare a basic financial statement or segment information and include it in the audit report when management omits such information. It would also not be considered practicable if the omitted information would be unduly voluminous in relation to the audit report.

(4) **Scope Limitation Explanation** If the modification results from an inability to obtain sufficient appropriate audit evidence, the reasons for that inability should be included.

Editor Note: When the auditor modifies the opinion due to scope limitation, it is not appropriate for the scope of the audit to be explained in a note to the financial statements because the description of the audit scope is the responsibility of the auditor and not that of management.

(5) **Other Matters** Even if an adverse opinion or disclaimer of opinion is expressed, a description of any other matters that would have otherwise required a modification to the opinion and their effects should also be included in the basis for modification paragraph.

5. **Opinion Paragraph**

a. **Heading** When the auditor modifies an opinion, a heading that includes *Qualified Opinion, Adverse Opinion*, or *Disclaimer of Opinion*, as applicable, should be used for the opinion paragraph.

b. **Use *Except for* Language for a Qualified Opinion**

(1) **Due to a Material Misstatement** When the auditor expresses a qualified opinion due to a material misstatement, the auditor should state in the opinion paragraph that, in the auditor's opinion, except for the effects of the matter(s) described in the basis for qualified opinion paragraph, the financial statements

are presented fairly, in all material respects, in accordance with the applicable financial reporting framework.

Editor Note: It would not be appropriate to use phrases such as *with the foregoing explanation* or *subject to* in the qualified opinion paragraph because these are not sufficiently clear or forceful. Because accompanying notes are part of the financial statements, wording such as *fairly presented, in all material respects, when read in conjunction with note 1* is likely to be misunderstood and would also not be appropriate.

(2) **Due to a Scope Limitation** When the modification arises from an inability to obtain sufficient appropriate audit evidence, the auditor should use the corresponding phrase "except for the possible effects of the matter(s)..." for the modified opinion. The language used refers to the possible effects of the matter on the financial statements rather than the scope limitation itself which would be unacceptable.

c. **Adverse Opinion Language** When the auditor expresses an adverse opinion, the auditor should state in the opinion paragraph that, in the auditor's opinion, because of the significance of the matter(s) described in the basis for adverse opinion paragraph, the financial statements are not presented fairly in accordance with the applicable financial reporting framework.

d. **Disclaimer of Opinion Language** When the auditor disclaims an opinion due to a scope limitation, the auditor should state in the opinion paragraph that:

(1) Because of the significance of the matter(s) described in the basis for disclaimer of opinion paragraph, the auditor has not been able to obtain sufficient appropriate audit evidence to provide a basis for an audit opinion

(2) Accordingly, the auditor does not express an opinion on the financial statements

6. **Emphasis-of-Matter or Other-Matter Paragraph(s)** Even if the auditor has expressed an adverse opinion or disclaimed an opinion on the financial statements, the auditor should consider the need to describe in an emphasis-of-matter or other-matter paragraph(s) any other matters of which the auditor is aware that would have resulted in additional communications in the audit report on the financial statements that are not modifications of the auditor's opinion.

J. **Communication With Those Charged With Governance**

When the auditor expects to modify the opinion in the audit report, the auditor should communicate with those charged with governance the reasons or circumstances that led to the expected modification and the proposed wording of the modification. This communication serves the following purposes.

1. **Notification** Notice is given to those charged with governance.

2. **Confirmation of Facts** The auditor can either seek the concurrence of those charged with governance regarding the facts of the matter or confirm matters of disagreement with management as such.

3. **Exchange of Information** Those charged with governance have an opportunity, when appropriate, to provide the auditor with further information and explanations.

Exhibit 5 ▸ Changes to Audit Report for Modified Opinions

Reason for Modification	Type of Modified Opinion	Basis of Modification Paragraph Added **Before** Opinion	Modified Opinion Paragraph
Financial statements misstated as to: amount, classification, presentation, or disclosure due to errors (including omissions) & fraud **F/S effect**: Material but **not** pervasive	Qualified *	Heading: *Basis for Qualified Opinion* Describe the departure; Include amount(s), if practicable; if not practicable, so state If disclosure misstated, paragraph should explain how the disclosure is misstated; If related to omission of presentation or disclosure, paragraph should explain nature of omitted information & include it if evidence obtained, if practicable	Heading: *Qualified Opinion* **Modify** opinion: use *except for...* language and refer to the *basis for qualified opinion* paragraph
Financial statements misstated as to: (same as preceding) **F/S effect**: Material **and** pervasive	Adverse *	Heading: *Basis for Adverse Opinion* (same as preceding)	Heading: *Adverse Opinion* **Modify** opinion: use *...because of...not presented fairly...* language and refer to the *basis for adverse opinion* paragraph
Scope limitation **F/S effect**: Material but **not** pervasive	Qualified *	Heading: *Basis for Qualified Opinion* Explain reasons for inability to obtain evidence	Heading: *Qualified Opinion* **Modify** opinion: use *except for the possible effects of the matter...* language and refer to the *basis for qualified opinion* paragraph
Scope limitation **F/S effect**: Material **and** pervasive	Disclaimer of Opinion **	Heading: *Basis for Disclaimer of Opinion* (same as preceding)	Heading: *Disclaimer of Opinion* **Modify** opinion: use *Because of the significance of...not been able...to provide a basis for* language and refer to the *basis for disclaimer of opinion* paragraph State that auditor does not express an opinion
Auditor is **not** independent, but is required by law or regulation to report on F/S	Disclaimer of Opinion **	Heading: *Basis for Disclaimer of Opinion* Auditor not required to nor precluded from providing reasons for lack of independence, but if elects to do so, should include all reasons	Heading: *Disclaimer of Opinion* **Modify** opinion: state specifically that auditor is not independent and disclaim opinion

* For qualified or adverse opinions, the last paragraph of the *Auditor's Responsibility* section is also modified to indicate the type of opinion.

** For a disclaimer of opinion, the introductory paragraph and the entire *Auditor's Responsibility* section are also modified.

Editor Note: For illustrative purposes only, the additions to the "standard" report required by the circumstances described in the following sample reports are underlined and the deletions are shown by strikethrough.

Exhibit 6 ▸ Audit Report on Financial Statements for a Single Year With a Qualified Opinion Due to a Material Misstatement & an Emphasis-of-Matter Paragraph Because There Is an Uncertainty

Independent Auditor's Report

[*Appropriate Addressee*]

We have audited the accompanying financial statements of ABC Company, which comprise the balance sheet as of December 31, 20X1, and the related statements of income, changes in stockholders' equity, and cash flows for the year then ended, and the related notes to the financial statements.

Management's Responsibility for the Financial Statements

Management is responsible for the preparation and fair presentation of these financial statements in accordance with accounting principles generally accepted in the United States of America; this includes the design, implementation, and maintenance of internal control relevant to the preparation and fair presentation of financial statements that are free from material misstatement, whether due to fraud or error.

Auditor's Responsibility

Our responsibility is to express an opinion on these financial statements based on our audit. We conducted our audit in accordance with auditing standards generally accepted in the United States of America. Those standards require that we plan and perform the audit to obtain reasonable assurance about whether the financial statements are free from material misstatement.

An audit involves performing procedures to obtain audit evidence about the amounts and disclosures in the financial statements. The procedures selected depend on the auditor's judgment, including the assessment of the risks of material misstatement of the financial statements, whether due to fraud or error. In making those risk assessments, the auditor considers internal control relevant to the entity's preparation and fair presentation of the financial statements in order to design audit procedures that are appropriate in the circumstances, but not for the purpose of expressing an opinion on the effectiveness of the entity's internal control. Accordingly, we express no such opinion. An audit also includes evaluating the appropriateness of accounting policies used and the reasonableness of significant accounting estimates made by management, as well as evaluating the overall presentation of the financial statements.

We believe that the audit evidence we have obtained is sufficient and appropriate to provide a basis for our qualified audit opinion.

Basis for Qualified Opinion

The Company has stated inventories at cost in the accompanying balance sheet. Accounting principles generally accepted in the United States of America require inventories to be stated at the lower of cost or market. If the Company stated inventories at the lower of cost or market, a write down of $XXX would have been required as of December 31, 20X1. Accordingly, cost of sales would have been increased by $XXX and net income, income taxes, and stockholders' equity would have been reduced by $XXX, $XXX, and $XXX, as of and for the year ended December 31, 20X1, respectively.

Qualified Opinion

In our opinion, except for the effects of the matter described in the Basis for Qualified Opinion paragraph, the financial statements referred to above present fairly, in all material respects, the financial position of ABC Company as of December 31, 20X1, and the results of its operations and its cash flows for the year then ended in accordance with accounting principles generally accepted in the United States of America.

Emphasis of Matter

As discussed in Note X to the financial statements, the Company is a defendant in a lawsuit [*briefly describe the nature of the litigation consistent with the Company's description in the note to the financial statements*]. Our opinion is not modified with respect to this matter.

[*Auditor's signature*]

[*Auditor's city and state*]

[*Date of the audit report*]

Exhibit 7 ▸ Audit Report on Financial Statements for a Single Year With a Qualified Opinion Due to a Scope Limitation

Independent Auditor's Report

[*Appropriate Addressee*]

We have audited the accompanying financial statements of ABC Company, which comprise the balance sheet as of December 31, 20X1, and the related statements of income, changes in stockholders' equity, and cash flows for the year then ended, and the related notes to the financial statements.

Management's Responsibility for the Financial Statements

Management is responsible for the preparation and fair presentation of these financial statements in accordance with accounting principles generally accepted in the United States of America; this includes the design, implementation, and maintenance of internal control relevant to the preparation and fair presentation of financial statements that are free from material misstatement, whether due to fraud or error.

Auditor's Responsibility

Our responsibility is to express an opinion on these financial statements based on our audit. We conducted our audit in accordance with auditing standards generally accepted in the United States of America. Those standards require that we plan and perform the audit to obtain reasonable assurance about whether the financial statements are free from material misstatement.

An audit involves performing procedures to obtain audit evidence about the amounts and disclosures in the financial statements. The procedures selected depend on the auditor's judgment, including the assessment of the risks of material misstatement of the financial statements, whether due to fraud or error. In making those risk assessments, the auditor considers internal control relevant to the entity's preparation and fair presentation of the financial statements in order to design audit procedures that are appropriate in the circumstances, but not for the purpose of expressing an opinion on the effectiveness of the entity's internal control. Accordingly, we express no such opinion. An audit also includes evaluating the appropriateness of accounting policies used and the reasonableness of significant accounting estimates made by management, as well as evaluating the overall presentation of the financial statements.

We believe that the audit evidence we have obtained is sufficient and appropriate to provide a basis for our qualified audit opinion.

Basis for Qualified Opinion

ABC Company's investment in XYZ Company, a foreign affiliate acquired during the year and accounted for under the equity method, is carried at $XXX on the balance sheet at December 31, 20X1, and ABC Company's share of XYZ Company's net income of $XXX is included in ABC Company's net income for the year then ended. We were unable to obtain sufficient appropriate audit evidence about the carrying amount of ABC Company's investment in XYZ Company as of December 31, 20X1, and ABC Company's share of XYZ Company's net income for the year then ended because we were denied access to the financial information, management, and the auditors of XYZ Company. Consequently, we were unable to determine whether any adjustments to these amounts were necessary.

Qualified Opinion

In our opinion, except for the possible effects of the matter described in the Basis for Qualified Opinion paragraph, the financial statements referred to above present fairly, in all material respects, the financial position of ABC Company as of December 31, 20X1, and the results of its operations and its cash flows for the year then ended in accordance with accounting principles generally accepted in the United States of America.

[*Auditor's signature*]

[*Auditor's city and state*]

[*Date of the audit report*]

Exhibit 8 ▶ Audit Report on Consolidated Financial Statements for a Single Year With an Adverse Opinion Due to a Material Misstatement

Independent Auditor's Report

[*Appropriate Addressee*]

We have audited the accompanying consolidated financial statements of ABC Company and its subsidiaries, which comprise the consolidated balance sheet as of December 31, 20X1, and the related consolidated statements of income, changes in stockholders' equity, and cash flows for the year then ended, and the related notes to the financial statements.

Management's Responsibility for the Financial Statements

Management is responsible for the preparation and fair presentation of these consolidated financial statements in accordance with accounting principles generally accepted in the United States of America; this includes the design, implementation, and maintenance of internal control relevant to the preparation and fair presentation of consolidated financial statements that are free from material misstatement, whether due to fraud or error.

Auditor's Responsibility

Our responsibility is to express an opinion on these consolidated financial statements based on our audit. We conducted our audit in accordance with auditing standards generally accepted in the United States of America. Those standards require that we plan and perform the audit to obtain reasonable assurance about whether the consolidated financial statements are free from material misstatement.

An audit involves performing procedures to obtain audit evidence about the amounts and disclosures in the consolidated financial statements. The procedures selected depend on the auditor's judgment, including the assessment of the risks of material misstatement of the consolidated financial statements, whether due to fraud or error. In making those risk assessments, the auditor considers internal control relevant to the entity's preparation and fair presentation of the consolidated financial statements in order to design audit procedures that are appropriate in the circumstances, but not for the purpose of expressing an opinion on the effectiveness of the entity's internal control. Accordingly, we express no such opinion. An audit also includes evaluating the appropriateness of accounting policies used and the reasonableness of significant accounting estimates made by management, as well as evaluating the overall presentation of the consolidated financial statements.

We believe that the audit evidence we have obtained is sufficient and appropriate to provide a basis for our adverse audit opinion.

Basis for Adverse Opinion

As described in Note X, the Company has not consolidated the financial statements of subsidiary XYZ Company that it acquired during 20X1 because it has not yet been able to ascertain the fair values of certain of the subsidiary's material assets and liabilities at the acquisition date. This investment is therefore accounted for on a cost basis by the Company. Under accounting principles generally accepted in the United States of America, the subsidiary should have been consolidated because it is controlled by the Company. Had XYZ Company been consolidated, many elements in the accompanying consolidated financial statements would have been materially affected. The effects on the consolidated financial statements of the failure to consolidate have not been determined.

Adverse Opinion

In our opinion, because of the significance of the matter discussed in the Basis for Adverse Opinion paragraph, the consolidated financial statements referred to above do not present fairly, ~~in all material respects,~~ the financial position of ABC Company and its subsidiaries as of December 31, 20X1, or ~~and~~ the results of their operations or ~~and~~ their cash flows for the year then ended in accordance with accounting principles generally accepted in the United States of America.

[*Auditor's signature*]

[*Auditor's city and state*]

[*Date of the audit report*]

Exhibit 9 ▸ Audit Report on Financial Statements for a Single Year With a Disclaimer of Opinion Due to a Scope Limitation

Independent Auditor's Report

[*Appropriate Addressee*]

We were engaged to audit ~~have audited~~ the accompanying financial statements of ABC Company, which comprise the balance sheet as of December 31, 20X1, and the related statements of income, changes in stockholders' equity, and cash flows for the year then ended, and the related notes to the financial statements.

Management's Responsibility for the Financial Statements

Management is responsible for the preparation and fair presentation of these financial statements in accordance with accounting principles generally accepted in the United States of America; this includes the design, implementation, and maintenance of internal control relevant to the preparation and fair presentation of financial statements that are free from material misstatement, whether due to fraud or error.

Auditor's Responsibility

Our responsibility is to express an opinion on these financial statements based on conducting the audit in accordance with auditing standards generally accepted in the United States of America. Because of the matter described in the Basis for Disclaimer of Opinion paragraph, however, we were not able to obtain sufficient appropriate audit evidence to provide a basis for an audit opinion. ~~our audit. We conducted our audit in accordance with auditing standards generally accepted in the United States of America. Those standards require that we plan and perform the audit to obtain reasonable assurance about whether the consolidated financial statements are free from material misstatement.~~

~~An audit involves performing procedures to obtain audit evidence about the amounts and disclosures in the consolidated financial statements. The procedures selected depend on the auditor's judgment, including the assessment of the risks of material misstatement of the consolidated financial statements, whether due to fraud or error. In making those risk assessments, the auditor considers internal control relevant to the entity's preparation and fair presentation of the consolidated financial statements in order to design audit procedures that are appropriate in the circumstances, but not for the purpose of expressing an opinion on the effectiveness of the entity's internal control. Accordingly, we express no such opinion. An audit also includes evaluating the appropriateness of accounting policies used and the reasonableness of significant accounting estimates made by management, as well as evaluating the overall presentation of the consolidated financial statements~~.

~~We believe that the audit evidence we have obtained is sufficient and appropriate to provide a basis for our audit opinion~~.

Basis for Disclaimer of Opinion

The Company's investment in XYZ Company, a joint venture, is carried at $XXX on the Company's balance sheet, which represents over 90 percent of the Company's net assets as of December 31, 20X1. We were not allowed access to the management and the auditors of XYZ Company. As a result, we were unable to determine whether any adjustments were necessary relating to the Company's proportional share of XYZ Company's assets that it controls jointly, its proportional share of XYZ Company's liabilities for which it is jointly responsible, its proportional share of XYZ Company's income and expenses for the year, and the elements making up the statements of changes in stockholders' equity and cash flows.

Disclaimer of Opinion

Because of the significance of the matter described in the Basis for Disclaimer of Opinion paragraph, we have not been able to obtain sufficient appropriate audit evidence to provide a basis for an audit opinion. Accordingly, we do not express an opinion on these financial statements. ~~In our opinion, the financial statements referred to above present fairly, in all material respects, the financial position of ABC Company as of December 31, 20X1, and the results of its operations and its cash flows for the year then ended in accordance with accounting principles generally accepted in the United States of America~~.

[*Auditor's signature*]

[*Auditor's city and state*]

[*Date of the audit report*]

V. Consistency of Financial Statements (AU 708)

A. Overview

1. **Add Emphasis-of-Matter Paragraph to Audit Report for Changes That Affect Consistency** The auditor should evaluate the consistency of the financial statements between periods, including changes to previously issued financial statements, and add an emphasis-of-matter paragraph to the audit report when the comparability of financial statements between periods has been *materially* affected by either:

   a. A change in accounting principle or

   b. Adjustments to correct a material misstatement in previously issued financial statements, i.e., those financial statements that have been restated for the correction of a misstatement in the respective period

   Editor Note: A material change in financial statement classification and the related disclosure should also be evaluated to determine if it is either a. or b. (See this topic in this section of this chapter.)

2. **Consistency Is Implied in Audit Report** Consistency is implied in the audit report, i.e., if satisfied, the auditor does **not** refer to consistency in the audit report. Even if there has been a change in accounting principle or an adjustment to previously issued financial statements, the auditor need not refer to consistency in the audit report when no material effect on comparability results from the change or adjustment.

B. Scope of the Evaluation of Consistency

The periods included in the auditor's evaluation of consistency depend on the periods covered by the auditor's opinion on the financial statements.

1. **When Opinion Covers Only Current Period** When the opinion covers only the current period, consistency is evaluated by a comparison to only the preceding period, *regardless of whether financial statements for the preceding period are presented*.

   C*urrent period* is defined as the most recent period upon which the auditor is reporting.

2. **When Opinion Covers Two or More Periods** When the opinion covers two or more periods, the auditor should evaluate:

   a. Consistency between the periods covered by the opinion

   b. Consistency of the earliest period covered by the auditor's opinion with the period prior to that, if that prior period is presented

   c. The auditor should evaluate whether the financial statements for the periods being reported upon are consistent with previously *issued* financial statements for the relevant periods.

   Editor Note: When an entity accounts for a change in accounting principle by applying the principle to one or more prior periods that were included in previously issued financial statements, as if that principle had always been used (commonly referred to as *retrospective application*), the financial statements *presented* generally will be consistent. However, in this case, the previous periods' financial statements *presented* will appear different from those same previous periods' financial statements *issued* on which the auditor previously reported. Thus, the standard stipulates that the auditor's evaluation of consistency should encompass previously *issued* financial statements for the relevant periods.

C. Changes in Accounting Principles

1. **Nature of a Change in Accounting Principle** A change in accounting principle may occur when two or more acceptable accounting principles apply or an accounting principle in use becomes unacceptable. Accounting principles are approved and superseded by the designated body for the applicable financial reporting framework (AFRF).

   Additionally the following situations should be evaluated by the auditor as a change in accounting principle.

   a. **Change in Method of Application** A change in the method of applying an accounting principle is also considered a change in accounting principle.

   b. **Change in Accounting Estimate Effected by a Change in Accounting Principle** A change in accounting estimate that is inseparable from the effect of a related change in accounting principle; for example, when a change is made to the method of depreciation of an asset to reflect a change in the estimated future benefit of the asset or the pattern of consumption for those benefits, such a change in accounting may be inseparable from a change in estimate

   c. **Investment Accounted for by Equity Method & Investee Changes Accounting Principle** A change in accounting principle by an investee, if an entity's financial statements contain an investment accounted for by the equity method

      Editor Note: The change must be material to the invest*ing* company's financial statements.

   d. **A Change in Reporting Entity That is *Not* the Result of Transaction or Event** A change in the reporting entity **except** when it is the result of a transaction or event

      (1) **Definition of a Change in Reporting Entity** A change in reporting entity is a change that results in financial statements that, in effect, are those of a different reporting entity.

      (2) **Examples of a Change in Reporting Entity That Require Recognition in Audit Report**

         - Presenting consolidated or combined financial statements in place of financial statements of individual entities
         - Changing specific subsidiaries that make up the group of entities for which consolidated financial statements are presented
         - Changing the entities included in combined financial statements

      (3) **Examples of a Change in Reporting Entity That Do *Not* Require Recognition in Audit Report** A change in reporting entity that results from a transaction or event, such as the creation, cessation, or complete or partial purchase or disposition of a subsidiary or other business unit, does **not** require recognition in the audit report.

         Editor Note: In these instances, the change to the financial statements is due to the occurrence of a transaction or an event; *not* to a change in reporting presentation or method. Recognition in the audit report relating to consistency is limited to consideration of changes in accounting principles (or their method of application) or the correction of misstatements in previously issued financial statements.

2. **Evaluation of a Change in Accounting Principle** The AFRF usually sets forth the method of accounting for the effects of a change in accounting principle and the related disclosures.

   The auditor should evaluate a change in accounting principle to determine whether the:

   a. Effect on the comparability of the financial statements is material

   b. Newly adopted accounting principle is in accordance with the AFRF

   c. Method of accounting for the effect of the change is in accordance with the AFRF

   d. Related disclosures are appropriate and adequate

   e. Entity has justified that the alternative accounting principle is preferable

      As long as the change in accounting principle is made in accordance with the AFRF, sufficient justification for a change in accounting principle is provided by the issuance of an accounting pronouncement that:

      (1) Requires the use of a new accounting principle

      (2) Interprets an existing principle

      (3) Expresses a preference for an accounting principle

      (4) Rejects a specific principle

   Editor Note: If b.–e. of the preceding criteria are *not* met, the auditor should evaluate whether a modified (qualified or adverse) opinion is appropriate. (See the coverage of modified opinions in this chapter.)

D. **Correction of a Material Misstatement in Previously Issued Financial Statements**

1. The audit report should recognize an entity's correction of a material misstatement *regardless of whether it involves the application of an accounting principle*.

2. *A change from an accounting principle that is not in accordance with the AFRF to one that is in accordance is **not** a change in accounting principle; it is a correction of a misstatement*.

3. If the related disclosures are not adequate, the auditor should evaluate whether a modified (qualified or adverse) opinion is appropriate.

4. See the coverage in this chapter of subsequently discovered facts for an auditor's responsibilities when adjustments have been made to correct a material misstatement in previously issued financial statements.

E. **Material Change in Financial Statement Classification**
The auditor is required to evaluate a material change in financial statement classification and the related disclosure to determine whether it is a change in accounting principle or a correction of a material misstatement in previously issued financial statements. For example, certain reclassifications, such as reclassifications of debt from long-term to short-term or reclassifications of cash flows from the operating activities category to the financing activities category, might occur because those items were classified incorrectly in the previously issued financial statements. In such situations, the reclassification is also the correction of a misstatement.

Exhibit 10 ▸ Consistency of Financial Statements

Should these changes be recognized in the audit report If they *materially* affect comparability? (by the addition of an emphasis-of-matter paragraph)	**Yes**	**No**
Change in accounting principle or the method of applying it	✓	
Change in accounting principle inseparable from a change in estimate	✓	
Investment accounted for by the equity method; investee makes a change in accounting principle	✓	
Change in reporting entity		
Not resulting from a transaction or event	✓	
Resulting from a transaction or event		✓
Change in accounting estimate		✓
Adjustments to correct a misstatement in previously issued financial statements	✓	
Change in classification if also either a change in accounting principle or the correction of a misstatement in previously issued financial statements	✓	
Change in classification		✓
Change expected to have a material future effect, but no material effect on current financial statements		✓

F. Emphasis-of-Matter Paragraph

This type of paragraph is not a qualification of the audit opinion; hence, the auditor's concurrence with the change in accounting principle or the correction of previously issued financial statements is implied.

1. Change in Accounting Principle

a. Content The emphasis-of-matter paragraph should:

(1) Describe the change

(2) Provide a reference to the entity's disclosure

(3) Indicate that the matter does **not** modify the opinion

Exhibit 11 ▸ Emphasis-of-Matter Paragraph for a Change in Accounting Principle Resulting From the Adoption of a New Accounting Pronouncement

> ***Emphasis of Matter***
>
> As discussed in Note X to the financial statements, in [*insert year(s) of financial statements that reflect the accounting method change*], the entity adopted new accounting guidance [*insert description of new accounting guidance*]. Our opinion is not modified with respect to this matter.

Exhibit 12 ▸ Emphasis-of-Matter Paragraph When the Entity Has Made a Voluntary Change in Accounting Principle

> ***Emphasis of Matter***
>
> As discussed in Note X to the financial statements, the entity has elected to change its method of accounting for [*describe accounting method change*] in [*insert year(s) of financial statements that reflect the accounting method change*]. Our opinion is not modified with respect to this matter.

b. **Criteria for Inclusion in Subsequent Period Audit Reports** The emphasis-of-matter paragraph relating to a change in accounting principle should be included in subsequent audit reports until it is applied in all periods presented. If the change is accounted for by retrospective application to the financial statements of all prior periods presented, the emphasis-of-matter paragraph is only needed in the period of the change.

c. **Recognition in Audit Report *Not* Required If Change *Only Materially Affects the Future*** If a change in accounting principle is not material in the current year, recognition in the audit report is **not** required even if a material effect is expected in later years.

2. **Correction of a Material Misstatement in Previously Issued Financial Statements** An emphasis-of-matter paragraph should be included in the audit report when the related financial statements are restated to correct a prior material misstatement. The paragraph need *not* be repeated in subsequent periods.

The emphasis-of-matter paragraph should include a/an:

a. Statement that the previously issued financial statements have been restated for the correction of a material misstatement in the respective period; this clearly distinguishes it from the reporting of a change in accounting principle

b. Reference to the entity's disclosure of the corrections of the material misstatement

c. Indication that the matter does **not** modify the opinion

Exhibit 13 ▸ Emphasis-of-Matter Paragraph for a Correction of a Material Misstatement in Previously Issued Financial Statements

> ***Emphasis of Matter***
>
> As discussed in Note X to the financial statements, the 20X2 financial statements have been restated to correct a misstatement. Our opinion is not modified with respect to this matter.

VI. Segment Information (AU 501 continued)

Depending on the applicable financial reporting framework (AFRF), the entity may be required or permitted to disclose segment information in the financial statements. The auditor's responsibility regarding the presentation and disclosure of segment information is in relation to the financial statements as a whole. Accordingly, the auditor is **not** required to perform audit procedures that would be necessary to express an opinion on the segment information presented on a stand-alone basis.

A. Objective

The objective of the auditor is to obtain sufficient appropriate audit evidence regarding the presentation and disclosure of segment information, in accordance with the AFRF.

B. Procedures

The auditor should obtain sufficient appropriate audit evidence regarding the presentation and disclosure of segment information, in accordance with the AFRF, by:

1. Obtaining an understanding of the methods used by management in determining segment information

   a. Evaluating whether such methods are likely to result in disclosure in accordance with the AFRF

   b. Testing the application of such methods, when appropriate

   Depending on the circumstances, examples of matters that *may* be relevant when obtaining an understanding of the methods used by management in determining segment information and evaluating whether such methods are likely to result in disclosure in accordance with the AFRF include:

   - Sales, transfers, and charges between segments and elimination of intersegment amounts
   - Comparisons with budgets and other expected results, for example, operating profits as a percentage of sales
   - The allocation of assets and costs among segments
   - Consistency with prior periods and the adequacy of the disclosures with respect to inconsistencies
   - Management's process for identifying those segments that require disclosure in accordance with the entity's financial reporting framework

2. Performing analytical procedures or other audit procedures appropriate in the circumstances

VII. Reports on Comparative Financial Statements (AU 700 continued & 560)

Comparative financial statements may be required by the applicable financial reporting framework (AFRF) or management may elect to provide them.

A. Definitions

1. **Comparative Financial Statements** A complete set of financial statements for one or more prior periods included for comparison with the financial statements of the current period

2. **Comparative Information** Prior period information presented for purposes of comparison with current period amounts or disclosures that is not in the form of a complete set of financial statements; comparative information includes prior period information presented as condensed financial statements or summarized financial information

3. **Condensed Financial Statements** Historical financial information that is presented in less detail than a complete set of financial statements, in accordance with an appropriate financial reporting framework; condensed financial statements may be separately presented as unaudited financial information or may be presented as comparative information

B. Procedures

The auditor should perform the following procedures if comparative financial statements or comparative information is presented for the prior period(s).

1. **In Accordance With AFRF** The auditor should determine whether the comparative financial statements or comparative information has been presented in accordance with the relevant requirements, if any, of the AFRF.

2. **Continuing Auditor**

   a. **Agree Comparative Statements or Information to Prior Presentation** The auditor should evaluate whether the comparative financial statements or information agree with the amounts and other disclosures presented in the prior period or, when appropriate, has been restated for the correction of a material misstatement or adjusted for the retrospective application of an accounting principle.

   b. **Evaluate the Consistency of Accounting Policies** The auditor should evaluate whether the accounting policies reflected in the comparative financial statements or information are consistent with those applied in the current period or if there have been changes in accounting policies, whether those changes have been properly accounted for and adequately presented and disclosed.

   c. **Perform Additional Procedures If Possible Material Misstatement Discovered** If the auditor becomes aware of a possible material misstatement in the comparative financial statements or information while performing the current period audit, the auditor should perform additional procedures. If the auditor audited the prior period financial statements and becomes aware of a material misstatement in those financial statements, the auditor should also follow the relevant requirements of AU 560, *Subsequent Events and Subsequently Discovered Facts*. If the prior period financial statements are restated, the auditor should determine that the comparative financial statements or information agree with the restated financial statements.

   d. **Written Representations** The auditor should request written representations from management for all periods referred to in the auditor's opinion. The auditor should also obtain a specific written representation regarding any restatement made to correct a material misstatement in a prior period that affects the comparative financial statements.

3. **Predecessor Auditor Whose Report Will Be Reissued (AU 560 continued)** Before reissuing an audit report on financial statements that are to be presented on a comparative basis with audited financial statements of a subsequent period, the predecessor should perform the following procedures to determine whether the previously issued audit report is still appropriate. (A predecessor auditor is *not* required to reissue an audit report.)

   a. **Agree Comparative Statements to Prior Presentation** Read the financial statements of the subsequent period to be presented on a comparative basis and compare them to the prior period financial statements that the predecessor auditor reported on

   b. **Request Written Representations From Management** Request written management representations, at or near the date of reissuance, about whether:

      (1) Any information has come to their attention that would cause them to believe that any of the previous representations should be modified

      (2) Any events have occurred subsequent to the date of the latest prior period financial statements reported on by the predecessor that would require adjustment to, or disclosure in, those financial statements

   c. **Obtain Representation Letter From Successor Auditor** Obtain a representation letter from the successor auditor stating whether the successor's audit revealed any matters that might have a material effect on, or require disclosure in, the financial statements reported on by the predecessor

   d. **Follow Procedures for Subsequently Discovered Facts If Applicable** See the coverage of subsequently discovered facts in this chapter for procedures required if any such facts become known to the predecessor auditor as a result of performing the preceding procedures.

C. General Reporting Requirements

1. **Audit Report Should Refer to Each Period Presented & Covered by Opinion** When comparative financial statements are presented, the audit report should refer to each period for which financial statements are presented and on which an audit opinion is expressed.

2. **Level of Information for Prior Periods Should Be Comparable to Current Period** The level of information included for the prior periods in comparative financial statements should be comparable with that of the financial statements of the current period.

3. **Comparative Information**

   a. **Comparative Information Presented *Not* Covered by Audit Opinion** If comparative information is presented but not covered by the auditor's opinion, the auditor should clearly indicate in the audit report the character of the auditor's work, if any, and the degree of responsibility the auditor is taking.

   b. **Comparative Information Presented & Entity Requests Auditor to Express Opinion on All Periods Presented** If comparative information is presented and the entity requests the auditor to express an opinion on all periods presented, the auditor should consider whether the information included for the prior period(s) contains sufficient detail to constitute a fair presentation in accordance with the AFRF.

   Editor Note: The guidance in AU 930, *Interim Financial Information*, may be adapted to report on condensed financial statements or prior period summarized financial information that is derived from audited financial statements and is presented comparatively with the complete set of financial statements of the current period. (See this topic in chapter 12 of this text.)

Exhibit 14 ▸ Audit Report on a Single Year When Comparative Summarized Financial Information Derived From Audited Financial Statements for Prior Year Is Presented

Independent Auditor's Report

[*Appropriate Addressee*]

We have audited the accompanying financial statements of XYZ Not-for-Profit Organization, which comprise the statement of financial position as of September 30, 20X1, and the related statements of activities and cash flows for the year then ended, and the related notes to the financial statements.

Management's Responsibility for the Financial Statements

Management is responsible for the preparation and fair presentation of these financial statements in accordance with accounting principles generally accepted in the United States of America; this includes the design, implementation, and maintenance of internal control relevant to the preparation and fair presentation of financial statements that are free from material misstatement, whether due to fraud or error.

Auditor's Responsibility

Our responsibility is to express an opinion on these financial statements based on our audit. We conducted our audit in accordance with auditing standards generally accepted in the United States of America. Those standards require that we plan and perform the audit to obtain reasonable assurance about whether the financial statements are free from material misstatement.

An audit involves performing procedures to obtain audit evidence about the amounts and disclosures in the financial statements. The procedures selected depend on the auditor's judgment, including the assessment of the risks of material misstatement of the financial statements, whether due to fraud or error. In making those risk assessments, the auditor considers internal control relevant to the entity's preparation and fair presentation of the financial statements in order to design audit procedures that are appropriate in the circumstances, but not for the purpose of expressing an opinion on the effectiveness of the entity's internal control. Accordingly, we express no such opinion. An audit also includes evaluating the appropriateness of accounting policies used and the reasonableness of significant accounting estimates made by management, as well as evaluating the overall presentation of the financial statements.

We believe that the audit evidence we have obtained is sufficient and appropriate to provide a basis for our audit opinion.

Opinion

In our opinion, the financial statements referred to above present fairly, in all material respects, the financial position of ABC Company as of December 31, 20X1, and the results of its operations and its cash flows for the year then ended in accordance with accounting principles generally accepted in the United States of America.

Report on Summarized Comparative Information

We have previously audited the XYZ Not-for-Profit Organization's 20X0 financial statements, and we expressed an unmodified audit opinion on those audited financial statements in our report dated December 15, 20X0. In our opinion, the summarized comparative information presented herein as of and for the year ended September 30, 20X0, is consistent, in all material respects, with the audited financial statements from which it has been derived.

[*Auditor's signature*]

[*Auditor's city and state*]

[*Date of the audit report*]

Exhibit 15 ▸ *Report on Summarized Comparative Information* Paragraph in Audit Report on a Single Year When Comparative Summarized Financial Information Derived From *Un*audited Financial Statements for Prior Year Is Presented

> ***Report on Summarized Comparative Information***
>
> The summarized comparative information presented herein as of and for the year ended September 30, 20X0, derived from those unaudited financial statements, has not been audited, reviewed, or compiled and, accordingly, we express no opinion on it.

D. **Reporting by Continuing Auditor**

1. **Update Audit Report on Prior Periods Presented** When expressing an opinion on all periods presented, a continuing auditor should update the report on the financial statements of one or more prior periods presented on a comparative basis.

   a. **Report Dated as of Current Audit** The audit report on comparative financial statements should not be dated earlier than the date on which the auditor has obtained sufficient appropriate audit evidence on which to support the opinion for the most recent audit.

   b. **Current Audit Information Considered** When issuing an updated report, the information considered by the continuing auditor is that which the auditor has become aware of during the audit of the current period financial statements.

2. **Auditor Can Express Different Opinions on Different Periods** Because the audit report on comparative financial statements applies to the financial statements for each of the periods presented, the auditor may express a qualified opinion or an adverse opinion, disclaim an opinion, or include an emphasis-of-matter paragraph with respect to one or more financial statements for one or more periods while expressing a different opinion on one or more financial statements of another period presented. (An illustration of this type of report is included in this section of this chapter.)

3. **Change of Opinion on Prior Period Financial Statements** When reporting on prior period financial statements in connection with the current period audit, if the auditor's opinion on such prior period financial statements differs from the opinion the auditor previously expressed, the auditor should disclose the following matters in an emphasis-of-matter or other-matter paragraph.

   a. The date of the auditor's previous report

   b. The type of opinion previously expressed

   c. The substantive reasons for the different opinion

   d. That the auditor's opinion on the amended financial statements is different from the auditor's previous opinion

   Editor Note: In some circumstances, the auditor may have additional reporting responsibilities designed to prevent future reliance on the auditor's previously issued report on the prior period financial statements. See the coverage of subsequent events and subsequently discovered facts in this chapter.

Editor Note: An updated report is issued in conjunction with the audit report on the current period financial statements. Depending on the circumstances, the continuing auditor will either re-express the previous opinion or express a different opinion on the prior period statements as of the date of the current report. The next two sample audit reports illustrate how the auditor updates the previous opinion by re-expressing it, followed by a report that illustrates when the auditor's opinion differs from the one the auditor previously expressed.

Exhibit 16 ▶ Audit Report on Consolidated Comparative Financial Statements With an Unmodified Opinion

Independent Auditor's Report

[*Appropriate Addressee*]

We have audited the accompanying consolidated financial statements of ABC Company and its subsidiaries, which comprise the consolidated balance sheets as of December 31, 20X1 and 20X0, and the related consolidated statements of income, changes in stockholders' equity, and cash flows for the years then ended, and the related notes to the financial statements.

Management's Responsibility for the Financial Statements

Management is responsible for the preparation and fair presentation of these consolidated financial statements in accordance with accounting principles generally accepted in the United States of America; this includes the design, implementation, and maintenance of internal control relevant to the preparation and fair presentation of consolidated financial statements that are free from material misstatement, whether due to fraud or error.

Auditor's Responsibility

Our responsibility is to express an opinion on these consolidated financial statements based on our audits. We conducted our audits in accordance with auditing standards generally accepted in the United States of America. Those standards require that we plan and perform the audit to obtain reasonable assurance about whether the consolidated financial statements are free from material misstatement.

An audit involves performing procedures to obtain audit evidence about the amounts and disclosures in the consolidated financial statements. The procedures selected depend on the auditor's judgment, including the assessment of the risks of material misstatement of the consolidated financial statements, whether due to fraud or error. In making those risk assessments, the auditor considers internal control relevant to the entity's preparation and fair presentation of the consolidated financial statements in order to design audit procedures that are appropriate in the circumstances, but not for the purpose of expressing an opinion on the effectiveness of the entity's internal control. Accordingly, we express no such opinion. An audit also includes evaluating the appropriateness of accounting policies used and the reasonableness of significant accounting estimates made by management, as well as evaluating the overall presentation of the consolidated financial statements.

We believe that the audit evidence we have obtained is sufficient and appropriate to provide a basis for our audit opinion.

Opinion

In our opinion, the consolidated financial statements referred to above present fairly, in all material respects, the financial position of ABC Company and its subsidiaries as of December 31, 20X1 and 20X0, and the results of their operations and their cash flows for the years then ended in accordance with accounting principles generally accepted in the United States of America.

[*Auditor's signature*]

[*Auditor's city and state*]

[*Date of the audit report*]

Editor Note: The changes to the "standard" report required by circumstances described are underlined for illustrative purposes only. All of the changes are additions, i.e., nothing is omitted from the "standard" report.

Exhibit 17 ▸ Audit Report on Comparative Financial Statements With Qualified Opinion on Current Year & Unmodified Opinion on Prior Year

Independent Auditor's Report

[*Appropriate Addressee*]

We have audited the accompanying financial statements of ABC Company, which comprise the balance sheets as of December 31, 20X1 and 20X0, and the related statements of income, changes in stockholders' equity, and cash flows for the years then ended, and the related notes to the financial statements.

Management's Responsibility for the Financial Statements

Management is responsible for the preparation and fair presentation of these financial statements in accordance with accounting principles generally accepted in the United States of America; this includes the design, implementation, and maintenance of internal control relevant to the preparation and fair presentation of financial statements that are free from material misstatement, whether due to fraud or error.

Auditor's Responsibility

Our responsibility is to express an opinion on these financial statements based on our audits. We conducted our audits in accordance with auditing standards generally accepted in the United States of America. Those standards require that we plan and perform the audit to obtain reasonable assurance about whether the financial statements are free from material misstatement.

An audit involves performing procedures to obtain audit evidence about the amounts and disclosures in the financial statements. The procedures selected depend on the auditor's judgment, including the assessment of the risks of material misstatement of the financial statements, whether due to fraud or error. In making those risk assessments, the auditor considers internal control relevant to the entity's preparation and fair presentation of the financial statements in order to design audit procedures that are appropriate in the circumstances, but not for the purpose of expressing an opinion on the effectiveness of the entity's internal control. Accordingly, we express no such opinion. An audit also includes evaluating the appropriateness of accounting policies used and the reasonableness of significant accounting estimates made by management, as well as evaluating the overall presentation of the financial statements.

We believe that the audit evidence we have obtained is sufficient and appropriate to provide a basis for our qualified audit opinion.

Basis for Qualified Opinion

The Company has excluded, from property and debt in the accompanying 20X1 balance sheet, certain lease obligations that were entered into in 20X1 which, in our opinion, should be capitalized in accordance with accounting principles generally accepted in the United States of America. If these lease obligations were capitalized, property would be increased by $XXX, long-term debt by $XXX, and retained earnings by $XXX as of December 31, 20X1, and net income and earnings per share would be increased (decreased) by $XXX and $XXX, respectively, for the year then ended.

Qualified Opinion

In our opinion, except for the effects on the 20X1 financial statements of not capitalizing certain lease obligations as described in the Basis for Qualified Opinion paragraph, the financial statements referred to above present fairly, in all material respects, the financial position of ABC Company as of December 31, 20X1 and 20X0, and the results of its operations and its cash flows for the years then ended in accordance with accounting principles generally accepted in the United States of America.

[*Auditor's signature*]

[*Auditor's city and state*]

[*Date of the audit report*]

Exhibit 18 ▶ Audit Report With Other-Matter Paragraph That May Be Appropriate When an Auditor Issues Updated Report on Financial Statements of Prior Period That Contains an Opinion Different From Opinion Previously Expressed

Independent Auditor's Report

[*Appropriate Addressee*]

We have audited the accompanying financial statements of ABC Company, which comprise the balance sheets as of December 31, 20X1 and 20X0, and the related statements of income, changes in stockholders' equity, and cash flows for the years then ended, and the related notes to the financial statements.

Management's Responsibility for the Financial Statements

Management is responsible for the preparation and fair presentation of these financial statements in accordance with accounting principles generally accepted in the United States of America; this includes the design, implementation, and maintenance of internal control relevant to the preparation and fair presentation of financial statements that are free from material misstatement, whether due to fraud or error.

Auditor's Responsibility

Our responsibility is to express an opinion on these financial statements based on our audits. We conducted our audits in accordance with auditing standards generally accepted in the United States of America. Those standards require that we plan and perform the audit to obtain reasonable assurance about whether the financial statements are free from material misstatement.

An audit involves performing procedures to obtain audit evidence about the amounts and disclosures in the financial statements. The procedures selected depend on the auditor's judgment, including the assessment of the risks of material misstatement of the financial statements, whether due to fraud or error. In making those risk assessments, the auditor considers internal control relevant to the entity's preparation and fair presentation of the financial statements in order to design audit procedures that are appropriate in the circumstances, but not for the purpose of expressing an opinion on the effectiveness of the entity's internal control. Accordingly, we express no such opinion. An audit also includes evaluating the appropriateness of accounting policies used and the reasonableness of significant accounting estimates made by management, as well as evaluating the overall presentation of the financial statements.

We believe that the audit evidence that we have obtained is sufficient and appropriate to provide a basis for our audit opinion.

Opinion

In our opinion, the financial statements referred to above present fairly, in all material respects, the financial position of ABC Company as of December 31, 20X1 and 20X0, and the results of its operations and its cash flows for the years then ended in accordance with accounting principles generally accepted in the United States of America.

Other Matter

In our report dated March 1, 20X1, we expressed an opinion that the 20X0 financial statements did not fairly present the financial position, results of operations, and cash flows of ABC Company in accordance with accounting principles generally accepted in the United States of America because of two departures from such principles: (1) ABC Company carried its property, plant, and equipment at appraisal values, and provided for depreciation on the basis of such values, and (2) ABC Company did not provide for deferred income taxes with respect to differences between income for financial reporting purposes and taxable income. As described in Note X, the Company has changed its method of accounting for these items and restated its 20X0 financial statements to conform with accounting principles generally accepted in the United States of America. Accordingly, our present opinion on the restated 20X0 financial statements, as presented herein, is different from that expressed in our previous report.

[*Auditor's signature*]

[*Auditor's city and state*]

[*Date of the audit report*]

E. Reporting by Successor Auditor

1. Predecessor's Report *Not* Reissued

a. **Prior Period Financial Statements *Not* Restated** If the financial statements of the prior period were audited by a predecessor auditor, and the predecessor's audit report is not reissued, in addition to expressing an opinion on the current period financial statements, the auditor should state the following in an other-matter paragraph:

(1) That the financial statements of the prior period were audited by a predecessor auditor

(2) The type of opinion expressed by the predecessor auditor and, if the opinion was modified, the reasons

(3) The nature of an emphasis-of-matter paragraph or other-matter paragraph included in the predecessor audit report, if any

(4) The date of that report

b. **Prior Period Financial Statements Restated** The predecessor auditor may be unable or unwilling to reissue the audit report on the prior period financial statements that have been restated. In this situation, provided that the auditor has audited the adjustments to the prior period financial statements, the auditor may include an other-matter paragraph indicating that the predecessor auditor reported on the financial statements of the prior period before restatement. In addition, if the auditor is engaged to audit and obtains sufficient appropriate audit evidence to be satisfied about the appropriateness of the restatement, the audit report may also include the following paragraph *within* the other-matter paragraph section:

> As part of our audit of the 20X2 financial statements, we also audited the adjustments described in Note X that were applied to restate the 20X1 financial statements. In our opinion, such adjustments are appropriate and have been properly applied. We were not engaged to audit, review, or apply any procedures to the 20X1 financial statements of the Company other than with respect to the adjustments and, accordingly, we do not express an opinion or any other form of assurance on the 20X1 financial statements as a whole.

2. Predecessor's Report Reissued

a. **Prior Period Financial Statements *Not* Restated** Before the report can be reissued, a predecessor auditor (who is requested to reissue an audit report on financial statements that are to be presented on a comparative basis with audited financial statements of a subsequent period) should perform specified procedures to determine whether the previously issued audit report is still appropriate. (See the coverage in this section on procedures for a predecessor auditor who reissues such a report.)

b. **Prior Period Financial Statements Restated** An auditor may conclude that a material misstatement exists that affects the prior period financial statements on which the predecessor auditor had previously reported without modification. In this situation, if the prior period financial statements are restated, and the predecessor agrees to reissue the audit report, the auditor should express an opinion only on the current period.

F. Reporting When Prior Period Statements *Not* Audited

1. **Prior Period Financial Statements Reviewed or Compiled** When current period financial statements are audited and presented in comparative form with compiled or reviewed financial statements for the prior period, *and the report on the prior period is not reissued*, the auditor should include an other-matter paragraph in the current period audit report that includes the following.

   a. The service performed in the prior period

   b. The date of the report on that service

   c. A description of any material modifications noted in that report

   d. A statement that the service was less in scope than an audit and does not provide the basis for the expression of an opinion on the financial statements

   Exhibit 19 ▶ Other-Matter Paragraph If Prior Period Financial Statements Were Reviewed

   Other Matter

   The 20X1 financial statements were reviewed by us (other accountants) and our (their) report thereon, dated March 1, 20X2, stated we (they) were not aware of any material modifications that should be made to those statements for them to be in conformity with accounting principles generally accepted in the United States of America. However, a review is substantially less in scope than an audit and does not provide a basis for the expression of an opinion on the financial statements.

   Exhibit 20 ▶ Other-Matter Paragraph If Prior Period Financial Statements Were Compiled

   Other Matter

   The 20X1 financial statements were compiled by us (other accountants) and our (their) report thereon, dated March 1, 20X2, stated we (they) did not audit or review those financial statements and, accordingly, express no opinion or other form of assurance on them.

2. **Prior Period Financial Statements *Not* Audited, Reviewed or Compiled** If the prior period financial statements were not audited, reviewed, or compiled, the financial statements should be clearly marked to indicate their status, and the audit report should include an other-matter paragraph to indicate that the auditor has not audited, reviewed, or compiled the prior period financial statements and assumes no responsibility for them.

   Exhibit 21 ▶ Other-Matter Paragraph If Prior Period Financial Statements Were *Not* Audited, Reviewed or Compiled

   Other Matter

   The accompanying balance sheet of X Company as of December 31, 20X1, and the related statements of income and cash flows for the year then ended were not audited, reviewed, or compiled by us and, accordingly, we do not express an opinion or any other form of assurance on them.

VIII. Subsequent Events & Subsequently Discovered Facts and Omitted Procedures

A. Subsequent Events & Subsequently Discovered Facts (AU 560 continued)

1. **Overview** This standard addresses:

   a. **Subsequent Events** The auditor's responsibilities to obtain sufficient appropriate audit evidence about whether subsequent events occurring between the date of the financial statements and the date of the audit report that require adjustment of, or disclosure in, the financial statements are reflected in accordance with the applicable financial reporting framework (AFRF)

   b. **Subsequently Discovered Facts** The auditor's responsibilities to respond appropriately to subsequently discovered facts that become known to the auditor after the date of the audit report that, had they been known to the auditor at that date, may have caused the auditor to revise the audit report

   c. **Audit Report Reissued by Predecessor Auditor** The responsibilities of a predecessor auditor who is requested to reissue an audit report on financial statements that are to be presented on a comparative basis with audited financial statements of a subsequent period to perform specified procedures to determine whether the previously issued audit report is still appropriate

   Editor Note: Coverage of the procedures the predecessor auditor is required to perform before reissuing an audit report is included in this chapter in the section on comparative financial statements. Note that these are only required procedures if the predecessor agrees to reissue the report; reissuing the report is *not* a requirement.

   Financial statements may be affected by certain events that occur after the date of the financial statements. Most financial reporting frameworks identify two types of such subsequent events. Those that provide evidence of conditions that:

   - Existed at the date of the financial statements
   - Arose after the date of the financial statements

   The date of the audit report informs the users of the audit report that the auditor has considered the effect of events and transactions of which the auditor becomes aware and that occurred up to that date.

   Subsequently discovered facts can be discovered either before (1st scenario, exhibit 22) or after the date of the release of the audit report (2nd scenario, exhibit 22). In both cases, if the financial statements are revised, the guidance provided related to their revision is the same.

   If the audit report has been released (2nd scenario, exhibit 22) additional guidance is provided regarding:

   - The notification (by management, or failing that, by the auditor) of third parties in receipt of the financial statements
   - When the audit opinion on the revised statements differs from the one previously expressed in the released report

Exhibit 22▸ Timetable for Subsequent Events & Subsequently Discovered Facts

Date of Financial Statements	*Subsequent Events*	**Date of Audit Report**	*1st Scenario: Subsequently Discovered Facts*	**Date of Audit Report Release**	*2nd Scenario: Subsequently Discovered Facts*

2. **Definitions**

   a. **Date of Financial Statements** The date of the end of the latest period covered by the financial statements

   b. **Date of Audit Report** The date of the audit report on the financial statements

   c. **Subsequent Events** Events occurring between the date of the financial statements and the date of the audit report

   d. **Subsequently Discovered Facts** Facts that become known to the auditor after the date of the audit report that, had they been known to the auditor at that date, may have caused the auditor to revise the report

3. **Procedures to Identify Subsequent Events**

   a. **Period Covered** The procedures should cover the period from the date of the financial statements to the date of the audit report (or as near to that as practicable).

   b. **Nature & Extent of Procedures** The nature and extent of the procedures performed should be based on the auditor's risk assessment.

   These procedures are in addition to those performed for other purposes that, nevertheless, may provide evidence about subsequent events. For example, procedures to obtain audit evidence for account balances as of the date of the financial statements, such as cut-off procedures or procedures regarding subsequent receipts of accounts receivable; inquiries of legal counsel; or procedures related to management representations about subsequent events.

   Additional procedures are *not* required for matters for which previous procedures provided satisfactory conclusions. However, if new information is inconsistent with the audit evidence obtained, the auditor is required to resolve the matter and consider its effect, if any, on other aspects of the audit.

   c. **Required Procedures** The procedures for the subsequent period should be designed to obtain sufficient appropriate audit evidence that all subsequent events that require adjustment of, or disclosure in, the financial statements have been identified. They should include:

      (1) Obtaining an understanding of any procedures that management has established to ensure that subsequent events are identified

      (2) Reading minutes, if any, of the meetings of the entity's owners, management, and those charged with governance that have been held after the date of the financial statements and inquiring about matters discussed at any such meetings for which minutes are not yet available

      (3) Reading the entity's latest subsequent interim financial statements, if any

(4) Inquiring of management and, when appropriate, those charged with governance about whether any subsequent events have occurred that might affect the financial statements

For example, this *may* include inquiring about the current status of items that were accounted for on the basis of preliminary or inconclusive data, for example, whether:

- New commitments, borrowings, or guarantees have been entered into
- Sales or acquisitions of assets have occurred or are planned
- There have been increases in capital or issuance of debt instruments, such as the issue of new shares or debentures, or an agreement to merge or liquidate has been made or is planned
- Any assets have been appropriated by the government or destroyed, for example, by fire or flood
- There have been any developments regarding contingencies
- Any unusual accounting adjustments have been made or are contemplated
- Any events have occurred or are likely to occur that will bring into question the appropriateness of accounting policies used in the financial statements, as would be the case, for example, if such events call into question the validity of the going concern assumption
- Any events have occurred that are relevant to the measurement of estimates or provisions made in the financial statements
- Any events have occurred that are relevant to the recoverability of assets

4. **Determine Whether Identified Subsequent Events Handled in Accordance With AFRF** If the auditor identifies subsequent events that require adjustment of, or disclosure in, the financial statements, the auditor should determine whether each such event is appropriately reflected in the financial statements in accordance with the AFRF.

Editor Note: The following guidance is also applicable when a subsequently discovered fact becomes known to a predecessor auditor when the predecessor is performing procedures required before reissuing a report on financial statements that are to be presented on a comparative basis with audited financial statements of a subsequent period.

5. **Procedures Required When Subsequently Discovered Facts Become Known *Before or After* Audit Report Is Released** The auditor is **not** required to perform any audit procedures regarding the financial statements after the date of the audit report*; however, if a subsequently discovered fact becomes known to the auditor before or after the report release date, the auditor should:

- Discuss the matter with management and, when appropriate, those charged with governance
- Determine whether the financial statements need revision and, if so, inquire how management intends to address the matter in the financial statements

  Editor Note: In determining whether the financial statements need revision, the auditor may consider, in addition to the requirements of the AFRF, whether there are persons currently relying or likely to rely on the financial statements who would attach importance to the subsequently discovered facts. Consideration may also be given to the issuance of audited financial statements for a subsequent period, the time elapsed since the financial statements were issued and the audit report was released, and any legal implications.

* Editor Note: The exception to this is legal or regulatory requirements involving offerings of securities to the public when audited financial statements are included, subsequent to their issuance, in other documents.

a. **When Management Revises Financial Statements** The auditor should perform the audit procedures necessary on the revision and then either change the date of the audit report or dual-date the report for the revision.

(1) **If Audit Report Date Is Changed to a Later Date (to include revision)**

(a) Extend the auditing procedures for subsequent events to the new date of the audit report on the revised financial statements

(b) Request management representations as of the new date

(2) **If Audit Report Is Dual Dated**

(a) Additional procedures subsequent to the original date of audit report are limited solely to the specific event described in the relevant note to the financial statements

(b) Request management representations as of the later date about whether any:

(i) Information has come to their attention that would cause them to believe that any of their previous representations should be modified

(ii) Other events have occurred subsequent to the date of the financial statements that would require adjustment to, or disclosure in, those financial statements

b. **When Management Does *Not* Revise Financial Statements & Audit Report Has *Not* Been Released** If financial statements that should be revised are not, the auditor should, of course, modify the opinion.

6. **Additional Procedures Required When Subsequently Discovered Facts Become Known *After* Audit Report Is Released**

a. **When Management Revises Financial Statements**

(1) **If Original Report Already Made Available to Third Parties**

(a) **When Management Takes Timely Steps to Notify & Prevent Reliance** The auditor should determine that the steps taken by management are timely and appropriate to ensure that anyone in receipt of those financial statements is informed of the situation, including that the audited financial statements are not to be relied upon.

Appropriate steps depend on the circumstances and *may* include the following.

- Notification to anyone who is known to be relying or who is likely to rely on the financial statements and the audit report that they are not to be relied upon and that revised financial statements, together with a new audit report, will be issued. This may be necessary when the issuance of revised financial statements and a new audit report is not imminent.

- Issuing, as soon as practicable, revised financial statements with appropriate disclosure of the matter.
- Issuing the subsequent period financial statements with appropriate disclosure of the matter. This may be appropriate when issuance of the subsequent period audited financial statements is imminent.

(b) **Management Does *Not* Appropriately Notify Third Parties** The following procedures are applicable whether or not management agrees to revise the financial statements. (Guidance when management does not agree to revise the statements follows.)

(i) **Warning** If management does not take the necessary steps to ensure that anyone in receipt of the financial statements and audit report is informed of the situation, the auditor should notify management and those charged with governance that the auditor will seek to prevent future reliance on the audit report.

(ii) **Warning *Not* Heeded** If, despite such notification, management or those charged with governance still do not take the necessary steps, the auditor should take appropriate action to seek to prevent reliance on the audit report. The auditor *may* consider it appropriate to seek legal advice.

In addition to seeking legal advice, the auditor *may* consider taking the following steps to the extent applicable:

- Notify regulatory agencies having jurisdiction over the entity that the audit report is not to be relied upon, including a request that the agency take whatever steps it may deem appropriate to accomplish the necessary disclosure.
- Notify anyone known to the auditor to be relying on the financial statements that the auditor's report is not to be relied upon. In some instances, it will not be practicable for the auditor to give appropriate individual notification to stockholders or investors at large whose identities are unknown to the auditor; notification to a regulatory agency having jurisdiction over the entity will usually be the only practical means for the auditor to provide appropriate disclosure, together with a request that the agency take whatever steps it may deem appropriate to accomplish the necessary disclosure.

Depending on the circumstances, if the auditor is able to determine that the financial statements need revision, the auditor's notification to anyone in receipt of the audited financial statements *may* (if permitted by law, regulation, and relevant ethical requirements):

- Include a description of the nature of the matter and of its effect on the financial statements, avoiding comments concerning the conduct or motives of any person

- Describe the effect that the matter would have had on the audit report if it had been known to the auditor at the date of the report and had not been reflected in the financial statements

If the auditor was not able to determine whether the financial statements need revision, the notification to anyone in receipt of the audited financial statements may indicate that information became known to the auditor and that, if the information is true, the auditor believes that the audit report is not to be relied upon. The specific matter need not be detailed in the notification.

(2) **When Opinion on Revised Financial Statements Differs from Original Opinion** If the auditor's opinion on the revised financial statements differs from the opinion the auditor previously expressed, the auditor should disclose the following matters in an emphasis-of-matter or other-matter paragraph.

(a) Date of previous report

(b) Type of opinion previously expressed

(c) Substantive reasons for the different opinion

(d) That the opinion on the revised financial statements is different from the previous opinion

b. When Management Does *Not* Revise Financial Statements If financial statements that should be revised are not, then:

(1) **If Original Report Already Made Available to Third Parties** Same as preceding (when management *has* revised the financial statements).

(2) **If Original Report Has *Not* Been Made Available to Third Parties** The auditor should notify management and those charged with governance not to make the audited financial statements available to third parties before the necessary revisions have been made and a new audit report on the revised financial statements has been provided.

B. Consideration of Omitted Procedures After the Report Release Date (AU 585)

1. **Overview** The auditor may become aware, after the report release date, that one or more auditing procedures were omitted. (After the report release date, the auditor has *no* responsibility to carry out any retrospective review of the audit work performed; however, the discovery of an omitted procedure may occur, for example, in connection with a firm's inspection or monitoring processes.

   The period of time during which the auditor considers whether this standard applies to the circumstances of a particular engagement and then takes the actions, if any, that are required may be important.

2. **Definition of Omitted Procedure** An auditing procedure that the auditor considered necessary in the circumstances existing at the time of the audit of the financial statements but which was not performed

3. **Procedures to Assess Effect on Support for Opinion** If, after the report release date, the auditor becomes aware of an omitted procedure, the auditor should assess the effect of the omitted procedure on the auditor's present ability to support the previously expressed opinion and respond appropriately.

The auditor's present ability to support the previously expressed opinion is dependent on whether the omitted procedure affects the auditor's conclusion that sufficient appropriate audit evidence was obtained.

The auditor *may* perform the following procedures to make such an assessment.

- Review the audit documentation
- Discuss the circumstances with engagement personnel and others within the firm
- Reevaluate the overall scope of the audit
- Seek legal advice to determine actions, if any, to take

The results of other audit procedures that were performed may tend to compensate for the omitted procedure or make the effect of its omission less significant. Additionally, subsequent audits may provide audit evidence in support of the previously expressed opinion.

4. **When Support for Opinion Is Impaired & There Is Current Reliance on Report** If the auditor concludes that an omitted procedure impairs the support for the opinion and there are users currently relying, or likely to rely, on the released report, the auditor should:

   a. **When Previously Omitted Procedures Can Be Performed**

      (1) Promptly perform the omitted procedure, or alternative procedures, to determine whether there is a satisfactory basis for the opinion

      (2) Document the procedures performed

      Editor Note: If, as a result of performing the omitted procedure, the auditor becomes aware of facts regarding the financial statements that existed at the report release date that, had they been known to the auditor at that date, may have caused the auditor to revise the audit report, the auditor should, of course, follow US GAAS for that circumstance. (See the section in this chapter on subsequently discovered facts.)

   b. **When Previously Omitted Procedures Can *Not* Be Performed** If unable to perform the omitted procedure or alternative procedures, the auditor *may* decide to consult an attorney to determine an appropriate course of action concerning responsibilities to the entity, regulatory authorities, if any, having jurisdiction, and users relying, or likely to rely, on the audit report.

IX. Consideration of an Entity's Ability to Continue as a Going Concern (AU 570)

A. Overview

1. **Going Concern Assumption** Continuation of an entity as a going concern is assumed in financial reporting in the absence of significant information to the contrary. Ordinarily, information that significantly contradicts the going concern assumption relates to the entity's inability to continue to meet its obligations as they become due without substantial disposition of assets outside the ordinary course of business; restructuring of debt; externally forced revisions of its operations; or similar actions.

2. **Auditor's Responsibility**

   a. **Evaluation of Relevant Conditions or Events** The auditor is responsible for evaluating information gathered during the audit about relevant conditions or events that exist at, or have occurred prior to, the date of the audit report to determine whether there is substantial doubt about the entity's ability to continue as a going concern for a reasonable period of time (hereafter referred to as substantial doubt).

b. **Financial Statements & Audit Report Effect** The auditor should also assess the financial statement effects, including the adequacy of disclosure, and determine the implications for the audit report regarding going concern uncertainties.

c. **Inherent Limitations of Audit** An auditor is not expected to predict future conditions or events. If an entity ceases to exist even within a year of receiving an audit report which does not refer to the auditor having substantial doubt, this does not, in itself, indicate an inadequate performance by the auditor. Likewise, the absence of a reference to substantial doubt should *not* be interpreted as a guarantee of the entity's ability to continue as a going concern.

3. **Definition of Reasonable Period of Time** A period not to exceed one year beyond the date of the financial statements being audited

B. **Procedures**

Based on the results of the audit procedures performed, the auditor should evaluate whether there is substantial doubt.

1. **Identifying Conditions or Events That Indicate Substantial Doubt Could Exist** The auditor should consider whether the results of the procedures performed during the course of the audit identify conditions or events that, when considered in the aggregate, indicate there could be substantial doubt. The auditor should consider the need to obtain additional information about such conditions or events, as well as the appropriate audit evidence to support information that mitigates the auditor's doubt.

Audit procedures do **not** need to be designed specifically to identify conditions or events that may indicate substantial doubt. The results of audit procedures designed and performed to identify and assess risk, gather audit evidence in response to assessed risks, and complete the audit are expected to be sufficient for that purpose. For example:

- Analytical procedures
- Review of subsequent events
- Review of compliance with the terms of debt and loan agreements
- Reading of minutes of meetings of stockholders, board of directors, and important committees of the board
- Inquiry of an entity's legal counsel about litigation, claims, and assessments
- Confirmation with related and third parties of the details of arrangements to provide or maintain financial support

In performing such audit procedures, the auditor may identify information about certain conditions or events that indicate there could be substantial doubt. The significance of these conditions or events depends on the circumstances, and some may only have significance when viewed in conjunction with others. For example:

- **Negative Trends** Recurring operating losses, working capital deficiencies, negative cash flows from operating activities, adverse key financial ratios
- **Other Indications of Possible Financial Difficulties** Default on loan or similar agreements, arrearages in dividends, denial of usual trade credit from suppliers, restructuring of debt, noncompliance with statutory capital requirements, need to seek new sources or methods of financing or to dispose of substantial assets
- **Internal Matters** Work stoppages or other labor difficulties, substantial dependence on the success of a particular project, uneconomic long-term commitments, need to significantly revise operations

- **External Matters That Have Occurred** Legal proceedings, legislation, or similar matters that might jeopardize an entity's ability to operate; loss of a key franchise, license, or patent; loss of a principal customer or supplier; uninsured or underinsured catastrophe such as a drought, earthquake, or flood

2. **Consideration of Management's Plans When There Is Substantial Doubt** If, after considering the identified conditions or events in the aggregate, the auditor believes there is substantial doubt, the auditor should obtain information about management's plans that are intended to mitigate the adverse effects of such conditions or events. The auditor should:

   a. Assess whether it is likely that the adverse effects would be mitigated by management's plans for a reasonable period of time

   b. Identify those elements of management's plans that are particularly significant to overcoming the adverse effects of the conditions or events and plan and perform procedures to obtain audit evidence about them, including, when applicable, considering the adequacy of support regarding the ability to obtain additional financing or the planned disposal of assets

   c. Assess whether it is likely that such plans can be effectively implemented

   d. When prospective financial information is particularly significant to management's plans, the auditor should request management to provide that information and should consider the adequacy of support for significant assumptions underlying that information. The auditor should give particular attention to assumptions that are:

   - Material to the prospective financial information
   - Especially sensitive or susceptible to change
   - Inconsistent with historical trends

   The auditor's consideration should be based on knowledge of the entity, its business, and its management and should include:

   (1) Reading the prospective financial information and the underlying assumptions

   (2) Comparing prospective financial information from prior periods with actual results

   (3) Comparing prospective information for the current period with results achieved to date

If the auditor becomes aware of factors, the effects of which are not reflected in such prospective financial information, the auditor should discuss those factors with management and, if necessary, request revision of the prospective financial information.

Other considerations by the auditor relating to management's plans in general *may* include:

- *Plans to Dispose of Assets*
  - Restrictions on disposal of assets, such as covenants limiting such transactions in loan or similar agreements or encumbrances against assets
  - Apparent marketability of assets that management plans to sell
  - Possible direct or indirect effects of disposal of assets

- *Plans to Borrow Money or Restructure Debt*
    - Availability of debt financing, including existing or committed credit arrangements, such as lines of credit or arrangements for factoring receivables or sale-leaseback of assets
    - Existing or committed arrangements to restructure or subordinate debt or to guarantee loans to the entity
    - Possible effects on management's borrowing plans of existing restrictions on additional borrowing or the sufficiency of available collateral
- *Plans to Reduce or Delay Expenditures*
    - Apparent feasibility of plans to reduce overhead or administrative expenditures, to postpone maintenance or research and development projects, or to lease rather than purchase assets
    - Possible direct or indirect effects of reduced or delayed expenditures
- *Plans to Increase Ownership Equity*
    - Apparent feasibility of plans to increase ownership equity, including existing or committed arrangements to raise additional capital
    - Existing or committed arrangements to reduce current dividend requirements or to accelerate cash distributions from affiliates or other investors

3. **Consideration of Financial Statement Effects**

a. **Consideration of Financial Statement Effects, Including Disclosure, If After Considering Management's Plans There Is Substantial Doubt** When, after considering management's plans, the auditor concludes there is substantial doubt, the auditor should consider the possible effects on the financial statements and the adequacy of the related disclosure.

b. **Consideration of Disclosure If After Considering Management's Plans Substantial Doubt Is Alleviated** When the auditor concludes, primarily because of the auditor's consideration of management's plans, that substantial doubt has been alleviated, the auditor should consider the need for, and evaluate the adequacy of, disclosure of the principal conditions or events that initially caused the auditor to believe there was substantial doubt. The auditor's consideration of disclosure should include the possible effects of such conditions or events, and any mitigating factors, including management's plans.

In considering the adequacy of disclosure, some of the information that might be disclosed includes:

- Principal conditions and events giving rise to the assessment of substantial doubt
- The possible effects of such conditions and events
- Management's evaluation of the significance of those conditions and events and any mitigating factors
- Possible discontinuance of operations
- Management's plans (including relevant prospective financial information)
- Information about the recoverability or classification of recorded asset amounts or the amounts or classification of liabilities

4. **Written Representations** If substantial doubt exists, *before consideration of management's plans*, the auditor should obtain the following written representations from management.

   a. Regarding its plans that are intended to mitigate the adverse effects of conditions or events that indicate there is substantial doubt and the likelihood that those plans can be effectively implemented

   b. That the financial statements disclose all the matters of which management is aware that are relevant to the entity's ability to continue as a going concern, including principal conditions or events and management's plans

C. **Consideration of the Effects on the Audit Report**

1. **Emphasis-of-Matter Paragraph** If, after considering identified conditions or events and management's plans, the auditor concludes that substantial doubt remains, the auditor should include an emphasis-of-matter paragraph in the audit report to reflect that conclusion.

   a. **Required Terms** The auditor's conclusion about the entity's ability to continue as a going concern should be expressed through the use of the phrase *substantial doubt about its ability to continue as a going concern* or similar wording that includes the terms:

      (1) *Substantial doubt*

      (2) *Going concern*

   b. **Conditional Language *Not* Allowed** The auditor should **not** use conditional language in expressing a conclusion concerning the existence of substantial doubt. Examples of inappropriate conditional language include:

      (1) ~~If the Company continues to suffer recurring losses from operations and continues to have a net capital deficiency, there may be substantial doubt about its ability to continue as a going concern~~.

      (2) ~~The Company has been unable to renegotiate its expiring credit agreements. Unless the Company is able to obtain financial support, there is substantial doubt about its ability to continue as a going concern~~.

Exhibit 23 ▸ Emphasis-of-Matter Paragraph

Emphasis of Matter Regarding Going Concern

The accompanying financial statements have been prepared assuming that the Company will continue as a going concern. As discussed in Note X to the financial statements, the Company has suffered recurring losses from operations and has a net capital deficiency that raise substantial doubt about its ability to continue as a going concern. Management's plans in regard to these matters are also described in Note X. The financial statements do not include any adjustments that might result from the outcome of this uncertainty. Our opinion is not modified with respect to this matter.

2. **Inadequate Disclosure** If the auditor concludes that the entity's disclosures with respect to substantial doubt are inadequate, the opinion should be modified (qualified or adverse).

3. **Disclaimer Allowed** An auditor is not precluded from disclaiming an opinion in cases involving uncertainties. When the auditor disclaims an opinion, the report should **not** include an emphasis-of-matter paragraph but, rather, describe the substantive reasons for the disclaimer of opinion in the *Basis for Disclaimer of Opinion* paragraph. The auditor should

consider the adequacy of disclosure of the uncertainties and their possible effects on the financial statements even when disclaiming an opinion.

4. **Comparison With Prior Financial Statements**

   a. **Substantial Doubt in Current Period** Substantial doubt that arose in the current period does not imply that the basis for such doubt existed in the prior period, and accordingly, does **not** affect the audit report on the financial statements of the prior period that are presented on a comparative basis.

   b. **Substantial Doubt in Prior Period** If substantial doubt existed at the date of prior period financial statements that are presented on a comparative basis and that doubt has been removed in the current period, the going-concern emphasis-of-matter paragraph included in the audit report of the prior period should **not** be repeated.

5. **Reissued Audit Report** When conditions or events that gave rise to the substantial doubt are resolved, the auditor may be requested to reissue an audit report and eliminate the going-concern emphasis-of-matter paragraph. (For example, an entity might obtain needed financing.)

   Although an auditor has no obligation to reissue the report, if the auditor decides to, the auditor should reassess the going-concern status of the entity by:

   a. Performing procedures related to the event or transaction that prompted the request to reissue the report without the going-concern emphasis-of-matter paragraph

   b. Performing the required procedures and considering the implications for the audit report related to subsequent events and subsequently discovered facts, at or near the date of reissuance

   c. Reconsidering the results of procedures previously performed related to the substantial doubt based on conditions or circumstances at the date of reissuance

D. **Communication With Those Charged With Governance**
When substantial doubt remains after considering identified conditions and events in the aggregate as well as management's plans, the auditor should communicate the following to those charged with governance:

1. The nature of the events or conditions identified

2. The possible effect on the financial statements and the adequacy of related disclosures in the financial statements

3. The effects on the audit report

E. **Audit Documentation**
If the auditor has substantial doubt about an entity *before consideration of management's plans to mitigate the adverse effects of identified conditions or events*, the auditor should document:

1. The conditions or events that led the auditor to believe that there were substantial doubt

2. The elements of management's plans that the auditor considered to be particularly significant to overcoming the adverse effects of the conditions or events

3. The audit procedures performed and evidence obtained to evaluate the significant elements of management's plans

4. The auditor's conclusion as to whether substantial doubt remains or is alleviated

   a. If substantial doubt remains, the auditor should also document the possible effects of the conditions or events on the financial statements and the adequacy of the related disclosures.

   b. If substantial doubt is alleviated, the auditor should also document the auditor's conclusion as to the need for, and, if applicable, the adequacy of, disclosure of the principal conditions or events that initially caused the auditor to believe there was substantial doubt.

5. The auditor's conclusion with respect to the audit report

X. Other Information in Documents Containing Audited Financial Statements (AU 720)

A. Overview

The auditor's opinion on the financial statements does **not** cover other information in documents containing audited financial statements and the audit report. Additionally, the auditor has **no** responsibility for determining whether such information is properly stated. (The exception being when there is a separate requirement to do so in the particular circumstances of an engagement.)

The auditor's purpose is to identify and attempt to resolve any possible material inconsistencies between the audited financial statements and the other information and any apparent material misstatements of fact in the other information that could undermine the credibility of the audited financial statements and the audit report. Failing a resolution on the revisions needed, the auditor should respond in a manner that is appropriate for the particular circumstances.

Editor Note: The auditor's responsibility for other information presented in a document containing audited financial statements that is *required* to be included per an accounting standard is addressed by AU 730, *Required Supplementary Information* (RSI). However, if the other information is prepared according to an accounting standard's guidance, but is presented *voluntarily*, then it is addressed by this standard—AU 720, *Other Information in Documents Containing Audited Financial Statements*. (See the coverage of RSI in this chapter.)

B. Definitions

1. Documents Containing Audited Financial Statements

   a. Annual reports (or similar documents) that are issued to owners (or similar stakeholders)

   b. Annual reports of governments and organizations for charitable or philanthropic purposes that are available to the public that contain audited financial statements and the audit report

   c. Other documents to which the auditor, at the client's request, devotes attention

2. **Other Information** Financial and nonfinancial information (other than the financial statements and the audit report) that is included in a document containing audited financial statements and the audit report, excluding RSI

   a. **Examples of Other Information**

   - A report by management or those charged with governance on operations
   - Financial summaries or highlights
   - Employment data
   - Planned capital expenditures

- Financial ratios
- Names of officers and directors
- Selected quarterly data

b. **Items *Not* Considered to Be Other Information** Other information does **not,** for example, include:

- A press release or similar memorandum or a cover letter accompanying the document containing audited financial statements and the audit report
- Information contained in analyst briefings
- Information contained on the entity's website

Editor Note: Websites are a means of distributing information and are not, themselves, documents containing audited financial statements.

3. **Inconsistency (With Financial Statements)** Other information that conflicts with information contained in the audited financial statements; a material inconsistency may raise doubt about the audit conclusions drawn from audit evidence previously obtained and, possibly, about the basis for the auditor's opinion

4. **Misstatements of Fact (Unrelated to Financial Statements)** Other information that is unrelated to matters appearing in the audited financial statements that is incorrectly stated or presented; material misstatements of fact may undermine the credibility of the document containing audited financial statements

C. **Procedures**

1. **Overall**

a. **Read Other Information Before Audit Report Release Date** The auditor should read the other information prior to the report release date, if possible, to identify any material inconsistencies with the audited financial statements. If the client does not make the other information available by then, the auditor should read it as soon as practicable.

The auditor *may* decide to delay the release of the report until the information is provided.

The auditor should also note any apparent material misstatements of fact in order to discuss them with management. (The specific procedures regarding the discovery of material misstatements of fact in the other information are covered later in this same section.)

b. **Determine Whether Financial Statements or Other Information Should Be Revised for Identified Inconsistencies** If the auditor identifies a material inconsistency, the auditor should determine whether the audited financial statements or the other information needs revision.

2. **When Financial Statements Should Be Revised**

a. **Identified *Before* Date of Audit Report** When the auditor identifies a material inconsistency prior to the date of the audit report that requires revision of the audited financial statements and management refuses to make the revision, the auditor should modify the auditor's opinion.

b. **Identified *After* Date of Audit Report or *After* Report Release Date** If the material inconsistency that requires revision of the financial statements is identified after the date of the audit report or after the report release date, the auditor should follow the guidance related to subsequently discovered facts. (See the coverage of subsequent events and subsequently discovered facts in this chapter.)

3. **When Other Information Should Be Revised**

a. **Identified *Before* Report Release Date** If the auditor determines, prior to the report release date, that the other information should be revised due to a material inconsistency and management refuses, the auditor should respond as follows.

(1) The auditor should communicate the matter to those charged with governance.

(2) Depending on the circumstances and the significance of the inconsistency, the auditor should do one of the following.

(a) Add an other-matter paragraph to the audit report describing the material inconsistency

or

(b) Withhold the audit report

or

(c) Withdraw from the engagement, if possible under applicable law or regulation

When management refuses to revise the other information, the auditor *may* base any decision on what further action to take on advice from legal counsel.

b. **Identified *After* Report Release Date & Management Agrees to Revise** When revision of the other information is necessary after the report release date and management agrees to make the revision, the auditor should carry out the procedures necessary under the circumstances.

The auditor's procedures *may* include reviewing the steps taken by management to ensure that individuals in receipt of the previously issued financial statements, the auditor's report, and the other information are informed of the need for revision.

c. **Identified *After* Report Release Date but Management Refuses to Revise** When revision of the other information is necessary after the report release date but management refuses to make the revision, the auditor should notify those charged with governance of the auditor's concerns regarding the other information and take any further appropriate action.

Appropriate further actions by the auditor *may* include obtaining legal advice.

4. **Material Misstatements of Fact**

a. **Discuss With Management** If, on reading the other information to identify material inconsistencies, the auditor discovers an apparent material misstatement of fact, the auditor should discuss the matter with management.

b. **Consultation With Third Party** If the discussion with management does not resolve the auditor's concerns, the auditor should request that management consult with a qualified third party, such as the entity's legal counsel. The auditor should consider the advice received by the entity from the third party in determining whether the matter is a material misstatement of fact. (The auditor may conclude that valid differences of judgment or opinion exist.)

c. **Management Refuses to Make Correction** When the auditor concludes there is a material misstatement of fact in the other information that management refuses to correct, the auditor should notify those charged with governance of the auditor's concerns regarding the other information and take any further appropriate action.

Appropriate further actions by the auditor *may* include obtaining advice from legal counsel, withholding the audit report (if it has not been released), or withdrawing from the engagement.

D. **Communication With Those Charged With Governance**
The auditor should communicate the following with those charged with governance.

1. **Auditor's Responsibilities** The auditor's responsibility with respect to the other information

2. **Procedures & Results** Any procedures performed relating to the other information and the results

3. **Management Refuses to Revise Other Information for a Material Inconsistency or to Correct a Material Misstatement of Fact** When the auditor identifies a material inconsistency that requires revision of the other information and management refuses to make the revision, the auditor should communicate this matter to those charged with governance. When the auditor concludes that there is a material misstatement of fact in the other information that management refuses to correct, the auditor should notify those charged with governance of the auditor's concerns regarding the other information.

E. **Audit Report**

1. **Audit Report Reference *Not* Required** The auditor is **not** required to reference the other information in the audit report on the financial statements.

2. **Optional Disclaimer** However, the auditor *may* include an other-matter paragraph disclaiming an opinion on the other information. For example, an auditor may choose to do so when the auditor could be associated with the information and the user may infer a level of assurance that is not intended.

Exhibit 24 ▸ Other-Matter Paragraph to Disclaim Opinion on Other Information

Other Matter

Our audit was conducted for the purpose of forming an opinion on the basic financial statements as a whole. The [*identify the other information*] is presented for purposes of additional analysis and is not a required part of the basic financial statements. Such information has not been subjected to the auditing procedures applied in the audit of the basic financial statements, and accordingly, we do not express an opinion or provide any assurance on it.

XI. Required Supplementary Information (AU 730)

A. Overview

1. **Auditor's Objectives** When a designated accounting standards setter requires information to accompany an entity's basic financial statements, the auditor's objectives are to perform specified (limited) procedures in order to:

   a. Describe, in the audit report in an other-matter paragraph, whether the required supplementary information (RSI) is presented

   b. Communicate in the audit report when

      (1) Some or all of the RSI has *not* been presented in accordance with guidelines established by a designated accounting standards setter

      (2) There are material modifications that should be made to the RSI for it to be in accordance with guidelines established by the designated accounting standards setter

2. **No Assurance Expressed on RSI** Because the RSI accompanies the basic financial statements, the audit report includes a discussion of the responsibility taken by the auditor on that information; however, no opinion is expressed nor is any assurance provided on the RSI.

3. **RSI Has No Effect on Opinion** Because the RSI is not part of the basic financial statements, the auditor's opinion is **not** affected by the presentation by the entity of the RSI or the failure to present some or all of it. Further, if the RSI is omitted by the entity, the auditor does not have a responsibility to present that information.

Editor Note: The auditor's responsibility for financial and nonfinancial information (other than the financial statements and the audit report) that is included in a document containing audited financial statements and the audit report that is **not** required by a designated accounting standards setter (even when the information is prepared in accordance with the standards-setter's guidance), but is presented *voluntarily* by the entity, is addressed in AU 720, *Other Information in Documents Containing Audited Financial Statements*. (See coverage of other information in this chapter.)

B. Definitions

1. **Designated Accounting Standards Setter** A body designated by the AICPA to promulgate GAAP pursuant to of the AICPA Code of Professional Conduct. They are the:

   - Financial Accounting Standards Board (FASB)
   - Governmental Accounting Standards Board (GASB)
   - Federal Accounting Standards Advisory Board (FASAB)
   - International Accounting Standards Board (IASB)

2. **Applicable Financial Reporting Framework (AFRF)** The financial reporting framework adopted by management and, when appropriate, those charged with governance in the preparation and fair presentation of the financial statements that is acceptable in view of the nature of the entity and the objective of the financial statements, or that is required by law or regulation

3. **Basic Financial Statements** Financial statements presented in accordance with an AFRF as established by a designated accounting standards setter, excluding RSI

4. **Required Supplementary Information** RSI is information that a designated accounting standards setter requires to accompany an entity's basic financial statements. RSI is **not** part of the basic financial statements; however, a standards setter considers the information to be an essential part of financial reporting for placing the basic financial statements in an appropriate operational, economic, or historical context. In addition, authoritative guidelines for the methods of measurement and presentation of the information have been established.

5. **Prescribed Guidelines** The authoritative guidelines established by the designated accounting standards setter for the methods of measurement and presentation of the RSI

C. Procedures

The auditor should apply the following procedures to RSI.

1. Inquire of management about the methods of preparing the information, including whether:

   a. It has been measured and presented in accordance with prescribed guidelines

   b. Methods of measurement or presentation have been changed from those used in the prior period and the reasons for any such changes

   c. There were any significant assumptions or interpretations underlying the measurement or presentation of the information

2. Compare the information for consistency with:

   a. Management's responses to the foregoing inquiries

   b. The basic financial statements

   c. Other knowledge obtained during the audit of the basic financial statements

3. Obtain written representations from management:

   a. That it acknowledges its responsibility for the RSI

   b. About whether the RSI is measured and presented in accordance with prescribed guidelines

   c. About whether the methods of measurement or presentation have changed from those used in the prior period and, if so, the reasons for such changes

   d. About any significant assumptions or interpretations underlying the measurement or presentation of the RSI

D. Communication With Those Charged With Governance

If the auditor is unable to complete the required procedures for RSI due to significant difficulties encountered in dealing with management, the auditor should inform those charged with governance.

E. Other-Matter Paragraph

1. **Overview** The auditor should include an other-matter paragraph in the audit report on the financial statements to refer to the RSI. It should explain the following circumstances, as applicable.

   a. Management has included the RSI and the auditor has applied the required procedures.

b. Management has omitted some of the RSI and presented some of the RSI in accordance with the prescribed guidelines.

c. The auditor is unable to complete the required procedures.

d. The auditor has identified material departures from the prescribed guidelines.

e. The auditor has unresolved doubts about whether the RSI is presented in accordance with prescribed guidelines.

f. Management has omitted *all* of the RSI.

2. **Content & Presentation**

   a. For all circumstances **except** when management omits *all* of the RSI

      (1) These two statements begin the paragraph.

         (a) A statement that [*identify the AFRF (for example, accounting principles generally accepted in the United States of America)*] require that the [*identify the RSI*] be presented to supplement the basic financial statements

         (b) A statement that such information, although not a part of the basic financial statements, is required by [*identify designated accounting standards setter*], who considers it to be an essential part of financial reporting for placing the basic financial statements in an appropriate operational, economic, or historical context

      (2) If the auditor *has* applied the required procedures to the RSI, then these two statements are added to the same paragraph.

         (a) A statement that the auditor has applied certain limited procedures to the RSI in accordance with auditing standards generally accepted in the United States of America, which consisted of inquiries of management about the methods of preparing the information and comparing the information for consistency with management's responses to the auditor's inquiries, the basic financial statements, and other knowledge the auditor obtained during the audit of the basic financial statements

         (b) A statement that the auditor does not express an opinion or provide any assurance on the information because the limited procedures do not provide the auditor with sufficient evidence to express an opinion or provide any assurance

Exhibit 25 ▸ RSI Is Included, Auditor Has Applied Required Procedures & No Material Departures From Prescribed Guidelines Have Been Identified

> ***Other Matter***
>
> [*Identify the applicable financial reporting framework (for example, accounting principles generally accepted in the United States of America)*] require that the [*identify the required supplementary information*] on page XX be presented to supplement the basic financial statements. Such information, although not a part of the basic financial statements, is required by [*identify designated accounting standards setter*] who considers it to be an essential part of financial reporting for placing the basic financial statements in an appropriate operational, economic, or historical context. We have applied certain limited procedures to the required supplementary information in accordance with auditing standards generally accepted in the United States of America, which consisted of inquiries of management about the methods of preparing the information and comparing the information for consistency with management's responses to our inquiries, the basic financial statements, and other knowledge we obtained during our audit of the basic financial statements. We do not express an opinion or provide any assurance on the information because the limited procedures do not provide us with sufficient evidence to express an opinion or provide any assurance.

(3) If the auditor is unable to complete the required procedures, then these two statements are, instead, added to the same paragraph.

- **(a)** A statement that the auditor was unable to apply certain limited procedures to the RSI in accordance with auditing standards generally accepted in the United States because [*state the reasons*]
- **(b)** A statement that the auditor does not express an opinion or provide any assurance on the information

Exhibit 26 ▸ Auditor Is *Not* Able to Complete Required Procedures

> ***Other Matter***
>
> [*Identify the applicable financial reporting framework (for example, accounting principles generally accepted in the United States of America)*] require that the [*identify the supplementary information*] on page XX be presented to supplement the basic financial statements. Such information, although not a part of the basic financial statements, is required by [*identify designated accounting standards setter*] who considers it to be an essential part of financial reporting for placing the basic financial statements in an appropriate operational, economic, or historical context. We were unable to apply certain limited procedures to the required supplementary information in accordance with auditing standards generally accepted in the United States of America because [*state the reasons*]. We do not express an opinion or provide any assurance on the information.

(4) A second paragraph is added if management has omitted some of the RSI. It is comprised of these three statements.

(a) A statement that management has omitted [*description of the missing RSI*] that [*identify the AFRF (for example, accounting principles generally accepted in the United States of America)*] require to be presented to supplement the basic financial statements

(b) A statement that such missing information, although not a part of the basic financial statements, is required by [*identify designated accounting standards setter*], who considers it to be an essential part of financial reporting for placing the basic financial statements in an appropriate operational, economic, or historical context

(c) A statement that the auditor's opinion on the basic financial statements is not affected by the missing information

Exhibit 27 ▸ Entity Has Omitted Some of RSI & Some Is Presented in Accordance With Prescribed Guidelines

Other Matter
[*Identify the applicable financial reporting framework (for example, accounting principles generally accepted in the United States of America)*] require that [*identify the included supplementary information*] be presented to supplement the basic financial statements. Such information, although not a part of the basic financial statements, is required by [*identify designated accounting standards setter*] who considers it to be an essential part of financial reporting for placing the basic financial statements in an appropriate operational, economic, or historical context. We have applied certain limited procedures to the required supplementary information in accordance with auditing standards generally accepted in the United States of America, which consisted of inquiries of management about the methods of preparing the information and comparing the information for consistency with management's responses to our inquiries, the basic financial statements, and other knowledge we obtained during our audit of the basic financial statements. We do not express an opinion or provide any assurance on the information because the limited procedures do not provide us with evidence sufficient to express an opinion or provide any assurance. Management has omitted [*describe the missing required supplementary information*] that [*identify the applicable financial reporting framework*] require to be presented to supplement the basic financial statements. Such missing information, although not a part of the basic financial statements, is required by [*identify designated accounting standards setter*] who considers it to be an essential part of financial reporting for placing the basic financial statements in an appropriate operational, economic, or historical context. Our opinion on the basic financial statements is not affected by this missing information.

(5) If the auditor has identified material departures from the prescribed guidelines, then the second paragraph described in (4) is *not* included. Instead, these two statements are added to the single paragraph format.

(a) A statement that although the auditor's opinion on the basic financial statements is not affected, material departures from prescribed guidelines exist [*identify the RSI and describe the material departures from the*

AFRF]; the auditor *may* consider including the reason(s) the doubts were not resolved

(b) A statement that the auditor does not express an opinion or provide any assurance on the information

Exhibit 28 ▸ Auditor Has Identified Material Departures From Prescribed Guidelines

Other Matter

[*Identify the applicable financial reporting framework (for example, accounting principles generally accepted in the United States of America)*] require that the [*identify the supplementary information*] on page XX be presented to supplement the basic financial statements. Such information, although not a part of the basic financial statements, is required by [*identify designated accounting standards setter*] who considers it to be an essential part of financial reporting for placing the basic financial statements in an appropriate operational, economic, or historical context. We have applied certain limited procedures to the required supplementary information in accordance with auditing standards generally accepted in the United States of America, which consisted of inquiries of management about the methods of preparing the information and comparing the information for consistency with management's responses to our inquiries, the basic financial statements, and other knowledge we obtained during our audit of the basic financial statements. Although our opinion on the basic financial statements is not affected, the following material departures from the prescribed guidelines exist [*identify the required supplementary information and describe the material departures from the prescribed guidelines*]. We do not express an opinion or provide any assurance on the information.

(6) If the auditor has unresolved doubts about whether the RSI is presented in accordance with prescribed guidelines, then, again, the second paragraph is *not* included. Instead the following statement is added to the single paragraph format. The auditor *may* consider including in the report the reason(s) the auditor was unable to resolve his or her doubts.

- A statement that although the auditor's opinion on the basic financial statements is not affected, the results of the limited procedures have raised doubts about whether material modifications should be made to the RSI for it to be presented in accordance with guidelines established by [*identify designated accounting standards setter*]

Exhibit 29 ▶ Auditor Has Unresolved Doubts About Whether RSI Is in Accordance With Prescribed Guidelines

> ***Other Matter***
>
> [*Identify the applicable financial reporting framework (for example, accounting principles generally accepted in the United States of America)*] require that the [*identify the supplementary information*] on page XX be presented to supplement the basic financial statements. Such information, although not a part of the basic financial statements, is required by [identify designated accounting standards setter] who considers it to be an essential part of financial reporting for placing the basic financial statements in an appropriate operational, economic, or historical context. We have applied certain limited procedures to the required supplementary information in accordance with auditing standards generally accepted in the United States of America, which consisted of inquiries of management about the methods of preparing the information and comparing the information for consistency with management's responses to our inquiries, the basic financial statements, and other knowledge we obtained during our audit of the basic financial statements. We do not express an opinion or provide any assurance on the information because the limited procedures do not provide us with sufficient evidence to express an opinion or provide any assurance. Although our opinion on the basic financial statements is not affected, the results of the limited procedures have raised doubts about whether material modifications should be made to the required supplementary information for it to be presented in accordance with guidelines established by [*identify designated accounting standards setter*].

b. If the entity has omitted *all* of the RSI, the other-matter paragraph is comprised of these statements.

(1) A statement that management has omitted [description of the missing RSI] that [identify the AFRF (for example, accounting principles generally accepted in the United States of America)] require to be presented to supplement the basic financial statements

(2) A statement that such missing information, although not a part of the basic financial statements, is required by [identify designated accounting standards setter], who considers it to be an essential part of financial reporting for placing the basic financial statements in an appropriate operational, economic, or historical context

(3) A statement that the auditor's opinion on the basic financial statements is not affected by the missing information

Exhibit 30 ▶ Entity Has Omitted All of RSI

> ***Other Matter***
>
> Management has omitted [*describe the missing required supplementary information*] that [*identify the applicable financial reporting framework (for example, accounting principles generally accepted in the United States of America)*] require to be presented to supplement the basic financial statements. Such missing information, although not a part of the basic financial statements, is required by [*identify designated accounting standards setter*] who considers it to be an essential part of financial reporting for placing the basic financial statements in an appropriate operational, economic, or historical context. Our opinion on the basic financial statements is not affected by this missing information.

CHAPTER 8—REPORTS ON AUDITED FINANCIAL STATEMENTS

Problem 8-1 MULTIPLE-CHOICE QUESTIONS

Forming an Opinion on the Financial Statements

1. In forming an opinion on whether the financial statements of a nonissuer achieve fair presentation, within the context of the applicable financial reporting framework, the auditor should evaluate all of the following **except**

   a. Whether the overall presentation, structure, and content of the financial statements is appropriate
   b. Whether the financial statements represent the underlying transactions and events in an appropriate manner
   c. Whether the notes to the financial statements represent the underlying transactions and events in an appropriate manner
   d. Whether the terminology used in the financial statements, including the title of each financial statement, is appropriate (ID: 90395)

Audit Report With an Unmodified Opinion

2. The description of management's responsibilities in the audit report on the financial statements of a nonissuer

   a. May reference a separate statement by management about such responsibilities if this statement is included in the document containing the financial statements
   b. Should be included in the first paragraph of the audit report
   c. Includes a description of management's responsibilities for the preparation and fair presentation of the financial statements and the related internal controls
   d. Identifies the entity that management represents (ID: 90393)

3. The description of the auditor's responsibilities in the audit report on the financial statements of a nonissuer

   a. Should include the name of the auditor with primary responsibility for the audit
   b. Should state that the audit was conducted in accordance with the applicable financial reporting framework
   c. Should include a reference to a footnote in the financial statements that describes an audit
   d. Should include the phrase *reasonable assurance* (ID: 90394)

4. Which paragraphs or sections of an audit report with an unmodified opinion for a nonissuer reference the applicable financial reporting framework?

	Introductory paragraph	Management's responsibility section	Opinion section
a.	No	Yes	No
b.	Yes	Yes	No
c.	Yes	No	Yes
d.	No	Yes	Yes

(ID: 89471)

Emphasis-of-Matter & Other-Matter Paragraphs

5. An emphasis-of-matter paragraph in an audit report prepared in accordance with US GAAS
   a. Refers to a matter other than those presented or disclosed in the financial statements that is relevant to users' understanding of the audit, the auditor's responsibilities, or the audit report
   b. Refers to a matter appropriately presented or disclosed in the financial statements that is of such importance that it is fundamental to users' understanding of the financial statements
   c. Includes an explanation for the modification of the audit opinion
   d. Is required to have the heading *Emphasis-of-Matter* (ID: 90396)

6. An emphasis-of-matter paragraph that is included in an audit report prepared in accordance with US GAAS
   a. May refer to disclosures in the financial statements required by the applicable financial reporting framework that management failed to include
   b. May, in rare circumstances, be used to avoid modifying the audit opinion when, according to the auditor's professional judgment, it is appropriate in the specific circumstances of the audit engagement
   c. May be used to explain why it is not possible for the auditor to withdraw from an engagement
   d. Should be communicated to those charged with governance (ID: 90397)

7. An other-matter paragraph that is included in an audit report prepared in accordance with US GAAS
   a. Should not address circumstances when the auditor has other reporting responsibilities that are in addition to the auditor's responsibility under US GAAS to report on the financial statements
   b. May be used to include information that management failed to provide
   c. May refer to significant transactions with related parties
   d. May refer to an uncertainty relating to the future outcome of unusually important litigation or regulatory action (ID: 90398)

Modified Opinions

8. All of the following describe the pervasive effects of misstatements on the financial statements of a nonissuer **except**
   a. Pervasive effects are not confined to specific elements, accounts, or items of the financial statements.
   b. Pervasive effects, with regard to disclosures, are fundamental to users' understanding of the financial statements.
   c. Pervasive effects, with regard to disclosures, would cause a reasonable person to misunderstand the nature of a significant component of the financial statements.
   d. Pervasive effects, if confined to specific elements, accounts, or items of the financial statements, represent or could represent a substantial proportion of the financial statements. (ID: 90043)

9. The auditor of a nonissuer should express an adverse opinion when, having obtained sufficient appropriate audit evidence, concludes that misstatements are
   a. Both qualitatively and quantitatively material to the financial statements
   b. Both material and pervasive to the financial statements
   c. Material to the financial statements
   d. Both material and significant to the financial statements as a whole (ID: 90041)

10. The factor considered by the auditor of a nonissuer when deciding whether to express a qualified opinion vs. an adverse opinion or a qualified opinion vs. a disclaimer of opinion is the
    a. Dollar magnitude of the effects or possible effects on the financial statements
    b. Significance of an item to a particular entity
    c. Pervasiveness of the effects or possible effects on the financial statements
    d. Effects or possible effects on the financial statements taken as a whole (ID: 90042)

11. When the auditor of a nonissuer disclaims an opinion due to an inability to obtain sufficient appropriate audit evidence, the auditor should

    a. Amend the introductory paragraph of the report to state that the auditor began, but was unable to complete, an audit of the financial statements
    b. Omit the auditor's responsibility section of the audit report
    c. Add a basis for disclaimer of opinion paragraph that clearly describes only the matter directly related to the disclaimer of opinion
    d. Add a basis for disclaimer of opinion paragraph that includes a description of other identified matters that would have otherwise required a modification of the auditor's opinion (ID: 90044)

Consistency of Financial Statements

12. Which of the following paragraphs of the audit report should include a description of a change in accounting principle that has a material effect on the comparability of financial statements of a nonissuer?

    a. Basis-for-modification paragraph
    b. Opinion paragraph
    c. Emphasis-of-matter paragraph
    d. Other-matter paragraph (ID: 89760)

13. The auditor of a nonissuer should evaluate the appropriateness of a change in accounting principle to determine whether

    a. Both the principle and the method of accounting for the effect of the change are in accordance with US generally accepted accounting principles
    b. The related disclosures are adequate
    c. The auditor can justify that the alternative accounting principle is preferable
    d. The effect of the change exceeds the auditor's planned level of materiality (ID: 90399)

14. When the comparability of financial statements between periods has been materially affected by adjustments to correct a material misstatement in previously issued financial statements the auditor should include an emphasis-of-matter paragraph in the audit report

    a. That includes a description of, and explains the reason for, the correction
    b. That includes a statement that the previously issued financial statements have been restated for the correction of a material misstatement in the respective period
    c. That should be repeated in the subsequent period
    d. That omits the statement that the opinion is not modified with respect to this matter, common to other emphasis-of-matter paragraphs (ID: 90400)

15. When considering whether the comparability of financial statements between periods has been materially affected, the auditor should evaluate and report on

    a. A change in accounting estimate that is inseparable from the effect of a related change in accounting principle like other changes in accounting principle
    b. A change from an accounting principle that is not in accordance with the applicable financial reporting framework to one that is in accordance like other changes in accounting principle
    c. A change in financial statement classification like other changes in accounting principle
    d. A change in reporting entity that results from a transaction or event like other changes in accounting principle (ID: 90436)

Segment Information

16. When an entity is required or permitted to disclose segment information in the financial statements
    a. The auditor should obtain an understanding of the related industry standards as the applicable financial reporting framework may not include requirements for this level of presentation
    b. The auditor is unlikely to perform analytical procedures on segment information
    c. The auditor's responsibility regarding the presentation and disclosure of segment information is in relation to the financial statements as a whole
    d. The auditor is required to perform audit procedures that would be necessary to express an opinion on the segment information presented on a stand-alone basis (ID: 90437)

Reporting on Comparative Financial Statements

17. When current period financial statements are audited and presented in comparative form with compiled or reviewed financial statements for the prior period, and the report on the prior period is not reissued, the auditor should include an other-matter paragraph in the current period audit report that includes all of the following **except**
    a. The service performed in the prior period and the date of the report on that service
    b. A description of any material modifications noted in that report
    c. A statement that the service was less in scope than an audit and does not provide the basis for the expression of an opinion on the financial statements
    d. The reasons an audit was not performed for the prior period (ID: 90438)

Subsequent Events & Subsequently Discovered Facts and Omitted Procedures

18. An auditor is concerned with completing various phases of the audit after the balance sheet date. This subsequent period extends to the date of the
    a. Final review of the audit working papers
    b. Delivery of the auditor's report to the client
    c. Public issuance of the financial statements
    d. Audit report (ID: 381)

19. After issuing an audit report, an auditor has **no** obligation to make continuing inquiries or perform other procedures concerning the audited financial statements, unless
    a. Information, which existed at the audit report date and may affect the audit report, comes to the auditor's attention.
    b. Management of the entity requests the auditor to reissue the audit report.
    c. Information about an event that occurred after the audit report date comes to the auditor's attention.
    d. Final determinations or resolutions are made about contingencies that were disclosed in the financial statements. (ID: 2288)

20. Which of the following procedures would an auditor most likely perform to obtain evidence about the occurrence of subsequent events?
    a. Confirming a sample of material accounts receivable established after year-end
    b. Comparing the financial statements being reported on with those of the prior period
    c. Investigating personnel changes in the accounting department occurring after year-end
    d. Inquiring as to whether any unusual adjustments were made after year-end (ID: 6003)

21. Which of the following procedures would an auditor most likely perform to obtain evidence about the occurrence of subsequent events?
    a. Determine whether inventory ordered before the year-end was included in the physical count.
    b. Inquire about payroll checks that were recorded before year-end but cashed after year-end.
    c. Investigate changes in capital stock recorded after year-end.
    d. Review tax returns prepared by management after year-end. (ID: 9906)

22. The definition of a subsequent event is an event

    a. Occurring between the date of the financial statements and the audit report release date
    b. That existed at the date of the financial statements
    c. Occurring between the date of the financial statements and the date of the audit report
    d. That arose after the date of the financial statements (ID: 89494)

23. Six months after issuing an unmodified opinion on financial statements, an auditor discovered that the engagement personnel failed to confirm several of the client's material accounts receivable balances. The auditor should first

    a. Request the client's permission to undertake the confirmation of such accounts receivable.
    b. Perform alternative procedures to provide a satisfactory basis for the unmodified opinion.
    c. Assess the importance of the omitted procedures to the auditor's ability to support the previously expressed opinion.
    d. Inquire whether there are persons currently relying, or likely to rely, on the opinion. (ID: 332)

24. An auditor concludes that an audit procedure considered necessary at the time of the audit was omitted. The auditor should assess the importance of the omitted procedure to the ability to support the previously expressed opinion. Which of the following would be **least** helpful in making that assessment?

    a. A discussion with the client about whether there are persons relying on the audit report
    b. A discussion of the circumstances with engagement personnel
    c. A review of the other audit procedures that were applied that might compensate for the one omitted
    d. A re-evaluation of the overall scope of the audit (ID: 371)

25. When an auditor becomes aware that one or more auditing procedures that the auditor considered necessary in the circumstances existing at the time of the audit were omitted from the audit of the financial statements,

    a. If the auditor needs to perform a previously omitted or alternative procedure, but is unable to do so, as long as the auditor documents the attempt, the auditor has discharged his or her responsibility.
    b. The US GAAS guidance relevant to this matter relates to the period subsequent to the audit report release date regarding when the auditor became aware of the omission.
    c. If the auditor needs to perform a previously omitted or alternative procedure, but is unable to do so, the auditor should seek legal advice to determine the appropriate course of action.
    d. The US GAAS guidance relevant to this matter relates to the period subsequent to the audit report date regarding when the auditor became aware of the omission. (ID: 89497)

Consideration of an Entity's Ability to Continue as a Going Concern

26. Which of the following auditing procedures most likely would assist an auditor in identifying conditions and events that may indicate substantial doubt about an entity's ability to continue as a going concern?

    a. Inspecting title documents to verify whether any assets are pledged as collateral
    b. Confirming with third parties the details of arrangements to maintain financial support
    c. Reconciling the cash balance per books with the cutoff bank statement and the bank confirmation
    d. Comparing the entity's depreciation and asset capitalization policies to other entities in the industry (ID: 4720)

27. After considering an entity's negative trends and financial difficulties, an auditor has substantial doubt about the entity's ability to continue as a going concern. The auditor's considerations relating to management's plans for dealing with the adverse effects of these conditions most likely would include management's plans to

    a. Increase current dividend distributions
    b. Reduce existing lines of credit
    c. Increase ownership equity
    d. Purchase assets formerly leased (ID: 7026)

28. Which of the following statements is correct with respect to the auditor's consideration of an entity's ability to continue as a going concern?

    a. The auditor's workpapers must include audit evidence which provides assurance that the entity will continue as a going concern.
    b. If there is absence of reference to substantial doubt in the auditor's report, this should be viewed as assurance as to an entity's ability to continue as a going concern.
    c. It is not necessary for the auditor to design audit procedures solely to identify conditions and events that, when considered in the aggregate, indicate there could be substantial doubt about the entity's ability to continue as a going concern for a reasonable period of time.
    d. The auditor has a responsibility to evaluate whether there is substantial doubt about the entity's ability to continue as a going concern for a reasonable period of time, not to exceed the date of the financial statements being audited. (ID: 7506)

29. Which of the following audit procedures most likely would assist an auditor in identifying conditions and events that may indicate substantial doubt about an entity's ability to continue as a going concern?

    a. Reading the minutes of meetings of the stockholders and the board of directors
    b. Comparing the market value of property to amounts owed on the property
    c. Reviewing lease agreements to determine whether leased assets should be capitalized
    d. Inspecting title documents to verify whether any assets are pledged as collateral (ID: 7807)

30. An auditor believes that there is substantial doubt about an entity's ability to continue as a going concern for a reasonable period of time. In evaluating the entity's plans for dealing with the adverse effects of future conditions and events, the auditor most likely would consider, as a mitigating factor, the entity's plans to

    a. Repurchase the entity's stock at a price below its book value
    b. Issue stock options to key executives
    c. Lease rather than purchase operating facilities
    d. Accelerate the due date of an existing mortgage (ID: 8129)

31. Which of the following procedures most likely would assist an auditor in identifying conditions and events that may indicate substantial doubt about an entity's ability to continue as a going concern?

    a. Performing cutoff tests of sales transactions with customers with long-standing receivable balances
    b. Evaluating the entity's procedures for identifying and recording related-party transactions
    c. Inspecting title documents to verify whether any real property is pledged as collateral
    d. Inquiring of the entity's legal counsel about litigation, claims, and assessments (ID: 8153)

32. When there is substantial doubt about the entity's ability to continue as a going concern for a reasonable period of time, the auditor should

    a. Disclaim an opinion
    b. Include an emphasis-of-matter paragraph before the opinion in the audit report to reflect that conclusion
    c. Include an other-matter paragraph in the audit report to reflect that conclusion
    d. Obtain written representations from management about management's related plans (ID: 89496)

33. Kane, CPA, concludes that there is substantial doubt about Lima Co.'s ability to continue as a going concern. If Lima's financial statements adequately disclose its financial difficulties, Kane's auditor's report is required to include an emphasis-of-matter paragraph that specifically uses the phrase(s)

	Possible discontinuance of operations	Reasonable period of time, not to exceed one year
a.	Yes	Yes
b.	Yes	No
c.	No	Yes
d.	No	No

(ID: 6019)

Other Information in Documents Containing Audited Financial Statement

34. What is an auditor's responsibility for information that is outside the basic financial statements, but presented in a document with the audited financial statements?

    a. The auditor should apply substantive tests of transactions to the other information and include an explanatory paragraph in the audit report to refer to the other information.
    b. The auditor should apply certain limited procedures to the other information and include an explanatory paragraph in the audit report to refer to the other information.
    c. The auditor's only responsibility for the other information is to read it and determine whether it has any material inconsistencies with the financial statements.
    d. The auditor has no responsibility for other information as long as it is outside the basic financial statements. (ID: 90029)

35. An auditor reads the cover letter accompanying the document containing the audit report and audited financial statements and identifies a material inconsistency with the financial statements. The auditor determines that the financial statements do **not** require revision. Which of the following actions should the auditor take?

    a. No action is required
    b. Include a other-matter paragraph in the audit report
    c. Consider withdrawing from the engagement
    d. Request a client representation letter acknowledging the inconsistency (ID: 8399)

36. An auditor concludes, prior to the audit report release date, that there is a material inconsistency in the other information in an annual report to shareholders containing audited financial statements. If the auditor concludes that the financial statements do **not** require revision, but the client refuses to revise the other information to eliminate the inconsistency, the auditor should communicate the matter to those charged with governance and may

    a. Revise the auditor's report to include an other-matter paragraph describing the material inconsistency
    b. Issue a qualified opinion after discussing the matter with the client's board of directors
    c. Consider the matter closed, because the other information is not in the audited financial statements
    d. Disclaim an opinion on the financial statements (ID: 5159)

Required Supplementary Information

37. What is an auditor's responsibility for supplementary information which is outside the basic financial statements but required by a standard setter designated by the AICPA to promulgate GAAP?

    a. The auditor should apply substantive tests of transactions to the supplementary information and verify its conformity with the designated standard setter's requirement.
    b. The auditor should apply certain limited procedures to the supplementary information and include an other-matter paragraph in the audit report to refer to the RSI.
    c. The auditor's only responsibility for the supplementary information is to determine that such information has not been omitted.
    d. The auditor has no responsibility for such supplementary information as long as it is outside the basic financial statements. (ID: 7642)

Problem 8-2 SIMULATION: Audit Reports

- The auditor is independent.
- The auditor previously expressed an unmodified opinion on the prior year's financial statements.
- Only single-year (not comparative) statements are presented for the current year.
- The conditions for an unmodified opinion exist unless contradicted in the factual situations.
- No report modifications are to be made except in response to the factual situation.

The following items present various independent factual situations an auditor might encounter in conducting an audit of financial statements. The list represents the types of opinions the auditor ordinarily would issue. For each situation, select one response—the action the auditor normally would take based on the information given. A selection may be used once, more than once, or not at all.

Situation	Type of Opinion
1. The auditor was unable to obtain sufficient appropriate evidence for an investment in a foreign affiliate. The possible effects of the inability to obtain sufficient appropriate audit evidence are deemed to be material but not pervasive to the financial statements.	
2. Due to recurring operating losses and working capital deficiencies, an auditor has substantial doubt about an entity's ability to continue as a going concern for a reasonable period of time. The financial statement disclosures concerning these matters are adequate.	
3. The financial statements have inadequate disclosures. The effects are material, but are not fundamental to users' understanding of the financial statements.	
4. An entity issues financial statements that present financial position and results of operations, but omits the required statement of cash flows. The auditor concludes that its omission has a material but not a pervasive effect on the financial statement presentation.	
5. An entity changes its method of inventory pricing from LIFO to FIFO. The auditor concurs with the change although it has a material effect on the comparability of the entity's financial statements.	
6. An entity is a defendant in a lawsuit alleging infringement of certain patent rights However, the ultimate outcome of the litigation cannot be reasonably estimated by management. The auditor believes there is a reasonable possibility of a significant material loss related to this unusually important matter. The lawsuit is adequately disclosed in the notes to the financial statements.	
7. Certain lease obligations have been excluded from the financial statements in the current year that should be capitalized in accordance with the entity's applicable financial reporting framework. The effect of the exclusion is material and pervasive.	
8. All required supplementary information has been omitted.	
9. The auditor was unable to obtain audit evidence about the entity's inventories and accounts receivable. The possible effects of this inability to obtain sufficient appropriate audit evidence are deemed to be both material and pervasive to the financial statements.	
10. The auditor has identified a material inconsistency prior to the audit report release date that requires revision of the other information in documents containing audited financial statements. Management refuses to make the revision. Based on advice from legal counsel, the auditor does not believe it is appropriate to either withhold the audit report or to withdraw from the engagement.	

(ID: 89472)

Types of Opinions

A. Unmodified opinion
B. Unmodified opinion with an emphasis-of-matter paragraph
C. Unmodified opinion with an other-matter paragraph
D. Qualified opinion due to a misstatement
E. Qualified opinion due to a scope limitation
F. Adverse opinion
G. Disclaimer of opinion

Problem 8-3 SIMULATION: Research

Which citation in the professional standards provides guidance regarding the condition that should be met in order for an auditor to refer in the audit report to having conducted an audit in accordance with another set of auditing standards in addition to US GAAS?

[ ] § [ ] . [ ] (ID: 90054)

Solution 8-1 MULTIPLE-CHOICE ANSWERS

1. (d) Whether the terminology used in the financial statements, including the title of each financial statement, is appropriate is part of the auditor's evaluation of the adherence of the financial statements to the requirements of the applicable financial reporting framework (AFRF) rather than the auditor's consideration of whether, in the context of the AFRF, the financial statements achieve fair presentation. (ID: 90395)

2. (c) The section on management's responsibilities in the audit report includes a description of both of these responsibilities (regarding the financial statements and the related internal controls) because it helps explain to users the premise on which an audit is conducted. Regarding incorrect answer a., in some instances, a document containing the audit report may include a separate statement by management regarding its responsibility for the preparation of the financial statements. The audit report should **not** make reference to such a separate statement in another document. This could lead users to erroneously believe that the auditor is providing assurances about representations made by management about their responsibilities for financial reporting, internal control, and other matters that might be discussed in such a management report. Regarding incorrect answer b., management's responsibilities should be described in a separate section headed *Management's Responsibility for the Financial Statements*; not included in the first [introductory] paragraph. Regarding incorrect answer d, the introductory paragraph, not the management responsibility section, identifies the entity whose financial statements have been audited. (ID: 90393)

3. (d) The auditor's responsibility section of the audit report should explain that US GAAS require that the auditor plan and perform the audit to obtain *reasonable assurance* about whether the financial statements are free from material misstatement. Regarding incorrect answer a., the name of the auditor is *not* required. Regarding incorrect answer b., the auditor's responsibility section of the report should state that the audit was conducted in accordance with generally accepted auditing standards (not the applicable financial reporting framework) and should identify the United States of America as the country of origin of those standards. (The opinion paragraph indicates whether the financial statements are presented fairly in accordance with the the applicable financial reporting framework.) Regarding incorrect answer c., it would be inappropriate for the financial statements to include a disclosure that describes an audit. The description on an audit is included in the auditor's responsibility section of the audit report. (ID: 90394)

4. (d) The management's responsibility and the opinion sections of an audit report with an unmodified opinion for a nonissuer refer to the applicable financial reporting framework (AFRF). The introductory paragraph does not mention the AFRF. This is true for audit reports with all types of opinions as well as a disclaimer of opinion. The *Management's Responsibility for the Financial Statements* section should include the explanation that management is responsible for the preparation and fair presentation of the financial statements in accordance with the AFRF, for example, accounting principles generally accepted in the United States of America. This is true for audit reports with all types of opinions as well as a disclaimer of opinion. When expressing an unmodified opinion on financial statements, the auditor's opinion should state that the financial statements present fairly, in all material respects, the financial position of the entity as of the balance sheet date and the results of its operations and its cash flows for the period then ended, in accordance with the AFRF. The opinion section of an audit report with either a qualified or an adverse opinion also refers to the AFRF. A disclaimer of opinion does *not* refer to the AFRF. (ID: 89471)

5 (b) An emphasis-of-matter paragraph in an audit report refers to a matter appropriately presented or disclosed in the financial statements that, in the auditor's professional judgment, is of such importance that it is fundamental to users' understanding of the financial statements. It is either required by US GAAS or is included at the auditor's discretion. Incorrect answer a., describes an other-matter paragraph. Regarding incorrect answer c., an emphasis-of-matter paragraph does not refer to a matter that modifies the audit opinion, i.e., it does **not** affect the audit opinion. Regarding incorrect answer d., the heading *Emphasis-of-Matter* is *not* required; however, either *Emphasis-of-Matter* or another appropriate heading should be used. (Another heading may be considered appropriate if it adequately describes the nature of the matter.) (ID: 90396)

6. (d) If the auditor expects to include an emphasis-of-matter or other-matter paragraph in the audit report, the auditor should communicate with those charged with governance regarding this expectation and the proposed wording. Regarding incorrect answers a. and b., an emphasis-of-matter paragraph is *not* a substitute

for either (1) disclosures in the financial statements that the applicable financial reporting framework requires management to make or (2) the auditor expressing a modified opinion, when required by the circumstances of a specific audit engagement. Regarding incorrect answer c., in the rare circumstance when the auditor is unable to withdraw from an engagement even though the possible effect of an inability to obtain sufficient appropriate audit evidence due to a scope limitation imposed by management is pervasive, the auditor may consider it necessary to include an other-matter paragraph, not an emphasis-of-matter paragraph, in the audit report to explain why it is not possible for the auditor to withdraw from the engagement. (ID: 90397)

7. (a) An other-matter paragraph should *not* address circumstances when the auditor has other reporting responsibilities that are in addition to the auditor's responsibility under US GAAS to report on the financial statements (these other reporting responsibilities should be addressed in a separate section in the audit report that should be subtitled in a manner appropriate to its content). Regarding incorrect answer b., an other-matter paragraph should *not* include information that is required to be provided by management. Incorrect answers c. and d. are examples of matters that an auditor may reference in an emphasis-of-matter paragraph, not an other-matter paragraph. (ID: 90398)

8. (c) *Pervasive*, used in the context of misstatements, is used to describe the effects on the financial statements of misstatements (or the possible effects on the financial statements of misstatements, if any), that are undetected due to an inability to obtain sufficient appropriate audit evidence. Pervasive effects on the financial statements are those that, in the auditor's professional judgment (1) are not confined to specific elements, accounts, or items of the financial statements; (2) if so confined, represent or could represent a substantial proportion of the financial statements; or (3) with regard to disclosures, are fundamental to users' understanding of the financial statements. Answer c., pervasive effects, with regard to disclosures, would cause a reasonable person to misunderstand the nature of a significant component of the financial statements is *not* part of the definition of pervasive per US GAAS. (ID: 90043)

9. (b) The auditor should express an adverse opinion when the auditor, having obtained sufficient appropriate audit evidence, concludes that misstatements, individually or in the aggregate, are both material and pervasive to the financial statements. (ID: 90041)

10. (c) The factor considered by the auditor when deciding whether to express a qualified opinion vs. an adverse opinion or a qualified opinion vs. a disclaimer of opinion is the pervasiveness of the effects or possible effects on the financial statements. A matter giving rise to a modified opinion is material for all types of modified opinions—qualified, adverse, and a disclaimer of opinion. Thus, when deciding whether to modify the opinion, the auditor must first either decide that the financial statements as a whole are materially misstated; or, if unable to obtain sufficient appropriate audit evidence, to determine that a conclusion that the financial statements as a whole are free from material misstatement cannot be reached. Then, it is the auditor's judgment about the pervasiveness of the effects (qualified vs. adverse) or the possible effects of undetected misstatements (qualified vs. a disclaimer of opinion) on the financial statements that determines whether an adverse opinion or a disclaimer of opinion should be expressed. (ID: 90042)

11. (d) When the auditor disclaims an opinion due to an inability to obtain sufficient appropriate audit evidence, the auditor should add a basis for disclaimer of opinion paragraph that includes a description of other identified matters that would have otherwise required a modification of the auditor's opinion. Regarding incorrect answer a., when the auditor disclaims an opinion due to an inability to obtain sufficient appropriate audit evidence, the auditor should change the beginning of the introductory paragraph from *We ~~have~~ audited*… to *We* ***were engaged*** *to audit*...; **not** *We began, but were unable to complete, an audit*…. Regarding incorrect answer b., the auditor should also amend (not omit) the the auditor's responsibility section of the report to state *only* the following: *Our responsibility is to express an opinion on the financial statements based on conducting the audit in accordance with auditing standards generally accepted in the United States of America. Because of the matter(s) described in the basis for disclaimer of opinion paragraph; however, we were not able to obtain sufficient appropriate audit evidence to provide a basis for an audit opinion.* Regarding incorrect answer c., a disclaimer of opinion (or an adverse opinion) relating to a specific matter described in the basis-for-modification paragraph does *not* justify the omission of a description of other identified matters that would have otherwise required a modification of the auditor's opinion. In such cases, their disclosure may be relevant to users of the financial statements. (ID: 90044)

12. (c) When a change in accounting principle that the auditor has determined was handled appropriately has a material effect on the financial statements, the auditor should include an emphasis-of-matter paragraph in the audit report that describes the change in accounting principle and provides a reference to the entity's disclosure. Regarding incorrect answer a., a matter described in an emphasis-of-matter paragraph does not affect [modify] the auditor's opinion. (ID: 89760)

13. (b) The auditor should evaluate a change in accounting principle to determine whether the disclosures related to the accounting change are appropriate and adequate. Regarding incorrect answer a., for a nonissuer, the principle and the effect of the change should be in accordance with the applicable financial reporting framework, which may or may not be US GAAP. Regarding incorrect answer c., management, not the auditor, justifies that the alternative accounting principle is preferable. The auditor evaluates management's justification. Editor Note: The issuance of an accounting pronouncement that requires the use of a new accounting principle, interprets an existing principle, expresses a preference for an accounting principle, or rejects a specific principle is sufficient justification for a change in accounting principle, as long as the change in accounting principle is made in accordance with the applicable financial reporting framework. Regarding incorrect answer d., the materiality limits set by the auditor for the audit are not relevant to the evaluation of the appropriateness of an entity's change in accounting principle. The auditor considers materiality in the evaluation of whether the comparability of financial statements between periods has been affected to a degree that it should be reflected in the audit report and related procedures performed. (ID: 90399)

14. (b) When the comparability of financial statements between periods has been materially affected by adjustments to correct a material misstatement in previously issued financial statements the auditor should include an emphasis-of-matter paragraph in the audit report that includes a statement that the previously issued financial statements have been restated for the correction of a material misstatement in the respective period. Regarding incorrect answer a., the paragraph should include a reference to the entity's disclosure of the correction of the material misstatement rather than a description and explanation of the correction. Regarding incorrect answer c., the paragraph need *not* be repeated in subsequent periods. Regarding incorrect answer d., *all* emphasis-of-matter paragraphs, there are no exceptions, should include a statement that the opinion is not modified with respect to this matter. (ID: 90400)

15. (a) The auditor should evaluate and report on a change in accounting estimate that is inseparable from the effect of a related change in accounting principle like other changes in accounting principle. For example, when a change is made to the method of depreciation of an asset to reflect a change in the estimated future benefit of the asset or the pattern of consumption for those benefits, such a change in accounting may be inseparable from a change in estimate. Regarding incorrect answer b., a change from an accounting principle that is *not* in accordance with the applicable financial reporting framework (AFRF) to one that is in accordance with the AFRF is a correction of a misstatement, not a change in accounting principle. Regarding incorrect answer c., the auditor should evaluate a material change in financial statement classification and the related disclosure to determine whether such a change is also *either* a change in accounting principle *or* an adjustment to correct a material misstatement in previously issued financial statements. Regarding incorrect answer d., when a change in the reporting entity results in financial statements that, in effect, are those of a different reporting entity, the auditor should include an emphasis-of-matter paragraph in the audit report that describes the change in the reporting entity and provides a reference to the entity's disclosure, *unless the change in reporting entity results from a transaction or event.* A change in reporting entity that results from a transaction or event, such as the creation, cessation, or complete or partial purchase or disposition of a subsidiary or other business unit, does *not* require recognition in the audit report. Examples of a change in reporting entity that *should* be recognized in the audit report because they are **not** the result of a transaction or event include (1) presenting consolidated or combined financial statements in place of financial statements of individual entities; (2) changing specific subsidiaries that make up the group of entities for which consolidated financial statements are presented; and (3) changing the entities included in combined financial statements. (ID: 90436)

16. (c) The auditor's responsibility regarding the presentation and disclosure of segment information is in relation to the financial statements as a whole. Accordingly (regarding incorrect answer d.), the auditor is *not* required to perform audit procedures that would be necessary to express an opinion on the segment information presented on a stand-alone basis. Regarding incorrect answer a., the applicable financial reporting framework (AFRF) is the likely source of guidance for management and the auditor. The AFRF may include requirements

to disclose segment information; thus, the auditor should, rather than looking to industry standards, obtain an understanding of the methods used by management in determining segment information and evaluate whether such methods are likely to result in disclosure and presentation in accordance with the AFRF. When appropriate, the auditor should test the application methods and perform audit procedures. For example, when obtaining an understanding of management's methods to determine segment information, the auditor may look at (1) the allocation of assets and costs among segments or (2) sales, transfers, and charges between segments and the elimination of intersegment amounts. Regarding incorrect answer b., the auditor may find it appropriate to perform analytical procedures or other audit procedures appropriate in the circumstances. Analytical procedures may help identify inconsistencies with prior period information. (ID: 90437)

17. (d) The other-matter paragraph should *not* include the reasons an audit was not performed for the prior period. (ID: 90438)

18. (d) The subsequent period extends to the date of the audit report. (ID: 381)

19. (a) After the date of the audit report, the auditor has no obligation to make any further or continuing inquiries or perform any other auditing procedures with respect to the audited financial statements covered by that report, unless new information which may affect the report becomes known by the auditor. (ID: 2288)

20. (d) One of the auditor's procedures to determine the occurrence of subsequent events that may require adjustment or disclosure is asking management if any unusual adjustments were made after year-end. Confirming a sample of accounts receivable established after year-end is usually done to determine if proper cutoff was made. Comparison between the current and the prior year financial statements is unlikely to uncover evidence about the occurrence of subsequent events — rather a comparison of the current statements to the latest interim statements and an analysis of those interim statements should be done. Investigating personnel changes in the accounting department occurring after year-end would be more likely when possible misconduct, rather than a subsequent event, is being considered. (ID: 6003)

21. (c) An auditor should perform auditing procedures with respect to the period after the balance sheet date for the purpose of ascertaining the occurrence of subsequent events that may require adjustment or disclosure. These procedures should cover the period from the date of the financial statements to as near as practicable to the audit report date. For example, the auditor generally should inquire of and discuss with officers and other executives having responsibility for financial and accounting matters as to whether there was any significant change in the capital stock, long-term debt, or working capital to the date of inquiry. Regarding incorrect answers a. and b., the determination of whether inventory ordered before the year-end was included in the physical count as well as inquiries about payroll checks recorded before year-end, but cashed after year-end are examples of procedures to determine proper cutoff, not the occurrence of subsequent events. Regarding incorrect answer d., a review of tax returns prepared after year-end would generally not be as likely to reveal the occurrence of subsequent events as would changes in capital stock after year-end. (ID: 9906)

22. (c) A subsequent event is an event occurring between the date of the financial statements and the date of the audit report; not incorrect answer a., the audit report release date. Incorrect answers b. and d., existed at the date of the financial statements and arose after the date of the financial statements, respectively, refer to the timing of conditions that gave rise to a particular event and are used in some financial reporting frameworks to determine the appropriate treatment (adjustment vs. disclosure) of the subsequent event in the financial statements. (ID: 89494)

23. (c) When the auditor concludes that an auditing procedure considered necessary at the time of the audit in the circumstances then existing was omitted from the audit, the auditor should assess the importance of the omitted procedure to the auditor's present ability to support the previously expressed opinion regarding those financial statements taken as a whole. The other answer alternatives are steps that should be performed after the required assessment. (ID: 332)

24. (a) A determination of whether or not there are persons relying on the report would provide no evidence to the auditor in assessing the impact of the omitted procedure on the ability to support the opinion. (When an auditor concludes that an audit procedure considered necessary has been omitted, the first concern should be

to determine whether the previously expressed opinion can still be supported.) A discussion of the circumstances with engagement personnel; a review of the working papers to determine if there were other audit procedures performed that might compensate for the one omitted; and a re-evaluation of the overall scope of the audit may be helpful in making this assessment. If the opinion can still be supported, no further action is necessary. Otherwise, if the auditor believes there are persons relying on the report, then the auditor must promptly undertake the omitted procedures or alternative procedures. (ID: 371)

25. (b) The relevant time period for US GAAS guidance for such omitted procedures begins subsequent to the audit report release date; not the audit report date. Regarding incorrect answer d., if the auditor becomes aware of the omission before the report is released, the auditor can withhold the report until the appropriate action is taken. Regarding incorrect answer c., if the auditor needs to perform a previously omitted or alternative procedure, but is unable to do so, the auditor may, but is not required, to seek legal advice to determine an appropriate course of action concerning the auditor's responsibilities to the entity; regulatory authorities having jurisdiction over the entity; and users relying, or likely to rely, on the audit report. Regarding incorrect answer a., the auditor cannot discharge his or her responsibility for an omitted procedure by documenting the attempt to perform it or alternate procedures. However, the auditor is required to document new or additional audit procedures performed after the date of the audit report for inclusion in the audit file. The auditor should document the (1) circumstances encountered; (2) the new or additional audit procedures performed, audit evidence obtained, and conclusions reached, and their effect on the audit report; and (3) when and by whom the resulting changes to audit documentation were made and reviewed. Editor Note: It is rare for the auditor to perform new or additional audit procedures or to draw new conclusions after the date of the audit report. The guidance provides only two examples of such circumstances, i.e., this one, omitted procedures, and subsequently discovered facts. (ID: 89497)

26. (b) Confirmation with related and third parties of the details of arrangements to provide or maintain financial support is an audit procedure which may identify conditions and events that may indicate substantial doubt about the entity's ability to continue as a going concern. Pledging assets as collateral does not indicate an inability to continue as a going concern. The other two auditing procedures described (c. and d.) would not provide evidence about an entity's ability to continue as a going concern. (ID: 4720)

27. (c) In this situation, an auditor's consideration of management's plans may include plans to increase ownership equity as well as reduce expenditures; dispose of assets; and restructure debt. (ID: 7026)

28 (c) It is not necessary to design audit procedures solely to identify conditions and events that, when considered in the aggregate, indicate there could be substantial doubt about the entity's ability to continue as a going concern for a reasonable period of time. The results of auditing procedures designed and performed to achieve other audit objectives should be sufficient for that purpose. There is no requirement that the auditor's workpapers include evidence which provides assurance that the entity will continue as a going concern. The fact that the entity may cease to exist as a going concern subsequent to receiving a report from the auditor that does not refer to substantial doubt, even within one year following the date of the financial statements, does not, in itself, indicate inadequate performance by the auditor. Accordingly, the absence of reference to substantial doubt in an auditor's report should not be viewed as providing assurance as to an entity's ability to continue as a going concern. (The auditor is not responsible for predicting future conditions or events.) *A reasonable period of time* is defined as not to exceed one year beyond the date of the financial statements. (ID: 7506)

29. (a) The minutes of meetings of stockholders and the board of directors are likely to contain clear indications of doubts about the entity's ability to continue as a going concern. Comparisons of market value of property and related loans don't focus on the financial condition of the entity as a whole; many assets—such as relationships with customers and suppliers—are very valuable, and yet do not appear on the balance sheet. Lease agreements rarely highlight financial distress. Assets often are pledged as collateral by entities in strong financial condition. (ID: 7807)

30. (c) Possible plans to mitigate the adverse effects of future conditions and events may include: reducing or delaying expenditures such as leasing instead of purchasing operating facilities; increasing ownership equity; and borrowing money or restructuring debt. Issuing stock options would only cost the company money if they were exercised rather than mitigate the situation. (ID: 8129)

31. (d) The entity's legal counsel may provide information about the probability of litigation, claims, and assessments that could possibly cause the company to cease to exist. The procedures in the other answer alternatives. would not provide evidence of an entity's inability to continue as a going concern. Performing cutoff tests provides evidence about whether account balances are stated accurately. Evaluating procedures concerning related-party transactions would provide evidence of proper disclosure of such transactions. Real property pledged as collateral does not necessarily indicate a cause for concern. (ID: 8153)

32. (d) If the auditor believes, before consideration of management's plans, there is substantial doubt about the entity's ability to continue as a going concern for a reasonable period of time (substantial doubt), the auditor should obtain written representations about management's plans and adequate disclosure in the financial statements (1) regarding its plans that are intended to mitigate the adverse effects of conditions or events and the likelihood that those plans can be effectively implemented; and (2) that the financial statements disclose all the matters of which management is aware that are relevant to the entity's ability to continue as a going concern, including principal conditions or events and management's plans. The auditor is not precluded from disclaiming an opinion in cases involving uncertainties, but it is not required. Emphasis-of-matter paragraphs should be placed immediately after, not before, the opinion paragraph in the audit report. If, after considering identified conditions or events and management's plans, the auditor concludes there is substantial doubt, the auditor should include an emphasis-of-matter paragraph, not an other-matter paragraph. (ID: 89496)

33. (d) The terms substantial doubt and going concern should be used in a phrase similar to substantial doubt about its [the entity's] ability to continue as a going concern. (ID: 6019)

34. (c) The auditor's only responsibility for the other information is to read it and determine whether it has any material inconsistencies with the financial statements. The auditor need not preform audit (substantive tests) or review (limited procedures) procedures related to the other information. (ID: 90029)

35. (a) For purposes of US GAAS, other information does not encompass a cover letter accompanying the document containing audited financial statements and the audit report. (ID: 8399)

36. (a) One of the auditor's alternatives in this situation is to include a other-matter paragraph in the audit report describing the material inconsistency. The addition of this paragraph would not affect the auditor's opinion. The auditor may also decide to withhold the audit report or withdraw from the engagement, if withdrawal is possible under applicable law or regulation. The auditor should not consider the matter closed. A qualified opinion or a disclaimer of opinion would not be appropriate. (ID: 5159)

37. (b) RSI differs from other types of information outside the basic financial statements because an accounting standard setter (FASB, GASB, FASAB, or IASB) designated by the AICPA to establish GAAP considers the information an essential part of the financial reporting of certain entities and because authoritative guidelines for the measurement and presentation of the information have been established. Accordingly, the auditor should apply certain limited procedures to the RSI and should include a other-matter paragraph after the opinion paragraph in the audit report to explain that the RSI is included and that limited audit procedures were applied. If there are problems with the RSI, the other-matter paragraph should describe whether some or all of the information has been omitted or has not been presented in accordance with the applicable guidelines; and whether the auditor was unable to complete the audit procedures or has unresolved doubts about whether the information is presented in accordance with prescribed guidelines. (ID: 7642)

Solution 8-2 SIMULATION ANSWER: Audit Reports

The following items present various independent factual situations an auditor might encounter in conducting an audit of financial statements. The list represents the types of opinions the auditor ordinarily would issue. For each situation, select one response—the action the auditor normally would take based on the information given. A selection may be used once, more than once, or not at all.

Situation	Type of Opinion
1. The auditor was unable to obtain sufficient appropriate evidence for an investment in a foreign affiliate. The possible effects of the inability to obtain sufficient appropriate audit evidence are deemed to be material but not pervasive to the financial statements.	E. Qualified/Scope limitation
2. Due to recurring operating losses and working capital deficiencies, an auditor has substantial doubt about an entity's ability to continue as a going concern for a reasonable period of time. The financial statement disclosures concerning these matters are adequate.	B. Unmodified/ Emphasis-of-matter paragraph
3. The financial statements have inadequate disclosures. The effects are material, but are not fundamental to users' understanding of the financial statements.	D. Qualified/ Misstatement
4. An entity issues financial statements that present financial position and results of operations, but omits the required statement of cash flows. The auditor concludes that its omission has a material but not a pervasive effect on the financial statement presentation.	D. Qualified/ Misstatement
5. An entity changes its method of inventory pricing from LIFO to FIFO. The auditor concurs with the change although it has a material effect on the comparability of the entity's financial statements.	B. Unmodified/ Emphasis-of-matter paragraph
6. An entity is a defendant in a lawsuit alleging infringement of certain patent rights However, the ultimate outcome of the litigation cannot be reasonably estimated by management. The auditor believes there is a reasonable possibility of a significant material loss related to this unusually important matter. The lawsuit is adequately disclosed in the notes to the financial statements.	B. Unmodified/ Emphasis-of-matter paragraph
7. Certain lease obligations have been excluded from the financial statements in the current year that should be capitalized in accordance with the entity's applicable financial reporting framework. The effect of the exclusion is material and pervasive.	F. Adverse opinion
8. All required supplementary information has been omitted.	C. Unmodified opinion with an other-matter paragraph
9. The auditor was unable to obtain audit evidence about the entity's inventories and accounts receivable. The possible effects of this inability to obtain sufficient appropriate audit evidence are deemed to be both material and pervasive to the financial statements.	G. Disclaimer of opinion
10. The auditor has identified a material inconsistency prior to the audit report release date that requires revision of the other information in documents containing audited financial statements. Management refuses to make the revision. Based on advice from legal counsel, the auditor does not believe it is appropriate to either withhold the audit report or to withdraw from the engagement.	C. Unmodified opinion with an other-matter paragraph

(ID: 89472)

1. E. Qualified opinion due to a scope limitation

The auditor should express a qualified opinion due to a scope limitation when the auditor is unable to obtain sufficient appropriate audit evidence on which to base the opinion, but concludes that the possible effects on the financial statements of undetected misstatements, if any, could be material but not pervasive.

2. B. Unmodified opinion with an emphasis-of-matter paragraph

If, after considering identified conditions or events and management's plans, the auditor concludes that substantial doubt about the entity's ability to continue as a going concern for a reasonable period of time remains, the auditor should include an emphasis-of-matter paragraph in the audit report to reflect that conclusion. An emphasis-of-matter paragraph refers to a matter appropriately presented or disclosed in the financial statements that, in the auditor's professional judgment, is of such importance that it is fundamental to users' understanding of the financial statements. The auditor's opinion is not modified with respect to the matter emphasized.

3. D. Qualified opinion due to a misstatement

The auditor should express a qualified opinion due to a misstatement when the auditor, having obtained sufficient appropriate audit evidence, concludes that misstatements, individually or in the aggregate, are material but not pervasive to the financial statements. With regard to disclosures, pervasive effects on the financial statements are those that are fundamental to users' understanding of the financial statements.

4. D. Qualified opinion due to a misstatement

The auditor should express a qualified opinion due to a misstatement when the auditor, having obtained sufficient appropriate audit evidence, concludes that misstatements, individually or in the aggregate, are material but not pervasive to the financial statements. With regard to the appropriateness of the financial statement presentation, material misstatements of the financial statements may arise when information required to be presented in accordance with the applicable financial reporting framework is omitted because a required statement has not been included.

5. B. Unmodified opinion with an emphasis-of-matter paragraph

If the auditor concurs with a change in accounting principle and the change has a material effect on the comparability of the financial statements between periods, the auditor should include an emphasis-of-matter paragraph in the audit report that describes the change in accounting principle and provides a reference to the entity's disclosure. An emphasis-of-matter paragraph refers to a matter appropriately presented or disclosed in the financial statements that, in the auditor's professional judgment, is of such importance that it is fundamental to users' understanding of the financial statements. The auditor's opinion is not modified with respect to the matter emphasized.

6. B. Unmodified opinion with an emphasis-of-matter paragraph

The situation described indicated this was an unusually important litigation matter. The auditor believed there was a reasonable possibility of a significant material loss. The required disclosures were adequate. Under such circumstances, an auditor would normally find it necessary to include an emphasis-of-matter paragraph; however, it is not required. An emphasis-of-matter paragraph refers to a matter appropriately presented or disclosed in the financial statements that, in the auditor's professional judgment, is of such importance that it is fundamental to users' understanding of the financial statements. The auditor's opinion is not modified with respect to the matter emphasized.

7. F. Adverse opinion

The auditor should express an adverse opinion when, having obtained sufficient appropriate audit evidence, concludes that misstatements, individually or in the aggregate, are both material and pervasive to the financial statements.

8. C. Unmodified opinion with an other-matter paragraph

The auditor should include an other-matter paragraph in the audit report on the financial statements to refer to the required supplementary information (RSI). The paragraph should be included whether or not there are departures from the prescribed guidelines for the RSI. (In the absence of any separate requirement in the particular circumstances of the engagement, the auditor's opinion on the basic financial statements does not cover required supplementary information.)

9. G. Disclaimer of opinion

The auditor should disclaim an opinion when the auditor is unable to obtain sufficient appropriate audit evidence on which to base the opinion, and the auditor concludes that the possible effects on the financial statements of undetected misstatements, if any, could be both material and pervasive.

10. C. Unmodified opinion with an other-matter paragraph

When the auditor identifies a material inconsistency prior to the report release date that requires revision of the other information and management refuses to make the revision, the auditor should communicate this matter to those charged with governance and include in the auditor's report an other-matter paragraph describing the material inconsistency. (ID: 89472)

Solution 8-3 SIMULATION ANSWER: Research

Which citation in the professional standards provides guidance regarding the condition that should be met in order for an auditor to refer in the audit report to having conducted an audit in accordance with another set of auditing standards in addition to US GAAS?

AU	§	700	42	(ID: 90054)

.42 Paragraph .31 requires that the auditor's report state that the audit was conducted in accordance with US GAAS and identify the United States of America as the country of origin of those standards. However, an auditor may indicate that the audit was also conducted in accordance with another set of auditing standards (for example, International Standards on Auditing (ISA), the standards of the Public Company Accounting Oversight Board, or *Government Auditing Standards*). The auditor should not refer to having conducted an audit in accordance with another set of auditing standards in addition to US GAAS, unless the audit was conducted in accordance with both sets of standards in their entirety.

CHAPTER 9

AUDITS OF GROUP FINANCIAL STATEMENTS

AU Identifier Used for Clarified US GAAS in This Textbook

We have not continued to use the temporary AU-C identifier for the clarified auditing standards issued by the American Institute of Certified Public Accountants (AICPA). In this textbook these standards have an AU identifier.

CHAPTER 9

AUDITS OF GROUP FINANCIAL STATEMENTS

I. Overview (AU 600)

This guidance addresses special considerations that apply to group audits, in particular those that involve component auditors. However, it also applies to *all* audits of group financial statements whether or not different auditors are involved in the audit.

A. Objectives

1. **Decision to Act as Auditor of Group Financial Statements** An auditor must first determine whether to act as the auditor of the group financial statements. Relevant factors for this determination may include the following.

    a. **Individual Financial Significance of Components** The individual financial significance of the components for which the auditor of the group financial statements will be assuming responsibility

    b. **Significant Risks Included in Components** The extent to which significant risks of material misstatement (RMM) of the group financial statements are included in the components for which the auditor of the group financial statements will be assuming responsibility

    c. **Group Engagement Team's Knowledge of Overall Financial Statements** The extent of the group engagement team's knowledge of the overall financial statements

2. **Auditor of Group Financial Statements Decides Whether to Reference Component Auditor** The auditor of the group financial statements is responsible for deciding, individually for each component, to *either*:

    a. **Assume Responsibility / No Reference** Assume responsibility for, and thus be required to be involved in, the work of a component auditor, insofar as that work relates to the expression of an opinion on the group financial statements; in this case no reference is made to the component auditor in the report on the group financial statements

        (1) **Additional Requirements** There are additional requirements that only apply when the auditor of the group financial statements assumes responsibility for the work of a component auditor. These stem from the requirement for the group auditor to be involved in the work of the component auditor for this situation.

        (2) **No Reference Made to Prevent Misinterpretation Regarding Responsibility** When responsibility is assumed for the work of the component auditor, no reference is made to the component auditor in the report on the group audit because to do so may cause a reader to misinterpret the degree of responsibility being assumed.

    b. ***Not* Assume Responsibility / Make Reference** *Not* assume responsibility for, and accordingly make reference to, the audit report of a component auditor in the report on the group financial statements

3. **Communication** Communicate clearly with component auditors

4. **Express Opinion on Group Financial Statements** Obtain sufficient appropriate audit evidence regarding the financial information of the components and the consolidation process to express a group audit opinion

B. Definitions

1. **Component** An entity or business activity for which group or component management prepares financial information that is required by the applicable financial reporting framework (AFRF) to be included in the group financial statements

   a. **Basis of Group Financial Reporting Affects Identification of Components** The structure of the group affects how components are identified. The group financial reporting system may be based on an organization structure, in which case a component may include a parent and one or more subsidiaries, investees, or joint ventures; or a head office and one or more divisions; or by a combination of both. Other groups may organize financial reporting by function; product or service; or geographical location, in which case these will constitute components.

      Various levels of components may exist within the group financial reporting system, in which case it may be more appropriate to identify components at certain levels of aggregation rather than individually.

   b. **Investments** An investment accounted for under the equity method constitutes a component. Investments accounted for under the cost method may be analogous to a component when the work and reports of other auditors constitute a major element of evidence for such investments.

2. **Component Auditor** An auditor who performs work on the financial information of a component that will be used as audit evidence for the group audit; a component auditor may be part of the group engagement partner's firm, a network firm of the group engagement partner's firm, or another firm

3. **Component Management** Management responsible for preparing the financial information of a component

4. **Component Materiality** The materiality for a component determined by the group engagement team for the purposes of the group audit

5. **Group** All the components whose financial information is included in the group financial statements; a group always has more than one component

6. **Group Audit** The audit of group financial statements

7. **Group Audit Opinion** The audit opinion on the group financial statements

8. **Group Engagement Partner** The partner or other person in the firm who is responsible for the group audit engagement and its performance and for the audit report on the group financial statements that is issued on behalf of the firm

9. **Group Engagement Team** Partners, including the group engagement partner, and staff who establish the overall group audit strategy; communicate with component auditors; perform work on the consolidation process; and evaluate the conclusions drawn from the audit evidence as the basis for forming an opinion on the group financial statements

10. **Group Financial Statements** Financial statements that include the financial information of more than one component; the concept of group financial statements is broader than consolidated or combined financial statements as it encompasses business activities as well as separate entities

    The term *group financial statements* also refers to combined financial statements aggregating the financial information prepared by components that are under common control.

    a. **Applicable Financial Reporting Framework (AFRF)** Reference in this guidance to the AFRF means the financial reporting framework that applies to the group financial statements.

    b. **Consolidation Process** Reference in this guidance to the consolidation process includes the following:

        (1) The recognition, measurement, presentation, and disclosure of the financial information of the components in the group financial statements by way of inclusion, consolidation, proportionate consolidation, or the equity or cost methods of accounting

        (2) The aggregation in combined financial statements of the financial information of components that are under common control

11. **Group Management** Management responsible for the preparation and fair presentation of the group financial statements

12. **Group-Wide Controls** Controls designed, implemented, and maintained by group management over group financial reporting

13. **Significant Component** A component identified by the group engagement team that:

    a. **Financially Significant** Is of individual financial significance to the group, or

        Editor note: As the individual financial significance of a component increases, the RMM of the group financial statements ordinarily increases. The group engagement team may apply a percentage to a chosen benchmark as an aid to identify components that are of individual financial significance. For example, the group engagement team may consider that components exceeding a specified percentage of the chosen benchmark are significant components.

    b. **Risk Significant** Due to its specific nature or circumstances, is likely to include significant RMM of the group financial statements

C. **Group Engagement Partner Responsibilities**
The group engagement partner is responsible for:

1. **Leadership** The direction, supervision, and performance of the group audit engagement in compliance with professional standards, applicable regulatory and legal requirements, and the firm's policies and procedures

2. **Audit Report** Determining whether the audit report that is issued is appropriate in the circumstances

D. Engagement Acceptance & Continuance

1. Preliminary Understanding of Consolidation Process & Financial Information of Components

a. **Availability of Evidence** The group engagement partner should determine whether sufficient appropriate audit evidence can reasonably be expected to be obtained regarding the consolidation process and the financial information of the components on which to base the group audit opinion.

b. **Identification of Significant Components** The group engagement team should obtain an understanding of the group, its components, and their environments that is sufficient to identify components that are likely to be significant.

(1) **New Engagement**

(a) **Sources** In the case of a new engagement, the group engagement team's understanding of the group, its components, and their environments may be obtained from the following.

(i) Information provided by and communication with group management

(ii) When applicable, communication with the previous group engagement team, component management, or component auditors

(b) **Understanding Obtained** The group engagement team's understanding may include matters such as the following.

(i) How the group financial reporting system is organized

(ii) Components' business activities that are significant to the group, including the industry and regulatory, economic, and political environments in which those activities take place

(iii) The use of service organizations, including shared service centers

(iv) A description of group-wide controls

(v) The complexity of the consolidation process

(vi) Whether component auditors that are not from the group engagement partner's firm or network will perform work on the financial information of any of the components and group management's rationale for engaging more than one auditor, if applicable

(vii) Whether the group engagement team will have unrestricted access to those charged with governance of the group, group management, those charged with governance of the component, component management, component information, and the component auditors (including relevant audit documentation sought by the group engagement team) and will be able to perform necessary work on the financial information of the components

(2) **Significant Changes Considered for Continuing Engagements** In the case of a continuing engagement, the group engagement team's ability to obtain sufficient appropriate audit evidence may be affected by significant changes, such as the following.

(a) Changes in the group structure, for example, acquisitions, disposals, reorganizations, or changes in how the group financial reporting system is organized

(b) Changes in components' business activities that are significant to the group

(c) Changes in the composition of those charged with governance of the group, group management, or key management of significant components

(d) Concerns the group engagement team has with regard to the integrity and competence of group or component management

(e) Changes in group-wide controls

(f) Changes in in the AFRF

2. **Scope Limitations**

a. **Material & Pervasive Scope Limitation Imposed by Management** When circumstances due to restrictions imposed by group management would result in a disclaimer of opinion on the group financial statements, the auditor of the group financial statements should, in the case of:

(1) **A New Engagement** *Not* accept the engagement

(2) **A Continuing Engagement** Withdraw when this is possible under applicable law or regulation

(3) **An Audit Required by Law or Regulation** After having performed the audit to the extent possible, disclaim an opinion on the group financial statements

b. **Access Restricted by Circumstances** When access to information is restricted by circumstances, the group engagement team may still be able to obtain sufficient appropriate audit evidence; however, this is less likely as the significance of the component increases.

c. **Access Restricted by Group Management** There will be a scope limitation if group management restricts the access to the information of a significant component. If it is not a significant component, the auditor of the group financial statements may be able to obtain sufficient appropriate audit evidence; however, the reason for the restriction may affect the group audit opinion (constitute a scope limitation). For example, the auditor may not be able to rely on group management's representations or responses to inquiries under such circumstances.

E. Terms of Engagement

The auditor of the group financial statements is required to agree upon the terms of the group audit engagement. Additional matters that may be included in the terms of a group audit engagement include:

1. **Whether the Audit Report Will Reference Audit of Component Auditor** The terms may include whether reference will be made to the audit of a component auditor in the audit report on the group financial statements.

2. **Matters That May Need to Be Facilitated** The terms may include, when relevant, the arrangements to facilitate the following.

   a. **Unrestricted Communication** Unrestricted communication between the group engagement team and component auditors to the extent permitted by law or regulation

   b. **Communication to the Group Engagement Team** Communication to the group engagement team of important communications between:

      (1) **Within the Component** The component auditors, those charged with governance of the component, and component management, including communications on significant deficiencies and material weaknesses in internal control

      (2) **Regulatory Authorities & Components** Regulatory authorities and components related to financial reporting matters

   c. **Access & Permissions** To the extent the group engagement team considers necessary

      (1) **Component Information & Personnel** Access to component information, those charged with governance of components, component management, and the component auditors, including relevant audit documentation

      (2) **Permission to Perform Work or Request Work From Component Auditors** Permission to perform work, or request a component auditor to perform work, on the financial information of the components

II. Planning (AU 600 continued)

A. Overall Audit Strategy & Audit Plan

1. **Engagement Team Develops Strategy & Plan** The group engagement team should establish an overall group audit strategy and should develop a group audit plan. In developing the group audit plan, the group engagement team should assess the extent to which the group engagement team will use the work of component auditors and whether the audit report on the group financial statements will make reference to the audit of a component auditor.

2. **Group Engagement Partner Approves Strategy & Plan** The group engagement partner should review and approve the overall group audit strategy and group audit plan.

B. Obtaining an Understanding of the Group and Its Components & Their Environments

1. **Obtain Understanding to Assess Risk** The auditor is required to identify and assess the RMM through obtaining an understanding of the entity and its environment. The group engagement team should:

   a. **Components & Environments, Including Group-Wide Controls** Enhance its understanding of the group, its components, and their environments, including group-wide controls, obtained during the acceptance or continuance stage

   b. **Consolidation Process** Obtain an understanding of the consolidation process, including the instructions issued by group management to components

   c. **Examples of Areas of Understanding** Examples of matters about which the group engagement team obtains an understanding are as follows.

      (1) **Group-Wide Controls** Group-wide controls may include a combination of the following.

         (a) Regular meetings between group and component management to discuss business developments and review performance

         (b) Monitoring of components' operations and their financial results, including regular reporting routines, which enables group management to monitor components' performance against budgets and take appropriate action

         (c) Group management's risk assessment process

         (d) Monitoring, controlling, reconciling, and eliminating intragroup account balances, transactions, and unrealized profits or losses at group level

         (e) A process for monitoring the timeliness and assessing the accuracy and completeness of financial information received from components

         (f) A central IT system controlled by the same general IT controls for all or part of the group

         (g) Control activities within an IT system that are common for all or some components

         (h) Monitoring of controls, including activities of internal audit and self-assessment programs

- **(i)** Consistent policies and procedures, including a group financial reporting procedures manual
- **(j)** Group-wide programs, such as codes of conduct and fraud prevention programs
- **(k)** Arrangements for assigning authority and responsibility to component management

(2) **Consolidation Process** The group engagement team's understanding of the consolidation process may include matters such as the following.

- **(a)** **AFRF Matters** Matters relating to the AFRF, such as the following.
  - **(i)** **Component Management's Understanding** The extent to which component management has an understanding of the AFRF
  - **(ii)** **Identification of & Accounting for Components** The process for identifying and accounting for components, in accordance with the AFRF
  - **(iii)** **Identification of Reportable Segments** The process for identifying reportable segments for segment reporting, in accordance with the AFRF
  - **(iv)** **Identification of Related-Party Relationships & Transactions** The process for identifying related-party relationships and related-party transactions for reporting, in accordance with the AFRF
  - **(v)** **Accounting Policies & Changes** The accounting policies applied to the group financial statements, changes from those of the previous financial year, and changes resulting from new or revised standards under the AFRF
  - **(vi)** **Components With Different Year-Ends** The procedures for dealing with components with financial year-ends different from the group's year-end
- **(b)** **Consolidation Process** Matters relating to the consolidation process, such as the following.
  - **(i)** **Differences in Accounting Policies Among Components** Group management's process for obtaining an understanding of the accounting policies used by components and, when applicable, ensuring that uniform accounting policies are used to prepare the financial information of the components for the group financial statements and that differences in accounting policies are identified and adjusted, when required, in terms of the AFRF
  - **(ii)** **Accurate & Timely Reporting Process** Group management's process for ensuring complete, accurate, and timely financial reporting by the components for the consolidation
  - **(iii)** **Currency Translation** The process for translating the financial information of foreign components into the currency of the group financial statements

(iv) **IT Organization & Controls** How IT is organized for the consolidation, including the manual and automated stages of the process and the manual and programmed controls in place at various stages of the consolidation process

(v) **Subsequent Events** Group management's process for obtaining information on subsequent events

(c) **Consolidation Adjustments** Matters relating to consolidation adjustments, such as the following

(i) **Recording Process** The process for recording consolidation adjustments, including the preparation, authorization, and processing of related journal entries and the experience of personnel responsible for the consolidation

(ii) **AFRF Adjustment Requirements** The consolidation adjustments required by the AFRF

(iii) **Business Rationale** Business rationale for the events and transactions that gave rise to the consolidation adjustments

(iv) **Transactions Between Components** Frequency, nature, and size of transactions between components

(v) **Procedures for Intragroup Transactions & Accounts** Procedures for monitoring, controlling, reconciling, and eliminating intragroup account balances, transactions, and unrealized profits or losses

(vi) **Fair Value & Goodwill Considerations** Steps taken to arrive at the fair value of acquired assets and liabilities, procedures for amortizing goodwill (when applicable), and impairment testing of goodwill, in accordance with the AFRF

(vii) **Controlling & Noncontrolling Interest Arrangements** Arrangements with a controlling interest or noncontrolling interest regarding losses incurred by a component (for example, an obligation of the noncontrolling interest to compensate such losses)

2. **Sufficiency of Understanding** The group engagement team should obtain an understanding that is sufficient to:

a. **Confirm or Revise Identification of Significant Components** Confirm or revise its initial identification of components that are likely to be significant

b. **Assess RMM** Assess the RMM of the group financial statements, whether due to fraud or error. Examples of conditions or events that, individually or together, may indicate RMM of the group financial statements, including risks due to fraud are as follows.

(1) A complex group structure, especially when there are frequent acquisitions, disposals, or reorganizations

(2) Poor corporate governance structures, including decision-making processes that are not transparent

(3) Nonexistent or ineffective group-wide controls, including inadequate group management information on monitoring of components' operations and their results

(4) Components operating in foreign jurisdictions that may be exposed to factors, such as unusual government intervention in areas such as trade and fiscal policy, restrictions on currency and dividend movements, and fluctuations in exchange rates

(5) Business activities of components that involve high risk, such as long-term contracts or trading in innovative or complex financial instruments

(6) Uncertainties regarding which components' financial information requires incorporation in the group financial statements, in accordance with the AFRF, for example, whether any special purpose entities or nontrading entities exist and require incorporation

(7) Unusual related-party relationships and transactions

(8) Prior occurrences of intragroup account balances that did not balance or reconcile on consolidation

(9) The existence of complex transactions that are accounted for in more than one component

(10) Components' application of accounting policies that differ from those applied to the group financial statements

(11) Components with different financial year-ends, which may be utilized to manipulate the timing of transactions

(12) Prior occurrences of unauthorized or incomplete consolidation adjustments

(13) Aggressive tax planning within the group or large cash transactions with entities in tax havens

(14) Frequent changes of auditors engaged to audit the financial statements of components

C. Materiality Considerations

1. **All Audits of Group Financial Statements** The group engagement team should determine the following.

   a. **Materiality & Performance Materiality for Group Financial Statements as a Whole** Materiality, including performance materiality, for the group financial statements as a whole when establishing the overall group audit strategy

   b. **Materiality for Particular Classes of Transactions, Account Balances, or Disclosures** Whether, in the specific circumstances of the group, particular classes of transactions, account balances, or disclosures in the group financial statements exist for which misstatements of lesser amounts than materiality for the group financial statements as a whole could reasonably be expected to influence the economic decisions of users taken on the basis of the group financial statements; in such circumstances, the group engagement team should determine materiality to be applied to those particular classes of transactions, account balances, or disclosures

c. **Component Materiality** Component materiality for those components on which the group engagement team will perform, or for which the auditor of the group financial statements will assume responsibility for the work of a component auditor who performs, an audit or a review; component materiality should be determined taking into account all components, regardless of whether reference is made in the audit report on the group financial statements to the audit of a component auditor; to reduce the risk that the aggregate of uncorrected and undetected misstatements in the group financial statements exceeds the materiality for the group financial statements as a whole, component materiality should be lower than the materiality for the group financial statements as a whole, and component performance materiality should be lower than performance materiality for the group financial statements as a whole

d. **Threshold** The threshold above which misstatements cannot be regarded as clearly trivial to the group financial statements

2. **Additional Considerations When Auditor Assumes Responsibility for the Work of Component Auditors** In the case of an audit of the financial information of a component in which the auditor of the group financial statements is assuming responsibility for the component auditor's work, the group engagement team should evaluate the appropriateness of performance materiality at the component level.

D. **Obtaining an Understanding of Component Auditors**

1. **Areas of Understanding** Regardless of whether reference will be made in the audit report on the group financial statements to the audit of a component auditor, the group engagement team should obtain an understanding of the following.

   a. **Ethics & Independence** Whether a component auditor understands and will comply with the ethical requirements that are relevant to the group audit and, in particular, is independent

   b. **Competence** A component auditor's professional competence

   c. **Extent of Engagement Team's Involvement in Work of Component Auditor** The extent, if any, to which the group engagement team will be able to be involved in the work of the component auditor

   d. **Whether Component Auditor Can Provide Information About Consolidation Process** Whether the group engagement team will be able to obtain information affecting the consolidation process from a component auditor

   e. **Whether Component Auditor Operates in a Regulatory Environment** Whether a component auditor operates in a regulatory environment that actively oversees auditors

2. **Other Factors to Consider Regarding Use of Component Auditor's Work and/or Whether to Reference Their Audit in Group Report** Other factors that *may* affect the decision to use the work of component auditors or make reference to their audit include the following.

   a. **Different Reporting Framework** Differences in the financial reporting framework of the component financial statements vs. the financial reporting framework of the group financial statements

   b. **Timing of Completion of Component Audit** Whether the audit of the financial statements of the component will be completed in time to meet the group reporting timetable

c. **Different Standards** Differences in the auditing and other standards applied by the component auditor and those applied in the audit of the group financial statements

d. **Practicality of Involvement in Work of Component Auditors** Whether it is impracticable for the group engagement team to be involved in the work of a component auditor

3. **After Review of Component Auditor Completed**

a. **Decide Whether to Reference Component Auditor in Audit Report on Group Financial Statement** Having gained an understanding of each component auditor, the group engagement partner should decide whether to make reference to a component auditor in the audit report on the group financial statements

b. **Group Auditor Should *Not* Make Reference in Report *or* Use Their Work When Component Auditor Fails to Meet Requirements for Independence, Ethics & Competence** When component auditors do not meet the independence requirements or there are serious concerns about other matters related to them (their ethics, competence, or when interaction with them or access to their work is limited or blocked, etc.), the group engagement team should not make reference to their audit in the audit report on the group financial statements or otherwise use their work.

E. **Determining Whether to Make Reference to a Component Auditor in the Audit Report**

1. **Separate Decision for Each Component Auditor** The decision to make reference to the audit of a component auditor is made individually for each component auditor, i.e., reference can be made to any, all, or none of them.

2. **Preconditions** Reference to the audit of a component auditor in the audit report on the group financial statements should *not* be made *unless* the following determinations are made.

a. **US GAAS Audit of Component Financial Statements Performed by Component Auditor** The component auditor has performed an audit of the financial statements of the component in accordance with the relevant requirements of US GAAS

(1) **US GAAS or PCAOB Audit Standards** A statement in a component audit report that the audit was conducted in accordance with US GAAS or PCAOB auditing standards is sufficient to make this determination

(2) **Group Partner May Exercise Professional Judgment** Otherwise, the group engagement partner may exercise professional judgment to evaluate whether the audit performed by the component auditor meets the relevant requirements of US GAAS

(a) **Only US GAAS Requirements Related to Planning & Performing Are Relevant** Relevant requirements of US GAAS are those that pertain to planning and performing the audit of the component financial statements and do not include those related to the form of the audit report

(b) **Component Auditor May Remedy Audit With Additional Procedures** If the component auditor has performed an audit in accordance with standards other than US GAAS, the component auditor may perform additional procedures, if needed, in order to meet the relevant requirements of US GAAS

b. **General Use Component Audit Report** Reference to the audit of a component auditor in the audit report on the group financial statements should not be made unless the component auditor has issued an audit report for general use, i.e., not restricted as to use

c. **Resolution of Different Financial Reporting Frameworks** If the component's financial statements are prepared using a different financial reporting framework from that used for the group financial statements, reference to the audit of a component auditor should *not* be made *unless* the:

(1) **Similar Criteria for All Material Items** Measurement, recognition, presentation, and disclosure criteria that are applicable to all material items in the component's financial statements under the component's financial reporting framework are similar to the criteria that are applicable to those in the group's financial statements under the group's financial reporting framework

(2) **Appropriateness of Adjustments Can Be Evaluated** Group engagement team has obtained sufficient appropriate audit evidence for purposes of evaluating the appropriateness of the adjustments to convert the component's financial statements to the financial reporting framework used by the group without the need to assume responsibility for, and, thus, be involved in, the work of the component auditor

Factors related to the conversion adjustments that *may* be considered when deciding whether to make reference to the audit of the component auditor when the component's financial statements are prepared using a different financial reporting framework include:

(a) **Effectiveness of Group-Wide Controls & Adequacy of Consolidation Process Related to Adjustments** Effectiveness of group-wide controls and the adequacy of the consolidation process specifically related to the adjustments to convert the component's financial statements to the group's financial reporting framework, including the financial reporting competencies of personnel involved in the adjustments

(b) **Understanding of Component & RMM Related to Adjustments** Depth of the group engagement team's understanding of the component and its environment, including the complexity of the events and transactions subject to the differing financial reporting requirements and the assessed RMM related to the adjustments

(c) **Knowledge of Component's Reporting Framework** Extent of the group engagement team's knowledge of the component's financial reporting framework

(d) **Access to Information of Component Relevant to Adjustments** Group engagement team's ability to obtain information from group or component management that is relevant to the adjustments

(e) **Need for Specialist's Assistance Regarding Adjustments** Need and ability to seek, as necessary, the assistance of professionals possessing specialized skills or knowledge related to the adjustments

Editor Note: Evaluating whether the financial statements of the component have been appropriately adjusted to conform with the financial reporting framework used by the group is based on a depth of understanding of the component's financial statements that ordinarily is *not* obtained unless the auditor of the group financial statements assumes responsibility for, and, thus, is involved in, the work of the component auditor.

In rare circumstances, however, the group engagement partner may conclude otherwise and thus, make reference.

F. Responding to Assessed Risks

1. **All Audits of Group Financial Statements Regarding Testing Operating Effectiveness of Group-Wide Controls** The auditor is required to design and implement appropriate responses to address the assessed RMM of the financial statements. If the nature, extent, and timing of the work to be performed on the consolidation process or the financial information of the components is based on an expectation that group-wide controls are operating effectively or when substantive procedures alone cannot provide sufficient appropriate audit evidence at the assertion level, the group engagement team should test, or have a component auditor test on the group engagement team's behalf, the operating effectiveness of those controls.

2. **Additional Considerations When Auditor Assumes Responsibility for the Work of Component Auditors—Procedures on Financial Information of Components** For components for which the auditor of the group financial statements is assuming responsibility for the work of component auditors, the group engagement team should determine the type of work to be performed by the group engagement team or by component auditors on its behalf on the financial information of the components. The group engagement team also should determine the nature, timing, and extent of its involvement in the work of component auditors.

   a. **Significant Components**

      (1) **Risk Assessment** When a component auditor performs an audit or other specified audit procedures of the financial information of a significant component for which the auditor of the group financial statements is assuming responsibility for the component auditor's work, the group engagement team should be involved in the risk assessment of the component to identify significant RMM of the group financial statements. The nature, extent, and timing of this involvement are affected by the group engagement team's understanding of the component auditor but, at a minimum, should include the following.

         (a) **Business Activities of Component** Discussing with the component auditor or component management the component's business activities of significance to the group

         (b) **Susceptibility of Component Financial Information to Material Misstatement** Discussing with the component auditor the susceptibility of the component to material misstatement of the financial information due to fraud or error

         (c) **Significant Risks Identified by Component** Reviewing the component auditor's documentation of identified significant RMM of the group financial statements; such documentation may take the form of a memorandum that reflects the component auditor's conclusion with regard to the identified significant risks

      (2) **Components That Are Individually Financially Significant** For a component that is significant due to its individual financial significance to the group, the group engagement team, or a component auditor on its behalf, should perform an audit of the financial information of the component, adapted as necessary to meet the needs of the group engagement team, using component materiality.

(3) **Components With Significant RMM** For a component that is significant not due to its individual financial significance but because it is likely to include significant RMM of the group financial statements due to its specific nature or circumstances, the group engagement team, or a component auditor on its behalf, should perform one or more of the following.

(a) **Perform Audit of Component Financial Information Using Component Materiality** An audit, adapted as necessary to meet the needs of the group engagement team, of the financial information of the component, using component materiality

(b) **Perform Audit of Specific Items With Highest RMM of Component** An audit, adapted as necessary to meet the needs of the group engagement team, of one or more account balances, classes of transactions, or disclosures relating to the likely significant RMM of the group financial statements

(c) **Perform Specific Audit Procedures Related to RMM** Specified audit procedures relating to the likely significant risks of material misstatement of the group financial statements

b. **Perform Analytical Procedures for Components That Are *Not* Significant** For components that are *not* significant components, the group engagement team should perform analytical procedures at the group level.

c. **Further Procedures If Additional Audit Evidence Is Needed** The group engagement team may determine that sufficient appropriate audit evidence will not be obtained from the procedures performed on group-wide controls, the consolidation process, the information of significant components, and the analytical procedures at the group level. In this case, the group engagement team should select additional components that are not significant components and should perform or request a component auditor to perform one or more of the following on the financial information of the individual components selected. The group engagement team should vary the selection of such individual components over a period of time.

(1) **Perform Audit of Component Financial Information Using Component Materiality** An audit, adapted as necessary to meet the needs of the group engagement team, of the financial information of the component, using component materiality

(2) **Perform Audit of Specific Items of Component** An audit, adapted as necessary to meet the needs of the group engagement team, of one or more account balances, classes of transactions, or disclosures

(3) **Perform Specific Audit Procedures** Specified audit procedures

Exhibit 1 ▸ How the Significance of the Components Affects the Group Engagement Team's Determination (Planning) of the Type of Work to Be Performed on the Components

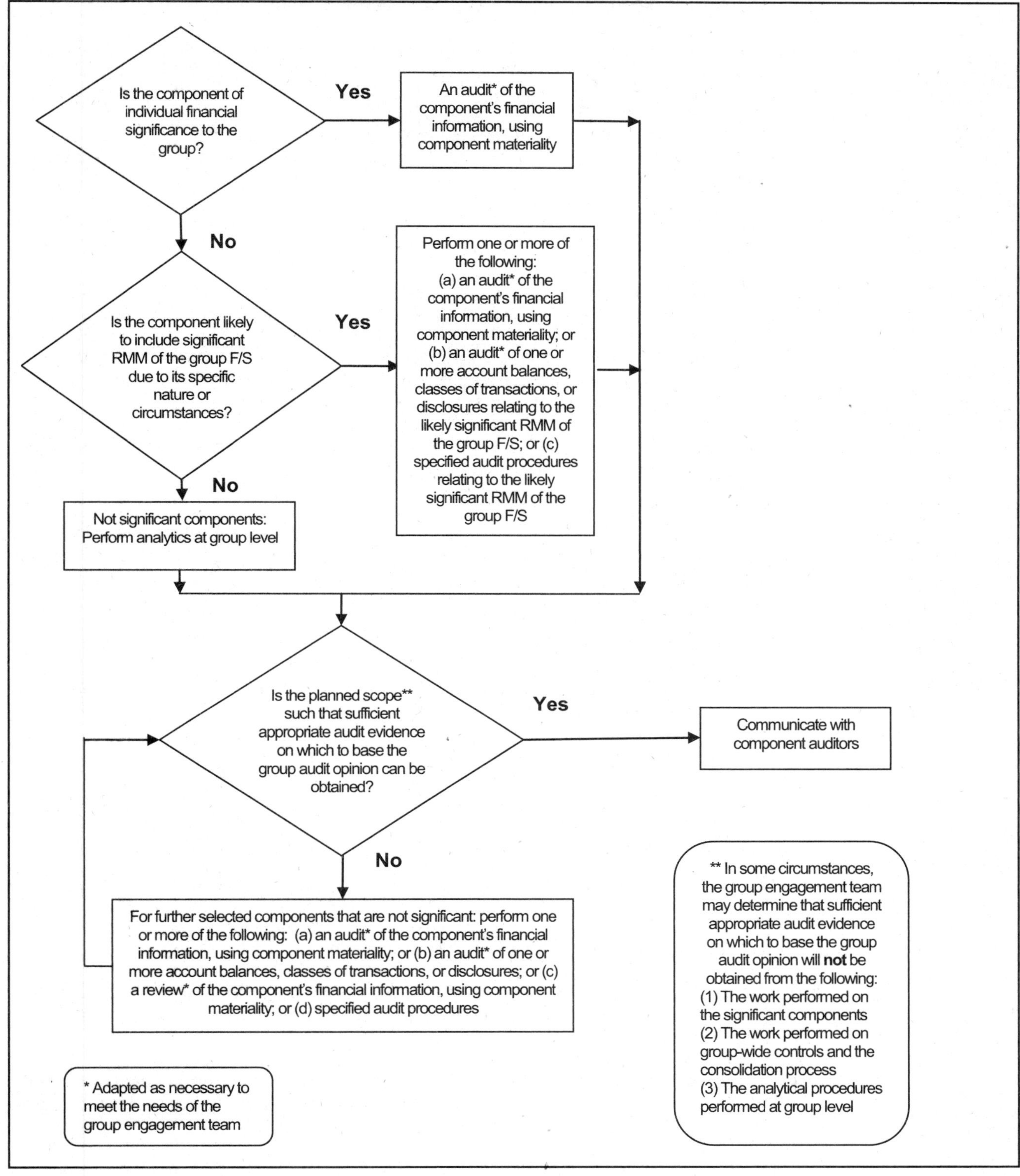

III. Communication With Component Auditor (AU 600 continued)

A. Communication of Requirements From Group Engagement Team

1. **All Audits of Group Financial Statements** The group engagement team should communicate its requirements to a component auditor on a timely basis. This communication should include the following.

   a. **Agreement to Cooperate** A request that the component auditor, knowing the context in which the group engagement team will use the work of the component auditor, confirm that the component auditor will cooperate with the group engagement team

   b. **Ethical Requirements, Including Independence** The ethical requirements that are relevant to the group audit and, in particular, the independence requirements

   c. **List of Related Parties** A list of related parties prepared by group management and any other related parties of which the group engagement team is aware; the group engagement team should request the component auditor to communicate on a timely basis related parties not previously identified by group management or the group engagement team; the group engagement team should identify such additional related parties to other component auditors

   d. **Significant RMM** Identified significant risks of material misstatement of the group financial statements, due to fraud or error that are relevant to the work of the component auditor

2. **Additional Considerations When Auditor Assumes Responsibility for the Work of Component Auditors** When the auditor of the group financial statements is assuming responsibility for the work of a component auditor, the communication of its requirements should also include the following.

   a. **Work to be Performed** Set out the work to be performed

   b. **Communication** Form and content of the component auditor's communication with the group engagement team

   c. **For Audit or Review of Component Financial Information**

      (1) **Materiality** Component materiality and the amount or amounts lower than the materiality for particular classes of transactions, account balances, or disclosures, if applicable

      (2) **Threshold** The threshold above which misstatements cannot be regarded as clearly trivial to the group financial statements

B. Communication Requested From Component Auditors

1. **All Audits of Group Financial Statements** The group engagement team should request a component auditor to communicate matters relevant to the group engagement team's conclusion, with regard to the group audit. Such communication should include the following.

   a. **Compliance With Ethical/Independence & Competence Requirements** Whether the component auditor has complied with ethical requirements relevant to the group audit, including independence and professional competence

   b. **Identification of Component Financial Information** Identification of the financial information of the component on which the component auditor is reporting

c. **Component Auditor's Conclusion** The component auditor's overall findings, conclusions, or opinion

2. **Additional Considerations When Auditor Assumes Responsibility for the Work of Component Auditors** When the auditor of the group financial statements is assuming responsibility for the work of a component auditor, the communication requested from the component auditor should also include the following.

   a. **Component Auditor's Compliance With Group Requirements** Whether the component auditor has complied with the group engagement team's requirements

   b. **Noncompliance by Component With Laws & Regulations** Information on instances of noncompliance with laws or regulations at the component or group level that could give rise to a material misstatement of the group financial statements

   c. **Significant RMM & Component Responses** Significant RMM of the group financial statements, due to fraud or error, identified by the component auditor in the component and the component auditor's responses to such risks; the group engagement team should request the component auditor to communicate such significant risks on a timely basis

   d. **Component Corrected & Uncorrected Misstatements** A list of corrected and uncorrected misstatements of the financial information of the component

   e. **Indicators of Possible Management Bias** Indicators of possible management bias regarding accounting estimates and the application of accounting principles

   f. **Material Weaknesses & Significant Deficiencies at Component** Description of any identified material weaknesses and significant deficiencies in internal control at the component level

   g. **Other Significant Findings, Including Fraud** Other significant findings and issues that the component auditor communicated or expects to communicate to those charged with governance of the component, including fraud or suspected fraud involving component management, employees who have significant roles in internal control at the component level, or others that resulted in a material misstatement of the financial information of the component

   h. **Other Relevant Matters** Any other matters that may be relevant to the group audit or that the component auditor wishes to draw to the attention of the group engagement team, including exceptions noted in the written representations that the component auditor requested from component management

IV. Further Audit Procedures (AU 600 continued)

A. Procedures When Making Reference vs. Assuming Responsibility

1. **Making Reference to Component Auditor in Group Audit Report** When the group engagement partner decides to make reference in the audit report on the group financial statements to the audit of a component auditor, the group engagement team should perform the following procedures.

   a. The procedures indicated for all audits of group financial statements, i.e., all procedures covered **except** the ones indicated as additional when the auditor assumes responsibility for the work of component auditors

b. Reading the component's financial statements and the related component auditor's report to identify significant findings and issues and, when considered necessary, communicating with the component auditor

2. **Assuming Responsibility for the Work of Component Auditors** When the group engagement partner assumes responsibility for the work of component auditors, the group engagement team should perform the procedures indicated for all group audits **plus** the ones indicated as additional when the the auditor assumes responsibility for the work of component auditors.

B. **Consolidation Process Considerations for All Audits of Group Financial Statements** The group engagement team should design and perform further audit procedures on the consolidation process to respond to the assessed RMM of the group financial statements arising from the consolidation process. Procedures should include the following.

1. **Confirm All Components Included** The group engagement team should evaluate whether all components have been included in the group financial statements.

2. **Consolidation Adjustments** The group engagement team should evaluate the appropriateness, completeness, and accuracy of consolidation adjustments and reclassifications and should evaluate whether any fraud risk factors or indicators of possible management bias exist.

   The consolidation process may require adjustments to amounts reported in the group financial statements that do not pass through the usual transaction processing systems and may not be subject to the same internal controls to which other financial information is subject. The group engagement team's evaluation of the appropriateness, completeness, and accuracy of the adjustments *may* include the following.

   a. Evaluating whether significant adjustments appropriately reflect the events and transactions underlying them

   b. Determining whether significant adjustments have been correctly calculated, processed, and authorized by group management and, when applicable, by component management

   c. Determining whether significant adjustments are properly supported and sufficiently documented

   d. Checking the reconciliation and elimination of intragroup account balances, transactions, and unrealized profits or losses

   e. Communicating with the component auditor, regardless of whether reference is made in the audit report on the group financial statements to the audit of the component auditor.

3. **Different Accounting Policies** If the financial information of a component has not been prepared in accordance with the same accounting policies applied to the group financial statements, the group engagement team should evaluate whether the financial information of that component has been appropriately adjusted for purposes of the preparation and fair presentation of the group financial statements in accordance with the AFRF.

4. **Verification of Component Financial Information Received** The group engagement team should determine whether the financial information identified in a component auditor's communication is the financial information that is incorporated in the group financial statements.

5. **Different Reporting Period** If the group financial statements include the financial statements of a component with a financial reporting period-end that differs from that of the group, the

group engagement team should evaluate whether appropriate adjustments have been made to those financial statements in accordance with the AFRF.

C. Subsequent Events

1. **All Audits of Group Financial Statements** When the group engagement team or component auditors perform audits on the financial information of components, the group engagement team or the component auditors should perform procedures designed to identify events at those components that occur between the dates of the financial information of the components and the date of the audit report on the group financial statements and that may require adjustment to, or disclosure in, the group financial statements.

2. **Additional Considerations When Auditor Assumes Responsibility for the Work of Component Auditors** When component auditors perform work other than audits of the financial information of components at the request of the group engagement team, the group engagement team should request the component auditors to notify the group engagement team if they become aware of events at those components that occur between the dates of the financial information of the components and the date of the audit report on the group financial statements that may require an adjustment to, or disclosure in, the group financial statements.

D. Significant RMM Identified in Component Not Referenced in Audit Report

When significant RMM of the group financial statements have been identified in a component for which the auditor of the group financial statements is assuming responsibility for the work of a component auditor, the group engagement team should evaluate the appropriateness of the further audit procedures to be performed to respond to the identified significant RMM of the group financial statements. Based on its understanding of the component auditor, the group engagement team should determine whether it is necessary to be involved in the further audit procedures.

V. Evaluating Sufficiency & Appropriateness of Audit Evidence (AU 600 continued)

A. Evaluating Component Auditors' Communication & Adequacy of Their Work

1. **All Audits of Group Financial Statements** The group engagement team should evaluate a component auditor's communication. The group engagement team should discuss significant findings and issues arising from that evaluation with the component auditor, component management, or group management, as appropriate.

2. **Additional Considerations When Auditor Assumes Responsibility for the Work of Component Auditors** The group engagement team should determine, based on the evaluation of a component auditor's communication, whether it is necessary to review other relevant parts of a component auditor's audit documentation. If the group engagement team concludes that the work of a component auditor is insufficient, the group engagement team should determine additional procedures to be performed and whether they are to be performed by the component auditor or by the group engagement team.

B. Evaluating Audit Evidence

1. **Overall** The auditor is required to obtain sufficient appropriate audit evidence on which to base the audit opinion. The group engagement team should evaluate whether sufficient appropriate audit evidence on which to base the group audit opinion has been obtained from the audit procedures performed on the consolidation process and the work performed by the group engagement team and the component auditors on the financial information of the components.

2. **Uncorrected Misstatements** The group engagement partner should evaluate the effect on the group audit opinion of any uncorrected misstatements.

VI. Communication With Management & Those Charged With Governance (AU 600 continued)

A. Communication With Group Management & Those Charged With Governance of Group

1. All Audits of Group Financial Statements

a. **Material Weaknesses & Significant Deficiencies in Internal Control** The group engagement team should communicate to group management and those charged with governance of the group material weaknesses and significant deficiencies in internal control that are relevant to the group.

b. **Fraud** If fraud has been identified or information indicates that a fraud may exist, the group engagement team should communicate this on a timely basis to the appropriate level of group management in order to inform those with primary responsibility for the prevention and detection of fraud of matters relevant to their responsibilities.

c. **Communication Between Group Management & Component Management** When a component auditor has been engaged to express an audit opinion on the financial statements of a component, the group engagement team should request group management to inform component management of any matter of which the group engagement team becomes aware that may be significant to the financial statements of the component, but of which component management may be unaware. If group management refuses to communicate the matter to component management, the group engagement team should discuss the matter with those charged with governance of the group. If the matter remains unresolved, the group engagement team, subject to legal and professional confidentiality considerations, should consider whether to advise the component auditor not to issue the audit report on the financial statements of the component until the matter is resolved and whether to withdraw from the engagement.

2. **Additional Considerations When Auditor Assumes Responsibility for the Work of Component Auditors** The group engagement team should determine which material weaknesses and significant deficiencies in internal control that component auditors have brought to the attention of the group engagement team should be communicated to group management and those charged with governance of the group.

B. Communication With Those Charged With Governance of the Group

The group engagement team should communicate the following matters with those charged with governance of the group, in addition to those required by other US GAAS guidance.

1. **Overview of Type of Work to Be Performed on Financial Information of Components** An overview of the type of work to be performed on the financial information of the components, including the basis for the decision to make reference to the audit of a component auditor in the audit report on the group financial statements

2. **Nature Of Group Engagement Team's Involvement In Component Auditor Work On Significant Components** An overview of the nature of the group engagement team's planned involvement in the work to be performed by the component auditors on the financial information of significant components

3. **Problems With Work of Component Auditors** Instances in which the group engagement team's evaluation of the work of a component auditor gave rise to a concern about the quality of that auditor's work

4. **Limitations on Group Audit** Any limitations on the group audit, for example, when the group engagement team's access to information may have been restricted

5. **Fraud or Suspected Fraud** Fraud or suspected fraud involving group management, component management, employees who have significant roles in group-wide controls, or others in which a material misstatement of the group financial statements has or may have resulted from fraud

VII. Making Reference to Audit of a Component in Audit Report (AU 600 continued)

A. Elements

When the group engagement partner decides to make reference to the audit of a component auditor, the report on the group financial statements should clearly indicate the following.

1. **Component Was Audited by a Component Auditor** That the component was not audited by the auditor of the group financial statements but was audited by the component auditor [whose report has been furnished to the auditor of the group financial statements, and that the opinion, insofar as it relates to the amounts included for the component, is based solely on the report of the other auditors]

2. **Portion Audited by Component Auditor** The magnitude of the portion of the financial statements audited by the component auditor

   a. The magnitude can be included by stating the dollar amounts or percentages of one or more of the following: total assets, total revenues, or other appropriate criteria, whichever most clearly describes the portion of the financial statements audited by a component auditor.

   b. When two or more component auditors participate in the audit, the dollar amounts or the percentages covered by the component auditors may be combined.

3. **Different Financial Reporting Framework** When the component's financial statements are prepared using a different financial reporting framework from that used for the group financial statements, the report should clearly indicate:

   a. The financial reporting framework used by the component

   b. That the auditor of the group financial statements is taking responsibility for evaluating the appropriateness of the adjustments to convert the component's financial statements to the group financial reporting framework

4. **Different Auditing Standards** When the component audit report on the component's financial statements does:

   - **Not** state that the audit of the component's financial statements was performed in accordance with US GAAS or PCAOB auditing standards, **and**

   - The group engagement partner has determined that the component auditor performed additional audit procedures in order to meet the relevant requirements of US GAAS

   The report should clearly indicate:

   a. The set of auditing standards used by the component auditor

   b. That additional audit procedures were performed by the component auditor to meet the relevant requirements of US GAAS

   Editor Note: If additional procedures were *not* necessary for the audit of the component auditor to meet the relevant requirements of US GAAS, then this requirement does not apply, i.e., nothing should be added to the report.

B. **Presentation**

1. **Elements Added to Auditor's Responsibility Section** These additional elements just described, as applicable, are added after the first sentence of the first paragraph of the auditor's responsibility section of the audit report.

2. **Change to Opinion Paragraph** The opinion paragraph is also changed to include the following phrase after the first three words (shown in boldface for illustrative purposes only): *In our opinion, **based on our audit and the report of the other auditors,** the consolidated financial statements referred to above present fairly,...*

C. **Component Auditor Named in Group Audit Report**
When the group engagement partner decides to name a component auditor in the audit report on the group financial statements:

1. **Named Only With Permission** The component auditor's express permission should be obtained.

2. **Component Audit Report Should Be Included** The component audit report should be presented together with that of the audit report on the group financial statements.

D. **Component Opinion Modified or Report Includes Additional Paragraphs**

1. **Modified Component Opinion** If the opinion of a component auditor is modified, the auditor of the group financial statements should determine if the effect of this is such that it is appropriate to modify the opinion on the group financial statements as well.

2. **Component Audit Report Has Emphasis-of-Matter or Other-Matter Paragraph** If the report of a component auditor includes an emphasis-of-matter or other-matter paragraph, the auditor of the group financial statements should determine if the effect of this is such that it is appropriate to include such a paragraph in the audit report of the group financial statements as well.

3. **If Such a Component Report Does *Not* Affect Report on Group Financial Statements**

   a. **Component Audit Report *Not* Presented** If the modified opinion, emphasis-of-matter paragraph, or other-matter paragraph in the component audit report does *not* affect the report on the group financial statements and the component audit report is *not* presented, the auditor of the group financial statements need not make reference to those paragraphs in the audit report on the group financial statements.

   b. **Component Audit Report *Is* Presented** If the component audit report is presented, the auditor of the group financial statements *may* make reference to those paragraphs and their disposition.

Editor note: The changes to the "standard" report required by the circumstances described for the following sample reports are underlined for illustrative purposes only. All of the changes are additions, i.e., nothing is omitted from the "standard" report.

Exhibit 2 ▸ Audit Report on Group Financial Statements; Reference Is Made to Audit of Financial Statements of a Component Prepared Using *Same* Financial Reporting Framework & Performed in Accordance With US GAAS

Independent Auditor's Report

[*Appropriate Addressee*]

We have audited the accompanying consolidated financial statements of ABC Company and its subsidiaries, which comprise the consolidated balance sheets as of December 31, 20X1 and 20X0, and the related consolidated statements of income, changes in stockholders' equity, and cash flows for the years then ended, and the related notes to the financial statements.

Management's Responsibility for the Financial Statements

Management is responsible for the preparation and fair presentation of these consolidated financial statements in accordance with accounting principles generally accepted in the United States of America; this includes the design, implementation, and maintenance of internal control relevant to the preparation and fair presentation of consolidated financial statements that are free from material misstatement, whether due to fraud or error.

Auditor's Responsibility

Our responsibility is to express an opinion on these consolidated financial statements based on our audits. <u>We did not audit the financial statements of B Company, a wholly-owned subsidiary, which statements reflect total assets constituting 20 percent and 22 percent, respectively, of consolidated total assets at December 31, 20X1 and 20X0, and total revenues constituting 18 percent and 20 percent, respectively, of consolidated total revenues for the years then ended. Those statements were audited by other auditors, whose report has been furnished to us, and our opinion, insofar as it relates to the amounts included for B Company, is based solely on the report of the other auditors.</u> We conducted our audits in accordance with auditing standards generally accepted in the United States of America. Those standards require that we plan and perform the audit to obtain reasonable assurance about whether the consolidated financial statements are free from material misstatement.

An audit involves performing procedures to obtain audit evidence about the amounts and disclosures in the consolidated financial statements. The procedures selected depend on the auditor's judgment, including the assessment of the risks of material misstatement of the consolidated financial statements, whether due to fraud or error. In making those risk assessments, the auditor considers internal control relevant to the entity's preparation and fair presentation of the consolidated financial statements in order to design audit procedures that are appropriate in the circumstances, but not for the purpose of expressing an opinion on the effectiveness of the entity's internal control. Accordingly, we express no such opinion. An audit also includes evaluating the appropriateness of accounting policies used and the reasonableness of significant accounting estimates made by management, as well as evaluating the overall presentation of the consolidated financial statements.

We believe that the audit evidence we have obtained is sufficient and appropriate to provide a basis for our audit opinion.

Opinion

In our opinion, <u>based on our audit and the report of the other auditors,</u> the consolidated financial statements referred to above present fairly, in all material respects, the financial position of ABC Company and its subsidiaries as of December 31, 20X1 and 20X0, and the results of their operations and their cash flows for the years then ended in accordance with accounting principles generally accepted in the United States of America.

[*Auditor's signature*]

[*Auditor's city and state*]

[*Date of the audit report*]

Exhibit 3 ▸ Audit Report on Group Financial Statements; Reference Is Made to Audit of Financial Statements of a Component Prepared Using a *Different* Financial Reporting Framework & Performed in Accordance With US GAAS

Independent Auditor's Report

[*Appropriate Addressee*]

We have audited the accompanying consolidated financial statements of ABC Company and its subsidiaries, which comprise the consolidated balance sheets as of December 31, 20X1 and 20X0, and the related consolidated statements of income, changes in stockholders' equity, and cash flows for the years then ended, and the related notes to the financial statements.

Management's Responsibility for the Financial Statements

Management is responsible for the preparation and fair presentation of these consolidated financial statements in accordance with accounting principles generally accepted in the United States of America; this includes the design, implementation, and maintenance of internal control relevant to the preparation and fair presentation of consolidated financial statements that are free from material misstatement, whether due to fraud or error.

Auditor's Responsibility

Our responsibility is to express an opinion on these consolidated financial statements based on our audits. We did not audit the financial statements of B Company, a wholly-owned subsidiary, which statements reflect total assets constituting 20 percent and 22 percent, respectively, of consolidated total assets at December 31, 20X1 and 20X0, and total revenues constituting 18 percent and 20 percent, respectively, of consolidated total revenues for the years then ended. Those statements, which were prepared in accordance with International Financial Reporting Standards as issued by the International Accounting Standards Board, were audited by other auditors, whose report has been furnished to us. We have applied audit procedures on the conversion adjustments to the financial statements of B Company, which conform those financial statements to accounting principles generally accepted in the United States of America. Our opinion, insofar as it relates to the amounts included for B Company, prior to these conversion adjustments, is based solely on the report of the other auditors. We conducted our audits in accordance with auditing standards generally accepted in the United States of America. Those standards require that we plan and perform the audit to obtain reasonable assurance about whether the consolidated financial statements are free from material misstatement.

An audit involves performing procedures to obtain audit evidence about the amounts and disclosures in the consolidated financial statements. The procedures selected depend on the auditor's judgment, including the assessment of the risks of material misstatement of the consolidated financial statements, whether due to fraud or error. In making those risk assessments, the auditor considers internal control relevant to the entity's preparation and fair presentation of the consolidated financial statements in order to design audit procedures that are appropriate in the circumstances, but not for the purpose of expressing an opinion on the effectiveness of the entity's internal control. Accordingly, we express no such opinion. An audit also includes evaluating the appropriateness of accounting policies used and the reasonableness of significant accounting estimates made by management, as well as evaluating the overall presentation of the consolidated financial statements.

We believe that the audit evidence we have obtained is sufficient and appropriate to provide a basis for our audit opinion.

Opinion

In our opinion, based on our audit and the report of the other auditors, the consolidated financial statements referred to above present fairly, in all material respects, the financial position of ABC Company and its subsidiaries as of December 31, 20X1 and 20X0, and the results of their operations and their cash flows for the years then ended in accordance with accounting principles generally accepted in the United States of America.

[*Auditor's signature*]

[*Auditor's city and state*]

[*Date of the audit report*]

Exhibit 4 ▸ Audit Report on Group Financial Statements; Reference Is Made to Audit of Financial Statements of a Component Prepared Using Same Financial Reporting Framework & Performed in Accordance With Standards *Other Than* US GAAS

Independent Auditor's Report

[*Appropriate Addressee*]

We have audited the accompanying consolidated financial statements of ABC Company and its subsidiaries, which comprise the consolidated balance sheets as of December 31, 20X1 and 20X0, and the related consolidated statements of income, changes in stockholders' equity, and cash flows for the years then ended, and the related notes to the financial statements.

Management's Responsibility for the Financial Statements

Management is responsible for the preparation and fair presentation of these consolidated financial statements in accordance with accounting principles generally accepted in the United States of America; this includes the design, implementation, and maintenance of internal control relevant to the preparation and fair presentation of consolidated financial statements that are free from material misstatement, whether due to fraud or error.

Auditor's Responsibility

Our responsibility is to express an opinion on these consolidated financial statements based on our audits. We did not audit the financial statements of B Company, a wholly-owned subsidiary, which statements reflect total assets constituting 20 percent and 22 percent, respectively, of consolidated total assets at December 31, 20X1 and 20X0, and total revenues constituting 18 percent and 20 percent, respectively, of consolidated total revenues for the years then ended. Those statements were audited by other auditors in accordance with [*describe the set of auditing standards*], whose report has been furnished to us, and our opinion, insofar as it relates to the amounts included for B Company, is based solely on the report of, and additional audit procedures to meet the relevant requirements of auditing standards generally accepted in the United States of America performed by, the other auditors. We conducted our audits in accordance with auditing standards generally accepted in the United States of America. Those standards require that we plan and perform the audit to obtain reasonable assurance about whether the consolidated financial statements are free from material misstatement.

An audit involves performing procedures to obtain audit evidence about the amounts and disclosures in the consolidated financial statements. The procedures selected depend on the auditor's judgment, including the assessment of the risks of material misstatement of the consolidated financial statements, whether due to fraud or error. In making those risk assessments, the auditor considers internal control relevant to the entity's preparation and fair presentation of the consolidated financial statements in order to design audit procedures that are appropriate in the circumstances, but not for the purpose of expressing an opinion on the effectiveness of the entity's internal control. Accordingly, we express no such opinion. An audit also includes evaluating the appropriateness of accounting policies used and the reasonableness of significant accounting estimates made by management, as well as evaluating the overall presentation of the consolidated financial statements.

We believe that the audit evidence we have obtained is sufficient and appropriate to provide a basis for our audit opinion.

Opinion

In our opinion, based on our audit and the report of, and additional audit procedures performed by, the other auditors, the consolidated financial statements referred to above present fairly, in all material respects, the financial position of ABC Company and its subsidiaries as of December 31, 20X1 and 20X0, and the results of their operations and their cash flows for the years then ended in accordance with accounting principles generally accepted in the United States of America.

[*Auditor's signature*]

[*Auditor's city and state*]

[*Date of the audit report*]

Exhibit 5 ▸ Audit Report on Group Financial Statements With a Qualified Opinion Due to a Scope Limitation; *No* Reference Is Made to Report of Component Auditor

Independent Auditor's Report

[*Appropriate Addressee*]

We have audited the accompanying consolidated financial statements of ABC Company and its subsidiaries, which comprise the consolidated balance sheets as of December 31, 20X1 and 20X0, and the related consolidated statements of income, changes in stockholders' equity, and cash flows for the years then ended, and the related notes to the financial statements.

Management's Responsibility for the Financial Statements

Management is responsible for the preparation and fair presentation of these consolidated financial statements in accordance with accounting principles generally accepted in the United States of America; this includes the design, implementation, and maintenance of internal control relevant to the preparation and fair presentation of consolidated financial statements that are free from material misstatement, whether due to fraud or error.

Auditor's Responsibility

Our responsibility is to express an opinion on these consolidated financial statements based on our audits. We conducted our audits in accordance with auditing standards generally accepted in the United States of America. Those standards require that we plan and perform the audit to obtain reasonable assurance whether the consolidated financial statements are free from material misstatement.

An audit involves performing procedures to obtain audit evidence about the amounts and disclosures in the consolidated financial statements. The procedures selected depend on the auditor's judgment, including the assessment of the risks of material misstatement of the consolidated financial statements, whether due to fraud or error. In making those risk assessments, the auditor considers internal control relevant to the entity's preparation and fair presentation of the consolidated financial statements in order to design audit procedures that are appropriate in the circumstances, but not for the purpose of expressing an opinion on the effectiveness of the entity's internal control. Accordingly, we express no such opinion. An audit also includes evaluating the appropriateness of accounting policies used and the reasonableness of significant accounting estimates made by management, as well as evaluating the overall presentation of the consolidated financial statements.

We believe that the audit evidence we have obtained is sufficient and appropriate to provide a basis for our qualified audit opinion.

Basis for Qualified Opinion

We were unable to obtain audited financial statements supporting the Company's investment in a foreign affiliate stated at $ ______ and $ ______ at December 31, 20X1 and 20X0, respectively, or its equity in earnings of that affiliate of $ ______ and $ ______, which is included in net income for the years then ended as described in Note X to the consolidated financial statements; nor were we able to satisfy ourselves as to the carrying value of the investment in the foreign affiliate or the equity in its earnings by other auditing procedures.

Qualified Opinion

In our opinion, except for the possible effects of the matter described in the Basis for Qualified Opinion paragraph, the consolidated financial statements referred to above present fairly, in all material respects, the financial position of ABC Company and its subsidiaries as of December 31, 20X1 and 20X0, and the results of their operations and their cash flows for the years then ended in accordance with accounting principles generally accepted in the United States of America.

[*Auditor's signature*]

[*Auditor's city and state*]

[*Date of the audit report*]

VIII. Documentation (AU 600 continued)

A. All Audits of Group Financial Statements

The group engagement team should include the following items in the audit documentation.

1. **Component Analysis** An analysis of components indicating those that are significant and the type of work performed on the financial information of the components

2. **Components Whose Audits Were Referenced in Group Audit Report** Those components for which reference to the reports of component auditors is made in the audit report on the group financial statements

   a. **Financial Statements & Audit Report of Component** The financial statements of the component and the related audit report

   b. **How Different Audit Standards Followed by Component Auditor Were Resolved** When the component audit report does not state that the audit was performed in accordance with US GAAS or the standards promulgated by the PCAOB, the basis for the group engagement partner's determination that the audit performed by the component auditor met the relevant requirements of US GAAS

3. **Written Communications** Written communications between the group engagement team and the component auditors about the group engagement team's requirements

B. Additional Documentation When Component Auditor Not Referenced in Audit Report

The group engagement team should include in the audit documentation the nature, extent, and timing of the group engagement team's involvement in the work performed by the component auditors on significant components, including, when applicable, the group engagement team's review of relevant parts of the component auditors' audit documentation and conclusions.

Registration Process

To sit for the exam, candidates must apply to the appropriate board of accountancy or its exam administrator. (Some boards contract with an exam administrator to handle candidate applications.) Once a board or its exam administrator determines that a candidate is eligible to sit for the exam, they inform the National Association of State Boards of Accountancy (NASBA) and NASBA adds the candidate to its database. With a national database, NASBA is able to ensure that no candidate can sit for the same exam section more than once during the same exam window. NASBA then sends Prometric a notice to schedule (NTS). (The exam is given at test centers operated by Prometric.) When you receive your NTS you can make your appointment with Prometric to sit for the exam.

Candidates may select any available date during the open window. If taking the exam on a particular day is important to you, it is advisable to schedule it at least 45 days in advance. No appointment can be made fewer than 5 days (10 days, if you have been approved for special testing accommodations) in advance of a desired test date. Your NTS will have an expiration date which is set by your board. After the expiration date, you must reapply and pay the fees again.

If any medical conditions exist or other special testing accommodations are needed, candidates must supply their information to their board or its exam administrator during the application process in order to obtain their approval so the information can be included on their NTS. Ordinarily, candidates may not bring anything into the exam room—including prescription medications.

See the AICPA's *Candidate Bulletin* for more information. To download a copy, visit the exam portion of the AICPA's website (aicpa.org) or NASBA's (nasba.org).

CHAPTER 9—AUDITS OF GROUP FINANCIAL STATEMENTS

Problem 9-1 MULTIPLE-CHOICE QUESTIONS

Planning

1. When developing the group audit plan, the group engagement team is required
   a. To determine the timing of the group engagement team's interaction with component auditors
   b. To determine whether the audit report on the group financial statements will make reference to the audit of each component auditor
   c. To determine whether the audit report on the group financial statements will make reference to the audit of either all or none of the component auditors
   d. To include the component auditors in a brainstorming session regarding the risks of material misstatement of the group financial statements, including the risks of fraud (ID: 90083)

2. Which of the following is the earliest determination to be made by an auditor for a group audit?
   a. The materiality for the group financial statements as a whole
   b. Whether to act as the auditor of the group financial statements
   c. Which components are significant components
   d. Whether to reference a component auditor in the audit report on the group financial statements (ID: 90445)

Materiality

3. In a group audit, both component materiality and component performance materiality should be ____________ the materiality and performance materiality for the group financial statements as a whole.
   a. Higher than
   b. Lower than
   c. Equal to
   d. Factored into (ID: 90098)

4. Regarding materiality considerations in group audits
   a. The group engagement team should set materiality for the group financial statements as a whole equal to that of the component with the lowest level when establishing the overall group audit strategy.
   b. Component materiality should be determined taking into account only those components referenced in the audit report on the group financial statements.
   c. A threshold for misstatements is determined in addition to component materiality.
   d. The group engagement team should review the component materiality determined by each component. (ID: 90099)

Responding to Assessed Risk

5. When the auditor of the group financial statements is assuming responsibility for the work of component auditors, for a component that is significant due to its individual financial significance to the group, the group engagement team, or a component auditor on its behalf, should perform
   a. Analytical procedures at the group level
   b. An audit using component materiality
   c. An audit of one or more account balances, classes of transactions, or disclosures relating to the likely significant risks of material misstatement of the group financial statements
   d. Specified audit procedures relating to the likely significant risks of material misstatement of the group financial statements (ID: 90441)

6. When the auditor of the group financial statements is assuming responsibility for the work of component auditors, for components that are **not** significant components, the group engagement team should perform
   a. Analytical procedures at the group level
   b. An audit using component materiality
   c. An audit of one or more account balances, classes of transactions, or disclosures relating to the likely significant risks of material misstatement of the group financial statements
   d. Specified audit procedures relating to the likely significant risks of material misstatement of the group financial statements (ID: 90440)

Consolidation Process

7. Audit procedures performed on the consolidation process should include all of the following **except**
   a. Evaluating whether all components have been included in the group financial statements
   b. Evaluating the appropriateness, completeness, and accuracy of consolidation adjustments and reclassifications
   c. Exclusion of any components with a financial reporting period-end that differs from that of the group
   d. Evaluating whether any fraud risk factors or indicators of possible management bias exist (ID: 90443)

Subsequent Events

8. When performing an audit on the financial information of a component, the group engagement team or the component auditor should perform procedures designed to identify relevant subsequent events at that component that occur between the date of the financial information of the component and
   a. The date when sufficient appropriate evidence on which to base the auditor's opinion on the component financial information has been obtained
   b. The date of the audit report on the group financial statements
   c. The date of the release of the audit report on the group financial statements
   d. As near as practicable to the date of the release of the audit report on the group financial statements (ID: 89495)

Communication With Those Charged With Governance of the Group

9. All of the following matters should be communicated by the group engagement team to those charged with governance of the group **except**
   a. An overview of the nature of the group engagement team's planned involvement in the work to be performed by the component auditors on the financial information of significant components
   b. Any limitations on the group audit
   c. Instances in which the group engagement team's evaluation of the work of a component auditor gave rise to a concern about the quality of that auditor's work
   d. Any internal control deficiencies that are relevant to the group (ID: 90444)

Reference to Component Auditor in Audit Report

10. If the group engagement partner decides to assume responsibility for the work of a component auditor, the group engagement partner
    a. Should make reference to the audit of the component auditor in the audit report on the group financial statements
    b. Should be involved in the work of the component auditor, insofar as that work relates to the expression of an opinion on the group financial statements
    c. Need not assess the component auditor's independence or professional competence
    d. Should make reference to the audit of the component auditor as well as name the component auditor in the audit report on the group financial statements. (ID: 90442)

11. All of the following are conditions that should be met to allow reference to the audit of a component auditor in the audit report on the group financial statements **except**

    a. The component auditor has performed an audit of the financial statements of the component in accordance with the relevant requirements of GAAS.
    b. The component auditor has issued an audit report that is not restricted as to use.
    c. If the component's financial statements are prepared using a different financial reporting framework from that used for the group financial statements, the measurement, recognition, presentation, and disclosure criteria that are applicable to all material items are similar.
    d. If the component's financial statements are prepared using a different financial reporting framework from that used for the group financial statements, the conversion adjustments needed are not material. (ID: 89498)

Problem 9-2 SIMULATION: Research

Which citation in the professional standards provides guidance when a group engagement partner who has decided to reference the audit of a component auditor also decides to name that component auditor in the audit report on the group financial statements?

[ ] § [ ] . [ ] (ID: 90439)

Solution 9-1 MULTIPLE-CHOICE ANSWERS

1. (b) When developing the group audit plan, the group engagement team is required to determine whether the audit report on the group financial statements will make reference to the audit of a component auditor. Editor Note: The group engagement team should also assess the extent to which the group engagement team will use the work of component auditors. Regarding incorrect answer a., when developing the group audit plan the group engagement team is required to assess the extent to which the group engagement team will use the work of component auditors; not determine the timing of the interaction. A determination of the nature, extent, and timing of its involvement in the work of component auditors [interaction] is required when the auditor of the group financial statements is assuming responsibility for the work of a component auditor and the engagement team is deciding the work to be performed by it or on its behalf by the component auditors on the financial information of the components. Regarding incorrect answer c., in group audits involving two or more component auditors, the decision to make reference to the audit of a component auditor is made individually for each component auditor, regardless of the decision whether to refer to any other component auditor. The auditor of the group financial statements may make reference to any, all, or none of the component auditors. Regarding incorrect answer d., the key members of the engagement team are required to discuss the susceptibility of an entity to material misstatement of the financial statements due to fraud or error, specifically emphasizing the risks due to fraud. In a group audit, these discussions also may include the component auditors, but their inclusion is not a requirement. The group engagement partner's determination of who to include in the discussions, how and when they occur, and their extent is affected by factors, such as prior experience with the group. (ID: 90083)

2. (b) One of the first determinations to be made by an auditor for a group audit is whether to act as the auditor of the group financial statements. Although the other answer alternatives are matters that are determined early in the audit, they are made by an auditor who has decided to act as auditor for the group financial statements. Relevant factors in determining whether to act as the auditor of the group financial statements include, among other things, the following: (1) the individual financial significant of the components for which the auditor of the group financial statements will be assuming responsibility; (2) the extent to which significant risks of material misstatement of the group financial statements are included in the components for which the auditor of the group financial statements will be assuming responsibility; and (3) the extent of the group engagement team's knowledge of the overall financial statements. (ID: 90445)

3. (b) To reduce the risk that the aggregate of uncorrected and undetected misstatements in the group financial statements exceeds the materiality for the group financial statements as a whole, component materiality should be lower than the materiality for the group financial statements as a whole, and component performance materiality should be lower than performance materiality for the group financial statements as a whole. Answer d. in may not be incorrect, but it is not the best answer. (ID: 90098)

4. (c) A threshold for misstatements is determined in addition to component materiality. This is a threshold above which misstatements cannot be regarded as clearly trivial to the group financial statements. (Misstatements identified in the financial information of the component that are above this threshold for misstatements of the group are communicated to the group engagement team.) The group engagement team should determine materiality, including performance materiality, for the group financial statements as a whole when establishing the overall group audit strategy. Regarding incorrect answer a., there is no such requirement to set materiality equal to the component with the lowest level. Regarding incorrect answer b., component materiality should be determined taking into account all components, regardless of whether reference is made in the audit report on the group financial statements to the audit of a component auditor. Regarding incorrect answer d., component materiality is the materiality for a component that is determined by the group engagement team for the purposes of the group audit. (ID: 90099)

5. (b) For a component that is significant due to its individual financial significance to the group, the group engagement team, or a component auditor on its behalf, should perform an audit of the financial information of the component, adapted as necessary to meet the needs of the group engagement team, using component materiality. Regarding incorrect answer a., for components that are *not* significant components, the group engagement team should perform analytical procedures at the group level. Regarding incorrect answers c. and d., these plus answer a. are the options, one or more of which, that should be performed for a component that is

significant not due to its individual financial significance but because it is likely to include significant risks of material misstatement of the group financial statements due to its specific nature or circumstances. (ID: 90441)

6. (a) When the auditor of the group financial statements is assuming responsibility for the work of component auditors, for components that are *not* significant components, the group engagement team should perform analytical procedures at the group level. The group engagement team, or a component auditor on its behalf, should perform one or more of the other answer alternatives for a component that is significant not due to its individual financial significance but because it is likely to include significant risks of material misstatement of the group financial statements due to its specific nature or circumstances. (ID: 90440)

7. (c) If the group financial statements include the financial statements of a component with a financial reporting period-end that differs from that of the group, the group engagement team should evaluate whether appropriate adjustments have been made to those financial statements in accordance with the applicable financial reporting framework. In addition to the other answer alternatives, the group engagement team should verify that the financial information that is incorporated in the group financial statements was the same as that received in the component auditors' communications. Also, if the financial information of a component has not been prepared in accordance with the same accounting policies applied to the group financial statements, the group engagement team should evaluate whether it has been appropriately adjusted for purposes of the preparation and fair presentation of the group financial statements in accordance with the applicable financial reporting framework. (ID: 90443)

8. (b) When the group engagement team or component auditors perform audits on the financial information of components, the group engagement team or the component auditors should perform procedures designed to identify events at those components that occur between the dates of the financial information of the components and the date of the audit report on the group financial statements and that may require adjustment to, or disclosure in, the group financial statements. (ID: 89495)

9. (d) The group engagement team should communicate to group management and those charged with governance of the group material weaknesses and significant deficiencies in internal control that are relevant to the group; not all internal control deficiencies. In addition to the other answer alternatives, the group engagement team should also communicate the following matters to those charged with governance of the group: (1) an overview of the type of work to be performed on the financial information of the components, including the basis for the decision to make reference to the audit of a component auditor in the audit report on the group financial statements and (2) fraud or suspected fraud involving group management, component management, employees who have significant roles in group-wide controls, or others in which a material misstatement of the group financial statements has or may have resulted from fraud. (ID: 90444)

10. (b) If the group engagement partner decides to assume responsibility for the work of a component auditor, the group engagement partner is required to be involved in the work of the component auditor, insofar as that work relates to the expression of an opinion on the group financial statements. Regarding incorrect answers a. and d., under these circumstances, *no* reference will be made to the component auditor in the group audit report. Further regarding incorrect answer d., if the group engagement auditor does *not* assume responsibility and thus, makes reference to the component auditor, the component auditor may also be named, but this is not a requirement. (Naming should only be done with the component auditor's express permission and the component auditor's report should be presented together with that of the audit report on the group financial statements.) Regarding incorrect answer c., regardless of whether reference to a component auditor will be made in the audit report, the group engagement team should obtain an understanding of the component auditor which includes determining whether the component auditor understands and will comply with the ethical requirements that are relevant to the group audit and, in particular, is independent. An assessment of the component auditor's professional competence should also be performed. There are other required elements of this understanding: (1) the extent, if any, to which the group engagement team will be able to be involved in the work of the component auditor; (2) whether the group engagement team will be able to obtain information affecting the consolidation process from a component auditor; and (3) whether a component auditor operates in a regulatory environment that actively oversees auditors. (ID: 90442)

11. (d) If the component's financial statements are prepared using a different financial reporting framework from that used for the group financial statements, reference to the audit of a component auditor in the audit report on the group financial statements should not be made unless, in addition to answer c., the group engagement team has obtained sufficient appropriate audit evidence for purposes of evaluating the appropriateness of the adjustments to convert the component's financial statements to the financial reporting framework used by the group without the need to assume responsibility for, and, thus, be involved in, the work of the component auditor. (ID: 89498)

Solution 9-2 SIMULATION ANSWER: Research

Which citation in the professional standards provides guidance when a group engagement partner who has decided to reference the audit of a component auditor also decides to name that component auditor in the audit report on the group financial statements?

AU	§	600	.	29	(ID: 90439)

.29

If the group engagement partner decides to name a component auditor in the auditor's report on the group financial statements

a. the component auditor's express permission should be obtained.

b. the component auditor's report should be presented together with that of the auditor's report on the group financial statements.

CHANGE ALERT

Title 2 of the Code of Federal Regulations (2 CFR)
Chapter I and Chapter II, Parts 200, 215, 220, 225, and 230
Uniform Administrative Requirements, Cost Principles, and Audit Requirements for Federal Awards
A Final Rule by the Office of Management and Budget on 12/26/2013

Summary

To deliver on the promise of a 21st-Century government that is more efficient, effective, and transparent, the Office of Management and Budget (OMB) is streamlining the Federal government's guidance on Administrative Requirements, Cost Principles, and Audit Requirements for Federal awards. This guidance provides a government-wide framework for grants management which will be complemented by additional efforts to strengthen program outcomes through innovative and effective use of grant-making models, performance metrics, and evaluation. This reform of OMB guidance will reduce administrative burden for non-Federal entities receiving Federal awards while reducing the risk of waste, fraud, and abuse.

This final guidance does not broaden the scope of applicability from existing government-wide requirements, affecting Federal awards to non-Federal entities including state and local governments, Indian tribes, institutions of higher education, and nonprofit organizations. Parts of it may also apply to for-profit entities in limited circumstances and to foreign entities as described in this guidance and the Federal Acquisition Regulation. This guidance does not change or modify any existing statute or guidance otherwise based on any existing statute. This guidance does not supersede any existing or future authority under law or by executive order or the Federal Acquisition Regulation.

Superseded Guidance

This final guidance supersedes and streamlines requirements from OMB Circulars A-21, A-87, A-110, and A-122 (which have been placed in OMB guidances); Circulars A-89, A-102, and A-133; and the guidance in Circular A-50 on Single Audit Act follow-up. Copies of the OMB Circulars that are superseded by this guidance are available on OMB's website at http://www.whitehouse.gov/omb/circulars_default/. The final guidance consolidates the guidance previously contained in the aforementioned citations into a streamlined format that aims to improve both the clarity and accessibility. This final guidance is located in Title 2 of the Code of Federal Regulations.

Main Issues for Candidates

References to OMB Circular A-133 on Audits of States, Local Governments and Non-Profit Organizations, and guidance in Circular A-50 on Single Audit Act follow-up should now reference Title 2 of the Code of Federal Regulations (2 CFR), particularly Subpart F on Audit Requirements. Perhaps the most noticeable change is that now a non-Federal entity that expends $750,000 or more in Federal awards during the non-Federal entity's fiscal year must have a single or program-specific audit conducted for that year. Previously the threshold for requiring a single or program-specific audit was $500,000 or more.

Effective and Applicability Dates

This guidance is effective December 26, 2013 (the issue date). It is applicable (goes into effect) for Federal agencies December 26, 2013 and for non-Federal entities December 26, 2014. Non-Federal entities wishing to implement entity-wide system changes to comply with guidance after the effective date will not be penalized for doing so (i.e., early application is permitted).

Eligibility for Testing

This final guidance became eligible to be tested beginning with the **July-August 2014** exam window.

CHAPTER 10

GOVERNMENT AUDITING

AU Identifier Used for Clarified GAAS in This Textbook

We have not continued to use the temporary AU-C identifier for the clarified auditing standards issued by the American Institute of Certified Public Accountants (AICPA). In this textbook these standards have an AU identifier.

CHAPTER 10

GOVERNMENT AUDITING

I. Government Auditing Standards

A. Foundation

Government auditing is essential in providing accountability to legislators, oversight bodies, those charged with governance, and the public. Audits provide an independent, objective, nonpartisan assessment of the stewardship, performance, or cost of government policies, programs, or operations, depending upon the type and scope of the audit.

1. **Purpose** The US Government Accountability Office (GAO) issues *Government Auditing Standards,* also known as Generally Accepted Government Auditing Standards (GAGAS) or the Yellow Book, to provide a framework for conducting high quality audits with competence, integrity, objectivity, and independence. GAGAS is used by auditors of government entities, entities that receive government awards, and other audit organizations for GAGAS audits.

2. **Applicability** Provisions of laws, regulations, contracts, grant agreements, or policies frequently require audits be conducted in accordance with GAGAS. In addition, many auditors and audit organizations voluntarily choose to perform their work in accordance with GAGAS. The requirements and guidance in GAGAS apply to audits of government entities, programs, activities, and functions, and of government assistance administered by contractors, nonprofit entities, and other nongovernmental entities when the use of GAGAS is required or is voluntarily followed.

3. **Ethical Principles** The ethical principles that provide the overall framework for application of GAGAS are the public interest, integrity, objectivity, proper use of government information, resources, and position, and professional behavior. The concept of accountability underlies decision makers' need to know whether resources are managed properly and used in compliance with laws and regulations, programs achieve their objectives and desired outcomes, services are provided effectively, efficiently, economically, ethically, and equitably, and managers are held accountable for their use of public resources.

4. **Management's Role** Managers have basic responsibilities for carrying out government functions. Management of the audited entity is responsible for the following:

   a. Using resources to achieve purposes for which the resources were furnished

   b. Complying with applicable laws and regulations (including identifying requirements with which the entity and official are responsible for compliance), along with implementing systems designed to achieve compliance with those laws and regulations

   c. Establishing and maintaining effective internal control to help ensure that appropriate goals and objectives are met, following laws and regulations, and ensuring that management and financial information is reliable and properly reported

   d. Following sound procurement practices when contracting for audits, including ensuring procedures are in place for monitoring contract performance

   e. Addressing the findings and recommendations of auditors, and for establishing and maintaining a process to track the status of such findings and recommendations

   f. Taking timely and appropriate steps to remedy fraud, noncompliance with provisions of laws, regulations, contracts or grant agreements, or abuse that auditors report

B. Standards for Use and Application of GAGAS

There are certain types of audits that may be performed in accordance with GAGAS, terminology that GAGAS uses to identify requirements relationships between GAGAS and other professional standards, and requirements for stating compliance with GAGAS in the auditors' report.

1. **Engagement Types** The types of audits covered by GAGAS, as defined by their objectives, are classified as financial audits, attestation engagements, and performance audits.

   a. **Financial Audits** GAGAS incorporates by reference AICPA Statements on Auditing Standards (SAS). Financial audits performed in accordance with GAGAS include financial statement audits and other related financial audits.

      (1) The primary purpose of a financial statement audit is to provide an opinion about whether an entity's financial statements are presented fairly in all material respects in conformity with an applicable financial reporting framework. Reporting on financial statement audits performed in accordance with GAGAS also includes reports on internal control over financial reporting and on compliance with provisions of laws, regulations, contracts, and grant agreements that have a material effect on the financial statements.

      (2) Other types of financial audits conducted in accordance with GAGAS entail various scopes of work, including: obtaining sufficient, appropriate evidence to form an opinion on single financial statements, specified elements, accounts, or items of a financial statement; issuing letters for underwriters and certain other requesting parties; and auditing compliance with applicable compliance requirements relating to one or more government programs.

   b. **Attestation Engagements** GAGAS incorporates by reference AICPA Statements on Standards for Attestation Engagements (SSAE). The AICPA's standards recognize attestation engagements that result in an examination, a review, or an agreed-upon procedures report on a subject matter or on an assertion about a subject matter that is the responsibility of another party.

      (1) An *examination* consists of obtaining sufficient, appropriate evidence to express an opinion on whether the subject matter is based on (or in conformity with) the criteria in all material respects or the assertion is presented (or fairly stated) in all material respects based on the criteria.

      (2) A *review* consists of sufficient testing to express a conclusion about whether any information came to the auditors' attention on the basis of the work performed that indicates the subject matter is not based on (or not in conformity with) the criteria or the assertion is not presented (or fairly stated) in all material respects based on the criteria. Auditors should not perform review-level work for reporting on internal control or compliance with provisions of laws and regulations.

      (3) An *agreed-upon procedures* engagement consists of auditors performing specific procedures on the subject matter and issuing a report of findings based on the agreed-upon procedures. The auditor does not express an opinion or conclusion, but only reports on agreed-upon procedures in the form of procedures and findings related to the specific procedures applied.

   c. **Performance Audits** Performance audits are defined as audits that provide findings or conclusions based on an evaluation of sufficient, appropriate evidence against criteria. The term "program" is used in GAGAS to include government entities, organizations, programs, activities, and functions. Performance audit objectives vary widely and include assessments of program effectiveness, economy, and efficiency; internal control; compliance; and prospective analyses.

(1) Program effectiveness and results audit objectives are frequently interrelated with economy and efficiency objectives. Audit objectives that focus on program effectiveness and results typically measure the extent to which a program is achieving its goals and objectives. Audit objectives that focus on economy and efficiency address the costs and resources used to achieve program results.

(2) Internal control audit objectives relate to an assessment of one or more components of an organization's system of internal control that is designed to provide reasonable assurance of achieving effective and efficient operations, reliable financial and performance reporting, or compliance with applicable laws and regulations.

(3) Compliance audit objectives relate to an assessment of compliance with criteria established by provisions of laws, regulations, contracts, or grant agreements, or other requirements that could affect the acquisition, protection, use, and disposition of the entity's resources and the quantity, quality, timeliness, and cost of services the entity produces and delivers. Compliance requirements can be either financial or nonfinancial.

(4) Prospective analysis audit objectives provide analysis or conclusions about information that is based on assumptions about events that may occur in the future, along with possible actions that the entity may take in response to the future events.

2. **Nonaudit Services** GAGAS does not cover nonaudit services, which are defined as professional services other than audits or attestation engagements. When performing nonaudit services for an entity for which the audit organization performs a GAGAS audit, audit organizations should communicate that the work performed does not constitute an audit conducted in accordance with GAGAS.

3. **Terminology Defining Requirements** GAGAS contains requirements indicating the degree of responsibility imposed in audits, identified through use of specific language. The two categories of requirements are: *unconditional requirements* (in which the words *must* or *is required* are used) and *presumptively mandatory requirements* (in which the word *should* is used). Explanatory material intended to provide guidance or to be descriptive rather than required is also included in the standards in which the words *may, might* and *could* are used.

   a. **Unconditional Requirement** Auditors and audit organizations must comply with an unconditional requirement in all cases where such requirement is relevant.

   b. **Presumptively Mandatory Requirement** Auditors and audit organizations must comply with a presumptively mandatory requirement in all cases where such a requirement is relevant except in rare circumstances. If auditors judge it necessary to depart from a relevant presumptively mandatory requirement, they must document their justification for the departure and how the alternative procedures performed in the circumstances were sufficient to achieve the intent of that requirement.

4. **GAGAS and Other Professional Standards** Auditors may use GAGAS in conjunction with professional standards issued by other authoritative bodies and cite its use in their reports.

5. **Stating Compliance with GAGAS** Auditors should include one of the following types of GAGAS compliance statements in reports on GAGAS audits, as appropriate:

   a. **Unmodified GAGAS Compliance Statement** Stating that the auditor performed the audit in accordance with GAGAS. Auditors should include an unmodified GAGAS compliance statement in the auditors' report when they have followed unconditional and applicable presumptively mandatory GAGAS requirements, *or* have followed unconditional requirements, and documented justification for any departures from applicable presumptively mandatory requirements and have achieved the objectives of those requirements through other means.

b. **Modified GAGAS Compliance Statement** Stating either that the auditor performed the audit in accordance with GAGAS, except for specific applicable requirements that were not followed, *or* because of the significance of the departure(s) from the requirements, the auditor was unable to and did not perform the audit in accordance with GAGAS. Situations when auditors use modified compliance statements also include scope limitations, such as restrictions on access to records, government officials, or other individuals needed to conduct the audit.

C. General Standards

General standards apply to financial audits, attestation engagements, and performance audits. General standards emphasize the importance of the independence, the exercise of professional judgment, the competence of staff; and quality control and assurance.

1. **Independence** In all matters relating to the audit work, the audit organization and the individual auditor, whether government or public, must be independent of mind and in appearance.

   a. **Conceptual Framework Approach** Auditors should identify threats to independence, evaluate the significance of the threats identified, and apply safeguards to eliminate the threats or reduce them to an acceptable level. Auditors should evaluate threats both individually and in the aggregate. If no safeguards are available to eliminate or acceptably reduce an unacceptable threat, independence is considered impaired.

   b. **Audit Organization Structure** The independence standard applies to auditors in government entities whether they report to third parties externally (external auditors), to senior management within the audited entity (internal auditors), or to both.

   c. **Nonaudit Services** Before an auditor agrees to provide a nonaudit service to an audited entity, the auditor should determine whether providing such a service would create a threat to independence, either by itself or in aggregate with other nonaudit services provided, with respect to any GAGAS audit it performs.

      (1) If an auditor were to assume management responsibilities for an audited entity, the management participation threats created would be so significant that no safeguards could reduce them to an acceptable level.

      (2) By their nature, certain nonaudit services directly support the entity's operations and impair auditors' ability to maintain independence in mind and appearance. Some services involving preparation of accounting records always impair an auditor's independence with respect to an audited entity.

      (3) GAGAS quality control and assurance requires appropriate documentation on threats to independence, safeguards required, management's ability to oversee a nonaudit service, and the auditor's understanding with an audited entity for which the auditor will perform a nonaudit service.

2. **Professional Judgment** Auditors must use professional judgment in planning and performing audits and attestation engagements and in reporting the results. Professional judgment includes exercising reasonable care and professional skepticism.

3. **Competence** The staff assigned to perform the audit must collectively possess adequate professional competence needed to address the audit objectives and perform the work in accordance with GAGAS. Competence is derived from a blending of education and experience. Competence enables an auditor to make sound professional judgments.

4. **Quality Control and Assurance** Each audit organization performing audits in accordance with GAGAS must establish a system of quality control that is designed to provide the audit organization with reasonable assurance that the organization and its personnel comply with professional standards and applicable legal and regulatory requirements, and have an external peer review at least once every 3 years.

D. **Financial Audit Standards**
GAGAS establishes requirements for performing and reporting on financial audits in addition to the requirements contained in the AICPA standards.

1. **Additional Performance Requirements** Additional requirements for performing financial audits relate to the following:

   a. **Auditor Communication** Auditors should communicate pertinent information to individuals contracting for or requesting the audit, and to cognizant legislative committees when auditors perform the audit pursuant to a law or regulation, or they conduct the work for the legislative committee that has oversight of the audited entity. This requirement does not apply if the law or regulation requiring an audit of the financial statements does not specifically identify the entities to be audited, such as audits required by the Single Audit Act Amendments of 1996.

   b. **Previous Audits and Attestation Engagements** Auditors should evaluate whether the audited entity has taken appropriate corrective action to address findings and recommendations from previous engagements that could have a material effect on the financial statements or other financial data significant to the audit objectives.

   c. **Fraud, Noncompliance, and Abuse** Auditors should extend AICPA requirements pertaining to the auditors' responsibilities for laws and regulations to also apply to consideration of compliance with provisions of contracts or grant agreements. The determination of abuse is subjective, and as such auditors are not required to detect abuse in financial audits. Auditors may find that the abuse represents potential fraud or noncompliance with provisions of laws, regulations, contracts, or grant agreements.

   d. **Elements of a Finding** In a financial audit, findings may involve deficiencies in internal control; noncompliance with provisions of laws, regulations, contracts, or grant agreements; fraud; or abuse. When auditors identify findings, auditors should plan and perform procedures to develop the elements of the findings that are relevant and necessary to achieve the audit objectives. The elements of a finding are as follows:

      (1) **Criteria** The laws, regulations, contracts, grant agreements, standards, measures, expected performance, defined business practices, and benchmarks against which performance is compared or evaluated.

      (2) **Condition** Condition is a situation that exists. The condition is determined and documented during the audit.

      (3) **Cause** The cause identifies the reason or explanation for the condition or the factor or factors responsible for the difference between the situation that exists (condition) and the required or desired state (criteria), which may also serve as a basis for recommendations for corrective actions.

      (4) **Effect or Potential Effect** The effect is a clear, logical link to establish the impact or potential impact of the difference between the situation that exists (condition) and the required or desired state (criteria). The effect or potential effect identifies the outcomes or consequences of the condition.

   e. **Audit Documentation** Auditors should document supervisory review, before the report release date, of the evidence that supports the findings, conclusions, and recommendations contained in the auditors' report. They should also document any departures from the GAGAS requirements and the impact on the audit and on the auditors' conclusions when the audit is not in compliance with GAGAS requirements.

2. **Additional Reporting Requirements** Additional requirements for reporting financial audits relate to the following:

   a. **Reporting Auditor's Compliance** When auditors comply with all applicable GAGAS requirements for financial audits, they should include a statement in the auditors' report that they performed the audit in accordance with GAGAS.

   b. **Reporting on Internal Control and Compliance** When providing an opinion or a disclaimer on financial statements, auditors should also report on internal control over financial reporting and on compliance with provisions of laws, regulations, contracts, or grant agreements that have a material effect on the financial statements. Auditors report on internal control and compliance, regardless of whether or not they identify internal control deficiencies or instances of noncompliance.

      (1) Auditors should include either in the same or separate report(s) a description of the scope of the auditors' testing of internal control over financial reporting and compliance with provisions of laws, regulations, contracts, or grant agreements.

      (2) Auditors should also state in the reports whether the tests they performed provided sufficient, appropriate evidence to support opinions on the effectiveness of internal control and on compliance with provisions of laws, regulations, contracts, or grant agreements.

   c. **Communication** Auditors should communicate the following in GAGAS reports:

      (1) Significant deficiencies and material weaknesses on internal control over financial reporting when deficiencies are identified during the audit.

      (2) Any instances of fraud, abuse, and noncompliance with provisions of laws, regulations, contracts and grant agreements that have a material effect on the financial statements. Instances of noncompliance and abuse that are less than material but warrant attention should have findings developed and communicated in writing to audited entity officials. If auditors sufficiently develop the elements of a finding, they may provide recommendations for corrective action.

      (3) Auditors should report known or likely fraud, noncompliance with provisions of laws, regulations, contracts, or grant agreements, or abuse directly to parties outside the audited entity when entity management and those charged with governance fail to satisfy legal/regulatory requirements to report such information to external parties specified in law/regulation *or* fail to take timely and appropriate steps to respond to known or likely fraud, noncompliance, or abuse that is material and involves funding from a governmental agency.

      (4) If the auditors' report discloses deficiencies, auditors should obtain and report the views of responsible officials of the audited entity concerning the findings, conclusions, and recommendations, as well as any planned corrective actions.

      (5) If certain pertinent information is prohibited from public disclosure or is excluded from a report due to the confidential or sensitive nature of the information, auditors should disclose in the report that certain information has been omitted and the reason or other circumstances that make the omission necessary.

      (6) Auditors should document any limitation on report distribution.

3. **Additional Considerations** Additional considerations relating to materiality in GAGAS financial audits and early communication of deficiencies for GAGAS financial audits may apply.

   a. **Materiality** In audits performed in accordance with GAGAS, auditors may find it appropriate to use lower materiality levels as compared with the materiality levels used in non-GAGAS audits.

   b. **Early Communication of Deficiencies** For some matters, early communication to those charged with governance or management may be important because of the relative significance and the urgency for corrective follow-up action. Further, when a control deficiency results in noncompliance with provisions of laws, regulations, contracts, or grant agreements, or abuse, early communication is important to allow management to take prompt corrective action to prevent further noncompliance.

      (1) Auditors should include either in the same or in separate report(s) a description of the scope of the auditors' testing of internal control over financial reporting and of compliance with provisions of laws, regulations, contracts, or grant agreements.

      (2) Auditors should also state in the reports whether the tests they performed provided sufficient, appropriate evidence to support opinions on the effectiveness of internal control and on compliance with provisions of laws, regulations, contracts, or grant agreements.

E. Attestation Engagement Standards

GAGAS establishes requirements for performing and reporting on attestation engagements in addition to the requirements contained in the AICPA standards. An attestation engagement can provide one of three levels of service: an examination engagement; a review engagement; or an agreed-upon procedures engagement.

1. **Additional Field Work Requirements for Examination Engagements** The additional field work requirements for examination engagements relate to the following:

   a. **Auditor Communication** Auditors should communicate pertinent information to individuals contracting for or requesting the audit, and to cognizant legislative committees when auditors perform the audit pursuant to a law or regulation, or they conduct the work for the legislative committee that has oversight of the audited entity.

   b. **Previous Audits and Attestation Engagements** Auditors should evaluate whether the audited entity has taken appropriate corrective action to address findings and recommendations from previous engagements that could have a material effect on (or an assertion about) the subject matter of the examination engagement.

   c. **Fraud, Noncompliance, and Abuse** Auditors should design the engagement to detect instances, and assess the risk and possible effects, of fraud and noncompliance with provisions of laws, regulations, contracts, and grant agreements that may have a material effect. Because the determination of abuse is subjective, auditors are not required to detect abuse in examination engagements. If auditors become aware of abuse that could be quantitatively or qualitatively material, auditors should apply procedures specifically directed to ascertain the potential effect.

   d. **Elements of a Finding** Findings may involve deficiencies in internal control; noncompliance with provisions of laws, regulations, contracts, or grant agreements; fraud; or abuse. When auditors identify findings, auditors should plan and perform procedures to develop the elements of the findings that are relevant and necessary to achieve the examination engagement objectives. The elements of a finding for an examination engagement are the same as for an audit.

e. **Examination Engagement Documentation** In performing a GAGAS examination engagement, auditors should prepare attest documentation in sufficient detail to enable an experienced auditor, having no previous connection to the examination engagement, to understand from the documentation the nature, timing, extent, and results of procedures performed and the evidence obtained and its source and the conclusions reached, including evidence that supports the auditors' significant judgments and conclusions.

2. **Additional Reporting Requirements for Examination Engagements** The additional requirements for reporting on examination engagements relate to the following:

a. **Reporting Auditor's Compliance** When auditors comply with all applicable GAGAS requirements for examination engagements, they should include a statement in the examination report that they performed the examination engagement in accordance with GAGAS.

b. **Reporting Deficiencies in Internal Control, Fraud, Noncompliance, and Abuse** When performing GAGAS examination engagements, auditors should report, based upon the work performed, the following:

(1) Related to internal control, auditors should include in the examination report all deficiencies, even those communicated early, that are considered to be significant deficiencies or material weaknesses.

(2) When presenting findings such as deficiencies in internal control, fraud, noncompliance with provisions of laws, regulations, contracts, or grant agreements, or abuse, auditors should develop the elements of the findings to the extent necessary.

(3) Auditors should report known or likely fraud, noncompliance with provisions of laws, regulations, contracts, or grant agreements, or abuse directly to parties outside the audited entity when entity management and those charged with governance fail to satisfy legal/regulatory requirements to report such information to external parties specified in law/regulation or fail to take timely and appropriate steps to respond to known or likely fraud, noncompliance, or abuse that is material and involves funding from a governmental agency.

c. **Reporting Views of Responsible Officials** If the examination report discloses deficiencies in internal control, fraud, noncompliance with provisions of laws, regulations, contracts, or grant agreements, or abuse, auditors should obtain and report the views of responsible officials of the audited entity concerning the findings, conclusions, and recommendations, as well as any planned corrective actions.

d. **Reporting Confidential and Sensitive Information** If certain pertinent information is prohibited from public disclosure or is excluded from a report due to the confidential or sensitive nature of the information, auditors should disclose in the report that certain information has been omitted and the reason or other circumstances that make the omission necessary.

e. **Distributing Reports** Distribution of reports depends on the relationship of the auditors to the audited organization and the nature of the information contained in the report. Auditors should document any limitation on report distribution.

3. **Additional Considerations for Examination Engagements** Additional considerations for examination engagements relating to materiality and early communication of deficiencies may apply.

a. **Materiality** In engagements performed in accordance with GAGAS, auditors may find it appropriate to use lower materiality levels as compared with the materiality levels used in non-GAGAS engagements.

b. **Early Communication of Deficiencies** For some matters, early communication to those charged with governance or management may be important because of the relative significance and the urgency for corrective follow-up action.

4. **Additional Field Work Requirements for Review Engagements** If, on the basis of conducting the procedures necessary to perform a review, significant deficiencies; material weaknesses; instances of fraud, noncompliance with provisions of laws, regulations, contracts, or grant agreements; or abuse come to the auditors' attention that warrant the attention of those charged with governance, GAGAS requires that auditors should communicate such matters to audited entity officials.

5. **Additional Reporting Requirements for Review Engagements** When auditors comply with all applicable requirements for a review engagement conducted in accordance with GAGAS, they should include a statement in the review report that they performed the engagement in accordance with GAGAS. If the subject matter or the assertion involves material that is classified for security purposes or contains confidential or sensitive information, auditors should limit the report distribution. Auditors should document any limitation on report distribution.

6. **Additional Considerations for Review Engagements** Additional considerations for review engagements completed in accordance with GAGAS may apply relating to establishing an understanding regarding services to be performed and reporting on review engagements.

   a. **Establishing an Understanding** Auditors often perform GAGAS engagements under a contract with a party other than the officials of the audited entity or pursuant to a third-party request. In such cases, auditors may also find it appropriate to communicate information regarding the services to be performed to the individuals contracting for or requesting the engagement.

   b. **Reporting** The AICPA standards require that the auditors' review report be in the form of a conclusion expressed in the form of negative assurance. Including only those elements that the AICPA reporting standards for review engagements require or permit ensures that auditors comply with the AICPA standards and that users of GAGAS reports have an understanding of the nature of the work performed and the results of the review engagement.

7. **Additional Field Work Requirements for Agreed-Upon Procedures Engagements** The additional field work requirement for review engagements is that if, on the basis of conducting the procedures necessary to perform an agreed-upon procedures engagement, significant deficiencies, material weaknesses, instances of fraud, noncompliance with provisions of laws, regulations, contracts, or grant agreements, or abuse come to the auditors' attention that warrant the attention of those charged with governance, GAGAS requires that auditors should communicate such matters to audited entity officials.

8. **Additional Reporting Requirements for Agreed-Upon Procedures Engagements** The additional reporting requirements for agreed-upon procedures engagements relate to reporting auditors' compliance with GAGAS and distributing reports.

   a. **Reporting Auditor's Compliance** When auditors comply with all applicable GAGAS requirements for agreed-upon procedures engagements, they should include a statement in the agreed-upon procedures engagement report that they performed the engagement in accordance with GAGAS.

b. **Distributing Reports** For GAGAS agreed-upon procedures engagements, if the subject matter or the assertion involves material that is classified for security purposes or contains confidential or sensitive information, auditors should limit the report distribution. Auditors should document any limitation on report distribution.

9. **Additional Considerations for Agreed-Upon Procedures Engagements** Additional considerations for agreed-upon procedures engagements completed in accordance with GAGAS may apply relating to establishing an understanding regarding services to be performed and reporting on agreed-upon procedures engagements.

   a. **Establishing an Understanding** Auditors often perform GAGAS engagements under a contract with a party other than the officials of the audited entity or pursuant to a third-party request. In such cases, auditors may also find it appropriate to communicate information regarding the services to be performed to the individuals contracting for or requesting the engagement.

   b. **Reporting** The AICPA standards require that the auditors' report on agreed-upon procedures engagements be in the form of procedures and findings and specifies the required elements to be contained in the report. A required element is a statement that the sufficiency of the procedures is solely the responsibility of the specified parties and a disclaimer of responsibility for the sufficiency of those procedures. Including only those elements ensures that auditors comply with the AICPA standards and that users of reports have an understanding of the nature of the work performed and the results of the agreed-upon procedures engagement.

F. Field Work Standards for Performance Audits

The field work requirements for performance audits relate to planning the audit; supervising staff; obtaining sufficient, appropriate evidence; and preparing audit documentation. Reasonable assurance, significance, and audit risk form a framework for applying these requirements.

1. **Reasonable Assurance** Auditors obtain reasonable assurance that evidence is sufficient and appropriate to support the auditors' findings and conclusions in relation to the audit objectives. The sufficiency and appropriateness of evidence needed and tests of evidence will vary based on the audit objectives, findings, and conclusions.

2. **Significance** The concept of significance assists auditors throughout a performance audit. Significance is defined as the relative importance of a matter within the context in which it is being considered, including quantitative and qualitative factors. In the performance audit requirements, the term "significant" is comparable to the term "material" as used in the context of financial statement engagements.

3. **Audit Risk** Audit risk is the possibility the auditors' findings, conclusions, recommendations, or assurance may be improper or incomplete, as a result of factors such as evidence that is not sufficient and/or appropriate, an inadequate audit process, or intentional omissions or misleading information due to misrepresentation or fraud. It includes the risk that auditors will not detect a mistake, inconsistency, significant error, or fraud in the evidence supporting the audit. The assessment of audit risk involves both qualitative and quantitative considerations.

4. **Planning** Auditors must plan the audit to reduce audit risk to an appropriate level for the auditors to obtain reasonable assurance that the evidence is sufficient and appropriate to support the auditors' findings and conclusions. In planning the audit, auditors should assess significance and audit risk. Planning is a continuous process throughout the audit.

   a. **Nature and Profile of Program** Auditors should obtain an understanding of the nature of the program or program component under audit and the potential use that will be made of the audit results or report as they plan a performance audit.

b. **User Needs** One group of users of the auditors' report is government officials who may have authorized or requested the audit. Other important users of the auditors' report are the audited entity, those responsible for acting on the auditors' recommendations, oversight organizations, and legislative bodies. Other potential users of the auditors' report include other government legislators or, the media, interest groups, and individual citizens.

c. **Internal Control** Auditors should obtain an understanding of internal control that is significant within the context of the audit objectives. Auditors should assess if internal control has been properly designed and implemented, and should perform procedures designed to obtain sufficient, appropriate evidence to support their assessment about the effectiveness of those controls. The effectiveness of significant internal controls is frequently dependent on the effectiveness of information systems controls.

   (1) In performance audits, a deficiency in internal control exists when the design or operation of a control does not allow management or employees, in the normal course of performing their assigned functions, to prevent, or detect and correct impairments of effectiveness or efficiency of operations, misstatements in financial or performance information, or noncompliance with provisions of laws, regulations, contracts, or grant agreements on a timely basis.

   (2) A key role of many internal audit organizations is to provide assurance that internal controls are in place to adequately mitigate risks and achieve program goals and objectives. The auditor may determine that it is appropriate to use the work of the internal auditors in the auditor's assessment of the effectiveness of design or operation of internal controls.

d. **Provisions of Laws, Regulations, Contracts, and Grant Agreements** Auditors should design and perform procedures to obtain reasonable assurance of detecting instances of noncompliance with provisions of laws, regulations, contracts, or grant agreements that are significant within the context of the audit objectives.

e. **Fraud** Fraud involves obtaining something of value through willful misrepresentation. When auditors identify factors or risks related to fraud that has occurred or is likely to have occurred that they believe are significant to the audit objectives, they should design procedures to obtain reasonable assurance of detecting any such fraud.

f. **Abuse** Abuse involves behavior that is deficient or improper when compared with behavior that a prudent person would consider reasonable and necessary business practice given the facts and circumstances. Because the determination of abuse is subjective, auditors are not required to detect abuse in performance audits. However, if auditors become aware of abuse that could be quantitatively or qualitatively significant to the program under audit, auditors should apply audit procedures specifically directed to ascertain the potential effect on the program under audit.

g. **Ongoing Investigations and Legal Proceedings** Laws, regulations, and policies may require auditors to report indications of certain types of fraud, noncompliance with provisions of laws, regulations contracts, or grant agreements, or abuse to law enforcement or investigatory authorities before performing additional audit procedures. In some cases, it may be appropriate for the auditors to work with investigators or legal authorities, or withdraw from or defer further work on the audit to avoid interfering with an ongoing investigation or legal proceeding.

h. **Previous Audits and Attestation Engagements** Auditors should evaluate whether the audited entity has taken appropriate corrective action to address findings and recommendations from previous engagements. Auditors should ask management of the audited entity to identify previous audits, attestation engagements, performance audits, or other studies that directly relate to the objectives of the audit, including whether related recommendations have been implemented.

i. **Identifying Audit Criteria** Auditors should identify audit criteria. Criteria represent the laws, regulations, contracts, grant agreements, standards, specific requirements, measures, expected performance, defined business practices, and benchmarks against which performance is compared or evaluated.

j. **Identifying Sources, Amount, and Type of Evidence** Auditors should identify potential sources of information that could be used as evidence. Auditors should determine the amount and type of evidence needed to obtain sufficient, appropriate evidence to address the audit objectives and adequately plan audit work.

k. **Using the Work of Others** Auditors should determine whether other auditors have conducted audits of the program that could be relevant to the current audit objectives. The results of other auditors' work may be useful sources of information for planning and performing the audit. If auditors intend to use the work of specialists, they should assess the professional qualifications and independence of the specialists.

l. **Assigning Staff and Other Resources** Audit management should assign sufficient staff and specialists with adequate collective professional competence to perform the audit. If planning to use the work of a specialist, auditors should document the nature and scope of the work to be performed by the specialist.

m. **Communication** Auditors should communicate an overview of the objectives, scope, methodology, and timing of the performance audit and planned reporting (including any potential restrictions on the report), unless doing so could significantly impair the auditors' ability to obtain sufficient, appropriate evidence in addressing the audit objectives, such as when the auditors plan to conduct unannounced cash counts or perform procedures related to indications of fraud. Auditors should communicate with the management of the audited entity, those charged with governance, the individuals contracting for or requesting audit services, and any cognizant legislative committee.

n. **Preparing Written Audit Plan** Auditors must prepare a written audit plan for each audit. A written audit plan provides an opportunity for audit organization management to supervise audit planning and assess the proposed audit.

5. **Obtaining Sufficient, Appropriate Evidence** Auditors must obtain sufficient, appropriate evidence to provide a reasonable basis for their findings and conclusions. The concept of sufficient, appropriate evidence is integral to an audit

a. **Appropriateness** Appropriateness is the measure of the quality of evidence that encompasses its relevance, validity, and reliability in providing support for findings and conclusions related to the audit objectives. Relevance refers to the extent to which evidence has a logical relationship with, and importance to, the issue being addressed. Validity refers to the extent to which evidence represents what it is purported to represent. Reliability refers to the consistency of results when information is measured or tested and includes the concepts of being verifiable or supported.

b. **Sufficiency** Sufficiency is a measure of the quantity of evidence used to support the findings and conclusions related to the audit objectives and supporting findings and conclusions. Sufficiency also depends on the appropriateness of the evidence.

c. **Overall Assessment of Evidence** Auditors should determine the overall sufficiency and appropriateness of evidence to provide a reasonable basis for the findings and conclusions, within the context of the audit objectives.

d. **Developing Elements of a Finding** Auditors should plan and perform procedures to develop the elements of a finding necessary to address the audit objectives. If auditors are able to sufficiently develop the elements of a finding, they should develop recommendations for corrective.

e. **Early Communication of Deficiencies** Auditors report deficiencies in internal control, fraud, noncompliance with provisions of laws, regulations, contracts, or grant agreements, or abuse. For some matters, early communication to those charged with governance or management may be important because of their relative significance and the urgency for corrective follow-up action. When a deficiency is communicated early, the reporting requirements for performance audits still apply.

6. **Audit Documentation** Auditors must prepare audit documentation related to planning, conducting, and reporting for each audit. Auditors should prepare audit documentation in sufficient detail to enable an experienced auditor, having no previous connection to the audit, to understand the nature, timing, extent, and results of audit procedures performed, the audit evidence obtained and its source, and the conclusions reached.

G. **Reporting Standards for Performance Audits**
The purpose of reporting requirements is to establish the overall approach for auditors to apply in communicating the results of the performance audit. The reporting requirements for performance audits relate to the form of the report, the report contents, and report issuance and distribution.

1. **Report Form** Auditors must issue audit reports communicating the results of each completed performance audit. Auditors should use a form of the audit report appropriate for its intended use and is in writing or in some other retrievable form. Different forms of audit reports include written reports, letters, briefing slides, or other presentation materials.

2. **Report Contents** Auditors should prepare audit reports that contain the following:

a. **Objectives, Scope, and Methodology** Auditors should communicate audit objectives in the audit report in a clear, specific, neutral, and unbiased manner that includes relevant assumptions. Auditors should describe the scope of the work performed and any limitations, including issues that would be relevant to likely users. In reporting audit methodology, auditors should explain how the completed audit work supports the audit objectives.

b. **Reporting Findings** In the audit report, auditors should present sufficient, appropriate evidence to support the findings and conclusions in relation to the audit objectives. If auditors are able to sufficiently develop the elements of a finding, they should provide recommendations for corrective action if they are significant. Auditors should describe limitations or uncertainties with the reliability or validity of evidence if the evidence is significant to the findings and conclusions within the context of the audit objectives.

c. **Deficiencies in Internal Control** Auditors should include in the audit report the scope of their work on internal control and any deficiencies in internal control that are significant. Deficiencies in internal control that are not significant but warrant the attention of those charged with governance, should be included in the report or communicated in writing to audited entity officials. Auditors should refer to that written communication in the audit report if the written communication is separate from the audit report. In a performance audit, auditors may conclude that identified deficiencies in internal control that are significant are the cause of deficient performance of the program or operations being audited. In reporting this type of finding, the internal control deficiency would be described as the cause.

(1) When auditors conclude, based on sufficient, appropriate evidence, that fraud, noncompliance with provisions of laws, regulations, contracts or grant agreements, or abuse either has occurred or is likely to have occurred which is significant within the context of the audit objectives, they should report the matter as a finding.

(2) When auditors detect instances of fraud, noncompliance with provisions of laws, regulations, contracts, or grant agreements, or abuse that are not significant within the context of the audit objectives but warrant the attention of those charged with governance, they should communicate those findings in writing to audited entity officials.

d. **Reporting Findings Directly to Outside Parties** Auditors should report known or likely fraud, noncompliance with provisions of laws, regulations, contracts, or grant agreements, or abuse directly to parties outside the audited entity when entity management fails to satisfy legal or regulatory requirements to report such information to external parties specified or fails to take timely and appropriate steps to respond to known or likely fraud noncompliance with provisions of laws, regulations, contracts, or grant agreements, or abuse that is significant to the findings and conclusions and involves funding received directly or indirectly from a government agency.

e. **Conclusions** Auditors should report conclusions based on the audit objectives and the audit findings. The strength of the auditors' conclusions depends on the sufficiency and appropriateness of the evidence supporting the findings and the soundness of the logic used to formulate the conclusions.

f. **Recommendations** Auditors should recommend actions to correct deficiencies and other findings identified during the audit and to improve programs and operations when the potential for improvement in programs, operations, and performance is substantiated by the reported findings and conclusions.

g. **Reporting Auditor's Compliance** When auditors comply with all applicable GAGAS requirements, they should use the following language, which represents an unmodified GAGAS compliance statement, in the audit report to indicate that they performed the audit in accordance with GAGAS:

> We conducted this performance audit in accordance with generally accepted government auditing standards. Those standards require that we plan and perform the audit to obtain sufficient, appropriate evidence to provide a reasonable basis for our findings and conclusions based on our audit objectives. We believe that the evidence obtained provides a reasonable basis for our findings and conclusions based on our audit objectives.

When auditors do not comply with all applicable GAGAS requirements, they should include a modified GAGAS compliance statement in the audit report. For performance audits, auditors should use the language just mentioned, but modified to indicate the requirements that were not followed, or language that the auditor did not follow GAGAS.

h. **Reporting Views of Responsible Officials** Auditors should report the views of responsible officials of the audited entity concerning the findings, conclusions, and recommendations included in the audit report, as well as planned corrective actions. When auditors receive written comments from the responsible officials, they should include in their report a copy of the officials' written comments, or a summary of the comments received. The auditors may issue the report without receiving comments from the audited entity. In such cases, the auditors should indicate in the report that the audited entity did not provide comments.

i. **Reporting Confidential and Sensitive Information** If certain pertinent information is prohibited from public disclosure or is excluded from a report due to the confidential or sensitive nature of the information, auditors should disclose in the report that certain information has been omitted and the reason or other circumstances that make the omission necessary.

3. **Distributing Reports** Distribution of reports completed in accordance with GAGAS depends on the relationship of the auditors to the audited organization and the nature of the information contained in the report. Auditors should document any limitation on report distribution. Audit organizations in government entities should distribute audit reports to those charged with governance, to the appropriate audited entity officials, and to the appropriate oversight bodies or organizations requiring or arranging for the audits.

II. Audit Requirements for Federal Awards

A. Single Audit Act

Entities receiving Federal funds are subject to audit requirements commonly referred to as "single audits" under the Single Audit Act of 1984, as amended in 1996. The Single Audit Act provides that grantees are subject to one audit of all their Federal programs, hence the term single audit, versus separate audits of each Federal program. The Act set a monetary awards threshold requiring the audit, which has been periodically increased by the Office of Management and Budget (OMB).

B. Guidance

The OMB has modified Title 2 of the Code of Federal Regulations (2 CFR) on the Federal government's guidance on Administrative Requirements, Cost Principles, and Audit Requirements for Federal awards. This guidance supersedes and streamlines requirements from OMB Circulars A-21, A-87, A-110, and A-122 (which have been placed in OMB guidances); Circulars A-89, A-102, and A-133; and the guidance in Circular A-50 on Single Audit Act follow-up.

C. Audit Requirements

Subpart F—Audit Requirements of 2 CFR sets forth standards for obtaining consistency and uniformity among Federal agencies for the audit of non-Federal entities expending Federal awards.

1. **Audit Required** A non-Federal entity that expends $750,000 or more during the non-Federal entity's fiscal year in Federal awards must have a single or program-specific audit conducted for that year in accordance with the provisions of this part.

2. **Single Audit** A non-Federal entity that expends $750,000 or more during the non-Federal entity's fiscal year in Federal awards must have a single audit conducted except when it elects to have a program-specific audit conducted.

3. **Program-Specific Audit Election** When an auditee expends Federal awards under only one Federal program (excluding R&D) and the Federal program's statutes, regulations, or the terms and conditions of the Federal award do not require a financial statement audit of the auditee, the auditee may elect to have a program-specific audit. A program-specific audit may not be elected for R&D unless all of the Federal awards expended were received from the same Federal agency, or the same Federal agency and the same pass-through entity, and that Federal agency, or pass-through entity in the case of a subrecipient, approves in advance a program-specific audit.

4. **Exemption** A non-Federal entity that expends less than $750,000 during the non-Federal entity's fiscal year in Federal awards is exempt from Federal audit requirements for that year, but records must be available for review or audit by appropriate officials of the Federal agency, pass-through entity, and Government Accountability Office (GAO). Even if exempt, a Federal agency, Inspectors General, or GAO may conduct or arrange for additional audits.

5. **Federally Funded Research and Development Centers (FFRDC)** Management of an auditee that owns or operates a FFRDC may elect to treat the FFRDC as a separate entity for purposes of this part.

6. **Subrecipients and Contractors** An auditee may simultaneously be a recipient, a subrecipient, and a contractor. Federal awards expended as a recipient or a subrecipient are subject to audit. Payments received for goods or services provided as a contractor are not Federal awards. Subrecipient and contractor determinations should be considered in determining whether payments constitute a Federal award or a contractor payment.

7. **Compliance Responsibility for Contractors** In most cases, the auditee's compliance responsibility for contractors is only to ensure that the procurement, receipt, and payment for goods and services comply with Federal statutes, regulations, and the terms and conditions of Federal awards. Federal award compliance requirements normally do not pass through to contractors. However, the auditee is responsible for ensuring compliance for procurement transactions which are structured such that the contractor is responsible for program compliance or the contractor's records must be reviewed to determine program compliance.

8. **For-Profit Subrecipient** The pass-through entity is responsible for establishing requirements, as necessary, to ensure compliance by for-profit subrecipients. The agreement with the for-profit subrecipient should describe applicable compliance requirements and the for-profit subrecipient's compliance responsibility.

9. **Basis for Determining Federal Awards Expended** The determination of when a Federal award is expended should be based on when the activity related to the Federal award occurs. Generally, the activity pertains to events that require the non-Federal entity to comply with Federal statutes, regulations, and the terms and conditions of Federal award.

D. Relation to Other Audit Requirements

An audit conducted in accordance with this part must be in lieu of any financial audit of Federal awards which a non-Federal entity is required to undergo under any other Federal statute or regulation. To the extent that such audit provides a Federal agency with the information it requires to carry out its responsibilities under Federal statute or regulation, a Federal agency must rely upon and use that information. A Federal agency, Inspectors General, or GAO may conduct or arrange for additional audits which are necessary to carry out its responsibilities.

1. **Constraints** The provisions do not authorize any non-Federal entity to constrain, in any manner, a Federal agency from carrying out or arranging for additional audits, except that the agency must plan such audits to not be duplicative of other audits of Federal awards.

2. **Authority** The provisions of this part do not limit the authority of Federal agencies to conduct, or arrange for the conduct of, audits and evaluations of Federal awards, nor limit the authority of any Federal agency Inspector General or other Federal official.

3. **Funding** A Federal agency that conducts or arranges for additional audits must, consistent with other applicable Federal statutes and regulations, arrange for funding the full cost of such additional audits.

4. **Major Program Request** A Federal awarding agency may request that an auditee have a particular Federal program audited as a major program. To allow for planning, such requests should be made at least 180 calendar days prior to the end of the fiscal year to be audited.

E. Frequency of Audits and Sanctions

Except for the provisions for biennial audits, audits required must be performed annually. Any biennial audit must cover both years within the biennial period. In cases of continued inability or unwillingness to have an audit conducted, Federal agencies and pass-through entities must take appropriate action for noncompliance.

F. **Program-Specific Audits**
In many cases, a program-specific audit guide will be available to provide specific guidance to the auditor with respect to internal controls, compliance requirements, suggested audit procedures, and audit reporting requirements. A listing of current program-specific audit guides can be found in the compliance supplement (beginning with the 2014 supplement).

1. **Audit Guide Available** When a current program-specific audit guide is available, the auditor must follow GAGAS and the guide when performing a program-specific audit.

2. **Audit Guide Not Available** When a program-specific audit guide is not available, the auditee and auditor must have basically the same responsibilities for the Federal program as they would have for an audit of a major program in a single audit. The auditor must:

   a. Perform an audit of the financial statement(s) for the Federal program in accordance with GAGAS

   b. Obtain an understanding of internal controls and perform tests of internal controls over the Federal program consistent with the audit scope requirements for a major program

   c. Perform procedures to determine whether the auditee has complied with Federal statutes, regulations, and the terms and conditions of Federal awards that could have a direct and material effect on the Federal program consistent with the requirements of a scope of audit for a major program

   d. Follow up on prior audit findings and report, as a current year audit finding, when the auditor concludes that the summary schedule of prior audit findings materially misrepresents the status of any prior audit finding

   e. Report any audit findings consistent with the requirements for audit findings

3. **Report Submission** The audit must be completed and the reporting required submitted within the earlier of 30 calendar days after receipt of the auditor's report(s), or nine months after the end of the audit period, unless a different period is specified in a program-specific audit guide. Unless restricted by Federal law or regulation, the auditee must make report copies available for public inspection. Auditees and auditors must ensure that their parts of the reporting package do not include protected personally identifiable information.

G. **Auditee Responsibilities**
The auditee must arrange for the audit and ensure it is properly performed and submitted when due. The auditee prepares appropriate financial statements, including the schedule of expenditures of Federal awards. The auditee also promptly follows up and takes corrective action on audit findings, including preparation of a summary schedule of prior audit findings and a corrective action plan. Finally, the auditee must provide the auditor with access to personnel, accounts, books, records, supporting documentation, and other information as needed to perform the audit required.

H. **Federal Agencies**

1. **Cognizant Agency for Audit** A non-Federal entity expending more than $50 million a year in Federal awards must have a cognizant agency for audit. The designated cognizant agency must be the Federal awarding agency that provides the predominant amount of direct funding to a non-Federal entity unless OMB designates a specific cognizant agency.

2. **Oversight Agency for Audit** The Federal awarding agency that provides the predominant amount of direct funding to a non-Federal entity not assigned a cognizant agency for audit. When there is no direct funding, the Federal awarding agency which is the predominant source of pass-through funding must assume the oversight responsibilities.

I. **Scope of Audit**

The audit must be conducted in accordance with GAGAS. The audit must cover the entire operations of the auditee, or, a series of audits that cover departments, agencies, and other organizational units that expended or otherwise administered Federal awards during such audit period, provided that each such audit must encompass the financial statements and schedule of expenditures of Federal awards for each such department, agency, and other organizational unit, which must be considered to be a non-Federal entity. The financial statements and schedule of expenditures of Federal awards must be for the same audit period.

1. **Financial Statements** The auditor must determine whether the financial statements of the auditee are presented fairly in all material respects in accordance with generally accepted accounting principles. The auditor must also determine whether the schedule of expenditures of Federal awards is stated fairly in all material respects in relation to the auditee's financial statements as a whole.

2. **Internal Control** In addition to GAGAS requirements, the auditor must perform procedures to obtain an understanding of internal control over Federal programs sufficient to plan the audit to support a low assessed level of control risk of noncompliance for major programs. When internal control over the compliance requirements for a major program are likely to be ineffective in preventing or detecting noncompliance, planning and performing testing are not required for those compliance requirements. The auditor must report a significant deficiency or material weakness, assess the related control risk at the maximum, and consider whether additional compliance tests are required because of ineffective internal control.

3. **Compliance** The auditor must also determine whether the auditee has complied with Federal statutes, regulations, and the terms and conditions of Federal awards that may have a direct and material effect on each of its major programs. The compliance testing must include tests of transactions and such other auditing procedures necessary to provide the auditor sufficient appropriate audit evidence to support an opinion on compliance. The principal compliance requirements applicable to most Federal programs and the compliance requirements of the largest Federal programs are included in the compliance supplement.

4. **Audit Follow-up** The auditor must follow-up on prior audit findings, perform procedures to assess the reasonableness of the summary schedule of prior audit findings prepared by the auditee and report, as a current year audit finding, when the auditor concludes that the summary schedule of prior audit findings materially misrepresents the status of any prior audit finding. The auditor must perform audit follow-up procedures regardless of whether a prior audit finding relates to a major program in the current year.

J. **Audit Reporting**

The auditor's report(s) may be in the form of either combined or separate reports and may be organized differently from the manner presented in this section. The auditor's report(s) must state that the audit was conducted in accordance with this part and include the following:

1. **Financial Statements** An opinion (or disclaimer of opinion) as to whether the financial statements are presented fairly in all material respects in accordance with generally accepted accounting principles and an opinion (or disclaimer of opinion) as to whether the schedule of expenditures of Federal awards is fairly stated in all material respects in relation to the financial statements as a whole.

2. **Internal Control** A report on internal control over financial reporting and compliance with Federal statutes, regulations, and the terms and conditions of the Federal award, noncompliance with which could have a material effect on the financial statements. This report must describe the scope of testing of internal control and compliance and the results of the tests, and, where applicable, it will refer to the separate schedule of findings and questioned costs.

3. **Compliance** A report on compliance for each major program and report and internal control over compliance. This report must describe the scope of testing of internal control over compliance, include an opinion or modified opinion as to whether the auditee complied with Federal statutes, regulations, and the terms and conditions of Federal awards which could have a direct and material effect on each major program and refer to the separate schedule of findings and questioned costs.

4. **Schedule of Findings and Questioned Costs** A schedule of findings and questioned costs, which must include a summary of the auditor's results, findings relating to the financial statements which are required to be reported in accordance with GAGAS, and findings and questioned costs for Federal awards which must include audit findings.

K. Audit Findings

Audit findings must be presented in sufficient detail and clarity for the auditee to prepare a corrective action plan and take corrective action, and for Federal agencies and pass-through entities to arrive at a management decision. The auditor must report the following as audit findings in a schedule of findings and questioned costs:

1. **Significant Items** Significant deficiencies and material weaknesses in internal control over major programs and significant instances of abuse relating to major programs. The auditor's determination of whether a deficiency in internal control is a significant deficiency or material weakness for the purpose of reporting an audit finding is in relation to a type of compliance requirement for a major program identified in the compliance supplement.

2. **Material Noncompliance** Material noncompliance with the provisions of Federal statutes, regulations, or the terms and conditions of Federal awards related to a major program. The auditor's determination of whether a noncompliance with the provisions of Federal statutes, regulations, or the terms and conditions of Federal awards is material for the purpose of reporting an audit finding is in relation to a type of compliance requirement for a major program identified in the compliance supplement.

3. **Major Program** Known questioned costs that are greater than $25,000 for a type of compliance requirement for a major program. Known questioned costs are those specifically identified by the auditor. In evaluating the effect of questioned costs on the opinion on compliance, the auditor considers the best estimate of total costs questioned (likely questioned costs), not just the questioned costs specifically identified (known questioned costs). The auditor must also report known questioned costs when likely questioned costs are greater than $25,000 for a type of compliance requirement for a major program. In reporting questioned costs, the auditor must include information to provide proper perspective for judging the prevalence and consequences of the questioned costs.

4. **Non-Major Program** Known questioned costs that are greater than $25,000 for a Federal program which is not audited as a major program. Except for audit follow-up, the auditor is not required under this part to perform audit procedures for such a Federal program; therefore, the auditor will normally not find questioned costs for a program that is not audited as a major program. However, if the auditor does become aware of questioned costs for a Federal program that is not audited as a major program (e.g., as part of audit follow-up or other audit procedures) and the known questioned costs are greater than $25,000, then the auditor must report this as an audit finding.

5. **Circumstances** The circumstances concerning why the auditor's report on compliance for each major program is other than an unmodified opinion, unless such circumstances are otherwise reported as audit findings in the schedule of findings and questioned.

6. **Fraud** Known or likely fraud affecting a Federal award, unless such fraud is otherwise reported as an audit finding in the schedule of findings and questioned costs.

7. **Follow-up Procedures** Instances where the results of audit follow-up procedures disclosed that the summary schedule of prior audit findings prepared by the auditee materially misrepresents the status of any prior audit finding.

L. **Audit Documentation**
The auditor must retain audit documentation and reports for a minimum of three years after the date of issuance of the auditor's report(s) to the auditee, unless the auditor is notified in writing by the cognizant agency for audit, oversight agency for audit, cognizant agency for indirect costs, or pass-through entity to extend the retention period. When the auditor is aware that the Federal agency, pass-through entity, or auditee is contesting an audit finding, the auditor must contact the parties contesting the audit finding for guidance prior to destruction of the audit documentation and reports. Audit documentation must be made available upon request to the cognizant or oversight agency for audit or its designee, cognizant agency for indirect cost, a Federal agency, or GAO at the completion of the audit, as part of a quality review, to resolve audit findings, or to carry out oversight responsibilities. Access to audit documentation includes the right of Federal agencies to obtain copies of audit documentation, as is reasonable and necessary.

M. **Major Program Determination**
The auditor must use a risk-based approach to determine which Federal programs are major programs. This risk-based approach must include consideration of: current and prior audit experience, oversight by Federal agencies and pass-through entities, and the inherent risk of the Federal program.

Exhibit 1 ▸ Major Program—Awards Expended and Thresholds

Total Federal Awards Expended	Type A/B Threshold
Equal to $750,000 but less than or equal to $25 million	$750,000.
Exceed $25 million but less than or equal to $100 million	Total Federal awards expended times .03.
Exceed $100 million but less than or equal to $1 billion	$3 million.
Exceed $1 billion but less than or equal to $10 billion	Total Federal awards expended times .003.
Exceed $10 billion but less than or equal to $20 billion	$30 million.
Exceed $20 billion	Total Federal awards expended times .0015.

1. **Step One** The auditor must identify the larger Federal programs, which must be labeled Type A programs. Type A programs are defined as Federal programs with Federal awards expended during the audit period exceeding the levels outlined in Exhibit 1. The inclusion of large loan and loan guarantees (loans) should not result in the exclusion of other programs as Type A programs. When a Federal program providing loans exceeds four times the largest non-loan program it is considered a large loan program, and the auditor must consider this Federal program as a Type A program and exclude its values in determining other Type A programs. For biennial audits permitted, the determination of Type A and Type B programs must be based upon the Federal awards expended during the two-year period.

2. **Step Two** The auditor must identify Type A programs which are low-risk. In making this determination, the auditor must consider whether the results of audit follow-up, or any changes in personnel or systems affecting the program indicate significantly increased risk and preclude the program from being low risk. For a Type A program to be considered low-risk, it must have been audited as a major program in at least one of the two most recent audit periods (in the most recent audit period in the case of a biennial audit), and, in the most recent audit period, the program must have not had internal control deficiencies which were

identified as material weaknesses in the auditor's report on internal control for major programs, a modified opinion on the program in the auditor's report on major programs, or known or likely questioned costs that exceed five percent of the total Federal awards expended for the program. OMB may approve a Federal awarding agency's request that a Type A program may not be considered low risk for a certain recipient. The Federal awarding agency must notify the recipient and, if known, the auditor of OMB's approval at least 180 calendar days prior to the end of the fiscal year to be audited.

3. **Step Three** The auditor must identify Type B programs which are high-risk using professional judgment and the criteria for Federal program risk. However, the auditor is not required to identify more high-risk Type B programs than at least one fourth the number of low-risk Type A programs identified as low-risk under Step Two. Except for known material weakness in internal control or compliance problems, a single criteria in risk would seldom cause a Type B program to be considered high-risk. When identifying which Type B programs to risk assess, the auditor is encouraged to use an approach which provides an opportunity for different high-risk Type B programs to be audited as major over a period of time. The auditor is not expected to perform risk assessments on relatively small Federal programs. The auditor is only required to perform risk assessments on Type B programs that exceed twenty-five percent (0.25) of the Type A threshold determined in Step One.

4. **Step Four** At a minimum, the auditor must audit all of the following as major programs:

   a. All Type A programs not identified as low risk under Step Two

   b. All Type B programs identified as high-risk under Step Three

   c. Such additional programs as may be necessary to comply with the percentage of coverage rule. This may require the auditor to audit more programs as major programs than the number of Type A programs.

5. **Percentage of Coverage Rule** If the auditee meets the criteria for a low-risk auditee, the auditor need only audit the major programs identified in Step Four and such additional Federal programs with Federal awards expended that, in aggregate, all major programs encompass at least 20 percent (0.20) of total Federal awards expended. Otherwise, the auditor must audit the major programs identified in Step Four and such additional Federal programs with Federal awards expended that, in aggregate, all major programs encompass at least 40 percent (0.40) of total Federal awards expended.

6. **Documentation of Risk** The auditor must include in the audit documentation the risk analysis process used in determining major programs.

7. **Auditor's Judgment** When the major program determination was performed and documented in accordance with this guidance, the auditor's judgment in applying the risk-based approach to determine major programs must be presumed correct. Federal agencies and pass-through entities may provide auditors guidance about the risk of a particular Federal program and the auditor must consider this guidance in determining major programs in audits not yet completed.

N. Criteria for Federal Program Risk

The auditor's determination should be based on an overall evaluation of the risk of noncompliance occurring that could be material to the Federal program. The auditor must consider criteria, such as described in this section, to identify risk in Federal programs.

1. **Current and Prior Audit Experience** Weaknesses in internal control over Federal programs would indicate higher risk. Prior audit findings would indicate higher risk, particularly when the situations identified in the audit findings could have a significant impact on a Federal program or have not been corrected. Federal programs not recently audited as major pro-

grams may be of higher risk than Federal programs recently audited as major programs without audit findings.

2. **Oversight Exercised by Federal Agencies and Pass-through Entities** Oversight exercised by Federal agencies or pass-through entities could be used to assess risk. Federal agencies, with the concurrence of OMB, may identify Federal programs that are higher risk. OMB will provide this identification in the compliance supplement.

3. **Inherent Risk of the Federal Program** The nature of a Federal program may indicate risk. Consideration should be given to the complexity of the program and extent to which the Federal program contracts for goods and services. The phase of a Federal program in its life cycle at the Federal agency or at the auditee may indicate risk. Type B programs with larger Federal awards expended would be of higher risk than programs with substantially smaller Federal awards expended.

O. Criteria for Low-Risk Auditee

An auditee that meets all of the following conditions for each of the preceding two audit periods must qualify as a low-risk auditee and be eligible for reduced audit coverage.

1. **Single Audits** Single audits were performed on an annual basis in accordance with the provisions of this guidance, including submitting the data collection form and the reporting package to the FAC within the timeframe specified. A non-Federal entity that has biennial audits does not qualify as a low-risk auditee.

2. **Auditor's Opinion** The auditor's opinion on whether the financial statements were prepared in accordance with GAAP, or a basis of accounting required by state law, and the auditor's in relation to opinion on the schedule of expenditures of Federal awards were unmodified.

3. **Internal Control** There were no deficiencies in internal control which were identified as material weaknesses under the requirements of GAGAS.

4. **Going Concern** The auditor did not report a substantial doubt about the auditee's ability to continue as a going concern.

5. **Audit Findings** None of the Federal programs had audit findings from any of the following in either of the preceding two audit periods in which they were classified as Type A programs: internal control deficiencies that were identified as material weaknesses in the auditor's report on internal control for major programs; a modified opinion on a major program in the auditor's report on major program; or, known or likely questioned costs that exceeded five percent of the total Federal awards expended for a Type A program during the audit period.

P. Management Decisions

The management decision must clearly state whether or not the audit finding is sustained, the reasons for the decision, and the expected auditee action to make financial adjustments or take other action. If the auditee has not completed corrective action, a timetable for follow-up should be given. While not required, the Federal agency or pass-through entity may also issue a management decision on findings relating to the financial statements which are required to be reported in accordance with GAGAS.

1. **Federal Agency** The cognizant agency for audit must be responsible for coordinating a management decision for audit findings that affect the programs of more than one Federal agency. A Federal awarding agency is responsible for issuing a management decision for findings that relate to Federal awards it makes to non-Federal entities.

2. **Pass-Through Entity** The pass-through entity must be responsible for issuing a management decision for audit findings that relate to Federal awards it makes to subrecipients.

3. **Time Requirements** The Federal awarding agency or pass-through entity responsible for issuing a management decision must do so within six months of acceptance of the audit report by the FAC. The auditee must initiate and proceed with corrective action as rapidly as possible and corrective action should begin no later than upon receipt of the audit report.

4. **Reference Numbers** Management decisions must include the reference numbers the auditor assigned to each audit finding.

III. Compliance Auditing Considerations in Governmental Audits (AU 935)

Governments often establish governmental audit requirements for entities to undergo an audit of their compliance with applicable compliance requirements. Compliance audits are usually performed in conjunction with a financial statement audit. AU 935 does **not** apply to the financial statement audit component of such engagements.

A. Applicability

AU 935, *Compliance Audits*, is applicable when an auditor is engaged, or required by law or regulation, to perform a compliance audit in accordance with generally accepted auditing standards (GAAS), standards for financial audits under *Government Auditing Standards,* and a governmental audit requirement that requires an auditor to express an opinion on compliance.

1. **Generally Accepted Auditing Standards (GAAS)** AU 935 requires the adaption and application of many of the AU sections (GAAS) to a compliance audit; however, some AU sections generally cannot be adapted because either they are not relevant to a compliance audit, the procedures and guidance would not contribute to meeting the objectives of a compliance audit, or the subject matter is specifically covered in AU 935. An appendix to AU 935 lists the specific AU sections/paragraphs that are not applicable.

   a. **AU Sections 200-800** Address audits of financial statements and can generally be adapted to the objectives of a compliance audit. This can be done with relative ease for some standards, for example, by simply replacing the word *misstatement* with the word *noncompliance*.

   b. **Sections Not Listed in the Appendix to AU 935** Are applicable to a compliance audit, however, the auditor is not required to make a literal translation of each procedure that might be performed in a financial statement, but rather to obtain sufficient appropriate audit evidence to support the auditor's opinion on compliance.

2. ***Government Auditing Standards*** The standards for financial audits under *Government Auditing Standards*, often referred to as generally accepted government auditing standards (GAGAS) or the "Yellow Book"

3. **Opinion on Compliance Required** A governmental audit requirement that requires an auditor to express an opinion on compliance

4. **Other** AU 935 is **not** applicable when the governmental audit requirement calls for an examination in accordance with Statements on Standards for Attestation Engagements of an entity's compliance with specified requirements or an examination of an entity's internal control over compliance. Statement on Standards for Attestation Engagements AT 601, *Compliance Attestation*, is applicable to these engagements.

B. Compliance Is Management's Responsibility

Management is responsible for ensuring that an entity complies with the compliance requirements. This includes: identifying the entity's government programs and understanding the compliance requirements of each program's administration; establishing internal controls to provide reasonable assurance of compliance; evaluating and monitoring the entity's compliance; and taking corrective action when instances of noncompliance are identified, including on compliance audit findings.

C. **Auditor's Objectives**

1. **Obtain Sufficient Appropriate Audit Evidence** The auditor should obtain sufficient appropriate audit evidence to form an opinion and report at the level specified in the governmental audit requirement—usually at the program level—on whether the entity complied in all material respects with the applicable compliance requirements.

2. **Identify Audit and Reporting Requirements** The auditor should identify audit and reporting requirements specified in the governmental audit requirement that are supplementary to GAAS and GAGAS, if any, and perform procedures to address those requirements.

D. **Definitions**
For purposes of adapting GAAS to a compliance audit, the following terms are defined:

1. **Applicable Compliance Requirements** Compliance requirements that are subject to the compliance audit.

2 **Audit Findings** The matters that are required to be reported by the auditor in accordance with the governmental audit requirement.

3. **Audit Risk of Noncompliance** The risk that the auditor expresses an inappropriate audit opinion on the entity's compliance when material noncompliance exists. Audit risk of noncompliance is a function of the risks of material noncompliance and detection risk of noncompliance.

4. **Compliance Audit** A program-specific audit or an organization-wide audit of an entity's compliance with applicable compliance requirements.

5. **Compliance Requirements** Laws, regulations, rules, and provisions of contracts or grant agreements applicable to government programs with which the entity is required to comply.

6. **Deficiency in Internal Control Over Compliance** This exists when the design or operation of a control over compliance does not allow management or employees performing their assigned functions to prevent, or detect and correct, noncompliance on a timely basis.

   a. **Deficiency in Design** This exists when a control necessary to meet the control objective is missing or an existing control is not properly designed so that, even if the control operates as designed, the control objective would not be met.

   b. **Deficiency in Operation** This exists when a properly designed control does not operate as designed or the person performing the control does not possess the necessary authority or competence to perform the control effectively.

7. **Detection Risk of Noncompliance** The risk that the procedures performed by the auditor to reduce audit risk of noncompliance to an acceptably low level will not detect noncompliance that exists and that could be material, either individually or when aggregated with other instances of noncompliance.

8. ***Government Auditing Standards*** Guidance issued by the US Government Accountability Office for financial audits, attestation engagements, and performance audits (also known as generally accepted government auditing standards (GAGAS) or the "Yellow Book").

9. **Government Program** The means by which governmental entities achieve their objectives. Government programs that are relevant to this section are those in which a grantor or pass-through entity provides an award to another entity, usually in the form of a grant, contract, or other agreement.

10. **Governmental Audit Requirement** A government requirement established by law, regulation, rule, or provision of contracts or grant agreements requiring that an entity undergo an audit of its compliance with applicable compliance requirements related to one or more government programs that the entity administers.

11. **Grantor** A government agency from which funding for the government program originates.

12. **Known Questioned Costs** Questioned costs specifically identified by the auditor; known questioned costs are a subset of likely questioned costs.

13. **Likely Questioned Costs** The auditor's best estimate of total questioned costs, not just the known questioned costs. Likely questioned costs are developed by extrapolating from audit evidence obtained, for example, by projecting known questioned costs identified in an audit sample to the entire population from which the sample was drawn.

14. **Material Noncompliance** In the absence of a definition of material noncompliance in the governmental audit requirement, a failure to follow compliance requirements or a violation of prohibitions included in the applicable compliance requirements that results in noncompliance that is quantitatively or qualitatively material to the affected government program.

15. **Material Weakness in Internal Control Over Compliance** A deficiency, or combination of deficiencies, in internal control over compliance, such that there is a reasonable possibility that material noncompliance with a compliance requirement will not be prevented, or detected and corrected, on a timely basis. A reasonable possibility exists when the likelihood of the event is either reasonably possible or probable as defined as follows:

    a. **Reasonably Possible** The chance of the future event or events occurring is more than remote but less than likely.

    b. **Remote** The chance of the future event or events occurring is slight.

    c. **Probable** The future event or events are likely to occur.

16. **Organization-Wide Audit** An audit of an entity's financial statements and an audit of its compliance with the applicable compliance requirements as they relate to one or more government programs that the entity administers.

17. **Pass-Through Entity** An entity that receives an award from a grantor or other entity and distributes all or part of it to another entity to administer a government program.

18. **Program-Specific Audit** An audit of an entity's compliance with applicable compliance requirements as they relate to one government program that the entity administers. The compliance audit portion of a program-specific audit is performed in conjunction with either an audit of the entity's or the program's financial statements.

19. **Questioned Costs** Costs that are questioned by the auditor due to:

    a. **Violations** A violation or possible violation of the applicable compliance requirements

    b. **Inadequate Documentation** The costs are not supported by adequate documentation

    c. **Unreasonableness** The incurred costs appear unreasonable and do not reflect the actions that a prudent person would take in the circumstances.

20. **Risk of Material Noncompliance** The risk that material noncompliance exists prior to the audit. This consists of two components, described as follows:

    a. **Inherent Risk of Noncompliance** The susceptibility of a compliance requirement to noncompliance that could be material, either individually or when aggregated with other instances of noncompliance, before consideration of any related controls over compliance.

b. **Control Risk of Noncompliance** The risk that noncompliance with a compliance requirement that could occur and that could be material, either individually or when aggregated with other instances of noncompliance, will not be prevented, or detected and corrected, on a timely basis by the entity's internal control over compliance.

21. **Significant Deficiency in Internal Control Over Compliance** A deficiency, or a combination of deficiencies, in internal control over compliance that is less severe than a material weakness in internal control over compliance, yet important enough to merit attention by those charged with governance.

E. Compliance Audit Requirements

1. **Adapting and Applying GAAS** When performing a compliance audit, the auditor, using professional judgment, should adapt and apply the AU sections that are relevant and necessary to meet the objectives of the compliance audit.

2. **Materiality Levels** The auditor should establish and apply materiality levels for the compliance audit based on the governmental audit requirement.

   a. **Auditor's Purpose** The auditor's purpose for establishing materiality levels is to:

      (1) Determine the nature and extent of risk assessment procedures.

      (2) Identify and assess the risks of material noncompliance.

      (3) Determine the nature, extent, and timing of further audit procedures.

      (4) Evaluate whether the entity complied with the applicable compliance requirements.

      (5) Report findings of noncompliance and other matters required to be reported by the governmental audit requirement.

   b. **Auditor's Consideration** Generally, for all of the purposes identified, the auditor's consideration of materiality is in relation to the government program taken as a whole; however, the governmental audit requirement may specify a different level of materiality for one or more of these purposes.

   c. **Auditor's Determination** The auditor's determination of materiality usually is influenced by the needs of the grantors because the governmental audit requirement usually is established by them and the auditor's report on compliance is primarily for their use; however, the auditor also considers the needs of users as a group, including grantors.

3. **Identifying Government Programs and Applicable Compliance Requirements** The auditor should determine which of the entity's government programs and compliance requirements to test, i.e., the *applicable compliance requirements*, in accordance with the governmental audit requirement.

   a. **Sources of Information About Applicable Compliance Requirements**

      (1) ***The Compliance Supplement*** Issued by the OMB, contains the compliance requirements that typically are applicable to federal government programs, as well as suggested audit procedures when compliance requirements are applicable and have a direct and material effect on the entity's compliance.

(2) **Program-Specific Audit Guides** The applicable program-specific audit guide issued by the grantor agency, which contains the compliance requirements pertaining to the government program and suggested audit procedures to test for compliance with the applicable compliance requirements.

b. **Procedures to Obtain Additional Information**

(1) Reading laws, regulations, rules, and provisions of contracts or grant agreements that pertain to the government program

(2) Making inquiries of management and other knowledgeable entity personnel

(3) Making inquiries of appropriate individuals outside the entity, such as other audit oversight organizations or regulators, about the laws and regulations applicable to entities within their jurisdiction

(4) Making inquiries of a third-party specialist, such as an attorney

(5) Reading the minutes of meetings of the governing board of the entity being audited

(6) Reading audit documentation about the applicable compliance requirements prepared during prior years' audits or other engagements

(7) Discussing the applicable compliance requirements with auditors who performed prior years' audits or other engagements

4. **Risk Assessment Procedures** For each of the government programs and applicable compliance requirements selected for testing, the auditor should perform risk assessment procedures to obtain a sufficient understanding of the applicable compliance requirements and the entity's related internal controls. This understanding establishes a frame of reference within which the auditor plans the compliance audit and exercises professional judgment about assessing risks of material noncompliance and responding to those risks throughout the compliance audit.

a. **Management's Response to Other Engagements' Findings** The auditor should inquire of management about whether there are findings and recommendations in reports or other written communications resulting from previous audits, attestation engagements, and internal or external monitoring that directly relate to the objectives of the compliance audit. The auditor should gain an understanding of management's response to findings and recommendations that could have a material effect on the entity's compliance with the applicable compliance requirements, for example, taking corrective action. The auditor should use this information to assess risk and determine the nature, extent, and timing of the audit procedures for the compliance audit, including determining the extent to which testing the implementation of any corrective actions is applicable to the audit objectives.

b. **Other Factors That Influence Nature and Extent of Risk Assessment Procedures**

(1) The newness and complexity of the applicable compliance requirements

(2) The nature of the applicable compliance requirements

(3) The services provided by the entity and how they are affected by external factors

(4) The level of oversight by the grantor or pass-through entity

c. **Evaluation of Controls** Performing risk assessment procedures to obtain an understanding of the entity's internal control over compliance includes an evaluation of the design of controls and whether the controls have been implemented.

5. **Assessing the Risks of Material Noncompliance** The auditor should assess the risks of material noncompliance whether due to fraud or error for each applicable compliance requirement.

   a. **Pervasive Risk** The auditor should consider whether any of those risks are pervasive to the entity's compliance because they may affect the entity's compliance with many compliance requirements.

   b. **Inherent Risk and Control Risk** In assessing the risks of material noncompliance, the auditor may evaluate inherent risk of noncompliance and control risk of noncompliance individually or in combination.

   c. **Factors to Consider** Factors the auditor may consider in assessing the risks of material noncompliance are as follows:

      (1) The complexity of the applicable compliance requirements

      (2) The susceptibility of the applicable compliance requirements to noncompliance

      (3) The length of time the entity has been subject to the applicable compliance requirements

      (4) The auditor's observations about how the entity has complied with the applicable compliance requirements in prior years

      (5) The potential effect on the entity of noncompliance with the applicable compliance requirements

      (6) The degree of judgment involved in adhering to the compliance requirements

      (7) The auditor's assessment of the risks of material misstatement in the financial statement audit

6. **Performing Further Audit Procedures in Response to Assessed Risks** If the auditor identifies risks of material noncompliance that are pervasive to the entity's compliance, the auditor should develop an overall response to such risks.

   a. **Tests of Details** The auditor should design and perform further audit procedures, including tests of details to obtain sufficient appropriate audit evidence about the entity's compliance with each of the applicable compliance requirements in response to the assessed risks of material noncompliance. Risk assessment procedures, tests of controls, and analytical procedures *alone* are **not** sufficient to address a risk of material noncompliance.

      (1) Examples of areas where tests of details may be performed include grant disbursements or expenditures; eligibility files; cost allocation plans; and periodic reports filed with grantor agencies.

      (2) A compliance audit includes designing procedures to detect both intentional and unintentional material noncompliance.

      (3) An auditor may decide to use audit sampling to obtain sufficient appropriate audit evidence in a compliance audit.

b. **Tests of Operating Effectiveness of Controls** If *any* of the following conditions are met, the auditor should test the operating effectiveness of controls over each applicable compliance requirement to which the conditions apply in each compliance audit. The use of audit evidence about the operating effectiveness of controls obtained in prior audits is **not** applicable to a compliance audit.

(1) The auditor's risk assessment includes an expectation of the operating effectiveness of controls over compliance related to the applicable compliance requirements.

(2) Substantive procedures alone do not provide sufficient appropriate audit evidence.

(3) Such tests of controls over compliance are required by the governmental audit requirement.

7. **Supplementary Audit Requirements** The auditor should determine whether audit requirements are specified in the governmental audit requirement that are supplementary to GAAS and GAGAS and perform procedures to address those requirements, if any. Examples of supplementary audit requirements are requirements that have the auditor perform specified procedures to identify major programs and to follow up on prior audit findings.

8. **Written Representations** The auditor should request from management written representations that are tailored to the entity and the governmental audit requirement. In some cases, management may include qualifying language to the effect that representations are made to the best of management's knowledge and belief. Such qualifying language is **not** appropriate for the representations in the first, second and last of the following statements:

a. Acknowledging management's responsibility for understanding and complying with the compliance requirements;

b. Acknowledging management's responsibility for establishing and maintaining controls that provide reasonable assurance that the entity administers government programs in accordance with the compliance requirements;

c. Stating that management has identified and disclosed to the auditor all of its government programs and related activities subject to the governmental audit requirement;

d. Stating that management has made available to the auditor all contracts and grant agreements, including amendments, if any, and any other correspondence relevant to the programs and related activities subject to the governmental audit requirement;

e. Stating that management has disclosed to the auditor all known noncompliance with the applicable compliance requirements or stating that there was no such noncompliance;

f. Stating whether management believes that the entity has complied with the applicable compliance requirements (except for noncompliance it has disclosed to the auditor);

g. Stating that management has made available to the auditor all documentation related to compliance with the applicable compliance requirements;

h. Identifying management's interpretation of any applicable compliance requirements that are subject to varying interpretations;

i. Stating that management has disclosed to the auditor any communications from grantors and pass-through entities concerning possible noncompliance with the applicable compliance requirements, including communications received from the end of the period covered by the compliance audit to the date of the auditor's report;

j. Stating that management has disclosed to the auditor the findings received and related corrective actions taken for previous audits, attestation engagements, and internal or external monitoring that directly relate to the objectives of the compliance audit, including findings received and corrective actions taken from the end of the period covered by the compliance audit to the date of the auditor's report;

k. Stating that management has disclosed to the auditor all known noncompliance with the applicable compliance requirements subsequent to the period covered by the auditor's report or stating that there were no such known instances; and

l. Stating that management is responsible for taking corrective action on audit findings of the compliance audit.

9. **Subsequent Events** The auditor should perform audit procedures up to the date of the auditor's report to obtain sufficient appropriate audit evidence that all subsequent events related to the entity's compliance during the period covered by the auditor's report on compliance have been identified.

   a. **Procedures** Audit procedures should include, but are not limited to, inquiring of management about and considering:

      (1) Relevant internal auditors' reports issued during the subsequent period;

      (2) Other auditors' reports identifying noncompliance that were issued during the **subsequent** period;

      (3) Reports from grantors and pass-through entities on the entity's noncompliance that were issued during the subsequent period; and

      (4) Information about the entity's noncompliance obtained through other professional engagements performed for that entity.

   b. **Period Subsequent to Auditor's Report** The auditor has no obligation to perform any audit procedures related to the entity's compliance during the period subsequent to the period covered by the auditor's report. However, if before the report release date, the auditor becomes aware of noncompliance in the period subsequent to the period covered by the auditor's report that is of such a nature and significance that its disclosure is needed to prevent report users from being misled, the auditor should discuss the matter with management and, if appropriate, those charged with governance, and should include an explanatory paragraph in the audit report describing the nature of the noncompliance.

10. **Evaluating Sufficiency and Appropriateness of Audit Evidence** The auditor should evaluate the sufficiency and appropriateness of the audit evidence obtained. Factors to consider in the determination of whether the entity materially complied with the applicable compliance requirements may include the following:

   a. The frequency and nature of the noncompliance;

   b. The adequacy of the entity's system for monitoring compliance and the possible effect of any noncompliance on the entity; and

   c. Whether any identified noncompliance with the applicable compliance requirements resulted in likely questioned costs that are material to the government program.

11. **Forming an Opinion** The auditor should form an opinion, at the level specified by the governmental audit requirement, on whether the entity complied in all material respects with the applicable compliance requirements, and report appropriately. When determining if the entity

materially complied with applicable compliance requirements, noncompliance identified by the auditor should be considered even if the entity corrected it once the auditor brought it to management's attention. In forming an opinion, the auditor should evaluate likely questioned costs, not just known questioned costs, as well as other material noncompliance that, by its nature, may not result in questioned costs.

12. Reporting Requirements

a. **Elements of a Report on Compliance Only** The auditor's report on compliance should include the following elements:

(1) A title that includes the word *independent*

(2) Identification of the one or more government programs covered by the compliance audit or reference to a separate schedule containing that information

(3) Identification of the applicable compliance requirements or a reference to where they can be found

(4) Identification of the period covered by the report

(5) A statement that compliance with the applicable compliance requirements is the responsibility of the entity's management

(6) A statement that the auditor's responsibility is to express an opinion on the entity's compliance with the applicable compliance requirements based on the compliance audit

(7) A statement that the compliance audit was conducted in accordance with auditing standards generally accepted in the United States of America, the standards applicable to financial audits contained in *Government Auditing Standards*, and the governmental audit requirement

(8) A statement that the compliance audit included examining, on a test basis, evidence about the entity's compliance with those requirements and performing such other procedures as the auditor considered necessary in the circumstances

(9) A statement that the auditor believes the compliance audit provides a reasonable basis for her/his opinion

(10) A statement that the compliance audit does not provide a legal determination of the entity's compliance

(11) The auditor's opinion, at the level specified by the governmental audit requirement, on whether the entity complied, in all material respects, with the applicable compliance requirements

(12) If noncompliance that results in an opinion modification is identified, a description of such noncompliance, or a reference to a description of such noncompliance in an accompanying schedule

(13) If other noncompliance that is required to be reported by the governmental audit requirement is identified (that is, noncompliance that does not result in an opinion modification), a description of such noncompliance or a reference to a description of such noncompliance in an accompanying schedule

(14) If the criteria used to evaluate compliance are determined by contractual agreement or regulatory provisions developed solely for the parties to the agreement or regulatory agency responsible for the provisions, or are available only to the specified parties, a separate paragraph should be prepared at the end of the report that includes a statement indicating that the report is intended solely for the information and use of the specified parties, an identification of the specified parties to whom use is restricted, and that the report is not intended to be and should not be used by anyone other than the specified parties

(15) The manual or printed signature of the auditor's firm

(16) The date of the auditor's report

b. Elements of a Combined Report on Compliance and Internal Control Over Compliance (See Exhibit 2) If the governmental audit requirement requires the auditor to report on internal control over compliance and the auditor combines the auditor's report on compliance with a report on internal control over compliance, the following elements should be *added* to the report elements listed previously:

(1) A statement that management is responsible for establishing and maintaining effective internal control over compliance with the requirements of laws, regulations, rules, and provisions of contracts or grant agreements applicable to government programs.

(2) A statement that in planning and performing the compliance audit, the auditor considered the entity's internal control over compliance with the applicable compliance requirements to determine the auditing procedures for the purpose of expressing an opinion on compliance, but not for the purpose of expressing an opinion on the effectiveness of internal control over compliance.

(3) A statement that the auditor is not expressing an opinion on internal control over compliance.

(4) A statement that the auditor's consideration of the entity's internal control over compliance was not designed to identify all deficiencies in internal control that might be significant deficiencies or material weaknesses in internal control over compliance.

(5) The definition of *deficiency in internal control over compliance* and *material weakness in internal control over compliance*.

(6) A description of any identified material weaknesses in internal control over compliance or a reference to an accompanying schedule containing such a description.

(7) If significant deficiencies in internal control over compliance were identified, the definition of *significant deficiency in internal control over compliance* and a description of the deficiencies or a reference to an accompanying schedule containing such a description.

(8) If no material weaknesses in internal control over compliance were identified, a statement to that effect.

(9) The restricted use paragraph should be included in all combined reports on the entity's compliance and internal control over compliance.

Exhibit 2 ▸ Combined Report on Compliance With Applicable Requirements and Internal Control Over Compliance

Independent Auditor's Report

[*Addressee*]

Compliance

We have audited Example Entity's compliance with the [*identify the applicable compliance requirements or refer to the document that describes the applicable compliance requirements*] applicable to Example Entity's [*identify the government program(s) audited or refer to a separate schedule that identifies the program(s)*] for the year ended June 30, 20X1. Compliance with the requirements referred to above is the responsibility of Example Entity's management. Our responsibility is to express an opinion on Example Entity's compliance based on our audit.

We conducted our audit of compliance in accordance with auditing standards generally accepted in the United States of America; the standards applicable to financial audits contained in *Government Auditing Standards* issued by the Comptroller General of the United States; and [*insert the name of the governmental audit requirement or program-specific audit guide*]. Those standards and [*insert the name of the governmental audit requirement or program-specific audit guide*] require that we plan and perform the audit to obtain reasonable assurance about whether noncompliance with the compliance requirements referred to above that could have a material effect on [*identify the government program(s) audited or refer to a separate schedule that identifies the program(s)*] occurred. An audit includes examining, on a test basis, evidence about Example Entity's compliance with those requirements and performing such other procedures as we considered necessary in the circumstances. We believe that our audit provides a reasonable basis for our opinion. Our audit does not provide a legal determination of Example Entity's compliance with those requirements.

In our opinion, Example Entity complied, in all material respects, with the compliance requirements referred to above that are applicable to [*identify the government program(s) audited*] for the year ended June 30, 20X1.

Internal Control Over Compliance

Management of Example Entity is responsible for establishing and maintaining effective internal control over compliance with the compliance requirements referred to above. In planning and performing our audit, we considered Example Entity's internal control over compliance to determine the auditing procedures for the purpose of expressing our opinion on compliance, but not for the purpose of expressing an opinion on the effectiveness of internal control over compliance. Accordingly, we do not express an opinion on the effectiveness of Example Entity's internal control over compliance.

A *deficiency in internal control over compliance* exists when the design or operation of a control does not allow management or employees, in the normal course of performing their assigned functions, to prevent, or detect and correct, noncompliance on a timely basis. A *material weakness in internal control over compliance* is a deficiency, or combination of deficiencies in internal control over compliance, such that there is a reasonable possibility that material noncompliance with a compliance requirement will not be prevented, or detected and corrected, on a timely basis.

> Our consideration of internal control over compliance was for the limited purpose described in the first paragraph of this section and was not designed to identify all deficiencies in internal control that might be deficiencies, significant deficiencies, or material weaknesses in internal control over compliance. We did not identify any deficiencies in internal control over compliance that we consider to be material weaknesses, as defined above.
>
> This report is intended solely for the information and use of management, [*identify the body or individuals charged with governance*], others within the entity, [*identify the legislative or regulatory body*], and [*identify the grantor agency(ies)*] and is not intended to be and should not be used by anyone other than these specified parties.
>
> [*Signature*]
>
> [*Date*]

c. **Elements of a Separate Report on Internal Control Over Compliance** If the governmental audit requirement requires the auditor to report on internal control over compliance and the auditor chooses to issue a separate report on internal control over compliance, the auditor should include in that separate report the previously listed elements and the following additional elements:

   (1) A title that includes the word *independent*

   (2) A statement that the auditor audited the entity's compliance with applicable compliance requirements pertaining to [*identify the government program(s) and the period audited*] and a reference to the auditor's report on compliance

   (3) A statement that the compliance audit was conducted in accordance with auditing standards generally accepted in the United States of America, the standards applicable to financial audits contained in *Government Auditing Standards*, and the governmental audit requirement

   (4) The manual or printed signature of the auditor's firm

   (5) The date of the auditor's report

d. **Other Reporting Requirements** The auditor should report noncompliance as well as other matters that are required to be reported by the governmental audit requirement in the manner specified by the governmental audit requirement. If the other matters required to be reported by the governmental audit requirement are not appropriate for the auditor to report on, the auditor should attach a separate report.

e. **Material Noncompliance or Scope Restriction** The auditor should modify her/his opinion on compliance if the compliance audit identifies noncompliance with the applicable compliance requirements that the auditor believes has a material effect on the entity's compliance or there is a restriction on the scope of the compliance audit.

f. **Reference to Another Auditor** The auditor should modify the report when the auditor makes reference to the report of another auditor as the basis, in part, for the auditor's report.

g. **Printed Forms** Printed forms, schedules, or reports designed or adopted by government agencies with which they are to be filed sometimes contain prescribed wording. If these require the auditor to make a statement that the auditor has no basis to make, the auditor should accordingly reword the form, schedule, or report or attach an appropriately worded separate report.

h. **Reissuance of a Compliance Report** If an auditor reissues a report, it should include an explanatory paragraph stating that the report is replacing a previously issued report and describing the reasons why it is being reissued, and any changes from the previously issued report.

(1) **Additional Procedures Performed for All Programs** If additional procedures are performed for all of the government programs being reported on, the auditor's report date should be updated to reflect the date the auditor obtained sufficient appropriate audit evidence regarding the events that caused the auditor to perform the new procedures.

(2) **Additional Procedures Performed for Only Some Programs** If additional procedures are performed for only some of the government programs, the auditor should dual date the report with the updated report date reflecting the date the auditor obtained sufficient appropriate audit evidence regarding the government programs affected by the circumstances and referencing the government programs for which additional audit procedures have been performed.

i. **Communication Requirements**

(1) In the absence of a governmental audit requirement to report on internal control over compliance, the auditor should, nevertheless, communicate in writing to management and those charged with governance identified significant deficiencies and material weaknesses in internal control over compliance. *Government Auditing Standards* require the auditor to obtain a response from responsible officials, preferably in writing.

(2) The auditor also should communicate to those charged with governance of the entity the auditor's responsibilities under GAAS, GAGAS, and the governmental audit requirement; an overview of the planned scope and timing of the compliance audit; and significant findings from the compliance audit.

13. **Documentation Requirements** The auditor should document the following:

a. The risk assessment procedures performed, including those related to gaining an understanding of internal control over compliance

b. The auditor's responses to the assessed risks of material noncompliance

c. The procedures performed to test compliance with the applicable compliance requirements and the results of those procedures, including any tests of controls over compliance

d. The materiality levels and the basis on which they were determined

e. How the auditor complied with the specific governmental audit requirements that are supplementary to GAAS and GAGAS

CHAPTER 10—GOVERNMENT AUDITING

Problem 10-1 MULTIPLE-CHOICE QUESTIONS

Government Auditing Standards

1. Which of the following bodies promulgates standards for audits of federal financial assistance recipients?
   a. Governmental Accounting Standards Board
   b. Financial Accounting Standards Board
   c. Governmental Auditing Standards Board
   d. Government Accountability Office (ID: 7513)

2. Because of the pervasive effects of laws and regulations on the financial statements of governmental units, an auditor may consider obtaining written management representations acknowledging that management has
   a. Identified and disclosed all laws and regulations that have a direct and material effect on its financial statements
   b. Implemented internal control policies and procedures designed to detect all illegal acts
   c. Expressed both positive and negative assurance to the auditor that the entity complied with all laws and regulations
   d. Employed internal auditors who can report their findings, opinions, and conclusions objectively without fear of political repercussion (ID: 4749)

3. Wolf is auditing an entity's compliance with requirements governing a major federal financial assistance program in accordance with *Government Auditing Standards.* Wolf detected noncompliance with requirements that have a material effect on the program. Wolf's report on compliance should express
   a. No assurance on the compliance tests
   b. An adverse or disclaimer of opinion
   c. A qualified or adverse opinion
   d. Reasonable assurance on the compliance tests (ID: 5158)

Financial Audits

4. For financial statement audits, generally accepted government auditing standards (GAGAS) incorporate the *Statements on Auditing Standards* (SAS) that are issued by the AICPA. GAGAS prescribe additional standards on

	Direct reporting of illegal acts	Reporting on internal controls
a.	Yes	Yes
b.	Yes	No
c.	No	Yes
d.	No	No

(ID: 7626)

5. The GAO standards of reporting for governmental financial audits incorporate the AICPA standards of reporting and prescribe supplemental standards to satisfy the unique needs of governmental audits. Which of the following is a supplemental reporting standard for governmental financial audits?
   a. Auditors should report the scope of their testing of compliance with laws and regulations and of internal controls.
   b. Material indications of illegal acts should be reported in a document distributed only to the entity's senior officials.
   c. All changes in the audit program from the prior year should be reported to the entity's audit committee.
   d. Any privileged or confidential information discovered should be reported to the organization that arranged for the audit. (ID: 8121)

6. When auditing an entity's financial statements in accordance with *Government Auditing Standards* (the "Yellow Book"), an auditor is required to report on

    I. Noteworthy accomplishments of the program
    II. The scope of the auditor's testing of internal controls

    a. I only
    b. II only
    c. Both I and II
    d. Neither I nor II (ID: 6943)

7. Which of the following statements is a standard applicable to financial statement audits in accordance with *Government Auditing Standards* (the "Yellow Book")?

    a. An auditor should report on the scope of the auditor's testing of compliance with laws and regulations.
    b. An auditor should assess whether the entity has reportable measures of economy and efficiency that are valid and reliable.
    c. An auditor should report recommendations for actions to correct problems and improve operations.
    d. An auditor should determine the extent to which the entity's programs achieve the desired results. (ID: 6844)

8. An enterprise engaged a CPA to audit its financial statements in accordance with *Government Auditing Standards* (the "Yellow Book") because of the provisions of government grant funding agreements. Under these circumstances, the CPA is required to report on the enterprise's internal controls either in the report on the financial statements or in

    a. The report on the performance audit
    b. The notes to the financial statements
    c. A letter to the government funding agency
    d. A separate report (ID: 8385)

9. Reporting standards for financial audits under *Government Auditing Standards* (the "Yellow Book") differ from reporting under generally accepted auditing standards in that *Government Auditing Standards* require the auditor to

    a. Provide positive assurance that control activities regarding segregation of duties are consistent with the entity's control objectives
    b. Present the results of the auditor's tests of controls
    c. Provide negative assurance that the auditor discovered no evidence of intentional override of internal controls
    d. Describe the scope of the auditor's principal substantive tests (ID: 8417)

10. An auditor notes significant deficiencies in a financial statement audit conducted in accordance with *Government Auditing Standards.* In reporting on internal control, the auditor should state that

    a. Expressing an opinion on the entity's financial statements provides no assurance on internal control.
    b. The auditor obtained an understanding of the design of relevant policies and procedures, and determined whether they have been placed in operation.
    c. The specified government funding or legislative body is responsible for reviewing internal control as a condition of continued funding.
    d. The auditor has not determined whether any of the significant deficiencies described in the report are so severe as to be material weaknesses. (ID: 4750)

11. Reporting on internal control under *Government Auditing Standards* differs from reporting under generally accepted auditing standards in that *Government Auditing Standards* requires a
    a. Statement of positive assurance that internal control procedures designed to detect material errors and fraud were tested
    b. Written report describing each significant deficiency observed including identification of those considered material weaknesses
    c. Statement of negative assurance that internal control procedures not tested have an immaterial effect on the entity's financial statements
    d. Written report describing the entity's internal control procedures specifically designed to prevent fraud, abuse, and illegal acts (ID: 3920)

12. In reporting on compliance with laws and regulations during a financial statement audit in accordance with *Government Auditing Standards,* an auditor should include in the auditor's report
    a. A statement of assurance that all controls over fraud and illegal acts were tested
    b. Material instances of fraud and illegal acts that were discovered
    c. The materiality criteria used by the auditor in considering whether instances of noncompliance were significant
    d. An opinion on whether compliance with laws and regulations affected the entity's goals and objectives (ID: 5707)

13. In reporting under *Government Auditing Standards*, an auditor most likely would be required to report a falsification of accounting records directly to a federal inspector general when the falsification is
    a. Discovered after the auditor's report has been made available to the federal inspector general and to the public
    b. Reported by the auditor to the audit committee as a significant deficiency in internal control
    c. Voluntarily disclosed to the auditor by low-level personnel as a result of the auditor's inquiries
    d. Communicated by the auditor to the auditee and the auditee fails to make a required report of the matter (ID: 6847)

14. In reporting under *Government Auditing Standards,* an auditor most likely would be required to communicate management's misappropriation of assets directly to a federal inspector general when the fraudulent activities are
    a. Concealed by management by circumventing specific internal controls designed to safeguard those assets
    b. Reported to the entity's governing body and the governing body fails to make a required report to the federal inspector general
    c. Accompanied by fraudulent financial reporting that results in material misstatements of asset balances
    d. Perpetrated by several levels of management in a scheme that is likely to continue in future years (ID: 6715)

Performance Audits

15. Which of the following is **not** one of the elements that form a framework for applying the field work requirements for a performance audit conducted in accordance with *Government Auditing Standards*?
    a. Sufficiency
    b. Significance
    c. Reasonable assurance
    d. Audit risk (ID: 90414)

16. In reporting on a performance audit under *Government Auditing Standards*, an auditor most likely would be required to report findings directly to outside parties under which of the following circumstances?
    a. When entity management fails to take the corrective action recommended by the auditor to resolve the findings
    b. When entity management fails to satisfy legal or regulatory requirements to report such information to external parties specified
    c. When auditors detect instances of fraud, noncompliance with provisions of laws, regulations, contracts, or grant agreements, or abuse that are not significant within the context of the audit objectives but warrant the attention of those charged with governance
    d. When auditors conclude, based on sufficient, appropriate evidence, that fraud, noncompliance with provisions of laws, regulations, contracts or grant agreements, or abuse either has occurred or is likely to have occurred which is significant within the context of the audit objectives (ID: 90415)

17. When auditors do not comply with applicable GAGAS requirements for a performance audit they should include which of the following in the audit report?
    a. A modified GAGAS performance statement
    b. An unmodified GAGAS performance statement
    c. A modified GAGAS compliance statement
    d. An unmodified GAGAS compliance statement (ID: 90416)

Audit Requirements for Federal Awards

18. The scope of audits of recipients of federal financial assistance in accordance with federal audit regulations varies. Which of the following elements do these audits have in common?
    a. The auditor is required to disclose all situations and transactions that could be indicative of fraud, abuse, and illegal acts to the federal inspector general.
    b. The materiality levels are higher and are determined by the government entities that provide the federal financial assistance to the recipients.
    c. The auditor is required to document an understanding of internal control established to ensure compliance with the applicable laws and regulations.
    d. The accounts should be 100% verified by substantive tests because certain statistical sampling applications are not permitted. (ID: 8149)

19. Although the scope of audits of recipients of federal financial assistance in accordance with federal audit regulations varies, these audits generally have which of the following elements in common?
    a. The auditor is to determine whether the federal financial assistance has been administered in accordance with applicable laws and regulations.
    b. The materiality levels are lower and are determined by the government entities that provided the federal financial assistance to the recipient.
    c. The auditor should obtain written management representations that the recipient's internal auditors will report their findings objectively without fear of political repercussion.
    d. The auditor is required to express both positive and negative assurance that illegal acts that could have a material effect on the recipient's financial statements are disclosed to the inspector general. (ID: 7597)

20. In auditing a not-for-profit entity that receives governmental financial assistance, the auditor has a responsibility to
    a. Issue a separate report that describes the expected benefits and related costs of the auditor's suggested changes to the entity's internal control
    b. Render an opinion concerning the entity's continued eligibility for the governmental financial assistance
    c. Notify the governmental agency providing the financial assistance that the audit is not designed to provide any assurance of detecting errors and fraud
    d. Assess whether management has identified laws and regulations that have a direct and material effect on the entity's financial statements (ID: 6035)

21. Hill, CPA, is auditing the financial statements of Helping Hand, a not-for-profit organization that receives financial assistance from governmental agencies. To detect misstatements in Helping Hand's financial statements resulting from violations of laws and regulations, Hill should focus on violations that

    a. Could result in criminal prosecution against the organization
    b. Involve significant deficiencies to be communicated to the organization's trustees and the funding agencies
    c. Have a direct and material effect on the amounts in the organization's financial statements
    d. Demonstrate the existence of material weaknesses in the organization's internal control (ID: 2990)

22. In auditing compliance with requirements governing major federal financial assistance programs under the Single Audit Act, the auditor's consideration of materiality differs from materiality under generally accepted auditing standards. Under the Single Audit Act, materiality is

    a. Calculated in relation to the financial statements taken as a whole
    b. Determined separately for each major federal financial assistance program
    c. Decided in conjunction with the auditor's risk assessment
    d. Ignored, because all account balances, regardless of size, are fully tested (ID: 6036)

Compliance Audits

23. The risk that material noncompliance exists prior to the compliance audit consists of

    I. Control risk of noncompliance
    II. Detection risk of noncompliance
    III. Inherent risk of noncompliance

    a. I only
    b. II only
    c. Both I and III
    d. I, II, and III (ID: 90417)

24. The auditor should test the operating effectiveness of controls over each applicable compliance requirement to which the condition applies in a compliance audit under which of the following conditions?

    a. The use of audit evidence about the operating effectiveness of controls applied to prior audits
    b. Substantive procedures alone do not provide sufficient appropriate audit evidence
    c. Tests of controls over compliance are not required by the governmental audit requirement
    d. The auditor's risk assessment includes no expectation of the operating effectiveness of controls over compliance related to the applicable compliance requirements (ID: 90418)

25. If the governmental audit requirement requires the auditor to report on internal control over compliance and the auditor combines the auditor's report on compliance with a report on internal control over compliance, which of the following statements should be added to the report?

    a. No material weaknesses in internal control over compliance were identified, if none were
    b. The compliance audit provides a legal determination of the entity's compliance
    c. That the auditor is expressing an opinion on internal control over compliance
    d. That the auditor's consideration of the entity's internal control over compliance was designed to identify all deficiencies in internal control that might be significant deficiencies material weaknesses in internal control over compliance (ID: 90419)

Problem 10-2 SIMULATION: Report on Compliance With Laws and Regulations

The auditors' separate report on compliance with laws and regulations that was drafted by a staff accountant of your firm at the completion of the engagement contained the statements below. The criteria used to evaluate compliance were determined by regulatory provisions that were developed solely for the regulatory agency responsible for the provisions. It was submitted to the engagement partner who reviewed matters thoroughly and properly concluded that no material instances of noncompliance were identified. For each of the statements below, indicate whether each is an appropriate (A) or inappropriate (I) element within the report on compliance with laws and regulations.

Report Elements	Appropriate (A) or Inappropriate (I)
1. A statement that the compliance audit was conducted in accordance with auditing standards generally accepted in the United States of America, the standards applicable to financial audits contained in *Government Auditing Standards*, and the governmental audit requirement.	
2. A statement that the compliance audit included examining, on a test basis, evidence about the entity's compliance with those requirements and performing such other procedures as the auditor considered necessary in the circumstances.	
3. A statement that it is the auditor's responsibility is to express an opinion on management's assertion that the entity is in compliance with the applicable compliance requirements based on the compliance audit.	
4. A statement that compliance with the applicable compliance requirements is the responsibility of the entity's management.	
5. Identification of the applicable compliance requirements or a reference to where they can be found.	
6. The auditor's opinion, at the level specified by the governmental audit requirement, on whether the entity complied, in all respects, with the applicable compliance requirements.	
7. A statement that the compliance audit provides a legal determination of the entity's compliance.	
8. A separate paragraph at the end of the report that includes (a) a statement indicating that the report is intended solely for the information and use of the specified parties (b) an identification of the specified parties to whom use is restricted, and (c) a statement that the report is not intended to be and should not be used by anyone other than the specified parties.	

(ID: 9213)

Problem 10-3 SIMULATION: Research

What authoritative reference describes the auditor's objectives in a compliance audit?

[   ] § [   ] [   ]

(ID: 9214)

Solution 10-1 MULTIPLE-CHOICE ANSWERS

1. (d) The standards for audits of federally assisted programs may be found in the publication of the US Government Accountability Office (GAO) entitled *Government Auditing Standards*. The Governmental Accounting Standards Board (GASB) establishes financial accounting principles for state and local government entities. The Financial Accounting Standards Board (FASB) establishes GAAP. The Governmental Auditing Standards Board does not exist. (ID: 7513)

2. (a) The auditor should assess whether management has identified laws and regulations that have a direct and material effect on the determination of amounts in the entity's financial statements. The auditor may consider obtaining written representation from management regarding the completeness of management's identification of applicable laws and regulations. The other items listed are not required. (ID: 4749)

3. (c) When an auditor detects noncompliance with requirements that have a material effect on a program, the auditor should express a qualified or adverse opinion. A disclaimer is appropriate only when an audit has not been completed. Reasonable assurance on tests is implicit, not explicit. (ID: 5158)

4. (a) According to GAGAS, when providing an opinion or a disclaimer on financial statements, auditors should include in their report on the financial statements either a description of the scope of the auditors' testing of internal control over financial reporting and compliance with laws, regulations, and provisions of contracts or grant agreements and the results of those tests or an opinion, if sufficient work was performed; or reference to the separate report(s) containing that information. In some circumstances, auditors should report fraud and illegal acts directly to parties external to the audited entity. (ID: 7626)

5. (a) GAGAS require auditors to include in their report either a description of the scope of the auditors' testing of internal control over financial reporting and compliance with laws, regulations, and provisions of contracts or grant agreements and the results of those tests or, if sufficient work was performed, an opinion; or a reference to the separate report(s) containing that information. In some circumstances, auditors must report illegal acts directly to parties external to the audited entity. Auditors are not required to disclose all changes in the audit program. Certain privileged or confidential information may be prohibited from disclosure; the report should state the nature of the omitted information and the requirement making omission necessary. (ID: 8121)

6. (b) GAGAS require a written report on the consideration of internal control in all audits; whereas GAAS require communication only when the auditor has noted significant deficiencies. Reporting on program accomplishments is not required of the auditor. (ID: 6943)

7. (a) The auditor must report on the scope of tests of compliance with laws and regulations. An auditor may report recommendations to correct problems and improve operations, but this is not the purpose of an audit. The auditor expresses an opinion on whether the information is correct; users of the report determine whether the measures of economy and efficiency are valid and reliable as well as the extent to which programs achieve the desired results. (ID: 6844)

8. (d) *Government Auditing Standards* require that when providing an opinion or a disclaimer on financial statements, auditors must also report on internal control over financial reporting and on compliance with laws, regulations, and provisions of contracts or grant agreements. Auditors should include either in the same or in a separate report(s) a description of the scope of the auditors' testing of internal control over financial reporting and compliance with laws, regulations, and provisions of contracts or grant agreements. An auditor sends a letter to a funding agency in certain circumstances; while the auditor may include this information in such a letter, the auditor still must include this information in an audit report. (ID: 8385)

9. (b) When providing an opinion or a disclaimer of opinion on financial statements in accordance with GAGAS, the audit must include in the report either a description of the scope of the auditor's testing of internal control over financial reporting and compliance with laws, regulations, and contractual provisions and the results of those tests (negative assurance) or, if sufficient work was performed, an opinion (positive assurance); or refer to a separate report containing that information. The auditor does not necessarily assure that no evidence of intentional override of controls was found, nor report the scope of the principal substantive tests. (ID: 8417)

10. (b) The auditor should obtain a sufficient understanding by performing risk assessment procedures to evaluate the design of controls relevant to an audit of financial statements and to determine whether they have been implemented. This includes governmental audits. GAGAS requires that the auditor include in their report on the financial statements either a description of the scope of the auditors' testing of internal control and the results of those tests or an opinion, if sufficient work was performed; or reference to the separate report(s) containing that information. GAGAS requires that auditors identify those significant deficiencies that are individually or in the aggregate considered to be material weaknesses. (ID: 4750)

11. (b) GAGAS require a written report on the consideration of internal control in all audits; whereas GAAS require communication only when the auditor has noted significant deficiencies. The auditor is not required to report on the description of the entity's internal control procedures. The auditor should not give negative assurance that internal control procedures not tested have an immaterial effect on the entity's financial statements or give positive assurance because of the potential for misinterpretation of the limited degree of assurance associated with the auditor's written report representing that no significant deficiencies were noted. (ID: 3920)

12. (b) AICPA standards and GAGAS require auditors to address the effect fraud or illegal acts may have on the audit report and to determine that the audit committee or others with equivalent authority and responsibility are adequately informed about the fraud or illegal acts. GAGAS further require that this information be in writing and also include reporting on significant violations of provisions of contracts or grant agreements and significant abuse. Therefore, when auditors conclude, on the basis of evidence obtained, that fraud, an illegal act, a significant violation of a contract or grant agreement, or significant abuse either has occurred or is likely to have occurred, they should include in their audit report the relevant information. GAGAS require auditors to place their findings in proper perspective and identify the condition, criteria, cause, and effect of noncompliance. There is no requirement that all controls be tested. There also is no requirement for an opinion on whether compliance with laws and regulations affected the entity's goals and objectives in a financial statement audit. (ID: 5707)

13. (d) Generally, the auditor need report a falsification of accounting records only to the audit committee (or equivalent). If auditors have communicated such irregularities or illegal acts to the auditee, and it fails to report them, then the auditors should communicate their awareness of that failure to the auditee's governing body. If the auditee does not make the required report as soon as practicable after the auditors' communication with its governing body, then the auditors should report the irregularities or illegal acts directly to the external party specified. (ID: 6847)

14. (b) It is the audit committee's (or its equivalent) responsibility to take appropriate action regarding fraudulent activities that are perpetrated or concealed by management. Only when the audit committee fails to take appropriate action (such as not filing a required report), is the auditor responsible to do so. The other responses are failings by management, not omissions of the governing body (the audit committee equivalent). (ID: 6715)

15. (a) Sufficiency is not one of the elements that form a framework for applying field work requirements for a performance audit, it is a measure of the quantity of evidence used to support the findings and conclusions related to the audit objectives and supporting findings and conclusions. Sufficiency also depends on the appropriateness of the evidence. Field work requirements for performance audits relate to planning the audit; supervising staff; obtaining sufficient, appropriate evidence; and preparing audit documentation. Reasonable assurance, significance, and audit risk form a framework for applying these requirements. (ID: 90414)

16. (b) Auditors should report known or likely fraud, noncompliance with provisions of laws, regulations, contracts, or grant agreements, or abuse directly to parties outside the audited entity when entity management fails to satisfy legal or regulatory requirements to report such information to external parties specified. Management should respond to known or likely fraud noncompliance, but is not required to use auditor recommended corrective actions. When auditors detect instances of fraud, noncompliance with provisions of laws, regulations, contracts, or grant agreements, or abuse that are not significant within the context of the audit objectives but warrant the attention of those charged with governance, they should communicate those findings in writing to audited entity officials. When auditors conclude, based on sufficient, appropriate evidence, that fraud, noncompliance with provisions of laws, regulations, contracts or grant agreements, or abuse either has occurred or is likely to have occurred which is significant within the context of the audit objectives, they merely report the matter as a finding in the report. (ID: 90415)

17. (c) When auditors do not comply with all applicable GAGAS requirements for a performance audit, they should include a modified GAGAS compliance statement in the audit report. For performance audits, auditors should use the language for an unmodified GAGAS compliance statement, but modified to indicate the requirements that were not followed, or language that the auditor did not follow GAGAS. (ID: 90416)

18. (c) All audits of recipients of federal financial assistance require the auditor to obtain and document an understanding of internal control established to ensure compliance with the laws and regulations applicable to the federal award. The auditor is not required to disclose all situations and transactions that could be indicative of fraud, abuse, and illegal acts to the federal inspector general. Materiality levels are determined by the auditor in relation to an entity's federal programs, not the government entities that provide the federal financial assistance to the recipients. Accounts need not be 100% verified by substantive tests because certain statistical sampling applications are in fact permitted. (ID: 8149)

19. (a) The auditor must design the audit to provide reasonable assurance that the financial statements are free of material misstatements resulting from violations of law and regulations that have a direct and material effect on the determination of financial statement amounts. Materiality levels are determined by the auditor in relation to an entity's federal programs, not the government entities that provide the federal financial assistance to the recipient. An auditor generally does not obtain representations regarding internal auditors' reports. An auditor usually does not express assurance on disclosures to an inspector general. (ID: 7597)

20. (d) The auditor, when auditing a nonprofit organization that receives governmental financial assistance should assess whether management has identified laws and regulations that have a direct and material effect on the entity's financial statements. The auditor issues a report on internal control over financial reporting and compliance with statutes, regulations, and terms and conditions of the financial assistance award, noncompliance with which could have a material effect on the financial statements. The auditor does not issue a separate report that describes the expected benefits and related costs of the auditor's suggested changes to the entity's internal control, render an opinion concerning the entity's continued eligibility for the governmental financial assistance, or notify the governmental agency providing the financial assistance that the audit is not designed to provide any assurance of detecting errors and fraud. (ID: 6035)

21. (c) Due to their acceptance of financial assistance from government agencies, not-for-profit organizations may be subject to laws and regulations. The audit should be designed to give reasonable assurance that the financial statements are free of misstatements resulting from violations of laws and regulations that have a direct and material effect on the determination of financial statement amounts. The audit should not be restricted to the consideration of violations that could result in criminal prosecution against the organization, involve significant deficiencies to be communicated to the organization's trustees and the funding agencies, or demonstrate the existence of material weaknesses in the organization's internal control. (ID: 2990)

22. (b) In auditing an entity's compliance with requirements governing each major federal financial assistance program in accordance with the Single Audit Act, the auditor considers materiality separately for each major federal financial assistance program, not in relation to the financial statements taken as a whole. Also, materiality is decided completely separate of the auditor's risk assessment. Materiality is not ignored because not all account balances need to fully tested. (ID: 6036)

23. (c) The risk that material noncompliance exists prior to the audit consists of two components, inherent risk of noncompliance and control risk of noncompliance. Inherent risk of noncompliance is the susceptibility of a compliance requirement to noncompliance that could be material, either individually or when aggregated with other instances of noncompliance, before consideration of any related controls over compliance. Inherent risk of noncompliance is the risk that noncompliance with a compliance requirement that could occur and that could be material, either individually or when aggregated with other instances of noncompliance, will not be prevented, or detected and corrected, on a timely basis by the entity's internal control over compliance. Detection risk of noncompliance is the risk that the procedures performed by the auditor to reduce audit risk of noncompliance to an acceptably low level will not detect noncompliance that exists and that could be material, either individually or when aggregated with other instances of noncompliance. (ID: 90417)

24. (b) The auditor should test the operating effectiveness of controls over each applicable compliance requirement to which the conditions apply in each compliance audit if any of the following conditions are met: the auditor's risk assessment includes an expectation of the operating effectiveness of controls over compliance related to the applicable compliance requirements; substantive procedures alone do not provide sufficient appropriate audit evidence; and such tests of controls over compliance are required by the governmental audit requirement. The use of audit evidence about the operating effectiveness of controls obtained in prior audits is not applicable to a compliance audit. (ID: 90418)

25. (a) If the governmental audit requirement requires the auditor to report on internal control over compliance and the auditor combines the auditor's report on compliance with a report on internal control over compliance, there are a number of elements that should be *added* to the report, including a statement that no material weaknesses in internal control over compliance were identified, if none were. Other statements would include: that in planning and performing the compliance audit, the auditor considered the entity's internal control over compliance with the applicable compliance requirements to determine the auditing procedures for the purpose of expressing an opinion on compliance, but **not** for the purpose of expressing an opinion on the effectiveness of internal control over compliance; that the auditor is **not** expressing an opinion on internal control over compliance; and that the auditor's consideration of the entity's internal control over compliance was **not** designed to identify all deficiencies in internal control that might be significant deficiencies or material weaknesses in internal control over compliance. (ID: 90419)

Solution 10-2 SIMULATION ANSWER: Report on Compliance With Laws and Regulations

1. A

2. A

3. I

The report should include a statement that the auditor's responsibility is to express an opinion [directly] on the entity's compliance with the applicable compliance requirements based on the compliance audit; not on management's assertion.

4. A

5. A

6. I

The report should contain the auditor's opinion, at the level specified by the governmental audit requirement, on whether the entity complied, in all *material* respects, with the applicable compliance requirements.

7. I

The report should include a statement that the compliance audit does *not* provide a legal determination of the entity's compliance.

8. A

This paragraph is required if the criteria used to evaluate compliance are (a) established or determined by contractual agreement or regulatory provisions that are developed solely for the parties to the agreement or regulatory agency responsible for the provisions or (b) available only to the specified parties. (ID: 9213)

Solution 10-3 SIMULATION ANSWER: Research

AU	§ 801	10

.10 The auditor's objectives in a compliance audit are to

a. obtain sufficient appropriate audit evidence to form an opinion and report at the level specified in the governmental audit requirement on whether the entity complied in all material respects with the applicable compliance requirements; and

b. identify audit and reporting requirements specified in the governmental audit requirement that are supplementary to GAAS and *Government Auditing Standards*, if any, and perform procedures to address those requirements. (ID: 9214)

CHANGE ALERT

PCAOB AS 17, *Auditing Supplemental Information Accompanying Audited Financial Statements*

On February 12, 2014, the Securities and Exchange Commission approved Public Company Accounting Oversight Board (PCAOB) Auditing Standard (AS) 17. It is effective for audit procedures and reports on supplemental information that accompany financial statements for fiscal years ending on or after June 1, 2014.

PCAOB AS 17 supersedes PCAOB interim standard AU 551, *Reporting on Information Accompanying the Basic Financial Statements in Auditor-Submitted Documents*.

This standard establishes the auditor's responsibilities when engaged to perform audit procedures and report on supplemental information that accompanies financial statements audited according to PCAOB standards. It is covered in topic X. of this chapter.

This statement will become eligible to be tested beginning with the January–February 2015 exam window—at this time only the new guidance will be eligible to be tested.

STUDY TIP

PCAOB Standards

PCAOB requirements tend to be similar to US GAAS in nature, but generally more stringent. The editors recommend that candidates thoroughly review US GAAS first, and then review PCAOB standards once US GAAS are well understood.

CHAPTER 11

OTHER AUDITING STANDARDS

AU Identifier Used for Clarified US GAAS in This Textbook

We have not continued to use the temporary AU-C identifier for the clarified auditing standards issued by the American Institute of Certified Public Accountants (AICPA). In this textbook these standards have an AU identifier.

CHAPTER 11

OTHER AUDITING STANDARDS

I. PCAOB Auditing Standards

A. Background

The Sarbanes-Oxley Act of 2002 established the Public Company Accounting Oversight Board (PCAOB). The term *public company* refers to an issuer of publicly traded securities. The Securities and Exchange Commission (SEC) has oversight authority over the PCAOB, including the approval of its rules, standards, and budget.

B. PCAOB Responsibilities

The PCAOB is charged with the responsibility of overseeing the audits of public companies, brokers, and dealers. Its four primary responsibilities are:

1. Registration of accounting firms

   a. Accounting firms are required to register with the PCAOB in order to prepare, issue, or participate in audit reports of issuers, brokers, and dealers. Non-US accounting firms that furnish, prepare, or play a substantial role in preparing an audit report for same are also subject to PCAOB rules.

   b. Each registered firm is required to file an annual report.

2. Inspections of registered firms' audits and quality control

3. Establishment of auditing and related attestation, quality control, ethics, and independence standards for registered public accounting firms

4. Investigation and discipline of registered public accounting firms and their associated persons for violations of specified laws or professional standards

C. Interim Auditing Guidance

The PCAOB adopted as interim standards, on an initial, transitional basis, the generally accepted auditing standards issued by the AICPA that were in existence on April 16, 2003. Each of these interim standards remains in effect to the extent not amended or superseded by PCAOB action.

II. PCAOB Interim Auditing Guidance With Substantive Differences From US GAAS

Editor Note: This section covers the auditing guidance based on adopted interim standards (see C. above) that is markedly different from US GAAS. (All auditing standards issued by the PCAOB and approved by the SEC are covered in the following sections of this chapter with the exception of AS 7, *Engagement Quality Review*, which is included in chapter 15, and AS 2 which was superseded by AS 5.)

A. The 10 Auditing Standards

Auditing standards provide a measure of audit quality and the objectives to be achieved in an audit. Auditing procedures differ from auditing standards. Auditing procedures are acts that the auditor performs during the course of an audit to comply with auditing standards.

1. **Overview**

   a. **General Standards**

      (1) **Technical Training & Proficiency** The audit is to be performed by a person or persons having adequate technical training and proficiency as an auditor.

(2) **Independence** In all matters relating to the assignment, an independence in mental attitude is to be maintained by the auditor or auditors.

(3) **Due Professional Care** Due professional care is to be exercised in the performance of the audit and the preparation of the report.

b. **Standards of Fieldwork** Audit documentation should be sufficient to show that the standards of fieldwork have been observed.

(1) **Adequate Planning & Supervision** The work is to be adequately planned and assistants, if any, are to be properly supervised.

(2) **Understanding of Internal Control** A sufficient understanding of internal control is to be obtained to plan the audit and to determine the nature, timing, and extent of tests to be performed.

(3) **Sufficient Appropriate Evidential Matter** Sufficient appropriate evidential matter is to be obtained through inspection, observation, inquiries, and confirmations to afford a reasonable basis for an opinion regarding the financial statements under audit.

c. **Standards of Reporting**

(1) **Accounting in Conformity With US GAAP** The report shall state whether the financial statements are presented in accordance with generally accepted accounting principles (GAAP).

(2) **Consistency** The report shall identify those circumstances in which such principles have not been consistently observed in the current period in relation to the preceding period.

(3) **Adequate Informative Disclosure** Informative disclosures in the financial statements are to be regarded as reasonably adequate unless otherwise stated in the report.

(4) **Expression of an Opinion** The report shall contain either an expression of opinion regarding the financial statements, taken as a whole, or an assertion to the effect that an opinion cannot be expressed. When an overall opinion cannot be expressed, the reasons therefor should be stated. In all cases where an auditor's name is associated with financial statements, the report should contain a clear-cut indication of the character of the auditor's work, if any, and the degree of responsibility the auditor is taking.

2. **Nature of the General Standards** The general standards are personal in nature. They relate to the qualifications of the auditor and the quality of the work performed. They apply alike to the areas of fieldwork and reporting.

a. **Technical Training & Proficiency** The audit is to be performed by a person or persons having adequate technical training and proficiency as an auditor.

In the performance of the audit which leads to an opinion, the independent auditor holds himself or herself out as one who is proficient in accounting and auditing. The attainment of that proficiency begins with the auditor's formal education and extends into his or her subsequent experience. The independent auditor must undergo training adequate to meet the requirements of a professional. This training must be adequate in technical scope and should include a commensurate measure of general education. The junior assistant, just entering upon an auditing career, must obtain his or her professional experience with the proper supervision and review of his or her work by a more experienced superior. The nature and extent of supervision and review must necessarily reflect wide variances in practice. The engagement partner must exercise seasoned judgment in the varying degrees of his or her supervision and review of the work done and judgments exercised by his or her subordinates, who in turn must meet the responsibilities attaching to the varying gradations and functions of their work.

b. **Independence** In all matters relating to the assignment, an independence in mental attitude is to be maintained by the auditor or auditors.

The attitude implied by independence is that of judicial impartiality or fairness toward clients and others who rely upon the independent auditor's report. The auditor's objective is to ensure that the general public maintains confidence in the independence of the auditor. Independence in attitude also implies the auditor is without bias towards the client.

c. **Due Professional Care** Due professional care is to be exercised in the performance of the audit and the preparation of the report.

An auditor should possess the degree of skill commonly possessed by other auditors. An auditor commits a type of fraud if the auditor alleges possessing the degree of skill commonly possessed by other auditors when that is not the case.

Each person within an independent auditor's organization has the responsibility to exercise due care and adhere to the standards of fieldwork and reporting. Auditors should be assigned to tasks and supervised commensurate with their level of knowledge, skill, and ability so that they can evaluate the audit evidence they are examining. The engagement partner should know, at a minimum, the relevant professional accounting and auditing standards and should be knowledgeable about the client. The engagement partner is responsible for the assignment of tasks to, and supervision of, the members of the engagement team.

(1) **Professional Skepticism** Due professional care requires the auditor to exercise professional skepticism. Professional skepticism is an attitude that includes a questioning mind and a critical assessment of audit evidence.

Gathering and objectively evaluating audit evidence requires the auditor to consider the appropriateness and sufficiency of the evidence. Since evidence is gathered and evaluated throughout the audit, professional skepticism should be exercised throughout the audit process.

The auditor neither assumes that management is dishonest nor assumes unquestioned honesty. In exercising professional skepticism, the auditor should not be satisfied with less than persuasive evidence because of a belief that management is honest.

(2) **Reasonable Assurance** The exercise of due professional care allows the auditor to obtain reasonable assurance about whether the financial statements are free of material misstatement, whether caused by error or fraud, or whether any material weaknesses exist as of the date of management's assessment. Absolute assurance is not attainable because of the nature of audit evidence and the characteristics of fraud. Although not absolute assurance, reasonable assurance is a high level of assurance. Therefore, an audit conducted in accordance with the standards of the PCAOB may *not* detect a material weakness in internal control over financial reporting or a material misstatement to the financial statements.

(a) **Inherent Limitations of an Audit** The independent auditor's objective is to obtain sufficient appropriate evidential matter to provide him or her with a reasonable basis for forming an opinion. The nature of most evidence derives, in part, from the concept of selective testing of the data being audited, which involves judgment regarding both the areas to be tested and the nature, extent, and timing of the tests to be performed. In addition, judgment is required in interpreting the results of audit testing and evaluating audit evidence. Even with good faith and integrity, mistakes and errors in judgment can be made. Furthermore, accounting presentations contain accounting estimates, the measurement of which is inherently uncertain and depends on the outcome of future events. The auditor exercises professional judgment in evaluating the reasonableness of accounting estimates based on information that could reasonably be expected to be available prior to the completion of field work. As a result of these factors, in the great majority of cases, the auditor has to rely on evidence that is persuasive rather than convincing.

(b) **Fraud** Because of the characteristics of fraud, a properly planned and performed audit may not detect a material misstatement. Characteristics of fraud include (*1*) concealment through collusion among management, employees, or third parties; (*2*) withheld, misrepresented, or falsified documentation; and (*3*) the ability of management to override or instruct others to override what otherwise appears to be effective controls. For example, auditing procedures may be ineffective for detecting an intentional misstatement that is concealed through collusion among personnel within the entity and third parties or among management or employees of the entity. Collusion may cause the auditor who has properly performed the audit to conclude that evidence provided is persuasive when it is, in fact, false. In addition, an audit conducted in accordance with PCAOB auditing standards rarely involves authentication of documentation, nor are auditors trained as or expected to be experts in such authentication. Furthermore, an auditor may not discover the existence of a modification of documentation through a side agreement that management or a third party has not disclosed. Finally, management has the ability to directly or indirectly manipulate accounting records and present fraudulent financial information by overriding controls in unpredictable ways.

B. Overall Opinion & Association With Financial Statements

Exhibit 1 ▸ The Fourth Standard of Reporting

The report shall contain either an expression of opinion regarding the financial statements, taken as a whole, or an assertion to the effect that an opinion cannot be expressed. When an overall opinion cannot be expressed, the reasons therefor should be stated. In all cases where an auditor's name is associated with financial statements, the report should contain a clear-cut indication of the character of the auditor's work, if any, and the degree of responsibility the auditor is taking.

1. **Overall Opinion** Reference to the financial statements *taken as a whole* applies equally to a complete set of financial statements and to an individual financial statement (such as a balance sheet) for one or more periods presented. Thus, an auditor may express an unqualified opinion on one of the financial statements and express a qualified or adverse opinion or disclaim an opinion on another if the circumstances warrant. For example, when an auditor of a new client cannot become satisfied with the accuracy of opening inventory balances, this scope limitation affects the income, retained earnings, and cash flow statements, but not the balance sheet. (This is because cost of goods sold cannot be verified.) Thus, an

unqualified opinion could be issued on the balance sheet and a disclaimer of opinion should be issued on the other financial statements.

2. **Association With Financial Statements** The objective of the fourth standard is to prevent any misinterpretation of the degree of responsibility the auditor is assuming when the auditor's name is associated with financial statements.

3. **Piecemeal Opinions** The auditor should not express an opinion on specified elements, accounts, or items included in financial statements on which the auditor has expressed an adverse opinion or disclaimed an opinion on the financial statements taken as a whole, *if* such reporting would be tantamount to expressing a piecemeal opinion on the financial statements. Piecemeal opinions are expressions of opinion as to certain identified items in financial statements and tend to overshadow or contradict a disclaimer of opinion or an adverse opinion. However, an auditor is able to express an opinion on one or more certain identified items of a financial statement, provided the identified items and the scope of the related audit do not encompass so many elements as to constitute a major portion of the financial statements. For example, it may be appropriate for an auditor to express an opinion on an entity's accounts receivable even if the auditor disclaimed an opinion on the financial statements taken as a whole. However, the report on the certain identified item should be presented separately from the report on the financial statements.

C. Types of Audit Opinions

1. **Unqualified Opinion, Standard Report**

   The standard report is issued when the auditor feels the financial statements fairly present, in all material respects, the financial position, results of operations, and cash flows in conformity with US GAAP or OCBOA (including adequate disclosure). The audit must have been conducted in accordance with the standards of the Public Company Accounting Oversight Board (PCAOB auditing standards).

2. **Explanatory Language Added to Standard Report** Certain circumstances, while not affecting the auditor's unqualified opinion on the financial statements, may require that the auditor add an explanatory paragraph (or other explanatory language) to the report. These circumstances include: part of the audit is performed by other auditors; substantial doubt about the entity's ability to continue as a going concern; a material lack of consistency; certain circumstances related to reports on comparative financial statements; certain circumstances related to interim financial information; required supplementary information (RSI) accompanies the financial statements; and other information in documents containing the financial statements is materially inconsistent with the financial statements.

   Additionally, the auditor may add an explanatory paragraph to emphasize a matter regarding the financial statements, but this is not required. Emphasis paragraphs are added solely at the auditor's discretion.

3. **Qualified Opinion** A qualified opinion states that, "except for" the effects of the matter to which the qualification relates, the financial statements present fairly, in all material respects, the financial position, results of operations, and cash flows of the entity in conformity with GAAP. A qualification may exist due to a scope limitation (and the auditor has decided not to express an unqualified opinion or disclaim an opinion) or a material departure from GAAP (and the auditor has decided not to express an adverse opinion).

4. **Adverse Opinion** An adverse opinion states that the financial statements do not present fairly the financial position, results of operations, or cash flows of the entity in conformity with GAAP. It is expressed when the financial statements taken as a whole are not presented fairly in conformity with GAAP.

5. **Disclaimer of Opinion** A disclaimer of opinion states that the auditor does not express an opinion on the financial statements. Usually an opinion is disclaimed due to scope limitations. It should **not** be expressed when there is a material departure from GAAP.

D. **Unqualified Opinions & the Standard Report**

1. **Implications of the Standard Report** The auditor's standard report states that the financial statements present fairly, in all material respects, an entity's financial position, results of operations, and cash flows in conformity with US GAAP. The auditor may express this opinion only when an audit conducted according to the standards of the Public Company Accounting Oversight Board (United States) has been completed and the necessary conditions are met. The auditor's standard report identifies the financial statements audited in an opening, introductory paragraph, describes the nature of an audit in a scope paragraph, and expresses the auditor's opinion in a separate opinion paragraph. The United States of America should be identified as the country of the origin of the PCAOB auditing standards and GAAP.

2. **Elements of the Standard Report** The basic elements of the report are:

   a. **Title** A title that includes the word "independent"

   b. **Address** Addressed to the company, to its board of directors, or to its stockholders (**not to management**). If the auditor is retained to audit the financial statements of a company that is **not** the auditor's client, the report would be addressed to the client and **not** to the directors or stockholders of the company being audited.

   c. **Introductory Paragraph**

      (1) A statement that identifies the financial statements that were audited

      (2) A statement that the financial statements are the responsibility of the company's management and that the auditor's responsibility is to express an opinion on the financial statements based on the audit

   d. **Scope Paragraph**

      (1) A statement that the audit was conducted in accordance with the standards of the Public Company Accounting Oversight Board (United States)

      (2) A statement that those standards require that the auditor plan and perform the audit to obtain reasonable assurance about whether the financial statements are free of material misstatement

      (3) Statements that an audit includes:

         (a) Examining, on a test basis, evidence supporting the amounts and disclosures in the financial statements

         (b) Assessing the accounting principles used and significant estimates made by management

         (c) Evaluating the overall financial statement presentation

      (4) A statement that the auditor believes that the audit provides a reasonable basis for the auditor's opinion

   e. **Opinion Paragraph** An opinion as to whether the financial statements present fairly, in all material respects, the financial position of the company as of the balance sheet date and the results of its operations and its cash flows for the period then ended in conformity with US GAAP

f. **Signature** The manual or printed signature of the auditor's firm

g. **City and State or Country** The city and state (or city and country, in the case of non-US auditors) from which the audit report has been issued

h. **Date** The date of the report should be no earlier than the date on which the auditor has obtained sufficient appropriate audit evidence to support the opinion.

Exhibit 2 ▸ The Form of the Auditor's Standard Report for a Single Year

Report of Independent Registered Public Accounting Firm

Address (The title and address should be included in all letters, but is not reproduced in all subsequent exhibits.)

(Introductory paragraph)

We have audited the accompanying balance sheet of X Company as of December 31, 20XX, and the related statements of income, retained earnings, and cash flows for the year then ended. These financial statements are the responsibility of the Company's management. Our responsibility is to express an opinion on these financial statements based on our audit.

(Scope paragraph)

We conducted our audit in accordance with the standards of the Public Company Accounting Oversight Board (United States). Those standards require that we plan and perform the audit to obtain reasonable assurance about whether the financial statements are free of material misstatement. An audit includes examining, on a test basis, evidence supporting the amounts and disclosures in the financial statements. An audit also includes assessing the accounting principles used and significant estimates made by management, as well as evaluating the overall financial statement presentation. We believe that our audit provides a reasonable basis for our opinion.

(Opinion paragraph)

In our opinion, the financial statements referred to above present fairly, in all material respects, the financial position of X Company as of (at) December 31, 20XX, and the results of its operations and its cash flows for the year then ended in conformity with US generally accepted accounting principles.

Signature, City and State or Country, and Date (These should be included in all letters, but are not reproduced in all subsequent exhibits.)

3. **Explanatory Language Added to Standard Report** There are certain circumstances which, while **not** affecting the auditor's unqualified opinion, may require that the auditor add explanatory language to the standard report. These circumstances include the following:

a. **Part of Audit Performed by Other Independent Auditors** Sometimes the auditor will be in a position where other independent auditors have audited the financial statements of subsidiaries, divisions, branches, components, or investments that are included in the financial statements the auditor is auditing. The auditor must first decide whether he or she has participated sufficiently to be the principal auditor, i.e., to report on the financial statements.

(1) **Whether Principal Auditor Makes Reference to Other Auditor** As principal auditor, the auditor must decide whether to assume responsibility for the work of the other auditor as it relates to the expression of an opinion on the financial statements taken as a whole.

(a) **Decision *Not* to Make Reference / Principal Auditor Assumes Responsibility** No reference should be made to the other auditor's work or report. If all other conditions for an unqualified opinion are met, a standard report can be issued.

The principal auditor must be satisfied of the other auditor's independence, professional reputation, and the quality and scope of the audit performed. This position is usually appropriate when (a) the other auditor is an associated or correspondent firm, (b) the other auditor was retained by the principal auditor, (c) the principal auditor takes steps necessary to be satisfied with the other auditor's work, or (d) the other auditor audited an immaterial portion of the financial statements.

The principal auditor must also obtain, and review and retain, the following information from the other auditor prior to the report release date.

(i) An engagement completion document

(ii) A list of significant risks, the auditor's responses, and the results of the auditor's related procedures

(iii) Sufficient information relating to significant findings or issues that are inconsistent with or contradict the auditor's final conclusions; the relevant records to be retained include, but are not limited to, procedures performed in response to the information, and records documenting consultations on, or resolutions of, differences in professional judgment among members of the engagement team or between the engagement team and others consulted

(iv) Any findings affecting the consolidating or combining of accounts in the consolidated financial statements

(v) Sufficient information to enable the office issuing the auditor's report to agree or reconcile the financial statement amounts audited by the other firm to the information underlying the consolidated financial statements

(vi) A schedule of accumulated misstatements, including a description of the nature and cause of each accumulated misstatement, and an evaluation of uncorrected misstatements, including the quantitative and qualitative factors the auditor considered to be relevant to the evaluation

(vii) All significant deficiencies and material weaknesses in internal control over financial reporting, including a clear distinction between those two categories

(viii) Letters of representations from management

(ix) All matters to be communicated to the audit committee

In addition, the principal auditor *should consider* performing one or more of the following procedures.

(x) Visit the other auditor and discuss the audit procedures followed and the results

(xi) Review the audit programs of the other auditor; in some cases, it may be appropriate to issue instructions to the other auditor as to the scope of the audit work

(xii) Review additional audit documentation of the other auditor relating to significant findings or issues in the engagement completion document

(b) **Decision to Make Reference / Principal Auditor Does *Not* Assume Responsibility** The principal auditor's report should clearly indicate, in the introductory, scope, and opinion paragraphs, the division of responsibility between the portion of the financial statements covered by the principal auditor's own audit and that covered by the audit of the other auditor. The portion examined by the other auditor should be indicated (e.g., dollar amounts or percentages of total assets, total revenues, etc.). The other auditor may be named only if (a) the other auditor has given permission, and (b) the other auditor's report is included.

Exhibit 3 ▶ Report Indicating Division of Responsibility

Report of Independent Registered Public Accounting Firm

We have audited the consolidated balance sheets of ABC Company and subsidiaries as of December 31, 20X2 and 20X1, and the related consolidated statements of income, retained earnings, and cash flows for the years then ended. These financial statements are the responsibility of the Company's management. Our responsibility is to express an opinion on these financial statements based on our audits. We did not audit the financial statements of B Company, a wholly owned subsidiary, which statements reflect total assets of $_____ and $_____ as of December 31, 20X2 and 20X1, respectively, and total revenues of $_____ and $_____ for the years then ended. Those statements were audited by other auditors whose report has been furnished to us, and our opinion, insofar as it relates to the amounts included for B Company, is based solely on the report of other auditors.

We conducted our audits in accordance with the standards of the Public Company Accounting Oversight Board (United States). Those standards require that we plan and perform the audit to obtain reasonable assurance about whether the financial statements are free of material misstatements. An audit includes examining on a test basis, evidence supporting the amounts and disclosures in the financial statements. An audit also includes assessing the accounting principles used and significant estimates made by management, as well as evaluating the overall financial statements presentation. We believe that our audits and the report of other auditors provide a reasonable basis for our opinion.

In our opinion, based on our audits and the report of other auditors, the consolidated financial statements referred to above present fairly, in all material respects, the financial position of ABC Company and subsidiaries as of December 31, 20X2 and 20X1, and the results of their operations and their cash flows for the years then ended in conformity with US generally accepted accounting principles.

(2) **Other Procedures** Regardless of whether or not reference is made, the principal auditor should inquire as to the professional reputation and independence of the other auditors and should attempt to achieve a proper coordination of their activities.

b. **Lack of Consistency** The auditor should recognize the following matters relating to the consistency of the company's financial statements in the auditor's report if those matters have a material effect on the financial statements:

(1) Change in accounting principle

(2) An adjustment to correct a misstatement in previously issued financial statements

Exhibit 4 ▸ Change in Accounting Principle (*after* opinion paragraph)

As discussed in Note X to the financial statements, the Company changed its method of computing depreciation in 20X1.

c. **Going Concern Doubt** The audit report should include an explanatory paragraph **after** the opinion paragraph if the auditor concludes that substantial doubt about the entity's ability to continue as a going concern does exist. This paragraph should **not** include any conditional language and should include the terms *substantial doubt* and *going concern.*

Exhibit 5 ▸ Going Concern Doubt: Explanatory Paragraph (*after* opinion paragraph)

The accompanying financial statements have been prepared assuming that the Company will continue as a going concern. As discussed in Note X to the financial statements, the Company has suffered recurring losses from operations and has a net capital deficiency, raising substantial doubt about its ability to continue as a going concern. Management's plans in regard to these matters are also described in Note X. The financial statements do not include any adjustments that might result from the outcome of this uncertainty.

Editor Note: If disclosure is inadequate, a qualified or adverse opinion should be expressed (GAAP departure).

d. **Emphasis of a Matter** The auditor may wish to emphasize a matter regarding the financial statements even though the auditor intends to express an unqualified opinion. For example, the auditor may wish to emphasize that the entity is a component of a larger business enterprise or that it has had significant transactions with related parties. The auditor may wish to mention an important subsequent event. This should be presented in a separate paragraph in the auditor's report **after** the opinion paragraph.

E. Departures From Unqualified Opinions

1. **Qualified Opinions** When the auditor expresses a qualified opinion, the auditor should disclose all of the substantive reasons in one or more separate explanatory paragraph(s) **before** the opinion paragraph of the report. A qualified opinion should include the word *except* or *exception* in a phrase such as *except for* or *with the exception of.* Phrases such as *subject to* and *with the foregoing explanation* are **not** clear or forceful enough and should **not** be used.

a. **Scope Limitations** Restrictions on the scope of an audit, whether imposed by the client or by circumstances, may require the auditor to express a qualified opinion. The decision depends upon the auditor's assessment of the importance of the omitted procedure(s) in relation to the financial statements. When a significant scope limitation is imposed by the client, the auditor normally would disclaim an opinion on the financial statements.

Exhibit 6 ▸ Scope Limitations

> <u>Report of Independent Registered Public Accounting Firm</u>
>
> (Same first paragraph as the standard report)
>
> Except as discussed in the following paragraph, we conducted our audits in accordance with the standards of the Public Company Accounting Oversight Board (United States). Those standards require that we plan and perform the audit to obtain reasonable assurance about whether the financial statements are free of material misstatement. An audit includes examining, on a test basis, evidence supporting the amounts and disclosures in the financial statements. An audit also includes assessing the accounting principles used and significant estimates made by management, as well as evaluating the overall financial statement presentation. We believe that our audits provide a reasonable basis for our opinion.
>
> We were unable to obtain audited financial statements supporting the Company's investment in a foreign affiliate stated at $_____ and $_____ at December 31, 20X2 and 20X1, respectively, or its equity in earnings of that affiliate of $_______ and $______, which is included in net income for the years then ended as described in Note X to the financial statements; nor were we able to satisfy ourselves as to the carrying value of the investment in the foreign affiliate or the equity in its earnings by other auditing procedures.
>
> In our opinion, except for the effects of such adjustments, if any, as might have been determined to be necessary had we been able to examine evidence regarding the foreign affiliate investment and earnings, the financial statements referred to in the first paragraph above present fairly, in all material respects, the financial position of X Company as of December 31, 20X2 and 20X1, and the results of its operations and its cash flows for the years then ended in conformity with US generally accepted accounting principles.

(1) **Qualified Opinion** If a qualified opinion is expressed, the reasons should be explained in the audit report in an explanatory paragraph (**before** the opinion paragraph) and referred to in both the scope and opinion paragraphs. The wording in the opinion paragraph should indicate that the qualification pertains to the possible effects on the financial statements and **not** to the scope limitation itself.

(2) **Scope Limitation Examples**

- (a) The auditor is unable to observe physical inventories or apply alternative procedures to verify their balances.
- (b) The client refuses to permit its attorney to furnish information requested in a letter of audit inquiry.

(3) **Uncertainties & Scope Limitations**

- (a) A matter involving an uncertainty is one that is expected to be resolved at a future date, at which time conclusive evidential matter concerning its outcome would be expected to become available. Uncertainties include, but are not limited to, contingencies and matters related to estimates.

(b) Conclusive evidential matter concerning the ultimate outcome of uncertainties cannot be expected to exist at the time of the audit because the outcome and related evidential matter are prospective. In these circumstances, management is responsible for estimating the effect of future events on the financial statements, or determining that a reasonable estimate cannot be made and making the required disclosures. An audit includes an assessment of whether the evidential matter is sufficient to support management's analysis and estimate.

(c) Absence of the existence of information related to the outcome of an uncertainty does not necessarily lead to a conclusion that the evidential matter supporting management's assertion is not sufficient. Rather, the auditor's judgment regarding the sufficiency of the evidential matter is based on the evidential matter that is, or should be, available. An unqualified opinion is appropriate if sufficient evidential matter supports management's assertions about the nature of a matter involving an uncertainty and its presentation or disclosure in the financial statements.

(d) If the auditor is unable to obtain sufficient evidential matter to support management's assertions, the auditor should consider the need to express a qualified opinion or to disclaim an opinion because of a scope limitation. A qualification or disclaimer of opinion because of a scope limitation is appropriate if sufficient evidential matter related to an uncertainty does or did exist but was not available to the auditor for reasons such as management's record retention policies or a restriction imposed by management.

(4) **Limited Reporting Engagements** The auditor is **not** precluded from reporting on only one of the basic financial statements and not the others. A scope limitation would **not** exist if the auditor is able to apply all the procedures to the one financial statement the auditor considers necessary. Such engagements involve limited reporting objectives.

b. **Departure From GAAP**

(1) **Qualified vs. Adverse Opinion** When financial statements are materially affected by a departure from GAAP, the auditor should express a qualified or an adverse opinion. Materiality, significance of an item to the entity, pervasiveness of the misstatement, and the effect of the misstatement on the financial statements as a whole, must be considered in deciding whether to express a qualified or an adverse opinion.

(2) **Explanatory Paragraph for Qualified Opinion** When the auditor expresses a qualified opinion, the auditor should disclose, in a separate explanatory paragraph(s) **before** the opinion paragraph, the substantive reasons that have led the auditor to conclude that there is a departure from GAAP. The opinion paragraph should include appropriate qualifying language and should refer to the explanatory paragraph(s). The explanatory paragraph(s) also should disclose the principal effects of the matter on the financial position, results of operations and cash flows, if practicable. If the effects cannot be determined, the report should so state.

Exhibit 7 ▸ Departure From GAAP

Report of Independent Registered Public Accounting Firm

(Same first and second paragraphs as the standard report)

The company has excluded, from property and debt in the accompanying balance sheets, certain lease obligations that, in our opinion, should be capitalized in order to conform with US generally accepted accounting principles. If these lease obligations were capitalized, property would be increased by $_____ and $_____, long-term debt by $_____ and $_____, and retained earnings by $_____ and $_____ as of December 31, 20X2 and 20X1, respectively. Additionally, net income would be increased (decreased) by $_____ and $_____, and earnings per share would be increased (decreased) by $_____ and $_____, respectively, for the years then ended.

In our opinion, except for the effects of not capitalizing certain lease obligations as discussed in the preceding paragraph, the financial statements referred to above present fairly, in all material respects, the financial position of X Company as of December 31, 20X2 and 20X1, and the results of its operations and its cash flows for the years then ended in conformity with US generally accepted accounting principles.

(3) Inadequate Disclosure

(a) If information that is essential for a fair presentation of financial statements in conformity with GAAP is **not** disclosed in the financial statements or accompanying notes, the auditor should express a qualified or an adverse opinion, and should provide the information in the report if practicable, unless its omission from the auditor's report is recognized as appropriate by a specific auditing standard.

Exhibit 8 ▸ Report Qualified for Inadequate Disclosure (Not Practicable to Present)

Report of Independent Registered Public Accounting Firm

(Same first and second paragraphs as the standard report)

The Company's financial statements do not disclose [*describe the nature of the omitted information that is not practicable to present in the auditor's report*]. In our opinion, disclosure of this information is required by US generally accepted accounting principles.

In our opinion, except for the omission of the information discussed in the preceding paragraph,...

(b) The auditor is **not** required to prepare a basic financial statement and include it in the report if the company's management declines to present the statement. In the case of, for example, the omission of a cash flow statement, a qualified opinion would be appropriate, with an explanatory paragraph added **before** the opinion paragraph.

Exhibit 9 ▸ Report Qualified: Lacking Basic Financial Statement

<u>Report of Independent Registered Public Accounting Firm</u>

We have audited the accompanying balance sheets of X Company as of December 31, 20X2 and 20X1, and the related statements of income and retained earnings for the years then ended. These financial statements are the responsibility of the Company's management. Our responsibility is to express an opinion on these financial statements based on our audit.

(Same second paragraph as the standard report)

The Company declined to present a statement of cash flows for the years ended December 31, 20X2 and 20X1. Presentation of such statement summarizing the Company's operating, investing, and financing activities is required by US generally accepted accounting principles.

In our opinion, except that the omission of a statement of cash flows results in an incomplete presentation as explained in the preceding paragraph, the financial statements referred to above present fairly, in all material respects, the financial position of X Company as of December 31, 20X2 and 20X1, and the results of its operations for the years then ended in conformity with US generally accepted accounting principles.

(4) **Uncertainties or Risks** Departures from GAAP involving uncertainties or risks (and related materiality considerations) generally fall into one of the following categories which result in the expression of an unqualified or adverse opinion:

(a) **Inadequate Disclosure** The auditor should consider materiality in evaluating the adequacy of disclosure of matters involving risks or uncertainties in the financial statements in the context of the financial statements taken as a whole. The auditor should evaluate the materiality of reasonably possible losses that may be incurred upon the resolution of uncertainties both individually and in the aggregate without regard to an evaluation of the materiality of known and likely misstatements in the financial statements.

(b) **Inappropriate Accounting Principles** In preparing financial statements, management estimates the outcome of certain types of future events. For example, estimates ordinarily are made about the useful lives of depreciable assets, the collectability of accounts receivable, the realizable value of inventory items, and the provision for product warranties. The inability to make a reasonable estimate may raise questions about the appropriateness of the accounting principles used. In those or other situations, the auditor may conclude that the accounting principles used cause the financial statements to be materially misstated.

(c) **Unreasonable Accounting Estimates** The auditor concludes that management's estimate is unreasonable and that its effect is to cause the financial statements to be materially misstated.

(5) **Accounting Changes** The auditor should evaluate a change in accounting principle to be satisfied that (a) the newly adopted accounting principle is a generally accepted accounting principle, (b) the method of accounting for the effect of the change is in conformity with GAAP, and (c) management's justification for the change is reasonable. If a change in accounting principle does **not** meet these conditions, the auditor should express a qualified opinion, or if the effect of the change is sufficiently material, an adverse opinion should be expressed.

Exhibit 10 ▶ Report Qualified: Accounting Change Not Justified by Management

Report of Independent Registered Public Accounting Firm

(Same first and second paragraphs as the standard report)

As disclosed in Note X to the financial statements, the Company adopted, in 20X2, the first-in, first-out method of accounting for its inventories, whereas it previously used the last-in, first-out method. Although use of the first-in, first-out method is in conformity with US generally accepted accounting principles, in our opinion, the Company has not provided reasonable justification for making this change as required by those principles.

In our opinion, except for the change in accounting principle discussed in the preceding paragraph, the financial statements referred to above present fairly, in all material respects, the financial position of X Company as of December 31, 20X2 and 20X1, and the results of its operations and its cash flows for the years then ended in conformity with US generally accepted accounting principles.

2. **Adverse Opinions** State that financial statements do **not** present fairly the financial position, the results of operations, or cash flows in conformity with GAAP.

Exhibit 11 ▶ Adverse Opinion

Report of Independent Registered Public Accounting Firm

(Same first and second paragraphs as the standard report)

As discussed in Note X to the financial statements, the Company carries its property, plant and equipment accounts at appraisal values, and provides depreciation on the basis of such values. Further, the Company does not provide for income taxes with respect to differences between financial income and taxable income arising because of the use, for income tax purposes, of the installment method of reporting gross profit from certain types of sales. US generally accepted accounting principles require that property, plant, and equipment be stated at an amount not in excess of cost, reduced by depreciation based on such amount, and that deferred income taxes be provided.

Because of the departures from US generally accepted accounting principles identified above, as of December 31, 20X2 and 20X1, inventories have been increased $_____ and $_____ by inclusion in manufacturing overhead of depreciation in excess of that based on cost; property, plant, and equipment, less accumulated depreciation, is carried at $_____ and $_____ in excess of an amount based on the cost to the Company; and deferred income taxes of $_____ and $_____ have not been recorded, resulting in an increase of $_____ and $_____ in retained earnings and in appraisal surplus of $_____ and $_____, respectively. For the years ended December 31, 20X2 and 20X1, cost of goods sold has been increased $_____ and $_____, respectively, because of the effects of the depreciation accounting referred to above and deferred income taxes of $_____ and $_____ have not been provided, resulting in an increase in net income of $_____ and $_____, respectively.

In our opinion, because of the effects of the matters discussed in the preceding paragraphs, the financial statements referred to above do not present fairly, in conformity with US generally accepted accounting principles, the financial position of X Company as of December 31, 20X2 and 20X1, or the results of its operations or its cash flows for the years then ended.

a. **Explanatory Paragraph** The auditor should disclose in a separate explanatory paragraph(s) **before** the opinion paragraph of the report (a) all the substantive reasons for the adverse opinion, and (b) the principal effects of the subject matter of the adverse opinion on financial position, results of operations, and cash flows, if practicable. If the effects are not reasonably determinable, the report should so state.

b. **Opinion Paragraph** The opinion paragraph should include a direct reference to a separate paragraph that discloses the basis for the adverse opinion.

3. **Disclaimer of Opinion** States that the auditor does **not** express an opinion on the financial statements. It is appropriate when the auditor has **not** performed an audit sufficient in scope to enable the auditor to form an opinion on the financial statements.

Exhibit 12 ▸ Disclaimer of Opinion Due to Scope Limitation

> Report of Independent Registered Public Accounting Firm
>
> We were engaged to audit the accompanying balance sheets of X Company as of December 31, 20X2 and 20X1, and the related statements of income, retained earnings, and cash flows for the years then ended. These financial statements are the responsibility of the Company's management.
>
> [Second (scope) paragraph of standard report should be omitted.]
>
> The Company did not make a count of its physical inventory in 20X2 or 20X1, stated in the accompanying financial statements at $_____ as of December 31, 20X2, and at $_____ as of December 31, 20X1. Further, evidence supporting the cost of property and equipment acquired prior to December 31, 20X1, is no longer available. The Company's records do not permit the application of other auditing procedures to inventories or property and equipment.
>
> The Company did not take physical inventories and we were not able to apply other auditing procedures to satisfy ourselves as to inventory quantities and the cost of property and equipment, thus, the scope of our work was not sufficient to enable us to express, and we do not express, an opinion on these financial statements.

a. **Scope Limitation** If a scope limitation is the reason for the disclaimer, the auditor should indicate in a separate paragraph the reasons for the disclaimer. The auditor should state that the scope of the audit was not sufficient to warrant the expression of an opinion, but the auditor should **not** identify the procedures that were performed nor include the paragraph describing the characteristics of an audit, i.e., the scope paragraph. In addition any other reservations regarding fair presentation in conformity with GAAP should be disclosed.

b. **Material GAAP Departures** A disclaimer of opinion should **not** be expressed when the auditor believes, on the basis of the audit, that there are material departures from GAAP.

F. Reports on Comparative Financial Statements

1. **Standard Report** An auditor's standard report covers statements of the current period and those of one or more prior periods that are presented on a comparative basis. Therefore, a continuing auditor, an auditor who has audited the current period's financial statements and those of one or more immediately preceding periods, will update the report (re-express an opinion) on the individual financial statements of those prior periods. The updated opinion may differ from that previously given if circumstances warrant a change. During the audit of the current period financial statements, the auditor should be alert for circumstances or events that affect the prior period financial statements. Generally, the date of the report should be dated as of the date of completion of fieldwork for the most recent audit.

Exhibit 13 ▸ Auditor's Standard Report: Comparative Financial Statements

> Report of Independent Registered Public Accounting Firm
>
> We have audited the accompanying balance sheets of X Company as of December 31, 20X2 and 20X1, and the related statements of income, retained earnings, and cash flows for the years then ended. These financial statements are the responsibility of the Company's management. Our responsibility is to express an opinion on these financial statements based on our audits.
>
> We conducted our audits in accordance with the standards of the Public Company Accounting Oversight Board (United States). Those standards require that we plan and perform the audit to obtain reasonable assurance about whether the financial statements are free of material misstatement. An audit includes examining, on a test basis, evidence supporting the amounts and disclosures in the financial statements. An audit also includes assessing the accounting principles used and significant estimates made by management, as well as evaluating the overall financial statement presentation. We believe that our audits provide a reasonable basis for our opinion.
>
> In our opinion, the financial statements referred to above present fairly, in all material respects, the financial position of X Company as of December 31, 20X2 and 20X1, and the results of its operations and its cash flows for the years then ended in conformity with US generally accepted accounting principles.

2. **Differing Opinions** The auditor's report on the comparative statements applies to the individual financial statements that are presented. Therefore, the same type of opinion is **not** required (qualified, unqualified, etc.) on all of the statements. When it is **not** the same, the auditor should (1) disclose all of the substantive reasons for the modified opinion (or for disclaiming an opinion) in a separate explanatory paragraph of the report, and (2) in the opinion paragraph, include an appropriate modification (or disclaimer of opinion) along with a reference to the explanation.

Exhibit 14 ▸ Different Opinions for Financial Statements Presented—Qualified Opinion on Current Year Financial Statements and an Unqualified Opinion on Prior Year Financial Statements

> Report of Independent Registered Public Accounting Firm
>
> (Same first and second paragraphs as the standard report)
>
> The Company has excluded, from property and debt in the accompanying 20X2 balance sheet, certain lease obligations that were entered into in 20X2 which, in our opinion, should be capitalized in order to conform with US generally accepted accounting principles. If these lease obligations were capitalized, property would be increased by $_____, long-term debt by $_____, and retained earnings by $_____ as of December 31, 20X2, and net income and earnings per share would be increased (decreased) by $_____ and $_____, respectively, for the year then ended.
>
> In our opinion, except for the effects on the 20X2 financial statements of not capitalizing certain lease obligations as described in the preceding paragraph, the financial statements referred to above present fairly, in all material respects, the financial position of ABC Company as of December 31, 20X2 and 20X1, and the results of its operations and its cash flows for the years then ended in conformity with US generally accepted accounting principles.

Exhibit 15 ▶ Different Opinions for Financial Statements Presented—Unqualified Opinion on Current Year Financial Statements and a Disclaimer of Opinion on Prior Year Statements of Income, Retained Earnings & Cash Flows

Report of Independent Registered Public Accounting Firm

(Same first paragraph as the standard report)

Except as explained in the following paragraph, we conducted our audits in accordance with the standards of the Public Company Accounting Oversight Board (United States).. Those standards require that we plan and perform our audit to obtain reasonable assurance about whether the financial statements are free of material misstatement. An audit includes examining, on a test basis, evidence supporting the amounts and disclosures in the financial statements. An audit also includes assessing the accounting principles used and significant estimates made by management, as well as evaluating the overall financial statement presentation. We believe that our audits provide a reasonable basis for our opinion.

We did not observe the taking of the physical inventory as of December 31, 20X0, since that date was prior to our appointment as auditors for the Company, and we were unable to satisfy ourselves regarding inventory quantities by means of other auditing procedures. Inventory amounts as of December 31, 20X0, enter into the determination of net income and cash flows for the year ended December 31, 20X1.

Because of the matter discussed in the preceding paragraph, the scope of our work was not sufficient to enable us to express, and we do not express, an opinion on the results of operations and cash flows for the year ended December 31, 20X1.

In our opinion, the balance sheets of ABC Company as of December 31, 20X2 and 20X1, and the related statements of income, retained earnings, and cash flows for the year ended December 31, 20X2, present fairly, in all material respects, the financial position of ABC Company as of December 31, 20X2 and 20X1, and the results of its operations and its cash flows for the year ended December 31, 20X2, in conformity with accounting principles generally accepted in the United States of America.

3. **Subsequent Restatement of Prior Period Statements to Conform With GAAP** If the auditor, during the current audit, becomes aware of circumstances or events that affect the financial statements of a prior period, the auditor should consider such matters when updating the report.

Exhibit 16 ▸ Changed Opinion

<u>Independent Auditor's Report</u>

(Same first and second paragraphs as the standard report)

In our report dated March 1, 20X2, we expressed an opinion that the 20X1 financial statements did not fairly present financial position, results of operations, and cash flows in conformity with US generally accepted accounting principles because of two departures from such principles: (1) the Company carried its property, plant and equipment at appraisal values, and provided for depreciation on the basis of such values, and (2) the Company did not provide for deferred income taxes with respect to differences between income for financial reporting purposes and taxable income. As described in Note X, the Company has changed its method of accounting for these items and restated its 20X1 financial statements to conform with US generally accepted accounting principles. Accordingly, our present opinion on the 20X1 financial statements, as presented herein, is different from that expressed in our previous report.

In our opinion, the financial statements referred to above present fairly, in all material respects, the financial position of X Company as of December 31, 20X2 and 20X1, and the results of its operations and its cash flows for the years then ended in conformity with US generally accepted accounting principles.

a. **Unqualified Opinion** If an auditor previously had qualified the opinion on the financial statements of a prior period because of a departure from GAAP, and the prior period financial statements are restated in the current period to conform with GAAP, the updated report of the prior period should indicate that the statements have been restated and should express an unqualified opinion with respect to the restated financial statements.

b. **Different Opinion From Previous** If the auditor decides to express a different opinion than that previously expressed, the auditor should disclose all the substantive reasons for the different opinion in a separate explanatory paragraph(s) **before** the opinion paragraph of the report. The explanatory paragraph should disclose (a) the date of the auditor's previous report, (b) the type of opinion previously expressed, (c) the circumstances or events that caused the auditor to express a different opinion, and (d) that the auditor's updated opinion on the financial statements of the prior period is different from the auditor's previous opinion on those statements.

4. **Report of Predecessor Auditor**

a. **Reissued** The predecessor auditor should consider whether the opinion previously issued on the financial statements of the prior period is still appropriate. This should include (a) reading the financial statements of the current period, (b) comparing the statements reported on with those that are being presented for comparative purposes, (c) obtaining a letter of representation from the successor auditor as to whether the successor's audit found anything that might have a material effect on (or require disclosure in) the prior period's statements, and (d) obtaining an updating representation letter from management.

(1) **Procedures** If the predecessor becomes aware of circumstances that may affect the predecessor's own previous opinion, the predecessor should inquire about the event and may want to perform tests such as reviewing the working

papers of the successor auditor in regard to the matter. The predecessor must then decide whether to revise the opinion.

(2) **Report** When the predecessor reissues the report, the predecessor should use the same date as that of the predecessor's own previous report to avoid any implication that the predecessor examined any records, transactions, or events after that date. The predecessor should **not** refer to the work or report of the successor auditor. If the predecessor revises the report or if the financial statements are restated, the report should be dual dated.

b. **Not Presented** If the financial statements of a prior period are presented for comparative purposes, but the report of the predecessor auditor is **not** presented, the successor auditor should modify the introductory paragraph of the report to indicate (a) that another auditor audited the prior period financial statements, (b) the date of the predecessor's report, (c) the type of report issued by the predecessor auditor, and (d) if the report was other than standard, and the substantive reasons.

Exhibit 17 ▸ Report When Predecessor's Report Is Not Presented

> We have audited the balance sheet of ABC Company as of December 31, 20X2, and the related statements of income, retained earnings, and cash flows for the year then ended. These financial statements are the responsibility of the Company's management. Our responsibility is to express an opinion on these financial statements based on our audit. The financial statements of ABC Company as of December 31, 20X1, were audited by other auditors whose report dated March 31, 20X2, expressed an unqualified opinion on those statements.
>
> (Same second paragraph as the standard report)
>
> In our opinion, the 20X2 financial statements referred to above present fairly, in all material respects, the financial position of ABC Company as of December 31, 20X2, and the results of its operations and its cash flows for the year then ended in conformity with US generally accepted accounting principles.

(1) If the predecessor auditor's opinion was other than a standard report, the successor auditor should describe the nature of and the reasons for the report modifications.

Exhibit 18 ▸ Predecessor Auditor's Report Not Standard

> ...were audited by other auditors whose report, dated March 1, 20X2, on those statements included an explanatory paragraph that described the change in the Company's method of computing depreciation discussed in Note X to the financial statements.

(2) If the financial statements of the prior period have been restated, the introductory paragraph should indicate that a predecessor auditor reported on the financial statements of the prior period before restatement. In addition, if the successor auditor applies sufficient procedures to satisfy the appropriateness of the restatement adjustments, the successor may also state this in the report.

Exhibit 19 ▸ Prior Period Is Restated

> We also audited the adjustments described in Note X that were applied to restate the 20X1 financial statements. In our opinion, such adjustments are appropriate and have been properly applied.

G. Summary of Various Audit Opinions & Corresponding Reports

1. Unqualified

a. **Standard Report** When all of the necessary conditions for an unqualified opinion are met and none of the situations described under the section below exist, the auditor may issue a standard report.

b. **Explanatory Language Added to Standard Report**

(1) **Doubt About Ability to Continue as a Going Concern** Add an explanatory paragraph **after** the opinion paragraph to describe the conclusion using the terms *substantial doubt* and *going concern*, referring the reader to the related note in the financial statements.

(2) **Lack of Consistency Resulting in a Material Effect on the Comparability of Financial Statements** Add an explanatory paragraph **after** the opinion paragraph to describe the change, referring the reader to the related note in the financial statements.

Editor Note: If the change is **not** properly accounted for and disclosed, this should be treated as a GAAP departure.

(3) **Principal Auditor Does *Not* Take Responsibility for an Other Auditor's Work** The principal auditor should make reference to an other auditor (the other auditor should not be named unless the other auditor gives permission and the other's report is included) and clearly indicate the division of responsibility. The introductory, scope, and opinion paragraphs should all be changed to reflect the division of responsibility; however, no explanatory paragraph is required.

Editor Note: If the principal auditor *does* take responsibility for the other auditor's work, no reference should be made to the other auditor's work or report. If all other conditions for an unqualified opinion are met, a standard report can be issued.

(4) **Prior Period Opinion Changed to Unqualified** If a qualified or adverse opinion was expressed on a prior period and those financial statements have been restated to conform to GAAP, an explanatory paragraph should be added **before** the opinion paragraph to update the prior report, describing the reason for the different opinion. The standard opinion paragraph should be used.

(5) **RSI Included** Add an explanatory paragraph **after** the opinion paragraph to refer to the required supplementary information (RSI) and explain the relevant circumstances.

(6) **Other Information Inconsistent With Financial Statements** Add an explanatory paragraph **after** the opinion paragraph to describe the inconsistency.

(7) **Emphasis of a Matter** An explanatory paragraph may be added **after** the opinion paragraph to emphasize a matter regarding the financial statements. This is solely at the auditor's discretion—it is never required.

2. **Qualified** An explanatory paragraph should be added **before** the opinion paragraph and words such as *except for* or *with the exception of* should be used in the opinion paragraph to refer to the added paragraph, thus qualifying the opinion.

   a. **Scope Limitation** The added paragraph should be referred to in the scope and opinion paragraphs.

      The auditor may, instead, choose to disclaim an opinion.

   b. **Material Departure From GAAP** The auditor may, instead, choose to issue an adverse opinion. This decision is based on materiality, significance of the item to the entity, pervasiveness of the misstatement, and the effect of the misstatement on the financial statements taken as a whole.

      Editor Note: Inadequate disclosure and inappropriate accounting changes are examples of departures from GAAP.

3. **Adverse** An explanatory paragraph should be added **before** the opinion paragraph and referred to in the opinion paragraph.

4. **Disclaimer** The introductory paragraph is modified and an explanatory paragraph should be added before the disclaimer paragraph and referred to in the disclaimer of opinion paragraph. If the disclaimer is due to a scope limitation, the scope paragraph should be omitted.

5. **Comparative** If there are different opinions for comparative financial statements presented, an explanatory paragraph should be added **before** the opinion paragraph and referred to in the opinion paragraph with "except for..." language.

6. **Predecessor Auditor** If a predecessor's report is **not** presented with comparative statements, the successor auditor should modify the introductory paragraph of his or her report and only express an opinion on current year financial statements (audited by the successor). The standard scope and opinion paragraphs should be used.

Exhibit 20 ▸ Most Common Conditions Requiring Modification of Audit Report

Reasons for Modification*	Opinion Expressed	Explanatory Paragraph	Opinion Paragraph
GAAP Departure	Qualified or Adverse	**Before** opinion paragraph to explain the departure and amount(s)	**Modified** to provide qualifying language and refer to explanatory paragraph(s)
Inadequate Disclosure (type of GAAP departure)	Qualified or Adverse	**Before** opinion paragraph to explain missing disclosure	**Modified** to provide qualifying language and refer to explanatory paragraph(s)
Scope Limitation	Qualified or Disclaimer	**Before** opinion paragraph to explain scope limitation and potential monetary effects	**Modified** to provide qualifying language or to provide disclaimer**
Going Concern Doubt	Explanatory Language Added to Standard Report (disclaimer is allowed)	**After** opinion paragraph to describe conclusion and referring reader to the note in the financial statements	**Not** modified
Lack of Consistency	Explanatory Language Added to Standard Report	**After** opinion paragraph describing change and referring reader to the note in the financial statements	**Not** modified
Reliance on Report of Another Auditor	Explanatory Language Added to Standard Report	NA	**Modified** to refer to report of other auditor ***
Prior Period Opinion Changed to Unqualified	Explanatory Language Added to Standard Report	**Before** opinion paragraph to describe reason	**Not** modified
Required supplementary information (RSI) included	Explanatory Language Added to Standard Report	**After** opinion paragraph to refer to RSI & explain relevant circumstances	**Not** modified
Other information inconsistent; management refuses to change	Explanatory Language Added to Standard Report	**After** opinion paragraph to describe inconsistency****	**Not** modified

NOTE: When **not** qualifying an opinion, an explanatory paragraph generally (but not always) comes **after** the opinion paragraph (which is **not** modified). When the opinion is other than unqualified and an explanatory paragraph is included, it comes **before** the opinion.

* Assuming item is material

** Qualified opinion requires modification of scope paragraph (using "except for" language). Disclaimer requires modification of introductory paragraph and the scope paragraph is OMITTED.

*** Division of responsibility indicated in introductory paragraph; scope paragraph is also modified to refer to report of other auditor—all 3 paragraphs modified

**** Auditor also has option to withhold report or, if not illegal or prohibited, to withdraw from engagement

H. Association With Financial Statements

1. **Association** The fourth standard of reporting seeks to avoid any misunderstanding as to the responsibility a CPA is assuming when a CPA's name is associated with financial statements.

Exhibit 21 ▸ From the Fourth Standard of Reporting

> "...In all cases where an auditor's name is associated with financial statements, the auditor should clearly indicate the character of the auditor's work, if any, and the degree of responsibility the auditor is taking in the auditor's report."

a. The CPA is associated with an entity's financial statements when the CPA (1) has agreed to the use of his or her name in a report, document, or written communication that contains the financial statements and/or (2) submits financial statements that the CPA has prepared (or assisted in preparing) to the client or to others (even if the CPA does not append his or her name to the financial statements).

b. Association does **not** occur when the CPA prepares data, such as tax returns, solely for submission to taxing authorities because these do not constitute financial statements.

2. **Disclaimer of Opinion on Unaudited Financial Statements** When associated with a public entity's financial statements that the CPA has not audited or reviewed, the CPA should issue the disclaimer shown in Exhibit 22. Note that this disclaimer is different from a disclaimer of opinion due to a scope limitation discussed earlier.

Exhibit 22 ▸ Disclaimer

The accompanying balance sheet of X Company as of December 31, 20X1, and the related statements of income, retained earnings, and cash flows for the year then ended were not audited by us and, accordingly, we do not express an opinion on them.

a. **Location** Disclaimer may accompany, or may be placed directly on, the unaudited financial statements.

b. **Markings** Each page of the statement should be marked as *unaudited.*

c. **Responsibility** CPA's only responsibility is to read the financial statements for obvious material misstatements.

d. **Procedures** The CPA should **not** describe any procedures that may have been applied, because to do so might give the impression that the CPA audited or reviewed the financial statements.

e. **Inclusion of Name** When a CPA learns that a client who is a public entity plans to include the CPA's name in a client-prepared written communication that will contain financial statements that the CPA has **not** audited or reviewed, the CPA should ask (a) that his or her name **not** be used or (b) that the client clearly mark the financial statements as *unaudited* and that a notation be made that the auditor does **not** express an opinion on them. If the client refuses, the CPA may need to consult legal counsel as to appropriate actions.

3. **Disclaimer of Opinion on Unaudited OCBOA Financial Statements**

Exhibit 23 ▸ OCBOA Financial Statements

The accompanying statement of assets and liabilities resulting from cash transactions of XYZ Corporation as of December 31, 20X1, and the related statement of revenues collected and expenses paid during the year then ended were not audited by us and, accordingly, we do not express an opinion on them.

a. **Modification of Disclaimer** The unaudited disclaimer applies except that the identification of the financial statements should be modified to conform to the PCAOB interim standard on special reports.

b. **Note to Financial Statements** Should describe the difference between the basis of presentation and GAAP. The monetary effect of such differences does **not** need to be stated.

4. **Disclaimer of Opinion When CPA Is Not Independent** The second general standard requires independence in mental attitude. The CPA cannot be in accordance with PCAOB auditing standards if the CPA is not independent, so the CPA should disclaim an opinion and clearly state that he or she is not independent (the CPA should **not** give the reasons for this lack of independence).

   Exhibit 24 ▸ Lack of Independence

We are not independent with respect to XYZ Company, and the accompanying balance sheet as of December 31, 20X1, and the related statements of income, retained earnings, and cash flows for the year then ended were not audited by us and, accordingly, we do not express an opinion on them.

   a. **Nonpublic Entity** The CPA should follow SSARS when the financial statements are those of a nonpublic entity.

   b. **Public Entity** Paragraphs a. through b. of 3., above, should be followed except that the disclaimer should be modified so that it clearly indicates the CPA is **not** independent. The reasons for lack of independence should **not** be described.

5. **Modified Disclaimer** If the CPA feels the unaudited financial statements do not conform to GAAP (which includes adequate disclosure), the CPA should ask the client to revise the statements. If the client refuses, the CPA should describe the departure in a disclaimer by (1) specifically referring to the nature of the departure and (2) if practicable, stating the effects of the departure on the financial statements or including the information that is needed in order to provide adequate disclosure.

   a. **Indeterminable or Impracticable** If the effects of the departure cannot be reasonably determined, the CPA should state this in the disclaimer. In the case of inadequate disclosure, it may not be practicable for the CPA to include the omitted disclosures in the disclaimer.

   b. **Withdrawal** If the client refuses to revise the statements or accept the disclaimer describing the departure, the CPA should refuse to be associated with the statements. The CPA may find it necessary to withdraw from the engagement.

   c. **Negative Assurance** The CPA should **not** include statements in the disclaimer that would give negative assurance except as specifically permitted by the AICPA. (One permissible area is letters for underwriters.)

6. **Comparative Financial Statements**

   a. **Documents Filed With the SEC** Unaudited financial statements presented in comparative form with audited financial statements should be clearly marked "unaudited." The auditor's report should **not** refer to the unaudited statements.

   b. **Documents Other Than Those Filed With the SEC** The unaudited financial statements should be clearly marked to indicate they have **not** been audited and either (a) the report on the prior period should be reissued or (b) the current period's report should contain a separate paragraph that describes the responsibility assumed for the financial statements of the prior period. In either case, the CPA should consider any information that has come to his or her attention during the CPA's current engagement that would help in evaluating the current form and presentation of the prior period information.

      (1) **Current Period Financial Statements Unaudited, Prior Period Financial Statements Audited** If a separate paragraph is to be used, it should state (1) the prior period's statements were previously audited, (2) the date of the previous report, (3) the type of opinion that was previously expressed, (4) if it

was **not** unqualified, the substantive reasons for this, and (5) that no auditing procedures have been performed after the date of the previous report.

Exhibit 25 ▸ Prior Audited, Current Unaudited

The financial statements for the year ended December 31, 20X1, were audited by us (other accountants) and we (they) expressed an unqualified opinion on them in our (their) report dated March 1, 20X2, but we (they) have not performed any auditing procedures since that date.

(2) **Prior Period Financial Statements Were Not Audited** If a separate paragraph is to be used, it should (1) state the service that was performed in the prior period, (2) state the date of the report on that service, (3) describe any material modifications noted in that report, and (4) state that the scope of the service was less than that of an audit and, therefore, does **not** provide a basis for the expression of an opinion on the financial statements taken as a whole. When the financial statements are those of a public entity, the separate paragraph should include a disclaimer of opinion or a description of a review. When the prior period statements are for a nonpublic entity and were compiled or reviewed, the separate paragraph should contain an appropriate description of the compilation or review. The unaudited financial statements should be clearly marked to indicate their status.

Exhibit 26 ▸ Review Performed on Prior Period Financial Statements & Current Year's Statements Audited

The 20X1 financial statements were reviewed by us (other accountants) and our (their) report thereon, dated March 1, 20X2, stated we (they) were not aware of any material modifications that should be made to those statements for them to be in conformity with generally accepted accounting principles. However, a review is substantially less in scope than an audit and does not provide a basis for the expression of an opinion on the financial statements taken as a whole.

Exhibit 27 ▸ Compiled Prior Period Financial Statements

The 20X1 financial statements were compiled by us (other accountants) and our (their) report thereon, dated March 1, 20X2, stated we (they) did not audit or review those financial statements and, accordingly, express no opinion or other form of assurance on them.

I. Required Supplementary Information

The most significant difference between the PCAOB's interim adopted interim auditing standard on required supplementary information (RSI) vs. US GAAS is that per US GAAS the auditor is required to include an other-matter paragraph in the audit report on the financial statements that refers to the RSI. The PCAOB only requires an explanatory paragraph in the audit report if there is a problem with the information, i.e., when it is omitted or materially departs from the prescribed guidelines; or the auditor is unable to complete the required procedures or to remove substantial doubts about whether the RSI conforms to the prescribed guidelines.

Other substantive differences include:

- US GAAS requires the auditor to obtain specific written representations from management about RSI
    - Per the PCAOB, the auditor is only required to *consider* whether representations on RSI should be included with written representations obtained from management

- US GAAS requires specific language for the audit report for each situation (see the reporting requirements and sample reports in chapter 8 on this topic)
    - The PCAOB's interim standard recommends different language than US GAAS for the same deficiencies and does not include guidance for the circumstance of an incomplete presentation of RSI. The PCAOB provides these examples of explanatory paragraphs an auditor might include in an audit report for these circumstances:
        - When RSI is omitted: The (Company or Governmental Unit) has not presented [*describe the supplementary information required by GAAP*] that accounting principles generally accepted in the United States has determined is necessary to supplement, although not required to be part of, the basic financial statements
        - When there are material departures from guidelines: The [*specifically identify the supplementary information*] on page XX is not a required part of the basic financial statements, and we did not audit and do not express an opinion on such information. However, we have applied certain limited procedures, which consisted principally of inquiries of management regarding the methods of measurement and presentation of the supplementary information. As a result of such limited procedures, we believe that the [*specifically identify the supplementary information*] is not in conformity with accounting principles generally accepted in the United States because [*describe the material departure(s) from the GAAP*].
        - When procedures are not completed: The [*specifically identify the supplementary information*] on page XX is not a required part of the basic financial statements, and we did not audit and do not express an opinion on such information. Further, we were unable to apply to the information certain procedures prescribed by professional standards because [*state the reasons*].
        - When the auditor has unresolved doubts about adherence to guidelines: The [*specifically identify the supplementary information*] on page XX is not a required part of the basic financial statements, and we did not audit and do not express an opinion on such information. However, we have applied certain limited procedures prescribed by professional standards that raised doubts that we were unable to resolve regarding whether material modifications should be made to the information for it to conform with guidelines established by accounting principles generally accepted in the United States. [*The auditor should consider including in the report the reason(s) he or she was unable to resolve his or her substantial doubts.*]
- Per US GAAS, the auditor is required to inform those charged with governance if the reason the auditor was unable to complete the procedures was due to significant difficulties encountered in dealing with management.
    - The PCAOB does not have a similar requirement.

J. Review of Interim Financial Information of Issuers

1. Overview

a. **Objective** The objective of the guidance covered by the PCAOB's adopted and amended interim standard on interim financial information, is to provide the CPA with a basis for communicating whether material modifications are needed to make the information conform with GAAP.

b. **Period Covered** The term *interim financial information* means financial information or statements covering a period less than a full year or for a 12-month period ending on a date other than the entity's fiscal year-end.

c. **SEC Filing Requirements** The Securities and Exchange Commission (SEC) requires a registrant to engage an independent accountant to review the registrant's interim financial information before the registrant files its quarterly report on Form 10-Q or Form 10-QSB. The SEC also requires management, with the participation of the principal executive and financial officers (the certifying officers) to make certain quarterly and annual certifications with respect to the company's internal control over financial reporting. An accountant is not required to issue a written report on a review of interim financial information, the SEC requires that an accountant's review report be filed with the interim financial information if, in any filing, the entity states that the interim financial information has been reviewed by an independent public accountant.

d. **Review vs. Audit** The objective of a review of interim financial information differs significantly from that of an audit conducted in accordance with GAAP. A review of interim financial information does not provide a basis for expressing an opinion about whether the financial statements are presented fairly, in all material respects, in conformity with generally accepted accounting principles. A review consists principally of performing analytical procedures and making inquiries of persons responsible for financial and accounting matters, and does not contemplate (a) tests of accounting records through inspection, observation, or confirmation; (b) tests of controls to evaluate their effectiveness; (c) obtaining corroborating evidence in response to inquiries; or (d) performing certain other procedures ordinarily performed in an audit. A review may bring to the accountant's attention significant matters affecting the interim financial information, but it does not provide assurance that the accountant will become aware of all significant matters that would be identified in an audit. Also, a review is not designed to provide assurance on internal control or to identify significant deficiencies. However, the accountant is responsible for communicating with the audit committee or others with equivalent authority or responsibility, regarding any significant deficiencies that come to the auditor's attention.

The auditor's responsibility as it relates to management's quarterly certifications on internal control over financial reporting is also different from the auditor's responsibility as it relates to management's annual assessment of internal control over financial reporting. The auditor should perform limited procedures quarterly to provide a basis for determining whether he or she has become aware of any material modifications that, in the auditor's judgment, should be made to the disclosures about changes in internal control over financial reporting.

2. **Procedures**

a. **Inquiries & Other Review Procedures**

(1) **Reading Minutes** Reading the available minutes of meetings of stockholders, directors, and appropriate committees, and inquiring about matters dealt with at meetings for which minutes are not available, to identify matters that may affect the interim financial information.

(2) **Obtaining Reports From Other Accountants** Obtaining reports from other accountants, if any, who have been engaged to perform a review of the interim financial information of significant components of the reporting entity, its subsidiaries, or its other investees, or inquiring of those accountants if reports have not been issued.

(3) **Inquiring of Members of Management** Inquiring of members of management who have responsibility for financial and accounting matters concerning

(a) Whether the interim financial information has been prepared in conformity with generally accepted accounting principles consistently applied

(b) Unusual or complex situations that may have an effect on the interim financial information

(c) Significant transactions occurring or recognized in the last several days of the interim period

(d) The status of uncorrected misstatements identified during the previous audit and interim review (that is, whether adjustments had been recorded subsequent to the prior audit or interim period and, if so, the amounts recorded and period in which such adjustments were recorded)

(e) Matters about which questions have arisen in the course of applying the review procedures

(f) Events subsequent to the date of the interim financial information that could have a material effect on the presentation of such information

(g) Their knowledge of any fraud or suspected fraud affecting the entity involving (a) management, (b) employees who have significant roles in internal control, or (c) others where the fraud could have a material effect on the financial statements

(h) Whether they are aware of allegations of fraud or suspected fraud affecting the entity, for example, received in communications from employees, former employees, analysts, regulators, short sellers, or others

(i) Significant journal entries and other adjustments

(j) Communications from regulatory agencies

(k) Significant deficiencies, including material weaknesses, in the design or operation of internal controls which could adversely affect the issuer's ability to record, process, summarize, and report financial data

(4) **Accounting Records** Obtaining evidence that the interim financial information agrees or reconciles with the accounting records. For example, the accountant may compare the interim financial information to

(a) The accounting records, such as the general ledger

(b) A consolidating schedule derived from the accounting records

(c) Other supporting data in the entity's records

In addition, the accountant should consider inquiring of management as to the reliability of the records to which the interim financial information was compared or reconciled.

(5) **Reading Interim Financial Information** To determine whether it conforms to GAAP.

(6) **Other Information** Reading other information that accompanies the interim financial information and is contained in reports (to consider whether such information or the manner of its presentation is materially inconsistent with the interim financial information)

(a) To holders of securities or beneficial interests

(b) Filed with regulatory authorities under the Securities Exchange Act of 1934 (such as Form 10-Q or 10-QSB)

If the accountant concludes that there is a material inconsistency, or becomes aware of information that he or she believes is a material misstatement of fact, the action taken will depend on his or her judgment in the particular circumstances.

(7) **Management's Quarterly Certifications About Internal Control** Evaluating management's quarterly certifications about internal control over financial reporting by performing the following procedures:

(a) Inquiring of management about significant changes in the design or operation of internal control over financial reporting as it relates to the preparation of annual as well as interim financial information that could have occurred subsequent to the preceding annual audit or prior review of interim financial information

(b) Evaluating the implications of misstatements identified by the auditor as part of the auditor's other interim review procedures as they relate to effective internal control over financial reporting

(c) Determining, through a combination of observation and inquiry, whether any change in internal control over financial reporting has materially affected, or is reasonably likely to materially affect, the company's internal control over financial reporting

(8) **Analytics** Applied to interim financial information to provide a basis for inquiring about unusual items. These procedures consist of

(a) Comparing the financial information with the immediately preceding interim period and with the corresponding previous period(s)

(b) Comparing actual results with anticipated results

(c) Studying the relationships of those elements that can be expected to conform to predictable patterns. The CPA should consider the types of matters that required accounting adjustments in the preceding year or quarters.

(9) **Obtaining Management's Written Representations** Management's responsibility for the financial information, completeness of the minutes, subsequent events, etc.

b. **Required Procedures**

(1) **Disaggregated Comparison** Comparing disaggregated revenue data, for example, comparing revenue reported by month and by product line or business segment for the current interim period with that of comparable prior periods.

(2) **Reconciliation** Obtaining evidence that the interim financial information agrees or reconciles with the accounting records.

(3) **Fraud Inquiry** Inquiring of members of management who have responsibility for financial and accounting matters as to their knowledge of any fraud or suspected fraud affecting the entity, and whether they are aware of allegations of fraud or suspected fraud, affecting the entity received in communications from employees, former employees, analysts, regulators, short sellers, or others.

If the auditor becomes aware of information indicating that fraud or an illegal act has or may have occurred, the auditor must also determine his or her responsibilities under the PCAOB auditing standards on fraud, illegal, and Section 10A of the Securities Exchange Act of 1934.

c. **Timing** Performing some of the work before the end of the interim period (a) usually permits the work to be carried out more efficiently, and (b) permits early consideration of accounting matters that affect the interim financial information.

d. **Extent** The extent to which the CPA applies procedures depends on the accountant's knowledge of changes in accounting practices or in the nature or volume of business activity; inquiry concerning litigation, claims, and assessments; questions raised in performing other procedures; and modification of review procedures.

e. **Understanding With Client** An accountant is required to establish an understanding with his or her client regarding the services to be performed in an engagement to review interim financial information. This understanding is usually in the form of an engagement letter that includes: a general description of the procedures; a statement that the procedures are substantially less in scope than an audit performed in accordance with PCAOB auditing standards; an explanation that the financial information is the responsibility of the company's management; and a description of the form of the report, if any.

f. **Knowledge of the Entity's Business & Internal Control** In order for an accountant to perform a review of interim financial information, there must exist a sufficient knowledge of the client's business and internal control policies and procedures as they relate to the preparation of both annual and interim financial information to: (a) identify types of potential material misstatements in the interim financial information and consider the likelihood of their occurrence; and (b) select the inquiries and analytics that will provide the accountant with a basis for reporting whether material modifications should be made for such information to conform with GAAP.

g. **Subsequent Events** Subsequent discovery of facts that existed at the date of the auditor's report should be handled in accordance with the PCAOB auditing standard on subsequent events.

h. **Quality of Principles & Estimates** An auditor is required to discuss the quality of accounting principles and accounting estimates, but limited to the impact of transactions, events, and changes considered in performing review procedures. The auditor should attempt a discussion with those charged with governance prior to filing the Form 10-Q. The discussion should occur before the filing or as soon thereafter as practicable.

3. **Communications to Management, Audit Committee & Others** As a result of conducting a review of interim financial information, the accountant may become aware of matters that cause him or her to believe that:

   a. Material modification should be made to the interim financial information for it to conform with generally accepted accounting principles

   b. Modification to the disclosures about changes in internal control over financial reporting is necessary for the certifications to be accurate and to comply with the requirements of Section 302 of the Act and Securities Exchange Act Rule 13a-14(a) or 15d-14(a), whichever applies

   c. The entity filed the Form 10-Q or Form 10-QSB before the completion of the review

   In such circumstances, the accountant should communicate the matter(s) to the appropriate level of management as soon as practicable.

   When conducting a review of interim financial information, the accountant may become aware of matters relating to internal control that may be of interest to the audit committee. Matters that should be reported to the audit committee are referred to as significant deficiencies. A significant deficiency is a deficiency, or a combination of deficiencies, in internal control over financial reporting, that is less severe than a material weakness yet important enough to merit attention by those responsible for oversight of the company's financial reporting.

4. **Report** The report should consist of: (a) a statement that the review conformed to the standards for a review of interim financial information; (b) an identification of the information reviewed; (c) a description of the procedures for a review; (d) a statement that the scope of a review is substantially less than that of an audit and that an opinion on the financial statements, taken as a whole, is **not** expressed; and (e) a statement as to whether the CPA is aware of any material modifications needed to make the financial information conform with GAAP.

   a. **Report Form** The report is addressed to the company, its board of directors, or its stockholders and is dated as of the completion of the review. Each page of the interim financial information should be clearly marked "unaudited." The CPA may use and make reference to the report of another accountant; such reference indicates a division of responsibility for performing the review.

Exhibit 28 ▶ Report on Interim Financial Information

We have reviewed the accompanying [*describe the interim financial information or statements reviewed*] of X Company as of September 30, 20X3 and 20X2, and for the three-month and nine-month periods then ended. This (these) interim financial information (statements) is (are) the responsibility of the Company's management.

We conducted our review in accordance with the standards of the Public Company Accounting Oversight Board (United States). A review of interim financial information consists principally of applying analytical procedures and making inquiries of persons responsible for financial and accounting matters. It is substantially less in scope than an audit conducted in accordance with the standards of the Public Company Accounting Oversight Board, the objective of which is the expression of an opinion regarding the financial statements taken as a whole. Accordingly, we do not express such an opinion.

Based on our review, we are not aware of any material modifications that should be made to the accompanying interim financial statement(s) for it (them) to be in conformity with US generally accepted accounting principles.

b. **Modification of CPA's Report** Neither an uncertainty **nor** a lack of consistency in applying accounting principles would result in a modified report as long as the matters are disclosed adequately in the interim financial information or statements. However, a modification is required if a change in accounting principle is **not** in conformity with GAAP.

(1) **Departure From GAAP** Report should be modified when the interim financial information is affected materially by a departure from GAAP. The nature of the departure and, if practicable, its effects should be disclosed.

Exhibit 29 ▸ Departure From GAAP

(Explanatory third paragraph)

Based on information furnished to us by management, we believe that the Company has excluded from property and debt in the accompanying balance sheet certain lease obligations that should be capitalized to conform with generally accepted accounting principles. This information indicates that if these lease obligations were capitalized at September 30, 20X1, property would be increased by $______, long-term debt by $______, and net income and earnings per share would be increased (decreased) by $_______, $_______, $_____, and $_______, respectively, for the three-month and nine-month periods then ended.

(Concluding paragraph)

Based on our review, with the exception of the matter(s) described in the preceding paragraph(s), we are not aware of any material modifications that should be made to the accompanying financial (information or statements) for them (it) to be in conformity with US generally accepted accounting principles.

(2) **Inadequate Disclosure** Report should be modified and, if practicable, the needed information should be included.

Exhibit 30 ▸ Inadequate Disclosure

(Explanatory third paragraph)

Management has informed us that the Company is presently contesting deficiencies in federal income taxes proposed by the Internal Revenue Service for the years 20X1 through 20X3 in the aggregate amount of approximately $_______, and that the extent of the company's liability, if any, and the effect on the accompanying (information or statements) are (is) not determinable at this time. The (information or statements) fail to disclose these matters, which we believe are required to be disclosed in conformity with generally accepted accounting principles.

(Concluding paragraph)

Based on our review, with the exception of the matter(s) described in the preceding paragraph(s), we are not aware of any material modifications that should be made to the accompanying financial (information or statements) for them (it) to be in conformity with US generally accepted accounting principles.

5. **Presented in Note to Audited Financial Statements** SEC Regulation S-K requires some companies to include a note containing selected quarterly financial information in their audited financial statements. In addition, other companies may choose to do so. If the quarterly data is presented voluntarily, the auditor should review it or the auditor should expand the report to state the data has not been reviewed. The interim financial information is **not** required by GAAP and has not been audited; therefore, the auditor ordinarily will **not** modify the report on the audited financial statements to refer to the quarterly data.

a. **Omission** If the CPA has audited the annual financial statements for which the quarterly information required by Regulation S-K is presented, the CPA should review the quarterly information. If unable to perform such review, the report on the audited financial statements may need to be modified. If the quarterly data either has been omitted **or** has not been reviewed, the auditor's report on the annual statements should be modified.

b. **Other** The auditor's report also should be expanded when the following occurs: the interim financial information is not marked "unaudited;" the interim information is presented voluntarily, but has not been reviewed and is not appropriately marked as such; the interim information does not conform to GAAP; or the information, although reviewed, fails to indicate that a review is substantially less in scope than an audit performed per PCAOB auditing standards.

III. References in Auditors' Reports to the Standards of the PCAOB (AS 1)

A. Requirements

1. **Reference to PCAOB Audit Standards** PCAOB AS 1 requires audit reports on engagements conducted in accordance with the PCAOB's standards (which include the adopted interim AICPA auditing standards to the extent not amended or superseded by actions of the PCAOB) to include a reference that the engagement was performed in accordance with the standards of the PCAOB, rather than US GAAS: *...the standards of the Public Company Accounting Oversight Board (United States).*

2. **Auditor Address** An auditor must also include the city and state (or city and country, in the case of non-US auditors) from which the audit report has been issued.

B. Report Illustrations

Exhibit 31 ▸ Report on an Audit of Financial Statements

Report of Independent Registered Public Accounting Firm

We have audited the accompanying balance sheets of X Company as of December 31, 20X3 and 20X2, and the related statements of operations, stockholders' equity, and cash flows for each of the three years in the period ended December 31, 20X3. These financial statements are the responsibility of the Company's management. Our responsibility is to express an opinion on these financial statements based on our audits.

We conducted our audits in accordance with the standards of the Public Company Accounting Oversight Board (United States). Those standards require that we plan and perform the audit to obtain reasonable assurance about whether the financial statements are free of material misstatement. An audit includes examining, on a test basis, evidence supporting the amounts and disclosures in the financial statements. An audit also includes assessing the accounting principles used and significant estimates made by management, as well as evaluating the overall financial statement presentation. We believe that our audits provide a reasonable basis for our opinion.

In our opinion, the financial statements referred to above present fairly, in all material respects, the financial position of the Company as of [at] December 31, 20X3 and 20X2, and the results of its operations and its cash flows for each of the three years in the period ended December 31, 20X3, in conformity with US generally accepted accounting principles.

[*Signature*]

[*City and State or Country*]

[*Date*]

Exhibit 32 ▸ Report on a Review of Interim Financial Information

> Report of Independent Registered Public Accounting Firm
>
> We have reviewed the accompanying [*describe the interim financial information or statements reviewed*] of X Company as of September 30, 20X3 and 20X2, and for the three-month and nine-month periods then ended. This (these) interim financial information (statements) is (are) the responsibility of the Company's management.
>
> We conducted our review in accordance with the standards of the Public Company Accounting Oversight Board (United States). A review of interim financial information consists principally of applying analytical procedures and making inquiries of persons responsible for financial and accounting matters. It is substantially less in scope than an audit conducted in accordance with the standards of the Public Company Accounting Oversight Board, the objective of which is the expression of an opinion regarding the financial statements taken as a whole. Accordingly, we do not express such an opinion.
>
> Based on our review, we are not aware of any material modifications that should be made to the accompanying interim financial (statements) for it (them) to be in conformity with US generally accepted accounting principles.
>
> [*Signature*]
>
> [*City and State or Country*]
>
> [*Date*]

IV. Audit Documentation (AS 3)

PCAOB AS 3, *Audit Documentation,* includes requirements and guidance similar to that addressed in AU 230 (US GAAS) of the same title (covered in chapter 4 of this text) with the exception of the following significant differences. Note that the PCAOB's requirements are more stringent.

A. PCAOB vs. US GAAS

1. **Documentation Completion Date** A complete and final set of audit documentation should be assembled for retention as of a date not more than 45 days after the report release date. Per US GAAS, this is required no later than 60 days following the report release date.

2. **Retention** Audit documentation must be retained for 7 years from the report release date unless a longer period of time is required by law. Per US GAAS, the retention period should not be shorter than 5 years from the report release date.

B. Additional PCAOB or US GAAS Requirements

1. **Engagement Completion Document** In addition to requirements similar to those in US GAAS pertaining to significant findings or issues, the PCAOB requires that significant findings or issues be identified in an engagement completion document. This document may include either all information necessary to understand the significant findings or issues or consist of cross-references to other supporting documentation. Per US GAAS, a similar document is highly recommended, but it is not required.

2. **Risk Assessment Procedures & Responses to Risks of Misstatement** In addition to requirements similar to those in US GAAS regarding the documentation of audit procedures, the PCAOB specifies that the documentation of risk assessment procedures and responses to risks of misstatement should include:

    a. A summary of the identified risks of misstatement and the auditor's assessment of risks of material misstatement (RMM) at the financial statement and assertion levels

    b. The auditor's responses to the risks of material misstatement, including linkage of the responses to those risks

3. **Audit Documentation Supporting the Work of Other Auditors**

   a. **PCAOB** The PCAOB requires that all supporting documentation prepared by other auditors must be retained by or accessible to the office issuing the audit report.

      In addition, *unless reference is made to the other auditor in the audit report*, the following specific documentation must be obtained, reviewed, and retained by the office issuing the audit report prior to the report release date:

      (1) An engagement completion document including any cross-referenced documentation

      (2) A list of significant risks and results of related audit procedures

      (3) Sufficient information concerning significant findings or issues that contradict or are inconsistent with final conclusions

      (4) Any findings affecting the consolidating or combining of accounts in the consolidated financial statements

      (5) Sufficient information to show that financial statement amounts audited by other auditors reconcile to the information underlying the consolidated financial statements

      (6) A schedule of accumulated misstatements, including descriptions of the nature and cause of each misstatement, and an evaluation of uncorrected misstatements, including the quantitative and qualitative factors

      (7) All significant deficiencies and material weaknesses in internal control over financial reporting, including a clear distinction between the two

      (8) Management representation letters

      (9) All matters to be communicated to the audit committee

   b. **US GAAS** US GAAS requires the group engagement team to include the following in the audit documentation. There is no similar explicit requirement regarding the role of the office that issued the audit report.

      (1) **Overall Requirements**

         (a) An analysis of components indicating those that are significant and the type of work performed on the financial information of the components

         (b) Written communications between the group engagement team and the component auditors about the group engagement team's requirements

      (2) **Requirements Related to Components for Which Reference Is Made in Group Audit Report to Component Auditor**

         (a) Those components referenced

         (b) The financial statements of those components

         (c) The audit reports of the component auditors

         (d) The basis for the group engagement partner's determination that the audit performed by the component auditor met the relevant requirements of US GAAS when the component audit reports do *not* state that their audit was performed in accordance with US GAAS or PCAOB auditing standards

(3) **Additional Requirements When Group Auditor Is Assuming Responsibility for Work of Component Auditor** The group engagement team should include in the audit documentation the nature, extent, and timing of the group engagement team's involvement in the work performed by the component auditors on significant components, including, when applicable, the group engagement team's review of relevant parts of the component auditors' audit documentation and related conclusions.

V. Audit of Internal Control Over Financial Reporting (AS 5)

A. Overview

PCAOB AS 5, *An Audit of Internal Control Over Financial That Is Integrated with An Audit of Financial Statements,* establishes requirements and provides guidance for auditors engaged to audit management's assessment of the effectiveness of internal control over financial reporting (ICFR) that is integrated with an audit of the financial statements. Effective ICFR provides reasonable assurance that the financial reporting process and the preparation of the financial statements are reliable for external purposes.

B. Auditor's Objective in an Audit of ICFR

The objective of the auditor for this type of engagement is to express an opinion on the effectiveness of the company's ICFR as of a point in time and taken as a whole. To express an opinion as of a point in time, the auditor must obtain evidence that ICFR has operated effectively for a sufficient period of time which may be less than the period covered by the company's financial statements. To express an opinion on ICFR as a whole, the auditor must obtain evidence about the effectiveness of selected controls over *all* relevant assertions. This involves testing the design and operating effectiveness of controls that in most cases would **not** be required if *only* expressing an opinion on the financial statements. During an audit of financial statements, when the auditor's risk assessment of specific financial statement assertions includes an expectation of the operating effectiveness of the relevant controls, evidence must be obtained that these controls were effective for a particular time (or throughout the period) upon which the auditor plans to rely on them. The auditor's risk assessment, during a financial statement audit, would ordinarily **not** include an expectation of the operating effectiveness of controls for *all* relevant assertions.

1. **Material Weaknesses** If one or more material weaknesses exist, a company's ICFR is not effective. Therefore, the auditor must plan and perform the audit to obtain evidence that is sufficient to obtain reasonable assurance about whether material weaknesses exist as of the date of management's assessment. There may be a material weakness in ICFR even when financial statements are not materially misstated. Indicators of material weaknesses include:

   a. Identification of fraud on the part of senior management, whether or not material

   b. Restatement of previously issued financial statements to reflect the correction of a material misstatement

   c. Auditor identification of a material misstatement of current period financial statements that would not have been detected by the company's ICFR

   d. Ineffective oversight by the company's audit committee of external financial reporting and ICFR

2. **Standards & Criteria** The three general standards per the PCAOB's interim standards are applicable to an audit of ICFR. PCAOB AS 5 establishes the applicable fieldwork and reporting standards. The auditor should use the same appropriate, established control framework to

perform an audit of ICFR as the company's management uses in its annual evaluation of the effectiveness of ICFR.

C. Definitions

This standard defines the following terms:

1. **Control Objective** A *control objective* provides a specific target against which to evaluate the effectiveness of controls. A control objective for internal control over financial reporting generally relates to a relevant assertion and states a criterion for evaluating whether the company's control procedures in a specific area provide reasonable assurance that a misstatement or omission in that relevant assertion is prevented or detected by controls on a timely basis.

2. **Deficiency** A *deficiency* in internal control over financial reporting exists when the design or operation of a control does not allow management or employees, in the normal course of performing their assigned functions, to prevent or detect misstatements on a timely basis.

   a. A deficiency in *design* exists when

   (1) A control necessary to meet the control objective is missing or

   (2) An existing control is not properly designed so that, even if the control operates as designed, the control objective would not be met.

   b. A deficiency in *operation* exists when a properly designed control does not operate as designed, or when the person performing the control does not possess the necessary authority or competence to perform the control effectively.

3. **Financial Statements & Related Disclosures** *Financial statements and related disclosures* refers to a company's financial statements and notes to the financial statements as presented in accordance with generally accepted accounting principles (GAAP). References to financial statements and related disclosures do not extend to the preparation of management's discussion and analysis or other similar financial information presented outside a company's GAAP-basis financial statements and notes.

4. **Internal Control Over Financial Reporting** *Internal control over financial reporting* is a process designed by, or under the supervision of, the company's principal executive and principal financial officers, or persons performing similar functions, and effected by the company's board of directors, management, and other personnel, to provide reasonable assurance regarding the reliability of financial reporting and preparation of financial statements for external purposes in accordance with GAAP and includes those policies and procedures that:

   a. Pertain to the maintenance of records that, in reasonable detail, accurately and fairly reflect the transactions and dispositions of the assets of the company;

   b. Provide reasonable assurance that transactions are recorded as necessary to permit preparation of financial statements in accordance with generally accepted accounting principles, and that receipts and expenditures of the company are being made only in accordance with authorizations of management and directors of the company; and

   c. Provide reasonable assurance regarding prevention or timely detection of unauthorized acquisition, use, or disposition of the company's assets that could have a material effect on the financial statements.

   Note: The auditor's procedures as part of either the audit of internal control over financial reporting or the audit of the financial statements are not part of a company's internal control over financial reporting.

Note: Internal control over financial reporting has inherent limitations. Internal control over financial reporting is a process that involves human diligence and compliance and thus, is subject to lapses in judgment and breakdowns resulting from human failures. Internal control over financial reporting also can be circumvented by collusion or improper management override. Because of such limitations, there is a risk that material misstatements will not be prevented or detected on a timely basis by internal control over financial reporting. However, these inherent limitations are known features of the financial reporting process. Therefore, it is possible to design into the process safeguards to reduce, though not eliminate, this risk.

5. **Management's Assessment** *Management assessment* is the assessment described in Item 308(a)(3) of Regulations S-B and S-K that is included in management's annual report on internal control over financial reporting." It is described therein as "Management's assessment of the effectiveness of the registrant's internal control over financial reporting as of the end of the registrant's most recent fiscal year, including a statement as to whether or not internal control over financial reporting is effective. This discussion must include disclosure of any material weakness in the registrant's internal control over financial reporting identified by management. Management is *not* permitted to conclude that the registrant's internal control over financial reporting is effective if there are one or more material weaknesses in the registrant's internal control over financial reporting.

6. **Material Weakness** A *material weakness* is a deficiency, or a combination of deficiencies, in internal control over financial reporting, such that there is a reasonable possibility that a material misstatement of the company's annual or interim financial statements will not be prevented or detected on a timely basis.

   Note: There is a reasonable possibility of an event, as used in this standard, when the likelihood of the event is either *reasonably possible* or *probable*, as those terms are defined in the Financial Accounting Standards Board *Accounting Standards Codification* glossary. *Reasonably possible* is defined therein as "...more than remote but less than likely." *Probable* is defined therein as "...likely to occur."

7. **Preventive or Detective Controls** Controls over financial reporting may be preventive controls or detective controls. Effective internal control over financial reporting often includes a combination of preventive and detective controls.

   a. Preventive controls have the objective of preventing errors or fraud that could result in a misstatement of the financial statements from occurring.

   b. Detective controls have the objective of detecting errors or fraud that has already occurred that could result in a misstatement of the financial statements.

8. **Relevant Assertion** A *relevant assertion* is a financial statement assertion that has a reasonable possibility of containing a misstatement or misstatements that would cause the financial statements to be materially misstated. The determination of whether an assertion is a relevant assertion is based on inherent risk, without regard to the effect of controls.

9. **Significant Account or Disclosure** An account or disclosure is a *significant account or disclosure* if there is a reasonable possibility that the account or disclosure could contain a misstatement that, individually or when aggregated with others, has a material effect on the financial statements, considering the risks of both overstatement and understatement. The determination of whether an account or disclosure is significant is based on inherent risk, without regard to the effect of controls.

10. **Significant Deficiency** A *significant deficiency* is a deficiency, or a combination of deficiencies, in internal control over financial reporting that is less severe than a material weakness,

yet important enough to merit attention by those responsible for oversight of the company's financial reporting.

D. **Integrating Audits of ICFR & Financial Statements**
Although an audit of ICFR and an audit of financial statements have distinct objectives, the auditor must plan an integrated approach and perform the work so that the objectives of both are achieved.

1. **Test of Controls** The tests of controls should be designed to simultaneously meet the objectives of both audits—to obtain sufficient evidence to support both the auditor's opinion on ICFR as of year-end and the auditor's control risk assessments during the audit of financial statements. During an audit of the financial statements, when making a determination of the effectiveness of controls to assess control risk, the auditor should consider the results of the additional tests of controls that were performed in order to express an opinion on ICFR. Likewise, during an audit of ICFR, the results of any additional tests of controls performed to support the opinion on the financial statements should be considered. And although the absence of misstatements verified by substantive procedures in an audit of financial statements is no substitute for the direct testing of controls required by an audit of ICFR, their absence should be taken into consideration by the auditor when making risk assessments that underlie the decisions about the testing needed to determine the effectiveness of controls in an audit of ICFR.

2. **Substantive Procedures** Although some procedures performed in an audit of ICFR may reduce the work needed during an audit of financial statements, the auditor must perform substantive procedures for all relevant assertions. This requirement for an audit of financial statements is **not** diminished by the procedures performed during an audit of ICFR.

E. **Planning**

1. **Audit Procedure Considerations** The following matters should be considered to determine if and if so, how, they will impact the auditor's procedures and risk assessment.

   a. **Previous Engagements** Knowledge of the company's ICFR obtained during previous engagements

   b. **Industry Issues** Industry issues such as financial reporting practices, economic conditions, laws and regulations, and technological changes

   c. **Company-Specific Issues** Company-specific issues such as its organization; operating system characteristics and degree of complexity; capital structure; ongoing legal or regulatory matters; any recent changes in the company and its operations or its ICFR; and public information about the company that is relevant to the evaluation of the likelihood of material financial statement misstatements and the effectiveness of its ICFR

   d. **Auditor's Preliminary Judgments** The auditor's preliminary judgments about the effectiveness of ICFR; and materiality, risk, and other factors related to the identification of material weaknesses

   e. **Auditor's Client Acceptance & Retention Evaluation** Consideration of any risks analyzed as part of the auditor's client acceptance and retention evaluation

   f. **Identified Control Deficiencies** Control deficiencies previously communicated to the audit committee or management

   g. **Other Available Evidence** Type and extent of available other evidence that is relevant to the effectiveness of the company's ICFR

2. **Role of Risk Assessment** The assessment of risk affects all the auditor's decisions. In assessing risk, the auditor should focus on the areas of highest risk—there is no need to test controls when their failure would not result in the reasonable possibility of a material misstatement to the financial statements. The risk that a company's ICFR will fail to prevent or detect a misstatement caused by fraud is usually greater than the risk that it will fail to prevent or detect an error.

3. **Scaling the Audit** The audit should be adjusted to fit the size and complexity of the company. Smaller and/or less complex companies may address the risks of misstatement and the needed controls differently than more complex companies.

4. **Risk of Fraud & Management Override** When selecting controls to test, the auditor should consider whether the company's controls sufficiently address the risk of material misstatement due to fraud and improper management override of other controls.

5. **Using the Work of Others** Assistance can be obtained from internal auditors, other company personnel and third parties. The auditor's decision to use others and the extent to use them should be based on an evaluation of their competence and objectivity. The auditor should also consider the risk associated with the control being tested—the higher the risk, the more important it becomes for the auditor to perform the work.

6. **Materiality** The standard directs the auditor of ICFR to use the same guidance for materiality considerations used in planning an audit of financial statements.

F. Selection of Controls to Test

The auditor should use a "top-down" approach to identify risks and select controls. The auditor should begin at the financial statement level and gain an understanding of the overall risks to ICFR. Then the auditor should evaluate the entity-level controls. Next, the auditor should identify the significant accounts and disclosures and their relevant assertions. The auditor should then verify his or her understanding of the risks in the company's processes and select for testing those controls that sufficiently address the assessed risk of misstatement to each relevant assertion.

1. **Entity-Level Controls** Entity-level controls that are important to the auditor's determination of the effectiveness of the company's ICFR must be tested. Depending on their nature and precision, the degree of effectiveness of the entity-level controls can impact both the selection of other controls to be tested as well as the nature, timing and extent of the testing of other controls. The entity-level controls include:

   a. Controls related to the control environment

   b. Controls over management override of other controls

   c. The company's risk assessment processes

   d. Centralized processing and controls, including shared service environments

   e. Controls to monitor results of operations

   f. Controls to monitor other controls, including activities of the internal audit function, the audit committee, and self-assessment programs

   g. Controls over the period-end financial reporting process

   h. Policies that address significant business control and risk management practices

2. **Assessment of Control Environment** The auditor must determine whether management's philosophy and operating style promote effective ICFR by reflecting their sound integrity and

ethical values. The auditor must also determine if the board or audit committee understands and exercises oversight responsibility over ICFR.

3. **Evaluation of Period-End Financial Reporting Process** The period-end financial reporting process evaluation by the auditor should include assessing:

   a. Inputs, procedures performed, and outputs of the processes the company uses to produce its annual and quarterly financial statements

   b. Types of adjusting and consolidating entries

   c. Effect of and the degree to which information technology (IT) is used

   d. Who participates from management

   e. Locations involved

   f. Nature and extent of the oversight by management, the board of directors, and the audit committee

4. **Identification of Significant Accounts & Disclosures and Their Relevant Assertions** The auditor should evaluate both the qualitative and quantitative risk factors related to the financial statement line items and disclosures in order to identify significant accounts and disclosures and their relevant assertions. These risk factors are the same for both an audit of ICFR and an audit of the financial statements as are the significant accounts and disclosures and their relevant assertions—however, for various reasons, the audit of financial statements may also involve performing substantive procedures on items that are not identified as part of this significant group. The components of an account or disclosure might be subject to different risks and thus may require different controls to address these separate risks. As part of this process, the auditor should also determine the likely sources of potential misstatements that would cause the financial statements to be materially misstated. The auditor should reflect on scenarios of what could go wrong.

5. **Multiple Locations or Business Units** Tests should only be performed at locations that present a reasonable possibility of material misstatement to the consolidated financial statements. For other locations or business units, the testing of entity-level controls may be sufficient to provide the needed assurance. Entities that are acquired on or before the date of management's assessment and operations that are accounted for as discontinued operations on the date of management's assessment should be included in the auditor's considerations. Testing of controls over the reporting of equity method investments would ordinarily **not** extend to the investee's controls.

6. **Understanding Likely Sources of Misstatement** The auditor should continue to develop a further understanding of the likely sources of misstatement which he or she started while identifying significant accounts and disclosures and their relevant assertions.

   a. **Auditor's Objectives** The auditor's objectives are to:

      (1) Understand the flow of transactions (including the effect of IT) related to the relevant assertions, including how these transactions are initiated, authorized, processed, and recorded

      (2) Confirm that all the points within the company's processes at which a material (individually or combined with other misstatements) misstatement could arise have been identified

(3) Identify the controls that management has implemented over the prevention or timely detection of unauthorized acquisition, use, or disposition of the company's assets that could result in a material misstatement of the financial statements

b. **Procedures** The procedures used to achieve these objectives should either be performed by the auditor or under his or her direct supervision due to the degree of judgment required.

c. **Walk-Throughs** An effective method to achieve these objectives is to perform walk-throughs. The auditor follows a transaction from its origin to its reflection in the financial statements, step-by-step, using the same documents and information technology that a company's personnel use. Walk-throughs usually involve a combination of procedures, including inquiry, observation, inspections of documentation and reperformance.

7. **Selection of Controls** The decision for selection is based on whether a control by itself (or in combination with other controls) sufficiently addresses the assessed risk of misstatement to a given relevant assertion. It is not necessary to test all the controls that address an assertion.

G. Testing Controls

1. **Testing Design Effectiveness** The auditor should test the design of a control by determining whether the control, if performed correctly by persons with the necessary authority and competence, meets the company's control objectives and can be expected to prevent or detect errors or fraud that could result in material misstatements in the financial statements. Walk-throughs that include inquiries of appropriate people, observation of the company's operations, and inspection of documentation will usually suffice.

2. **Testing Operating Effectiveness** The auditor should test the operating effectiveness of a control by determining if the control is operating as designed and confirming that it is being performed by a person with the necessary authority and competence. Procedures for this test would include reperformance of the control in addition to inquiries of appropriate people, observation of the company's operations, and inspection of documentation.

3. **Evidence to Be Obtained** The evidence obtained is dependent on the nature, timing, and extent of audit procedures performed. Generally, more evidence is required to support the conclusion that a control is operating effectively than is needed when a control is deemed ineffective. The auditor should increase the amount of evidence gathered as the risk associated with a control increases. The following factors affect the risk associated with a control:

   a. The nature and materiality of misstatements that the control is intended to prevent or detect

   b. The inherent risk associated with the related account(s) and assertion(s)

   c. Whether there have been changes in the volume or nature of transactions that might adversely affect control design or operating effectiveness

   d. Whether the account has a history of errors

   e. The effectiveness of entity-level controls, especially controls that monitor other controls

   f. The nature of the control and the frequency with which it operates

   g. The degree to which the control relies on the effectiveness of other controls

h. The competence of the personnel who perform the control or monitor its performance and whether there have been changes in these key personnel

i. Whether the control relies on performance by an individual or is automated, i.e., an automated control would generally be expected to be lower risk if relevant information technology general controls are effective

j. The complexity of the control and the significance of the judgments that must be made in connection with its operation

4. **Deviations From Controls** When deviations from controls are discovered, the auditor should determine the impact on the assessment of the risk associated with the control, the evidence being gathered, and the operating effectiveness of the control. Any *one* control does not necessarily have to operate without any deviation to be considered effective because effective ICFR does **not** provide absolute assurance.

5. **Special Considerations to Reduce Testing for Subsequent Years' Audits** The auditor should incorporate knowledge gained in prior years' audits of ICFR into the determination of the nature, timing, and extent of audit procedures selected to test controls.

   a. **Risk Factors** After taking into account various risk factors, the additional information provided in subsequent years' audits may allow the auditor to assess the risk as lower than in the first year and thus reduce the testing in the subsequent audits. The factors affecting the risk associated with a control in subsequent years' audits includes those listed in the previous "Evidence to Be Obtained" section of this topic plus the following factors:

      (1) The nature, extent, and timing of procedures performed in previous audits

      (2) The results of the previous years' testing of the control

      (3) Whether there have been changes in the control or the process in which it operates since the previous audit

   b. **Benchmarking** The standard specifically allows the use of a benchmarking strategy (establishment of a baseline) under certain conditions for automated (IT) application controls in subsequent years' audits because of their inherent reliability. If the auditor is able to obtain evidence that general controls over program changes, access to programs, and computer operations are effective and continue to be tested; and that there have been no changes to the automated application controls since they were last tested, the auditor may conclude that the automated application controls continue to be effective.

6. **Vary the Testing** The auditor should vary the nature, timing, and extent of the testing of controls from one year to another to allow for changes in circumstances as well as to make the audit unpredictable.

7. **Service Organizations** The relevant concepts in the PCAOB auditing standard on service organizations (concerning a company that obtains services from another organization that are part of the company's information system) are applicable to ICFR audits. If the services provided are part of the company's information system, then it follows that they are part of the information and communications component of the company's ICFR. Thus, the auditor should include the activities of the service organization in the determination of what evidence is needed to support his or her opinion. The auditor should gain an understanding of both the controls of the service organization that are relevant to the company's internal control and the controls of the company over the activities of the service organization. Then the auditor should obtain evidence that the relevant controls are operating effectively. The auditor may use a service auditor's report on controls placed in operation and tests of operating effective-

ness if the auditor judges that the report provides sufficient evidence and is satisfied as to the professional reputation, competence and independence of the service auditor. However, the auditor should **not** refer to the service auditor's report in his or her opinion of ICFR.

8. **Superseded Controls** Sometimes management changes controls during the period being audited. The auditor must use professional judgment to determine if testing of the superseded controls is needed.

H. **Evaluating Identified Deficiencies**

1. **Severity of the Deficiency** The auditor must determine if each control deficiency identified, either individually or in combination, is a material weakness as of the date of management's assessment by evaluating its severity. However, the auditor is **not** required to search for deficiencies that do not constitute a material weakness. The severity of a deficiency is dependent on whether there is a reasonable possibility that the company's controls will fail to prevent or detect a misstatement and the magnitude of the potential misstatement. Severity is not dependent on whether a misstatement has actually occurred. What matters is the lack of effectiveness of a company's controls, i.e., if there is a reasonable possibility that a deficiency, or a combination of deficiencies, will result in a misstatement of an account balance or disclosure.

2. **Prudent Official Standard** The auditor should set and use a *prudent official* standard to help evaluate the severity of a deficiency, or combination of deficiencies. To do so, the auditor must determine the level of detail and degree of assurance that would satisfy prudent officials in the conduct of their own affairs that they have reasonable assurance that transactions are recorded as necessary to permit the preparation of financial statements in conformity with GAAP. If this standard is not met, the auditor should consider the deficiency, or combination of deficiencies, to be an indicator of a material weakness.

3. **Compensating Controls** The auditor should consider the effect of compensating controls when determining if a deficiency, or combination of deficiencies, constitutes a material weakness. The compensating control should be judged effective enough to prevent or detect a misstatement that could be material in order to be considered to have a mitigating effect.

I. **Management's Written Representations**

The standard refers the auditor to the PCAOB auditing standard on management representations for further guidance on the management representation letter such as who should sign it, the period it covers, and when to obtain an updated letter as these are the same as for an audit of the financial statements. The auditor should obtain the following written representations from management:

1. Acknowledgment of management's responsibility for establishing and maintaining effective ICFR

2. Statement that management has performed an evaluation and made an assessment of the effectiveness of the company's ICFR and specifying the control criteria

3. Statement that management did not use the auditor's procedures performed during either the audit of ICFR or the financial statements as part of the basis for management's assessment of the effectiveness of the company's ICFR

4. Statement of management's conclusion, as set forth in its assessment, about the effectiveness of the company's ICFR based on the control criteria as of a specified date

5. Statement that management disclosed to the auditor all deficiencies in the design or operation of ICFR identified as part of management's evaluation, including separately disclosing all such deficiencies that it believes to be significant deficiencies or material weaknesses in ICFR

6. Description of any fraud resulting in a material misstatement to the company's financial statements and any other fraud that involves senior management or management or other employees who have a significant role in the company's ICFR

7. Statement of whether control deficiencies identified and communicated to the audit committee during previous engagements have been resolved, and specifically identifying any that have not

8. Statement whether there were, subsequent to the date being reported on, any changes in ICFR or other factors that might significantly affect ICFR, including any corrective actions taken by management with regard to significant deficiencies and material weaknesses

J. Communications

1. **Ineffective Oversight** In the case where the auditor concludes that oversight by the company's audit committee of external financial reporting and ICFR is ineffective, the auditor must communicate that conclusion, in writing, to the board of directors.

2. **Material Weaknesses** The auditor must communicate, in writing, to management and the audit committee all material weaknesses identified during the audit. This should be done prior to the issuance of the audit report on ICFR. If a material weakness has **not** been included in management's assessment, the auditor should also communicate this fact, in writing, to the audit committee.

3. **Significant Deficiencies** The auditor must also communicate, in writing, all significant deficiencies to the audit committee.

4. **Deficiencies** The auditor should communicate, in writing, all deficiencies in ICFR to management of which he or she is *aware*—the auditor is **not** required to perform procedures that are sufficient to identify *all* control deficiencies. The audit committee should be informed by the auditor when this communication to management has been made.

5. **Scope Limitation** If the auditor concludes that he or she cannot express an opinion because there has been a scope limitation, the auditor should communicate, in writing, to management and the audit committee that the audit of ICFR cannot be completed. See the "Disclaiming an Opinion or Withdrawing From the Engagement" section of this topic for further information.

6. **Material Misstatement in Additional Information Included With Management's Report** If the auditor determines that the other information included with management's annual report on ICFR contains a material misstatement of fact and if after a discussion with management, management does not remedy it, the auditor should communicate his or her concerns, in writing, to management and the audit committee. See the "Report Modifications" section of this topic for additional information.

7. **Fraud & Illegal Acts** The standard refers the auditor to the PCAOB auditing standards on fraud, illegal acts, and §10A of the Securities Exchange Act of 1934 for guidance regarding the auditor's responsibilities if he or she becomes aware of fraud or possible illegal acts.

8. **Management's Annual Certification Is Misstated** The standard refers the auditor to the PCAOB auditing standard on interim financial information, for guidance as to communication responsibilities in this instance.

9. **Auditor Disagrees With Management's Exclusion of Certain Entities** The auditor may disagree with management's application of the SEC's criteria for exclusion of certain entities from the assessment of ICFR or find their disclosure of the exclusion inadequate. The standard refers the auditor to the PCAOB auditing standard on interim financial information for guidance as to communication responsibilities in this instance.

K. Reporting

1. **Forming an Opinion** The auditor should form an opinion of the effectiveness of ICFR after considering the evidence obtained from all sources. In addition to the evidence from the auditor's testing of controls and identification of control deficiencies, this would include misstatements identified during the financial statement audit and the evidence in current reports on ICFR issued by internal auditors or others. The auditor should **not** issue a report stating that no deficiencies exist because an audit of ICFR does not provide assurance that all deficiencies less severe than a material weakness have been identified.

2. **Required Elements of Audit Report** The following must be included in the auditor's report on ICFR:

   a. A title that includes the word *independent*

   b. A statement that management is responsible for maintaining effective ICFR and for assessing the effectiveness of ICFR

   c. An identification of management's report on internal control

   d. A statement that the auditor's responsibility is to express an opinion on the company's ICFR based on his or her audit

   e. A definition of ICFR as stated in paragraph A5 of the standard (see the "Definitions" section of this topic)

   f. A statement that the audit was conducted in accordance with the standards of the PCAOB (United States)

   g. A statement that the standards of the PCAOB require that the auditor plan and perform the audit to obtain reasonable assurance about whether effective ICFR was maintained in all material respects

   h. A statement that an audit includes obtaining an understanding of ICFR, assessing the risk that a material weakness exists, testing and evaluating the design and operating effectiveness of internal control based on the assessed risk, and performing such other procedures as the auditor considered necessary in the circumstances

   i. A statement that the auditor believes the audit provides a reasonable basis for his or her opinion

   j. A paragraph stating that because of inherent limitations, ICFR may not prevent or detect misstatements and that projections of any evaluation of effectiveness to future periods are subject to the risk that controls may become inadequate because of changes in conditions, or that the degree of compliance with the policies or procedures may deteriorate

   k. The auditor's opinion on whether the company maintained, in all material respects, effective ICFR as of the specified date, based on the control criteria

   l. The manual or printed signature of the auditor's firm

   m. The city, and state (or city and country, in the case of non-US auditors) from which the auditor's report has been issued

   n. The date of the audit report

Exhibit 33 ▶ Combined Report Expressing an Unqualified Opinion on Financial Statements & An Unqualified Opinion On Internal Control Over Financial Reporting

Report of Independent Registered Public Accounting Firm

We have audited the accompanying balance sheets of W Company as of December 31, 20X8 and 20X7, and the related statements of income, stockholders' equity and comprehensive income, and cash flows for each of the years in the three-year period ended December 31, 20X8. We also have audited W Company's internal control over financial reporting as of December 31, 20X8, based on [*Identify control criteria, for example, "criteria established in Internal Control—Integrated Framework issued by the Committee of Sponsoring Organizations of the Treadway Commission (COSO)."*]. W Company's management is responsible for these financial statements, for maintaining effective internal control over financial reporting, and for its assessment of the effectiveness of internal control over financial reporting, included in the accompanying [*title of management's report*]. Our responsibility is to express an opinion on these financial statements and an opinion on the company's internal control over financial reporting based on our audits.

We conducted our audits in accordance with the standards of the Public Company Accounting Oversight Board (United States). Those standards require that we plan and perform the audits to obtain reasonable assurance about whether the financial statements are free of material misstatement and whether effective internal control over financial reporting was maintained in all material respects. Our audits of the financial statements included examining, on a test basis, evidence supporting the amounts and disclosures in the financial statements, assessing the accounting principles used and significant estimates made by management, and evaluating the overall financial statement presentation. Our audit of internal control over financial reporting included obtaining an understanding of internal control over financial reporting, assessing the risk that a material weakness exists, and testing and evaluating the design and operating effectiveness of internal control based on the assessed risk. Our audits also included performing such other procedures as we considered necessary in the circumstances. We believe that our audits provide a reasonable basis for our opinions.

A company's internal control over financial reporting is a process designed to provide reasonable assurance regarding the reliability of financial reporting and the preparation of financial statements for external purposes in accordance with generally accepted accounting principles. A company's internal control over financial reporting includes those policies and procedures that (1) pertain to the maintenance of records that, in reasonable detail, accurately and fairly reflect the transactions and dispositions of the assets of the company; (2) provide reasonable assurance that transactions are recorded as necessary to permit preparation of financial statements in accordance with generally accepted accounting principles, and that receipts and expenditures of the company are being made only in accordance with authorizations of management and directors of the company; and (3) provide reasonable assurance regarding prevention or timely detection of unauthorized acquisition, use, or disposition of the company's assets that could have a material effect on the financial statements.

Because of its inherent limitations, internal control over financial reporting may not prevent or detect misstatements. Also, projections of any evaluation of effectiveness to future periods are subject to the risk that controls may become inadequate because of changes in conditions, or that the degree of compliance with the policies or procedures may deteriorate.

In our opinion, the financial statements referred to above present fairly, in all material respects, the financial position of W Company as of December 31, 20X8 and 20X7, and the results of its operations and its cash flows for each of the years in the three-year period ended December 31, 20X8, in conformity with accounting principles generally accepted in the United States of America. Also in our opinion, W Company maintained, in all material respects, effective internal control over financial reporting as of December 31, 20X8, based on [*Identify control criteria, for example, "criteria established in Internal Control—Integrated Framework issued by the Committee of Sponsoring Organizations of the Treadway Commission (COSO)."*].

[*Signature*]

[*City and State or Country*]

[*Date*]

3. **Separate or Combined Reports** The auditor may choose to issue separate reports on the company's financial statements and ICFR or to issue a combined report containing both opinions. If the auditor issues separate reports, a separate paragraph should be added to each report that cross-references the other report, giving the date and nature of its opinion. The reference in the financial statement report to the ICFR report should also identify the control criteria on which the ICFR opinion is based.

4. **Date of Report** The auditor should date the audit report(s) no earlier than the date on which the auditor has obtained sufficient competent evidence to support the auditor's opinion. If separate reports on the financial statements and ICFR are issued, the date of the reports should be the same, as the auditor cannot audit ICFR without also auditing the financial statements.

5. **Audit Report on ICFR Included With Filings Under Federal Securities Statutes** The PCAOB auditing standard on filings under federal securities statutes is applicable when the auditor's report is included in registration statements, proxy statements, or periodic reports filed under federal securities statutes.

6. **Report Modifications** The auditor should modify the report if any of the following conditions exist:

   a. **Elements of Management's Annual Report on ICFR Are Incomplete or Improperly Presented** After forming an opinion on the effectiveness of ICFR, the auditor should review management's presentation on the elements that is required by the SEC to be included in the company's annual report on ICFR. If the auditor determines that any of these elements are incomplete or not properly presented the auditor should add an explanatory paragraph that describes the reasons why the auditor found management's report unsatisfactory.

   b. **Scope Limitation** See the "Disclaiming an Opinion or Withdrawing From the Engagement" section of this topic.

   c. **Auditor Decides to Refer to the Report of Other Auditors** When another auditor has audited the financial statements and ICFR of one or more components of a company, the auditor needs to determine whether he or she may serve as the principal auditor and use the work and reports of another auditor as a basis, in part, for his or her opinion on ICFR. The standard states that the PCAOB auditing standard related to a part of an audit performed by other independent auditors is applicable to this determination by the auditor. If the auditor decides that he or she should be the principal auditor of the financial statements, then he or she must also be the principal auditor for ICFR. The principal auditor's decision whether to make reference in the report on ICFR to the audit of ICFR performed by another auditor is similar to the same decision for financial reporting, so again, the same standard is applicable. When the auditor decides to make this reference, the auditor should refer to the report of the other auditor when describing the scope of the audit and when expressing the opinion.

   d. **Other Information in Management's Annual Report on ICFR** If the additional information included by management appears to be part of management's annual report on ICFR, then the auditor should disclaim an opinion on the other information. If the auditor determines that the other information contains a material misstatement of fact and if after a discussion with management, management does not remedy it, the auditor should communicate his or her concerns, in writing, to management and the audit committee. This standard also refers the auditor to the PCAOB auditing standard on illegal acts by clients, and §10A of the Securities Exchange Act of 1934 for further direction because in some circumstances additional action may be required.

e. **Management's Annual Certification Is Misstated** The standard refers the auditor to the PCAOB auditing standard on interim financial information for guidance as to communication requirements if matters come to the auditor's attention that convince the auditor that modifications to the disclosures about changes in ICFR are needed for the annual certifications to be accurate and to be in compliance with either the requirements of §302 of Sarbanes-Oxley Act of 2002 or Securities Exchange Act rules for any interim period. If management and the audit committee fail to respond satisfactorily, the auditor (in addition to the requirements described in the PCAOB auditing standard on interim financial information) should add an explanatory paragraph to his or her report on ICFR which explains the reasons he or she believes management's disclosures should be modified.

f. **Assessment of ICFR Excludes Certain Entities** The SEC allows management to limit its assessment of ICFR by excluding certain entities and the auditor may choose to do likewise. This situation is **not** considered a scope limitation. However, the auditor should include, either in an additional explanatory paragraph or as part of the scope paragraph in his or her report, a disclosure similar to management's concerning the exclusion of an entity from both the scope of management's assessment and the auditor's audit of ICFR. If the auditor considers management's application of the SEC's exclusion criteria to be unreasonable or management's disclosure inadequate, the auditor should follow the guidance in the PCAOB auditing standard on interim financial information as to communication requirements. In addition, the auditor should add in explanatory paragraph to his or her report on ICFR which describes the reasons why the auditor believes management's disclosures should be modified.

g. **Subsequent Events** The auditor may obtain knowledge about subsequent events with respect to conditions that did *not* exist at the date of the assessment, but arose subsequent to that date and before issuance of the auditor's report and had a material effect on the company's ICFR. The auditor should add an explanatory paragraph to his or her report describing the event and its effects or a reference to the disclosure in management's report. (If the effect cannot be determined, the auditor should disclaim an opinion. For additional information see the "Subsequent Events" section of this topic.)

7. **Adverse Opinion** If there are one or more material weaknesses, the auditor must express an adverse opinion on the company's ICFR unless the scope of the audit has been limited. (The auditor must either withdraw from the engagement or disclaim an opinion if there are restrictions on the scope of the engagement. See the "Disclaiming an Opinion or Withdrawing From the Engagement" section of this topic.)

   a. **Disclosure** The auditor should include a disclosure in the report as to whether the opinion on the financial statements was affected by the adverse opinion on ICFR.

   b. **Material Weakness** An adverse opinion report resulting from a material weakness must include the definition of a material weakness (see the "Definitions" section of this topic). The remaining modifications to the report and required actions depend on if the material weakness was also included in management's assessment, and if so, how it was included:

      (1) When a material weakness was identified and was included in management's assessment, the report must include a statement that a material weakness was identified and an identification of the material weakness described in management's assessment. If the auditor finds that the disclosure is not fairly presented in all material respects, the auditor's report should describe this conclusion and the information needed to fairly describe the material weakness.

(2) When a material weakness was identified, but was **not** included in management's assessment the following items must be included in the auditor's report:

(a) A statement that a material weakness was identified, but not included in management's assessment

(b) A description of the material weakness that includes specific information about its nature plus the actual and potential effect on the financial statements issued during its existence

(c) Additionally, the auditor should communicate, in writing, to the audit committee that the material weakness was not identified or disclosed in management's assessment.

8. **Disclaiming an Opinion or Withdrawing From the Engagement**

a. **Scope Limitation** The auditor may not form an opinion on the effectiveness of ICFR if there have been restrictions on the scope of the auditor's work to the degree that the auditor was unable to apply the procedures necessary under the circumstances. If there has been such a scope limitation the auditor is required to disclaim an opinion or withdraw from the engagement. One example of a scope limitation is when the auditor is unable to obtain written representations from management. In this case, the auditor should also consider the effects of management's refusal on his or her ability to rely on other representations made by management, including those made in conjunction with the audit of the financial statements. The auditor may issue a disclaimer as soon as he or she determines that a scope limitation will prevent the attainment of evidence sufficient to gain the reasonable assurance needed to express an opinion. No additional work is required by the auditor at this point. The report date is the date that the auditor has gained sufficient competent evidence to support the representations contained in his or her report. The auditor should communicate, in writing, to management and the audit committee that he or she is unable to satisfactorily complete the audit of ICFR. When disclaiming an opinion due to a scope limitation, the auditor's report should:

(1) Include a statement that the scope of the audit was not sufficient to warrant the expression of an opinion

(2) Include a separate paragraph(s) that gives the substantive reasons for the disclaimer

(3) **Not** identify the procedures that were performed **nor** include the description of the characteristics of an audit of ICFR to avoid overshadowing the disclaimer

(4) Include a description of any material weakness that was identified in the company's ICFR (if the auditor was able to conclude it existed based on the limited procedures applied); this should include specifics about the nature of the material weakness and its actual and potential effect on the presentation of the company's financial statements issued during the existence of the material weakness—this description should conform to the requirements of the standard for the issuance of an adverse opinion due to a material weakness (covered in the previous "Adverse Opinion" section of this topic); the definition of the term material weakness per the standard (see the "Definitions" section of this topic) should also be included

b. **Effect of Subsequent Event Not Determinable** The auditor should disclaim an opinion when he or she cannot determine the effect that a subsequent event (with respect to conditions that existed at the date of the assessment) had on a company's ICFR. For additional information see the "Subsequent Events" section of this topic.

L. Subsequent Events

1. **Procedures to Identify Subsequent Events** Changes in ICFR or other factors that have a material impact on ICFR may occur subsequent to the date that ICFR is being audited but before the date of the auditor's report. The PCAOB auditing standard on subsequent events provides direction on subsequent events for a financial statement audit that may also be helpful during an audit of ICFR. As previously covered, the auditor should attain written representations from management relating to subsequent events. The auditor should review, for this subsequent period, the following:

   a. Internal audit reports

   b. Other independent auditor reports of deficiencies in internal control

   c. Regulatory agency reports on the company's ICFR

   d. Information about the company's ICFR obtained via other engagements

2. **When the Subsequent Event Became Known or Arose *Before* the Issuance of the Auditor's Report:**

   a. **And *Did* Exist As of the Date of Management's Assessment** If the auditor becomes aware of subsequent events that materially and adversely affect ICFR as of the date of the assessment, the auditor should issue an adverse opinion. If management's assessment states that ICFR is effective, the auditor should follow the guidance described previously under "Adverse Opinion" in this topic. If the auditor cannot determine the effect of the event on the company's ICFR, the auditor should disclaim an opinion.

   b. **And Did *Not* Exist As of the Date of Management's Assessment** The auditor may become aware of a subsequent event with respect to conditions that did **not** exist as of the date specified in management's assessment, but arose subsequent to that date and before issuance of the auditor's report. If the subsequent event had a material effect on ICFR, the auditor should add an explanatory paragraph to his or her report that either describes the event and its effect or includes a referral to the disclosure in management's report.

3. **When the Subsequent Event Became Known *After* the Issuance of the Auditor's Report** If after the auditor issues the report, he or she becomes aware of a subsequent event that existed as of the report date and that might have affected his or her opinion, the auditor should follow the guidance in the PCAOB auditing standard on subsequent discovery of facts existing at the date of the auditor's report.

VI. Reporting on Whether a Previously Reported Material Weakness Continues to Exist (AS 4)

A. Overview

PCAOB AS 4, *Reporting on Whether a Previously Reported Material Weakness Continues to Exist*, applies when an auditor is engaged to report on whether a previously reported material weakness in ICFR continues to exist as of a date specified by management. The PCAOB does not require this type of engagement. A *previously reported material weakness* means a material weakness that was described previously in an auditor's report on ICFR as required by PCAOB AS 5. The auditor may report on more than one previously reported material weakness in a single engagement.

B. **Conditions**

There may be certain material weaknesses that are not suitable for this type of engagement; that is, if identifying *all* stated control objectives affected by the material weakness is difficult, then the material weakness should be addressed, instead, in the annual audit of ICFR. The following conditions must all be met for an auditor to complete this type of engagement:

1. Management has accepted responsibility for the effectiveness of ICFR.
2. Management has evaluated the effectiveness of the specific control(s) using the same stated control objectives and control criteria it used for its most recent annual assessment of ICFR.
3. Management has asserted that the specific control(s) identified is/are effective in achieving the stated control objective.
4. Management has supported its assertion with sufficient evidence, including documentation.
5. Management has presented a written report that will accompany the audit report that contains all required elements.

C. **Opinion**

In order to render an *unqualified opinion, the auditor must have (1) obtained evidence about the design and operating effectiveness of the specifically identified controls, (2) determined that the material weakness no longer exists, and (3) determined that there were no scope limitations. If a scope limitation exists, the auditor is required to either disclaim an opinion or withdraw from the engagement.

*Editor Note: The auditor's opinion on whether a previously reported material weakness continues to exist may be expressed as *the material weakness no longer exists* or *the material weakness exists*. The PCAOB's guidance does **not** use the terms *unqualified opinion* or *adverse opinion*; instead, it refers simply to "an opinion" or "the auditor's opinion." However, it does explicitly state that a qualified opinion is **not** permitted.

D. **Material Weakness Continues to Exist**

If an auditor determines that a material weakness continues to exist, the following should be considered:

1. If the auditor issues a report, it must state that the material weakness continues to exist as of the date specified by management.
2. If the auditor does not issue a report (which is not required), he or she must communicate to the audit committee, in writing, his or her conclusion that the material weakness continues to exist. If another material weakness is discovered during the engagement, it must also be communicated to the audit committee in writing.
3. The auditor must consider the conclusion that the material weakness continues to exist as part of his or her evaluation of management's quarterly disclosures about ICFR, as required by PCAOB AS 5.
4. If an auditor is engaged to report on two previously reported material weaknesses and only one of them continues to exist, the auditor can report in either of two ways: (1) the auditor can issue one report that contains two different opinions on each material weakness; or (2) the auditor can issue a report that contains a single opinion on the material weakness that no longer exists if management modifies its assertion to address only that material weakness. The auditor will still need to communicate in writing to the audit committee, the conclusion regarding the second material weakness that continues to exist.

VII. Evaluating Consistency of Financial Statements (AS 6)

Editor Note: This standard is essentially the same as AU 708, *Consistency of Financial Statements,* except for the different reporting terminology. If comparability is materially affected, an *explanatory* paragraph is added per PCAOB auditing standards, whereas per US GAAS, the same is termed an *emphasis-of-matter* paragraph and an *emphasis-of-matter* heading is required for the paragraph. However, in both cases, the paragraph should be placed below the opinion paragraph.

A. Consistency & the Audit Report

1. **Objective** PCAOB Auditing Standard (AS) 6 establishes requirements and provides direction for the auditor's evaluation of the consistency of the financial statements, including changes to previously issued financial statements, and the effect of that evaluation on the auditor's report on the financial statements.

2. **Comparability of Financial Statements Between Periods** To identify consistency matters that might affect the report, the auditor should evaluate whether the comparability of the financial statements between periods has been materially affected by changes in accounting principles or by material adjustments to previously issued financial statements for the relevant periods.

3. **Periods to Evaluate** The periods covered in the auditor's evaluation of consistency depend on the periods covered by the auditor's report on the financial statements. When reporting only on the current period, the auditor should evaluate whether the current period financial statements are consistent with those of the preceding period. When reporting on two or more periods, the auditor should evaluate consistency between such periods and the consistency of such periods with the period prior thereto if such prior period is presented with the financial statements being reported upon.

4. **Recognition in Audit Report** The auditor should recognize the following matters relating to the consistency of the company's financial statements in the auditor's report if those matters have a material effect on the financial statements.

   a. A change in accounting principle

   b. An adjustment to correct a misstatement in previously issued financial statements

   An explanatory paragraph should be added, following the opinion paragraph, as discussed in the following topics.

B. Change in Accounting Principle

1. **Definition** A change in accounting principle is a change from one generally accepted accounting principle to another generally accepted accounting principle when

   (a) There are two or more generally accepted accounting principles that apply

   (b) The accounting principle formerly used is no longer generally accepted

   (c) A change in the method of applying an accounting principle has occurred

2. **Change in Accounting Estimate Effected by a Change in Accounting Principle** The auditor should evaluate and report on a change in accounting estimate effected by a change in accounting principle like other changes in accounting principles.

3. **Change in Reporting Entity** The auditor should recognize a change in the reporting entity like other changes in accounting principles unless the change in reporting entity results from a transaction or event. (A change in reporting entity that results from a transaction or event,

such as the creation, cessation, or complete or partial purchase or disposition of a subsidiary or other business unit does not require recognition in the auditor's report.)

4. **Investee's Change in Accounting Principle** If a company's financial statements contain an investment accounted for by the equity method, the auditor's evaluation of consistency should include consideration of the investee. If the investee makes a change in accounting principle that is material to the investing company's financial statements, the auditor should add an explanatory paragraph (following the opinion paragraph) to the auditor's report.

5. **Auditor's Evaluation** The auditor should evaluate a change in accounting principle to determine whether

   a. The newly adopted accounting principle is a generally accepted accounting principle

   b. The method of accounting for the effect of the change is in conformity with generally accepted accounting principles

   c. The disclosures related to the accounting change are adequate

   d. The company has justified that the alternative accounting principle is preferable

   Editor Note: If the above criteria are not met, the auditor should consider the matter to be a departure from GAAP and, if the effect of the change in accounting principle is material, issue a qualified or adverse opinion.

6. **Explanatory Paragraph** If the auditor concludes that the above criteria have been met, the auditor should add an explanatory paragraph to the auditor's report, through the addition of an explanatory paragraph **following** the opinion paragraph. The explanatory paragraph should include identification of the nature of the change and a reference to the note disclosure describing the change.

   a. **Adoption of a New Pronouncement Example** "As discussed in Note X to the financial statements, the company has changed its method of accounting for [*describe accounting method change*] in [*year(s) of financial statements that reflect the accounting method change*] due to the adoption of [*name of accounting pronouncement*]."

   b. **Change in Accounting Principle Not Involving a New Pronouncement Example** "As discussed in Note X to the financial statements, the company has elected to change its method of accounting for [*describe accounting method change*] in [*year(s) of financial statements that reflect the accounting method change*]."

   c. **Report Recognition Periods Required** The explanatory paragraph relating to a change in accounting principle should be included in reports on financial statements in the year of the change and in subsequent years until the new accounting principle is applied in all periods presented. If the accounting change is accounted for by retrospective application to the financial statements of all prior periods presented, the additional paragraph is needed only in the year of the change.

C. **Correction of a Material Misstatement in Previously Issued Financial Statements**

1. **Explanatory Paragraph** The correction of a material misstatement in previously issued financial statements should be recognized in the auditor's report through the addition of an explanatory paragraph **following** the opinion paragraph. The explanatory paragraph should include the following.

   a. A statement that the previously issued financial statements have been restated for the correction of a misstatement in the respective period

b. A reference to the company's disclosure of the correction of the misstatement.

c. **Example** "As discussed in Note X to the financial statements, the 20X2 financial statements have been restated to correct a misstatement."

2. **Report Recognition Periods Required** This type of explanatory paragraph in the auditor's report should be included in reports on financial statements when the related financial statements are restated to correct the prior material misstatement. The paragraph need not be repeated in subsequent years.

Editor Note: A change from an accounting principle that is not generally accepted to one that is generally accepted is a correction of a misstatement.

D. Change in Classification

Changes in classification in previously issued financial statements do **not** require recognition in the auditor's report, unless the change represents the correction of a material misstatement or a change in accounting principle. Accordingly, the auditor should evaluate a material change in financial statement classification and the related disclosure to determine whether such a change also is a change in accounting principle or a correction of a material misstatement. For example, certain reclassifications in previously issued financial statements, such as reclassifications of debt from long-term to short-term or reclassifications of cash flows from the operating activities category to the financing activities category, might occur because those items were incorrectly classified in the previously issued financial statements. In such situations, the reclassification also is the correction of a misstatement.

VIII. PCAOB Risk Assessment Standards vs. US GAAS & ISA

A. PCAOB AS 8, *Audit Risk*

1. **Overview** This standard discusses the auditor's consideration of audit risk in an audit of financial statements as part of an integrated audit or an audit of financial statements only. It describes the components of audit risk and the auditor's responsibilities for reducing audit risk to an appropriately low level in order to obtain reasonable assurance that the financial statements are free of material misstatement.

2. **Inverse Relationship of Detection Risk & Substantive Procedures** PCAOB standards include an explicit requirement that as the appropriate level of detection risk decreases, the evidence from substantive procedures that the auditor should obtain increases.

   US GAAS and ISA include a discussion about the inverse relationship and guidance that the auditor can act accordingly. Put another way, US GAAS and ISA include an implicit rather than an explicit requirement regarding this matter because risk assessment is required and its purpose is to allow auditors to vary the amount of audit attention related to particular areas based on the risks presented by them.

   Editor Note: Detection risk relates to the substantive audit procedures and is managed by the auditor's response to the risk of material misstatement (RMM). As the assessed RMM increases, the evidence from substantive procedures that the auditor should obtain also increases. The auditor reduces detection risk through the nature, extent, and timing of substantive procedures performed. However, the auditor should perform substantive procedures for all relevant assertions related to material classes of transactions, account balances, and disclosures.

B. PCAOB AS 9, *Audit Planning*

1. **Overview** This standard establishes requirements regarding planning an audit, including assessing matters that are important to the audit, and establishing an appropriate audit strategy and audit plan.

2. **Development of the Audit Strategy & Audit Plan** PCAOB standards include a requirement to evaluate whether the following matters are important to the company's financial statements and internal control over financial reporting and, if so, how they will affect the auditor's procedures. These matters were adapted from PCAOB AS 5, *An Audit of Internal Control Over Financial Reporting That Is Integrated with An Audit of Financial Statements.*

   a. Knowledge of the company's internal control over financial reporting obtained during other engagements performed by the auditor

   b. Matters affecting the industry in which the company operates, such as financial reporting practices, economic conditions, laws and regulations, and technological changes

   c. Matters relating to the company's business, including its organization, operating characteristics, and capital structure

   d. The extent of recent changes, if any, in the company, its operations, or its internal control over financial reporting

   e. The auditor's preliminary judgments about materiality, risk, and, in integrated audits, other factors relating to the determination of material weaknesses

   f. Control deficiencies previously communicated to the audit committee or management

   g. Legal or regulatory matters of which the company is aware

   h. The type and extent of available evidence related to the effectiveness of the company's internal control over financial reporting

   i. Preliminary judgments about the effectiveness of internal control over financial reporting

   j. Public information about the company relevant to the evaluation of the likelihood of material financial statement misstatements and the effectiveness of the company's internal control over financial reporting

   k. Knowledge about risks related to the company evaluated as part of the auditor's client acceptance and retention evaluation

   l. The relative complexity of the company's operations

   US GAAS and ISA advise the auditor to consider similar matters with less emphasis on internal control.

3. **Documentation of the Audit Plan & Audit Strategy** PCAOB standards do not include the phrase *at the relevant assertion level for each material class of transactions, account balance, and disclosure* when describing the documentation requirements for audit procedures as do US GAAS and ISA. This is not a difference between the standards regarding documentation of audit procedures. US GAAS and ISA use the phrase to indicate the level of detail of the coverage while the PCAOB omits it for clarity reasons because not all audit procedures relate to the assertion level, i.e., some are performed at the entity level.

4. **Multilocation Engagements** PCAOB standards state that the auditor should determine the extent to which auditing procedures should be performed at selected locations or business units to obtain sufficient appropriate evidence to obtain reasonable assurance about whether the consolidated financial statements are free of material misstatement. This includes determining the locations or business units at which to perform audit procedures, as well as the nature, extent, and timing of the audit procedures to be performed at those individual locations or business units. The auditor should assess the RMM to the consolidated financial statements associated with the location or business unit and correlate the amount of audit

attention devoted to the location or business unit with the degree of RMM associated with that location or business unit.

Factors that are relevant to the assessment of the RMM associated with a particular location or business unit and the determination of the necessary audit procedures include:

a. The nature and amount of assets, liabilities, and transactions executed at the location or business unit, including, e.g., significant transactions executed at the location or business unit that are outside the normal course of business for the company, or that otherwise appear to be unusual given the auditor's understanding of the company and its environment

b. The materiality of the location or business unit

c. The specific risks associated with the location or business unit that present a reasonable possibility of material misstatement to the company's consolidated financial statements

d. Whether the RMM associated with the location or business unit apply to other locations or business units such that, in combination, they present a reasonable possibility of material misstatement to the company's consolidated financial statements

e. The degree of centralization of records or information processing

f. The effectiveness of the control environment, particularly with respect to management's control over the exercise of authority delegated to others and its ability to effectively supervise activities at the location or business unit

g. The frequency, timing, and scope of monitoring activities by the company or others at the location or business unit

US GAAS advise consideration of different locations and business components when establishing the scope of an audit, but do not include a detailed discussion like the PCAOB standards. ISA address some of the same aspects of this matter in a separate standard on audits of group financial statements (including the work of component auditors) mainly in relation to the impact on the scope of the audit. The focus in ISA is on the determination of whether a component is significant (mainly based on materiality) and, if so, the applicable audit procedures. Risk assessment is an important factor but not to the degree or specificity as described in the PCAOB approach.

C. PCAOB AS 10, *Supervision of the Audit Engagement*

1. Overview This standard sets forth requirements for supervision of the audit engagement, including, in particular, supervising the work of engagement team members. It applies to the engagement partner and to other engagement team members who assist the engagement partner with supervision.

2. Supervision by Other Engagement Team Members PCAOB standards state that the engagement partners may seek assistance from appropriate engagement team members in fulfilling their responsibilities. US GAAS and ISA mention delegation of review responsibilities only.

3. Extent of Supervision Needed Factors Per PCAOB standards, to determine the extent of supervision necessary for engagement team members to perform their work as directed and form appropriate conclusions, the engagement partner and other engagement team members performing supervisory activities should take into account:

a. The nature of the company, including its size and complexity

b. The nature of the assigned work for each engagement team member, including the procedures to be performed, and the controls or accounts and disclosures to be tested

c. The knowledge, skill, and ability of each engagement team member.

ISA list essentially the same factors. US GAAS explain that many factors are involved in determining the extent of the supervision that is appropriate and give two examples: the complexity of the subject matter and the qualifications of the persons performing the work, including knowledge of the client's business and industry.

D. PCAOB AS 11, *Consideration of Materiality in Planning and Performing an Audit*

1. **Overview** This standard describes the auditor's responsibilities for consideration of materiality in planning and performing an audit.

2. **Materiality for Financial Statements as a Whole** PCAOB standards require the auditor to establish a materiality level for the financial statements as a whole that is appropriate in light of the particular circumstances, including consideration of the company's earnings and other relevant factors.

   US GAAS and ISA have essentially the same requirement. US GAAS and ISA state that the determination of what is material to the users is a matter of professional judgment. The auditor often may apply a percentage to a chosen benchmark as a step in determining materiality for the financial statements taken as a whole. To identify an appropriate benchmark, factors, e.g., earnings should be considered.

3. **Definition of Materiality** The PCAOB's requirement for establishing a materiality level for the financial statements as a whole is based on the concept of materiality that is articulated by the courts in interpreting the federal securities laws. In interpreting the federal securities laws, the Supreme Court of the United States has held that a fact is material if there is "a substantial likelihood that the...fact would have been viewed by the reasonable investor as having significantly altered the 'total mix' of information made available." As the Supreme Court has noted, determinations of materiality require "delicate assessments of the inferences a 'reasonable shareholder' would draw from a given set of facts and the significance of those inferences to him [*sic*]."

   The US GAAS requirement is based on the definition of materiality similarly articulated by the FASB: "...the magnitude of an omission or misstatement of accounting information that, in the light of surrounding circumstances, makes it probable that the judgment of a reasonable person relying on the information would have been changed or influenced by the omission or misstatement."

4. **Tolerable Misstatement** PCAOB standards contain a requirement to take into account the nature, cause (if known), and amount of misstatements that were accumulated in audits of the financial statements of prior periods when determining tolerable misstatement and planning and performing audit procedures.

   US GAAS and ISA do not have such a requirement.

   Editor Note: *Tolerable misstatement* is the maximum error in a population (e.g., the class of transactions, account balance, or disclosure) that the auditor is willing to accept. When assessing the RMM and designing and performing further audit procedures to respond to the assessed risks, the auditor should allow for the possibility that some misstatements of lesser amounts than the materiality levels could, in the aggregate, result in a material misstatement of the financial statements.

E. PCAOB AS 12, *Identifying and Assessing Risks of Material Misstatement*

1. **Overview** This standard establishes requirements regarding the process of identifying and assessing RMM of the financial statements. The risk assessment process discussed in the standard includes information-gathering procedures to identify risks and an analysis of the identified risks.

2. **Additional Procedures for Obtaining an Understanding** PCAOB standards require the auditor to consider performing certain procedures as part of obtaining an understanding of the company. These procedures include reading public information about the company, observing or reading transcripts of earnings calls, obtaining an understanding of compensation arrangements with senior management, and obtaining information about trading activity in the company's securities and holdings in the company's securities by significant holders.

   With the exception of the first item, US GAAS and ISA do not have such a requirement.

3. **Disclosures** PCAOB standards require the auditor to develop expectations about the disclosures that are necessary for the company's financial statements to be presented fairly in conformity with the applicable financial reporting framework to identify and assess the RMM related to omitted, incomplete, or inaccurate disclosures. Additionally, the engagement team members should discuss how fraud might be perpetrated or concealed by omitting or presenting incomplete or inaccurate disclosures. The auditor's evaluation of fraud risk factors should include how fraud could be perpetrated or concealed by presenting incomplete or inaccurate disclosures or by omitting disclosures that are necessary for the financial statements to be presented fairly in conformity with the applicable financial reporting framework.

   Although consideration of appropriate disclosure is included throughout the US GAAS and ISA, they do not include a risk assessment requirement similar to this for disclosures.

4. **Control Deficiencies Identified** PCAOB standards state that if the auditor identifies a control deficiency in the company's control environment, the auditor should evaluate the extent to which this control deficiency is indicative of a fraud risk factor.

   US GAAS and ISA do not have such a requirement.

5. **Relationship of Understanding of Internal Control to Tests of Controls** PCAOB standards require the auditor to take into account the evidence obtained from understanding internal control when assessing control risk and, in the audit of internal control, forming conclusions about the effectiveness of controls. The auditor should also take into account the evidence obtained from understanding internal control when determining the nature, extent, and timing of procedures necessary to support the auditor's conclusions about the effectiveness of entity-level controls in the audit of internal control.

   US GAAS and ISA do not have such a requirement linking tests of controls to the audit of internal control.

6. **Review of Interim Financial Information** When the auditor has performed a review of interim financial information in accordance with the PCAOB auditing standard on interim financial information, PCAOB standards require the auditor to evaluate whether information obtained during the review is relevant to identifying RMM in the year-end audit.

   US GAAS and ISA do not have such a requirement.

7. **Analytical Procedures** Per PCAOB standards, when the auditor has performed a review of interim financial information in accordance with the PCAOB auditing standard on interim financial information the auditor should take into account the analytical procedures applied in that review when designing and applying analytical procedures as risk assessment procedures.

   US GAAS and ISA do not have such a requirement.

8. **Discussion Among Engagement Team** Per PCAOB standards, communication among the engagement team members about significant matters affecting the RMM should continue throughout the audit, including when conditions change.

   US GAAS and ISA do not have such a requirement to continue the discussion throughout the audit. US GAAS state that depending on the circumstances of the audit, there *may* be multiple discussions in order to facilitate the ongoing exchange of information between audit team members regarding the susceptibility of the entity's financial statements to material misstatements. The purpose is for audit team members to communicate and share information obtained throughout the audit that may affect the assessment of the RMM due to fraud or error or the audit procedures performed to address the risks.

F. **PCAOB AS 13, *The Auditor's Responses to the Risks of Material Misstatement***

1. **Overview** This standard establishes requirements for responding to the RMM in financial statements through the general conduct of the audit and performing audit procedures regarding significant accounts and disclosures.

2. **Determination of Need for Pervasive Changes** PCAOB standards require the auditor to determine whether it is necessary to make pervasive changes to the nature, timing, or extent of audit procedures to adequately address the assessed RMM. Examples of such pervasive changes include modifying the audit strategy to:

   a. Increase the substantive testing of the valuation of numerous significant accounts at year-end because of significantly deteriorating market conditions

   b. Obtain more persuasive audit evidence from substantive procedures due to the identification of pervasive weaknesses in the company's control environment

   US GAAS and ISA require the adjustment of the audit strategy and plan to changes in circumstances which would cover the events described above, but they do not have this specific requirement.

3. **More Persuasive Evidence Required** PCAOB standards require the auditor to obtain more persuasive evidence about the effectiveness of controls for each relevant assertion for which the audit approach consists primarily of tests of controls.

   US GAAS and ISA do not have such a requirement.

4. **Evaluating Operating Effectiveness of Controls** PCAOB standards and US GAAS require the auditor to determine whether the person performing the control possesses the necessary authority and competence to perform the control effectively.

   ISA do not have such a requirement.

5. **Tests of Controls in an Integrated Audit** PCAOB standards require the auditor to perform tests of controls in integrated audits to meet the objectives of both the audit of financial statements and the audit of internal control.

   US GAAS and ISA do not have such a requirement.

6. **Testing of Controls That Have Not Changed** When the auditor is relying on controls, US GAAS and ISA allow the testing of the operating effectiveness of controls that have not changed to be performed at least every third annual audit.

   PCAOB standards require the auditor to test controls during the period of reliance, i.e., the period covered by the financial statements or the portion of that period for which the auditor plans to rely on them in order to modify the nature, extent, and timing of substantive procedures—they do **not** allow rotational testing.

7. **Assessment of Control Risk** PCAOB standards require the assessment of control risk.

   US GAAS and ISA do not require the separate specific assessment of control risk—how to consider the components of audit risk is left up to the auditor's judgment.

8. **Substantive Procedures** PCAOB standards require the auditor to perform substantive procedures for each relevant assertion of each significant account and disclosure, regardless of the assessed level of control risk.

   US GAAS and ISA have essentially the same requirement; however, they require it regardless of the assessed RMM rather than the assessed level of control risk and require it for each material class of transactions, account balance, and disclosure.

9. **Confirmation Procedures** PCAOB standards and US GAAS do not specifically address confirmation procedures in their risk assessment standards; however, in their respective standards dedicated to confirmations, an auditor who has not requested confirmations in the examination of accounts receivable is required to document the justification for not doing so.

   ISA address confirmation procedures in their risk assessment standards, requiring the auditor to consider whether confirmation procedures are to be performed as substantive audit procedures.

10. **Interim Substantive Procedures** PCAOB standards and US GAAS list various factors the auditor is required to consider when determining whether to perform substantive procedures at an interim date.

    ISA do not have such a requirement; however, they do provide a list of similar factors that may influence the auditor's decision.

11. **Substantive Procedures to Cover Remaining Period if Interim Testing Performed** All three sets of standards include requirements to cover the remaining period. PCAOB standards require that such procedures include comparing relevant information about the account balance at the interim date with comparable information at the end of the period to identify amounts that appear unusual and investigating such amounts; and performing audit procedures to test the remaining period. US GAAS and ISA contain essentially the same guidance; however, they use the term *may*, i.e., specific procedures are not required for covering the remaining period.

12. **Dual-Purpose Tests** PCAOB standards define a dual-purpose test as a substantive test of a transaction and a test of a control relevant to that transaction that are performed concurrently, e.g., a substantive test of sales transactions performed concurrently with a test of controls over those transactions. PCAOB standards state that when dual-purpose tests are performed, the auditor should design the dual-purpose test to achieve the objectives of both the test of the control and the substantive test. Also, when performing a dual-purpose test, the auditor should evaluate the results of the test in forming conclusions about both the assertion and the effectiveness of the control being tested.

    US GAAS and ISA do not have such requirements.

G. PCAOB AS 14, *Evaluating Audit Results*

1. **Overview** This standard establishes requirements regarding the auditor's evaluation of audit results and determination of whether the auditor has obtained sufficient appropriate audit evidence. The evaluation process set forth in this standard includes, among other things, evaluation of misstatements identified during the audit; the overall presentation of the finan-

cial statements, including disclosures; and the potential for management bias in the financial statements.

2. **Analytical Procedures Regarding Revenue** All three sets of standards require the auditor to perform analytical procedures relating to revenue; however, only the PCAOB standards require them to be performed through the end of the period.

3. **Timely Communication of Accumulated Misstatements** All three sets of standards require the auditor to communicate misstatements accumulated during the audit to management and follow up on their correction; however, PCAOB standards do not include a specific requirement for the auditor to request their correction as US GAAS and ISA do.

4. **Evaluation of Effect of Misstatements on Assessed RMM** PCAOB standards require the auditor to evaluate the nature and effects of the individual misstatements accumulated during the audit on the assessed risks of material misstatement.

   US GAAS and ISA do not have an explicit requirement to evaluate the effect of accumulated misstatements on risk assessment; however, US GAAS and ISA do have a requirement for the auditor to consider whether the overall audit strategy and audit plan need to be revised if the nature of identified misstatements and the circumstances of their occurrence are indicative that other misstatements may exist that, when aggregated with identified misstatements, could be material.

5. **Misstatements Indicative of Fraud** PCAOB standards and US GAAS require the auditor to perform procedures to obtain additional audit evidence to determine whether fraud has occurred or is likely to have occurred, and, if so, its effect on the financial statements and the auditor's report if the auditor believes that a misstatement is or might be intentional, and if the effect on the financial statement cannot be readily determined.

   ISA have similar requirements; however, they do not explicitly require the auditor to perform audit procedures to obtain additional audit evidence to determine the effect of the misstatement on the financial statements.

6. **Communications Regarding Fraud** If the auditor becomes aware of information indicating that fraud or another illegal act has occurred or might have occurred, PCAOB standards require the auditor to determine the auditor's responsibility for communications under their adopted interim standards on (a) fraud and (b) illegal acts by clients; and federal securities laws and regulations. The auditor is required, whenever the auditor has determined that there is evidence that fraud may exist, to bring the matter to the attention of an appropriate level of management.

   US GAAS and ISA have essentially the same requirement for communication with management and those charged with governance. As for communication outside the entity, their guidance requires the auditor to determine when the auditor should communicate. US GAAS state that the auditor may wish to consult with legal counsel beforehand.

7. **Adjusting Entries by Management That Offset Accumulated Misstatements** If management identifies adjusting entries that offset misstatements accumulated by the auditor, PCAOB standards require the auditor to perform procedures to determine why the misstatements were not identified previously and to evaluate the implications on the integrity of management and the auditor's risk assessments, including fraud risk assessments. The auditor should also perform additional procedures as necessary to address the risk of further undetected misstatements.

   US GAAS and ISA do not have such a requirement.

H. PCAOB AS 15, *Audit Evidence*

This standard explains what constitutes audit evidence and establishes requirements for designing and performing audit procedures to obtain sufficient appropriate audit evidence to support the opinion expressed in the auditor's report.

There are no substantive differences between the three sets of standards regarding audit evidence.

IX. Communications With Audit Committees (AS 16)

A. Overview

PCAOB AS 16 requires the auditor to communicate with a company's audit committee certain matters about an audit and to obtain certain information from the audit committee relevant to the audit. This standard also requires the auditor to establish an understanding of the terms of the audit engagement with the audit committee and to record that understanding in an engagement letter.

Other PCAOB rules and standards and various laws and regulations require the auditor to communicate certain matters to the audit committee. This standard does not modify or replace those requirements.

Nothing in this standard precludes the auditor from communicating other matters to the audit committee.

B. Objectives

The objectives of the auditor are to:

1. Communicate to the audit committee (communicate) the responsibilities of the auditor and establish an understanding of the terms of the audit engagement with the audit committee
2. Obtain information from the audit committee relevant to the audit
3. Communicate an overview of the overall audit strategy and timing of the audit
4. Provide the audit committee with timely observations arising from the audit that are significant to the financial reporting process

C. Definitions

1. **Audit Committee** An *audit committee* is a committee established by and among the board of directors of a company for the purpose of overseeing the accounting and financial reporting processes of the company and audits of its financial statements.
2. **Communicate To** *Communicate to*, as used in this standard, is meant to encourage effective two-way communication between the auditor and the audit committee throughout the audit to assist in understanding matters relevant to the audit.
3. **Critical Accounting Estimate** A *critical accounting estimate* is an accounting estimate where the:
   - Nature of the estimate is material due to the levels of subjectivity and judgment necessary to account for highly uncertain matters or the susceptibility of such matters to change
   - Impact of the estimate on financial condition or operating performance is material
4. **Critical Accounting Policies & Practices** The *critical accounting policies and practices* of a company are the accounting policies and practices that are most important to the portrayal of the company's financial condition and results, and require management's most difficult, subjective, or complex judgments, often as a result of the need to make estimates about the effects of matters that are inherently uncertain. *Critical accounting policies and practices* are

tailored to specific events in the current year; thus, accounting policies and practices that are considered critical might change from year to year.

5. **Other Independent Public Accounting Firms** *Other independent public accounting firms* includes firms that perform audit procedures in the current period audit regardless of whether they otherwise have any relationship with the auditor.

D. Appointment & Retention

1. **Significant Issues Discussed With Management in Connection With the Auditor's Appointment or Retention** The auditor should discuss with the audit committee any significant issues that the auditor discussed with management in connection with the appointment or retention of the auditor, including significant discussions regarding the application of accounting principles and auditing standards.

2. **Establish an Understanding of the Terms of the Audit** The auditor should establish an understanding of the terms of the audit engagement with the audit committee. This understanding includes communicating the following.

   - The objective of the audit
   - The responsibilities of the auditor
   - The responsibilities of management

   If the auditor cannot establish an understanding of the terms of the audit engagement with the audit committee, the auditor should decline to accept, continue, or perform the engagement.

3. **Engagement Letter Required** The auditor should record the understanding of the terms of the audit engagement in an engagement letter and provide this letter to the audit committee annually. The auditor should have the letter executed by the appropriate parties on behalf of the company. If this is other than the audit committee (or its chair on its behalf), the auditor should obtain the audit committee's acknowledgement that it has agreed to the terms of the engagement.

4. **Terms of the Engagement for an Audit of Financial Statements Included in the Engagement Letter** The auditor should include the following matters about the terms of the engagement for an audit of financial statements in the engagement letter.

   a. The objective of the audit is the expression of an opinion on the financial statements.

   b. Auditor's responsibilities:

   (1) The auditor is responsible for conducting the audit in accordance with the standards of the Public Company Accounting Oversight Board.

   (2) Those standards require that the auditor plan and perform the audit to obtain reasonable assurance about whether the financial statements are free of material misstatement, whether caused by error or fraud.

   (a) Accordingly, there is some risk that a material misstatement would remain undetected.

   (b) Although not absolute assurance, reasonable assurance is a high level of assurance.

   (c) Also, a financial statement audit is not designed to detect error or fraud that is immaterial to the financial statements.

(3) If, for any reason, the auditor is unable to complete the audit or is unable to form or has not formed an opinion, the auditor may decline to express an opinion or decline to issue a report as a result of the engagement.

(4) An audit includes obtaining an understanding of internal control sufficient to plan the audit and to determine the nature, extent, and timing of audit procedures to be performed. An audit of financial statements is not designed to provide assurance on internal control or to identify internal control deficiencies. However, the auditor is responsible for communicating:

(a) To the audit committee and management: all significant deficiencies and material weaknesses identified during the audit, in writing

(b) To the board of directors: if the auditor becomes aware that the oversight of the company's external financial reporting and internal control over financial reporting by the audit committee is ineffective, that conclusion, in writing

c. Management's responsibilities:

(1) The company's financial statements, including disclosures

(2) Establishing and maintaining effective internal control over financial reporting

(3) Identifying and ensuring that the company complies with the laws and regulations applicable to its activities

(4) Making all financial records and relevant information available to the auditor

(5) Providing the auditor, at the conclusion of the engagement, with a letter that confirms certain representations made during the audit

(6) Adjusting the financial statements to correct material misstatements relating to accounts or disclosures

(7) Affirming to the auditor in the representation letter that the effects of any uncorrected misstatements aggregated by the auditor are immaterial, both individually and in the aggregate, to the financial statements taken as a whole

5. Terms of the Engagement for an Audit of Internal Control Over Financial Reporting That Is Integrated With an Audit of Financial Statements Included in the Engagement Letter The auditor should include the following matters about the terms of the engagement for an audit of internal control over financial reporting that is integrated with an audit of financial statements in the engagement letter.

a. The objective of the audit is the expression of an opinion on both the effectiveness of internal control over financial reporting and the financial statements.

b. Auditor's responsibilities:

(1) The auditor is responsible for conducting the audit in accordance with the standards of the Public Company Accounting Oversight Board.

(2) Those standards require that the auditor plan and perform the audit to obtain reasonable assurance about whether the financial statements are free of material misstatement, whether caused by error or fraud, and whether effective internal control over financial reporting was maintained in all material respects.

(a) Accordingly, there is some risk that a material misstatement of the financial statements or a material weakness in internal control over financial reporting would remain undetected.

(b) Although not absolute assurance, reasonable assurance is a high level of assurance.

(c) Also, an integrated audit is not designed to detect error or fraud that is immaterial to the financial statements or deficiencies in internal control over financial reporting that, individually or in combination, are less severe than a material weakness.

(3) If, for any reason, the auditor is unable to complete the audit or is unable to form or has not formed an opinion, the auditor may decline to express an opinion or decline to issue a report as a result of the engagement.

(4) In fulfillment of the responsibilities noted above, the auditor communicates:

(a) To the audit committee and management: all material weaknesses in internal control over financial reporting identified during the audit, in writing

(b) To the audit committee: all significant deficiencies identified during the audit, in writing, and informs the audit committee when the auditor has informed management of all internal control deficiencies

(c) To management: all internal control deficiencies identified during the audit and not previously communicated in writing by the auditor or by others, including internal auditors or others within the company

(d) To the board of directors: any conclusion that the audit committee's oversight of the company's external financial reporting and internal control over financial reporting is ineffective, in writing

c. Management's responsibilities (same as above, i.e., for an audit of just the financial statements)

6. **Terms of the Engagement for a Review of Interim Information Included in the Engagement Letter** In connection with a review of interim financial information, to confirm and document the understanding, the auditor should either:

- Document in the audit engagement letter the nature and objectives of the engagement to review interim financial information and the responsibilities of management and the auditor

  or

- Issue a separate engagement letter that addresses such matters

E. Obtaining Information & Communicating the Audit Strategy

1. **Obtaining Information Relevant to the Audit** The auditor should inquire of the audit committee about whether it is aware of matters relevant to the audit, including, but not limited to, violations or possible violations of laws or regulations.

2. **Overall Audit Strategy, Timing of the Audit & Significant Risks** The auditor should communicate an overview of the overall audit strategy, including the timing of the audit, and discuss the significant risks identified with the audit committee. This overview should **not** include specific details that would compromise the effectiveness of the audit.

   As part of communicating the overall audit strategy, the auditor should, if applicable, communicate:

   a. The nature and extent of specialized skill or knowledge needed to perform the planned audit procedures or evaluate the audit results related to significant risks

   b. The extent to which the auditor plans to use the work of the company's internal auditors in an audit of financial statements

   c. The extent to which the auditor plans to use the work of internal auditors, company personnel (in addition to internal auditors), and third parties working under the direction of management or the audit committee when performing an audit of internal control over financial reporting

   d. The names, locations, and planned responsibilities of other independent public accounting firms or other persons, who are not employed by the auditor, that perform audit procedures in the current period audit

   e. The basis for the auditor's determination that the auditor can serve as principal auditor, if significant parts of the audit are to be performed by other auditors

   f. Significant changes to the planned audit strategy or the significant risks initially identified and the reasons for such changes

F. **Results of the Audit**

1. **Accounting Policies and Practices, Estimates & Significant Unusual Transactions** The auditor should communicate:

   a. Significant accounting policies and practices:

      (1) Management's initial selection of, or changes in, significant accounting policies or their application in the current period

      (2) The effect on financial statements or disclosures of significant accounting policies in:

         (a) Controversial areas

         (b) Areas for which there is diversity in practice (lack of consensus) or a lack of authoritative guidance

   b. All critical accounting policies and practices to be used, including:

      (1) The reasons they are considered critical

      (2) How current and anticipated future events might affect the determination of which policies and practices are considered critical

   c. Critical accounting estimates:

      (1) A description of the process management used to develop them

(2) Management's significant assumptions used in critical accounting estimates that are highly subjective

(3) Any significant changes management made to the processes used to develop critical accounting estimates or significant assumptions

(a) A description of management's reasons for the changes

(b) The effects of the changes on the financial statements

d. Significant unusual transactions:

(1) Significant transactions that are outside the company's normal course of business or that otherwise appear to be unusual due to their timing, size, or nature

(2) The policies and practices management used to account for significant unusual transactions

e. When management communicates any of the preceding matters, the auditor does **not** need to communicate them *at the same level of detail* as management, as long as the auditor:

- Participated in management's discussion with the audit committee
- Confirmed to the audit committee that management has adequately communicated these matters
- Identified for the audit committee those accounting policies and practices that the auditor considers critical
- Communicates any omitted or inadequately described matters to the audit committee

Editor Note: If management communicates these matters to the audit committee and, as a result, the auditor did not communicate these matters at the same level of detail as management, the auditor must include a copy or a summary of management's communications provided to the audit committee in the audit documentation.

2. Auditor's Evaluation of the Quality of the Company's Financial Reporting The auditor should communicate:

a. Qualitative aspects of significant accounting policies and practices:

(1) The auditor's conclusions about the qualitative aspects of the company's significant accounting policies and practices, including situations in which the auditor identified bias in management's judgments about the amounts and disclosures in the financial statements

(2) The results of the auditor's evaluation of the differences between:

(a) Estimates best supported by the audit evidence

and

(b) Estimates included in the financial statements, which are individually reasonable, that indicate a possible bias on the part of the company's management

b. The auditor's assessment of management's disclosures related to the critical accounting policies and practices, along with any significant modifications to the disclosure of those policies and practices proposed by the auditor that management did **not** make

c. The basis for the auditor's conclusions regarding the reasonableness of the critical accounting estimates

d. The auditor's understanding of the business rationale for significant unusual transactions

e. The results of the auditor's evaluation of whether the presentation of the financial statements and the related disclosures are in conformity with the applicable financial reporting framework (AFRF), including the auditor's consideration of the form, arrangement, and content of the financial statements (including the accompanying notes), encompassing matters such as the terminology used, the amount of detail given, the classification of items, and the bases of amounts set forth

f. Situations in which the auditor identified a concern regarding management's anticipated application of accounting pronouncements that have been issued, but are not yet effective and might have a significant effect on future financial reporting

g. All alternative accounting treatments permissible under the AFRF for policies and practices related to material items that have been discussed with management, including the ramifications of their use and the treatment preferred by the auditor

3. **Other Information in Documents Containing Audited Financial Statements** When other information is presented in documents containing audited financial statements, the auditor should communicate the auditor's responsibility for such information; any related procedures performed; and the results of such procedures.

4. **Difficult or Contentious Matters for Which the Auditor Consulted** The auditor should communicate matters that are difficult or contentious for which the auditor consulted outside the engagement team and that the auditor reasonably determined are relevant to the audit committee's oversight of the financial reporting process.

5. **Management Consultation With Other Accountants** When the auditor has concerns about significant auditing or accounting matters about which management has consulted with other accountants, the auditor should communicate the auditor's views about such matters.

6. **Going Concern Issues** The auditor should communicate, if applicable, the following matters relating to the auditor's evaluation of the company's ability to continue as a going concern:

   a. If the auditor believes there is substantial doubt about the company's ability to continue as a going concern for a reasonable period of time, the conditions and events that, when considered in the aggregate, indicate there is substantial doubt

   b. If the auditor concludes, after consideration of management's plans, that substantial doubt about the company's ability to continue as a going concern is alleviated, the basis for the auditor's conclusion, including elements within management's plans that are significant to overcoming the adverse effects of the conditions and events

   c. If the auditor concludes, after consideration of management's plans, that substantial doubt about the company's ability to continue as a going concern for a reasonable period of time remains:

      (1) The effects, if any, on the financial statements and the adequacy of the related disclosure

(2) The effects on the audit report

7. **Uncorrected & Corrected Misstatements** The auditor should:

   a. Provide the audit committee with the schedule of uncorrected misstatements related to accounts and disclosures that the auditor presented to management

   b. Discuss with the audit committee (or determine that management has adequately discussed with them) the basis for the determination that the uncorrected misstatements were immaterial, including the qualitative factors considered

      Editor Note: If management communicates these matters to the audit committee and, as a result, the auditor did not communicate these matters at the same level of detail as management, the auditor must include a copy or a summary of management's communications provided to the audit committee in the audit documentation.

   c. Communicate that uncorrected misstatements or matters underlying them could potentially cause future financial statements to be materially misstated, even if the auditor has concluded that the uncorrected misstatements are immaterial to the current financial statements

   d. Communicate those corrected misstatements, other than those that are clearly trivial, related to accounts and disclosures that were brought to management's attention as a result of audit procedures, and discuss with the audit committee the implications that such corrected misstatements might have on the company's financial reporting process

8. **Material Written Communications** The auditor should communicate other material written communications between the auditor and management.

9. **Departure from the Standard Audit Report** The auditor should communicate the following matters related to the audit report.

   a. When the auditor expects to modify the opinion in the audit report, the reasons for the modification, and the wording of the report

   b. When the auditor expects to include explanatory language or an explanatory paragraph in the audit report, the reasons for the explanatory language or paragraph, and the wording of the explanatory language or paragraph.

10. **Disagreements With Management** The auditor should communicate any disagreements with management about matters, whether or not satisfactorily resolved, that individually or in the aggregate could be significant to the company's financial statements or the audit report. (Disagreements with management do *not* include differences of opinion based on incomplete facts or preliminary information that are later resolved by the auditor obtaining additional relevant facts or information prior to the issuance of the audit report.)

11. **Difficulties Encountered in Performing the Audit** The auditor should communicate any significant difficulties encountered during the audit. (Difficulties encountered by the auditor could represent a scope limitation, which may result in the auditor modifying the opinion or withdrawing from the engagement.)

    Significant difficulties encountered during the audit include, but are not limited to:

    a. Significant delays by management, the unavailability of company personnel, or unwillingness by management to provide information needed by the auditor

    b. An unreasonably brief time within which to complete the audit

c. Unexpected extensive effort required by the auditor to obtain sufficient appropriate audit evidence

d. Unreasonable management restrictions encountered by the auditor

e. Management's unwillingness to make or extend its assessment of the company's ability to continue as a going concern

12. **Other Matters** The auditor should communicate other matters arising from the audit that are significant to the oversight of the company's financial reporting process. This communication includes, among other matters, complaints or concerns regarding accounting or auditing matters that have come to the auditor's attention during the audit and the results of the auditor's procedures regarding such matters.

G. Form & Documentation of Communications

Unless otherwise specified, these required audit committee communications can be done orally or in writing. Regardless of the method of communication, the auditor must document the communications in the workpapers.

If management communicated any of the required matters related to:

- Accounting policies and practices, estimates, and significant unusual transactions
- Uncorrected and corrected misstatements

And, as a result, the auditor did not communicate these matters at the same level of detail as management, the auditor must include a copy or a summary of management's communications provided to the audit committee in the audit documentation.

H. Timing

All required audit committee communications should be made:

- In a timely manner
- Prior to the issuance of the audit report

An auditor may communicate to only the chair of the audit committee if done in order to communicate matters in a timely manner during the audit. The auditor, however, should communicate such matters to the entire audit committee prior to the issuance of the audit report.

The appropriate timing of a particular communication depends on factors such as the significance of the matters to be communicated and corrective or follow-up action needed, unless other timing requirements are specified by PCAOB rules or standards or the securities laws.

I. PCAOB Auditing Standards vs. US GAAS vs. ISA

1. Objectives

- AU 210, *Terms of Engagement*, / ISA 210 (similarly titled) both include an objective (and requirement) to establish whether the preconditions for an audit are present.
  - PCAOB AS 16 does *not* include this objective or requirement.

2. Appointment & Retention

a. Significant Issues Discussed With Management in Connection With the Auditor's Appointment or Retention

- PCAOB AS 16 requires the auditor to discuss with the audit committee any significant issues that the auditor discussed with management in connection with the appointment or retention of the auditor, including significant discussions regarding the application of accounting principles and auditing standards.

- AU 210 / ISA 210 do not include a similar requirement.

b. Establish an Understanding of the Terms of the Audit / Engagement Letter

- PCAOB AS 16 requires the auditor to establish an understanding of the terms of the audit engagement with the audit committee. PCAOB AS 16 requires the auditor to decline to accept, continue, or perform the engagement if the auditor cannot establish an understanding of the terms of the audit engagement with the audit committee.
    - AU 210 / ISA 210 require the auditor to agree on the terms of the audit engagement with management and, where appropriate, those charged with governance.
- PCAOB AS 16 requires the auditor to provide the engagement letter to the audit committee annually.
    - AU 210 / ISA 210 do not require that the engagement letter be given to the audit committee
        - Per AU 210, if the auditor concludes that the terms of the preceding engagement need not be revised for the current engagement, the auditor should remind management of the terms of the engagement, and the reminder should be documented.
        - Per ISA 210, the auditor is not required to send a new audit engagement letter or other written agreement each period (for recurring audits) unless circumstances require the terms of the audit engagement to be revised. And the auditor decides whether there is a need to remind the entity of the existing terms of the audit engagement.
- PCAOB AS 16 requires the auditor to have the engagement letter executed by the appropriate parties on behalf of the company. If this is other than the audit committee, the auditor should determine that the audit committee has acknowledged and agreed to the terms of the engagement.
    - AU 210 / ISA 210 do not require that the engagement letter be signed by the audit committee or that it otherwise be acknowledged by the audit committee.
- ISA 210 requires the auditor to determine whether there are any conflicts between the financial reporting standards and additional requirements supplemented by law or regulation.
    - PCAOB AS 16 and AU 210 do not have a similar requirement.
- AU 210 / ISA 210 include requirements regarding the limitation of scope prior to audit engagement acceptance, other factors affecting audit engagement acceptance, and acceptance of a change in the terms of the audit engagement.
    - PCAOB AS 16 does *not* have a similar requirement.
- AU 210 includes requirements regarding initial audits and re-audits.
    - PCAOB AS 16 does not include similar requirements, but its interim standard on communications between predecessor and successor auditors does.

- ISA 210 does not include similar requirements.

- AU 260, *The Auditor's Communication With Those Charged With Governance* / ISA 260 (similarly titled) include a requirement for the auditor to communicate with those charged with governance the form, timing, and expected general content of communications.
  - PCAOB AS 16 does not have a similar requirement, but it does not preclude it.

3. Obtaining Information & Communicating the Audit Strategy

a. Obtaining Information Relevant to the Audit

- PCAOB AS 16 requires the auditor to inquire of the audit committee about whether it is aware of matters relevant to the audit, including, but not limited to, violations, or possible violations of laws or regulations.
  - AU 260 / ISA 260 do *not* include a similar requirement; however, AU 240, *Consideration of Fraud in a Financial* Statement *Audit* / ISA 240 (similarly titled) require the auditor to make inquiries of those charged with governance to determine whether they have knowledge of any actual, suspected, or alleged fraud affecting the entity.

b. Overall Audit Strategy, Timing of the Audit & Significant Risks

- PCAOB AS 16 requires the auditor to communicate an overview of the overall audit strategy, including the timing of the audit, and discuss the significant risks identified. Significant changes to the planned audit strategy or the significant risks initially identified and the reasons for such changes should also be communicated.
  - AU 260 / ISA 260 require the auditor to communicate an overview of the planned scope and timing of the audit; however, they do not require the auditor to communicate significant changes to the planned scope and timing of the audit.

- PCAOB AS 16 requires the auditor to communicate the nature and extent of specialized skill or knowledge needed to perform the planned audit procedures or evaluate the audit results related to significant risks.
  - AU 260 / ISA 260 do not have a similar requirement.

- PCAOB AS 16 requires the auditor to communicate the extent to which the auditor plans to use the work of the company's internal auditors, other company personnel, and third parties.
  - AU 260 / ISA 260 do not have a similar requirement.

- PCAOB AS 16 requires the auditor to communicate the names, locations, and planned responsibilities of other independent public accounting firms or other persons, who are not employed by the auditor, that perform audit procedures in the current period audit.
  - AU 260 / ISA 260 do not have a similar requirement, however, AU 600, *Special Considerations—Audits of Group Financial Statements (Including the Work of Component Auditors)* / ISA 600 (similarly titled) include requirements for the auditor to communicate to those charged with governance information about the work of component auditors.

4. Results of the Audit

a. Accounting Policies and Practices, Estimates & Significant Unusual Transactions

- PCAOB AS 16 includes a requirement to communicate certain matters related to significant unusual transactions.
  - AU 260 / ISA 260 do not have a similar requirement.

b. Auditor's Evaluation of the Quality of the Company's Financial Reporting

- PCAOB AS 16 includes a requirement to communicate the auditor's understanding of the business rationale for significant unusual transactions.
  - AU 260 / ISA 260 do *not* have a similar requirement.

c. Other Information in Documents Containing Audited Financial Statements

- PCAOB AS 16 includes a requirement to communicate the auditor's responsibilities when other information is presented in documents containing audited financial statements; any related procedures performed; and the results of such procedures.
  - AU 260 / ISA 260 do *not* have a similar requirement; however, US GAAS and ISA include requirements in other standards for communication to those charged with governance when there are material inconsistencies or misstatements in the other information that management refuses to revise.

d. Difficult or Contentious Matters for Which the Auditor Consulted

- PCAOB AS 16 requires the auditor to communicate matters that are difficult or contentious for which the auditor consulted outside the engagement team and that the auditor reasonably determined are relevant to the audit committee's oversight of the financial reporting process.
  - AU 260 / ISA 260 do not have a similar requirement.

e. Management Consultation With Other Accountants

- PCAOB AS 16 requires the auditor to communicate the auditor's concerns, if any, regarding management's consultation with other accountants about significant auditing or accounting matters.
  - AU 260 requires the auditor to do the same regarding significant matters rather than identified concerns about significant matters.
  - ISA 260 does not have a similar requirement.

f. Going Concern Issues

- PCAOB AS 16 requires the auditor to communicate, when applicable, certain matters relating to the auditor's evaluation of the company's ability to continue as a going concern.
  - AU 260 / ISA 260 do not have similar requirements; however, US GAAS and ISA include similar communication requirements in their standards dedicated to going concern issues.

g. Uncorrected & Corrected Misstatements

- PCAOB AS 16 requires the auditor to provide the audit committee with the schedule of uncorrected misstatements related to accounts and disclosures that the auditor presented to management.
  - AU 260 / ISA 450, *Evaluation of Misstatements Identified During the Audit*, include requirements for the auditor to communicate uncorrected misstatements plus an additional requirement to communicate the effect that they, individually or in aggregate, may have on the audit report opinion.
- PCAOB AS 16 and AU 260 require the auditor to communicate those corrected misstatements that were brought to management's attention as a result of audit procedures.
  - ISA 450 does not have a similar requirement.
- AU 260 / ISA 450 include requirements for the auditor to communicate the effect of uncorrected misstatements related to prior periods on the relevant classes of transactions, account balances or disclosures, and the financial statements as a whole.
  - PCAOB AS 16 does not have a similar requirement.
- AU 450 (same title as ISA) / ISA 450 require the auditor to request that uncorrected misstatements be corrected.
  - PCAOB AS 16 does *not* have a similar requirement because under SEC rules the financial statements are required to reflect all material correcting adjustments identified by the auditor.

h. Material Written Communications

- PCAOB AS 16 requires the auditor to communicate other material written communications between the auditor and management.
  - AU 260 / ISA 260 require the auditor to communicate to those charged with governance written representations the auditor is requesting.

i. Disagreements With Management

- PCAOB AS 16 and AU 260 require the auditor to communicate disagreements with management that could be significant to the financial statements or audit report.
  - ISA 260 does not include a similar requirement.

5. Form & Documentation of Communications

- PCAOB AS 16 requires the auditor to include a copy or a summary of management's communication provided to the audit committee in the audit documentation, if as part of its communications to the audit committee, management communicated any of the matters related to accounting policies and practices, estimates, significant unusual transactions, or uncorrected misstatements to the audit committee, and, as a result, the auditor did not communicate these matters at the same level of detail as management.
  - AU 260 / ISA 260 do not have a similar requirement.

6. **Timing**

    - PCAOB AS 16 requires communications to the audit committee to be made in a timely manner and prior to the issuance of the audit report.

        - AU 260 / ISA 260 do not include the requirement that the communications be made prior to the issuance of the audit report, i.e., they only require that the communications be made in a timely manner.

X. Auditing Supplemental Information Accompanying Audited Financial Statements (AS 17)

A. Overview

PCAOB AS 17 provides guidance when the auditor of the company's financial statements is engaged to perform audit procedures and report on supplemental information that accompanies financial statements audited in accordance with PCAOB standards.

1. **Objective** The objective of the auditor of the financial statements is to obtain sufficient appropriate audit evidence to express an opinion on whether the supplemental information is fairly stated, in all material respects, in relation to the financial statements as a whole.

2. **Definition of Supplemental Information** Supplemental information refers to the following information when it accompanies audited financial statements.

    a. **Supporting Schedules Required of Brokers & Dealers** Supporting schedules that brokers and dealers are required to file under the Securities Exchange Act of 1934

    b. **Supplemental Information Required by Regulatory Authorities** Supplemental information required to be presented by a regulatory authority and covered by an CPA's report on that information in relation to financial statements that are audited in accordance with PCAOB standards

    c. **Other** Information that is:

        (1) Ancillary to the audited financial statements;

        (2) Derived from the company's accounting books and records; and

        (3) Covered by a CPA's report on that information in relation to the financial statements that are audited in accordance with PCAOB standards

    Editor Note: Thus the standard covers supplemental information that is required (by regulatory authorities) as well as information that is voluntarily provided when the auditor of the company's financial statements is engaged to report on the information in relation to those financial statements.

B. Audit Procedures

1. **Nature, Timing & Extent of Audit Procedures** The nature, timing, and extent of audit procedures necessary to obtain sufficient appropriate audit evidence and to report on the supplemental information depends on, but is not limited to, the following factors.

    a. **Risk of Material Misstatement (RMM)** The RMM of the supplemental information

    b. **Materiality Considerations** The materiality considerations relevant to the information presented; generally, the auditor should use the same materiality considerations as those used in the audit of the related financial statements; however, in the case of information required by a regulatory authority that specifies a lower amount, the auditor should apply that prescribed materiality level in planning and performing audit procedures for the supplemental information

c. **Evidence Obtained in the Financial Statement Audit** The evidence obtained from the audit of financial statements and, if applicable, other engagements by the auditor for the period presented; the procedures performed regarding the supplemental information should be planned and performed in conjunction with the audit of the financial statements

d. **Audit Opinion Expressed on the Financial Statements** Whether a qualified or adverse opinion or a disclaimer of opinion was issued on the financial statements

2. **Required Procedures** The auditor should:

a. **Understand Purpose & Criteria** Obtain an understanding of the purpose of the supplemental information and the criteria management used to prepare the supplemental information, including relevant regulatory requirements

b. **Understand & Evaluate Methodology and Changes, If Any, in Methodology** Obtain an understanding of the methods of preparing the supplemental information, evaluate the appropriateness of those methods, and determine whether those methods have changed from the methods used in the prior period and, if the methods have changed, determine the reasons for and evaluate the appropriateness of such changes

c. **Make Inquiries Regarding Significant Assumptions or Interpretations** Inquire of management about any significant assumptions or interpretations underlying the measurement or presentation of the supplemental information

d. **Reconcile to Accounting Records/Financial Statements** Determine that the supplemental information reconciles to the underlying accounting and other records or to the financial statements, as applicable

e. **Test Completeness/Accuracy** Perform procedures to test the completeness and accuracy of the information presented in the supplemental information to the extent that it was not tested as part of the audit of financial statements

f. **Test Compliance With Criteria** Evaluate whether the supplemental information, including its form and content, complies with relevant regulatory requirements or other applicable criteria, if any

g. **Obtain Management Representations** The auditor should obtain the following written representations from management.

(1) A statement that management acknowledges its responsibility for the fair presentation of the supplemental information and, if applicable, the form and content of that supplemental information, in conformity with relevant regulatory requirements or other applicable criteria

(2) A statement that management believes the supplemental information, including its form and content, is fairly stated, in all material respects

(3) A statement that the methods of measurement or presentation have not changed from those used in the prior period or, if the methods of measurement or presentation have changed, the reasons for such changes and why those changes are appropriate

(4) If the form and content of the supplemental information is prescribed by regulatory requirements or other applicable criteria, a statement that the supplemental information complies, in all material respects, with the regulatory requirements or other applicable criteria, and identification of those requirements or other applicable criteria

(5) A description of any significant assumptions or interpretations underlying the measurement or presentation of the supplemental information, and a statement that management believes that such assumptions or interpretations are appropriate

C. **Evaluation of Audit Results**
To form an opinion on the supplemental information, the auditor should evaluate whether the supplemental information, including its form and content, is fairly stated, in all material respects, in relation to the financial statements as a whole, including whether the supplemental information is presented in conformity, in all material respects, with the relevant regulatory requirements or other applicable criteria.

1. **Misstatements**

a. **Communicate Accumulated Misstatements to Management for Correction** The auditor should accumulate misstatements regarding the supplemental information identified during the performance of audit procedures on the supplemental information and in the audit of the financial statements. The auditor should communicate accumulated misstatements regarding the supplemental information to management on a timely basis to provide management with an opportunity to correct them.

b. **Evaluate Materiality of Uncorrected Misstatements** The auditor should evaluate whether uncorrected misstatements related to the supplemental information are material, either individually or in combination with other misstatements, taking into account relevant quantitative and qualitative factors. The auditor should evaluate the effect of uncorrected misstatements related to the supplemental information in evaluating the results of the financial statement audit.

2. **Evaluate Effect of Modifications to the Audit Report on the Financial Statements on the Opinion on the Supplemental Information** The auditor should evaluate the effect of any modifications to the audit report on the financial statements when forming an opinion on the supplemental information.

a. **Qualified Opinion on the Financial Statements** When the auditor expresses a qualified opinion on the financial statements and the basis for the qualification also applies to the supplemental information, the auditor should describe the effects of the qualification on the supplemental information in the report on supplemental information and should express a qualified opinion on the supplemental information.

b. **Adverse Opinion or Disclaimer of Opinion on the Financial Statements** When the auditor expresses an adverse opinion, or disclaims an opinion on the financial statements, the auditor should express an adverse opinion, or disclaim an opinion, on the supplemental information, whichever is appropriate.

D. **Reporting**

1. **Elements** The elements of the auditor's report on supplemental information are as follows.

a. **Identification** Identification of the supplemental information; this may be by descriptive title or a reference to the page number and document where it is located

b. **Management Is Responsible** A statement that the supplemental information is the responsibility of management

c. **Audit Procedures Performed in Conjunction With Financial Statement Audit** A statement that the supplemental information has been subjected to audit procedures performed in conjunction with the audit of the financial statements; if the financial statements are presented in a separate document from the supplemental information or otherwise are not readily identifiable to the user of the supplemental information, the auditor's report on supplemental information should identify the document containing the company's financial statements

d. **Reconciled to the Accounting Records/Financial Statements & Tested for Completeness/Accuracy** A statement that the audit procedures performed included determining whether the supplemental information reconciles to the financial statements or the underlying accounting and other records, as applicable, and performing procedures to test the completeness and accuracy of the information presented in the supplemental information

e. **Compliance With Criteria** A statement that in forming the auditor's opinion, the auditor evaluated whether supplemental information, including its form and content, complies, in all material respects, with the specified regulatory requirements or other criteria, if applicable

f. **If Applicable, Basis of Presentation Different From Financial Statements** A statement, if applicable, that the supplemental information is presented on a basis that differs from the financial statements and is not prescribed by regulatory requirements. When such a statement is made, the report should describe the basis for the supplemental information presentation.

g. **Opinion** An opinion on whether the supplemental information is fairly stated, in all material respects, in relation to the financial statements as a whole, or a disclaimer of opinion.

2. **Combined or Separate Reports** Unless prescribed by regulatory requirements, the auditor may either include the auditor's report on the supplemental information in the auditor's report on the financial statements or issue a separate report on the supplemental information. If the auditor issues a separate report on the supplemental information, that report should identify the auditor's report on the financial statements.

Exhibit 34 ▸ Report on Supplemental Information Included in Audit Report on the Financial Statements

> The [identify supplemental information] has been subjected to audit procedures performed in conjunction with the audit of [Company's] financial statements. The [supplemental information] is the responsibility of the Company's management. Our audit procedures included determining whether the [supplemental information] reconciles to the financial statements or the underlying accounting and other records, as applicable, and performing procedures to test the completeness and accuracy of the information presented in the [supplemental information]. In forming our opinion on the [supplemental information], we evaluated whether the [supplemental information], including its form and content, is presented in conformity with [specify the relevant regulatory requirement or other criteria, if any]. In our opinion, the [identify supplemental information] is fairly stated, in all material respects, in relation to the financial statements as a whole.

3. **Date of Report on Supplemental Information** The report on the supplemental information should not be dated earlier than the auditor's report on the financial statements from which the supplemental information was derived. It should also, of course, not be dated earlier than the date on which the auditor obtained sufficient appropriate audit evidence to support the auditor's opinion on the supplemental information.

4. **Supplemental Information Materially Misstated** If the the supplemental information is materially misstated in relation to the financial statements as a whole, the auditor should describe the material misstatement in the auditor's report on the supplemental information and express a qualified or adverse opinion on the supplemental information.

5. **Insufficient Evidence** If the auditor is unable to obtain sufficient appropriate audit evidence to support an opinion on the supplemental information, the auditor should disclaim an opinion on the supplemental information. In those situations, the auditor's report on the supplemental information should describe the reason for the disclaimer and state that the auditor is unable to and does not express an opinion on the supplemental information. If the auditor is able to obtain sufficient appropriate audit evidence to support an opinion on some but not all schedules, the auditor may express an opinion on only those schedules for which the auditor obtained sufficient appropriate evidence but should disclaim an opinion on the other schedules.

E. PCAOB Auditing Standards vs. US GAAS

Editor Note: There is no corresponding International Standard on Auditing.

This PCAOB auditing standard addresses the same subject matter as AU 725, *Supplementary Information in Relation to the Financial Statements as a Whole*, covered in the first section of chapter 12 of this text. Some of the differences between the two standards result from the fact that, although PCAOB AS 17 encompasses supplemental information that is provided voluntarily, its main focus is on supplemental information required by the SEC and other regulatory agencies. Some of the requirements included in US GAAS are covered by the various regulatory authorities' requirements; thus, the PCAOB did not feel the need to include such requirements in their standard.

1. Conditions in Order to Opine on Supplemental Information

- US GAAS establishes certain preconditions in order to opine on whether the supplementary information is fairly stated.
  - The PCAOB standard does not include such conditions.

2. Management Representations

- US GAAS requires the auditor to obtain a representation that when the supplementary information is not presented with the audited financial statements, management will make the statements readily available no later than the date of issuance of the supplementary information and the related audit report.
  - The PCAOB standard does *not* require this particular representation.

3. Evaluation of Audit Results

- US GAAS requires the auditor to evaluate the appropriateness and completeness of the supplementary information
  - The PCAOB includes more extensive and explicit requirements for the evaluation of audit results; see the matters discussed in level C. of this section's outline.

4. Reporting

- US GAAS requires the auditor to include a statement in the report that the audit was conducted for the purpose of forming an opinion on the financial statements as a whole and a statement that the supplementary information is presented for purposes of additional analysis and is not a required part of the financial statements.

- The PCAOB standard does not require similar language.

- The PCAOB standard includes a requirement that if the supplemental information is presented on a basis that differs from the financial statements and that basis is not prescribed by regulatory requirements, the report should state that and describe the basis for the presentation; and a requirement to include a statement that in forming the auditor's opinion, the auditor evaluated whether supplemental information, including its form and content, complies, in all material respects, with the specified regulatory requirements or other criteria, if applicable.

  - US GAAS does not require similar language.

XI. International Standards on Auditing

A. Overview

The International Auditing and Assurance Standards Board (IAASB) of the International Federation of Accountants (IFAC) issues International Standards on Auditing (ISA) and assurance standards.

A CPA practicing in the United States may be engaged to audit the financial statements of a client in accordance with the ISA. In those circumstances where the auditor's report states that the audit was conducted in accordance with International Auditing Standards, the US auditor should comply with both the ISA and, as required by the AICPA Code of Professional Conduct, auditing standards generally accepted in the United States of America for a nonissuer or the standards of the Public Company Accounting Oversight Board (United States) for an issuer. An engagement of this nature is normally conducted by performing an audit in accordance with auditing standards generally accepted in the United States of America or the PCAOB standards plus performing the additional procedures required by the ISA.

B. ISA vs. US GAAS vs. PCAOB Auditing Standards

The substantive differences between the standards include the following.

1. **ISA 200, *Overall Objectives of the Independent Auditor and the Conduct of an Audit in Accordance With International Standards on Auditing* vs. AU 210, *Overall...in Accordance With Generally Accepted Auditing Standards* vs. PCAOB Auditing Standards & Rule 3101**

   a. **Two Categories of Professional Responsibilities—Unconditional & Presumptively Mandatory** ISA do **not** use these terms. US GAAS and PCAOB auditing standards (AS) use them, but define a presumptively mandatory responsibility differently.

      (1) **ISA** Essentially, the IAASB did not see the need for labeling any requirements as *unconditional*. ISA have only one category—relevant requirements, accordingly there was no need to specify language to differentiate requirements. All ISA requirements are mandatory unless, in the circumstances of the audit, the entire standard is not relevant (for example, ISA 610, *Using the Work of Internal Auditors*, when an entity does not have an internal audit function) or a particular requirement is not relevant because it is conditional and the condition does not exist. In exceptional circumstances, i.e., when a specific procedure would be ineffective, an auditor may depart from a relevant requirement by performing alternate procedures that achieve the aim of the requirement.

      (2) **US GAAS** In an attempt to meet part of its stated goal of the clarification of its auditing standards, i.e., to converge with ISA while avoiding unnecessary conflict with PCAOB AS, the AICPA kept the two terms, but requires them both only when they are relevant which differs from the definition of a presumptively mandatory requirement per the PCAOB AS (see the next paragraph). Further, US GAAS use only the word *must* to indicate an unconditional requirement and *must* is very rarely used. US GAAS define a presumptively mandatory require-

ment in the same way they do an unconditional requirement, except they allow a departure under rare circumstances. US GAAS have the same criteria for allowing such a departure as ISA do for all of their requirements, i.e., when a required procedure would be ineffective. (US GAAS use only the word *should* to indicate a presumptively mandatory requirement.)

(3) **PCAOB Auditing Standards** PCAOB AS use both terms, but instead of using the word *relevant*, the Board requires compliance with an unconditional requirement in all cases in which the circumstances exist to which the requirement applies—same meaning as *relevant*—and uses *must*, *shall*, and *is required* to indicate it. (Like US GAAS, the PCAOB AS only use the word *should* to indicate a presumptively mandatory requirement.)

PCAOB AS have a different definition for a presumptively mandatory requirement than US GAAS, i.e., the auditor must comply unless the auditor demonstrates that alternative actions followed in the circumstances were sufficient to achieve the objectives of the standard; and thus, different criteria for allowing a departure. Instead of mandating that the requirement not used be judged as ineffective in the circumstances, if the auditor demonstrates the sufficiency of alternative procedures, the auditor is allowed to deviate. Obviously, this allows a great deal more latitude for auditors following PCAOB AS.

Editor Note: In their specified circumstances, all three sets of standards require the auditor to include in the audit documentation how the alternative procedure(s) achieved the intent of the requirement. Additionally, per ISA and US GAAS, the inclusion of the justification for the departure is required.

b. **Fair Presentation Framework** ISA provide for reporting on financial statements that are prepared in accordance with both fair presentation and compliance financial reporting frameworks. Per ISA, compliance frameworks do not necessarily require fair presentation. US GAAS explicitly addresses reporting on financial statements that are prepared in accordance with fair presentation frameworks only; PCAOB AS implicitly does so.

An example of where this difference is demonstrated is in the first component of the definition of the premise of an audit, [Management is responsible for]:

(1) **Per ISA** ...the preparation of the financial statements in accordance with the applicable financial reporting framework, including, where relevant, their fair presentation...

(2) **Per US GAAS** ...the preparation and fair presentation of the financial statements in accordance with the applicable financial reporting framework...

2. **ISA 210, *Agreeing the Terms of Audit Engagements* vs. AU 210, *Terms of Engagement* vs. PCAOB Adopted Interim Standards**

a. **Communication With Predecessor Prior to Engagement Acceptance** US GAAS require making inquiries of predecessor auditors regarding the auditor's decision to accept an initial or reaudit engagement. PCAOB AS include this requirement in the adopted interim standard on communications between predecessor and successor auditors under the same circumstances and for the same purpose. ISA does not have this requirement.

b. **Engagement Terms for Recurring Audits** Per US GAAS, if the auditor concludes that the terms of the preceding engagement need not be revised for the current engagement, the auditor should remind management of the terms of the engagement, and the reminder should be documented. Per ISA, the auditor is only required to consider the need to remind the entity of the existing terms.

3. **ISA 230, *Audit Documentation* vs. AU 230 & PCAOB AS 3 of the Same Title**

   a. **Abstracts or Copies of Significant Contracts or Agreements Inspected** For audit procedures related to the inspection of significant contracts or agreements, US GAAS and PCAOB AS require the auditor to include abstracts or copies of those contracts or agreements in the audit documentation. ISA does **not** have this requirement.

   b. **Documentation Completion Date** Per US GAAS and PCAOB AS, this date is measured from the report release date. Per US GAAS, the auditor should assemble the audit documentation in an audit file and complete the administrative process of assembling the final audit file on a timely basis, no later than 60 days following the report release date (the documentation completion date). Per PCAOB AS, the documentation completion date should not be more than 45 days after report release date. Per ISA, the auditor is only required to accomplish the same in a timely fashion. Per ISA, an appropriate time limit is ordinarily not more than 60 days after the date of the audit report, instead of the report release date.

4. **ISA 240, *The Auditor's Responsibilities Relating to Fraud in an Audit of Financial Statements* vs. AU 240, *Consideration of Fraud in a Financial Statement Audit* vs. PCAOB AS 12, *Identifying and Assessing Risks of Material Misstatement* & Adopted Interim Standards**

   a. **Definition of Fraud** All three standards define fraud differently; however, the ISA definition is the only one that is significantly different; however, note that US GAAS does *not* define fraud as a material misstatement, while PCAOB does.

      (1) **Per ISA** An intentional act by one or more individuals among management, those charged with governance, employees, or third parties, involving the use of deception *to obtain an unjust or illegal advantage*

      (2) **US GAAS** An intentional act by one or more individuals among management, those charged with governance, employees, or third parties, involving the use of deception *that results in a misstatement in financial statements that are the subject of an audit*

      (3) **PCAOB** An intentional act that results in a *material* misstatement in financial statements that are the subject of an audit

   b. **US GAAS Requirements Expanded Beyond Similar ISA Requirements**

      (1) **Investigation of Inconsistent Responses** US GAAS requires the auditor to further investigate, not only inconsistencies in responses from management, those charged with governance, or others, but also those that are otherwise unsatisfactory, for example, vague or implausible. ISA only require further investigation of inconsistent responses.

      (2) **Engagement Team Discussion on Fraud** Compare the following requirements for this discussion per ISA to the expanded requirements per US GAAS covered in chapter in chapter 2 of this text. (The requirements in PCAOB AS 12 for the discussion are similar to US GAAS.) Per ISA, a discussion is required among the engagement team members and a determination by the engagement partner of which matters are to be communicated to those team members not involved in the discussion. This discussion shall place particular emphasis on how and where the entity's financial statements may be susceptible to material misstatement due to fraud, including how fraud might occur. The discussion

shall occur setting aside beliefs that the engagement team members may have that management and those charged with governance are honest and have integrity.

In addition to the inclusion of the significant decisions reached during the discussion required by ISA, both the PCAOB's amended interim adopted standard on fraud and US GAAS requires the inclusion of how and when the discussion occurred and the audit team members who participated.

(3) **Inquiries of Internal Audit** In addition to the ISA requirements for the auditor to make inquiries of internal audit to determine whether it has knowledge of any actual, suspected or alleged fraud affecting the entity, and to obtain its views about the risks of fraud, US GAAS requires the auditor to make inquiries of internal audit to determine whether it has performed any procedures to identify or detect fraud during the year; and whether management has satisfactorily responded to any findings resulting from these procedures. PCAOB AS requirements include all of these plus they require that the auditor inquire whether internal auditors are aware of instances of management override of controls and the nature and circumstances of such overrides.

(4) **Analytical Procedures Related to the Evaluation of Evidence** Per ISA, the auditor is required to evaluate whether analytical procedures that are performed near the end of the audit, when forming an overall conclusion as to whether the financial statements are consistent with the auditor's understanding of the entity, indicate a previously unrecognized RMM due to fraud. US GAAS enhances this requirement by requiring the auditor to evaluate whether the accumulated results of auditing procedures (including analytical procedures that were performed as substantive tests or when forming an overall conclusion) affect the assessment of the RMM due to fraud made earlier in the audit or indicate a previously unrecognized risk of material misstatement due to fraud. Additionally, US GAAS specifically requires that analytical procedures relating to revenue be performed through the end of the reporting period. PCAOB standards do not include this explicit requirements related to fraud risk.

(5) **Testing Journal Entries Related to Responding to Risks of Management Override of Controls**

(a) **ISA** The auditor is required to test the appropriateness of journal entries recorded in the general ledger and other adjustments made in the preparation of the financial statements. In designing and performing audit procedures for such tests, the auditor shall:

- Make inquiries of individuals involved in the financial reporting process about inappropriate or unusual activity relating to the processing of journal entries and other adjustments
- Select journal entries and other adjustments made at the end of a reporting period
- Consider the need to test journal entries and other adjustments throughout the period

(b) **US GAAS & PCAOB** In addition to the preceding ISA requirements, US GAAS and PCAOB amended interim standards require the auditor to:

- Obtain an understanding of the entity's financial reporting process and controls over journal entries and other adjustments, and the suitability of design and implementation of such controls
- Consider fraud risk indicators, the nature and complexity of accounts, and entries processed outside the normal course of business

(6) **Review of Accounting Estimates for Biases Related to Responding to Risks of Management Override of Controls** Per ISA, the auditor is required to perform a retrospective review of management judgments and assumptions related to significant accounting estimates reflected in the financial statements of the prior year. In addition, both US GAAS and PCAOB amended interim standards require the auditor to include in such a review estimates that are based on highly sensitive assumptions or are otherwise significantly affected by judgments made by management.

5. **ISA 260, *Communication With Those Charged With Governance* vs. AU 260, *The Auditor's Communication With Those Charged With Governance*** US GAAS has these additional requirements that are **not** included in ISA; the auditor is required to:

- Determine that those charged with governance are informed about the process used by management in formulating particularly sensitive accounting estimates, including fair value estimates, and about the basis for the auditor's conclusions regarding the reasonableness of those estimates
- Disagreements with management
- Restrict the communication
- Unless all of those charged with governance are involved in managing the entity, the auditor also should communicate:
  - Material, corrected misstatements that were brought to the attention of management as a result of audit procedures
  - The auditor's views about significant matters that were the subject of management's consultations with other accountants on accounting or auditing matters when the auditor is aware that such consultation has occurred

Editor Note: Please see the section in this chapter on PCAOB AS 16, *Communications with Audit Committees*, for comparison of its requirements to the other two sets of standards.

6. **ISA 265, *Communicating Deficiencies In Internal Control To Those Charged With Governance And Management* vs. AU 265, *Communicating Internal Control Related Matters Identified in an Audit*** Both US GAAS and PCAOB standards prohibit the issuance of a written communication stating that no significant deficiencies were identified during the audit. ISA do not address this issue. US GAAS has these additional requirements that are **not** included in ISA; the auditor is required to:

- Communicate significant deficiencies and material weaknesses to management and those charged with governance. (ISA do not include or define the term *material weakness,* thus, it does not contain a requirement to separately identify or communicate material weaknesses)

- Consider, if the auditor determines that a deficiency, or a combination of deficiencies, in internal control is not a material weakness, whether prudent officials, having knowledge of the same facts and circumstances, would likely reach the same conclusion
- Document the communication of other deficiencies in internal control that are communicated orally to management
- Communicate to those charged with governance and management no later than 60 days following the report release date, instead of on a timely basis per ISA
- Include these additional elements in the communication:
    - The definition of material weakness and, when relevant, the definition of significant deficiency
    - An explanation that the auditor is not expressing an opinion on the effectiveness of internal control
    - An explanation that the auditor's consideration of internal control was not designed to identify all deficiencies in internal control that might be material weaknesses or significant deficiencies
    - A statement restricting the use of the communication to management, those charged with governance, others within the organization, and any governmental authority to which the auditor is required to report

7. **ISA 300, *Planning an Audit of Financial Statements* vs. AU 300, *Planning an Audit*** Both US GAAS and PCAOB AS 9, *Audit Planning*, include the requirement for the auditor to consider / determine, respectively, whether specialized skills are needed in performing the audit. The ISA do not include this requirement.

8. **ISA 501, *Audit Evidence—Specific Considerations for Selected Items* vs. AU 501, of the Same Title**

    a. **Investments in Securities & Derivative Instruments** Both US GAAS and the PCAOB interim standards include a section in this standard / a standard, respectively, for requirements for obtaining audit evidence for the valuation of investments in securities and derivative instruments. The ISA do not include this guidance.

    b. **Litigation & Claims** Both US GAAS and the PCAOB interim standard include requirements, in part, due to an agreement between the AICPA and the American Bar Association that are **not** in the ISA. The following are the ISA requirements. Compare them to the requirements for this topic in chapter 4 of this text.

    - The auditor shall design and perform audit procedures in order to identify litigation and claims involving the entity which may give rise to a RMM, including:
        - Inquiry of management and, where applicable, others within the entity, including in-house legal counsel
        - Reviewing minutes of meetings of those charged with governance and correspondence between the entity and its external legal counsel
        - Reviewing legal expense accounts
    - If the auditor assesses a RMM regarding litigation or claims that have been identified, or when audit procedures performed indicate that other material litigation or claims may exist, the auditor shall, in addition to the procedures required by other ISA, seek direct communication with the entity's external legal counsel. The auditor shall do so through a letter of inquiry, prepared by management and sent by the auditor, requesting the entity's external legal counsel to communicate directly with the auditor. If law, regulation or the respective

legal professional body prohibits the entity's external legal counsel from communicating directly with the auditor, the auditor shall perform alternative audit procedures.

- If either of the following occurs, the auditor shall modify the opinion in the auditor's report.
  - Management refuses to give the auditor permission to communicate or meet with the entity's external legal counsel, or the entity's external legal counsel refuses to respond appropriately to the letter of inquiry, or is prohibited from responding; and
  - The auditor is unable to obtain sufficient appropriate audit evidence by performing alternative audit procedures
- The auditor shall request management and, where appropriate, those charged with governance to provide written representations that all known actual or possible litigation and claims whose effects should be considered when preparing the financial statements have been disclosed to the auditor and accounted for and disclosed in accordance with the AFRF.

9. **ISA 510, *Initial Audit Engagements—Opening Balances* vs. AU 510, *Opening Balances—Initial Audit Engagements, Including Reaudit Engagements***

   a. **Predecessor Auditor Protocol** Both US GAAS and PCAOB standards state that the auditor, when the prior period financial statements were audited by a predecessor auditor, should request management to authorize the predecessor to allow a review of the predecessor's audit documentation and to respond fully to inquiries by the auditor. ISA do **not** include this statement; however, the other requirements related to reviewing the predecessor's audit documentation do not differ.

   b. **Procedures for Opening Balances** In addition to other procedures to obtain evidence about whether opening balances contain material misstatement, ISA require *one* of the following procedures to be performed:

      - Evaluating whether audit procedures performed in the current period provide evidence relevant to the opening balances
      - Where the prior year financial statements were audited, reviewing the predecessor auditor's working papers to obtain evidence regarding the opening balances
      - Performing specific audit procedures to obtain evidence regarding the opening balances

      US GAAS strengthens the ISA requirement by requiring the first option of the preceding three options and one or both of the other two options to be performed.

   c. **Discovery of Possible Need for Predecessor to Revise Report** The ISA do **not** address this issue.

   d. **Auditor is Precluded From Making Reference in Audit Report to Predecessor** Both US GAAS and PCAOB standards state that he auditor should not make reference to the report or work of the predecessor auditor as the basis, in part, for the auditor's own opinion. ISA do **not** address this issue.

10. **ISA 520, *Analytical Procedures* vs. AU 520, of the Same Title** ISA do **not** include the specific documentation requirements for substantive analytical procedures that are included in both US GAAS and the PCAOB interim standards.

11. **ISA 560, *Subsequent Events* vs. AU 560, *Subsequent Events and Subsequently Discovered Facts***

    a. **Definition of Subsequent Events** US GAAS separates the terms as indicated in its title of this standard; the ISA defines subsequent events to include facts that become known after the date of the audit report.

    b. **Reissuance of Predecessor Audit Report** US GAAS includes requirements and guidance related to a predecessor auditor's responsibilities when reissuing the audit report on previously issued financial statements that are to be presented on a comparative basis with audited financial statements of a subsequent period. ISA do **not** include such requirements.

    c. **Written Representations When Financial Statements Are Subsequently Revised** ISA do **not** include the specific additional requirements included in US GAAS for written representations when the auditor either dates the audit report as of a later date or dual dates the audit report for that revision.

12. **ISA 580, *Written Representations* vs. AU 580, of the Same Title** Per ISA the date of the written representations shall be as near as practicable to, but not after, the date of the auditor's report on the financial statements. Both US GAAS and the PCAOB interim standard require them to be as of the date of the audit report.

13. **ISA 600, *Special Considerations—Audits of Group Financial Statements (Including the Work of Component Auditors)* vs. AU 600, of the Same Title** ISA do **not** permit the audit report on the group financial statements to make reference to a component auditor unless required by law or regulation to include such reference. Both US GAAS and the PCAOB interim standard do **not** include this prohibition.

14. **ISA 705, *Modifications to the Opinion in the Independent Auditor's Report* vs. AU 705, of the Same Title** ISA state that the auditor shall disclaim an opinion when, in extremely rare circumstances involving multiple uncertainties, the auditor concludes that, notwithstanding having obtained sufficient appropriate audit evidence regarding each of the individual uncertainties, it is not possible to form an opinion on the financial statements due to the potential interaction of the uncertainties and their possible cumulative effect on the financial statements. US GAAS does **not** include this requirement because the AICPA believes that a disclaimer of opinion is appropriate only when the auditor is not able to obtain sufficient appropriate audit evidence.

15. **ISA 710, *Comparative Information—Corresponding Figures and Comparative Financial Statements* vs. AU 700, *Forming an Opinion and Reporting on Financial Statements*** The AICPA elected not in create a separate section for comparative financial statements. (ISA 710 includes a considerable amount of guidance that was not applicable to reporting in the United States.)

    a. **Comparative Information** US GAAS requires that when expressing an opinion on all periods presented, the auditor should update the report on the individual financial statements of one or more prior periods presented on a comparative basis with those of the current period. The auditor's report on comparative financial statements should not be dated earlier than the date on which the auditor has obtained sufficient appropriate audit evidence on which to support the opinion for the most recent audit. ISA do **not** include this requirement.

       US GAAS contain a requirement that if comparative information is presented, and the entity requests the auditor to express an opinion on all periods presented, the auditor should consider whether the information included for the prior period contains sufficient detail to constitute a fair presentation in accordance with the AFRF. ISA do **not** include this requirement.

b. **Audit Procedures** US GAAS includes a requirement that specific procedures be performed whenever either comparative financial statements or comparative information is presented for the prior periods. ISA do **not** include such a requirement.

c. **Prior Period Financial Statements** US GAAS includes requirements on what to disclose in an other-matter paragraph when reporting on prior period financial statements in connection with the current period's audit, and the auditor's opinion on such prior period financial statements differs from the opinion the auditor previously expressed. ISA do **not** include this requirement.

US GAAS includes a requirement that when the financial statements of the prior period were audited by a predecessor auditor, and the predecessor auditor's report on the prior period's financial statements is not reissued, the auditor should include in the other-matter paragraph the nature of any emphasis-of-matter paragraph or other-matter paragraph included in the predecessor audit report, if any. ISA do **not** include this requirement.

d. **Prior Period Financial Statements Not Audited** US GAAS include requirements on how to report when prior period financial statements were not audited, reviewed, or compiled. ISA do **not** include this requirement.

16. **ISA 800, *Special Considerations—Audits of Financial Statements Prepared in Accordance With Special Purpose Frameworks* vs. AU 800, of the Same Title**

a. **Engagement Acceptance** US GAAS include a requirement for the auditor, when accepting the engagement, to obtain the agreement of management that it acknowledges and understands its responsibility to include all informative disclosures, including specified disclosures, that are appropriate for the special-purpose framework used to prepare the entity's financial statements. ISA do **not** include this requirement.

b. **Description of the Applicable Financial Reporting Framework** US GAAS require the auditor to evaluate whether the financial statements are suitably titled, include a summary of significant accounting policies, and adequately describe how the special purpose framework differs from GAAP. ISA do **not** include these requirements with their similar requirement to evaluate whether the financial statements adequately refer to or describe the AFRF.

c. **Fair Presentation** If the special-purpose financial statements contain items that are the same as, or similar to, those in financial statements prepared in accordance with GAAP, US GAAS include a requirement for the auditor to evaluate whether the financial statements include informative disclosures similar to those required by GAAP. US GAAS also require the auditor to evaluate whether additional disclosures, beyond those specifically required by the framework, related to matters that are not specifically identified on the face of the financial statements or other disclosures may be necessary for the financial statements to achieve fair presentation. ISA do **not** include these requirements.

d. **Restricting the Use of the Auditor's Report** US GAAS require the audit report to include an other-matter paragraph that restricts the use of the audit report when the special-purpose financial statements are prepared in accordance with a contractual basis of accounting, a regulatory basis of accounting, or an other basis of accounting, except when the regulatory basis financial statements and the related audit report are intended for general use. In this circumstance, the auditor is required to express an opinion on whether the financial statements are prepared in accordance with GAAP and, in a separate paragraph, an opinion on whether the financial statements are prepared in accordance with the special-purpose framework. ISA do **not** include these requirements.

e. **Auditor's Report Prescribed by Law or Regulation** US GAAS include requirements when the auditor is required by law or regulation to use a specific layout, form, or wording of the auditor's report. ISA do **not** include these requirements.

f. **Audit Report** ISA require the auditor's report to describe the purpose for which the financial statements are prepared and, if necessary, the intended users, or refer to a note in the special-purpose financial statements that contains that information. US GAAS does **not** require this description when the special-purpose financial statements are prepared in accordance with the cash or tax basis of accounting.

g. **Alerting Readers That the Financial Statements Are Prepared in Accordance With a Special Purpose Framework** ISA requires the audit report to include an emphasis-of-matter paragraph alerting users of the audit report that the financial statements are prepared in accordance with a special-purpose framework and that, as a result, the financial statements may not be suitable for another purpose. US GAAS does **not** require the audit report to state that the financial statements may not be suitable for another purpose; however, US GAAS requires (and ISA do **not**), the emphasis-of-matter paragraph to state that the special-purpose framework is a basis of accounting other than GAAP. And per US GAAS, the emphasis-of-matter paragraph is **not** required when the special-purpose financial statements are prepared in accordance with a regulatory basis of accounting and the special-purpose financial statements together with the audit report are intended for general use.

17. **ISA 805, *Special Considerations—Audits of Single Financial Statements and Specific Elements, Accounts, or Items of a Financial Statement* vs. AU 805, of the Same Title**

a. **Procedures on Interrelated Items** As a consideration when accepting the engagement, US GAAS requires the auditor determine whether the auditor will be able to perform procedures on interrelated items. US GAAS includes a requirement for the auditor to perform procedures on interrelated items as necessary to meet the objective of the audit. In the case of an audit of a specific element that is, or is based upon, the entity's stockholders' equity or net income (or the equivalents thereto), US GAAS further requires the auditor to perform procedures necessary to obtain sufficient appropriate audit evidence about financial position, or financial position and results of operations, respectively, because of the interrelationship between the element and the balance sheet accounts and the income statement accounts. ISA do **not** include these requirements.

b. **Acceptability of the Financial Reporting Framework** US GAAS require the auditor to obtain an understanding of (a) the purpose for which the single financial statement or specific element of a financial statement is prepared, (b) the intended users, and (c) the steps taken by management to determine that the application of the financial reporting framework is acceptable in the circumstances. ISA do **not** include these requirements.

c. **Materiality** US GAAS require the auditor to determine materiality for the single financial statement being reported on, and in the case of an audit of one or more specific elements of a financial statement, materiality for each individual element reported on. ISA do **not** include these requirements.

d. **Reporting on an Incomplete Presentation but One That Is Otherwise in Accordance With GAAP** When the auditor reports on an incomplete presentation but one that is otherwise in accordance with GAAP, US GAAS require the auditor to include an emphasis-of-matter paragraph in the audit report, alerting users as to the purpose of the presentation and that the presentation is incomplete. ISA do not address reporting on incomplete presentations that are otherwise in accordance with the AFRF.

e. **Reporting on the Entity's Complete Set of Financial Statements and a Single Financial Statement or a Specific Element of Those Financial Statements** ISA require the auditor to express a separate opinion for each engagement when undertaking an engagement to report on a single financial statement or a specific element of a financial statement in conjunction with an engagement to audit the entity's complete set of financial statements. US GAAS require that the separate opinions be in separate audit reports and that the report on a specific element includes the date of the audit report on the complete set of financial statements and the nature of opinion expressed on those financial statements under an appropriate heading.

US GAAS address the case of an audit of a specific element of a financial statement when the opinion in the audit report on an entity's complete set of financial statements is modified and the modification of the audit opinion is relevant to the audit of the specific element. In such cases, the auditor is required to express either an adverse opinion or disclaim an opinion on the specific element, depending on the reasons for the modification of the auditor's opinion on the complete set of financial statements. ISA do not specifically require an adverse opinion or disclaimer of opinion in such circumstances.

ISA address situations when the auditor concludes that it is necessary to express an adverse opinion or disclaim an opinion on the entity's complete set of financial statements as a whole, but in the context of a separate audit of a specific element that is included in those financial statements, the auditor nevertheless considers it appropriate to express an unmodified opinion on that element. In addition to the requirements in ISA regarding this circumstance, US GAAS precludes such reporting when the specific element is, or is based upon, the entity's stockholders' equity or net income (or the equivalent).

18. **ISA 810, *Engagements to Report on Summary Financial Statements* vs. AU 810, of the Same Title**

a. **Management's Acknowledgement of Written Representations Required** Before accepting an engagement to report on summary financial statements, US GAAS require the auditor to obtain the agreement of management, in writing, that it acknowledges and understands its responsibility to provide the auditor with written representations regarding the summary financial statements. ISA do **not** include this requirement; neither do they include the requirement for the specific written representations

b. **Audit Report on Audited Financial Statements Contains an Adverse Opinion or A Disclaimer of Opinion** US GAAS require the auditor to withdraw from the engagement to report on the summary financial statements when withdrawal is possible under applicable law or regulation and when the audit report on the audited financial statements contains an adverse opinion or a disclaimer of opinion. US GAAS further clarifies the reporting elements when the auditor issues a report on the summary financial statements in those situations when it is not possible to withdraw from the engagement. ISA do **not** include these requirements.

c. **Additional Report Elements Regarding Nature & Cutoff of Procedures Performed** US GAAS require additional elements for the audit report on the summary financial statements with regard to the nature of the procedures that were performed by the auditor on the summary financial statements, including that the auditor did not perform audit procedures regarding the audited financial statements after the date of the report on those financial statements if the date of the auditor's report on the summary financial statements is later than the date of the audit report on the audited financial statements. ISA do **not** include these requirements.

d. **Audit Report on Audited Financial Statements Contains a Modified Opinion, Emphasis-of-Matter Paragraph, or Other-Matter Paragraph** ISA address the reporting elements when the audit report on the audited financial statements contains a qualified opinion, an emphasis-of-matter paragraph, or an other-matter paragraph and the auditor expresses an unmodified opinion on the summary financial statements.

Per ISA, under these circumstances, the auditor is required to:

- State that the auditor's report on the audited financial statements contains a qualified opinion, an emphasis-of-matter paragraph, or an other-matter paragraph
- Describe the basis for the qualified opinion on the audited financial statements and that qualified opinion; or the emphasis-of-matter or other-matter paragraph in the auditor's report on the audited financial statements
- Describe the effect on the summary financial statements, if any

Per US GAAS, the preceding requirements apply when the auditor expresses an either an unmodified or an adverse opinion on the summary financial statements.

e. **Comparatives** US GAAS contain the additional requirement that if the summary financial statements contain comparatives that were not reported on by the auditor or another auditor, the audit report on the summary financial statements should state that the comparative summary financial statements were not reported on by the auditor and, accordingly, the auditor does not express an opinion on the comparative summary financial statements. ISA do **not** include this requirement.

f. **Other Information in Documents Containing Summary Financial Statements** US GAAS contain an additional requirement that if, upon reading the other information, the auditor identifies a material inconsistency or becomes aware of an apparent material misstatement of fact, the auditor should discuss the matter with management and should consider appropriate further action in the circumstances. For an identified material inconsistency, the auditor should also determine whether the summary financial statements or the other information needs to be revised.

Editor Note: The individual ISA or the entire handbook of pronouncements can be viewed or downloaded for no charge on IFAC's website (http://www.ifac.org/publications-resources/2013-handbook-international-quality-control-auditing-review-other-assurance-a).

CHAPTER 11—OTHER AUDITING STANDARDS

Problem 11-1 MULTIPLE-CHOICE QUESTIONS

Sarbanes-Oxley Act of 2002

1. Which of the following statements is correct concerning the Public Company Accounting Oversight Board (PCAOB)?
   a. It was established by the Sarbanes-Oxley Act of 2002.
   b. It was established by the Dodd-Frank Wall Street Reform and Consumer Protection Act.
   c. It has oversight authority over the Securities and Exchange Commission (SEC).
   d. It was established by the Securities Exchange Act of 2002. (ID: 90354)

2. All of the following statements regarding the Public Company Accounting Oversight Board's (PCAOB) adopted interim auditing standards are true **except**
   a. The PCAOB adopted GAAS that were in existence on April 16, 2003 as its interim standards.
   b. The interim standards provide guidance, but they are not authoritative.
   c. Each of the interim standards remains in effect to the extent not amended or superseded by PCAOB action.
   d. The interim standards had been previously issued by the AICPA. (ID: 90355)

3. The Public Company Accounting Oversight Board's responsibilities include
   a. Investigation and enforcement of registered public accounting firms for violations of specified laws or professional standards.
   b. Investigation of violations committed by registered public accounting firms; enforcement is left to the Securities and Exchange Commission (SEC).
   c. Final approval of auditing and related attestation, quality control, ethics, and independence standards for registered public accounting firms established by the SEC.
   d. Registration of companies that issue publicly traded securities. (ID: 90356)

PCAOB Audit Documentation

4. Which of the following is **not** a documentation requirement for an engagement conducted pursuant to the standards of the PCAOB?
   a. The auditor must identify all significant findings or issues in an engagement completion document.
   b. The auditor must retain audit documentation for at least seven years from the report release date.
   c. Audit documentation must contain sufficient information to enable an experienced auditor, having no previous connection with the engagement, to understand the nature, extent, timing, and results of procedures performed; evidence obtained; and conclusions reached.
   d. A complete and final set of audit documentation should be assembled for retention not more than 60 days after the report release date. (ID: 8268)

5. The office issuing the auditor's report on a public company must obtain, and review and retain, prior to the report release date, the following documentation related to the work performed by other auditors, **except for**
   a. Any findings affecting the consolidating or combining of accounts in the consolidated financial statements
   b. All internal controls over financial reporting found to be ineffective by other auditors
   c. Letters of representations from management
   d. Sufficient information to allow the reconciliation of the financial statement amounts audited by the other auditors to the information underlying the consolidated financial statements (ID: 89470)

PCAOB Audit of Internal Control Over Financial Reporting

6. The Public Company Accounting Oversight Board (PCAOB) uses the term *internal control over financial reporting* to describe a process that does **not** include which of the following?
   a. Procedures performed by the auditor
   b. Procedures that pertain to the maintenance of reasonably detailed records that accurately and fairly reflect the transactions and dispositions of the company's assets
   c. Procedures that provide reasonable assurance that transactions are recorded as necessary to permit preparation of the financial statements in accordance with GAAP and that receipts and expenditures are made only in accordance with company management and director authorization
   d. Procedures that provide reasonable assurance regarding prevention or timely detection of unauthorized acquisition, use, or disposition of company assets that could have a material effect on the financial statements (ID: 7938)

7. The Public Company Accounting Oversight Board's auditing standards recognize that effective internal control over financial reporting (ICFR) cannot, and does not, provide absolute assurance of achieving the company's reporting objectives in large part due to inherent limitations. Which of the following is **not** such an inherent limitation?
   a. Lapses in judgment and breakdowns resulting from human failures
   b. Circumvention by collusion
   c. Circumvention by improper management override
   d. Lack of controls over information technology (ID: 7941)

8. Which of the following statements apply to an audit of internal control over financial reporting conducted in accordance with the standards of the Public Company Accounting Oversight Board (PCAOB)?
   I. The auditor should consider the effect of compensating controls in assessing whether the objectives of internal control over financial reporting have been achieved.
   II. While management is responsible for the company's internal control, the auditor should also assess the effectiveness of the board of directors' and audit committee's oversight as part of evaluating the control environment.

   a. I. only
   b. II. only
   c. Both I. and II.
   d. Neither I. nor II. (ID: 7943)

9. Mammoth Co. plans to present comparative financial statements for the years ended December 31, year 5, and year 6, respectively. Brown, CPA, audited Mammoth's financial statements for both years and plans to report on the comparative financial statements on March 1, year 7. Brown's audit is subject to the requirements of the Public Company Accounting Oversight Board (PCAOB). Mammoth's current management team was not present until January 1, year 6. What period of time should be covered by Mammoth's management representation letter?
   a. January 1, year 5, through December 31, year 6
   b. January 1, year 5, through March 1, year 7
   c. January 1, year 6, through December 31, year 6
   d. January 1, year 6, through March 1, year 7 (ID: 7944)

10. Wale Company plans to present comparative financial statements for the years ended December 31, year 7, and year 8, respectively. Dauphin, CPA, audited Wale's financial statements for both years and plans to report on the comparative financial statements on March 1, year 9. Dauphin's audit is subject to the requirements of the Public Company Accounting Oversight Board (PCAOB). What time is covered by Dauphin's opinion on internal control over financial reporting (ICFR)?

    a. The end of year 7 and the end of year 8
    b. The end of year 8
    c. Year 7 and year 8
    d. Year 8 (ID: 7947)

11. In an audit of internal control over financial reporting conducted in accordance with the standards of the Public Company Accounting Oversight Board (PCAOB), the auditor must communicate in writing to the audit committee

    a. Significant deficiencies only
    b. Material weaknesses only
    c. All deficiencies in internal control over financial reporting
    d. Significant deficiencies and material weaknesses (ID: 7949)

12. What is the term for an internal control deficiency such that there is a reasonable possibility that a material misstatement of the company's financial statements will not be prevented or detected on a timely basis?

    a. Deficiency in internal control
    b. Material deficiency
    c. Material weakness
    d. Significant deficiency (ID: 7950)

13. The conceptual definition of materiality that applies to an audit of a public company's internal control over financial reporting includes which of the following considerations?

	Qualitative	Quantitative
a.	Yes	Yes
b.	Yes	No
c.	No	Yes
d.	No	No

(ID: 7951)

14. In an audit of internal control over financial reporting conducted in accordance with the standards of the Public Company Accounting Oversight Board (PCAOB), which procedure is insufficient by itself to test the effectiveness of a control?

    a. Inquiries of appropriate personnel
    b. Inspection of relevant documents
    c. Observation of operations
    d. Reperformance of the control procedure (ID: 7953)

15. Which of the following statements is **false** in regard to an audit of internal control over financial reporting conducted in accordance with the standards of the Public Company Accounting Oversight Board (PCAOB)?

    a. The auditor may rely upon the judgments of others regarding the sufficiency of evidence.
    b. The auditor may use the work of others to alter the nature, timing, or extent of the work that the auditor performs.
    c. The extent to which the auditor may use the work of others depends on their objectivity.
    d. As the risk associated with a control increases, the need for the auditor to perform his or her own work on the control increases. (ID: 7954)

16. Each of the following types of controls is considered to be an entity-level control, **except** those
    a. Relating to the control environment
    b. Pertaining to the company's risk assessment process
    c. Regarding the company's annual stockholder meeting
    d. Addressing policies over significant risk management practices (ID: 9920)

PCAOB Previously Reported Material Weakness

17. In accordance with the standards of the PCAOB, which of the following conditions must be met in order for an auditor to report on whether a previously reported material weakness continues to exist?
    I. Management supports its assertion with sufficient evidence, including documentation.
    II. Management accepts responsibility for the effectiveness of internal control over operations.
    III. Management evaluates the effectiveness of the specific control(s) that address the material weakness using the same control criteria management used for its most recent annual assessment of internal control over financial reporting and its stated control objective(s).

    a. Only I
    b. Only II
    c. Only I and III
    d. I, II, and III (ID: 8269)

18. Which of the following statements is **false** in regard to an engagement conducted in accordance with the standards of the PCAOB to report on whether a previously reported material weakness continues to exist?
    a. The auditor may report on more than one previously reported material weakness as part of a single engagement.
    b. This type of engagement is voluntary, i.e., the standards of the PCAOB do not require an auditor to undertake an engagement to report on whether a previously reported material weakness continues to exist.
    c. A qualified opinion is not permitted.
    d. The auditor's opinion on whether a previously reported material weakness continues to exist may be expressed as "the material weakness exists" or "the material weakness has been eliminated". (ID: 89465)

PCAOB Consistency

19. Which of the following circumstances does **not** describe when a change in accounting principle is a change from one generally accepted accounting principle to another generally accepted accounting principle?
    a. There are two or more generally accepted accounting principles that apply.
    b. The accounting principle formerly used is no longer generally accepted.
    c. There is a change in accounting estimate.
    d. There is a change in the method of applying an accounting principle. (ID: 9282)

20. The auditor should evaluate a change in accounting principle to determine whether the newly adopted accounting principle is a generally accepted accounting principle. All of the following conditions must also be met **except for**
    a. The method of accounting for the effect of the change is in conformity with generally accepted accounting principles.
    b. The disclosures related to the accounting change are adequate.
    c. The company has justified that the alternative accounting principle is preferable.
    d. The company has prepared pro forma financial statements with and without the change (ID: 9283)

21. The correction of a material misstatement in the previously issued financial statements of an issuer
    a. Should be recognized in the auditor's report through the addition of an explanatory paragraph following the opinion paragraph
    b. Should be recognized in the auditor's report through the addition of an explanatory paragraph preceding the opinion paragraph
    c. Should be recognized in the auditor's report through the addition of an explanatory paragraph following the opinion paragraph if the correction involved an error in accounting principle
    d. Should be recognized in the auditor's report through the addition of an explanatory paragraph preceding the opinion paragraph if the correction involved an error in accounting principle (ID: 9281)

Reviews for Issuers

22. Which of the following statements is **not** true of both an engagement to review interim financial statements according to PCAOB auditing standards and SSARS?
    a. The objective of a review differs significantly from that of an audit.
    b. A review includes primarily applying analytical procedures and making inquiries.
    c. A review requires obtaining an understanding of the entity's internal control over financial reporting.
    d. The CPA should possess an understanding of the entity's industry, including the accounting principles and practices generally used. (ID: 9284)

23. During an engagement to review the interim financial statements of a public entity, a CPA becomes aware that several leases that should be capitalized are not capitalized. The CPA considers these leases to be material to the financial statements. The CPA decides to modify the standard review report because management will not capitalize the leases. Under these circumstances, the CPA should
    a. Issue an adverse opinion because of the departure from GAAP.
    b. Express no assurance of any kind on the entity's financial statements.
    c. Disclose the departure from GAAP in a separate paragraph after the limited assurance paragraph of the review report.
    d. Disclose the departure from GAAP in a separate paragraph before the limited assurance paragraph of the review report. (ID: 9285)

PCAOB Risk Assessment Standards

24. When developing the audit strategy and audit plan for an issuer, the auditor should evaluate whether the following matters are important to the company's financial statements and internal control over financial reporting and, if so, how they will affect the auditor's procedures, **except for**
    a. The relative complexity of the company's operations
    b. The response to the auditor's letter of audit inquiry to the client's lawyer for the current audit
    c. Matters relating to the company's business, including its organization, operating characteristics, and capital structure
    d. The extent of recent changes, if any, in the company, its operations, or its internal control over financial reporting (ID: 89466)

25. When the auditor is relying on controls in a financial statement audit, GAAS and ISA allow the testing of the operating effectiveness of controls that have not changed to be performed at least every third annual audit. How do PCAOB auditing standards differ?
    a. Such controls must be tested every other annual audit.
    b. The auditor should not rely on the testing of controls; substantive procedures alone provide sufficient, appropriate evidence.
    c. Evidence must be obtained that such controls were effective during the entire period of reliance.
    d. The every third annual audit rule only applies to automated controls. (ID: 89467)

PCAOB Auditing Supplemental Information Accompanying Audited Financial Statements

26. When engaged to report on supplemental information that accompanies a public company's financial statements that is required by a regulatory authority that prescribes a lower materiality level than the one used for the audit of the financial statements, the auditor should

    a. Withdraw from the engagement to report on the supplemental information
    b. Use the same level as for the financial statements and add an explanatory paragraph to the report on the supplemental information
    c. Use the regulatory authority's level in planning and performing the audit procedures for the supplemental information
    d. File an exception report with the regulatory authority (ID: 90446)

ISA

27. Which of the following boards is responsible for promulgating International Standards on Auditing?

    a. International Accounting Standards Board
    b. International Auditing and Assurance Standards Board
    c. International Ethics Standards Board for Accountants
    d. International Auditing and Attestation Standards Board (ID: 9286)

28. Primary differences between International Standards on Auditing (ISA) and Public Company Accounting Oversight Board (PCAOB) auditing standards include all of the following **except**

    a. PCAOB auditing standards, unlike ISA, do not include a requirement to put changes to the terms of an engagement in writing.
    b. ISA do not have a requirement similar to PCAOB auditing standards for an audit of internal control over financial reporting that is integrated with an audit of financial statements.
    c. ISA, unlike PCAOB auditing standards, do not allow the principal auditor to share responsibility with another auditor and accordingly, do not allow a reference in the audit report to another auditor
    d. There are significant differences per PCAOB auditing standards vs. ISA regarding requirements for written representations from management. (ID: 9287)

29. Both the AICPA's Statements on Auditing Standards and the PCAOB's auditing standards limit the period of evaluation by an auditor of an entity's ability to continue as a going concern to 12 months from the date of the financial statements. The International Standards on Auditing differ in that they

    a. Require that it be at least 12 months from the date of the release of the audit report
    b. Require that it be at least 12 months from the date of the financial statements, but do not limit it to 12 months
    c. Require that it be at least 12 months from the date of the management representation letter
    d. Require that it be at least 12 months from the date of the financial statements if the previous audit report contained an unqualified opinion, otherwise the evaluation should be for at least 18 months from the date of the financial statements (ID: 9288)

Problem 11-2 SIMULATION: Research

Which citation in the professional standards explains why the audit report on internal control over financial reporting should be dated the same as the audit report on the financial statements for a public company?

[ ] [ ] . [ ] (ID: 89469)

Problem 11-3 SIMULATION: Management Representations in an Audit of Internal Control Over Financial Reporting

The table below lists possible management representations that should be obtained in an audit of internal control over financial reporting. For each item, indicate whether it is appropriate or inappropriate.

Management Representations	Appropriate or Inappropriate?
1. Acknowledgment of management's responsibility for establishing and maintaining effective internal control over financial reporting.	
2. A statement that management has performed an evaluation and made an assessment of the effectiveness of the company's internal control over financial reporting and specifying the control criteria.	
3. A statement that management agreed to and relied on the auditor's procedures performed during the audits of internal control over financial reporting or the financial statements as part of the basis for management's assessment of the effectiveness of internal control over financial reporting.	
4. Management's conclusion, as set forth in its assessment, about the effectiveness of the company's internal control over financial reporting based on the control criteria for the same period covered by audit.	
5. A statement that management has disclosed to the auditor all deficiencies in the design or operation of internal control over financial reporting identified as part of management's evaluation, including separately disclosing to the auditor all such deficiencies that it believes to be significant deficiencies or material weaknesses in internal control over financial reporting.	
6. A description of any fraud resulting in a material misstatement to the company's financial statements and any other fraud that does not result in a material misstatement to the company's financial statements but involves senior management or management or other employees who have a significant role in the company's internal control over financial reporting.	
7. A statement as to whether control deficiencies identified and communicated to management during previous engagements have been resolved, and specifically identifying any that have not.	
8. A statement as to whether there were, subsequent to the date being reported on, any changes in internal control over financial reporting or other factors that might significantly affect internal control over financial reporting, including any corrective actions taken by management with regard to significant deficiencies and material weaknesses.	

(ID: 89468)

Problem 11-4 SIMULATION: Audit Report

Webb & Weber, CPAs, audited the consolidated financial statements of Quest Co., a public company, and all but one of its subsidiaries for the year ended September 30, year 1, and expressed a qualified opinion because Quest capitalized certain research and development expenditures that should have been expensed.

Webb & Weber also audited Quest's consolidated financial statements and all but one of its subsidiaries for the year ended September 30, year 2. These consolidated financial statements are being presented on a comparative basis with those of the prior year and an unqualified opinion is being expressed.

Webb, the engagement partner, instructed Perry, an assistant on the engagement, to draft the auditor's report on November 4, year 2, the date of completion of the audit. In drafting the report, Perry considered the following:

- In preparing its year 2 financial statements, Quest changed its method of accounting for research and development costs and properly expensed these amounts. Quest also restated its year 1 financial statements to conform with GAAP. Consequently, Webb & Weber's present opinion on the year 1 financial statements is different (unqualified) from the opinion expressed on November 5, year 1.
- Hill & Hall, CPAs, audited the financial statements of Biotherm, Inc., a consolidated subsidiary of Quest, for the years ended September 30, year 2 and year 1. The subsidiary's financial statements reflect total assets constituting 23% and 22% at September 30, year 2 and year 1, respectively, and total revenues constituting 21% and 20% in year 2 and year 1, respectively, of the consolidated totals. Hill & Hall expressed an unqualified opinion each year and furnished Webb & Weber with a copy of each year's audit report. Webb & Weber have decided not to assume responsibility for the work of Hill & Hall insofar as it relates to the expression of an opinion on the consolidated financial statements taken as a whole because of the materiality of Biotherm's financial statements to the consolidated financial statements. Hill & Hall's report will not be presented together with that of Webb & Weber.
- Quest is the subject of a grand jury investigation into possible violations of federal antitrust laws and possible related crimes. Related civil class actions are pending. This is adequately disclosed in Note 12 to Quest's consolidated financial statements. Because of the early stage of the investigation, the ultimate outcome of these matters cannot presently be determined. Therefore, no provision for any liability that may result has been recorded.
- Quest experienced a net loss in year 2 and is currently in default under substantially all of its debt agreements. Management's plans in regard to these matters are adequately disclosed in Note 14 to Quest's consolidated financial statements, although the financial statements do not include any adjustments that might result from the outcome of this uncertainty. These matters raise substantial doubt about Quest's ability to continue as a going concern.

<u>Report of Independent Registered Public Accounting Firm</u>

We have audited the consolidated financial statements of Quest Co. and subsidiaries as of September 30, year 2 and year 1, and the related consolidated statements of income, changes in stockholders' equity, and cash flows for the years then ended. These financial statements are the responsibility of the Company's management. Our responsibility is to express an opinion on these financial statements based on our audits. We did not audit the financial statements of Biotherm, Inc., a wholly owned subsidiary, which statements reflect total assets constituting 23% and 22% at September 30, year 2 and year 1, respectively, and total revenues constituting 21% and 20% in year 2 and year 1, respectively, of the consolidated totals. Those statements were audited by Hill & Hall, CPAs, whose reports have been furnished to us, and our opinion, insofar as it relates to the amounts included for Biotherm, Inc., is based solely on their reports.

We conducted our audits in accordance with the standards of the Public Company Accounting Oversight Board (United States). Those standards require that we plan and perform the audit to obtain reasonable assurance about whether the financial statements are free of material misstatement. An audit includes examining, on a test basis, evidence supporting the amounts and disclosures in the financial statement. An audit also includes assessing the accounting principles used, as well as assessing control risk. We believe that our audits provide a reasonable basis for our opinion.

In our previous report dated November 5, year 1, we expressed a qualified opinion that, except for the effects on the year 1 financial statements of not expensing certain research and development costs, the year 1 financial statements present fairly, in all material respects, the financial position of Quest Co. and subsidiaries as of September 30, year 1, and the results of its operations and its cash flows for the year then ended in conformity with generally accepted accounting principles. As described in Note 10, the Company has changed its method of accounting for these items and restated its year 1 financial statements to conform with generally accepted accounting principles. Accordingly, our present opinion on the year 1 financial statements, as presented herein, is different from that expressed in our previous report.

In our opinion, based on our audits and the reports of the other auditors, the consolidated financial statements referred to above present fairly, in all material respects, the financial position of Quest Co. as of September 30, year 2 and year 1, in conformity with generally accepted accounting principles, except for the uncertainty, which is discussed in Note 12 to the consolidated financial statements.

The accompanying consolidated financial statements have been prepared assuming that the Company will continue in existence for a reasonable period of time. As discussed in Note 14 to the consolidated financial statements, the Company suffered a net loss in year 2 and is currently in default under substantially all of its debt agreements. Management's plans in regard to these matters are also described in Note 14. The consolidated financial statements do not include any adjustments that might result from the outcome of this uncertainty.

Webb & Weber, CPAs
Seattle, Washington
November 4, year 2

Webb reviewed Perry's draft and indicated there were many deficiencies in Perry's draft. The following items are the deficiencies noted by Webb. For each deficiency indicate whether:

- W—Webb's review note is correct.
- P—Perry's draft is correct.
- B—Both Webb's review note and Perry's draft are incorrect.

Webb's Review Notes	**W / P / B**
1. The reference to the subsidiary, Biotherm, and the magnitude of its financial statements should be in the scope paragraph rather than in the opening (introductory) paragraph.	
2. The other independent auditors, Hill & Hall, should be named in the scope paragraph rather than in the opening (introductory) paragraph.	
3. The reference in the scope paragraph to "the financial statements are free of material misstatement" should be followed by the phrase "whether caused by error or fraud."	
4. The required reference in the scope paragraph to assessing "significant estimates made by management" has been omitted.	
5. The reference in the scope paragraph to "assessing control risk" is inappropriate and should be omitted from the report.	
6. The required reference in the scope paragraph to "evaluating the overall financial statement presentation" has been omitted.	
7. A separate explanatory paragraph describing the grand jury investigation into possible violations of federal antitrust laws should to be placed between the scope and opinion paragraphs.	
8. The reference in the first explanatory paragraph (between the scope and opinion paragraphs) to the qualified opinion on the year 1 financial statements is not properly placed. It should be placed in the opinion paragraph.	

(ID: 9237)

Problem 11-5 SIMULATION: Audit Report Modifications

- The entity is a public company.
- The auditor is independent.
- The auditor previously expressed an unqualified opinion on the prior year's financial statements.
- Only single year (not comparative) statements are presented for the current year.
- The conditions for an unqualified opinion exist unless contradicted in the factual situations.
- The conditions stated in the factual situations are material.
- No report modifications are to be made except in response to the factual situation.

The following items present various independent factual situations an auditor might encounter in conducting an audit. The list represents the report modifications (if any) that would be necessary. For each situation, select one response—the action the auditor normally would take, based on the information above and in each situation.

Situation	Report Modification
1. In auditing the long-term investments account, an auditor is unable to obtain audited financial statements for an investee located in a foreign country. The auditor concludes that sufficient appropriate audit evidence regarding this investment cannot be obtained.	
2. Due to recurring operating losses and working capital deficiencies, an auditor has substantial doubt about an entity's ability to continue as a going concern for a reasonable period of time. However, the financial statement disclosures concerning these matters are adequate.	
3. A principal auditor decides to take responsibility for the work of another CPA who audited a wholly owned subsidiary of the entity and issued an unqualified opinion.	
4. An entity issues financial statements that present financial position and results of operations but omits the related statement of cash flows. Management discloses in the notes to the financial statements that it does not believe the statement of cash flows to be a useful financial statement.	
5. An entity changes its method of inventory pricing from LIFO to FIFO. The auditor concurs with the change although it has a material effect on the comparability of the entity's financial statements.	
6. An entity is a defendant in a lawsuit alleging infringement of certain patent rights. However, the ultimate outcome of the litigation cannot be reasonably estimated by management. The auditor believes there is a reasonable possibility of a significant material loss, but the lawsuit is adequately disclosed in the notes to the financial statements.	
7. An entity discloses in the notes to the financial statements certain lease obligations. The auditor believes that the failure to capitalize these leases is a departure from generally accepted accounting principles.	

(ID: 9238)

Report Modifications

A. Describe the circumstances in an explanatory paragraph preceding the opinion paragraph without modifying the three standard paragraphs.

B. Describe the circumstances in an explanatory paragraph following the opinion paragraph without modifying the three standard paragraphs.

C. Describe the circumstances in an explanatory paragraph preceding the opinion paragraph and modify the opinion paragraph.

D. Describe the circumstances in an explanatory paragraph following the opinion paragraph and modify the opinion paragraph.

E. Describe the circumstances in an explanatory paragraph preceding the opinion paragraph and modify the scope and opinion paragraphs.

F. Describe the circumstances in an explanatory paragraph following the opinion paragraph and modify the scope and opinion paragraphs.

G. Describe the circumstances within the scope paragraph without adding an explanatory paragraph.

H. Describe the circumstances within the opinion paragraph without adding an explanatory paragraph.

I. Describe the circumstances within the scope and opinion paragraphs without adding an explanatory paragraph.

J. Issue the standard auditor's report without modification.

Problem 11-6 SIMULATION: Audit Report

Webb & Weber, CPAs, audited the consolidated financial statements of Quest Co, a public company, and all but one of its subsidiaries for the year ended September 30, year 1, and expressed a qualified opinion because Quest capitalized certain research and development expenditures that should have been expensed.

Webb & Weber also audited Quest's consolidated financial statements and all but one of its subsidiaries for the year ended September 30, year 2. These consolidated financial statements are being presented on a comparative basis with those of the prior year and an unqualified opinion is being expressed.

Webb, the engagement partner, instructed Perry, an assistant on the engagement, to draft the auditor's report on November 4, year 2, the date of completion of the audit. In drafting the report, Perry considered the following:

- In preparing its year 2 financial statements, Quest changed its method of accounting for research and development costs and properly expensed these amounts. Quest also restated its year 1 financial statements to conform with GAAP. Consequently, Webb & Weber's present opinion on the year 1 financial statements is different (unqualified) from the opinion expressed on November 5, year 1.
- Hill & Hall, CPAs, audited the financial statements of Biotherm, Inc., a consolidated subsidiary of Quest, for the years ended September 30, year 2 and year 1. The subsidiary's financial statements reflect total assets constituting 23% and 22% at September 30, year 2 and year 1, respectively, and total revenues constituting 21% and 20% in year 2 and year 1, respectively, of the consolidated totals. Hill & Hall expressed an unqualified opinion each year and furnished Webb & Weber with a copy of each year's auditor's report. Webb & Weber have decided not to assume responsibility for the work of Hill & Hall insofar as it relates to the expression of an opinion on the consolidated financial statements taken as a whole because of the materiality of Biotherm's financial statements to the consolidated financial statements. Hill & Hall's report will not be presented together with that of Webb & Weber.
- Quest is the subject of a grand jury investigation into possible violations of federal antitrust laws and possible related crimes. Related civil class actions are pending. This is adequately disclosed in Note 12 to Quest's consolidated financial statements. Because of the early stage of the investigation, the ultimate outcome of these matters cannot presently be determined. Therefore, no provision for any liability that may result has been recorded.
- Quest experienced a net loss in year 2 and is currently in default under substantially all of its debt agreements. Management's plans in regard to these matters are adequately disclosed in Note 14 to Quest's consolidated financial statements, although the financial statements do not include any adjustments that might result from the outcome of this uncertainty. These matters raise substantial doubt about Quest's ability to continue as a going concern.

<u>Report of Independent Registered Public Accounting Firm</u>

We have audited the consolidated financial statements of Quest Co. and subsidiaries as of September 30, year 2 and year 1, and the related consolidated statements of income, changes in stockholders' equity, and cash flows for the years then ended. These financial statements are the responsibility of the Company's management. Our responsibility is to express an opinion on these financial statements based on our audits. We did not audit the financial statements of Biotherm, Inc., a wholly owned subsidiary, which statements reflect total assets constituting 23% and 22% at September 30, year 2 and year 1, respectively, and total revenues constituting 21% and 20% in year 2 and year 1, respectively, of the consolidated totals. Those statements were audited by Hill & Hall, CPAs, whose reports have been furnished to us, and our opinion, insofar as it relates to the amounts included for Biotherm, Inc., is based solely on their reports.

We conducted our audits in accordance with the standards of the Public Company Accounting Oversight Board (United States). Those standards require that we plan and perform the audit to obtain reasonable assurance about whether the financial statements are free of material misstatement. An audit includes examining, on a test basis, evidence supporting the amounts and disclosures in the financial statements. An audit also includes assessing the accounting principles used, as well as assessing control risk. We believe that our audits provide a reasonable basis for our opinion.

In our previous report dated November 5, year 1, we expressed a qualified opinion that, except for the effects on the year 1 financial statements of not expensing certain research and development costs, the year 1 financial statements present fairly, in all material respects, the financial position of Quest Co. and subsidiaries as of September 30, year 1, and the results of its operations and its cash flows for the year then ended in conformity with generally accepted accounting principles. As described in Note 10, the Company has changed its method of accounting for these items and restated its year 1 financial statements to conform with generally accepted accounting principles. Accordingly, our present opinion on the year 1 financial statements, as presented herein, is different from that expressed in our previous report.

In our opinion, based on our audits and the reports of the other auditors, the consolidated financial statements referred to above present fairly, in all material respects, the financial position of Quest Co. as of September 30, year 2 and year 1, in conformity with generally accepted accounting principles, except for the uncertainty, which is discussed in Note 12 to the consolidated financial statements.

The accompanying consolidated financial statements have been prepared assuming that the Company will continue in existence for a reasonable period of time. As discussed in Note 14 to the consolidated financial statements, the Company suffered a net loss in year 2 and is currently in default under substantially all of its debt agreements. Management's plans in regard to these matters are also described in Note 14. The consolidated financial statements do not include any adjustments that might result from the outcome of this uncertainty.

Webb & Weber, CPAs
Seattle, Washington
November 4, year 2

Webb reviewed Perry's draft and indicated there were many deficiencies in Perry's draft. The following items are the deficiencies noted by Webb. For each deficiency, indicate whether:

- W—Webb's review note is correct.
- P—Perry's draft is correct.
- B—Both Webb's review note and Perry's draft are incorrect.

Webb's Review Notes	W / P / B
1. The reference in the first explanatory paragraph (between the scope and opinion paragraphs) to Note 10 does not express our concurrence with Quest's change in accounting principle. Our concurrence should be specifically expressed in this paragraph.	
2. The reference to the other auditors in the opinion paragraph is incomplete. It should specifically include the words "unqualified opinion" to describe the type of opinion expressed by Hill & Hall.	
3. The opinion paragraph should extend the auditor's opinion beyond financial position to include the results of Quest's operations and its changes in stockholders' equity.	
4. The reference to the uncertainty in the opinion paragraph is incomplete. It should describe the nature of the uncertainty as pertaining to the grand jury investigation into possible violations of federal antitrust laws.	
5. The explanatory paragraph following the opinion paragraph does not include the term "substantial doubt." This term is required to be used in this paragraph under these circumstances.	
6. The explanatory paragraph following the opinion paragraph does not include the term "going concern." This term is required to be used in this paragraph under these circumstances.	
7. The explanatory paragraph following the opinion paragraph includes an inappropriate statement that "the consolidated financial statements do not include any adjustments that might result from the outcome of this uncertainty." This statement is misleading and should be omitted.	
8. The auditor's report is not correctly dated. It should be dual dated because of Note 12, the grand jury investigation, and also because of Note 14, the going concern uncertainty.	

(ID: 9239)

Problem 11-7 SIMULATION: Types of Opinions

- The entity is a public company.
- The auditor is independent.
- The auditor previously expressed an unqualified opinion on the prior year's financial statements.
- Only single year (not comparative) statements are presented for the current year.
- The conditions for an unqualified opinion exist unless contradicted in the factual situations.
- The conditions stated in the factual situations are material.
- No report modifications are to be made except in response to the factual situation.

The following items present various independent factual situations an auditor might encounter in conducting an audit. The list represents the types of opinions the auditor ordinarily would issue. For each situation, select one response—the action the auditor normally would take based on the information above and in each situation. A selection may be used once, more than once, or not at all.

Situation	Type of Opinion
1. In auditing the long-term investments account, an auditor is unable to obtain audited financial statements for an investee located in a foreign country. The auditor concludes that sufficient appropriate audit evidence regarding this investment cannot be obtained.	
2. Due to recurring operating losses and working capital deficiencies, an auditor has substantial doubt about an entity's ability to continue as a going concern for a reasonable period of time. However, the financial statement disclosures concerning these matters are adequate.	
3. A principal auditor decides to take responsibility for the work of another CPA who audited a wholly owned subsidiary of the entity and issued an unqualified opinion.	
4. An entity issues financial statements that present financial position and results of operations but omits the related statement of cash flows. Management discloses in the notes to the financial statements that it does not believe the statement of cash flows to be a useful financial statement.	
5. An entity changes its method of inventory pricing from LIFO to FIFO. The auditor concurs with the change although it has a material effect on the comparability of the entity's financial statements.	
6. An entity is a defendant in a lawsuit alleging infringement of certain patent rights. However, the ultimate outcome of the litigation cannot be reasonably estimated by management. The auditor believes there is a reasonable possibility of a significant material loss, but the lawsuit is adequately disclosed in the notes to the financial statements.	
7. An entity discloses in the notes to the financial statements certain lease obligations. The auditor believes that the failure to capitalize these leases is a departure from generally accepted accounting principles.	

(ID: 9236)

Types of Opinions

A. Qualified opinion

B. Unqualified opinion

C. Adverse opinion

D. Disclaimer of opinion

E. Explanatory language added to standard report

Solution 11-1 MULTIPLE-CHOICE ANSWERS

1. (a) The Sarbanes-Oxley Act of 2002 established the Public Company Accounting Oversight Board (PCAOB). The Dodd-Frank Wall Street Reform and Consumer Protection Act amended the Sarbanes-Oxley Act of 2002, but it did not establish the PCAOB. The SEC has oversight authority over the PCAOB, not vice versa. There is no Securities Exchange Act of 2002. (ID: 90354)

2. (b) The Public Company Accounting Oversight Board's adopted interim auditing standards are authoritative. All of the other answers are true. (ID: 90355)

3. (a) The Public Company Accounting Oversight Board's (PCAOB) responsibilities include investigation and enforcement of registered public accounting firms for violations of specified laws or professional standards; they do not rely on the Securities and Exchange Commission (SEC) to take enforcement or disciplinary action. The SEC approves auditing and related attestation, quality control, ethics, and independence standards for registered public accounting firms established by the PCAOB, not vice versa. The PCAOB registers accounting firms, not the companies audited by the accounting firms. (ID: 90356)

4. (d) A complete and final set of audit documentation should be assembled for retention not more than 45, not 60, days after the report release date. According to GAAS, not PCAOB auditing standards, the assembly of the final audit file should be completed within 60 days following the report release date. The alternative answers are all audit documentation requirements for public companies. (ID: 8268)

5. (b) The office issuing the auditor's report on a public company is not required to obtain records of all internal controls over financial reporting found to be ineffective by other auditors; however, documentation regarding all significant deficiencies and material weaknesses in internal control over financial reporting, including a clear distinction between those two categories is required. In addition to this and the items in the other three answer alternatives, the following documentation related to the work performed by other auditors must be obtained, and reviewed and retained, prior to the report release date by the office issuing the auditor's report: an engagement completion document; a list of significant risks, the auditor's responses, and the results of the auditor's related procedures; sufficient information relating to any significant findings or issues that are inconsistent with or contradict the final conclusions; a schedule of accumulated misstatements, including a description of the nature and cause of each accumulated misstatement, and an evaluation of uncorrected misstatements, including the quantitative and qualitative factors the auditor considered to be relevant to the evaluation; and all matters to be communicated to the audit committee. (ID: 89470)

6. (a) An auditor's procedures performed during either an audit of ICFR or an audit of financial statements are not part of a company's internal control over financial reporting (ICFR). The term *internal control over financial reporting* is defined as a process designed by, or under the supervision of, the company's principal executive and principal financial officers, or persons performing similar functions, and effected by the company's board of directors, management, and other personnel, to provide reasonable assurance regarding the reliability of financial reporting and the preparation of financial statements for external purposes in accordance with GAAP. Answers b, c, and d describe what its policies and procedures pertain to or provide. (ID: 7938)

7. (d) Lack of information technology (IT) controls is not an inherent limitation of an internal control system. A combination of manual and automated controls may be designed for systems that use IT. All of the other answers are examples of inherent limitations of ICFR. However, because these inherent limitations are known features of the financial reporting process, it is possible to design into the process safeguards to reduce, though not eliminate, this risk. (ID: 7941)

8. (c) The auditor should consider the effect of compensating controls when determining if a deficiency constitutes a material weakness. The compensating control should be judged effective enough to prevent or detect a material misstatement in order to be considered to have a mitigating effect. Ineffective oversight by the audit committee of the company's external financial reporting and internal control over financial reporting (ICFR) should be regarded as an indication of a material weakness in ICFR. (ID: 7943)

9. (b) Issues such as who should sign the letter, the period to be covered by the letter, and when an updated letter should be obtained are the same as in a financial statement audit under GAAS. If comparative financial statements are reported on, the written representations obtained at the completion of the most recent audit should address all periods being reported on. The representations should be made as of the date of the auditor's report. If current management was not present during all periods covered by the auditor's report, the auditor should nevertheless obtain written representations from current management on all such periods. (ID: 7944)

10. (b) The auditor's opinion on ICFR is as of a specified date rather than a period of time. When the auditor elects to issue a combined report, the audit opinion will address multiple periods for the financial statements presented, but only the end of the most recent fiscal year for the effectiveness of ICFR. (ID: 7947)

11. (d) The auditor must communicate, in writing, to the audit committee, all significant deficiencies and material weaknesses identified during the audit. (ID: 7949)

12. (c) A *material weakness* is a deficiency or combination of deficiencies, in internal control over financial reporting such that there is a reasonable possibility that a material misstatement of the company's financial statements will not be prevented or detected on a timely basis. A *significant deficiency* is a deficiency or a combination of deficiencies, in internal control that is less severe than a material weakness, yet important enough to merit attention by those responsible for oversight of the company's financial reporting. A *deficiency in internal control* exists when the design or operation of a control does not allow management or employees, in the normal course of performing their assigned functions, to prevent or detect misstatements on a timely basis. The various standards don't use the term material deficiency. (ID: 7950)

13. (a) In planning the audit of ICFR, the auditor should use the same materiality considerations used in planning the audit of a entity's annual financial statements. Materiality judgments are made in the light of surrounding circumstances and necessarily involve both quantitative and qualitative considerations. (ID: 7951)

14. (a) Inquiry alone does not provide sufficient evidence to support a conclusion about the effectiveness of a control. Some tests, by their nature, provide greater evidence than others. The following tests that an auditor might perform are listed in the order of least to most evidence that they ordinarily produce: inquiry, observation, inspection of relevant documentation, and reperformance of a control. Auditors normally use a mix of these procedures. (ID: 7953)

15. (a) Judgments about evidence sufficiency and other factors affecting the opinion must be the auditor's. The other statements are true. (ID: 7954)

16. (c) Controls regarding the company's annual stockholder meeting are not entity-level. Entity-level controls include: controls related to the control environment; controls over management override of other controls; the company's risk assessment processes; centralized processing and controls, including shared service environments; controls to monitor results of operations; controls to monitor other controls, including activities of the internal audit function, the audit committee, and self-assessment programs; controls over the period-end financial reporting process; and policies that address significant business control and risk management practices. (ID: 9920)

17. (c) According to PCAOB standards, *all* of the following conditions must be met for an auditor to complete this type of engagement: (1) management accepts responsibility for the effectiveness of internal control over *financial reporting* (ICFR) (**not** over operations); (2) management evaluates the effectiveness of the specific control(s) that it believes addresses the material weakness using the same control criteria that management used for its most recent annual assessment of ICFR and management's stated control objective(s); (3) management asserts that the specific control(s) identified is effective in achieving the stated control objective; (4) management supports its assertion with sufficient evidence, including documentation; and (5) management presents a written report that will accompany the auditor's report that contains all the required elements. (ID: 8269)

18. (d) The auditor's opinion on whether a previously reported material weakness continues to exist may be expressed as *the material weakness no longer exists*, not *has been eliminated*, or *the material weakness exists*. The PCAOB's guidance does not use the terms *unqualified* opinion and *adverse* opinion, instead, it refers simply to "an opinion" or "the auditor's opinion." The other answer alternatives are true. (ID: 89465)

19. (c) A change in accounting estimate is not a change in accounting principle. Editor Note: However, the auditor should evaluate and report on a change in accounting estimate effected by a change in accounting principle like other changes in accounting principle. (A change in accounting estimate effected by a change in accounting principle is a change in accounting estimate that is inseparable from the effect of a related change in accounting principle.) This guidance is the same for issuers (PCAOB audit standards) and nonissuers (GAAS). (ID: 9282)

20. (d) Preparation of pro forma financial statements is not required. (ID: 9283)

21. (a) The correction of a material misstatement in the previously issued financial statements of an *issuer* should be recognized in the auditor's report through the addition of an explanatory paragraph following the opinion paragraph. If the entity was a *non*issuer, the correction should be recognized in the auditor's report through the addition of an explanatory paragraph following the opinion paragraph *if the correction involved an error in accounting principle*. If no element of a principle or its application is included in the error, then its correction would *not* be recognized in the auditor's report for a nonissuer. Examples of such errors are mathematical mistakes, oversights, or misuse of facts that existed at the time the financial statements were originally prepared. (ID: 9281)

22. (c) A review performed in accordance with SSARS does **not** contemplate obtaining an understanding of the entity's internal control. (ID: 9284)

23. (d) If the CPA becomes aware that the interim financial information of a public entity is materially affected by a departure from GAAP, the CPA should modify the report. The modification should describe the nature of the departure and, if practicable, should state the effects on the interim financial information. It should *precede* the limited assurance paragraph. If the client was a *non*issuer and the CPA was following the SSARS, the separate paragraph should *follow* the limited assurance paragraph. (ID: 9285)

24. (b) The auditor should evaluate legal or regulatory matters of which the company is aware; however, the response to the auditor's letter of inquiry to the client's lawyer would not be available in the planning stage; it should be dated as close as possible to the date of the audit report. Additional matters for evaluation during the planning stage are knowledge of the company's internal control over financial reporting obtained during other engagements performed by the auditor; matters affecting the industry in which the company operates, such as financial reporting practices, economic conditions, laws and regulations, and technological changes; the auditor's preliminary judgments about materiality, risk, and, in integrated audits, other factors relating to the determination of material weaknesses; control deficiencies previously communicated to the audit committee or management; the type and extent of available evidence related to the effectiveness of the company's internal control over financial reporting; preliminary judgments about the effectiveness of internal control over financial reporting; public information about the company relevant to the evaluation of the likelihood of material financial statement misstatements and the effectiveness of the company's internal control over financial reporting; and knowledge about risks related to the company evaluated as part of the auditor's client acceptance and retention evaluation. (ID: 89466)

25. (c) If the auditor plans to assess control risk at less than the maximum by relying on controls, and the nature, extent, and timing of planned substantive procedures are based on that lower assessment, the auditor must obtain evidence that the controls selected for testing are designed effectively and operated effectively during the entire *period of reliance*, i.e., the period being covered by the company's financial statements, or the portion of that period, for which the auditor plans to rely on controls in order to modify the nature, timing, and extent of planned substantive procedures. Rotational testing is not allowed. (ID: 89467)

26. (c) When engaged to report on supplemental information that accompanies a public company's financial statements that is required by a regulatory authority that prescribes a lower materiality level than the one

used for the audit of the financial statements, the auditor should use the regulatory authority's level in planning and performing the audit procedures for the supplemental information. (ID: 90446)

27. (b) The International Auditing and Assurance Standards Board (IAASB) of the International Federation of Accountants issues International Standards on Auditing (ISA). (ID: 9286)

28. (d) There are no substantive differences per PCAOB auditing standards vs. ISA regarding requirements for written representations from management. (ID: 9287)

29. (b) The International Standards on Auditing require that the period of the auditor's evaluation of an entity's ability to continue as a going concern be at least 12 months from the date of the financial statements, but do not limit it to 12 months. (ID: 9288)

Solution 11-2 SIMULATION ANSWER: Research

Which citation in the professional standards explains why the audit report on internal control over financial reporting should be dated the same as the audit report on the financial statements for a public company?

PCAOB	AS	5	.	89	(ID: 89469)

.89 The auditor should date the audit report no earlier than the date on which the auditor has obtained sufficient appropriate evidence to support the auditor's opinion. Because the auditor cannot audit internal control over financial reporting without also auditing the financial statements, the reports should be dated the same.

Solution 11-3 SIMULATION ANSWER: Management Representations in an Audit of Internal Control Over Financial Reporting

Management Representations	Appropriate or Inappropriate?
1. Acknowledgment of management's responsibility for establishing and maintaining effective internal control over financial reporting.	Appropriate
2. A statement that management has performed an evaluation and made an assessment of the effectiveness of the company's internal control over financial reporting and specifying the control criteria.	Appropriate
3. A statement that management agreed to and relied on the auditor's procedures performed during the audits of internal control over financial reporting or the financial statements as part of the basis for management's assessment of the effectiveness of internal control over financial reporting.	Inappropriate
4. Management's conclusion, as set forth in its assessment, about the effectiveness of the company's internal control over financial reporting based on the control criteria for the same period covered by audit.	Inappropriate
5. A statement that management has disclosed to the auditor all deficiencies in the design or operation of internal control over financial reporting identified as part of management's evaluation, including separately disclosing to the auditor all such deficiencies that it believes to be significant deficiencies or material weaknesses in internal control over financial reporting.	Appropriate
6. A description of any fraud resulting in a material misstatement to the company's financial statements and any other fraud that does not result in a material misstatement to the company's financial statements but involves senior management or management or other employees who have a significant role in the company's internal control over financial reporting.	Appropriate
7. A statement as to whether control deficiencies identified and communicated to management during previous engagements have been resolved, and specifically identifying any that have not.	Inappropriate
8. A statement as to whether there were, subsequent to the date being reported on, any changes in internal control over financial reporting or other factors that might significantly affect internal control over financial reporting, including any corrective actions taken by management with regard to significant deficiencies and material weaknesses.	Appropriate

(ID: 89468)

1. Appropriate

Self-explanatory

2. Appropriate

Self-explanatory

3. Inappropriate

A statement that management *did not use*, not *agreed to and relied on*, the auditor's procedures performed during the audits of internal control over financial reporting or the financial statements as part of the basis for management's assessment of the effectiveness of internal control over financial reporting should be included.

4. Inappropriate

Management's conclusion, as set forth in its assessment, about the effectiveness of the company's internal control over financial reporting based on the control criteria *as of a specified date*, not *for the same period covered by audit* should be included.

5. Appropriate

Self-explanatory

6. Appropriate

Self-explanatory

7. Inappropriate

A statement as to whether control deficiencies identified and communicated to *the audit committee*, not *management*, during previous engagements have been resolved, and specifically identifying any that have not should be included.

8. Appropriate

Self-explanatory

Solution 11-4 SIMULATION ANSWER: Audit Report

1. P

A division of responsibility is indicated in the introductory paragraph. The report should disclose the magnitude of the portion of the financial statements audited by the other auditor. This may be done by stating the dollar amounts or percentages of one or more of the following: total assets, total revenues, or other appropriate criteria, whichever most clearly reveals the portion of the financial statements audited by the other auditor.

2. B

The report should indicate clearly, in the introductory, scope and opinion paragraphs, the division of responsibility as between that portion of the financial statements covered by the principal auditor's audit and that covered by the audit of the other auditor. The report should disclose the magnitude of the portion of the financial statements audited by the other auditor in the introductory paragraph. The other auditor may be named but only with his or her express permission and provided his or her report is presented together with that of the principal auditor. The question stated the other auditor's report would not be presented.

3. P

The phrase, "whether caused by error or fraud," is not part of the standard auditor's report.

4. W

The phrase, "significant estimates made by management," is included in the scope paragraph of the standard report.

5. W

Control risk is not mentioned in the standard report.

6. W

The phrase, "evaluating the overall financial statement presentation" is included in the scope paragraph of the standard report.

7. P

As the investigation is adequately disclosed in the notes to the financial statements, it need not be mentioned in the auditor's report. If the auditor wanted to emphasize this matter and yet still issue an unqualified opinion, the auditor would mention it in an explanatory paragraph following the opinion paragraph.

8. P

If an auditor had previously qualified the opinion on the financial statements of a prior period because of a departure from GAAP, and the prior period financial statements are restated in the current period, the updating report should indicate that the statements have been restated in a paragraph preceding the opinion paragraph. (ID: 9237)

Solution 11-5 SIMULATION ANSWER: Audit Report Modifications

1. E

When a qualified opinion results from a limitation on the scope of the audit or an insufficiency of audit evidence, the situation should be described in an explanatory paragraph preceding the opinion paragraph and referred to in both the scope and opinion paragraphs of the auditor's report.

2. B

If, after considering identified conditions and events and management's plans, the auditor concludes that substantial doubt about the entity's ability to continue as a going concern for a reasonable period of time remains, the audit report should include an explanatory paragraph (following the opinion paragraph) to reflect that conclusion. Inadequate disclosure with respect to an entity's ability to continue as a going concern is a departure from GAAP, resulting in either a qualified opinion or an adverse opinion. In this case, however, because it was concluded that financial statement disclosures were adequate, an unqualified opinion with an explanatory paragraph is appropriate.

3. J

If the auditor decides that it is appropriate to serve as the principal auditor, the auditor must then decide whether to make reference in the report to the audit performed by another auditor. If the principal auditor decides to assume responsibility for the work of the other auditor insofar as that work relates to the principal auditor's expression of an opinion taken as a whole, no reference should be made to the other auditor's work or report.

4. C

If a company issues financial statements that purport to present financial position and results of operations but omits the related statement of cash flows, the auditor will normally conclude that the omission requires qualification of his opinion. The auditor is not required to prepare a basic financial statement and include it in the audit report if the company's management declines to present the statement. The circumstances surrounding the qualification are to be reported in a separate paragraph preceding the opinion paragraph. The opinion paragraph should then be modified using the appropriate "except for" wording, making reference to the separate explanatory paragraph.

5. B

Changes in accounting principle having a material effect on the financial statements require recognition in the independent auditor's report through the addition of an explanatory paragraph (following the opinion paragraph). Such an explanatory paragraph should identify the nature of the change and refer the reader to the note in the financial statements that discusses the change in detail.

6. J

Circumstances that may require the auditor to add an explanatory paragraph to a standard report, while not precluding an unqualified opinion, do not include an uncertainty. An emphasis paragraph may be added; however, emphasis paragraphs are never required—they are added solely at the auditor's discretion.

7. C

The auditor should disclose, in a separate explanatory paragraph preceding the opinion paragraph, all the substantive reasons for a departure from generally accepted accounting principles. The opinion paragraph should then be modified using the appropriate "except for" wording, making reference to the separate explanatory paragraph. (ID: 9238)

Solution 11-6 SIMULATION ANSWER: Audit Report

1. P

Concurrence with a change in accounting principle is implicit and need not be explicitly stated. If management does not provide reasonable justification for a change, the auditor's opinion would be qualified.

2. P

Such a reference is not required.

3. B

The opinion paragraph should extend the auditor's opinion beyond the statement of financial position to include the results of operations and cash flows, not changes in stockholders' equity.

4. B

If an auditor elects to emphasize an uncertainty, it should be in a paragraph following the opinion paragraph. No reference should be made to the uncertainty in the introductory, scope, or opinion paragraphs.

5. W

If the auditor concludes that substantial doubt about the entity's ability to continue as a going concern exists, the terms *substantial doubt* and *going concern* are required to be used in an explanatory paragraph.

6. W

If the auditor concludes that substantial doubt about the entity's ability to continue as a going concern exists, the terms *substantial doubt* and *going concern* are required to be used in an explanatory paragraph.

7. P

This sentence is the last sentence in the standard going concern explanatory paragraph.

8. P

Auditors use dual dates when subsequent events, not going concern uncertainties, are mentioned. (ID: 9239)

Solution 11-7 SIMULATION ANSWER: Types of Opinions

1. A. Qualified opinion

Restrictions on the scope of an audit, whether imposed by the client or by the circumstances, such as an inability to obtain sufficient appropriate audit evidence, or an inadequacy in the accounting records, may require the auditor to qualify the opinion, if material, or to disclaim an opinion, if very material. The problem stated that the conditions in all the situations were material, not very material.

2. E. Explanatory language added to standard report

Substantial doubt about an entity's ability to continue as a going concern is one of the circumstances which does not affect the auditor's unqualified opinion (if financial statement disclosure is adequate), but does require the addition of an explanatory paragraph after the opinion paragraph.

3. B. Unqualified opinion

If the principal auditor is satisfied as to the independence and professional reputation of the other auditor and the audit performed by the other auditor; and adopts appropriate measures to assure the coordination of activities with those of the other auditor in order to achieve a proper review of matters affecting the consolidating or combining of accounts in the financial statements, the principal auditor may express an unqualified opinion on the financial statements taken as a whole.

4. A. Qualified opinion

If a company issues financial statements that purport to present financial position and results of operations but omits the related statement of cash flows, the auditor will normally conclude that the omission requires qualification of the opinion. The auditor is not required to prepare a basic financial statement and include it in the report if the company's management declines to present the statement.

5. E. Explanatory language added to standard report

The auditor concurs with the change in accounting principle. Therefore, the auditor may express an unqualified opinion; however, the addition of an explanatory paragraph, following the opinion paragraph, is required.

6. B. Unqualified opinion

If, after considering existing conditions and available evidence, the auditor concludes that sufficient audit evidence supports management's assertions about an uncertainty and its presentation or disclosure, an unqualified opinion ordinarily is appropriate. An emphasis paragraph may be added, after the opinion paragraph, but it is not required (emphasis paragraphs are added solely at the auditor's discretion).

7. A. Qualified opinion

When financial statements are affected by a departure from generally accepted accounting principles the auditor should express a qualified opinion (if it's material) or an adverse opinion (if it's very material). Factors to consider when deciding which of these opinions to issue include the dollar magnitude of the effect; the qualitative and quantitative aspects of the departure; the pervasiveness of the misstatement; and the effects on the other financial statements. In this case, the problem stated that the conditions in all the situations were material, not very material. (ID: 9236)

CHAPTER 12

OTHER TYPES OF REPORTS

AU Identifier Used for Clarified US GAAS in This Textbook

We have not continued to use the temporary AU-C identifier for the clarified auditing standards issued by the American Institute of Certified Public Accountants (AICPA). In this textbook these standards have an AU identifier.

CHAPTER 12

OTHER TYPES OF REPORTS

I. Engagement to Report on Supplementary Information (AU 725)

A. Overview

1. **Definition of Supplementary Information** Supplementary information is defined as information presented outside the basic financial statements, excluding required supplementary information, that is not considered necessary for the financial statements to be fairly presented in accordance with the applicable financial reporting framework (AFRF). Such information may be presented in a document containing the audited financial statements or separate from the financial statements. Examples include:

   - Additional details or explanations of items in or related to the basic financial statements
   - Consolidating information
   - Historical summaries of items extracted from the basic financial statements
   - Statistical data
   - Other material, some of which may be from sources outside the accounting system or outside the entity

   Editor Note: The auditor's responsibility for financial and nonfinancial information (other than the financial statements and the related audit report) that is included in a document containing audited financial statements and the related audit report, excluding required supplementary information, is addressed in AU 720, *Other Information in Documents Containing Audited Financial Statements*; see chapter 8 of this text.

2. **Engagement Objective** Evaluate the presentation of the supplementary information and report on whether it is fairly stated, in all material respects, in relation to the financial statements as a whole.

3. **Required Conditions** The auditor should determine that all of the following conditions are met in order to opine on supplementary information.

   a. The supplementary information was derived from, and relates directly to, the underlying accounting and other records used to prepare the financial statements.

   b. The supplementary information relates to the same period as the financial statements.

   c. The auditor issued an audit report on the financial statements that contained neither an adverse opinion nor a disclaimer of opinion.

   d. The supplementary information will accompany the entity's audited financial statements, or such audited financial statements will be made readily available by the entity.

   Editor Note: Audited financial statements are deemed to be readily available if a third-party user can obtain the audited financial statements without any further action by the entity. For example, financial statements on an entity's website may be considered readily available, but being available upon request is *not* considered readily available.

B. **Management's Responsibilities**
The auditor should obtain the agreement of management that it acknowledges and understands its responsibility:

1. For the preparation of the supplementary information in accordance with the applicable criteria

2. To provide the auditor with certain written representations

3. To include the audit report on the supplementary information in any document that contains the supplementary information and indicates that the auditor has reported on such supplementary information

4. To present the supplementary information with the audited financial statements or, if the supplementary information will not be presented with the audited financial statements, to make the audited financial statements readily available to the intended users of the supplementary information no later than the date of issuance by the entity of the supplementary information and the related audit report

C. **Procedures**

1. **Written Management Representations** The auditor should obtain written representations from management:

   a. That it acknowledges its responsibility for the presentation of the supplementary information in accordance with the applicable criteria

   b. That it believes the supplementary information, including its form and content, is fairly presented in accordance with the applicable criteria

   c. That the methods of measurement or presentation have not changed from those used in the prior period or, if they have, the reasons for such changes

   d. About any significant assumptions or interpretations underlying the measurement or presentation of the supplementary information

   e. That when the supplementary information is not presented with the audited financial statements, management will make the audited financial statements readily available to the intended users of the supplementary information no later than the date of issuance by the entity of the supplementary information and the related audit report

2. **Other Procedures** In addition to the procedures performed during the audit of the financial statements and obtaining the preceding written representations from management, the auditor should perform the following procedures *using the same materiality level used in the audit of the financial statements*:

   a. Inquire of management about the purpose of the supplementary information and the criteria used by management to prepare it, such as an AFRF; criteria established by a regulator; a contractual agreement; or other requirements.

   b. Determine whether the form and content of the supplementary information complies with the applicable criteria.

   c. Obtain an understanding about the methods of preparing the supplementary information and determine whether these methods have changed from those used in the prior period and, if so, the reasons for such changes.

d. Compare and reconcile the supplementary information to the underlying accounting and other records used in preparing the financial statements or to the financial statements themselves.

e. Inquire of management about any significant assumptions or interpretations underlying the measurement or presentation of the supplementary information.

f. Evaluate the appropriateness and completeness of the supplementary information.

Editor Note: With respect to the supplementary information, the auditor is **not** required to obtain a separate understanding of the entity's internal control or to assess fraud risk.

3. **Subsequent Events** The auditor has no responsibility for the consideration of subsequent events with respect to the supplementary information. However, if information comes to the auditor's attention prior to or after the release of the audit report on the financial statements regarding subsequent events or subsequently discovered facts that affect the financial statements, the auditor should apply the relevant requirements in AU 560, *Subsequent Events and Subsequently Discovered Facts* (see chapter 8 of this text).

D. **Reporting**
The guidance in this standard may also be applied, with the report wording adapted as necessary, when an auditor has been engaged to report on whether required supplementary information is fairly stated, in all material respects, in relation to the financial statements as a whole.

1. **Reporting When Supplementary Information Presented With Financial Statements** The auditor should report on the supplementary information in *either*:

- An other-matter paragraph in the audit report on the financial statements or
- A separate report on the supplementary information

The other-matter paragraph or separate report should include the following elements:

a. A statement that the audit was conducted for the purpose of forming an opinion on the financial statements as a whole.

b. A statement that the supplementary information is presented for purposes of additional analysis and is not a required part of the financial statements.

c. A statement that the supplementary information is the responsibility of management and was derived from, and relates directly to, the underlying accounting and other records used to prepare the financial statements.

d. A statement that the supplementary information has been subjected to the auditing procedures applied in the audit of the financial statements and certain additional procedures, including comparing and reconciling such information directly to the underlying accounting and other records used to prepare the financial statements or to the financial statements themselves and other additional procedures, in accordance with auditing standards generally accepted in the United States of America.

e. If the auditor issues an unmodified opinion on the financial statements and the auditor has concluded that the supplementary information is fairly stated, in all material respects, in relation to the financial statements as a whole, a statement that, in the auditor's opinion, the supplementary information is fairly stated, in all material respects, in relation to the financial statements as a whole.

Exhibit 1 ▸ Supplementary Information Other-Matter Paragraph / Unmodified Opinion Issued on Both Financial Statements & Supplementary Information

> Our audit was conducted for the purpose of forming an opinion on the financial statements as a whole. The [*identify accompanying supplementary information*] is presented for purposes of additional analysis and is not a required part of the financial statements. Such information is the responsibility of management and was derived from and relates directly to the underlying accounting and other records used to prepare the financial statements. The information has been subjected to the auditing procedures applied in the audit of the financial statements and certain additional procedures, including comparing and reconciling such information directly to the underlying accounting and other records used to prepare the financial statements or to the financial statements themselves, and other additional procedures in accordance with auditing standards generally accepted in the United States of America. In our opinion, the information is fairly stated in all material respects in relation to the financial statements as a whole.

f. If the auditor issues a qualified opinion on the financial statements and the qualification has an effect on the supplementary information, a statement that, in the auditor's opinion, except for the effects on the supplementary information of (refer to the paragraph in the auditor's report explaining the qualification), such information is fairly stated, in all material respects, in relation to the financial statements as a whole.

Exhibit 2 ▸ Supplementary Information Other-Matter Paragraph / Qualified Opinion Issued on Both Financial Statements & Supplementary Information

> Our audit was conducted for the purpose of forming an opinion on the financial statements as a whole. The [*identify accompanying supplementary information*] is presented for purposes of additional analysis and is not a required part of the financial statements. Such information is the responsibility of management and was derived from and relates directly to the underlying accounting and other records used to prepare the financial statements. The information has been subjected to the auditing procedures applied in the audit of the financial statements and certain additional procedures, including comparing and reconciling such information directly to the underlying accounting and other records used to prepare the financial statements or to the financial statements themselves, and other additional procedures in accordance with auditing standards generally accepted in the United States of America. In our opinion, except for the effect on the supplementary information of [*describe reason for qualification of the auditor's opinion on the financial statements and reference the other-matter paragraph*], the information is fairly stated in all material respects in relation to the financial statements as a whole.

2. **Separate Report on Supplementary Information When Supplementary Information Is *Not* Presented With Financial Statements**

   a. **Additional Reporting Elements for Separate Report** When the audited financial statements are not presented with the supplementary information, the auditor should report on the supplementary information in a separate report. This report should include, in addition to the preceding elements:

      (1) A reference to the report on the financial statements

      (2) The date of that report

      (3) The nature of the opinion expressed on the financial statements

      (4) Any report modifications

b. **Separate Report May Be Restricted Use** When reporting in a separate report, the auditor may consider including an alert that restricts its use solely to the appropriate specified parties to avoid potential misinterpretation or misunderstanding of the supplementary information that is not presented with the financial statements.

Exhibit 3 ▸ Separate Report on Supplementary Information / Unmodified Opinion Issued on Both Financial Statements & Supplementary Information

> We have audited the financial statements of XYZ Entity as of and for the year ended June 30, 20X1, and have issued our report thereon dated [*date of the auditor's report on the financial statements*] which contained an unmodified opinion on those financial statements. Our audit was performed for the purpose of forming an opinion on the financial statements as a whole. The [*identify supplementary information*] is presented for the purposes of additional analysis and is not a required part of the financial statements. Such information is the responsibility of management and was derived from and relates directly to the underlying accounting and other records used to prepare the financial statements. The information has been subjected to the auditing procedures applied in the audit of the financial statements and certain additional procedures, including comparing and reconciling such information directly to the underlying accounting and other records used to prepare the financial statements or to the financial statements themselves, and other additional procedures in accordance with auditing standards generally accepted in the United States of America. In our opinion, the information is fairly stated in all material respects in relation to the financial statements as a whole.

3. **Adverse Opinion or Disclaimer of Opinion on Financial Statements Precludes Reporting on Supplementary Information** When the audit report on the financial statements contains an adverse opinion or a disclaimer of opinion, the auditor is precluded from expressing an opinion on whether supplementary information is fairly stated. When permitted by law or regulation, the auditor may withdraw from an engagement to report on the supplementary information. If the auditor does not withdraw, the audit report on the supplementary information should state that because of the significance of the matter disclosed in the audit report, it is inappropriate to, and the auditor does not, express an opinion on the supplementary information.

Exhibit 4 ▸ Other-Matter Paragraph for No Opinion on Supplementary Information Due to Adverse Opinion Issued on Financial Statements

> Our audit was conducted for the purpose of forming an opinion on the financial statements as a whole. The [*identify accompanying supplementary information*] is presented for the purposes of additional analysis and is not a required part of the financial statements. Because of the significance of the matter described above [*the auditor may describe the basis for the adverse opinion*], it is inappropriate to and we do not express an opinion on the supplementary information referred to above.

Exhibit 5 ▸ Other-Matter Paragraph for No Opinion on Supplementary Information Due to a Disclaimer of Opinion Issued on Financial Statements

> We were engaged for the purpose of forming an opinion on the basic financial statements as a whole. The [*identify accompanying supplementary information*] is presented for the purposes of additional analysis and is not a required part of the financial statements. Because of the significance of the matter described above [*the auditor may describe the basis for the disclaimer of opinion*], it is inappropriate to and we do not express an opinion on the supplementary information referred to above.

4. **Date of Audit Report on Supplementary Information** The date of the audit report on the supplementary information should not be earlier than the date on which the auditor completed the procedures required to render an opinion on it.

5. **Supplementary Information Materially Misstated** The auditor should discuss the matter with management and propose appropriate revision of the supplementary information.

   If management does **not** revise the supplementary information, the auditor should either:

   a. Modify the auditor's opinion on the supplementary information and describe the misstatement in the audit report (this does not affect the opinion on the financial statements) or

   b. If a separate report is being issued on the supplementary information, withhold the audit report on the supplementary information

6. **Additional Reporting Illustrations**

Exhibit 6 ▶ Separate Report on Supplementary Information / Qualified Opinion Issued on Both Financial Statements & Supplementary Information

> We have audited the financial statements of XYZ Entity as of and for the year ended June 30, 20X1, and have issued our report thereon dated [*date of the auditor's report on the financial statements, the nature of the opinion expressed on the financial statements, and a description of the report modifications*]. Our audit was performed for the purpose of forming an opinion on the financial statements as a whole. The [*identify supplementary information*] is presented for the purposes of additional analysis and is not a required part of the financial statements. Such information is the responsibility of management and was derived from and relates directly to the underlying accounting and other records used to prepare the financial statements. The information has been subjected to the auditing procedures applied in the audit of the financial statements and certain additional procedures, including comparing and reconciling such information directly to the underlying accounting and other records used to prepare the financial statements or to the financial statements themselves, and other additional procedures in accordance with auditing standards generally accepted in the United States of America. In our opinion, except for the effect on the accompanying information of the qualified opinion on the financial statements as described above, the information is fairly stated in all material respects in relation to the financial statements as a whole.

Exhibit 7 ▶ Separate Report for No Opinion on Supplementary Information Due to Adverse Opinion Issued on Financial Statements

> We have audited the financial statements of XYZ Entity as of and for the year ended June 30, 20X1, and have issued our report thereon dated [*date of the auditor's report on the financial statements*] which stated that the financial statements are not presented fairly in accordance with [*identify the applicable financial reporting framework (for example, accounting principles generally accepted in the United States of America [GAAP])*] because [*describe reasons*]. The [*identify the supplementary information*] is presented for purposes of additional analysis and is not a required part of the basic financial statements. Because of the significance of the matter discussed above, it is inappropriate to and we do not express an opinion on the supplementary information referred to above.

Exhibit 8 ▸ Separate Report for No Opinion on Supplementary Information Due to Disclaimer of Opinion Issued on Financial Statements

> We were engaged to audit the financial statements of XYZ Entity as of and for the year ended June 30, 20X1, and have issued our report thereon dated [*date of the auditor's report on the financial statements*]. However, the scope of our audit of the financial statements was not sufficient to enable us to express an opinion because [*describe reasons*] and accordingly we did not express an opinion on such financial statements. The [*identify the supplementary information*] is presented for purposes of additional analysis and is not a required part of the basic financial statements. Because of the significance of the matter discussed above, it is inappropriate to and we do not express an opinion on the supplementary information referred to above.

II. Audits of Special-Purpose Financial Statements (AU 800)

A. Overview

This standard addresses some special considerations in the application of US GAAS to an audit of a *complete set* of financial statements, including the related notes, prepared in accordance with a special-purpose framework.

The requirements of the applicable financial reporting framework (AFRF) determine the form and content of the financial statements and what constitutes a complete set of financial statements.

Special-purpose frameworks include:

- Cash
- Tax
- Regulatory
- An other basis of accounting
- Contractual

The contractual basis is **not** considered an other comprehensive basis of accounting; however, it is included along with the other comprehensive bases of accounting (cash, tax, regulatory, and other) as a type of special-purpose framework.

There is an exception to this standard's application to a complete set of financial statements. When the auditor reports on an incomplete presentation, but one that is otherwise in accordance with GAAP, it is addressed by AU 805, *Special Considerations—Audits of Single Financial Statements and Specific Elements, Accounts, or Items of a Financial Statement*, with the following exception. If the incomplete presentation is prepared in accordance with a regulatory or contractual basis of accounting, then this standard (AU 800) is applicable.

1. **Objective** The objective of the auditor, when applying US GAAS in an audit of financial statements prepared in accordance with a special-purpose framework, is to appropriately address the special considerations that are relevant to:

   a. The acceptance of the engagement

   b. The planning and performance of that engagement

   c. Forming an opinion and reporting on the financial statements

2. **Definitions**

   a. **Special-Purpose Financial Statements** Financial statements prepared in accordance with a special-purpose framework.

   b. **Special-Purpose Framework** A financial reporting framework other than GAAP that is one of the following bases of accounting:

      (1) **Cash Basis** A basis of accounting that the entity uses to record cash receipts and disbursements and modifications of the cash basis having substantial support (for example, recording depreciation on fixed assets)

      (2) **Tax Basis** A basis of accounting that the entity uses to file its tax return for the period covered by the financial statements

      (3) **Regulatory Basis** A basis of accounting that the entity uses to comply with the requirements or financial reporting provisions of a regulatory agency to whose jurisdiction the entity is subject (for example, a basis of accounting that insurance companies use pursuant to the accounting practices prescribed or permitted by a state insurance commission)

      (4) **Other Basis** A basis of accounting that uses a definite set of logical, reasonable criteria that is applied to all material items appearing in the financial statements

      (5) **Contractual Basis** A basis of accounting that the entity uses to comply with an agreement between the entity and one or more third parties other than the auditor

B. **Considerations When Accepting the Engagement**

1. **Acceptability of Financial Reporting Framework** US GAAS requires the auditor to determine the acceptability of the financial reporting framework applied in the preparation of the financial statements. In an audit of special-purpose financial statements, the auditor should obtain an understanding of the:

   a. Purpose for which the financial statements are prepared

   b. Intended users

   c. Steps taken by management to determine that the AFRF is acceptable in the circumstances

2. **Preconditions for Audit** US GAAS requires the auditor to establish whether the preconditions for an audit are present, including determining whether the financial reporting framework to be applied in the preparation of the financial statements is acceptable. In an audit of special-purpose financial statements, the auditor should obtain the agreement of management that it acknowledges and understands its responsibility to include all informative disclosures that are appropriate for the special-purpose framework used to prepare the entity's financial statements, including:

   a. A description of the special-purpose framework, including a summary of significant accounting policies, and how the framework differs from GAAP, the effects of which need *not* be quantified

   b. Informative disclosures similar to those required by GAAP, in the case of special-purpose financial statements that contain items that are the same as, or similar to, those in financial statements prepared in accordance with GAAP

c. A description of any significant interpretations of the contract on which the special-purpose financial statements are based, in the case of special-purpose financial statements prepared in accordance with a contractual basis of accounting

d. Additional disclosures beyond those specifically required by the framework that may be necessary for the special-purpose financial statements to achieve fair presentation

C. Considerations When Planning & Performing Audit

1. In planning and performing an audit of special-purpose financial statements, the auditor should adapt and apply all US GAAS relevant to the audit as necessary in the circumstances of the engagement.

   Editor Note: For example, according to US GAAS, judgments about matters that are material to users of the financial statements are based on a consideration of the common financial information needs of users as a group. In an audit of special-purpose financial statements, those judgments may be based on a consideration of the financial information needs of the intended users.

2. US GAAS requires the auditor to obtain an understanding of the entity's selection and application of accounting policies.

   In the case of special-purpose financial statements prepared in accordance with a contractual basis of accounting, the auditor should obtain an understanding of any significant interpretations of the contract that management made in the preparation of those financial statements. An interpretation is significant when adoption of another reasonable interpretation would have produced a material difference in the information presented in the financial statements.

D. Forming an Opinion & Reporting Considerations

When forming an opinion and reporting on special-purpose financial statements, the auditor should apply the requirements in AU 700, *Forming an Opinion and Reporting on Financial Statements*. When the auditor concludes that a modification to the auditor's opinion is necessary, the auditor should apply the requirements in AU 705, *Modifications to the Opinion in the Independent Auditor's Report*.

1. Description of AFRF

a. **Evaluation of Financial Statement Description of AFRF** US GAAS requires the auditor to evaluate whether the financial statements adequately refer to or describe the AFRF. In an audit of special-purpose financial statements, the auditor should evaluate the following.

   (1) **Financial Statement Titles** Whether the statements are suitably titled

   (2) **Significant Accounting Policies** Whether the statements include a summary of significant accounting policies

   (3) **AFRF vs. GAAP** Whether the statements adequately describe how the special-purpose framework differs from GAAP; the description of how the special-purpose framework differs from GAAP ordinarily only includes the material differences and the effects of these differences need *not* be quantified

   Editor Note: Terms such as *balance sheet*, *statement of financial position*, *statement of income*, *statement of operations*, and *statement of cash flows*, or similar unmodified titles, are generally understood to be applicable only to financial statements that are intended to present financial position, results of operations, or cash flows in accordance with GAAP. Accordingly, the auditor is required to evaluate whether the financial statements are suitably titled. For example, cash basis financial statements might be titled *statement of assets and liabilities arising from cash transactions* or *statement of revenue collected and expenses paid*; a financial statement prepared on a regulatory basis of accounting might be titled *statement of income—regulatory basis*.

b. **Contractual Basis Interpretations** In the case of special-purpose financial statements prepared in accordance with a contractual basis of accounting, the auditor should also evaluate whether the financial statements adequately describe any significant interpretations of the contract on which the financial statements are based.

2. **Fair Presentation** US GAAS requires the auditor to evaluate whether the financial statements achieve fair presentation. In an audit of special-purpose financial statements when the special-purpose financial statements contain items that are the same as, or similar to, those in financial statements prepared in accordance with GAAP, the auditor should evaluate whether the financial statements include informative disclosures similar to those required by GAAP.

   The auditor should also evaluate whether additional disclosures, beyond those specifically required by the framework, related to matters that are not specifically identified on the face of the financial statements or other disclosures are necessary for the financial statements to achieve fair presentation. This requires consideration of:

   a. The overall presentation, structure and content of the financial statements

   b. Whether the financial statements, including the related notes, represent the underlying transactions and events in a manner that achieves fair presentation

3. **Audit Report** In addition to the requirements addressed in AU 700, *Forming an Opinion and Reporting on Financial Statements*, in an audit report on special-purpose financial statements, the:

   a. Explanation of management's responsibility for the financial statements should also make reference to its responsibility for determining that the AFRF is acceptable in the circumstances, *when management has a choice* of financial reporting frameworks

   b. Audit report should also describe the purpose for which the financial statements are prepared or refer to a note in the special-purpose financial statements that contains that information, when the financial statements are prepared in accordance with:

      (1) A regulatory or contractual basis of accounting

      (2) An other basis of accounting, and the auditor is required to restrict use of the audit report because the subject matter is based on:

         (a) Measurement or disclosure criteria that are determined by the auditor to be suitable only for a limited number of users who can be presumed to have an adequate understanding of the criteria

         (b) Measurement or disclosure criteria that are available only to the specified parties

4. **Alerting Readers in Emphasis-of-Matter Paragraph That Financial Statements Are Prepared in Accordance With Special-Purpose Framework** Except when the financial statements are prepared in accordance with a regulatory basis of accounting and the financial statements together with the audit report are intended for general use, the audit report on special-purpose financial statements should include an emphasis-of-matter paragraph, under an appropriate heading, that:

   a. Indicates that the financial statements are prepared in accordance with the applicable special-purpose framework

   b. Refers to the note to the financial statements that describes that framework

   c. States that the special-purpose framework is a basis of accounting other than GAAP

5. **Restricting Use of Auditor's Report in Other-Matter Paragraph** Except when the financial statements are prepared in accordance with a regulatory basis of accounting and the financial statements together with the audit report are intended for general use, the audit report on special-purpose financial statements should include an other-matter paragraph, under an appropriate heading, that restricts the use of the audit report when the special-purpose financial statements are prepared in accordance with:

   a. A regulatory or contractual basis of accounting

   b. An other basis of accounting when the subject matter is based on:

      (1) Measurement or disclosure criteria that are determined by the auditor to be suitable only for a limited number of users who can be presumed to have an adequate understanding of the criteria

      (2) Measurement or disclosure criteria that are available only to the specified parties

6. **Regulatory Basis Financial Statements Intended for General Use** If the special-purpose financial statements are prepared in accordance with a regulatory basis of accounting, and the special-purpose financial statements together with the audit report are intended for general use, the auditor should **not** include the emphasis-of-matter or other-matter paragraphs just described.

   Instead, the auditor should express an opinion about whether the special-purpose financial statements are presented fairly, in all material respects, in accordance with GAAP. The auditor should also, in a separate paragraph, express an opinion about whether the financial statements are prepared in accordance with the special-purpose framework.

7. **Audit Report Prescribed by Law or Regulation** If the prescribed specific layout, form, or wording of the audit report is not acceptable or would cause an auditor to make a statement that the auditor has no basis to make, the auditor should reword the prescribed form of report or attach an appropriately worded separate report.

   If the auditor is required by law or regulation to use a specific layout, form, or wording of the audit report, the report should refer to US GAAS *only if* the report includes, at a minimum, *each* of the elements given below.

   a. A title

   b. An addressee

   c. An introductory paragraph that identifies the special-purpose financial statements audited

d. A description of the responsibility of management for the preparation and fair presentation of the special-purpose financial statements

e. A reference to management's responsibility for determining that the AFRF is acceptable in the circumstances when management has a choice of financial reporting frameworks in the preparation of such financial statements

f. A description of the purpose for which the financial statements are prepared when the financial statements are prepared in accordance with

   (1) A regulatory or contractual basis of accounting

   (2) An other basis of accounting, and the auditor is required to restrict use of the auditor's report because the subject matter is based on:

      (a) Measurement or disclosure criteria that are determined by the auditor to be suitable only for a limited number of users who can be presumed to have an adequate understanding of the criteria

      (b) Measurement or disclosure criteria that are available only to the specified parties

g. A description of the auditor's responsibility to express an opinion on the special-purpose financial statements and the scope of the audit, that includes:

   (1) A reference to US GAAS and, if applicable, the law or regulation

   (2) A description of an audit in accordance with those standards

h. An opinion paragraph containing an expression of opinion on the special-purpose financial statements and a reference to the special-purpose framework used to prepare the financial statements (including identifying the origin of the framework) and, if applicable, an opinion on whether the special-purpose financial statements are presented fairly, in all material respects, in accordance with GAAP when the financial statements are prepared in accordance with a regulatory basis of accounting and the financial statements together with the audit report are intended for general use.

i. An emphasis-of-matter paragraph that indicates that the financial statements are prepared in accordance with a special-purpose framework except when the financial statements are prepared in accordance with a regulatory basis of accounting and the financial statements together with the audit report are intended for general use.

j. An other-matter paragraph that restricts the use of the auditor's report except when the financial statements are prepared in accordance with a regulatory basis of accounting and the financial statements together with the audit report are intended for general use.

k. The auditor's signature

l. The auditor's city and state

m. The date of the audit report

Exhibit 9 ▸ Summary of Special-Purpose Framework Reporting Requirements

	Cash Basis	Tax Basis	Regulatory Basis	Contractual Basis	Other Basis	Regulatory Basis (General Use)
Opinion(s)	Single opinion on special-purpose framework	Same	Same	Same	Same	Dual opinion on special-purpose framework and GAAP
Description of purpose for which financial statements are prepared	No	No	Yes	Yes	When subject matter criteria is suitable/ available only to limited/specified parties	Yes
Emphasis-of-matter paragraph regarding special-purpose framework	Yes	Yes	Yes	Yes	Yes	No
Other-matter paragraph restricting use of audit report	No	No	Yes	Yes	When subject matter criteria is suitable/ available only to limited/specified parties	No

Editor Note: The changes to the "standard" report required by the use of special-purpose reporting frameworks in the following exhibits are underlined for illustrative purposes only. The content omitted from the "standard" report is shown with strikethrough.

Exhibit 10 ▸ Audit Report on Financial Statements Prepared in Accordance With *Cash* Basis of Accounting; Management Has *Choice* of Financial Reporting Frameworks

Independent Auditor's Report

[*Appropriate Addressee*]

We have audited the accompanying financial statements of ABC Partnership, which comprise the ~~balance sheet~~ statement of assets and liabilities arising from cash transactions as of December 31, 20X1, and the related statement~~s of income, changes in stockholders' equity, and cash flows~~ of revenue collected and expenses paid for the year then ended, and the related notes to the financial statements.

Management's Responsibility for the Financial Statements

Management is responsible for the preparation and fair presentation of these financial statements in accordance with ~~accounting principles generally accepted in the United States of America;~~ the cash basis of accounting described in Note X; this includes determining that the cash basis of accounting is an acceptable basis for the preparation of the financial statements in the circumstances. ~~this includes~~ Management is also responsible for the design, implementation, and maintenance of internal control relevant to the preparation and fair presentation of financial statements that are free from material misstatement, whether due to fraud or error.

Auditor's Responsibility

Our responsibility is to express an opinion on these financial statements based on our audit. We conducted our audit in accordance with auditing standards generally accepted in the United States of America. Those standards require that we plan and perform the audit to obtain reasonable assurance about whether the financial statements are free from material misstatement.

An audit involves performing procedures to obtain audit evidence about the amounts and disclosures in the financial statements. The procedures selected depend on the auditor's judgment, including the assessment of the risks of material misstatement of the financial statements, whether due to fraud or error. In making those risk assessments, the auditor considers internal control relevant to the partnership's preparation and fair presentation of the financial statements in order to design audit procedures that are appropriate in the circumstances, but not for the purpose of expressing an opinion on the effectiveness of the partnership's internal control. Accordingly, we express no such opinion. An audit also includes evaluating the appropriateness of accounting policies used and the reasonableness of significant accounting estimates made by management, as well as evaluating the overall presentation of the financial statements.

We believe that the audit evidence we have obtained is sufficient and appropriate to provide a basis for our audit opinion.

Opinion

In our opinion, the financial statements referred to above present fairly, in all material respects, the ~~financial position~~ assets and liabilities arising from cash transactions of ABC Partnership as of December 31, 20X1, and ~~the results of its operations and its cash flows~~ its revenue collected and expenses paid during ~~for~~ the year then ended in accordance with ~~accounting principles generally accepted in the United States of America~~ the cash basis of accounting described in Note X.

Basis of Accounting

We draw attention to Note X of the financial statements, which describes the basis of accounting. The financial statements are prepared on the cash basis of accounting, which is a basis of accounting other than accounting principles generally accepted in the United States of America. Our opinion is not modified with respect to this matter.

[*Auditor's signature*]

[*Auditor's city and state*]

[*Date of the audit report*]

Exhibit 11 ▸ Audit Report on Financial Statements Prepared in Accordance With *Tax* Basis of Accounting; Management Does *Not* Have Choice of Financial Reporting Frameworks

Independent Auditor's Report

[*Appropriate Addressee*]

We have audited the accompanying financial statements of ABC Partnership, which comprise the ~~balance sheet~~ statements of assets, liabilities, and capital-income tax basis as of December 31, 20X1, and the related statements of ~~income, changes in stockholders' equity, and cash flows~~ revenue and expenses—income tax basis and of changes in partners' capital accounts—income tax basis for the year then ended, and the related notes to the financial statements.

Management's Responsibility for the Financial Statements

Management is responsible for the preparation and fair presentation of these financial statements in accordance with ~~accounting principles generally accepted in the United States of America;~~ the basis of accounting the Partnership uses for income tax purposes; this includes the design, implementation, and maintenance of internal control relevant to the preparation and fair presentation of financial statements that are free from material misstatement, whether due to fraud or error.

Auditor's Responsibility

Our responsibility is to express an opinion on these financial statements based on our audit. We conducted our audit in accordance with auditing standards generally accepted in the United States of America. Those standards require that we plan and perform the audit to obtain reasonable assurance about whether the financial statements are free from material misstatement.

An audit involves performing procedures to obtain audit evidence about the amounts and disclosures in the financial statements. The procedures selected depend on the auditor's judgment, including the assessment of the risks of material misstatement of the financial statements, whether due to fraud or error. In making those risk assessments, the auditor considers internal control relevant to the partnership's preparation and fair presentation of the financial statements in order to design audit procedures that are appropriate in the circumstances, but not for the purpose of expressing an opinion on the effectiveness of the partnership's internal control. Accordingly, we express no such opinion. An audit also includes evaluating the appropriateness of accounting policies used and the reasonableness of significant accounting estimates made by management, as well as evaluating the overall presentation of the financial statements.

We believe that the audit evidence we have obtained is sufficient and appropriate to provide a basis for our audit opinion.

Opinion

In our opinion, the financial statements referred to above present fairly, in all material respects, the ~~financial position~~ assets, liabilities, and capital of ABC Partnership as of December 31, 20X1, and ~~the results of its operations and its cash flows~~ its revenue and expenses and changes in partners' capital accounts for the year then ended in accordance with ~~accounting principles generally accepted in the United States of America~~ the basis of accounting the Partnership uses for income tax purposes described in Note X.

Basis of Accounting

We draw attention to Note X of the financial statements, which describes the basis of accounting. The financial statements are prepared on the basis of accounting the Partnership uses for income tax purposes, which is a basis of accounting other than accounting principles generally accepted in the United States of America. Our opinion is not modified with respect to this matter.

[*Auditor's signature*]

[*Auditor's city and state*]

[*Date of the audit report*]

Exhibit 12 ▸ Audit Report on Financial Statements Prepared in Accordance With *Regulatory* Basis of Accounting; Management Does *Not* Have Choice of Financial Reporting Frameworks; *Restricted* as to Use

Independent Auditor's Report

[*Appropriate Addressee*]

We have audited the accompanying financial statements of ABC City, Any State, which comprise ~~the balance sheet~~ cash and unencumbered cash for each fund as of December 31, 20X1, and the related statements of ~~income, changes in stockholders' equity, and cash flows~~ cash receipts and disbursements and disbursements—budget and actual for the year then ended, and the related notes to the financial statements.

Management's Responsibility for the Financial Statements

Management is responsible for the preparation and fair presentation of these financial statements in accordance with ~~accounting principles generally accepted in the United States of America;~~ the financial reporting provisions of Section Y of Regulation Z of Any State; ~~this includes~~ Management is also responsible for the design, implementation, and maintenance of internal control relevant to the preparation and fair presentation of financial statements that are free from material misstatement, whether due to fraud or error.

Auditor's Responsibility

Our responsibility is to express an opinion on these financial statements based on our audit. We conducted our audit in accordance with auditing standards generally accepted in the United States of America. Those standards require that we plan and perform the audit to obtain reasonable assurance about whether the financial statements are free from material misstatement.

An audit involves performing procedures to obtain audit evidence about the amounts and disclosures in the financial statements. The procedures selected depend on the auditor's judgment, including the assessment of the risks of material misstatement of the financial statements, whether due to fraud or error. In making those risk assessments, the auditor considers internal control relevant to the entity's preparation and fair presentation of the financial statements in order to design audit procedures that are appropriate in the circumstances, but not for the purpose of expressing an opinion on the effectiveness of the entity's internal control. Accordingly, we express no such opinion. An audit also includes evaluating the appropriateness of accounting policies used and the reasonableness of significant accounting estimates made by management, as well as evaluating the overall presentation of the financial statements.

We believe that the audit evidence we have obtained is sufficient and appropriate to provide a basis for our audit opinion.

Opinion

In our opinion, the financial statements referred to above present fairly, in all material respects, the ~~financial position~~ cash and unencumbered cash of each fund of ABC City as of December 31, 20X1, and ~~the results of its operations and its cash flows~~ their respective cash receipts and disbursements, and budgetary results for the year then ended in accordance with ~~accounting principles generally accepted in the United States of America~~ the financial reporting provisions of Section Y of Regulation Z of Any State described in Note X.

Basis of Accounting

We draw attention to Note X of the financial statements, which describes the basis of accounting. As described in Note X to the financial statements, the financial statements are prepared by ABC City on the basis of the financial reporting provisions of Section Y of Regulation Z of Any State, which is a basis of accounting other than accounting principles generally accepted in the United States of America, to meet the requirements of Any State. Our opinion is not modified with respect to this matter.

Restriction on Use

Our report is intended solely for the information and use of ABC City and Any State and is not intended to be and should not be used by anyone other than these specified parties.

[*Auditor's signature*]

[*Auditor's city and state*]

[*Date of the audit report*]

Exhibit 13 ▸ Audit Report on Financial Statements Prepared in Accordance With *Contractual* Basis of Accounting; Management Does *Not* Have Choice of Financial Reporting Frameworks

Independent Auditor's Report

[*Appropriate Addressee*]

We have audited the accompanying financial statements of ABC Company, which comprise ~~the balance sheet~~ the assets and liabilities-contractual basis as of December 31, 20X1, and the ~~related statements of income, changes in stockholders' equity, and cash flows~~ revenues and expenses—contractual basis, changes in equity—contractual basis, and cash flows—contractual basis for the year then ended, and the related notes to the financial statements.

Management's Responsibility for the Financial Statements

Management is responsible for the preparation and fair presentation of these financial statements in accordance with ~~accounting principles generally accepted in the United States of America;~~ the financial reporting provisions of Section Z of the contract between ABC Company and DEF Company dated January 1, 20X1 (the contract) ~~this includes~~ Management is also responsible for the design, implementation, and maintenance of internal control relevant to the preparation and fair presentation of financial statements that are free from material misstatement, whether due to fraud or error.

Auditor's Responsibility

Our responsibility is to express an opinion on these financial statements based on our audit. We conducted our audit in accordance with auditing standards generally accepted in the United States of America. Those standards require that we plan and perform the audit to obtain reasonable assurance about whether the financial statements are free from material misstatement.

An audit involves performing procedures to obtain audit evidence about the amounts and disclosures in the financial statements. The procedures selected depend on the auditor's judgment, including the assessment of the risks of material misstatement of the financial statements, whether due to fraud or error. In making those risk assessments, the auditor considers internal control relevant to the entity's preparation and fair presentation of the financial statements in order to design audit procedures that are appropriate in the circumstances, but not for the purpose of expressing an opinion on the effectiveness of the entity's internal control. Accordingly, we express no such opinion. An audit also includes evaluating the appropriateness of accounting policies used and the reasonableness of significant accounting estimates made by management, as well as evaluating the overall presentation of the financial statements.

We believe that the audit evidence we have obtained is sufficient and appropriate to provide a basis for our audit opinion.

Opinion

In our opinion, the financial statements referred to above present fairly, in all material respects, the ~~financial position~~ assets and liabilities of ABC Company as of December 31, 20X1, and ~~the results of its operations and its cash flows~~ revenues, expenses, changes in equity, and cash flows for the year then ended in accordance with ~~accounting principles generally accepted in the United States of America~~ the financial reporting provisions of Section Z of the contract.

Basis of Accounting

We draw attention to Note X of the financial statements, which describes the basis of accounting. The financial statements are prepared by ABC Company on the basis of the financial reporting provisions of Section Z of the contract, which is a basis of accounting other than accounting principles generally accepted in the United States of America, to comply with the financial reporting provisions of the contract referred to above. Our opinion is not modified with respect to this matter.

Restriction on Use

Our report is intended solely for the information and use of ABC Company and DEF Company and is not intended to be and should not be used by anyone other than these specified parties.

[*Auditor's signature*]

[*Auditor's city and state*]

[*Date of the audit report*]

III. Audits of Single Financial Statements & Specific Elements, Accounts, or Items (AU 805)

A. Overview

This standard addresses some special considerations in the application of US GAAS to an audit of a single financial statement or a specific element, account, or item of a financial statement (element). The single financial statement or specific element may be prepared in accordance with a general-purpose or special-purpose framework. If prepared in accordance with a special-purpose framework, AU 800, *Special Considerations—Audits of Financial Statements Prepared in Accordance With Special Purpose Frameworks*, also applies to the audit.

1. **Objective** The objective of the auditor, when applying US GAAS in an audit of a single financial statement or specific element, is to address appropriately the special considerations that are relevant to:

   a. The acceptance of the engagement

   b. The planning and performance of that engagement

   c. Forming an opinion and reporting on the single financial statement or specific element

2. **Definitions**

   a. **Element** An *element of a financial statement* or an *element* means an element, account, or item of a financial statement.

   b. **Single Financial Statement or Specific Element of Financial Statement** A single financial statement or a specific element of a financial statement *includes the related notes*. The related notes ordinarily comprise a summary of significant accounting policies and other explanatory information relevant to the financial statement or specific element.

      Examples of single financial statements, each of which would include related notes:

      - Balance sheet
      - Statement of income or statement of operations
      - Statement of retained earnings
      - Statement of cash flows
      - Statement of assets and liabilities
      - Statement of changes in owner's equity
      - Statement of revenue and expenses
      - Statement of operations by product lines

      Examples of specific elements, accounts, or items of a financial statement:

      - Accounts receivable; allowance for doubtful accounts receivable; inventory; the liability for accrued benefits of a private benefit plan; the recorded value of identified intangible assets; or the liability for incurred but not reported claims in an insurance portfolio, including related notes
      - A schedule of externally managed assets and income of a private benefit plan, including related notes
      - A schedule of disbursements regarding a lease property, including related notes
      - A schedule of profit participation or employee bonuses, including related notes

B. Considerations When Accepting the Engagement

1. Application of US GAAS

a. An auditor is required to comply with all US GAAS relevant to the audit. In the case of an audit of a single financial statement or specific element, this requirement applies irrespective of whether the auditor is also engaged to audit the entity's complete set of financial statements.

b. If the auditor is not also engaged to audit the entity's complete set of financial statements, the auditor should determine whether the:

(1) Audit of a single financial statement or specific element in accordance with US GAAS is practicable

(2) Auditor will be able to perform procedures on interrelated items

2. Acceptability of Financial Reporting Framework

a. US GAAS requires the auditor to determine the acceptability of the financial reporting framework. In an audit of a single financial statement or specific element, the auditor should obtain an understanding of the:

(1) Purpose for which the single financial statement or specific element is prepared

(2) Intended users

(3) Steps taken by management to determine that the application of the financial reporting framework is acceptable

b. The auditor should also consider whether the application of the financial reporting framework will result in a presentation that provides adequate disclosures to enable the intended users to understand the information conveyed in the financial statement or specific element and the effect of material transactions and events on the information conveyed in the financial statement or specific element.

C. Considerations When Planning & Performing the Audit

In planning and performing an audit of a single financial statement or specific element, the auditor should adapt all US GAAS relevant to the audit.

1. **Interrelated Items** The auditor should perform procedures on interrelated items as necessary to meet the objective of the audit.

In the case of an audit of a specific element, the auditor should:

a **Specific Element Based on Stockholders' Equity** If the specific element is, or is based upon, the entity's stockholders' equity or the equivalent, perform procedures necessary to obtain sufficient appropriate audit evidence to enable the auditor to express an opinion about financial position, excluding matters related to classification or disclosure that are not relevant to the audit of the specific element.

b. **Specific Element Based on Net Income** If the specific element is, or is based upon, the entity's net income or the equivalent, perform procedures necessary to obtain sufficient appropriate audit evidence to enable the auditor to express an opinion about financial position *and results of operations*, excluding matters related to classification or disclosure that are not relevant to the audit of the specific element

2. **Appropriate Level of Materiality** US GAAS requires the auditor to determine, when establishing the overall audit strategy, materiality for the financial statements as a whole. In the case of an audit of a single financial statement, the auditor should determine materiality for the single financial statement being reported on rather than for the complete set of financial statements. In the case of an audit of one or more specific elements, the auditor should determine materiality for each individual element reported on rather than the aggregate of all elements or the complete set of financial statements.

D. Forming an Opinion & Reporting Considerations

When forming an opinion and reporting on a single financial statement or specific element, the auditor should apply the requirements in AU 700, *Forming an Opinion and Reporting on Financial Statements*, adapted as necessary.

1. **Reporting on Complete Set of Financial Statements & Single Financial Statement or Specific Element**

   a. If, in conjunction with an audit of a complete set of financial statements, the auditor undertakes an audit of a single financial statement or a specific element, the auditor should:

      (1) **Separate Reports** Issue a separate audit report and express a separate opinion for each engagement

      (2) **Reference Report on Complete Set of Financial Statements** Indicate in the report on a specific element the:

         (a) **Date of Report** Date of the audit report on the complete set of financial statements

         (b) **Opinion** Nature of opinion expressed on those financial statements under an appropriate heading

         Editor Note: This reference can be made in an other-matter paragraph; see exhibit 16.

   b. **When Opinion on Complete Set of Financial Statements Is *Not* Adverse or Disclaimed—May Publish Together If Differentiated From Each Other** As long as an adverse or disclaimer of opinion has not been expressed on the complete set of financial statements, an audited single financial statement or specific element may be published together with an audited complete set of financial statements, provided that the presentation of the single financial statement or specific element is sufficiently differentiated from the complete set of financial statements. If management does not present the statements or specific element appropriately, the auditor should not release the audit report containing the opinion on the single financial statement or specific element until satisfied with management's differentiation.

      The auditor should also differentiate the report on the single financial statement or specific element from the report on the complete set of financial statements.

2. **Modified Opinion, Emphasis-of-Matter Paragraph, or Other-Matter Paragraph in Audit Report on Complete Set of Financial Statements**

   a. **Determine Effect on Single Financial Statement or Specific Element** If the auditor's opinion on the complete set of financial statements is modified, the auditor should determine the effect this may have on the opinion on a single financial statement or specific element.

   b. **When Modified Opinion Is Relevant to Specific Element** In the case of an audit of a specific element, if the auditor's modified opinion on the complete set of financial statements is relevant to the audit of the specific element, the auditor should:

      (1) **Express Adverse Opinion on Element If Complete Set Misstated** Express an adverse opinion on the specific element when the modification of the auditor's opinion on the complete set of financial statements arises from a material misstatement

      (2) **Disclaim Opinion on Element If Scope Limitation on Complete Set** Disclaim an opinion on the specific element when the modification of the auditor's opinion on the complete set of financial statements arises from an inability to obtain sufficient appropriate audit evidence

      Editor Note: Thus, even if the auditor's modified opinion on the complete set of financial statements is only qualified, if it is relevant to the specific element, then the auditor should issue either an adverse opinion or a disclaimer of opinion on the element, depending on the reason for the qualification. The assumption is that if the opinion is qualified for the complete set of financial statements, it follows that it is both material and pervasive with respect to the related element.

   c. **Exception to Piecemeal Opinion Prohibition for Specific Element When Adverse Opinion or Disclaimer Issued on Complete Set** If the auditor expresses an adverse opinion or disclaims an opinion on the complete set of financial statements, an unmodified opinion on a specific element in the same audit report would contradict the adverse opinion or disclaimer of opinion on the complete set of financial statements and would be tantamount to expressing a piecemeal opinion. In the context of a separate audit of a specific element that is included in those financial statements, when the auditor nevertheless considers it appropriate to express an unmodified opinion on that specific element, the auditor should only do so if:

      (1) **Can*not* Publish Specific Element With Complete Set** That opinion is expressed in an audit report that is neither published together with nor otherwise accompanies the audit report containing the adverse opinion or disclaimer of opinion;

      and

      (2) **Specific Element Does *Not* Comprise Major Portion of Complete Set** The specific element does not constitute a major portion of the complete set of financial statements

      or

      (3) **Specific Element Is *Not*, or Is *Not* Based On, Stockholders' Equity or Net Income** The specific element is not, or is not based upon, the entity's stockholders' equity or net income or the equivalent

d. **Adverse Opinion or Disclaimer Issued on Complete Set Precludes Unmodified Opinion on Single Financial Statement** A single financial statement is deemed to constitute a major portion of a complete set of financial statements. Therefore, the auditor should not express an unmodified opinion on a single financial statement of a complete set of financial statements if the auditor has expressed an adverse opinion or disclaimed an opinion on the complete set of financial statements as a whole, even if the audit report on the single financial statement is neither published together with nor otherwise accompanies the audit report containing the adverse opinion or disclaimer of opinion.

Editor Note: In the audit report on a complete set of financial statements, the expression of a disclaimer of opinion regarding the results of operations and cash flows, when relevant, and an unmodified opinion regarding the financial position are permitted because the disclaimer of opinion is being issued on the results of operations and cash flows only and not on the financial statements as a whole.

e. **Add Similar Paragraph to Single Financial Statement or Element Report If Emphasis-of-Matter or Other-Matter Paragraph in Audit Report on Complete Set Is Relevant** If the audit report on a complete set of financial statements includes an emphasis-of-matter or an other-matter paragraph that is relevant to the audit of the single financial statement or specific element, the auditor should include a similar paragraph in the audit report on the single financial statement or specific element.

Editor Note: Even when the modified opinion, emphasis-of-matter paragraph, or other-matter paragraph in the audit report on a complete set of financial statements does *not* relate to the audited single financial statement or specific element, the auditor may nevertheless deem it appropriate to refer to the modification in an other-matter paragraph in an audit report on the single financial statement or the specific element because the auditor judges it to be relevant to the users' understanding of the audited single financial statement or the audited element or the related audit report.

3. **Reporting on Incomplete Presentation Otherwise in Accordance With GAAP**

a. **Emphasis-of-Matter Paragraph Required** When the auditor reports on an incomplete presentation that is otherwise in accordance with GAAP, the auditor should include an emphasis-of-matter paragraph in the audit report that:

(1) **Purpose & Reference to Note on Basis of Presentation** States the purpose for which the presentation is prepared and refers to a note in the financial statements that describes the basis of presentation

(2) **Caveat—Not Intended to Be Complete Presentation** Indicates that the presentation is not intended to be a complete presentation of the entity's assets, liabilities, revenues, or expenses

b. **Exception for Regulatory or Contractual Bases** If the presentation is prepared in accordance with a regulatory or contractual basis of accounting, this requirement does **not** apply. In such circumstances, the guidance in AU 800 applies.

Editor Note: The changes to the "standard" report required by reporting on a single financial statement or a specific element in the following exhibits are <u>underlined</u> *for illustrative purposes only*. The content omitted from the "standard" report is shown with strikethrough.

Exhibit 14 ▸ Audit Report on Single Financial Statement (Balance Sheet) Prepared in Accordance With GAAP (General-Purpose Framework)

Independent Auditor's Report

[*Appropriate Addressee*]

We have audited the accompanying ~~financial statements~~ <u>balance sheet</u> of ABC Company, ~~which comprise the balance sheet~~ as of December 31, 20X1, ~~and the related statements of income, changes in stockholders' equity, and cash flows for the year then ended,~~ and the related notes to the financial statement~~s~~.

Management's Responsibility for the Financial Statement~~s~~

Management is responsible for the preparation and fair presentation of ~~these~~ <u>this</u> financial statement~~s~~ in accordance with accounting principles generally accepted in the United States of America; this includes the design, implementation, and maintenance of internal control relevant to the preparation and fair presentation of <u>the</u> financial statement~~s~~ that ~~are~~ is free from material misstatement, whether due to fraud or error.

Auditor's Responsibility

Our responsibility is to express an opinion on ~~these~~ <u>the</u> financial statement~~s~~ based on our audit. We conducted our audit in accordance with auditing standards generally accepted in the United States of America. Those standards require that we plan and perform the audit to obtain reasonable assurance about whether the financial statement~~s~~ ~~are~~ is free from material misstatement.

An audit involves performing procedures to obtain audit evidence about the amounts and disclosures in the financial statement~~s~~. The procedures selected depend on the auditor's judgment, including the assessment of the risks of material misstatement of the financial statement~~s~~, whether due to fraud or error. In making those risk assessments, the auditor considers internal control relevant to the entity's preparation and fair presentation of the financial statement~~s~~ in order to design audit procedures that are appropriate in the circumstances, but not for the purpose of expressing an opinion on the effectiveness of the entity's internal control. Accordingly, we express no such opinion. An audit also includes evaluating the appropriateness of accounting policies used and the reasonableness of significant accounting estimates made by management, as well as evaluating the overall presentation of the financial statement~~s~~.

We believe that the audit evidence we have obtained is sufficient and appropriate to provide a basis for our audit opinion.

Opinion

In our opinion, the financial statement~~s~~ referred to above present<u>s</u> fairly, in all material respects, the financial position of ABC Company as of December 31, 20X1, ~~and the results of its operations and its cash flows for the year then ended~~ in accordance with accounting principles generally accepted in the United States of America.

[*Auditor's signature*]

[*Auditor's city and state*]

[*Date of the audit report*]

Exhibit 15 ▶ Audit Report on Single Financial Statement (Statement of Cash Receipts & Disbursements) Prepared in Accordance With Cash Basis of Accounting (Special-Purpose Framework); Management Has Choice of Financial Reporting Frameworks

Independent Auditor's Report

[*Appropriate Addressee*]

We have audited the accompanying ~~financial~~ statement~~s~~ of cash receipts and disbursements of ABC Company, ~~which comprise the balance sheet as of~~ for the year ended December 31, 20X1, ~~and the related statements of income, changes in stockholders' equity, and cash flows for the year then ended,~~ and the related notes to the financia~~l~~ statement~~s~~.

Management's Responsibility for the Financial Statement~~s~~

Management is responsible for the preparation and fair presentation of ~~these~~ this financial statement~~s~~ in accordance with ~~accounting principles generally accepted in the United States of America;~~ the cash basis of accounting described in Note X; this includes determining that the cash basis of accounting is an acceptable basis for the preparation of the financial statement in the circumstances. ~~this includes~~ Management is also responsible for the design, implementation, and maintenance of internal control relevant to the preparation and fair presentation of the financial statement~~s~~ that ~~are~~ is free from material misstatement, whether due to fraud or error.

Auditor's Responsibility

Our responsibility is to express an opinion on ~~these~~ the financial statement~~s~~ based on our audit. We conducted our audit in accordance with auditing standards generally accepted in the United States of America. Those standards require that we plan and perform the audit to obtain reasonable assurance about whether the financial statement~~s~~ ~~are~~ is free from material misstatement.

An audit involves performing procedures to obtain audit evidence about the amounts and disclosures in the financial statement~~s~~. The procedures selected depend on the auditor's judgment, including the assessment of the risks of material misstatement of the financial statement~~s~~, whether due to fraud or error. In making those risk assessments, the auditor considers internal control relevant to the entity's preparation and fair presentation of the financial statement~~s~~ in order to design audit procedures that are appropriate in the circumstances, but not for the purpose of expressing an opinion on the effectiveness of the entity's internal control. Accordingly, we express no such opinion. An audit also includes evaluating the appropriateness of accounting policies used and the reasonableness of significant accounting estimates made by management, as well as evaluating the overall presentation of the financial statement~~s~~.

We believe that the audit evidence we have obtained is sufficient and appropriate to provide a basis for our audit opinion.

Opinion

In our opinion, the financial statement~~s~~ referred to above presents fairly, in all material respects, the ~~financial position~~ cash receipts and disbursements of ABC Company ~~as of~~ for the year ended December 31, 20X1, ~~and the results of its operations and its cash flows for the year then ended~~ in accordance with ~~accounting principles generally accepted in the United States of America~~ the cash basis of accounting described in Note X.

Basis of Accounting

We draw attention to Note X to the financial statement, which describes the basis of accounting. The financial statement is prepared on the cash basis of accounting, which is a basis of accounting other than accounting principles generally accepted in the United States of America. Our opinion is not modified with respect to this matter.

[*Auditor's signature*]

[*Auditor's city and state*]

[*Date of the audit report*]

Exhibit 16 ▶ Audit Report on Specific Element (Schedule of Accounts Receivable) Prepared in Accordance With GAAP (General-Purpose Framework); Audit Performed in Conjunction With Audit of Financial Statements

Independent Auditor's Report

[*Appropriate Addressee*]

We have audited the accompanying ~~financial statements~~ schedule of accounts receivable of ABC Company, ~~which comprise~~ ~~the balance sheet~~ as of December 31, 20X1, ~~and the~~ ~~related statements of income, changes in stockholders' equity, and cash flows for the year then ended,~~ and the related notes to the ~~financial statements~~ schedule.

Management's Responsibility for the ~~Financial Statements~~ Schedule

Management is responsible for the preparation and fair presentation of ~~these financial statements~~ this schedule in accordance with accounting principles generally accepted in the United States of America; this includes the design, implementation, and maintenance of internal control relevant to the preparation and fair presentation of ~~financial statements~~ the schedule that ~~are~~ is free from material misstatement, whether due to fraud or error.

Auditor's Responsibility

Our responsibility is to express an opinion on ~~these financial statements~~ the schedule based on our audit. We conducted our audit in accordance with auditing standards generally accepted in the United States of America. Those standards require that we plan and perform the audit to obtain reasonable assurance about whether the ~~financial statements~~ schedule ~~are~~ is free from material misstatement.

An audit involves performing procedures to obtain audit evidence about the amounts and disclosures in the ~~financial statements~~ schedule. The procedures selected depend on the auditor's judgment, including the assessment of the risks of material misstatement of the schedule ~~financial statements~~, whether due to fraud or error. In making those risk assessments, the auditor considers internal control relevant to the entity's preparation and fair presentation of the ~~financial statements~~ schedule in order to design audit procedures that are appropriate in the circumstances, but not for the purpose of expressing an opinion on the effectiveness of the entity's internal control. Accordingly, we express no such opinion. An audit also includes evaluating the appropriateness of accounting policies used and the reasonableness of significant accounting estimates made by management, as well as evaluating the overall presentation of the ~~financial statements~~ schedule.

We believe that the audit evidence we have obtained is sufficient and appropriate to provide a basis for our audit opinion.

Opinion

In our opinion, the ~~financial statements~~ schedule referred to above presents fairly, in all material respects, the ~~financial position~~ accounts receivable of ABC Company as of December 31, 20X1, ~~and the results of its operations and its cash flows~~ ~~for the year then ended~~ in accordance with accounting principles generally accepted in the United States of America.

Other Matter

We have audited, in accordance with auditing standards generally accepted in the United States of America, the financial statements of ABC Company as of and for the year ended December 31, 20X1, and our report thereon, dated March 15, 20X2, expressed an unmodified opinion on those financial statements.

[*Auditor's signature*]

[*Auditor's city and state*]

[*Date of the audit report*]

Exhibit 17 ▸ Audit Report on Specific Element (Schedule of Royalties) Prepared in Accordance With Contractual Basis of Accounting (Special-Purpose Framework); Management Does *Not* Have Choice of Financial Reporting Frameworks

Independent Auditor's Report

[*Appropriate Addressee*]

We have audited the accompanying ~~financial statements~~ schedule of royalties applicable to engine production of the Q Division of ABC Company, ~~which comprise~~ ~~the balance sheet as of~~ for the year then ended December 31, 20X1, ~~and the related statements of income, changes in stockholders' equity, and cash flows for the year then ended,~~ and the related notes to the ~~financial statements~~ schedule.

Management's Responsibility for the ~~Financial Statements~~ Schedule

Management is responsible for the preparation and fair presentation of ~~these financial statements~~ the schedule in accordance with ~~accounting principles generally accepted in the United States of America~~ the financial reporting provisions of Section Z of the license agreement between ABC Company and XYZ Corporation dated January 1, 20X1 (the contract). ~~this includes~~ Management is also responsible for the design, implementation, and maintenance of internal control relevant to the preparation and fair presentation of ~~financial statements~~ the schedule that ~~are~~ is free from material misstatement, whether due to fraud or error.

Auditor's Responsibility

Our responsibility is to express an opinion on ~~these financial statements~~ the schedule based on our audit. We conducted our audit in accordance with auditing standards generally accepted in the United States of America. Those standards require that we plan and perform the audit to obtain reasonable assurance about whether the ~~financial statements~~ schedule ~~are~~ is free from material misstatement.

An audit involves performing procedures to obtain audit evidence about the amounts and disclosures in the ~~financial statements~~ schedule. The procedures selected depend on the auditor's judgment, including the assessment of the risks of material misstatement of the schedule ~~financial statements~~, whether due to fraud or error. In making those risk assessments, the auditor considers internal control relevant to the entity's preparation and fair presentation of the ~~financial statements~~ schedule in order to design audit procedures that are appropriate in the circumstances, but not for the purpose of expressing an opinion on the effectiveness of the entity's internal control. Accordingly, we express no such opinion. An audit also includes evaluating the appropriateness of accounting policies used and the reasonableness of significant accounting estimates made by management, as well as evaluating the overall presentation of the ~~financial statements~~ schedule.

We believe that the audit evidence we have obtained is sufficient and appropriate to provide a basis for our audit opinion.

Opinion

In our opinion, the ~~financial statements~~ schedule referred to above presents fairly, in all material respects, the ~~financial position~~ royalties applicable to engine production of the Q Division of ABC Company for the year then ended ~~as of~~ December 31, 20X1, ~~and the results of its operations and its cash flows for the year then ended~~ in accordance with ~~accounting principles generally accepted in the United States of America~~ the financial reporting provisions of Section Z of the contract.

Basis of Accounting

We draw attention to Note X to the schedule, which describes the basis of accounting. The schedule was prepared by ABC Company on the basis of the financial reporting provisions of Section Z of the contract, which is a basis of accounting other than accounting principles generally accepted in the United States of America, to comply with the financial reporting provisions of the contract referred to above. Our opinion is not modified with respect to this matter.

Restriction on Use

Our report is intended solely for the information and use of ABC Company and XYZ Corporation and is not intended to be and should not be used by anyone other than these specified parties.

[*Auditor's signature*]

[*Auditor's city and state*]

[*Date of the audit report*]

Exhibit 18 ▸ Audit Report on Incomplete Presentation (Single Financial Statement) That Is Otherwise in Accordance With GAAP

Independent Auditor's Report

[*Appropriate Addressee*]

We have audited the accompanying ~~financial statements~~ Historical Summaries of Gross Income and Direct Operating Expenses of ABC Apartments, ~~which comprise~~ ~~the balance sheet as of~~ for each of the three years in the period ended December 31, 20X1, ~~and the related statements of income, changes in stockholders' equity, and cash flows for the year then ended,~~ and the related notes to the ~~financial statements~~ historical summaries.

Management's Responsibility for the Historical Summaries

Management is responsible for the preparation and fair presentation of these ~~financial statements~~ historical summaries in accordance with accounting principles generally accepted in the United States of America; this includes the design, implementation, and maintenance of internal control relevant to the preparation and fair presentation of ~~financial statements~~ the historical summaries that are free from material misstatement, whether due to fraud or error.

Auditor's Responsibility

Our responsibility is to express an opinion on ~~these financial statements~~ the historical summaries based on our audit. We conducted our audit in accordance with auditing standards generally accepted in the United States of America. Those standards require that we plan and perform the audit to obtain reasonable assurance about whether the ~~financial statements~~ historical summaries are free from material misstatement.

An audit involves performing procedures to obtain audit evidence about the amounts and disclosures in the ~~financial statements~~ historical summaries. The procedures selected depend on the auditor's judgment, including the assessment of the risks of material misstatement of the ~~financial statements~~ historical summaries, whether due to fraud or error. In making those risk assessments, the auditor considers internal control relevant to the entity's preparation and fair presentation of the ~~financial statements~~ historical summaries in order to design audit procedures that are appropriate in the circumstances, but not for the purpose of expressing an opinion on the effectiveness of the entity's internal control. Accordingly, we express no such opinion. An audit also includes evaluating the appropriateness of accounting policies used and the reasonableness of significant accounting estimates made by management, as well as evaluating the overall presentation of the ~~financial statements~~ historical summaries.

We believe that the audit evidence we have obtained is sufficient and appropriate to provide a basis for our audit opinion.

Opinion

In our opinion, the ~~financial statements~~ historical summaries referred to above present fairly, in all material respects, the ~~financial position~~ gross income and direct operating expenses described in Note X of ABC Apartments ~~as of~~ for each of the three years in the period ended December 31, 20X1, ~~and the results of its operations and its cash flows~~ ~~for the year then ended~~ in accordance with accounting principles generally accepted in the United States of America.

Emphasis of Matter

We draw attention to Note X to the historical summaries, which describes that the accompanying historical summaries were prepared for the purpose of complying with the rules and regulations of Regulator DEF (for inclusion in the filing of Form Z of ABC Company) and are not intended to be a complete presentation of the Company's revenues and expenses. Our opinion is not modified with respect to this matter.

[*Auditor's signature*]

[*Auditor's city and state*]

[*Date of the audit report*]

IV. Reports on Compliance in Connection With Audited Financial Statements (AU 806)

A. Overview

Entities may be required by covenants of contractual agreements, such as certain bond indentures and loan agreements, or regulatory requirements to provide an audit report on compliance. For example, loan agreements may impose a variety of obligations on borrowers involving matters such as payments into sinking funds; payments of interest; maintenance of current ratios; and restrictions of dividend payments. Loan agreements may also require the borrower to provide annual financial statements that have been audited. In some instances, the lenders or their trustees may request the auditor to report that the borrower has complied with certain covenants of the agreement relating to accounting matters.

This standard addresses the auditor's responsibility when the auditor is requested to report on an entity's compliance with aspects of contractual agreements or regulatory requirements, insofar as they relate to accounting matters, in connection with an audit of financial statements. Such a report on compliance is commonly referred to as a by-product report.

The financial statements being audited may be either general-purpose or special-purpose financial statements.

Editor Note: When the auditor is engaged or required by law or regulation to perform a compliance audit in accordance with US GAAS, the standards for financial audits under *Government Auditing Standards*, and a governmental audit requirement that requires the auditor to express an opinion on compliance with applicable compliance requirements, AU 935, *Compliance Audits*, applies (see chapter 10 of this text).

B. Reports on Compliance

1. Nature of Report on Compliance

a. **Conditions for Negative Assurance** The auditor's report on compliance should include a statement that nothing came to the auditor's attention that caused the auditor to believe that the entity failed to comply with specified aspects of the contractual agreements or regulatory requirements, insofar as they relate to accounting matters, *only* when the:

   (1) **No Instances of Noncompliance** Auditor has not identified any instances of noncompliance

   (2) **Unmodified or Qualified Opinion on Related Audited Financial Statements** Auditor has expressed an unmodified or qualified opinion on the related financial statements to which the applicable covenants of such contractual agreements or regulatory requirements relate

   (3) **Applicable Covenants or Regulatory Requirements Covered During Audit** Applicable covenants or regulatory requirements relate to accounting matters that have been subjected to the audit procedures applied in the audit of financial statements

   Editor Note: If there are instances of noncompliance, the auditor should still issue a compliance report which describes the noncompliance even when an adverse opinion or a disclaimer of opinion has been expressed on the financial statements; the auditor is only precluded from issuing a compliance report that offers negative assurance under these circumstances.

b. **All Instances of Noncompliance Should Be Described in Report** All instances of noncompliance are required to be described in the report on compliance, including those for which a waiver has been obtained. (The entity may have obtained a waiver for such noncompliance which the auditor may state in the report—the determination of whether to include such a statement is based on the procedures performed by the auditor to evaluate the waiver for the purposes of obtaining sufficient appropriate audit evidence in connection with the audit of the financial statements.)

c. **Only Report Noncompliance When Adverse Opinion or Disclaimer of Opinion Expressed on Financial Statements** When the auditor has expressed an adverse opinion or disclaimed an opinion on the financial statements, the auditor should issue a report on compliance *only when instances of noncompliance are identified.*

d. **Other Auditing Standards' Requirements to Issue Report on Compliance Trump US GAAS Restrictions** Regardless of the aforementioned US GAAS requirements, an auditor is **not** precluded from issuing a report on compliance if such a report is required by another set of auditing standards, for example, *Government Auditing Standards,* and the auditor has been engaged to audit the financial statements in accordance with both US GAAS and those other standards.

e. **Report Format**

(1) **In Writing** The report on compliance should be in writing.

(2) **Date** The date of the report should be the same date at the audit report on the related financial statements.

(3) **Separate Report or Combined With Audit Report on Financial Statements** The report should be provided either in a separate report or in one or more paragraphs included in the audit report on the related financial statements.

(4) **Restricted Use** The report should contain an alert that restricts its use whether it is issued separately or combined with the audit report on the financial statements; however, only the report on compliance is restricted. Accordingly, if combined, the intended use of the audit report on the financial statements is *not* affected.

2. **Elements of Separate Report on Compliance** When the auditor reports on compliance in a separate report, the report should include the following:

a. A title that includes the word *independent* to clearly indicate that it is the report of an independent auditor

b. An appropriate addressee

c. A paragraph that states that the financial statements were audited in accordance with generally accepted auditing standards and an identification of the United States of America as the country of origin of those standards and the date of the audit report on those financial statements

d. If the auditor expressed a modified opinion on the financial statements, a statement describing the nature of the modification

e. When no instances of noncompliance are identified by the auditor, a reference to the specific covenants or paragraphs of the contractual agreement or regulatory requirement and a statement that nothing came to the auditor's attention that caused the auditor to believe that the entity failed to comply with specified aspects of the contractual agreements or regulatory requirements, insofar as they relate to accounting matters

f. When instances of noncompliance are identified by the auditor, a reference to the specific covenants or paragraphs of the contractual agreement or regulatory requirement, insofar as they relate to accounting matters, and a description of the identified instances of noncompliance

g. A statement that the report is being provided in connection with the audit of the financial statements

h. A statement that the audit was not directed primarily toward obtaining knowledge regarding compliance, and accordingly, had the auditor performed additional procedures, other matters may have come to the auditor's attention regarding noncompliance with the specific covenants or paragraphs of the contractual agreement or regulatory requirement, insofar as they relate to accounting matters

i. A paragraph that includes a description and the source of significant interpretations made by the entity's management relating to the provisions of the relevant contractual agreement or regulatory requirement

j. A paragraph that includes an appropriate alert, i.e., a restriction as to the use of the report

k. The manual or printed signature of the auditor's firm and the city and state where the auditor practices

l. The date of the report, which should be the same date as the audit report on the financial statements

3. **Report on Compliance Included in Audit Report**

a. **Elements of Other-Matter Paragraph on Compliance** When a report on compliance is included in the audit report on the financial statements, the audit report should include an other-matter paragraph that includes:

(1) Reference to the specific covenants or paragraphs of the contractual agreement or regulatory requirement, insofar as they relate to accounting matters

(2) When no instances of noncompliance are identified by the auditor, a statement that nothing came to the auditor's attention that caused the auditor to believe that the entity failed to comply with specified aspects of the contractual agreements or regulatory requirements, insofar as they relate to accounting matters

(3) When instances of noncompliance are identified by the auditor, a description of the identified instances of noncompliance

(4) A statement that the communication is being provided in connection with the audit of the financial statements

(5) A statement that the audit was not directed primarily toward obtaining knowledge regarding compliance, and accordingly, had the auditor performed additional procedures, other matters may have come to the auditor's attention regarding noncompliance with the specific covenants or paragraphs of the contractual agreement or regulatory requirement, insofar as they relate to accounting matter

(6) A paragraph that includes a description and the source of significant interpretations, if any, made by the entity's management relating to the provisions of the relevant contractual agreement or regulatory requirement

b. A paragraph that includes an appropriate alert, i.e., a restriction as to the use of the report

Exhibit 19 ▸ Separate Report on Compliance When *No* Instances of Noncompliance Are Identified

Independent Auditor's Report

[*Appropriate Addressee*]

We have audited, in accordance with auditing standards generally accepted in the United States of America, the financial statements of XYZ Company, which comprise the balance sheet as of December 31, 20X2, and the related statements of income, changes in stockholders' equity, and cash flows for the year then ended, and the related notes to the financial statements, and have issued our report thereon dated February 16, 20X3.

In connection with our audit, nothing came to our attention that caused us to believe that XYZ Company failed to comply with the terms, covenants, provisions, or conditions of sections XX to YY, inclusive, of the Indenture dated July 21, 20X0, with ABC Bank, insofar as they relate to accounting matters. However, our audit was not directed primarily toward obtaining knowledge of such noncompliance. Accordingly, had we performed additional procedures, other matters may have come to our attention regarding the Company's noncompliance with the above-referenced terms, covenants, provisions, or conditions of the Indenture, insofar as they relate to accounting matters.

This report is intended solely for the information and use of the board of directors and management of XYZ Company and ABC Bank and is not intended to be and should not be used by anyone other than these specified parties.

[*Auditor's signature*]

[*Auditor's city and state*]

[*Date of the audit report*]

Exhibit 20 ▸ Separate Report on Compliance When Instances of Noncompliance *Are* Identified

Independent Auditor's Report

[*Appropriate Addressee*]

We have audited, in accordance with auditing standards generally accepted in the United States of America, the financial statements of XYZ Company, which comprise the balance sheet as of December 31, 20X2, and the related statements of income, changes in stockholders' equity, and cash flows for the year then ended, and the related notes to the financial statements, and have issued our report thereon dated March 5, 20X3.

In connection with our audit, we noted that XYZ Company failed to comply with the "Working Capital" provision of section XX of the Loan Agreement dated March 1, 20X2, with ABC Bank. Our audit was not directed primarily toward obtaining knowledge as to whether XYZ Company failed to comply with the terms, covenants, provisions, or conditions of sections XX to YY, inclusive, of the Loan Agreement, insofar as they relate to accounting matters. Accordingly, had we performed additional procedures, other matters may have come to our attention regarding noncompliance with the above-referenced terms, covenants, provisions, or conditions of the Loan Agreement, insofar as they relate to accounting matters.

This report is intended solely for the information and use of the board of directors and management of XYZ Company and ABC Bank and is not intended to be and should not be used by anyone other than these specified parties.

[*Auditor's signature*]

[*Auditor's city and state*]

[*Date of the audit report*]

Exhibit 21 ▸ Separate Report on Compliance When Instances of Noncompliance *Are* Identified & Waiver Has Been Obtained

Independent Auditor's Report

[*Appropriate Addressee*]

We have audited, in accordance with auditing standards generally accepted in the United States of America, the financial statements of XYZ Company, which comprise the balance sheet as of December 31, 20X2, and the related statements of income, changes in stockholders' equity, and cash flows for the year then ended, and the related notes to the financial statements, and have issued our report thereon dated March 5, 20X3.

In connection with our audit, we noted that XYZ Company failed to comply with the "Working Capital" provision of section XX of the Loan Agreement dated March 1, 20X2, with ABC Bank. The Company has received a waiver dated February 5, 20X3, from ABC Bank. Our audit was not directed primarily toward obtaining knowledge as to whether XYZ Company failed to comply with the terms, covenants, provisions, or conditions of sections XX to YY, inclusive, of the Loan Agreement, insofar as they relate to accounting matters. Accordingly, had we performed additional procedures, other matters may have come to our attention regarding noncompliance with the above-referenced terms, covenants, provisions, or conditions of the Loan Agreement, insofar as they relate to accounting matters.

This report is intended solely for the information and use of the board of directors and management of XYZ Company and ABC Bank and is not intended to be and should not be used by anyone other than these specified parties.

[*Auditor's signature*]
[*Auditor's city and state*]
[*Date of the audit report*]

Exhibit 22 ▸ Separate Report on Compliance When Instances of Noncompliance *Are* Identified & Disclaimer of Opinion Has Been Expressed on Related Financial Statements

Independent Auditor's Report

[*Appropriate Addressee*]

We were engaged to audit, in accordance with auditing standards generally accepted in the United States of America, the financial statements of XYZ Company, which comprise the balance sheet as of December 31, 20X2, and the related statements of income, changes in stockholders' equity, and cash flows for the year then ended, and the related notes to the financial statements, and have issued our report thereon dated March 5, 20X3. Our report disclaims an opinion on such financial statements because of [*describe the scope limitation or matter causing the disclaimer*].

In connection with our engagement, we noted that XYZ Company failed to comply with the "Working Capital" provision of section XX of the Loan Agreement dated March 1, 20X2, with ABC Bank. Our engagement was not directed primarily toward obtaining knowledge as to whether XYZ Company failed to comply with the terms, covenants, provisions, or conditions of sections XX to YY, inclusive, of the Loan Agreement, insofar as they relate to accounting matters. Accordingly, had we been able to complete the audit, other matters may have come to our attention regarding noncompliance with the above-referenced terms, covenants, provisions, or conditions of the Loan Agreement, insofar as they relate to accounting matters.

This report is intended solely for the information and use of the board of directors and management of XYZ Company and ABC Bank and is not intended to be and should not be used by anyone other than these specified parties.

[*Auditor's signature*]
[*Auditor's city and state*]
[*Date of the audit report*]

Exhibit 23 ▸ Combined Report on Compliance When *No* Instances of Noncompliance Are Identified

Independent Auditor's Report

[*Appropriate Addressee*]

We have audited the accompanying financial statements of ABC Company, which comprise the balance sheet as of December 31, 20X1, and the related statements of income, changes in stockholders' equity, and cash flows for the year then ended, and the related notes to the financial statements.

Management's Responsibility for the Financial Statements

Management is responsible for the preparation and fair presentation of these financial statements in accordance with accounting principles generally accepted in the United States of America; this includes the design, implementation, and maintenance of internal control relevant to the preparation and fair presentation of financial statements that are free from material misstatement, whether due to fraud or error.

Auditor's Responsibility

Our responsibility is to express an opinion on these financial statements based on our audit. We conducted our audit in accordance with auditing standards generally accepted in the United States of America. Those standards require that we plan and perform the audit to obtain reasonable assurance about whether the financial statements are free from material misstatement.

An audit involves performing procedures to obtain audit evidence about the amounts and disclosures in the financial statements. The procedures selected depend on the auditor's judgment, including the assessment of the risks of material misstatement of the financial statements, whether due to fraud or error. In making those risk assessments, the auditor considers internal control relevant to the entity's preparation and fair presentation of the financial statements in order to design audit procedures that are appropriate in the circumstances, but not for the purpose of expressing an opinion on the effectiveness of the entity's internal control. Accordingly, we express no such opinion. An audit also includes evaluating the appropriateness of accounting policies used and the reasonableness of significant accounting estimates made by management, as well as evaluating the overall presentation of the financial statements.

We believe that the audit evidence we have obtained is sufficient and appropriate to provide a basis for our audit opinion.

Opinion

In our opinion, the financial statements referred to above present fairly, in all material respects, the financial position of ABC Company as of December 31, 20X1, and the results of its operations and its cash flows for the year then ended in accordance with accounting principles generally accepted in the United States of America.

Other Matter

In connection with our audit, nothing came to our attention that caused us to believe that ABC Company failed to comply with the terms, covenants, provisions, or conditions of sections XX to YY, inclusive, of the Indenture dated July 21, 20X0 with XYZ Bank, insofar as they relate to accounting matters. However, our audit was not directed primarily toward obtaining knowledge of such noncompliance. Accordingly, had we performed additional procedures, other matters may have come to our attention regarding the Company's noncompliance with the above-referenced terms, covenants, provisions, or conditions of the Indenture, insofar as they relate to accounting matters.

Restricted Use Relating to the Other Matter

The communication related to compliance with the aforementioned Indenture described in the Other Matter paragraph is intended solely for the information and use of the boards of directors and management of ABC Company and XYZ Bank and is not intended to be and should not be used by anyone other than these specified parties.

[*Auditor's signature*]

[*Auditor's city and state*]

[*Date of the audit report*]

V. Filings With the US Securities and Exchange Commission (AU 925)

A. Overview

1. **Objective** The objective of the auditor, in connection with audited financial statements of a nonissuer that are separately included or incorporated by reference in a registration statement filed under the Securities Act of 1933 (the 1933 Act), is to perform specified procedures at or shortly before the effective date of the registration statement to sustain the burden of proof that the auditor has performed a reasonable investigation, per the 1933 Act.

2. **Definitions**

   a. **Auditor's Consent** A statement signed and dated by the auditor that indicates that the auditor consents to the use of the audit report, and other references to the auditor, in a registration statement filed under the 1933 Act.

   b. **Awareness Letter** A letter signed and dated by the auditor to acknowledge the auditor's awareness that the auditor's review report on unaudited interim financial information is being used in a registration statement filed under the 1933 Act. This letter is not considered to be part of the registration statement and is also commonly referred to as an *acknowledgment letter*.

   c. **Effective Date of Registration Statement** The date on which the registration statement filed under the 1933 Act becomes effective for purposes of evaluating the auditor's liability under Section 11 of the 1933 Act.

   Editor Note: References to *included* or *the inclusion of* in a registration statement in this section means *included* or *incorporated by reference* in a registration statement filed under the 1933 Act.

3. **Effective Date of Registration Statement** Because the effective date of a registration statement filed under the 1933 Act may not necessarily coincide with the filing date, the auditor should request management to keep the auditor advised of the progress of the registration proceedings through the effective date of the registration statement.

4. **The Prospectus & Other Information**

   a. When the auditor's report on audited financial statements is included in a registration statement filed under the 1933 Act, the auditor should perform the procedures described in AU 720, *Other Information in Documents Containing Audited Financial Statements*, (see chapter 8 of this text) on the prospectus and pertinent portions of the registration statement (including material that is incorporated by reference).

   b. In connection with the procedures required by AU 720, the auditor should determine that the auditor's name is not being used in a way that indicates that the auditor's responsibility is greater than the auditor intends.

B. Subsequent Events Procedures

1. When the most recent separate financial statements of the entity and related audit report are included in the registration statement, the auditor should perform the following procedures described in AU 560, *Subsequent Events and Subsequently Discovered Facts*, at or shortly before the effective date of the registration statement:

   a. Audit procedures designed to identify events occurring between the date of the audit report and the effective date of the registration statement that require adjustment to, or disclosure in, the financial statements. Such procedures, which take into account the auditor's risk assessment in determining the nature and extent of such audit procedures, should include:

(1) Obtaining an understanding of any procedures that management has established to ensure that such events are identified

(2) Inquiring of management and, when appropriate, those charged with governance about whether any such events have occurred that might affect the financial statements

(3) Reading minutes, if any, of the meetings of the entity's owners, management, and those charged with governance that have been held after the date of the financial statements and inquiring about matters discussed at any such meetings for which minutes are not yet available

(4) Reading the entity's latest subsequent interim financial statements, if any

b. Obtain updated written representations from management at or shortly before the effective date of the registration statement, about whether:

(1) Any information has come to management's attention that would cause management to believe that any of the previous representations should be modified

(2) Any events have occurred subsequent to the date of the financial statements that would require adjustment to, or disclosure in, those financial statements

2. The auditor may be unable to perform all of the preceding subsequent events procedures when the auditor has audited the most recent period for which separate audited financial statements of the entity are included in the registration statement and *all* of the following are true:

a. The entity has been acquired by another entity;

b. The acquirer's audited financial statements included in the registration statement reflect a period that includes the date of acquisition; and

c. The auditor is a predecessor auditor because the auditor is not the continuing auditor of the entity

In such circumstances, the auditor should obtain written representations from management and the successor auditor as described in AU 560 at or shortly before the effective date of the registration statement.

3. If a predecessor auditor audited the entity's separate financial statements for a prior period included in the registration statement, but has not audited the entity's separate financial statements for the most recent audited period for which the entity's audited financial statements are included in the registration statement, then the predecessor auditor should perform the following procedures described in AU 560 through a date at or shortly before the effective date of the registration statement:

a. Read the financial statements of the subsequent period to be presented on a comparative basis

b. Compare the prior period financial statements that the predecessor auditor reported on with the financial statements of the subsequent period to be presented on a comparative basis

c. Obtain written representations from management at or shortly before the effective date

d. Obtain a representation letter from the successor auditor stating whether the successor auditor's audit revealed any matters that, in the successor auditor's opinion, might have a material effect on, or require disclosure in, the financial statements reported on by the predecessor auditor

4. If the auditor becomes aware of subsequently discovered facts, the auditor should not provide the auditor's consent until the auditor's consideration of subsequently discovered facts, including the effect on the audit report on the financial statements, has been satisfactorily completed in accordance with AU 560. If management does not revise the audited financial statements in circumstances in which the auditor believes they need to be revised, then the auditor should determine whether to withhold the auditor's consent (and the awareness letter, if applicable).

C. Unaudited Annual Financial Statements or Unaudited Interim Financial Information

1. If the auditor concludes, based on known facts, that unaudited annual financial statements or unaudited interim financial information included in a registration statement filed under the 1933 Act is not in conformity with the requirements of the AFRF, then the auditor should request that management revise the unaudited annual financial statements or unaudited interim financial information appropriately.

2. If management does not revise the unaudited annual financial statements or unaudited interim financial information appropriately and

   a. The auditor has reported on a review of the unaudited annual financial statements or unaudited interim financial information;

   b. The auditor's review report is included in the registration statement; and

   c. The subsequently discovered facts are such that they would have affected the report had they been known to the auditor at the date of the report

   —the auditor should perform the applicable procedures described in AU 560.

3. If management does not revise the unaudited annual financial statements or unaudited interim financial information appropriately and

   a. The auditor has not reported on a review of the unaudited annual financial statements or unaudited interim financial information; or

   b. The auditor's review report is not included in the registration statement

   —the auditor should modify the report on the audited financial statements to describe the departure from the requirements of the AFRF contained in the unaudited annual financial statements or unaudited interim financial information, as described in AU 930, *Interim Financial Information.* (See the section of this chapter on the review of interim financial information.)

4. Additionally, the auditor should determine whether to withhold the auditor's consent (and the awareness letter, if applicable).

VI. Letters for Underwriters & Certain Other Requesting Parties (AU 920)

A. Overview

1. **Scope** This standard addresses the auditor's responsibilities when engaged to issue comfort letters to requesting parties in connection with a nonissuer's financial statements included in registration statements filed with the Securities and Exchange Commission (SEC) under the Securities Act of 1933 (the 1933 Act) or included in other securities offerings.

    a. **Auditor's Services** Auditors' services include audits or reviews of financial statements included in securities offerings. In connection with the securities offerings, auditors are often requested to issue comfort letters to certain requesting parties.

    b. **Support for Underwriter's Claim of Reasonable Investigation** The service of providing letters for underwriters developed following the passing of the 1933 Act. Section 11 of the 1933 Act provides that underwriters, among others, could be liable if any part of a registration statement contains material omissions or misstatements. The 1933 Act also provides for an affirmative defense for underwriters if it can be demonstrated that, after a reasonable investigation, the underwriter has reasonable grounds to believe that no material omissions or misstatements existed in a securities offering. An auditor issuing a comfort letter is one of a number of procedures that may be used to establish that an underwriter has conducted a reasonable investigation. Consequently, underwriters may request auditors to assist them in developing a record of reasonable investigation.

        Editor Note: An affirmative defense is a defense in which the defendant introduces evidence, which, if found to be credible, will negate criminal or civil liability, even if it is proven that the defendant committed the alleged acts.

    c. **Comfort Letter Subjects** The subjects that may be covered in a comfort letter include:

        - The independence of the auditor
        - Whether the audited financial statements included in the securities offering comply regarding form, in all material respects, with the applicable accounting requirements of the 1933 Act and the related rules and regulations adopted by the SEC
        - Unaudited financial statements, condensed interim financial information, capsule financial information, pro forma financial information, financial forecasts, management's discussion and analysis (MD&A), and changes in selected financial statement items during a period subsequent to the date and period of the latest financial statements included in the securities offering
        - Tables, statistics, and other financial information included in the securities offering
        - Negative assurance about whether certain nonfinancial statement information included in the securities offering complies regarding form, in all material respects, with Regulation S-K

2. **Objectives** The objectives of the auditor, when engaged to issue a letter to a requesting party in connection with an entity's financial statements included in a securities offering, are to:

    a. Address appropriately the acceptance of the engagement and the scope of services

    b. Issue a letter with the appropriate form and content

3. **Definitions**

   a. **Capsule Financial Information** Unaudited summarized interim financial information for periods subsequent to the periods covered by the audited financial statements or unaudited interim financial information included in the securities offering; capsule financial information may be presented in narrative or tabular form and is often provided for the most recent interim period and for the corresponding period of the prior year

   b. **Change Period** The period ending on the cutoff date and ordinarily beginning, for balance sheet items, immediately after the date of the latest balance sheet in the securities offering and, for income statement items, immediately after the latest period for which such items are presented in the securities offering

   c. **Closing Date** The date on which the issuer of the securities or selling security holder delivers the securities to the underwriter in exchange for the proceeds of the offering

   d. **Comfort Letter** A letter issued by an auditor in accordance with this standard to requesting parties in connection with an entity's financial statements included in a securities offering

   e. **Comparison Date & Comparison Period** The date as of which, and period for which, data at the cutoff date and data for the change period are to be compared

   f. **Cutoff Date** The date through which certain procedures described in the comfort letter are to relate

   g. **Effective Date** The date on which the securities offering becomes effective

   h. **Entity** The party whose financial statements are the subject of the engagement

   i. **Negative Assurance** A statement that, based on the procedures performed, nothing has come to the auditor's attention that caused the auditor to believe that specified matters do not meet specified criteria (for example, that nothing came to the auditor's attention that caused the auditor to believe that any material modifications should be made to the unaudited interim financial information for it to be in accordance with GAAP).

   j. **Requesting Party** One of the following specified parties requesting a comfort letter, which has negotiated an agreement with the entity:

      - An underwriter
      - Other parties that are conducting a review process that is, or will be, substantially consistent with the due diligence process performed when the securities offering is, or if the securities offering was, being registered pursuant to the 1933 Act, as follows:
        - A selling shareholder, sales agent, or other party with a statutory due diligence defense under Section 11 of the 1933 Act
        - A broker-dealer or other financial intermediary acting as principal or agent in a securities offering in connection with the following types of securities offerings:
          - Foreign offerings, including Regulation S, Eurodollar, and other offshore offerings
          - Transactions that are exempt from the registration requirements of Section 5 of the 1933 Act, including those pursuant to Regulation A, Regulation D, and Rule 144A

- Offerings of securities issued or backed by governmental, municipal, banking, tax-exempt, or other entities that are exempt from registration under the 1933 Act
- The buyer or seller in connection with acquisition transactions in which there is an exchange of stock

k. **Securities Offerings** One of the following types of securities offerings:

- Registration of securities with the SEC under the 1933 Act
- Foreign offerings, including Regulation S, Eurodollar, and other offshore offerings
- Transactions that are exempt from the registration requirements of Section 5 of the 1933 Act, including those pursuant to Regulation A, Regulation D, and Rule 144A
- Offerings of securities issued or backed by governmental, municipal, banking, tax-exempt, or other entities that are exempt from registration under the 1933 Act
- Acquisition transactions in which there is an exchange of stock

l. **Underwriter** As defined in the 1933 Act: any person who has purchased from an issuer with a view to, or offers or sells for an issuer in connection with, the distribution of any security, or participates or has a direct or indirect participation in any such undertaking, or participates or has a participation in the direct or indirect underwriting of any such undertaking; but such term shall not include a person whose interest is limited to a commission from an underwriter or dealer not in excess of the usual and customary distributors' or sellers' commission. As used in this paragraph, the term *issuer* shall include, in addition to an issuer, any person directly or indirectly controlling or controlled by the issuer, or any person under direct or indirect common control with the issuer.

Except when the context otherwise requires, the word *underwriter*, as used in this standard, refers to the managing, or lead, underwriter, who typically negotiates the underwriting agreement or purchase agreement (hereafter referred to as the *underwriting agreement*) for a group of underwriters whose exact composition is not determined until shortly before a securities offering becomes effective.

Editor Note: References in this standard to information that is *included* in a document are to be read to also encompass information that is *incorporated by reference* in that document.

B. **Engagement Acceptance**

The auditor should determine whether to accept an engagement to issue a comfort letter in connection with financial statements included in a securities offering. (The auditor is *not* required to accept such an engagement.)

1. **Acceptable Addressee** The auditor should provide a comfort letter in connection with financial statements included in a securities offering **only** to:

a. Underwriters

b. Requesting parties (that meet the preceding definition)

Further, when issuing a letter in accordance with this standard, the auditor should not circumvent the requirements of this standard by issuing any additional letters or reports to a requesting party in connection with the securities offering in which the auditor comments on items for which commenting is otherwise precluded by this standard.

2. **Requesting Party Should Provide Either Proof of Due Diligence Defense Legal Opinion or Representation Letter** The auditor should request the requesting party to provide either:

   a. A *written* opinion from external legal counsel that the requesting party has a statutory due diligence defense under Section 11 of the 1933 Act

   or

   b. A representation letter that:

      (1) Is addressed to the auditor

      (2) Contains the statement, "The review process applied to the information relating to the issuer, is, or will be, substantially consistent with the due diligence process that we would perform if this securities offering were being registered pursuant to the Securities Act of 1933. We are knowledgeable with respect to that due diligence process."

      (3) Is signed by the requesting party

C. **Agreeing Upon the Scope of Services**
The auditor should obtain an understanding of the specific matters to be addressed in the comfort letter.

1. **Meeting With Requesting Party & Entity** The auditor should ask to meet with the requesting party and the entity to discuss the procedures to be followed.

2. **No Assurance on Sufficiency of Procedures** The auditor should clearly state in any discussion of procedures that the auditor cannot provide any assurance regarding the sufficiency of the procedures for the requesting party's purposes.

3. **Draft of Form of Letter Provided** The auditor should provide a draft of the form of the letter the auditor expects to furnish. To the extent possible, the draft should deal with all matters to be covered in the final letter and should use exactly the same terms as those to be used in the final letter, subject to the understanding that the comments in the final letter cannot be determined until the procedures underlying it have been performed.

   a. **Letter Should Be Marked Draft** The draft letter should be identified as a draft to avoid giving the impression that the procedures described have been performed.

   b. **Procedures Included Should Be Clearly Stated** In both the draft and final forms of the comfort letter, the auditor should clearly describe the procedures performed by the auditor—the auditor should **not** state or imply that the auditor is carrying out such procedures *as the auditor considers necessary* because such statements or implications may lead to misunderstanding about the responsibility for the sufficiency of the procedures for the requesting party purposes.

   c. **If No Meeting Takes Place Include Procedures in Underwriting Agreement in Draft Letter** If the auditor has been unable to have a discussion with the requesting party about the auditor's planned procedures, the auditor should describe in the draft letter those procedures specified in the draft underwriting agreement that the auditor is willing to perform.

4. **Group Financial Statements** When the comfort letter relates to group financial statements, the auditor of the group financial statements should read the comfort letters of the component auditors reporting on significant components. The auditor of the group financial statements should state in the comfort letter that:

   a. Reading the component auditors' letters was one of the procedures followed

   b. The procedures, other than reading the component auditors' letters, performed by the auditor of the group financial statements, relate solely to entities audited by the auditor of the group financial statements and to the group financial statements

5. **Requested From More Than One Auditor** When comfort letters are requested from more than one auditor, the requirements of this standard apply to each auditor.

6. **Competitive Bidding Situations** In competitive bidding situations in which legal counsel for the requesting party acts as the requesting party's representative prior to opening and acceptance of the bid, the auditor should carry out the discussions and other communications required by this standard with the legal counsel until the requesting party is selected. In such circumstances, the auditor should *not* agree to provide a comfort letter addressed to the entity, legal counsel, or a nonspecific addressee, such as "any or all underwriters to be selected." If the auditor agrees to provide a draft comfort letter, the draft comfort letter should include a legend describing the letter's purpose and limitations.

D. Format & Contents of Comfort Letters

1. **Dating**

   a. The letter should state that the inquiries and other procedures described in the letter did *not* cover the period from the cutoff date to the date of the letter.

   b. When an additional letter, dated at or shortly before the closing date, is requested, the auditor should carry out the specified procedures and inquiries as of the cutoff date for each letter. The subsequent letter should relate only to information in the securities offering as most recently amended.

2. **Addressee** The letter should be addressed only to the requesting party, or both the requesting party and the entity, and should *not* be provided to any other parties.

3. **Introductory Paragraph** The letter should contain an introductory paragraph that identifies the financial statements and the securities offering.

4. **Audit Report on Audited Financial Statements Included in Securities Offering**

   a. The auditor should, in the comfort letter, make reference to, but not repeat, the audit report.

   b. When the audit report contains an emphasis-of-matter or other-matter paragraph addressing matters *other than* consistency of application of accounting policies, the auditor should refer to that fact in the comfort letter and discuss the subject matter of the paragraph. In those instances in which the SEC accepts a modified opinion on historical financial statements, the auditor should refer to the modification in the opening paragraph of the comfort letter and discuss the subject matter of the modification.

   c. The auditor should **not** provide negative assurance regarding the audit report or regarding financial statements that have been audited and are reported on in the securities offering by other auditors.

d. In the introductory paragraph of the comfort letter, if the auditor refers to reports that the auditor has previously issued other than the audit report on the audited financial statements included in the securities offering, the auditor should not repeat the reports in the comfort letter or otherwise imply that the auditor is reporting as of the date of the comfort letter or assuming responsibility for the sufficiency of the procedures for the requesting party's purposes.

e. The auditor should not mention, refer to, or attach to the comfort letter any report or other auditor's written communication that includes an alert that restricts the use of the auditor's written communication, or any other restricted use reports.

5. **Representations** The auditor should refer in the comfort letter to the requesting party's representations when a representation letter regarding knowledge of and consistency with the 1933 Act's due diligence process has been provided.

6. **Independence** The auditor should state in the comfort letter that the auditor is independent, or the date through which the auditor was independent, with respect to the entity, and identify the applicable independence rules.

7. **Compliance With SEC Requirements**

a. **1933 Act Compliance** If the auditor is requested to include an opinion in the comfort letter on whether the financial statements covered by the audit report comply as to form with the pertinent accounting requirements adopted by the SEC, the auditor's opinion should refer to compliance as to form, in all material respects, with the applicable accounting requirements of the 1933 Act and the related rules and regulations adopted by the SEC.

b. **1934 Act Compliance Except Internal Control Over Financial Reporting** Certain financial statements may be incorporated in a registration statement under the 1933 Act by reference to filings under the Securities Exchange Act of 1934 (the 1934 Act). If the auditor is requested to include an opinion in the comfort letter on whether the financial statements covered by the audit report comply as to form with the pertinent accounting requirements adopted by the SEC, the auditor's opinion should refer to whether the audited financial statements incorporated by reference in the registration statement comply as to form, in all material respects, with the applicable accounting requirements of the 1934 Act and the related rules and regulations adopted by the SEC. However, the auditor should **not** opine on compliance with the provisions of the 1934 Act regarding internal control over financial reporting.

c. **Material Departure** If the auditor has been requested to include an opinion in the comfort letter on whether the financial statements covered by the audit report comply as to form with the pertinent accounting requirements adopted by the SEC, and a material departure from the pertinent rules and regulations adopted by the SEC exists, the auditor should disclose the departure in the comfort letter.

d. **Opinion on Compliance Limited to Audited Financial Statements** The auditor should express an opinion on compliance as to form with requirements under the rules and regulations adopted by the SEC only with respect to those rules and regulations applicable to the form and content of financial statements that the auditor has audited. When the financial statements or financial statement schedules have not been audited, the auditor is limited to providing negative assurance on compliance as to form.

The auditor should **not** comment in a comfort letter on compliance as to form of MD&A with rules and regulations adopted by the SEC.

8. **When Legal Opinion or Representation Letter *Not* Provided** If a requesting party, other than an underwriter, requests a comfort letter but does not provide a legal opinion affirming that the requesting party has a statutory due diligence defense or a representation letter regarding knowledge of and consistency with the 1933 Act's due diligence process, the auditor should **not** provide negative assurance on the financial statements as a whole, or on any of the specified elements, accounts, or items. In such circumstances, the comfort letter should include the following statements:

   a. It should be understood that we have no responsibility for establishing (and did not establish) the scope and nature of the procedures enumerated in the preceding paragraphs; rather, the procedures enumerated therein are those that the requesting party asked us to perform. Accordingly, we make no representations regarding questions of legal interpretation or regarding the sufficiency for your purposes of the procedures enumerated in the preceding paragraphs; also, such procedures would not necessarily reveal any material misstatement of the amounts or percentages previously listed as set forth in the [*offering circular*]. Further, we have addressed ourselves solely to the foregoing data and make no representations regarding the adequacy of disclosures or whether any material facts have been omitted. This letter relates only to the financial statement items previously specified and does not extend to any financial statement of the company as a whole.

   b. The foregoing procedures do not constitute an audit conducted in accordance with generally accepted auditing standards. Had we performed additional procedures or had we conducted an audit or a review of the company's [*give dates of any interim financial statements*] consolidated financial statements in accordance with auditing standards generally accepted in the United States of America, other matters might have come to our attention that would have been reported to you.

   c. These procedures should not be taken to supplant any additional inquiries or procedures that you would undertake in your consideration of the proposed offering.

   d. This letter is solely for your information and to assist you in your inquiries in connection with the offering of the securities covered by the [*offering circular*]. It is not to be used, circulated, quoted, or otherwise referred to for any other purpose, including but not limited to, the registration, purchase, or sale of securities, nor is it to be filed with or referred to in whole or in part in the offering document or any other document, except that reference may be made to it in any list of closing documents pertaining to the offering of the securities covered by the offering document.

   e. We have no responsibility to update this letter for events and circumstances occurring after [*cutoff date*].

E. Commenting in a Comfort Letter on Information Other Than Audited Financial Statements

1. General

   a. When commenting in a comfort letter on information other than audited financial statements, the auditor should:

      (1) Describe the procedures performed by the auditor

      (2) Describe the criteria specified by the requesting party

      (3) State that the procedures performed with respect to interim periods may not disclose matters of significance regarding certain matters about which negative assurance is requested

b. The auditor should **not**, in the comfort letter:

(1) Make any statements, or imply, that the auditor has applied procedures that the auditor determined to be necessary or sufficient for the requesting party's purposes

(2) Use terms of uncertain meaning (such as *general review*, *limited review*, *reconcile*, *check*, or *test*) in describing the work *unless* the procedures encompassed by these terms are described in the comfort letter

(3) Make a statement that nothing else has come to the auditor's attention that would be of interest to the requesting party as a result of carrying out the specified procedures

c. When the report on the audited financial statements in the securities offering is a modified report, the auditor should consider the effect on providing negative assurance in the comfort letter regarding subsequent interim financial information included in the securities offering or regarding an absence of specified subsequent changes.

When the audit report contains an emphasis-of-matter or other-matter paragraph addressing matters *other than* consistency of application of accounting policies, the auditor should refer to that fact in the comfort letter and discuss the subject matter of the paragraph. In those instances in which the SEC accepts a modified opinion on historical financial statements, the auditor should refer to the modification in the opening paragraph of the comfort letter and discuss the subject matter of the modification.

2. **Knowledge of Internal Control** The auditor should obtain an understanding of the entity's internal control over financial reporting for both annual and interim periods when commenting in a comfort letter on:

a. Unaudited interim financial information, including unaudited condensed interim financial information

b. Capsule financial information

c. A financial forecast when historical financial statements provide a basis for one or more significant assumptions for the forecast

d. Subsequent changes in specified financial statement items

3. **Unaudited Interim Financial Information**

a. The auditor should provide negative assurance on unaudited interim financial information included in the securities offering only if the auditor has conducted a review of the interim financial information in accordance with US GAAS applicable to reviews of interim financial information.

If the auditor has not conducted a review in accordance with US GAAS applicable to reviews of interim financial information, the auditor is limited to reporting procedures performed and findings obtained.

b. The negative assurance provided regarding such unaudited interim information should be about whether:

(1) Any material modifications should be made to the unaudited interim financial information for it to be in accordance with the AFRF

(2) The unaudited interim financial information complies as to form in all material respects with the applicable accounting requirements of the 1933 Act and the related rules and regulations adopted by the SEC, if applicable

c. If the auditor states in the comfort letter that the auditor has performed a review of the unaudited interim financial information, the auditor should attach the review report to the letter unless the review report is already included in the securities offering.

d. The auditor should specifically identify, in the comfort letter, any unaudited interim financial information and should state that the auditor has not audited the interim financial information in accordance with US GAAS and does not express an opinion concerning such information.

e. When the auditor is requested by the requesting party to provide negative assurance on the unaudited interim financial information, or information extracted from it, for a monthly period ending after the latest financial statements included in the securities offering, the preceding requirements regarding unaudited interim financial information apply. In such a circumstance, a copy of the unaudited interim financial information should be attached to the comfort letter.

4. Capsule Financial Information

a. The auditor should **not** provide negative assurance regarding whether the selected capsule financial information is in accordance with the AFRF *unless*:

(1) The auditor has performed a review of the financial statements underlying the capsule financial information in accordance with US GAAS applicable to reviews of interim financial information

(2) The selected capsule financial information is in accordance with minimum disclosure requirements of the AFRF for interim financial information

If these conditions have not been met, the auditor is limited to reporting procedures performed and findings obtained.

b. The auditor should **not** provide negative assurance on selected capsule financial information regarding whether the dollar amounts were determined on a basis substantially consistent with that of the corresponding amounts in the audited financial statements *unless* the auditor has performed a review of the financial statements underlying the capsule financial information in accordance with US GAAS applicable to reviews of interim financial information.

Otherwise, the auditor is limited to reporting procedures performed and findings obtained.

5. **Pro Forma Financial Information**

   a. The auditor should **not** comment in a comfort letter on pro forma financial information *unless* the auditor has an appropriate level of knowledge of the accounting and financial reporting practices of the entity.

   b. The auditor should **not** provide negative assurance in a comfort letter on pro forma financial information, including negative assurance on:

      - The application of pro forma adjustments to historical amounts
      - The compilation of pro forma financial information
      - Whether the pro forma financial information complies as to form in all material respects with the applicable accounting requirements of Rule 11-02 of Regulation S-X

      Unless the auditor has an appropriate level of knowledge of the accounting and financial reporting practices of the entity and has performed either:

      (1) An audit of the annual financial statements

      or

      (2) A review of the interim financial statements, in accordance with US GAAS applicable to reviews of interim financial information of the entity (or, in the case of a business combination, of a significant constituent part of the combined entity) to which the pro forma adjustments were applied. In the case of a business combination, the historical financial statements of each constituent part of the combined entity on which the pro forma financial information is based should be audited or reviewed.

      If these conditions are not met, the auditor is limited to reporting procedures performed and findings obtained.

6. **Financial Forecasts**

   a. When performing procedures agreed to with the requesting party on a financial forecast and commenting on it in a comfort letter, the auditor should:

      (1) Obtain an understanding of the entity's internal control over financial reporting for both annual and interim periods

      (2) Perform procedures required by AT 301, *Financial Forecasts and Projections*, for reporting on the compilation of a forecast

      (3) Issue a report on the compilation of prospective financial information in accordance with AT 301 and attach the report thereon to the comfort letter

      (4) Perform additional procedures as requested by the requesting party and report the findings in the comfort letter

   b. The auditor should **not** provide negative assurance on the results of procedures performed on a financial forecast.

   c. The auditor should **not** provide negative assurance with respect to compliance of the financial forecast with Rule 11-03 of Regulation S-X *unless* the auditor has performed an examination of the financial forecast in accordance with AT 301.

- **d.** If the financial forecast is included in the securities offering, the auditor should **not** issue a comfort letter *unless* the financial forecast is accompanied by an indication that the auditor has not examined the financial forecast and, therefore, does not express an opinion on it.

7. Subsequent Changes

- **a.** The auditor should base comments regarding subsequent changes in specified financial statement items solely on the limited procedures performed with respect to the change period as determined by the requesting party.
- **b.** The auditor should provide negative assurance in the comfort letter regarding subsequent changes in specified financial statement items only as of a date less than 135 days from the end of the most recent period for which the auditor has performed an audit or a review.
- **c.** When the requesting party requests negative assurance regarding subsequent changes in specified financial statement items as of a date 135 days or more from the end of the most recent period for which the auditor has performed an audit or a review, the auditor is limited to reporting procedures performed and findings obtained.
- **d.** In commenting on subsequent changes, the auditor should **not** characterize subsequent changes using ambiguous terms, such as referring to the change as *adverse*. The auditor should note in the comfort letter if there has been a change in the application of the requirements of the AFRF.
- **e.** The auditor should comment only on the occurrence of subsequent changes in specified financial statement items that are not disclosed in the securities offering. Accordingly, the auditor should include the phrase *except for changes, increases, or decreases that the securities offering discloses have occurred or may occur* in the comfort letter when it has come to the auditor's attention that a change, increase, or decrease has occurred during the change period, and the amount of such change, increase, or decrease is disclosed in the securities offering. This phrase need not be included in the letter when no changes, increases, or decreases in the specified financial statement items are disclosed in the securities offering.
- **f.** The auditor should identify in the comfort letter in both draft and final form the dates as of which, and periods for which, data at the cutoff date and data for the change period are to be compared, whether or not specified in the underwriting agreement.
- **g.** If the requesting party requests the use of a change period or periods other than those defined per this standard, the auditor should explain to the requesting party the implications of using an earlier date. If the requesting party, nonetheless, requests the use of a change period or periods other than those defined per this standard, the auditor is permitted to use the period or periods requested.

8. **Tables, Statistics & Other Financial Information**

   a. The auditor should **not** comment in a comfort letter on tables, statistics, and other financial information appearing in the securities offering *unless* the information:

      (1) Is expressed in dollars (or percentages derived from such dollar amounts) and has been obtained from accounting records that are subject to internal control over financial reporting

      or

      (2) Has been derived directly from such accounting records by analysis or computation

   b. The auditor should **not** comment in a comfort letter on quantitative information that has been obtained from accounting records *unless* the information is subject to the same controls over financial reporting as the dollar amounts.

   c. The auditor should **not** comment in a comfort letter on tables, statistics, and other financial information relating to an unaudited period *unless* the auditor has:

      (1) Performed an audit of the entity's financial statements for a period including, or immediately prior to, the unaudited period or completed an audit for a later period

      or

      (2) Otherwise obtained knowledge of the entity's internal control over financial reporting

   d. The auditor should **not** use the term *presents fairly* in comments concerning tables, statistics, and other financial information and should **not** comment on:

      (1) Information subject to legal interpretation, such as beneficial share ownership

      (2) Nonfinancial data presented in MD&A, *unless* the auditor has conducted an examination or review of MD&A in accordance with AT 701, *Management's Discussion and Analysis*

      (3) Matters merely because the auditor is capable of reading, counting, measuring, or performing other functions that might be applicable

   e. The auditor's comments in the comfort letter concerning tables, statistics, and other financial information included in the securities offering should include:

      (1) A clear identification of the specific information commented on

      (2) A description of the procedures performed

      (3) The findings, expressed in terms of agreement between items compared

   f. With respect to the acceptability of methods of allocation used in deriving the figures commented on, the auditor should comment only to the extent to which such allocation is made in, or can be derived directly by analysis or computation from, the entity's accounting records. Such comments, if made, should make clear that:

      (1) Such allocations may be, to a substantial extent, arbitrary

      (2) The method of allocation used is not the only acceptable method

(3) Other acceptable methods of allocation might produce significantly different results.

g. The comfort letter should state that the auditor makes no representations regarding:

(1) Any matter of legal interpretation

(2) The completeness or adequacy of disclosure

(3) The adequacy of the procedures followed, and that such procedures would not necessarily disclose material misstatements or omissions in the information to which the comments relate

9. **Compliance as to Form With Regulation S-K**

a. The auditor should **not** provide negative assurance about whether certain financial information in registration statements, included because of specific requirements of Regulation S-K, is in conformity with the disclosure requirements of Regulation S-K *unless* the following conditions are met:

(1) The information is derived, directly or by analysis or computation, from the accounting records subject to internal control over financial reporting

(2) The information is capable of evaluation against reasonable criteria that have been established by the SEC

b. The auditor should **not** express an opinion on conformity with the disclosure requirements of Regulation S-K.

10. **Restriction as to Use in Concluding Paragraph** The comfort letter should include a concluding paragraph restricting the use of the comfort letter for the information of the addressees and to assist the requesting parties in connection with the securities offering.

11. **Disclosure of Subsequently Discovered Matters** The auditor should inform the entity when the auditor has discovered matters that require mention in the final comfort letter but were not mentioned in the draft letter that has been furnished to the requesting party. If the entity decides that disclosure will not be made in the securities offering, the auditor should inform the entity that the matters will be mentioned in the comfort letter and should recommend that the requesting party be informed promptly.

F. Summary Format of a Comfort Letter

A typical comfort letter includes:

1. A statement regarding the independence of the auditor

2. If applicable, an opinion regarding whether the audited financial statements included in the securities offering comply as to form in all material respects with the applicable accounting requirements of the 1933 Act and related rules and regulations adopted by the SEC.

3. Negative assurance on whether:

   a. If applicable, the unaudited interim financial information included in the registration statement complies as to form in all material respects with the applicable accounting requirements of the 1933 Act and the related rules and regulations adopted by the SEC

   b. Any material modifications should be made to the unaudited financial information included in the securities offering for them to be in conformity with the AFRF

4. Negative assurance on whether, during a specified period following the date of the latest financial statements in the securities offering and prospectus, there has been any change in capital stock, increase in long-term debt, or any decrease in other specified financial statement items

5. Assumptions for Illustration of a Typical Comfort Letter

   The illustration of a comfort letter that follows is an example of a letter that the auditor of a nonissuer may provide when a registrant is including the nonissuer's financial statements in the securities offering to be filed with the SEC. Appropriate modifications would be made if additional financial information is covered by the comfort letter. The following circumstances are assumed:

   - The prospectus includes audited consolidated balance sheets as of December 31, 20X5 and 20X4, and audited consolidated statements of income, stockholders' equity, and cash flows for each year in the three-year period ended December 31, 20X5. Note that the example assumes all the net income is attributable to the company. If that were not the case, the references to net income would be modified, or additional references would be included as appropriate.

   - The prospectus also includes an unaudited condensed consolidated balance sheet as of March 31, 20X6, and unaudited condensed consolidated statements of income, stockholders' equity, and cash flows for the three-month periods ended March 31, 20X6 and 20X5, reviewed in accordance with generally accepted auditing standards applicable to reviews of interim financial information but not previously reported on by the auditor. The example also assumes that the auditor has not previously reported on the interim financial information. If the auditor has previously reported on the interim financial information, that fact may be referred to in the introductory paragraph of the comfort letter as follows:

     > Also, we have reviewed the unaudited condensed consolidated financial statements as of March 31, 20X6 and 20X5, and for the three-month periods then ended, as indicated in our report dated May 15, 20X6, which is included (incorporated by reference) in the registration statement.

   - The cutoff date is June 23, 20X6, and the letter is dated June 28, 20X6. The effective date is June 28, 20X6.

   - The auditors are reporting independence under the SEC rules and regulations.

Exhibit 24 ▸ Typical Comfort Letter for 1933 Act Securities Offering

June 28, 20X6

[*Appropriate Addressee*]

Dear Ladies and Gentlemen:

We have audited the consolidated financial statements of The Nonissuer Company, Inc. (the company) and subsidiaries, which comprise the consolidated balance sheets as of December 31, 20X5 and 20X4, and the related consolidated statements of income, changes in stockholders' equity, and cash flows for each of the years in the three-year period ended December 31, 20X5, and the related notes to the consolidated financial statements, all included in The Issuer Company's (the registrant) registration statement (no. 33-00000) on Form S-1 filed by the registrant under the Securities Act of 1933 (the Act); our report with respect thereto is also included in that registration statement. The registration statement, as amended on June 28, 20X6, is herein referred to as the registration statement.

In connection with the registration statement:

1. We are independent certified public accountants with respect to the company within the meaning of the 1933 Act and the applicable rules and regulations thereunder adopted by the SEC.
2. In our opinion [*include the phrase* except as disclosed in the registration statement *if applicable*], the consolidated financial statements audited by us and included in the registration statement comply as to form in all material respects with the applicable accounting requirements of the Act and the related rules and regulations adopted by the SEC.
3. We have not audited any financial statements of the company as of any date or for any period subsequent to December 31, 20X5; although, we have conducted an audit for the year ended December 31, 20X5, the purpose (and, therefore, the scope) of the audit was to enable us to express our opinion on the consolidated financial statements as of December 31, 20X5, and for the year then ended, but not on the financial statements for any interim period within that year. Therefore, we are unable to and do not express any opinion on the unaudited condensed consolidated balance sheet as of March 31, 20X6, and the unaudited condensed consolidated statements of income, stockholders' equity, and cash flows for the three-month periods ended March 31, 20X6 and 20X5, included in the registration statement, or on the financial position, results of operations, or cash flows as of any date or for any period subsequent to December 31, 20X5.
4. For purposes of this letter we have read the 20X6 minutes of meetings of the stockholders, the board of directors, and [*include other appropriate committees, if any*] of the company and its subsidiaries as set forth in the minute books at June 23, 20X6, officials of the company having advised us that the minutes of all such meetings through that date were set forth therein and having discussed with us the unapproved minutes of meetings held on [*dates*]; we have carried out other procedures to June 23, 20X6, as follows (our work did not extend to the period from June 24, 20X6 to June 28, 20X6, inclusive):
   a. With respect to the three-month periods ended March 31, 20X6 and 20X5, we have:
      (i) Performed the procedures specified for a review in accordance with auditing standards generally accepted in the United States of America applicable to reviews of interim financial information, on the unaudited condensed consolidated balance sheet as of March 31, 20X6, and the unaudited condensed consolidated statements of income, stockholders' equity, and cash flows for the three-month periods ended March 31, 20X6 and 20X5, included in the registration statement.
      (ii) Inquired of certain officials of the company who have responsibility for financial and accounting matters whether the unaudited condensed consolidated financial statements referred to in *a*(i) comply as to form in all material respects with the applicable accounting requirements of the Act and the related rules and regulations adopted by the SEC.

b. With respect to the period from April 1, 20X6 to May 31, 20X6, we have:
   (i) Read the unaudited consolidated financial statements of the company and subsidiaries for April and May of both 20X5 and 20X6 furnished us by the company, officials of the company having advised us that no such financial statements as of any date or for any period subsequent to May 31, 20X6, were available. [*If applicable:* The financial information for April and May of both 20X5 and 20X6 is incomplete in that it omits the statements of cash flows and other disclosures.]

   (ii) Inquired of certain officials of the company who have responsibility for financial and accounting matters whether the unaudited consolidated financial statements referred to in *b*(i) are stated on a basis substantially consistent with that of the audited consolidated financial statements included in the registration statement.

The foregoing procedures do not constitute an audit conducted in accordance with generally accepted auditing standards. Also, they would not necessarily reveal matters of significance with respect to the comments in the following paragraph. Accordingly, we make no representations regarding the sufficiency of the foregoing procedures for your purposes.

5. Nothing came to our attention as a result of the foregoing procedures, however, that caused us to believe that:
   a. (i) Any material modifications should be made to the unaudited condensed consolidated financial statements described in 4*a*(i), included in the registration statement, for them to be in conformity with generally accepted accounting principles.
      (ii) The unaudited condensed consolidated financial statements described in 4*a*(i) do not comply as to form in all material respects with the applicable accounting requirements of the Act and the related rules and regulations adopted by the SEC.
   b. (i) At May 31, 20X6, there was any change in the capital stock, increase in long-term debt, or decrease in consolidated net current assets or stockholders' equity of the consolidated companies as compared with amounts shown in the March 31, 20X6, unaudited condensed consolidated balance sheet included in the registration statement, or
      (ii) For the period from April 1, 20X6 to May 31, 20X6, there were any decreases, as compared to the corresponding period in the preceding year, in consolidated net sales or in income before extraordinary items or of net income, except in all instances for changes, increases, or decreases that the registration statement discloses have occurred or may occur.
6. As mentioned in 4*b*, company officials have advised us that no consolidated financial statements as of any date or for any period subsequent to May 31, 20X6, are available; accordingly, the procedures carried out by us with respect to changes in financial statement items after May 31, 20X6, have, of necessity, been even more limited than those with respect to the periods referred to in 4. We have inquired of certain officials of the company who have responsibility for financial and accounting matters whether (*a*) at June 23, 20X6, there was any change in the capital stock, increase in long-term debt, or any decreases in consolidated net current assets or stockholders' equity of the consolidated companies as compared with amounts shown on the March 31, 20X6, unaudited condensed consolidated balance sheet included in the registration statement, or (*b*) for the period from April 1, 20X6 to June 23, 20X6, there were any decreases, as compared with the corresponding period in the preceding year, in consolidated net sales, or in income before extraordinary items or of net income. On the basis of these inquiries and our reading of the minutes as described in 4, nothing came to our attention that caused us to believe that there was any such change, increase, or decrease, except in all instances for changes, increases, or decreases that the registration statement discloses have occurred or may occur.
7. This letter is solely for the information of the addressees and to assist the underwriters in conducting and documenting their investigation of the affairs of the company in connection with the offering of the securities covered by the registration statement, and it is not to be used, circulated, quoted, or otherwise referred to within or without the underwriting group for any other purpose, including but not limited to the registration, purchase, or sale of securities, nor is it to be filed with or referred to in whole or in part in the registration statement or any other document, except that reference may be made to it in the underwriting agreement or in any list of closing documents pertaining to the offering of the securities covered by the registration statement.

[*Auditor's signature*]

[*Date*]

VII. Review of Interim Financial Information (AU 930)

Editor Note: The term *auditor* is used throughout this section, not because the auditor is performing an audit but because the scope of this section is limited to a review of interim financial information performed by an auditor of the financial statements of the entity.

A. Overview

1. **Scope** This standard applies to a review of interim financial information when:

    a. The entity's latest annual financial statements have been audited

    and

    b. The auditor has *either*

        (1) Been engaged to audit the entity's current year financial statements

        or

        (2) Audited the latest annual financial statements and although an audit of the current year financial statements is expected, the engagement of another auditor to audit them is not effective prior to the beginning of the period to be reviewed

    and

    c. The same financial reporting framework used to prepare the annual financial statements is used for the interim financial information

    d. The interim financial information is condensed information, if *all* of the following conditions are met. The condensed interim financial information:

        (1) Purports to be in accordance with an appropriate financial reporting framework, which includes appropriate form and content of interim financial information

        (2) Includes a note that the financial information does not represent complete financial statements and is to be read in conjunction with the entity's latest annual audited financial statements

        (3) Accompanies the entity's latest audited annual financial statements or such audited annual financial statements are made readily available by the entity. (Audited financial statements are deemed to be readily available if a third-party user can obtain the financial statements without any further action by the entity, for example, financial statements on an entity's website may be considered readily available, but being available upon request is *not* considered readily available.)

    Editor Note: The preceding conditions are an acknowledgement of the difference between a review performed by an accountant with an audit base of knowledge versus that performed by an accountant who is not the entity's auditor. Further, when these conditions are met, generally the review engagement is intended to provide a periodic update to the year-end reporting and is considered an extension of the annual audit. Thus, the standard setters decided the requirements and guidance should reside in the auditing literature. Accordingly, if these conditions are *not* met, reviews of interim financial information of nonissuers should be performed in accordance with Statements on Standards for Accounting and Review Services.

2. **Objective** The objective of the auditor is to obtain a basis for reporting whether the auditor is aware of any material modifications that should be made to the interim financial information for it to be in accordance with the applicable financial reporting framework (AFRF) through performing limited procedures.

   Editor Note: The objective of a review of interim financial information differs significantly from that of an audit conducted in accordance with US GAAS. Although a review may bring to the auditor's attention significant findings or issues affecting the interim financial information, a review:

   - Does **not** provide a basis for expressing an opinion about whether the interim financial information is presented fairly, in all material respects, in accordance with the AFRF
   - Is **not** designed to provide the auditor with a basis for obtaining reasonable assurance that the interim financial information is free from material misstatement
   - Consists principally of performing analytical procedures and making inquiries of persons responsible for financial and accounting matters and does **not** contemplate:
     - Tests of accounting records through inspection, observation, or confirmation
     - Tests of controls to evaluate their effectiveness

       Editor Note: However, the auditor should have an *understanding* of the entity and its environment, including its internal control.
     - The obtainment of corroborating evidence in response to inquiries
     - The performance of certain other procedures ordinarily performed in an audit
   - Does **not** provide assurance that the auditor will become aware of all significant findings or issues that would be identified in an audit

3. **Definitions**

   a. **Interim Financial Information** Financial information prepared and presented in accordance with an AFRF that comprises either a complete or condensed set of financial statements covering a period or periods less than one full year or covering a 12-month period ending on a date other than the entity's fiscal year-end

   b. **Applicable Financial Reporting Framework** The financial reporting framework adopted by management and, when appropriate, those charged with governance in the preparation and fair presentation of the financial statements that is acceptable in view of the nature of the entity and the objective of the financial statements, or that is required by law or regulation

B. Acceptance & Agreement on Terms of Engagement

1. Acceptance of Engagement

a. **New Client** Before accepting an engagement to review an entity's interim financial information for a new client, the auditor should request management to authorize the predecessor auditor to respond fully to the auditor's inquiries regarding matters that will assist the auditor in determining whether to accept the engagement. If management refuses to authorize the predecessor auditor to respond, or limits the response, the auditor should inquire about the reasons and consider the implications of that refusal in deciding whether to accept the engagement.

   The auditor should evaluate the predecessor auditor's response, or consider the implications if the predecessor auditor provides no response or a limited response, in determining whether to accept the engagement.

b. **Conditions for Engagement Acceptance** If the following conditions are not met the auditor should not accept the engagement.

Before accepting an engagement to perform a review of interim financial information, the auditor should:

(1) Determine whether the financial reporting framework to be applied in the preparation of the interim financial information is acceptable

(2) Obtain the agreement of management that it acknowledges and understands its responsibility:

(a) For the preparation and fair presentation of the interim financial information in accordance with the AFRF

(b) For the design, implementation, and maintenance of internal control sufficient to provide a reasonable basis for the preparation and fair presentation of interim financial information in accordance with the AFRF

(c) To provide the auditor with:

(i) Access to all information of which management is aware that is relevant to the preparation and fair presentation of the interim financial information, such as records, documentation, and other matters

(ii) Additional information that the auditor may request from management for the purpose of the review

(iii) Unrestricted access to persons within the entity of whom the auditor determines it necessary to make inquiries

(d) To include the auditor's review report in any document containing interim financial information that indicates that such information has been reviewed by the entity's auditor

2. **Agreement on Engagement Terms** The auditor should agree upon the terms of the engagement with management or those charged with governance, as appropriate. The agreed-upon terms of the engagement should be recorded in an engagement letter or other suitable form of *written* agreement and should include the following matters.

a. **Objectives & Scope** The wording the auditor *may* use in the written agreement is as follows.

- The objective of a review of interim financial information is to provide the auditor with a basis for reporting whether the auditor is aware of any material modifications that should be made to the interim financial information for it to be in accordance with the applicable financial reporting framework.
- A review includes obtaining sufficient knowledge of the entity's business and internal control, as it relates to the preparation and fair presentation of both annual and interim financial information, to enable the auditor to:
  - Identify the types of potential material misstatements in the interim financial information and consider the likelihood of their occurrence
  - Select the inquiries and analytical procedures that will provide the auditor with a basis for reporting whether the auditor is aware of any material

modifications that should be made to the interim financial information for it to conform with the applicable financial reporting framework

b. **Management's Responsibilities** These should include those responsibilities described previously as conditions for the acceptance of the engagement.

Management's responsibilities *may* be worded in the written agreement as follows.

- Preparing and presenting the interim financial information in accordance with the applicable financial reporting framework
- Designing, implementing, and maintaining internal control sufficient to provide a reasonable basis for the preparation and fair presentation of interim financial information in accordance with the applicable financial reporting framework
- Providing the auditor with:
  - Access to all information of which management is aware that is relevant to the preparation and fair presentation of the interim financial information, such as records, documentation, and other matters
  - Additional information that the auditor may request from management for the purpose of the review
  - Unrestricted access to persons within the entity of whom the auditor determines it necessary to make inquiries
- Including the auditor's review report in any document containing interim financial information that indicates that such information has been reviewed by the entity's auditor
- Identifying and ensuring that the entity complies with the laws and regulations applicable to its activities
- Providing the auditor, at the conclusion of the engagement, with a letter confirming certain representations made during the review
- Adjusting the interim financial information to correct material misstatements; although a review of interim financial information is not designed to provide the auditor with reasonable assurance that the interim financial information is free from material misstatement, management nonetheless is responsible for affirming in its representation letter to the auditor that the effects of any uncorrected misstatements aggregated by the auditor during the current engagement and pertaining to the current year period(s) under review are immaterial, both individually and in the aggregate, to the interim financial information as a whole

c. **Auditor's Responsibilities** The wording the auditor *may* use in the written agreement is as follows.

- The auditor is responsible for conducting the review in accordance with auditing standards generally accepted in the United States of America applicable to reviews of interim financial information.
- A review of interim financial information consists principally of performing analytical procedures and making inquiries of persons responsible for financial and accounting matters.
- A review is substantially less in scope than an audit conducted in accordance with auditing standards generally accepted in the United States of America, the objective of which is the expression of an opinion regarding the financial information as a whole. Accordingly, the auditor will not express an opinion on the interim financial information.

d. **Limitations of a Review Engagement** The wording the auditor *may* use in the written agreement is as follows.

- A review does not provide a basis for expressing an opinion about whether the interim financial information is presented fairly, in all material respects, in accordance with the applicable financial reporting framework.
- A review does not provide the auditor with a basis for obtaining reasonable assurance that the auditor will become aware of all significant findings or issues that would be identified in an audit.
- A review is not designed to provide the auditor with a basis for obtaining reasonable assurance on internal control or to identify significant deficiencies or material weaknesses in internal control; however, the auditor is responsible for communicating to management and those charged with governance any significant deficiencies or material weaknesses in internal control that the auditor identifies during the performance of review procedures.

e. **Identification of AFRF for Preparation of Interim Financial Information**

C. Procedures

1. Understanding the Entity & Its Environment, Including Its Internal Control

a. **Required Understanding** To plan and conduct the engagement, the auditor should have an understanding of the entity and its environment, *including its internal control* as it relates to the preparation and fair presentation of both annual and interim financial information, sufficient to be able to:

(1) Identify the types of potential material misstatements in the interim financial information and consider the likelihood of their occurrence

(2) Select the inquiries and analytics that will provide the auditor with a basis for reporting whether material modifications should be made to the interim financial information for it to be in accordance with the AFRF

b. **Procedures to Obtain or Update Understanding** The auditor should perform the following procedures.

(1) Read documentation of the preceding year's audit and of reviews of prior interim periods to identify matters that may be relevant to the current review—the accountant should specifically consider the nature of any:

(a) Corrected material misstatements

(b) Matters identified in any summary of uncorrected misstatements

(c) Identified risks of material misstatement due to fraud, including the risk of management override of controls

(d) Significant financial accounting and reporting matters that may be of continuing significance, such as significant deficiencies and material weaknesses

(2) Read the most recent annual and comparable prior interim period financial information.

(3) Consider the results of any audit procedures performed with respect to the current year's financial statements.

(4) Inquire of management about changes in the entity's business activities.

(5) Inquire of management about whether relevant significant changes in internal control, as it relates to the preparation and fair presentation of interim financial information, have occurred subsequent to the preceding annual audit or prior review of interim financial information, including changes in the entity's policies, procedures, and personnel, as well as the nature and extent of such changes.

Editor Note: For a new client, the auditor *may* also consider requesting access to review the predecessor auditor's documentation related to reviews of an interim period or interim periods in the prior year; however, the auditor is **not** permitted to make reference to the report or work of the predecessor auditor as the basis, in part, for the auditor's own report. If the predecessor auditor does not respond to the auditor's inquiries or does not allow the auditor to review the predecessor auditor's documentation, the auditor *may* inquire why and use alternative procedures to obtain the understanding required.

2. **Analytical Procedures, Inquiries & Other Review Procedures** Procedures for conducting a review of interim financial information generally are limited to analytical procedures, inquiries, and other procedures that address significant accounting and disclosure matters relating to the interim financial information.

a. **Analytical Procedures** The auditor should apply analytical procedures to the interim financial information to identify and provide a basis for inquiry about the relationships and individual items that appear to be unusual and that may indicate a material misstatement. Such analytical procedures should include the following.

(1) Comparing the interim financial information with comparable information for the immediately preceding interim period, if applicable, and with the corresponding period(s) in the previous year, giving consideration to knowledge about changes in the entity's business and specific transactions

(2) Considering plausible relationships among both financial and, when relevant, nonfinancial information

Editor Note: In considering plausible relationships, the auditor *may* consider information developed and used by the entity, for example, analyses prepared for management or those charged with governance.

(3) Comparing recorded amounts, or ratios developed from recorded amounts, to expectations developed by the auditor through identifying and using relationships that are reasonably expected to exist, based on the auditor's understanding of the entity and the industry in which the entity operates

(4) Comparing disaggregated *revenue* data

Editor Note: To compare disaggregated revenue data, the auditor may compare, for example, revenue reported by month and product line or operating segment during the current interim period with that of comparable prior periods.

Editor Note: Expectations developed by the accountant in performing analytical procedures in connection with a review of interim financial information ordinarily are less precise than those developed in an audit.

Analytical procedures *may* include such statistical techniques as trend analysis or regression analysis and may be performed manually or with the use of computer-assisted techniques. Examples of other analytical procedures that an auditor *may* consider performing when conducting a review of interim financial information include:

- Comparing current interim financial information with anticipated results, such as budgets or forecasts (for example, comparing tax balances and the relationship between the provision for income taxes and pretax income in the current interim financial information with corresponding information in (a) budgets, using expected rates, and (b) financial information for prior periods). Caution is necessary when comparing and evaluating current interim financial information with budgets, forecasts, or other anticipated results because of the inherent lack of precision in estimating the future and the susceptibility of such information to manipulation and misstatement by management to reflect desired interim results.
- Comparing relationships among elements in the current interim financial information with corresponding relationships in the interim financial information of prior periods (for example, expense by type as a percentage of sales, assets by type as a percentage of total assets, and percentage of change in sales to percentage of change in receivables).

b. **Inquiries & Other Review Procedures** The auditor should make the following inquiries and perform the following other review procedures when conducting a review of interim financial information.

(1) Read the available minutes of meetings of stockholders, directors, and appropriate committees, and inquire about matters dealt with at meetings for which minutes are not available, to identify matters that may affect the interim financial information.

(2) Obtain reports from component auditors, if any, related to reviews performed of the interim financial information of significant components of the reporting entity, including its investees, or inquire of those auditors if reports have not been issued

(3) Inquire of management about:

(a) Whether the interim financial information has been prepared and fairly presented in accordance with the AFRF consistently applied

(b) *Unusual or complex situations that may have an effect on the interim financial information

(c) Significant transactions occurring or recognized in the interim period, particularly those in the last several days of the interim period

(d) The status of uncorrected misstatements identified during the previous audit and interim review, i.e., whether adjustments had been recorded subsequent to the periods covered by the prior audit or interim review and, if so, the amounts recorded and period in which such adjustments were recorded

(e) Matters about which questions have arisen in the course of applying the review procedures

(f) Events subsequent to the date of the interim financial information that could have a material effect on the fair presentation of such information

(g) Their knowledge of any fraud or suspected fraud affecting the entity involving:

(i) Management

(ii) Employees who have significant roles in internal control

(iii) Others where the fraud could have a material effect on the financial information

(h) Whether they are aware of allegations of fraud or suspected fraud affecting the entity communicated by employees, former employees, regulators, or others

(i) Significant journal entries and other adjustments

(j) Communications from regulatory agencies

(k) Significant deficiencies, including material weaknesses, in the design or operation of internal control as it relates to the preparation of both annual and interim financial information

(l) Changes in related parties or significant new related-party transactions

(4) Obtain evidence that the interim financial information agrees or reconciles with the accounting records. In addition, the auditor should inquire of management about the reliability of the records to which the interim financial information was compared or reconciled.

(5) Read the interim financial information to consider whether, based on the results of the review procedures performed and other information that has come to the auditor's attention, the information to be reported conforms with the AFRF.

(6) Read other information in documents containing the interim financial information to consider whether such information or the manner of its presentation is materially inconsistent with the interim financial information. If the auditor concludes that a material inconsistency exists or becomes aware of information that the auditor believes is a material misstatement of fact, the auditor should take action based on the auditor's professional judgment.

*Examples of unusual or complex situations about which the auditor *may* inquire of management:

- Business combinations
- New or complex revenue recognition methods
- Impairment of assets
- Disposal of a segment of a business
- Use of derivative instruments and hedging activities
- Sales and transfers that may call into question the classification of investments in securities, including management's intent and ability with respect to the remaining securities classified as held to maturity
- Adoption of new stock compensation plans or changes to existing plans
- Restructuring charges taken in the current and prior quarters
- Significant, unusual, or infrequently occurring transactions

- Changes in litigation or contingencies
- Changes in major contracts with customers or suppliers
- Application of new accounting principles
- Changes in accounting principles or the methods of applying them
- Trends and developments affecting accounting estimates, such as allowances for bad debts and excess or obsolete inventories, provisions for warranties and employee benefits, and realization of unearned income and deferred charges
- Compliance with debt covenants
- Changes in related parties or significant new related-party transactions
- Material off-balance-sheet transactions, special purpose entities, and other equity investments
- Unique terms for debt or capital stock that could affect classification

c. **Inquiry Concerning Litigation, Claims & Assessments** If information comes to the auditor's attention regarding litigation, claims, or assessments that leads the auditor to question whether the interim financial information has been prepared, in all material respects, in accordance with the AFRF, and the auditor believes that the entity's internal or external legal counsel may have relevant information, the auditor should inquire of such legal counsel concerning litigation, claims, and assessments.

Editor Note: A review of interim financial information does **not** contemplate obtaining corroborating evidence for responses to inquiries. Consequently, the auditor is **not** required to send an inquiry letter to an entity's legal counsel concerning litigation, claims, and assessments.

d. **Inquiry Concerning an Entity's Ability to Continue as a Going Concern** If (1) conditions or events that may indicate substantial doubt about an entity's ability to continue as a going concern existed at the date of prior period financial statements, regardless of whether the substantial doubt was alleviated by the auditor's consideration of management's plans, or (2) in the course of performing review procedures on the current period interim financial information, the auditor becomes aware of conditions or events that might be indicative of the entity's possible inability to continue as a going concern, the auditor should:

(1) Inquire of management about its plans for dealing with the adverse effects of the conditions and events

(2) Consider the adequacy of the disclosure about such matters in the interim financial information

Editor Note: If the auditor determines that the disclosure is inadequate, the auditor is required to modify the review report due to this departure from the AFRF.

Editor Note: When performing a review engagement, the auditor is **not** required to obtain evidence in support of the information that mitigates the effects of the conditions and events.

e. **Consideration of Management's Responses & Extension of Interim Review Procedures**

(1) The auditor should consider the reasonableness and consistency of management's responses in light of the results of other review procedures and the auditor's knowledge of the entity's business and its internal control. However, the auditor is **not** required to corroborate management's responses with other evidence.

(2) When a matter comes to the auditor's attention that leads the auditor to question whether the interim financial information has been prepared in accordance with the AFRF in all material respects, the auditor should make additional inquiries of management or others or perform other procedures to provide a basis for reporting whether the auditor is aware of any material modifications that should be made to the interim financial information.

f. **Evaluating Results of Interim Review Procedures** The auditor should accumulate misstatements, including inadequate disclosure, and evaluate them, individually and in the aggregate, to determine whether material modification should be made to the interim financial information for it to be in accordance with the AFRF.

Considerations that *may* affect the evaluation of whether uncorrected misstatements, individually or in the aggregate, are material include:

- The nature, cause (if known), and amount of the misstatements
- Whether the misstatements originated in the preceding year or interim periods of the current year
- Materiality judgments made in conjunction with the current or prior year's annual audit
- The potential effect of the misstatements on future interim or annual periods
- The appropriateness of offsetting a misstatement of an estimated amount with a misstatement of an item capable of precise measurement
- Recognition that an accumulation of immaterial misstatements in the balance sheet could contribute to material misstatements in future periods

g. **Obtain Written Representations From Management** For all interim financial information presented and for all periods covered by the review, the auditor should request management to provide the following written representations, as of the date of the auditor's review report.

When management does not provide the first 5 written representations, the auditor should withdraw from the engagement to review the interim financial information.

(1) **That management has fulfilled its responsibility for the preparation and fair presentation of the interim financial information, in accordance with the AFRF, as set out in the terms of the engagement**

(2) **That management acknowledges its responsibility for designing, implementing, and maintaining internal control relevant to the preparation and fair presentation of interim financial statements, including its responsibility to prevent and detect fraud**

(3) **That management has disclosed to the auditor all significant deficiencies and material weaknesses in the design or operation of internal control of**

which management is aware as it relates to the preparation and fair presentation of both annual and interim financial information

(4) **That management has provided the auditor with all relevant information and access, as agreed upon in the terms of the engagement**

(5) **That all transactions have been recorded and are reflected in the interim financial information**

(6) That management has disclosed to the auditor the results of its assessment of the risk that the interim financial information may be materially misstated as a result of fraud

(7) That management has disclosed to the auditor its knowledge of fraud or suspected fraud affecting the entity involving:

- Management
- Employees who have significant roles in internal control
- Others when the fraud could have a material effect on the interim financial information

(8) That management has disclosed to the auditor its knowledge of any allegations of fraud or suspected fraud affecting the entity's interim financial information communicated by employees, former employees, regulators, or others

(9) That management has disclosed to the auditor all known instances of noncompliance or suspected noncompliance with laws and regulations whose effects should be considered when preparing interim financial information

(10) About whether management believes that the effects of uncorrected misstatements are immaterial, individually and in the aggregate, to the interim financial information as a whole; a summary of such items should be included in, or attached to, the written representation

(11) That management has disclosed to the auditor all known actual or possible litigation and claims whose effects should be considered when preparing the interim financial information, and it has appropriately accounted for and disclosed such litigation and claims in accordance with the AFRF

(12) About whether management believes that significant assumptions used by it in making accounting estimates are reasonable

(13) That management has disclosed to the auditor the identity of the entity's related parties and all the related-party relationships and transactions of which it is aware, and it has appropriately accounted for and disclosed such relationships and transactions

(14) That all events occurring subsequent to the date of the interim financial information and for which the AFRF requires adjustment or disclosure have been adjusted or disclosed

If the auditor has concerns about the reliability of the representations or if management does not provide the requested written representations, the auditor should take appropriate action.

The auditor *may* request additional representations regarding matters specific to the entity's business or industry.

This representation letter is to be used in conjunction with the representation letter for the audit of the financial statements of the prior year. Management confirms the representations made in the representation letter for the audit of the financial statements of the prior year-end, as they apply to the interim financial information, and makes additional representations that may be needed for the interim financial information.

Exhibit 25 ▸ Short Form Representation Letter for Review of Interim Financial Information Used in Conjunction with the Letter for the Prior Year Audit

[Entity Letterhead]

[*Date*]

To [*Auditor*]

This representation letter is provided in connection with your review of the [*consolidated*] balance sheet as of June 30, 20X1 and the related [*consolidated*] statements of income, changes in equity, and cash flows for the six-month period then ended of ABC Company for the purpose of reporting whether any material modifications should be made to the [*consolidated*] interim financial information for it to be in accordance with accounting principles generally accepted in the United States of America (US GAAP) [*including, if appropriate, an indication as to the appropriate form and content of interim financial information (for example, Article 10 of SEC Regulation S-X)*].

We confirm that [, *to the best of our knowledge and belief, having made such inquiries as we considered necessary for the purpose of appropriately informing ourselves*] [*as of (date of auditor's review report),*]:

Interim Financial Information

1. We have fulfilled our responsibilities, as set out in the terms of the engagement letter dated [insert date] for the preparation and fair presentation of interim financial information in accordance with US GAAP; in particular the interim financial information is presented in accordance therewith.
2. We acknowledge our responsibility for the design, implementation, and maintenance of internal control relevant to the preparation and fair presentation of interim financial information that is free from material misstatement, whether due to fraud or error.
3. The interim financial information has been adjusted or includes disclosures for all events subsequent to the date of the interim financial information for which US GAAP requires adjustment or disclosure.
4. The effects of uncorrected misstatements are immaterial, both individually and in the aggregate, to the interim financial information as a whole. A list of the uncorrected misstatements is attached to the representation letter.

[*Any other matters that the auditor may consider appropriate.*]

Information Provided

5. We have provided you with:
   - Access to all information of which we are aware that is relevant to the preparation and fair presentation of the interim financial information such as records, documentation, and other matters;
   - Minutes of the meetings of stockholders, directors, and committees of directors, or summaries of actions of recent meetings for which minutes have not yet been prepared;
   - Additional information that you have requested from us for the purpose of the review; and
   - Unrestricted access to persons within the entity of whom you determined it necessary to make inquiries.
6. We have disclosed to you all significant deficiencies or material weaknesses in the design or operation of internal control of which we are aware, as it relates to the preparation and fair presentation of both annual and interim financial information.
7. We have disclosed to you the results of our assessment of the risk that the interim financial information may be materially misstated as a result of fraud.
8. We have [*no knowledge of any*] [*disclosed to you all information of which we are aware in relation to*] fraud or suspected fraud that affects the entity and involves:
   - Management;
   - Employees who have significant roles in internal control; or
   - Others when the fraud could have a material effect on the interim financial information.
9. We have [*no knowledge of any*] [*disclosed to you all information in relation to*] allegations of fraud, or suspected fraud, affecting the entity's interim financial information communicated by employees, former employees, analysts, regulators, or others.
10. We have disclosed to you the identity of the entity's related parties and all the related-party relationships and transactions of which we are aware.

[*Any other matters that the auditor may consider necessary.*]

11. We have reviewed our representation letter to you dated [*date of representation letter relating to most recent audit*] with respect to the audited consolidated financial statements as of and for the year ended [*prior year-end date*]. We believe that representations [*references to applicable representations*] within that representation letter do not apply to the interim financial information referred to above. We now confirm those representations [*references to applicable representations*], as they apply to the interim financial information referred to above, and incorporate them herein, with the following changes:

[*Indicate any changes.*]

12. [*Add any representations related to new accounting or auditing standards that are being implemented for the first time.*]

____

[*Name of Chief Executive Officer and Title*]

____

[*Name of Chief Financial Officer and Title*]

This next representation letter is similar in detail to the management representation letter used for the audit of the financial statements of the prior year and, thus, need not refer to the written management representations received in the most recent audit.

Exhibit 26 ▸ Detailed Representation Letter for Review of Interim Financial Information

[Entity Letterhead]

[*Date*]

To [*Auditor*]

This representation letter is provided in connection with your review of the [consolidated] balance sheet as of June 30, 20X1 and the related [consolidated] statements of income, changes in equity, and cash flows for the six-month period then ended of ABC Company for the purpose of reporting whether any material modifications should be made to the [consolidated] interim financial information for it to be in accordance with accounting principles generally accepted in the United States of America (US GAAP) [including, if appropriate, an indication as to the appropriate form and content of interim financial information (for example, Article 10 of SEC Regulation S-X)].

We confirm that [, to the best of our knowledge and belief, having made such inquiries as we considered necessary for the purpose of appropriately informing ourselves] [as of (date of auditor's review report),]:

Interim Financial Information

1. We have fulfilled our responsibilities, as set out in the terms of the engagement letter dated [*insert date*] for the preparation and fair presentation of the interim financial information in accordance with US GAAP; in particular the interim financial information is presented in accordance therewith.
2. We acknowledge our responsibility for the design, implementation, and maintenance of internal control relevant to the preparation and fair presentation of interim financial information that is free from material misstatement, whether due to fraud or error.
3. Significant assumptions used by us in making accounting estimates, including those measured at fair value, are reasonable.
4. Related-party relationships and transactions have been appropriately accounted for and disclosed in accordance with the requirements of US GAAP.
5. The interim financial information has been adjusted or includes disclosures for all events subsequent to the date of the interim financial information for which US GAAP requires adjustment or disclosure.
6. The effects of uncorrected misstatements are immaterial, both individually and in the aggregate, to the interim financial information as a whole. A list of the uncorrected misstatements is attached to the representation letter.

[*Any other matters that the auditor may consider appropriate*.]

Information Provided

7. We have provided you with:
   - Access to all information of which we are aware that is relevant to the preparation and fair presentation of the interim financial information such as records, documentation, and other matters;
   - Minutes of the meetings of stockholders, directors, and committees of directors, or summaries of actions of recent meetings for which minutes have not yet been prepared;
   - Additional information that you have requested from us for the purpose of the review; and
   - Unrestricted access to persons within the entity of whom you determined it necessary to make inquiries.
8. All transactions have been recorded in the accounting records and are reflected in the interim financial information.
9. We have disclosed to you all significant deficiencies or material weaknesses in the design or operation of internal control of which we are aware, as it relates to the preparation and fair presentation of both annual and interim financial information.
10. We have disclosed to you the results of our assessment of the risk that the interim financial information may be materially misstated as a result of fraud.
11. We have [*no knowledge of any*][*disclosed to you all information of which we are aware in relation to*] fraud or suspected fraud that affects the entity and involves:
    - Management;
    - Employees who have significant roles in internal control; or
    - Others when the fraud could have a material effect on the interim financial information.
12. We have [*no knowledge of any*][*disclosed to you all information in relation to*] allegations of fraud, or suspected fraud, affecting the entity's interim financial information communicated by employees, former employees, analysts, regulators, or others.
13. We have disclosed to you all known instances of non-compliance or suspected non-compliance with laws and regulations whose effects should be considered when preparing interim financial information.
14. There have been no communications from regulatory agencies concerning noncompliance with or deficiencies in financial reporting practices.
15. We have disclosed to you the identity of the entity's related parties and all the related-party relationships and transactions of which we are aware.

[*Any other matters that the auditor may consider necessary.*]

____

[*Name of Chief Executive Officer and Title*]

____

[*Name of Chief Financial Officer and Title*]

D. **Communications With Management & Those Charged With Governance**
These required communications may be oral or written. (The communications are most helpful when made on a sufficiently timely basis to enable management or those charged with governance to take appropriate action.)

1. **Communication—Auditor Cannot Complete Review** If the auditor cannot complete the review, the auditor should communicate to the appropriate level of management and those charged with governance:

   a. **Reason** The reason why the review cannot be completed

   b. **Issuance of Review Report Is Precluded** That an incomplete review does not provide a basis for reporting and, accordingly, that the auditor is precluded from issuing a review report

   c. **Material Modifications Needed** Any material modifications of which the auditor has become aware that should be made to the interim financial information for it to be in accordance with the AFRF

   Editor Note: When an auditor is unable to perform the procedures that the auditor considers necessary to achieve the objective of a review, or management does not provide the auditor with the written representations that the auditor believes are necessary, the review will be incomplete.

2. **Communication—Material Modifications to Interim Financial Information Needed** The auditor should communicate to the appropriate level of management, as soon as practicable, matters that cause the auditor to believe that material modification should be made to the interim financial information for it to be in accordance with the AFRF.

3. **Communication—Interim Financial Statements Issued Prior to Completion of Review** The auditor should communicate to the appropriate level of management, as soon as practicable, matters that cause the auditor to believe that the entity issued the interim financial information before the completion of the review.

4. **Communication—Other Matters**

   a. **Fraud**

      (1) **Management** If the auditor becomes aware that fraud may have occurred, the auditor should communicate the matter as soon as practicable to the appropriate level of management.

      (2) **Those Charged With Governance** If the fraud involves senior management or results in a material misstatement of the interim financial information, the auditor should communicate the matter directly to those charged with governance.

   b. **Communicate Noncompliance With Laws or Regulations to Those Charged With Governance** If the auditor becomes aware of matters involving identified or suspected noncompliance with laws and regulations whose effects should be considered when preparing interim financial information, the auditor should communicate the matters to those charged with governance, other than when the matters are clearly inconsequential.

c. **Communicate Other Relevant Matters to Those Charged With Governance** The auditor should communicate relevant matters of governance interest arising from the review of interim financial information to those charged with governance, including the following.

(1) **Significant Deficiencies or Material Weaknesses in Internal Control** Significant deficiencies or material weaknesses in internal control as it relates to the preparation and fair presentation of annual and interim financial information

(2) **Matters Required by AU 260** Any of the matters described in AU 260, *The Auditor's Communication With Those Charged With Governance*, that have been identified, as they relate to the interim financial information (see chapter 2 of this text)

5. **Evaluation of Entity's Response to Communications**

a. **Management** If management does not respond appropriately to the auditor's communication within a reasonable period of time, the auditor should inform those charged with governance of the matters as soon as practicable.

b. **Those Charged With Governance** If those charged with governance do not respond appropriately to the auditor's communication within a reasonable period of time, the auditor should consider whether to withdraw from the engagement and, if applicable, from serving as the entity's auditor.

Editor Note: The auditor may seek legal advice when considering whether to withdraw from the engagement to review the interim financial information and as the entity's auditor.

E. Auditor's Review Report

1. **In Writing** The auditor's review report should be in writing.

2. **Each Page of Interim Financial Information Marked as Unaudited** The auditor should determine that management has clearly marked as unaudited each page of the interim financial information accompanying the review report.

3. **Review Report Elements**

   a. A title that includes the word *independent* to clearly indicate that it is the report of an independent auditor

   b. An addressee as appropriate for the circumstances of the engagement

   c. An introductory paragraph that:

      (1) Identifies the entity whose interim financial information has been reviewed

      (2) States that the interim financial information identified in the report was reviewed

      (3) Identifies the interim financial information

      (4) Specifies the date or period covered by each financial statement comprising the interim financial information

   d. A section with the heading *Management's Responsibility for the Financial Statements* that includes an explanation that management is responsible for the preparation and fair presentation of the interim financial information in accordance with the AFRF; this responsibility includes the design, implementation, and maintenance of internal control sufficient to provide a reasonable basis for the preparation and fair presentation of interim financial information in accordance with the AFRF

   e. A section with the heading *Auditor's Responsibility* that includes the following statements:

      (1) The auditor's responsibility is to conduct the review of interim financial information in accordance with auditing standards generally accepted in the United States of America applicable to reviews of interim financial information.

      (2) A review of interim financial information consists principally of applying analytical procedures and making inquiries of persons responsible for financial and accounting matters.

      (3) A review of interim financial information is substantially less in scope than an audit conducted in accordance with auditing standards generally accepted in the United States of America, the objective of which is an expression of an opinion regarding the financial information as a whole, and accordingly, no such opinion is expressed.

   f. A concluding section with an appropriate heading that includes a statement about whether the auditor is aware of any material modifications that should be made to the accompanying interim financial information for it to be in accordance with the applicable financial reporting framework and that identifies the country of origin of those accounting principles, if applicable

   g. The manual or printed signature of the auditor's firm

h. The city and state where the auditor practices

i. The date of the review report, which should be dated as of the date of completion of the review procedures

Exhibit 27 ▸ Review Report on Interim Financial Information

Independent Auditor's Review Report

[*Appropriate Addressee*]

We have reviewed the accompanying [*describe the interim financial information or statements reviewed*] of ABC Company and subsidiaries as of September 30, 20X1, and for the three-month and nine-month periods then ended.

Management's Responsibility

The Company's management is responsible for the preparation and fair presentation of the interim financial information in accordance with [*identify the applicable financial reporting framework; for example, accounting principles generally accepted in the United States of America*]; this responsibility includes the design, implementation, and maintenance of internal control sufficient to provide a reasonable basis for the preparation and fair presentation of interim financial information in accordance with [*identify the applicable financial reporting framework; for example, accounting principles generally accepted in the United States of America*].

Auditor's Responsibility

Our responsibility is to conduct our review in accordance with auditing standards generally accepted in the United States of America applicable to reviews of interim financial information. A review of interim financial information consists principally of applying analytical procedures and making inquiries of persons responsible for financial and accounting matters. It is substantially less in scope than an audit conducted in accordance with auditing standards generally accepted in the United States of America, the objective of which is the expression of an opinion regarding the financial information. Accordingly, we do not express such an opinion.

Conclusion

Based on our review, we are not aware of any material modifications that should be made to the accompanying interim financial information for it to be in accordance with [*identify the applicable financial reporting framework; for example, accounting principles generally accepted in the United States of America*].

[*Auditor's signature*]

[*Auditor's city and state*]

[*Date of the auditor's report*]

Exhibit 28 ▸ Review Report That Refers to a Component Auditor's Review Report on Interim Financial Information of a Significant Component of the Reporting Entity

Independent Auditor's Review Report

[*Appropriate Addressee*]

We have reviewed the accompanying [*describe the interim financial information or statements reviewed*] of ABC Company and subsidiaries as of September 30, 20X1, and for the three-month and nine-month periods then ended.

Management's Responsibility

The Company's management is responsible for the preparation and fair presentation of the interim financial information in accordance with [*identify the applicable financial reporting framework; for example, accounting principles generally accepted in the United States of America*]; this responsibility includes the design, implementation, and maintenance of internal control sufficient to provide a reasonable basis for the preparation and fair presentation of interim financial information in accordance with [*identify the applicable financial reporting framework; for example, accounting principles generally accepted in the United States of America*].

Auditor's Responsibility

Our responsibility is to conduct our review in accordance with auditing standards generally accepted in the United States of America applicable to reviews of interim financial information. A review of interim financial information consists principally of applying analytical procedures and making inquiries of persons responsible for financial and accounting matters. It is substantially less in scope than an audit conducted in accordance with auditing standards generally accepted in the United States of America, the objective of which is the expression of an opinion regarding the financial information. Accordingly, we do not express such an opinion.

We were furnished with the report of other auditors on their review of the interim financial information of DEF subsidiary, whose total assets as of September 30, 20X1, and whose revenues for the three-month and nine-month periods then ended, constituted 15 percent, 20 percent, and 22 percent, respectively, of the related consolidated totals.

Conclusion

Based on our review and the review report of other auditors, we are not aware of any material modifications that should be made to the accompanying interim financial information for it to be in accordance with [*identify the applicable financial reporting framework; for example, accounting principles generally accepted in the United States of America*].

[*Auditor's signature*]

[*Auditor's city and state*]

[*Date of the auditor's report*]

Exhibit 29 ▶ Review Report on Comparative Interim Financial Information When the Prior Period Was Reviewed by Another Auditor

Independent Auditor's Review Report

[*Appropriate Addressee*]

We have reviewed the accompanying [*describe the interim financial information or statements reviewed*] of ABC Company and subsidiaries as of March 31, 20X1, and for the three-month period then ended. The consolidated statements of income and cash flows of ABC Company and subsidiaries for the three-month period ended March 31, 20X0, were reviewed by other auditors whose report dated June 1, 20X0, stated that based on their review, they were not aware of any material modifications that should be made to those statements in order for them to be in conformity with [*identify the applicable financial reporting framework; for example, accounting principles generally accepted in the United States of America*]. The consolidated balance sheet of the Company as of December 31, 20X0, and the related consolidated statements of income, changes in stockholders' equity, and cash flows for the year then ended (not presented herein), were audited by other auditors whose report dated March 15, 20X1, expressed an unmodified opinion on that statement.

Management's Responsibility

The Company's management is responsible for the preparation and fair presentation of the interim financial information in accordance with [*identify the applicable financial reporting framework; for example, accounting principles generally accepted in the United States of America*]; this responsibility includes the design, implementation, and maintenance of internal control sufficient to provide a reasonable basis for the preparation and fair presentation of interim financial information in accordance with [*identify the applicable financial reporting framework; for example, accounting principles generally accepted in the United States of America*].

Auditor's Responsibility

Our responsibility is to conduct our review in accordance with auditing standards generally accepted in the United States of America applicable to reviews of interim financial information. A review of interim financial information consists principally of applying analytical procedures and making inquiries of persons responsible for financial and accounting matters. It is substantially less in scope than an audit conducted in accordance with auditing standards generally accepted in the United States of America, the objective of which is the expression of an opinion regarding the financial information. Accordingly, we do not express such an opinion.

Conclusion

Based on our review, we are not aware of any material modifications that should be made to the accompanying interim financial information as of and for the three months ended March 31, 20X1, for it to be in accordance with [*identify the applicable financial reporting framework; for example, accounting principles generally accepted in the United States of America*].

[*Auditor's signature*]

[*Auditor's city and state*]

[*Date of the auditor's report*]

Editor Note: The auditor is **not** required to modify the review report if there is adequate and appropriate disclosure about going concern conditions or events in the interim financial information; however, the auditor *may* include an emphasis-of-matter paragraph in the auditor's review report.

Exhibit 30 ▸ Emphasis-of-Matter Paragraph When a Going Concern Emphasis-of-Matter Paragraph Was Included in the Prior Year's Audit Report & Conditions Giving Rise to the Emphasis-of-Matter Paragraph Continue to Exist

Emphasis of Matter Regarding Going Concern

Note 4 of the Company's audited financial statements as of December 31, 20X1, and for the year then ended, discloses that the Company was unable to renew its line of credit or obtain alternative financing at December 31, 20X1. Our auditor's report on those financial statements includes an emphasis-of-matter paragraph referring to the matters in note 4 of those financial statements and indicating that these matters raised substantial doubt about the Company's ability to continue as a going concern. As indicated in note 3 of the Company's unaudited interim financial information as of March 31, 20X2, and for the three months then ended, the Company was still unable to renew its line of credit or obtain alternative financing as of March 31, 20X2. The accompanying interim financial information does not include any adjustments that might result from the outcome of this uncertainty.

Exhibit 31 ▸ Emphasis-of-Matter Paragraph When a Going Concern Emphasis-of-Matter Paragraph Was *Not* Included in the Prior Year's Audit Report & Conditions or Events Exist as of the Interim Reporting Date Covered by Review That Might Be Indicative of the Entity's Possible Inability to Continue as a Going Concern

Emphasis of Matter Regarding Going Concern

As indicated in note 3, certain conditions indicate that the Company may be unable to continue as a going concern. The accompanying interim financial information does not include any adjustments that might result from the outcome of this uncertainty.

4. **Comparative Interim Financial Information That Has Not Been Reviewed Presented With Reviewed Interim Financial Information** If reviewed interim financial information will be presented in comparative form with prior period interim financial information that has not been reviewed, the auditor's review report should indicate that the auditor has not reviewed the prior period and that the auditor assumes no responsibility for it. This *may* be worded, for example, as follows:

   > The accompanying [*describe the interim financial information or statements*] of ABC Company and subsidiaries as of September 30, 20X1, and for the three-month period then ended were not reviewed by us, and accordingly, we do not express any form of assurance on it.

5. **Interim Financial Information Presented on a Comparative Basis With Condensed Balance Sheet Information for the Most Recent Year-End** When a condensed balance sheet derived from audited financial statements is presented on a comparative basis with the interim financial information, the auditor should report on the condensed balance sheet only when the auditor audited the financial statements from which the condensed balance sheet was derived. The auditor should compare the condensed balance sheet with the related information in the audited financial statements to determine whether the condensed balance sheet agrees with, or can be recalculated from, the related information in the audited financial statements. The auditor's report on the interim financial information should include a paragraph addressing the condensed balance sheet that:

   a. Identifies the condensed balance sheet on which the auditor is reporting

   b. Identifies the audited financial statements from which the condensed balance sheet was derived and indicates that such financial statements are not separately presented

   c. Refers to the auditor's report on the audited financial statements, the date of that report, and the type of opinion expressed and, if the opinion is modified, the basis for the modification

   d. Describes the nature of any emphasis-of-matter paragraph or other-matter paragraph included in the auditor's report

   e. Includes an opinion about whether the condensed balance sheet is consistent, in all material respects, in relation to the audited financial statements from which it has been derived

Exhibit 32 ▸ Review Report on Condensed Comparative Interim Financial Information

Independent Auditor's Review Report

[*Appropriate Addressee*]

We have reviewed the condensed consolidated financial statements of ABC Company and subsidiaries, which comprise the balance sheet as of March 31, 20X1, and the related condensed consolidated statements of income and cash flows for the three-month periods ended March 31, 20X1 and 20X0.

Management's Responsibility

The Company's management is responsible for the preparation and fair presentation of the condensed financial information in accordance with [*identify the applicable financial reporting framework; for example, accounting principles generally accepted in the United States of America*]; this responsibility includes the design, implementation, and maintenance of internal control sufficient to provide a reasonable basis for the preparation and fair presentation of interim financial information in accordance with [*identify the applicable financial reporting framework; for example, accounting principles generally accepted in the United States of America*].

Auditor's Responsibility

Our responsibility is to conduct our reviews in accordance with auditing standards generally accepted in the United States of America applicable to reviews of interim financial information. A review of interim financial information consists principally of applying analytical procedures and making inquiries of persons responsible for financial and accounting matters. It is substantially less in scope than an audit conducted in accordance with auditing standards generally accepted in the United States of America, the objective of which is the expression of an opinion regarding the financial information. Accordingly, we do not express such an opinion.

Conclusion

Based on our reviews, we are not aware of any material modifications that should be made to the condensed financial information referred to above for it to be in accordance with [*identify the applicable financial reporting framework; for example, accounting principles generally accepted in the United States of America*].

***Report on Condensed Balance Sheet as of* [*Date*]**

We have previously audited, in accordance with auditing standards generally accepted in the United States of America, the consolidated balance sheet as of December 31, 20X0, and the related consolidated statements of income, changes in stockholders' equity, and cash flows for the year then ended (not presented herein); and we expressed an unmodified audit opinion on those audited consolidated financial statements in our report dated February 15, 20X1. In our opinion, the accompanying condensed consolidated balance sheet of ABC Company and subsidiaries as of December 31, 20X0, is consistent, in all material respects, with the audited consolidated financial statements from which it has been derived.

[*Auditor's signature*]

[*Auditor's city and state*]

[*Date of the auditor's report*]

6. **Interim Financial Information *Not* in Accordance With AFRF** When the interim financial information has **not** been prepared in accordance with the AFRF in all material respects, the auditor should consider whether modification of the auditor's review report is sufficient to address the departure from the AFRF.

   a. **When Departure Can Be Addressed by Modification of Review Report** If the auditor concludes that modification of the standard review report is sufficient to address the departure, the auditor should modify the review report. The modification should:

      (1) Describe the nature of the departure

      (2) If practicable, should state the effects on the interim financial information

      (3) If the departure is due to inadequate disclosure, the auditor should, if practicable, include the information in the report that the auditor believes is necessary for adequate disclosure in accordance with the AFRF

   b. **Withdraw When Modification of Review Report *Not* Sufficient to Address Departure** If the auditor believes that modification of the review report is **not** sufficient to address the deficiencies in the interim financial information, the auditor should withdraw from the review engagement and provide no further services with respect to such interim financial information.

   Editor Note: Departures from the AFRF include inadequate disclosure and changes in accounting policies that are not in accordance with the AFRF.

Exhibit 33 ▸ Modification to Review Report on Interim Financial Information Due to a Departure From the Applicable Financial Reporting Framework

Basis for Modification of Conclusion

Based on information furnished to us by management, we believe that the Company has excluded from property and debt in the accompanying balance sheet certain lease obligations that we believe should be capitalized to be in accordance with [*identify the applicable financial reporting framework; for example, accounting principles generally accepted in the United States of America*]. This information indicates that if these lease obligations were capitalized at September 30, 20X1, property would be increased by $______, long-term debt would be increased by $______, and net income would be increased (decreased) by $________ and $________, respectively, for the three-month and nine-month periods then ended.

Conclusion

Based on our review, with the exception of the matter(s) described in the preceding paragraph(s), we are not aware of any material modifications that should be made to the accompanying interim financial information for it to be in accordance with [*identify the applicable financial reporting framework; for example, accounting principles generally accepted in the United States of America*].

Exhibit 34 ▸ Modification to Review Report on Interim Financial Information Due to a Departure From the Applicable Financial Reporting Framework (Inadequate Disclosure)

Basis for Modification of Conclusion

Management has informed us that the Company is presently defending a claim regarding [*describe the nature of the loss contingency*] and that the extent of the Company's liability, if any, and the effect on the accompanying interim financial information is not determinable at this time. The interim financial information fails to disclose these matters, which we believe are required to be disclosed in accordance with [*identify the applicable financial reporting framework; for example, accounting principles generally accepted in the United States of America*].

Conclusion

Based on our review, with the exception of the matter(s) described in the preceding paragraph(s), we are not aware of any material modifications that should be made to the accompanying interim financial information for it to be in accordance with [*identify the applicable financial reporting framework; for example, accounting principles generally accepted in the United States of America*].

7. **Subsequent Discovery of Facts Existing at Date of Review Report** If, subsequent to the date of the auditor's review report, the auditor becomes aware that facts existed at the date of the review report that might have affected the auditor's review report had the auditor then been aware of those matters, the auditor should apply the requirements and guidance, adapted as necessary, in AU 560, *Subsequent Events and Subsequently Discovered Facts* (see chapter 8 of this text).

8. **Entity Does *Not* Include Review Report With Reviewed Interim Financial Information** If management does **not** include the auditor's review report in a report, document, or written communication (document) containing the reviewed interim financial information *that indicates that such information has been reviewed by the entity's auditor*, despite having agreed in the terms of the engagement to do so, the auditor should perform the following procedures.

    a. **Include Report & Reissue Document** Request that management amend the document to include the auditor's review report and reissue the document.

    b. **Reissue Document Without Reference to Auditor** If management does not comply with the request to amend and reissue the document, request that the auditor's name not be associated with the interim financial information or referred to in the document because the auditor will not permit either the use of the auditor's name or reference to the auditor unless the auditor's review report is included.

    c. **Communicate Matter to Those Charged With Governance** Communicate management's noncompliance with the requests to those charged with governance.

    d. **Recommend Entity Consult Legal Counsel** When appropriate, recommend that the entity consult with its legal counsel about the application of relevant laws and regulations.

    e. **Consider Other Actions** Consider what other actions might be appropriate.

    f. **When Review Report *Not* Included Is Modified Due to Departure From AFRF** In the case of an entity's failure to include a review report modified due to a departure from the AFRF, the auditor should determine the appropriate course of action, *including whether to withdraw from the engagement to audit the annual financial statements*.

9. When Interim Financial Information Accompanies Audited Financial Statements

a. **When to Include Other-Matter Paragraph About Interim Financial Information in Audit Report** The auditor should include an other-matter paragraph in the audit report on the audited financial statements when *all* the following conditions exist.

(1) The interim financial information that has been reviewed in accordance with this standard is included in a document containing audited financial statements.

(2) The interim financial information accompanying audited financial statements does **not** appear to be presented in accordance with the AFRF.

(3) The auditor's separate review report, which refers to the departure from the applicable financial reporting framework, is **not** presented with the interim financial information.

b. **When to Include Disclaimer of Opinion on Interim Financial Information in Audit Report**

(1) **Requirement—Clear Differentiation** The auditor is required to address in the audit report on the audited financial statements information that is *not* required by the AFRF but is nevertheless presented as part of the basic financial statements if it cannot be clearly differentiated.

(2) **Interim Financial Information Included in Note to Audited Financial Statements** When the interim financial information included in a note to the financial statements, including information that has been reviewed in accordance with this standard, is not appropriately marked as unaudited, the auditor should, in the audit report on the audited financial statements, disclaim an opinion on the interim financial information.

Editor Note: If management chooses or is required to present interim financial information in a note to the audited financial statements, management is responsible for clearly marking the information as unaudited in the note.

F. Documentation

1. **Review Procedures & Results and Significant Findings** The auditor should prepare documentation in connection with a review of interim financial information that will enable an experienced auditor, having no previous connection to the review, to understand:

a. The nature, extent, and timing of the review procedures performed

b. The results of the review procedures performed and the evidence obtained

c. Significant findings or issues arising during the review, the conclusions reached thereon, and significant professional judgments made in reaching those conclusions

Editor Note: Examples of findings or issues that, in the auditor's judgment, are significant include the results of review procedures that indicate that the interim financial information could be materially misstated, including actions taken to address such findings, and the basis for the final conclusions reached.

2. **Communications** The documentation should include the communications required by this standard, whether written or oral.

VIII. Engagements to Report on Summary Financial Statements (AU 810)

This standard does **not** provide guidance on condensed financial statements or summarized financial information presented as comparative information; or summary financial statements required, i.e., RSI, by a designated accounting standards setter (for example, GASB). Comparative information and RSI are addressed by AU 700, *Forming an Opinion and Reporting on Financial Statements*, and AU 730, *Required Supplementary Information*, respectively; see chapter 8 of this text.

Editor Note: Summary financial statements differ from summarized comparative information. Summary financial statements may be presented in a document containing financial statements or in a separate document—comparative information is presented *within* the financial statements.

A. Overview

1. **Objective** The objectives of the auditor are:

   a. **Determine If Engagement Is Appropriate** To determine whether it is appropriate to accept the engagement

   b. **If Engaged** If engaged to report on summary financial statements, to:

      (1) **Perform Procedures** Perform the procedures necessary as the basis for the auditor's opinion on the summary financial statements

      (2) **Form An Opinion** Form an opinion on whether the summary financial statements are consistent, in all material respects, with the audited financial statements from which they have been derived, in accordance with the applied criteria, based on an evaluation of the conclusions drawn from the evidence obtained

      (3) **Write Report** Express clearly that opinion through a written report that also describes the basis for that opinion

2. **Definitions**

   a. **Applied Criteria** The criteria applied by management in the preparation of the summary financial statements

   b. **Summary Financial Statements** Historical financial information that is derived from financial statements but that contains less detail, while still providing a structured representation, consistent with that provided by the financial statements, of the entity's economic resources or obligations at a point in time or the changes therein for a period of time

      Summary financial statements are:

      (1) Separately presented

      (2) *Not* presented as comparative information

      Editor Note: In addition to being considerably less detailed than a complete set of financial statements, summary financial statements do *not* contain all their required disclosures. Thus, reading the summary financial statements is not a substitute for reading the audited financial statements. Accordingly, before accepting an engagement to report on summary financial statements, the auditor is required (see the topic on preconditions for engagement acceptance that follows) to obtain management's agreement that it acknowledges and understands its responsibility to make the audited financial statements readily available to the intended users of the summary financial statements, when the summary financial statements will not be accompanied by the audited financial statements.

c. **Audited Financial Statements** For the purposes of this standard, the term *audited financial statements* refers to those financial statements audited by the auditor in accordance with US GAAS and from which the summary financial statements are derived.

B. Preconditions for Engagement Acceptance

The auditor should **not** accept the engagement unless these conditions are met.

1. **Must Have Audited Financial Statements on Which Summary Financial Statements Are Based** The auditor should not accept an engagement to report on summary financial statements unless the auditor has been engaged to conduct an audit in accordance with US GAAS of the financial statements from which the summary financial statements are derived.

2. **Adverse Opinion or Disclaimer of Opinion on Audited Financial Statements Precludes Acceptance of Engagement** When the audit report on the audited financial statements contains an adverse opinion or a disclaimer of opinion, the auditor should either not accept or withdraw from the engagement to report on the summary financial statements. If withdrawal is not possible, the report on the summary financial statements should not express an opinion (the standard does not use the phrase *disclaim an opinion;* see the topic on the form of opinion that follows later in this section).

3. **Procedures Before Acceptance of Engagement** Before accepting the engagement, the auditor should perform the following procedures.

   a. **Determine Acceptability of Applied Criteria** Determine whether the applied criteria is acceptable, including determining that the applied criteria:

      (1) **Free From Bias** Is free from bias so that the summary financial statements are not misleading

      (2) **Methodology Permits Reconciliation With Audited Financial Statements** Permits reasonably consistent qualitative or quantitative measurements so that the information in the summary financial statements agrees with or can be recalculated from the related information in the audited financial statements

      (3) **Allows for Sufficiently Complete Summary Financial Statements** Is sufficiently complete so that the summary financial statements contain the information necessary and are at an appropriate level of aggregation, so that they are not misleading

      (4) **Relevance** Is relevant to the summary financial statements in view of their purpose

   Editor Note: When the criteria is established by an authorized or recognized standards-setting organization or by law or regulation, the auditor *may* be able to presume that it is acceptable. Otherwise, it may be developed by management, for example, based on practice in a particular industry.

   b. **Obtain Agreement That Management Acknowledges & Understands Its Responsibility** Obtain the agreement of management, *in writing*, that it acknowledges and understands its responsibility:

      (1) **Prepare Summary Financial Statements** For the preparation of the summary financial statements in accordance with the applied criteria

Editor Note: The preparation of summary financial statements requires management to determine the information that needs to be reflected in the summary financial statements so that they are consistent, in all material respects, with the audited financial statements. Because summary financial statements by their nature contain aggregated information and limited disclosure, there is an increased risk that they may not contain the information necessary so that they are not misleading. This risk increases when established criteria for the preparation of summary financial statements does not exist.

(2) **Make Audited Financial Statements Readily Available** To clearly describe in the summary financial statements where the audited financial statements are available and to make the audited financial statements readily available to the intended users, when the summary financial statements will not be accompanied by the audited financial statements

Editor Note: Audited financial statements are deemed to be readily available if a third-party user can obtain them without any further action by the entity, for example, financial statements on an entity's website may be considered readily available, but being available upon request is *not* considered readily available.

(3) **Provide Written Representations** To provide the auditor with written representations (obtaining written representations is included with the descriptions of the other procedures that are covered in the next topic of this section)

(4) **Include Auditor's Report on Summary Financial Statements When Appropriate** To include the auditor's report on the summary financial statements in any document that contains the summary financial statements and indicates the auditor has reported on them

c. **Obtain Agreement on Form & Content of Auditor's Report On Summary Financial Statements** Obtain the agreement of management, *in writing*, about the expected form and content of the report on the summary financial statements, including the agreement that there may be circumstances in which the report may differ from its expected form and content

Editor Note: This may include a description of the types of opinions the auditor may express. It is *not* necessary to describe the type of opinion expected to be issued.

C. Required Procedures for Basis of Opinion

The auditor should perform the following procedures, and any other procedures that the auditor may consider necessary, as the basis for the auditor's opinion on the summary financial statements.

1. **Appropriate Title** Evaluate whether the summary financial statements adequately disclose their summarized nature and identify the audited financial statements. (This may be accomplished with an appropriate title such as *Summary Financial Statements Prepared From the Audited Financial Statements as of and for the Year Ended December 31, 20X1.*)

2. **Location & Availability of Audited Financial Statements** When the summary financial statements are not accompanied by the audited financial statements, evaluate whether the:

   a. Summary financial statements clearly describe where the audited financial statements are available

   b. Audited financial statements are readily available to the intended users of the summary financial statements

3. **Disclosure of Criteria** Evaluate whether the summary financial statements adequately disclose the applied criteria.

4. **Agreement With Audited Financial Statements** Compare the summary financial statements with the related information in the audited financial statements to determine whether they agree with or can be recalculated from the related information in the audited financial statements.

5. **In Accordance With Criteria** Evaluate whether the summary financial statements are prepared in accordance with the applied criteria.

6. **Not Misleading** Evaluate, in view of the purpose of the summary financial statements, whether they contain the information necessary, and are at an appropriate level of aggregation, so that they are not misleading in the circumstances.

7. **Written Representations** The auditor should request management to provide written representations, in the form of a representation letter addressed to the auditor, for all summary financial statements and periods referred to in the auditor's report on the summary financial statements.

   The date of the written representations should be as of the date of the auditor's report on the summary financial statements.

   The written representations should regard the following matters.

   a. Management has fulfilled its responsibility for the preparation of the summary financial statements in accordance with the applied criteria and believes the applied criteria is acceptable.

   b. Management has made the audited financial statements readily available to the intended users of the summary financial statements, when the summary financial statements will not be accompanied by the audited financial statements.

   c. If the date of the auditor's report on the summary financial statements is later than the date of the audit report on the audited financial statements, whether any:

      (1) Information has come to management's attention that would cause management to believe that any of the previous representations on the audited financial statements need to be modified

      (2) Events have occurred subsequent to the date of the audited financial statements that may require adjustment of, or disclosure in, the audited financial statements

D. Form of Opinion

1. **Unmodified Opinion** When the auditor has concluded that an unmodified opinion on the summary financial statements is appropriate, the auditor's opinion should state that the summary financial statements are consistent, in all material respects, with the audited financial statements from which they have been derived, in accordance with the applied criteria.

2. ***No* Qualified Opinion Allowed for Summary Financial Statements** Due to their nature, a qualified opinion is **not** appropriate for summary financial statements—the summary financial statements either are or are not consistent, in all material respects, with the audited financial statements, in accordance with the applied criteria.

3. **Adverse Opinion** If the summary financial statements are not consistent, in all material respects, with the audited financial statements, in accordance with the applied criteria, and management does not agree to make the necessary changes, the auditor should express an adverse opinion on the summary financial statements.

   The auditor should state in the opinion paragraph that, in the auditor's opinion, because of the significance of the matter(s) described in the basis for adverse opinion paragraph, the summary financial statements are not consistent, in all material respects, with the audited financial statements from which they have been derived, in accordance with the applied criteria.

4. **No Opinion Expressed** When the audit report on the audited financial statements contains an adverse opinion or a disclaimer of opinion, the auditor should withdraw from the engagement to report on the summary financial statements, when withdrawal is possible under applicable law or regulation.

   If it is not possible for the auditor to withdraw from the engagement, the auditor's report on the summary financial statements should not express an opinion. The auditor should state that, because of the significance of the matter described above (the adverse opinion or disclaimer of opinion on the audited financial statements), it is inappropriate to express, and the auditor does not express, an opinion on the summary financial statements. (The elements of this type of report are covered in the next topic on the auditor's report on summary financial statements and there is an illustration of this report that follows its list of elements.)

E. **Auditor's Report on Summary Financial Statements**
The auditor does not report in the same manner as the auditor reported on the complete set of financial statements from which they are derived. To do so might lead users to assume, erroneously, that the summary financial statements include all the disclosures necessary for the complete set of financial statements.

1. **Elements of Auditor's Report on Summary Financial Statements With Unmodified or Adverse Opinion**

   a. Title that includes the word *independent* to clearly indicate that it is the report of an independent auditor

   b. Addressee

   c. Introductory paragraph that:

      (1) Identifies the summary financial statements on which the auditor is reporting, including the title of each statement included in the summary financial statements

      (2) Identifies the audited financial statements from which the summary financial statements have been derived

      (3) Refers to the audit report on the audited financial statements, the date of that report, and that the opinion on those statements was unmodified, if applicable (see below for when the opinion is modified)

      (4) If the date of the auditor's report on the summary financial statements is later than the date of the audit report on the audited financial statements, states that the summary financial statements and the audited financial statements do not reflect the effects of events, if any, that occurred subsequent to the date of the audit report on the audited financial statements

Editor Note: When the auditor's report on the summary financial statements is dated later than the date of the audit report on the audited financial statements, the auditor may become aware of subsequently discovered facts (see coverage of AU 560, *Subsequent Events and Subsequently Discovered Facts*, in the chapter 8 of this text). If so, the auditor should *not* release the auditor's report on the summary financial statements until the auditor's consideration of subsequently discovered facts in relation to the audited financial statements has been completed—the statements may need to be revised and the auditor's opinion on the revised statements may differ from the one previously expressed.

(5) Indicates that the summary financial statements do not contain all the disclosures required by the [*financial reporting framework applied in the preparation of the financial statements*] and that reading the summary financial statements is not a substitute for reading the audited financial statements

d. Description of management's responsibility for the summary financial statements, explaining that management is responsible for the preparation of the summary financial statements in accordance with the applied criteria

e. Statement that the auditor is responsible for expressing an opinion about whether the summary financial statements are consistent, in all material respects, with the audited financial statements based on the procedures required by US GAAS and an identification of the United States of America as the country of origin of those standards, including the following:

(1) The procedures consisted principally of comparing the summary financial statements with the related information in the audited financial statements from which the summary financial statements have been derived and evaluating whether the summary financial statements are prepared in accordance with the applied criteria

(2) If the date of the auditor's report on the summary financial statements is later than the date of the audit report on the audited financial statements, the auditor did not perform any audit procedures regarding the audited financial statements after the date of the report on those financial statements.

Editor Note: The auditor is **not** required to obtain additional audit evidence on the audited financial statements, or report on the effects of events that occurred subsequent to the date of the audit report on the audited financial statements because the summary financial statements are derived from the audited financial statements and do *not* update them.

f. A paragraph that clearly expresses either an unmodified or adverse opinion

g. Auditor's signature

h. Auditor's city and state

i. Date of the auditor's report; the auditor should date the auditor's report on the summary financial statements *no earlier than* the date:

- On which the auditor has obtained sufficient appropriate evidence on which to base the opinion, including evidence that the summary financial statements have been prepared and that management and, when appropriate, those charged with governance, have asserted that they have taken responsibility for them; and
- Of the audit report on the audited financial statements

Editor Note: In other words, the auditor's report on the summary financial statements may be dated as of the same date or later than the date of the auditor's report on the audited financial statements.

Exhibit 35 ▸ Report on Summary Financial Statements With Unmodified Opinion; Auditor's Report on Summary Financial Statements Is Dated Later Than Date of Audit Report on Financial Statements From Which Summary Financial Statements Are Derived

Independent Auditor's Report on Summary Financial Statements

[*Appropriate Addressee*]

The accompanying summary financial statements, which comprise the summary balance sheet as of December 31, 20X1, the summary income statement, summary statement of changes in stockholders' equity, and summary cash flow statement for the year then ended, and the related notes, are derived from the audited financial statements of ABC Company as of and for the year ended December 31, 20X1. We expressed an unmodified audit opinion on those audited financial statements in our report dated February 15, 20X2. The audited financial statements, and the summary financial statements derived therefrom, do not reflect the effects of events, if any, that occurred subsequent to the date of our report on the audited financial statements.

The summary financial statements do not contain all the disclosures required by [*describe financial reporting framework applied in the preparation of the financial statements of ABC Company*]. Reading the summary financial statements, therefore, is not a substitute for reading the audited financial statements of ABC Company.

Management's Responsibility for the Summary Financial Statements

Management is responsible for the preparation of the summary financial statements on the basis described in Note X.

Auditor's Responsibility

Our responsibility is to express an opinion about whether the summary financial statements are consistent, in all material respects, with the audited financial statements based on our procedures, which were conducted in accordance with auditing standards generally accepted in the United States of America. The procedures consisted principally of comparing the summary financial statements with the related information in the audited financial statements from which the summary financial statements have been derived, and evaluating whether the summary financial statements are prepared in accordance with the basis described in Note X. We did not perform any audit procedures regarding the audited financial statements after the date of our report on those financial statements.

Opinion

In our opinion, the summary financial statements of ABC Company as of and for the year ended December 31, 20X1, referred to above are consistent, in all material respects, with the audited financial statements from which they have been derived, on the basis described in Note X.

[*Auditor's signature*]

[*Auditor's city and state*]

[*Date of the auditor's report*]

Exhibit 36 ▶ Report on Summary Financial Statements With Adverse Opinion

Independent Auditor's Report on Summary Financial Statements

[*Appropriate Addressee*]

The accompanying summary financial statements, which comprise the summary balance sheet as of December 31, 20X1, the summary income statement, summary statement of changes in stockholders' equity, and summary cash flow statement for the year then ended, and the related notes, are derived from the audited financial statements of ABC Company as of and for the year ended December 31, 20X1. We expressed an unmodified audit opinion on those audited financial statements in our report dated February 15, 20X2

The summary financial statements do not contain all the disclosures required by [*describe financial reporting framework applied in the preparation of the financial statements of ABC Company*]. Reading the summary financial statements, therefore, is not a substitute for reading the audited financial statements of ABC Company.

Management's Responsibility for the Summary Financial Statements

Management is responsible for the preparation of the summary financial statements on the basis described in Note X.

Auditor's Responsibility

Our responsibility is to express an opinion about whether the summary financial statements are consistent, in all material respects, with the audited financial statements based on our procedures, which were conducted in accordance with auditing standards generally accepted in the United States of America. The procedures consisted principally of comparing the summary financial statements with the related information in the audited financial statements from which the summary financial statements have been derived, and evaluating whether the summary financial statements are prepared in accordance with the basis described in Note X.

Basis for Adverse Opinion

[*Describe matter that caused the summary financial statements not to be consistent, in all material respects, with the audited financial statements, in accordance with the applied criteria.*]

Adverse Opinion

In our opinion, because of the significance of the matter discussed in the *Basis for Adverse Opinion* paragraph, the summary financial statements of ABC Company as of and for the year ended December 31, 20X1, referred to above are not consistent with the audited financial statements from which they have been derived, on the basis described in Note X.

[*Auditor's signature*]

[*Auditor's city and state*]

[*Date of the auditor's report*]

2. **Additional Elements of Auditor's Report on Summary Financial Statements When Audit Report on Audited Financial Statements Contains Qualified Opinion, Emphasis-of-Matter, or Other Matter Paragraph** If the audit report on the audited financial statements contains a qualified opinion, an emphasis-of-matter paragraph, or an other-matter paragraph, and the auditor expresses an unmodified opinion or an adverse opinion on the summary financial statements, in addition to the elements just listed, the auditor's report on the summary financial statements should:

   a. State that the audit report on the audited financial statements contains a qualified opinion, an emphasis-of-matter paragraph, or an other-matter paragraph

   b. Describe:

      (1) The basis for the qualified opinion on the audited financial statements and that qualified opinion; or the emphasis-of-matter or other-matter paragraph in the audit report on the audited financial statements

      (2) The effect on the summary financial statements, if any

   Editor Note: Alternatively, the auditor may determine that, due to the effect of the qualified opinion, it is inappropriate to express an opinion on the summary financial statements. In this case, the auditor may adapt and apply the requirements for when there is an adverse opinion or a disclaimer of opinion on the audited financial statements.

Exhibit 37 ▶ Report on Summary Financial Statements With Unmodified Opinion; Qualified Opinion Is Expressed on Audited Financial Statements

Independent Auditor's Report on Summary Financial Statements

[*Appropriate Addressee*]

The accompanying summary financial statements, which comprise the summary balance sheet as of December 31, 20X1, the summary income statement, summary statement of changes in stockholders' equity, and summary cash flow statement for the year then ended, and the related notes, are derived from the audited financial statements of ABC Company as of and for the year ended December 31, 20X1. We expressed a qualified audit opinion on those audited financial statements in our report dated February 15, 20X2 (see below).

The summary financial statements do not contain all the disclosures required by [*describe financial reporting framework applied in the preparation of the financial statements of ABC Company*]. Reading the summary financial statements, therefore, is not a substitute for reading the audited financial statements of ABC Company.

Management's Responsibility for the Summary Financial Statements

Management is responsible for the preparation of the summary financial statements on the basis described in Note X.

Auditor's Responsibility

Our responsibility is to express an opinion about whether the summary financial statements are consistent, in all material respects, with the audited financial statements based on our procedures, which were conducted in accordance with auditing standards generally accepted in the United States of America. The procedures consisted principally of comparing the summary financial statements with the related information in the audited financial statements from which the summary financial statements have been derived, and evaluating whether the summary financial statements are prepared in accordance with the basis described in Note X.

Opinion

In our opinion, the summary financial statements of ABC Company as of and for the year ended December 31, 20X1, referred to above are consistent, in all material respects, with the audited financial statements from which they have been derived, on the basis described in Note X.

The summary financial statements are misstated to the equivalent extent as the audited financial statements of ABC Company as of and for the year ended December 31, 20X1. The misstatement of the audited financial statements is described in our qualified audit opinion in our report dated February 15, 20X2. Our qualified audit opinion is based on the fact that the Company's inventories are carried in the balance sheet in those audited financial statements at $XXX. Management has not stated the inventories at the lower of cost or net realizable value but has stated them solely at cost, which constitutes a departure from [*describe financial reporting framework applied in the preparation of the financial statements of ABC Company*]. The Company's records indicate that, had management stated the inventories at the lower of cost or net realizable value, an amount of $XXX would have been required to write the inventories down to their net realizable value. Accordingly, cost of sales would have been increased by $XXX, and income tax, net income, and stockholders' equity would have been reduced by $XXX, $XXX, and $XXX, respectively. Our qualified audit opinion states that, except for the effects of the described matter, those financial statements present fairly, in all material respects, the financial position of ABC Company as of December 31, 20X1, and the results of its operations and its cash flows for the year then ended in accordance with [*describe financial reporting framework applied in the preparation of the financial statements of ABC Company*].

[*Auditor's signature*]

[*Auditor's city and state*]

[*Date of the auditor's report*]

3. **Elements of Auditor's Report on Summary Financial Statements When Audit Report on Audited Financial Statements Contains Adverse Opinion or Disclaimer of Opinion & Withdrawal From Engagement To Report on Summary Financial Statements Is *Not* Possible** The auditor's report on the summary financial statements should:

   a. State that the audit report on the audited financial statements contains an adverse opinion or disclaimer of opinion

   b. Describe the basis for that adverse opinion or disclaimer of opinion

   c. State that, as a result of the adverse opinion or disclaimer of opinion, it is inappropriate to express, and the auditor does not express, an opinion on the summary financial statements

   d. Include the report elements described previously for a report when the auditor expresses an unmodified or adverse opinion on the summary financial statements, *except for* the elements regarding subsequent events, disclosures, the auditor's responsibilities, and, of course, the opinion.

Exhibit 38 ▸ Adverse Opinion on Audited Financial Statements; as a Result, It Is Inappropriate to Express Opinion on Summary Financial Statements

Independent Auditor's Report on Summary Financial Statements

[*Appropriate Addressee*]

Management derived the accompanying summary financial statements, which comprise the summary balance sheet as of December 31, 20X1, the summary income statement, summary statement of changes in stockholders' equity, and summary cash flow statement for the year then ended, and the related notes, from the audited financial statements of ABC Company as of and for the year ended December 31, 20X1. Management is responsible for the preparation of these summary financial statements on the basis described in Note X.

In our report dated February 15, 20X2, we expressed an adverse audit opinion on the financial statements of ABC Company as of and for the year ended December 31, 20X1. The basis for our adverse audit opinion was [*describe basis for adverse audit opinion*]. Our adverse audit opinion stated that [*describe adverse audit opinion*].

Because of the significance of the matter discussed above, it is inappropriate to express, and we do not express, an opinion on the summary financial statements of ABC Company as of and for the year ended December 31, 20X1.

[*Auditor's signature*]

[*Auditor's city and state*]

[*Date of the auditor's report*]

4. **Repeat Restriction on Use or Alert for Basis of Accounting** When use of the audit report on the audited financial statements is restricted or it alerts readers that the audited financial statements are prepared in accordance with a special-purpose framework, the auditor should include a similar restriction or alert in the auditor's report on the summary financial statements.

5. **Comparatives**

   a. **Evaluation of Omission of Comparatives From Summary Financial Statements** If the audited financial statements contain comparative financial statements, a presumption exists that the summary financial statements also would contain comparatives. If that is not the case, the auditor should determine whether such omission is reasonable. And the auditor should determine the effect of an unreasonable omission on the auditor's report on the summary financial statements.

   b. **Predecessor Auditor's Report on Summary Financial Statements** Unless the predecessor auditor's report on the prior period's summary financial statements is reissued with the summary financial statements, if the summary financial statements contain comparatives that were reported on by another auditor, the auditor's report on the summary financial statements should state:

      (1) That the summary financial statements of the prior period were audited by a predecessor auditor

      (2) The type of opinion expressed by the predecessor auditor and, if the opinion was modified, the reasons for the modification

      (3) The date of that report

   c. **Comparatives *Not* Reported On** If the prior year summary financial statements contain comparatives that were not reported on by the auditor or another auditor, the auditor's report on the summary financial statements should state that the comparative summary financial statements were not reported on by the auditor and, accordingly, the auditor does not express an opinion on the comparative summary financial statements.

F. Other Information Presented or Included With Summary Financial Statements

1. **Unaudited Information Presented With Summary Financial Statements** The auditor should evaluate whether any unaudited information presented with the summary financial statements is clearly differentiated from the summary financial statements. If this is not the case, the auditor should ask management to change the presentation of the unaudited information. If management refuses to do so, the auditor should explain in the auditor's report on the summary financial statements that such information is not covered by that report and accordingly, the auditor does not express an opinion on the information.

2. **Other Information in Documents Containing Summary Financial Statements** The auditor should read other information included in a document containing the summary financial statements and related auditor's report to identify material inconsistencies, if any, with the summary financial statements and the audited financial statements.

   If, upon reading the other information, the auditor identifies a material inconsistency or becomes aware of an apparent material misstatement of fact, the auditor should discuss the matter with management and should consider appropriate further action. For an identified material inconsistency, the auditor should also determine whether the summary financial statements or the other information needs to be revised.

G. **Auditor Association**

1. **Entity Refers to Auditor but Fails to Include Auditor's Report** If the auditor becomes aware that the entity plans to state that the auditor has reported on summary financial statements in a document containing the summary financial statements, but does *not* plan to include the related auditor's report, the auditor should request management to include the auditor's report in the document. If management does not do so, the auditor should determine and carry out other appropriate actions designed to prevent management from inappropriately associating the auditor with the summary financial statements in that document.

2. **Entity Refers to Auditor When Auditor Did *Not* Report on Summary Financial Statements** The auditor may be engaged to report on the financial statements of an entity, while *not* engaged to report on the summary financial statements. If, in this case, the auditor becomes aware that the entity plans to make a statement in a document that refers to the auditor and the fact that summary financial statements are derived from the financial statements audited by the auditor, the auditor should be satisfied that the:

   a. Reference to the auditor is made in the context of the audit report on the audited financial statements

   b. Statement does not give the impression that the auditor has reported on the summary financial statements

   If not satisfied, the auditor should request management to change the statement to meet both of the above criteria or not to refer to the auditor in the document. Alternatively, the entity may engage the auditor to report on the summary financial statements and include the related auditor's report in the document.

   If management does not change the statement, delete the reference to the auditor, or include the auditor's report on the summary financial statements in the document containing the summary financial statements, the auditor should advise management that the auditor disagrees with the reference to the auditor, and the auditor should determine and carry out other appropriate actions designed to prevent management from inappropriately associating the auditor with the summary financial statements in that document. Such appropriate actions *may* include informing the intended users and other known third-party users of the inappropriate reference to the auditor, including that the auditor did not report, and does not express an opinion on, the summary financial statements. (The auditor's course of action depends on the auditor's association with the misleading information and the auditor's legal rights and obligations; consequently, the auditor may consider it appropriate to seek legal advice.)

IX. Reports on Application of Requirements of an AFRF (AU 915)

Differing interpretations may exist concerning whether and, if so, how existing accounting policies in an applicable financial reporting framework (AFRF) apply to new transactions or how new accounting policies in an AFRF apply to existing transactions. Management and others may consult with accountants on the application of the requirements of an AFRF to those transactions or to increase their knowledge of specific financial reporting issues.

This standard does **not** apply to:

- A continuing accountant with respect to the specific entity whose financial statements the continuing accountant has been engaged to report on
- Engagements either to assist in litigation involving accounting or auditing matters or to provide expert testimony in connection with such litigation
- Professional advice provided to another accountant in public practice

- Communications such as position papers prepared by an accountant for the purpose of presenting views on an issue involving the application of the requirements of an AFRF, provided that these communications are *not* intended to provide guidance on the application of these requirements to a specific transaction

A. Overview

1. **Objective** The objective of the reporting accountant, when engaged to issue a written report or provide oral advice on the application of the requirements of an AFRF to a specific transaction or on the type of report that may be issued on a specific entity's financial statements, is to address appropriately:

   a. The acceptance of the engagement

   b. The planning and performance of the engagement

   c. Reporting on the specific transaction or type of report

2. **Definitions**

   a. **Continuing Accountant** An accountant who has been engaged to report on the financial statements of a specific entity or entities of which the specific entity is a component

   b. **Hypothetical Transaction** A transaction or financial reporting issue that does **not** involve facts or circumstances of a specific entity.

   c. **Reporting Accountant** An accountant, other than a continuing accountant, in the practice of public accounting who prepares a written report or provides oral advice on the application of the requirements of an AFRF to a specific transaction or on the type of report that may be issued on a specific entity's financial statements

   d. **Advisory Accountant** A reporting accountant who is also engaged to provide accounting and reporting advice to a specific entity on a recurring basis

   e. **Specific Transaction** A completed or proposed transaction or group of related transactions or a financial reporting issue involving facts and circumstances of a specific entity

   f. **Written Report** Any written communication that provides a conclusion on the appropriate application of the requirements of an AFRF to a specific transaction or on the type of report that may be issued on a specific entity's financial statements

B. Engagement Acceptance Considerations

1. **Decision to Accept Engagement** In determining whether to accept the engagement, the reporting accountant should consider:

   a. The circumstances under which the written report or oral advice is requested

   b. The purpose of the request

   c. The intended use of the written report or oral advice

   d. Whether the transaction involves facts or circumstances of a specific entity; the reporting accountant should **not** accept an engagement to issue a written report on hypothetical transactions

   Editor Note: Independence is **not** required.

2. **Understanding With Requesting Party** If acceptance of the engagement is appropriate, the reporting accountant should establish an understanding with the requesting party that:

   a. **Management's Responsibility for Proper Accounting Treatment** Responsibility for the proper accounting treatment rests with management, *who is expected to consult with its continuing accountant*

   b. **Consultation With Continuing Accountant** Management acknowledges that the reporting accountant may need to consult with the continuing accountant and that, upon request, management will authorize the continuing accountant to respond fully to the reporting accountant's inquiries

      (1) **Same Degree of Cooperation as Predecessor Auditor** The responsibilities of an entity's continuing accountant to respond to inquiries by the reporting accountant are the same as the responsibilities of a predecessor auditor to respond to inquiries by the auditor.

      (2) **When Management Refuses to Authorize Full Response** If management refuses to agree to authorize the continuing accountant to respond fully to the reporting accountant's inquiries, the reporting accountant should inquire about the reasons and consider the implications of that refusal when determining whether to accept the engagement.

   c. **Management's Responsibility to Notify Others About Nature of Engagement** Concerning the nature of the engagement, management will notify:

      (1) Those charged with governance

      (2) Continuing accountant

C. **Engagement Planning & Performance**

1. **Procedures** The reporting accountant should:

   a. Obtain an understanding of the form and substance of the specific transaction(s) or the conditions relevant to the type of report that may be issued on a specific entity's financial statements

   b. Review the relevant requirements of the AFRF, if appropriate

   c. Consult with other professionals, experts, or regulatory authorities, if appropriate

   d. Perform research or other procedures, as appropriate, to identify and consider existing creditable precedents or analogies

   e. Request permission from the entity's management to consult with the continuing accountant and request the entity's management to authorize the continuing accountant to respond fully to the reporting accountant's inquiries

   f. Consult with the continuing accountant to determine the available facts relevant to forming a conclusion

   The continuing accountant *may* provide information related to the form and substance of the specific transaction that is not otherwise available to the reporting accountant regarding, for example:

   - How management has applied the requirements of an AFRF to similar transactions

- Whether the method of accounting recommended by the continuing accountant is disputed by management
- The continuing accountant's conclusion on the application of the requirements of an AFRF to the specific transaction or the type of report that may be issued on the entity's financial statements

2. **Document Rationale for Decision *Not* to Consult With Continuing Accountant** If the reporting accountant determines it is not necessary to consult with the continuing accountant, the reporting accountant should document the rationale for not consulting.

   The reporting accountant *should* consult with the continuing accountant to determine whether the reporting accountant has obtained the available facts relevant to form a conclusion, **unless** *all of the following are true.*

   a. **Specific Transaction** The reporting accountant is engaged to issue a written report or provide oral advice on the application of the requirements of an AFRF to a specific transaction.

   b. **Reporting Accountant Is Advisory Accountant** The reporting accountant is engaged to provide recurring accounting and reporting advice and all of the following are true. The reporting accountant:

      (1) Does not believe that a second opinion is being requested

      (2) Has full access to management

      (3) Believes that the relevant information has been obtained in order to issue a written report or provide oral advice regarding the application of the requirements of an AFRF to an entity's specific transaction.

D. **Written Report**

The reporting accountant's written report should be addressed to the requesting party (for example, management or those charged with governance) and should include the following:

1. A brief description of the nature of the engagement
2. A statement that the engagement was performed in accordance with this standard, i.e., per AU 915, *Reports on Application of Requirements of an Applicable Financial Reporting Framework*
3. Identification of the specific entity
4. Description of the specific transaction(s), if applicable
5. A statement of the relevant facts, circumstances, and assumptions
6. A statement about the source of the preceding information
7. A statement describing the appropriate application of the requirements of an AFRF (including the country of origin) to the specific transaction or type of report that may be issued on the entity's financial statements
8. A description of the reasons for the reporting accountant's conclusion, if appropriate
9. A statement that the responsibility for the proper accounting treatment rests with the preparers of the financial statements, who should consult with their continuing accountant

10. A statement that any difference in the facts, circumstances, or assumptions presented may change the report

11. An alert that restricts the use of the report solely to the specified parties

    Editor Note: This alert is not intended to preclude distribution of the report to the continuing accountant.

12. If the reporting accountant is not independent of the entity, a statement indicating the reporting accountant's lack of independence—the reporting accountant is neither required to provide, nor precluded from providing, the reasons for the lack of independence; however, if the reporting accountant chooses to provide the reasons, all them should be included

Exhibit 39 ▸ Written Report on Application of Requirements of US GAAP to a Specific Transaction

[*Appropriate Addressee*]

Introduction

We have been engaged to report on the appropriate application of the requirements of accounting principles generally accepted in the United States of America to the specific transaction described below. This report is being issued to ABC Company for assistance in evaluating accounting policies for the described specific transaction. Our engagement has been conducted in accordance with Statement on Auditing Standards 122 section 915, *Reports on Application of Requirements of an Applicable Financial Reporting Framework*.

Description of Transaction

The facts, circumstances, and assumptions relevant to the specific transaction as provided to us by the management of ABC Company are as follows:

[*Text discussing the facts, circumstances, and assumptions relevant to the specific transaction*]

Appropriate Accounting Principles

[*Text discussing accounting principles generally accepted in the United States of America and how they apply to the described transaction*]

Concluding Comments

The ultimate responsibility for the decision on the appropriate application of the requirements of accounting principles generally accepted in the United States of America for an actual transaction rests with the preparers of financial statements, who should consult with their continuing accountant. Our conclusion on the appropriate application of the requirements of accounting principles generally accepted in the United States of America for the described specific transaction is based solely on the facts provided to us as previously described; should these facts and circumstances differ, our conclusion may change.

Restricted Use

This report is intended solely for the information and use of those charged with governance and management of ABC Company and is not intended to be and should not be used by anyone other than these specified parties.

X. Use of a Reporting Framework Generally Accepted in Another Country (AU 910)

An auditor practicing in the United States may be engaged to report on financial statements that have been prepared in accordance with a financial reporting framework generally accepted in another country when such audited statements are generally intended for use outside the United States, but *may* also be used within the United States.

These are financial reporting frameworks **not** adopted by a body designated by the AICPA to establish generally accepted accounting principles.

A. Overview

1. **Objective** The objective of the auditor, when engaged to report on financial statements prepared in accordance with a financial reporting framework generally accepted in another country, when such audited financial statements are intended for use outside the United States, is to address appropriately the special considerations that are relevant to:

   a. The acceptance of the engagement

   b. The planning and performance of the engagement

   c. Forming an opinion and reporting on the financial statements

2. **Definitions**

   a. **Financial Reporting Framework** A set of criteria used to determine measurement, recognition, presentation, and disclosure of all material items in the financial statements; for example, US GAAP, International Financial Reporting Standards, or a special-purpose framework

   b. **Applicable Financial Reporting Framework** The financial reporting framework adopted by management and those charged with governance in the preparation and fair presentation of the financial statements that is acceptable in view of the nature of the entity and the objective of the financial statements, or that is required by law or regulation

B. Engagement Acceptance Considerations

1. **Financial Statements** The auditor should obtain an understanding of the:

   a. Purpose for which the financial statements are prepared and whether the financial reporting framework applied in the preparation of the financial statements is a fair presentation framework

   b. Intended users of the financial statements

   c. Steps taken by management to determine that the AFRF is acceptable in the circumstances

2. **Report** When the auditor plans to use the form and content of the audit report of another country, the auditor should obtain an understanding of the applicable legal responsibilities involved.

C. Performance

1. **Financial Statements Intended for Use *Only* Outside United States** When auditing financial statements prepared in accordance with a financial reporting framework generally accepted in another country that are intended for use *only* outside the United States, the auditor should:

   a. Comply with US GAAS, **except** the auditor should follow the reporting requirements described in the next topic in this section (reporting for use *only* outside the United States)

   b. Determine whether the application of US GAAS requires special consideration in the circumstances of the engagement

   c. Obtain an understanding of the entity's selection and application of accounting policies

2. **Terms of Engagement Are to Apply Auditing Standards Other Than US GAAS** If the terms of an engagement require the auditor to apply auditing standards other than US GAAS, the auditor should obtain an understanding of and apply those relevant auditing standards, *as well as US GAAS*, **except** the auditor should follow the reporting requirements described in the next topic in this section (reporting for use *only* outside the United States).

D. Reporting

1. **Financial Statements Intended for Use *Only* Outside United States** The auditor should report using *either*:

   a. A US form of report that reflects that the financial statements have been prepared in accordance with a financial reporting framework generally accepted in another country which would, in addition to the "standard" format:

      (1) Include a statement that refers to the note to the financial statements that describes the basis of presentation of the financial statements (AFRF), including the identification of the country of origin of the accounting principles (shown added to the end of the introductory paragraph in the report illustrations at the end of this section)

      Editor Note: Mention of the AFRF and its country of origin are included in the management's responsibility and opinion sections in the "standard" US audit report. This form of report also requires their inclusion (along with the reference to the note to the financial statements) in the introductory paragraph.

      (2) When the terms of engagement require the application of auditing standards other than US GAAS, indicate the country of origin of those auditing standards along with the statement about adherence to US GAAS (shown added to the first paragraph of the auditor's responsibility section in the report illustrations at the end of this section)

   or

   b. The report form and content of the other country if *all* of these conditions are met:

      (1) Such a report would be issued by auditors in the other country in similar circumstances

      (2) The auditor understands and has obtained sufficient appropriate audit evidence to support the statements contained in such a report

(3) The auditor has complied with the reporting standards of that country and identifies the other country in the report

(4) The auditor has obtained an understanding of the applicable legal responsibilities involved

2. **Financial Statements Are Intended for Use Both Outside & Inside the United States**

a. **When One Report Is Issued** When financial statements prepared in accordance with a financial reporting framework generally accepted in another country are *also* intended for use in the United States, the auditor should report using the US form of report described as the first option in the preceding topic of this section (when the financial statements are intended *only* for use outside the United States) **except** that an emphasis-of-matter paragraph should be added that:

(1) Identifies the AFRF

(2) Refers to the note to the financial statements that describes that framework

(3) Indicates that such framework differs from US GAAP

b. **When Two Reports Are Issued** Alternatively, the auditor *may* issue two reports:

(1) **For Use Outside the United States** The auditor should issue one of the two reports previously described when the financial statements are only intended for use outside the United States.

(2) **For Use Within the United States**: The auditor should issue the first report described when the financial statements are only intended for use outside the United States (the US form of report) with the inclusion of the emphasis-of-matter paragraph just described.

3. **GAAP Financial Statements & Another Reporting Framework** An entity that prepares financial statements in accordance with GAAP also may prepare financial statements in accordance with a financial reporting framework generally accepted in another country for use outside the United States. For the financial statements prepared in accordance with a financial reporting framework generally accepted in another country, the auditor may issue one of the two reports previously described when the financial statements are only intended for use outside the United States. The auditor may include in one or both of the reports a statement that another report has been issued on the financial statements for the entity that have been prepared in accordance with a financial reporting framework generally accepted in another country. The auditor's statement may also reference any note disclosure in the financial statements that describes significant differences between the accounting principles used and GAAP. An example of such a statement, which may be included in an emphasis-of-matter paragraph, is as follows:

We also have reported separately on the financial statements of ABC Company for the same period presented in accordance with [*specify the financial reporting framework generally accepted*] in [*name of country*]. (The significant differences between the [*specify the financial reporting framework generally accepted*] in [*name of country*] and accounting principles generally accepted in the United States of America are summarized in Note X.)

Editor Note: The changes to the "standard" report are underlined and text from the "standard' report that is not included is shown with strikethrough in the following report illustrations.

Exhibit 40 ▶ US Form of Audit Report on Financial Statements Prepared in Accordance With Financial Reporting Framework Generally Accepted in Another Country That Are Intended for Use *Only* Outside United States

Independent Auditor's Report

[*Appropriate Addressee*]

We have audited the accompanying financial statements of ABC Company, which comprise the balance sheet as of December 31, 20X1, and the related statements of income, changes in stockholders' equity, and cash flows for the year then ended, and the related notes to the financial statements, which, as described in note X to the financial statements, have been prepared on the basis of [*specify the financial reporting framework generally accepted*] in [*name of country*].

Management's Responsibility for the Financial Statements

Management is responsible for the preparation and fair presentation of these financial statements in accordance with ~~accounting principles generally accepted~~ [*specify the financial reporting framework generally accepted*] in ~~the United States of America~~ [*name of country*]; this includes the design, implementation, and maintenance of internal control relevant to the preparation and fair presentation of financial statements that are free from material misstatement, whether due to fraud or error.

Auditor's Responsibility

Our responsibility is to express an opinion on these financial statements based on our audit. We conducted our audit in accordance with auditing standards generally accepted in the United States of America *(and [*in name of country*]). Those standards require that we plan and perform the audit to obtain reasonable assurance about whether the financial statements are free from material misstatement.

An audit involves performing procedures to obtain audit evidence about the amounts and disclosures in the financial statements. The procedures selected depend on the auditor's judgment, including the assessment of the risks of material misstatement of the financial statements, whether due to fraud or error. In making those risk assessments, the auditor considers internal control relevant to the entity's preparation and fair presentation of the financial statements in order to design audit procedures that are appropriate in the circumstances, but not for the purpose of expressing an opinion on the effectiveness of the entity's internal control. Accordingly, we express no such opinion. An audit also includes evaluating the appropriateness of accounting policies used and the reasonableness of significant accounting estimates made by management, as well as evaluating the overall presentation of the financial statements.

We believe that the audit evidence we have obtained is sufficient and appropriate to provide a basis for our audit opinion.

Opinion

In our opinion, the financial statements referred to above present fairly, in all material respects, the financial position of ABC Company as of December 31, 20X1, and the results of its operations and its cash flows for the year then ended in accordance with ~~accounting principles generally accepted~~ [*specify the financial reporting framework generally accepted*] in ~~the United States of America~~ [*name of country*].

[*Auditor's signature*]

[*Auditor's city and state*]

[*Date of the audit report*]

* Only included if the terms of engagement require the application of auditing standards other than US GAAS; the auditor must also apply US GAAS under these circumstances.

Exhibit 41 ▶ US Form of Audit Report on Financial Statements Prepared in Accordance With Financial Reporting Framework Generally Accepted in Another Country That Are Intended for Use Both Inside & Outside United States

Independent Auditor's Report

[*Appropriate Addressee*]

We have audited the accompanying financial statements of ABC Company, which comprise the balance sheet as of December 31, 20X1, and the related statements of income, changes in stockholders' equity, and cash flows for the year then ended, and the related notes to the financial statements, which, as described in note X to the financial statements, have been prepared on the basis of [*specify the financial reporting framework generally accepted*] in [*name of country*].

Management's Responsibility for the Financial Statements

Management is responsible for the preparation and fair presentation of these financial statements in accordance with ~~accounting principles generally accepted~~ [*specify the financial reporting framework generally accepted*] in ~~the United States of America~~ [*name of country*]; this includes the design, implementation, and maintenance of internal control relevant to the preparation and fair presentation of financial statements that are free from material misstatement, whether due to fraud or error.

Auditor's Responsibility

Our responsibility is to express an opinion on these financial statements based on our audit. We conducted our audit in accordance with auditing standards generally accepted in the United States of America *(and [*in name of country*]). Those standards require that we plan and perform the audit to obtain reasonable assurance about whether the financial statements are free from material misstatement.

An audit involves performing procedures to obtain audit evidence about the amounts and disclosures in the financial statements. The procedures selected depend on the auditor's judgment, including the assessment of the risks of material misstatement of the financial statements, whether due to fraud or error. In making those risk assessments, the auditor considers internal control relevant to the entity's preparation and fair presentation of the financial statements in order to design audit procedures that are appropriate in the circumstances, but not for the purpose of expressing an opinion on the effectiveness of the entity's internal control. Accordingly, we express no such opinion. An audit also includes evaluating the appropriateness of accounting policies used and the reasonableness of significant accounting estimates made by management, as well as evaluating the overall presentation of the financial statements.

We believe that the audit evidence we have obtained is sufficient and appropriate to provide a basis for our audit opinion.

Opinion

In our opinion, the financial statements referred to above present fairly, in all material respects, the financial position of ABC Company as of December 31, 20X1, and the results of its operations and its cash flows for the year then ended in accordance with ~~accounting principles generally accepted~~ [*specify the financial reporting framework generally accepted*] in ~~the United States of America~~ [*name of country*].

Emphasis of Matter

As discussed in Note X to the financial statements, the Company prepares its financial statements in accordance with [*specify the financial reporting framework generally accepted*] in [*name of country*], which differ(s) from accounting principles generally accepted in the United States of America. Our opinion is not modified with respect to this matter.

[*Auditor's signature*]

[*Auditor's city and state*]

[*Date of the audit report*]

* Only included if the terms of engagement require the application of auditing standards other than US GAAS; the auditor must also apply US GAAS under these circumstances.

XI. Alert That Restricts the Use of the Auditor's Written Communication (AU 905)

A. Overview

An auditor should restrict the use of an auditor's written communication by including an alert when the communication has the potential to be misunderstood if taken out of context. This standard contains guidance regarding the form of such an alert when US GAAS require its inclusion. This standard also applies when the auditor decides to voluntarily restrict a communication.

Editor Note: Audit reports on financial statements prepared in accordance with a general-purpose framework ordinarily do **not** include an alert that restricts their use. However, nothing in US GAAS precludes an auditor from voluntarily including such an alert in any audit report or other auditor's written communication.

B. Definitions

1. **Auditor's Written Communication** An auditor's written communications include audit reports and letters; or presentation materials. For example, letters communicating internal control related matters or presentations addressing communications with those charged with governance.

2. **Alert** An alert is language that restricts the use of the auditor's written communication. It is designed to avoid misunderstandings related to its use. In an audit report, such language is included in an other-matter paragraph.

3. **Specified Parties** Specified parties are the intended users of the auditor's written communication.

4. **By-Product Report** A by-product report is an auditor's written communication that is based solely on matters identified by the auditor during the course of an audit engagement when the identification of such matters is *not* the primary objective of the audit engagement.

5. **General-Purpose Framework** A general-purpose framework is a financial reporting framework designed to meet the common financial information needs of a wide range of users.

C. Conditions for the Restriction of an Auditor's Written Communication

The auditor's written communication should include an alert that restricts its use when the subject matter is based on:

1. Measurement or disclosure criteria that are:

   a. Suitable only for a limited number of users with an adequate understanding of the criteria

   b. Available only to the specified parties

2. Matters in a by-product report (because a by-product report can generally only be understood in relation to the primary objective of the audit engagement)

D. Elements of an Alert That Restricts the Use of an Auditor's Written Communication

Unless specified otherwise by other US GAAS, the alert should include the following *in a separate paragraph*.

1. A statement that the auditor's written communication is intended solely for the information and use of the specified parties

2. The identification of the specified parties (the alert may contain a list or a reference to a list elsewhere in the communication); in the case of a by-product report, the specified parties should *only* include:

   a. Management

   b. Those charged with governance

   c. Others within the entity

   d. Parties to the contract or agreement

   e. Relevant regulatory agencies

3. A statement that the auditor's written communication is not intended to be and should not be used by anyone other than the specified parties

Exhibit 42 ▸ Alert Paragraph

This [*report, letter, presentation, or communication*] is intended solely for the information and use of [*list or refer to the specified parties*] and is not intended to be and should not be used by anyone other than these specified parties.

Editor Note: If the alert is included in an audit report, it should be in an other-matter paragraph and have an appropriate heading, for example, *Restriction on Use*.

4. The alert language just described should **not** be used when the engagement is performed in accordance with *Government Auditing Standards and* the auditor's written communication is related to requirements in:

   - AU 265, *Communicating Internal Control Related Matters Identified in an Audit*
   - AU 806, *Reporting on Compliance With Aspects of Contractual Agreements or Regulatory Requirements in Connection With Audited Financial Statements*
   - AU 935, *Compliance Audits*

   Instead, the alert should describe the purpose of the auditor's written communication and state that the auditor's written communication is not suitable for any other purpose. (No specified parties are identified in this type of alert.)

   Editor Note: *Government Auditing Standards* regard the auditor's written communications issued related to these sections to be an integral part of the audit engagement for the purpose of assessing the results of the engagement; accordingly, different language is used.

E. When Restricted-Use & General-Use Communications Are Combined

1. **Combined in Same Document** When a restricted-use communication is included in a document that also contains a general-use communication, the use of the general-use communication is *not* affected, i.e., the restriction is limited to the communication with the alert.

2. **Combined in Same Communication** An auditor may also issue a written communication that includes both types. As long as the two are clearly differentiated within the combined communication, for example, by the use of headings, the use of the general-use communication is *not* affected, i.e., the restriction is limited to the communication with the alert.

F. Adding Other Specified Parties to an Alert

1. The auditor should determine whether to agree to add other specified parties; in the case of a by-product report, the auditor should only agree to add parties from the groups listed in the previous topic.

   Editor Note: In considering whether to add others, the auditor's decision *may* be based on, for example, their identity or the intended use of the communication.

2. If the auditor agrees to add them, the auditor should obtain their acknowledgment, *in writing*, that they understand the:

   a. Nature of the engagement

   b. Measurement or disclosure criteria related to the subject matter

   c. Auditor's written communication

3. When the other parties are added *after* the release of the auditor's written communication, the auditor should *also* either:

   a. Amend the communication to add the other parties, in which case the original date of the auditor's written communication should be used

   or

   b. Provide to management and the other parties a *written* acknowledgment of the specified parties that have been added. The auditor should state in the acknowledgment that no procedures were performed subsequent to the original date of the auditor's written communication or the date that the engagement was completed, as appropriate.

G. Distribution of an Auditor's Written Communication

An auditor is **not** responsible for controlling the distribution of the auditor's written communication after its release. An auditor *may* consider informing the entity or other specified parties that the auditor's written communication is not intended for distribution to parties other than those specified. If an auditor deems a stauncher approach is needed, the terms of the engagement *may* state that the use of the auditor's written communication will be restricted and include the entity's agreement that the entity and the specified parties will not distribute it to parties other than those specified in the communication.

CHAPTER 12—OTHER TYPES OF REPORTS

Problem 12-1 MULTIPLE-CHOICE QUESTIONS

Engagement to Report on Supplementary Information

1. An auditor is engaged to report on selected financial data that are included in a client-prepared document containing audited financial statements. Under these circumstances, the report on the selected data should

   a. Be limited to data derived from the audited financial statements
   b. Be distributed only to senior management and the board of directors
   c. State that the presentation is a comprehensive basis of accounting other than GAAP
   d. Indicate that the data is not fairly stated in all material respects (ID: 6034)

2. In order to opine on whether supplementary information is fairly stated, in all material respects, in relation to the financial statements as a whole, all of the following conditions must be met **except for**

   a. The supplementary information was derived from, and relates directly to, the underlying accounting and other records used to prepare the financial statements.
   b. The supplementary information relates to the same period as the financial statements.
   c. The auditor issued an audit report on the financial statements that contained neither an adverse opinion nor a disclaimer of opinion.
   d. The supplementary information will accompany the entity's audited financial statements, or such audited financial statements will be made available upon request. (ID: 9271)

3. Which of the following is **not** a condition that should be met in order for an auditor to opine on whether supplementary information is fairly stated, in all material respects, in relation to the financial statements as a whole?

   a. The supplementary information was derived from, and relates directly to, the underlying accounting and other records used to prepare the financial statements.
   b. The supplementary information relates to the same period as the financial statements.
   c. The auditor issued an audit report on the financial statements that contained an unmodified opinion.
   d. The supplementary information will accompany the entity's audited financial statements, or such audited financial statements will be made readily available by the entity. (ID: 9289)

4. Which of the following is **not** an acknowledgement an auditor should obtain from management regarding management's responsibilities when an auditor is engaged to report on whether supplementary information is fairly stated, in all material respects, in relation to the financial statements as a whole?

   a. Management is responsible for the preparation of the supplementary information in accordance with the applicable criteria.
   b. Management is responsible for including the auditor's report on the supplementary information in any document that contains the supplementary information and that indicates that the auditor has reported on such supplementary information.
   c. Management is responsible for providing the auditor with certain written representations.
   d. Management is responsible for presenting the supplementary information with the audited financial statements or making the statements available no later than 30 days after the date of issuance of the auditor's report on the supplementary information. (ID: 9290)

5. When performing procedures in an engagement to report on whether supplementary information is fairly stated, in all material respects, in relation to the financial statements as a whole, the auditor should
   a. Use the same materiality level used in the audit of the financial statements.
   b. Obtain a separate understanding of the entity's internal control and assess fraud risk.
   c. Apply procedures as extensive as would be necessary to express an opinion on the information on a stand-alone basis.
   d. Not consider materiality in determining which information to compare and reconcile to the underlying accounting and other records used in preparing the financial statements or to the financial statements themselves. (ID: 9291)

6. When an auditor is engaged to report on whether supplementary information is fairly stated, in all material respects, in relation to the financial statements as a whole, and the audited financial statements are **not** presented with the supplementary information, the auditor should
   a. Include a copy of the audit report on the financial statements
   b. Report on the accompanying information only if the auditor participated in its preparation
   c. Determine a materiality level that is appropriate for the subject of the supplementary information
   d. Report on the supplementary information in a separate report (ID: 9270)

7. When an auditor is engaged to report on whether supplementary information is fairly stated, in all material respects, in relation to the financial statements as a whole and the entity presents the supplementary information with the financial statements, the auditor should
   a. Include a statement in the report that the supplementary information is presented for purposes of additional analysis and is a required part of the financial statements.
   b. Include an explanation in the report if the auditor expressed an adverse opinion or disclaimed an opinion on the financial statements.
   c. Report on the supplementary information in either an other-matter paragraph in the audit report on the financial statements or in a separate report
   d. Restrict the distribution of the report (ID: 9292)

8. An auditor is engaged to report on supplementary information in relation to the financial statements as a whole that is included in a client-prepared document containing audited financial statements. Under these circumstances, the auditor has elected to report on the supplementary information in an other-matter paragraph in the audit report on the financial statements. The other-matter paragraph should
   a. State that the presentation is a comprehensive basis of accounting other than GAAP
   b. State that the supplementary information has not been subjected to the auditing procedures
   c. State that the information is limited to data derived from records used to prepare the entity's financial statements
   d. Restrict the use of the report to appropriate specified parties (ID: 89782)

Audits of Special-Purpose Financial Statements

9. Helpful Co., a nonprofit entity, prepared its financial statements in accordance with an accounting basis prescribed by a regulatory agency solely for filing with that agency. Green audited the financial statements in accordance with US GAAS and concluded that the financial statements were fairly presented. Green should issue an audit report
   a. With a qualified opinion
   b. With an unmodified opinion with reference to the footnote disclosure
   c. With a disclaimer of opinion
   d. On special-purpose financial statements (ID: 2285)

10. Financial statements are considered special-purpose financial statements when
    a. Prepared in accordance with either a regulatory or contractual basis of accounting
    b. Restricted as to use
    c. Prepared in accordance with either a contractual or an other comprehensive basis of accounting
    d. Prepared on a pro forma basis designed to demonstrate the effects of hypothetical transactions

(ID: 9375)

11. An audit report on special-purpose financial statements (except for a report on regulatory basis financial statements intended for general use) should include an emphasis-of-matter paragraph that
    a. Indicates that the financial statements are prepared in accordance with an other comprehensive basis of accounting
    b. States that the special-purpose framework is a basis of accounting other than GAAP
    c. Has the heading *Basis of Accounting*
    d. Describes the framework

(ID: 392)

12. When an auditor reports on financial statements prepared on the tax basis of accounting, the audit report should
    a. Disclaim an opinion on whether the statements were examined in accordance with generally accepted auditing standards
    b. Not express an opinion on whether the statements are presented in conformity with the basis of accounting used
    c. Include an explanation of how the results of operations differ from the cash basis of accounting
    d. State that the basis of accounting is other than GAAP

(ID: 4748)

13. Which of the following titles would be considered suitable for financial statements that are prepared on a cash basis?
    a. Income statement
    b. Statement of operations
    c. Statement of revenue collected and expenses paid
    d. Statement of cash flows

(ID: 8815)

14. Which of the following would be an appropriate title for a statement of revenue and expenses prepared using a special-purpose framework?
    a. Statement of operations
    b. Statement of income—statutory basis
    c. Income statement
    d. Statement of activities

(ID: 9351)

Audits of Single Financial Statements & Specific Elements, Accounts, or Items

15. A CPA is permitted to accept a separate engagement (**not** in conjunction with an audit of financial statements) to audit an entity's schedule of

	Accounts receivable	Royalties
a.	Yes	Yes
b.	Yes	No
c.	No	Yes
d.	No	No

(ID: 7694)

16. An auditor may express an unmodified opinion on an entity's accounts receivable balance even if the auditor has disclaimed an opinion on the entity's complete set of financial statements as a whole, provided certain conditions are met and the
    a. Audit report on the accounts receivable discloses the reason for the disclaimer of opinion on the complete set of financial statements
    b. Distribution of the audit report on the accounts receivable is restricted to internal use only
    c. Auditor also reports on the current asset portion of the entity's balance sheet
    d. Audit report on the accounts receivable is presented separately from the disclaimer of opinion on the complete set of financial statements (ID: 6240)

Reports on Compliance in Connection With Audited Financial Statements

17. When the auditor reports on compliance with aspects of contractual agreements or regulatory requirements, in connection with the audit of financial statements, in a separate report, the report should
    a. Be a general-use report
    b. Be dated the same date as the audit report on the financial statements
    c. Not reference the audit report on the financial statements
    d. Not include negative assurance (ID: 90390)

Filings With the US Securities and Exchange Commission

18. Because the effective date of a registration statement filed under the Securities Act of 1933 may not necessarily coincide with the filing date, the auditor should request management to keep the auditor advised of the progress of the registration proceedings through
    a. The effective date of the registration statement
    b. The date of the referenced financial statements
    c. The date of the audit report on the referenced financial statements
    d. The date of the entity's latest interim financial statements (ID: 90387)

Letters for Underwriters & Certain Other Requesting Parties

19. Comfort letters ordinarily are

	Addressed to the	Signed by the
a.	Audit committee	Independent auditor
b.	Underwriter of securities	Senior management
c.	Audit committee	Senior management
d.	Underwriter of securities	Independent auditor

(ID: 8387)

20. When commenting in a comfort letter on information other than audited financial statements, an auditor should
    a. State that nothing else has come to the auditor's attention that would be of interest to the requesting party as a result of carrying out the specified procedures
    b. State that the auditor has applied procedures that the auditor determined to be necessary or sufficient for the requesting party's purposes
    c. Describe the criteria specified by the requesting party
    d. Use universally understood and accepted terms such as *reconcile*, *check*, or *test* (ID: 90388}

Review of Interim Financial Information

21. The objective of a review of interim financial information of a nonissuer is to provide an auditor with a basis for communicating whether
    a. Material modifications should be made to conform with the applicable financial reporting framework
    b. A reasonable basis exists for expressing an updated opinion regarding the financial statements that were previously audited
    c. Condensed financial statements or pro forma financial information should be included in a registration statement
    d. The financial information is presented fairly in accordance with the applicable financial reporting framework (ID: 5701)

22. Which of the following procedures ordinarily should be applied when an auditor conducts a review of interim financial information of a nonissuer?
    a. Verify changes in key account balances
    b. Read the minutes of the board of directors' meeting
    c. Inspect the open purchase order file
    d. Perform cutoff tests for cash receipts and disbursements (ID: 2985)

23. Which of the following circumstances requires modification of the auditor's report on a review of interim financial information of a nonissuer?

	An uncertainty	Inadequate disclosure
a.	No	No
b.	Yes	Yes
c.	Yes	No
d.	No	Yes

(ID: 410)

Engagements to Report on Summary Financial Statements

24. An auditor should not accept an engagement to report separately on summary financial statements unless
    a. The auditor's report on the financial statements from which the summary financial statements are derived contains an unmodified opinion.
    b. The auditor has been engaged to conduct an audit in accordance with US GAAS of the financial statements from which the summary financial statements are derived.
    c. The auditor's report on the financial statements from which the summary financial statements are derived was released less than six months previous to the start of the engagement to report on the summary financial statements.
    d. Management agrees not to distribute the report or statements outside the entity. (ID: 90383)

Reports on Application of Requirements of an Applicable Financial Reporting Framework

25. A CPA is asked to prepare a report on the application of the requirements of an applicable financial reporting framework to a specific transaction. The CPA's report should include a statement that
    a. The engagement was performed in accordance with auditing standards generally accepted in the United States of America.
    b. Responsibility for the proper accounting treatment rests with the preparers of the financial statements.
    c. The CPA is independent of the entity.
    d. The evaluation of the requirements is based on a hypothetical transaction. (ID: 90384)

Use of a Reporting Framework Generally Accepted in Another Country

26. In an audit of financial statements prepared in accordance with a financial reporting framework generally accepted in another country, the auditor should obtain an understanding of all of the following **except**

    a. The purpose for which the financial statements are prepared
    b. The certification required by the appropriate auditing or accountancy board of the other country
    c. The intended users of the financial statements
    d. The steps taken by management to determine that the applicable financial reporting framework is acceptable in the circumstances (ID: 90385)

27. When the auditor plans to use the form and content of the audit report of another country, the auditor should

    a. Notify management of the US entity that the auditor is required to disclaim an opinion on the financial statements
    b. Receive a waiver to report on the US entity from the appropriate accountancy authority in the other country
    c. Obtain an understanding of the applicable legal responsibilities involved
    d. Communicate with the auditor of the non-US parent regarding the level of assurance to be provided (ID: 90386)

Alert that Restricts the Use of the Auditor's Written Communication

28. The auditor's written communication should include an alert, in a separate paragraph, that restricts its use **except**

    a. When the subject matter is based on measurement or disclosure criteria that are available only to the specified parties
    b. When the subject matter is based on measurement or disclosure criteria that are determined by the auditor to be suitable only for a limited number of users who can be presumed to have an adequate understanding of the criteria
    c. When it relates to special-purpose financial statements
    d. When it relates to matters identified by the auditor during the course of the audit engagement when the identification of such matters is not the primary objective of the audit engagement (ID: 90389)

Problem 12-2 SIMULATION: Audit Report on Financial Statements Prepared in Accordance with the Cash Basis of Accounting

The audit report on financial statements prepared in accordance with the cash basis of accounting was drafted by a staff accountant of your firm at the completion of the engagement. It contained the elements below. Indicate whether each item is an appropriate (A) or an inappropriate (I) element within the report.

Report Elements	Appropriate (A) or Inappropriate (I)
1. A title that includes the word independent.	
2. A statement that management is responsible for the preparation and fair presentation of these financial statements in accordance with the cash basis of accounting.	
3. A statement that the audit was conducted in accordance with standards established by the American Institute of Certified Public Accountants and includes an identification of the United States of America as the country of origin of those standards.	
4. When management has a choice of financial reporting frameworks, a statement that management is responsible for determining that the cash basis of accounting is an acceptable basis for the preparation of the financial statements in the circumstances.	
5. A statement that the cash basis of accounting is not a fair presentation framework.	
6. A statement that an audit also includes: (a) Evaluating the appropriateness of accounting policies used; (b) The reasonableness of significant accounting estimates made by management; and (c) Evaluating the overall presentation of the financial statements.	
7. An other-matter paragraph that restricts the use of the report.	

(ID: 9246)

Problem 12-3 SIMULATION: Research

When engaged to report on supplementary information in relation to the financial statements as a whole, the auditor need not apply procedures as extensive as would be necessary to express an opinion on the information on a stand-alone basis. Which citation in the professional standards provides guidance on whether or not the auditor is required to obtain a separate understanding of the entity's internal control or to assess fraud risk?

[ ] § [ ] . [ ] (ID: 90382)

Solution 12-1 MULTIPLE-CHOICE ANSWERS

1. (a) The selected data accompanying the basic financial statements (supplementary information) should be derived from, and related directly to, the underlying accounting and other records used to prepare the financial statements. Regarding incorrect answer b., the report is not required to be restricted. Regarding incorrect answer c., the basis of accounting is not necessarily other than GAAP. Supplementary information may be prepared in accordance with various criteria or other requirements. Regarding incorrect answer d., ordinarily, the opinion on whether the supplementary information is fairly stated, in all material respects, in relation to the financial statements as a whole, is that it is fairly stated. However, if a qualified opinion on the financial statements affects the supplementary information, the opinion on the supplementary information will refer to the explanation about the qualification that either appears in the audit report on the financial statements or if the auditor reports on the supplementary information in a separate report, the explanation described in that separate report. (When the audit report on the financial statements contains an adverse opinion or a disclaimer of opinion, the auditor is precluded from expressing an opinion on the supplementary information.) If the supplementary information is materially misstated, the auditor should discuss the matter with management and propose appropriate revision of the supplementary information. If management does not revise the supplementary information, the auditor should either (1) modify the auditor's opinion on the supplementary information and describe the misstatement in the audit report or (2) if a separate report is being issued on the supplementary information, withhold the report on the supplementary information. (ID: 6034)

2. (d) Being available upon request is not considered readily available. One of the conditions that must be met is that the supplementary information will accompany the entity's audited financial statements, or such audited financial statements will be made readily available by the entity. Audited financial statements are deemed to be readily available if a third party user can obtain the audited financial statements without any further action by the entity. For example, financial statements on an entity's website may be considered readily available, but being available upon request is not considered readily available. (ID: 9271)

3. (c) An unmodified opinion on the financial statements is **not** required; instead, the auditor should have issued an audit report on the financial statements that contained neither an adverse opinion nor a disclaimer of opinion (the report can contain a qualified opinion). The other answer alternatives cover the other conditions. (ID: 9289)

4. (d) All of the answers are correct regarding the responsibilities of management except the last one. Instead of answer d., the correct statement is as follows: Management is responsible for presenting the supplementary information with the audited financial statements or, if the supplementary information will not be presented with the audited financial statements, to make the audited financial statements readily available to the intended users of the supplementary information no later than the date of issuance by the entity of the supplementary information and the auditor's report thereon. (ID: 9290)

5. (a) When performing procedures in an engagement to report on whether supplementary information is fairly stated, in all material respects, in relation to the financial statements as a whole, the auditor should use the same materiality level used in the audit of the financial statements. Regarding incorrect answer b., with respect to the supplementary information, the auditor is *not* required to obtain a separate understanding of the entity's internal control or assess fraud risk. Regarding incorrect answer c., the auditor need *not* apply procedures as extensive as would be necessary to express an opinion on the information on a stand-alone basis. Regarding incorrect answer d., the auditor *should* consider materiality in determining which information to compare and reconcile to the underlying accounting and other records used in preparing the financial statements or to the financial statements themselves. (ID: 9291)

6. (d) When an auditor is engaged to report on whether supplementary information is fairly stated, in all material respects, in relation to the financial statements as a whole, and the audited financial statements are *not* presented with the supplementary information, the auditor should report on the supplementary information in a separate report. Regarding incorrect answer a., a copy of the audit report on the financial statements would *not* be included. Regarding incorrect answer b., the preparation of the supplementary information is the responsibility of management. Regarding incorrect answer c., the materiality level should be the same level used in the audit of the financial statements. Editor Note: When reporting separately on the supplementary information, the

report should include (in addition to the elements required in the other-matter paragraph when not presented separately), a reference to the report on the financial statements; the date of that report; the nature of the opinion expressed on the financial statements; and any report modifications. Also, the auditor may consider including an alert that restricts the use of the separate report solely to the appropriate specified parties to avoid potential misinterpretation or misunderstanding of the supplementary information that is not presented with the financial statements. (ID: 9270)

7. (c) When the entity presents the supplementary information *with* the financial statements, the auditor should report on the supplementary information in either an other-matter paragraph in the audit report on the financial statements or in a separate report. Regarding incorrect answer a., the auditor should include a statement that the supplementary information is presented for purposes of additional analysis and is *not* a required part of the financial statements. Regarding incorrect answer b., when the audit report on the financial statements contains an adverse opinion or a disclaimer of opinion the auditor is precluded from expressing an opinion on the supplementary information. In this case, when permitted by law or regulation, the auditor may withdraw from the engagement to report on the supplementary information. If the auditor does not withdraw, the report on the supplementary information (or the other-matter paragraph in the audit report) should state that because of the significance of the matter disclosed in the audit report, it is inappropriate to, and the auditor does not, express an opinion on the supplementary information. Regarding incorrect answer d., the auditor is most likely to consider restricting the use of a separate report on supplementary information to the appropriate specified parties to avoid potential misinterpretation or misunderstanding of the supplementary information that is *not* presented with the financial statements, but it is not required in either case. (ID: 9292)

8. (c) When an auditor is engaged to report on supplementary information that is included in a client-prepared document containing audited financial statements, the other-matter paragraph or separate report should include a statement that the supplementary information is the responsibility of management and was derived from, and relates directly to, the underlying accounting and other records used to prepare the financial statements. None of the other answers are required report elements. Regarding incorrect answer a., supplementary information is presented outside the basic financial statements; thus, an explanation concerning the framework is *not* required. And, the basis of accounting used for supplementary information is not necessarily other than GAAP. Supplementary information may be prepared in accordance with various criteria or other requirements. Regarding incorrect answer b., the report should state that the supplementary information has been subjected to the auditing procedures applied in the audit of the financial statements and certain additional procedures, including comparing and reconciling such information directly to the underlying accounting and other records used to prepare the financial statements or to the financial statements themselves and other additional procedures, in accordance with US GAAS. Regarding incorrect answer d., note that the question stipulates that the selected financial data is in a document containing the financial statements and the auditor is reporting via an other-matter paragraph included in the audit report on the financial statements. If the auditor had elected to issue a separate report on the supplementary information (or had been required to report separately because the audited financial statements were not presented with the supplementary information), the auditor *may* consider including an alert that restricts the use of the separate report solely to the appropriate specified parties to avoid potential misinterpretation or misunderstanding of the supplementary information that is not presented with the financial statements. Further, as nothing in US GAAS precludes an auditor from restricting a report or other written communication, such a restriction would be presented in a separate other-matter paragraph. Editor Note: When the entity presents the supplementary information with the financial statements, the auditor should report on the supplementary information in either an other-matter paragraph in the audit report on the financial statements or in a separate report. When the audited financial statements are *not* presented with the supplementary information, the auditor should report on the supplementary information in a separate report. When reporting separately, the report should include a reference to the report on the financial statements, the date of that report, the nature of the opinion expressed on the financial statements, and any report modifications. (ID: 89782)

9. (d) Special-purpose financial statements include those prepared in accordance with a regulatory basis of accounting (basis of accounting that the entity uses to comply with the requirements or financial reporting provisions of a regulatory agency to whose jurisdiction the entity is subject). (ID: 2285)

10. (c) Special-purpose financial statements are financial statements prepared in accordance with a special-purpose framework. A special-purpose framework is a financial reporting framework other than GAAP that is

one of the following bases of accounting: contractual or an other comprehensive basis of accounting, i.e., cash, tax, regulatory, or other (a basis of accounting having substantial support that is applied to all material financial statement items). (ID: 9375)

11. (b) The purpose of the emphasis-of-matter paragraph is to alert readers that the financial statements are prepared in accordance with a special-purpose framework. The emphasis-of-matter paragraph should state that the special-purpose framework is a basis of accounting other than GAAP. Regarding incorrect answer a., the phrase *other comprehensive basis of accounting* is not used. The emphasis-of-matter paragraph should indicate that the financial statements are prepared in accordance with the applicable special-purpose framework, for example, "The financial statements are prepared on the cash basis of accounting, which is a basis of accounting other than accounting principles generally accepted in the United States of America." Regarding incorrect answer c., *Basis of Accounting* is an appropriate heading for the emphasis-of-matter paragraph included in an audit report on special-purpose financial statements; however, another appropriate heading may be used. Regarding incorrect answer d., the framework should *not* be described in the emphasis-of-matter paragraph; instead, the paragraph should refer to the note to the financial statements that describes that framework. Editor Note: And, as with all emphasis-of-matter paragraphs, it should state that the opinion is not modified with respect to this matter. (ID: 392)

12. (d) The audit report should state that the special-purpose framework is a basis of accounting other than GAAP. Except for general-use regulatory basis financial statements, the audit report on special-purpose financial statements should include an emphasis-of-matter paragraph that (1) indicates that the financial statements are prepared in accordance with the applicable financial reporting framework; (2) refers to the note to the financial statements that describes that framework; and (3) states that the special-purpose framework is a basis of accounting other than GAAP. Regarding incorrect answer a., the auditor disclaims an opinion based on the inability to obtain sufficient appropriate audit evidence as to whether the financial statements are in accordance with the applicable special-purpose framework, in this case, the tax basis—an opinion is *not* disclaimed because an audit was not conducted in accordance with GAAS. Regarding incorrect answer b., when an audit is performed an opinion or disclaimer of opinion should be expressed on whether the financial statements are prepared in accordance with the applicable special-purpose framework, in this case, the tax basis, unless the auditor withdraws from the engagement which was not indicated in this question. Regarding incorrect answer c., the auditor is not required to compare any aspect of the tax basis of accounting with the cash basis of accounting. The auditor should evaluate whether the financial statements adequately describe how the special-purpose framework, in this case, the tax basis, differs from GAAP—the effects of these differences need not be quantified. (ID: 4748)

13. (c) Examples of suitable titles for cash basis financial statements are *statement of revenue collected and expenses paid* or *statement of assets and liabilities arising from cash transactions*. Regarding the incorrect answers, titles such as *statement of income*, *statement of operations*, *statement of cash flows*, *balance sheet*, and *statement of financial position* are generally understood to be applicable only to financial statements that are presented in accordance with GAAP. Financial statements prepared in conformity with a special-purpose framework should *not* use these GAAP titles. (ID: 8815)

14. (b) *Statement of income–statutory basis* is an example of an appropriate format for a title of a financial statement prepared in accordance with a basis of accounting used by insurance companies prescribed by a state insurance commission, i.e., a regulatory basis of accounting. Regarding incorrect answers a. and c., terms such as *statement of operations* and *statement of income* are generally understood to be applicable only to financial statements that are intended to present results of operations in conformity with GAAP. Regarding incorrect answer d., a *statement of activities* is a financial statement prepared in accordance with GAAP by a not-for-profit organization. (ID: 9351)

15. (a) An engagement to express an opinion on a single financial statement or one or more specified elements, accounts, or items of a financial statement may be undertaken either as a separate engagement or in conjunction with an audit of financial statements. (ID: 7694)

16. (d) The report on the accounts receivable should be presented separately. Generally, the auditor should not express an unmodified opinion on specified elements, accounts, or items included in financial statements on

which the auditor has disclaimed an opinion or expressed an adverse opinion because such reporting would be tantamount to expressing a piecemeal opinion on the financial statements. However, when the auditor nevertheless considers it appropriate to express an unmodified opinion on that specific element, the auditor should only do so if (1) the report on the specified element is presented separately from the report on the financial statements, i.e., is neither published together or otherwise accompanies the audit report containing the adverse opinion or disclaimer of opinion and (2) the specific element does not constitute a major portion of an entity's complete set of financial statements or the specific element is not, or is not based on, the entity's stockholders' equity or net income or the equivalent. None of the other answers represent conditions that would allow this exception. Editor Note: A single financial statement is considered to be a major portion of a complete set of financial statements, so this exception does not apply to it—an adverse opinion or disclaimer of opinion issued on a complete set of financial statements precludes an unmodified opinion on a single financial statement. (ID: 6240)

17. (b) The date of the report on compliance should be the same date as the audit report on the related financial statements. Regarding incorrect answer a., the use of report should be restricted. Regarding incorrect answer c., the report *should* state that the report is being provided in connection with the audit of the financial statements. Regarding incorrect answer d., if the auditor has *not* identified any instances of noncompliance the report should include a statement that nothing came to the auditor's attention [negative assurance] that caused the auditor to believe that the entity failed to comply with specified aspects of the contractual agreements or regulatory requirements, insofar as they relate to accounting matters, but only when (1) the audit report on the related financial statements contains an unmodified or qualified opinion and (2) the the applicable covenants or regulatory requirements relate to accounting matters that have been subjected to the audit procedures applied in the audit of financial statements. Editor Note: When the auditor has expressed an adverse opinion or disclaimed an opinion on the financial statements, the auditor should issue a report on compliance *only* when instances of *non*compliance are identified. (ID: 90390)

18. (a) Because the effective date of a registration statement filed under the Securities Act of 1933 may not necessarily coincide with the filing date, the auditor should request management to keep the auditor advised of the progress of the registration proceedings through the effective date of the registration statement. The effective date of the registration statement is the date on which the registration statement becomes effective for purposes of evaluating the auditor's liability. Requesting management to keep the auditor advised of the progress of the registration proceedings through the effective date is important so that the auditor's consideration of events occurring after the date of the audit report up to the effective date, or as close to it as reasonable and practicable, can be completed by the effective date of the registration statement. Generally, the filing date of a registration statement will precede the effective date. In addition to performing the procedures required by US GAAS at or shortly before the effective date, the auditor may also perform some or all of such procedures at or shortly before the filing date. (ID: 90387)

19. (d) In connection with an entity's financial statements included in a securities offering, auditors are often requested to issue comfort letters to underwriters. The comfort letter is ordinarily addressed to the underwriter and signed by the auditor. (ID: 8387)

20. (c) When commenting in a comfort letter on information other than audited financial statements, the auditor should describe the criteria specified by the underwriter or other requesting party. The auditor should *not* make the statements or use the terms (which are of uncertain meaning; they are *not* universally understood) described in the other answer alternatives. (ID: 90388)

21. (a) The objective of a review of the interim financial information of a nonissuer is to obtain a basis for reporting whether any material modifications should be made for such information to be in accordance with the applicable financial reporting framework by performing limited procedures. It is not to update the opinion on the previously audited financial statements nor to determine whether condensed statements or pro forma information should be included. In a review, the accountant supplies only limited assurance and would not provide an opinion stating the financial information is presented fairly. (ID: 5701)

22. (b) The procedures for a review of the interim financial information should include reading the available minutes of meetings of stockholders, directors, and appropriate committees and inquiring about matters dealt

with at meetings for which minutes are not available to identify matters that may affect the interim financial information. Answers a., c., and d. are not procedures ordinarily applied in a review of interim financial information. (ID: 2985)

23. (d) The accountant's report on a review of the interim financial information should be modified for departures from the applicable financial reporting framework, which include inadequate disclosure and changes in accounting principles that are not in conformity with the applicable financial reporting framework. The existence of an uncertainty or a lack of consistency in the application of accounting principles affecting interim financial information would not require the accountant to include an additional paragraph in the report, provided that the interim financial information appropriately discloses such matters. (ID: 410)

24. (b) The auditor should not accept an engagement to report separately on summary financial statements unless the auditor has been engaged to conduct an audit in accordance with US GAAS of the financial statements from which the summary financial statements are derived. Regarding incorrect answer a., when the auditor's report on the audited financial statements contains an adverse opinion or a disclaimer of opinion, the auditor should withdraw from the engagement to report on the summary financial statements, when withdrawal is possible under applicable law or regulation; however, the auditor may accept an engagement if a qualified opinion was expressed on the audited financial statements. Regarding incorrect answer c., there is no constraint related to engagement acceptance based on the report release date of the audited financial statements. Regarding incorrect answer d., the audit report on summary financial statements is *not* required to be restricted. (ID: 90383)

25. (b) The report should include a statement that the responsibility for the proper accounting treatment rests with the preparers of the financial statements, who should consult with their continuing accountant. Regarding incorrect answer a., it should include a statement that that the engagement was performed in accordance with Statement on Auditing Standards No. 122 §915, *Reports on Application of Requirements of an Applicable Financial Reporting Framework*, not US GAAS. Regarding incorrect answer c., the CPA is not required to be independent of the entity, but if the CPA is not, the report should include a statement indicating the CPA's lack of independence. The CPA is neither required to provide, nor precluded from providing, the reasons for the lack of independence; however, if the CPA chooses to provide the reasons for the lack of independence, the CPA should include *all* the reasons. Regarding incorrect answer d., the CPA should only accept an engagement to issue a written report on the application of the requirements of an applicable financial reporting framework to a specific transaction when the transaction involves facts or circumstances of a specific entity. The CPA should *not* accept an engagement to issue a written report on hypothetical transactions. (ID: 90384)

26. (b) The auditor is *not* required to have an understanding of the certification required by the appropriate auditing or accountancy board of the other country. (ID: 90385)

27. (c) When the auditor plans to use the form and content of the audit report of another country, the auditor should obtain an understanding of the applicable legal responsibilities involved. (ID: 90386)

28. (c) Some special-purpose financial statements and related audit reports are intended for general use (see exhibit 9 in this chapter) and thus, do *not* require an alert that restricts their use. (ID: 90389)

Solution 12-2 SIMULATION ANSWER: Audit Report on Financial Statements Prepared in Accordance with the Cash Basis of Accounting

Report Elements	Appropriate (A) or Inappropriate (I)
1. A title that includes the word independent.	A
2. A statement that management is responsible for the preparation and fair presentation of these financial statements in accordance with the cash basis of accounting.	A
3. A statement that the audit was conducted in accordance with standards established by the American Institute of Certified Public Accountants and includes an identification of the United States of America as the country of origin of those standards.	I
4. When management has a choice of financial reporting frameworks, a statement that management is responsible for determining that the cash basis of accounting is an acceptable basis for the preparation of the financial statements in the circumstances.	A
5. A statement that the cash basis of accounting is not a fair presentation framework.	I
6. A statement that an audit also includes: (a) Evaluating the appropriateness of accounting policies used; (b) The reasonableness of significant accounting estimates made by management; and (c) Evaluating the overall presentation of the financial statements.	A
7. An other-matter paragraph that restricts the use of the report.	I

(ID: 9246)

1. A

2. A

3. I

The report should include a statement that the audit was conducted in accordance with *generally accepted auditing standards* (not standards established by the American Institute of Certified Public Accountants) and includes an identification of the United States of America as the country of origin of those standards.

4. A

5. I

The basis of accounting paragraph, an emphasis-of-matter paragraph, should include a statement that the financial statements are prepared on the cash basis of accounting, which is a basis of accounting other than accounting principles generally accepted in the United States of America.

6. A

7. I

The report is not required to be restricted as to use.

Solution 12-3 SIMULATION ANSWER: Research

When engaged to report on supplementary information in relation to the financial statements as a whole, the auditor need not apply procedures as extensive as would be necessary to express an opinion on the information on a stand-alone basis. Which citation in the professional standards provides guidance on whether or not the auditor is required to obtain a separate understanding of the entity's internal control or to assess fraud risk?

AU	§	725	.	.A11	(ID: 90382)

.A11 With respect to the supplementary information, the auditor is not required to obtain a separate understanding of the entity's internal control or to assess fraud risk.

CHAPTER 13

ACCOUNTING AND REVIEW SERVICES

AU Identifier Used for Clarified GAAS in This Textbook

We have not continued to use the temporary AU-C identifier for the clarified auditing standards issued by the American Institute of Certified Public Accountants (AICPA). In this textbook these standards have an AU identifier.

CHAPTER 13

ACCOUNTING AND REVIEW SERVICES

I. Compilation and Review Engagements For Nonissuers

A. Authoritative Guidance Hierarchy

1. **Authoritative Body** The Accounting and Review Services Committee of the AICPA issues Statements on Standards for Accounting and Review Services (SSARS) and provides performance and reporting guidance for compilations and reviews of unaudited financial statements or other unaudited financial information of nonissuers.

   a. **Compilation** A compilation assists management in presenting financial information in the form of financial statements without providing any assurance on the statements. A compilation does not involve making inquiries or performing analytical or other review procedures. A compilation does not provide any level of assurance. A CPA need not be independent to perform a compilation; however, the lack of independence must be stated in the report. Independence is required for a review.

   b. **Review** A review provides only limited assurance that there are no material modifications that should be made to the financial statements for them to be in conformity with the applicable financial reporting framework. A CPA must be independent to perform a review as some form of assurance is provided

   c. **Nonissuer** An entity whose securities are not registered with the SEC; who is not required to file reports with the SEC; and who has not filed a pending registration statement with the SEC.

   d. **Submission** Presenting to management or a third party financial statements that a CPA has prepared (manually or electronically).

2. **Interpretative Publications** Interpretative publications provide guidance on the application of SSARS. They consist of Interpretations of SSARS; appendices to SSARS; and compilation and review guidance included in AICPA Audit and Accounting Guides and Statements of Position. CPAs should be aware of and consider applicable interpretive publications. Interpretations are recommendations, not standards; however, if a CPA does not apply the applicable interpretative guidance, the CPA should be prepared to justify the departure.

3. **Other Publications** Other compilation and review publications have no authoritative status. A CPA is not expected to be aware of the full body of other publications. A CPA should be satisfied that the guidance is both relevant and appropriate. Other publications include AICPA compilation and review publications not listed above; the AICPA annual *Compilation and Review Alert*; compilation and review articles in the *Journal of Accountancy*, and other professional journals and instructional materials.

4. **Professional Requirements** SSARS use two categories of professional requirements, identified by specific terms to describe the degree of responsibility they impose on CPAs.

   a. **Unconditional Requirements** The accountant is required to comply with an unconditional requirement in all cases in which the circumstances exist to which the unconditional requirement applies. The words *must* or *is required* are used to indicate an unconditional requirement.

b. **Presumptively Mandatory Requirements** The accountant also is required to comply with a presumptively mandatory requirement in all cases in which the circumstances exist to which the presumptively mandatory requirement applies; however, in rare circumstances, the accountant may depart from a presumptively mandatory requirement provided that the accountant documents his or her justification for the departure. The word *should* is used to indicate a presumptively mandatory requirement.

5. **SSARS Applicability** An accountant who submits unaudited financial statements of a nonissuer should comply with SSARS. SSARS also applies to engagements to issue a compilation report on specified elements, accounts, or items of a nonissuer's financial statements, or on a nonissuer's pro forma financial information. SSARS does not apply to other accounting services, such as preparing adjusting entries, consulting on financial matters, or preparing tax returns.

6. **Interim Reviews** When all of the following conditions are met, interim reviews should be performed in accordance with GAAS (AU 930, *Interim Financial Information*) instead of SSARS (i.e., the review engagement is generally considered an extension of the annual audit, and the standard setters decided the guidance should reside in the auditing literature.)

   - The entity's latest annual financial statements have been audited
   - The CPA has either been engaged to audit the entity's current year financial statements or audited the latest annual financial statements and although an audit of the current year financial statements is expected, the appointment of another auditor to audit them is not effective prior to the beginning of the period to be reviewed
   - The same financial reporting framework used to prepare the annual financial statements is used for the interim financial information
   - The interim financial information is in a condensed format, it conforms with an appropriate financial reporting framework, and it accompanies the latest audited financial statements

   When these conditions are met, the review engagement is generally intended to provide a periodic update to the year-end reporting and is considered an extension of the annual audit. Thus, the standard setters decided the guidance should reside in the auditing literature.

7. **Compilation and Review vs. Audit** Neither a review nor a compilation involves obtaining an understanding of internal control, assessing fraud risk, testing accounting records, examining source documents, or other procedures ordinarily performed in an audit.

B. Elements of a Compilation or Review Engagement

1. **Three-Party Relationship** A compilation or review engagement involves three parties: management (or the responsible party); a CPA; and intended users, who may be from different entities or the same entity. Sometimes management is the intended user.

   a. **Management (Responsible Party)** Management is responsible for the preparation and fair presentation of the financial statements in accordance with the applicable financial reporting framework. Management is also responsible for the design, implementation, and maintenance of internal control.

   A CPA is precluded from issuing an unmodified compilation or review report unless management accepts these responsibilities. The CPA may make suggestions about the form or content of the financial statements or prepare them, in whole or in part; however this service is based on information that is the representation of management.

b. **CPA** A CPA (an accountant in the practice of public accounting) should possess a level of knowledge of the accounting principles and practices of the entity's industry needed to compile or review financial statements that are appropriate in form.

c. **Intended Users** The intended users are the person(s) who understand the limitations of the compilation or review engagement and financial statements or financial information. Management and intended users may be the same. The CPA has no responsibility to identify the intended users. Sometimes intended users (for example, bankers or regulators) will impose additional requirements. The CPA may perform these additional services as long as the CPA adheres to professional standards.

2. **Financial Reporting Framework** Management is responsible for the selection of the entity's applicable financial reporting framework, as well as individual accounting policies when the reporting framework contains acceptable alternatives.

   a. **Examples** US GAAP, as promulgated by the FASB, GASB, or FASAB; IFRS issued by the IASB; and OCBOA are examples of financial reporting frameworks.

   b. **OCBOA** Financial statements prepared under OCBOA must include: a description of the OCBOA; a summary of significant accounting policies; and a description of the primary differences from US GAAP.

3. **Financial Statements or Financial Information** The applicable financial reporting framework determines what constitutes a complete set of financial statements. A CPA may be engaged to compile or review a complete set of financial statements or an individual financial statement. The financial statements may be for an annual period or for a shorter or longer period, depending on management's needs.

4. **Sufficient Appropriate Evidence** When performing a compilation engagement, the CPA has no responsibility to obtain any evidence about the accuracy or completeness of the financial statements. In a review engagement, the CPA should apply professional judgment in determining the specific nature, extent, and timing of review procedures (i.e., analytical procedures and inquiries) to provide the CPA with a reasonable basis for obtaining limited assurance.

5. **Written Report Objective** The CPA's objective in reporting is to prevent misinterpretation of the degree of responsibility the CPA is assuming when the CPA's name is associated with the financial statements.

C. Materiality

A CPA's determination of materiality is a matter of professional judgment and is affected by the CPA's perception of the financial information needs of users of the financial statements. Misstatements, including omissions, are considered to be material if they, individually or in the aggregate, could reasonably be expected to influence the economic decisions of users taken on the basis of the financial statements. Judgments about materiality are made in light of surrounding circumstances and are affected by the size or nature of a misstatement or a combination of both.

D. Compilation of Financial Statements (AR 80)

1. **Objective** A compilation is an attest engagement, but not an assurance engagement. The objective is limited to assisting management in presenting financial information in the form of financial statements without undertaking to obtain or provide any assurance that there are no material modifications that should be made to the financial statements in order for the statements to be in conformity with the applicable financial reporting framework.

2. **Establish and Document an Understanding With the Client** The CPA should establish an understanding with the client regarding the services to be performed and should document the understanding through a written communication with management, i.e., an engagement letter.

   a. **Contents** The engagement letter should include the objectives and limitations of the engagement as well as management's and the CPA's responsibilities, and should address the following items:

      - The objectives of the compilation
      - Management's responsibilities
      - The accountant's responsibilities
      - Limitations of the engagement
      - A description of the accounting services to be performed, if any
      - Communications with management or third party
      - The effect of any independence impairments on the expected form of the CPA's compilation report

   b. **Additional Matters If Applicable** The engagement letter should also address the following matters if applicable:

      - Material departures from the applicable financial reporting framework may exist, and the effects of those departures, if any, on the financial statements may not be disclosed.
      - Substantially all disclosures (and statement of cash flows, if applicable) required by the applicable financial reporting framework may be omitted.
      - Reference to supplementary information

   c. **If Report Not Issued** If the compiled financial statements are not expected to be used by a third party and the CPA does not expect to issue a compilation report, the CPA should include in the engagement letter an acknowledgment of management's representation and agreement that the financial statements are not to be used by a third party.

3. **Compilation Requirements**

   a. **Understanding of the Industry** A CPA should understand the accounting principles and practices of the client's industry. A CPA can accept an engagement for an entity in an industry in which the CPA has no previous experience as long as the CPA can acquire said knowledge.

   b. **Knowledge of the Client**

      (1) **Business** A CPA should obtain a general understanding of the client's organization; operating characteristics; and the nature of its assets, liabilities, revenues, and expenses. This knowledge is usually acquired through experience with the client or its industry and inquiry of its personnel.

      (2) **Accounting Principles and Practices** The CPA should obtain an understanding of the accounting principles and practices used by the client in measuring, recognizing, recording, and disclosing all significant accounts and disclosures in the financial statements. The CPA should be alert to accounting policies and procedures that are unusual as compared with normal practices within the industry.

c. **Read the Financial Statements** Before submission, the CPA should read the financial statements to consider if they appear to be appropriate in form and are free from obvious material errors. This would encompass detection of math or clerical errors and misapplication of accounting principles, including inadequate disclosure.

d. **Other Issues** A CPA may become aware that information is unsatisfactory or that fraud or an illegal act may have occurred, that there is a going concern issue, or that there may have been a subsequent event. The CPA should request that management consider the effect of these matters on the financial statements, consider the effect of management's conclusions, and evaluate the impact on the compilation report. If the financial statements may be materially misstated and the client refuses to supply additional or revised information, the CPA should withdraw from the engagement.

4. **Documentation** Documentation provides the primary support that the CPA conducted the engagement in accordance with SSARS. The CPA should prepare documentation in sufficient detail to provide a clear understanding of the work performed, including

   a. The engagement letter;

   b. Significant findings or issues and their resolution; and

   c. Communications, oral or written, to management about fraud or illegal acts.

5. **Reporting**

   a. **Report Not Required** When a CPA submits compiled financial statements to a client that are not expected to be used by a third party, a report is not required; however, each page of the financial statements should include a reference restricting their use, such as *Restricted for Management's Use Only*.

   b. **Report Is Required** When a CPA is engaged to report on compiled financial statements or submits financial statements that are to be used by a third party, the statements should be accompanied by a written report. Procedures that may have been performed as part of the compilation engagement should not be described in the report.

      (1) **Title** The title may be *Independent's Accountant's Compilation Report* or *Accountant's Compilation Report*

      (2) **Introductory Paragraph** This paragraph should

      - Identify the entity
      - Identify the financial statements and state that they were compiled
      - State the date or period covered by the financial statements
      - State that the accountant did not review or audit the statements, and that the accountant does not express an opinion or provide any assurance about whether the statements are in accordance with the applicable financial reporting framework

      (3) **Management's Responsibility Paragraph** State that management is responsible for the preparation and fair presentation of the financial statements in accordance with the applicable financial reporting framework, and for the design, implementation, and maintenance of internal controls

(4) **Accountant's Responsibility Paragraph** State that

- The accountant's responsibility is to conduct the compilation in accordance with SSARS
- The objective of a compilation is to assist management in presenting financial information in the form of financial statements without obtaining or providing any assurance that there are no material modifications that should be made to the financial statements

(5) **Emphasis of a Matter Paragraph** As long as the matter is disclosed in the financial statements (emphasis paragraphs should not be used in lieu of management disclosures), a CPA may add a separate explanatory paragraph to the report to emphasize a matter. Emphasis paragraphs are never required.

(6) **Signature and Date** Date is the completion of the compilation

c. **Financial Statements' Reference to Report** Each page of the financial statements should include a reference, such as *See Accountant's Compilation Report*.

Exhibit 1 ▸ Standard Compilation Report

Accountant's Compilation Report

[*Appropriate salutation*]

We have compiled the accompanying balance sheet of XYZ Company as of December 31, 20XX, and the related statements of income, retained earnings, and cash flows for the year then ended. We have not audited or reviewed the accompanying financial statements and, accordingly, do not express an opinion or provide any assurance about whether the financial statements are in accordance with accounting principles generally accepted in the United States of America.

Management is responsible for the preparation and fair presentation of the financial statements in accordance with accounting principles generally accepted in the United States of America and for designing, implementing, and maintaining internal control relevant to the preparation and fair presentation of the financial statements.

Our responsibility is to conduct the compilation in accordance with Statements on Standards for Accounting and Review Services issued by the American Institute of Certified Public Accountants. The objective of a compilation is to assist management in presenting financial information in the form of financial statements without undertaking to obtain or provide any assurance that there are no material modifications that should be made to the financial statements.

[*Signature of accounting firm or accountant, as appropriate*]

[*Date*]

6. **Compilation Reports in Certain Prescribed Forms** A prescribed form is any standard preprinted form adopted by the body to which it is to be submitted, e.g., forms used by governmental and regulatory bodies other than those concerned with the sale or trading of securities, industry trade associations, etc.

a. **Applicability** SSARS provides guidance when the prescribed form or related instructions call for a departure from the applicable financial reporting framework in a compilation engagement.

b. **Departures From the Reporting Framework Required by the Prescribed Form** There is a presumption that the information required by a prescribed form is sufficient to meet the needs of the body that adopted the form; thus, there is no need to advise that body about departures from the applicable financial reporting framework. However, the report should be a restricted use report.

7. **Financial Statements With Limited Disclosures** When the entity wishes to include disclosures about only a few matters in the form of notes to the financial statements, such disclosures should be labeled *Selected Information—Substantially All Disclosures Required by* [identify the applicable financial reporting framework] *Are Not Included*.

8. **Financial Statements That Omit Substantially All Disclosures** A CPA may be requested to compile financial statements that omit substantially all disclosures required by an applicable financial reporting framework. This is permissible as long as the intent is not to mislead. A fourth paragraph should be added after the accountant's responsibilities paragraph, disclosing said omissions.

9. **Material Departures From Applicable Financial Reporting Framework / Financial Statements Not Revised**

   a. **When Modification of the Report Is Adequate** The departure should be disclosed in a separate paragraph of the report, including disclosure of the effects on the financial statements. If the effects have not been determined by management or are not known as the result of the CPA's procedures, the CPA is not required to determine them; however, the report should include a statement that such determination has not been made.

   b. **When Modification of the Report Is Not Adequate** If modification of the report is not adequate to indicate the deficiencies in the financial statements as a whole, the CPA should withdraw from the engagement and provide no further services with respect to those financial statements. The CPA may wish to consult with legal counsel.

10. **Reporting When Not Independent** A CPA is not required to be independent of an entity to issue a compilation report; however, the report must be modified by adding a final paragraph that specifically discloses the lack of independence. The CPA may disclose the reason(s) the CPA's independence is impaired in the same final paragraph. If the CPA elects to do this, all the reasons should be included.

11. **Personal Financial Statements** A CPA may submit a written personal financial plan containing unaudited personal financial statements to a client without complying with SSARS guidance on compilations (AR 80) if the CPA establishes an understanding with the client and documents through a written communication that the financial statements will be used solely to develop the client's personal financial goals and objectives, and will not be used to obtain credit or for any purposes other than developing these goals and objectives. Nothing comes to the CPA's attention during the engagement that would cause the CPA to believe that the financial statements will be used to obtain credit or for any purposes other than developing the client's financial goals and objectives. A written report must be issued.

E. **Other Compilations**

1. **Compilation of Specified Elements, Accounts, or Items of a Financial Statement (AR 110)**

   a. **Applicability** A CPA is required to comply with this guidance whenever the CPA is engaged to report on one or more compiled specified elements, accounts, or items of a financial statement (items) or submits same to a client or to third parties. However, if the item is included as supplementary information, the CPA should refer to that topic (supplementary information) in AR 80.

b. **Reporting**

(1) **Whether to Issue a Report** A report is not required for this engagement unless the CPA has been engaged to report on the item. However, if it is likely that the CPA's name will be associated with the presentation and because of that a user may inappropriately infer an unintended level of assurance, the CPA should consider issuing a report. Procedures that the may have been performed as part of the compilation engagement should not be described in the report.

(2) **Report Structure** Guidance for the title, date, and financial statements referenced to the report is essentially the same as for a compilation of financial statements (AR 80).

(3) **Engagement in Conjunction With a Compilation of Financial Statements** If this compilation was performed in conjunction with a compilation of financial statements, the introductory paragraph should so state and indicate the date of the compilation report on the financial statements. Any departure from the standard report on those statements should also be disclosed if considered relevant to the presentation of the item.

c. **Communications Regarding Fraud or Illegal Acts** The guidance is essentially the same as for a compilation of financial statements (AR 80) also covered in this chapter.

2. **Compilation of Pro Forma Financial Information (AR 120)**

a. **Applicability** A CPA is required to comply with this guidance whenever the CPA is engaged to report on pro forma financial information or submits same to a client or to third parties. However, if the pro forma financial information is included as supplementary information, the CPA should refer to that topic (supplementary information) in AR 80.

b. **Objective** The objective of pro forma financial information is to show what the significant effects on historical financial information might have been had a consummated or proposed transaction (or event) occurred at an earlier date. This is achieved by applying pro forma adjustments to historical financial information. These adjustments should be based on management's assumptions and give effect to all significant effects directly attributable to the transaction (or event). Pro forma financial information is commonly used to show the effects of transactions such as the following:

- Business combination
- Change in capitalization
- Disposition of a significant portion of the business
- Change in the form of business organization or status as an autonomous entity
- Proposed sale of securities and the application of the proceeds

c. **Presentation**

(1) **Labeling** Pro forma financial information should be labeled as such to distinguish it from historical financial information.

(2) **Description** This presentation should describe:

- The transaction (or event) that is reflected in the pro forma financial information
- The source of the historical financial information on which it is based
- The significant assumptions used in developing the pro forma adjustments
- Any significant uncertainties about those assumptions

(3) **Cautions** The presentation should also indicate that the pro forma financial information should be read in conjunction with the related historical financial information and that the pro forma financial information is not necessarily indicative of the results (such as financial position and results of operations, as applicable) that would have been attained had the transaction (or event) actually taken place earlier.

d. **Conditions for Compiling Pro Forma Financial Information**

(1) **Historical Financial Statements Included** A CPA may only compile pro forma financial information if the document that contains it includes (or incorporates by reference) the historical financial statements of the entity on which the pro forma financial information is based. Historical interim financial information may be presented in condensed form. In the case of a business combination, the document should include (or incorporate by reference) the appropriate historical financial information for the significant constituent parts of the combined entity.

(2) **Audit, Review, or Compilation of Historical Financial Statements Required** The historical financial statements of the entity (or, in the case of a business combination, of each significant constituent part of the combined entity) on which the pro forma financial information is based must have been compiled, reviewed, or audited.

(3) **Report on Historical Financial Statements Included** The CPA's compilation, review, or audit report on the historical financial statements should be included (or incorporated by reference) in the document containing the pro forma financial information.

e. **Performance Requirements** The guidance is essentially the same as for a compilation of financial statements (AR 80) also covered in this chapter. The requirement to read the pro forma financial information to consider if it appears to be appropriate in form and free of obvious material errors includes the summary of significant assumptions.

f. **Reporting** This guidance is the same as for a compilation of specified elements, accounts, or items of a financial statement (AR 110). The report on pro forma financial information should also refer (in the introductory paragraph) to any modifications in the CPA's report on the historical financial statements.

g. **Pro Forma Financial Information That Omits Substantially All Disclosures** The explanatory paragraph required when management has elected to omit substantially all disclosures, but the pro forma financial information is otherwise in conformity with the applicable financial reporting framework, should be added after the paragraph on the objectives and limitations of the pro forma financial information.

F. Review of Financial Statements (AR 90)

1. **Objective** A review is both an assurance engagement and an attest engagement. The objective is to obtain limited assurance that there are no material modifications that should be made to the financial statements in order for the statements to be in conformity with the applicable financial reporting framework. It is a higher level of service than a compilation, but a lower level of service than an audit. A CPA is precluded from performing a review engagement if the CPA's independence is impaired for any reason.

2. **Applicability** A CPA is required to comply with this guidance whenever the CPA has been engaged to review financial statements, except for reviews of interim financial information if the following are true:

   a. The entity's latest annual financial statements have been audited;

   b. The CPA has been engaged to audit the entity's current year financial statements, or audited the latest annual statements and another CPA's appointment to audit the current year statements is not effective prior to the beginning of the period covered by the review; and

   c. The same financial reporting framework used to prepare the annual financial statements is used for the interim financial information.

   When all of these conditions are met, interim reviews should be performed in accordance with GAAS (AU 930, *Interim Financial Information*) instead of SSARS. In this circumstance, the review engagement is generally intended to provide a periodic update to the year-end reporting and is considered an extension of the annual audit. Thus, the standard setters decided the guidance should reside in the auditing literature.

3. **Client Understanding** The CPA should establish an understanding with the client regarding the services to be performed and should document the understanding through a written communication with management, i.e., an engagement letter.

   a. **Contents** The engagement letter should include the objectives and limitations of the engagement as well as management's and the CPA's responsibilities. Thus, the understanding should address the following items:

      - The objectives of the review
      - Management's responsibilities
      - The accountant's responsibilities
      - Limitations of the engagement

   b. **Material Departures** Material departures from the applicable financial reporting framework may exist, and the effects of those departures, if any, on the financial statements may not be disclosed.

4. **Requirements** The design and performance of review procedures should be based on the CPA's understanding of the industry and the client as well as awareness of the risk that the financial statements may be materially misstated. The CPA should focus the analytical procedures and inquiries in areas of increased risk of misstatement.

   a. **Understanding of the Industry** A CPA should understand the accounting principles and practices of the client's industry. A CPA can accept an engagement for an entity in an industry in which the CPA has no previous experience as long as the CPA can acquire said knowledge

   b. **Knowledge of the Client** A CPA should obtain a general understanding of the client's organization; operating characteristics; the nature of its assets, liabilities, revenues, and expenses; the accounting principles and practices used by the client in measuring, recognizing, recording, and disclosing all significant accounts and disclosures in the financial statements.

   c. **Analytical Procedures** If analytical procedures performed identify fluctuations or relationships that are inconsistent with other relevant information or that differ from expected values by a significant amount, the CPA should investigate these differences by inquiring of management and performing other procedures. Analytical procedures include

      - Compare current financial statements to prior period financial statements, or current ratios to prior period ratios
      - Compare client's ratios to other entities in the same industry
      - Compare actual financial statements to budgets or forecasts
      - Compare current financial statement elements to those of prior periods

   d. **Inquiries of Financial Management** The CPA should consider making the following inquiries of financial management:

      - Whether the financial statements have been prepared in conformity with the applicable financial reporting framework
      - The client's accounting principles and practices and the methods followed in applying them
      - Procedures for recording, classifying, and summarizing transactions, and accumulating information for disclosure in the financial statements
      - Unusual or complex situations that may have an effect on the financial statements
      - Significant transactions occurring or recognized near the end of the reporting period
      - The status of uncorrected misstatements identified during the previous engagement
      - Questions that have arisen in the course of applying the review procedures
      - Events subsequent to the date of the financial statements that could have a material effect on the financial statements
      - Their knowledge of any fraud or suspected fraud affecting the entity involving management or others where the fraud could have a material effect on the financial statements
      - Significant journal entries and other adjustments
      - Communications from regulatory agencies

e. **Other Procedures** The CPA should also consider making these inquiries or performing these procedures:

(1) Make inquiries concerning actions taken at meetings of stockholders, board of directors, committees of the board of directors, or comparable meetings that may affect the financial statements

(2) Read the financial statements to consider whether they appear to conform with the applicable financial reporting framework

(3) Obtain reports from other accountants, if any, who have been engaged to audit or review the financial statements of significant components of the entity, its subsidiaries and other investees

Again, the CPA is not required to corroborate management's responses with other evidence; however, the CPA should consider the reasonableness and consistency of management's responses in light of the results of other review procedures and the accountant's knowledge of the client's business and the industry in which it operates.

f. **Management Representations** The CPA must obtain representations from management for all financial statements and periods covered by the review report.

(1) **Content** The CPA should request that management provide written representations related to the following matters; however, the representation letter ordinarily should be tailored to include additional appropriate representations relating to matters specific to the entity's business or industry.

- Management's acknowledgment of its responsibility for the preparation and fair presentation of the financial statements in accordance with the applicable financial reporting framework
- Management's belief that the financial statements are fairly presented in conformity with the applicable financial reporting framework
- Management's acknowledgment of its responsibility for designing, implementing, and maintaining internal control relevant to the preparation and fair presentation of the financial statements
- Management's acknowledgment of its responsibility to prevent and detect fraud
- Knowledge of any fraud or suspected fraud affecting the entity involving management or others where the fraud could have a material effect on the financial statements, including any communications received from employees, former employees, or others
- Management's full and truthful response to all inquiries
- Completeness of information
- Information concerning subsequent events

(2) **Date** The letter should be dated as of the date of the CPA's review report.

(3) **Address** The letter should be addressed to the CPA.

(4) **Signatures** The letter should be signed by the members of management that are responsible for and knowledgeable about the matters covered.

g. **Updating Management Representations** Circumstances exist in which the accountant should consider obtaining an updating representation letter from management, including

(1) A material subsequent event occurs after the completion of inquiry and analytical review procedures, but before the issuance of the report

(2) There is a significant delay in the issuance of the review report

(3) If a predecessor accountant is requested to reissue the report on the financial statements of a prior period and those financial statements are to be presented on a comparative basis with reviewed financial statements of a subsequent period, the predecessor accountant should obtain an updating representation letter from the management of the former client. The updated letter should state whether:

- Any information has come to management's attention that would cause management to believe that any of the previous representations should be modified
- Any events have occurred subsequent to the balance-sheet date of the latest financial statements reported on by the accountant that would require adjustment to or disclosure in those financial statements

5. **Documentation** Documentation is the CPA's primary support for both the representation in the CPA's review report that the engagement was performed in accordance with SSARS and for the limited assurance expressed in the report. The CPA should prepare documentation in sufficient detail to provide a clear understanding of the work performed; the evidence obtained and its source; and the conclusions reached. Because of differing circumstances, it is not possible to specify the form, content, or extent of the documentation that a CPA should prepare for each engagement; however it should include the following:

a. The engagement letter

b. Analytical procedures performed, including: the expectations and the factors considered in their development; the results of the comparison of the expectations to the recorded amounts or ratios; and management's responses to the CPA's inquiries regarding fluctuations or relationships that are inconsistent with other relevant information or that differ from expected values by a significant amount

c. A description and the results of any additional procedures performed in response to significant unexpected differences arising from analytical procedures

d. Significant matters covered by the CPA's inquiries and the responses

e. Significant findings or issues including actions taken and final conclusions

f. Significant unusual matters that the CPA considered while performing the review procedures, including their disposition

g. Communications (oral and written) to management about fraud or illegal acts

h. Management's representation letter

6. **Incomplete Review** When the CPA is unable to perform the inquiry and analytical procedures necessary to obtain limited assurance or the client does not provide the CPA with a representation letter, the review will be incomplete and a review report should not be issued. In such a situation, the CPA should consider whether it is appropriate to issue a compilation report on the financial statements.

7. **Reporting** Financial statements reviewed by a CPA should be accompanied by a written report. The standard report is comprised of four paragraphs: introductory paragraph; management's responsibilities paragraph (same as for the standard compilation of financial statements report); accountant's responsibilities paragraph; and results of engagement paragraph

    a. **Title** The title should include the word Independent, such as *Independent's Accountant's Review Report*

    b. **Introductory Paragraph** This paragraph should

        (1) Identify the entity

        (2) Identify the financial statements and state that they were reviewed

        (3) State the date or period covered by the financial statements

        (4) State that a review includes primarily applying analytical procedures to management's financial data and making inquiries of company management

        (5) State that a review is substantially less in scope than an audit, the objective of which is the expression of an opinion regarding the financial statements as a whole, and that, accordingly, the accountant does not express such an opinion

    c. **Management's Responsibility Paragraph** State that management is responsible for the preparation and fair presentation of the financial statements in accordance with the applicable financial reporting framework, and for the design, implementation, and maintenance of internal controls

    d. **Accountant's Responsibility Paragraph** State that the accountant's responsibility is to conduct the review in accordance with SSARS; those standards require the accountant to perform procedures to obtain limited assurance that no material modifications should be made to the financial statements; and the accountant believes that the results of the engagement procedures provide a reasonable basis for the report

    e. **Results of Engagement Paragraph**

    f. **Signature and Date** Date is the completion of the review

    g. **Financial Statements' Reference to Report** Each page of the financial statements should include a reference, such as See *Independent Accountant's Review Report.*

Exhibit 2 ▸ Standard Review Report

Independent Accountant's Review Report

[*Appropriate salutation*]

We have reviewed the accompanying balance sheet of XYZ Company as of December 31, 20XX, and the related statements of income, retained earnings, and cash flows for the year then ended. A review includes primarily applying analytical procedures to management's financial data and making inquiries of company management. A review is substantially less in scope than an audit, the objective of which is the expression of an opinion regarding the financial statements as a whole. Accordingly, we do not express such an opinion.

Management is responsible for the preparation and fair presentation of the financial statements in accordance with accounting principles generally accepted in the United States of America and for designing, implementing, and maintaining internal control relevant to the preparation and fair presentation of the financial statements.

Our responsibility is to conduct the review in accordance with Statements on Standards for Accounting and Review Services issued by the American Institute of Certified Public Accountants. Those standards require us to perform procedures to obtain limited assurance that there are no material modifications that should be made to the financial statements. We believe that the results of our procedures provide a reasonable basis for our report.

Based on our review, we are not aware of any material modifications that should be made to the accompanying financial statements in order for them to be in conformity with accounting principles generally accepted in the United States of America.

[*Signature of accounting firm or accountant, as appropriate*]

[*Date*]

8. **Limited Reporting Engagement** A CPA may be asked to issue a review report on one financial statement, such as a balance sheet, and not on other related financial statements, such as the statements of income, retained earnings, and cash flows. The CPA may do so if the scope of the CPA's inquiries and analytical procedures has not been restricted.

G. **Subsequent Discovery of Facts Existing at the Date of the Report**
The accountant has no obligation to make inquiries after the date of the compilation or review report. If an accountant does become aware of material information that existed at the date of the report, and the subsequent event is not adequately accounted for in the financial statements or disclosed in the notes, it should be handled in the CPA's report like any other material departure from an applicable financial reporting framework.

1. **Actions** The CPA should advise the client to disclose the information and its effect on the financial statements. If disclosed, the CPA may elect to include an emphasis of matter paragraph.

2. **Client Refusal** If the client refuses to comply with the accountant, the CPA should notify: management or the appropriate level of governance; an regulatory agencies that may have jurisdiction over the client; and persons known to be relying or likely to rely on the financial statements that the accountant's report should no longer be relied upon.

H. Supplementary Information
When the financial statements are accompanied by information presented for supplementary analysis purposes, the CPA should clearly indicate the degree of responsibility, if any, that the CPA is taking with respect to such information.

1. **Compilations** When the CPA has compiled both the financial statements and other data presented only for supplementary analysis purposes, the report should refer to the other data, or the CPA can issue a separate report on the other data. If a separate report is issued, the report should state that the other data accompanying the financial statements is presented only for the purposes of additional analysis, and that it has been compiled from information that is the representation of management, without audit or review, and that the CPA does not express an opinion or provide any assurance on such data.

2. **Review** When the CPA has reviewed the financial statements, an explanation should be included in the review report or in a separate report on the other data. The report should state that the review has been made for the purpose of expressing a conclusion that there are no material modifications that should be made to the statements in order for them to be in conformity with the applicable financial reporting framework and the other data accompanying the statements is presented only for purposes of additional analysis and that it either

   a. Has been subjected to the inquiry and analytical procedures applied in the review of the statements, and the CPA did not become aware of any material modifications that should be made to such data, or

   b. Has not been subjected to the inquiry and analytical procedures applied in the review of the statements, but was compiled from information that is the representation of management, without audit or review, and the CPA does not express an opinion or provide any assurance on such data.

I. Restricted Use Reports
The term *restricted use* applies to reports intended only for one or more specified third parties. The need for restriction may result from the purpose of the report and the potential for the report to be misunderstood when taken out of the context. A CPA should restrict the use of a report when the subject matter or the presentation being reported on is based on measurement or disclosure criteria contained in contractual agreements or regulatory provisions that are not in conformity with an applicable financial reporting framework.

If a general and restricted subject matter are combined into one report, the combined report should be restricted. A paragraph should be added to the end of the report and should include: a statement that the report is intended solely for the use of the specified parties; identification of the specified parties; and a statement that the report is not intended to be and should not be used by anyone other than the specified parties

J. Communications Regarding Fraud or Illegal Acts
If, during a compilation or review, information comes to the CPA's attention that fraud or an illegal act may have occurred, it should be brought to the attention of the appropriate level of management or governance. The CPA should also consider consulting with legal counsel.

1. **Inconsequential** The CPA need not report matters that are clearly inconsequential and may reach agreement in advance with the entity on the nature of such items to be communicated.

2. **Communication** Communication can be oral or written; if oral, the CPA should document it.

3. **Owner Implicated** When matters involve an owner of the business, the CPA should consider withdrawing from the engagement.

4. **Confidentiality** Disclosure is precluded outside the entity except in certain limited circumstances.

K. **Change in Engagement**
Before the completion of the audit or review, a CPA may be requested to change the engagement to a compilation.

1. **Considerations** Before the CPA agrees to change the engagement to a compilation, the following should be considered:

   a. The client's reason for the request, particularly the implications of a restriction on the scope of the audit or review

   b. The additional effort required to complete the audit or review

   c. The estimated additional cost to complete the audit or review

   If the additional cost or effort to complete the audit or review is minimal, the CPA should consider the propriety of accepting a change in the engagement. The report should not refer to the original engagement, any procedures performed as part of the engagement, or any scope limitations.

2. **Acceptable Reasons** A change in circumstances affecting the entity's requirement for an audit or review, or a misunderstanding regarding the nature of an audit, review, or compilation are acceptable reasons for a change in the engagement

3. **Scope Restriction of Audit or Review** If the reason for the request is due to a restriction on the scope of the audit or review, whether imposed by the client or caused by circumstance, the decision to change the engagement can be more problematic. The CPA should evaluate the possibility that information affected by the scope restriction may be incorrect, incomplete, or otherwise unsatisfactory. Ordinarily, the CPA is precluded from issuing a compilation report when

   a. During an audit, the CPA has been prohibited by the client from corresponding with the entity's legal counsel; or

   b. During an audit or review, a management representation letter is not provided.

II. Reporting on Comparative Financial Statements (AR 200)

A. **Overview**
Comparative financial statements are financial statements of two or more periods which are presented in a columnar format. AR 200 applies when reporting on comparative financial statements of a nonissuer when the financial statements of one or more periods presented have been compiled and reported on or reviewed per AR 80 or 90, respectively. The CPA should issue an appropriate report that covers each of the periods presented in the comparative financial statements.

1. **Report Structure** The same common report elements/paragraphs required for compilation and review reports on financial statements of a single period are applicable to comparative financial statements.

2. **Continuing Accountant** A CPA engaged to audit, review, or compile the current period's financial statements who has audited, reviewed, or compiled those of one or more consecutive periods immediately prior to the current period.

3. **Updated Report** A report issued by a continuing accountant. It takes into consideration information the continuing accountant becomes aware of during the current engagement. In it, depending on the circumstances, the continuing accountant will either re-express the previous conclusion on the prior period statements or express a different conclusion on the prior period statements as of the date of the current report.

4. **Reissued Report** A report issued after the date of the original report, but bearing the same date as the original report. If it must be revised because of the effects of specific events, it should be dual-dated, using the original date and a separate date that applies to the effects of such events.

5. **Client-Prepared Financial Statements Included on Separate Pages** It is permissible for the client to include client-prepared financial statements of some periods that have not been audited, reviewed, or compiled by the CPA on separate pages of a document containing financial statements of other periods on which the CPA has reported, if they are accompanied by an indication by the client that the CPA has not audited, reviewed, or compiled those statements and does not assume any responsibility for them.

6. **Modified and Unmodified Reports** A CPA may modify a report with respect to one or more financial statements for one or more periods while issuing an unmodified report on the other financial statements presented.

7. **Omission of Disclosures** Statements that omit substantially all disclosures are not comparable to financial statements that include such disclosures. Therefore, the CPA should not issue a report on comparative financial statements when statements for some, but not all, of the periods presented omit substantially all required disclosures.

8. **Financial Statements' Reference to Report** Each page of the comparative financial statements compiled or reviewed by the CPA should include a reference such as *See Accountant's Compilation Report* or *See Independent Accountant's Review Report*.

B. Continuing Accountant's Standard Report

1. **Same or Higher Level of Service in Current Period** A continuing accountant who performs the same or a higher level of service with respect to the financial statements of the current period should update the report on the prior period financial statements and presented as the last paragraph of the current period's report.

2. **Lower Level of Service in Current Period** A continuing accountant who performs a lower level of service with respect to the financial statements of the current period should either (a) include as a separate paragraph of the report a description of the responsibility assumed for the financial statements of the prior period or (b) reissue the report on the financial statements of the prior period. The reissued review report may be:

    a. **Combined** The CPA can combine the current compilation report with the reissued review report on the financial statements of the prior period or present them separately. The combined report should state that the CPA has not performed any procedures in connection with that review engagement after the date of the review report.

    b. **Presented Separately** The CPA can issue a compilation report on the current period financial statements that includes a description of the responsibility assumed for the financial statements of the prior period. The description should include the original date of the CPA's report and should also state that the CPA has not performed any procedures in connection with that review engagement after that date.

C. Departure From the Applicable Financial Reporting Framework

When the CPA's report on the prior period financial statements contains a changed reference to a departure from the applicable financial reporting framework, the report should include a separate explanatory paragraph indicating:

1. The date of the CPA's previous report

2. The circumstances or events that caused the reference to be changed

3. That the prior period financial statements have been changed, when applicable

D. Predecessor's Compilation or Review Report Reissued
At the client's request, a predecessor CPA may reissue the compilation or review report on the prior period financial statements; however, a predecessor is not required to do so.

1. The predecessor accountant should consider

   a. The current form and manner of presentation of the prior period financial statements

   b. Subsequent events not previously known

   c. Changes in the financial statements that require the addition or deletion of modifications to the standard report

2. The predecessor accountant should perform the following procedures before reissuing a compilation or review report of a prior period:

   a. Read the current period financial statements and the report of the successor.

   b. Compare the prior period financial statements with those previously issued and with those of the current period.

   c. Obtain a letter from the successor that indicates whether the successor is aware of any matter that might have a material effect on the financial statements, including disclosures, reported on by the predecessor. The predecessor should not refer in the reissued report to this letter or to the report of the successor.

3. **Directed Procedures Prior to Reissue** If the predecessor becomes aware of information that may affect the financial statements of the prior period or the report on them, the predecessor should make inquiries or perform analytics similar to the ones the predecessor would have performed at the date of the report on the prior period statements had the predecessor been aware of the information, and perform any other necessary procedures.

4. **Date of Reissued Report** The date of the previous report should be used when reissuing a report. Dual dating is appropriate if the predecessor revised the report or if the financial statements are restated. The predecessor should also obtain a written statement from the former client setting forth the information currently acquired and its effect on the prior period financial statements and, if applicable, expressing an understanding of its effect on the predecessor's reissued report.

E. Predecessor's Report Not Reissued
When a predecessor does not reissue the compilation or review report, the successor should either

1. Perform a compilation, review, or audit of the prior period financial statements and issue an appropriate report, or

2. Include an additional paragraph in the current report that makes reference to the predecessor's report on the prior period financial statements. The reference should either be added to the end of the introductory paragraph or placed in a separate paragraph and should include:

   a. A statement that other accountants compiled or reviewed the prior period financial statements (generally, the predecessor should not be named)

   b. The date of the predecessor's report

   c. The disclaimer (for a compilation) or limited assurance (for a review) statement that appeared in the report

   d. A description of any modifications that were made to the standard report and of any paragraphs that were included to emphasize any matter in the financial statements

3. **Restated Prior Period Financial Statements** When prior period financial statements have been restated

   a. The predecessor may reissue the report (normally, this is what should happen as covered above); or

   b. The predecessor may not reissue the report and the successor may be engaged to report on the prior year financial statements; or

   c. The predecessor may not reissue the report and the successor may not be engaged to report on the prior year financial statements.

   d. **Predecessor's Report Not Presented (Not Reissued) / Successor Engaged to Report on Prior Year** The successor should indicate in the introductory paragraph of the compilation or review report that a predecessor reported on the financial statements of the prior period before restatement. The successor may also indicate in the report that the successor compiled or reviewed the adjustments that were applied to restate prior year financial statements.

   e. **Predecessor's Report Not Presented (Not Reissued) / Successor Not Engaged to Report on Prior Year** The successor should indicate in the introductory paragraph of the compilation or review report that a predecessor reported on the financial statements of the prior period before restatement.

F. **Current Period Unaudited and Prior Period Audited**
When the current period financial statements of a nonissuer have been compiled or reviewed and those of the prior period have been audited, the CPA should issue an appropriate compilation or review report on the current period financial statements and either

1. The report on the prior period should be reissued; or

2. The report on the current period should include as a separate paragraph a description of the responsibility assumed for the financial statements of the prior period. The separate paragraph should indicate

   a. That the financial statements of the prior period were audited previously

   b. The date of the previous report

   c. The type of opinion expressed previously

   d. If the opinion was other than unqualified, the substantive reasons

   e. That no auditing procedures were performed after the date of the previous report

G. **Current Period Audited and Prior Period Unaudited**
When the current period financial statements of a nonissuer have been audited and those of the prior period are unaudited (i.e., compiled or reviewed), the CPA should include an other-matter paragraph that includes

1. The service that was performed in the prior period

2. The date of the prior period report

3. A description of any material modifications described in the report

4. A statement that the compilation/review was less in scope than an audit and did not provide the basis for an opinion

III. Communications Between Predecessor and Successor Accountants (AR 400)

A. Purpose

This standard provides guidance to a successor CPA who decides to communicate with a predecessor CPA about the acceptance or performance of a compilation or review engagement. The successor should bear in mind that the predecessor and the client may have disagreed about accounting principles, procedures applied by the predecessor, or similarly significant matters.

B. Definitions

1. **Successor** The successor is either considering making a proposal to compile or review financial statements or has accepted the engagement.

2. **Predecessor** The predecessor may have reported on the most recent financial statements or been engaged to perform, but did not complete, a review or compilation and has either resigned or been terminated.

C. Client Consent

As with an audit, a successor should obtain specific consent from a prospective client to make any inquiries of a predecessor and request that the client authorize the predecessor to respond fully. If the prospective client refuses to permit the predecessor to respond or limits the response, the successor should inquire about the reasons and consider the implications regarding the pursuance of the engagement.

D. Communication With Predecessor Regarding Engagement Acceptance

1. **Circumstances When Communication Is Recommended** Unlike an audit, a successor is not required to communicate with a predecessor regarding the acceptance of a compilation or review engagement, but may deem it prudent to do so when, for example, information obtained about the prospective client is limited or appears to require special attention; the change in CPAs takes place substantially after the end of the accounting period; or there have been frequent changes in CPAs.

2. **Inquiries** When the successor accountant decides to communicate with the predecessor accountant, the inquiries may be oral or written. The inquiries should be specific and reasonable regarding matters that will assist the successor accountant in determining whether to accept the engagement. Matters subject to inquiry might include: information that might bear on the integrity of management, or disagreements with management about accounting principles, or the necessity for the performance of certain procedures, or similarly significant matters.

3. **Responses** The successor accountant should consider the implications of a limited response in connection with acceptance of the engagement.

E. Other Inquiries

1. **Engagement Documentation** The successor accountant also may wish to review the predecessor's engagement documentation. If so, the successor accountant should request the client to authorize the predecessor accountant to allow access—ordinarily, this would be documentation relating to contingencies and other matters of continuing accounting significance.

2. **Reference** The successor should not refer to the report or work of the predecessor in the report, except as specifically permitted by AR 200 with respect to the financial statements of a prior period.

CHAPTER 13—ACCOUNTING & REVIEW SERVICES

Problem 13-1 MULTIPLE-CHOICE QUESTIONS

Framework

1. The authoritative body designated to promulgate standards that provide performance and reporting guidance for compilations and reviews of the unaudited financial statements of a nonissuer is the
   a. Financial Accounting Standards Board
   b. Government Accountability Office
   c. American Institute of Certified Public Accountants
   d. Auditing Standards Board (ID: 6)

2. SSARS guidance for compilations of unaudited financial statements establishes standards and procedures for which of the following engagements?
   a. Assisting in adjusting the books of account for a partnership
   b. Compiling an individual's personal financial statements which will be used solely to assist the client and the client's advisors to develop the clients' personal financial goals
   c. Processing financial data for clients of other accounting firms
   d. Compiling an individual's personal financial statements to be used to obtain a mortgage (ID: 2281)

3. An accountant is required to comply with the provisions of the Statements on Standards for Accounting and Review Services for compilations when performing which of the following tasks?
   a. Preparing monthly journal entries
   b. Providing the client with software to generate financial statements
   c. Generating financial statements of a nonissuer
   d. Providing a blank financial statement format or template (ID: 8628)

4. An accountant is required to comply with the provisions of Statements on Standards for Accounting and Review Services (SSARS) when

	Compiling financial statements generated through the use of computer software	Reproducing client prepared financial statements, without modification, for the client
a.	Yes	Yes
b.	Yes	No
c.	No	Yes
d.	No	No

(ID: 9376)

5. Which of the following describes how the objective of a review of financial statements differs from the objective of a compilation engagement?
   a. The primary objective of a review engagement is to test the completeness of the financial statements prepared, but a compilation tests for reasonableness.
   b. The primary objective of a review engagement is to provide positive assurance that the financial statements are fairly presented, but a compilation provides no such assurance.
   c. In a review engagement, accountants provide limited assurance, but a compilation expresses no assurance.
   d. In a review engagement, accountants provide reasonable or positive assurance that the financial statements are fairly presented, but a compilation provides limited assurance. (ID: 8381)

6. Which of the following services, if any, may an accountant who is not independent provide?
   a. Compilations, but not reviews
   b. Reviews, but not compilations
   c. Both compilations and reviews
   d. No services (ID: 9397)

Compilations

7. Which of the following is correct regarding a compilation of financial statements engagement in accordance with *Statement on Standards for Accounting and Review Services*?

   a. If the accountant's independence is impaired, a qualified opinion must be issued.
   b. The accountant may not base the report on information obtained from prior engagements with the same client.
   c. The accountant is not required to make inquiries nor perform procedures to corroborate the information provided by the client.
   d. The accountant should perform analytical procedures to financial data. (ID: 90166)

8. Which of the following would not be included in an accountant's documentation of a compilation of a client's financial statements?

   a. Discussion with the client regarding the proper presentation of gross cash flows for investment purchases
   b. An engagement letter
   c. A memo to the CFO about a potentially significant fraud revealed during compilation procedures
   d. A review of the segregation of duties in the cash disbursement process (ID: 90174)

9. If requested to perform a compilation engagement for a nonissuer in which an accountant has an immaterial direct financial interest, the accountant is

   a. Independent because the financial interest in the nonissuer is immaterial
   b. Not independent and, therefore, may not be associated with the financial statements
   c. Not independent and, therefore, may not issue a compilation report
   d. Not independent and, therefore, may issue a compilation report, but may not issue a review report (ID: 90175)

10. An accountant compiles the financial statements of a nonissuer and issues the standard compilation report. Although not specifically stated in this report, it is implied that

    a. The accountant has not audited or reviewed the financial statements.
    b. Substantially all disclosures required by GAAP are included in the financial statements.
    c. The financial statements should not be used to obtain credit.
    d. The compilation is limited to presenting information that is the representation of management. (ID: 90199)

11. The standard compilation report includes which statement or phrase?

    a. A compilation is substantially less in scope than a review or an audit.
    b. The accountant does not express an opinion but expresses only limited assurance on the compiled financial statements.
    c. The objective of a compilation is to assist management in presenting financial information in the form of financial statements.
    d. The accountant has compiled the financial statements in accordance with standards established by the Auditing Standards Board. (ID: 4743)

12. When the accountant is engaged to report on compiled financial statements or submits financial statements that are reasonably expected to be used by a third party, the financial statements should be accompanied by a written report stating that

    a. The scope of the accountant's procedures has not been restricted in testing the financial information that is the representation of management.
    b. The accountant assessed the accounting principles used and significant estimates made by management.
    c. The accountant does not express an opinion or any other form of assurance on the financial statements.
    d. A compilation consists principally of inquiries of entity personnel and analytical procedures applied to financial data. (ID: 6027)

13. When compiling the financial statements of a nonissuer, an accountant should
    a. Review agreements with financial institutions for restrictions on cash balances
    b. Understand the accounting principles and practices of the entity's industry
    c. Inquire of key personnel concerning related parties and subsequent events
    d. Perform ratio analyses of the financial data of comparable prior periods (ID: 2978)

14. How does an accountant make the following representations when issuing the standard report for the compilation of a nonissuer's financial statements?

	The financial statements have not been audited	The accountant has compiled the financial statements
a.	Implicitly	Implicitly
b.	Explicitly	Explicitly
c.	Implicitly	Explicitly
d.	Explicitly	Implicitly

(ID: 2294)

15. Which of the following procedures is ordinarily performed by an accountant during an engagement to compile financial statements?
    a. Make inquiries of the employees and senior management regarding transactions with related parties.
    b. Determine whether there is substantial doubt about the entity's ability to continue as a going concern.
    c. Scan the entity's records for the period just after the balance sheet date to identify subsequent events requiring disclosure.
    d. Consider whether the financial statements are free from obvious material mistakes in the application of accounting principles. (ID: 8611)

16. Which of the following statements is correct regarding a compilation report on financial statements issued in accordance with Statements on Standards for Accounting and Review Services (SSARS)?
    a. The report should not be issued if the accountant is not independent from the entity.
    b. The report should include a statement indicating that the information is the representation of the accountant.
    c. The report should include a description of other procedures performed during the compilation.
    d. The date on the report should be the date of completion of the compilation. (ID: 8624)

17. Which of the following statements would be appropriate in an accountant's report on compiled financial statements of a nonissuer prepared in accordance with Statements on Standards for Accounting and Review Services (SSARS)?
    a. We are not aware of any material modifications that should be made to the accompanying financial statements.
    b. A compilation is substantially less in scope than an audit, the objective of which is the expression of an opinion regarding the financial statements as a whole.
    c. The objective of a compilation is to assist management in presenting financial information in the form of financial statements.
    d. A compilation is performed to obtain reasonable assurance about whether the financial statements are free from material misstatement. (ID: 8629)

18. When an accountant is not independent with respect to an entity, which of the following types of compilation reports may be issued?
    a. The standard compilation report may be issued, regardless of independence.
    b. A compilation report with negative assurance may be issued.
    c. A compilation report with special wording that notes the accountant's lack of independence may be issued.
    d. A compilation report may be issued if the engagement is upgraded to a review. (ID: 8653)

19. Independence is not required on which of the following types of engagements?

    a. Audit
    b. Review
    c. Compilation
    d. Agreed-upon procedures (ID: 8819)

20. An accountant compiled the financial statements of a nonissuer in accordance with Statements on Standards for Accounting and Review Services (SSARS). If the accountant has an ownership interest in the entity, which of the following statements is correct?

    a. The accountant should refuse the compilation engagement.
    b. A report need not be issued for a compilation of a nonissuer.
    c. The accountant should include the disclaimer "I am an owner of the entity" in the report.
    d. The accountant should include the statement "I am not independent with respect to the entity" in the compilation report. (ID: 9373)

21. General Retailing, a nonissuer, has asked Ford, CPA, to compile its financial statements that omit substantially all disclosures required by GAAP. Ford may comply with General's request provided the omission is clearly indicated in Ford's report and the

    a. Distribution of the financial statements and Ford's report is restricted to internal use only.
    b. Reason for omitting the disclosures is acknowledged in the notes to the financial statements.
    c. Omitted disclosures would not influence any potential creditor's conclusions about General's financial position.
    d. Omission is not undertaken with the intention of misleading the users of General's financial statements. (ID: 9932)

22. An accountant has been engaged to compile the financial statements of a nonpublic entity. The financial statements contain many departures from GAAP because of inadequacies in the accounting records. The accountant believes that modification of the compilation report is not adequate to indicate the deficiencies. Under these circumstances, the accountant should

    a. Inform management that the engagement can proceed only if distribution of the accountant's report is restricted to internal use
    b. Withdraw from the engagement and provide no further service concerning these financial statements
    c. Quantify the effects of the departures from GAAP and describe the departures from GAAP in a special report
    d. Obtain written representations from management that the financial statements will not be used to obtain credit from financial institutions (ID: 8828)

23. An accountant agrees to the client's request to change an engagement from a review to a compilation of financial statements. The compilation report should include

    a. No reference to the original engagement
    b. Reference to a departure from GAAS
    c. Scope limitations that may have resulted in the change of engagement
    d. Information about review procedures already performed (ID: 8806)

Reviews

24. An entity engaged an accountant to review its financial statements in accordance with *Statements on Standards for Accounting and Review Services*. The accountant determined that the entity maintained its accounts on a comprehensive basis of accounting other than generally accepted accounting principles (GAAP). In this situation, the accountant most likely would have taken which of the following actions?

    a. Withdrawn from the engagement because the entity has not been following GAAP
    b. Advised management to make the adjustments necessary for the account balances to conform with GAAP
    c. Modified the review report to reflect the fact that the financial statements were presented on another comprehensive basis of accounting
    d. Requested that management justify the use of the other comprehensive basis of accounting in the management representation letter (ID: 90156)

25. What type of analytical procedure would an auditor most likely use in developing relationships among balance sheet accounts when reviewing the financial statements of a nonissuer?

    a. Trend analysis
    b. Regression analysis
    c. Ratio analysis
    d. Risk analysis (ID: 5692)

26. Each page of a nonissuer's financial statements reviewed by an accountant should include the following reference:

    a. See Accompanying Accountant's Footnotes
    b. Reviewed, No Material Modifications Required
    c. See Accountant's Review Report
    d. Reviewed, No Accountant's Assurance Expressed (ID: 5699)

27. Which of the following would be performed during a review engagement?

    a. Examination of board minutes
    b. Confirmation of cash and accounts receivable
    c. Comparison of current-year to prior-year account balances
    d. Recalculation of depreciation expense (ID: 8168)

28. During an engagement to review the financial statements of a nonissuer, an accountant becomes aware that several leases that should be capitalized are not capitalized. The accountant considers these leases to be material to the financial statements. The accountant decides to modify the standard review report because management will not capitalize the leases. Under these circumstances, the accountant should

    a. Issue an adverse opinion because of the departure from GAAP
    b. Express no assurance of any kind on the entity's financial statements
    c. Emphasize that the financial statements are for limited use only
    d. Disclose the departure from GAAP in a separate paragraph of the accountant's report (ID: 6239)

29. In reviewing the annual financial statements of a nonissuer, an accountant is required to modify the standard review report for which of the following matters?

	Inability to assess the risk of material misstatement due to fraud	Discovery of significant deficiencies in the design of the entity's internal control
a.	Yes	Yes
b.	Yes	No
c.	No	Yes
d.	No	No

(ID: 7023)

30. If requested to perform a review engagement for a nonissuer in which an accountant has an immaterial direct financial interest, the accountant is

    a. Not independent and, therefore, may not be associated with the financial statements
    b. Not independent and, therefore, may not issue a review report
    c. Not independent and, therefore, may issue a review report, but may not issue an auditor's opinion
    d. Independent because the financial interest is immaterial and, therefore, may issue a review report

(ID: 5638)

31. Under which of the following circumstances would an accountant most likely conclude that it is necessary to withdraw from an engagement to review a nonissuer's financial statements?

    a. The entity does not have reasonable justification for making a change in accounting principle.
    b. The entity prepares its financial statements on the income tax basis of accounting.
    c. The entity requests the accountant to report only on the balance sheet, and not on the other financial statements.
    d. The entity declines to provide the accountant with a signed representation letter. (ID: 7627)

32. Which of the following procedures would an accountant least likely perform during an engagement to review the financial statements of a nonissuer?

    a. Observing the safeguards over access to and use of assets and records
    b. Comparing the financial statements with anticipated results in budgets and forecasts
    c. Inquiring of management about actions taken at the board of directors' meetings
    d. Studying the relationships of financial statement elements expected to conform to predictable patterns (ID: 5147)

33. An accountant has been asked to issue a review report on the balance sheet of a nonissuer without reporting on the related statements of income, retained earnings, and cash flows. The accountant may issue the requested review report only if

    a. The balance sheet is not to be used to obtain credit or distributed to the entity's creditors.
    b. The balance sheet is part of a comprehensive personal financial plan developed to assist the entity.
    c. There have been no material changes during the year in the entity's accounting principles.
    d. The scope of the accountant's inquiry and analytical procedures has not been restricted. (ID: 7825)

34. Which of the following statements is correct regarding both a compilation and a review engagement of a nonpublic company's financial statements performed in accordance with SSARS?

    a. The CPA should assess fraud risk.
    b. The CPA must obtain an understanding of the client's internal control.
    c. The CPA must establish an understanding with the client regarding the services to be performed and document it in an engagement letter.
    d. The reports contain a statement that the engagement is substantially less in scope than an audit.

(ID: 8378)

35. Which of the following procedures does a CPA normally perform first in a review engagement in accordance with Statements on Standards for Accounting and Review Services (SSARS)?

    a. Inquiry regarding the client's principles and practices and the method of applying them
    b. Inquiry concerning the effectiveness of the client's system of internal control
    c. Inquiry to identify transactions between related parties and management
    d. Inquiry of the client's professional advisors, including bankers, insurance agents, and consultants

(ID: 8379)

36. The standard report issued by an accountant after reviewing the financial statements of a nonissuer according to SSARS should state that

    a. The objective of a review is to assist management in presenting financial information in the form of financial statements.
    b. A review includes primarily applying analytical procedures to management's financial data and making inquiries of company management.
    c. The accountant does not express an opinion or any other form of assurance on the financial statements.
    d. The accountant did not obtain an understanding of the entity's internal control or assess fraud risk.

    (ID: 8410)

37. In an engagement to review the annual financial statements of a nonissuer, the accountant most likely would perform which of the following procedures?

    a. Physical inspection of inventory
    b. Vouching of inventory purchase transactions
    c. Analysis of inventory turnover
    d. Evaluation of internal control over inventory (ID: 8619)

38. Which of the following statements is true regarding analytical procedures in a review engagement?

    a. Analytical procedures are not required to be used as a substantive test.
    b. Analytical procedures do not involve comparisons of recorded amounts to expected amounts.
    c. Analytical procedures are required to be used in the final review stage.
    d. Analytical procedures involve the use of both financial and nonfinancial data. (ID: 8634)

39. To obtain a reasonable basis for the expression of limited assurance in a review engagement, the accountant is required to do all of the following except

    a. Apply analytical procedures to the financial statements
    b. Make inquiries of management and, when deemed appropriate, other company personnel
    c. Send a letter of inquiry to the client's attorney
    d. Obtain representations from management for all financial statements and periods covered by the accountant's review report (ID: 8635)

40. Which of the following procedures would an accountant most likely perform during an engagement to review the annual financial statements of a nonissuer?

    a. Review the predecessor accountant's working papers.
    b. Inquire of management about related-party transactions.
    c. Corroborate litigation information with the entity's attorney.
    d. Communicate internal control deficiencies to senior management. (ID: 8645)

41. When reviewing the financial statements of a nonissuer in accordance with *Statements on Standards for Accounting and Review Services*, an accountant's procedures should include

    a. Obtaining an understanding of internal control
    b. Assessing fraud risk
    c. Applying substantive tests of transactions
    d. Inquiring into actions taken at meetings of the board of directors (ID: 90182)

42. Which of the following procedures is an accountant required to perform when reviewing the financial statements of a nonpublic entity in accordance with Statements on Standards for Accounting and Review Services (SSARS)?

    a. Assess control risk
    b. Obtain a management representation letter
    c. Confirm account balances
    d. Perform a physical inventory observation (ID: 8803)

43. Which of the following statements is correct regarding a review of a nonpublic entity's financial statements in accordance with Statements on Standards for Accounting and Review Services (SSARS)?
    a. The accountant is required to assess the risk of fraud.
    b. It is not necessary for the accountant to obtain a management representation letter.
    c. An opinion is expressed in the review report.
    d. The accountant must be independent to issue the review report. (ID: 8825)

44. An accountant has been engaged to review a nonissuer's financial statements that contain several departures from GAAP. Management is unwilling to revise the financial statements, and the accountant believes that modification of the standard review report is inadequate to communicate the deficiencies. Under these circumstances, the accountant should
    a. Determine the effects of the departures from GAAP and issue a special report on the financial statements
    b. Express a disclaimer of opinion on the financial statements and advise the board of directors that the financial statements should not be relied on
    c. Inform management that a review of the financial statements cannot be completed and request a change from a review to a compilation engagement
    d. Withdraw from the engagement and provide no further services concerning these financial statements (ID: 9352)

45. Which of the following procedures would a CPA ordinarily perform when reviewing the financial statements of a nonissuer in accordance with Statements on Standards for Accounting and Review Services (SSARS)?
    a. Apply year-end cutoff tests for the sales and purchasing functions
    b. Compare the financial statements with budgets or forecasts
    c. Obtain an understanding of the entity's internal control components
    d. Document whether control risk is assessed at or below the maximum level (ID: 9368)

46. Which of the following is required of an accountant in reviewing a company's financial statements under Statements on Standards for Accounting and Review Services (SSARS)?
    a. Obtain knowledge of the client's industry
    b. Send bank confirmations
    c. Corroboration of management's responses to inquiries
    d. Observe client's physical inventory (ID: 9392)

47. Which of the following situations would preclude an accountant from issuing a review report on a company's financial statements in accordance with Statements on Standards for Accounting and Review Services (SSARS)?
    a. The owner of a company is the accountant's father.
    b. The accountant was engaged to review only the balance sheet.
    c. Land has been recorded at appraisal value instead of historical cost.
    d. Finished-goods inventory does not include any overhead amounts. (ID: 9398)

48. Which of the following statements would not normally be included in a representation letter for a review of interim financial information?
    a. To the best of our knowledge and belief, no events have occurred subsequent to the balance sheet and through the date of this letter that would require adjustment to or disclosure in the interim financial information.
    b. We acknowledge our responsibility for the design and implementation of programs and controls to prevent and detect fraud.
    c. We understand that a review consists principally of performing analytical procedures and making inquiries about the interim financial information.
    d. We have made available to you all financial records and related data. (ID: 9921)

49. When performing a review of interim financial information, an accountant would typically do each of the following, except
    a. Consider the results from the latest audit
    b. Test controls related to the preparation of annual financial information
    c. Perform analytical procedures
    d. Make inquiries of management (ID: 9922)

50. In an accountant's review of interim financial information, the accountant typically performs each of the following, except
    a. Reading the available minutes of the latest stockholders' meeting
    b. Applying financial ratios to the interim financial information
    c. Inquiring of the Accounting Department's management
    d. Obtaining corroborating external evidence (ID: 9949)

51. Which of the following applies to an accountant conducting a review of interim financial information?
    a. The accountant must indicate in the report those circumstances in which generally accepted accounting principles have not been consistently observed in the current period in relation to the preceding period.
    b. The accountant must express an opinion on the financial statements taken as a whole.
    c. The accountant must maintain independence in mental attitude in all matters relating to the engagement.
    d. The accountant must obtain sufficient appropriate evidence by performing procedures to afford a reasonable basis for an opinion. (ID: 90196)

52. A CPA started to audit the financial statements of a nonissuer. After completing certain audit procedures, the client requested the CPA to change the engagement to a review because of a scope limitation. The CPA concludes that there is reasonable justification for the change. Under these circumstances, the CPA's review report should include a
    a. Statement that a review is substantially less in scope than an audit
    b. Reference to the scope limitation that caused the changed engagement
    c. Description of the auditing procedures that were completed before the engagement was changed
    d. Reference to the CPA's justification for agreeing to change the engagement (ID: 9909)

Comparative Financial Statements

53. Clark, CPA, compiled and properly reported on the financial statements of Green Co., a nonissuer, for the year ended March 31, year 1. These financial statements omitted substantially all disclosures required by generally accepted accounting principles (GAAP). Green asked Clark to compile the statements for the year ended March 31, year 2, and to include all GAAP disclosures for year 2 statements only, but otherwise present both years' financial statements in comparative form. What is Clark's responsibility concerning the proposed engagement?
    a. Clark may not report on the comparative financial statements because the year 1 statements are not comparable to the year 2 statements that include the GAAP disclosures.
    b. Clark may report on the comparative financial statements provided Clark updates the report on the year 1 statements that do not include the GAAP disclosures.
    c. Clark may report on the comparative financial statements provided an explanatory paragraph is added to Clark's report on the comparative financial statements.
    d. Clark may report on the comparative financial statements provided the year 1 statements do not contain any obvious material misstatements. (ID: 2757)

54. Gole, CPA, is engaged to review the year 4 financial statements of North Co., a nonissuer. Previously, Gole audited North's year 3 financial statements and expressed an unqualified opinion. Gole decides to include a separate paragraph in the year 4 review report because North plans to present comparative financial statements for year 4 and year 3. This separate paragraph should indicate that

a. The year 4 review report is intended solely for the information of management and the board of directors.
b. There are justifiable reasons for changing the level of service from an audit to a review.
c. No auditing procedures were performed after the date of the year 3 auditor's report.
d. The year 3 auditor's report may no longer be relied on. (ID: 5152)

55. When unaudited financial statements of a nonissuer are presented in comparative form with audited financial statements in the subsequent year, the unaudited financial statements should be clearly marked to indicate their status and

I. The report on the unaudited financial statements should be reissued.
II. The report on the audited financial statements should include a separate paragraph describing the responsibility assumed for the unaudited financial statements.

a. I only
b. II only
c. Both I and II
d. Either I or II (ID: 4754)

56. Before reissuing a compilation report on the financial statements of a nonissuer for the prior year, the predecessor accountant is required to

a. Make inquiries about actions taken at meetings of the board of directors during the current year
b. Verify that the reissued report will not be used to obtain credit from a financial institution
c. Review the successor accountant's working papers for matters affecting the prior year
d. Compare the prior year's financial statements with those of the current year (ID: 9367)

57. A CPA is reporting on comparative financial statements of a nonissuer. The CPA audited the prior year's financial statements and reviewed those of the current year in accordance with Statements on Standards for Accounting and Review Services (SSARS). The CPA has added a separate paragraph to the review report to describe the responsibility assumed for the prior year's audited financial statements. This separate paragraph should indicate

a. The type of opinion expressed previously
b. That the CPA did not update the assessment of control risk
c. The reasons for the change from an audit to a review
d. That the audit report should no longer be relied on (ID: 9908)

Problem 13-2 SIMULATION: Compilation & Review Requirements

Each of the following items represents a series of unrelated procedures that an accountant may consider performing in separate engagements to review the financial statements of a nonissuer (a review) and to compile the financial statements of a nonissuer (a compilation) according to SSARS. Select, as the best answer for each item, whether the procedure is required (R) or not required (N) for **both** review and compilation engagements.

Procedures	Required / Not Required	
	Compilation	**Review**
1. The accountant should establish an understanding with the entity regarding the nature and limitations of the services to be performed.		
2. The accountant should make inquiries concerning actions taken at the board of directors' meetings.		
3. The accountant, as the entity's successor accountant, should communicate with the predecessor accountant to obtain access to the predecessor's working papers.		
4. The accountant should obtain a level of knowledge of the accounting principles and practices of the entity's industry.		
5. The accountant should obtain an understanding of the entity's internal control structure.		
6. The accountant should perform analytical procedures designed to identify relationships that appear to be unusual.		
7. The accountant should make an assessment of the fraud risk.		

(ID: 9243)

Problem 13-3 SIMULATION: Review Report

Wallace & Wallace, CPAs, audited the financial statements of West Co., a nonissuer, for the year ended September 30, 20X1, and expressed an unqualified opinion. For the year ended September 30, 20X2, West issued comparative financial statements. Wallace & Wallace reviewed West's year 2 financial statements and Gordon, an assistant on the engagement, drafted the review report below. Martin, the engagement supervisor, decided not to reissue the prior year's audit report, but instructed Gordon to include a separate paragraph in the current year's review report describing the responsibility assumed for the prior year's audited financial statements.

Martin reviewed Gordon's draft and indicated that there were many deficiencies in Gordon's draft.

Accountant's Review Report

We have reviewed the accompanying balance sheet of West Company as of September 30, 20X2, and the related statements of income and cash flows for the year then ended. A review includes primarily applying analytical procedures to management's financial data and making inquiries of company management. A review also includes assessing the accounting principles used and significant estimates made by management, as well as evaluating the overall financial statement presentation.

Management is responsible for the preparation and fair presentation of the financial statements in accordance with accounting principles generally accepted in the United States of America.

Our responsibility is to conduct the review in accordance with standards issued by the American Institute of Certified Public Accountants. Those standards require us to perform procedures to obtain limited assurance that there are no material modifications that should be made to the financial statements. We believe that the results of our procedures provide a reasonable basis for our report.

Based on our review, we are not aware of any material modifications that should be made to the accompanying financial statements. Accordingly, the accompanying financial statements have been prepared assuming that the company will continue as a going concern. Furthermore, we have no responsibility to update this report for events and circumstances occurring after the date of this report.

The financial statements for the year ended September 30, 20X1, were audited by us and we expressed an unqualified opinion on them in our report dated November 7, 20X1, but we have not performed any auditing procedures since that date. In our opinion, the financial statements referred to above are presented fairly, in all material respects, for the year then ended in conformity with generally accepted accounting principles.

Wallace & Wallace, CPAs

November 6, 20X2

Each of the following items represents a deficiency noted by Martin. For each deficiency, indicate whether Martin is correct (M); Gordon is correct (G); or both Martin and Gordon are incorrect (B).

Report Deficiencies Noted by Martin	M / G / B
1. There should be a reference to the prior year's audited financial statements in the first (introductory) paragraph.	
2. All of the current year's basic financial statements are not properly identified in the first (introductory) paragraph.	
3. The standards referred to in the third (accountant's responsibilities) paragraph should not be standards issued by the American Institute of Certified Public Accountants, but should be Standards for the Compilation and Review of Financial Statements.	
4. The title of the report should be Independent Accountant's Review Report.	
5. The statement in the third paragraph that the accountant is required to perform procedures to obtain limited assurance that there are no material modifications that should be made to the financial statements should be in the introductory paragraph following the description of a review.	
6. There should be a statement in the second (management's responsibilities) paragraph that describes management's responsibilities relative to internal control.	
7. There should be a comparison of the scope of a review to an audit in the introductory paragraph.	
8. There should be no reference to "assessing the accounting principles used," "significant estimates made by management," and "evaluating the overall financial statement presentation" in the introductory paragraph.	

(ID: 9241)

Problem 13-4 SIMULATION: Review Report

Wallace & Wallace, CPAs, audited the financial statements of West Co., a nonissuer, for the year ended September 30, 20X1, and expressed an unqualified opinion. For the year ended September 30, 20X2, West issued comparative financial statements. Wallace & Wallace reviewed West's year 2 financial statements and Gordon, an assistant on the engagement, drafted the review report below. Martin, the engagement supervisor, decided not to reissue the prior year's audit report, but instructed Gordon to include a separate paragraph in the current year's review report describing the responsibility assumed for the prior year's audited financial statements.

Martin reviewed Gordon's draft and indicated that there were many deficiencies in Gordon's draft.

Accountant's Review Report

We have reviewed the accompanying balance sheet of West Company as of September 30, 20X2, and the related statements of income and cash flows for the year then ended. A review includes primarily applying analytical procedures to management's financial data and making inquiries of company management. A review also includes assessing the accounting principles used and significant estimates made by management, as well as evaluating the overall financial statement presentation.

Management is responsible for the preparation and fair presentation of the financial statements in accordance with accounting principles generally accepted in the United States of America.

Our responsibility is to conduct the review in accordance with standards issued by the American Institute of Certified Public Accountants. Those standards require us to perform procedures to obtain limited assurance that there are no material modifications that should be made to the financial statements. We believe that the results of our procedures provide a reasonable basis for our report.

Based on our review, we are not aware of any material modifications that should be made to the accompanying financial statements. Accordingly, the accompanying financial statements have been prepared assuming that the company will continue as a going concern. Furthermore, we have no responsibility to update this report for events and circumstances occurring after the date of this report.

The financial statements for the year ended September 30, 20X1, were audited by us and we expressed an unqualified opinion on them in our report dated November 7, 20X1, but we have not performed any auditing procedures since that date. In our opinion, the financial statements referred to above are presented fairly, in all material respects, for the year then ended in conformity with generally accepted accounting principles.

Wallace & Wallace, CPAs

November 6, 20X2

Each of the following items represents a deficiency noted by Martin. For each deficiency, indicate whether Martin is correct and Gordon is incorrect (M); Gordon is correct and Martin is incorrect (G); or both Martin and Gordon are incorrect (B).

Report Deficiencies Noted by Martin	M / G / B
1. There should be a reference to "conformity with generally accepted accounting principles" in the fourth paragraph.	
2. There should be a reference to consistency in the fourth paragraph.	
3. There should be a restriction on the distribution of the accountant's review report in the fourth paragraph.	
4. The reference to "going concern" in the fourth paragraph should be in the first paragraph.	
5. The accountant's lack of responsibility to update the report in the fourth paragraph should be in the first paragraph.	
6. There should be no mention of the type of opinion expressed on the prior year's audited financial statements in the fifth paragraph.	
7. All of the prior year's basic financial statements are not properly identified in the fifth paragraph.	
8. The reference in the fifth paragraph to the fair presentation of the prior year's audited financial statements in accordance with generally accepted accounting principles should be omitted.	
9. The report should be dual dated to indicate the date of the prior year's auditor's report.	

(ID: 9245)

Problem 13-5 SIMULATION: Research

Before submission of compiled financial statements, the accountant should read the financial statements and consider whether such financial statements appear to be appropriate in form and free from obvious material errors. Which section of the professional standards defines the term *error* in this context?

Reminder: On the actual exam, you will use an electronic database of authoritative literature to find and select the reference (appropriate section and paragraph of the relevant guidance). Please see the AICPA's tutorial and sample test on the exam section of their website.

[ ] § [ ] [ ] (ID: 89463)

Solution 13-1 MULTIPLE-CHOICE ANSWERS

1. (c) Statements on Standards for Accounting and Review Services (SSARS) are issued by the AICPA's Accounting and Review Services Committee, the senior technical committee of the Institute designated to issue pronouncements in connection with the unaudited financial statements or other unaudited financial information of a nonissuer. (ID: 6)

2. (d) An engagement to compile an individual's personal financial statements to be used to obtain a mortgage must be performed in compliance with AR 80, Compilations of Financial Statements. AR 600, Reporting on Personal Financial Statements Included in Written Personal Financial Plans provides an exemption from AR 80 for such personal financial statements and guidance on reporting if the statements will not be used to obtain credit or for any other purpose than developing the client's personal financial goals. (However, AR 600 does not preclude an accountant from complying with AR 80 in such engagements.) Answers a. and c. do not meet the SSARS definition of submission of financial statements. (ID: 2281)

3. (c) The accountant is required to comply with the provisions of SSARS for compilations whenever he or she is engaged to report on compiled financial statements or submits financial statements to a client or to third parties. *Submission of financial statements* is defined as presenting to management financial statements that an accountant has prepared. Only answer c. meets this definition. (ID: 8628)

4. (b) The accountant is required to comply with the provisions of SSARS for compilations whenever he or she is engaged to report on compiled financial statements or submits financial statements to a client or to third parties. *Submission of financial statements* is defined as presenting to management financial statements that an accountant has prepared. Reproducing client-prepared financial statements, without modification, for the client is not considered a submission of financial statements. (ID: 9376)

5. (c) The objective of a review differs significantly from the objective of a compilation. The inquiry and analytical procedures performed in a review should provide the accountant with a reasonable basis for expressing limited assurance that there are no material modifications that should be made to the financial statements. No expression of assurance is contemplated in a compilation. (ID: 8381)

6. (a) An accountant who is not independent may perform compilations, but not reviews. (ID: 9397)

7. (c) An accountant is not required to corroborate information provided by the client or perform analytics for a compilation engagement. An accountant is prohibited from issuing any opinion for a compilation. An accountant may use information obtained from prior engagements with the same client in connection with a compilation engagement. (ID: 90166)

8. (d) A compilation engagement involves assisting the client in presenting financial information in the form of financial statements without undertaking to provide any assurance. Generally, no review of internal control is performed for a compilation engagement; therefore, the accountant generally would not review the segregation of duties in the cash disbursement process. Documentation should be sufficiently detailed to provide a clear understanding of the work performed. Any discussion with the client regarding gross cash flows for investment purchases should be documented; such a discussion is appropriate to a compilation engagement. An engagement letter is part of the minimal required documentation for a compilation engagement. While an accountant need not look for fraud during a compilation engagement, any potentially significant fraud revealed during the procedures should be reported to the appropriate level of management or those charged with governance. (ID: 90174)

9. (d) A direct financial interest, even if immaterial, impairs an accountant's independence; however, independence is not required to issue a compilation report. Independence is required to issue a review report. (ID: 90175)

10. (b) The disclosures in the notes to the financial statements are an integral element of the financial statements; any omission of disclosures must be noted in the compilation report to keep it from being misleading. The standard compilation report explicitly states that the accountant has not audited or reviewed the financial statements as well as that a compilation is limited to presenting information that is the representation of management. Compiled financial statements may be used to obtain credit if acceptable to the creditor. (ID: 90199)

11. (c) The only phrase (of the alternatives) that is included in the standard compilation report is: The objective of a compilation is to assist management in presenting financial information in the form of financial statements. (ID: 4743)

12. (c) When the accountant is engaged to report on compiled financial statements or submits financial statements that are reasonably expected to be used by a third party, the financial statements should be accompanied by a written report that states that the accountant does not express an opinion or any other form of assurance on the financial statements. No reference to testing the financial information or to assessing the principles and estimates used is made in the report nor is testing the information supplied required in a compilation. A review consists primarily of inquiries of entity personnel and analytics. (ID: 6027)

13. (b) The accountant should possess a level of knowledge of the accounting principles and practices of the industry in which the entity operates that will enable the accountant to compile financial statements that are appropriate in form for an entity operating in that industry. Answers a., c., and d. represent procedures beyond the scope of a compilation. (ID: 2978)

14. (b) Both are explicitly stated in the introductory paragraph of the standard compilation report. The introductory paragraph begins: We have compiled the accompanying balance sheet of XYZ Company...and includes this statement: We have not audited or reviewed the accompanying financial statements.... (ID: 2294)

15. (d) When engaged to compile the financial statements of a nonissuer, an accountant should read the financial statements and consider whether they appear to be appropriate in form and free from obvious material errors. This would include mistakes in the compilation of the financial statements, including arithmetical or clerical mistakes; and mistakes in the application of accounting principles, including inadequate disclosure. A compilation does not contemplate performing inquiries, analytical procedures or other procedures performed in a review. Accordingly, it would not include performing procedures regarding related-party transactions, going concern issues, or subsequent events. (A compilation does not provide a basis for expressing any level of assurance on the financial statements.) Note: Even though an accountant is not required to perform these procedures, if going concern or subsequent event issues come to the accountant's attention, the accountant should request that management consider the possible effects on the financial statements. The accountant should then evaluate management's response and consider its effect on the compilation report. (ID: 8611)

16. (d) The date on the report should be the date of completion of the compilation. An accountant need not be independent with respect to an entity to issue a compilation report; however, the report should be modified. The accountant should specifically disclose the lack of independence in the last paragraph of the report. The accountant is not precluded from including a description of the reasons(s) that the accountant's independence is impaired; however, if the accountant elects to do so, all the reasons should be included. The accountant utilizes information that is the representation of management. Any other procedures that the accountant might have performed as part of the compilation engagement should not be described in the report. (ID: 8624)

17. (c) One of the basic elements of a report on compiled financial statements is a statement that the objective of a compilation is to assist management in presenting financial information in the form of financial statements without undertaking to obtain or provide any assurance that there are no material modifications that should be made to the financial statements. A statement that a review is substantially less in scope than an audit, the objective of which is the expression of an opinion regarding the financial statements taken as a whole is an element of a review report rather than a compilation report. The last answer is similar to the statement included in the scope paragraph of the standard audit report rather than a compilation report. (ID: 8629)

18. (c) When an accountant is not independent with respect to an entity, a compilation report with special wording that notes the accountant's lack of independence may be issued. The accountant should specifically disclose the lack of independence in the last paragraph of the report. The accountant is not precluded from disclosing the reason(s) for the impairment. If this election is made, all reasons should be included. Regardless of the accountant's independence, a compilation does not provide a basis for expressing any level of assurance on the financial statements being compiled. There is no point in upgrading the engagement when the accountant lacks independence. An accountant is precluded from issuing a review report for an entity with respect to which the accountant is not independent. (ID: 8653)

19. (c) An accountant is not required to be independent to perform a compilation engagement. The lack of independence should be specifically disclosed by adding a statement in the final paragraph of the report. The accountant is not precluded from disclosing the reason(s) for the impairment. If this election is made, all reasons should be included. Independence is required for the other answers. (ID: 8819)

20. (d) If an accountant compiles the financial statements of a nonissuer in accordance with SSARS for a client with which the accountant has an ownership interest, the accountant should include the statement "I am not independent with respect to the entity." in the compilation report. An accountant is not precluded from issuing a compilation report for an entity with respect to which the accountant is not independent. The accountant is also not precluded from disclosing the reason(s) that independence is impaired—in this case ownership—however, there is no requirement to disclose the reasons for the lack of independence as indicated by answer c. (ID: 9373)

21. (d) An entity may request the accountant to compile financial statements that omit substantially all the disclosures required by an applicable financial reporting framework, including disclosures that might appear in the body of the financial statements. The accountant may compile such financial statements, provided that the omission of substantially all disclosures is not undertaken with the intention of misleading those who might reasonably be expected to use such financial statements. Distribution is not restricted to internal use; however, the compilation report should include a paragraph, after the accountant's responsibilities paragraph, that states that management has elected to omit the disclosures; that if the disclosures were included, they might influence the user's conclusions about the company's financial position, results of operations, and cash flows (or equivalent presentations for OCBOA statements); and that, accordingly, the statements are not designed for those who are not informed about such matters. Acknowledgement in the notes to the financial statements is not sufficient. Whether the omission would influence a creditor is not a consideration. (ID: 9932)

22. (b) If the accountant believes that modification of the standard report is not adequate to indicate the deficiencies in the financial statements, taken as whole, the accountant should withdraw from the compilation (or review) engagement and provide no further services concerning those financial statements. It may also be advisable for the accountant to consult with an attorney. (ID: 8828)

23. (a) The compilation report should not include a reference to the original engagement, any review procedures that may have been performed, or scope limitations that resulted in the changed engagement. A reference to a departure from GAAS is not related to the question because an accountant must perform a compilation or review of a nonpublic entity in accordance with SSARS, not GAAS. (ID: 8806)

24. (c) The review report should reflect the basis of accounting used in the corresponding financial statements. There is no requirement that financial statements be prepared in accordance with GAAP; nor must management justify the use of a comprehensive basis of accounting other than GAAP to the accountant. (ID: 90156)

25. (c) In reviewing the financial statements of a nonissuer, the auditor would most likely use ratio analysis as an analytic for developing relationships among balance sheet accounts. Ratios are useful in evaluating an entity's solvency. Ratio analysis that includes relationships between income statement and balance sheet accounts are useful in evaluating operational efficiency and profitability. Ratio analysis provides an indication of the firm's financial strengths and weaknesses. (ID: 5692)

26. (c) Each page of the financial statements reviewed by the accountant should include a reference, such as "See Accountant's Review Report." (ID: 5699)

27. (c) Review engagement procedures generally are limited to inquiries and analytics. Comparison of current-year to prior-year account balances is an analytical procedure. Answers a., b., and d. are audit procedures. (ID: 8168)

28. (d) When a CPA becomes aware of a departure from the applicable financial reporting framework that is material to the financial statements, if the financial statements are not revised, the CPA should consider whether modification of the standard report is adequate to disclose the departure. If the CPA concludes that modification of the standard report is appropriate, the departure should be disclosed in a separate paragraph, including disclosure of the effects of the departure on the financial statements, if such effects have been determined by management or are known as the result of the CPA's procedures. The CPA is not required to determine the effects of a departure if management has not done so, provided the CPA states in the report that such determination has not been made. If modification of the report is not adequate to indicate the deficiencies in the financial statements as a whole, the CPA should withdraw from the engagement and provide no further services with respect to those financial statements. The CPA may also wish to consult with legal counsel. (ID: 6239)

29. (d) A review does not include assessing fraud risk nor does it contemplate obtaining an understanding of the entity's internal control, so the report would not speak to these matters. (ID: 7023)

30. (b) An accountant is precluded from performing a review engagement if the accountant's independence is impaired for any reason. (ID: 5638)

31. (d) A CPA must obtain a representation letter from management to complete a review. If a CPA becomes aware of a departure from GAAP (such as a lack of justification for a change in accounting principles) in the financial statements, the CPA should consider whether the departure can be adequately disclosed by modifying the standard report. If it can, a separate paragraph should be used to disclose the departure. An accountant may review financial statements prepared in accordance with a basis of accounting other than GAAP, such as the income tax basis. A CPA may issue a review report on one financial statement and not on other related financial statements if the scope of the CPA's inquiries and analytical procedures has not been restricted. (ID: 7627)

32. (a) Procedures for conducting a review of financial statements generally are limited to analytical procedures and inquiries. The practitioner does not need to observe internal controls. (ID: 5147)

33. (d) The accountant may be asked to issue a review report on one financial statement, such as a balance sheet, and not on other related financial statements, such as the statements of income, retained earnings, and cash flows. The accountant may do so if the scope of his or her inquiry and analytical procedures has not been restricted. (ID: 7825)

34. (c) The CPA must establish an understanding with the client regarding the services to be performed and document it in an engagement letter for both engagements. Neither engagement contemplates obtaining an understanding of internal control or assessing fraud risk. Only the review report includes a statement that a review is substantially less in scope than an audit, the objective of which is the expression of an opinion regarding the financial statements as a whole. (ID: 8378)

35. (a) A review provides an accountant with a basis for expressing limited assurance on financial statements. Inquiries should be made regarding the client's principles and practices, including the methods used in applying them. In performing a review, it is not intended that the CPA will obtain an understanding of internal control; assess fraud risk; test accounting records; or other procedures normally performed during an audit (such as identifying related-party transactions). (ID: 8379)

36. (b) The standard review report states that a review includes primarily applying analytical procedures to management's financial data and making inquiries of company management. The objective of a compilation is to assist management in presenting financial information in the form of financial statements. In a review, a CPA expresses limited assurance on the financial statements. A CPA is not required to obtain an understanding of the entity's internal control or assess fraud risk in a SSARS review so it would not be included in the report. (ID: 8410)

37. (c) In a review, the accountant must apply analytical procedures, such as the analysis of inventory turnover. A review does not include tests of accounting records through inspection, observation, confirmation, or examination of source documents; or other procedures ordinarily performed in an audit. So the accountant would not perform a physical inspection of inventory or vouch inventory purchase transactions. Nor does a review according to SSARS include obtaining an understanding of the entity's internal control, so the accountant would not evaluate internal control over inventory. (ID: 8619)

38. (d) The analytical procedures the accountant may consider performing when conducting a review of financial statements include comparing current financial information with relevant nonfinancial information. In order to obtain a reasonable basis for the expression of limited assurance, the accountant must apply analytical procedures to the financial statements, as well as make inquiries and obtain representations from management. Analytical procedures include comparing recorded amounts, or ratios developed from recorded amounts, to expectations developed by the accountant. Although analytical procedures are required by GAAS to be included in the both the planning and the final review stage of an audit, this is not a requirement of a review. (ID: 8634)

39. (c) The attainment of corroborating evidence, such as sending a letter of inquiry to the client's attorney, is not a requirement of a review. The other answers make up the performance requirements of a review. (ID: 8635)

40. (b) A review does include making inquiries of management which should include asking about related-party transactions. The successor accountant may wish to review the predecessor's working papers relating to matters of continuing accounting significance and those relating to contingencies. As this is not a requirement, as are inquiries of management, it is not as likely to be performed. In a review the accountant is ordinarily not required to corroborate management's responses with other evidence, so it is not likely that the accountant would contact the entity's attorney. A review according to SSARS does not contemplate obtaining an understanding of the entity's internal control, thus communication of internal control deficiencies to senior management would not be likely. (ID: 8645)

41. (d) A review engagement consists mainly of analytics and inquires of management. Generally, neither a review nor a compilation involves obtaining an understanding of internal control, assessing fraud risk, testing accounting records, or examining source documents. (ID: 90182)

42. (b) When reviewing the financial statements of a nonpublic entity in accordance with SSARS, the accountant is required to obtain a management representation letter. A review differs significantly from an audit of financial statements in which the auditor provides reasonable assurance that the financial statements, taken as a whole, are free of material misstatement. The objective of a review is to express limited assurance that there are no material modifications that should be made to the financial statements in order for them to be in conformity with the applicable financial reporting framework. A review does not contemplate obtaining an understanding of the entity's internal control, thus assessing control risk is not required. Nor does it involve tests of accounting records by obtaining sufficient, appropriate audit evidence via inspection, observation, confirmation or examination of source documents or other procedures usually performed in an audit, so confirmation of account balances and observation of the physical inventory would also not be required. (ID: 8803)

43. (d) The accountant must be independent to issue the review report because although the accountant is not expressing an opinion, limited assurance is being given. The other answers are not true. (ID: 8825)

44. (d) If modification of the standard review (or compilation) report is inadequate to communicate the deficiencies in the financial statements due to departures from GAAP, the accountant should withdraw from the engagement and provide no further services concerning these financial statements. The accountant may wish to consult with legal counsel. Under these circumstances it would not be an option for the accountant to determine the effects of the departures and issue a special report; disclaim an opinion; or change from a review engagement to a compilation engagement because the accountant is precluded from providing further services with respect to these financial statements. (ID: 9352)

45. (b) When reviewing the financial statements of a nonissuer in accordance with SSARS, a CPA would ordinarily compare the financial statements with budgets or forecasts. A review does not contemplate obtaining an understanding of the entity's internal control or assessing control risk; assessing fraud risk; tests of accounting records by obtaining sufficient appropriate audit evidence through inspection, observation, confirmation, or the examination of source documents or other procedures ordinarily performed in an audit. (ID: 9368)

46. (a) An accountant reviewing a company's financial statements in accordance with SSARS is required to obtain knowledge of the client's industry. Sending bank confirmations, observing a client's physical inventory, and corroboration of management's responses to inquiries with other evidence are audit procedures which are not required in a review engagement. (ID: 9392)

47. (a) If the owner of a company is the accountant's father, the accountant would be precluded from issuing a review report on a company's financial statements in accordance with SSARS because independence is required. The other answers would not preclude an accountant from performing a review. Note: The accountant engaged to review only the balance sheet may do so if the scope of the accountant's inquiry and analytical procedures has not been restricted. (ID: 9398)

48. (c) The statement that a review consists principally of performing analytical procedures and making inquiries about the interim financial information is not appropriate for inclusion in a management representation letter; rather, it should be included in the engagement letter to provide information about the CPA's responsibilities. Written representations from management ordinarily confirm representations explicitly or implicitly given to the auditor; indicate and document the continuing appropriateness of such representations; and reduce the possibility of misunderstanding concerning the matters that are the subject of the representations. The other answers are appropriate statements for inclusion in a management representation letter for all reviews. (ID: 9921)

49. (b) No review, interim or annual, performed according to the SSARS contemplates obtaining an understanding of the client's internal controls, much less testing controls to evaluate their effectiveness. An interim review performed according to GAAS for a nonissuer or PCAOB audit standards for an issuer does require obtaining an understanding of the client's internal control as it relates to the preparation of both annual and interim financial information, but does not involve testing controls. The other answers would typically be done during a review engagement which consists principally of performing analytical procedures and making inquiries of person responsible for financial and accounting matters. (ID: 9922)

50. (d) Reviews consist principally of performing analytical procedures and making inquiries of persons within the entity responsible for financial and accounting matters. Reviews do not contemplate the obtainment of corroborating evidence. The other answers describe procedures typically performed during a review engagement. (ID: 9949)

51. (c) Independence is required to issue a review report. While the notes to the financial statements must disclose the change in accounting principles, the accountant is not required to mention the change in accounting principles in the review report, although an explanatory paragraph emphasizing the matter is permissible. A review report must disclaim an opinion on the interim financial statements taken as a whole and then state whether the accountant is aware of any material modification that should be made to the accompanying interim financial statements for them to be in conformity with the applicable financial reporting framework. An accountant need not obtain sufficient evidence to afford a reasonable basis for an opinion; the accountant may not express an opinion in a review report. (ID: 90196)

52. (a) When a CPA concludes that there is reasonable justification to change the engagement, the CPA should comply with the standards applicable to a review engagement and issue an appropriate review report which would include a statement that a review is substantially less in scope than an audit, the objective of which is the expression of an opinion regarding the financial statements as a whole, and that, accordingly, the CPA does not express such an opinion. The report should not include a reference to: the scope limitation that caused the changed engagement; any description of audit procedures that may have been performed before the engagement was changed; nor the original engagement—reference to the CPA's justification for agreeing to change the engagement would constitute a reference to the original engagement. (ID: 9909)

53. (a) Compiled financial statements that omit substantially all of the disclosures required by GAAP are not comparable to financial statements that include such disclosures. Accordingly, the accountant should not issue a report on the comparative financial statements when statements for one or more, but not all, of the periods presented omit substantially all of the disclosures required by GAAP. (ID: 2757)

54. (c) When the current period financial statements of a nonissuer have been compiled or reviewed and those of the prior period have been audited, the accountant should issue an appropriate compilation or review report on the current period financial statements and either the report on the prior period should be reissued or the report on the current period should include as a separate paragraph an appropriate description of the responsibility assumed for the financial statements of the prior period. In the latter case, the separate paragraph should indicate (a) that the financial statements of the prior period were audited previously, (b) the date of the previous report, (c) the type of opinion expressed previously, (d) if the opinion was other than unqualified, the substantive reasons therefore, and (e) that no auditing procedures were performed after the date of the previous report. (ID: 5152)

55. (d) Either reissuance or reference in a separate paragraph is acceptable. (ID: 4754)

56. (d) Before reissuing a compilation (or review) report on the financial statements of a nonissuer for the prior year, the predecessor accountant is required to (1) read the financial statements of the current period and the successor's report; (2) compare the prior period financial statements with those previously issued and with those of the current period; and (3) obtain a letter from the successor that indicates whether the successor is aware of any matter that might have a material effect on the financial statements, including disclosures, reported on by the predecessor—the predecessor should not refer in the reissued report to this letter or to the report of the successor. In a compilation engagement the accountant is not required to make inquiries or perform other procedures to verify, corroborate, or review information supplied by the entity. The predecessor is not required to review the successor's working papers for matters affecting the prior year—the predecessor may rely on a review of the financial statements of the current period and the successor's report as well as the letter from the successor just described in (3) to identify any matters affecting the prior year. The predecessor is not required to verify that the reissued report will not be used to obtain credit from a financial institution. (ID: 9367)

57. (a) When the current period financial statements of a nonissuer have been compiled or reviewed and those of the prior period have been audited, the CPA should issue an appropriate compilation or review report on the current period financial statements and either the report on the prior period should be reissued or the report on the current period should include, as a separate paragraph, an appropriate description of the responsibility assumed for the financial statements of the prior period. In the latter case, the separate paragraph should indicate (1) that the financial statements of the prior period were audited previously; (2) the date of the previous report; (3) the type of opinion expressed previously; (4) if the opinion was other than unqualified, the substantive reasons; and (5) that no auditing procedures were performed after the date of the previous report. The reasons for a review in the current period vs. the audit in the prior period should not be included and neither should the fact that the assessment of control risk (an audit procedure) was not updated. There is nothing in the question that indicates that the prior year's audit report should no longer be relied on. (ID: 9908)

Solution 13-2 SIMULATION ANSWER: Compilation & Review Requirements

Each of the following items represents a series of unrelated procedures that an accountant may consider performing in separate engagements to review the financial statements of a nonissuer (a review) and to compile the financial statements of a nonissuer (a compilation) according to SSARS. Select, as the best answer for each item, whether the procedure is required (R) or not required (N) for **both** review and compilation engagements.

Procedures	Required / Not Required	
	Compilation	**Review**
1. The accountant should establish an understanding with the entity regarding the nature and limitations of the services to be performed.	R	R
2. The accountant should make inquiries concerning actions taken at the board of directors' meetings.	N	R
3. The accountant, as the entity's successor accountant, should communicate with the predecessor accountant to obtain access to the predecessor's working papers.	N	N
4. The accountant should obtain a level of knowledge of the accounting principles and practices of the entity's industry.	R	R
5. The accountant should obtain an understanding of the entity's internal control structure.	N	N
6. The accountant should perform analytical procedures designed to identify relationships that appear to be unusual.	N	R
7. The accountant should make an assessment of the fraud risk.	N	N

1. R, R

The accountant should establish an understanding with management regarding the services to be performed for both engagements and should document the understanding through a written communication (in the form of an engagement letter) with management.

2. N, R

The accountant is not required to make inquiries about information supplied by the client in a compilation engagement. Inquiries concerning actions taken at meetings of stockholders, board of directors, committees of the board of directors, or comparable meetings that may affect the financial statements should be made in a review engagement.

3. N, N

The successor accountant may wish to review the predecessor's working papers. This step is not required in either a compilation or a review.

4. R, R

For both engagements, the accountant should possess a level of knowledge of the accounting principles and practices of the industry in which the entity operates.

5. N, N

Neither engagement contemplates obtaining an understanding of the entity's internal control structure.

6. N, R

The accountant is not required to perform such procedures for a compilation; however, such analytics are required for a review.

7. N, N

Neither engagement contemplates assessing fraud risk. (ID: 9243)

Solution 13-3 SIMULATION ANSWER: Review Report

Wallace & Wallace, CPAs, audited the financial statements of West Co., a nonissuer, for the year ended September 30, 20X1, and expressed an unqualified opinion. For the year ended September 30, 20X2, West issued comparative financial statements. Wallace & Wallace reviewed West's year 2 financial statements and Gordon, an assistant on the engagement, drafted the review report below. Martin, the engagement supervisor, decided not to reissue the prior year's audit report, but instructed Gordon to include a separate paragraph in the current year's review report describing the responsibility assumed for the prior year's audited financial statements.

Martin reviewed Gordon's draft and indicated that there were many deficiencies in Gordon's draft.

Accountant's Review Report

We have reviewed the accompanying balance sheet of West Company as of September 30, 20X2, and the related statements of income and cash flows for the year then ended. A review includes primarily applying analytical procedures to management's financial data and making inquiries of company management. A review also includes assessing the accounting principles used and significant estimates made by management, as well as evaluating the overall financial statement presentation.

Management is responsible for the preparation and fair presentation of the financial statements in accordance with accounting principles generally accepted in the United States of America.

Our responsibility is to conduct the review in accordance with standards issued by the American Institute of Certified Public Accountants. Those standards require us to perform procedures to obtain limited assurance that there are no material modifications that should be made to the financial statements. We believe that the results of our procedures provide a reasonable basis for our report.

Based on our review, we are not aware of any material modifications that should be made to the accompanying financial statements. Accordingly, the accompanying financial statements have been prepared assuming that the company will continue as a going concern. Furthermore, we have no responsibility to update this report for events and circumstances occurring after the date of this report.

The financial statements for the year ended September 30, 20X1, were audited by us and we expressed an unqualified opinion on them in our report dated November 7, 20X1, but we have not performed any auditing procedures since that date. In our opinion, the financial statements referred to above are presented fairly, in all material respects, for the year then ended in conformity with generally accepted accounting principles.

Wallace & Wallace, CPAs

November 6, 20X2

Each of the following items represents a deficiency noted by Martin. For each deficiency, indicate whether Martin is correct (M); Gordon is correct (G); or both Martin and Gordon are incorrect (B).

Report Deficiencies Noted by Martin	M / G / B
1. There should be a reference to the prior year's audited financial statements in the first (introductory) paragraph.	G
2. All of the current year's basic financial statements are not properly identified in the first (introductory) paragraph.	M
3. The standards referred to in the third (accountant's responsibilities) paragraph should not be standards issued by the American Institute of Certified Public Accountants, but should be Standards for the Compilation and Review of Financial Statements.	B
4. The title of the report should be Independent Accountant's Review Report.	B
5. The statement in the third paragraph that the accountant is required to perform procedures to obtain limited assurance that there are no material modifications that should be made to the financial statements should be in the introductory paragraph following the description of a review.	G
6. There should be a statement in the second (management's responsibilities) paragraph that describes management's responsibilities relative to internal control.	M
7. There should be a comparison of the scope of a review to an audit in the introductory paragraph.	M
8. There should be no reference to "assessing the accounting principles used," "significant estimates made by management," and "evaluating the overall financial statement presentation" in the introductory paragraph.	M

1. G Gordon is correct. The first paragraph of the report should not include a reference to the prior year's audited financial statements. The standard review report should be issued on the current period statements and the prior period report should be reissued or a separate paragraph should be added to the current period report which describes the responsibility assumed for the financial statements of the prior period.

2. M Martin is correct. The statement of retained earnings should be listed in the first paragraph.

3. B Both are incorrect. The review should be conducted in accordance with Statements on Standards for Accounting and Review Services which are issued by the AICPA.

4. B Both are incorrect. The title should clearly indicate that it is the accountant's review repot and should include the word *independent*.

5. G Gordon is correct. The statement should be in the third (accountant's responsibilities) paragraph.

6. M Martin is correct. The following should be part of the statement regarding management's responsibilities: "...and for designing, implementing, and maintaining internal control relevant to the preparation and fair presentation of the financial statements."

7. M Martin is correct. The introductory paragraph of the review report should include the following comparison of the scope of a review to an audit: "A review is substantially less in scope than an audit, the objective of which is the expression of an opinion regarding the financial statements as a whole."

8. M Martin is correct. These phrases are part of the scope paragraph of the standard audit report. This is a review report. (ID: 9241)

Solution 13-4 SIMULATION ANSWER: Review Report

Wallace & Wallace, CPAs, audited the financial statements of West Co., a nonissuer, for the year ended September 30, 20X1, and expressed an unqualified opinion. For the year ended September 30, 20X2, West issued comparative financial statements. Wallace & Wallace reviewed West's year 2 financial statements and Gordon, an assistant on the engagement, drafted the review report below. Martin, the engagement supervisor, decided not to reissue the prior year's audit report, but instructed Gordon to include a separate paragraph in the current year's review report describing the responsibility assumed for the prior year's audited financial statements.

Martin reviewed Gordon's draft and indicated that there were many deficiencies in Gordon's draft.

Accountant's Review Report

We have reviewed the accompanying balance sheet of West Company as of September 30, 20X2, and the related statements of income and cash flows for the year then ended. A review includes primarily applying analytical procedures to management's financial data and making inquiries of company management. A review also includes assessing the accounting principles used and significant estimates made by management, as well as evaluating the overall financial statement presentation.

Management is responsible for the preparation and fair presentation of the financial statements in accordance with accounting principles generally accepted in the United States of America.

Our responsibility is to conduct the review in accordance with standards issued by the American Institute of Certified Public Accountants. Those standards require us to perform procedures to obtain limited assurance that there are no material modifications that should be made to the financial statements. We believe that the results of our procedures provide a reasonable basis for our report.

Based on our review, we are not aware of any material modifications that should be made to the accompanying financial statements. Accordingly, the accompanying financial statements have been prepared assuming that the company will continue as a going concern. Furthermore, we have no responsibility to update this report for events and circumstances occurring after the date of this report.

The financial statements for the year ended September 30, 20X1, were audited by us and we expressed an unqualified opinion on them in our report dated November 7, 20X1, but we have not performed any auditing procedures since that date. In our opinion, the financial statements referred to above are presented fairly, in all material respects, for the year then ended in conformity with generally accepted accounting principles.

Wallace & Wallace, CPAs

November 6, 20X2

Each of the following items represents a deficiency noted by Martin. For each deficiency, indicate whether Martin is correct and Gordon is incorrect (M); Gordon is correct and Martin is incorrect (G); or both Martin and Gordon are incorrect (B).

Report Deficiencies Noted by Martin	M / G / B
1. There should be a reference to "conformity with generally accepted accounting principles" in the fourth paragraph.	M
2. There should be a reference to consistency in the fourth paragraph.	G
3. There should be a restriction on the distribution of the accountant's review report in the fourth paragraph.	G
4. The reference to "going concern" in the fourth paragraph should be in the first paragraph.	B
5. The accountant's lack of responsibility to update the report in the fourth paragraph should be in the first paragraph.	B
6. There should be no mention of the type of opinion expressed on the prior year's audited financial statements in the fifth (separate) paragraph.	G
7. All of the prior year's basic financial statements are not properly identified in the fifth (separate) paragraph.	G
8. The reference in the fifth (separate) paragraph to the fair presentation of the prior year's audited financial statements in accordance with generally accepted accounting principles should be omitted.	M
9. The report should be dual dated to indicate the date of the prior year's auditor's report.	G

1. M Martin is correct. The fourth paragraph should include a reference to "conformity with generally accepted accounting principles."

2. G Gordon is correct. The standard review report does not refer to consistency.

3. G Gordon is correct. The standard review report does not contain a restriction on distribution.

4. B Both are incorrect. The standard review report does not contain a reference to a "going concern."

5. B Both are incorrect. The statement regarding responsibility to update the report should be omitted.

6. G Gordon is correct. The fifth paragraph should describe the responsibility the CPA is assuming for the financial statements of the prior period. Specifically, it should indicate (1) that the prior period's financial statements were audited previously; (2) the date of the previous report; (3) the type of opinion that was previously expressed; (4) if the opinion was other than qualified, the reasons; and (5) that no auditing procedures have been performed since the date of the previous report.

7. G Gordon is correct. A list of the basic financial statements is not required in the fifth paragraph.

8. M Martin is correct. The reference in the fifth paragraph to the fair presentation of the prior year's audited financial statements in accordance with generally accepted accounting principles should be omitted.

9. G Gordon is correct. The report should be dated as of the completion of the inquiry and analytical procedures; the report should not be dual dated. The fifth paragraph correctly indicates the date of the audit report for the prior year's financial statements. (ID: 9245)

Solution 13-5 SIMULATION ANSWER: Research

Before submission of compiled financial statements, the accountant should read the financial statements and consider whether such financial statements appear to be appropriate in form and free from obvious material errors. Which section of the professional standards defines the term *error* in this context?

AR	§ 80	12	(ID: 89463)

.12 Before submission, the accountant should read the financial statements and consider whether such financial statements appear to be appropriate in form and free from obvious material errors. In this context, the term *error* refers to mistakes in the preparation of financial statements, including arithmetical or clerical mistakes, and mistakes in the application of accounting principles, including inadequate disclosure.

CHAPTER 14

ATTESTATION ENGAGEMENTS

AU Identifier Used for Clarified GAAS in This Textbook

We have not continued to use the temporary AU-C identifier for the clarified auditing standards issued by the American Institute of Certified Public Accountants (AICPA). In this textbook these standards have an AU identifier.

CHAPTER 14

ATTESTATION ENGAGEMENTS

I. Overview of Attestation Standards

A. Attestation Engagements

1. **Attestation** An attest engagement is one in which a CPA in public practice (i.e., practitioner) is engaged to, or does, issue an examination, review, compilation or agreed-upon procedures report on subject matter, or an assertion about subject matter, that is the responsibility of another party (usually management). An attest engagement may be part of a larger engagement, for example, a feasibility study or business acquisition study that includes an examination of prospective financial information.

2. **Applicability** Attestation services include: agreed-upon procedures (excluding letters to underwriters and consulting services or any attest engagement concerning assertions about solvency); financial forecasts and projections; pro forma financial statements; internal control over financial reporting; compliance reporting (regulatory or contractual); and Management's Discussion and Analysis. An attest engagement can be: an audit or other engagement under SAS; a review of financial statements under SSARS; an examination of prospective financial information under SSAE; or any engagement under PCAOB. It does not include any other SSAE engagement (such as a review or agreed-upon procedure), nor does it include compilations under SSARS.

3. **Degrees of Responsibility** AT 20, *Defining Professional Requirements in Statements on Standards for Attestation Engagements*, defines two kinds of requirements that describe the practitioner's degrees of responsibility.

   a. **Unconditional Requirements** The practitioner is required to comply with an unconditional requirement in all cases in which the requirement applies. The words *must* or *is required* indicate an unconditional requirement.

   b. **Presumptively Mandatory Requirements** The practitioner is also required to comply with a presumptively mandatory requirement in all cases in which the requirement applies. However, in rare circumstances, the practitioner may depart from such a requirement provided the practitioner documents the justification in the workpapers and the alternative procedures performed to achieve the objectives of that requirement. The word *should* indicates a presumptively mandatory requirement.

4. **Subsequent Events** Attest standards define subsequent events in essentially the manner as for audits performed in accordance with GAAS. While the practitioner has no responsibility to detect subsequent events, the practitioner should inquire of the responsible party (and the client, if different) as to whether they are aware of any subsequent events through the report date. The representation letter ordinarily contains a representation about subsequent events.

5. **Subject Matter** The subject matter of an attest engagement may take many forms, including: (a) historical or prospective financial information, performance measurements, backlog data; (b) physical characteristics, e.g., descriptions, square footage of facilities; (c) historical events, e.g., the market price of products or services at a specific time; (d) analyses, e.g., break-even analyses, target profit levels; (e) systems and processes, e.g., internal control; and (f) behavior, e.g., corporate governance, compliance with laws and regulations, human resource practices.

6. **Written Assertion** An assertion is any declaration(s) about whether subject matter is based on, or in conformity with, selected criteria. A CPA may attest to a written assertion or directly on the subject matter. In either situation, the CPA typically obtains a written assertion in an examination or a review engagement. A written assertion may be presented to the CPA in several ways, including: a narrative description, a schedule, or as part of a representation letter which clearly identifies what is being presented and the point in time or period of time covered. Without a written assertion, the CPA still may report on the subject matter; however, the CPA needs to exercise caution and ensure that interested parties clearly understand the subject matter in question, including restricting use of the report, when appropriate.

7. **Trust Services** Trust Services are a set of professional assurance services based on a framework comprised of a core set of principles and criteria. The framework addresses risk and opportunities associated with information technology. SysTrust and WebTrust are two specific services jointly developed by the AICPA and the Canadian Institute of Chartered Accountants. Engagements use the following five principles and criteria: security; availability; processing integrity; online privacy; and confidentiality.

   a. **WebTrust** Practitioners who obtain a WebTrust business license from can provide assurance services to evaluate and test whether a particular eCommerce service meets the selected principles and criteria. The WebTrust seal of assurance is placed on the organization's web site following the engagement and signifies the practitioner's unqualified opinion.

   b. **SysTrust** A SysTrust engagement allows practitioners to provide assurance on the reliability of a system.

B. Attestation Standards

The AICPA Code of Professional Conduct requires an AICPA member who performs an attestation engagement to comply with Statements on Standards for Attestation Engagements (SSAE). SSAE are codified within the framework of the 11 attestation standards. Attestation interpretations are recommendations on the application of SSAE in specific circumstances. The practitioner should be aware of and consider attestation interpretations applicable to the attestation engagement. If the practitioner does not apply the attestation guidance included in an applicable attestation interpretation, the practitioner should be prepared to explain how he or she complied with SSAE provisions addressed by such attestation guidance.

1. **Applicability** SSAE do not apply to: audits; reviews and compilations of financial statements of nonissuers under SSARS; tax return preparation; advocating, consulting, or advisory services; or operational audits.

2. **General Standards**

   a. **Training and Proficiency** The practitioner must have adequate technical training and proficiency to perform the attestation engagement.

   b. **Knowledge** The practitioner must have adequate knowledge in the subject matter. The CPA may use specialists, provided that the CPA has enough knowledge of the subject matter (1) to communicate to the specialist the objectives of the work, and (2) to evaluate the specialist's work to determine if the objectives were achieved.

   c. **Criteria** The practitioner must have reason to believe that the subject matter is capable of evaluation against criteria that are suitable and available to users. Suitable criteria must be objective, measurable, complete, and relevant.

   d. **Independence** The practitioner must maintain independence in mental attitude in all matters relating to the engagement.

   e. **Due Professional Care** The practitioner must exercise due professional care in the planning and performance of the engagement and the preparation of the report.

3. **Fieldwork Standards**

   a. **Planning and Supervision** The practitioner must adequately plan the work and must properly supervise any assistants.

   b. **Evidence** The practitioner must obtain appropriate sufficient evidence to provide a reasonable basis for the conclusion that is expressed in the report.

4. **Reporting Standards**

   a. **Identification** The practitioner must identify the subject matter or the assertion being reported on and state the character of the engagement in the report. If the attestation is on an assertion, the assertion must accompany, or be restated within, the CPA's report. The statement of the character of an attest engagement designed to result in a general-use report (i.e., an examination or a review) includes two elements: (1) a description of the nature and scope of the work performed, and (2) a reference to the professional (AICPA) standards governing the engagement.

   b. **Disclose Reservations** The practitioner must state all of the practitioner's significant reservations about the engagement subject matter and, if applicable, the assertion related thereto in the report.

      (1) **Unresolved Problem** Reservations about the engagement refers to any unresolved problem the CPA had in complying with the standards and guidance applicable to attestation services or procedures agreed to by the specified parties. An unqualified conclusion should not be expressed if the CPA has been unable to apply all the procedures considered necessary to comply with attestation standards.

      (2) **Scope Restrictions** Restrictions on the scope of the engagement, whether imposed by the client or by other circumstances, may require the CPA to qualify the report, to disclaim any assurance, or to withdraw from the engagement. When restrictions that significantly limit the scope of the engagement are imposed by the client, the CPA generally should either withdraw from the engagement or disclaim any assurance on the subject matter, assertions, or presentation. An incomplete review engagement requires the CPA to withdraw.

   c. **Conclusion** The practitioner must state the practitioner's conclusion about the subject matter or the assertion in relation to the criteria against which the subject matter was evaluated in the report.

      (1) **Misstatements** If deviations from the criteria or material misstatements exist, the practitioner should modify the report, directly expressing an opinion on the subject matter, rather than the assertion.

      (2) **Materiality** The CPA should consider the idea of materiality in applying this standard. Materiality is determined by the relative size of a misstated or omitted fact, rather than by its absolute amount. Materiality considerations include whether a reasonable person relying on the presentation of assertions would be influenced by the inclusion or correction of an individual assertion.

   d. **Restrictions** The practitioner must state in the report that the report is intended solely for the information and use of the specified parties under the following circumstances

      (1) When the criteria used to evaluate the subject matter are available only to specified parties

      (2) When reporting on subject matter and a written assertion has not been provided by the responsible party

(3) When the report is on an attestation engagement to apply agreed-upon procedures to the subject matter

When a report is restricted as to use, it contains a separate final paragraph that includes the following types of statements: (1) indicate the report is intended solely for the use of the specified parties, (2) identify the specified parties, and (3) indicate the report is not intended to be, and should not be, used by anyone other than the specified parties.

C. **Report Components**
Standard reports for examinations and reviews share some elements:

1. **Title** The title includes the word *independent*, a signature, and a date.

2. **Responsible Party's Responsibility** A statement that the subject matter [or, assertion] is the responsible party's responsibility.

3. **Identification** An identification of the subject matter [or, assertion] and the responsible party. If the assertion doesn't accompany the practitioner's report, the first paragraph of the report also contains a statement of the assertion.

4. **Restriction** A statement restricting the report use to specified parties

D. **Conclusions**
Three types of conclusions can be issued by the accountant:

1. **Examination** Examinations represent the highest level of assurance. They usually include: search; verification; inquiry; and analysis procedures.

   a. **Report** When CPAs are engaged to express an opinion as the result of an attestation engagement, they should state clearly whether: (1) management's assertion is presented (or fairly stated), in all material respects, based on (or in conformity with) the established/stated criteria, or (2) the subject matter of the assertion is based on (or in conformity with) the established or stated criteria in all material respects.

   b. **Modifications** Reports expressing a positive opinion on the reliability of an assertion may be qualified or modified for an aspect of the subject matter, assertion, or the engagement. In addition, examination reports may emphasize certain matters relating to the attest engagement, subject matter, or assertion. Remember, if deviations from the criteria or material misstatements exist, the practitioner should modify the report, directly expressing an opinion on the subject matter, rather than the assertion.

2. **Review** A review report provides limited assurance. They usually include: inquiry and analysis procedures. The CPA's report states whether any information came to the CPA's attention on the basis of the work performed that indicates that the subject matter is materially misstated or divergent from criteria; or that assertions are not presented in all material respects in conformity with criteria. The report: (a) indicates that the work performed was less in scope than an examination, (b) disclaims a positive opinion on the assertions, and (c) contains a statement of limitations on the use of the report when it has been prepared in conformity with specified criteria that have been agreed upon by the specified parties because it is intended solely for specified parties.

Exhibit 1 ▶ Examination Report on a Subject Matter

Independent Accountant's Report

We have examined the [*identify the subject matter—for example, the accompanying schedule of investment returns of XYZ Company for the year ended December 31, 20XX*]. XYZ Company's management is responsible for the schedule of investment returns. Our responsibility is to express an opinion based on our examination.

Our examination was conducted in accordance with attestation standards established by the American Institute of Certified Public Accountants and, accordingly, included examining, on a test basis, evidence supporting [*identify the subject matter—for example, XYZ Company's schedule of investment returns*] and performing such other procedures as we considered necessary in the circumstances. We believe that our examination provides a reasonable basis for our opinion.

[*Additional paragraph(s) may be added to emphasize certain matters relating to the attest engagement or the subject matter.*]

In our opinion, the schedule referred to above presents, in all material respects, [*identify the subject matter—for example, the investment returns of XYZ Company for the year ended December 31, 20XX*] based on [*identify criteria—for example, the ABC criteria set forth in Note 1*].

[*Signature*]

[*Date*]

Exhibit 2 ▶ Review Report on an Assertion About a Subject Matter (Restricted)

Independent Accountant's Report

We have reviewed management's assertion that [*identify the assertion—for example, the accompanying schedule of investment returns of XYZ Company for the year ended December 31, 20XX is presented in accordance with the ABC criteria referred to in Note 1*]. XYZ Company's management is responsible for the assertion.

Our review was conducted in accordance with attestation standards established by the American Institute of Certified Public Accountants. A review is substantially less in scope than an examination, the objective of which is the expression of an opinion on management's assertion. Accordingly, we do not express such an opinion.

[*Additional paragraph(s) may be added to emphasize certain matters relating to the attest engagement or the assertion.*]

Based on our review, nothing came to our attention that caused us to believe that management's assertion referred to above is not fairly stated, in all material respects, based on [*identify the criteria—for example, the ABC criteria referred to in the investment management agreement between XYZ Company and DEF Investment Managers, Ltd., dated November 15, 20X1*].

This report is intended solely for the information and use of XYZ Company and [*identify other specified parties—for example, DEF Investment Managers, Ltd.*] and is not intended to be and should not be used by anyone other than these specified parties.

[*Signature*]

[*Date*]

Editor Note: Although suitable criteria exist for the subject matter, the report in exhibit 2 is restricted as to use because the criteria are available only to specified parties; otherwise, the paragraph restricting the use of the report would be omitted.

3. **Agreed-upon Procedures** No assurance is provided, but procedures and findings are listed. See next section for more detailed information.

II. Agreed-Upon Procedures

A. Definition

An agreed-upon procedures engagement is one in which a practitioner is engaged to issue a report of findings based on specific procedures performed on subject matter; a written assertion is not required. The nature, extent, and timing of procedures may vary widely. The specified parties assume responsibility for the sufficiency of the procedures since they best understand their own needs.

B. Required Conditions

To satisfy the agreement and responsibility requirements listed here, the practitioner ordinarily communicates directly with, and obtains affirming acknowledgments from, each specified party.

1. **Independence** The practitioner must be independent
2. **Responsibility** The client takes responsibility for the sufficiency of the agreed-upon procedures for their purpose, or a third party assumes responsible for the subject matter
3. **Procedures and Criteria** The specified parties and the practitioner agree upon procedures to be performed by the practitioner, the criteria to be used in the determination of findings, and any materiality limits
4. **Measurement** The specific subject matter is subject to reasonably consistent measurement. The procedures are expected to result in reasonably consistent findings using the criteria. Evidential matter related to the specific subject matter is expected to exist to provide a reasonable basis for expressing findings in the practitioner's report
5. **Restricted Report** Use of the report is restricted to the specified parties
6. **Disclosure** For engagements involving prospective financial information, the prospective financial statements must include a summary of significant assumptions
7. **Specialist** The specified parties and the practitioner must agree explicitly on the involvement of a specialist.
8. **Internal Auditors and Other Personnel** The agreed-upon procedures are to be performed entirely by the practitioner and any assisting specialists; however, internal auditors or other client personnel may prepare schedules or provide other information for the practitioner's use in performing the procedures.

C Report Components

The practitioner reports all findings from applying the agreed-upon procedures. The concept of materiality is inapplicable unless the specified parties and the practitioner have established a definition of materiality. The practitioner's report should contain the following elements:

1. A title, including the word *independent*, a signature, and a date
2. An identification of the character of the engagement, the subject matter, and the parties
3. A statement that the procedures performed were those agreed to by the specified parties, and that the engagement was conducted in accordance with attestation standards established by the AICPA
4. A statement that the sufficiency of the procedures is solely the specified parties' responsibility and a disclaimer of responsibility on the part of the practitioner for the sufficiency of the procedures
5. A list of, or reference to, the procedures performed and related findings
6. Where applicable, a description of any agreed-upon materiality limits

7. A statement that the practitioner did not conduct an examination of the subject matter, the objective of which would be the expression of an opinion on the subject matter; and a statement that if the practitioner had performed additional procedures, other matters might have come to his or her attention that would have been reported

8. A statement restricting the report use because it is intended solely for the use of specified parties

9. Where applicable, a description of the assistance provided by a specialist

Exhibit 3 ▶ Report on Agreed-Upon Procedures

Independent Accountant's Report on Applying Agreed-Upon Procedures

To the Board of Directors and Management of X Company:

We have performed the procedures enumerated below, which were agreed to by the Board of Directors and Management of X Company, solely to assist you in connection with the proposed acquisition of Y Company as of December 31, 20XX. Y Company is responsible for its cash and accounts receivable records. This agreed-upon procedures engagement was conducted in accordance with attestation standards established by the American Institute of Certified Public Accountants. The sufficiency of these procedures is solely the responsibility of the parties specified in this report. Consequently, we make no representation regarding the sufficiency of the procedures described below either for the purpose for which this report has been requested or for any other purpose.

[include paragraphs to enumerate procedures and findings]

We were not engaged to and did not conduct an audit, the objective of which would be the expression of an opinion on cash and accounts receivable. Accordingly, we do not express such an opinion. Had we performed additional procedures, other matters might have come to our attention that would have been reported to you.

This report is intended solely for the information and use of the board of directors and management of X Company and is not intended to be and should not be used by anyone other than these specified parties.

[*Signature*]

[*Date*]

D. Other Requirements

1. **Explanatory Language** The practitioner may include explanations about issues such as the following: (a) disclosures of stipulated facts, assumptions, or interpretations used in applying procedures; (b) condition of records, controls, or data; (c) a statement that the practitioner has no responsibility to update the report.

2. **Scope Limitations** When the situation imposes restrictions on the performance of procedures, the practitioner should obtain agreement from the specified parties to modify the agreed-upon procedures, describe any restrictions in the report, or withdraw from the engagement.

3. **Outside Knowledge** The practitioner need not perform additional procedures, but if a matter comes to the practitioner's attention that significantly contradicts the subject matter, the practitioner should include this matter in the report.

4. **Request to Change Engagement Type** If the practitioner concludes, based on professional judgment, that there is reasonable justification to change the engagement, and provided the practitioner complies with the standards applicable to that engagement, the practitioner issues the report appropriate to the new engagement type. This report should not include reference to either the original engagement or performance limitations that resulted in a different engagement.

III. Financial Forecasts and Projections

A. Guidance

AT 301, *Financial Forecasts and Projections*, establishes guidance concerning performance and reporting for engagements to examine, compile, or apply agreed-upon procedures to prospective financial statements (PFS). Pro Forma financial statements show what past financial results would have been if something had been different; they are not considered to be PFS.

B. Definitions

1. **Financial Forecast** PFS that present, to the best of the responsible party's knowledge and belief, an entity's expected financial position, results of operations, and cash flows. A financial forecast may be expressed in specific monetary amounts as a single-point estimate of forecasted results or as a range.

2. **Financial Projection** PFS that present, to the best of the responsible party's knowledge and belief, given one or more hypothetical assumptions, an entity's expected financial position, results of operations, and cash flows. A financial projection sometimes is prepared to present one or more hypothetical courses of action for evaluation. It answers the question, "What would happen if...?" It may also contain a range.

C. Restrictions

1. **General Use** Refers to the use of PFS by persons with whom the responsible party is not negotiating directly. Since users are unable to ask questions of the responsible party, the presentation most useful to them is one that portrays, to the best of the responsible party's knowledge and belief, the expected results. Only a financial forecast is appropriate for general use.

2. **Limited Use** Refers to the use of PFS by the responsible party alone or by the responsible party and third parties with whom the responsible party is negotiating directly. Third-party recipients of PFS intended for limited use can ask questions of the responsible party and directly negotiate terms with it. Any type of PFS that would be useful in the circumstances normally is appropriate for limited use. The presentation may be a financial forecast or a financial projection.

D. Report Components

1. **Formats** The practitioner may perform a compilation report, an examination (usually to be used by a third party), or an agreed-upon procedures report. A review of PFS is not permitted.

2. **Common Elements** Standard reports for the three engagements share some elements: (a) a caveat that the prospective results might not be achieved; (b) a statement that the CPA assumes no responsibility to update the report for events and circumstances occurring after the date of the report; (c) the practitioner's signature; and (d) the date of the completion of the CPA's procedures.

3. **Compilation of PFS** A compilation of PFS involves (a) assembling the PFS based on the responsible party's assumptions, (b) performing the required compilation procedures, including reading the statements and considering whether they are appropriate and are presented in conformity with AICPA presentation guidelines, and (c) issuing a compilation report. Independence is **not** necessary for a compilation engagement.

   a. **Limited Procedures** A compilation is not intended to provide assurance on the PFS or the assumptions underlying such statements. Because of the limited nature of the CPA's procedures, a compilation does not provide assurance that the CPA will become aware of significant matters that might be disclosed by more extensive procedures.

   b. **Assumptions** Since this summary is essential to the reader's understanding of PFS, the CPA should not compile PFS that exclude disclosure of the summary of significant assumptions. Also, the CPA should not compile a financial projection that omits (1) an identification of the hypothetical assumptions or (2) a description of the limitations on the usefulness of the presentation.

   c. **Obviously Inappropriate** The practitioner should consider when representations or other information appear to be obviously inappropriate, incomplete, etc., and if so, should attempt to clarify the matter. If the matter is not clarified, the practitioner ordinarily withdraws from the engagement.

4. **Compilation Reports** In addition to the previously discussed elements, the standard compilation report includes: (a) identification of the PFS presented by the responsible party; (b) a statement that the CPA has compiled the PFS in accordance with attestation standards established by the AICPA; and (c) a statement that a compilation is limited in scope and does not enable the CPA to express an opinion or any other form of assurance on the PFS or the assumptions.

Exhibit 4 ▸ Compilation Report on a Forecast / Projection

We have compiled the accompanying forecasted [projected] balance sheet, statements of income, retained earnings, and cash flows of XYZ Company as of December 31, 20X1, and for the year then ending, in accordance with attestation standards established by the American Institute of Certified Public Accountants. [*If for a projection add:* The accompanying projection was prepared for *(state special purpose, for example, "the purpose of negotiating a loan to expand XYZ Company's plant")*.]

A compilation is limited to presenting in the form of a forecast [projection] information that is the representation of management and does not include evaluation of the support for the assumptions underlying the projection. We have not examined the forecast [projection] and, accordingly, do not express an opinion or any other form of assurance on the accompanying statements or assumptions. Furthermore, [*If for a projection, add:* even if (*describe hypothetical assumption, for example, "the loan is granted and the plant is expanded,"*)] there will usually be differences between the forecasted [projected] and actual results, because events and circumstances frequently do not occur as expected, and those differences may be material. We have no responsibility to update this report for events and circumstances occurring after the date of this report.

<Additional paragraph for a projection>

The accompanying projection and this report are intended solely for the information and use of [*identify specified parties, for example*, "*XYZ Company and DEF National Bank*"] and is not intended to be and should not be used by anyone other than these specified parties.

[*Signature*]

[*Date*]

a. **Projection Presentation** The practitioner's report should include a separate paragraph that describes the limitations on the usefulness of the presentation.

b. **Range** When the PFS contain a range, the practitioner's report also should include a separate paragraph that states that the responsible party has elected to portray the expected results of one or more assumptions as a range.

c. **Emphasis** In some circumstances, a CPA may wish to expand the report to emphasize a matter regarding the PFSs. Such information may be presented in a separate paragraph of the CPA's report. However, the CPA should exercise care that emphasizing such a matter does not give the impression that the CPA is expressing assurance or expanding the degree of responsibility the CPA is taking regarding such information.

d. **Historical Financial Information** PFS may be included in a document that also includes historical financial statements (HFS) with a related practitioner's report. Additionally, HFS may be summarized and presented with PFS for comparative purposes.

e. **Independence *Not* Required** A CPA may compile PFS for an entity with respect to which a CPA is not independent. When the CPA is not independent, the CPA should include the following as a separate paragraph in the report, "We are not independent with respect to XYZ Company." The CPA is permitted, but not required, to disclose (in the same paragraph) the reason(s) for the independence impairment. If the CPA elects to do this, *all* the reasons should be included.

5. **Examination of PFS** An examination of PFS is substantially more in scope and responsibility than a compilation or an agreed-upon procedures engagement. The practitioner must be independent, and follow the general, fieldwork, and reporting standards outlined in AT 101 as applicable to examination engagements.

a. **Examination Reports** As a result of the examination, the CPA has a basis for reporting on whether, in the CPA's opinion, (1) the assumptions provide a reasonable basis for the responsible party's forecast or projection, given the hypothetical assumptions, and (2) whether the PFS are presented in accordance with AICPA guidelines.

b. **Standard Report** In addition to the previously listed elements, the CPA's standard report on an examination of PFS includes the following:

- A title which includes independent; a signature, and a date
- Identification of the PFS presented
- Identification of the responsible parties and a statement that the PFS are the responsibility of said parties
- A statement that the practitioner's responsibility is to express an opinion on the PFS based on an examination
- A brief description of the nature of an examination of PFS
- The CPA's opinion that the PFS are presented in accordance with AICPA presentation guidelines and that the underlying assumptions provide a reasonable basis for the forecast (or projection, given the hypothetical assumptions).

c. **Projection** The CPA should express an opinion on whether the assumptions provide a reasonable basis for the projection given the hypothetical assumptions. A reference should be included to the hypothetical assumption(s), and the report should include a separate paragraph that limits the use to specified parties.

d. **Emphasis** The practitioner may wish to emphasize a matter regarding the PFS, but issue an unmodified opinion. The practitioner may present other information and comments, such as explanatory comments or other informative material, in a separate paragraph of the report.

e. **Evaluation Based in Part on Report of Another Accountant** When the principal practitioner decides to refer to the report of another CPA as a basis, in part, for the principal's own opinion, the principal practitioner should disclose that fact in stating the scope of the examination and refer to the report of the other CPA in expressing the opinion. Such a reference indicates the division of responsibility for the performance of the examination.

f. **Part of Larger Engagement** When the practitioner's examination of PFS is part of a larger engagement, for example, a financial feasibility study or business acquisition study, it is appropriate to expand the report on the examination of the PFS to describe the entire engagement.

Exhibit 5 ▸ Standard Report on an Examination of Forecast / Projection

Independent Accountant's Report

We have examined the accompanying forecasted [projected] balance sheet, statements of income, retained earnings, and cash flows of XYZ Company as of December 31, 20X1, and for the year then ending. XYZ Company is responsible for the forecast [*projection*]. Our responsibility is to express an opinion on the forecast [*projection*] based on our examination.

Our examination was made in accordance with attestation standards established by the American Institute of Certified Public Accountants and, accordingly, included such procedures as we considered necessary to evaluate both the assumptions used by management and the preparation and presentation of the forecast [projection]. We believe our examination provides a reasonable basis for our opinion.

<Opinion paragraph for a forecast>

In our opinion, the accompanying forecast is presented in conformity with guidelines for presentation of a forecast established by the American Institute of Certified Public Accountants, and the underlying assumptions provide a reasonable basis for management's forecast. However, there will usually be differences between the forecasted and actual results, because events and circumstances frequently do not occur as expected, and those differences may be material. We have no responsibility to update this report for events and circumstances occurring after the date of this report.

<Opinion paragraph for a projection>

In our opinion, the accompanying projection is presented in conformity with guidelines for presentation of a projection established by the American Institute of Certified Public Accountants, and the underlying assumptions provide a reasonable basis for management's projection [*describe the hypothetical assumption, for example, "assuming the granting of the requested loan to expand XYZ Company's plant as described in the summary of significant assumptions."*]. However, even if [*describe hypothetical assumption, for example, "the loan is granted and the plant is expanded,"*] there will usually be differences between the projected and actual results, because events and circumstances frequently do not occur as expected, and those differences may be material. We have no responsibility to update this report for events and circumstances occurring after the date of this report.

<Additional paragraph for a projection report>

The accompanying projection and this report were prepared for [*identify specified parties, for example, "XYZ Company and DEF National Bank"*] and are not intended to be and should not be used by anyone other than these specified parties.

[*Signature*]

[*Date*]

g. **Qualified Opinion** In a qualified report, the CPA states, in a separate paragraph, all the substantive reasons for modifying the opinion, and describes the departure from AICPA presentation guidelines. The opinion includes the words *except* or *exception* as the qualifying language and refers to the separate explanatory paragraph.

h. **Adverse Opinion** In an adverse opinion, the CPA states, in a separate paragraph, all the substantive reasons for the adverse opinion. The opinion should state that the presentation is not in conformity with presentation guidelines and should refer to the explanatory paragraph. When applicable, the opinion paragraph also should state that, in the accountant's opinion, the assumptions do not provide a reasonable basis for the prospective financial statements.

  (1) If the presentation, including the summary of significant assumptions, fails to disclose assumptions that, at the time, appear to be significant, the CPA should describe the assumptions in the report and issue an adverse opinion.

  (2) The CPA should not examine a presentation that omits all disclosures of assumptions. Also, the CPA should not examine a financial projection that omits: (a) an identification of the hypothetical assumptions or (b) a description of the limitations on the usefulness of the presentation.

i. **Disclaimer of Opinion** The CPA's report should indicate, in a separate paragraph, the respects in which the examination did not comply with standards for an examination. The CPA should state that the scope of the examination was not sufficient to enable an opinion to be expressed concerning the presentation or the underlying assumptions, and the CPA's disclaimer of opinion should include a direct reference to the explanatory paragraph. When there is a scope limitation and the CPA also believes there are material departures from the presentation guidelines, those departures should be described in the CPA's report.

6. **Agreed-Upon Procedures**

a. **Standards** The guidance in AT 101 (including general, fieldwork, and reporting standards) and AT 201 applies to engagements to apply agreed-upon procedures to PFS. This includes the extent of procedures and agreement among the parties regarding the procedures.

b. **Conditions** A practitioner may accept an engagement to apply agreed-upon procedures to PFS provided that: (1) the practitioner is independent; (2) the practitioner and the specified users agree upon the procedures and criteria; (3) the specified users take responsibility for the sufficiency of the agreed-upon procedures for their purposes; (4) the PFS include a summary of significant assumptions; (5) the PFS are subject to reasonably consistent evaluation against criteria that are suitable and available to the specified parties; (6) the procedures are expected to result in reasonably consistent findings using the criteria; (7) evidential matter related to the PFS is expected to exist to provide a reasonable basis for expressing the findings in the practitioner's report; (8) where applicable, the practitioner and the specified user agree on any materiality limits for reporting purposes; and (9) use of the report is restricted to the specified parties.

c. **Reports on Results** When the CPA reports on the results of applying agreed-upon procedures, the CPA should not express any form of negative assurance on the PFS. In addition to the previously discussed elements, the practitioner's report must include:

- A title that includes the word independent
- Identification of the specified parties
- Reference to the PFS and the character of the engagement
- A statement that the procedures performed were those agreed to by the specified parties identified in the report
- Identification of the responsible party and a statement that the PFS are the responsible party's responsibility

- A statement that the engagement was conducted in accordance with attestation standards established by the AICPA
- A statement that the sufficiency of the procedures is solely the responsibility of the specified parties and a disclaimer of responsibility for the sufficiency of those procedures
- A list of (or reference to) procedures performed and related findings
- Where applicable, a description of any agreed-upon materiality limits
- A statement that the practitioner was not engaged to and did not conduct an examination of PFS
- A disclaimer of opinion on whether the presentation of the PFS is in conformity with AICPA presentation guidelines and on whether the underlying assumptions provide a reasonable basis for the forecast or a reasonable basis for the projection given the hypothetical assumptions
- A statement that if the practitioner had performed additional procedures, other matters might have come to his or her attention that would have been reported
- A restriction on the use of the report, because it is intended to be used solely by the specified parties, and should not be used by others
- Where applicable, reservations or restrictions concerning procedures or findings
- Where applicable, a description of assistance provided by a specialist

IV. Pro Forma Financial Information

A. Purpose

Pro forma financial information is used to show what the significant effects on historical financial information might have been if a consummated or proposed transaction or event had occurred at an earlier date. Pro forma financial information generally is used to show the effects of transactions such as a business combination, a change in capitalization, the disposition of a significant portion of a business, a change in the form of business organization, or the proposed sale of securities and the application of proceeds.

1. **Examination Objective** Examination procedures applied to pro forma financial information are to provide reasonable assurance as to whether the following exists: (a) management's assumptions provide a reasonable basis for presenting the significant effects directly attributable to the underlying transaction or event; (b) the related pro forma adjustments give appropriate effect to those assumptions; and (c) the pro forma column reflects the proper application of those adjustments to the historical financial statements.

2. **Review Objective** Review procedures are to provide negative assurance as to whether any information came to the CPA's attention to cause a belief that: (a) management's assumptions do not provide a reasonable basis for presenting the significant effects directly attributable to the transaction or event; (b) the related pro forma adjustments do not give appropriate effect to those assumptions; and (c) the related pro forma column does not reflect the proper application of those adjustments to the historical financial statements.

B. Guidance

Engagements to report on an examination or review of pro forma financial information are covered by AT 101 and AT 401, *Reporting on Pro Forma Financial Information*. When pro forma financial information is presented outside the basic financial statements but within the same document, and the CPA is not engaged to report on the pro forma financial information, the CPA's responsibilities are described in AU 720, *Other Information in Documents Containing Audited Financial Statements* and in AU 925, *Filings With the US Securities and Exchange Commission Under the Securities Act of 1933*.

C. **Requirements**
A CPA may agree to report on an examination or a review of pro forma financial information under certain conditions. The presentation should indicate that the pro forma information should be read in conjunction with the historical data, make reference to the financial statements from which the historical data is derived, and state whether those statements were audited or reviewed. The presentation also should state that the pro forma financial information does not necessarily indicate the results that would have been attained had the transaction actually taken place earlier.

1. **Procedures** The procedures the CPA applies to the assumptions and pro forma adjustments for either an examination or a review engagement, other than those applied to the historical financial statements, include:

    a. Obtain an understanding of the underlying transaction or event; obtain a level of knowledge of each significant constituent part of the combined entity in a business combination; and discuss with management its assumptions regarding the effects of the transaction or event.

    b. Evaluate whether pro forma adjustments are included for all significant effects directly attributable to the transaction or event.

    c. Obtain sufficient evidence in support of adjustments. The evidence required to support the level of assurance given is a matter of professional judgment.

    d. Evaluate whether management's assumptions that underlie the pro forma adjustments are presented in a sufficiently clear and comprehensive manner.

    e. Determine that computations of pro forma adjustments are mathematically correct.

    f. Obtain written representations from management acknowledging responsibility for the assumptions used in determining the pro forma adjustments.

2. **Report** The report on pro forma financial information may be added to the CPA's report on historical financial information, or it may appear separately.

    a. **Contents** In addition to the previously listed items, a report on pro forma financial information includes the following: a separate paragraph explaining the objective of pro forma financial information and its limitations; and reference to the financial statements from which the historical financial information is derived and any modification in the practitioner's report on the historical financial information.

    b. **Date** The practitioner's report on pro forma financial information should be dated as of the completion of the appropriate procedures. If the reports are combined and the date of completion of the procedures for the examination or review of the pro forma financial information is after the date of completion of the fieldwork for the audit or review of the historical financial information, the combined report should be dual-dated.

    c. **Modifications** Restrictions on the scope of the engagement, significant uncertainties about the assumptions that could affect the transaction or event materially, reservations about the propriety of the assumptions and the conformity of the presentation with those assumptions (including inadequate disclosure of significant matters), or other reservations may require the CPA to qualify the opinion, render an adverse opinion, disclaim an opinion, or withdraw from the engagement. The CPA should disclose all substantive reasons for any report modifications. Uncertainty as to whether the transaction or event will be consummated ordinarily would not require a report modification.

d. **Examination** In addition to the previously listed elements, an examination report also includes the following:

(1) **Reference** A statement that the historical financial statements were audited.

(2) **Responsibility** A statement that the practitioner's responsibility is to express an opinion on the pro forma financial information based on his or her examination.

(3) **Standards** A statement that the examination was made in accordance with attestation standards established by the AICPA, and accordingly, included such procedures as the practitioner considered necessary in the circumstances.

(4) **Basis** A statement that the practitioner believes the examination provides a reasonable basis for his or her opinion.

(5) **Opinion** The practitioner's opinion as to whether management's assumptions provide a reasonable basis for presenting the significant effects directly attributable to the transaction or event, whether the related pro forma adjustments give appropriate effect to those assumptions, and whether the pro forma column reflects the proper application of those adjustments to the historical financial statements.

e. **Review** In addition to the previously listed elements, a review report also includes the following:

(1) **Reference** A statement as to whether the historical financial statements were audited or reviewed.

(2) **Disclaimer** A statement that a review is substantially less in scope than an examination, the objective of which is the expression of an opinion on the pro forma financial information, and accordingly, the practitioner does not express such an opinion.

3. **Conclusion** The practitioner's conclusion as to whether any information came to the CPA's attention to cause a belief that management's assumptions do not provide a reasonable basis for presenting the significant effects directly attributable to the transaction or event, or that the related pro forma adjustments do not give appropriate effect to those assumptions, or that the pro forma column does not reflect the proper application of those adjustments to the historical financial statements.

Exhibit 6 ▸ Report on an Examination of Pro Forma Financial Information

Independent Accountant's Report

We have examined the pro forma adjustments reflecting the transaction [*or event*] described in Note 1 and the application of those adjustments to the historical amounts in [*the assembly of*] the accompanying pro forma condensed balance sheet of X Company as of December 31, 20X1, and the pro forma condensed statement of income for the year then ended. The historical condensed financial statements are derived from the historical financial statements of X Company, which were audited by us, and of Y Company, which were audited by other accountants, appearing elsewhere herein [*or incorporated by reference*]. Such pro forma adjustments are based upon management's assumptions described in Note 2. X Company's management is responsible for the pro forma financial statements. Our responsibility is to express an opinion on the pro forma financial information based on our examination.

Our examination was made in accordance with attestation standards established by the American Institute of Certified Public Accountants and, accordingly, included such procedures as we considered necessary under the circumstances. We believe our examination provides a reasonable basis for our opinion.

The objective of this pro forma financial information is to show what the significant effects on the historical financial information might have been had the transaction [*or event*] occurred at an earlier date. However, the pro forma condensed financial statements are not necessarily indicative of the results of operations or related effects on financial position that would have been attained had the above-mentioned transaction [*or event*] occurred earlier.

[*Additional paragraph(s) may be added to emphasize certain matters relating to the engagement.*]

In our opinion, management's assumptions provide a reasonable basis for presenting the significant efforts directly attributable to the above-mentioned transaction [*or event*] described in Note 1, the related pro forma adjustments give appropriate effect to those assumptions, and the pro forma column reflects the proper application of those adjustments to the historical financial statement amounts in the pro forma condensed balance sheet as of December 31, 20X1, and the pro forma condensed statement of income for the year then ended.

[*Signature*]

[*Date*]

Exhibit 7 ▸ Report on a Review of Pro Forma Financial Information

Independent Accountant's Report

We have reviewed the pro forma adjustments reflecting the transaction [*or event*] described in Note 1 and the application of those adjustments to the historical amounts in [*the assembly of*] the accompanying pro forma condensed balance sheet of X Company as of March 31, 20X2, and the pro forma condensed statement of income for the three months then ended. These historical condensed financial statements are derived from the historical unaudited financial statements of X Company, which were reviewed by us, and of Y Company, which were reviewed by other accountants, appearing elsewhere herein [*or incorporated by reference*]. Such pro forma adjustments are based on management's assumptions as described in Note 2. X Company's management is responsible for the pro forma financial statements.

Our review was conducted in accordance with attestation standards established by the American Institute of Certified Public Accountants. A review is substantially less in scope than an examination, the objective of which is the expression of an opinion on management's assumptions, the pro forma adjustments, and the application of those adjustments to historical financial information. Accordingly, we do not express such an opinion.

<Same third paragraph as in an examination report.>

[*Additional paragraph(s) may be added to emphasize certain matters relating to the engagement.*]

Based on our review, nothing came to our attention that caused us to believe that management's assumptions do not provide a reasonable basis for presenting the significant effects directly attributable to the above-mentioned transaction [*or event*] described in Note 1, that the related pro forma adjustments do not give appropriate effect to those assumptions, or that the pro forma column does not reflect the proper application of those adjustments to the historical financial statement amounts in the pro forma condensed balance sheet as of March 31, 20X2, and the pro forma condensed statement of income for the three months then ended.

[*Signature*]

[*Date*]

V. Examination of Internal Control Over Financial Reporting

AT 501, *An Examination of an Entity's Internal Control Over Financial Reporting That Is Integrated With an Audit of Its Financial Statements*, establishes requirements and provides guidance for the performance of an examination of a nonissuer's internal control over financial reporting (internal control) that is integrated with an audit of financial statements. (An auditor should **not** accept an engagement to review an entity's internal control or a written assertion thereon.) It aligns the definitions and related guidance for evaluating deficiencies in internal control with PCAOB AS 5, *An Audit of Internal Control Over Financial Reporting That is Integrated with an Audit of Financial Statements* (see Chapter 11).

A. Applicability

AT 501 does not provide guidance for the following engagements:

1. As covered under AT 101, *Attest Engagements*:
2. Performance of agreed-upon procedures on controls covered under AT 201, *Agreed-Upon Procedures Engagements*
3. Examining controls over compliance with laws and regulations covered under AT 601, *Compliance Attestation*
4. Reporting on controls at a service organization covered under AT 801, *Reporting on Controls at a Service Organization*

B. Definitions

1. **Control Objective** The aim or purpose of specified controls. Control objectives ordinarily address the risks that the controls are intended to mitigate. In the context of internal control, a control objective generally relates to a relevant assertion for a significant account or disclosure and addresses the risk that the controls in a specific area will not provide reasonable assurance that a misstatement or omission in that relevant assertion is prevented, or detected and corrected on a timely basis.

2. **Deficiency** A deficiency in internal control exists when the design or operation of a control does not allow management or employees, in the normal course of performing their assigned functions, to prevent, or detect and correct misstatements on a timely basis.

   a. A deficiency in design exists when

      (1) A control necessary to meet the control objective is missing or

      (2) An existing control is not properly designed so that, even if the control operates as designed, the control objective would not be met.

   b. A deficiency in operation exists when a properly designed control does not operate as designed, or when the person performing the control does not possess the necessary authority or competence to perform the control effectively.

3. **Detective Control** A control that has the objective of detecting and correcting errors or fraud that have already occurred that could result in a misstatement of the financial statements.

4. **Financial Statements and Related Disclosures** An entity's financial statements and notes to the financial statements as presented in accordance with the applicable financial reporting framework. References to financial statements and related disclosures do not extend to the preparation of other financial information presented outside an entity's basic financial statements and notes.

5. **Internal Control Over Financial Reporting** A process effected by those charged with governance, management, and other personnel, designed to provide reasonable assurance regarding the preparation of reliable financial statements for external purposes in accordance with the applicable financial reporting framework and includes those policies and procedures that

   a. Pertain to the maintenance of records that, in reasonable detail, accurately and fairly reflect the transactions and dispositions of the assets of an entity

   b. Provide reasonable assurance that transactions are recorded as necessary to permit preparation of financial statements in accordance with the applicable financial reporting framework, and that receipts and expenditures of an entity are being made only in accordance with authorizations of management and those charged with governance

   c. Provide reasonable assurance regarding prevention, or timely detection and correction of unauthorized acquisition, use, or disposition of an entity's assets that could have a material effect on the financial statements

   d. Internal control has inherent limitations. Internal control is a process that involves human diligence and compliance and is subject to lapses in judgment and breakdowns resulting from human failures. Internal control also can be circumvented by collusion or improper management override.

6. **Material Weakness** A deficiency, or a combination of deficiencies, in internal control such that there is a reasonable possibility (per the FASB's definition regarding accounting for contingencies) that a material misstatement of an entity's financial statements will not be prevented, or detected and corrected on a timely basis.

7. **Preventive Control** A control that has the objective of preventing errors or fraud that could result in a misstatement of the financial statements.

8. **Relevant Assertion** A financial statement assertion that has a reasonable possibility of containing a misstatement or misstatements that would cause the financial statements to be materially misstated. The determination of whether an assertion is a relevant assertion is made without regard to the effect of controls.

9. **Significant Account or Disclosure** An account balance or disclosure that has a reasonable possibility that it could contain a misstatement that, individually or when aggregated with others, has a material effect on the financial statements, considering the risks of both overstatement and understatement. The determination of whether an account balance or disclosure is a significant account or disclosure is made without regard to the effect of controls.

10. **Significant Deficiency** A deficiency, or a combination of deficiencies, in internal control that is less severe than a material weakness, yet important enough to merit attention by those charged with governance.

C. **Engagement Objective**
The auditor's objective is to form an opinion on the effectiveness of an entity's internal control as of a point in time and taken as a whole. To express an opinion *as of a point in time*, the auditor should obtain evidence that internal control has operated effectively for a sufficient period of time which may be less than the period covered by the company's financial statements. To express an opinion on internal control *taken as a whole*, the auditor should obtain evidence about the effectiveness of selected controls over all relevant assertions. This involves testing the design and operating effectiveness of controls that in most cases would not be required if only expressing an opinion on the financial statements.

D. **Examination Requirements**
Management must: (1) accept responsibility for the effectiveness of the entity's internal control; (2) evaluate the effectiveness of the entity's internal control using suitable and available criteria; (3) support its assertion about the effectiveness of the entity's internal control with sufficient appropriate evidence, including documentation of the controls and their objectives and evidence of monitoring activities; and (4) provide its assertion about the effectiveness of the entity's internal control in a report that accompanies the audit report.

E. **Material Weaknesses**
If one or more material weaknesses exist, an entity's internal control cannot be considered effective, thus the auditor must obtain sufficient appropriate evidence to obtain reasonable assurance about whether material weaknesses exist as of the date specified in management's assertion. There may be a material weakness in internal control even when financial statements are not materially misstated. An auditor is not required to search for deficiencies that are less severe than a material weakness.

F. Integrating the Examination With the Financial Statement Audit

1. **Significant Accounts and Disclosures and Their Relevant Assertions** The significant accounts and disclosures and their relevant assertions and the risk factors used to identify them are the same in the examination of internal control (examination) as in an audit of financial statements (audit).

2. **Tests of Controls** The tests of controls should be designed to achieve the objectives of both engagements simultaneously, i.e., to obtain sufficient appropriate evidence to support the auditor's opinion on internal control as well as the auditor's risk assessment for purposes of the audit. As previously mentioned, for the purposes of the audit, the auditor is not required to test the controls of all relevant assertions as is required in the examination. Consideration of the results of the additional tests of controls performed for the purposes of the examination may affect the auditor's decisions about the nature, timing and extent of substantive procedures and further tests of controls for the purposes of the audit. Obviously, this would be particularly true if deficiencies were identified in the examination.

3. **Substantive Procedures** Likewise, the results of substantive procedures performed for purposes of the audit should be evaluated to determine their effect on the auditor's risk assessments regarding the testing necessary to form a conclusion about the effectiveness of a control in the examination. Results of substantive tests of particular interest include those related to fraud, illegal acts, related-party transactions, and those that detect misstatements or indicate management bias in making accounting estimates or selecting accounting principles.

4. **Period End Reporting Process** As part of the examination, the auditor should evaluate the procedures that make up the period end reporting process because of its importance to financial reporting and the integrated approach.

5. **Risk Assessment and Materiality** The same materiality should be used for planning and performing both engagements and the same risk assessment process supports both.

6. **Fraud Risk Assessment** The results of the fraud risk assessment for the purposes the audit should be incorporated into the examination. The auditor should consider whether the identified risks due to fraud and inappropriate management override of other controls are sufficiently addressed by the internal control system.

7. **As of Date or Period Covered** The date specified in management's assertion (the as of date of the examination) should correspond to the balance sheet date of the period covered by the financial statements. If management chooses an as of date for the examination that is different than the end of the entity's fiscal year, the examination and the audit should still be integrated. If the auditor is engaged to examine the effectiveness of internal control for a period of time (rather than an as of date), the examination should be integrated with an audit that covers the same period.

8. **Audit Report Date** Because the examination is integrated with the audit, the dates of the reports should be the same.

G. Communications

Significant deficiencies and material weaknesses should be communicated, in writing by the audit report release date, to the entity's management and those charged with governance, including those previously communicated, but not remediated. In the case where the nature of some matters directs their early communication, even if such significant deficiencies or material weaknesses are remediated during the audit, they should still be included in this formal written communication.

H. Adverse Opinion

If there a material weakness, the auditor should express an adverse opinion. Under these circumstances, the auditor is prohibited from expressing an opinion on management's assertion and should report directly on the effectiveness of internal control. The auditor should determine the effect of an adverse opinion on the auditor's opinion on the financial statements and disclose whether the auditor's opinion on the financial statements was affected by the material weakness. The adverse report should include:

1. A definition of material weakness

2. A statement that one or more material weaknesses have been identified and an identification of the material weaknesses described in management's report; the audit report does not need to include a description of the material weaknesses as long as each material weakness is included and fairly presented in all material respects in management's report

3. If management's report does not include a fair presentation of all material weaknesses, the audit report should include a statement that one or more material weaknesses have been identified and not included in management's report, along with a description of all such material weaknesses which contains specific information about the nature of each, and its actual and potential effect on the presentation of the entity's financial statements.

I. Disclaimer of Opinion or Withdrawal

1. If there are restrictions on the scope of an engagement, for example, if management refuses to provide written representations, the auditor should either withdraw from the engagement or disclaim an opinion. The auditor may issue the disclaimer of opinion as soon as the auditor concludes that the scope limitation will prevent the auditor from obtaining the reasonable assurance necessary to express an opinion. No additional work is required.

2. The auditor should disclaim an opinion when the auditor discovers a material weakness subsequent to the as of date of the examination, but before the date of the audit report that existed as of the date in management's assertion and whose effect on internal control can not be determined. (If its effect can be determined, the auditor should issue an adverse opinion.)

3. A disclaimer of opinion should include: a statement that the auditor does not express an opinion on the effectiveness of internal control; an explanation in a separate paragraph that includes the substantive reasons for the disclaimer. The auditor should not identify the procedures that were performed nor include the statements describing the characteristics of an examination.

VI. Compliance Attestation

AT 601, *Compliance Attestation*, provides guidance for engagements related to an entity's compliance with requirements of specified laws, regulations, rules, contracts, or grants, as well as the effectiveness of an entity's internal control (IC) over compliance with specified requirements. An attest engagement must comply with the general, fieldwork, and reporting standards delineated in AT 101 as well as specific standards established in AT 601.

A. Applicability

CPAs may be engaged to perform agreed-upon procedures to assist users in evaluating compliance with specified requirements (or related assertions) and/or the effectiveness of an entity's IC over compliance. These engagements also are subject to the requirements of AT 201. CPAs also may be engaged to examine, but not review, an entity's compliance with specified requirements, or related written assertions. CPAs may provide nonattest services connected with compliance; however, these services adhere to professional consulting standards, rather than SSAE.

1. **Agreed-Upon Procedures** The objective is to present specific findings to assist users in evaluating an entity's assertion about compliance with specified requirements or about the effectiveness of an entity's IC over compliance based on procedures agreed-upon by the report users. The CPA's procedures generally may be as limited or as extensive as the specified parties desire as long as the specified users participate in establishing the procedures to be performed, and take responsibility for the adequacy of such procedures for their purposes. Prior to performing procedures, the practitioner should obtain an understanding of the specified compliance requirements.

2. **Examination** The objective is to express an opinion on an entity's compliance with specified requirements (or related assertion) based on specified criteria. To express such an opinion, the practitioner accumulates sufficient evidence regarding the entity's compliance with specified requirements, thereby limiting attestation risk to an appropriately low level. Among other procedures, the practitioner considers subsequent events. The practitioner considers issues that parallel those in a financial statement audit, but the perspective may be different. Some of these issues are risk, materiality, planning, professional skepticism, relevant internal controls and internal audit functions, use of specialists, and obtaining sufficient evidence.

3. **Conditions for Engagement** For both types of engagements, the responsible party must accept responsibility for the entity's compliance with specified requirements and the effectiveness of IC over compliance, and provide a written assertion about compliance with specified requirements or IC over compliance in either: (a) a separate report to accompany the practitioner's report; or (b) a representation letter to the practitioner.

   a. **Agreed-Upon Procedures** The responsible party evaluates compliance with specified requirements or the effectiveness of the entity's IC over compliance.

   b. **Examinations** The responsible party evaluates compliance with specified requirements, and sufficient evidential matter exists, or could be developed, to support that evaluation.

B. **Report Components**

The practitioner modifies the report if: (1) material noncompliance with specified requirements exists; (2) a restriction on the engagement scope exists; or (3) the practitioner refers to another practitioner's report as the basis, in part, for the report.

1. When a situation imposes restrictions on the engagement scope, the practitioner attempts to obtain agreement to modify the procedures. If such agreement is not obtained, the practitioner should describe the restrictions in the report or withdraw from the engagement.

2. The practitioner has no obligation to perform beyond the agreed-upon procedures and no responsibility to perform procedures to detect noncompliance in the subsequent period, beyond obtaining the responsible party's representation about noncompliance in the subsequent period.

3. The practitioner's report should not provide negative assurance about whether management's assertion is fairly stated.

VII. **Management's Discussion & Analysis**

Management is responsible for the preparation of management's discussion & analysis (MD&A). AT 701, *Management's Discussion and Analysis*, provides specific guidance to CPAs related to the performance of an attest engagement with respect to MD&A prepared pursuant to Securities and Exchange Commission (SEC) regulations. This guidance does not change an auditor's responsibility in a financial statement audit, or apply to situations where CPAs provide recommendations rather than assurance. (SSAE require an auditor to read the MD&A and consider whether it is materially inconsistent with information appearing in the financial statements.) A practitioner engaged to examine or review MD&A complies with AT 101 plus the specific standards in AT 701. A practitioner engaged to perform agreed-upon procedures on MD&A follows the guidance in AT 201.

A. **Objectives**
The objective is to report on MD&A taken as a whole. An examination of MD&A provides users with an independent opinion regarding whether: (a) the presentation meets SEC criteria; (b) the historical financial information is derived accurately from the financial statements; and (c) the underlying information and assumptions provide a reasonable basis for the disclosures contained therein. A review of MD&A provides users and preparers with negative assurance concerning such matters.

B. **Engagement Acceptance**
A CPA may perform an examination or review of MD&A for an annual period, an interim period, or a combined annual and interim period. A base knowledge of the entity gained through a financial statement audit is necessary to provide the CPA with sufficient knowledge to evaluate the results of procedures. For nonpublic entities, the CPA also must receive a written assertion from management that MD&A was prepared using SEC criteria.

1. **Annual Period** A CPA may accept an engagement to examine or review MD&A of an entity for an annual period, provided the practitioner audits the financial statements for at least the latest period to which MD&A relates and the financial statements for the other periods covered by MD&A have been audited.

2. **Review of Interim Period** A CPA may accept an engagement to review MD&A for an interim period provided that MD&A for the most recent fiscal year has been (or will be) examined or reviewed (by either the CPA or a predecessor) and the CPA performs either an audit of the interim financial statements or a review for either of the following:

   a. **Public Entity** A review of the financial statements for the related comparative interim periods and issues a review report in accordance with AU 930, *Interim Financial Information.*

   b. **Nonpublic Entity** A review of either (1) the financial statements for the related interim periods under SSARSs and issues a review report, or (2) the related condensed interim financial information in accordance with AU 930 and issues a review report, and such information is accompanied by complete financial statements for the most recent audited fiscal year.

3. **Predecessor** If a predecessor audited prior period financial statements, the successor must acquire sufficient knowledge of the entity and apply appropriate procedures relating to prior years included in the MD&A presentation.

C. **Scope**
The practitioner considers the following as well as historical financial information:

1. **Pro Forma Information** The guidance in AT 401 when performing procedures with respect to any pro forma information, even if MD&A indicates that certain information is derived from unaudited financial statements

2. **External Information** For example, debt ratings of a rating agency

3. **Forward-Looking Information** Tested only for the purpose of expressing an opinion or providing limited assurance on MD&A taken as a whole; the CPA considers whether cautionary language concerning achievability is included

4. **Voluntary Information** When the entity includes other information in MD&A required by other SEC regulations, the CPA also considers those other SEC criteria in subjecting such information to procedures

D. **Engagement Procedures**
The CPA obtains an understanding of the SEC criteria for MD&A and management's MD&A preparation method; plans the engagement; considers materiality; considers relevant portions of the entity's internal control; considers subsequent events; and obtains appropriate written representations from management. The misstatement of an individual assertion is material if the magnitude of the misstatement (individually or aggregated) is such that a reasonable person would be influenced by its correction. A practitioner also considers whether management (and any assistants) has appropriate knowledge of rules and regulations of the SEC to prepare MD&A. Because the objective of an audit of financial statements is different from that of an examination of MD&A, additional procedures typically are performed in an examination of MD&A.

1. **Examination** The CPA obtains sufficient evidence, including testing completeness, and forms an opinion consistent with examination objectives. The CPA considers the results of financial statement audits for the periods covered by MD&A, including the possible impact on the examination engagement scope of a modified audit report.

2. **Review** Procedures generally are limited to inquiries and analytics concerning factors that have a material effect on financial condition, results of operations, and cash flows. The CPA also forms a conclusion consistent with review objectives.

E. **Control Risk**
After obtaining an understanding of the entity's internal controls over preparation of the MD&A section, the CPA assesses control risk for the content in the MD&A. Control risk may be assessed at the maximum level (the greatest probability that a material misstatement could occur in an assertion and will not be prevented or detected in a timely manner) if the CPA believes controls are ineffective.

F. **Review Performance**
The CPA develops an overall strategy for analytics and inquiries. The CPA considers factors such as matters affecting the entity's industry; matters relating to the entity's business; the types of relevant information that management reports to external analysts; the extent of management's knowledge of, and experience with, SEC criteria for MD&A; if the entity is a nonpublic entity, the intended use of MD&A; matters identified during other engagements; and, the nature of complex or subjective matters that may require special skill or knowledge.

G. **Reports**
A report on a examination or review of MD&A includes the date of the completion of the CPA's procedures, which should not precede the date of the audit (or review) report on the latest historical financial statements covered by the MD&A. An entity should not name the practitioner in a client-prepared document as having examined or reviewed MD&A unless the MD&A presentation and related practitioner's report and the related financial statements and auditor's (or accountant's review) report are included in the document (or, in the case of a public entity, incorporated by reference to such information filed with a regulatory agency). The practitioner's report on an examination or review of MD&A should include the following:

1. **Both:** a title that includes the word independent

2. **Both (introductory paragraph):** an identification of the MD&A presentation, including the period covered

3. **Responsibility (introductory paragraph contd.)**

   a. **Both:** a statement that management is responsible for the preparation of the MD&A pursuant to the rules and regulations adopted by the SEC

   b. **Examination only:** and a statement that the practitioner's responsibility is to express an opinion on the presentation based on his or her examination

4. **Both (introductory paragraph concluded):** a reference to the audit report on the related financial statements, and, if the report was other than a "standard" report, the substantive reasons

5. **Both (scope paragraph):** a statement that the examination or review was conducted in accordance with attestation standards established by the AICPA

6. **Scope (scope paragraph contd.)**

   a. **Examination only:** a description of the scope of an examination of MD&A

   b. **Review only:** a description of the procedures for a review of MD&A

7. **Nature of engagement (scope paragraph concluded)**

   a. **Examination only:** a statement that the practitioner believes the examination provides a reasonable basis for his or her opinion

   b. **Review only:** a statement that a review of MD&A is substantially less in scope than an examination, the objective of which is an expression of opinion regarding the MD&A presentation, and accordingly, no such opinion is expressed

8. **Both: Explanation of MD&A (explanatory paragraph)**

   a. The preparation of MD&A requires management to interpret the criteria, make determinations as to the relevancy of information to be included, and make estimates and assumptions that affect reported information

   b. Actual results in the future may differ materially from management's present assessment of information regarding the estimated future impact of transactions and events that have occurred or are expected to occur, expected sources of liquidity and capital resources, operating trends, commitments, and uncertainties

   c. If the entity is a nonpublic entity, a statement that although the entity is not subject to the rules and regulations of the SEC, the MD&A presentation is intended to be a presentation in accordance with the rules and regulations adopted by the SEC

9. **Examination only (opinion paragraph):** the practitioner's opinion on whether:

   a. The presentation includes, in all material respects, the required elements of the rules and regulations adopted by the SEC

   b. The historical financial amounts have been accurately derived, in all material respects, from the entity's financial statements

   c. The underlying information, determinations, estimates, and assumptions of the entity provide a reasonable basis for the disclosures contained therein

10. **Review only (concluding—negative assurance—paragraph):** a statement about whether any information came to the practitioner's attention that caused him or her to believe that:

    a. The MD&A presentation does not include, in all material respects, the required elements of the rules and regulations adopted by the SEC

    b. The historical financial amounts included therein have not been accurately derived, in all material respects, from the entity's financial statements

    c. The underlying information, determinations, estimates, and assumptions of the entity do not provide a reasonable basis for the disclosures contained therein

11. **Review only (restricted use paragraph):** if the entity is a public entity or a nonpublic entity that is making or has made an offering of securities and it appears that the securities may subsequently be registered or subject to a filing with the SEC or other regulatory agency, a statement of restrictions on the use of the report to specified parties, because it is not intended to be filed with the SEC as a report under the 1933 Act or the 1934 Act

12. **Both:** the manual or printed signature of the practitioner's firm

13. **Both:** the date of the report

H. Review Presentation

In order for a CPA to issue a report on a review of MD&A, the financial statements for the periods covered by MD&A and the related auditor's or practitioner's report(s) should accompany MD&A (or be incorporated by reference to information filed with a regulatory agency). There are additional requirements in the following circumstances:

1. **Interim Periods** The comparative financial statements for the most recent annual period and the related MD&A should accompany the interim MD&A (or be incorporated by reference). Generally, this requirement is satisfied by a public entity that has filed its annual financial statements and MD&A in its annual Form 10-K.

2. **Nonpublic Entity** The MD&A should include a statement that it was prepared using SEC criteria or a separate written assertion should accompany MD&A.

VIII. Reporting on Controls at a Service Organization

A. Guidance

Service Organization Controls (SOC) are a series of accounting standards that measure the control of financial information for a service organization. SOC 1 reports are examination engagements prepared in accordance with SSAE No. 16, and are undertaken by a service auditor to report on controls at an organization that provides services to user entities when those controls are likely to be relevant to user entities' internal control over financial reporting. For reports that are not specifically focused on internal controls over financial reporting, SOC 2 and SOC 3 reports should be used, which focus on controls at a service organization relevant to

1. **Security** The system is protected against unauthorized access

2. **Availability** The system is available for operation and use as committed and agreed

3. **Processing Integrity** The system processing is complete, accurate, timely, and authorized

4. **Confidentiality** Information classified as confidential is protected as committed or agreed

5. **Privacy** Personal information is collected, used, retained, disclosed, and destroyed in conformity with the commitments in the entity's privacy notice and with criteria set forth in the AICPA's generally accepted privacy principles

B. Objective

The objectives of the service auditor are to:

1. Obtain reasonable assurance about whether, in all material respects, based on suitable criteria

   a. Management's description of the service organization's system fairly presents the system that was designed and implemented throughout the specified period (or in the case of a type 1 report, as of a specified date)

b. The controls related to the control objectives stated in management's description of the service organization's system were suitably designed throughout the specified period (or in the case of a type 1 report, as of a specified date)

c. When included in the scope of the engagement, the controls operated effectively to provide reasonable assurance that the control objectives stated in management's description of the service organization's system were achieved throughout the specified period

2. Report on the preceding matters in accordance with the service auditor's findings

C. Engagement Acceptance

1. **Auditor Responsibilities** The service auditor has the capabilities and competence to perform the engagement. The service auditor should obtain an understanding of the service organization's system, including controls that are included in the scope of the engagement. The service auditor's preliminary knowledge of the engagement circumstances indicates that the

   a. Criteria to be used will be suitable and available to the intended user entities and their auditors

   b. Service auditor will have access to sufficient appropriate evidence to the extent necessary

   c. Scope of the engagement and management's description of the service organization's system will not be so limited that they are unlikely to be useful to user entities and their auditors.

2. **Management's Responsibilities** Management agrees to the terms of the engagement by acknowledging and accepting its responsibility in that they have used suitable criteria in:

   a. Preparing its description of the service organization's system

   b. Evaluating whether controls were suitably designed to achieve the control objectives stated in the description

   c. Evaluating whether controls operated effectively throughout the specified period to achieve the control objectives stated in the description of the service organization's system

3. **Materiality** In an engagement to report on controls at a service organization, the concept of materiality relates to the information being reported on, not the financial statements of user entities.

4. **Internal Audit** If the work of the internal audit function has been used, the service auditor should not make reference to that work in the service auditor's *opinion*; however, in the case of a type 2 report, if the work of the internal audit function has been used in performing tests of controls, that part of the service auditor's report that describes the service auditor's tests of controls and results thereof should include a description of the internal auditor's work and of the service auditor's procedures with respect to that work.

D. Report Components

1. **Date** The service auditor should date the service auditor's report no earlier than the date on which the service auditor has obtained sufficient appropriate evidence to support the service auditor's opinion.

2. **Time Frame** A Type 1 Report is a report on management's description of a service organization's system and the suitability of the design of controls for a specific date. A Type 2 Report expands on the Type 1 Report and includes the operating effectiveness of controls as well as the suitability of their design for a period of time.

3. **Elements** A Type 1 Report will include:

   a. A description of the service organization's system prepared by management

   b. A written assertion by management about whether, in all material respects, and based on suitable criteria:

      (1) The description of the service organization's system fairly presents the design and implementation of the system as of a specified period/date.

      (2) The controls related to the control objectives stated in management's description were suitably designed to achieve those control objectives as of the specified period/date.

      (3) For Type 2 Reports only, the controls that were tested were operating effectively to provide reasonable, but not absolute, assurance that the control objectives were achieved during the period specified.

   c. A service auditor's opinion on management's assertions.

4. **Modified Opinion** The service auditor's opinion should be modified and the service auditor's report should contain a clear description of all the reasons for the modification, if the service auditor concludes that:

   a. Management's description of the service organization's system is not fairly presented, in all material respects

   b. The controls are not suitably designed to provide reasonable assurance that the control objectives stated in management's description of the service organization's system would be achieved if the controls operated as described

   c. In the case of a type 2 report, the controls did not operate effectively throughout the specified period to achieve the related control objectives stated in management's description of the service organization's system

   d. The service auditor is unable to obtain sufficient appropriate evidence

5. **Disclaimer** If the service auditor plans to disclaim an opinion because of the inability to obtain sufficient appropriate evidence, and, based on the limited procedures performed, has concluded that:

   a. Certain aspects of management's description of the service organization's system are not fairly presented, in all material respects

   b. Certain controls were not suitably designed to provide reasonable assurance that the control objectives stated in management's description of the service organization's system would be achieved if the controls operated as described

   c. In the case of a type 2 report, certain controls did not operate effectively throughout the specified period to achieve the related control objectives stated in management's description of the service organization's system

   The service auditor should not identify the procedures that were performed nor include statements describing the characteristics of a service auditor's engagement in the service auditor's report; to do so might overshadow the disclaimer.

CHAPTER 14—ATTESTATION ENGAGEMENTS

Problem 14-1 MULTIPLE-CHOICE QUESTIONS

Attestation Standards

1. A practitioner is engaged to express an opinion on management's assertion that the square footage of a warehouse offered for sale is 150,000 square feet. The practitioner should refer to which of the following sources for professional guidance?

   a. Statements on Auditing Standards
   b. Statements on Standards for Attestation Engagements
   c. Statements on Standards for Accounting and Review Services
   d. Statements on Standards for Consulting Services (ID: 90184)

2. A CPA is required to comply with the provisions of Statements on Standards for Attestation Engagements when engaged to

   a. Report on financial statements that the CPA generated through the use of computer software
   b. Review management's discussion and analysis (MD&A) prepared pursuant to rules and regulations adopted by the SEC
   c. Provide the client with a financial statement format that does not include dollar amounts
   d. Audit financial statements that the client prepared for use in another country (ID: 7103)

3. Which of the following activities would most likely be considered an attestation engagement?

   a. Consulting with management representatives of a firm to provide advice
   b. Issuing a report about a firm's compliance with laws and regulations
   c. Advocating a client's position on tax matters that are being reviewed by the IRS
   d. Preparing a client's tax returns (ID: 7835)

4. Which of the following is not an attestation standard?

   a. The practitioner must obtain sufficient evidence to provide a reasonable basis for the conclusion that is expressed in the report.
   b. The practitioner must identify the subject matter or the assertion being reported on and state the character of the engagement in the report.
   c. The practitioner must adequately plan the work and must properly supervise any assistants.
   d. A sufficient understanding of internal control shall be obtained to plan the engagement. (ID: 3900)

5. A CPA in public practice is required to comply with the provisions of the Statements on Standards for Attestation Engagements when

	Testifying as an expert witness in accounting and auditing matters given stipulated facts	Compiling a client's financial projection that presents a hypothetical course of action
a.	Yes	Yes
b.	Yes	No
c.	No	Yes
d.	No	No

(ID: 7016)

6. Which of the following professional services would be considered an attestation engagement?

   a. Advocating on behalf of a client about trust tax matters under review by the Internal Revenue Service
   b. Providing financial analysis, planning, and capital acquisition services as a part-time, in-house controller
   c. Advising management in the selection of a computer system to meet business needs
   d. Preparing the income statement and balance sheet for one year in the future based on client expectations and predictions (ID: 7838)

7. Which of the following procedures would be most effective in reducing attestation risk?
   a. Discussion with responsible individuals
   b. Examination of evidence
   c. Inquiries of senior management
   d. Analytical procedures (ID: 8376)

8. A CPA is engaged to examine management's assertion that the entity's schedule of investment returns is presented in accordance with specific criteria. In performing this engagement, the CPA should comply with the provisions of
   a. Statements on Standards for Accounting and Review Services (SSARS)
   b. Statements on Auditing Standards (SAS)
   c. Statements on Standards for Consulting Services (SSCS)
   d. Statements on Standards for Attestation Engagements (SSAE) (ID: 8415)

9. Which of the following is a conceptual similarity between generally accepted auditing standards and the attestation standards?
   a. Both sets of standards require the CPA to report on the adequacy of disclosure in the financial statements.
   b. All of the standards of fieldwork in generally accepted auditing standards are included in the attestation standards.
   c. The requirement that the CPA be independent in mental attitude is included in both sets of standards.
   d. Both sets of standards are applicable to engagements regarding financial forecasts and projections. (ID: 8849)

10. What type of evidence would provide the highest level of assurance in an attestation engagement?
    a. Evidence secured solely from within the entity
    b. Evidence obtained from independent sources
    c. Evidence obtained indirectly
    d. Evidence obtained from multiple internal inquiries (ID: 9369)

Agreed-Upon Procedures

11. An accountant may accept an engagement to apply agreed-upon procedures to prospective financial statements provided that
    a. Use of the report is restricted to the specified users.
    b. The prospective financial statements are also examined.
    c. Responsibility for the adequacy of the procedures performed is taken by the accountant.
    d. Negative assurance is expressed on the prospective financial statements taken as a whole. (ID: 5096)

12. Which of the following statements should be included in a practitioner's report on the application of agreed-upon procedures?
    a. A statement that the practitioner performed an examination of prospective financial statements
    b. A statement of scope limitation that will qualify the practitioner's opinion
    c. A statement referring to standards established by the AICPA
    d. A statement of negative assurance based on procedures performed (ID: 90180)

13. A practitioner has been engaged to apply agreed-upon procedures in accordance with Statements on Standards for Attestation Engagements to prospective financial statements. Which of the following conditions must be met for the practitioner to perform the engagement?
    a. The prospective financial statement includes a summary of significant accounting policies.
    b. The practitioner takes responsibility for the sufficiency of the agreed-upon procedures.
    c. The practitioner and specified parties agree upon the procedures to be performed by the practitioner.
    d. The practitioner reports on the criteria to be used in the determination of findings. (ID: 8811)

14. A CPA's report on agreed-upon procedures related to management's assertion about an entity's compliance with specified requirements should contain
    a. A statement of restrictions on the use of the report
    b. An opinion about whether management's assertion is fairly stated
    c. Negative assurance that control risk has not been assessed
    d. An acknowledgment of responsibility for the sufficiency of the procedures (ID: 6028)

15. A practitioner's report on agreed-upon procedures that is in the form of procedures and findings should contain
    a. Negative assurance that the procedures did not necessarily disclose all reportable conditions
    b. An acknowledgment of the practitioner's responsibility for the sufficiency of the procedures
    c. A statement of restrictions on the use of the report
    d. A disclaimer of opinion on the entity's financial statements (ID: 8132)

16. An accountant's report on a review of pro forma financial information should include a
    a. Statement that the entity's internal control was not relied on in the review
    b. Disclaimer of opinion on the financial statements from which the pro forma financial information is derived
    c. Caveat that it is uncertain whether the transaction or event reflected in the pro forma financial information will ever occur
    d. Reference to the financial statements from which the historical financial information is derived (ID: 4733)

17. Which of the following components is appropriate in a practitioner's report on the results of applying agreed-upon procedures?
    a. A list of the procedures performed, as agreed to by the specified parties identified in the report.
    b. A statement that management is responsible for expressing an opinion.
    c. A title that includes the phrase "independent audit."
    d. A statement that the report is unrestricted in its use. (ID: 9399)

18. Which of the following should a practitioner perform as part of an engagement for agreed-upon procedures in accordance with Statements on Standards for Attestation Engagements?
    a. Issue a report on findings based on specified procedures performed
    b. Assess whether the procedures meet the needs of the parties
    c. Express negative assurance on findings of work performed
    d. Report the differences between agreed-upon and audit procedures (ID: 90159)

19. An accountant may accept an engagement to apply agreed-upon procedures to prospective financial statements provided the
    a. Provisions of Statements on Standards for Accounting and Review Services (SSARS) are followed.
    b. Accountant also examines the prospective financial statements.
    c. Distribution of the report is restricted to the specified users.
    d. The accountant takes responsibility for the adequacy of the procedures performed. (ID: 8421)

Financial Forecasts and Projections

20. An accountant's standard report on a compilation of a projection should not include a
    a. Statement that a compilation of a projection is limited in scope
    b. Disclaimer of responsibility to update the report for events occurring after the report's date
    c. Statement that the accountant expresses only limited assurance that the results may be achieved
    d. Caveat that the prospective results may not be achieved (ID: 4294)

21. When a CPA examines a client's projected financial statements, the CPA's report should
    a. Explain the principal differences between historical and projected financial statements
    b. State that the CPA performed procedures to evaluate management's assumptions
    c. Refer to the CPA's auditor's report on the historical financial statements
    d. Include the CPA's opinion on the client's ability to continue as a going concern (ID: 7091)

22. When an accountant compiles a financial forecast, the accountant's report should include a(an)
    a. Explanation of the differences between a financial forecast and a financial projection
    b. Caveat that the prospective results of the financial forecast may not be achieved
    c. Statement that the accountant's responsibility to update the report is limited to one year
    d. Disclaimer of opinion on the reliability of the entity's internal controls (ID: 8150)

23. Which of the following is a prospective financial statement for general use upon which an accountant may appropriately report?
    a. Pro forma financial statement
    b. Partial presentation
    c. Financial projection
    d. Financial forecast (ID: 7511)

24. When an accountant compiles projected financial statements, the accountant's report should include a separate paragraph that
    a. Disclaims any form of assurance on the historical financial statements
    b. Expresses limited assurance that the results will be within the projected range
    c. Describes the limitations on the usefulness of the projection
    d. Evaluates the hypothetical assumptions used to prepare the projection (ID: 90178)

25. Accepting an engagement to examine an entity's financial projection most likely would be appropriate if the projection were to be used by
    a. All employees who work for the entity
    b. Potential stockholders who request a prospectus or a registration statement
    c. All stockholders of record as of the report date
    d. A bank with which the entity is negotiating for a loan (ID: 4679)

26. An examination of a financial forecast is a professional service that involves
    a. Compiling or assembling a financial forecast that is based on management's assumptions
    b. Evaluating the preparation of a financial forecast and the support underlying management's assumptions
    c. Assuming responsibility to update management on key events for one year after the report's date
    d. Limiting the distribution of the accountant's report to management and the board of directors (ID: 5640)

27. An accountant's compilation report on a financial forecast should include a statement that
    a. The hypothetical assumptions used in the forecast are reasonable in the circumstances.
    b. The forecast should be read only in conjunction with the audited historical financial statements.
    c. The accountant expresses only limited assurance on the forecasted statements and their assumptions.
    d. There will usually be differences between the forecasted and actual results. (ID: 8820)

28. A CPA is engaged to examine an entity's financial forecast. The CPA believes that several significant assumptions do **not** provide a reasonable basis for the forecast. Under these circumstances, the CPA should issue a(an)

    a. Adverse opinion
    b. Pro forma opinion
    c. Qualified opinion
    d. Unqualified opinion with an explanatory paragraph (ID: 8835)

29. Which of the following prospective financial statements is(are) appropriate for general use?

	Financial forecast	Financial projection
a.	Yes	Yes
b.	Yes	No
c.	No	Yes
d.	No	No

(ID: 8838)

30. Which of the following procedures should an accountant perform during an engagement to compile prospective financial statements?

    a. Test the entity's internal controls to determine if adequate controls exist so that financial projections can be reasonably achieved
    b. Make inquiries prior to the date of the report about possible future transactions that may impact the forecast once the report is issued
    c. Make inquiries about the accounting principles used in the preparation of the prospective financial statements
    d. Compare the prospective financial statements with the entity's historical results for the prior year (ID: 9393)

31. Accepting an engagement to compile a financial projection most likely would be inappropriate if the projection is to be distributed to

    a. The entity's principal stockholder, to the exclusion of the other stockholders
    b. Potential stockholders in an offering statement
    c. A financial institution in a loan application
    d. A state or federal regulatory agency (ID: 9903)

Reporting on Internal Control

32. In reporting on a nonissuer's internal control over financial reporting, an auditor should include a paragraph that describes the

    a. Documentary evidence regarding the control environment factors
    b. Changes in internal control since the prior report
    c. Potential benefits from the auditor's suggested improvements
    d. Inherent limitations of any internal control structure (ID: 5702)

33. Brown, CPA, has accepted an engagement to examine the effectiveness of internal control over financial reporting of Crow Company (a nonissuer). Crow Company's written assertion about the effectiveness of internal control should be presented

    I. In a separate report that will accompany Brown's report
    II. In a representation letter to Brown

    a. Neither I nor II
    b. Either I or II
    c. I only
    d. II only (ID: 5983)

34. How do the scope, procedures, and objective of an engagement to examine the design and operating effectiveness of an entity's internal control over financial reporting compare to those for obtaining an understanding of internal control and assessing control risk as part of an audit?

	Scope	Procedures	Objective
a.	Similar	Different	Similar
b.	Different	Similar	Similar
c.	Different	Different	Different
d.	Different	Similar	Different

(ID: 400)

Problem 14-2 SIMULATION: Research

Which section of the professional standards provides guidance for dating a practitioner's report on agreed-upon procedures?

Reminder: On the actual exam, you will use an electronic database of authoritative literature to find and select the reference (appropriate section and paragraph of the relevant guidance). Please see the AICPA's tutorial and sample test on the exam section of their website.

[ ] § [ ] [ ] (ID: 9242)

Problem 14-3 SIMULATION: Attestation Standards Terminology

The items in the table below are definitions of terms used in the attestation standards. Select, from the accompanying list of terms, the term each item defines.

Definitions	Terms
1. Any declaration or set of declarations about whether the subject matter is based on or in conformity with the criteria selected.	
2. Any unresolved problem that the practitioner had in complying with the attestation standards, interpretive standards, or the specific procedures agreed to by the specified parties.	
3. A presentation that shows, given one or more hypothetical assumptions, an entity's expected financial position, results of operations, and cash flows.	
4. A deficiency, or a combination of deficiencies, in internal control such that there is a reasonable possibility that a material misstatement of the entity's financial statements will not be prevented, or detected and corrected on a timely basis.	
5. A financial statement assertion that has a reasonable possibility of containing a misstatement or misstatements that would cause the financial statements to be materially misstated.	
6. Exists when the design or operation of a control does not allow management or employees, in the normal course of performing their assigned functions, to prevent, or detect and correct misstatements on a timely basis.	
7. A presentation that shows an entity's expected financial position, results of operations, and cash flows.	
8. The person or persons, either as individuals or representatives of the entity, responsible for the subject matter.	
9. A presentation that shows what the significant effects on historical financial information might have been had a consummated or proposed transaction (or event) occurred at an earlier date.	
10. A deficiency, or a combination of deficiencies, in internal control that is important enough to merit attention by those charged with governance.	

Selection List of Terms

A.	Responsible party	L.	Assertion
B.	Deficiency in internal control	M.	Weakness
C.	Affirmation	N.	Assurance
D.	Significant deficiency	O.	Accountable party
E.	Client	P.	Assessment
F.	Material weakness	Q.	Material limitation
G.	Exception	R.	Material assertion
H.	Financial projection	S.	Evaluation
I.	Reservation	T.	Finding
J.	Relevant assertion	U.	Financial forecast
K.	Pro forma financial information	V.	Significant limitation

(ID: 89464)

Solution 14-1 MULTIPLE-CHOICE ANSWERS

1. (a) The Statements on Standards for Attestation Engagements are applicable to engagements to issue an assertion about subject matter that is the responsibly of another party; these engagements exclude audits of historical financial statements (HFS). The Statements on Auditing Standards provide guidance for audits of HFS and reviews of interim HFS when the corresponding annual HFS are expected to be audited by the same auditor. The Statements on Standards for Accounting and Review Services are applicable to engagements to compile and review HFS. The Statements on Standards for Consulting Services provide guidance for a wide array of services with little relation to financial statements, including information technology selection and implementation, support services, and business plan preparation. (ID: 90184)

2. (b) An attest engagement is one in which a CPA in public practice (or practitioner) is engaged to, or does, issue an examination, review, or agreed-upon procedures report on subject matter or an assertion about subject matter that is the responsibility of another party. Reports on financial statements are subject to the guidance of Statements on Auditing Standards (SAS) and Statements on Standards for Accounting & Review Services (SSARS). Supplying a client with a blank financial statement format is a service exempt from SAS and SSARS; SSAE do not apply to financial statements. (ID: 7103)

3. (b) An attest engagement is one in which a CPA in public practice is engaged to issue an examination, review, or agreed-upon procedures report on subject matter or an assertion about subject matter that is the responsibility of another party. AT 600 established guidance concerning attest engagements on an entity's compliance with requirements of specified laws, regulations, rules, contracts, etc. AT 100 specifically lists, as engagements to which attest standards are inapplicable, engagements performed in accordance with Statements on Standards for Consulting Services, client advocacy engagements, and tax return preparation services. (ID: 7835)

4. (d) A sufficient understanding of internal control for planning an engagement is not an attestation standard. The other answers are attestation standards. Answer a. is the second standard of fieldwork; answer b. is the first standard of reporting; and answer c. is the first standard of fieldwork. (ID: 3900)

5. (c) SSAE do not apply to client advocacy engagements, but they do apply to engagements to examine, compile, or apply agreed-upon procedures to financial forecasts and projections. (ID: 7016)

6. (d) The SSAEs provide guidance concerning attest engagements on prospective financial statements. The other answers would not be considered attest engagements. (ID: 7838)

7. (b) Examination of evidence is the most effective procedure. In the hierarchy of available attest procedures, those that involve search and verification (for example, inspection, confirmation, or observation), particularly when using independent sources outside the entity, are generally more effective in restricting attestation risk than those involving internal inquiries and comparisons of internal information (for example, analytical procedures and discussions with individuals responsible for the subject matter or the assertion). (ID: 8376)

8. (d) SSAE apply when a CPA in public practice is engaged to issue an examination, review, or agreed-upon procedures report on subject matter or an assertion about subject matter that is the responsibility of another party. SSARS apply to compilations and reviews of financial statements. SAS apply to audits to financial statements. SSCS apply to consulting engagements. (ID: 8415)

9. (c) The requirement that the CPA be independent in mental attitude is included in both sets of standards. Only GAAS require the CPA to report on the adequacy of disclosure in the financial statements. The attestation standards do not include a standard similar the GAAS second standard of fieldwork: "The auditor must obtain a sufficient understanding of the entity and its environment, including its internal control, to assess the risk of material misstatement of the financial statements whether due to error or fraud, and to design the nature, timing, and extent of further audit procedures." Only the attestation standards are applicable to engagements regarding financial forecasts and projections. (ID: 8849)

10. (b) Evidence obtained from independent sources outside an entity provides the highest level of assurance. Evidence obtained from independent sources outside an entity provides greater assurance about the subject matter or the assertion than evidence secured solely from within the entity even if it is obtained from multiple inquiries. Information obtained from the independent attester's direct personal knowledge (such as through physical examination, observation, computation, operating tests, or inspection) is more persuasive than information obtained indirectly. (ID: 9369)

11. (a) A practitioner may perform an agreed-upon procedures attestation engagement on prospective financial statements provided that use of the report is to be restricted to the specified parties. SSAE 10 merely requires the subject matter to be subject to reasonably consistent estimation or measurement. Responsibility for adequacy for the procedures performed is taken by the specified users, not the accountant. The practitioner should not provide negative assurance. (ID: 5096)

12. (c) For an engagement to report on agreed-upon procedures, the accountant issues a report on findings based on the specific procedures performed; in this report, the accountant mentions that the engagement was performed in accordance with the attestation standards of the AICPA. If the engagement was to examine prospective financial statements, the practitioner would not issue a report on the application of agreed-upon procedures. In a report on agreed-upon procedures, the accountant explicitly disclaims the expression of any opinion—including both a qualified opinion and negative assurance. (ID: 90180)

13. (c) One of the conditions that must be met by a practitioner who accepts an engagement to apply agreed-upon procedures in accordance with SSAE to prospective financial statements is that the practitioner and specified parties agree upon the procedures to be performed by the practitioner. The prospective financial statements must include a summary of significant assumptions, not account ting policies. The specified parties, not the practitioner, must take responsibility for the sufficiency of the agreed-upon procedures for their purpose. The practitioner does not report on the criteria to be used in the determination of findings, rather the criteria must be agreed upon between the practitioner and the specified parties. (ID: 8811)

14. (a) A report on an engagement consisting of applying agreed-upon procedures should include a statement of restrictions on the use of the report because it is intended to be used solely by the specified parties. The practitioner does not provide an opinion; instead the report should be presented in the form of procedures and findings. Negative assurance is not allowed. The sufficiency of the procedures is solely the responsibility of the specified parties who agreed to those procedures; the practitioner should disclaim responsibility for the sufficiency of the procedures. (ID: 6028)

15. (c) In an agreed-upon procedures engagement, a client engages the practitioner to assist specified parties in evaluating subject matter or an assertion as a result of needs of the specified parties. The specified parties assume responsibility for the sufficiency of the procedures since they best understand their own needs. The practitioner does not provide an opinion or negative assurance; the report should be in the form of procedures and findings. A practitioner's report on such engagements should indicate clearly that its use is restricted to those specified parties. (ID: 8132)

16. (d) The practitioner's report on pro forma financial information should include reference to the financial statements from which the historical financial information is derived. The statement in answer a. should not be made in any review engagement. The report on pro forma information is a different engagement from reporting on the financial statements from which the pro forma information was derived; thus, the practitioner would not issue an opinion or disclaimer of opinion on those statements. No reference to uncertainty should be made as that is assumed, based upon the nature of the engagement, and the accountant need only provide a conclusion as to whether any information came to the accountant's attention to cause the accountant to believe management's assumptions do not provide a reasonable basis for the effects directly attributable to the transaction or event or that the pro forma column does not reflect the proper application of those adjustments to the historical financial statements. (ID: 4733)

17. (a) A list of the procedures performed (or reference thereto) and related findings is an appropriate component of a practitioner's report on the results of applying agreed-upon procedures. Neither management nor the practitioner is responsible for expressing an opinion. The report includes a disclaimer of opinion on the subject matter. An appropriate title for the report is *Independent Accountant's Report on Applying Agreed-Upon Procedures*; it would not include the term *audit*. The report should include a statement of restrictions on the use of the report because it is intended to be used solely by the specified parties, not a statement that it is unrestricted in its use. (ID: 9399)

18. (a) For an engagement to report on agreed-upon procedures, the accountant issues a report on findings based on the specific procedures performed. The client must take responsibility for determining whether the agreed-upon procedures are sufficient for the intended purpose. An accountant rarely gives negative assurance; in a report on agreed-upon procedures, the accountant explicitly disclaims the expression of any opinion. Generally, no mention is made regarding audit procedures in a report on an attestation engagement. (ID: 90159)

19. (c) Among other things, a report on the results of applying agreed-upon procedures to financial forecasts and projections must include a restriction on the use of the report. The Statements on Standards for Attestation Engagements (SSAE) apply to engagements to apply agreed-upon procedures to prospective financial statements, not SSARS. A CPA may perform agreed-upon procedures without examining or compiling the related prospective financial statements. The client must accept responsibility for the adequacy of the procedures performed in an agreed-upon procedures engagement. (ID: 8421)

20. (c) The practitioner's standard report on a compilation of prospective financial statements should include a statement that a compilation is limited in scope and does not enable the practitioner to express an opinion or any other form of assurance on the prospective financial statements or the assumptions; a statement that the practitioner assumes no responsibility to update the report for events and circumstances occurring after the date of the report; and a caveat that the prospective results may not be achieved. It should also include an identification of the prospective financial statements presented by the responsible party and a statement that the practitioner compiled the prospective financial statements in accordance with attestation standards established by the AICPA. (ID: 4294)

21. (b) When a CPA examines a projection, the CPA should express an opinion on whether the assumptions provide a reasonable basis for the projection given the hypothetical assumptions. The standard report includes language such as the following in the scope paragraph, ...included such procedures as we considered necessary to evaluate both the assumptions used by management and the preparation and presentation of the projection. (ID: 7091)

22. (b) A standard compilation report of prospective financial statements requires a caveat that the prospective results may not be achieved. An explanation of the difference between a financial forecast and a financial projection is not needed. The practitioner assumes no responsibility to update the report for events and circumstances occurring after the date of the report. A compilation does not consider the entity's internal controls. (ID: 8150)

23. (d) Prospective financial statements are for either general use or limited use. General use of prospective financial statements refers to use of the statements by persons with whom the responsible party is not negotiating directly, for example, in an offering statement of an entity's debt or equity interests. Because recipients of prospective financial statements distributed for general use are unable to ask the responsible party directly about the presentation, the presentation most useful to them is one that portrays, to the best of the responsible party's knowledge and belief, the expected results. Thus, only a financial forecast is appropriate for general use. (ID: 7511)

24. (c) For a projection, a practitioner's compilation report must include a separate paragraph that describes the limitations on the usefulness of the presentation. A report for an engagement to compile a projection would be unlikely to reference historical financial statements. A compilation engagement involves assisting the client in presenting financial information in the form of financial statements without undertaking to provide any assurance. An evaluation of the assumptions used to prepare a projection is a form of assurance. (ID: 90178)

25. (d) A projection, since it is not meant for general use, would be inappropriate for all stockholders of record and employees, as it would be unreasonable to expect these groups to be familiar with the basis of the projection or to be involved closely with those preparing it. (ID: 4679)

26. (b) An examination of prospective financial statements...involves evaluating the preparation of the prospective financial statements, evaluating the support underlying the assumptions, evaluating the presentation of the prospective financial statements for conformity with AICPA presentation guidelines, and issuing an examination report. This service does not include compiling the forecast, or assuming responsibility to update management on key events afterwards. The report may be for general use, in which case the distribution need not be limited. (ID: 5640)

27. (d) An accountant's compilation report on a financial forecast should include a caveat that the prospective results may not be achieved, such as there will usually be differences between the forecasted and actual results because events and circumstances frequently do not occur as expected, and those differences may be material. Answers a. and c. are not correct because the report should also include a statement that a compilation is limited in scope and does not enable the accountant to express an opinion or any other form of assurance on the prospective financial statements or the assumptions. There is no requirement that the forecast be read in conjunction with the audited historical financial statements. (ID: 8820)

28. (a) If the CPA believes the assumptions do not provide a reasonable basis for the forecast, the CPA should issue an adverse opinion. The opinion paragraph should include a statement to that effect. (ID: 8835)

29. (b) A financial forecast is the only type of prospective financial statement appropriate for general use. General use refers to use of the statements by parties who are not negotiating directly with the responsible party. Because recipients of prospective financial statements distributed for general use are unable to ask the responsible party directly about the presentation, the presentation most useful to them is one that portrays, to the best of the responsible party's knowledge and belief, the expected results, i.e., a financial forecast. Any type of prospective financial statements that would be useful in the circumstances would normally be appropriate for limited use. Thus, a limited use distribution could include either a financial forecast or a projection. (ID: 8838)

30. (c) During an engagement to compile prospective financial statements, an accountant should make inquiries about the accounting principles used in the preparation of the prospective financial statements. The other answers are not required procedures. (ID: 9393)

31. (b) A CPA should not accept an engagement if the CPA's name will be used in conjunction with a financial projection that will be distributed to those who will not be negotiating directly with the responsible party (unless the projection is used to supplement a financial forecast which was not indicated by this question). The responsible party is the person(s) who are responsible for the assumptions underlying the prospective financial information. The responsible party is usually management, but it can be persons outside the entity, for example, a party considering acquiring the entity. The attestation standards for prospective financial statements distinguish between forecasts and projections. Relevant to this question, a financial projection is not appropriate for general use. General use refers to the use of the statements by persons with whom the responsible party is not negotiating directly, for example, in an offering statement of an entity's debt or equity interests. Because recipients of prospective financial statements distributed for general use are unable to ask the responsible party directly about the presentation, the presentation most useful to them is one that portrays, to the best of the responsible party's knowledge and belief, the expected results. Thus, only a financial forecast is appropriate for general use. Limited use refers to the use of the statements by the responsible party alone or by the responsible party and third parties with whom the responsible party is negotiating directly. Examples include use in negotiations for a bank loan, submission to a regulatory agency (submission to a regulatory agency is considered limited use even though, by law or regulation, it may be a matter of public record), and use solely within the entity. Thus, the other answers describe acceptable engagements as long as the report includes an appropriately worded restriction limiting its use. (ID: 9903)

32. (d) A paragraph describing the inherent limitations of any internal control structure is one of required elements of the auditor's report on the examination of internal control. The other answers are not required elements. (ID: 5702)

33. (c) Management must present its written assertion about the effectiveness of the entity's internal control in a report that accompanies the auditor's report. (ID: 5983)

34. (d) Although the examination of an entity's internal control over financial reporting should be integrated with the audit of financial statements, the two engagements have different objectives and generally differ in scope. However, the procedures are similar in nature. (ID: 400)

Solution 14-2 SIMULATION ANSWER: Research

Which section of the professional standards provides guidance for dating a practitioner's report on agreed-upon procedures?

AT	§	201	34	(ID: 9242)

.34 The date of completion of the agreed-upon procedures should be used as the date of the practitioner's report.

Solution 14-3 SIMULATION ANSWER: Attestation Standards Terminology

Definitions	Terms
1. Any declaration or set of declarations about whether the subject matter is based on or in conformity with the criteria selected.	L. Assertion
2. Any unresolved problem that the practitioner had in complying with the attestation standards, interpretive standards, or the specific procedures agreed to by the specified parties.	I. Reservation
3. A presentation that shows, given one or more hypothetical assumptions, an entity's expected financial position, results of operations, and cash flows.	H. Financial projection
4. A deficiency, or a combination of deficiencies, in internal control such that there is a reasonable possibility that a material misstatement of the entity's financial statements will not be prevented, or detected and corrected on a timely basis.	F. Material weakness
5. A financial statement assertion that has a reasonable possibility of containing a misstatement or misstatements that would cause the financial statements to be materially misstated.	J. Relevant assertion
6. Exists when the design or operation of a control does not allow management or employees, in the normal course of performing their assigned functions, to prevent, or detect and correct misstatements on a timely basis.	B. Deficiency in internal control
7. A presentation that shows an entity's expected financial position, results of operations, and cash flows.	U. Financial forecast
8. The person or persons, either as individuals or representatives of the entity, responsible for the subject matter.	A. Responsible party
9. A presentation that shows what the significant effects on historical financial information might have been had a consummated or proposed transaction (or event) occurred at an earlier date.	K. Pro forma financial information
10. A deficiency, or a combination of deficiencies, in internal control that is important enough to merit attention by those charged with governance. Note: A significant deficiency is less severe than a material weakness.	D. Significant deficiency

(ID: 89464)

CHANGE ALERT

AICPA Code of Professional Conduct; issued electronically 5/15/14

The AICPA membership adopted the *Code of Professional Conduct* (Code) to provide guidance and rules to all members in the performance of their professional responsibilities. The Code consists of principles and rules as well as interpretations and other guidance. The principles provide the framework for the rules that govern the performance of their professional responsibilities.

A revised version of the AICPA *Code of Professional Conduct* (Revised Code) was adopted by the Professional Ethics Executive Committee on January 28, 2014. It will be issued in electronic format by the third quarter of 2014; and it will become effective December 15, 2014, with delayed implementation of the two conceptual frameworks (effective December 15, 2015). The delayed effective date permits members sufficient time to become familiar with the new conceptual frameworks and update their internal policies and procedures.

The most significant change to the Revised Code is the inclusion of two conceptual frameworks; one for members in public practice, and one for members in business. The conceptual framework approach is based on a "threats and safeguards" approach, the purpose of which is to assist members in analyzing relationships and circumstances not specifically addressed in the Revised Code that may threaten compliance with the Revised Code's principles, rules and interpretations. In other words, in situations where no specific guidance is provided, the member will now need to apply the conceptual framework approach to determine if the relationship or circumstance could result in noncompliance.

In addition to inclusion of the conceptual frameworks, the original Code was reformatted to be more intuitively organized. The Revised Code separates guidance by line of business. Part 1 applies to AICPA members in public practice; Part 2 to members in business; and Part 3 to all other members, including those who are retired or between jobs. Content is then organized by topic, subtopic, and sections.

All ethical rulings have been redrafted as interpretations and codified under the appropriate topic. All non-authoritative guidance issued by the Professional Ethics Division is also included in the Revised Code. The electronic format allows for easy navigation and advanced search capabilities. Access to the Revised Code is free (pub.aicpa.org/codeofconduct).

Since early implementation is permitted for both the Revised Code and conceptual frameworks, it will become testable in the window beginning six months after the issuance date, which was May 15, 2014; in other words, the **January-February 2015** test window.

CHAPTER 15

ACCOUNTANTS' PROFESSIONAL RESPONSIBILITIES

CHAPTER 15

ACCOUNTANTS' PROFESSIONAL RESPONSIBILITIES

I. AICPA Code of Professional Conduct

A. Introduction

The AICPA recognizes that a distinguishing mark of a profession is its acceptance of a high degree of responsibility to the public. The Code of Professional Conduct (the Code) requires an unswerving commitment to honorable behavior even if it means sacrificing personal advantages, and consists of two sections—Principles and Rules. The Code applies to all types of engagements, including: audits, reviews, compilations, special reports; and attestation engagements.

1. **Adoption** The original Code was adopted in 1988 (and periodically revised) to provide guidance and rules to all members—those in public practice, in industry, in government, and in education—in the performance of all their professional responsibilities.

2. **Revised Code** A revised version AICPA Code (Revised Code) will become effective December 15, 2014. The Revised Code will have three parts. Part 1 applies to AICPA members in public practice; Part 2 to members in business; and Part 3 to all other members, including those who are retired or between jobs.

   The most significant change to the Revised Code is the inclusion of two conceptual frameworks, one for members in public practice, and one for members in business. The conceptual framework approach is a way of identifying, evaluating, and addressing threats to compliance with the rules. The conceptual framework and related interpretations are not effective until December 15, 2015. See Section X for the revised code.

3. **Other Changes** In addition to inclusion of the conceptual frameworks, the original Code was revised to reflect the conceptual framework approach, with the intent to aid the user if understanding potential threats. The Code was also expanded to include references to nonauthoritative guidance. The Revised Code will be available in electronic format, with basic and advanced search capabilities.

4. **Testability** Since early implementation is permitted, the Revised Code will become testable in the window beginning six months after the **issuance** date, which was June 30, 2014; in other words, the January-February 2015 test window.

B. Principles of Conduct

Six articles compose the Principles of Conduct section of the Code. They stress the CPA's responsibility to the public, to clients, and to colleagues, and provide a basis for the Rules of Conduct.

1. **Article I—Responsibilities** In carrying out their responsibilities as professionals, members should exercise sensitive professional and moral judgments in all their activities. Members also have a responsibility to cooperate with each other to continually improve the art of accounting, maintain the public's confidence, and carry out the responsibilities of self-governance.

2. **Article II—Public Interest** Members should accept the obligation to act in a way that will serve the public interest, honor the public trust, and demonstrate a commitment to professionalism. Members have a duty to discharge their responsibilities with integrity, objectivity, due professional care, and a genuine interest in serving the public.

3. **Article III—Integrity** To maintain and broaden public confidence, members should perform all professional responsibilities with the highest sense of integrity. Integrity requires a member to be honest and candid within the constraints of client confidentiality. Integrity also requires a member to observe the principles of objectivity and independence and of due care.

4. **Article IV—Objectivity and Independence** Independence is required for audit and attest services only. Objectivity is always required. A member in public practice should be independent in fact and appearance when providing auditing and other attestation services. Public confidence would be impaired by evidence that independence was actually impaired and it might also be impaired by the existence of circumstances that reasonable people might believe likely to influence independence.

5. **Article V—Due Care** A member should observe the profession's technical and ethical standards, strive continually to improve competence and the quality of services, and discharge professional responsibility to the best of the member's ability. Demonstrating competency requires a commitment to learning and professional improvement throughout a member's professional life. A member is required to plan and supervise adequately all professional activities for which the member has responsibility.

6. **Article VI—Scope and Nature of Services** A member in public practice should observe the Principles of the Code in determining the scope and nature of services to be provided. Members of the AICPA should practice in firms that maintain adequate internal quality control procedures, determine whether the scope and nature of other services provided to an audit client would create a conflict of interest, and assess whether an activity is consistent with their role as professionals.

C. Independence, Integrity, and Objectivity

1. **Rule 101—Independence** A member in public practice shall be independent in the performance of professional services as required by standards promulgated by bodies designated by council.

   a. **Impairment** Independence shall be considered impaired if, during the period of professional engagement

      (1) **Financial Interest** A member had a direct or material indirect financial interest in the client. A direct financial interest will impair independence even if it is immaterial. Under certain circumstances, this applies also to situations where the member or the member's firm is trustee, executor, or administrator of any estate that had acquired or was committed to acquire any direct or material indirect financial interest in the client; ownership in a mutual fund; and partnerships.

      (2) **Shareholder** A partner or professional employee of the firm, his or her immediate family, or any group of such persons acting together owned more than 5 percent of a client's outstanding equity securities or other ownership interests.

      (3) **Relationships** During the period covered by the financial statements, a firm, or partner or professional employee of the firm was simultaneously associated with the client as a(n): director, officer, or employee, or in any capacity equivalent to that of a member of management; promoter, underwriter, or voting trustee; or trustee for any pension or profit-sharing trust of the client.

b. **Key Position** A key position is one in which an individual has: primary responsibility for significant accounting functions that support material components of the financial statements; primary responsibility for the preparation of the financial statements; or the ability to exercise influence over the contents of the financial statements, including when the individual is a member of the board of directors or similar governing body, chief executive officer, president, chief financial officer, chief operating officer, general counsel, chief accounting officer, controller, director of internal audit, director of financial reporting, treasurer, or any equivalent position.

(1) **Members Formerly Employed by or Otherwise Associated With a Client** An individual who formerly was employed by a client or associated with a client as an officer, director, promoter, underwriter, voting trustee, or trustee for a pension or profit-sharing trust of the client would impair the firm's independence if the individual fails to dissociates from the client, or participates on the attest engagement team or is an individual in a position to influence the attest engagement for the client, when the attest engagement covers any period that includes his or her former employment or association with that client.

(2) **Member's Immediate Family** A member's immediate family (spouse, spousal equivalent, or dependent) is subject to Rule 101 (and its interpretations and rulings), but with the following exceptions: an individual in a member's immediate family was employed by the client in a position other than a key position; or in connection with her/his permitted employment, an immediate family member may participate in a certain retirement, savings, compensation, or similar plans under certain circumstances.

(3) **Close Relatives** Independence would be considered impaired with respect to close relatives (parent, sibling, or nondependent child) if:

(a) An individual participating on the attest engagement team has a close relative who had a key position with the client, or a financial interest in the client that was material to the close relative and of which the individual has knowledge or enabled the close relative to exercise significant influence over the client.

(b) An individual in a position to influence the attest engagement or any partner in the office in which the lead attest engagement partner primarily practices in connection with the attest engagement has a close relative who had a key position with the client, or a financial interest in the client that was material to the close relative and of which the individual or partner has knowledge and enabled the close relative to exercise significant influence over the client.

c. **Employment or Association With Attest Clients** If a partner or professional employee leaves the firm and subsequently is employed by or associated with that client in a key position, then the firm's independence would be impaired, unless all of these conditions are met

(1) **Payments for Prior Services** Payment of amounts owed to a former partner or professional employee for a prior interest in the firm or for unfunded, vested retirement benefits. The amounts may not be material to the firm and the formula used to calculate the payments should be fixed during the payout period.

(2) **No Influence in Firm's Operations** The former partner and professional employee is not in a position to influence the accounting firm's operations or financial policies.

(3) **No Participation With Former Firm** The former partner and professional employee may not participate or appear to participate, and is not associated with, the firm.

(4) **Engagement Procedure Modification** The ongoing attest engagement team considers the appropriateness or necessity of engagement procedures modification to adjust for the risk that audit effectiveness could be reduced as a result of the former partner or professional employee's prior knowledge of the audit plan.

(5) **Assessment** Attestation engagement team members must determine their effectiveness in dealing with the former partner or professional employee when that person will have significant interaction with the attest engagement team.

(6) **Review** Subsequent to the attestation engagement members must determine whether the engagement team members maintained the appropriate level of skepticism when evaluating the representations and work of the former partner or professional employee, when the person joins the client in a key position within one year of disassociating from the firm.

d. **Considering Employment or Association With Client** When a covered member becomes aware that a member of the attest engagement team or an individual in a position to influence the attest engagement is considering employment or association with a client, the covered member should notify an appropriate person in the firm.

e. **Performance of Nonattest Services** A member in public practice or the member's firm who performs attest services for a client (which requires independence) also may perform other nonattest services for the same client. A member's independence would not be impaired if all the following conditions exist: the nonattest services were provided prior to the period of the professional engagement; the nonattest services related to periods prior to the period covered by the financial statements; and the financial statements for the period to which the nonattest services relate were audited by another firm (or in the case of a review engagement, reviewed or audited by another firm).

(1) **General Activities** Some of the activities that would impair a member's independence include

- Setting policies or strategic direction for the client
- Having or exercising authority on behalf of the client to authorize, execute or consummate a transaction
- Preparing source documents in electronic form evidencing the occurrence of a transaction
- Having custody of client assets
- Supervising client employees in the performance of their normal recurring activities
- Determining which recommendations of the member should be implemented
- Reporting to the board of directors on behalf of management
- Serving as a client's stock transfer or escrow agent, registrar, general counsel or its equivalent
- Establishing or maintaining internal controls, including performing ongoing monitoring activities for a client

(2) **Specific Examples** The following list includes examples of certain nonattest services for an attest client that could impair independence under certain circumstances

- Bookkeeping
- Nontax disbursements (e.g., payroll)
- Benefit plan administration
- Investment—advisory or management
- Corporate finance—consulting or advisory
- Executive or employee search
- Business risk consulting
- Information systems—design, installation, or integration
- Appraisal, valuation, or actuarial service
- Forensic accounting services
- Internal audit assistance services

f. **Honorary Directorships and Trusteeships of NPOs** A not-for-profit organization that limits its activities to performing charitable, religious, civic, or similar functions may seek to gain the prestige of a member's name by asking the member to serve on its board of directors or trustees. The member may do so and be associated with the organization's financial statements as long as the position is purely honorary, all letterheads and material circulated to outside parties that identify the member as a director or trustee clearly indicate that the position is honorary, and the member does not vote or in any other way participate in management functions.

g. **Permitted Loans From Financial Institution Clients** Generally, independence shall be considered to be impaired if a covered member has any loan to or from a client, any officer or director of the client, or any individual owning 10 percent or more of the client's outstanding equity securities or other ownership interests.

(1) **Grandfathered Loans** Certain loans are grandfathered in the interpretations and are not considered to impair independence. The grandfathered loans must have been obtained from a financial institution under its normal lending procedures, terms, and requirements, and be current as to all terms. The types of grandfathered loans include home mortgages, other fully collateralized, secured loans and unsecured loans that are immaterial to the member's net worth.

(2) **Other Permitted Loans** Some personal loans are permitted from a financial institution client for which independence is required. These loans and leases must be obtained under normal lending procedures, terms, and requirements, and must be kept current as to all terms, at all times.

h. **Actual or Threatened Litigation** In some circumstances, independence may be considered to be impaired as a result of litigation or the expressed intention to commence litigation. When the auditor concludes that independence is impaired, the auditor should either resign from the engagement or cease any audit work then in progress until the issues can be resolved between the parties, or disclaim an opinion because of a lack of independence. Independence is no longer impaired when a resolution is reached and the matters at issue no longer have any effect on the relationship between the auditor and the client.

2. **Rule 102—Integrity and Objectivity** In the performance of any professional service, a member shall maintain objectivity and integrity, shall be free of conflicts of interest, and shall not knowingly misrepresent facts or subordinate her/his judgment to others.

   a. **Knowing Misrepresentations in Preparation** Knowingly making, permitting, or directing another to make materially false and misleading entries in an entity's financial statements or records is in violation of Rule 102. So too is knowingly failing to correct materially false and misleading financial statements or records while having the authority to do so. Knowingly signing, or permitting or directing another to sign a document containing materially false and misleading information is also a violation.

   b. **Conflicts of Interest** A conflict of interest may occur if a member performs a professional service for a client or employer and the member or the member's firm has a relationship that could be viewed as impairing the member's objectivity. If the member believes that objectivity can be maintained, discloses the relationship to the client, and obtains consent from the client, the rule shall not prohibit the performance of the professional service.

   c. **Obligations to Employer's External Accountant** A member must be candid and not knowingly misrepresent facts or knowingly fail to disclose material facts in dealing with her/his employer's external accountant.

   d. **Subordination of Judgment** If a member and the member's supervisor have a disagreement or dispute relating to the preparation of financial statements or the recording of transactions, the member should make her/his concerns known to the appropriate level of management within the organization. If appropriate action is not taken, the member should consider her/his continuing relationship with the employer, and any responsibility to communicate to third parties, such as regulatory authorities. The member may wish to consult with legal counsel.

   e. **Educational Services** Educational services are professional services and are subject to the rules of objectivity and integrity. This includes teaching at a university, teaching a continuing professional education course, and engaging in research and scholarship.

   f. **Client Advocacy** A member may be requested by a client to perform a tax or consulting services engagement that involves acting as an advocate for the client or the client's position on accounting or financial reporting issues. These services are considered professional services and the member shall comply with the rules of objectivity and integrity.

D. **General Standards—Accounting Principles**

1. **Rule 201—Professional Competence** A member will undertake only those professional services that the CPA or the CPA's firm has reasonable expectations of being able to complete with professional competence. Competence involves the technical knowledge of the CPA and the staff, the ability to apply this knowledge to the particular engagement, and the ability to supervise and evaluate the work performed.

   a. **Due Professional Care** A member must exercise due professional care in the performance of professional services.

   b. **Planning and Supervision** A member will adequately plan and supervise the performance of professional services.

   c. **Sufficient Relevant Data** A member must obtain sufficient relevant data to provide a reasonable basis for reaching conclusions or making recommendations in relation to any professional services performed.

2. **Rule 202—Compliance With Standards** A member who performs auditing, review, compilation, management consulting, tax, or other professional services shall comply with standards promulgated by bodies designated by Council of the AICPA.

3. **Rule 203—Accounting Principles** A member will not express an opinion that financial statements are presented in conformity with GAAP or state that the member is not aware of any material modifications that should be made to such statements or data in order for them to be in conformity with GAAP, if the statements contain a deviation from GAAP that has a material effect on the financial statements taken as a whole.

   a. **Departures From GAAP** Proper accounting treatment is that which will render the financial statements not misleading. The member must use professional judgment in deciding when a deviation from GAAP is appropriate. Circumstances justifying a departure include new legislation or the evolution of a new form of business transaction.

   b. **Status of FASB and GASB Interpretations** The Financial Accounting Standards Board (FASB) has been designated as the body to establish accounting principles, and the FASB Accounting Standards Codification constitutes accounting principles. The Governmental Accounting Standards Board (GASB) has been designated as the body to establish accounting principles for state and local governmental entities.

   c. **Financial Frameworks Other Than GAAP** Rule 203 does not preclude a member from preparing or reporting on financial statements that have been prepared pursuant to financial reporting frameworks other than GAAP, such as (1) financial reporting frameworks generally accepted in another country, including International Financial Reporting Standards (IFRSs) (2) financial reporting frameworks prescribed by an agreement or a contract; or (3) any other comprehensive basis of accounting. The financial statements or reports on those financial statements should make clear the financial reporting framework(s) used.

E. **Responsibilities to Clients**

1. **Rule 301—Confidential Client Information** A member in public practice will not disclose confidential information obtained in the course of the professional engagement without the consent of the client.

   a. **Exceptions** Confidential client information that may be disclosed without the client's permission include the following

      - To comply with a validly issued and enforceable subpoena or summons.
      - To comply with applicable laws and government regulations.
      - To comply with professional practice review procedures under AICPA or state CPA society or Board of Accountancy authorization.
      - To initiate a complaint with the professional ethics division or trial board of the AICPA or other appropriate investigative or disciplinary body.

   b. **Purchase, Sale, or Merger of Practice** A review of a member's professional practice is authorized in conjunction with a prospective purchase, sale, or merger of all or part of a member's practice. The member must take appropriate precautions, such as through a written confidentiality agreement, so that the prospective purchaser does not disclose any confidential client information obtained in the course of the review.

2. **Rule 302—Contingent Fees** A member in public practice shall not offer or render services under an agreement whereby the fee is contingent upon the findings or results. Specified services that a member in public practice or the member's firm shall not perform for a contingent fee include an audit or review of a financial statement, a compilation of a financial statement when the member reasonably might expect that a third party will use the statement, or an examination of prospective financial information. A member also is precluded from preparing an original or amended tax return or claim for a tax refund for a contingent fee.

   a. A CPA's fees may depend on the complexity of the service rendered. Fees that are fixed by the courts or public authorities or which are determined in tax matters by judicial proceedings or governmental agency findings are not considered contingent and, therefore, are permitted.

   b. In some cases, contingent fees in certain tax matters are permitted. A contingent fee would be permitted when a member represents a client in an examination by a revenue agent of the client's federal or state income tax return, when the member represents a client in connection with obtaining a private letter ruling, when filing an amended return claiming a refund that exceeds the threshold for review by the appropriate taxing authority, or when filing an amended return based on a tax issue that is the subject of a test case involving a different taxpayer or on which the taxing authority is developing a position.

F. **Other Responsibilities**

1. **Rule 501—Acts Discreditable** A member will not commit an act that is discreditable to the profession. The following acts would be considered discreditable to the profession.

   a. Refusing to return a client's records after the client has demanded them. A member's audit documentation, or working papers, are the member's property, not client records, and need not be made available to the client.

   b. Violation of any anti-discrimination law, including sexual and other forms of harassment.

   c. Failure to follow standards and/or procedures in government audits unless the member discloses the fact that such requirements were not followed and includes the reasons in the report.

   d. Negligence in preparation of financial statements or records

   e. Failure to follow requirements of governmental bodies unless the CPA discloses that such requirements were not followed and includes the reasons in the report. Examples of governmental bodies, commissions, or other regulatory agencies include the SEC, Federal Communications Commission (FCC), state insurance commissions, and other regulatory agencies, such as the Public Company Accounting Oversight Board (PCAOB).

   f. Solicitation or disclosure of CPA examination questions and answers

   g. Failure to file tax return or pay tax liability

   h. Failure to follow requirements of governmental bodies, commissions, or other regulatory agencies on indemnification and limitation of liability provisions

   i. Failure to maintain confidential information obtained from employment or volunteer activities

   j. Making false, misleading, or deceptive acts in promoting or marketing professional services

2. **Rule 502—Advertising and Other Forms of Solicitation** A member in public practice will not seek to obtain clients by advertising or other forms of solicitation in a manner that is false, misleading, or deceptive. Solicitation by the use of coercion, over-reaching, or harassing conduct is prohibited.

   a. **Advertising** Advertising or other forms of solicitation that are false, misleading, or deceptive are prohibited since they are not in the public interest. Examples of such activities include those that

      - Create false or unjustified expectations of favorable results
      - Imply the ability to influence any court, tribunal, regulatory agency, or similar body or official
      - Contain a representation that specific professional services will be performed for a stated fee, estimated fee, or fee range when it was likely at the time of representation that such fees would be substantially increased and the prospective client was not advised of that likelihood
      - Contain any other representations that would be likely to cause a reasonable person to misunderstand or be deceived

   b. **Engagements Obtained Through Efforts of Third Parties** Members are permitted to render professional services to clients or customers of third parties who were obtained through the advertising and solicitation efforts of the third parties. The member has the responsibility to determine that all promotional efforts are consistent with the Code of Professional Conduct.

3. **Rule 503—Commissions and Referral Fees** A member in public practice is prohibited from recommending or referring, for a commission, any product or service to a client or to be supplied by a client, when that member or member's firm provides certain services to the client. Specified services include an audit or review of a financial statement, a compilation of a financial statement when the member might reasonably expect that a third party will use the statement, or an examination of prospective financial information.

   a. **Disclosure** A member who receives or expects to receive a commission from a non-prohibited act should disclose that fact to the client

   b. **Referral Fees** Any member who accepts or pays a referral fee in relation to a client must disclose such acceptance or payment to the client

4. **Rule 505—Form of Organization and Name** A member may practice public accounting only in the form of organization permitted by law whose characteristics conform to resolutions of the Council of the AICPA.

   a. The name of the firm may not be misleading. A firm name would be considered misleading if the name contains any representation that would be likely to cause a reasonable person to misunderstand the legal form of the firm or who the owners or members of the firm are. The names of one or more past owners may be included in the firm name

   b. A firm cannot designate itself as Members of the AICPA unless all of its CPA owners are members of the AICPA

c. A member in public practice may own an interest in a separate business that performs for clients any of the professional services of accounting, tax, personal financial planning, or litigation support services

   (1) If the member, individually or collectively with members of his or her firm, controls the separate business, the entity and all its owners and employees must comply with all of the provisions of the Code

   (2) If the member, individually or collectively members of his or her firm, does not control the separate business, the provisions of the code would apply to the member but not to the entity, its other owners, and employees

d. The overriding focus is that CPAs remain responsible, financially and otherwise, for the attest work performed to protect the public interest. The Council Resolution requires that a majority of the financial interests in a firm engaged in attest services be owned by CPAs

II. AICPA Statement on Quality Control Standards (SQCS No. 8)

A. Scope and Authority

Statements on Quality Control Standards (SQCS) are issued by the Auditing Standards Board to provide guidance with respect to quality control. SQCS No. 8, *A Firm's System of Quality Control*, applies to quality control for a CPA firm's accounting and auditing practice; it does not apply to government audit organizations. It describes the elements of a quality control system and provides guidance for the design, implementation, and maintenance of the system.

1. **System of Quality Control** A system of quality control consists of policies and procedures designed to meet these objectives and monitor compliance. The nature and extent of the policies and procedures depend on the firm's size and operating characteristics. SQCSs use two categories of professional requirements to describe the degree of responsibility they impose on firms, as follows

   a. **Unconditional Requirements** A firm is required to comply with an unconditional requirement in all cases in which such a requirement is relevant. SQCSs use the word *must* to indicate an unconditional requirement.

   b. **Presumptively Mandatory Requirements** A firm is also required to comply with a presumptively mandatory requirement in all cases in which such a requirement is relevant; however, in rare circumstances, the firm may depart from a presumptively mandatory requirement, provided that the firm documents the justification for the departure and how the alternative policies established, or procedures performed, in the circumstances were sufficient to achieve the objectives of the presumptively mandatory requirement. SQCSs use the word *should* to indicate a presumptively mandatory requirement.

2. **GAAS vs SQCS** GAAS relate to the conduct of individual audit engagements. Quality control relates to the conduct of a CPA firm's accounting and audit practice as a whole, thus GAAS and quality control are related. A firm's quality control system may affect the conduct of individual engagements as well as a firm's practice as a whole. However, deficiencies in individual engagements or instances of noncompliance with a firm's quality control system do not, in and of themselves, indicate that a particular audit engagement was not performed in accordance with GAAS.

B. Elements of a Quality Control System

The firm must establish and maintain a system of quality control. The firm should document its policies and procedures and communicate them to the firm's personnel. The system of quality control should include policies and procedures addressing each of the following elements:

1. **Leadership Responsibilities** The firm should establish policies and procedures designed to promote an internal culture based on the recognition that quality is essential in performing engagements. The firm's leadership should assume ultimate responsibility for the firm's system of quality control. Any person(s) assigned operational responsibility for the firm's system of quality control should have sufficient and appropriate experience and ability, and the necessary authority, to assume that responsibility.

2. **Relevant Ethical Requirements** Policies and procedures should be designed to obtain reasonable assurance that the firm and its personnel maintain independence when required by relevant ethical requirements.

    a. **Policy Objectives** These policies allow for

        (1) Communication of the firm's independence requirements to its personnel and, as needed, to others

        (2) The identification and evaluation of circumstances and relationships that put independence at risk and the elimination of those risks with safeguards, if possible, and if not, withdrawal from the engagement

    b. **Policy Requirements** Such policies should require

        (1) Engagement partners to provide sufficient information about client engagements to enable the firm to evaluate any effect on independence

        (2) Personnel to promptly notify the firm of any threats to independence

        (3) The accumulation and communication of information to personnel so that it can be determined: if independence requirements are met; independence information can be maintained and updated; and appropriate action can be taken regarding threats to independence that are at an unacceptable level

    c. **Breaches** The firm's policies and procedures should provide reasonable assurance that breaches of independence requirements are promptly communicated and addressed.

    d. **Written Confirmation** At least annually, the firm should obtain written confirmation from relevant personnel of compliance with independence policies

3. **Acceptance and Continuance of Clients and Engagements**

    a. **Requirements** A firm should accept and continue relationships and engagements only when it

        (1) Is competent to perform the engagement and has the resources to do so

        (2) Can comply with legal and ethical requirements

        (3) Has considered the integrity of the client and does not have information that would lead it to conclude that the client lack integrity

b. **Obtaining Information** The firm should obtain such information as it considers necessary in the circumstances before: accepting an engagement with a new client; when deciding whether to continue an existing engagement; and when considering acceptance of a new engagement with an existing client.

c. **Conflict of Interest** If a conflict of interest issue has been identified, the firm should document the resolution of the issue

d. **Understanding** The firm should establish policies and procedures that provide for obtaining an understanding with the client regarding services to be performed to minimize the risk of misunderstandings regarding the nature, scope, and limitations of the services

e. **Continuance** Firm procedures addressing situations where the firm obtains information that would have caused it to decline the engagement had it known that information earlier. Such procedures should address if there is a need to report the circumstances to regulatory authorities, and whether the firm should withdraw from the engagement

4. **Human Resources** The firm should establish policies and procedures designed to provide it with reasonable assurance that

   a. It has sufficient personnel with the competence, capabilities, and commitment to ethical principles necessary to perform engagements in accordance with professional standards and applicable legal and regulatory requirements

   b. It can issue reports that are appropriate in the circumstances

   c. Ensure personnel selected for advancement have the qualifications necessary for fulfillment of the responsibilities that they will be called on to assume

   d. The firm should assign responsibility for each engagement to an engagement partner and should establish policies and procedures such that

      (1) The identity and role of the engagement partner is communicated to management and those charged with governance; the engagement partner has the appropriate competence, capabilities, and authority to perform the role; and the responsibilities of the engagement partner are clearly defined and communicated to that individual.

      (2) Personnel perform engagements in accordance with professional standards and applicable legal and regulatory requirements, the firm can issue reports that are appropriate in the circumstances

5. **Engagement Performance** Policies and procedures should be designed to provide the firm with reasonable assurance that engagements are performed in accordance with professional standards and applicable regulatory and legal requirements and that appropriate reports are issued, and should: promote consistency in the quality of performance; supervision responsibilities; and review responsibilities

   a. **Consultation** Policies and procedures should ensure that consultation takes place on difficult issues when appropriate; sufficient resources are available to enable consultation to take place; all relevant facts are provided to those consulted; and the conclusions reached are documented and implemented.

b. **Engagement Quality Control Review** Criteria should be developed to determine when an engagement quality control review should be performed. The review should be completed before the engagement report is released. The review should be conducted in a timely manner and may be done at appropriate stages during the engagement. The extent of the review may depend, among other things, on the complexity of the engagement and the degree of risk that the report may not be appropriate.

(1) **Components** The review should include:

- Discussing with the engagement partner any significant findings and issues
- Reading the financial statements or other subject matter information to determine if the report is appropriate
- Reviewing selected engagement documentation relating to significant judgments and conclusions
- Evaluating the appropriateness of conclusions reached and determining the appropriateness of the proposed report

(2) **Reviewer Criteria** The reviewer should satisfy the independence and objectivity requirements relating to the engagements reviewed. Additionally, the reviewer should

- Possess the technical qualifications, experience, and authority required to perform the role
- Not to selected by the engagement partner
- Not participate in, or make decisions for, the engagement
- Be replaced if his/her ability to perform the review is impaired

(3) **Documentation of the Review** There should be documentation that the:

- Firm's engagement quality control review procedures have been followed
- Review was completed before the engagement report was released
- Reviewer is not aware of any significant unresolved matters.

c. **Differences of Opinion** A firm should have policies and procedures in place for resolving differences of opinion within the engagement team and between the team and others, including the engagement quality control reviewer.

d. **Engagement Documentation** Policies and procedures should be established to

(1) Ensure assembly of the final engagement file on a timely basis

(2) Maintain the confidentiality, safe custody, integrity, accessibility, retention, and retrievability of engagement documentation

(3) Retain engagement documentation for a sufficient period of time to comply with laws and regulations

6. **Monitoring**

   a. **Process** The firm should establish a monitoring process such that reasonable assurance that the policies and procedures relating to the system of quality control are relevant, adequate, and operating effectively. This process should

      (1) Include inspection and periodic review of engagement documentation, reports, and clients' financial statements

      (2) Require assignment of the responsibility for monitoring to a partner with sufficient and appropriate authority and experience and assign the performance of monitoring tasks to qualified personnel

   b. **Deficiencies** Any system of quality control has inherent limitations that can reduce its effectiveness. Deficiencies in individual engagements do not, in and of themselves, indicate that the firm's system of quality control is insufficient to provide it with reasonable assurance that its personnel comply with applicable standards.

      (1) **Nature of Deficiencies** The firm should determine if deficiencies identified by the monitoring activities are systemic, repetitive, or significant and thus merit prompt corrective action.

      (2) **Communication** The firm should communicate to relevant engagement partners and other appropriate personnel deficiencies noted as a result of the monitoring process and recommendations for remedial action.

      (3) **Recommendations** Actions for identified deficiencies should include

         - Taking appropriate remedial steps in relation to an individual engagement or member of the firm
         - Communicating the findings to those responsible for training
         - Changes to the quality control policies and procedures
         - Disciplinary action against those who fail to comply

      (4) **Inappropriate Report or Omitted Engagement Procedures** If the deficiencies resulted in an inappropriate report or procedures were omitted during an engagement, in addition to determining what further action is needed to comply with professional standards and regulatory and legal requirements, the firm may consider obtaining legal advice.

      (5) **Communication of Monitoring Results** At least annually, the firm should communicate the results of the monitoring of its quality control process to engagement partners and other appropriate personnel, including the firm's leadership. The information should include:

         - A description of the monitoring procedures performed
         - The conclusions drawn from the monitoring procedures
         - A description of any systemic, repetitive, or other significant deficiencies and of the corrective actions taken

c. **Complaints and Allegations** Policies and procedures should be established for dealing with complaints and allegations of noncompliance with professional standards and applicable legal and regulatory requirements or with the firm's system of quality control.

(1) There should be clearly defined channels for personnel to use to communicate concerns without fear of reprisal.

(2) The firm should take appropriate action for any deficiencies or instances of noncompliance.

C. **Documentation of the Operation of a Quality Control System**
The firm should establish policies and procedures requiring

1. **Provide Evidence** Appropriate documentation to provide evidence of the operation of each element of the quality control system

2. **Evaluate Compliance** Retention of documentation for a sufficient period of time to permit those performing monitoring procedures and peer reviews to evaluate compliance with the quality control system

3. **Complaints** Documentation of complaints and allegations and the responses to them

III. Engagement Quality Review (PCAOB AS 7)

A. **Overview**

1. **Applicability of Standard** An engagement quality review and concurring approval of issuance are required for each audit engagement and for each engagement to review interim financial information conducted pursuant to the standards of the PCAOB.

2. **Objective** The objective of the engagement quality reviewer is to perform an evaluation of the significant judgments made by the engagement team and the related conclusions reached in forming the overall conclusion on the engagement and in preparing the engagement report, if a report is to be issued, in order to determine whether to provide concurring approval of issuance.

B. **Qualifications of Reviewer**

1. **Associated Person** The engagement quality reviewer must be an associated person of a registered public accounting firm. An engagement quality reviewer must be a partner or another individual in an equivalent position, or an individual from outside the firm. An outside reviewer who is not already associated with a registered public accounting firm would become associated with the firm issuing the report if he/she receives compensation from the firm issuing the report for performing the review or performs the review as agent for the firm issuing the report.

2. **Competence, Independence, Integrity and Objectivity** An engagement quality reviewer must

a. Possess the level of knowledge and competence related to accounting, auditing, and financial reporting required to serve as the engagement partner on the engagement under review.

b. Be independent of the company, perform the engagement quality review with integrity, and maintain objectivity in performing the review. To maintain objectivity, the engagement quality reviewer and others who assist the reviewer should not make decisions on behalf of the engagement team or assume any of the responsibilities of the engagement team. The engagement partner remains responsible for the engagement and its performance, notwithstanding the involvement of the engagement quality reviewer and others who assist the reviewer.

3. **"Cooling-Off" Period** The person who served as the engagement partner during either of the two audits preceding the audit subject to the engagement quality review may not be the engagement quality reviewer.

C. **Audit Engagement Quality Review**

1. **Process** In an audit engagement, the engagement quality reviewer should evaluate the significant judgments made by the engagement team and the related conclusions reached in forming the overall conclusion on the engagement and in preparing the engagement report. To evaluate such judgments and conclusions, the engagement quality reviewer should (a) hold discussions with the engagement partner and other members of the engagement team, and (b) review documentation. The engagement quality reviewer should:

a. Evaluate the significant judgments that relate to engagement planning

b. Evaluate the engagement team's assessment of, and audit responses to significant risks identified by the engagement team, including fraud risks

c. Evaluate the significant judgments made about (1) the materiality and disposition of corrected and uncorrected identified misstatements and (2) the severity and disposition of identified control deficiencies.

d. Review the engagement team's evaluation of the firm's independence in relation to the engagement.

e. Review the engagement completion document and confirm with the engagement partner that there are no significant unresolved matters.

f. Review the financial statements, management's report on internal control, and the related engagement report.

g. Read other information in documents containing the financial statements to be filed with the SEC and evaluate whether the engagement team has taken appropriate action with respect to any material inconsistencies with the financial statements or material misstatements of fact of which the engagement quality reviewer is aware.

h. Based on the procedures required by this standard, evaluate whether appropriate consultations have taken place on difficult or contentious matters. Review the documentation, including conclusions, of such consultations.

i. Based on the procedures required by this standard, evaluate whether appropriate matters have been communicated, or identified for communication, to the audit committee, management, and other parties, such as regulatory bodies.

2. **Evaluation of Engagement Documentation** The engagement quality reviewer should evaluate whether the engagement documentation that s/he reviewed when performing the procedures described above indicates that the engagement team responded appropriately to significant risks and supports the conclusions reached by the engagement team with respect to the matters reviewed.

3. **Concurring Approval of Issuance** The engagement quality reviewer may provide concurring approval of issuance only if, after performing with due professional care the review required by this standard, s/he is not aware of a significant engagement deficiency. The firm may grant permission to the client to use the engagement report only after the engagement quality reviewer provides concurring approval of issuance.

D. **Interim Engagement Quality Review**

1. **Process** The engagement quality reviewer should evaluate the significant judgments made by the engagement team and the related conclusions reached in forming the overall conclusion on the engagement and in preparing the engagement report, if a report is to be issued. To evaluate such judgments and conclusions, the engagement quality reviewer should, to the extent necessary to satisfy the requirements described below: (a) hold discussions with the engagement partner and other members of the engagement team, and (b) review documentation. The engagement quality reviewer should

   a. Evaluate the significant judgments that relate to engagement planning, including the consideration of

      (1) The firm's recent engagement experience with the company and risks identified in connection with the firm's client acceptance and retention process

      (2) The company's business, recent significant activities, and related financial reporting issues and risks

      (3) The nature of identified risks of material misstatement due to fraud

   b. Evaluate the significant judgments made about (1) the materiality and disposition of corrected and uncorrected identified misstatements and (2) any material modifications that should be made to the disclosures about changes in internal control over financial reporting.

   c. Perform the procedures described in paragraphs C.1.d. and e. above.

   d. Review the interim financial information for all periods presented and for the immediately preceding interim period, management's disclosure for the period under review, if any, about changes in internal control over financial reporting, and the related engagement report, if a report is to be issued.

   e. Read other information in documents containing interim financial information to be filed with the SEC and evaluate whether the engagement team has taken appropriate action with respect to material inconsistencies with the interim financial information or material misstatements of fact of which the engagement quality reviewer is aware.

   f. Perform the procedures discussed above.

2. **Evaluation of Engagement Documentation** The engagement quality reviewer should evaluate whether the engagement documentation that s/he reviewed when performing the required procedures supports the conclusions reached by the engagement team with respect to the matters reviewed.

3. **Concurring Approval of Issuance** The engagement quality reviewer may provide concurring approval of issuance only if, after performing with due professional care the review required by this standard, s/he is not aware of a significant engagement deficiency. In a review of interim financial information, the firm may grant permission to the client to use the engagement report (or communicate an engagement conclusion to its client, if no report is issued) only after the engagement quality reviewer provides concurring approval of issuance.

E. **Documentation**

Documentation of an engagement quality review should contain sufficient information to enable an experienced auditor, having no previous connection with the engagement, to understand the procedures performed by the engagement quality reviewer, and others who assisted the reviewer, to comply with the provisions of this standard, including information that identifies:

1. The engagement quality reviewer, and others who assisted the reviewer

2. The documents reviewed by the engagement quality reviewer, and others who assisted the reviewer

3. The date the engagement quality reviewer provided concurring approval of issuance or, if no concurring approval of issuance was provided, the reasons for not providing the approval

Documentation of an engagement quality review should be included in the engagement documentation. The requirements related to retention of and subsequent changes to audit documentation in PCAOB Auditing Standard No. 3, *Audit Documentation*, apply with respect to the documentation of the engagement quality review.

IV. The Sarbanes-Oxley Act (SOX)

A. **Title I—Public Company Accounting Oversight Board (PCAOB)**

Title I consists of nine sections and establishes the Public Company Accounting Oversight Board (PCAOB), to provide independent oversight of public accounting firms providing audit services. It also creates a central oversight board tasked with registering auditors, defining the specific processes and procedures for compliance audits, inspecting and policing conduct and quality control, and enforcing compliance with the specific mandates of SOX.

1. **PCAOB Responsibilities** The PCAOB is subject to oversight by the SEC and its four primary responsibilities are the: registration of accounting firms; inspections of registered firms' audits and quality control; establishment of auditing and related attestation, quality control, ethics, and independence standards for registered public accounting firms; and investigation and discipline of registered public accounting firms and their associated persons for violations of specified laws or professional standards. Public accounting firms are required to

   a. Register with the PCAOB before auditing an SEC issuer. The registration must be updated annually and include

      - Names of issuers audited in the preceding and current year, including fee information
      - A statement of the firm's quality control procedures
      - A list of all firm accountants who will work on the audit
      - Legal or disciplinary proceedings pending against the firm
      - Disclosures filed by the issuers concerning accounting disagreements between the issuer and the firm

   b. Prepare and maintain audit workpapers, and other information related to any audit report, in sufficient detail to support the conclusions reached in the report for a period not less than seven years

   c. Provide for a concurring or second partner review and approval of audit reports

   d. Adopt quality control standards and monitor professional ethics

   e. Report on auditor's evaluation of the internal control structure and include a description of any material weaknesses in internal control

f. Rotate off the lead audit or coordinating partner and the reviewing partner every five years

g. Report to the audit committee all critical accounting policies and practices to be used, all alternative treatments of financial information within GAAP that have been discussed with management, and the possible effects of the use of such alternative disclosures and treatments on the financial statements as well as the treatment preferred by the firm

2. **PCAOB Sanctions** If a firm or person has violated the provisions of SOX or PCAOB, the following sanctions can be imposed

   a. Temporary suspension or permanent revocation of PCAOB registration

   b. Temporary or permanent suspension of a person associating with a registered firm

   c. Temporary or permanent limitation on the activities, functions, or operations of a firm or person

   d. Civil monetary fines of no more than $750,000 for individuals and $15,000,000 for registered firms for intentional or knowing conduct; and penalties of no more than $100,000 for individuals and $2,000,000 for registered firms for other violations

   e. Censure; professional training/education; and any other PCAOB approved sanction

B. **Title II—Auditor Independence**

Title II consists of nine sections and establishes standards for external auditor independence, to limit conflicts of interest. It also addresses new auditor approval requirements, audit partner rotation, and auditor reporting requirements. It restricts auditing companies from providing non-audit services (e.g., consulting) for the same clients (firms may provide any non-audit service, including tax services, to audit clients that is not specifically prohibited in the following section, as long as the activity is approved in advance by the audit committee of the issuer).

1. **Prohibited Activities** It is unlawful for a registered public accounting firm that performs audits for issuers to contemporaneously provide with the audit any non-audit service, including: bookkeeping; financial information systems design and implementation; appraisal or valuation services; actuarial services; internal audit outsourcing services; or management functions or human resources.

2. **Preapproval Requirements** All auditing services and non-audit services, except for certain exclusions, provided to an issuer by the auditor of the issuer shall be preapproved by the audit committee of the issuer.

3. **Audit Partner Rotation** The lead (or coordinating) partner, or the reviewing partner, must rotate off the audit every five years.

4. **Auditor Reports to Audit Committees** Each registered accounting firm that performs audits must report to the issuer's audit committee all

   a. Critical accounting policies and practices to be used

   b. Alternative treatments of financial information within GAAP that have been discussed with management officials, ramifications of the use of such alternative disclosures and treatments, and the treatment preferred by the accounting firm

   c. Other material written communications between the firm and the management of the issuer, such as any management letter or schedule of unadjusted differences

5. **Conflicts of Interest** It is illegal for an accounting firm to perform an issuer audit service if a chief executive officer, controller, chief financial officer, chief accounting officer, or any person serving in an equivalent position for the issuer, was employed by that accounting firm and participated in any capacity in the audit of that issuer during the 1-year period preceding the date of the initiation of the audit.

C. **Title III, Section 303—Improper Influence on Conduct of Audits**
It is illegal for any officer or director of an issuer, or any other person acting under the direction thereof, to take any action to fraudulently influence, coerce, manipulate, or mislead any independent public or certified accountant engaged in the performance of an audit of the financial statements of that issuer for the purpose of rendering such financial statements materially misleading.

D. **Title IV—Enhanced Financial Disclosures**

1. **Disclosures in Periodic Reports** Each financial report that contains financial statements prepared in accordance with GAAP shall reflect all material correcting adjustments that have been identified by the registered public accounting firm.

   a. **Off-Balance Sheet Transactions** Annual and quarterly financial reports shall disclose all material off-balance sheet transactions, arrangements, obligations (including contingent obligations), and other relationships of the issuer with unconsolidated entities or other persons, that may have a material current or future effect on financial condition, changes in financial condition, results of operations, liquidity, capital expenditures, capital resources, or significant components of revenues or expenses.

   b. **Pro Forma Financial Information** Pro forma financial information shall not contain an untrue statement of a material fact or omit to state a material fact necessary in order to make the pro forma financial information not misleading, and reconciles it with the financial condition and results of operations of the issuer under GAAP.

2. **Enhanced Conflict of Interest Provisions** Personal loans to executives are prohibited.

   a. **In General** It shall be unlawful for any issuer, directly or indirectly, including through any subsidiary, to extend or maintain credit, to arrange for the extension of credit, or to renew an extension of credit, in the form of a personal loan to or for any director or executive officer.

   b. **Exclusions** Certain loans are permitted that are made or provided in the ordinary course of the consumer credit business of such issuer; of a type that is generally made available by such issuer to the public; and made by such issuer on market terms, or terms that are no more favorable than those offered by the issuer to the general public for such extensions of credit.

3. **Directors, Officers, and Principle Stockholders** An individual who is directly or indirectly the beneficial owner of more than 10 percent of a registered equity security, or who is a director or an officer of the issuer of such security shall file a statement with the SEC within 10 days after he/she becomes such beneficial owner, director, or officer, and before the end of the second business day following the day on which there has been a change in such ownership.

4. **Management Assessment of Internal Control** Each required annual report must contain an internal control report stating: it is management's responsibility for establishing and maintaining an adequate internal control structure and procedures for financial reporting. It must also contain an assessment, as of the end of the most recent fiscal year of the issuer, of the effectiveness of the internal control structure and procedures of the issuer for financial reporting. Each public accounting firm that prepares or issues the audit report for the issuer shall attest to, and report on, the assessment made by management of the issuer.

5. **Code of Ethics for Senior Financial Officers** Each issuer shall disclose in its periodic reports if they have adopted a code of ethics for senior financial officers, applicable to its principal financial officer and comptroller or principal accounting officer, or persons performing similar functions. If there is no code, the issuer must disclose the reasons. Any change in or waiver of the code of ethics for senior financial officers must be promptly disclosed on a Form 8-K, or by dissemination on the Internet or by other electronic means.

6. **Disclosure of Audit Committee Financial Expert** The SEC requires each issuer, together with periodic reports, to disclose whether or not, and if not, the reasons therefore, the issuer's audit committee of that issuer is comprised of at least 1 member who is a financial expert. In defining the term "financial expert" the SEC considers whether a person has, through education and experience: an understanding of generally accepted accounting principles and financial statements; experience in both the preparation or auditing of financial statements of generally comparable issuers; and the application of such principles in connection with the accounting for estimates, accruals, and reserves; experience with internal accounting controls; and an understanding of audit committee functions. The individual does not have to be a CPA.

7. **Real Time Issuer Disclosures** Each issuer shall disclose to the public on a rapid and current basis any additional information concerning material changes in the financial condition or operations of the issuer.

V. Securities and Exchange Commission (SEC)

A. Covered Person

Under the SEC rules, a Covered Person includes

1. The audit engagement team, including individuals who consult with the attest engagement team on technical or industry matters

2. The audit chain of command, which includes persons who

   a. Supervise or have direct management responsibility for the audit, including at all successively senior levels through the firm's chief executive

   b. Evaluate performance or recommend compensation of the audit engagement partner

   c. Provide quality control or other oversight of the audit

3. Partners or managers who provide 10 or more hours of non-audit services to the client

4. Other partners from an office of the firm in which the lead audit engagement partner primarily practices in connection with the audit

B. Applicability

Immediate family (i.e., covered person's spouse, spousal equivalent, or dependent) must comply with the same rules as covered persons, except that

1. The immediate family of a partner or manager providing non-attest services, or other partners in the lead attest engagement partner's primary office, may have a financial interest in a client that resulted as an unavoidable consequence of participation in his or her employer's compensation or benefits program, and the interest is disposed of as soon as practicable, but no later than 30 days after the person has the right to dispose of the financial interest

2. The immediate family of persons on the audit engagement team or those in a position to influence the engagement may not use the exception

C. **Relationships That Impair Independence**
Independence is impaired if covered members or their immediate families

1. Have a direct or indirect material financial interest in a client
2. Serve as a voting trustee of a trust, executor of an estate, containing the securities of a client, unless the trustee or executor has no authority to make investment decisions for the trust or estate
3. Have any direct or material indirect business relationship with a client or with persons associated with the client's officers, directors, or substantial shareholders
4. Have any loan to or from the client, or a client's officers, directors, or beneficial owners of more than 10 percent of the client's equity securities
5. Any partner, professional employee, or his/her immediate family has filed a Schedule 13D or 13G with the SEC indicating beneficial ownership of more than 5% of a client's equity securities
6. A covered person's close family has filed a Schedule 13D or 13G with the SEC indicating beneficial ownership of more than 5% of a client's equity securities or controls an audit client
7. A partner's close family controls a client

D. **Interests That Impair Independence**
Independence is considered to be impaired for an accounting firm, any covered person in the firm, or any of his/her immediate family if they have

1. Any direct or material indirect investment in an entity which an audit client has a material investment and the ability to exercise significant influence
2. Any direct or material indirect investment in an entity that has a material investment in an audit client and that enables that entity to exercise significant influence over the audit client
3. A material investment in an entity over which the audit client has the ability to exercise significant influence
4. The ability to exercise significant influence over an entity that has the ability to exercise significant influence over an audit client.

E. **Other Relationships That May Impair Independence**

1. A current partner or professional employee is employed by a client or serves as a member of the board of directors or similar management body of the client
2. A covered person's immediate family, parent, nondependent child, or sibling is in an accounting role or financial reporting oversight role at a client
    a. Accounting role is a role in which a person is in a position to or does exercise more than minimal influence over the contents of the accounting records or anyone who prepares them

b. Financial reporting oversight role means a role in which a person is in a position to or does exercise influence over the contents of the financial statements or anyone who prepares them, such as when the person is a member of the board of directors or similar management or governing body, chief executive officer, president, chief financial officer, chief operating officer, general counsel, chief accounting officer, controller, director of internal audit, director of financial reporting, treasurer, or any equivalent position

3. Former officer, director, or employee of a client who becomes a partner or professional employee of the firm impairs independence unless he or she does not participate in, and is not in a position to influence, the audit of the client's financial statements covering any period during which he or she was employed by or associated with that client.

4. An accountant is not independent when a former partner, principal, shareholder, or professional employee of an accounting firm is in an accounting role or financial reporting oversight role at an audit client, unless the individual meets all of the following:

   a. Does not influence the accounting firm's operations or financial policies

   b. Has no capital balances in the accounting firm

   c. Has no financial arrangement with the accounting firm other than one providing for regular payment of a fixed dollar amount (which is not dependent on the revenues, profits, or earnings of the accounting firm)

5. An accountant is not independent when a former partner, principal, shareholder, or professional employee of an accounting firm is in a financial reporting oversight role at an issuer unless the individual employed by the issuer was not a member of the audit engagement team of the issuer during the one year period preceding the date that audit procedures commenced for the fiscal period that included the date of initial employment of the audit engagement team member by the issuer

6. An accountant is not independent if the accountant provides the following non-audit services to an audit client

   - Management functions
   - Bookkeeping or other services related to the accounting records or financial statements of the audit client
   - Financial information systems design and implementation
   - Human resources
   - Appraisal or valuation services, fairness opinions, or contributions-in-kind reports
   - Actuarial services
   - Broker-dealer, investment advisor, or investment banking services
   - Internal audit outsourcing services
   - Legal services
   - Expert services unrelated to the audit

VI. Public Company Accounting Oversight Board (PCAOB)

A. Overview

Section 103 of the Sarbanes-Oxley Act of 2002 (SOX) directs the Public Company Accounting Oversight Board (PCAOB) to establish ethics standards to be used by registered public accounting firms in the preparation and issuance of audit reports, and directs the PCAOB to establish rules on auditor independence. SOX effectively eliminated self-regulation for the accounting profession, with the PCAOB assuming functions previously administered through the AICPA for public companies that are required to register with the SEC (issuers of securities).

B. Provisions Affecting Public Accounting Firms

The PCAOB has adopted Rules 101 (Independence) and 102 (Integrity and Objectivity) from the AICPA Code of Professional Conduct on an interim basis. In addition, the PCAOB has issued the following independence rules, which apply to all registered public accounting firms (defined as "RPA firm" for the following section).

1. **Rule 3502 Violations** A person associated with a RPA firm shall not take or omit to take an action knowing, or recklessly not knowing, that the act or omission would directly and substantially contribute to a violation by that RPA firm of the SOX Act, the rules of the PCAOB, the relevant provisions of the securities laws, or professional standards.

2. **Rule 3520 Independence** A RPA firm and its personnel must be independent of the firm's audit client throughout the audit and professional engagement period.

3. **Rule 3521 Contingent Fees** A RPA firm is not independent of its audit client if the firm, or any affiliate of the firm, during the audit and professional engagement period, provides any service or product to the audit client for a contingent fee or a commission, or receives from the audit client, directly or indirectly, a contingent fee or commission.

4. **Rule 3522 Tax Transactions** A RPA firm is not independent of its audit client if the firm, or any affiliate of the firm, during the audit and professional engagement period, provides any non-audit service to the audit client related to marketing, planning, or opining in favor of the tax treatment of, a confidential transaction or an aggressive tax position transaction.

5. **Rule 3523 Tax Services for Persons in Financial Reporting Oversight Roles** A RPA firm is not independent of its audit client if the firm, or any affiliate of the firm, during the professional engagement period provides any tax service to a person in a financial reporting oversight role at the audit client, or an immediate family member of such person, unless certain conditions are met.

6. **Rule 3524 Audit Committee Preapproval of Certain Tax Services** A RPA firm shall describe to the audit committee, in writing, any permissible tax service to be provided to an audit client, and include, among other things, the scope of the engagement, the fee structure or compensation arrangement, and any referral fee arrangements. The firm will discuss and document with the audit committee any potential effects on independence.

7. **Rule 3525 Audit Committee Preapproval of Non-Audit Services Related to Internal Control Over Financial Reporting** A RPA firm shall describe to the audit committee, in writing, any non-audit services related to internal control over financial reporting to be provided to an audit client, and will discuss and document with the audit committee any potential effects on independence.

8. **Rule 3526 Communication With Audit Committees Concerning Independence** Prior to accepting an initial engagement, and at least annually with respect to its issuer audit clients, a RPA firm must

   a. Describe in writing to the audit committee of the issuer, all relationships between the RPA firm and the potential/current audit client or persons in financial reporting oversight roles at the client that may be thought to bear on independence

b. Discuss the potential effects of the relationship with the audit committee, and document said discussion

c. In conjunction with the annual communication, the RPA firm must affirm to the audit committee, in writing, that, as of the date of the communication, the RPA firm is independent and in compliance with Rule 3520; and must document the discussion

VII. Department of Labor (DOL)

A. Overview

The Department of Labor (DOL) has guidelines for determining when a qualified public accountant is independent for purposes of auditing and rendering an opinion on the financial information required to be included in an Employee Benefit Plan annual report filed with the DOL.

A member includes all partners or shareholder equivalents in the firm and all professional employees participating in the audit or located in an office of the firm participating in a significant portion of the audit.

B. Impairment

An accountant will not be considered independent with respect to a plan if a member (1) had, or was committed to acquire, any direct or material indirect financial interest in the plan or plan sponsor; (2) was connected to the plan or plan sponsor as a promoter, underwriter, investment advisor, voting trustee, director, officer, or employee during the period of engagement, at the date of the opinion, or during the period covered by the financial statements; and (3) maintains financial records for the employee benefit plan.

C. Independence

An accountant will be considered independent with respect to a plan if a (1) member is retained or engaged on a professional basis by the plan sponsor, provided the accountant does not violate the items listed in V.B. above; (2) member is an actuary and renders actuarial services to the plan; and (3) former officer or employee of the plan or plan sponsor is employed by the auditing firm, as long as the individual has completely disassociated himself from the plan or plan sponsor and does not participate in auditing financial statements of the plan covering any period of his/her employment by the plan or plan sponsor.

VIII. IFAC Code of Ethics

A. Overview

The International Ethics Standards Board for Accountants (IESBA) is an independent standard-setting body that develops an internationally appropriate *Code of Ethics for Professional Accountants* (the Code). The IESBA's long-term objective is convergence of the Code's ethical standards for professional accountants, including auditor independence standards, with those issued by regulators and national standard setters.

B. Principles

The Code requires accountants to adhere to five fundamental principles

1. **Integrity** Be straightforward and honest in all professional and business relationships.

2. **Objectivity** Do not allow bias, conflict of interest, or undue influence of others to override professional or business judgments.

3. **Professional Competence and Due Care** Maintain professional knowledge and skill at the level required to ensure that a client or employer receives competent professional services based on current developments in practice, legislation and techniques and act diligently and in accordance with applicable technical and professional standards.

4. **Confidentiality** Respect the confidentiality of information acquired as a result of professional and business relationships and do not disclose such information to third parties without proper and specific authority, unless there is a legal or professional right or duty to disclose. Do not use the information for personal advantage.

5. **Professional Behavior** Comply with relevant laws and regulations and avoid any action that discredits the profession.

C. **Conceptual Framework**
The Code establishes a conceptual framework that requires a professional accountant to identify, evaluate, and address threats to compliance with the fundamental principles. When threats to compliance are identified, and the accountant determines that they are not at an acceptable level, s/he shall determine whether appropriate safeguards are available and can be applied to eliminate the threats or reduce them to an acceptable level.

1. **Threats** A circumstance or relationship may create more than one threat, and a threat may affect compliance with more than one fundamental principle. Threats fall into one or more of the following categories

   a. **Self-Interest** The threat that a financial or other interest will inappropriately influence the professional accountant's judgment or behavior

   b. **Self-Review** The threat that a professional accountant will not appropriately evaluate the results of a previous judgment made or service performed by the professional accountant, or by another individual within the professional accountant's firm, on which the accountant will rely when forming a judgment as part of providing a current service

   c. **Advocacy** The threat that a professional accountant will promote a client's or employer's position to the point that the professional accountant's objectivity is compromised

   d. **Familiarity** The threat that due to a long or close relationship with a client or employer, a professional accountant will be too sympathetic to their interests or too accepting of their work

   e. **Intimidation** The threat that a professional accountant will be deterred from acting objectively because of actual or perceived pressures, including attempts to exercise undue influence over the professional accountant

2. **Safeguards** Safeguards are actions or other measures that may eliminate threats or reduce them to an acceptable level. They fall into two broad categories

   a. Safeguards created by the profession, legislation or regulation, such as: educational, training, and experience requirements for entry into the profession; continuing professional development requirements; corporate governance regulations; etc.

   b. Safeguards in the work environment

D. **Professional Accountants in Public Practice**

1. **Conceptual Framework Approach** This Part of the Code describes how the conceptual framework contained in Part A applies in certain situations to professional accountants in public practice. A professional accountant in public practice shall not knowingly engage in any business, occupation, or activity that impairs or might impair integrity, objectivity or the good reputation of the profession and as a result would be incompatible with the fundamental principles.

2. **Professional Appointment Principles**

   a. **Client Acceptance** Before accepting a new client relationship, a professional accountant in public practice shall determine whether acceptance would create any threats to compliance with the fundamental principles.

   b. **Engagement Acceptance** Before accepting a specific client engagement, a professional accountant in public practice shall determine whether acceptance would create any threats to compliance with the fundamental principles.

3. **Conflicts of Interest** Where a conflict of interest creates a threat to one or more of the fundamental principles, including objectivity, confidentiality, or professional behavior, that cannot be eliminated or reduced to an acceptable level through the application of safeguards, the professional accountant in public practice shall not accept a specific engagement or shall resign from one or more conflicting engagements.

4. **Independence** This section addresses the independence requirements for audit and review engagements. Members of audit teams, firms and network firms shall be independent of audit clients. Independence comprises

   a. **Independence of Mind** The state of mind that permits the expression of a conclusion without being affected by influences that compromise professional judgment, thereby allowing an individual to act with integrity and exercise objectivity and professional skepticism.

   b. **Independence in Appearance** The avoidance of facts and circumstances that are so significant that a reasonable and informed third party would be likely to conclude, weighing all the specific facts and circumstances, that a firm's, or a member of the audit team's, integrity, objectivity or professional skepticism has been compromised.

5. **Threats to Independence** The threats listed below may contain references to the materiality of a financial interest, loan, or guarantee, or to the significance of a business relationship. For the purpose of determining whether such an interest is material to an individual, the combined net worth of the individual and the individual's immediate family members may be taken into account.

   a. **Financial Interests** Holding a financial interest in an audit client may create a self-interest threat. The existence and significance of any threat created depends on: the role of the person holding the financial interest; whether the financial interest is direct or indirect; and the materiality of the financial interest. The significance of any threat shall be evaluated and safeguards applied when necessary to eliminate the threat or reduce it to an acceptable level.

   b. **Loans and Guarantees** A loan, or a guarantee of a loan, to a member of the audit team, or a member of that individual's immediate family, or the firm from an audit client that is a bank or a similar institution, not made under normal lending procedures, terms and conditions, could create a self-interest threat that would be so significant that no safeguards could reduce the threat to an acceptable level. Therefore, neither a member of the audit team, a member of that individual's immediate family, nor a firm shall accept such a loan or guarantee.

   c. **Close Business Relationships** Unless the financial interest is immaterial and the business relationship is insignificant to the firm and the client or its management, the threat created from such a relationship could be so significant that no safeguards would reduce the threat to an acceptable level. Therefore, unless immaterial and insignificant, no business relationship shall be entered into between a firm, a member of the audit team (or member of the individual's immediate family), and the audit client or its management.

d. **Family and Personal Relationships** When an immediate family member of a member of the audit team is a director, officer, or employee (depending on their role) of the client, self-interest, familiarity or intimidation threats may be created. The existence and significance of any threats will depend on a number of factors, including the individual's responsibilities on the audit team, the role of the family member or other individual within the client and the closeness of the relationship. Generally, these threats to independence can only be reduced to an acceptable level by removing the individual from the audit team.

e. **Employment With Clients** Independence could be compromised if a former member of the audit team or partner joins the audit client as a director or officer, or as an employee in a position to exert significant influence over the preparation of the client's accounting records or the financial statements on which the firm will express an opinion, unless

(1) The individual is not entitled to any benefits or payments from the firm, except those made in accordance with fixed pre-determined arrangements, and any amount owed to the individual is not material to the firm; and

(2) The individual does not continue to participate or appear to participate in the firm's business or professional activities.

Firm members of an audit team are required to notify the firm when entering employment negotiations with the client, and said members should be removed from the engagement.

f. **Recent Service With Client** Self-interest, self-review or familiarity threats may be created if a member of the audit team has recently served as a director, officer, or employee of the audit client. Said members should be removed from the engagement.

g. **Serving as Director or Officer of Client** If a partner or employee of the firm serves as a director or officer of an audit client, the self-review and self-interest threats created would be so significant that no safeguards could reduce the threats to an acceptable level. Accordingly, no partner or employee shall serve as a director or officer of an audit client.

h. **Partner Rotation** Familiarity and self-interest threats are created by using the same senior personnel on an audit engagement over a long period of time. The significance of the threats depends on a number of factors. For audits of a public entity, an individual shall not be a key audit partner for more than seven years. After such time, the individual shall not be a member of the engagement team or be a key audit partner for the client for two years.

i. **Non-Assurance Services to Audit Clients** Providing non-assurance services may create self-review, self-interest, and advocacy threats to the independence of the firm or members of the audit team. Before the firm accepts such an engagement, a determination shall be made as to whether providing said service would create an independence threat. If a threat is created that cannot be reduced to an acceptable level by the application of safeguards, the non-assurance service shall not be provided.

j. **Fees** When the total fees from an audit client represent a large proportion of the total fees of the firm, the dependence on that client and concern about losing the client creates a self-interest or intimidation threat. A self-interest threat may also be created if fees due from an audit client remain unpaid for a long time, especially if a significant part is not paid before the issue of the audit report for the following year. A contingent fee may create such a self-interest threat that no safeguards could reduce the threat to an acceptable level. Accordingly, a firm shall not enter into any such fee arrangement.

k. **Compensation and Evaluation Policies** A self-interest threat is created when a member of the audit team is evaluated on or compensated for selling non-assurance services to an audit client. If the threat is not at an acceptable level, the firm shall either revise the compensation plan or evaluation process for that individual or apply safeguards to eliminate the threat or reduce it to an acceptable level.

l. **Gifts and Hospitality** If a firm or a member of the audit team accepts gifts or hospitality, unless the value is trivial and inconsequential, the threats created would be so significant that no safeguards could reduce the threats to an acceptable level. Consequently, a firm or a member of the audit team shall not accept such gifts or hospitality.

m. **Actual or Threatened Litigation** When the firm and the client's management are placed in adversarial positions by actual or threatened litigation, affecting management's willingness to make complete disclosures, self-interest and intimidation threats are created. If appropriate safeguards do not reduce the threats to an acceptable level, the firm should withdraw from, or decline, the audit engagement.

6. **Independence—Other Assurance Engagements** This section addresses independence requirements for assurance engagements that are not audit or review engagements.

a. **Objective** Assurance engagements are designed to enhance intended users' degree of confidence about the outcome of the evaluation or measurement of a subject matter against criteria. In the case of assurance engagements, it is in the public interest and, therefore, required by this Code of Ethics, that members of assurance teams and firms be independent of assurance clients and that any threats that the firm has reason to believe are created by a network firm's interests and relationships be evaluated.

b. **Relationships** When the assurance team knows or has reason to believe that a relationship or circumstance involving a related entity of the assurance client is relevant to the evaluation of the firm's independence from the client, the assurance team shall include that related entity when identifying and evaluating threats to independence and applying appropriate safeguards.

IX. Government Accountability Office (GAO)

A. Overview

The Government Accountability Office (GAO) issues independence and ethics rules that apply to auditors who perform attest services under Generally Accepted Government Auditing Standards (GAGAS). The GAO Independence Standards employ a principles-based approach to independence supplemented with certain safeguards for matters such as the performance of nonaudit services. In this regard the approach is not unlike the AICPA conceptual framework and the SEC's principles-based foundation for its independence standards.

B. Principles

The standard for nonaudit services employs two primary principles: (1) audit organizations should not provide nonaudit services that involve performing management functions or making management decisions; and (2) audit organizations should not audit their own work or provide nonaudit services in situations where the nonaudit services are significant or material to the subject matter of the audits.

C. Safeguards

If the nonaudit service meets both principles, the audit organization must then comply with a list of safeguards in order to perform the nonaudit service, including: precluding personnel who provided the nonaudit services from planning, conducting, or reviewing audit work related to the nonaudit service; and documenting its consideration of the nonaudit services including documentation for its rationale that providing the nonaudit services does not violate the two overarching principles.

D. **Impairment**
Independence would be considered to be impaired if the audit organization: maintains or prepares the audited entity's basic accounting records or maintain or take responsibility for basic financial or other records that the audit organization will audit; posts transactions (whether coded or not coded) to the entity's financial records or to other records that subsequently provide data to the entity's financial records; recommends a single individual for a specific position; or conducts an executive search or a recruiting program for the audited entity.

E. **Independence**
Independence would not be considered to be impaired if the audit organization provided basic accounting assistance *provided that such services were deemed not to be significant/material to the subject matter of the audit* and are limited to services such as: preparing draft financial statements that are based on management's chart of accounts and trial balance and any adjusting, correcting, and closing entries that have been approved by management; or preparing draft notes to the financial statements based on information determined and approved by management.

X. Consulting Services

A. **Overview**
Consulting services include a tremendous range of technical disciplines, industry knowledge, and consulting skills. Independence is not required for consulting services. These services are composed of professional services that use the CPA's technical skills, education, observations and experience, and knowledge of the consulting process. Examples include:

1. **Consultations** The practitioner provides advice or information based mostly, if not entirely, on existing personal knowledge about the client, the circumstances, the technical matters involved, and the mutual intent of the parties.

2. **Advisory Services** The practitioner develops findings, conclusions, and recommendations for client consideration and decision making.

3. **Implementation Services** The practitioner puts an action plan into effect. In an engagement of this type, client personnel may be pooled with those of the practitioners. The overall responsibility of all the activities rests with the practitioner.

4. **Staff & Other Support Services** The practitioner provides staff and other support, as needed, to accomplish tasks specified by the client.

B. **General Standards**
The AICPA issues Statements on Standards for Consulting Services (SSCS). Professional judgment is to be used in applying the SSCS to specific situations, since the understanding established with the client may impose some constraints within which the services are to be performed. The CPA is not required to decline or withdraw from a consulting engagement when such limitations are imposed.

C. **Additional Standards**
The following additional general standards address the distinctive nature of consulting services. These Standards are established under Rule 202 of the AICPA Code of Professional Conduct.

1. **Client Interest** The member shall serve the client's interest by seeking to accomplish the objectives established by the understanding with the client while maintaining integrity and objectivity.

2. **Understanding With Client** An oral or written understanding should be reached with the client concerning the nature, scope, and limitations of the services to be performed, and modifications should be made to the understanding if circumstances require a significant change during the engagement.

3. **Communication With Client** The client should be informed of the following: conflicts of interest that may occur that could be viewed as impairing the CPA's objectivity; significant reservations concerning the scope or benefits of the engagement; and significant engagement findings or events

D. **Attest Clients**
The performance of consulting services for an attest client does not impair independence. Members performing attest services for a client should comply with applicable independence standards, rules and regulations issued by the AICPA, the state boards of accountancy, state CPA societies, and other regulatory agencies.

XI. Revised AICPA Code of Professional Conduct

A. **Adoption**
The revised AICPA *Code of Professional Conduct* (Revised Code) was adopted by the Professional Ethics Executive Committee in January, 2014. It will be effective December 15, 2014, with a delayed effective date for the implementation of the two conceptual frameworks (this is to ensure that users have adequate time to become familiar with the new frameworks and update their policies and procedures accordingly). The Revised Code applies to all professional services performed, with limited exceptions.

B. **Other Guidance**
Interpretations of the rules of conduct are adopted after exposure to the membership, state societies, state boards, and other interested parties. The interpretations provide guidelines about the scope and application of the rules but are not intended to limit such scope or application. Members who do not comply with the interpretations have the burden of justifying the departure in any disciplinary hearing. Interpretations that existed before the adoption of the Code on January 12, 1988, will remain in effect until further action is deemed necessary by the appropriate senior committee. If applicable, members should also refer to guidance from: the SEC; the PCAOB; the GAO; the DOL; and state CPA societies.

C. **Code Organization**
The Revised Code separates guidance by line of business (i.e., separate parts for members in public practice, business, or other), and then by topic, and, where relevant, topics are further broken down into subtopics and sections. These conceptual frameworks use a "threats and safeguards" approach, and are designed to assist users in addressing threats to compliance that the Revised Code does not specifically address. The Revised Code begins with a Preface, which applies to all members. This is followed by three parts: Part 1 is for members in public practice; Part 2 is for members in business; and Part 3 is for all other members.

D. **Conceptual Frameworks**
The AICPA recognizes that a distinguishing mark of a profession is its acceptance of a high degree of responsibility to the public. The Code requires an unswerving commitment to honorable behavior even if it means sacrificing personal advantages. Under the conceptual framework approach, users should identify treats to compliance with the rules; determine if the threat is at an acceptable level. In some cases, the threat may be so significant that no safeguards will eliminate or reduce it to an acceptable level, in which case, a member would need to determine if they should decline or discontinue the professional service(s) or resign from the engagement.

E. **Terms**
The Revised Code contains an extensive definition section; key terms are provided below.

1. **Acceptable Level** A level at which a reasonable and informed third party who is aware of the relevant information would be expected to conclude that a member's compliance with the rules is not compromised.

2. **Member** A member, associate member, affiliate member, or international associate of the AICPA. When the term *member* is used in Part 1 of the Revised Code, it means a member in public practice; when used in Part 2 of the code, it means a member in business; and when used in Part 3 of the code, it means all other members.

3. **Threats** Relationships or circumstances that could compromise a member's compliance with the rules.

4. **Safeguards** Actions or other measures that may eliminate a threat or reduce a threat to an acceptable level.

F. **Principles of Professional Conduct**
Members in the AICPA assume an obligation of self-discipline, in addition to legal and regulatory requirements. The Principles stress the CPA's responsibility to the public, to clients, and to colleagues, and call for an unswerving commitment to honorable behavior, even at the sacrifice of personal advantage. The principles apply to all members.

1. **Responsibilities Principle** In carrying out their responsibilities as professionals, members should exercise sensitive professional and moral judgments in all their activities. Members also have a responsibility to cooperate with each other to continually improve the art of accounting, maintain the public's confidence, and carry out the responsibilities of self-governance.

2. **Public Interest Principle** Members should accept the obligation to act in a way that will serve the public interest, honor the public trust, and demonstrate a commitment to professionalism. Members have a duty to discharge their responsibilities with integrity, objectivity, due professional care, and a genuine interest in serving the public. "Public" is defined to include: clients; credit grantors; governments; employers; investors; the business and financial community; and others.

3. **Integrity Principle** To maintain and broaden public confidence, members should perform all professional responsibilities with the highest sense of integrity. Integrity requires a member to be honest and candid within the constraints of client confidentiality. Integrity also requires a member to observe the principles of objectivity and independence and of due care. Integrity expects a member to comply with both the form and the spirit of technical and ethical standards.

4. **Objectivity and Independence Principle** Objectivity is always required; independence is required for audit and attest services only.

   a. **Maintain Objectivity** A member should maintain objectivity and be free of conflicts of interest in discharging professional responsibilities. Objectivity is a state of mind; members should be impartial, intellectually honest, and free of conflicts of interest.

   b. **Independence in Fact and Appearance** A member in public practice should be independent in fact and appearance when providing auditing and other attestation services. They must avoid subordination of their judgment. Public confidence would be impaired by evidence that independence was actually impaired and it might also be impaired by the existence of circumstances that reasonable people might believe likely to influence independence.

5. **Due Care Principle** A member should observe the profession's technical and ethical standards, strive continually to improve competence and the quality of services, and discharge professional responsibility to the best of the member's ability, rendering services promptly, carefully, and thoroughly. Demonstrating competency requires a commitment to learning and professional improvement throughout a member's professional life. A member is required to plan and supervise adequately all professional activities for which the member has responsibility.

6. **Scope and Nature of Services Principle** A member in public practice should observe each of the above described principles in determining the scope and nature of services to be provided, and in assessing whether services would create a conflict of interest. Members should:

   a. **Firms** Practice in firms that maintain adequate internal quality control procedures to ensure that services are competently provided and supervised

   b. **Conflict of Interest** Individually determine whether the scope and nature of other services provided to an audit client would create a conflict of interest in the performance of the audit function for that client

   c. **Professionalism** Individually assess whether an activity is consistent with their role as professionals

G. **Part 1: Members in Public Practice**

Part 1 of the Revised Code applies to members in public practice. When the term *member* is used in part 1, the requirements apply only to members in public practice. When a member in public practice is also a member in business (for example, serves as a member of an entity's board of directors), the member should also consult part (i.e., member in business). Government auditors who audit federal, state, or local governments or component units, that are structurally located within the government audit organization, are considered in public practice as long as the head of the audit organization meets one of the organizational structures described in the Revised Code's definition of "client."

1. **Conceptual Framework** Members may have relationships or circumstances that create threats to the member's compliance with the rules. If there is not an interpretation that addresses that relationship or circumstance, a member should evaluate whether the relationship or circumstance would lead a reasonable and informed third party who is aware of the relevant information to conclude that there is a threat to the member's compliance with the rules that is not at an acceptable level.

   a. **Threats** Under the conceptual framework approach, members should evaluate identified threats both individually and in the aggregate because threats can have a cumulative effect on a member's compliance. The existence of a threat does not mean that the member is in violation of the rules; however, the member should evaluate the significance of the threat, considering both qualitative and quantitative factors. If the member concludes that the threat is not at an acceptable level, the member should apply safeguards to eliminate the threat or reduce it to an acceptable level. There are seven broad categories of threats:

      (1) **Adverse Interest Threat** The threat that a member will not act with objectivity because the member's interests are opposed to the client's interests. For example, the client has expressed an intention to begin litigation against the member; or a class action lawsuit has been filed against the client.

      (2) **Advocacy Threat** The threat that a member will promote a client's interests or position to the point that his or her objectivity or independence is compromised. For example, a member provides forensic accounting services to a client in litigation or in a dispute with third parties; or a member acts as an investment adviser for an officer, a director, or a 10 percent shareholder of a client.

(3) **Familiarity Threat** The threat that, due to a long or close relationship with a client, a member will become too sympathetic to the client's interests or too accepting of the client's work or product. Examples include: a member's immediate family or close relative is employed by the client; a member's close friend is employed by the client; a former partner or professional employee joins the client in a key position and has knowledge of the firm's policies and practices for the professional services engagement; senior personnel have a long association with a client; a member has a significant close business relationship with the client.

(4) **Management Participation Threat** The threat that a member will take on the role of client management or otherwise assume management responsibilities.

(5) **Self-Interest Threat** The threat that a member could benefit, financially or otherwise, from an interest in, or relationship with, a client or persons associated with the client. Examples include: the member's spouse enters into employment negotiations with the client; or there is excessive reliance on revenue from a single client.

(6) **Self-Review Threat** The threat that a member will not appropriately evaluate the results of a previous judgment made or service performed or supervised by the member and that the member will rely on that service in forming a judgment as part of another service. Examples of self-review threats include: the member relies on the work product of the member's firm; the member performs bookkeeping services for a client; or a partner was associated with the client as an employee, an officer, a director, or a contractor.

(7) **Undue Influence Threat** The threat that a member will subordinate his or her judgment to an individual associated with a client or any relevant third party due to that individual's reputation or expertise, aggressive or dominant personality, or attempts to coerce or exercise excessive influence over the member. For example, the client states that it will not award additional engagements to the firm if the firm continues to disagree with the client on an accounting or tax matter.

b. **Safeguards** Safeguards may partially or completely eliminate a threat or reduce it to an acceptable level, and fall into three broad categories:

(1) Those created by the profession, legislation, or regulation.

(2) Those implemented by the client that would operate in combination with other safeguards.

(3) Those implemented by the firm.

c. **Effectiveness** The effectiveness of a safeguard can depend upon many factors, including: the facts and circumstances specific to a particular situation; the proper identification of threats; whether the safeguard is suitably designed and consistently applied; how the safeguard interacts with a safeguard from another category; and whether the client is a public interest entity.

2. **Ethical Conflicts** An ethical conflict arises when a member encounters one or both of the following: obstacles to following an appropriate course of action due to internal or external pressures; and/or conflicts in applying relevant professional standards or legal standards For example, a member suspects a fraud may have occurred, but reporting the suspected fraud would violate the member's responsibility to maintain client confidentiality. Once an ethical conflict is encountered, a member may need to take steps to achieve compliance with the rules and law, justifying any departures that the member believes were appropriate in applying those rules and law. If the ethical conflict remains unresolved, the member may be in violation of one or more rules. Accordingly, the member should consider his or her continuing relationship with the engagement team, specific assignment, client, firm, or employer.

3. **Integrity and Objectivity Rule** In performing any professional service, a member shall maintain objectivity and integrity, be free of conflicts of interest, and not knowingly misrepresent facts or subordinate his or her judgment to others. In the absence of an interpretation that addresses a particular relationship or circumstance, a member should apply the *Conceptual Framework for Members in Public Practice*. If a member cannot demonstrate that any applied safeguards eliminated or reduced significant threats to an acceptable level, the member would be considered in violation of the *Integrity and Objectivity Rule*. When addressing ethical conflicts, a member should consider the guidance in *Ethical Conflicts* for determining an appropriate course of action.

   a. **Conflicts of Interest** A conflict of interest may arise during the performance of a professional service if a member or the member's firm has a relationship with another person, entity, product, or service that, in the member's professional judgment, the client or other appropriate parties may view as impairing the member's objectivity. In such situations, adverse interest or self-interest threats may exist to the member's compliance with the *Integrity and Objectivity Rule*.

      (1) **Unacceptable Threat Level** If identified threats to objectivity are so significant that no safeguards could eliminate or reduce the threat to an acceptable level, the member should either not perform the professional service or should terminate one or more of the relationships causing the conflict.

      (2) **Acceptable Threat Level** Threats to objectivity would be at an acceptable level and objectivity would not be impaired if both of the following safeguards are met before performing the professional service: the member notifies the client or other appropriate parties of the relevant facts and circumstances; and the member obtains consent from the client or other appropriate parties to perform the professional service. If consent is refused, the member either should not perform the professional service or should terminate one or more of the relationships causing the conflict.

   b. **Gifts and Entertainment** For purposes of this interpretation, a *client* includes: the client; an individual in a key position with the client; or an individual owning 10 percent or more of the client's outstanding equity securities or other ownership interests.

      (1) **Unacceptable Threat Level** Threats to compliance with the *Integrity and Objectivity Rule* would not be at an acceptable level and could not be reduced to an acceptable level by the application of safeguards if: the member offers to a client or accepts gifts or entertainment from a client that either: (a) violate the member's or client's policies or applicable laws, rules, and regulations; and the member knows of the violation or demonstrates recklessness in not knowing; or (b) a member offers to a client or accepts gifts or entertainment from a client that is not reasonable in the circumstances.

(2) **Acceptable Threat Level** Threats are at an acceptable level when gifts or entertainment are reasonable in the circumstances. The member should exercise judgment in determining whether gifts or entertainment would be considered reasonable in the circumstances.

c. **Preparing and Reporting Information** The member would be considered to have knowingly misrepresented facts in violation of the *Integrity and Objectivity Rule,* if the member: makes, or permits or directs another to make, materially false and misleading entries in an entity's financial statements or records; fails to correct an entity's financial statements or records that are materially false and misleading when the member has the authority to record the entries; or signs, or permits or directs another to sign, a document containing materially false and misleading information.

(1) **Subordination of Judgment** Self-interest, familiarity, and undue influence threats to the member's compliance with the *Integrity and Objectivity Rule* may exist when a member and his or her supervisor or any other person within the member's organization have a difference of opinion relating to the application of accounting principles, auditing standards, or other relevant professional standards, including standards applicable to tax and consulting services or applicable laws or regulations.

(2) **Resolution** For identified, significant threats, if the member concludes that no safeguards can eliminate or reduce the threats to an acceptable level or if the member concludes that appropriate action was not taken, then he or she should consider the continuing relationship with the member's organization and take appropriate steps to eliminate his or her exposure to subordination of judgment. Resignation may not relieve the member of responsibilities in the situation, including any responsibility to disclose concerns to third parties, such as regulatory authorities or the employer's (former employer's) external accountant.

d. **Client Advocacy** An advocacy threat to compliance with the *Integrity and Objectivity Rule* may exist when a member or the member's firm is engaged to perform nonattest services, such as tax and consulting services, that involve acting as an advocate for the client or to support a client's position on accounting or financial reporting issues either within the firm or outside the firm with standard setters, regulators, or others. If such circumstances exist, the member and member's firm should determine whether it is appropriate to perform the professional services.

e. **Use of a Third-Party Service Provider** When a member uses a third-party service provider to assist the member in providing professional services, threats to compliance with the *Integrity and Objectivity Rule* may exist. Clients might not have an expectation that a member would use a third-party service provider to assist the member in providing the professional services. Therefore, before disclosing confidential client information to a third-party service provider, the member should inform the client, preferably in writing, that the member may use a third-party service provider. If the client objects, the member either should not use the third-party service provider to perform the professional services or should decline to perform the engagement.

4. **Independence Rule** A member in public practice shall be independent in the performance of professional services as required by standards promulgated by bodies designated by Council.

   a. **Conceptual Framework Approach** It is impossible to list all relationships or circumstances in which the appearance of independence might be questioned. Thus, in the absence of an independence interpretation that addresses a particular relationship or circumstance, a member should evaluate whether that relationship or circumstance would lead a reasonable and informed third party who is aware of the relevant information to conclude that there is a threat to either the member's or firm's independence, or both, that is not at an acceptable level. When making that evaluation, a member should apply the conceptual framework approach.

      (1) **Threats** Many threats fall into one of the following seven broad categories: adverse interest, advocacy, familiarity, management participation, self-interest, self-review, and undue influence. Examples of threats associated with a specific relationship or circumstance are identified in the interpretations of the code.

      (2) **Safeguards** Safeguards may partially or completely eliminate a threat or diminish the potential influence of a threat. The nature and extent of the safeguards applied will depend on many factors, including the size of the firm and whether the attest client is a public interest entity. There are three broad categories of safeguards: those created by the profession; those implemented by the attest client; and those implemented by the firm. The effectiveness of a safeguard depends on a variety of factors, enumerated in the Revised Code.

   b. **Accounting Firms** To enhance their capabilities to provide professional services, accounting firms frequently join larger groups, which typically are membership associations that are separate legal entities and otherwise unrelated to their members. The associations do not themselves typically engage in public practice or provide professional services to their members' clients or other third parties.

      (1) **Audits and Reviews** If an association is considered a network (as defined in the Revised Code), and an entity is considered a network firm, it must comply with the *Independence Rule* with respect to the financial statement audit and review clients of the other network firms if the use of the audit or review report for the client is not restricted.

      (2) **Other Attest Clients** For all other attest clients, the covered member should consider any threats that may be created by another network firm's interests and relationships. If safeguards cannot be applied to eliminate or reduce the threats to an acceptable level, independence will be impaired.

      (3) **Network Characteristics** Associations that meet one of the following characteristics are considered to be a network:

         - Sharing a common brand name
         - Sharing common control
         - Sharing profits or costs
         - Sharing a common business strategy
         - Sharing significant professional resources
         - Sharing common quality control policies and procedures

(4) **Alternative Practice Structures (APS)** An alternative practice structure (APS) is a form of organization in which a firm that provides attest services is closely aligned with another public or private organization that performs other professional services. Members practicing public accounting in an APS should determine whether they are in compliance with the *Independence Rule*.

c. **Fees** The existence of unpaid fees from an attest client for professional services provided more than one year prior to the date of the current-year report may create unacceptable self-interest, undue influence, or advocacy threats to the covered member's compliance with the *Independence Rule.* Unpaid fees include fees that are unbilled or a note receivable arising from such fees; they do not include fees outstanding from an attest client in bankruptcy.

d. **Financial Interests** Independence would be impaired, and the self-interest threat to compliance would not be at an acceptable level and could not be reduced to an acceptable level by the application of safeguards, if

(1) A covered member had or was committed to acquire any direct financial interest or indirect financial interest in an attest client during the period of the professional engagement

(2) A partner or professional employee of the firm, his or her immediate family, or any group of such persons acting together owned more than 5 percent of an attest client's outstanding equity securities or other ownership interests during the period of the professional engagement

e. **Unsolicited Financial Interests** When a covered member becomes aware that he or she will receive, or has received, an unsolicited financial interest in an attest client during the period of the professional engagement, such as through a gift or an inheritance, the self-interest threat would be at an acceptable level and independence would not be impaired if both of the following safeguards are met:

(1) The member disposes of the financial interest as soon as practicable but no later than 30 days after the member has knowledge of and obtains the right to dispose of the financial interest

(2) The member does not participate on the attest engagement team during the period in which the member does not have the right to dispose of the financial interest, and the direct financial interest or indirect financial interest is not material to the covered member.

f. **Mutual Funds** A member who owns shares in a mutual fund has a direct financial interest in the mutual fund. However, whether the underlying investments in the mutual fund are considered to be the member's direct or indirect financial interests depends on the proportion of the mutual fund's outstanding shares that the member owns and whether the mutual fund is diversified.

(1) If a covered member owns 5 percent or less of the outstanding shares of a diversified mutual fund, the underlying investments would be considered immaterial indirect financial interests.

(2) If a covered member owns more than 5 percent of a diversified mutual fund's outstanding shares, or if a covered member owns a financial interest in a non-diversified mutual fund, the covered member should evaluate the mutual fund's underlying investments to determine whether the covered member holds a material indirect financial interest in any of the underlying investments.

g. **Trusts and Estates** Serving as a trustee of a trust or an executor or administrator of an estate that held, or was committed to acquire, any direct financial interest or any material indirect financial interest in an attest client during the period of the professional engagement, does not in itself create a self-interest threat. Independence would be impaired if:

(1) The member (individually or with others) has the authority to make investment decisions for the trust or estate

(2) The trust or estate owned or was committed to acquire more than 10 percent of the attest client's outstanding equity securities or other ownership interests

(3) The value of the trust's or estate's holdings in the attest client exceeds 10 percent of the total assets of the trust or estate

h. **Depository Accounts** If a member maintains checking, savings, certificates of deposit, money market, or other depository accounts (depository accounts) at a bank or similar depository institution that is an attest client during the period of the professional engagement, there may be a self-interest threat. When the member is a firm, the threat would be at an acceptable level if the firm concludes that the likelihood is remote that the bank or similar depository institution will experience financial difficulties

i. **Brokerage Accounts** If an attest client in the financial services industry, such as an insurance company, an investment adviser, a broker-dealer, a bank, or similar depository institution, has custody of a member's assets other than depository accounts, including retirement plan assets, during the period of the professional engagement, a self-interest threat may exist, unless: the attest client's services were rendered under the attest client's normal terms, procedures, and requirements; or any covered member's assets subject to the risk of loss are immaterial to the covered member's net worth.

j. **Loans and Leases** Independence would be impaired if a member had a loan to or from an attest client, any officer or director of the attest client, or any individual owning 10 percent or more of the attest client's outstanding equity securities or other ownership interests, except as follows:

(1) **Home Mortgages, Secured Loans, and Immaterial Unsecured Loans**. Independence would not be impaired if a member or his or her immediate family has an unsecured loan that is not material to the covered member's net worth (that is, immaterial unsecured loan), a home mortgage, or a secured loan from a lending institution attest client, provided certain safeguards are met.

(2) **Loans to Partnerships** For purposes of applying the provisions of section (1) above, when the member is a partner in a partnership, a loan to a limited partnership (or similar type of entity) or general partnership would be ascribed to each covered member who is a partner in the partnership on the basis of his or her legal liability as a limited or general partner if: the covered member's interest in the limited partnership, either individually or combined with the interest of one or more covered members, exceeds 50 percent of the total limited partnership interest; or the covered member, either individually or together with one or more covered members, can control the general partnership.

(3) **Other Loans and Leases** Independence would not be impaired if a member obtains one of the following types of loans or leases under the lending institution's normal lending procedures, terms, and requirements, provided the member complies with the terms of the loan or lease agreement at all times.

(4) **Leases** If a member enters into a leasing agreement with an attest client during the period of the professional engagement, independence would not be impaired if all the following safeguards are met: the lease meets the criteria of an operating lease (as described in GAAP); the terms and conditions set forth in the lease agreement are comparable with other leases of a similar nature; and all amounts are paid in accordance with the lease terms or provisions.

j. **Family Relationships With Attest Clients** If a member's immediate family is employed by an attest client but is not in a key position, independence would not be impaired. If they are in a key position during the period covered by the financial statements or during the period of the professional engagement, threats to compliance would not be at an acceptable level and could not be reduced to an acceptable level by the application of safeguard; independence would be impaired. There are a number of additional specific instances regarding immediate family and close relative relationships in regards to potential impairment of independence in the Revised Code.

k. **Current Employment With an Attest Client** Simultaneous employment or association with an attest client is defined to be: serving as a director, an officer, an employee, a promoter, an underwriter, a voting trustee, a trustee for any pension or profit-sharing trust of the attest client, or in any capacity equivalent to that of a member of management of an attest client during the period covered by the financial statements or the period of the professional engagement.

(1) **Impairment** If a partner or professional employee of the member's firm is simultaneously employed or associated with an attest client, familiarity, management participation, advocacy, or self-review threats could not be reduced to an acceptable level by the application of safeguards. Accordingly, independence would be impaired.

(2) **Exceptions** Independence will not be impaired if a partner or professional employee of a firm serves as an adjunct faculty member of an educational institution that is an attest client of the firm, provided that the partner or professional employee meets certain safeguards listed in the Revised Code.

l. **Memberships** When a partner or professional employee of a member's firm is asked to lend the prestige of his or her name to a not-for-profit organization (the assumption is that the organization limits its activities to charitable, religious, or civic or other matters of a similar nature) by serving as an honorary director or trustee of the organization during the period covered by the financial statements or during the period of the professional engagement, familiarity, self-review, or management participation threats may exist. However, threats would be at an acceptable level and independence would not be impaired if all of the following safeguards are met.

(1) The position is clearly honorary and the individual holds the position in name only

(2) The individual cannot vote or otherwise participate in board or management responsibilities

(3) If the individual is named in letterheads and externally circulated materials, the individual is identified as an honorary director or honorary trustee

m. **Former Employment With Attest Client** This applies to members who were formerly employed by or associated with an entity as an officer, director, promoter, underwriter, or trustee, and subsequently became employed by a firm that provides attest service to that entity.

(1) If the member participates on the client's attest engagement or can influence the attest engagement covering any period that includes the covered member's former employment or association with the attest client, independence would be impaired.

(2) If a member fails to disassociate from the attest client before becoming a covered member, independence would be impaired unless a number of safeguards (as detailed in the Revised Code) are met.

n. **Future Employment With Attest Client** This applies to a member of the attest engagement team, or an individual in a position to influence the attest engagement, who intends to seek or discuss potential employment or association with an attest client or is in receipt of a specific offer of employment from an attest client.

(1) Independence would not be impaired if a number of safeguards are met, including prompt reporting of such consideration to an appropriate person in the firm and immediate cessation of participation in the engagement.

(2) If a member becomes aware that an individual is considering employment or association with an attest client, the member should notify an appropriate person in the firm.

(3) The appropriate person in the firm should consider whether, based on the nature of the engagement and the individual involved, the firm should perform additional procedures to provide reasonable assurance that any work that the individual performed for the attest client was performed in compliance with the *Integrity and Objectivity Rule.*

o. **Subsequent Employment With Attest Client** This applies to partners and professional employees who leave their firms and are subsequently employed by, or associated with, one of the firm's attest clients in a key position. Independence would be impaired unless all of the following safeguards are met.

(1) **Individual Safeguards**

- Amounts due to the former partner/employee for his or her previous interest in the firm and unfunded, vested retirement benefits cannot be material to the firm, and the underlying formula used to calculate the payments remain fixed during the payout period.
- The former partner or professional employee is not in a position to influence the firm's operations or financial policies.
- The former partner or professional employee does not participate or appear to participate in the firm's business and is not otherwise associated with the firm.

(2) **Attest Engagement Team Safeguards**

- Consider modifying engagement procedures to adjust for the risk that the former partner's or professional employee's prior knowledge of the audit plan could reduce audit effectiveness. In addition, if the individual will have significant interaction with the attest engagement team, whether team members have sufficient experience and stature to deal effectively with the individual in conducting the engagement.

- If the former partner or professional employee joins the attest client in a key position within *one year* of disassociating from the firm and has significant interaction with the attest engagement team, review the subsequent attest engagement to determine whether the team maintained the appropriate level of skepticism when evaluating the individual's representations and work. The professional applying this safeguard should have appropriate stature, expertise, and objectivity.

p. **Memberships** If a member belongs to a social club (e.g., a country club) that is an attest client, and is required to acquire a pro rata share of the club's equity or debt securities, then threats to independence would be at an acceptable level if the club membership is essentially a social matter, because such equity or debt ownership would not be considered to be a direct financial interest. A number of other memberships and independence threats are discussed in the Revised Code.

q. **Gifts and Entertainment** If a member's firm, a member of the attest engagement team, or an individual in a position to influence the attest engagement, accepts a gift from an attest client and the value is not clearly insignificant to the recipient, independence would be impaired. Similarly, if a covered member accepts entertainment from an attest client that is not reasonable in the circumstances, independence would be impaired. Conversely, if a member offers a gift or entertainment to an attest client that is not reasonable in the circumstances, independence would be impaired.

r. **Actual or Threatened Litigation** Litigation or the expressed intention to commence litigation between a member and an attest client or its management, requires the member to assess the materiality of the litigation to the member, the member's firm, and the attest client. The covered member's assessment should include an evaluation of the nature of the matter(s) underlying the litigation and all other relevant factors.

(1) Situations involving threatened or actual litigation are complex and diverse, making it difficult to identify precise points at which threats become unacceptable. The Revised Code provides the following examples where independence would be impaired:

- An attest client's present management commences litigation alleging deficiencies in audit work performed for the attest client or expresses its intention to commence such litigation, and the member concludes that it is probable that such a claim will be filed.

- A member commences litigation against an attest client's present management alleging management fraud or deceit.

(2) If threatened or actual litigation is unrelated to the performance of a client's attest engagement and is for an amount that is not material to the member's firm or the attest client, independence would not be impaired. Such claims may from immaterial disputes regarding billings for services, or results of tax or management services advice.

s. **Nonattest Services** A member's independence would not be impaired if the member performed nonattest services that would have otherwise impaired independence during the period covered by the financial statements if all of the following conditions exist: the nonattest services were provided prior to period of the professional engagement; the nonattest services related to periods prior to the period covered by the financial statements; and the financial statements for the period to which the nonattest services relate were audited by another firm (or in the case of a review engagement, reviewed or audited by another firm).

(1) **Multiple Services** Performing multiple nonattest services can increase the significance of threats to independence. The member should evaluate whether the performance of multiple nonattest services by the member or member's firm in the aggregate creates a significant threat to the member's independence that cannot be reduced to an acceptable level by the application of the safeguards. In such cases, independence would be impaired.

(2) **Management Responsibilities** If a member were to assume a management responsibility for an attest client, independence would be impaired. Examples of management responsibilities include: leading and directing an entity; and making significant decisions regarding the acquisition, deployment, and control of human, financial, physical, and intangible resources.

(3) **General Requirements** When a member performs a nonattest service for an attest client, independence would not be impaired when all the following safeguards are met:

- Management assumes all management responsibilities (as defined in the Revised Code), including overseeing the service, evaluate the adequacy and results of the service, and accept responsibility for the results of the service.
- Management: will meet all of the criteria listed in the first bullet; will make an informed judgment on the results of the member's nonattest service; and will accept responsibility for significant judgments and decisions.
- The member establishes and documents in writing his or her understanding with the attest client regarding: engagement objectives; services to be performed; the attest client's acceptance of their responsibilities; and any limitations of the engagement.

(4) **Advisory Services** If the member's services are only advisory in nature and the member does not assume any management responsibilities, independence would not be impaired.

(5) **Appraisal, Valuation, and Actuarial Services** If the member performs an appraisal, a valuation, or an actuarial service for an attest client when (a) the services involve a significant degree of subjectivity and (b) the results of the service, individually or when combined with other valuation, appraisal, or actuarial services, are material to the attest client's financial statements, independence would be impaired.

(6) **Forensic Accounting** Forensic accounting services are nonattest services that involve the application of (a) special skills in accounting, auditing, finance, quantitative methods or certain areas of the law, and research and (b) investigative skills to collect, analyze, and evaluate evidential matter and to interpret and communicate findings. Forensic accounting services consist of investigative services and litigation services. Litigation services include: expert witness services, litigation consulting services, and other litigation services.

- When a member provides investigative services to an attest client, independence will not be impaired if the member applies the *General Requirements* criteria.
- Expert witness services create the appearance that a member is advocating or promoting an attest client's position. Accordingly, if a member is engaged conditionally or unconditionally to provide expert witness services or expert testimony for an attest client, independence would be impaired, except for certain exceptions permitted in the Revised Code.
- As long as the member applies the *General Requirements* criteria, independence would not be impaired when providing litigation consulting services.
- If a member serves as a trier of fact, a special master, a court-appointed expert, or an arbitrator (including serving on an arbitration panel) in a matter involving an attest client, independence would be impaired because these services create the appearance that the member is not independent.

(7) **Information Systems Design, Implementation or Integration** When a member provides information systems design, implementation, or integration services to an attest client, independence would not be impaired if the member applies the *General Requirements* criteria. Acceptable engagements include:

- Install or integrate an attest client's financial information system that the member did not design or develop
- Assist in setting up the attest client's chart of accounts and financial statement format with respect to the attest client's financial information system
- Design, develop, install, or integrate an attest client's information system that is unrelated to the attest client's financial statements or accounting records
- Provide training and instruction to an attest client's employees on an information and control system
- Perform network maintenance, such as updating virus protection, applying routine updates and patches, or configuring user settings consistent with management's request

Independence would be impaired if the member:

- Designs or develops an attest client's financial information system
- Makes other than insignificant modifications to source code underlying an attest client's existing financial information system
- Supervises attest client personnel in the daily operation of an attest client's information system
- Operates an attest client's network

(8) **Tax Services** Tax services include preparation of a tax return, transmittal of a tax return, and transmittal of any related tax payment to the taxing authority, signing and filing a tax return, having a power of attorney limited strictly to tax matters; and authorized representation of attest clients in administrative proceedings before a taxing authority. When a member prepares a tax return, and transmits the tax return and related tax payment to a taxing authority in paper or electronic form, independence will not be impaired. Additionally, the individual designated by the attest client to oversee the tax services must: review and approve the tax return and related tax payment; and if required for filing, signs the tax return prior to the member transmitting the return to the taxing authority.

t. **Independence Standards for SSAE Engagements** The *Independence Rule* and its interpretations apply to all attest engagements. However, when performing engagements to issue reports in accordance with Statements on Standards for Attestation Engagements (SSAEs), when independence is required or when the member's compilation report does not disclose a lack of independence, the covered member needs to be independent with respect to the responsible party(ies), as defined in the SSAEs. When providing nonattest services that would otherwise impair independence, independence will not be impaired provided that the nonattest services do not relate to the specific subject matter of the SSAE engagement.

5. **General Standards Rule** In the absence of an interpretation of the *General Standards Rule* that addresses a particular relationship or circumstance, a member should apply the *Conceptual Framework for Members in Public* A member would be considered in violation of the *General Standards Rule* if the member cannot demonstrate that safeguards were applied that eliminated or reduced significant threats to an acceptable level. A member shall comply with the following standards:

a. **Professional Competence** Undertake only those professional services that the member or the member's firm can reasonably expect to be completed with professional competence. Competence means that the member possesses the appropriate technical qualifications to perform professional services and that the member supervises and evaluates the quality of work performed. Competence encompasses knowledge of the profession's standards, the techniques and technical subject matter involved, and the ability to exercise sound judgment in applying such knowledge in the performance of professional services.

b. **Due Professional Care** Exercise due professional care in the performance of professional services.

c. **Planning and Supervision** Adequately plan and supervise the performance of professional services. A member who employs a specialist to perform consulting services for the member's clients must be qualified to supervise and evaluate the work of that specialist.

d. **Sufficient Relevant Data** Obtain sufficient relevant data to afford a reasonable basis for conclusions or recommendations in relation to any professional services performed.

e. **Third-Party Provider** The member should ensure that any third-party service provider has the required professional qualifications, technical skills, and other resources. The member must adequately plan and supervise the third-party service provider's professional services so that the member ensures that the services are performed with competence and due professional care. The member must also obtain sufficient relevant data to support the work product and comply with all technical standards applicable to the professional services.

6. **Compliance With Standards Rule** A member who performs auditing, review, compilation, management consulting, tax, or other professional services shall comply with standards promulgated by bodies designated by Council. In the absence of an interpretation of the *Compliance With Standards Rule* that addresses a particular relationship or circumstance, a member should apply the *Conceptual Framework for Members in Public Practice.* A member would be considered in violation of the *Compliance With Standards Rule* if the member cannot demonstrate that safeguards were applied that eliminated or reduced significant threats to an acceptable level.

7. **Accounting Principles Rule** A member shall not (a) express an opinion or state affirmatively that the financial statements or other financial data of any entity are presented in conformity with accounting principles promulgated by bodies designated by the Council (e.g., FASB, GASB, FASAB, IASB) or (b) state that he or she is not aware of any material modifications that should be made to such statements or data in order for them to be in conformity with generally accepted accounting principles, if such statements or data contain any departure from an accounting principle promulgated by bodies designated by Council to establish such principles that has a material effect on the statements or data taken as a whole.

   a. If the statements or data contain such a departure and the member can demonstrate that due to unusual circumstances the financial statements or data would otherwise have been misleading, the member can comply with the rule by describing the departure, its approximate effects, if practicable, and the reasons why compliance with the principle would result in a misleading statement.

   b. In the absence of an interpretation of the *Accounting Principles Rule* that addresses a particular relationship or circumstance, a member should apply the *Conceptual Framework for Members in Public Practice.* A member would be considered in violation of the *Accounting Principles Rule* if the member cannot demonstrate that safeguards were applied that eliminated or reduced significant threats to an acceptable level.

8. **Acts Discreditable Rule** A member shall not commit an act discreditable to the profession. In the absence of an interpretation of the *Acts Discreditable Rule* that addresses a particular relationship or circumstance, a member should apply the *Conceptual Framework for Members in Public Practice*. A member would be considered in violation of the *Acts Discreditable Rule* if the member cannot demonstrate that safeguards were applied that eliminated or reduced significant threats to an acceptable level. A member would be presumed to have committed an act discreditable to the profession if:

   a. **Discrimination/Harassment** A final determination, no longer subject to appeal, is made by a court or an administrative agency of competent jurisdiction that a member has violated any antidiscrimination laws of the US, a state, or a municipality, including those related to sexual and other forms of harassment.

   b. **Solicitation of CPA Exam Information** A member who solicits or knowingly discloses the Uniform CPA Examination question(s) or answer(s), or both, without the AICPA's written authorization.

   c. **Failure to File a Tax Return** A member who fails to comply with applicable federal, state, or local laws or regulations regarding (1) the timely filing of the member's personal tax returns or tax returns of the member's firm that the member has the authority to timely file or (2) the timely remittance of all payroll and other taxes collected on behalf of others.

d. **Negligence in Financial Statement Preparation** A member makes or permits materially false and misleading entries in the financial statements or records of an entity; fails to correct an entity's financial statements that are materially false and misleading when the member has the authority to record an entry; or signs, or permits or directs another to sign, a document containing materially false and misleading information.

e. **Governmental Audits** A member fails to follow specified government audit standards, guides, procedures, statutes, rules, and regulations, unless the member discloses in his or her report that such requirements were not followed and the applicable reasons for not following the requirements.

f. **Confidential Information** A member discloses or uses any confidential employer information acquired as a result of employment or volunteer relationships without the proper authority or specific consent of the employer or organization for whom the member may work in a volunteer capacity, unless there is a legal or professional responsibility to use or disclose such information. The following are examples of situations when such disclosure may be appropriate:

- Disclosure is permitted by law and authorized by the employer
- Disclosure is required by law to comply with a subpoena or summons or inform the appropriate public authorities of violations of law that have been discovered
- There is a professional responsibility or right to disclose information to: initiate a complaint with, or respond to any inquiry made by, a duly constituted investigative or disciplinary body; protect the member's professional interests in legal proceedings; comply with professional standards and other ethics requirements; or report potential concerns regarding questionable accounting, auditing, or other matters to the employer's confidential complaint hotline or those charged with governance.
- Disclosure is permitted on behalf of the employer to: obtain financing with lenders; communicate with vendors, clients, and customers; or to communicate with the employer's external accountant, attorneys, regulators, and other business professionals.

g. **Marketing Professional Services** A member would be in violation of the Acts Discreditable Rule if the member promotes or markets the member's abilities to provide professional services or makes claims about the member's experience or qualifications in a manner that is false, misleading, or deceptive (i.e., they contain any claim or representation that would likely cause a reasonable person to be misled or deceived. This includes any representation about CPA licensure or any other professional certification or accreditation that is not in compliance with the requirements of the relevant licensing authority or designating body.)

h. **Removing Client Files** A member whose employment relationship is terminated would be considered in violation of the *Acts Discreditable Rule* if the member takes or retains (1) originals or copies (in any format) from the firm's client files or (2) proprietary information without the firm's permission, unless the member has a contractual arrangement with the firm allowing such action. This interpretation does not apply to owners of firms as the firm's ownership agreement would govern ownership of client files and proprietary information.

9. **Contingent Fees Rule** A contingent fee is a fee established for the performance of any service pursuant to an arrangement in which no fee will be charged unless a specified finding or result is attained, or in which the amount of the fee is otherwise dependent upon the finding or result of such service. A member's fees may vary depending on the complexity of services rendered. For purposes of this rule only, fees are not regarded as being contingent if fixed by courts or other public authorities, or, in tax matters, if determined based on the results of judicial proceedings or the findings of governmental agencies. A member in public practice shall not.

   a. Perform for a contingent fee any professional services for, or receive such a fee from a client for whom the member or the member's firm performs: an audit or review of a financial statement; or a compilation of a financial statement when the member expects that a third party will use the financial statement and the member's compilation report does not disclose a lack of independence; or an examination of prospective financial information

   b. Prepare an original or amended tax return or claim for a tax refund for a contingent fee for any client.

   In the absence of an interpretation of the *Contingent Fee Rule* that addresses a particular relationship or circumstance, a member should apply the *Conceptual Framework for Members in Public Practice*. A member would be considered in violation of the *Contingent Fee Rule* if the member cannot demonstrate that safeguards were applied that eliminated or reduced significant threats to an acceptable level.

10. **Commissions and Referral Fees Rule** A member in public practice shall not for a commission recommend or refer to a client any product or service, or for a commission recommend or refer any product or service to be supplied by a client, or receive a commission, when the member or member's firm also performs for that client: an audit or review of a financial statement; a compilation of a financial statement when the member expects that a third party might use the financial statement and the member's compilation report does not disclose a lack of independence; or an examination of prospective financial information.

    Any member who accepts a referral fee for recommending or referring any service of a CPA to any person or entity or who pays a referral fee to obtain a client shall disclose such acceptance or payment to the client.

    In the absence of an interpretation of the *Commissions and Referral Fees Rule* that addresses a particular relationship or circumstance, a member should apply the *Conceptual Framework for Members in Public Practice*. A member would be considered in violation of the *Commissions and Referral Fees Rule* if the member cannot demonstrate that safeguards were applied that eliminated or reduced significant threats to an acceptable level.

11. **Advertising/Solicitations Rule** A member in public practice shall not seek to obtain clients by advertising or other forms of solicitation in a manner that is false, misleading, or deceptive. Solicitation by the use of coercion, over-reaching, or harassing conduct is prohibited. In the absence of an interpretation of the *Advertising/Solicitations Rule* that addresses a particular relationship or circumstance, a member should apply the *Conceptual Framework for Members in Public Practice*. A member would be considered in violation of the *Advertising/Solicitations Rule* if the member cannot demonstrate that safeguards were applied that eliminated or reduced significant threats to an acceptable level.

12. **Confidential Client Information Rule** A member in public practice shall not disclose any confidential client information without the specific consent of the client.

    a. This rule shall not be construed to affect in any way the member's obligation to: comply with a validly issued and enforceable subpoena or summons; prohibit a member's compliance with applicable laws and government regulations; prohibit review of a member's professional practice under AICPA or state CPA society or Board of Accountancy authorization; or preclude a member from initiating a complaint with, or responding to any inquiry made by, the professional ethics division or trial board of the Institute or a duly constituted investigative or disciplinary body of a state CPA society or Board of Accountancy.

    b. Members involved with professional practice reviews shall not use to their own advantage or disclose any member's confidential client information that comes to their attention in carrying out those activities. This prohibition shall not restrict members' exchange of information in connection with the investigative or disciplinary proceedings.

    c. In the absence of an interpretation of the *Confidential Client Information Rule* that addresses a particular relationship or circumstance, a member should apply the *Conceptual Framework for Members in Public Practice*. A member would be considered in violation of the *Confidential Client Information Rule* if the member cannot demonstrate that safeguards were applied that eliminated or reduced significant threats to an acceptable level.

13. **Form of Organization and Name Rule** A member may practice public accounting only in a form of organization permitted by law or regulation whose characteristics conform to resolutions of Council. A member shall not practice public accounting under a firm name that is misleading. Names of one or more past owners may be included in the firm name of a successor organization. A firm may not designate itself as "Members of the American Institute of Certified Public Accountants" unless all its CPA owners are members of the AICPA.

    a. In the absence of an interpretation of the *Form of Organization and Name Rule* that addresses a particular relationship or circumstance, a member should apply the *Conceptual Framework for Members in Public Practice*. A member would be considered in violation of the *Form of Organization and Name Rule* if the member cannot demonstrate that safeguards were applied that eliminated or reduced significant threats to an acceptable level.

    b. A member may own an interest in a separate business that performs for clients accounting, tax, personal financial planning, or litigation support services or other services for which standards are promulgated by bodies designated by Council. If the member, either individually or collectively with the member's firm or others in the firm, controls the separate business, then the separate business, its owners (including the member), and its professional employees must comply with the code.

H. **Part 2: Members in Business**
Part 2 of the Revised Code applies to members in business. Accordingly, when the term *member* is used in Part 2, the requirements apply only to members in business. When a member in business is also a member in public practice (for example, a member has a part-time tax practice), the member should also consult Part 1.

1. **Conceptual Framework** Members may have relationships or circumstances that create threats to the member's compliance with the rules. If there is not an interpretation that addresses that relationship or circumstance, a member should evaluate whether the relationship or circumstance would lead a reasonable and informed third party who is aware of the relevant information to conclude that there is a threat to the member's compliance with the rules that is not at an acceptable level.

   a. **Threats** Under the conceptual framework approach, members should evaluate identified threats both individually and in the aggregate because threats can have a cumulative effect on a member's compliance. The existence of a threat does not mean that the member is in violation of the rules; however, the member should evaluate the significance of the threat, considering both qualitative and quantitative factors. If the member concludes that the threat is not at an acceptable level, the member should apply safeguards to eliminate the threat or reduce it to an acceptable level. There are six broad categories of threats:

      (1) **Adverse Interest Threat** The threat that a member will not act with objectivity because the member's interests are opposed to the employing organization. For example, a member has charged the employing organization with violations of law.

      (2) **Advocacy Threat** The threat that a member will promote an employing organization's interests or position to the point that his or her objectivity or independence is compromised. For example, a member gives or fails to give information that the member knows will unduly influence the conclusions reached by an external service provider or other third party.

      (3) **Familiarity Threat** The threat that, due to a long or close relationship with a person or employing organization, a member will become too sympathetic to their interests or too accepting of the person's work or employing organization's product or service. Examples include: a member uses an immediate family's or a close relative's company as a supplier to the employing organization; or a member may accept an individual's work product with little or no review because the individual has been producing an acceptable work product for an extended period of time.

      (4) **Self-Interest Threat** The threat that a member could benefit, financially or otherwise, from an interest in, or relationship with, an employing organization or persons associated with the employing organization. Examples include: a member's immediate family or close relative has a financial interest in the employing organization; or a member holds a financial interest (for example, shares or share options) in the employing organization, and the value of that financial interest is directly affected by the member's decisions.

(5) **Self-Review Threat** The threat that a member will not appropriately evaluate the results of a previous judgment made or service performed or supervised by the member or an individual in the employing organization and that the member will rely on that service in forming a judgment as part of another service. Examples of self-review threats include: when performing an internal audit procedure, an internal auditor accepts work that he or she previously performed in a different position; or the member accepts the work previously performed by the member, alone or with others, that will be the basis for providing another professional service.

(6) **Undue Influence Threat** The threat that a member will subordinate his or her judgment to an individual associated with an employing organization or any relevant third party due to that individual's reputation or expertise, aggressive or dominant personality, or attempts to coerce or exercise excessive influence over the member. For example, a member is pressured to: become associated with misleading information; deviate from a company policy; change a conclusion regarding an accounting or a tax position; or hire an unqualified individual.

b. **Safeguards** Safeguards may partially or completely eliminate a threat or reduce it to an acceptable level, and fall into two broad categories:

(1) Those created by the profession, legislation, or regulation; including education and training requirements on ethics and professional responsibilities; professional standards and the threat of discipline; and competency and experience requirements for licensure.

(2) Those implemented by the employing organization. Examples include: a tone at the top emphasizing a commitment to fair financial reporting and compliance with applicable laws, rules, regulations, and corporate governance policies; policies and procedures addressing ethical conduct and compliance with laws, rules, and regulations; an audit committee charter, including independent audit committee members; and internal policies and procedures requiring disclosure of identified interests or relationships among the employing organization, its directors or officers, and vendors, suppliers, or customers (Editor note: many more examples are provided in the Revised Code.)

c. **Effectiveness** The effectiveness of a safeguard can depend upon many factors, including: the facts and circumstances specific to a particular situation; the proper identification of threats; whether the safeguard is suitably designed and consistently applied; how the safeguard interacts with a safeguard from another category; and whether the client is a public interest entity.

2. **Ethical Conflicts** An ethical conflict arises when a member encounters one or both of the following: obstacles to following an appropriate course of action due to internal or external pressures; and/or conflicts in applying relevant professional and legal standards. Once an ethical conflict is encountered, a member may need to take steps to achieve compliance with the rules and law, justifying any departures that the member believes were appropriate in applying those rules and law. If the ethical conflict remains unresolved, the member should consider his or her continuing relationship with the specific assignment or employer.

3. **Integrity and Objectivity Rule** In performing any professional service, a member shall maintain objectivity and integrity, be free of conflicts of interest, and not knowingly misrepresent facts or subordinate his or her judgment to others. In the absence of an interpretation that addresses a particular relationship or circumstance, a member should apply the *Conceptual Framework for Members in Public Practice.* If a member cannot demonstrate that any applied safeguards eliminated or reduced significant threats to an acceptable level, the member would be considered in violation of the *Integrity and Objectivity Rule*.

   a. **Conflicts of Interest** A conflict of interest may arise during the performance of a professional service for an employer if a member or the member's employer has a relationship with another person, entity, product, or service that, in the member's professional judgment, the employer or other appropriate parties may view as impairing the member's objectivity. In such situations, adverse interest or self-interest threats may exist to the member's compliance with the *Integrity and Objectivity Rule*.

      (1) **Unacceptable Threat Level** If identified threats to objectivity are so significant that no safeguards could eliminate or reduce the threat to an acceptable level, the member should either not perform the professional service or should terminate one or more of the relationships causing the conflict.

      (2) **Acceptable Threat Level** Threats to objectivity would be at an acceptable level and objectivity would not be impaired if both of the following safeguards are met before performing the professional service: the member notifies the employer or other appropriate parties of the relevant facts and circumstances; and the member obtains consent from the employer or other appropriate parties to perform the professional service. If consent is refused, the member either should not perform the professional service or should terminate one or more of the relationships causing the conflict.

   b. **Gifts and Entertainment** For purposes of this interpretation, a customer or vendor of the member's employer includes a representative of the customer or vendor.

      (1) **Unacceptable Threat Level** Threats to compliance with the *Integrity and Objectivity Rule* would not be at an acceptable level and could not be reduced to an acceptable level by the application of safeguards if: the member offers to, or accepts gifts or entertainment from, a customer or vendor of the member's employer that violate applicable laws, rules, or regulations or the policies of the member's employer, customer, or vender; and the member knows of the violation or demonstrates recklessness in not knowing.

      (2) **Acceptable Threat Level** Threats are at an acceptable level when gifts or entertainment are reasonable in the circumstances. The member should exercise judgment in determining whether gifts or entertainment would be considered reasonable in the circumstances.

   c. **Preparing and Reporting Information** The member would be considered to have knowingly misrepresented facts in violation of the *Integrity and Objectivity Rule,* if the member: makes, or permits or directs another to make, materially false and misleading entries in an entity's financial statements or records; fails to correct an entity's financial statements or records that are materially false and misleading when the member has the authority to record the entries; or signs, or permits or directs another to sign, a document containing materially false and misleading information.

      (1) **Subordination of Judgment** Self-interest, familiarity, and undue influence threats to the member's compliance with the *Integrity and Objectivity Rule* may exist when a member and his or her supervisor or any other person within the member's organization have a difference of opinion relating to the application of accounting principles, auditing standards, or other relevant professional standards, including standards applicable to tax and consulting services or applicable laws or regulations.

(2) **Resolution** For identified, significant threats, if the member concludes that no safeguards can eliminate or reduce the threats to an acceptable level or if the member concludes that appropriate action was not taken, then he or she should consider, in no specific order, the following safeguards:

- Determine whether the organization's internal policies and procedures have any additional requirements for reporting differences of opinion.
- Determine whether he or she is responsible for communicating to third parties, such as regulatory authorities or the organization's (former organization's) external accountant.
- Consult with his or her legal counsel regarding his or her responsibilities.

If the member concludes that no safeguards can eliminate or reduce the threats to an acceptable level or if the member concludes that appropriate action was not taken, then he or she should consider the continuing relationship with the member's organization and take appropriate steps to eliminate his or her exposure to subordination of judgment.

4. **General Standards Rule** In the absence of an interpretation of the *General Standards Rule* that addresses a particular relationship or circumstance, a member should apply the *Conceptual Framework for Members in Public* A member would be considered in violation of the *General Standards Rule* if the member cannot demonstrate that safeguards were applied that eliminated or reduced significant threats to an acceptable level. A member shall comply with the following standards:

   a. **Professional Competence** Undertake only those professional services that the member or the member's firm can reasonably expect to be completed with professional competence. Competence means that the member possesses the appropriate technical qualifications to perform professional services and that the member supervises and evaluates the quality of work performed. Competence encompasses knowledge of the profession's standards, the techniques and technical subject matter involved, and the ability to exercise sound judgment in applying such knowledge in the performance of professional services.

   b. **Due Professional Care** Exercise due professional care in the performance of professional services.

   c. **Planning and Supervision** Adequately plan and supervise the performance of professional services.

   d. **Sufficient Relevant Data** Obtain sufficient relevant data to afford a reasonable basis for conclusions or recommendations in relation to any professional services performed.

5. **Compliance With Standards Rule** A member who performs auditing, review, compilation, management consulting, tax, or other professional services shall comply with standards promulgated by bodies designated by Council. In the absence of an interpretation of the *Compliance With Standards Rule* that addresses a particular relationship or circumstance, a member should apply the *Conceptual Framework for Members in Public Practice.* A member would be considered in violation of the *Compliance With Standards Rule* if the member cannot demonstrate that safeguards were applied that eliminated or reduced significant threats to an acceptable level.

6. **Accounting Principles Rule** A member shall not (a) express an opinion or state affirmatively that the financial statements or other financial data of any entity are presented in conformity with accounting principles promulgated by bodies designated by the Council (e.g. FASB, GASB, FASAB, IASB) or (b) state that he or she is not aware of any material modifications that should be made to such statements or data in order for them to be in conformity with generally accepted accounting principles, if such statements or data contain any departure from an accounting principle promulgated by bodies designated by Council to establish such principles that has a material effect on the statements or data taken as a whole.

   a. If the statements or data contain such a departure and the member can demonstrate that due to unusual circumstances the financial statements or data would otherwise have been misleading, the member can comply with the rule by describing the departure, its approximate effects, if practicable, and the reasons why compliance with the principle would result in a misleading statement.

   b. In the absence of an interpretation of the *Accounting Principles Rule* that addresses a particular relationship or circumstance, a member should apply the *Conceptual Framework for Members in Public Practice.* A member would be considered in violation of the *Accounting Principles Rule* if the member cannot demonstrate that safeguards were applied that eliminated or reduced significant threats to an acceptable level.

7. **Acts Discreditable Rule** A member shall not commit an act discreditable to the profession. In the absence of an interpretation of the *Acts Discreditable Rule* that addresses a particular relationship or circumstance, a member should apply the *Conceptual Framework for Members in Public Practice.* A member would be considered in violation of the *Acts Discreditable Rule* if the member cannot demonstrate that safeguards were applied that eliminated or reduced significant threats to an acceptable level. A member would be presumed to have committed an act discreditable to the profession if:

   a. **Discrimination/Harassment** A final determination, no longer subject to appeal, is made by a court or an administrative agency of competent jurisdiction that a member has violated any antidiscrimination laws of the US, a state, or a municipality, including those related to sexual and other forms of harassment.

   b. **Solicitation of CPA Exam Information** A member who solicits or knowingly discloses the Uniform CPA Examination question(s) or answer(s), or both, without the AICPA's written authorization.

   c. **Failure to File a Tax Return** A member who fails to comply with applicable federal, state, or local laws or regulations regarding (1) the timely filing of the member's personal tax returns or tax returns of the member's firm that the member has the authority to timely file or (2) the timely remittance of all payroll and other taxes collected on behalf of others.

   d. **Negligence in Financial Statement Preparation** A member makes or permits materially false and misleading entries in the financial statements or records of an entity; fails to correct an entity's financial statements that are materially false and misleading when the member has the authority to record an entry; or signs, or permits or directs another to sign, a document containing materially false and misleading information.

e. **Confidential Information** A member should maintain the confidentiality of his or her employer's confidential information and should not use or disclose any confidential employer information obtained as a result of an employment relationship, such as discussions with the employer's vendors, customers, or lenders. Confidential employer information is any proprietary information pertaining to the employer or any organization for whom the member may work in a volunteer capacity that is not known to be available to the public and is obtained as a result of such relationships.

The following are examples of situations when such disclosure may be appropriate:

- Disclosure is permitted by law and authorized by the employer
- Disclosure is required by law to comply with a subpoena or summons or inform the appropriate public authorities of violations of law that have been discovered
- There is a professional responsibility or right to disclose information to: initiate a complaint with, or respond to any inquiry made by, a duly constituted investigative or disciplinary body; protect the member's professional interests in legal proceedings; comply with professional standards and other ethics requirements; or report potential concerns regarding questionable accounting, auditing, or other matters to the employer's confidential complaint hotline or those charged with governance.
- Disclosure is permitted on behalf of the employer to: obtain financing with lenders; communicate with vendors, clients, and customers; or to communicate with the employer's external accountant, attorneys, regulators, and other business professionals.

f. **Marketing Professional Services** A member would be in violation of the *Acts Discreditable Rule* if the member promotes or markets the member's abilities to provide professional services or makes claims about the member's experience or qualifications in a manner that is false, misleading, or deceptive (i.e., they contain any claim or representation that would likely cause a reasonable person to be misled or deceived. This includes any representation about CPA licensure or any other professional certification or accreditation that is not in compliance with the requirements of the relevant licensing authority or designating body.)

I. **Part 3: Other Members**

Part 3 of the Revised Code applies to members who are not in public practice and are not members in business (e.g., members who are retired or not currently employed). Accordingly, when the term member is used in Part 3 of the code, the requirements apply only to such members. A member shall not commit an act discreditable to the profession. A member would be presumed to have committed an act discreditable to the profession if:

1. **Discrimination/Harassment** A final determination, no longer subject to appeal, is made by a court or an administrative agency of competent jurisdiction that a member has violated any antidiscrimination laws of the US, a state, or a municipality, including those related to sexual and other forms of harassment.

2. **Solicitation of CPA Exam Information** A member who solicits or knowingly discloses the Uniform CPA Examination question(s) or answer(s), or both, without the AICPA's written authorization.

3. **Failure to File a Tax Return** A member who fails to comply with applicable federal, state, or local laws or regulations regarding (a) the timely filing of the member's personal tax returns or tax returns of the member's firm that the member has the authority to timely file or (b) the timely remittance of all payroll and other taxes collected on behalf of others.

4. **Confidential Information** A member should maintain the confidentiality of his or her former employer's confidential information and should not use or disclose any confidential employer information obtained as a result of an employment relationship.. Confidential employer information is any proprietary information pertaining to the former employer or any organization for whom the member may have worked in a volunteer capacity that is not known to be available to the public and is obtained as a result of such relationships. The following are examples of situations when such disclosure may be appropriate:

   a. Disclosure is permitted by law and authorized by the former employer

   b. Disclosure is required by law to comply with a subpoena or summons or inform the appropriate public authorities of violations of law that have been discovered

   c. There is a professional responsibility or right to disclose information to: initiate a complaint with, or respond to any inquiry made by, a duly constituted investigative or disciplinary body; protect the member's professional interests in legal requirements; or report potential concerns regarding questionable accounting, auditing, or other matters to the former employer's confidential complaint hotline or those charged with governance.

   d. Disclosure is permitted on behalf of the former employer to: obtain financing with lenders; communicate with vendors, clients, and customers; or to communicate with the employer's external accountant, attorneys, regulators, and other business professionals.

5. **Marketing Professional Services** A member would be in violation of the Acts Discreditable Rule if the member promotes or markets the member's abilities to provide professional services or makes claims about the member's experience or qualifications in a manner that is false, misleading, or deceptive (i.e., they contain any claim or representation that would likely cause a reasonable person to be misled or deceived. This includes any representation about CPA licensure or any other professional certification or accreditation that is not in compliance with the requirements of the relevant licensing authority or designating body.)

CHAPTER 15—ACCOUNTANTS' PROFESSIONAL RESPONSIBILITIES

Problem 15-1 MULTIPLE-CHOICE QUESTIONS

Independence

1. Which of the following is a correct statement regarding the nature and timing of communications between an accounting firm performing an initial audit of an issuer and the issuer's audit committee?
   a. Prior to accepting the engagement, the firm must orally affirm its independence to the audit committee with all members present.
   b. The firm must address all independence impairment issues on the date of the audit opinion.
   c. Communications related to independence may occur in any form prior to issuance of the financial statements.
   d. Prior to accepting the engagement, the firm should describe in writing all relationships that, as of the date of the communication, may reasonably be thought to bear on independence. (ID: 9923)

2. Which of the following situations would not impair objectivity, integrity, or independence with respect to an audit client?
   a. An auditor takes the client's audit committee to Las Vegas for the weekend.
   b. An out-of-town client takes the audit engagement team out to dinner at a renowned local restaurant.
   c. An auditor provides client management with box seats for the season at a major league baseball franchise.
   d. A client takes the audit engagement team on a two-day ski trip after the audit team worked for two consecutive weekends. (ID: 90170)

3. Which of the following rules of the AICPA Code of Professional Conduct must be observed even by a member who is not in public practice?
   a. Independence in Fact and Appearance
   b. Integrity and Objectivity
   c. Professional Competence
   d. Compliance with Standards (ID: 90183)

4. While performing certain nonaudit services for an insurance company, a professional accountant is asked to recommend the appropriate accounting treatment for a weather hedge transaction. The accountant has worked with financial hedges but has no experience with weather hedges. Which of the following actions by the accountant would be in compliance with the IFAC Code of Ethics for Professional Accountants?
   a. Agree to recommend the appropriate accounting treatment after performing sufficient research on weather hedges
   b. Refuse to conduct the research and make a recommendation, because of insufficient experience
   c. Refuse to conduct the research and make a recommendation, because of a conflict of interest
   d. Agree with the accounting treatment recommended by the company's hedge fund trader (ID: 90172)

5. An auditor may provide an issuer client any of the following nonaudit services without impairing independence and without obtaining the preapproval of the audit committee, except
   a. Nonaudit services with revenues in aggregate of less than 5% of the total revenues paid by the issuer to the auditor during the fiscal year in which the nonaudit services are provided
   b. Nonaudit services that were promptly brought to the attention of, and approved by, the audit committee prior to the completion of the audit
   c. Nonaudit services to perform financial information systems design and implementation
   d. Services that the issuer did not recognize as nonaudit services at the time of the engagement (ID: 90198)

6. The concept of materiality would be least important to an auditor when considering the
   a. Adequacy of disclosure of a client's illegal act
   b. Discovery of weaknesses in a client's internal control structure
   c. Effects of a direct financial interest in the client on the CPA's independence
   d. Decision whether to use positive or negative confirmations of accounts receivable (ID: 0003)

7. The controller of a small utility company has interviewed audit firms proposing to perform the annual audit of their employee benefit plan. According to the guidelines of the Department of Labor (DOL), the selected auditor must be
   a. The firm that proposes the lowest fee for the work required
   b. Independent for purposes of examining financial information required to be filed annually with the DOL
   c. Included on the list of firms approved by the DOL
   d. Independent of the utility company and not relying on its services (ID: 89773)

8. On June 1, Year 1, a CPA obtained a $100,000 personal loan from a financial institution client for whom the CPA provided compilation services. The loan was fully secured and considered material to the CPA's net worth. The CPA paid the loan in full on December 31, Year 1. On April 3, Year 2, the client asked the CPA to audit the client's financial statements for the year ended December 31, Year 2. Is the CPA considered independent with respect to the audit of the client's December 31, Year 2, financial statements?
   a. Yes, because the loan was fully secured
   b. Yes, because the CPA was not required to be independent at the time the loan was granted
   c. No, because the CPA had a loan with the client during the period of a professional engagement
   d. No, because the CPA had a loan with the client during the period covered by the financial statements (ID: 7037)

9. A CPA audits the financial statements of a client. The CPA has also been asked to perform bookkeeping functions for the client. Under the AICPA Code of Professional Conduct, which of the following activities would impair the CPA's independence with respect to the client?
   a. The CPA records transactions in accordance with classifications determined by management.
   b. The CPA prepares financial statements from a trial balance provided by management.
   c. The CPA posts adjusting journal entries prepared by management to the trial balance.
   d. The CPA authorizes client transactions and reports them to management. (ID: 9913)

10. In which of the following situations would a CPA's independence be considered to be impaired?
    I. The CPA maintains a checking account that is fully insured by a government deposit insurance agency at an audit-client financial institution.
    II. The CPA has a direct financial interest in an audit client, but the interest is maintained in a blind trust.
    III. The CPA owns a commercial building and leases it to an audit client. The lease qualifies as a capital lease.

    a. I and II
    b. II and III
    c. I and III
    d. I, II, and III (ID: 2936)

11. A cooling-off period of how many years is required before a member of an issuer's audit engagement team may begin working for the registrant in a key position?
    a. One year
    b. Two years
    c. Three years
    d. Four years (ID: 89797)

12. An accountant can perform, with preapproval of the audit committee of the board of directors, which of the following nonaudit services during the audit of an issuer?
    a. Bookkeeping services
    b. Human resource services
    c. Tax planning services
    d. Internal audit outsourcing services (ID: 89772)

13. A company hires one of its board members, a CPA, to issue accounting reports for the company. Assuming any required disclosures are made, which of the following reports may the CPA issue without violating independence rules?
    a. Compilations
    b. Reviews
    c. Audits
    d. Agreed-upon procedures (ID: 9940)

14. An accountant has been engaged to compile *pro forma* financial statements. During the accountant's acceptance procedures, it is discovered that the accountant is not independent with respect to the company. What action should the accountant take with regard to the compilation?
    a. The accountant should discuss the lack of independence with legal counsel to determine whether it is appropriate to accept the engagement.
    b. The accountant should disclose the lack of independence in the accountant's compilation report.
    c. The accountant should withdraw from the engagement.
    d. The accountant should compile the *pro forma* financial statements but should not provide a compilation report. (ID: 9948)

15. Under the ethical standards of the profession, which of the following is a "permitted loan" regardless of the date it was obtained?
    a. Home mortgage loan
    b. Student loan
    c. Secured automobile loan
    d. Personal loan (ID: 89780)

16. Under the ethical standards of the profession, which of the following investments by a CPA in a corporate client is an indirect financial interest?
    a. An investment held in a retirement plan
    b. An investment held in a blind trust
    c. An investment held through a regulated mutual fund
    d. An investment held through participation in an investment club (ID: 8682)

17. According to the AICPA Code of Professional Conduct, which of the following financial interests in the client during the period of the engagement impairs a CPA's independence?
    a. All direct and indirect financial interests
    b. Only direct financial interests
    c. Only direct and material indirect financial interests
    d. Only material financial interests (ID: 8890)

18. A CPA purchased stock in a client corporation and placed it in a trust as an educational fund for the CPA's minor child. The trust securities are not material to the CPA's wealth but are material to the child's personal net worth. According to the AICPA Code of Professional Conduct, would this action impair the CPA's independence with the client?
    a. No, because the CPA would not have a direct financial interest in the client.
    b. Yes, because the stock would be a direct financial interest and materiality is a factor.
    c. Yes, because the stock would be an indirect financial interest and materiality is not a factor.
    d. Yes, because the stock would be a direct financial interest and materiality is not a factor. (ID: 9941)

19. In which of the following circumstances would a covered member's independence be impaired with respect to a nonissuer client?
    a. The member is designated to serve as guardian of a friend's children if the need arises, and the friend's estate, which would be held in trust for the children, holds significant stock ownership in a client entity.
    b. The member's spouse qualifies because of geographical residence to belong to a client's credit union, and all transactions with the credit union are conducted under normal operating practices.
    c. The member owns municipal utility bonds issued by a client, and the bonds are not material to the member's wealth.
    d. The member belongs to a client golf club that requires members to acquire a share of the club's debt securities. (ID: 89795)

Responsibilities to Client

20. According to the standards of the profession, which of the following activities may be required in exercising due care?

	Consulting with experts	Obtaining specialty accreditation
a.	Yes	Yes
b.	Yes	No
c.	No	Yes
d.	No	No

(ID: 5872)

21. Assuming appropriate disclosure is made, which of the following fee arrangements generally would be permitted under the ethical standards of the profession?
    a. A fee paid to the client's audit firm for recommending investment advisory services to the client
    b. A fee paid to the client's tax accountant for recommending a computer system to the client
    c. A contingent fee paid to the CPA for preparing the client's amended income tax return
    d. A contingent fee paid to the CPA for reviewing the client's financial statements (ID: 8875)

22. A CPA is permitted to accept a separate engagement (not in conjunction with an audit of financial statements) to audit an entity's

	Schedule of accounts receivable	Schedule of royalties
a.	Yes	Yes
b.	Yes	No
c.	No	Yes
d.	No	No

(ID: 4293)

23. According to the profession's ethical standards, which of the following events may justify a departure from a Statement of Financial Accounting Standards?

	New legislation	Evolution of a new form of business transaction
a.	No	Yes
b.	Yes	No
c.	Yes	Yes
d.	No	No

(ID: 5181)

24. According to the Code of Professional Conduct of the AICPA, for which type of service may a CPA receive a contingent fee?
    a. Performing an audit of a financial statement
    b. Performing a review of a financial statement
    c. Performing an examination of prospective financial information
    d. Seeking a private letter ruling (RID: 89784)

25. A CPA is permitted to disclose confidential client information without the consent of the client to

    I. Another CPA firm if the information concerns suspected tax return irregularities
    II. A state CPA society voluntary quality control review board

    a. I only
    b. II only
    c. Both I and II
    d. Neither I nor II (ID: 5339)

26. The profession's ethical standards most likely would be considered to have been violated when a CPA represents that specific consulting services will be performed for a stated fee, and it is apparent at the time of the representation that the

    a. Actual fee would be substantially higher.
    b. Actual fee would be substantially lower than the fees charged by other CPAs for comparable services.
    c. CPA would not be independent.
    d. Fee was a competitive bid. (ID: 5180)

27. Which of the following fee arrangements generally would not be permitted under the ethical standards of the profession?

    a. A referral fee paid by a CPA to obtain a client
    b. A commission for compiling a client's internal-use financial statements
    c. A contingent fee for preparing a client's income tax return
    d. A contingent fee for representing a client in tax court (ID: 7660)

28. Under which of the following circumstances may a CPA charge fees that are contingent upon finding a specific result?

    a. For an examination of prospective financial statements
    b. For an audit or a review if agreed upon by both the CPA and the client
    c. For a compilation if a third party will use the financial statement and disclosure is not made in the report
    d. If fixed by courts, other public authorities, or in tax matters if based on the results of judicial proceedings (ID: 8442)

29. According to the ethical standards of the profession, which of the following acts is generally prohibited?

    a. Purchasing a product from a third party and reselling it to a client
    b. Writing a financial management newsletter promoted and sold by a publishing company
    c. Accepting a commission for recommending a product to an audit client without informing the client's management
    d. Accepting engagements obtained through the efforts of third parties (ID: 5870)

30. According to the AICPA Code of Professional Conduct, which of the following actions by a CPA most likely involves an act discreditable to the profession?

    a. Refusing to provide the client with copies of the CPA's workpapers
    b. Auditing financial statements according to governmental standards despite the client's preferences
    c. Accepting a commission from a nonattest function client
    d. Retaining client records after the client demands their return (ID: 9946)

31. Which of the following acts by a CPA is a violation of professional standards regarding the confidentiality of client information?

    a. Releasing financial information to a local bank with the approval of the client's mail clerk
    b. Allowing a review of professional practice without client authorization
    c. Responding to an enforceable subpoena
    d. Faxing a tax return to a loan officer at the request of the client (ID: 8675)

32. According to the SEC, members of an issuer's audit committee may not

    a. Establish procedures for employees to anonymously report fraud
    b. Be responsible for the compensation of any registered public accounting firm employed by the registrant to provide an audit report
    c. Accept any consulting, advisory, or other compensatory fee from the registrant for services other than as a member of the board
    d. Engage independent counsel as deemed necessary to carry out their duties (ID: 90173)

Quality Control Standards

33. Which of the following factors most likely would cause a CPA not to accept a new audit engagement?

    a. The prospective client's unwillingness to permit inquiry of its legal counsel
    b. The inability to review the predecessor auditor's working papers
    c. The CPA's lack of understanding of the prospective client's operations and industry
    d. The indications that management has not investigated employees in key positions before hiring them (ID: 7633)

34. Which of the following is not a factor a CPA firm should take into consideration when deciding whether to undertake or continue client relationships and engagements?

    a. The possibility of the existence of related party transactions
    b. The client's integrity
    c. The firm's ability to perform the engagement
    d. The firm's ability to comply with legal and ethical requirements (ID: 9046)

35. Would the following factors ordinarily be considered in planning an audit engagement's personnel requirements?

	Opportunities or on-the-job training	Continuity and periodic rotation of personnel
a.	Yes	Yes
b.	Yes	No
c.	No	Yes
d.	No	No

(ID: 5624)

36. Which of the following factors most likely would lead a CPA to conclude that a potential audit engagement should be rejected?

    a. The details of most recorded transactions are not available after a specified period of time.
    b. Internal control activities requiring the segregation of duties are subject to management override.
    c. It is unlikely that sufficient appropriate audit evidence is available to support an opinion on the financial statements.
    d. Management has a reputation for consulting with several accounting firms about significant accounting issues. (ID: 6927)

37. The nature and extent of a CPA firm's quality control policies and procedures will depend on various factors including its

	Size	Operating Characteristics
a.	Yes	Yes
b.	Yes	No
c.	No	Yes
d.	No	No

(ID: 5623)

38. A CPA firm would best provide itself reasonable assurance of meeting its responsibility to offer professional services that conform with professional standards by
    a. Establishing an understanding with each client concerning individual responsibilities in a signed engagement letter
    b. Assessing the risk that errors and fraud may cause the financial statements to contain material misstatements
    c. Developing specific audit objectives to support management's assertions that are embodied in the financial statements
    d. Maintaining a comprehensive system of quality control that is suitably designed in relation to its organizational structure (ID: 89776)

39. Which of the following is an element of a CPA firm's quality control policies and procedures applicable to the firm's accounting and auditing practice?
    a. Information processing
    b. Engagement performance
    c. Technology selection
    d. Professional skepticism (ID: 8655)

40. The purpose of establishing quality control policies and procedures for deciding whether to accept or continue a client relationship is to
    a. Monitor the risk factors concerning misstatements arising from the misappropriation of assets
    b. Provide reasonable assurance that personnel are adequately trained to fulfill their responsibilities
    c. Minimize the likelihood of associating with clients whose management lacks integrity
    d. Document objective criteria for the CPA firm's responses to peer review comments (ID: 8817)

41. Which of the following conditions most likely would pose the greatest risk in accepting a new audit engagement?
    a. Staff will need to be rescheduled to cover this new client.
    b. There will be a client-imposed scope limitation.
    c. The firm will have to hire a specialist in one audit area.
    d. The client's financial reporting system has been in place for 10 years. (ID: 9354)

42. In an audit engagement, the engagement quality reviewer should evaluate the significant judgments made by the engagement team and the related conclusions reached in forming the overall conclusion on the engagement and in preparing the engagement report. To evaluate such judgments and conclusions, the engagement quality reviewer should
    a. Hold discussions with the engagement partner and other members of the engagement team and review documentation.
    b. Reperform audit procedures performed regarding significant risks identified during the audit.
    c. Interview members of the client's audit committee regarding the audit team's performance.
    d. Confirm material revenue account balances. (ID: 9274)

43. An engagement quality review and concurring approval of issuance are required for engagements (conducted pursuant to the standards of the PCAOB) to perform audits and for engagements to
    a. Prepare tax returns.
    b. Prepare prospective financial statements.
    c. Provide consulting services.
    d. Review interim financial information. (ID: 9276)

Consulting Services

44. According to the Sarbanes-Oxley Act of 2002, which of the following nonaudit services can be provided by a registered public accounting firm to the client contemporaneously with the audit when preapproval is granted by audit committee action?

    a. Internal audit outsourcing services
    b. Tax services
    c. Actuarial services related to the audit
    d. Advice on financial information system design (ID: 90169)

45. According to the profession's standards, which of the following would be considered consulting services?

	Advisory services	Implementation services	Product services
a.	Yes	Yes	Yes
b.	Yes	Yes	No
c.	Yes	No	Yes
d.	No	Yes	Yes

(ID: 5184)

46. A pervasive characteristic of a CPA's role in a consulting services engagement is that of being a(n)

    a. Objective advisor
    b. Independent practitioner
    c. Computer specialist
    d. Confidential reviewer (ID: 3901)

47. According to the standards of the profession, which of the following would be considered a part of a consulting services engagement?

    I. Expressing a conclusion about the reliability of a client's financial statements
    II. Reviewing and commenting on a client-prepared business plan

    a. I only
    b. II only
    c. Both I and II
    d. Neither I nor II (ID: 6618)

48. Nile, CPA, on completing an audit, was asked by the client to provide technical assistance in integrating a new IT system. The set of pronouncements designed to guide Nile in this engagement is the Statement(s) on

    a. Quality Control Standards
    b. Auditing Standards
    c. Standards for Accountants' IT Services
    d. Standards for Consulting Services (ID: 4761)

49. According to the standards of the profession, which of the following events would require a CPA performing a consulting services engagement for a nonaudit client to withdraw from the engagement?

    I. The CPA has a conflict of interest that is disclosed to the client and the client consents to the CPA continuing the engagement.
    II. The CPA fails to obtain a written understanding from the client concerning the scope of the engagement.

    a. I only
    b. II only
    c. Both I and II
    d. Neither I nor II (ID: 5337)

50. According to the profession's standards, which of the following is not required of a CPA performing a consulting engagement?

    a. Complying with Statements on Standards for Consulting Services
    b. Obtaining an understanding of the nature, scope, and limitations of the engagement
    c. Supervising staff who are assigned to the engagement
    d. Maintaining independence from the client (ID: 5183)

51. A member of the International Federation of Accountants (IFAC) may practice in a jurisdiction or belong to another professional organization that has less stringent requirements than the IESBA Code of Ethics for Professional Accountants (Code). Which set of requirements should the member follow under these circumstances?

    a. A member of IFAC shall not apply less stringent standards from those stated in the code under any circumstances.
    b. A member of IFAC shall not apply less stringent standards from those stated in the code unless prohibited from complying by law or regulation.
    c. A member of IFAC is allowed to comply with the less stringent requirements if these are imposed by an organization recognized by IFAC.
    d. A member of IFAC shall request a ruling from IESBA regarding a conflict between its standards and those of another organization. (ID: 9298)

52. Which of the following is not one of the five fundamental principles of the International Federation of Accountant's Code of Ethics for Professional Accountants?

    a. Integrity
    b. Objectivity
    c. Professional behavior
    d. Independence (ID: 9296)

53. The use of which of the following word(s) in the IESBA Code of Ethics for Professional Accountants imposes a requirement?

    a. Must
    b. Shall
    c. Should
    d. Is required (ID: 9297)

54. Under the Sarbanes-Oxley Act of 2002, exactly how many consecutive years may an audit partner lead an audit for an issuer?

    a. Four years
    b. Five years
    c. Six years
    d. Seven years (ID: 89769)

55. The Public Company Accounting Oversight Board was established by which of the following?

    a. The Financial Accounting Standards Board
    b. The American Institute of Certified Public Accountants
    c. The Sarbanes-Oxley Act of 2002
    d. The International Accounting Standards Board (ID: 90195)

Problem 15-2 SIMULATION: Request by Client for CPA's Workpapers

Poole & Sterns, CPAs, performed an audit of Flight, a privately held corporation. Poole & Sterns are AICPA members.

While performing the audit, Poole & Sterns, developed and included in its electronic working papers adjusting and closing journal entries, without which Flight's financial information is incomplete.

Flight's management requested copies of the adjusting and closing journal entries in XBRL format. Poole & Sterns' audit software prints adjusting and closing journal entries to *.txt files, but doesn't provide them in XBRL format.

Indicate whether the following statements are true or false.

	Statement	True/False
1.	Poole & Sterns, CPAs', working papers must be made available to Flight.	
2.	Poole & Sterns, CPAs, should provide the adjusting and closing journal entries to Flight regardless of whether the fees related to the audit are unpaid.	
3.	Poole & Sterns, CPAs, must provide the adjusting and closing journal entries to Flight regardless of whether any fees related to other work are unpaid.	
4.	Poole & Sterns, CPAs, must provide the adjusting and closing journal entries to Flight in XBRL format.	
5.	Once Poole & Sterns, CPAs, have provided the adjusting and closing journal entries to Flight, it need not comply with subsequent requests for the same information.	
6.	If the engagement is ended before completion and fees incurred to that point are paid, Poole & Sterns, CPAs, must provide such adjusting and closing journal entries to Flight as are known to it at that point.	
7.	As Flight is a privately held corporation, Poole & Sterns, CPAs, must keep working papers related to the audit for one year and no longer.	
8.	Poole & Sterns, CPAs, may disclose information in the working papers without Flight's consent to comply with professional practice review procedures under AICPA authorization.	

(ID: 9248)

Problem 15-3 SIMULATION: Research

The AICPA Code of Professional Conduct has been revised by codifying the principles, rules, interpretations, and rulings. These revisions are effective December 15, 2014. To facilitate implementation of the revised code, the prior ET references from the professional standards of the AICPA will be included in bracketed text at the end of standards for how long? For this question only, use the Revised Code references.

Reminder: On the actual exam, you will use an electronic database of authoritative literature to find and select the reference (appropriate section and paragraph of the relevant guidance). Please see the AICPA's tutorial and sample test on the exam section of their website.

	§		

Solution 15-1 MULTIPLE-CHOICE ANSWERS

1. (d) Under the Independence Standards Board Statement 1 (ISB 1) the auditor must disclose, in writing, to the audit committee, all relationships between the auditor and its related entities and the client entity and its related entities that, in the auditor's judgment, may be considered to bear on independence. (ID: 9923)

2. (b) When gifts or hospitality are offered that a reasonable and informed third party would consider trivial and inconsequential, a professional accountant in public practice may conclude that the offer is made without the specific intent to influence decision making or to obtain information. In such cases, the professional accountant in public practice generally may conclude that any threat to compliance with the fundamental principles is at an acceptable level. The hospitality of an out-of-town client taking the audit engagement team out to dinner at a renowned local restaurant generally would be considered trivial. Rarely would overnight trips or season tickets be considered trivial. (ID: 90170)

3. (b) Members not in public practice are held to the same standards covering integrity and competence as members in public practice. The rules for independence, professional competence, and compliance with standards are specifically pertinent to members in public practice. Members not in public practice need not be independent; generally they are employed by the entity in question. Members need not be competent in all aspects of their employer's accounting and financial systems; their employers may contract with public accounting firms for that reason. Management accounting may depart from compliance with standards intentionally. (ID: 90183)

4. (a) An accountant has a duty to maintain knowledge and skill at the level required to ensure that a client or employer receives competent professional services based on current developments. As such, a professional accountant can agree to recommend the appropriate accounting treatment, but only after performing sufficient research on weather hedges. This situation does not involve a conflict of interest. An accountant's recommendation may agree with the hedge fund trader's recommendation, but the accountant must arrive at an independent recommendation; the hedge fund trader's recommendation is neither objective nor sufficient to provide support for the accountant. (ID: 90172)

5. (c) The Sarbanes-Oxley Act of 2002 prohibits an auditor performing financial information systems design and implementation, even if the audit committee approves of the services to an issuer audit client; this is deemed to impair independence. Minor services will not impair independence and do not require pre-approval. These include relatively small revenue services, services approved prior to completion of the audit, and services that the issuer did not recognize as needing audit committee approval. (ID: 90198)

6. (c) Independence will be considered to be impaired if during the period of the professional engagement, or at the time of expressing an opinion, the member or the member's firm had or was committed to acquire any direct or material indirect financial interest in the enterprise (ET 101-1). In other words, if a direct financial interest exists, materiality is not a factor. (ID: 0003)

7. (b) According to the guidelines of the Department of Labor (DOL), the selected auditor performing the annual audit of the company's employee benefit plan must be independent for purposes of examining financial information required to be filed annually with the DOL. The selected auditor may be a customer of the utility company, does not have to be on any approved list of firms, and does not have to be the lowest fee bidder for the work required. (ID: 89773)

8. (b) Independence is impaired if a member obtains a loan from an entity that, at the time of obtaining the loan, is a client requiring independence, except for certain personal loans obtained under normal lending procedures, terms, and requirements, and kept current as to terms. (ID: 7037)

9. (d) Under the AICPA Code of Professional Conduct, Rule 101-3 states that the CPA's independence with respect to the client would be impaired if the CPA authorized or approved transactions. The CPA's independence would not be impaired if they recorded transactions in accordance with classifications determined by management, prepared financial statements from a trial balance provided by management, or posted journal entries prepared by management to the trial balance. (ID: 9913)

10. (b) A CPA's independence would not be considered to be impaired by her/his maintaining a checking account that is fully insured by a government deposit insurance agency at an audit-client financial institution (ET 191-70). Independence is considered impaired if a CPA has a direct financial interest, or a material indirect financial interest in a client, whether or not it is placed in a blind trust (ET 191-68). Independence generally is considered impaired if a lease meets the criteria of a capital lease as defined by GAAP and independence is not considered impaired if a lease meets the criteria of an operating lease as long as the terms and conditions are comparable with other leases of a similar nature and all amounts are paid in accordance with the terms of the lease (ET 191-91). (ID: 2936)

11. (a) A cooling-off period of one year is required before a member of an issuer's audit engagement team may begin working for the registrant in a key position. (ID: 89797)

12. (c) Tax-planning services is an acceptable nonaudit service that an accountant can perform, with pre-approval of the audit committee of the board of directors, during the audit of an issuer. (ID: 89772)

13. (a) Audit reports, audit reviews, and audit procedures all require a level of independence that would necessitate that they be done by an independent accountant outside of the organization. However, compilation reports do not require that high level of independence and could be prepared by a board member without violating independence rules. (ID: 9940)

14. (b) A CPA does not have to be independent to perform a compilation engagement, but a separate paragraph should be added to the report that discloses the lack of independence. Additionally, the CPA may include the reasons for the lack of independence in the same paragraph. The disclosure of the reason(s) is not required, but if the CPA elects to do so, all the reasons must be included. (ID: 9948)

15. (c) A car loan that is collateralized by the vehicle is a permitted loan which will not impair independence, regardless of the date it was obtained. (ID: 89780)

16. (c) If a member does not have the ability to direct investments, an investment in a client through a financial service product (such as a mutual fund) is considered an indirect financial interest and, hence, does not necessarily impair independence. Independence is considered impaired if a covered member owns stock in a client through an investment club, where presumably the member has the ability to direct investments, whether or not exercised, resulting in a direct financial interest. Independence is considered impaired even if a CPA has a material indirect financial interest in a client, whether or not it is placed in a blind trust. (ID: 8682)

17. (c) Direct or material indirect financial interest in an audit client during the period of a professional engagement is held to impair a CPA's independence. (ID: 8890)

18. (d) According to the AICPA Code of Professional Conduct, any direct financial interest in a client corporation would impair a CPA's independence even if it is immaterial. (ID: 9941)

19. (c) Independence is impaired if the member has a direct or material indirect financial interest in the client. A direct financial interest will impair independence even if it is immaterial. (ID: 89795)

20. (b) According to the standards of the profession, exercise in due care may require consulting with experts, but would not require obtaining specialty accreditation. (ID: 5872)

21. (b) A CPA may recommend a product to a tax client, provided the fee paid to the CPA is disclosed to the client. A CPA may not recommend or refer any product or service to an audit client, for a fee. A CPA may not accept a fee contingent upon the outcome of an original or amended tax return or claim for refund or an audit or review of financial statements. (ID: 8875)

22. (a) An engagement to express an opinion on one or more specified elements, accounts, or items of a financial statement may be undertaken as a separate engagement (not in conjunction with an audit of financial statements). (ID: 4293)

23. (c) ET 203 provides that a CPA must use professional judgment in deciding when a deviation from GAAP is appropriate. Circumstances that may justify a departure include new legislation or the evolution of a new form of business. (ID: 5181)

24. (d) In some cases, contingent fees in certain tax matters are permitted. A contingent fee would be permitted when a member represents a client in an examination by a revenue agent of the client's tax return, or when a member represents a client with obtaining a private letter ruling. (ID: 89784)

25. (b) ET 301 prohibits the disclosure of confidential information obtained in the course of the professional engagement without the consent of the client, but does not prohibit review of a CPA's professional practices (including pertinent information) as a part of an AICPA authorized voluntary quality review program. (ID: 5339)

26. (a) ET 502-2 provides, "Advertising or other forms of solicitation that are false, misleading, or deceptive are not in the public interest and are prohibited." A prohibited activity is one that contains a representation that specific professional services in current or future periods will be performed for a stated fee, estimated fee, or fee range when it is likely at the time of representation that such fees would be substantially increased and the prospective client was not advised of such likelihood. (ID: 5180)

27. (c) A contingent fee for preparing a client's income tax return would not be permitted under the ethical standards of the profession. However, a contingent fee for representing a client in tax court would be permitted under the ethical standards, because the tax authority initiated the proceedings. A member who accepts or pays a referral fee in relation to a client must disclose such acceptance or payment to the client. A member is prohibited from recommending or referring, for a commission, any product or service to a client when that member or member's firm performs a financial statement compilation where the member might reasonably expect that a third party will use the statement. Since the financial statement compilation was for internal use only, it would be permitted under the ethical standards. (ID: 7660)

28. (d) An AICPA member in public practice shall not offer or render services under an agreement whereby the fee is contingent upon the findings or results, specifically including an examination of prospective financial information; an audit or review or financial statements; or a compilation of financial statements, when the member reasonably might expect that a third party will use the statement. Fees that are fixed by the courts or public authorities or which are determined in tax matters by judicial proceedings or governmental agency findings are not considered contingent and, therefore, are permitted. (ID: 8442)

29. (c) ET 503 prohibits a CPA from accepting a commission for recommending a product to a client, unless the CPA informs management. The other activities are not prohibited. (ID: 5870)

30. (d) According to the AICPA Code of Professional Conduct, client records are the property of the client and cannot be retained by a CPA when the client demands their return. This is specifically identified as an act discreditable to the profession. (ID: 9946)

31. (a) ET 301 prohibits the disclosure of confidential information obtained in the course of a professional engagement without consent of the client, but does not prohibit review of a CPA's professional practices (including pertinent information) as a part of an AICPA authorized voluntary quality review program. While disclosing information at a client's request is allowed, mail clerks typically do not have authority to approve releases of financial information. ET 301 shall not be construed to affect in any way the member's obligation to comply with a validly issued and enforceable subpoena or summons, or to prohibit a member's compliance with applicable laws and government regulations. (ID: 8675)

32. (c) As audit committee members are also members of the board of directors, they are restricted to receiving only the normal compensation provided to a board member. They cannot accept any additional consulting, advisory, or other compensatory fees from the registrant for services other than as a member of the board. There are no SEC rules restricting the establishment of procedures for employees to anonymously report fraud; being responsible for the compensation of any registered public accounting firm employed by the registrant to provide an audit report; or engaging independent counsel as deemed necessary to carry out their duties. (ID: 90173)

33. (a) Auditors typically inquire of the client's legal counsel regarding litigation, claims, and assessments. The prospective client's unwillingness to permit such inquiry casts doubt on the reliability of management representations. Further, such a scope limitation usually results in a disclaimer of opinion; ethics require auditors to accept only engagements they can reasonably expect to complete. There may be legitimate reasons why an auditor is unable to review a predecessor's working papers or why management doesn't investigate employees in key positions before hiring them. There is no need for the auditor to understand the prospective client's industry before the audit is begun as long as the auditor can reasonably expect to gain such understanding in a timely manner. (ID: 7633)

34. (a) The standards require that a firm's quality control policies and procedures regarding the acceptance and continuance of clients and engagements take answers b., c., and d. into consideration. In the absence of evidence to the contrary, related party transactions should not be assumed to be outside of the ordinary course of business. The auditor is concerned with complying with GAAS to identify related party transactions and determining that they are accounted for and disclosed according to GAAP. (ID: 9046)

35. (a) The auditor uses professional judgment in planning an audit engagement's personnel requirements; the auditor has final responsibility and may delegate portions of the audit functions to other firm personnel, referred to in the code as "assistants." Opportunities for on-the-job training as well as continuity and periodic rotation of personnel are all valid factors the auditor may consider in this task. (ID: 5624)

36. (c) If sufficient appropriate audit evidence is not available to support an opinion, an audit cannot be performed. In many online systems, most routine transaction details are not available after a specified period of time. Internal control is usually subject to management override. Consultation with several accounting firms reflects management's concern over proper accounting and reporting. (ID: 6927)

37. (a) Factors which impact the nature and extent of a firm's quality control policies and procedures depend on various factors including its size and operating characteristics. (ID: 5623)

38. (d) The best way a CPA firm could best provide reasonable assurance of meeting its responsibility to offer professional services that conform with professional standards is by maintaining a comprehensive system of quality control that is suitably designed in relation to its organizational structure. (ID: 89776)

39. (b) Engagement performance is one of the elements of a firm's system of quality control. The firm's quality control system should include policies and procedures addressing it and the other elements which are: leadership responsibilities for quality within the firm; relevant ethical requirements; acceptance and continuance of client relationships and specific engagements; human resources; and monitoring. Information processing, technology selection, and professional skepticism are not defined elements of a firm's quality control system. (ID: 8655)

40. (c) One of the purposes of establishing quality control policies and procedures for deciding whether to accept or continue a client relationship is to minimize the likelihood of associating with clients whose management lacks integrity. Monitoring the risk factors concerning misstatements arising from the misappropriation of assets is not an aspect of a CPA's firm quality control system. Providing reasonable assurance that personnel are adequately trained to fulfill their responsibilities is part of both the human resources element and the engagement performance element of a quality control system rather than the acceptance and continuance of client relationships and specific engagements element. Documenting objective criteria for the CPA firm's responses to peer review comments is part of the engagement performance element of a firm's quality control system. (ID: 8817)

41. (b) A client-imposed scope limitation poses the greatest risk in accepting a new audit engagement. The other answer alternatives involve fairly routine planning considerations. Restrictions on the scope of the audit, whether imposed by the client or by circumstances, may require the auditor to qualify the opinion or to disclaim an opinion. When restrictions that significantly limit the scope of the audit are imposed by the client, ordinarily the auditor should disclaim an opinion. (ID: 9354)

42. (a) To evaluate such judgments and conclusions, the engagement quality reviewer should hold discussions with the engagement partner and other members of the engagement team and review documentation. (ID: 9274)

43. (d) An engagement quality review and concurring approval of issuance are required for each audit engagement and for each engagement to review interim financial information conducted pursuant to the standards of the Public Company Accounting Oversight Board (PCAOB). (ID: 9276)

44. (b) Tax services are a non-audit service that can be provided by a registered public accounting firm to the client contemporaneously with the audit when preapproval is granted by the audit committee. The Sarbanes-Oxley Act of 2002 prohibits registered public accounting firms from providing the following nonaudit services to an audit client that issues publicly traded securities: bookkeeping; financial information system design and implementation; appraisal or valuation services; actuarial services; internal audit outsourcing services; management functions or human resources; broker or dealer investment advisor or investment bank services; and legal and expert services. (ID: 90169)

45. (a) The Statement of Standards for Consulting Services (SSCS 1) defines advisory services, implementation services, and product services as consulting services. (ID: 5184)

46. (a) The Bylaws of the AICPA include general definitions which state that in addition to furnishing advice in conjunction with their independent examinations of financial statements, CPAs are engaged to provide objective advice and consultation on various management problems (BL 921.09). Statements on Standards for Consulting Services (CS 100.07) state that the CPA is to serve the client interest by seeking to accomplish the objectives established by the understanding with the client while maintaining integrity and objectivity. (ID: 3901)

47. (b) According to the Statement on Standards for Consulting Services, consulting services include reviewing and commenting on a client-prepared business plan. Expressing a conclusion about the reliability of a client's financial statements is an attest engagement, not a consulting services engagement. (ID: 6618)

48. (d) Under the Standards for Consulting Services, advisory services are used to develop findings, conclusions and recommendations for client consideration and decision making. A stated example of advisory services is the defining of requirements for an information system. (ID: 4761)

49. (d) ET 202 requires that the client be informed of any conflict of interest or significant reservations concerning the scope or benefits of the engagement. However, independence is *not* required. This Rule also requires a written *or oral* understanding between consultant and client. (ID: 5337)

50. (d) ET 201 requires a CPA performing a consulting engagement to comply with Standards on Consulting Services and to supervise staff assigned to the engagement. ET 202 requires that the CPA obtain an understanding of the nature, scope, and limitations of the engagement. ET 202 also states that performing a consulting service does not, of itself, impair independence. (ID: 5183)

51. (b) A member of IFAC shall not apply less stringent standards from those stated in the code unless prohibited from complying by law or regulation. In this situation, the member shall comply with all other parts of the Code. (ID: 9298)

52. (d) The five fundamental principles that the International Ethics Standards Board for Accountants (IESBA) requires professional accountants to comply with per the IESBA Code of Ethics for Professional Accountants are integrity; objectivity; professional competence and due care; confidentiality; and professional behavior. (ID: 9296)

53. (b) The word *shall* is used to impose a requirement in the IESBA Code of Ethics for Professional Accountants. (ID: 9297)

54. (b) Under the Sarbanes-Oxley Act of 2002, the lead audit or coordinating partner and the reviewing partner must rotate off the audit every five years. (ID: 89769)

55. (c) The Sarbanes-Oxley Act of 2002 directed the SEC to establish the PCAOB. The Financial Accounting Standards Board (FASB) and the American Institute of Certified Public Accountants (AICPA) are non-governmental, nonprofit organizations. The FASB sets US GAAP. The AICPA supports and governs its members. The International Accounting Standards Board (IASB) is an international non-governmental, nonprofit organization. The IASB sets international GAAP. (ID: 90195)

Solution 15-2 SIMULATION ANSWER: Request by Client for CPA's Workpapers

1. False

All of an auditor's working papers need not be made available to a client. Information in an auditor's working papers that completes the client's incomplete financial information need not be made available to the client in all circumstances.

2. False

Information in an auditor's workpapers that completes the client's incomplete financial information need not be made available to the client if any fees from that client are unpaid.

3. False

Information in an auditor's workpapers that completes the client's incomplete financial information need not be made available to the client if any fees from that client are unpaid.

4. False

Information in an auditor's workpapers that completes the client's incomplete financial information need not be converted into another medium when providing it to the client.

5. True

Once an AICPA member has complied with an initial request for information from an auditor's workpapers that completes the client's incomplete financial information, the member need not comply with subsequent requests to provide such information again.

6. False

If an engagement has been completed, ordinarily a member should provide information in the workpapers that completes the client's incomplete financial information to the client upon request. There is no requirement to do so for an incomplete engagement.

7. False

The auditor should adopt reasonable procedures to retain and access audit documentation for a period of time sufficient to meet the needs of the auditor's practice and to satisfy any applicable legal or regulatory requirements for records retention. Such retention period, however, should not be shorter than five years from the report release date. Statutes, regulations, or the audit firm's quality control policies may specify a longer retention period.

8. True

Auditors may disclose information in workpapers without the client's consent in select circumstances only; compliance with professional practice review procedures under AICPA authorization is one of these circumstances.
(ID: 9248)

Solution 15-3 SIMULATION ANSWER: Research

0	§	200	.030

.030 The code has been revised by codifying the principles, rules, interpretations, and rulings. These revisions are effective December 15, 2014. To facilitate implementation of the revised code, the prior ET references from the professional standards of the AICPA will be included for a four-year period (until December 15, 2018) in Appendix D, "Mapping Document," and in bracketed text at the end of standards, where applicable.

Post-Exam Diagnostics

The AICPA Board of Examiners' Advisory Grading Service provides state boards of accountancy with individual diagnostic reports for all candidates along with the candidates' grades. The diagnostic reports show a candidate's level of proficiency on each examination section. The boards of accountancy **may** mail the diagnostic reports to candidates along with their scores, approximately **45 days** after examinations. Candidates should contact the state board in the relevant jurisdiction to find out its policies on score disclosures.

Each exam generally includes an undisclosed percentage of pretest questions that are not scored. Candidates do not know which questions will not be scored. This makes self-evaluation of exam performance without an individual diagnostic report extremely difficult.

Remember that candidates are required to sign a statement of confidentiality in which they promise not to reveal questions or answers. Due to the nondisclosure requirements, Bisk CPA Review editors are no longer able to address questions about specific examination questions, although we continue to supply help with similar study problems and questions in our texts.

See the **Exam Preparation Tips** appendix for more information.

APPENDIX A
PRACTICE EXAM

Editor Note: If a question pertains to an issuer (public company) it will indicate that; if there is no such indication, the question pertains to a nonissuer. There is only one practice (or final) exam. It's best to wait until you are ready before you take it.

Testlet 1 MULTIPLE-CHOICE QUESTIONS

1. An auditor ordinarily should request to review the predecessor's working papers relating to

	Contingencies	Risk Assessments
a.	Yes	Yes
b.	Yes	No
c.	No	Yes
d.	No	No

(ID: 7092)

2. Holding other planning considerations equal, a decrease in the amount of misstatements in a class of transactions that an auditor could tolerate most likely would cause the auditor to

   a. Apply the planned substantive tests prior to the balance sheet date
   b. Perform the planned auditing procedures closer to the balance sheet date
   c. Increase the assessed level of control risk for relevant financial statement assertions
   d. Decrease the extent of auditing procedures to be applied to the class of transactions (ID: 6574)

3. In a probability-proportional-to-size sample with a sampling interval of $10,000, an auditor discovered that a selected account receivable with a recorded amount of $5,000 had an audited amount of $4,000. If this were the only misstatement discovered by the auditor, the projected misstatement of this sample would be

   a. $ 1,000
   b. $ 2,000
   c. $ 5,000
   d. $10,000 (ID: 6935)

4. Morris, CPA, suspects that a pervasive scheme of illegal bribes exists throughout the operations of Worldwide Import-Export Inc., a new audit client, a nonissuer. Morris notified the audit committee and Worldwide's legal counsel, but neither could assist Morris in determining whether the amounts involved were material to the financial statements. Under these circumstances, Morris should

   a. Express an unmodified opinion with a other-matter paragraph
   b. Disclaim an opinion on the financial statements
   c. Express an adverse opinion of the financial statements
   d. Issue a special report regarding the illegal bribes (ID: 165)

5. An accountant may compile a nonissuer's financial statements that omit all of the disclosures required by GAAP only if the omission is

   I. Clearly indicated in the accountant's report
   II. Not undertaken with the intention of misleading the financial statement users

   a. I only
   b. II only
   c. Both I and II
   d. Either I or II (ID: 4744)

6. Under the ethical standards of the profession, which of the following positions would be considered a position of significant influence in an audit client?
   a. A marketing position related to the client's primary products
   b. A policy-making position in the client's finance division
   c. A staff position in the client's research and development division
   d. A senior position in the client's human resources division (ID: 7883)

7. Quality control, as referred to in Statements on Quality Control Standards (SQCS), applies to a CPA firm's responsibilities for its system of quality control for its
   a. Auditing services only
   b. Auditing and management advisory services
   c. Auditing and tax services
   d. Accounting and auditing practice (ID: 33)

8. Which of the following statements is **not** correct about materiality?
   a. The concept of materiality recognizes that some matters are important for fair presentation of financial statements in conformity with GAAP, while other matters are not important.
   b. An auditor considers materiality for planning purposes in terms of the largest aggregate level of misstatements that could be material to any one of the financial statements.
   c. An auditor's consideration of materiality is influenced by the auditor's perception of the needs of a reasonable person who will rely on the financial statements.
   d. Materiality judgments are made in light of surrounding circumstances and necessarily involve both quantitative and qualitative judgments. (ID: 5084)

9. The theoretical distribution of means from all possible samples of a given size is a normal distribution and this distribution is the basis for statistical sampling. Which of the following statements is **not** true with respect to the sampling distribution of sample means?
   a. Approximately 68% of the sample means will be within one standard deviation of the mean for the normal distribution.
   b. The distribution is defined in terms of its mean and its standard error of the mean.
   c. An auditor can be approximately 95% confident that the mean for a sample is within two standard deviations of the population mean.
   d. The items drawn in an auditor's sample will have a normal distribution. (ID: 8973)

10. For audits of financial statements made in accordance with generally accepted auditing standards, the use of analytical procedures is required to some extent

	As a substantive test	In the final review stage
a.	Yes	Yes
b.	Yes	No
c.	No	Yes
d.	No	No

(ID: 8952)

11. Miller, CPA, is engaged to compile the financial statements of Web Co., a nonissuer, in conformity with the income tax basis of accounting. If Web's financial statements do not disclose the basis of accounting used, Miller should
   a. Disclose the basis of accounting in the accountant's compilation report
   b. Clearly label each page "Distribution Restricted—Material Modifications Required"
   c. Issue a special report describing the effect of the incomplete presentation
   d. Withdraw from the engagement and provide no further services to Web (ID: 5154)

12. Kar, CPA, is a staff auditor participating in the audit engagement of Fort, Inc. Which of the following circumstances impairs Kar's independence?
    a. During the period of the professional engagement, Fort gives Kar tickets to a football game worth $25.
    b. Kar owns stock in a corporation that Fort's 401(k) plan also invests in.
    c. Kar's friend, an employee of another local accounting firm, prepares Fort's tax returns.
    d. Kar's sibling is an internal auditor employed part-time by Fort. (ID: 7036)

13. Prior to the acceptance of an audit engagement with a client who has terminated the services of the predecessor auditor, the CPA should
    a. Contact the predecessor auditor without advising the prospective client and request a complete report of the circumstances leading to the termination, with the understanding that all information disclosed will be kept confidential
    b. Accept the engagement without contacting the predecessor auditor since the CPA can include audit procedures to verify the reason given by the client for the termination
    c. Not communicate with the predecessor auditor because this would violate the confidential relationship between auditor and client
    d. Advise the client of the intention to contact the predecessor auditor and request permission for the contact (ID: 8947)

14. Which of the following statements best describes the auditor's responsibility regarding the detection of material errors and fraud?
    a. The auditor is responsible for the failure to detect material errors and fraud only when such failure results from the nonapplication of generally accepted accounting principles.
    b. The auditor is responsible for obtaining reasonable assurance that the financial statements as a whole are free from material misstatement, whether caused by fraud or error.
    c. The auditor is responsible for the failure to detect material errors and fraud only when the auditor fails to confirm receivables or observe inventories.
    d. Extended auditing procedures are required to detect unrecorded transactions even if there is no evidence that material errors and fraud may exist. (ID: 8948)

15. According to the guidance in the attestation standards regarding using the work of others, in an engagement to examine a nonissuer's internal control over financial reporting that is integrated with an audit of its financial statements, the auditor may consider using the work of any of the following as evidence about the effectiveness of internal control, **except**
    a. Internal auditors
    b. Entity personnel who are not internal auditors
    c. Third parties working under the direction of management
    d. Previous auditors (ID: 89456)

16. Analytical procedures used in the overall review stage of an audit generally include
    a. Gathering evidence concerning account balances that have not changed from the prior year
    b. Retesting control procedures that appeared to be ineffective during the assessment of control risk
    c. Considering unusual or unexpected account balances that were not previously identified
    d. Performing tests of transactions to corroborate management's financial statement assertions (ID: 5665)

17. The standard report on compiled financial statements includes which of the following statements or phrases?
    a. A compilation includes assessing the accounting principles used and significant management estimates, as well as evaluating the overall financial statement presentation.
    b. The accountant compiled the financial statements in accordance with Statements on Standards for Accounting and Review Services.
    c. A compilation is substantially less in scope than an audit, the objective of which is the expression of an opinion.
    d. The accountant is not aware of any material modifications that should be made to the accompanying financial statements in order for them to be in conformity with GAAP. (ID: 5696)

18. According to the ethical standards of the profession, which of the following acts generally is prohibited?
    a. Accepting a contingent fee for representing a client in connection with obtaining a private letter ruling from the Internal Revenue Service
    b. Retaining client records after the client has demanded their return
    c. Revealing client tax returns to a prospective purchaser of the CPA's practice
    d. Issuing a modified report explaining the CPA's failure to follow a governmental regulatory agency's standards when conducting an attest service for a client (ID: 7862)

19. The senior auditor responsible for coordinating the fieldwork usually schedules a preaudit conference with the audit team primarily to
    a. Give guidance to the staff regarding both technical and personnel aspects of the audit
    b. Provide an opportunity to document staff disagreements regarding technical issues
    c. Establish the need for using the work of specialists and internal auditors
    d. Discuss staff suggestions concerning the establishment and maintenance of time budgets (ID: 5077)

20. Management's attitude toward aggressive financial reporting and its emphasis on meeting projected profit goals most likely would significantly influence an entity's control environment when
    a. External policies established by parties outside the entity affect its accounting practices.
    b. Management is dominated by one individual who is also a shareholder.
    c. Internal auditors have direct access to the board of directors and the entity's management.
    d. The audit committee is active in overseeing the entity's financial reporting policies. (ID: 6390)

21. Written representations from a client's management which, among other matters, acknowledges responsibility for the fair presentation of financial statements, are normally signed by the
    a. Chief executive officer and the chief financial officer
    b. Chief financial officer and the chairman of the board of directors
    c. Chairman of the audit committee of the board of directors
    d. Chief executive officer, the chairman of the board of directors, and the client's lawyer (ID: 8954)

22. After issuing a report an auditor concludes that an auditing procedure considered necessary at the time of the audit was omitted from the audit. The auditor should first
    a. Undertake to apply the omitted procedure or alternative procedures that would provide a satisfactory basis for the auditor's opinion
    b. Assess the importance of the omitted procedure to the auditor's ability to support the opinion expressed on the financial statements taken as a whole
    c. Notify the audit committee or the board of director's that the auditor's opinion can no longer be relied upon
    d. Review the results of other procedures that were applied to compensate for the one omitted or to make its omission less important (ID: 8956)

23. Which of the following procedures is ordinarily performed by an accountant in a compilation engagement of a nonissuer?
    a. Reading the financial statements to consider whether they are free of obvious mistakes in the application of accounting principles
    b. Obtaining written representations from management indicating that the compiled financial statements will not be used to obtain credit
    c. Making inquiries of management concerning actions taken at meetings of the stockholders and the board of directors
    d. Applying analytical procedures designed to corroborate management's assertions that are embodied in the financial statement components (ID: 5693)

24. Under the ethical standards of the profession, which of the following business relationships would generally **not** impair an auditor's independence?
    a. Promoter of a client's securities
    b. Member of a client's board of directors
    c. Client's general counsel
    d. Advisor to a client's board of trustees (ID: 8175)

25. In obtaining an understanding of an entity's internal control, the auditor should obtain an understanding of control activities relevant to the audit, which are those judged necessary to understand in order to
    a. Assess whether operational efficiency has been achieved in accordance with management plans.
    b. Assess the risk of material misstatement at the assertion level and design further audit procedures responsive to assessed risks.
    c. Determine that management cannot override the controls.
    d. Determine that controls have not been circumvented by collusion. (ID: 7488)

26. The auditor is most likely to seek information from the plant manager with respect to the
    a. Adequacy of the provision for uncollectible accounts
    b. Appropriateness of physical inventory observation procedures
    c. Existence of obsolete machinery
    d. Deferral of procurement of certain necessary insurance coverage (ID: 8955)

27. The auditor concludes, prior to the report release date, that there is a material inconsistency that requires revision of the other information in an annual report to shareholders containing audited financial statements. If the client refuses to revise or eliminate the material inconsistency, the auditor should notify those charged with governance and
    a. Revise the audit report to include an other-matter paragraph describing the material inconsistency.
    b. Consult with a party whose advice might influence the client, such as the client's legal counsel.
    c. Issue a qualified opinion after discussing the matter with the client's board of directors.
    d. Consider the matter closed since the other information is not in the audited financial statements. (ID: 8957)

28. Under the ethical standards of the profession, which of the following investments in a client is **not** considered to be a direct financial interest?
    a. An investment held through a nonregulated mutual fund
    b. An investment held through a nonclient investment club
    c. An investment held in a blind trust
    d. An investment held by the trustee of a trust (ID: 7113)

29. An auditor would be most likely to consider expressing a qualified opinion if the client's financial statements include a footnote on related-party transactions that
    a. Lists the amounts due from related parties including the terms and manner of settlement
    b. Discloses compensating balance arrangements maintained for the benefit of related parties
    c. Represents that certain transactions with related parties were consummated on terms equally as favorable as would have been obtained in transactions with unrelated parties
    d. Presents the dollar volume of related-party transactions and the effects of any change in the method of establishing terms from that of the prior period (ID: 8958)

30. May a CPA hire for the CPA's public accounting firm a non-CPA systems analyst who specializes in developing computer systems?
    a. Yes, provided the CPA is qualified to perform each of the specialist's tasks
    b. Yes, provided the CPA is able to supervise the specialist and evaluate the specialist's end product
    c. No, because non-CPA professionals are not permitted to be associated with CPA firms in public practice
    d. No, because developing computer systems is not recognized as a service performed by public accountants (ID: 4240)

Testlet 2 MULTIPLE-CHOICE QUESTIONS

1. Which of the following factors most likely would cause an auditor to question the integrity of management?
    a. Management has an aggressive attitude toward financial reporting and meeting profit goals.
    b. Audit tests detect material fraud that was known to management, but not disclosed to the auditor.
    c. Managerial decisions are dominated by one person who is also a stockholder.
    d. Weaknesses in internal control reported to the audit committee are not corrected by management. (ID: 7631)

2. The auditor's knowledge about the design of relevant internal control policies and procedures primarily assists the auditor in
    a. Identifying the types of potential misstatements that could occur
    b. Assessing the operational efficiency of the internal control structure
    c. Determining whether controls have been circumvented by collusion
    d. Documenting the assessed level of control risk (ID: 5951)

3. A weakness in internal control over recording retirements of equipment may cause an auditor to
    a. Trace additions to the "other assets" account to search for equipment that is still on hand but no longer being used.
    b. Select certain items of equipment from the accounting records and locate them in the plant.
    c. Review the subsidiary ledger to ascertain whether depreciation was taken on each item of equipment during the year.
    d. Inspect certain items of equipment in the plant and trace those items to the accounting records. (ID: 81)

4. An auditor's working papers serve mainly to
    a. Provide the principal support for the audit report.
    b. Satisfy the auditor's responsibilities concerning the Code of Professional Conduct.
    c. Monitor the effectiveness of the CPA firm's quality control procedures.
    d. Document the level of independence maintained by the auditor. (ID: 5689)

5. When an accountant is engaged to compile a nonissuer's financial statements that omit substantially all disclosures required by GAAP, the accountant should indicate in the compilation report that the financial statements are

   a. Not designed for those who are uninformed about the omitted disclosures
   b. Prepared in conformity with a comprehensive basis of accounting other than GAAP
   c. Not compiled in accordance with Statements on Standards for Accounting and Review Services
   d. Special-purpose financial statements that are not comparable to those of prior periods (ID: 5155)

6. Must a CPA, in public practice, be independent in fact and appearance when providing the following services?

	Compilation of personal financial statements	Preparation of a tax return	Compilation of a financial forecast
a.	Yes	No	No
b.	No	Yes	No
c.	No	No	Yes
d.	No	No	No

(ID: 5182)

7. In developing a preliminary audit strategy, an auditor should consider

   a. Whether the allowance for sampling risk exceeds the achieved upper precision limit
   b. Findings from substantive tests performed at interim dates
   c. Whether the inquiry of the client's attorney identifies any litigation, claims, or assessments not disclosed in the financial statements
   d. The potential risks of material misstatement (ID: 2276)

8. Which of the following conditions is necessary for an auditor to accept an engagement to examine the design and operating effectiveness of a nonissuer's internal control over financial reporting that is integrated with an audit of financial statements?

   a. The auditor anticipates relying on the entity's internal control in a financial statement audit.
   b. Management provides its assertion about the effectiveness of internal control in a report that accompanies the auditor's report.
   c. The auditor is a continuing auditor who previously has audited the entity's financial statements.
   d. Management agrees not to present the auditor's report in a general-use document to stockholders. (ID: 5091)

9. Independent internal verification of inventory occurs when employees who

   a. Issue raw materials, obtain material requisitions for each issue and prepare daily totals of materials issued
   b. Compare records of goods on hand with physical quantities, do not maintain the records or have custody of the inventory
   c. Are independent of issuing production orders, update records from completed job cost sheets and production cost reports on a timely basis
   d. Obtain receipts for the transfer of completed work to finished goods, prepare a completed production report (ID: 89)

10. When a auditor of an issuer qualifies an opinion because of an insufficiency of audit evidence, an auditor should refer to the situation in the

	Scope paragraph	Notes to the financial statements
a.	Yes	Yes
b.	Yes	No
c.	No	Yes
d.	No	No

(ID: 7100)

11. Which of the following procedures would a CPA most likely perform when reviewing the annual financial statements of a nonissuer?
    a. Verify that the accounting estimates that could be material to the financial statements have been developed.
    b. Obtain an understanding of the entity's internal control components.
    c. Assess the entity's ability to continue as a going concern for a reasonable period of time.
    d. Make inquiries about actions taken at the board of directors meetings. (ID: 8648)

12. A CPA who is not in public practice is obligated to follow which of the following rules of conduct?
    a. Independence
    b. Integrity and objectivity
    c. Contingent fees
    d. Commissions (ID: 7885)

13. In assessing the objectivity of internal auditors, an external auditor may
    a. Evaluate the quality control program in effect for the internal auditors.
    b. Examine documentary evidence of the work performed by the internal auditors.
    c. Test a sample of the transactions and balances that the internal auditors examined.
    d. Determine the organizational level to which the internal auditors report. (ID: 5950)

14. Inherent risk and control risk differ from detection risk in that they
    a. Arise from the misapplication of auditing procedures
    b. May be assessed in either quantitative or nonquantitative terms
    c. Exist independently of the financial statement audit
    d. Can be changed at the auditor's discretion (ID: 5081)

15. An internal control questionnaire indicates that an approved receiving report is required to accompany every check request for payment of merchandise. Which of the following procedures provides the greatest assurance that this control is operating effectively?
    a. Select and examine canceled checks and ascertain that the related receiving reports are dated no earlier than the checks.
    b. Select and examine canceled checks and ascertain that the related receiving reports are dated no later than the checks.
    c. Select and examine receiving reports and ascertain that the related canceled checks are dated no earlier than the receiving reports.
    d. Select and examine receiving reports and ascertain that the related canceled checks are dated no later than the receiving reports. (ID: 8960)

16. When using the work of a specialist, the auditor may make reference to the work of the specialist in the audit report if
    a. The auditor decides to express a qualified opinion.
    b. The specialist's reputation or professional certification is being emphasized.
    c. The auditor wishes to indicate a division of responsibility.
    d. The specialist's work provides the auditor greater assurance of reliability. (ID: 8968)

17. An accountant is asked to issue a review report on the balance sheet, but not on other related statements. The scope of the inquiry and analytical procedures has not been restricted, but the client failed to provide a representation letter. Which of the following should the accountant issue under these circumstances?
    a. Review report with a qualification
    b. Review report with a disclaimer
    c. Review report and footnote exceptions
    d. Compilation report with the client's consent (ID: 7844)

18. Under the Code of Professional Conduct of the AICPA, which of the following is required to be independent in fact and appearance when discharging professional responsibilities?

    a. A CPA in public practice providing tax and management advisory services
    b. A CPA in public practice providing auditing and other attestation services
    c. A CPA not in public practice
    d. All CPAs (ID: 8668)

19. Which of the following factors would **least** influence an auditor's consideration of the reliability of data for purposes of substantive analytical procedures?

    a. Whether the data was processed in an IT system or in a manual accounting system
    b. Whether there were controls over the preparation of the data
    c. Whether the data used was comparable
    d. Whether the data was obtained from independent sources outside the entity or from sources within the entity (ID: 151)

20. A client erroneously recorded a large purchase twice. Which of the following internal control measures would be most likely to detect this error in a timely and efficient manner?

    a. Footing the purchases journal
    b. Reconciling vendors' monthly statements with subsidiary payable ledger accounts
    c. Tracing totals from the purchases journal to the ledger accounts
    d. Sending written quarterly confirmations to all vendors (ID: 8959)

21. In designing written audit programs, an auditor should establish specific audit objectives that relate primarily to the

    a. Timing of audit procedures
    b. Cost-benefit of gathering evidence
    c. Selected audit techniques
    d. Financial statement assertions (ID: 4673)

22. When comparative financial statements are presented, but the predecessor auditor's report is **not** presented, the auditor should do which of the following in the audit report?

    a. Disclaim an opinion on the prior year's financial statements.
    b. Identify the predecessor auditor who audited the financial statements of the prior year.
    c. Make no comment with respect to the predecessor audit.
    d. Indicate the type of opinion expressed by the predecessor auditor. (ID: 8969)

23. When developing the group audit plan, the group engagement team is required

    a. To determine the timing of the group engagement team's interaction with component auditors
    b. To determine whether the audit report on the group financial statements will make reference to the audit of each component auditor
    c. To determine whether the audit report on the group financial statements will make reference to the audit of either all or none of the component auditors
    d. To include the component auditors in a brainstorming session regarding the risks of material misstatement of the group financial statements, including the risks of fraud (ID: 90083)

24. A violation of the profession's ethical standards most likely would have occurred when a CPA

    a. Issued an unqualified opinion on the Year 3 financial statements of an issuer when fees for the Year 1 audit were unpaid
    b. Recommended a controller's position description with candidate specifications to an audit client
    c. Purchased a CPA firm's practice of monthly write-ups for a percentage of fees to be received over a three-year period
    d. Made arrangements with a financial institution to collect notes issued by a client in payment of fees due for the current year's audit (ID: 3897)

25. An auditor is required to attempt communication with the predecessor auditor prior to

    a. Performing tests of controls
    b. Developing an overall audit strategy
    c. Making a proposal for an audit engagement
    d. Accepting an engagement for an initial audit (ID: 8137)

26. The Accounts Payable Department receives the purchase order form to accomplish all of the following **except**

    a. Compare invoice price to purchase order price.
    b. Ensure the purchase had been properly authorized.
    c. Ensure the goods had been received by the party requesting the goods.
    d. Compare quantity ordered to quantity purchased. (ID: 8967)

27. The auditor will most likely perform extensive tests for possible understatement of

    a. Revenues
    b. Assets
    c. Liabilities
    d. Capital (ID: 8962)

28. Which of the following is a documentation requirement that an auditor should follow when auditing in accordance with *Government Auditing Standards?*

    a. The auditor should obtain written representations from management acknowledging responsibility for correcting instances of fraud, abuse, and waste.
    b. The auditor's working papers should contain sufficient information so that supplementary oral explanations are not required.
    c. The auditor's working papers should contain a caveat that all instances of material errors and fraud may not be identified.
    d. The auditor should document the procedures that assure discovery of all illegal acts and contingent liabilities resulting from noncompliance. (ID: 4281)

29. According to the standards of the profession, which of the following activities would most likely **not** impair a CPA's independence?

    a. Providing extensive advisory services for a client
    b. Contracting with a client to supervise the client's office personnel
    c. Signing a client's checks in emergency situations
    d. Accepting a luxurious gift from a client (ID: 5873)

30. An auditor's independence is considered impaired if the auditor has

    a. An immaterial, indirect financial interest in a client
    b. An automobile loan from a client bank, collateralized by the automobile
    c. A joint, closely held business investment with the client that is material to the auditor's net worth
    d. A mortgage loan, executed with a financial institution client on March 1,1990, that is material to the auditor's net worth (ID: 7864)

Testlet 3 MULTIPLE-CHOICE QUESTIONS

1. According the PCAOB's auditing standard for engagement quality reviews, the reviewer should evaluate the significant judgments that relate to engagement planning, including all of the following **except**
   a. The consideration of the firm's recent engagement experience with the company and risks identified in connection with the firm's client acceptance and retention process
   b. The consideration of the company's business, recent significant activities, and related financial reporting issues and risks
   c. The judgments made about materiality and the effect of those judgments on the engagement strategy
   d. Review the engagement completion document and confirm with the engagement partner that there are no significant unresolved matters (ID: 89457)

2. The justification for a request by management to change the terms of an audit engagement is most likely to be considered reasonable when
   a. It relates to information that is incorrect, incomplete, or otherwise unsatisfactory.
   b. Management imposes a scope limitation.
   c. Circumstances change that affect management's need for the service.
   d. Management decides it is unwilling to dedicate the resources promised to support the auditors. (ID: 90378)

3. The date of the representation letter should be as of the date of the
   a. Balance sheet
   b. Latest interim financial information
   c. Audit report
   d. Audit report release date (ID: 5685)

4. Which of the following procedures would the principal auditor of an issuer most likely perform after deciding to make reference to another CPA who audited a subsidiary of the entity?
   a. Review the working papers and the audit programs of the other CPA.
   b. Visit the other CPA and discuss the results of the other CPA's audit procedures.
   c. Make inquiries about the professional reputation and independence of the other CPA.
   d. Determine that the other CPA has a sufficient understanding of the subsidiary's internal control. (ID: 6831)

5. May an accountant accept an engagement to compile or review the financial statements of a not-for-profit entity if the accountant is unfamiliar with the specialized industry accounting principles, but plans to obtain the required level of knowledge before compiling or reviewing the financial statements?

	Compilation	Review
a.	No	No
b.	Yes	No
c.	No	Yes
d.	Yes	Yes

(ID: 4711)

6. Under the ethical standards of the profession, which of the following situations involving nondependent members of an auditor's family is most likely to impair the auditor's independence?
   a. A parent's immaterial investment in a client
   b. A first cousin's loan from a client
   c. A spouse's employment with a client
   d. A sibling's loan to a marketing manager of a client (ID: 7112)

7. Which of the following strategies would a CPA most likely consider in auditing an entity that processes most of its financial data only in electronic form, such as a paperless system?
   a. Continuous monitoring and analysis of transaction processing with an embedded audit module
   b. Increased reliance on internal control activities that emphasize the segregation of duties
   c. Verification of encrypted digital certificates used to monitor the authorization of transactions
   d. Extensive testing of firewall boundaries that restrict the recording of outside network traffic (ID: 6839)

8. The auditor would **least** likely be concerned about internal control as it relates to
   a. Land and buildings
   b. Common stock
   c. Shareholder meetings
   d. Minutes of board of directors meetings (ID: 8971)

9. Which of the following statements extracted from an entity's external legal counsel's response to an auditor's letter of inquiry concerning litigation, claims, and assessments most likely would cause the auditor to request clarification?
   a. "I believe that the possible liability to the company is nominal in amount."
   b. "I believe that the action can be settled for less than the damages claimed."
   c. "I believe that the plaintiff's case against the company is without merit."
   d. "I believe that the company will be able to defend this action successfully." (ID: 6364)

10. When an auditor concludes there is substantial doubt about a client's ability to continue as a going concern for a reasonable period of time, the auditor's responsibilities include
    a. Issuance of an adverse opinion
    b. Consideration of the adequacy of disclosure about the client's possible inability to continue as a going concern
    c. Reporting to those charged with governance that management's accounting estimates may need to be adjusted
    d. Reissuing the prior year's audit report with an emphasis-of-matter paragraph that includes the terms *substantial doubt* and *going concern* (ID: 4727)

11. An accountant should perform analytical procedures during an engagement to

	Compile a nonissuer's financial statements	Review a nonissuer's financial statements
a.	No	No
b.	Yes	Yes
c.	Yes	No
d.	No	Yes

(ID: 4724)

12. Which of the following is(are) a correct definition of auditing standards?
    I. Procedures used by an auditor to gather evidence on which to base an opinion
    II. Measures of the quality of the auditor's performance

    a. I only
    b. II only
    c. Both I and II
    d. Neither I nor II (ID: 7645)

13. Harris, CPA, has been asked to audit and report on the balance sheet of Fox Co. but not on the statements of income, retained earnings, or cash flows. Harris will have access to all information underlying the basic financial statements. Under these circumstances, Harris may

    a. Not accept the engagement because it would constitute a violation of the profession's ethical standards
    b. Not accept the engagement because it would be tantamount to rendering a piecemeal opinion
    c. Accept the engagement because such engagements merely involve limited reporting objectives
    d. Accept the engagement, but should disclaim an opinion because of an inability to apply the procedures considered necessary (ID: 6008)

14. Planning includes consideration of the timing of certain activities and audit procedures that need to be completed prior to the performance of further audit procedures. For example, prior to the auditor's identification and assessment of the risks of material misstatement, all of the following matters need to be considered **except for**

    a. The determination of materiality
    b. The identification of the controls to be tested
    c. The involvement of specialists
    d. A general understanding of the entity's legal and regulatory framework and how the entity is complying with that framework (ID: 90377)

15. "There have been no communications from regulatory agencies concerning noncompliance with, or deficiencies in, financial reporting practices that could have a material effect on the financial statements." The foregoing passage is most likely from a

    a. Report on internal control
    b. Special report
    c. Representation letter
    d. Letter for underwriters (ID: 6397)

16. An audit report on financial statements prepared on the cash basis of accounting should include all of the following **except**

    a. A reference to the note to the financial statements that describes the basis of accounting
    b. A statement that the cash basis of accounting is not a basis of accounting other than GAAP
    c. An opinion as to whether the financial statements are presented fairly in accordance with the cash basis of accounting
    d. A statement that the audit was conducted in accordance with generally accepted auditing standards (ID: 5700)

17. Which of the following procedures is **not** usually performed by the accountant during an annual review engagement of a nonissuer?

    a. Inquiring about actions taken at meetings of the board of directors that may affect the financial statements
    b. Issuing a report stating that the review was performed in accordance with standards issued by the AICPA
    c. Reading the financial statements to consider whether they conform with generally accepted accounting principles
    d. Communicating any material weaknesses discovered during the consideration of internal control (ID: 2979)

18. Which of the following statements best describes the ethical standard of the profession pertaining to advertising and solicitation?

    a. All forms of advertising and solicitation are prohibited.
    b. There are no prohibitions regarding the manner in which CPAs may solicit new business.
    c. A CPA may advertise in any manner that is not false, misleading, or deceptive.
    d. A CPA may only solicit new clients through mass mailings. (ID: 7111)

19. Which of the following relatively small misstatements most likely could have a material effect on an entity's financial statements?

    a. An illegal payment to a foreign official that was not recorded
    b. A piece of obsolete office equipment that was not retired
    c. A petty cash fund disbursement that was not properly authorized
    d. An uncollectible account receivable that was not written off (ID: 5627)

20. A significant deficiency in internal control exists when

    a. The design or operation of a control does not allow management or employees, in the normal course of performing their assigned functions, to be able to prevent, or detect and correct misstatements on a timely basis.
    b. The person performing the control does not possess the necessary authority or competence to perform the control effectively.
    c. There is a deficiency, or a combination of deficiencies, that is less severe than a material weakness, yet important enough to merit attention by those charged with governance.
    d. The auditor finds evidence that a misstatement of the financial statements actually occurred as a direct result of a missing control. (ID: 90376)

21. In the confirmation of accounts receivable, the auditor would most likely

    a. Request confirmation of a sample of the inactive accounts
    b. Seek to obtain positive confirmations for at least 50% of the total dollar amount of the receivables
    c. Require confirmation of all receivables from agencies of the federal government
    d. Require that confirmation requests be sent within one month of the fiscal year-end (ID: 8963)

22. An audit report issued in connection with which of the following is generally **not** considered to be a report on financial statements prepared in accordance with a special-purpose framework?

    a. Compliance with requirements of government programs administered by an entity
    b. Financial statements prepared in accordance with a cash basis of accounting
    c. Financial statements prepared in accordance with a tax basis of accounting
    d. Financial statements prepared in accordance with a contractual basis of accounting (ID: 8977)

23. Which of the following procedures is usually performed by the accountant in an annual review engagement of a nonissuer?

    a. Sending a letter of inquiry to the entity's lawyer
    b. Comparing the financial statements with statements for comparable prior periods
    c. Confirming a significant percentage of receivables by direct communication with debtors
    d. Communicating significant deficiencies discovered during the study of internal control (ID: 2787)

24. Burrow & Co., CPAs, have provided annual audit and tax compliance services to Mare Corp. for several years. Mare has been unable to pay Burrow in full for services Burrow rendered 19 months ago. Burrow is ready to begin fieldwork for the current year's audit. Under the ethical standards of the profession, which of the following arrangements will permit Burrow to begin the fieldwork on Mare's audit?

    a. Mare sets up a two-year payment plan with Burrow to settle the unpaid fee balance.
    b. Mare commits to pay the past due fee in full before the audit report is issued.
    c. Mare gives Burrow an 18-month note payable for the full amount of the past due fees before Burrow begins the audit.
    d. Mare engages another firm to perform the fieldwork, and Burrow is limited to reviewing the workpapers and issuing the audit report. (ID: 7114)

25. Which of the following statements is correct concerning deficiencies in internal control identified in an audit of financial statements?

    a. An auditor is required to search for control deficiencies during an audit.
    b. All significant deficiencies are also considered to be material weaknesses.
    c. An auditor may communicate deficiencies during an audit or after the audit's completion.
    d. An auditor may report that no significant deficiencies were noted during an audit. (ID: 5656)

26. Which of the following might be detected by an auditor's review of the client's sales cut-off?

    a. Excessive goods returned for credit
    b. Unrecorded sales discounts
    c. Lapping of year-end accounts receivable
    d. Inflated sales for the year (ID: 8964)

27. When auditing an entity's financial statements in accordance with *Government Auditing Standards,* an auditor should prepare a written report on the auditor's

    a. Identification of the causes of performance problems and recommendations for actions to improve operations
    b. Understanding of internal control and assessment of control risk
    c. Field work and procedures that substantiated the auditor's specific findings and conclusions
    d. Opinion on the entity's attainment of the goals and objectives specified by applicable laws and regulations (ID: 4282)

28. Which of the following inquiry or analytical procedures ordinarily is performed in a review engagement?

    a. Analytical procedures designed to test the accounting records by obtaining corroborating evidential matter
    b. Inquiries concerning the entity's procedures for recording and summarizing transactions
    c. Analytical procedures designed to test management's assertions regarding continued existence
    d. Inquiries of the entity's attorney concerning contingent liabilities (ID: 2977)

29. According to the SEC, an auditor is not independent of its issuer audit client in which of the following situations?

    a. The auditor's cousin has an insurance policy obtained from the issuer before it became an audit client.
    b. The auditor has an automobile loan at standard terms from the audit client that is collateralized by the automobile.
    c. The auditor has an investment in an entity that has the ability to exercise significant influence over the audit client.
    d. The auditor's grandparent was in an accounting role at the audit client and ended employment before the period under audit began. (ID: 9950)

30. Which of the following boards is responsible for establishing requirements for professional accountants for the International Federation of Accountants?

    a. International Accounting Standards Board
    b. International Ethics Standards Board for Accountants
    c. International Code of Ethics for Accountants Board
    d. International Code of Professional Conduct Board (ID: 9295)

Testlet 4 SIMULATIONS

Simulation 1 Compilation and Review Requirements

Each of the following items represents a series of unrelated procedures that an accountant may consider performing in separate engagements to review the financial statements of a nonissuer (a review) and to compile the financial statements of a nonissuer (a compilation) according to SSARS. Select, as the best answer for each item, whether the procedure is required (R) or not required (N) for **both** review and compilation engagements.

Procedures	Required / Not Required	
	Compilation	**Review**
1. The accountant should send a letter of inquiry to the entity's attorney to corroborate the information furnished by management concerning litigation.		
2. The accountant should obtain a management representation letter from the entity.		
3. The accountant should compare recorded amounts, or ratios developed from recorded amounts, to expectations developed by the accountant.		
4. The accountant should communicate to the entity's senior management illegal employee acts discovered by the accountant that are clearly inconsequential.		
5. The accountant should make inquiries about events subsequent to the date of the financial statements that would have a material effect on the financial statements.		
6. The accountant should modify the accountant's report if there is a change in accounting principles that is adequately disclosed.		
7. The accountant should submit a hard copy of the financial statements and accountant's report when the financial statements and accountant's report are submitted on a computer disk.		
8. The accountant should perform specific procedures to evaluate whether there is substantial doubt about the entity's ability to continue as a going concern.		

(ID: 9244)

Simulation 2 Independence

Peirce & Hinds, CPAs, are reviewing issues of independence with regard to potential audit clients. Each of these potential clients are privately held companies. Peirce & Hinds are AICPA members. Except as noted, Peirce & Hinds do not have any other association with these potential clients.

Indicate whether Peirce & Hinds, CPAs, may accept an engagement to audit each potential client.

Statement	Yes/No
1. Hinds was the controller of Amos, Inc., resigning in January, Year 3, to partner with Peirce. Amos, Inc. is seeking an auditor for its Year 3 financial statements. Hinds no longer has any financial interest in Amos' pension plan.	
2. Worth, a former audit employee of Peirce & Hinds, quit last year and now is internal auditor at Claire Cosmetics. Worth is not owed any payments by Peirce & Hinds. Worth does not influence or participate in any of Peirce & Hinds, CPAs' activities. Peirce & Hinds, CPAs' ongoing attest engagement team plans to consider the appropriateness and necessity of engagement procedures modification to adjust for the risk that audit effectiveness could be reduced as a result of Worth's prior knowledge of the audit plan.	
3. Elegance, Inc. authorized Peirce & Hinds to sign payroll checks for it in emergency situations.	
4. Yost, a professional employee of Peirce & Hinds, is a motorcycle enthusiast. This year, he received the gift of a prototype motorcycle from Gremlin Motors, Inc. When he realized Gremlin was seeking a new auditor, Yost suggested Peirce & Hinds as auditors to Gremlin and promptly reported the gift to Peirce & Hinds.	
5. Peirce & Hinds operate a local area network for Ingot, Inc.	
6. Peirce's husband is Director of Marketing at Kelpie, Inc., but does not influence the financial reporting process in this position.	
7. Hinds interviewed applicants for controller and recommended qualified candidates to Mole, Inc.	
8. Within the last year, Peirce & Hinds performed an engagement to provide assistance in assessing business risks and control processes for Optimal Solutions, Inc.	

(ID: 9249)

Simulation 3 Errors and Fraud

Field, CPA, is auditing the financial statements of Miller Mailorder, Inc. (MMI) for the year ended January 31, 20X1. Field has compiled a list of possible errors and fraud that may result in the misstatement of MMI's financial statements.

For each possible error and fraud listed, select one internal control procedure from the answer list that, if properly designed and implemented, most likely could assist MMI in preventing or detecting the errors and fraud. A procedure may be used once, more than once, or not at all.

Possible Errors & Fraud	Internal Control Procedure
1. Customers' checks are received for less than the customers' full account balances, but the customers' full account balances are credited.	
2. Customers' checks are misappropriated before being forwarded to the cashier for deposit.	
3. Customers' checks are credited to incorrect customer accounts.	
4. Different customer accounts are each credited for the same cash receipt.	
5. Customers' checks are properly credited to customer accounts and are properly deposited, but errors are made in recording receipts in the cash receipts journal.	
6. Customers' checks are misappropriated after being forwarded to the cashier for deposit.	
7. Invalid transactions granting credit for sales returns are recorded.	

(ID: 9254)

Internal Control Procedures

A. Shipping clerks compare goods received from the warehouse with the details on the shipping documents.

B. Approved sales orders are required for goods to be released from the warehouse.

C. Monthly statements are mailed to all customers with outstanding balances.

D. Shipping clerks compare goods received from the warehouse with approved sales orders.

E. Customer orders are compared with the inventory master file to determine whether items ordered are in stock.

F. Daily sales summaries are compared with control totals of invoices.

G. Shipping documents are compared with sales invoices when goods are shipped.

H. Sales invoices are compared with the master price file.

I. Customer orders are compared with an approved customer list.

J. Sales orders are prepared for each customer order.

K. Control amounts posted to the accounts receivable ledger are compared with control totals of invoices.

L. Sales invoices are compared with shipping documents and approved customer orders before invoices are mailed.

M. Prenumbered credit memos are used for granting credit for goods returned.

N. Goods returned for credit are approved by the supervisor of the Sales Department.

O. Remittance advices are separated from the checks in the mailroom and forwarded to the Accounting Department.

P. Total amounts posted to the accounts receivable ledger from remittance advices are compared with the validated bank deposit slip.

Q. The cashier examines each check for proper endorsement.

R. Validated deposit slips are compared with the cashier's daily cash summaries.

S. An employee, other than the bookkeeper, periodically prepares a bank reconciliation.

T. Sales returns are approved by the same employee who issues receiving reports evidencing actual return of goods.

Simulation 4 Unrecorded Liabilities

Based on the company and its environment, including its internal control, the auditors assessed the risk of material misstatements to the financial statements, whether due to error or fraud, and designed the nature, extent, and timing of further audit procedures to be performed.

As a result of conducting the above risk assessment procedures, the audit program for year 2 includes the following changes from the audit program for year 1. The company has a calendar year-end and operates only on weekdays.

In conducting the audit procedures for the search for unrecorded liabilities, the materiality/scope for this area was assessed by the auditors at $6,000. Adjustments are only recorded for items equal to, or exceeding materiality.

For the items reflected in the following check register, which are **not** recorded in the accounts payable subsidiary ledger at December 31, year 2, determine if each potential liability is recorded in the proper accounting period and also determine the amount that should be journalized, if any.

Check Register

Vendor	Check #	Check Date	Amount	Nature of Expense
Water World Distributors, Inc.	1333	1/6/year 3	$ 3,500	Water coolers in office and warehouse delivered 12/31/year 2
Daniel Breen, Esquire	1334	1/6/year 3	$ 6,000	Corporate legal services for December, year 2
Telephone Services, Inc.	1335	1/8/year 3	$ 6,500	December, year 2 telephone and computer services
Payroll processing—Paychecks	1336	1/10/year 3	$25,500	Biweekly payroll (12/25/year 2 -1/7/year 3)
Pitt Ohio Trucking Company	1337	1/10/year 3	$45,601	Trucking services 12/4/year 2 - 1/3/year 3, deliveries made evenly throughout the period
Petty cash	1338	1/17/year 3	$ 2,002	Replenish petty cash box
Smith's Forklift Repairs	1339	1/22/year 3	$11,000	Received new forklift on 12/29/year 2, ordered on 12/18/year 2
Glenn's Glass Distribution Center	1340	1/23/year 3	$12,230	Specialty goods ordered 12/20/year 2, delivered 12/31/year 2
Payroll processing—Paychecks	1341	1/24/year 3	$25,500	Biweekly payroll (1/8/year 3 -1/15/year 3)
Daniel Breen, Esquire	1342	2/6/year 3	$ 6,800	Corporate legal services for January, year 3

For each of the check numbers in the table below, indicate if an adjustment is required and if so, select its amount from the list below. Each selection may be used once, more than once, or not at all. If no adjustment is required, select $0.

Check #	**Adjustment needed?**		**Amount**
	Yes	**No**	
1333			
1334			
1335			
1336			
1337			
1338			
1339			
1340			
1341			
1342			

(ID: 9255)

Selection List for Amount

$0	$7,650
$2,002	$9,900
$2,970	$11,000
$3,500	$12,230
$4,413	$12,750
$6,000	$25,500
$6,500	$41,188
$6,800	$45,601

Simulation 5 Cutoff Procedures

For each of the potential December 31, year 2, sales cutoff problems listed below, select the appropriate adjustment for year 2 from the list provided. Each item in the list may be used once, more than once, or not at all.

Potential cutoff problem	Adjustment
A. The company shipped merchandise (f.o.b. destination) to a customer on December 29, year 2, and recorded the sale but not the relief of inventory. The customer received the merchandise on December 31, year 2.	
B. The company shipped merchandise (f.o.b. shipping point) on December 3, year 2, to a customer, and recorded the sale and relief of inventory. The customer, unhappy with the merchandise, returned the goods on December 29, year 2. The company records the following entry upon receipt of the goods: Inventory (dr.), Cost of Sales (cr.)	
C. The company shipped merchandise to a consignee on December 16, year 2, and did not record the transaction. The consignee returned the merchandise on December 28, year 2. Upon receipt of the goods, the company made the following entry: Inventory (dr.), Sales (cr.)	
D. The company shipped merchandise (f.o.b. shipping point) on December 29, year 2, and recorded relief of inventory, but not the sale, on that date. The customer has not received the merchandise and the company has not recorded the sale as of January 3, year 3.	

(ID: 9253)

Selection List

1. No adjustment necessary.	6. Accounts Receivable (dr.) Inventory (cr.)
2. Accounts Receivable (dr.) Sales (cr.)	7. Sales (dr.) Accounts Receivable (cr.) Inventory (dr.) Cost of Sales (cr.)
3. Sales (dr.) Accounts Receivable (cr.)	8. Sales (dr.) Inventory (cr.)
4. Inventory (dr.) Cost of Sales (cr.)	9. Accounts Receivable (dr.) Sales (cr.) Cost of Sales (dr.) Inventory (cr.)
5. Cost of Sales (dr.) Inventory (cr.)	10. Sales (dr.) Cost of Sales (cr.)

Simulation 6 Substantive Tests

An auditor determines that each of the following objectives will be part of a company's audit. For each objective, select **two** different substantive tests that provide the best support for the audit objective. A substantive test may be used once, more than once, or not at all.

Audit Objective	Substantive Tests
1. Receivables at the end of year 2 are properly cut off with respect to sales made in year 2.	
2. The aggregate of net receivables in the balance sheet is fairly stated at estimated net realizable value.	
3. Depreciation expense is fairly stated.	
4. Fixed assets included in the balance sheet exist.	

(ID: 9256)

Selection List

A. Request positive confirmation directly from the customer of its balance owed to the company.	I. From the fixed assets subledger, vouch a selection of fully depreciated assets from the ledger to the manufacturing floor and check the associated identification number.
B. Test that the income statement agrees to the change of assets minus liabilities and owner's equity.	J. Recalculate the year's depreciation expense.
C. Test the aging in the accounts receivable trial balance.	K. Review the process of assigning expected useful life to machinery with the controller and ask if any assumptions have changed.
D. Match shipping documents to the related sales invoices and orders, and trace them to entries in the sales journal and accounts receivable subsidiary ledger.	L. Foot the fixed asset subledger.
E. Analyze the historical relationship of bad debt write-offs in comparison with sales and accounts receivable.	M. Vouch additions from the property, plant and equipment subsidiary ledger.
F. Foot the accounts receivable trial balance.	N. Make a physical inspection of major property, plant and equipment acquisitions
G. Foot and cross-foot the sales journal.	O. Foot and cross-foot the purchases journal
H. Identify the last number used in year 2 and the first number used in year 3 for prenumbered shipping documents and prenumbered sales invoices. Trace the respective numbers to postings in the sales journal and accounts receivable subsidiary ledger.	P. Investigate and review cash receipts related to retirements and sales of property, plant and equipment during the year.

Simulation 7 Research

Which citation in the professional standards provides guidance on how to evaluate and report on a change in accounting estimate that is inseparable from the effect of a related change in accounting principle?

[ ] § [ ] . [ ] (ID: 90064)

PERFORMANCE BY TOPIC

The practice exam testlet and question numbers corresponding to each chapter of this textbook are listed below. To assess your preparedness for the exam, record the number and percentage of questions you answered correctly in each topic area.

Chapter 1: An Audit Conducted in Accordance With US GAAS

Question #	Correct √
3:12	
# Questions	1
# Correct	______
% Correct	______

Chapter 2: Planning

Question #	Correct √
1:2	
1:4	
1:8	
1:13	
1:14	
1:19	
2:1	
2:2	
2:7	
2:25	
3:2	
3:14	
3:19	
# Questions	13
# Correct	______
% Correct	______

Chapter 3: Internal Control

Question #	Correct √
1:20	
1:25	
2:3	
2:9	
2:14	
2:15	
2:20	
3:8	
3:20	
3:25	
# Questions	10
# Correct	______
% Correct	______

Chapter 4: Evidence & Procedures

Question #	Correct √
1:1	
1:10	
1:16	
1:21	
1:26	
1:29	
2:4	
2:13	
2:16	
2:19	
3:3	
3:9	
3:15	
# Questions	13
# Correct	______
% Correct	______

Chapter 5: Audit Programs

Question #	Correct √
2:21	
2:26	
2:27	
3:21	
3:26	
# Questions	5
# Correct	______
% Correct	______

Chapter 6: Audit Sampling

Question #	Correct √
1:3	
1:9	
# Questions	2
# Correct	______
% Correct	______

Chapter 7: Auditing IT Systems

Question #	Correct √
3:7	
# Questions	1
# Correct	______
% Correct	______

Chapter 8: Reports on Audited Financial Statements

Question #	Correct √
1:22	
1:27	
2:22	
3:10	
3:13	
# Questions	5
# Correct	______
% Correct	______

Chapter 9: Audits of Group Financial Statements

Question #	Correct √
2:23	
# Questions	1
# Correct	______
% Correct	______

Chapter 10: Government Auditing

Question #	Correct √
2:28	
3:27	
# Questions	2
# Correct	______
% Correct	______

Chapter 11: Other Auditing Standards

Question #	Correct √
2:10	
3:4	
# Questions	2
# Correct	______
% Correct	______

Chapter 12: Other Types of Reports

Question #	Correct √
3:16	
3:22	
# Questions	2
# Correct	______
% Correct	______

Chapter 13: Accounting & Review Services

Question #	Correct √
1:5	
1:11	
1:17	
1:23	
2:5	
2:6	
2:11	
2:17	
3:5	
3:11	
3:17	
3:23	
3:28	
# Questions	13
# Correct	______
% Correct	______

Chapter 14: Attestation Engagements

Question #	Correct √
1:15	
2:8	
# Questions	2
# Correct	______
% Correct	______

Chapter 15: Accountants' Professional Responsibilities

Question #	Correct √
1:6	
1:7	
1:12	
1:18	
1:24	
1:28	
1:30	
2:12	
2:18	
2:24	
2:29	
2:30	
3:1	
3:6	
3:18	
3:24	
3:29	
3:30	
# Questions	18
# Correct	______
% Correct	______

PERFORMANCE BY AICPA CONTENT SPECIFICATION OUTLINE

The practice exam testlet and question numbers corresponding to each area of the AICPA content specification outline (CSO) are listed below. To assess your preparedness for the exam, record the number and percentage of questions you answered correctly in each CSO area.

CSO I Auditing and Attestation: Engagement Acceptance and Understanding the Assignment (12% - 16%)

Question #	Correct √
1:13	
1:15	
1:19	
2:8	
2:13	
2:23	
2:25	
3:2	
3:12	
3:13	
3:14	
# Questions	11
# Correct	______
% Correct	______

CSO II Auditing and Attestation: Understanding the Entity and Its Environment (including Internal Control) (16% - 20%)

Question #	Correct √
1:2	
1:8	
1:14	
1:20	
1:25	
2:1	
2:2	
2:7	
2:9	
2:14	
2:20	
2:26	
3:7	
3:8	
3:19	
# Questions	15
# Correct	______
% Correct	______

CSO III Auditing and Attestation: Performing Audit Procedures and Evaluating Evidence (16% - 20%)

Question #	Correct √
1:1	
1:3	
1:9	
1:21	
1:26	
2:3	
2:15	
2:19	
2:21	
2:27	
3:3	
3:9	
3:15	
3:21	
3:26	
# Questions	15
# Correct	______
% Correct	______

CSO IV Auditing and Attestation: Evaluating Audit Findings, Communications, and Reporting (16% - 20%)

Question #	Correct √
1:4	
1:10	
1:16	
1:22	
1:27	
1:29	
2:4	
2:10	
2:16	
2:22	
2:28	
3:4	
3:10	
3:16	
3:20	
3:22	
3:25	
3:27	
# Questions	18
# Correct	______
% Correct	______

CSO V Accounting and Review Services Engagements (12% - 16%)

Question #	Correct √
1:5	
1:11	
1:17	
1:23	
2:5	
2:6	
2:11	
2:17	
3:5	
3:11	
3:17	
3:23	
3:28	
# Questions	13
# Correct	______
% Correct	______

CSO VI Professional Responsibilities (16% - 20%)

Question #	Correct √
1:6	
1:7	
1:12	
1:18	
1:24	
1:28	
1:30	
2:12	
2:18	
2:24	
2:29	
2:30	
3:1	
3:6	
3:18	
3:24	
3:29	
3:30	
# Questions	18
# Correct	______
% Correct	______

MULTIPLE-CHOICE ANSWERS

Testlet 1 Answers

1. (a) The predecessor auditor ordinarily permits the auditor to review audit documentation [working papers], including documentation of planning; risk assessment procedures; audit results; and other matters of continuing accounting and auditing significance, such as the schedule of uncorrected misstatements, working paper analysis of balance sheet accounts, and those relating to contingencies. (ID: 7092)

2. (b) If an auditor must decrease detection risk, the auditor should change the nature, extent, or timing of audit procedures. Performing procedures closer to the balance sheet date allows less opportunity for misstatements due to roll-forward adjustments to the auditor's interim work. An increase in the assessed level of control risk will cause a decrease in the amount of misstatements that an auditor can tolerate. A decrease in the tolerable amount of misstatements would increase, not decrease, the extent of auditing procedures. (ID: 6574)

3. (b) Book value less audit value divided by book value is the tainting percentage. [($5,000 – $4,000) / $5,000 = 0.2] The tainting percentage times the sampling interval is the projected error. 0.2 × $10,000 = $2,000 The sum of all the projected errors is the projected misstatement; there was only one error in this sample. (ID: 6935)

4. (b) The auditor should disclaim an opinion. If the auditor is precluded by management or those charged with governance from obtaining sufficient appropriate audit evidence to evaluate whether noncompliance that may be material to the financial statements has, or is likely to have, occurred, the auditor should express a qualified opinion or disclaim an opinion on the financial statements on the basis of a scope limitation. A qualified opinion was not one of the answer alternatives. (ID: 165)

5. (c) Both provisions are required by the SSARS. (ID: 4744)

6. (b) Independence is considered impaired if a spouse or dependent person (immediate family) of the member is employed in a position that allows significant influence over the client's operating, financial, or accounting policies. Independence is considered impaired if the position with the client involves activities that are audit-sensitive, even though the position is not one that allows significant influence. A person's activities would be considered audit sensitive if such activities are normally an element of, or subject to, significant internal controls; for example, the positions of cashier, internal auditor, accounting or finance supervisor, purchasing agent, or inventory warehouse supervisor. (ID: 7883)

7. (d) SQCS address a CPA's firm's responsibilities for its system of quality control for its accounting and auditing practice. (ID: 33)

8. (b) The auditor must determine a materiality level for the financial statements taken as a whole. The concept of materiality recognizes that some matters affect the fair presentation of financial statements, while others do not. Materiality judgments involve both quantitative and qualitative considerations. In making the assessment of materiality, an auditor should consider the needs of a reasonable person who would rely on the financial statements. (ID: 5084)

9. (d) Upon repeated random samples of a given size from a population, the distribution of the means of those samples will be a normal distribution. The mean of the distribution is equal to the population mean and the standard error of the mean of the distribution equals the population standard deviation divided by the square root of the sample size. Approximately 68% and 95% of the sample means will be within one and two standard deviations, respectively, of the mean of the distribution. All of these characteristics relate to the distribution of sample means that results from repeated samples of a given size from a population. However, the distribution of the items drawn by the auditor in a particular sample may take any form; such a sample does not necessarily have a normal distribution. (ID: 8973)

10. (c) Analytics should be applied to some extent to assist the auditor in planning the procedures to be performed and as an overall review in the final review stage. (ID: 8952)

11. (a) If financial statements compiled in conformity with OCBOA do not include disclosure of the basis, the accountant must modify the report by adding a separate paragraph that discloses the basis. Answers b., c., and d. are not options mentioned in the Standards. (ID: 5154)

12. (d) The independence of a member or firm may be impaired because of nondependent close relatives, which includes parent, sibling, or nondependent children that are in a position to influence the attest arrangement. (ID: 7036)

13. (d) The auditor should explain to the prospective client the need to make an inquiry of the predecessor and should request permission to do so. The predecessor should be contacted prior to final engagement acceptance. The predecessor may communicate with the successor provided that the client grants permission; such communication does not violate the auditor-client confidentiality. (ID: 8947)

14. (b) The auditor has a responsibility to plan and perform the audit to obtain reasonable assurance about whether the financial statements are free of material misstatements, whether caused by error or fraud. The auditor satisfies this responsibility by exercising due care in the performance of procedures appropriate under the circumstances. If procedures indicate that material errors or fraud may exist, the auditor should extend procedures. (ID: 8948)

15. (d) The auditor may use the work performed by, or receive direct assistance from, internal auditors, entity personnel (in addition to internal auditors), and third parties working under the direction of management or those charged with governance that provide evidence about the effectiveness of internal control. In the planning stage, the auditor may review the workpapers of the predecessor auditor to obtain knowledge of the entity's internal control; however, the information obtained is not considered to be evidence for the current audit. (ID: 89456)

16. (c) The objective of analytical procedures used in the overall review stage of the audit is to assist the auditor in assessing the conclusions reached and in the evaluation of the overall financial statement presentation. The overall review would generally include reading the financial statements and notes and considering unusual or unexpected balances or relationships that were not previously identified. The other answers describe procedures performed before the overall review stage. (ID: 5665)

17. (b) The compilation report should include a statement that the accountant's responsibility is to conduct the compilation in accordance with Statements on Standards for Accounting and Review Services issued by the AICPA. A compilation report does not include a statement that the accounting principles and significant estimates were assessed and an evaluation of the overall financial statement presentation was done; this statement is part of the standard audit report. The other answer alternatives are both statements, in part, that should be included in a review report rather than a compilation report. (ID: 5696)

18. (b) An auditor is required to return a client's records after the client has demanded them. Representing a client in connection with obtaining a private letter ruling is one of the specific tax matters for which an accountant may charge a contingent fee. Confidential client information may be disclosed without the client's permission in conjunction with a prospective purchase, sale, or merger of the accountant's practice. If an auditor does not follow requirements of government audits, this lapse must be disclosed in the auditor's report. (ID: 7862)

19. (a) In a preaudit conference, a senior auditor would most likely discuss the technical and personnel aspects of a job. Feedback from the staff would occur later. Establishing the need for specialists and the use of internal auditors is done during the planning stage. Answer b. is done during fieldwork. (ID: 5077)

20. (b) The control environment reflects the overall attitude, awareness, and actions of the board of directors, management, owners, and others concerning the importance of control and its emphasis in the entity. If management is dominated by one individual who is also a shareholder, aggressive reporting and the achievement of profit goals may be overemphasized to the detriment of proper reporting. Answers a., c., and d. represent examples of positive control environment influences. (ID: 6390)

21. (a) The auditor should request written representations from management with appropriate responsibilities for the financial statements and knowledge of the matters concerned. Those individuals may vary depending on the governance structure of the entity; however, management (rather than those charged with governance) is often the responsible party. Written representations may therefore be requested from the entity's chief executive officer and chief financial officer or other equivalent persons in entities that do not use such titles. In some circumstances, however, other parties, such as those charged with governance, also are responsible for the preparation and fair presentation of the financial statements. (ID: 8954)

22. (b) The omission of a procedure that was considered necessary at the time of the audit does not necessarily imply that the original opinion is faulty, or that not enough procedures were performed. Thus, the auditor should first assess the importance of the omitted procedure to the auditor's present ability to support the previously expressed opinion. The results of other procedures originally applied or the results of subsequent audits may provide evidence for the original audit opinion. If, at this point, the auditor concludes that the omitted procedure is indeed necessary to support the opinion and the auditor believes that there are users currently relying, or likely to rely, on the previously released report, then the auditor should promptly perform the omitted or an alternative procedure to determine whether there is a satisfactory basis for the previously expressed opinion. (ID: 8956)

23. (a) Before submission, the accountant should read the compiled financial statements and consider whether such financial statements appear to be appropriate in form and free from obvious material errors. In this context, the term *error* refers to mistakes in the compilation of financial statements, including arithmetical or clerical mistakes, and mistakes in the application of accounting principles, including inadequate disclosure. A representation letter from members of management usually is not obtained in a compilation engagement. Inquiry of management concerning actions taken at meetings of the stockholders and the board of directors is a procedure normally used in a review engagement, and is not necessary in a compilation engagement. The accountant is not required to make inquiries or perform other procedures to verify, corroborate, or review information supplied by the entity. (ID: 5693)

24. (d) Several relationships impair independence, including being a member of management (including the board of directors) or promoter. Serving as a client's general counsel, stock transfer, escrow agent, or registrar also impairs independence. Under the ethical standards of the profession, an advisor relationship in and of itself doesn't impair an auditor's independence. (ID: 8175)

25. (b) The auditor should obtain an understanding of controls relevant to the audit, which are those judged necessary to understand in order to assess the risks of material misstatement at the assertion level and design further audit procedures responsive to assessed risks. An auditor performs tests of controls later in the audit to obtain sufficient appropriate audit evidence about the operating *effectiveness* of controls as opposed to their operating efficiency. Collusion and management override are inherent limitations of internal control. (ID: 7488)

26. (c) The plant manager has a thorough knowledge of factory operations. This knowledge includes an awareness of the productive capability of the plant machinery, as well as new machinery on the market. As a result, the plant manager would know whether a particular machine is obsolete. The plant manager has no contact with accounts receivable and, thus, is not in a position to know about the adequacy of the provision for uncollectible accounts. The auditor determines the appropriateness of inventory observation procedures. The plant manager would be helpful in identifying the location of inventory. The plant manager is not responsible for procuring necessary insurance coverage and, therefore, would not be aware that such procurement was deferred. (ID: 8955)

27. (a) When the auditor identifies a material inconsistency prior to the report release date that requires revision of the other information and management refuses to make the revision, the auditor should communicate this matter to those charged with governance and take one of the following actions: (1) include in the audit report an other-matter paragraph describing the material inconsistency; or (2) withhold the audit report; or (3) when withdrawal is possible under applicable law or regulation, withdraw from the engagement. Incorrect answer b. relates to the auditor's discovery, when reading the other information, of an apparent material misstatement of fact. An *inconsistency* is defined as other information that conflicts with information contained in the audited **financial statements**; a *misstatement of fact* is defined as other information that is *unrelated* to matters appear-

ing in the financial statements that is incorrectly stated or presented. (A material misstatement of fact may undermine the credibility of the document containing audited financial statements.) The auditor should discuss an apparent material misstatement of fact with management; however, after doing so, the auditor may conclude that valid differences of judgment exist. If so, the auditor should *request management* to consult with a qualified third party, such as the entity's legal counsel (not go directly to the third party/client's legal counsel), and the auditor should consider the advice received by the entity. (When the auditor concludes that there is a material misstatement of fact in the other information that management refuses to correct, the auditor should notify those charged with governance and take any further appropriate action. Such actions may include obtaining legal advice, withholding the auditor's report if such report has not been released, or withdrawing from the engagement.) Regarding incorrect answer c., a qualified opinion is not warranted under these circumstances—the audit opinion on the financial statements does *not* cover other information (in the absence of any separate requirement in the particular circumstances of the engagement). However, the auditor is required to read the other information to identify material inconsistencies, if any, with the audited financial statements (because the credibility of the statements may be undermined by material inconsistencies between them and the other information) and respond appropriately. Regarding incorrect answer d., a material inconsistency may raise doubt about the audit conclusions drawn from audit evidence previously obtained and, possibly, about the basis for the auditor's opinion on the financial statements; thus, it should not be ignored [considered closed]. (ID: 8957)

28. (a) If a member does not have the ability to direct investments, an investment in a client through a financial service product (such as a mutual fund) is considered an indirect financial interest and, hence, doesn't necessarily impair independence. Direct or material indirect financial interest in a client impairs independence. In addition, if a member has significant influence over the nonregulated mutual investment fund, independence would be considered to be impaired. Independence is considered impaired if a covered member owns stock in a client through an investment club, where presumably the member has the ability to direct investments, whether or not exercised, resulting in a direct financial interest. Accordingly, any of the club's investments in a client are deemed to impair independence regardless of materiality. Independence is considered impaired even if a CPA has a material indirect financial interest in a client, whether or not it is placed in a blind trust. Furthermore, the member should ensure that any blind trust that s/he is a beneficiary of does not hold a direct or material indirect financial interest in any of the member's client's. The requirements for independence with regard to ordinary trusts are not less restrictive. (ID: 7113)

29. (c) It is difficult to substantiate representations that a related-party transaction was consummated on terms equivalent to those that prevail in arm's-length transactions. Thus, if a footnote includes such an assertion by management, there may be a risk of a material misstatement that could result in a qualified opinion. In such cases, the auditor should obtain sufficient appropriate audit evidence about the assertion. The other answer alternatives are all appropriate disclosures with respect to related-party transactions. (ID: 8958)

30. (b) The service in question constitutes a type of service performed by public accountants, and the member may hire such an employee as long as the CPA is able to supervise the specialist and evaluate her/his results. The CPA is not required to be a specialist outside of the realm of accounting and tax services. The CPA is permitted to be associated with non-CPA professionals, as long as the association is not misleading and the client is aware of the relationship. (ID: 4240)

Testlet 2 Answers

1. (b) As management signs a representation letter that includes a statement that all known fraud has been reported to the auditor, if an auditor discovers fraud known to management, but undisclosed to the auditor, the auditor has evidence that management has lied regarding audit information at least once. This impairs reliance on other management statements. While an aggressive attitude toward meeting profit goals is suggestive of incentive and management decision dominated by one person may provide opportunity to commit fraud, they are not as important as actual known management deception. Some weaknesses in internal control may be knowingly left uncorrected due to cost-benefit considerations. (ID: 7631)

2. (a) The auditor primarily uses the knowledge obtained in evaluating the design and implementation of controls [gaining an understanding of internal control] to (1) identify types of potential misstatements and factors that affect the risks of material misstatement; and (2) in designing the nature, extent, and timing of further audit procedures. (ID: 5951)

3. (b) The auditor may test controls over the recording of retirements by tracing certain items of equipment from the accounting records and locating them in the plant to make sure that they have not been retired. Additions to the "other assets" account should have nothing to do with the failure to record retirements of equipment. Tracing from the plant assets to the books would not locate assets which appear on the books even though they have been retired because none of the equipment traced would be retired equipment. If retired equipment that was not fully depreciated was not removed from the records, the related depreciation calculation would not reveal its retirement; further, fully depreciated equipment may or may not still be in use. (ID: 81)

4. (a) Audit documentation provides the principal support for the representation in the auditor's report that the auditor performed the audit in accordance with generally accepted auditing standards; and provides the principal support for the opinion expressed regarding the financial information or the assertion to the effect that an opinion cannot be expressed. (ID: 5689)

5. (a) When compiled financial statements omit substantially all disclosures, the accountant should indicate this in the report. The SSARS include the following as an example of an appropriate additional paragraph: "Management has elected to omit substantially all the disclosures required by accounting principles generally accepted in the United States of America. If the omitted disclosures were included in the financial statements, they might influence the user's conclusions about the company's financial position, results of operations, and cash flows. Accordingly, these financial statements are not designed for those who are not informed about such matters." The accountant must conclude that the omission was not made with the intention of misleading those who might reasonably be expected to use such financial statements. Answer b., indicating that the statements are prepared in conformity with OCBOA is an inappropriate remedy for the omission of disclosures required by GAAP. However, it should be noted that if financial statements compiled in conformity with a comprehensive basis of accounting other than GAAP do not include disclosure of the basis of accounting used, the basis should be disclosed in the accountant's report. Answers c. and d. are not acceptable statements for inclusion in the report. (ID: 5155)

6. (d) A CPA who provides auditing and other attestation services should be independent in fact and appearance. In providing all other services, an accountant should maintain objectivity and avoid conflicts of interest. Thus, an accountant need not be independent when providing compilation services or when preparing a tax return. (ID: 5182)

7. (d) In planning the scope of the audit, the auditor should consider, among other matters, the effect of the assessed risk of material misstatement at the overall financial statement level. When the auditor is developing a preliminary audit strategy, the auditor has not performed sampling procedures, interim tests, nor inquiry of the client's attorney. (ID: 2276)

8. (b) An auditor may perform an examination of internal control only if (1) management provides its assertion about the effectiveness of the entity's internal control in a report that accompanies the auditor's report; (2) management accepts responsibility for the effectiveness of the entity's internal control; (3) management evaluates the effectiveness of the entity's internal control using suitable and available criteria; and (4) management supports its assertion about the effectiveness of the entity's internal control with sufficient appropriate evidence. The other answers are not required conditions for acceptance of the engagement. (ID: 5091)

9. (b) Incompatible functions are those that place any person in a position to both perpetrate and conceal errors or fraud in the normal course of their duties. A well-designed plan of organization separates the duties of authorization, recordkeeping, and custody of assets. Answers a. and d. do not separate custody and recordkeeping. Answer c. does not provide verification of inventory. (ID: 89)

10. (b) When qualifying an opinion on the financial statements of an issuer because of insufficiency of audit evidence, an auditor refers to the situation in the scope and opinion paragraphs and includes an explanatory

paragraph before the opinion paragraph. Management is responsible for the financial statements, including the notes; an auditor merely recommends changes. (ID: 7100)

11. (d) When reviewing the financial statements of a nonissuer, an accountant should make inquiries about actions taken at the board of directors meetings. Making inquiries of management along with applying analytical procedures and obtaining representations from management are required in order to obtain a reasonable basis for the expression of limited assurance. A review does not include verification of accounting estimates or tests of accounting records and procedures ordinarily performed in an audit. A review according to SSARS does not contemplate obtaining an understanding of an entity's internal control. A review does not include the assessment of an entity's ability to continue as a going concern; however, during the performance of a review (or a compilation) it may come to the attention of the accountant that there may be such an uncertainty. If so, the accountant should request that management consider the possible effects on the financial statements, including related disclosures. (ID: 8648)

12. (b) A CPA who is not in public practice is obligated to integrity and objectivity, as well as the discreditable acts, rules of conduct. (ID: 7885)

13. (d) When assessing the internal auditors' objectivity, the external auditor may obtain information about the organizational status of the internal auditors, including the organizational level to which they report. The other answer alternatives do not directly relate to their objectivity. (ID: 5950)

14. (c) Inherent risk and control risk exist independently of the financial statement audit. They are the entity's risks and cannot be changed at the auditor's discretion. Detection risk is the risk that an auditor will not detect a material misstatement—it, not inherent risk or control risk, can arise from the misapplication of auditing procedures. All three risks can be assessed in quantitative terms, such as percentages, or nonquantitative terms, such as high, medium, or low risk. (ID: 5081)

15. (b) The requirement is to determine the best test of controls for a procedure that calls for an approved receiving report to accompany every check. This control can be tested by selecting canceled checks and ascertaining that the related receiving reports are dated no later than the check. (In addition, the auditor probably would want to ascertain that the check amounts correspond to the price of the goods received.) If the auditor selects receiving reports (rather than checks) to test the control, the auditor will not become aware of instances of checks with no related receiving report. (ID: 8960)

16. (a) The auditor should *not* refer to the work of a specialist in an audit report containing an unmodified opinion. However, it may be appropriate to refer to the specialist in an audit report containing a modified opinion to explain the nature of the modification. If so, the auditor should indicate in the audit report that such reference does *not* reduce the auditor's responsibility for that opinion. (ID: 8968)

17. (d) Failure by the client's management to provide a representation letter covering all of the periods under review precludes the completion of a review. The accountant may issue a compilation report as an accountant is not required to verify, corroborate, or review information supplied for a compilation. (ID: 7844)

18. (b) A CPA who provides auditing and other attestation services should be independent in fact and appearance. In providing all other services, an accountant should maintain objectivity and avoid conflicts of interest. A CPA need not be independent when providing tax and management advisory services. A CPA need not be independent when not in public practice. (ID: 8668)

19. (a) Whether the data was processed in an IT system or in a manual accounting system generally would not influence the auditor's consideration of the reliability of data for purposes of analytics. The reliability of data is influenced by its source and nature and is dependent on the circumstances under which it is obtained. Accordingly, the following are relevant when determining whether data is reliable for purposes of designing substantive analytical procedures: (1) the source of the information available, e.g., information may be more reliable when it is obtained from independent sources outside the entity; (2) the comparability of the information available, e.g., broad industry data may need to be supplemented to be comparable to that of an entity that produces and sells specialized products; (3) the nature and relevance of the information available, e.g., whether

budgets have been established as results to be expected rather than as goals to be achieved; and (4) controls over the preparation of the information that are designed to ensure its completeness, accuracy, and validity. (ID: 151)

20. (b) By reconciling vendors' monthly statements with the subsidiary payable ledger accounts, the error would be corrected in, at most, a month's time. Footing the purchases journal only verifies its mathematical accuracy. Answer c. is incorrect because the erroneous purchase amount in the purchases journal was originally carried through from the client's ledger accounts. Vendors might not confirm the fact that the client is overstating its liability for purchases. (ID: 8959)

21. (d) Once the audit strategy has been established, the auditor is able to start the development of a more detailed audit plan [audit programs] to address the various matters identified in the audit strategy, taking into account the need to achieve the audit objectives. The documentation of the audit plan via audit programs should include descriptions of the nature, extent, and timing of planned further audit procedures at the relevant assertion level. The other answer alternatives are all considerations of the procedures necessary to satisfy the audit objectives. Editor Note: The audit plan should also describe the nature and extent of planned risk assessment procedures and other planned audit procedures that are required to be performed so that the engagement complies with GAAS. (ID: 4673)

22. (d) The auditor should indicate in an other-matter paragraph (1) that the financial statements of the prior period were audited by a predecessor auditor; (2) the type of opinion expressed by the predecessor auditor and if the opinion was modified, the reasons for the modification; (3) the nature of an emphasis-of-matter paragraph or other-matter paragraph included in the predecessor auditor's report, if any, and; (4) the date of that prior report. (ID: 8969)

23. (b) When developing the group audit plan, the group engagement team is required to determine whether the audit report on the group financial statements will make reference to the audit of a component auditor. Editor Note: The group engagement team should also assess the extent to which the group engagement team will use the work of component auditors. Regarding incorrect answer a., when developing the group audit plan the group engagement team is required to assess the extent to which the group engagement team will use the work of component auditors; not determine the timing of the interaction. A determination of the nature, timing, and extent of its involvement in the work of component auditors [interaction] is required when the auditor of the group financial statements is assuming responsibility for the work of a component auditor and the engagement team is deciding the work to be performed by it or on its behalf by the component auditors on the financial information of the components. Regarding incorrect answer c., in group audits involving two or more component auditors, the decision to make reference to the audit of a component auditor is made individually for each component auditor, regardless of the decision whether to refer to any other component auditor. The auditor of the group financial statements may make reference to any, all, or none of the component auditors. Regarding incorrect answer d., the key members of the engagement team are required to discuss the susceptibility of an entity to material misstatement of the financial statements due to fraud or error, specifically emphasizing the risks due to fraud. In a group audit, these discussions also *may* include the component auditors, but their inclusion is not a requirement. The group engagement partner's determination of who to include in the discussions, how and when they occur, and their extent is affected by factors, such as prior experience with the group. (ID: 90083)

24. (a) Independence is considered to be impaired if, when the report on the client's current year is issued, fees remain unpaid for professional services provided more than one year prior to the date of the report. Such amounts assume the characteristics of a loan within the meaning of Rule 101. Recommending a controller's position description is not a violation of the ethical standards as long as the final hiring decision is made by management of the client. Purchasing a CPA firm's practice of monthly write-ups does not violate any provisions of the Code or client confidentiality. A member firm may make arrangements with a bank to collect notes issued by a client in payment of fees due. (ID: 3897)

25. (d) Before accepting an engagement for an initial audit, including a reaudit engagement, the auditor should request management to authorize the predecessor auditor to respond fully to the auditor's inquiries regarding matters that will assist the auditor in determining whether to accept the engagement. (ID: 8137)

26. (c) The Accounts Payable Department receives the vendor's invoice with quantities, descriptions, and prices of purchases. A copy of the purchase order enables them to (1) compare the invoice and purchase order price; (2) ensure that the purchase was authorized; and (3) compare the quantity ordered and purchased. Their review of the purchase order will not ensure that the goods were received by the party requesting the goods. (ID: 8967)

27. (c) The financial statements are the representations of management, who generally would like the financial position of the entity to appear as sound as possible. Thus, the auditor is concerned with possible overstatements of revenues, income, assets, and capital. Conversely, the auditor is concerned with the possible understatement of any losses, expenses, and liabilities. (ID: 8962)

28. (b) Included in the fieldwork standards of supplemental working paper requirements for financial audits is the statement that working papers should contain sufficient information so that supplementary oral explanations are not required. Written representations from management are not required. An audit does not ensure that all illegal acts and contingent liabilities resulting from noncompliance will be discovered by the auditor. The auditor's workpapers should include positive statements about the procedures applied and the results of those procedures; thus, there is no requirement that the working papers contain a caveat statement. (ID: 4281)

29. (a) According to the standards of the profession, providing extensive advisory services for a client would not impair the CPA's independence. Contracting with a client to supervise the client's office personnel, signing client checks, and accepting luxurious gifts would all impair a CPA's independence. (ID: 5873)

30. (c) A direct financial interest (business investment) always impairs an accountant's independence, regardless of materiality. Independence is impaired when a CPA holds a direct or material indirect financial interest. A loan to or from a client generally impairs independence; however, certain loans are permitted. These loans include car loans collateralized by the vehicles from financial institution clients when the loans are current as to all terms at all times and obtained under normal lending terms, requirements, and procedures. Grandfathered mortgages that are current as to all terms obtained under normal lending procedures, terms, and requirements before the institution became a client requiring independence are also permitted. With a twenty-first century question mentioning a 1990 date, the candidate may assume this loan meets these requirements. Candidates may have to make similar assumptions to answer other exam questions. (ID: 7864)

Testlet 3 Answers

1. (d) Reviewing the engagement completion document and confirming with the engagement partner that there are no significant unresolved matters is not a significant judgment related to engagement planning. (ID: 89457)

2. (c) The auditor should not agree to a change in the terms of the audit engagement when no reasonable justification for doing so exists. A change in circumstances that affects management's requirements or a misunderstanding concerning the nature of the service originally requested may be considered a reasonable basis for requesting a change. On the other hand, a change may not be considered reasonable if it relates to information that is incorrect, incomplete, or otherwise unsatisfactory. An example might be when the auditor is unable to obtain sufficient appropriate audit evidence regarding receivables and management asks for the audit engagement to be changed to a review engagement to avoid a qualified opinion or a disclaimer of opinion. Editor Note: If the auditor concludes that no reasonable justification for a change exists and is not permitted by management to continue the original audit engagement, the auditor should (1) withdraw, if possible under applicable law or regulation; (2) communicate the circumstances to those charged with governance; and (3) determine whether any obligation, either legal, contractual, or otherwise, exists to report the circumstances to other parties, such as owners, or regulators. (ID: 90378)

3. (c) The representation letter should be dated as of the date of the audit report. (ID: 5685)

4. (c) When the principal auditor of an issuer makes reference to the audit of another auditor, the principal auditor doesn't assume responsibility for the other auditor's work. Whether or not the principal auditor decides to make reference, the principal auditor should inquire about the professional reputation and independence of the other CPA. The other answer alternatives describe procedures that may be performed when the principal auditor decides *not* to make reference to the audit of the other auditor. (ID: 6831)

5. (d) For a compilation or review engagement, the requirement that the CPA possess a level of knowledge of the accounting principles and practices of the industry in which the entity operates does not prevent a CPA from accepting a compilation or review engagement for an entity. However, it does place upon the CPA a responsibility to obtain the required level of knowledge. (ID: 4711)

6. (c) Independence is considered impaired if a spouse or dependent person (immediate family) of the member is employed in a position that allows significant influence over the client's operating, financial, or accounting policies. Independence is considered impaired if the position with the client involves activities that are audit-sensitive, even though the position is not one that allows significant influence. A person's activities would be considered audit sensitive if such activities are normally an element of, or subject to, significant internal controls; for example, the positions of cashier, internal auditor, accounting supervisor, purchasing agent, or inventory warehouse supervisor. (ID: 7112)

7. (a) When a client processes financial data in electronic form without paper documentation, the auditor may audit on a more continuous basis than a traditional system, as a convenience, and may be required to audit on a more continuous basis to obtain sufficient, competent evidence as documentation for some transactions may be available only for a limited time. An embedded audit module can facilitate this continuous auditing. If anything, an auditor may rely less on controls that emphasize segregation of duties. Digital certificate verification and testing of firewall boundaries are more concerned with security than internal control. (ID: 6839)

8. (c) The auditor is concerned primarily with those policies and procedures that are relevant to the audit. Generally, controls that are relevant to the audit pertain to an entity's objective of preparing financial statements for external purposes that are fairly presented. Controls over land and buildings and common stock are of primary concern to the auditor because they relate directly to financial statement assertions. Control over meetings of shareholders and the minutes of board of directors (BOD) meetings are in the nature of administrative controls. Although these controls are of secondary concern to the auditor, the controls over the minutes of BOD meetings are more important than those over shareholder meetings because they relate directly to transaction authorization. Shareholder meetings have only an indirect impact on such authorization. (ID: 8971)

9. (b) The response in answer b. is vague and probably would need clarification. The other answers indicate that the client probably doesn't have any material liability concerning the matters discussed. (ID: 6364)

10. (b) When the auditor concludes there is substantial doubt about the entity's ability to continue as a going concern for a reasonable period of time, the auditor should assess the possible effects on the financial statements, including the adequacy of the related disclosure and determine the implications for the audit report. The auditor would only issue a qualified or adverse opinion if the auditor concludes that the entity's disclosure with respect to the ability to continue as a going concern is inadequate. The auditor may report adjustments to those charged with governance; however, further communication is required to deal specifically with the going concern issue, regardless of changes to accounting estimates. Substantial doubt about the entity's ability to continue as a going concern for a reasonable period of time that arose in the current period does not imply that a basis for such doubt existed in the prior period and should not affect the audit report on the prior-period statements presented on a comparative basis. (ID: 4727)

11. (d) For a financial statement compilation, the accountant is not required to make inquiries or perform other procedures to verify, corroborate, or review information supplied by the entity. A financial statement review involves performing inquiries and analytics that provide a reasonable basis for expressing limited assurance that there are no material modifications that should be made to the statements in order for them to be in conformity with the applicable financial reporting framework. (ID: 4724)

12. (b) Auditing standards differ from auditing procedures in that procedures relate to acts to be performed, whereas standards deal with measures of the quality of the performance of those acts and the objectives to be attained by the use of the procedures undertaken. (ID: 7645)

13. (c) An auditor is not precluded from reporting on only one of the basic financial statements and not the others. Such engagements involve limited reporting objectives. (Limited reporting engagements do not involve scope limitations if the auditor's access to information underlying the basic financial statements is not limited and if the auditor applies all the procedures considered necessary in the circumstances.) Regarding incorrect answer a., nothing in the question's scenario indicates a violation of professional ethics. Regarding incorrect answer b., a piecemeal opinion is an opinion on specific elements, i.e., a portion, of a financial statement; it is not relevant to an opinion on an entire individual financial statement. Regarding incorrect answer d., nothing in the question's scenario indicates an inability to apply necessary procedures—the question stated that the auditor will have access to all information underlying the basic financial statements. (ID: 6008)

14. (b) The identification of which controls will be tested for operating effectiveness is performed in response to the assessed risk of material misstatement (RMM) at the assertion level; thus, this is, of course, *not* an example of a matter that should be considered prior the identification and assessment of the RMM. In addition to the other answer alternatives, other examples of matters that do need to be considered prior to the identification and assessment of RMM include the analytical procedures to be applied as risk assessment procedures and the performance of other risk assessment procedures. (ID: 90377)

15. (c) Whether there have been communications from regulatory agencies concerning noncompliance with or deficiencies in financial reporting practices should be addressed in a representation letter. A report on internal control or another special report generally would not discuss communications from other entities. Letters for underwriters concentrate on financial statements more than internal control. (ID: 6397)

16. (b) The cash basis of accounting *is* a basis of accounting other than GAAP. The audit report should include an emphasis-of-matter paragraph that indicates the financial statements are prepared in accordance with the cash basis of accounting; refers to the note to the financial statements that describes the basis of accounting; and states that the cash basis of accounting is a basis of accounting other than GAAP. The report should include an opinion paragraph that indicates whether the financial statements are presented fairly in accordance with the cash basis of accounting. The report should include a statement that the audit was conducted in accordance with GAAS. (ID: 5700)

17. (d) An annual review does *not* contemplate obtaining an understanding of the internal control or assessing control risk, tests of accounting records and of responses to inquiries by obtaining corroborating evidential matter, and certain other procedures ordinarily performed during an audit. Answers a., b., and c. are usually performed by the accountant in an annual review. (ID: 2979)

18. (c) Advertising or other forms of solicitation that are false, misleading, or deceptive are prohibited since they are not in the public interest. (ID: 7111)

19. (a) The auditor should consider the implications of an illegal act in relation to other aspects of the audit, particularly on the auditor's risk assessment and the reliability of the written representations. A relatively small misstatement of unretired fixed assets, improperly authorized petty cash fund disbursement, or uncollectible account receivable that was not written off have less impact on the financial statements taken as a whole and, by themselves, do not tend to place doubt on the integrity of management. (ID: 5627)

20. (c) A significant deficiency is a deficiency in internal control, or combination of deficiencies in internal control, that is less severe than a material weakness, yet important enough to merit attention by those charged with governance. Answer a. is the definition of a deficiency in internal control. Answer b. describes one of the conditions for a deficiency in the operation of a control to exist (the other condition is when a properly designed control does not operate as designed). Answer d. is false; the severity of a deficiency in internal control (taken into consideration by the auditor in the determination of whether a deficiency is either a significant deficiency or a material weakness) does *not* depend on whether a misstatement actually occurred. (ID: 90376)

21. (a) By requesting confirmation of a sample of inactive accounts, the auditor seeks to determine the accuracy of records relating to those accounts. Due to their inactive nature, defalcations could occur in these accounts, e.g., through lapping or an improper write-off. The cost of obtaining positive confirmations for at least 50% of the total dollar value of receivables generally would outweigh the benefits derived from such confirmations. The auditor does not treat receivables from federal agencies differently than other receivables, i.e., they are also subject to selective testing. Receivable confirmations can be sent as of any date. (ID: 8963)

22. (a) A report issued in connection with an entity's compliance with requirements of government programs it administers is *not* considered to be a report on financial statements prepared in accordance with a special-purpose framework. Special-purpose frameworks include the other answer alternatives plus *regulatory* and *other* bases of accounting. (ID: 8977)

23. (b) An accountant's review procedures will include inquiry and analytical procedures. Analytics are designed to identify relationships and individual items that appear to be unusual, and consist of (1) comparison of the financial statements with statements for comparable prior period(s), (2) comparison of the statements with anticipated results, if available, and (3) study of the relationships of the elements of the statements that would be expected to conform with a predictable pattern based on the entity's experience. Answers a., c., and d. are procedures that should be performed in an audit. (ID: 2787)

24. (b) Independence is considered impaired if fees for professional services rendered for more than one year prior are not collected before the issuance of the CPA's report for the current year. This includes billed and unbilled fees and notes receivable arising from such fees (ET 191-52). (ID: 7114)

25. (c) An auditor may communicate some deficiencies in internal control during an audit of financial statements (in addition to after the audit's completion) due to their significance and the need for timely corrective action. Such early communication is not required to be in writing. However, all significant deficiencies and material weaknesses should ultimately be reported in the required written communication to management and those charged with governance even if they were communicated earlier or remediated during the audit. For a non-issuer, the required written communication is best made by the audit report *release* date, but should be made no later than 60 days following this date. For a public company (an issuer), it is required to be made *prior* to the issuance of the audit report. Regarding incorrect answer a., in an audit of financial statements, the auditor is *not* required to search for deficiencies in internal control. The objective of the auditor is to appropriately communicate to those charged with governance and management deficiencies in internal control that the auditor has identified during the audit—*on the basis of the audit work performed*—and that, in the auditor's professional judgment, are of sufficient importance to merit their respective attentions. Regarding incorrect answer b., all material weaknesses are significant deficiencies, but not all significant deficiencies are material weaknesses. Regarding incorrect answer d., an auditor should **not** issue a written communication stating that no significant deficiencies were identified during the audit. However, management or those charged with governance may request that the auditor issue a communication indicating that no *material weaknesses* were identified (this may be required by a governmental authority). This is allowable. Such a communication should include all the same elements as the written communication of significant deficiencies and material weaknesses, except it should omit the description of significant deficiencies and an explanation of their potential effects. (ID: 5656)

26. (d) The main objective of the sales cutoff test is to determine that sales are recorded in the proper period. The auditor would test for excessive sales returns and discounts from a sample encompassing the entire period, not just the year-end. Lapping of A/R would be detected by tracing payments received to postings in the appropriate receivable subsidiary ledger. (ID: 8964)

27. (b) In accordance with *Government Auditing Standards,* an auditor must also report on internal control over financial reporting and on compliance with laws, regulations, and provisions of contracts or grant agreements when providing an opinion or a disclaimer on financial statements. Answer a. represents procedures to be reported in a performance audit. Specific procedures performed are not included in the auditor's report. The auditor provides an opinion on the fairness of the presentation of the financial statements taken as a whole rather than an opinion on an entity's attainment of goals and objectives. (ID: 4282)

28. (b) Procedures ordinarily performed during a review include inquiries concerning the entity's procedures for recording and summarizing transactions. They are not concerned with corroborating evidential matter, management's assertions concerning continued existence, or the entity's attorney's opinion concerning contingent liabilities or other audit procedures. (ID: 2977)

29. (c) According to the AICPA Code of Professional Conduct, a CPA's independence is considered impaired if the CPA has a financial interest in the audit client or has a financial interest in an entity that has the ability to exercise significant influence over the audit client. Having a relative who obtained an insurance policy from the issuer before it became an audit client or who was in an accounting role at the audit client and ended employment before the period under audit began would not be considered an impairment to independence. The auditor having an automobile loan at standard terms from the audit client that is collateralized by the automobile is not considered to have their independence impaired. (ID: 9950)

30. (b) The International Ethics Standards Board for Accountants (IESBA) of the International Federation of Accountants (IFAC) issues the Code of Ethics for Professional Accountants. (ID: 9295)

TESTLET 4 SIMULATION ANSWERS

Simulation 1 Compilation and Review Requirements

Each of the following items represents a series of unrelated procedures that an accountant may consider performing in separate engagements to review the financial statements of a nonissuer (a review) and to compile the financial statements of a nonissuer (a compilation) according to SSARS. Select, as the best answer for each item, whether the procedure is required (R) or not required (N) for **both** review and compilation engagements.

Procedures	**Required / Not Required**	
	Compilation	**Review**
1. The accountant should send a letter of inquiry to the entity's attorney to corroborate the information furnished by management concerning litigation.	N	N
2. The accountant should obtain a management representation letter from the entity.	N	R
3. The accountant should compare recorded amounts, or ratios developed from recorded amounts, to expectations developed by the accountant.	N	R
4. The accountant should communicate to the entity's senior management illegal employee acts discovered by the accountant that are clearly inconsequential.	N	N
5. The accountant should make inquiries about events subsequent to the date of the financial statements that would have a material effect on the financial statements.	N	R
6. The accountant should modify the accountant's report if there is a change in accounting principles that is adequately disclosed.	N	N
7. The accountant should submit a hard copy of the financial statements and accountant's report when the financial statements and accountant's report are submitted on a computer disk.	N	N
8. The accountant should perform specific procedures to evaluate whether there is substantial doubt about the entity's ability to continue as a going concern.	N	N

1. N, N

Neither engagement requires sending a letter of inquiry to the entity's attorney.

2. N, R

An accountant is not required to make inquiries or perform other procedures to verify, corroborate, or review information supplied by the entity in a compilation engagement. An accountant is required to obtain a written representation from members of management in a review engagement.

3. N, R

Analytical procedures such as this are required for a review, but not for a compilation.

4. N, N

When evidence comes to the accountant's attention during the performance of compilation or review procedures that fraud or an illegal act may have occurred, that matter should be brought to the attention of the appropriate level of management. The accountant need not report matters regarding illegal acts that are clearly inconsequential.

5. N, R

A compilation does not require inquiries about subsequent events. A review includes inquiries to members of management who have responsibility for financial and accounting matters concerning events subsequent to the date of the financial statements that could have a material effect on the financial statements.

6. N, N

As long as the change is appropriate and is appropriately disclosed in the financial statements, there is no requirement to alter the report for a compilation or review.

7. N, N

There is no professional requirement that the accountant submit a hard copy of financial statements or the accountant's report for a review or a compilation.

8. N, N

During the performance of compilation or review procedures, evidence *may* come to the accountant's attention indicating there may be an uncertainty about the entity's ability to continue as a going concern. Specific procedures for the evaluation of an entity's ability to continue as a going concern are not required for either type of engagement. (ID: 9244)

Simulation 2 Independence

	Statement	Yes/No
1.	Hinds was the controller of Amos, Inc., resigning in January, Year 3, to partner with Peirce. Amos, Inc. is seeking an auditor for its Year 3 financial statements. Hinds no longer has any financial interest in Amos' pension plan.	No
2.	Worth, a former audit employee of Peirce & Hinds, quit last year and now is internal auditor at Claire Cosmetics. Worth is not owed any payments by Peirce & Hinds. Worth does not influence or participate in any of Peirce & Hinds, CPAs' activities. Peirce & Hinds, CPAs' ongoing attest engagement team plans to consider the appropriateness and necessity of engagement procedures modification to adjust for the risk that audit effectiveness could be reduced as a result of Worth's prior knowledge of the audit plan.	Yes
3.	Elegance, Inc. authorized Peirce & Hinds to sign payroll checks for it in emergency situations.	No
4.	Yost, a professional employee of Peirce & Hinds, is a motorcycle enthusiast. This year, he received the gift of a prototype motorcycle from Gremlin Motors, Inc. When he realized Gremlin was seeking a new auditor, Yost suggested Peirce & Hinds as auditors to Gremlin and promptly reported the gift to Peirce & Hinds.	No
5.	Peirce & Hinds operate a local area network for Ingot, Inc.	No
6.	Peirce's husband is Director of Marketing at Kelpie, Inc., but does not influence the financial reporting process in this position.	Yes
7.	Hinds interviewed applicants for controller and recommended qualified candidates to Mole, Inc.	Yes
8.	Within the last year, Peirce & Hinds performed an engagement to provide assistance in assessing business risks and control processes for Optimal Solutions, Inc.	Yes

1. No

Independence would be impaired. An individual who formerly was employed by a client or associated with a client as an officer, director, promoter, underwriter, voting trustee, or trustee for a pension or profit-sharing trust of the client would impair the firm's independence if the individual was in a position to influence the attest engagement for the client when the attest engagement covers any period that includes the former employment or association with that client. By accepting this engagement, Hinds would be auditing her/his own work. A key position is a position in which an individual has: primary responsibility for significant accounting functions that support material components of the financial statements; primary responsibility for the preparation of the financial statements; or the ability to exercise influence over the contents of the financial statements, including when the individual is a controller or any equivalent position.

2. Yes

Independence would **not** be impaired. If a partner or professional employee leaves the firm and subsequently is employed by or associated with that client in a key position, then the firm's independence would be impaired, unless among other conditions, the ongoing attest engagement team considers the appropriateness or necessity of engagement procedures modification to adjust for the risk that audit effectiveness could be reduced as a result of the former partner or professional employee's prior knowledge of the audit plan.

3. No

Independence would be impaired if the CPA accepted responsibility to sign or co-sign client checks, even only in emergency situations.

4. No

Independence would be impaired if an employee or partner accepts more than a token gift from a client, even with the knowledge of the firm.

5. No

Independence would be impaired if the CPA designed or developed a client's financial information system, made other than insignificant modifications to source code underlying a client's existing financial information system, supervised client personnel in the daily operation of a client's information system, or operated a client's local area network (LAN) system.

6. Yes

Independence would **not** be impaired. A member's independence is not considered impaired solely as a result of the following: (1) an individual in a member's immediate family was employed by the client in a position other than a key position; or (2) in connection with her/his employment, an individual in the immediate family of one of the following members participated in a retirement, savings, compensation, or similar plan that is a client, is sponsored by a client, or that invests in a client, provided such plan normally is offered to all employees in similar positions: (a) a partner or manager who provides ten or more hours of nonattest services to the client; or (b) any partner in the office in which the lead attest engagement partner primarily practices in connection with the attest engagement.

7. Yes

Independence would **not** be impaired if the CPA recommended a position description or candidate specifications, solicited and performed screening of candidates, and recommended qualified candidates to a client based on the client-approved criteria, or participated in employee hiring or compensation discussions in an advisory capacity.

8. Yes

Independence would **not** be impaired if the CPA either provided assistance in assessing the client's business risks and control processes or recommended a plan for making improvements to a client's control processes and assisted in implementing these improvements. Independence would be impaired if the CPA either made or approved business risk decisions or presented business risk considerations to the board or others on behalf of management. (ID: 9249)

Simulation 3 Errors & Fraud

Possible Errors & Fraud	Internal Control Procedure
1. Customers' checks are received for less than the customers' full account balances, but the customers' full account balances are credited.	P
2. Customers' checks are misappropriated before being forwarded to the cashier for deposit.	C
3. Customers' checks are credited to incorrect customer accounts.	C
4. Different customer accounts are each credited for the same cash receipt.	P
5. Customers' checks are properly credited to customer accounts and are properly deposited, but errors are made in recording receipts in the cash receipts journal.	S
6. Customers' checks are misappropriated after being forwarded to the cashier for deposit.	P
7. Invalid transactions granting credit for sales returns are recorded.	N

1. P

The company would be able to detect errors in postings to customer accounts by placing certain control procedures in place. For example, by comparing the validated bank deposit slip total to the A/R posting total for the day, a difference in the amount posted from the remittance advices to the A/R ledger and the amount of checks actually received and deposited would be discovered.

2. C

Mailing monthly statements to all customers with outstanding balances would most likely detect customers' checks that are misappropriated before being forwarded to the cashier for deposit. The customers would be billed for invoices already paid and would let MMI know.

3. C

The company should implement control procedures to detect errors in postings to customer accounts. For example, mailing monthly statements to all customers with outstanding balances would detect errors as customers who had paid (but receive statements indicating a balance due) most likely would call the company to report the error.

4. P

By comparing the A/R postings to the validated deposit slip total, the difference resulting from posting one cash receipt remittance advice amount to two accounts in the A/R ledger would be detected.

5. S

Errors made in recording receipts in the cash receipts journal would most likely be detected if bank statements are reconciled periodically as the deposit amounts on the bank statements would be compared to the receipts as listed in the cash receipts journal. For internal control purposes, the person preparing the bank reconciliation should be someone other than the bookkeeper who is preparing the cash receipts journal.

6. P

The company should implement control procedures to prevent customer checks from being misappropriated before being deposited by the cashier. One procedure would compare the total amount posted to the accounts receivable ledger from the remittance advice to the validated deposit slip. Differences may indicate misappropriation of checks because they were not deposited or were deposited to incorrect bank accounts.

7. N

To prevent invalid transactions granting credit for sales returns from being recorded, control procedures should be implemented to require proper authorization of any sales returns. Authorization by the Sales Department supervisor would be appropriate, especially as the supervisor's goals are generally higher sales, and thus, the supervisor would not likely have a motivation for approving invalid sales returns. (ID: 9254)

Simulation 4 Unrecorded Liabilities

Check Register				
Vendor	**Check #**	**Check Date**	**Amount**	**Nature of Expense**
Water World Distributors, Inc.	1333	1/6/year 3	$ 3,500	Water coolers in office and warehouse delivered 12/31/year 2
Daniel Breen, Esquire	1334	1/6/year 3	$ 6,000	Corporate legal services for December, year 2
Telephone Services, Inc.	1335	1/8/year 3	$ 6,500	December, year 2 telephone and computer services
Payroll processing—Paychecks	1336	1/10/year 3	$25,500	Biweekly payroll (12/25/year 2 -1/7/year 3)
Pitt Ohio Trucking Company	1337	1/10/year 3	$45,601	Trucking services 12/4/year 2 - 1/3/year 3, deliveries made evenly throughout the period
Petty cash	1338	1/17/year 3	$ 2,002	Replenish petty cash box
Smith's Forklift Repairs	1339	1/22/year 3	$11,000	Received new forklift on 12/29/year 2, ordered on 12/18/year 2
Glenn's Glass Distribution Center	1340	1/23/year 3	$12,230	Specialty goods ordered 12/20/year 2, delivered 12/31/year 2
Payroll processing—Paychecks	1341	1/24/year 3	$25,500	Biweekly payroll (1/8/year 3 -1/15/year 3)
Daniel Breen, Esquire	1342	2/6/year 3	$ 6,800	Corporate legal services for January, year 3

Check # 1333: No adjustment needed

The amount of this check ($3,500) is lower than the $6,000 materiality level for adjustments set by the auditors for unrecorded liabilities; otherwise an adjustment would have been needed.

Check # 1334: Amount of adjustment: $6,000

This represents an expense for year 2, paid in year 3, which is equal to the materiality level; an adjustment (accrual of expense) is needed.

Check # 1335: Amount of adjustment: $6,500

This represents an expense for year 2, paid in year 3, which exceeds the materiality level; an adjustment (accrual of expense) is needed.

Check # 1336: Amount of adjustment: $12,750

The portion of this check that represents the salary expense for the period December 25 through December 31, year 2 is an expense for year 2, paid in year 3. The only information the problem gives you is that it is a biweekly payroll. Halving the amount of the check ($25,500/2 = $12,750) is a reasonable assumption to arrive at the amount of the adjustment (accrual of expense) needed.

Check # 1337: Amount of adjustment: $41,188

The portion of this check that represents the delivery expense for the period December 4 through December 31, year 2 is an expense for year 2, paid in year 3. The problem states that deliveries are made evenly throughout the period. The expense covers a period of 31 days (December 4, year 2 through January 3, year 3), 28 of which were part of year 2; thus, the calculation for the amount of the adjustment (accrual of expense) needed would be (($45,601 / 31) × 28) = $41,188.

Check # 1338: No adjustment is needed

This amount of this check ($2,002) is lower than the $6,000 materiality level for adjustments set by the auditors for unrecorded liabilities; no adjustment is needed.

Check # 1339: Amount of adjustment: $11,000

This represents an unrecorded liability for year 2 (when the forklift was ordered and received), which exceeds the materiality level; an adjustment (recording of the asset and related payable) is needed.

Check # 1340: Amount of adjustment: $12,230

This represents an unrecorded liability for year 2 (when the goods were ordered and received) which exceeds the materiality level; an adjustment (recording of the purchase and related payable) is needed.

Check # 1341: No adjustment needed

No adjustment is needed; this represents year 3 salary expense, paid in year 3.

Check # 1342: No adjustment needed

No adjustment is needed; this represents an expense for year 3, paid in year 3. (ID: 9255)

Simulation 5 Cutoff Procedures

Potential cutoff problem	Adjustment
A. The company shipped merchandise (f.o.b. destination) to a customer on December 29, year 2, and recorded the sale but not the relief of inventory. The customer received the merchandise on December 31, year 2.	5
B. The company shipped merchandise (f.o.b. shipping point) on December 3, year 2, to a customer, and recorded the sale and relief of inventory. The customer, unhappy with the merchandise, returned the goods on December 29, year 2. The company records the following entry upon receipt of the goods: Inventory (dr.), Cost of Sales (cr.)	3
C. The company shipped merchandise to a consignee on December 16, year 2, and did not record the transaction. The consignee returned the merchandise on December 28, year 2. Upon receipt of the goods, the company made the following entry: Inventory (dr.), Sales (cr.)	8
D. The company shipped merchandise (f.o.b. shipping point) on December 29, year 2, and recorded relief of inventory, but not the sale, on that date. The customer has not received the merchandise and the company has not recorded the sale as of January 3, year 3.	2

Selection List

1. No adjustment necessary.	6. Accounts Receivable (dr.) Inventory (cr.)
2. Accounts Receivable (dr.) Sales (cr.)	7. Sales (dr.) Accounts Receivable (cr.) Inventory (dr.) Cost of Sales (cr.)
3. Sales (dr.) Accounts Receivable (cr.)	8. Sales (dr.) Inventory (cr.)
4. Inventory (dr.) Cost of Sales (cr.)	9. Accounts Receivable (dr.) Sales (cr.) Cost of Sales (dr.) Inventory (cr.)
5. Cost of Sales (dr.) Inventory (cr.)	10. Sales (dr.) Cost of Sales (cr.)

A. 5

The only adjustment needed is for the client to record the relief of inventory because the title passed to the client's customer when it received the merchandise from the common carrier (f.o.b. destination point) on December 31, year 2. The client has already recorded the sale.

B. 3

The only adjustment needed is for the client to reduce "sales" (dr.) and "accounts receivable" (cr.) for the merchandise that was returned on December 29, year 2. The client has already made the entry to include the merchandise in the inventory account.

C. 8

Merchandise out on consignment remains the property of the consignor, in this case, the client. The client handled the shipment correctly by **not** recording a sale or relief of inventory. However, they did not handle the subsequent return/receipt of the merchandise from the consignee correctly. The client needs to make an adjustment to reverse the entry it made, i.e., debit "accounts receivable" and credit "inventory."

D. 2

The only adjustment needed is for the client to record the sale because the title passed to the client's customer when the merchandise was delivered to the common carrier (f.o.b. shipping point) on December 29, year 2. The client has already recorded the relief of inventory. (ID: 9253)

Simulation 6 Substantive Tests

Audit Objective	Substantive Tests
1. Receivables at the end of year 2 are properly cut off with respect to sales made in year 2.	D, H
2. The aggregate of net receivables in the balance sheet is fairly stated at estimated net realizable value.	C, E
3. Depreciation expense is fairly stated.	J, K
4. Fixed assets included in the balance sheet exist.	N, M

1. D, H
   - Any shipping documents dated year 3 should not be invoiced (recorded as sales) in year 2; any shipping documents dated year 2 should be posted to the year 2 sales journal and accounts receivable subsidiary ledger.
   - Accounting for the prenumbered documents in each year's postings will determine if proper cutoff occurred.

2. C, E
   - If the aging of accounts receivable is not accurate, the allowance for uncollectible accounts receivable won't be either; thus, the net realizable value of receivables will not be fairly stated.
   - Comparison and the resulting analysis of the current year's relationship to prior years is a test of the reasonableness of the current year's relationship.

3. J, K
   - The recalculation of depreciation expense will confirm its mathematical accuracy and that the expense is allocated to the correct year.
   - This review will confirm that the methods and estimates are appropriate, reasonable, and consistently applied.

4. N, M
   - Testing (vouching) for existence by physically inspecting the acquisitions which are included in the balance sheet will confirm that fixed assets are not overstated.
   - This is another procedure to determine if the assets included in the balance sheet actually exist.

(ID: 9256)

Simulation 7 Research

Which citation in the professional standards provides guidance on how to evaluate and report on a change in accounting estimate that is inseparable from the effect of a related change in accounting principle?

AU	§	708	.	10

(ID: 90064)

.10 The auditor should evaluate and report on a change in accounting estimate that is inseparable from the effect of a related change in accounting principle like other changes in accounting principle, as required by paragraphs .08–.09.

APPENDIX B
EXAM PREPARATION TIPS

Your first step toward an effective review program is to carefully read the material in this appendix. It contains essential information about the nature of the exam. Effective techniques and strategies for taking the exam are also included.

SECTION	CONTENTS	PAGE

SECTION ONE:
AICPA CONTENT & SKILL SPECIFICATION OUTLINE

The Board of Examiners (BOE) of the American Institute of Certified Public Accountants (AICPA) has developed a content and skill specification outline (CSO/SSO) for each section of the exam. Each section's CSO identifies the extent of the technical content to be tested.

In October 2013, the BOE approved changes to the content outlines for all exam sections, except REG which was brought forward unchanged.

This combined CSO/SSO is effective beginning with the January–February 2015 exam window for all exam sections.

There were *no* substantive changes for the AUD exam section.

See our other exam section volumes for their outlines or go the exam section of the AICPA's website (aicpa.org). (Select *CPA Exam* from the drop-down menu under *Become a CPA*; then click on *What's on the CPA Exam* to download the outlines for all sections.)

AUD SKILL SPECIFICATION OUTLINE

The AUD section tests knowledge and understanding of the following professional standards: auditing standards promulgated in the United States of America (related to audits of an *issuer* (a public company), a *nonissuer* (an entity that is not a public company), governmental entities, not-for-profit entities, and employee benefit plans; standards related to attestation and assurance engagements; and standards for performing accounting and review services.

Candidates are expected to demonstrate an awareness of: (1) the International Auditing and Assurance Standards Board (IAASB) and its role in establishing International Standards on Auditing (ISA); (2) the differences between ISA and US auditing standards; and (3) the audit requirements under US auditing standards that apply when they perform audit procedures on a US company that supports an audit report based upon the auditing standards of another country, or the ISA.

This section also tests knowledge of professional responsibilities of certified public accountants, including ethics and independence.

Candidates are also expected to demonstrate an awareness of: (1) the International Ethics Standards Board for Accountants (IESBA) and its role in establishing the requirements of the International Federation of Accountants (IFAC) *Code of Ethics for Professional Accountants*; and (2) the independence requirements that apply when they perform audit procedures on a US company that supports an audit report based upon the auditing standards of another country, or the ISA.

In addition to demonstrating knowledge and understanding of the professional standards, candidates are required to demonstrate the skills required to apply that knowledge in performing auditing and attestation tasks as certified public accountants.

Candidates are also expected to perform the following tasks:

- Demonstrate an awareness and understanding of the process by which standards and professional requirements are established for audit, attestation, and other services performed by CPAs, including the role of standard-setting bodies within the US and those bodies with the authority to promulgate international standards.
- Differentiate between audits; attestation and assurance services; compilations; and reviews.
- Differentiate between the professional standards for issuers and nonissuers.

- Identify situations that might be unethical or a violation of professional standards; perform research and consultations as appropriate; and determine the appropriate action.
- Recognize potentially unethical behavior of clients and determine the impact on the services being performed.
- Demonstrate the importance of identifying and adhering to requirements, rules, and standards that are established by licensing boards within their states and which may place additional professional requirements specific to their state of practice.
- Appropriately apply professional requirements in practice and differentiate between unconditional requirements and presumptively mandatory requirements.
- Exercise due care in the performance of work.
- Demonstrate an appropriate level of professional skepticism in the performance of work.
- Maintain independence in mental attitude in all matters relating to the audit.
- Research relevant professional literature.

The outline that follows specifies the tasks and related knowledge in which candidates are required to demonstrate proficiency.

AUD CONTENT SPECIFICATION OUTLINE

The content outline lists the areas (Roman numerals), groups (capital letters), and topics (Arabic numerals) to be tested and indicates the approximate percentage of the total questions associated with each area. The AICPA does *not* provide such percentages for groups or topics, i.e., the levels of the outline under each content area. Further, the presence of several groups within [under] an area or several topics within a group does *not* imply equal importance or weight will be given to these groups or topics on an exam.

These are the six content areas covered by the AUD CSO (the complete outline follows):

Auditing and Attestation:

I. Engagement Acceptance and Understanding the Assignment (12% – 16%)

II. Understanding the Entity and Its Environment (Including Internal Control) (16% – 20%)

III. Performing Audit Procedures and Evaluating Evidence (16% – 20%)

IV. Evaluating Audit Findings, Communications, and Reporting (16% – 20%)

Other:

V. Accounting and Review Services Engagements (12% – 16%)

VI. Professional Responsibilities (16% – 20%)

I. Auditing and Attestation: Engagement Acceptance and Understanding the Assignment (12% – 16%)

A. Determine Nature and Scope of Engagement

B. Consider the Firm's Policies and Procedures Pertaining to Client Acceptance and Continuance

C. Communicate With the Predecessor Auditor

D. Establish an Understanding With the Client and Document the Understanding Through an Engagement Letter or Other Written Communication With the Client

E. Consider Other Planning Matters

1. Consider using the work of other independent auditors

2. Determine the extent of the involvement of professionals possessing specialized skills
3. Consider the independence, objectivity, and competency of the internal audit function

F. Identify Matters Related to Planning and Prepare Documentation for Communications With Those Charged With Governance

II. Auditing and Attestation: Understanding the Entity and Its Environment (Including Internal Control) (16% – 20%)

A. Determine and Document Materiality

B. Conduct and Document Risk Assessment Discussions Among Audit Team, Concurrently With Discussion on Susceptibility of the Entity's Financial Statements to Material Misstatement Due to Fraud

C. Consideration of Fraud

1. Identify characteristics of fraud
2. Document required discussions regarding risk of fraud
3. Document inquiries of management about fraud
4. Identify and assess risks that may result in material misstatements due to fraud

D. Perform and Document Risk Assessment Procedures

1. Identify, conduct, and document appropriate inquiries of management and others within the entity
2. Perform appropriate analytical procedures to understand the entity and identify areas of risk
3. Obtain information to support inquiries through observation and inspection (including reading corporate minutes, etc.)

E. Consider Additional Aspects of the Entity and Its Environment, Including: Industry, Regulatory, and Other External Factors; Strategies and Business Risks; Financial Performance

F. Consider Internal Control

1. Perform procedures to assess the control environment, including consideration of the COSO [Committee of Sponsoring Organizations of the Treadway Commission] framework and identifying entity-level controls
2. Obtain and document an understanding of business processes and information flows
3. Determine the effect of information technology on the effectiveness of an entity's internal control
4. Perform risk assessment procedures to evaluate the design and implementation of internal controls relevant to an audit of financial statements
5. Identify key risks associated with general controls in a financial IT environment
6. Identify key risks associated with application controls in a financial IT environment
7. Assess whether the entity has designed controls to mitigate key risks associated with general controls or application functionality
8. Identify controls relevant to reliable financial reporting and the period-end financial reporting process

9. Consider limitations of internal control
10. Consider the effects of service organizations on internal control
11. Consider the risk of management override of internal controls

G. Document an Understanding of the Entity and Its Environment, Including Each Component of the Entity's Internal Control, in Order to Assess Risks

H. Assess and Document the Risk of Material Misstatements

1. Identify and document financial statement assertions and formulate audit objectives, including significant financial statement balances, classes of transactions, disclosures, and accounting estimates
2. Relate the identified risks to relevant assertions and consider whether the risks could result in a material misstatement to the financial statements
3. Assess and document the risk of material misstatement that relates to both financial statement level and specific assertions
4. Identify and document conditions and events that may indicate the risks of material misstatement

I. Identify and Document Significant Risks That Require Special Audit Consideration

1. Significant recent economic, accounting, or other developments
2. Related parties and related-party transactions
3. Improper revenue recognition
4. Nonroutine or complex transactions
5. Significant accounting estimates
6. Noncompliance with laws and regulations, including illegal acts

III. Auditing and Attestation: Performing Audit Procedures and Evaluating Evidence (16% – 20%)

A. Develop Overall Responses to Risks

1. Develop overall responses to risks identified and use the risks of material misstatement to drive the nature, timing, and extent of further audit procedures
2. Document significant risks identified, related controls evaluated, and overall responses to address assessed risks
3. Determine and document performance materiality/level(s) of tolerable misstatement

B. Perform Audit Procedures Responsive to the Risks of Material Misstatement; Obtain and Document Evidence to Form a Basis for Conclusions

1. Design and perform audit procedures whose nature, timing, and extent are responsive to the assessed risk of material misstatement
2. Integrating audits: in an integrated audit of internal control over financial reporting and the financial statements, design and perform testing of controls to accomplish the objectives of both audits simultaneously
3. Design, perform, and document tests of controls to evaluate design effectiveness
4. Design, perform, and document tests of controls to evaluate operating effectiveness
5. Perform substantive procedures

6. Perform audit sampling
7. Perform analytical procedures
8. Confirm balances and/or transactions with third parties
9. Examine inventories and other assets
10. Perform other tests of details, balances, and journal entries
11. Perform audit procedures on significant accounting estimates
12. Auditing fair value measurements and disclosures, including the use of specialists in evaluating estimates
13. Perform tests on unusual year-end transactions
14. Audits performed in accordance with International Standards on Auditing or auditing standards of another country: determine if differences exist and whether additional audit procedures are required
15. Evaluate contingencies
16. Obtain and evaluate lawyers' letters
17. Review subsequent events
18. Obtaining and placing reliance on representations from management
19. Identify material weaknesses, significant deficiencies, and other control deficiencies

IV. Auditing and Attestation: Evaluating Audit Findings, Communications, and Reporting (16% – 20%)

A. Perform Overall Analytical Procedures

B. Evaluate the Sufficiency and Appropriateness of Audit Evidence and Document Engagement Conclusions

C. Evaluate Whether Audit Documentation Is in Accordance With Professional Standards

D. Review the Work Performed by Others, Including Specialists and Other Auditors, to Provide Reasonable Assurance That Objectives Are Achieved

E. Document the Summary of Uncorrected Misstatements and Related Conclusions

F. Evaluate Whether Financial Statements Are Free of Material Misstatements

G. Consider the Entity's Ability to Continue as a Going Concern

H. Consider Other Information in Documents Containing Audited Financial Statements, e.g., Supplemental Information and Management's Discussion and Analysis

I. Retain Audit Documentation as Required by Standards and Regulations

J. Prepare Communications

1. Reports on audited financial statements
2. Reports required by government auditing standards
3. Reports on compliance with laws and regulations
4. Reports on internal control
5. Reports on the processing of transactions by service organizations

6. Reports on agreed-upon procedures
7. Reports on financial forecasts and projections
8. Reports on pro forma financial information
9. Special reports
10. Reissue reports
11. Communicate internal control related matters identified in the audit
12. Communications with those charged with governance
13. Subsequent discovery of facts existing at the date of the auditor's report
14. Consideration after the report date of omitted procedures

V. Accounting and Review Services Engagements (12% – 16%)

A. Plan the Engagement

1. Determine nature and scope of engagement
2. Decide whether to accept or continue the client and engagement, including determining the appropriateness of the engagement to meet the client's needs and consideration of independence standards
3. Establish an understanding with the client and document the understanding through an engagement letter or other written communication with the client
4. Consider change in engagement
5. Determine if reports are to be used by third parties

B. Obtain and Document Evidence to Form a Basis for Conclusions

1. Obtain an understanding of the client's operations, business, and industry
2. Obtain knowledge of accounting principles and practices in the industry and the client
3. Perform analytical procedures for review services
4. Obtain representations from management for review services
5. Perform other engagement procedures
6. Consider departures from generally accepted accounting principles (GAAP) or other comprehensive basis of accounting (OCBOA)
7. Prepare documentation from evidence gathered
8. Retain documentation as required by standards
9. Review the work performed to provide reasonable assurance that objectives are achieved

C. Prepare Communications

1. Reports on compilations
2. Reports on reviews
3. Restricted use of reports
4. Communicating to management and others
5. Subsequent discovery of facts existing at the date of the report
6. Consider degree of responsibility for supplementary information

VI. Professional Responsibilities (16% – 20%)

A. Ethics and Independence

1. Code of Professional Conduct (AICPA)
2. Requirements related to issuers, including the PCAOB, the SEC, and the Sarbanes-Oxley Act of 2002, Titles II and III, Section 303
3. Government Accountability Office (GAO)
4. Department of Labor (DOL)
5. Code of Ethics for Professional Accountants (IFAC)

B. Other Professional Responsibilities

1. A firm's system of quality control
2. General role, structure, and requirements of the PCAOB (Title I and Title IV of the Sarbanes-Oxley Act of 2002)

SECTION TWO: GENERAL COMMENTS ON THE EXAM

OVERVIEW

The exam is one component of the CPA licensing requirements—it is designed to measure the technical competence of candidates.

Although licensing occurs at the state or territory level (usually by a board of accountancy), the exam is uniform at all sites and has national acceptance. Passing the exam in one jurisdiction generally allows you to obtain a reciprocal certificate or license in another jurisdiction if you meet that jurisdiction's other requirements.

It is to your advantage to take the exam as soon as possible after completing the formal education requirements because it is essentially an academic exam that tests the breadth of material covered by a good accounting curriculum.

One of the first things you should do is review the AUD content and skill specification outline (CSO/SSO) developed by the examiners (see the first section of this appendix). The outline identifies the topics covered by the exam. The CSO/SSO emphasizes the body of knowledge and entry-level skills required for the practice of public accounting.

Exam Partners

The exam is offered jointly by three organizations on behalf of the boards of accountancy:

- The American Institute of Certified Public Accountants (AICPA) develops and scores the exam.
- The National Association of the State Boards of Accountancy (NASBA) maintains a database of exam candidates' information.
- Prometric, a commercial test provider, delivers the exam to eligible candidates at its computer-based test centers across the United States and its territories as well as select international locations.

Exam Content and Structure

The AUD exam section covers knowledge and application of auditing procedures; generally accepted auditing standards (GAAS); other standards and procedures for other types of engagements; and ethics, independence, and other professional responsibilities. It consists of 3 multiple-choice question testlets (groups of questions) containing a total of 90 questions and 1 simulation testlet containing 7 task-based simulations (TBS), including at least 1 research question. (See the "Exam Format" section of this appendix for more information about these testlets.) It is a 4-hour exam.

Exam Availability—Testing Windows

There are four exam windows each year; the first one starts in January. Each window covers the first two months of each calendar quarter. Between windows—during the third month of each quarter—the exam is not given.

Testing Windows	No Testing
January–February	March
April–May	June
July–August	September
October–November	December

You can take any or all sections (in any order) during any testing window; however, **you may *not* take the same exam section more than once during any one testing window**.

Time Limit for Passing All Four Sections

Generally, candidates must pass all four sections of the exam within a rolling time frame (typically 18 months), which begins on the date that the first section passed is taken. If all four sections are not passed within the required time frame, credit for the first section passed is lost and the time frame rolls to the date that the next section passed was taken and so on. Candidates should check with their board of accountancy regarding time limits.

Computer-Based Testing (CBT)/Tutorial and Sample Tests

The exam is fully computerized and is offered only in English.

It is extremely important that you become familiar with the latest version of the exam's software. The AICPA provides a tutorial and sample tests (aicpa.org/becomeacpa/cpaexam/forcandidates/tutorialandsampletest) on their website. You must review these before the exam because neither is available at the test centers. Before the beginning of any exam session, candidates must attest to the fact that they have had the opportunity to review the tutorial and the sample test. This requirement is intended to ensure that *before* candidates report to the test centers, they are knowledgeable about the exam process and thoroughly familiar with its functionality, format, and directions.

You should review the tutorial before taking the sample test. The time you spend with these materials will prevent you from losing any points on the exam due to unfamiliarity with the CBT system. The exam uses both a word processor and a spreadsheet program that are similar, but not identical, to common commercial applications. Even if you are completely comfortable with the commercial applications, you may find it unsettling to encounter different or missing functionalities on your exam day.

View the tutorial and take the sample test right before you begin studying for AUD and then again a week before the exam.

Exam Confidentiality / Nondisclosure Policy

The Uniform CPA Examination is nondisclosed. This means that candidates are not allowed to receive a copy of their exam questions after taking the exam. Also, candidates are required to accept the terms of the exam which include a promise not to reveal questions or answers. The AICPA no longer discloses the exam in order to increase consistency, facilitate computer administration of the exam, and improve exam quality by pretesting questions. (See the "Exam Scoring" section of this appendix for more information about pretest questions.) Because the exam is no longer completely changed every year, statistical equating methods are more relevant and the usefulness of specific questions as indicators of candidates' knowledge can be tested.

Editor Note: Only the AICPA has access to the exam questions and answers. For the past several years the AICPA has released (usually annually) a small number of questions with unofficial answers that it has removed from its pool of questions, i.e., it is their policy that released questions will not appear on future exams. The questions in Bisk CPA Review materials are based on questions from previously disclosed exams, questions released by the AICPA, and the teaching expertise of our editors. They are updated based upon content changes. (Due to the nondisclosure requirements, our editors cannot address questions from candidates about specific questions that appeared on their exams.)

Testing of New Pronouncements

Accounting and auditing pronouncements are eligible to be tested on the exam in the testing window beginning six months after a pronouncement's *effective* date, unless early application is permitted. When early application is permitted, a new pronouncement may be tested in the window beginning 6 months after the *issue* date. In this case, beginning with that exam window, both the extant [still existing] and the new pronouncement can be tested until the new pronouncement becomes effective. Regarding new US GAAS pronouncements, early application is permitted if the new or updated AU section does not expressly prohibit it.

Reference Materials

All the content you need to review to pass the exam is in your Bisk CPA Review texts; however, if you would like more detailed coverage in any area, you can consult the actual authoritative literature. Pronouncements are available from the American Institute of Certified Public Accountants (AICPA), Public Company Accounting Oversight Board (PCAOB), and the International Federation of Accountants (IFAC).

The AICPA offers candidates with their Notice to Schedule (NTS) a *free* six-month subscription to online access to authoritative literature used in the AUD section of the exam. Visit their website (aicpa.org/becomeacpa/cpaexam/forcandidates/howtoprepare/pages/literature.aspx) for more information and to subscribe.

IFAC makes the majority of their material available for download free of charge—printed copies must be purchased.

The PCAOB's standards can be viewed on their website (pcaobus.org).

To order materials from the AICPA or IFAC contact:

AICPA's Service Center
220 Leigh Farm Road
Durham, NC 27707-8110
US telephone: (888) 777-7077
Outside United States:
(919) 402-4500
service@cpa2biz.com
cpa2biz.com

IFAC
529 Fifth Avenue, 6th Floor
New York, NY 10017 USA
Telephone: (212) 286-9344
Communications@ifac.org
ifac.org

THE UNIFORM CPA EXAMINATION PROCESS

The information presented here is intended to give you an overall idea of what the exam will be like. It is **not** intended to take the place of *The Candidate Bulletin* available from the AICPA's website (aicpa.org). (See the specific page's web address under the next heading or select *CPA Exam* from the drop-down menu under *Become a CPA*; then click on *CPA Exam* in the bullet list on the left near the top of the screen; then click on *For Candidates* on the next screen's bullet list; then click on *Candidate Bulletin* on the next screen's bullet list.) *The Candidate Bulletin* will provide you with more detailed instructions and the most current information.

The Candidate Bulletin

The Candidate Bulletin provides important general information about the entire process, including the requirements for taking the exam. Read it. At the test center you will be required to affirm that you have had the opportunity to read it and that you agree to all of its terms and conditions. *The Candidate Bulletin* is available for download on the websites of both the AICPA (aicpa.org/becomeacpa/cpaexam/forcandidates/candidatebulletin) and NASBA (nasba.org/exams/cpaexam).

Forty-five days before your exam, you should check one of the above websites to confirm you have the most recent version.

In addition to understanding the basic process as described in *The Candidate Bulletin*, **you need to know your board of accountancy's requirements for each step in the exam process**.

Contacting Your Board of Accountancy

Certified public accountants are licensed to practice by the individual boards of accountancy of the states and territories (jurisdictions) of the United States. Each jurisdiction sets its own requirements for education, examination, and experience. The NASBA website (nasba.org) has links to all of the board sites.

Applying to Take the Exam

Both US applicants and those from outside the United States must select the US jurisdiction in which they wish to qualify for the exam and to be subsequently licensed.

In addition to the exam, boards of accountancy rely upon other means to ensure that candidates possess the necessary attributes, including background checks, interviews, letters of reference, affidavits of employment, ethics exams, and educational requirements.

Depending on your jurisdiction, you should either apply online at cpacentral.nasba.org or contact your board of accountancy directly to apply—see *The Candidate Bulletin* for the approach required by your jurisdiction.

You must apply and submit any required documents and fees each time you want to take one or more exam sections. (Some jurisdictions arrange for an exam administrator, such as CPA Examination Services, a division of NASBA, to handle the review of applications, collection of fees, etc.)

It is extremely important that you complete the application correctly and submit it before the deadline. Errors or omissions may result in the delay of approval or rejection of your application. Be sure to enclose all required materials. Requirements vary as to education, experience, and other matters, as do cutoff dates to apply to receive approval in time to sit for a particular testing window. If you have not already done so, call or visit the website of the appropriate board for their specific and current requirements.

Pay special attention to the *form of your name on your application*. Your application information will be used to generate your Notice to Schedule (NTS) and the *order* and *spelling* of your name on your NTS must appear exactly the same as it appears on your 2 ids—the 3 items you must bring to the test center to gain admission. (See the topic on personal identification in this same section.)

International Applicants

The exam given at select international locations is offered only in English and is the same computerized test as the one administered in the United States. Please see the exam's website (aicpa.org/becomeacpa/cpaexam) for specific locations and schedules.

Applicants from countries other than the United States must follow the same basic steps as US applicants. They must select a US jurisdiction in which they wish to qualify (that participates in the International CPA Examination Administration Program) and file an application with its board of accountancy or exam administrator. Any special instructions for candidates who have completed their education outside the United States are included in the board of accountancy requirements.

Regardless of which board of accountancy has declared you eligible for the exam, in addition to paying any domestic testing fees, you must pay additional nonrefundable fees for each exam section you plan to take at an international test center.

For more information on the international administration of the exam, visit the international section of the NASBA website (nasba.org/international/international-exam).

Fees

The amount and types of fees as well as the timing for their payment vary by jurisdiction. You may be required to pay all or some of the fees when you submit your application. Your board or its exam administrator may instruct you to pay some of the fees to different entities. There are additional fees for taking the exam in Guam or international locations.

It is best not to apply for a section of the exam until you are ready to take it because refunds of fees are usually not available—check with your board or its exam administrator regarding their specific refund policy. Generally, if you fail to make an appointment during the period your NTS is valid or need to cancel your appointment and do not wish to reschedule it, you will not receive a refund or a credit; nor will you receive a refund or a credit if you fail to appear for your appointment at the test center or give less than 24 hours notice for a cancellation. In either case, you will probably have to reapply for the exam and pay the fees again.

Notice to Schedule (NTS)

The Candidate Bulletin includes a sample NTS.

Once a board or its exam administrator determines that a candidate is eligible to sit for the exam (and all fees are paid), they inform NASBA and NASBA adds the candidate to its database. (Thus, NASBA is able to ensure that no candidate can sit for the same exam section more than once during a single exam window.)

When you receive your NTS, listing the exam section(s) you have been approved to take, you can make your appointment to sit for the exam(s) with Prometric. **You can *not* schedule an exam without an NTS**. (From whom you receive your NTS varies by jurisdiction.)

You should verify the accuracy of your NTS *before* making your appointment. You must present your NTS and proper identification to be admitted to the exam room at the testing center. Make sure that your name as it appears on your NTS exactly matches your name on the IDs you will be using to check in at the testing center. If your name on your NTS is different in any way (the order or spelling) from your IDs, you will not be permitted to test; however, see the following section on personal identification for two exceptions to this "exact match" rule. If any information on your NTS is incorrect or your name doesn't match your IDs, immediately contact your board or its exam administrator to request a correction.

Your NTS will include an expiration date; it is only valid for a set period of time (determined by your board—usually 6 months) during which you must schedule and take the approved exam section(s) it lists. Your NTS is valid for one testing event or until the expiration date, whichever is first exhausted for each exam section. Cancelling an exam appointment does *not* change the expiration date of your NTS. If you do not take all sections for which you are registered before your NTS expires, you will **not** be able to extend it or receive a refund of any of the fees you have paid. Fees submitted for an expired NTS can **not** be applied to future exams.

You can **not** have more than one open NTS for the same exam section. You must receive the score or allow the NTS to expire before you can apply for the same exam section again and receive a new NTS for that exam section.

Your NTS also contains your exam section identification number which is your *launch code* [password] that you will enter as part of the log-on process once you are seated at a testing center.

Personal Identification

You must have **two forms of identification. One of them must contain a recent photograph. (Your photograph ID must not appear to be damaged or altered in any way.) Both IDs must bear your signature. Neither can be expired. If you do not present acceptable identification along with your NTS, you will *not* be allowed to take the exam and you will forfeit all fees for that section.**

See *The Candidate Bulletin* to review a list of examples of acceptable forms of *primary* and *secondary* identification—**one of your IDs must appear on their *primary* list**. (There is also a list of *un*acceptable forms of ID.)

The same form of your name must appear on your NTS and the identification you present at the test center with the following exceptions:

- The middle initial can be substituted for the middle name, for example, the NTS reads Michael A. Smith, but the name on the candidate's ID reads Michael Albert Smith, or vice versa.
- Truncated (shortened) names are allowable on a candidate's driver's license (a primary form of ID), as long as the name on the signature [secondary] ID exactly matches the name on the NTS.

If the test center staff has questions about the identification presented, you may be asked for additional proof of identity. Editor Note: Bring an extra acceptable ID, just in case.

Admittance to the test center and examination does *not* imply that your identification is valid or that your scores will be reported if subsequent investigations reveal impersonation or forgery.

There are separate requirements listed in *The Candidate Bulletin* for identification for international test centers.

Testing Accommodations

Testing accommodations must be requested as part of the application process. Unfortunately, some types of accommodations are only available at a limited number of test centers. If you need testing accommodations, check with your board or its exam administrator and give them your information to request their approval. If approved, the type of accommodation needed will be sent to NASBA. NASBA will ensure that the information is included on your NTS and sent to Prometric.

When you receive your NTS, if the accommodations indicated are not correct, you will need to contact your board or its exam administrator again *before* scheduling your appointment—changes to testing accommodations can **not** be made by Prometric.

Candidates are advised that they may receive limited or no accommodations if they choose to test in an international location. The testing accommodations on the NTS are applicable for testing in the United States and US territories only—approved testing accommodations for international locations will be detailed in an e-mail from NASBA.

Scheduling Your Exam Appointment With Prometric if *No* Testing Accommodations Are Needed

The exam is offered 5 days (and at some test centers, 7 days) per week.

Generally, you will be allowed to take the exam at any one of the authorized Prometric test centers in the United States and designated international locations, whether or not the test center is located in the jurisdiction where you are seeking your initial license. Check with your board of accountancy or their exam administrator to find out if there are any restrictions on the location where you can take the exam.

You may select any available date during the open window; however, **you must schedule your exam appointment at least five days in advance** of the day you would like to sit for the exam. (For example, if you call or go online to schedule an appointment on Monday, the first possible available date will be Saturday of the same week.) If taking the exam on a particular day, time, and/or location is important to you, you should schedule it at least 45 days in advance to increase your chances of getting your first choice. And remember, you must take each exam section listed on your NTS by the expiration date on your NTS.

Have your NTS in front of you when you contact Prometric (you will need to provide information from it) and also have your second and third choices for test dates, times, and locations ready, in case your first choice is not available. Some large cities have more than one test center, in this case, double-check the location of your test center.

You may schedule, confirm, reschedule, or cancel an exam appointment or change its location as well as find a preferred testing location online (prometric.com/cpa; 24-hour access) or by calling (800) 580-9648 Monday through Friday from 8:00 a.m. to 8:00 p.m. eastern time. The AICPA recommends using the Internet option. See *The Candidate Bulletin* for deadlines and fees associated with changes to appointments—depending on when you notify Prometric of a change or cancellation, you may be required to pay a rescheduling fee or you may forfeit the exam fees.

You must schedule a separate appointment for each exam section you are planning to take. It is not necessary to make all appointments during the same online visit or phone call. If you schedule more than one exam section for the same day, you must make sure the times don't overlap and that you have allowed enough time between exams to check in (at least 30 minutes before your appointment time). Unfortunately, the online system will not warn you if your appointments overlap.

You should receive an e-mail confirmation of your appointment from Prometric whether you made your appointment via the website or phone. If you do not receive an e-mail, you should print a confirmation via the Prometric website. This is available to you even if you made the appointment using the phone.

Refer to *The Candidate Bulletin* for more detailed information about scheduling your appointment or if you are planning on taking the exam in Guam or an international location.

Scheduling Your Exam Appointment With Prometric if Testing Accommodations Have Been Preapproved

Candidates with testing accommodations preapproved by their board or exam administrator (and indicated on their NTS) **must call Prometic at least 10 days in advance** of the desired date **and must call (800) 967-1139 to schedule** their appointment. Changes to appointments must be made by calling this same number. You should receive an e-mail confirmation of your appointment from Prometric.

Candidates approved for testing accommodations can *not* use the Prometric website to schedule or make changes to their appointments—if they use the website, they will **not** be provided with testing accommodations. Refer to *The Candidate Bulletin* for more detailed information about scheduling your appointment.

See *The Candidate Bulletin* for more information about testing accommodations in international testing locations. It is highly recommended to call Prometric at least 30 days in advance of the desired date for these locations. Further, you may receive limited or no accommodations if you choose to test in an international location.

Exam Appointment Time

The appointment time on the confirmation you receive from Prometric will reflect the exam testing time plus 30 minutes. The additional 30 minutes is **not** additional testing time—it is the time allowed to enter your password, respond to the introductory screens, and take the survey at the end of the exam. For example, the *testing* time for the AUD exam is 4 hours; thus, the *appointment* time will be for 4½ hours.

You will also need to plan for *another* 30 minutes **before** your *appointment* time to allow time for check-in and seating procedures. This extra 30 minutes is **not** reflected in your appointment time.

Checking In on Exam Day

You must arrive at least 30 minutes before your scheduled appointment to allow enough time for check-in and seating procedures. (If you arrive after your scheduled appointment time, you may be denied permission to test and you will not receive a refund.)

You will not be admitted without your **NTS** and **2 acceptable forms of identification** and you will forfeit all fees for that exam section. Security measures include the following.

- Your ID will be scanned and swiped in a magnetic strip and barcode reader.
    - An electronic image of your photo ID will be captured
- A digital photograph of your face will be taken.
- Biometrics will be used to capture your fingerprint—this is also required before and after breaks.
- You will be asked to turn your pockets out and then you will be scanned with a hand-held metal detector wand prior to each entry into the exam room, including returns from breaks.

You will be lent a key to a very *small* locker for storage of a few belongings, such as your purse/wallet and cell phone, because you are not allowed to take these items into the exam room. (You should only bring what is absolutely necessary to the test center. Test center staff will **not** be responsible for lost or stolen items.)

In lieu of scratch paper and pencils, candidates will be provided with 2 double-sided, laminated, colored sheets called *note boards*, as well as a fine point marker for making notations. You will be directed to write your launch code (from your NTS) on your note boards. If you need additional writing space, you may request additional note boards from the test center staff, but you must first turn in the ones you initially received. You will be required to return the note boards to the test center staff when your exam is over.

<table>
<tr><th></th><th>Time Allocation</th><th>Activity</th></tr>
<tr><td>Before
exam appointment</td><td>At least
30 minutes</td><td>Check in and get seated.
(Late arrivals may not be allowed to take the exam.)</td></tr>
<tr><td rowspan="3">AUD exam
appointment
↓
4 ½ hours
↓</td><td>10-minute limit
enforced</td><td>Respond to the introductory screens after log-in.</td></tr>
<tr><td>4-hour limit
enforced</td><td>Take the AUD exam and discretionary break(s) between testlets—
no more than
10 minutes for any break.</td></tr>
<tr><td>20 minutes
or less</td><td>Complete
voluntary survey.</td></tr>
</table>

Exam Room Regulations

There are very strict rules for the exam room.

Absolutely *no* visitors are allowed into the test center.

You must *not* communicate, orally or otherwise, with other candidates when in the exam room. To avoid even the appearance of cheating, you must not look at another candidate's materials or workstation.

During the exam, you must not read or process your thoughts out loud. Any conduct that unnecessarily disturbs other candidates is prohibited.

No cell phones, calculators, or other electronic devices are allowed. No purses or wallets are allowed. No food, beverages, or tobacco products are allowed. **See *The Candidate Bulletin* for a long list of prohibited items and other restrictions. Don't assume they will be what you may expect**. For example, you are **not** allowed to have a watch (a countdown of the time remaining to complete the exam will display on your computer screen during the exam); jewelry—a pendant necklace or large earrings; an eyeglass case; or a container of any kind—not even a transparent, plastic bag. (Keyed lockers large enough for a few small personal belongings will be available—only bring what is absolutely necessary to the test center.)

You *are* allowed to bring soft, foam earplugs with no strings attached, subject to an inspection by the test center staff.

Jackets, coats, and sweaters are also prohibited; however, iIf you require a separate sweater or a light jacket due to room temperature, it must be worn at all times.

All exam sessions are audio/video taped to document any unusual activity.

After checking in, you will be escorted to your workstation (seating is assigned by Prometric) where you must remain seated during the exam except when given permission to leave the exam room for an authorized break.

Exam's Introductory Screens

After you enter your password (launch code from your NTS), you have only 10 minutes to read and respond to the introductory screens. A 10-minute countdown timer will display on these screens. You should move through these screens quickly—ten minutes is enough time to review them and respond, but there is no time to do anything else.

If the 10-minute time limit is exceeded, your exam session will automatically terminate and you will not be allowed to restart the exam. (In this case, you must leave the test center, forfeit fees, reapply to test in the next exam window, and receive a score of zero.)

One of these screens presents the *Policy Statement and Agreement Regarding Exam Confidentiality and the Taking of Breaks*. A copy of this statement is included in *The Candidate Bulletin* so you can review it beforehand. If you do not accept it, you will not be allowed to take the exam and your fees will be forfeited.

If you encounter a problem with your computer or the testing environment, you should immediately report it to the test center staff.

Exam Timer

The time remaining to complete the exam (displayed on the title bar of your computer screen) begins to count down after you have moved from the introductory screens to the first testlet. **The countdown does *not* pause while you are taking a break**.

Breaks

Breaks are only allowed between testlets—after a break, you can *not* return to a testlet you were working on prior to your break. If you leave the exam room at any other time, you will not be allowed to return, and the incident will be reported to your board of accountancy. (A testlet is a segment of the exam—see the "Exam Format" section of this appendix.)

You do **not** have to take a break. After each testlet, a candidate has the option to take a break, but the exam's countdown will continue so you should use any break time sparingly and judiciously. Also, breaks over 10 minutes may be reported to your board of accountancy.

If you choose to take a break, the test center staff will confirm that you have completed a testlet and you will be asked to provide a fingerprint prior to leaving and again on your return. You will also be scanned again with the metal detector wand upon your return.

When you return to your computer you will be required to enter your exam launch code (password) in order to continue the exam.

Checking Out

After you have completed your exam you will be asked to respond to a survey about your exam experience. When you finish, simply exit the room quietly. You must turn in your note boards, sign a log book, and complete other procedures as directed by the test center staff. They will then dismiss you. You will receive a *Confirmation of Attendance* which you should keep in case you need the contact information it provides if you have a question or concern.

Candidate Requests for Question Review

Candidates who believe they have identified a problem with an exam question should contact the AICPA Examinations Team in writing by fax or letter. See *The Candidate Bulletin* for the fax number or mailing address and the AICPA's specific instructions. Your fax or letter must be *received* within *four* days of taking the exam. Include your exam section identification number (exam launch code or password); however, you should **not** include the exact wording or attempt to outline the question—simply provide enough information for the examiners to identify the question, such as "question number 12 in the first testlet" or "the *Interest Expense* tab in the 1st simulation." You should include the nature of your concern, your rationale, and, if possible, references to support your position. According to *The Candidate Bulletin*, the AICPA is unable to respond directly to candidates, but reviews every fax or letter received by the deadline.

Receipt of Scores

The exam is scored by the AICPA. Each exam section is scored separately. (See this appendix's section on "Exam Scoring" for more information.) The AICPA does *not* have access to candidate identities—candidates' anonymity is preserved throughout the exam and scoring process. (Exam responses are identified by exam section identification number only—this is the same number as your exam launch code or password.) The AICPA forwards the advisory scores to NASBA. NASBA matches the scores to the candidates and forwards the scores to the boards of accountancy. *After the boards approve the scores*, they are released to the candidates by NASBA. (The AICPA and Prometric do **not** provide score information to candidates.) NASBA will **not** give out scores over the phone.

See *The Candidate Bulletin* for NASBA's current estimated time line for release of scores to the boards. Scores are generally released during regular business hours. Be aware that some boards need at least a day beyond these target dates to process and approve the scores after they receive them from NASBA.

Postexam Diagnostics

If you fail an exam section you will receive a *Candidate Performance Report*. It will compare your performance by content area and question type to those who scored between 75 and 80 (the "just passed" category). This is intended to serve as a study aid for retaking the exam.

Contact your board or their exam administrator about their specific re-examination policy. Remember, you may only retake that section in a *future* testing window. You may **not** repeat any exam section within the same testing window.

Score Review and Appeal Processes

See *The Candidate Bulletin* for information about both of these separate processes. You will need to contact your board or its exam administrator if you decide to apply for either. If you obtain their approval, you must pay the required fees.

A score review is **not** a regrading, i.e., it is *not* an opportunity to find additional points; review content; or to have alternate responses considered. It is simply an independent verification of a candidate's score. For the AUD exam, it involves making certain that the approved answer key was used and that it was applied correctly.

You may only apply for a review for a short period of time after your score has been reported to you; check with your board or its exam administrator regarding the deadline. The AICPA cautions candidates that a score change after a review is very unlikely due to the quality checks that take place prior to their reporting of scores.

An appeal is the opportunity to appeal a failing score because you would like to challenge an exam question. For the AUD exam, an appeal allows you to review the multiple-choice questions and simulations you answered incorrectly together with your responses and submit your comments online. It is conducted in an authorized location in the presence of a representative of your board or its exam administrator.

Be aware that some jurisdictions do **not** permit appeals (see *The Candidate Bulletin* for a list; you should also check with your board or its exam administrator).

The option to apply for an appeal in jurisdictions that allow it is only available for a short period of time after your score has been reported to you; check with your board or its exam administrator regarding the deadline.

SECTION THREE: EXAM STRATEGIES

OVERVIEW

The exam is more than a test of your knowledge and technical competence. It is also a test of your ability to function under psychological pressure. Your objective is to avoid surprises and eliminate hassles and distractions. You want to be in complete control so you can concentrate on the exam material, rather than the exam situation. By taking charge of the exam, you will be able to handle pressure in a constructive manner. The keys to control are adequate preparation and an effective exam strategy.

Preparation

Advance preparation will arm you with the confidence you need to overcome the psychological pressure of the exam. As you complete your review, you will cover most of the material that will be tested; it is unlikely that any question will deal with a topic you have not studied. However, if an unfamiliar topic is tested, you will not be dismayed because you will have learned to use our Solutions Approach™ to derive the best possible answer from the knowledge you possess.

The components of your advance preparation include the following.

- Comprehensive review materials such as your Bisk CPA Review program
- A study plan that enables you to review each subject area methodically and thoroughly
- A method for ongoing self-evaluation of your level of proficiency
- An understanding of the scoring process
- A Solutions Approach™ for answering exam questions

Exam Strategies

Another key to controlling the exam is to develop effective strategies for the days you take the exam. Your objective is to avoid surprises and frustrations so you can focus your full concentration on the questions and your answers.

You should be familiar with the format of the exam and know exactly what you will do when you enter the exam room. Remember to read all instructions carefully, whether general or specific to a particular question. Disregarding the instructions could result in a loss of points.

Knowing in advance what to expect while taking the exam and planning how you will spend your exam time will help you avoid any confusion and save you valuable time while answering questions. This will greatly enhance your probability of passing.

EXAM FORMAT

The exam is fully computerized and is offered only in English.

Reviewing the tutorial and taking the sample test on the AICPA's website (aicpa.org/becomeacpa/cpaexam /forcandidates/tutorialandsampletest) will allow you to:

- Become familiar with the exam's directions and navigation system
- See how the questions are formatted
- Use the exam's software while answering a few practice questions

It is important for you to take advantage of this opportunity. Moreover, *The Candidate Bulletin* states that thorough familiarity with the exam's functionality, format, and directions is required before candidates report to test centers.

Four Testlets

Questions are grouped into 4 testlets (groups of questions). For the AUD section, the testing software presents 3 multiple-choice testlets followed by 1 testlet of simulations. You can **not** pick the order of the testlets to answer, but *within* a testlet, you can answer the questions in any order and you can return to questions. **Once you indicate you have completed a testlet, you can *not* return to it**.

Multiple-Choice Questions

Each exam section has 3 multiple-choice testlets. The AUD multiple-choice testlets have 30 questions each (a total of 90 questions). The questions in each testlet are in random order, i.e., they are *not* presented in the same order as the AUD content specification outline (CSO). (The AUD CSO is in the first section of this appendix.)

Multi-Stage Testing for Multiple-Choice Testlets

There are 2 levels of multiple-choice testlets, labeled *medium* and *difficult*. Within the testlets, questions often vary substantially in their level of difficulty, but across testlets, those testlets labeled *difficult* contain more difficult questions than those labeled *medium*.

The first testlet is always at the *medium* level. After you finish a multiple-choice question testlet, the software will select the next testlet based on your performance on the previous testlet(s). If you do well, the next testlet will be *difficult*. Otherwise, you will receive another *medium* testlet. Thus, if you find the questions are becoming more challenging, you should be encouraged rather than discouraged—this is probably an indication that you are doing well. (The exam will *not* indicate the level of your testlets.)

This testing model is **not** used with the simulations. Nor are the simulations chosen based on your performance on the multiple-choice questions—the simulations are preassigned.

The scoring procedures incorporate the difficulty of the testlets so candidates are scored fairly regardless of the difficulty of the testlets they take.

The examiners' intent is that analysis of the testing statistics will eventually allow them to reduce the number of questions, resulting in more time for testing skills.

Simulations

The AUD section has one simulation testlet containing 7 task-based simulations (TBS), including at least 1 research question.

A TBS is a condensed case study that tests accounting knowledge and skills using real life work-related situations. Each is expected to take approximately 8 to 15 minutes. All TBS are intended to assess knowledge and skills appropriate for an entry-level accountant. Accounting knowledge is tested through a variety of tasks, for example, you may be required to select answers from lists or enter numbers into worksheets.

See "Appendix C: Research Skills" in this text for information about the research questions.

Authoritative Literature

The AUD exam's fourth testlet of TBS includes access to a database of certain portions of the professional standards issued by the AICPA and PCAOB.

EXAM SCORING

Each exam section is scored separately.

Generally, boards of accountancy report scores on a numeric scale of 0-99, with 75 as a passing score.

All questions on the AUD exam are scored electronically by the AICPA.

An understanding of the scoring procedure will help you maximize points on the exam. Remember that your objective is to pass the exam. You cannot afford to spend time on activities that will not affect your score or to ignore opportunities to increase it.

Pretest Questions

Any of the four testlets can include pretest questions which are used to develop future exams. **Pretest questions are *not* included in your score**. Instead, your responses to pretest questions are used to evaluate the questions' statistical performance.

You will **not** be able to distinguish the pretest questions from the questions that will be scored. On the AUD exam it is possible that as many as 15 of the 90 multiple-choice questions will be pretest questions and, likewise, 1 of the 7 simulations.

Scoring Weights

In AUD, the multiple-choice questions make up 60% of the total score and the simulations make up 40%. Thus, you can **not** pass AUD just by doing well on the multiple-choice questions.

Scoring Implications

It is important to understand that your score for these questions is based solely on your *correct* answers. In other words, you receive credit for correct answers and **you are *not* penalized for incorrect responses**. Thus, **you should answer every question**. If you do not know the answer, make an intelligent guess.

You should avoid getting "bogged down" on any one question. Move along and answer all the questions in a testlet. This helps to avoid leaving any questions unanswered or answering in a panic due to poor budgeting of test time.

To summarize:

- Attempt an answer on every question.
- Respond directly to the requirements of the questions.
- Answer all requirements.
- Develop a Solutions Approach™ for answering the questions.
- Allocate your exam time based on the exam's scoring weights.

More Information

If you would like more information on how the exam is scored, visit the AICPA's website to read "How Is the CPA Exam Scored?" (aicpa.org/becomeacpa/cpaexam/psychometricsandscoring/scoringinformation/pages/default.aspx).

THE SOLUTIONS APPROACH™

The Bisk CPA Review Solutions Approach™ is an efficient, systematic method of organizing and solving exam questions. Even a little knowledge can go a long way if you use a sound approach. Our approach, when properly developed and practiced, can make the difference between passing and failing.

Recommended Approach

We suggest a number of steps for deriving a solution that will help maximize your score on the exam. Although you should remember the important steps in our approach, you should adapt them to your own taste and requirements. When you work the questions at the conclusion of each chapter, make sure to use your adapted version of our approach.

It is very important that you attempt to answer a question and formulate your solution *before* looking at the answer. The worst thing you can do is look at a question and then turn to the answer without working it. This will build false confidence and will not help you to develop a Solutions Approach™.

Solutions Approach™ for Multiple-Choice Question Testlets

We recommend the following approach for the 3 multiple-choice question testlets. (The timing suggested is based on the exam's scoring weight of 60% for the multiple-choice questions.)

- Read the directions at the beginning of the testlet to ensure you know what is expected. You should have already become familiar with the format via the AICPA's tutorial and sample test on their website (aicpa.org/becomeacpa/cpaexam/forcandidates/tutorialandsampletest).
- Answer the questions in order. This is a proven, systematic approach. You should limit yourself to a maximum of 1½ minutes per question for this first pass. Under no circumstances should you allow yourself to fall behind schedule. If a question is difficult or long, be sure to remain cognizant of the passage of time. If after a minute or so you feel that it is too costly to continue, select the answer you tentatively feel is the best, flag the question for review, and go on to the next question.
- Read each question carefully, so you know exactly what is being asked. Note key words. Be alert for negative requirements which are easily missed ("Which of the following does *not*...") and when the requirement is an exception ("...except for..."). The examiners normally use boldface type for "not" and "except," but you should not rely on that practice.
- Perform any intermediate calculations necessary for the determination of the correct answer.
- *Before looking at the possible responses, anticipate the answer if you can.* Many incorrect responses are based on the erroneous application of one or more items in the text of the question; thus, it is extremely helpful to anticipate the answer before you read the alternatives and are possibly led astray.
- Read the alternatives given.
- Select the best alternative. Very often, one or two possible responses will be clearly incorrect. Of the other alternatives, be sure to select the one that best answers the question asked—sometimes more than one alternative is a correct statement, *but only one answers the question*. If there are two close possibilities, make sure you select the best one in light of the facts and requirements of the question.
- After you have completed your first pass, return to the questions you flagged for review and attempt to better answer them if you have time remaining from what you allocated for that testlet. If you cannot find a better answer, use your preliminary answer because your first impressions are often correct.
- After completing all of the individual questions in a testlet, go back and make sure that you have answered each question. Your score will be based on the number of correct answers with *no penalty for incorrect responses*. Double-check your answers if time permits—remember, you can **not** go back to a previously completed testlet.

Solutions Approach™ for the Simulation Testlet

The last testlet in AUD consists of 7 task-based simulations (TBS), including at least 1 research question.

A TBS is a group of objective questions, based on a hypothetical situation. What differentiates it from a multiple-choice question is the various formats that may be used to answer the TBS. The formats include, but are not limited to, the following: selecting the correct answer from a list of possible choices (somewhat like a multiple-choice question); typing a response into a designated area; or doing some spreadsheet calculations. The point being no matter what type of format that may be used in a TBS; remember, that it is merely another type of objective question.

We recommend the following approach for the simulation testlet. (The timing suggested is based on the exam's scoring weight of 40% for the simulations.)

- Read the directions at the beginning of the testlet to ensure you know what is expected. You should have already become familiar with the format of the exam via the AICPA's tutorial and sample test on their website (aicpa.org/becomeacpa/cpaexam/forcandidates/tutorialandsampletest).
- Answer the research question first. Try to complete it within 5 or 6 minutes. (See "Appendix C: Research Skills" in this text for information about the research questions.)
- Read the titles (taking the AICPA's sample test will allow you to see how to locate the titles) to each of the TBS and work the one with the subject matter you believe you are most knowledgeable about first. By working the TBS you are most knowledgeable about first, you will save time and become more confident as you proceed.
- Read all the information provided in the TBS and the requirements very carefully, noting exactly what is being asked.
- Perform any intermediate calculations necessary to the determination of the correct answers.
- Read the alternatives given and select the ones that best answer the questions asked.
- After completing all of the individual responses required, go back and double-check that you have, in fact, answered each question in the TBS. Your score will be based on the number of correct answers *with no penalty for incorrect responses*.
- Do **not** answer the rest of the TBS in order. Reread the titles for the remaining TBS and and continue to work them in the order of the subject matter you are *most* knowledgeable about until you have completed the last one—the one you believe you are the *least* knowledgeable about.
- You generally should limit yourself to a maximum of 14 minutes per TBS. Under no circumstances should you allow yourself to fall behind schedule. If a TBS seems difficult or long, be sure to remain cognizant of the passage of time. If after a few minutes or so you feel that it is too costly to continue, answer all requirements with the response you tentatively feel is best, flag it for review, and go on to the next TBS.
- Return to any TBS you flagged and attempt to better answer it if you have time remaining. (Remember that you can **not** go back to any of the multiple-choice testlets.) If you cannot come up with any better answers, use your preliminary choices because your first impressions are often correct.

Note Boards

Identify and label your notations to avoid confusing yourself during the stress of the exam.

EXAM TIME MANAGEMENT

You must plan how you will use your exam time and adhere to your schedule. If you budget your time carefully, you should be able to answer all questions. Work quickly but efficiently, i.e., use the Solutions Approach™ discussed in this appendix.

Remember, you must complete each testlet in the order it is presented—the 3 multiple-choice testlets are presented first, followed by the simulation testlet. This sample schedule has been prepared based on the AUD exam's scoring weights—60% for the multiple-choice questions and 40% for the simulations.

Be sure to adjust your time budget to accommodate your individual needs and strengths, for example, you may prefer a different allocation of time between the multiple-choice testlets and the simulation testlet; however, **under no circumstance should you allow yourself less than 1 hour for the simulation [last] testlet**.

	Minutes
Answer the first multiple-choice question testlet.	46
Answer the second multiple-choice question testlet.	46
Answer the third multiple-choice question testlet.	46
Take a break, if you have time.	5
Review the simulation titles to pick the first one to answer.	1
Answer the simulations.	96
Total exam time	240

You should use **all** the allotted time. If you finish a testlet ahead of your schedule, go back and reconsider the more difficult questions.

EXAM CHECKLISTS

What to have on hand for each exam section:

- Your NTS and 2 forms of acceptable matching identification; see *The Candidate Bulletin*
- Cash and/or a major credit card
- An inexpensive watch (not allowed in the exam room) to facilitate your timely arrival at the testing center
- Comfortable clothing that can be loosened to suit varying temperatures (what is worn into the exam room must be worn throughout the testing period; once at the testing center, you can remove a jacket or sweater and place it in a small locker before entering the exam room)
- Appropriate review materials and tools for final reviews during the last days before the exam
- Healthy snack foods (not allowed in exam room)

If you will be staying overnight:

- Make travel arrangements, including contingency plans, well in advance.
- Reserve a room for the preceding night so you can check in, locate the testing center well before the exam, and get a good night's rest.
- Bring your hotel (and any other) confirmations.
- Use your own alarm device—don't rely on a hotel wake-up call.
- If crossing time zones, plan to compensate accordingly.
- International candidates should apply for passports and visas well in advance.

Evenings before exam sections:

- Briefly review your Bisk CPA Review chapter outlines for the next day's exam section(s).
- Eat lightly and monitor your intake of alcohol and caffeine.
- Get a good night's rest.
- Do **not** try to cram. A brief review of your notes will help to focus your attention on important points and remind you that you are well prepared, but too much cramming can undermine your self-confidence.

The morning of each exam section:

- Eat a satisfying meal before your exam. It will be several hours before your next meal. Eat enough to ward off hunger, but not so much that you feel uncomfortable.
- Dress appropriately. Wear layers you can loosen to suit varying temperatures in the room. If you require a separate sweater or a jacket due to room temperature, it must be worn at all times.
- Arrive at the exam center at least 30 minutes early.

What to bring to the testing center:

- Your NTS and 2 forms of acceptable matching identification; see *The Candidate Bulletin*
- An inexpensive watch (to be left outside the exam room; the exam's computer screen displays the time remaining to complete the exam) to ensure you arrive **at least 30 minutes early**
- Take only those articles that you need to get to and from the testing center; avoid taking any articles that are not allowed in the exam room, especially valuable ones (test center staff will **not** be held responsible for lost or stolen items); see *The Candidate Bulletin* for a list of prohibited items

---

TEN ATTRIBUTES OF EXAM SUCCESS

We believe that successful CPA candidates possess these ten characteristics that contribute to their ability to pass the exam.

1. Positive Mental Attitude

Preparation for the exam is a long, intense process. A positive mental attitude can be the difference between passing and failing.

2. Development of a Plan

The significant commitment involved in preparing for the exam requires a plan. A sample study plan is included in the foreword to this text. Whether you use our study plan or create your own, the importance of this attribute should not be overlooked.

3. Adherence to the Plan

You cannot expect to accomplish a successful review without adherence to your study plan.

4. Time Management

We all lead busy lives and the ability to budget study time is a key to success. We have outlined steps to budgeting study time in the foreword to this text.

5. Knowledge

There is a distinct difference between understanding material and knowing material. A superficial understanding of the exam content is **not** enough. You must *know* the material well. Your Bisk CPA Review text is designed to help you acquire the knowledge that is essential to exam success.

6. Exam Strategies

You should be familiar with the exam format and know exactly what you will do in the exam room. In this appendix, we discuss the steps you should take from the time you enter the exam room until you hand in your note boards. Advance planning will save you time and confusion on exam day.

7. Solutions Approach™

The Solutions Approach™ is an efficient, systematic method of organizing and solving exam questions. It will permit you to organize your approach in a logical manner that will maximize your exam score.

8. Exam Scoring

Remember that your objective is to score 75 points. An understanding of the scoring procedures described in this appendix will help you to maximize points.

9. Focus on the Ultimate Objective—Passing!

Your primary goal in preparing for the exam is to attain a score of 75. Your review should be focused on this goal. Other objectives, such as learning new material or reviewing old material, are important only insofar as they assist you in passing the exam.

10. Exam Confidence

Exam confidence is actually a function of the other nine attributes. If you have acquired a good working knowledge of the material, an understanding of the grading system, a tactic for answering simulations, and a plan for taking the exam; you can go into the exam room confident that you are in control.

APPENDIX C
RESEARCH SKILLS

The final testlet in AUD consists of 7 task-based simulations (TBS), including at least 1 research question.

If you are familiar with researching electronic databases, this appendix contains several research questions for practice. Make sure your speed is sufficient for the exam's time constraints.

If you have not developed electronic database research skills, your first step is to study the material in this appendix.

SECTION	CONTENTS	PAGE

If you have your Notice to Schedule for the exam, you can visit the website (aicpa.org/becomeacpa/cpaexam /forcandidates/howtoprepare/pages/literature.aspx) of the American Institute of Certified Public Accountants (AICPA) to get a *free* six-month subscription to online access to the professional [authoritative] literature used on the AUD exam; however, they caution candidates that **the interface used by their online package is *not* exactly the same as that used in the exam**. Candidates must also review the tutorial and take the AUD sample test provided (go to aicpa.org/becomeacpa/cpaexam/forcandidates/tutorialandsampletest) because the sample test reflects the functionality and interfaces used in the actual exam.

It is very important for you to utilize the AICPA's materials (tutorial, sample test, and authoritative literature subscription) to prepare for the exam's research questions.

Editor Note: If you are enrolled in one of our AUD online courses, please note that some of the questions included in our textbook are **not** included in our online course and vice versa. The authoritative literature provided for answering our online research questions may **not** include sections covered by the research questions that *only* appear in this textbook. (The authoritative literature provided in our AUD online courses is only a portion of the actual databases maintained by the standard-setting organizations. Our purpose in providing this was not to duplicate their databases (which would be cost prohibitive), but rather to provide a tool for candidates to use in answering research questions in our online courses.)

SECTION ONE: GENERAL RESEARCH SKILLS

OVERVIEW

The final testlet in AUD consists of 7 task-based simulations (TBS), including at least 1 research question.

Nature of Research Questions

A research question involves a search of an electronic database of authoritative literature for the guidance that contains the answer to the question posed. Your research is complete when you narrow your search down to a single paragraph in the authoritative literature. No analysis of the guidance is required. The *only* response accepted is the citation of a reference to the paragraph in the authoritative literature. You cannot avoid the research by writing a response that answers the question—*the examiners are testing your electronic database research skills.*

AUD Exam's Database of Authoritative Literature

The AUD exam's database of authoritative literature you will search to answer research questions includes certain portions of the professional standards issued by the American Institute of Certified Public Accountants (AICPA) and the Public Company Accounting Oversight Board (PCAOB).

Split Screen

The AICPA's testing software allows you to split the screen, so you can view the question/response screen and the authoritative literature database screen concurrently. You can search the authoritative literature on one portion of the screen and then enter the appropriate citation on the other portion of the same split screen.

Search Method

The search can be made by using the table-of-contents feature; the search engine with Boolean operators; or the advanced-search feature. Many candidates, once they become familiar with the authoritative literature and how it is organized, find that the table-of-contents approach is the easiest and most efficient method.

Additional Comments

Research skills are not something you can acquire overnight. You must become familiar with the authoritative literature and practice researching it to become proficient. It's best to do this well before you take the exam.

You should review the tutorial and take the AUD sample test on the AICPA's website (aicpa.org/becomeacpa/cpaexam/forcandidates/tutorialandsampletest/Pages/exam_tutorial_parallel.aspx) to become familiar with the exam's most current research interface.

In many instances, research questions are relatively easy; however, should you get a difficult one on your exam, move on after a few minutes; answer a TBS; and then return. Often a simple break helps avoid frustration and allows you to start again with a fresh perspective.

In addition to the research questions in this text's chapters, this appendix contains AUD research questions for you to use to practice your skills.

BOOLEAN SEARCH APPROACH

Boolean operators [commands] combined with key words or phrases are used to direct a search engine. The exam's Boolean operators include *or*, *and*, *not*, *near*, and quotation marks ("xx"). A review of these basic Boolean operators is provided here. (The exam's advanced-search feature allows you to define more types of parameters than it allows via a search using its Boolean operators plus you don't have to remember the operators.)

Or Operator

A search using *accounting or auditing* will find all documents containing the word *accounting* or the word *auditing* or both words. *Or* can be used to search for terms that are used as synonyms within the literature, such as *management*, *client*, and *entity*. As more terms are combined in an *or* search, more documents are included in the results.

And Operator

A search using *accounting and auditing* will only find documents containing both the word *accounting* and the word *auditing*. All things being equal, a search using *and* typically will find fewer documents than a search using *or*. As more terms are combined in an *and* search, fewer documents are included in the results.

Not Operator

A search using *accounting not auditing* will find all documents containing the word *accounting* except those that also contain the word *auditing*. *Not* searches can be helpful when using a word in a search that has more than one meaning or connection.

Near Operator

A search using *subsequent near subsequently* would generate results in which the words *subsequent* and *subsequently* appear close together.

Quotation Marks

A search using *"subsequent events"* would generate results in which the word(s) between the quotation marks appear exactly as entered.

Constructing Search Phrases

Avoid using a search phrase such as *guidance on materially false and misleading entries in records*. Anything you find in the standards will be guidance; further, the term *guidance* might not be in the reference that you seek. Also, eliminate words such as *on* and *in* unless you are seeking an exact phrase that you are sure includes them.

This leaves *materially false misleading entries records*. Typically, search engines default to the Boolean search operator *or* for all words, which probably would result in many irrelevant responses (hits), so modify it to *materially and false and statements*.

Why not include *misleading* in this search phrase? If *false* is in the reference, *misleading* probably will be there also; if *misleading* is in the reference without *materially*, that reference is likely irrelevant. In other words, the word *misleading* does little to narrow the search. If you get too many or too few hits from a search, refine your search parameters until you find what you need.

Answer Selection

Once you have narrowed the search response to a few hits, read through the most likely ones to determine which contains the answer to the research question.

SECTION TWO: AUD RESEARCH SKILLS

The AUD research questions test your ability to select the applicable set of standards; structure a search of it; navigate it; and select the relevant guidance.

Free Subscription to Online Access to Authoritative Literature vs. Sample Tests

If you have your Notice to Schedule for the exam, you can visit the AICPA's website (aicpa.org/becomeacpa /cpaexam/forcandidates/howtoprepare/pages/literature.aspx) to get a *free* six-month subscription to online access to professional [authoritative] literature used on the AUD exam; however, they caution candidates that **the interface used by the online package is *not* exactly the same as that used in the exam**. You must also review the tutorial and take the sample test provided (go to aicpa.org/becomeacpa/cpaexam/forcandidates /tutorialandsampletest) because the sample test reflects the functionality and interfaces used in the actual exam.

In other words, by all means, take advantage of the free subscription offered by the AICPA and use it to become familiar with the authoritative literature and to practice researching questions, but make sure you complement this by answering the sample test's research question so you know what to expect on the exam.

It is very important for you to utilize the AICPA's materials (tutorial, sample test, and authoritative literature subscription) to prepare for the exam's research questions.

Entering Your Response

The response must be entered into three separate fields on the AUD exam: the abbreviation for the applicable set of standards (selected from a drop-down list); the section number within those standards; and the paragraph number within that section. Prompts are provided that define the fields and give examples of acceptable answer formats.

Search Method

As mentioned previously, many candidates find the table-of-contents approach easier and more efficient than the other search methods once they become familiar with the AUD authoritative literature. If you are just beginning your review of AUD, you may find the most challenging aspect of this method to be the selection of the applicable set of standards. As your review progresses, you will find this becomes easier. (You may discover that practicing research questions provides more synergy with your preparation for the entire AUD exam than it does for the other exam sections. Becoming more comfortable with which set of standards is applicable is often an important aspect of successfully answering multiple-choice questions and TBS as well.)

How to Begin

First, obtain your free subscription to online access to the AUD authoritative literature from the AICPA. Then become familiar with it by going online and locating the various sets of standards associated with the topics in our text (most of the individual chapter table-of-contents pages include these references). Then scroll through a particular section of a set of standards to locate the various concepts covered in our text. After you have gained some familiarity with the authoritative literature, review the AICPA's tutorial and practice the sample research question within the simulation portion of their sample test. Then practice answering research questions using the AICPA's online database until you are satisfied with your level of skill.

SECTION THREE: AUD RESEARCH PRACTICE

RESEARCH SIMULATION QUESTIONS

All applicable research questions in this appendix use the June 1, 2013 AICPA Code of Professional Conduct (updated through April 30, 2014), not the revised Code, which becomes partially effective December 15, 2014. Chapter 15 includes a research question which uses the Revised Code.

C-1 Which citation in the professional standards provides guidance on obtaining sufficient appropriate audit evidence about whether the opening balance for inventory contains material misstatements for a non-issuer?

[ ] § [ ] . [ ] (ID: 90050)

C-2 Which citation in the professional standards provides a list of matters that may be subject to the auditor's inquiry of the predecessor auditor for a nonissuer?

[ ] § [ ] . [ ] (ID: 9260)

C-3 Which section of the professional standards requires a practitioner to prohibit the use of the practitioner's name in connection with a financial projection distributed to parties not negotiating directly with the party responsible for the projection?

[ ] § [ ] . [ ] (ID: 60532)

C-4 Which section of the professional standards provides guidance on reporting when an accountant is engaged to compile financial statements that omit substantially all the disclosures required by an applicable financial reporting framework, including disclosures that might appear in the body of the financial statements?

[ ] § [ ] . [ ] (ID: 9262)

C-5 Which citation in the professional standards provides guidance when a user auditor is unable to obtain a sufficient understanding from the user entity (a nonissuer) about the nature and significance of the services provided by a service organization?

[ ] § [ ] . [ ] (ID: 90051)

C-6 Which citation in the professional standards for a nonissuer provides guidance for preventing the undue use by the external auditor of the internal audit function in obtaining audit evidence?

[ ] § [ ] . [ ] (ID: 9264)

C-7 Which citation in the professional standards provides guidance as to when a complete and final set of audit documentation should be assembled for the audit of the financial statements of a public company?

[ ] § [ ] . [ ] (ID: 9266)

C-8 What authoritative reference describes the level of knowledge and competence the engagement quality reviewer must possess to perform an engagement quality review of a public company?

[ ] § [ ] . [ ] (ID: 9267)

C-9 Which citation in the professional standards provides guidance when an auditor is not independent but is required by law or regulation to report on the financial statements of a nonissuer?

[ ] § [ ] . [ ] (ID: 90052)

C-10 What authoritative reference provides guidance as to when a member's independence shall be considered to be impaired if during the period of a professional engagement a covered member had or was committed to acquire a material indirect financial interest in the client?

[ ] § [ ] . [ ] (ID: 89890)

C-11 What authoritative reference provides guidance as to how in the performance of any professional service, a member shall be free of conflicts of interest?

[ ] § [ ] . [ ] (ID: 89891)

C-12 What authoritative reference provides guidance for a member in public practice to obtain clients by advertising or other forms of solicitation in a manner that is misleading?

[ ] § [ ] . [ ] (ID: 89892)

C-13 Which citation in the professional standards provides guidance if an auditor is asked to issue a written communication stating that no significant deficiencies were identified during an audit of a nonissuer?

[ ] § [ ] . [ ] (ID: 89459)

C-14 Which citation in the professional standards provides guidance regarding the procedures the auditor should perform if the auditor identifies related parties or significant related-party transactions that management of a nonissuer has not previously identified or disclosed to the auditor?

[ ] § [ ] . [ ] (ID: 90053)

C-15 What authoritative reference discusses the qualitative aspects of misstatements that an auditor should consider when misstatements are discovered in a sample during substantive tests?

[ ] § [ ] . [ ] (ID: 27792)

RESEARCH SIMULATION ANSWERS

AU Identifier Used for Clarified US GAAS in This Textbook

We have not continued to use the temporary AU-C identifier for the clarified auditing standards issued by the American Institute of Certified Public Accountants (AICPA). In this textbook these standards have an AU identifier.

C-1

Which citation in the professional standards provides guidance on obtaining sufficient appropriate audit evidence about whether the opening balance for inventory contains material misstatements for a nonissuer?

AU	§	510	.	A13	(ID: 90050)

.A13 For current assets and liabilities, some audit evidence about opening balances may be obtained as part of the current period's audit procedures. For example, the collection (payment) of opening accounts receivable (accounts payable) during the current period will provide some audit evidence of their existence, rights and obligations, completeness, and valuation at the beginning of the period. In the case of inventories, however, the current period's audit procedures on the closing inventory balance provide little audit evidence regarding inventory on hand at the beginning of the period. Therefore, additional audit procedures, such as one or more of the following, may be necessary to obtain sufficient appropriate audit evidence:

- Observing a current physical inventory count and reconciling it to the opening inventory quantities
- Performing audit procedures on the valuation of the opening inventory items
- Performing audit procedures on gross profit and cutoff

C-2

Which citation in the professional standards provides a list of matters that may be subject to the auditor's inquiry of the predecessor auditor for a nonissuer?

AU	§	210	.	A31	(ID: 9260)

.A31 The communication with the predecessor auditor may be either written or oral. Matters subject to the auditor's inquiry of the predecessor auditor may include the following:

- Information that might bear on the integrity of management
- Disagreements with management about accounting policies, auditing procedures, or other similarly significant matters
- Communications to those charged with governance regarding fraud and noncompliance with laws or regulations by the entity
- Communications to management and those charged with governance regarding significant deficiencies and material weaknesses in internal control
- The predecessor auditor's understanding about the reasons for the change of auditors

---

C-3

Which section of the professional standards requires a practitioner to prohibit the use of the practitioner's name in connection with a financial projection distributed to parties not negotiating directly with the party responsible for the projection?

AT	§	301	.	11	(ID: 60532)

.11 Because a financial projection is not appropriate for general use, a practitioner should not consent to the use of his or her name in conjunction with a financial projection that he or she believes will be distributed to those who will not be negotiating directly with the responsible party, for example, in an offering statement of an entity's debt or equity interests, unless the projection is used to supplement a financial forecast.

C-4

Which section of the professional standards provides guidance on reporting when an accountant is engaged to compile financial statements that omit substantially all the disclosures required by an applicable financial reporting framework, including disclosures that might appear in the body of the financial statements?

AR	§	80	.	20	(ID: 9262)

.20 An entity may request the accountant to compile financial statements that omit substantially all the disclosures required by an applicable financial reporting framework, including disclosures that might appear in the body of the financial statements. The accountant may compile such financial statements, provided that the omission of substantially all disclosures is not, to his or her knowledge, undertaken with the intention of misleading those who might reasonably be expected to use such financial statements. When reporting on financial statements that omit substantially all disclosures, the accountant should include, after the paragraph describing the accountant's responsibility, a paragraph in the compilation report that includes the following elements:

a. A statement that management has elected to omit substantially all the disclosures (and the statement of cash flows, if applicable) required by the applicable financial reporting framework (or ordinarily included in the financial statements if the financial statements are prepared in accordance with an OCBOA)

b. A statement that if the omitted disclosures (and statement of cash flows, if applicable) were included in the financial statements, they might influence the user's conclusions about the company's financial position, results of operations, and cash flows (or equivalent for presentations other than accounting principles generally accepted in the United States of America)

c. A statement that, accordingly, the financial statements are not designed for those who are not informed about such matters

When the entity wishes to include disclosures about only a few matters in the form of notes to such financial statements, such disclosures should be labeled "Selected Information—Substantially All Disclosures Required by [*identify the applicable financial reporting framework (for example "Accepted Accounting Principles Generally Accepted in the United States of America")*] Are Not Included."

See Compilation Exhibit B for examples of compilation reports when substantially all disclosures required by an applicable financial reporting framework are omitted.

C-5

Which citation in the professional standards provides guidance when a user auditor is unable to obtain a sufficient understanding from the user entity (a nonissuer) about the nature and significance of the services provided by a service organization?

AU	§	402	.	12	(ID: 90051)

.12 If the user auditor is unable to obtain a sufficient understanding from the user entity, the user auditor should obtain that understanding from one or more of the following procedures:

a. Obtaining and reading a type 1 or type 2 report, if available

b. Contacting the service organization, through the user entity, to obtain specific information

c. Visiting the service organization and performing procedures that will provide the necessary information about the relevant controls at the service organization

d. Using another auditor to perform procedures that will provide the necessary information about the relevant controls at the service organization

---

C-6

Which citation in the professional standards for a nonissuer provides guidance for preventing the undue use by the external auditor of the internal audit function in obtaining audit evidence?

AU	§	610	.	17	(ID: 9264)

.17 To prevent undue use of the internal audit function in obtaining audit evidence, the external auditor should plan to use less of the work of the function and perform more of the work directly:

a. The more judgment is involved in

(i) planning and performing relevant audit procedures or

(ii) evaluating the audit evidence obtained

b. the higher the assessed risk of material misstatement at the assertion level, with special consideration given to significant risks;

c. the less the internal audit function's organizational status and relevant policies and procedures adequately support the objectivity of the internal auditors; and

d. the lower the level of competence of the internal audit function.

C-7

Which citation in the professional standards provides guidance as to when a complete and final set of audit documentation should be assembled for the audit of the financial statements of a public company?

PCAOB	AS	3	Par.	15	(ID: 9266)

15. Prior to the report release date, the auditor must have completed all necessary auditing procedures and obtained sufficient evidence to support the representations in the auditor's report. A complete and final set of audit documentation should be assembled for retention as of a date not more than 45 days after the report release date (*documentation completion date*). If a report is not issued in connection with an engagement, then the documentation completion date should not be more than 45 days from the date that fieldwork was substantially completed. If the auditor was unable to complete the engagement, then the documentation completion date should not be more than 45 days from the date the engagement ceased.

C-8

What authoritative reference describes the level of knowledge and competence the engagement quality reviewer must possess to perform an engagement quality review of a public company?

PCAOB	AS	7	Par.	5	(ID: 9267)

5. The engagement quality reviewer must possess the level of knowledge and competence related to accounting, auditing, and financial reporting required to serve as the engagement partner on the engagement under review.

C-9

Which citation in the professional standards provides guidance when an auditor is not independent but is required by law or regulation to report on the financial statements of a nonissuer?

AU	§	705	.	16	(ID: 90052)

.16 When the auditor is not independent but is required by law or regulation to report on the financial statements, the auditor should disclaim an opinion and should specifically state that the auditor is not independent. The auditor is neither required to provide, nor precluded from providing, the reasons for the lack of independence; however, if the auditor chooses to provide the reasons for the lack of independence, the auditor should include all the reasons therefor.

C-10

What authoritative reference provides guidance as to when a member's independence shall be considered to be impaired if during the period of a professional engagement a covered member had or was committed to acquire a material indirect financial interest in the client?

ET	§	101-1	.	02	(ID: 89890)

.02 Independence shall be considered to be impaired if:

During the period of the professional engagement a covered member

1. Had or was committed to acquire any direct or material indirect financial interest in the client.

2. Was a trustee of any trust or executor or administrator of any estate if such trust or estate had or was committed to acquire any direct or material indirect financial interest in the client and

   (i) The covered member (individually or with others) had the authority to make investment decisions for the trust or estate; or

   (ii) The trust or estate owned or was committed to acquire more than 10 percent of the client's outstanding equity securities or other ownership interests; or

   (iii) The value of the trust's or estate's holdings in the client exceeded 10 percent of the total assets of the trust or estate.

3. Had a joint closely held investment that was material to the covered member.

4. Except as specifically permitted in interpretation 101-5, had any loan to or from the client, any officer or director of the client, or any individual owning 10 percent or more of the client's outstanding equity securities or other ownership interests.

C-11

What authoritative reference provides guidance as to how in the performance of any professional service, a member shall be free of conflicts of interest?

ET	§	102-1	.	02	(ID: 89891)

.02 In the performance of any professional service, a member shall maintain objectivity and integrity, shall be free of conflicts of interest, and shall not knowingly misrepresent facts or subordinate his or her judgment to others.

A member shall be considered to have knowingly misrepresented facts in violation of rule 102 when he or she knowingly—

1. Makes, or permits or directs another to make, materially false and misleading entries in an entity's financial statements or records; or

2. Fails to correct an entity's financial statements or records that are materially false and misleading when he or she has the authority to record an entry; or

3. Signs, or permits or directs another to sign, a document containing materially false and misleading information.

C-12

What authoritative reference provides guidance for a member in public practice to obtain clients by advertising or other forms of solicitation in a manner that is misleading?

ET	§	502-2	.	03	(ID: 89892)

.01 Advertising or other forms of solicitation that are false, misleading, or deceptive are not in the public interest and are prohibited. Such activities include those that—

1. Create false or unjustified expectations of favorable results.

2. Imply the ability to influence any court, tribunal, regulatory agency, or similar body or official.

3. Contain a representation that specific professional services in current or future periods will be performed for a stated fee, estimated fee or fee range when it was likely at the time of the representation that such fees would be substantially increased and the prospective client was not advised of that likelihood.

4. Contain any other representations that would be likely to cause a reasonable person to misunderstand or be deceived.

C-13

Which citation in the professional standards provides guidance if an auditor is asked to issue a written communication stating that no significant deficiencies were identified during an audit of a nonissuer?

AU	§	265	.	16	(ID: 89459)

.16 The auditor should not issue a written communication stating that no significant deficiencies were identified during the audit.

C-14

Which citation in the professional standards provides guidance regarding the procedures the auditor should perform if the auditor identifies related parties or significant related party transactions that management of a nonissuer has not previously identified or disclosed to the auditor?

AU § 550 . 23 (ID: 90053)

.23 If the auditor identifies related parties or significant related party transactions that management has not previously identified or disclosed to the auditor, the auditor should

a. promptly communicate the relevant information to the other members of the engagement team.

b. request management to identify all transactions with the newly identified related parties for the auditor's further evaluation.

c. inquire why the entity's controls over related party relationships and transactions failed to enable the identification or disclosure of the related party relationships or transactions.

d. perform appropriate substantive audit procedures relating to such newly identified related parties or significant related party transactions.

e. reconsider the risk that other related parties or significant related party transactions may exist that management has not previously identified or disclosed to the auditor and perform additional audit procedures as necessary.

f. evaluate the implications for the audit if the nondisclosure by management appears intentional (and, therefore, indicative of a risk of material misstatement due to fraud).

C-15

What authoritative reference discusses the qualitative aspects of misstatements that an auditor should consider when misstatements are discovered in a sample during substantive tests?

AU § 530 . A23 (ID: 27792)

.27 In addition to the evaluation of the frequency and amounts of monetary misstatements, section 450 requires the auditor to consider the qualitative aspects of the misstatements. These include (a) the nature and cause of misstatements, such as whether they are differences in principle or in application, are errors, or are caused by fraud or are due to misunderstanding of instructions or to carelessness, and (b) the possible relationship of the misstatements to other phases of the audit. The discovery of fraud ordinarily requires a broader consideration of possible implications than does the discovery of an error.

APPENDIX D
FINANCIAL RATIOS

Analytical procedures consist of evaluations of financial information made by a study of plausible relationships among both financial and nonfinancial data. Plausible relationships among data may reasonably be expected to exist and continue in the absence of changes in conditions. Several common financial ratios are shown here for your reference.

Working Capital

Current Assets – Current Liabilities

Comments: Represents the liquid portion of resources or enterprise capital. The greater the amount of working capital, the greater the cushion of protection available to short-term creditors, and the greater assurance that short-term debts will be paid when due.

Current Ratio

$$\frac{\textit{Current Assets}}{\textit{Current Liabilities}}$$

Comments: This is a primary test of the overall solvency of the enterprise and its ability to meet current obligations from current assets. When the current ratio exceeds 1 to 1, an equal increase in current assets and current liabilities decreases the ratio. When the current ratio is less than 1 to 1, an equal increase in current assets and current liabilities increases the ratio.

Acid-Test or Quick Ratio

$$\frac{\textit{Cash + Marketable Securities + Net Receivables}}{\textit{Current Liabilities}}$$

Comments: This ratio provides a more severe test of immediate solvency by eliminating inventories and prepaid expenses (current assets that cannot be quickly converted into cash).

Defensive-Interval Ratio

$$\frac{\textit{Cash + Marketable Securities + Net Receivables}}{\textit{Average Daily Cash Expenditures}}$$

Comments: This ratio estimates the number of days that the company can meet its basic operational costs. The average daily cash expenditures can be approximated by reducing total expenses for the year by non-cash charges, e.g., depreciation or amortization of intangibles and dividing this amount by 365.

Debt to Equity

$$\frac{\textit{Total Liabilities}}{\textit{Owners' Equity}}$$

Comments: This ratio provides a measure of the relative amounts of resources provided by creditors and owners.

Times Interest Earned

$$\frac{\textit{Income Before Income Taxes and Interest Charges}}{\textit{Interest Charges}}$$

Comments: Measures the ability of the firm to meet its interest payments. Income taxes are added back to net income. (The ability to pay interest is not dependent on the amount of income taxes to be paid because interest is tax deductible.)

Times Preferred Dividends Earned

$$\frac{\textit{Net Income}}{\textit{Annual Preferred Dividend Requirement}}$$

Comments: Measures the adequacy of current earnings for the payment of preferred dividends.

Total Asset Turnover

$$\frac{\textit{Total Sales (Revenue)}}{\textit{Average Total Assets}}$$

Comments: This ratio is used to determine the amount of sales that are generated from each dollar of assets. Average total assets is generally determined by adding the beginning and ending total assets and dividing by two.

Receivables Turnover

$$\frac{\textit{Net Credit Sales}}{\textit{Average Net Receivables}}$$

Comments: This ratio provides an indication of the efficiency of credit policies and collection procedures, and the quality of the receivables. Average net receivables include trade notes receivable. Average net receivables is generally determined by adding the beginning and ending net receivables and dividing by two.

Number of Days' Sales in Average Receivables

$$\frac{\textit{360}}{\textit{Receivables Turnover}}$$

Comments: Tests the average number of days required to collect receivables. Some analysts prefer to use 365, 300, or 250 as the number of business days in a year.

Inventory Turnover

$$\frac{\textit{Cost of Goods Sold}}{\textit{Average Inventory}}$$

Comments: Indicates the number of times inventory was acquired and sold (or used in production) during the period. It can be used to detect inventory obsolescence or pricing problems. Average inventory is generally determined by adding the beginning and ending inventories and dividing by two.

Gross Margin Percentage

$$\frac{\textit{Sales} - \textit{Cost of Goods Sold}}{\textit{Sales}}$$

Comments: Represents the percentage of sales revenue that the company retains after incurring the direct costs associated with producing the goods and services sold by a company. The higher the percentage, the more the company retains on each dollar of sales to cover its other costs and obligations.

Net Operating Margin Percentage

$$\frac{\text{Operating Income}}{\text{Sales}}$$

Comments: Represents the percentage of sales revenue that the company makes before interest and taxes on each dollar of sales.

Number of Days' Supply in Average Inventory

$$\frac{360}{\text{Inventory Turnover}} \quad \text{or} \quad \frac{\text{Average (Ending) Inventory}}{\text{Average Daily Cost of Goods Sold}}$$

Comments: Indicates the number of days inventory is held before it is sold. Some analysts prefer to use 365, 300, or 250 as the number of business days in the year. Average daily cost of goods sold is determined by dividing cost of goods sold by the number of business days.

Length of Operating Cycle

Number of days' sales in average receivables + *Number of days' supply in average inventory*

Comments: Measures the average length of time from the purchase of inventory to the collection of cash from its sale.

Book Value Per Common Share

$$\frac{\text{Common Stockholders' Equity}}{\text{Number of Common Shares Outstanding}}$$

To determine common stockholders' equity, preferred stock is subtracted from total stockholders' equity at the greater of its liquidation, par, or stated value. Cumulative preferred stock dividends in arrears are also similarly subtracted. Treasury stock affects the denominator as the number of common shares outstanding is reduced.

Comments: This ratio measures the amount that common shareholders would receive if all assets were sold at their carrying amounts and all creditors were paid. When balance sheet valuations do not approximate fair values, the importance of this ratio is diminished.

Book Value Per Preferred Share

$$\frac{\text{Preferred Stockholders' Equity}}{\text{Number of Preferred Shares Outstanding}}$$

Preferred stockholders' equity is comprised of (a) preferred stock at the greater of its liquidation, par, or stated value and (b) cumulative preferred stock dividends in arrears.

Comments: This ratio measures the amount that preferred shareholders would receive if the company were liquidated on the basis of the amounts reported on the balance sheet.

Return on Total Assets

$$\frac{\text{Net Income + Interest Expense (Net of Tax)}}{\text{Average Total Assets}}$$

Comments: This ratio provides a measure of the degree of efficiency with which resources (total assets) are used to generate earnings.

Return on Common Stockholders' Equity

$$\frac{\text{Net Income – Preferred Dividends}}{\text{Average Common Stockholders' Equity}}$$

Comments: Measures the rate of earnings on resources provided by common stockholders. Common stockholders' equity is measured as indicated in the explanation for the book value per common share calculation on the previous page. Average common stockholders' equity is generally determined by adding beginning and ending common stockholders' equity and dividing by two.

Successful use of leverage occurs when a company earns more by the use of borrowed money than it costs to use the borrowed funds. When compared to the return on total assets, the return on common stockholders' equity measures the extent to which leverage is being employed for or against the common stockholders. When the return on common stockholders' equity is greater than the return on total assets, leverage is positive and common stockholders benefit.

Return on Stockholders' Equity

$$\frac{\text{Net Income}}{\text{Average Stockholders' Equity}}$$

Comments: Measures the rate of earnings on resources provided by all stockholders, i.e., common and preferred. Average stockholders' equity is generally determined by adding beginning and ending stockholders' equity and dividing by two.

Earnings Per Share (EPS)

$$\frac{\text{Net Income – Preferred Dividends}}{\text{Average Number of Common Shares Outstanding}}$$

Comments: Measures the ability to pay dividends to common stockholders by measuring profit earned per share of common stock.

Price Earnings Ratio

$$\frac{\text{Market Price Per Common Share}}{\text{Earnings Per Common Share}}$$

Comments: A measure of whether a stock is relatively cheap or relatively expensive based on its present earnings.

Dividend Payout Ratio

$$\frac{\text{Cash Dividend Per Common Share}}{\text{Earnings Per Common Share}}$$

Comments: This ratio represents the percentage of earnings per share distributed to common stockholders in cash dividends. A low ratio would probably indicate the reinvestment of profits by a growth-oriented firm.

Yield on Common Stock

$$\frac{\text{Dividend Per Common Share}}{\text{Market Price Per Common Share}}$$

Comments: Measures cash flow return on common stock investment.

APPENDIX E
RECENTLY RELEASED AICPA QUESTIONS

In April 2014, the AICPA released fifty multiple-choice questions, one research question; and two task-based simulations related to the AUD section of the CPA Examination. These questions and their unofficial answers are reproduced here as received from the AICPA examiners, along with Bisk CPA Review's explanations. The multiple-choice questions in Problems 1 and 2 were labeled *medium* and *difficult*, respectively, by the AICPA examiners. The AICPA did not state if these questions ever appeared on any exam; whether they were assigned points or were merely being pretested (and earned no points) if they did appear on an exam; or if they were now obsolete for some reason. These questions are intended only as a study aid and should not be used to predict the content of future exams. It is the AICPA's policy that released questions will not appear on future exams.

Problem E-1 MULTIPLE-CHOICE QUESTIONS

1. Which of the following would be considered an analytical procedure?

   a. Examining a sample of paid vendors' invoices for proper approval by an authorized supervisor
   b. Developing the current year's expected net sales based on the entity's sales trend of prior years
   c. Projecting a deviation rate by comparing the results of a sample with the actual population characteristics
   d. Evaluating management's plans for dealing with the adverse effects of recurring operating losses

   (ID: 90501)

2. Which of the following events occurring after the issuance of the audit report most likely would cause the auditor to make further inquiries about the previously issued financial statements?

   a. The auditor discovers that the entity intends to present comparative financial statements in subsequent years.
   b. Litigation that had been disclosed in the financial statements is resolved.
   c. A subsidiary that accounts for 30% of the entity's consolidated net revenue is sold.
   d. New information regarding significant unrecorded transactions from the year under audit is discovered.

   (ID: 90502)

3. Under which of the following circumstances would using the blank form of confirmation of accounts receivable most likely be preferable to other types of positive confirmations?

   a. The auditor's combined assessed level of control risk and inherent risk is low.
   b. Prior years' audits indicate a pattern of overstatement of account balances.
   c. Recipients are likely to sign other types of positive confirmations without careful investigation.
   d. Accounts receivable are immaterial to the entity's financial statements. (ID: 90503)

4. Which of the following procedures most likely would be performed in an engagement to review financial statements of a nonissuer?

   a. Analytical review of payroll tax expense
   b. Testing of internal controls over cash receipts
   c. Testing the aging of accounts payable
   d. Confirmation of notes receivable (ID: 90504)

5. When performing an audit, a CPA notes that bad-debt expense is unusually high relative to similar firms in the industry. The CPA should recommend which of the following controls?

   a. Use approved price lists for customer billing.
   b. Send monthly statements of account to customers with outstanding balances.
   c. Require credit checks on all new customers.
   d. Reconcile accounts receivable in the general ledger with the subsidiary ledger. (ID: 90505)

6. Which of the following steps should be performed first in applying analytical procedures?

   a. Determine whether the difference between the expectation and the recorded amount is reasonable.
   b. Investigate and evaluate significant differences from the expectation.
   c. Develop an expectation of a balance or ratio by using relationships that are expected to exist.
   d. Compare the client's recorded balance or ratio with the expectation. (ID: 90506)

7. Which of the following actions is an analytical procedure that an auditor most likely would use while auditing a company's notes payable?

   a. Multiplying the average outstanding loan balance by the interest rate and comparing the result to interest expense actually recorded
   b. Performing calculations to determine if the company is in compliance with debt covenants
   c. Sending a confirmation to the lender requesting verification of the loan's outstanding balance
   d. Reviewing the details of the company's loan and interest expense accounts to determine that all payments were properly recorded (ID: 90507)

8. Which of the following items is an example of an inherent limitation in an internal control system?

   a. Segregation of employee duties
   b. Human error in decision making
   c. Ineffective board of directors
   d. Understaffed internal audit functions (ID: 90508)

9. Which of the following circumstances would generally require an accountant to decline to perform a compilation of financial statements under *Statements on Standards for Accounting and Review Services*?

   a. A substantial portion of generally accepted accounting principles disclosures was omitted.
   b. There was a lack of independence between the accountant and client.
   c. The accountant had **no** prior experience with similar organizations within the industry.
   d. The accountant was **not** able to come to an understanding with representatives of the organization for services to be performed. (ID: 90509)

10. Which of the following types of risks most likely would increase if accounts receivable are confirmed three months before year-end?

    a. Inherent
    b. Control
    c. Detection
    d. Business (ID: 90510)

11. Which of the following statements is correct regarding an independent auditor's reliance on a client's internal audit staff?

    a. An independent auditor should **not** reduce the amount of audit testing based on the work of internal auditors.
    b. An independent auditor should assess the organizational status of the director of internal audit.
    c. An internal auditor should provide direct assistance to the independent auditor during preparation of audit workpapers.
    d. An independent auditor should use internal audit workpapers when available. (ID: 90511)

12. Which of the following parties should an auditor notify first when discovering an immaterial fraud is committed by an accounting clerk?

    a. The audit committee
    b. An appropriate level of management
    c. The client's legal counsel
    d. The client's internal auditor (ID: 90512)

13. Which of the following circumstances most likely would require an auditor to apply an omitted procedure after the audit report issuance date?

    a. The audit report is unsupported as a result of the omitted procedure.
    b. Generally accepted accounting principles are violated.
    c. The client has requested that the procedure be performed.
    d. The engagement letter requires the procedure to be performed. (ID: 90513)

14. Analytical procedures are required for which of the following?

    a. Audit planning
    b. Tests of balances
    c. Client retention decision
    d. Internal control evaluation (ID: 90514)

15. Which of the following is correct regarding the communication between successor and predecessor auditors?

    a. The successor and predecessor auditors should communicate with each other in writing regarding potential problems.
    b. The successor auditor should contact the predecessor auditor prior to proposing an audit engagement.
    c. The client should be present during the communications between the predecessor auditor and the successor auditor.
    d. The successor auditor should request permission from the prospective client to make an inquiry of the predecessor auditor. (ID: 90515)

16. Which of the following would an auditor most likely consider in evaluating the control environment of an audit client?

    a. Overall employee satisfaction with assigned duties
    b. The number of CPAs in the accounting department
    c. Management reviews of monthly financial statements
    d. Management's operating style (ID: 90516)

17. Which of the following statements is true with regard to review services performed under *Statements on Standards for Accounting and Review Services*?

    a. To perform a review, an accountant need **not** be independent but should disclose that fact.
    b. In a review, an accountant will express limited assurance as to generally accepted accounting principles on the financial statements.
    c. An accountant must have extensive knowledge of the client's business, industry, and the economy to perform a review.
    d. In a review, an accountant gives **no** assurance as to generally accepted accounting principles on the financial statements. (ID: 90517)

18. Each of the following broker-dealer relationships impairs auditor independence with respect to a broker-dealer issuer audit client, **except**:

    a. The auditor has a brokerage account that holds both US securities and assets other than cash or securities.
    b. The auditor has a brokerage account that holds US securities in excess of Securities Investor Protection Corporation coverage limits.
    c. The auditor has a brokerage account that includes assets other than cash or securities.
    d. The auditor has a cash balance in a brokerage account that is fully covered by the Securities Investor Protection Corporation. (ID: 90518)

19. When a former partner of a registered public accounting firm who left the firm two years ago accepts a financial reporting oversight role at an issuer audit client, the independence of the registered public accounting firm is considered impaired **unless** which of the following is true?

    a. The former partner discloses the relationship to the issuer audit client's board of directors.
    b. The former partner was employed by the registered public accounting firm for a period of 2 years or **less**.
    c. The former partner has **no** remaining capital balance in the registered public accounting firm.
    d. The former partner exerts only limited influence over the registered public accounting firm's operations and financial policies. (ID: 90519)

20. Each of the following is a required attribute of an issuer's audit committee financial expert, **except**

    a. The ability to assess the application of accounting principles in connection with estimates, accruals, and reserves
    b. Significant audit experience as a certified public accountant
    c. An understanding of internal controls related to financial reporting
    d. An understanding of generally accepted accounting principles (ID: 90520)

21. West, CPA, is engaged to compile the financial statements of Lake Co., a nonissuer. Lake's financial statements are prepared in conformity with the cash basis of accounting. If Lake's financial statements do **not** disclose the basis of accounting used, which of the following statements best describes West's reporting responsibility concerning this matter?

    a. West should disclose the basis of accounting used in the notes to Lake's financial statements.
    b. West should disclose the basis of accounting used in West's compilation report.
    c. West should quantify the effects of the differences between GAAP and the cash basis and disclose them in West's compilation report.
    d. West should quantify the effects of the differences between GAAP and the cash basis and disclose them in the notes to Lake's financial statements. (ID: 90521)

22. According to the AICPA Code of Professional Conduct, which of the following disclosures of client information by a member CPA to an outside party would normally require client consent?

    a. Disclosure of confidential client information to a third-party service provider when the member does **not** enter into a confidentiality agreement with the provider
    b. Disclosure to a potential client of the name of a client for whom the member or member's firm performed professional services
    c. Disclosure of confidential client information to the member's liability insurance carrier in response to a potential claim
    d. Disclosure of confidential client information to a court or in documents in connection with a subpoena (ID: 90522)

23. In accordance with Office of Management and Budget audit requirements for audits of non-Federal entities expending Federal awards, which of the following statements is accurate regarding Federal awards expended?

    a. Donated surplus property **cannot** be valued at the assessed value provided by the federal agency.
    b. Food stamps **cannot** be valued at fair market value at the time of receipt.
    c. Government loans are classified as noncash assistance programs.
    d. Free rents received as part of an award to carry out a federal program are treated as federal funds expended. (ID: 90523)

24. In the integrated audit of an issuer, which of the following would **not** be considered an entity-level control?

    a. Management's established controls to monitor results of operations
    b. The executive committee's process for assessing business risk
    c. The board of directors' controls to monitor the activities of the audit committee
    d. The outside auditor's assessment process of internal auditor competence and objectivity (ID: 90524)

25. For which of the following judgments may an independent auditor share responsibility with an entity's internal auditor who is assessed to be both competent and objective?

	Evaluation of significant accounting estimates	Materiality of misstatements
a.	Yes	Yes
b.	Yes	No
c.	Yes	Yes
d.	No	No

(ID: 90525)

Problem E-2 MULTIPLE-CHOICE QUESTIONS

26. Which of the following procedures would an auditor most likely perform in searching for unrecorded payables?
    a. Reconcile receiving reports with related cash payments made just prior to the year-end.
    b. Review the responses of accounts receivable confirmations for indications of disputes with customers.
    c. Compare cash payments made after the balance sheet date with the accounts payable trial balance.
    d. Examine a sample of creditor balances to supporting invoices, receiving reports, and purchase orders. (ID: 90526)

27. Which of the following procedures would an accountant most likely perform when reviewing the financial statements of a nonissuer?
    a. Ask management about the entity's procedures for recording transactions.
    b. Obtain an understanding of the entity's internal control components.
    c. Send a letter of inquiry to the entity's attorney regarding pending litigation.
    d. Assess the risk of material misstatement arising from fraudulent financial reporting. (ID: 90527)

28. A CPA is required to comply with the provisions of *Statements on Standards for Attestation Engagements* when engaged to
    a. Provide assurance on investment performance statistics prepared by an investment company on established criteria.
    b. Issue a letter for an underwriter, also known as a comfort letter, to a broker or dealer of securities.
    c. Compile financial statements in conformity with a comprehensive basis of accounting other than GAAP.
    d. Communicate with an audit committee regarding management's consultations with another CPA. (ID: 90528)

29. Which of the following is a component of internal control?
    a. Financial reporting
    b. Operating effectiveness
    c. Risk assessment
    d. Organizational structure (ID: 90529)

30. Which of the following statements is correct regarding the predictability of analytical procedures in a financial statement audit?
    a. Relationships involving only balance sheet accounts tend to be more predictable than relationships involving income statement accounts.
    b. Relationships involving income statement accounts tend to be more predictable than relationships involving only balance sheet accounts.
    c. Relationships involving transactions subject to management discretion tend to be more predictable than automated transactions.
    d. Relationships in a dynamic environment tend to be more predictable than relationships in a stable environment. (ID: 90530)

31. According to the PCAOB, which of the following tax services may be provided jointly with the audit of an issuer's financial statements without impairing independence?
    a. Planning and issuing an opinion in favor of the tax treatment of an aggressive tax position
    b. Reviewing a proposed transaction and informing the client of the tax consequences
    c. Providing consultations under a contingency fee arrangement
    d. Preparing tax returns for an individual in a financial oversight reporting role during the audit period (ID: 90531)

32. A CPA firm has decided to rely on the audit work performed by another audit firm. Which of the following procedures should the CPA firm perform when taking responsibility for the other firm's audit work?
    a. Review the other firm's audit workpapers and reperform a subset of audit testing to validate the firm's conclusions.
    b. Reference the reliance on the other firm's work in a footnote disclosure to the financial statements.
    c. Reference the reliance on the other firm's work in the first paragraph of the opinion in the audit report.
    d. Obtain and attach a copy of the other firm's representation letter and audit report to the opinion that the CPA firm issues. (ID: 90532)

33. Which of the following characteristics of prospective financial statements would require the practitioner to include in a report on the prospective financial statements a paragraph that restricts the use and distribution of the report?
    a. They are considered a financial projection.
    b. They are considered a financial forecast.
    c. They contain a range of forecasted results.
    d. They are prepared by a practitioner who lacks independence. (ID: 90533)

34. The degree of audit risk always present in an audit engagement is referred to as a combination of nonsampling and sampling risk. Which of the following is an example of nonsampling risk?
    a. The auditor selecting inappropriate auditing procedures
    b. The internal control being more effective than the auditor believes
    c. The auditor concluding the account balance is **not** materially misstated, but is, in fact, materially misstated
    d. The internal control **not** being as effective as the auditor believes (ID: 90534)

35. How would an auditor of a nonissuer most appropriately respond to a heightened assessed risk of material misstatement?
    a. By obtaining a management representation letter
    b. By performing analytical procedures, but **not** substantive procedures, at period end
    c. By assigning more experienced staff or those with specialized skills to high-risk areas
    d. By performing tests of controls at interim-end and period-end dates (ID: 90535)

36. Generally accepted government auditing standards use which of the following terms to describe a professional requirement to comply with a standard or provide a special explanation for **not** doing so?
    a. Explanatory requirement
    b. Conditional requirement
    c. Unconditional requirement
    d. Presumptively mandatory requirement (ID: 90536)

37. Which of the following statements is **least** likely to be included in a practitioner's report on agreed-upon procedures?

    a. The use of the report is subject to specified restrictions.
    b. The report has provided limited assurance.
    c. The subject matter is the responsibility of the responsible party.
    d. The procedures performed were agreed to by the specified parties. (ID: 90537)

38. According to the AICPA Code of Professional Conduct, under which of the following circumstances may a CPA receive a contingent fee for services?

    a. Examining a client's prospective financial information
    b. Preparing a client's federal income tax return
    c. Representing a client in an IRS examination of the client's federal income tax return
    d. Reviewing a client's financial statements (ID: 90538)

39. In an engagement to examine management's discussion and analysis (MD&A), which of the following best defines control risk?

    a. The risk that an assertion within the MD&A will lead to a material misstatement
    b. The risk of detecting misstatements that are material to the MD&A presentation taken as a whole
    c. The risk that the practitioner will **not** uncover a material misstatement within an MD&A assertion
    d. The risk that material misstatements in the MD&A presentation will **not** be prevented in a timely manner (ID: 90539)

40. Section 404 of the Sarbanes-Oxley Act of 2002 requires each annual report of an issuer to include which of the following?

    a. Representations from the company's external auditors that the company has effective internal control over operations
    b. Management representations that the company's external auditors have examined its internal control over compliance with laws and regulations
    c. Reasonable assurances that fraud will be identified before the issuance of the company's annual report
    d. Management's assessment of the effectiveness of internal control over financial reporting (ID: 90540)

41. To ensure that the audit report for an issuer is prepared in accordance with Section 404 of the Sarbanes-Oxley Act of 2002, the report must

    a. Be prepared within 60 days of the end of the issuer's fiscal year-end **unless** extenuating circumstances, as outlined in the act, are publicly disclosed
    b. Attest to and report on the internal control assessment made by the management of the issuer
    c. Be prepared within 60 days of the issuer's fiscal year-end, be certified by the Public Company Accounting Oversight Board, and be publicly disclosed
    d. Attest to, and report on, the efficiency and effectiveness of the issuer's system of internal control (ID: 90541)

42. In an integrated audit of a nonissuer, an auditor should issue an adverse opinion on the effectiveness of an entity's internal control in which of the following situations?

    a. The financial statements are misstated.
    b. A material weakness exists.
    c. The entity may **not** continue as a going concern.
    d. The auditor was asked by the client to provide the report to another practitioner. (ID: 90542)

43. In order to obtain an initial understanding of internal control sufficient to assess the risk of material misstatement of the financial statements, an auditor would most likely perform which of the following procedures?

    a. Tests of key controls to determine whether they are effective
    b. Expanded substantive testing to identify relevant controls
    c. Analytical procedures to determine the need for specific controls
    d. Risk assessment procedures to evaluate the design of relevant controls (ID: 90543)

44. Which of the following procedures regarding accounts payable would an accountant most likely perform during a nonissuer's review engagement?

    a. Obtaining an understanding of the entity's internal control over accounts payable
    b. Assessing fraud risk within the accounts payable function
    c. Comparing ratios developed from recorded amounts to expectations developed by the accountant
    d. Obtaining confirmations of the year-end accounts payable amounts from the client's five largest vendors (ID: 90544)

45. Each of the following statements is correct regarding the likely sources of potential misstatements in an integrated audit of a nonissuer, **except**:

    a. An evaluation of the entity's information technology risk and controls should be performed separately from the top-down approach.
    b. The controls that management has implemented to address potential sources of misstatements should be identified.
    c. An understanding of how transactions are initiated, authorized, processed, and recorded should be achieved.
    d. Walkthroughs are frequently the most effective way of understanding sources of potential misstatements. (ID: 90545)

46. During an audit of the financial statements of a company, the CFO provides a spreadsheet to the audit team that contains a number of errors that are material to the financial statements. Under what circumstances would this situation be a violation of the rules of the Sarbanes-Oxley Act of 2002 on improper influence on the conduct of audits?

    a. The CFO discovers and corrects most of the errors in the spreadsheet, which was prepared by a staff accountant. One immaterial error remains of which the CFO is aware, and this error remains undetected by the audit team, but the financial statements end up being fairly presented.
    b. The audit team discovers the errors through alternate procedures when they discern that the spreadsheet was improperly manipulated by the CFO. This intentional conduct of the CFO does **not** succeed in affecting the audit.
    c. The CFO had the spreadsheet prepared by a vendor of the company; the vendor intentionally misstates information in the spreadsheet, and the CFO does **not** discover the misstatements. The errors remain undetected by the audit team, and the financial statements are materially misleading.
    d. The CFO was unaware of the errors in the spreadsheet, which was prepared by a staff accountant and reviewed by the CFO. The errors remain undetected by the audit team, and the financial statements are materially misleading. (ID: 90546)

47. A nonissuer has asked an accountant to compile its financial statements that omit substantially all disclosures required by generally accepted accounting principles (GAAP). The accountant may comply with the entity's request provided that the

    a. Financial statements are compiled in conformity with a comprehensive basis of accounting other than GAAP.
    b. Financial statements will **not** be used to obtain credit from a third-party financial institution.
    c. Omission is **not** employed in order to mislead the users of the financial statements and is properly disclosed in the accountant's report.
    d. Omission is acknowledged in the notes to the financial statements and is consistent with the prior-year's financial statements. (ID: 90547)

48. Which of the following strategies most likely could improve the response rate of the confirmation of accounts receivable?

    a. Including a list of items or invoices that constitute the account balance
    b. Restricting the selection of accounts to be confirmed to those customers with relatively large balances
    c. Requesting customers to respond to the confirmation requests directly to the auditor by fax or e-mail
    d. Notifying the recipients that second requests will be mailed if they fail to respond in a timely manner

    (ID: 90548)

49. Under which of the following circumstances would the expression of a disclaimer of opinion be inappropriate?

    a. The chief financial officer and the chief executive officer are unwilling to sign the management representation letter.
    b. The auditor is unable to determine the extent of or the amounts associated with a pervasive employee fraud scheme.
    c. Management refuses to produce documentation verifying the ownership of its equipment and production facilities.
    d. The company issues financial statements that purport to present financial position and results of operations, but refuses to include the related statement of cash flows. (ID: 90549)

50. A CPA in public practice is required to comply with the provisions of the *Statements on Standards for Accounting and Review Services* when

	Advising a client regarding the selection of computer software	Materiality of misstatements
a.	Yes	Yes
b.	Yes	No
c.	No	Yes
d.	No	No

(ID: 90550)

Problem E-3 SIMULATION: Inherent Risk

For each independent situation below, select from the lists provided the appropriate inherent risk factor and the effect of the inherent risk, if any, on the company's net income. A response may be used once, more than once, or not at all.

		Column I		Column II
Situation		**Inherent risk factor**		**The effect of inherent risk on the company's net income**
Sales orders for an internet textbook distributor increased 100% over the last year. Additionally, the company's asset turnover has doubled since the previous year.	1.		2.	
JRM Co. recorded its first hedging transaction for mortgage-backed securities in year 1. At the end of year 1, the fair value of mortgage-backed securities had decreased significantly.	3.		4.	
Metal, Inc. supplies copper pipes to home builders. During year 1, copper prices doubled. At any given time, a significant amount of inventory is in transit or located at job sites.	5.		6.	
Joe's Computers provides three-year money back warranties on all laptops. During year 1, warranty claims decreased significantly and the company has not reduced the warranty reserve.	7.		8.	
Global Co. imports most of its products from a foreign supplier. During year 1, a new technology made part of the Global Co. inventory obsolete.	9.		10.	

(ID: 90443)

Selection List of Inherent Risk Factors (Column I)

A. Complexity	D. Other external circumstances
B. Estimates	E. Susceptibility of asset to theft
C. Industry circumstances	F. Volume

Selection List for the Effect of Inherent Risk on Net Income (Column II)

A. Overstatement	C. No impact
B. Understatement	

Problem E-4 SIMULATION: Review Draft Report Wording

Tucker Co. hired Dabies and Co., CPAs, to perform a review of their annual financial statements for the year ended December 31, year 1. A staff associate prepared the draft report in the Draft Report tab and has questions about the correct wording of the report based on the relevant professional standards.

For each of the questions below, select from the list provided the appropriate word or phrase to complete the indicated sentence in the accountant's report.

Date of report:

We have reviewed the accompanying balance sheet of Tucker Co. as of December 31, year 1, and the related statements of income, retained earnings, and cash flows for the year then ended. A review includes primarily **Question 1** management's financial data and making inquiries of company management. A review is substantially less in scope than an audit, the objective of which is the expression of an opinion regarding the financial statements as a whole. Accordingly, we do not express such an opinion.

Management is responsible for the **Question 2** of the financial statements in accordance with accounting principles generally accepted in the United States of America and for **Question 3** internal control relevant to the preparation and fair presentation of the financial statements.

Our responsibility is to **Question 4** in accordance with **Question 5** issued by the American Institute of Certified Public Accountants. Those standards require us to perform procedures to obtain **Question 6** that there are no material modifications that should be made to the financial statements. We believe that the results of our procedures provide a reasonable basis for our report.

Based on our review, we are not aware of any material modifications that should be made to the accompanying financial statements in order for them to be in conformity with **Question 7** generally accepted in the United States of America.

Dabies and Co., CPAs

March 1, year 2

(ID: 90444)

Response Selection List

Selection List – MO#1	Selection List – MO#4
Analyzing	Assemble the financial statements
Analyzing and assembling	Compile the financial statements
Applying analytical procedures to	Conduct the review
Assembling	Evaluate management's assertions
Compiling	Perform examination procedures
Performing substantive tests of	Provide an opinion
Preparing financial statements using	Report on our examination
Reviewing	**Selection List – MO#5**
Selection List – MO#2	International Standards on Auditing
Accuracy	Statements on Auditing Standards
Accuracy and completeness	Statements on Quality Control Standards
Compilation	Statements on Standards for Accounting and Review Services
Compilation and review	Statements on Standards for Attestation Engagements
Fair presentation	**Selection List – MO#6**
Preparation	Assurance
Preparation and fair presentation	Comfort
Review	Evidence
Selection List – MO#3	Limited assurance
Designing and communicating	Moderate assurance
Designing and implementing	Reasonable assurance
Designing and maintaining	Reasonable comfort
Implementing, and communicating	Reasonable evidence
Designing, implementing, and communicating	**Selection List – MO#7**
Designing, implementing, and maintaining	Accounting and review principles
Designing, maintaining, and communicating	Accounting principles
Implementing, maintaining, and communicating	Accounting review standards
	Accounting standards
	Review principles
	Review standards

Problem E-5 SIMULATION: Research

At the beginning of an engagement to compile Locomotiv Co.'s financial statements for year 1, Stiles, CPA, asked you, as an engagement team member, to prepare a workpaper suggesting materiality in relationship to potential misstatements found while preparing the financial statements. Which section of the authoritative literature provides a list of reasonable assumptions you can make in regard to the users of the compiled statements for purposes of materiality?

Reminder: On the actual exam, you will use an electronic database of authoritative literature to find and select the reference (appropriate section and paragraph of the relevant guidance). Please see the AICPA's tutorial and sample test on the exam section of their website.

[ ] § [ ] [ ] (ID: 90445)

Solution E-1 MULTIPLE-CHOICE ANSWERS

1. (b) Answer b., developing the current year's expected net sales based on the entity's sales trend of prior years, is an analytical procedure. Analytical procedures include the consideration of comparisons of the entity's financial information with comparable information for prior periods. Regarding incorrect answer a., examining a sample of paid vendors' invoices for proper approval by an authorized supervisor, is a test of controls. Regarding incorrect answer c., projecting a deviation rate by comparing the results of a sample with the actual population characteristics, is an audit sampling procedure. Regarding incorrect answer d., evaluating management's plans for dealing with the adverse effects of recurring operating losses, is required when there is substantial doubt about an entity's ability to continue as a going concern for a reasonable period of time. This evaluation includes various procedures and is required to include analytical procedures when prospective financial information is particularly significant to management's plans, but that may not always be the case.
(Chapter: 4-II-A; CSO: III.B.7; ID: 90501)

2. (d) Answer d., new information regarding significant unrecorded transactions from the year under audit is discovered [after the issuance of the audit report], is a subsequently discovered fact—defined as a fact that become known to the auditor after the date of the audit report that, had it been known to the auditor at that date, may have caused the auditor to revise the report. When this occurs the auditor should make further inquiries to determine whether the financial statements need revision, and if so, how the entity intends to address it. Regarding incorrect answer a., if a continuing auditor becomes aware of a possible material misstatement in the comparative financial statements while performing the *current* period audit, the auditor should perform additional procedures; however, simply learning after the issuance of the audit report that the entity intends to present comparative financial statements in *subsequent* years would not trigger a need for further inquiries. Regarding incorrect answer b., the resolution of litigation after the issuance of the audit report, would not require further inquiries if the disclosure of what was then known about the litigation was appropriate—and nothing in the question indicates otherwise. Regarding incorrect answer c., the sale of a subsidiary would not trigger additional procedures if disclosure requirements, if applicable, were met because the sale occurred after the date of the audit report. (Chapter: 8-IX-A; CSO: IV.J.13; ID: 90502)

3. (c) A positive confirmation request is a request that the confirming party respond directly to the auditor by indicating whether they agree or disagree with the information in the request or, if the request is the "blank" form of a positive confirmation, by providing the requested information. A blank confirmation request provides more persuasive evidence than a positive confirmation request that includes an amount or other information. Using the blank form of confirmation of accounts receivable would most likely be preferable when answer c., recipients are likely to sign other types of positive confirmations without careful investigation. Regarding incorrect answer a., when the auditor's combined assessed level of control risk and inherent risk [risk of material misstatement] is low and other conditions are present, the auditor may not need the more persuasive audit evidence provided by the blank form of a positive confirmation request. Regarding incorrect answer b., when prior years' audits indicate a pattern of overstatement of account balances, the blank form is less likely to be used because confirming parties are more likely to respond indicating their disagreement with an amount that is not in their favor. Regarding incorrect answer d., when accounts receivable are immaterial, the auditor may not need the more persuasive audit evidence provided by the blank form. (Chapter: 5-II-A; CSO: III.B.8; ID: 90503)

4. (a) A review is a service, the objective of which is to obtain limited assurance that there are no material modifications that should be made to the financial statements in order for the statements to be in conformity with the applicable financial reporting framework. Review evidence obtained through the performance of analytical procedures and inquires will ordinarily provide the CPA with a reasonable basis for expressing limited assurance. A CPA is not required to: test internal control; perform audit tests; assess fraud risk; or communicate with a predecessor auditor. (Chapter: 12-I-C; CSO: V.B.3: ID: 90504)

5. (c) When an auditor notes that bad-debt expense is unusually high relative to similar firms in the industry, the auditor *may* recommend answer c., require credit checks on all new customers. The other controls given would not have a direct impact on reducing bad-debt expense. Editor Note: This question erroneously indicates that when performing an audit, a CPA should make recommendations to the entity regarding its internal controls. The auditor may make oral suggestions for remedial action, i.e., recommend controls, or include

recommendations in the written communication of significant deficiencies and material weaknesses, but such recommendations are *not* required. (Chapter: 3-III-D; CSO: IV.J.11; ID: 90505)

6. (c) The first step of those given that should be performed in applying analytical procedures is answer c., develop an expectation of a balance or ratio by using relationships that are expected to exist. Next, the auditor should compare the client's recorded balance or ratio with the expectation (answer d.). Then, the auditor should determine whether the difference between the expectation and the recorded amount is reasonable (answer a.). And finally, the auditor should investigate and evaluate significant differences from the expectation (answer b.). Editor Note: The guidance lists the following required steps for *substantive* analytical procedures: (1) determine the suitability of the analytical procedures for given assertions; (2) evaluate the reliability of data from which the auditor's expectation of recorded amounts or ratios is developed; (3) develop an expectation of recorded amounts or ratios; (4) evaluate whether the expectation is sufficiently precise to identify a misstatement that, individually or when aggregated with other misstatements, may cause the financial statements to be materially misstated; (5) determine the amount of any difference of recorded amounts from expected values that is acceptable, i.e., does not merit investigation; (6) compare the recorded amounts, or ratios developed from recorded amounts, with the expectations; and finally, (7) the auditor should investigate any instances that significantly differ from the expectations. (Chapter: 4-II-B; CSO: III.B.7; ID: 90506)

7. (a) The most likely analytical procedure that an auditor would use while auditing notes payable is answer a., multiplying the average outstanding loan balance by the interest rate and comparing the result to interest expense actually recorded. The other answer alternatives do not describe analytical procedures.
(Chapter: 4-II-A; CSO: III.B.7; ID: 90507)

8. (b) An example of an inherent limitation in an internal control system is answer b., human error in decision making. Other examples include human errors that cause breakdowns in internal control; controls circumvented by the collusion of two or more people; and inappropriate management override of controls. Incorrect answer a., segregation of [incompatible] employee duties is an example of a control. Incorrect answers c. and d., an ineffective board of directors and understaffed internal audit functions, respectively, are not inherent limitations. These are problems that can be solved, i.e., they are not part of the essential nature of an internal control system. (Chapter: 3-I-A; CSO: II.F.9; ID: 90508)

9. (d) The objective of a compilation is limited to assisting management in presenting financial information in the form of financial statements without obtaining or providing any assurance that there are no material modifications that should be made to the financial statements in order for the statements to be in conformity with the applicable financial reporting framework. Substantially all required disclosures can be omitted, as long as the intent is not to mislead. The CPA must establish and document (in an engagement letter) an understanding with the client regarding the services to be performed; if an understanding cannot be reached, the CPA should not accept the engagement. A CPA should possess a level of knowledge of the accounting principles and practices of the entity's industry, but does not need to have prior experience with similar organizations within the industry. A CPA does not need to be independent, since no assurance is provided.
(Chapter: 12-I-B; CSO: V.A.2; ID: 90509)

10. (c) Detection risk is the risk that the procedures performed by the auditor will not detect a misstatement that exists—detection risk is a function of the effectiveness of an audit procedure and of its application by the auditor. Detection risk, would most likely increase if accounts receivable are confirmed three months before year-end. Performing substantive procedures, such as the confirmation of accounts receivable, at an interim date without undertaking additional procedures at a later date increases the risk that the auditor will not detect misstatements that may exist at the period-end. This risk increases as the remaining period is lengthened. (If substantive procedures are performed at an interim date, the auditor should cover the remaining period by performing either substantive procedures combined with tests of controls or further substantive procedures only—whichever provides a reasonable basis for extending the audit conclusions from the interim date to the period-end.) Incorrect answers a. and b., inherent risk and control risk, respectively, are the entity's risks—they exist independently of the audit and thus, are not affected by the auditor's procedures. Incorrect answer d., business risk, is also not affected by the auditor's procedures; it is affected by matters external to the entity and within the entity. (Chapter: 5-I-C; CSO: III.B.8; ID: 90510)

11. (b) Regarding an independent [external] auditor's reliance on a client's internal audit staff, answer b., an external auditor should assess the organizational status of the director of internal audit [if, after gaining an understanding of the work of the internal audit function, the external auditor concludes that their work is relevant to the audit and it would be efficient to consider using their work]. In this case, the external auditor should assess the objectivity of the internal audit function by evaluating *both* the organizational status of its director and the entity's policies to maintain their internal auditors' objectivity about the areas audited. This assessment of the organizational status of the director is required to include consideration of whether (1) the director reports to an officer of sufficient status to ensure broad audit coverage and adequate consideration of, and action on, the findings and recommendations of the internal auditors; (2) the director has direct access and reports regularly to those charged with governance; and (3) those charged with governance oversee employment decisions regarding the position. Editor Note: The preceding explanation is based on the guidance for public companies. The guidance for nonissuers for using the work of internal auditors requires both the evaluation of the extent to which the internal audit function's organizational status and relevant policies and procedures support the objectivity of the internal auditors, but it does *not* require specific procedures such as the ones just listed per the public company guidance. Regarding incorrect answer a., an external auditor *can* reduce the amount of audit testing based on the work of internal auditors. The guidance for both public companies and nonissuers allows the external auditor to determine whether, and if so, how and to what extent, the work of internal auditors can be used, i.e., can reduce the amount of audit testing performed by external auditors. Regarding incorrect answer c., an internal auditor would *not* provide direct assistance to the external auditor during preparation of audit workpapers. The external auditor's workpapers are the primary support for the opinion which is solely the responsibility of the external auditors. The external auditors and internal auditors should each maintain their own workpapers. Further, nothing in the guidance for public companies or nonissuers requires the external auditor to use any of the work of the internal auditors. Regarding incorrect answer d., an external auditor is *not* required to use internal audit workpapers when available; however, if the work of the internal auditors is expected to have an effect on the external auditor's procedures, the guidance for public companies recommends that it *may* be efficient for the external auditor to have access to the internal auditors' workpapers as a means to coordinating the work. And the guidance for public companies and nonissuers recommends reviewing the internal audit workpapers as part of the external auditor's evaluation of the internal audit function. Editor Note: The guidance for nonissuers requires that the workpapers prepared by the internal auditors who provided direct assistance on the audit engagement be included in the external auditor's documentation for the audit. (Chapter: 4-V-B; CSO: I.E.3; ID: 90511)

12. (b) If the auditor has identified a fraud or has obtained information that indicates that a fraud may exist, the auditor should communicate these matters on a timely basis to the appropriate level of management in order to inform those with primary responsibility for the prevention and detection of fraud of matters relevant to their responsibilities. (Ordinarily, the appropriate level of management is at least one level above the persons who appear to be involved with the suspected fraud.) (Chapter: 2-VII-K; CSO: IV.J.11; ID: 90512)

13. (a) An auditor would most likely be required to apply an omitted procedure after the audit report issuance date when answer a., the audit report is unsupported as a result of the omitted procedure. The auditor may become aware, after the report release date that one or more auditing procedures were omitted. (After the report release date, the auditor has no responsibility to carry out any retrospective review of the audit work performed; however, the discovery of an omitted procedure may occur, for example, in connection with a firm's inspection or monitoring processes.) An omitted procedure is defined as one that the auditor considered necessary in the circumstances existing at the time of the audit but which was not performed. The auditor is required to assess the effect of its omission on the auditor's present ability to support the previously expressed opinion and respond appropriately. If the auditor concludes that an omitted procedure impairs the auditor's present ability to support a previously expressed opinion and the auditor believes that there are users currently relying, or likely to rely, on the previously released report, the auditor should promptly perform the omitted procedure, or alternative procedures, to determine whether there is a satisfactory basis for the auditor's previously expressed opinion. The auditor should include the procedures performed in the audit documentation.
(Chapter: 8-IX-B; CSO: IV.J.14; ID: 90513)

14. (a) Analytical procedures are required for answer a., audit planning, i.e., analytical procedures performed as risk assessment procedures. They may include both financial and nonfinancial information. Such analytical procedures may enhance the auditor's understanding of the entity's business and the significant transactions and events that have occurred since the prior audit and also may help to identify unusual transactions or events

and amounts, ratios, and trends that might have audit implications. Unusual or unexpected relationships that are identified may assist in identifying the the risks of material misstatement (RMM), especially the RMM due to fraud; thus, providing a basis for designing and implementing responses to the assessed risks. However, because such analytical procedures may use data aggregated at a high level, they may only provide a broad initial indication about whether a material misstatement may exist. Accordingly, in such cases, other information may need to be considered in conjunction with the results of such analytical procedures. Editor Note: The auditor is also required to perform analytical procedures near the end of the audit when forming an overall conclusion on the financial statements. And analytical procedures *may* be performed as substantive procedures in response to assessed risks, but they are *not* required for this purpose. (Chapter: 2-V-D CSO: II.D.2; ID: 90514)

15. (d) The successor auditor (auditor) should request permission from the prospective client to make an inquiry of the predecessor auditor [about matters that will assist the auditor in determining whether to accept the engagement]. Regarding incorrect answer a., the communication with the predecessor auditor may be either oral or written. Regarding incorrect answer b., the auditor should contact the predecessor auditor prior to accepting, not prior to proposing, an audit engagement. (The auditor may advise management that the auditor's acceptance of the engagement cannot be final until the inquiries have been made and the responses of the predecessor auditor have been evaluated.) Regarding incorrect answer c., the client is not required to be present during the communications between the predecessor auditor and the auditor prior to the acceptance of an engagement. Editor Note: However, after the acceptance of the engagement, the need for the client to be involved with the communication between the auditor and the predecessor auditor could arise. Once the engagement is accepted, the auditor should request management to authorize the predecessor auditor to allow a review of the predecessor auditor's audit documentation and for the predecessor auditor to respond fully to inquiries by the auditor. The purpose of these communications and procedures is to help the auditor in planning and performing the audit; however, if the auditor determines that the opening balances contain misstatements that could materially affect the current period's financial statements or that the financial statements reported on by the predecessor auditor may require revision; then, the client should be included in the discussion to resolve such matters. (Chapter: 2-I-C; CSO: I.C.0; ID: 90515)

16. (d) Internal control consists of five interrelated components: the entity's (1) control environment; (2) risk assessment process; (3) information system, including the related business processes relevant to financial reporting and communication; (4) control activities relevant to the audit; and (5) monitoring of controls. The division of internal control into these components provides a useful framework for auditors when considering how different aspects of an entity's internal control may affect the audit. An auditor would most likely consider answer d., management's operating style, when evaluating the control environment component of an audit client. The control environment is the foundation for the other four components; it sets the tone of the entity. It includes the governance and management functions and the attitudes, awareness, and actions of those charged with governance and management concerning the entity's internal control and its importance in the entity. Incorrect answers a. and b., overall employee satisfaction with assigned duties (partially a result of human resource policies and procedures) and the number of CPAs in the accounting department (evidence of a commitment to competence), respectively, could also be factors related to the control environment, but management's operating style is clearly the best answer. Incorrect answer c., management reviews of monthly financial statements, would most likely be considered by the auditor in gaining an understanding of the entity's control activities component. (Chapter: 3-I-C; CSO: II.F.1; ID: 90516)

17. (b) A review provides limited assurance that there are no material modifications that should be made to the financial statements for them to be in conformity with the applicable financial reporting framework. A CPA must be independent to perform a review as some form of assurance is provided. A CPA should understand the accounting principles and practices of the client's industry; a CPA can accept an engagement for an entity in an industry in which the CPA has no previous experience as long as the CPA can acquire said knowledge. (Chapter: 12-I-C; CSO: V.A.1; ID: 90517)

18. (d) SEC rules state that independence is impaired if the accounting firm, covered persons, and his or her immediate family members have a broker-dealer account with an audit client if the account includes any asset other than cash or securities that are covered by the Securities Investor Protection Act. (Chapter: 14-I-D;CSO: VI.A.2; ID: 90518)

19. (c) If a partner or professional employee leaves the firm and subsequently is employed by or associated with that client in a key position, then the firm's independence would be impaired, unless a number of conditions are met, including: there are no amounts owed to a former partner or professional employee for a prior interest in the firm or for unfunded, vested retirement benefits; the former partner is not in a position to exert any influence over the accounting firm's operations or financial policies; and the former partner may not participate or appear to participate, and is not associated with, the firm. It is irrelevant how long the former partner was employed with the firm. Disclosure of the relationship is not adequate. (Chapter: 14-I-C; CSO: VI.A.2; ID: 90519)

20. (b) The SEC requires each issuer, together with periodic reports, to disclose whether or not, and if not, the reasons therefore, the issuer's audit committee of that issuer is comprised of at least 1 member who is a financial expert. In defining the term "financial expert" the SEC considers whether a person has, through education and experience: an understanding of generally accepted accounting principles and financial statements; experience in both the preparation or auditing of financial statements of generally comparable issuers; and the application of such principles in connection with the accounting for estimates, accruals, and reserves; experience with internal accounting controls; and an understanding of audit committee functions. The individual does not have to be a CPA. (Chapter: 14-IX-B; CSO: VI.B.2; ID: 90520)

21. (b) The objective of a compilation is limited to assisting management in presenting financial information in the form of financial statements without obtaining or providing any assurance that there are no material modifications that should be made to the financial statements in order for the statements to be in conformity with the applicable financial reporting framework. Management is responsible for the selection of the entity's applicable financial reporting framework. Financial statements must include: a description of the basis of accounting used; a summary of significant accounting policies; and a description of the primary differences from US GAAP. If the basis is not disclosed, West should include it in his report. (Chapter: 5-III-A; CSO: V.C.1; ID: 90521)

22. (a) Rule 301 states that a member in public practice will not disclose confidential information obtained in the course of the professional engagement without the consent of the client except to comply with: a validly issued and enforceable subpoena or summons; applicable laws and government regulations; professional practice review procedures under AICPA or state CPA society or Board of Accountancy authorization; or to initiate a complaint with the professional ethics division or trial board of the AICPA or other appropriate investigative or disciplinary body. Although answers "c" and "d" are confidential information, they fall within the exempt categories, and do not require consent. Answer "b" is not confidential, and therefore does not require consent either. Only answer "a" is both confidential and not listed as a specific exemption; thus requiring client consent.
(Chapter: 14-III-A; CSO: VI.A.1; ID: 90522)

23. (d) The determination of when an award is expended should be based on when the activity related to the award occurs. Generally, the activity pertains to events that require the non-Federal entity to comply with laws, regulations, and the provisions of contracts or grant agreements, such as: the receipt of surplus property; the distribution or consumption of food commodities; and the use of loan proceeds under loan and loan guarantee programs. Free rent received by itself is not considered a Federal award expended; however, free rent received as part of an award to carry out a Federal program shall be included in determining Federal awards expended and subject to audit. (Chapter: 9-III-C; CSO: I.A.0; ID: 90523)

24. (d) The audit of a public company's internal control over financial reporting (ICFR) should be integrated with the audit of the financial statements. The top-down approach in an audit of ICFR requires the auditor to test those entity-level controls that are important to the auditor's conclusion about whether the company's ICFR is effective. Other entity-level controls, in addition to those listed in the incorrect answers, include controls related to the control environment; controls over management override of other controls; the company's risk assessment process; centralized processing and controls; and controls over the period-end financial reporting process. In the integrated audit of a public company (an issuer), answer d., the outside auditor's assessment process of internal auditor competence and objectivity, would not be considered an entity-level control. It's not even one of the entity's controls—the external auditor assesses the competence and objectivity of the entity's internal audit function to determine if their work can be used to obtain audit evidence or if internal auditors can be used to provide direct assistance on the audit. (Chapter: 10-V-F; CSO: II.F.1; ID: 90524)

25. (d) An independent [external] auditor may *not* share responsibility with an entity's internal auditor in the evaluation of significant accounting estimates or the materiality of misstatements. Because the external auditor has sole responsibility for the audit opinion expressed (internal auditors are not independent of the entity as is required of the external auditor), the external auditor is required to make the significant judgments in the audit engagement. According to the guidance for public companies on using the work of internal auditors, in addition to the matters in this question, judgments about assessments of inherent and control risks [i.e., the risks of material misstatement]; the sufficiency of tests performed; and other matters affecting the audit report should always be those of the auditor. Editor Note: The guidance for nonissuers is essentially the same on this matter. It includes additional examples of significant judgments, such as, evaluating the appropriateness of management's use of the going concern assumption and whether substantial doubt exists about the entity's ability to continue as a going concern for a reasonable period of time; and evaluating the adequacy of disclosures in the financial statements. (Chapter: 4-V-C; CSO: I.E.3; ID: 90525)

Solution E-2 MULTIPLE-CHOICE ANSWERS

26. (c) When searching for unrecorded payables, the auditor would most likely, answer c., compare cash payments made *after* the balance sheet date with the [year-end] accounts payable trial balance. Analysis of unmatched cash payments would reveal unrecorded payables at the balance sheet date, unless they could be resolved by matching them to obligations incurred after the balance sheet date. Regarding incorrect answer a., matching receiving reports to related cash payments made *just prior* to year-end would not result in locating an unrecorded payable that was due at year-end because it would have already been paid. Regarding incorrect answer b., customers are most likely to dispute the balance of their account when it is overstated per an account receivable confirmation. In this case, payments may have been received from customers, but not correctly applied to their account; however, such cash receipts would not represent unrecorded payables. In the case where a customer reported [disputed] an understated account balance, deposits from customers may have erroneously been credited to their account. Such a deposit would represent an unrecorded payable; however, this procedure, reviewing accounts receivable confirmations disputed due to understatement, is not as likely to be performed for the purpose of locating unrecorded payables as is the analysis of cash payments made after the balance sheet date (answer c.). Regarding incorrect answer d., to obtain a sample of creditor balances [accounts payable] to match to supporting documentation (invoices, receiving reports, etc.), the auditor would have to access *recorded* payables—unrecorded payables, of course, will never be found on a list of recorded payables. (Chapter: 5-VI-F; CSO: III.B.10; ID: 90526)

27. (a) A nonissuer is essentially an entity whose securities are not registered with the SEC. The CPA should apply professional judgment in determining the specific nature, extent, and timing of review procedures (i.e., analytical procedures and inquiries) to provide the CPA with a reasonable basis for obtaining limited assurance that there are no material modifications that should be made to the financial statements for them to be in conformity with the applicable financial reporting framework; therefore, a CPA should ask management about the entity's procedures for recording transactions. A review does not involve obtaining an understanding of internal control, assessing fraud risk, testing accounting records, examining source documents, or other procedures ordinarily performed in an audit. (Chapter: 13-I-B; CSO: V.B.5; ID: 90527)

28. (a) The AICPA *Code of Professional Conduct* requires an AICPA member who performs an attestation engagement to comply with *Statements on Standards for Attestation Engagements* (SSAE). An attest engagement is one in which a member is engaged to issue an examination, review, compilation or agreed-upon procedures report on subject matter, or an assertion about subject matter, that is the responsibility of another party (usually management). Attestation services include: agreed-upon procedures (excluding letters to underwriters and consulting services or any attest engagement concerning assertions about solvency); financial forecasts and projections; pro forma financial statements; internal control over financial reporting; compliance reporting (regulatory or contractual); and Management's Discussion and Analysis. SSAE do not apply to: audits; reviews and compilations of financial statements of nonissuers under SSARS; tax return preparation; advocating, consulting, or advisory services; or operational audits. (Chapter: 13-I-A; CSO: I.A.0; ID: 90528)

29. (c) One of the five interrelated components of an entity's internal control is answer c., [the entity's] risk assessment [process]. The other answer alternatives do not include the other four which are the entity's: control environment; information system, including the related business processes relevant to financial reporting and communication; control activities relevant to the audit; and monitoring of controls. Editor Note: See the mnemonic *CRIME* in our text in section I.C. of chapter 3 for a memorization aide for these five components. (Chapter: 3-I-C; CSO: II.F.1; ID: 90529)

30. (b) Regarding the predictability of analytical procedures, it is true that answer b., relationships involving income statement accounts tend to be more predictable than relationships involving only balance sheet accounts. This is because income statement accounts represent transactions over a period of time, whereas balance sheet accounts represent amounts as of a point in time; thus, incorrect answer a., the reverse of this statement, is *not* true. Regarding incorrect answer c., relationships involving transactions subject to management discretion may be less, not more, predictable than automated transactions. For example, management may elect to incur maintenance expense rather than replace plant and equipment, or they may delay advertising expenditures. Regarding incorrect answer d., relationships in a dynamic [or unstable] environment are usually less, not more, predictable than relationships in a stable environment. (Chapter: 4-II-B; CSO: III.B.7; ID: 90530)

31. (b) A public accounting firm is not independent if the firm provides: any non-audit service to the audit client related to marketing, planning, or opining in favor of the tax treatment of, a confidential transaction or an aggressive tax position transaction; during the period of engagement, any tax service to a person in a financial reporting oversight; during the audit period any service or product to the audit client for a contingent fee or a commission. Reviewing a proposed transaction and informing the client of the tax consequences would not impair independence. (Chapter: 14-I-C; CSO: VI.A.2; ID: 90531)

32. (a) If an auditor decides to rely on the audit work performed by another firm, i.e., to assume responsibility for their work [and thus, *not* reference them in the audit report], the best answer is a., the auditor should review the other firm's audit workpapers and reperform a subset of audit testing to validate the firm's conclusions. If the entity is a public company, the principal auditor is explicitly required to obtain, and review and retain, the following information from the other auditor prior to the report release date: (1) an engagement completion document; (2) a list of significant risks, the auditor's responses, and the results of the auditor's related procedures; (3) sufficient information relating to significant findings or issues that are inconsistent with or contradict the auditor's final conclusions; the relevant records to be retained include, but are not limited to, procedures performed in response to the information, and records documenting consultations on, or resolutions of, differences in professional judgment among members of the engagement team or between the engagement team and others consulted; (4) any findings affecting the consolidating or combining of accounts in the consolidated financial statements; (5) sufficient information to enable the office issuing the audit report to agree or reconcile the financial statement amounts audited by the other firm to the information underlying the consolidated financial statements; (6) a schedule of accumulated misstatements, including a description of the nature and cause of each accumulated misstatement, and an evaluation of uncorrected misstatements, including the quantitative and qualitative factors the auditor considered to be relevant to the evaluation; (7) all significant deficiencies and material weaknesses in internal control over financial reporting, including a clear distinction between those two categories; (8) letters of representations from management; and (9) all matters to be communicated to the audit committee. In addition, the principal auditor should consider performing one or more of the following procedures: (1) visiting the other auditor and discussing the audit procedures followed and results; (2) reviewing the audit programs of the other auditor; in some cases, it may be appropriate to issue instructions to the other auditor as to the scope of the audit work; and/or (3) reviewing additional audit documentation of the other auditor relating to significant findings or issues in the engagement completion document. If the entity is a nonissuer, the auditor is required to follow the guidance for audits of group financial statements which directs the auditor to be involved in essentially all of the work of the component auditors that is related to the group audit opinion; see the topics related to group audits in our text chapters 2, 3, and 4. (According to the guidance for nonissuers and per the international auditing standards (ISA), the other auditor is termed a *component auditor* and the principal auditor is termed the *group engagement partner* or the *auditor of the group financial statements*.) Regarding incorrect answer b., according to all sets of auditing standards [eligible for testing, i.e., GAAS, PCAOB AS, and ISA], the financial statements are the responsibility of the entity; thus, the auditor would *not* include matters pertaining to the audit, such as this, in the notes to the financial statements. Regarding incorrect answer c., if the auditor of either a nonissuer or an issuer decides to assume responsibility for the work of the other auditor, *no* reference

should be made to the other auditor's work or report. According to ISA, sharing responsibility for an audit is not an option; thus, the audit report on the group financial statements should *not* refer to a component auditor in either situation, unless required by law or regulation to include such reference. (If such reference is required by law or regulation, the audit report per ISA should indicate that the reference does not diminish the group engagement partner's or the group engagement partner's firm's responsibility for the group audit opinion.) Regarding incorrect answer d., according to both PCAOB AS for issuers and GAAS for nonissuers, when an auditor assumes responsibility for the other firm's audit work, for the same reason that no reference should be made to the other auditor in the report on those financial statements, neither should the other firm's letter and report be attached to the report, i.e., because to do so may cause a reader to misinterpret the degree of responsibility being assumed. Editor Note: Normally, the CPA examiners will indicate whether the entity is an issuer or a nonissuer or if ISA apply if it is relevant to the question. (Chapter: 8-VIII-B; CSO: I.E.1; ID: 90532)

33. (a) Prospective financial statements (PFS) are either a forecast or a projection. A financial forecast presents, to the best of the responsible party's knowledge and belief, an entity's expected financial position, results of operations, and cash flows. A financial forecast can be a general-use or limited-use report. A financial projection presents, to the best of the responsible party's knowledge and belief, given one or more hypothetical assumptions, an entity's expected financial position, results of operations, and cash flows. It answers the question, "What would happen if…?" A financial projection must be labeled a limited-use report. Independence is not required for either type of engagement. (Chapter: 13-II-B; CSO: IV.J.7; ID: 90533)

34. (a) Audit sampling is the application of an audit procedure to less than 100 percent of the items within an account balance or class of transactions (the population) with the intent of drawing conclusions about the population based on the results of the sample. Attribute sampling is used for testing internal controls (i.e., are the controls effective), and variable sampling is used in substantive testing of account balances (i.e., is the balance not materially misstated). Sampling risk results from the possibility that if a test is restricted to a sample, the conclusions reached may be different than the conclusions that would have resulted if the entire population was examined. Nonsampling risk includes all aspects of audit risk not due to sampling. Examples of nonsampling risks include failure to select appropriate audit procedures for a given objective, and failure to recognize misstatements, thus making a procedure ineffective. (Chapter: 6-I-B; CSO: III.B.6: ID: 90534)

35. (c) An auditor of a nonissuer would most appropriately respond to a heightened assessed risk of material misstatement (RMM) by, answer c., assigning more experienced staff or those with specialized skills to high-risk areas. This is an example of an overall response to the RMM at the financial statement level. Other examples of overall responses include emphasizing the importance of maintaining professional skepticism; providing more supervision; incorporating more unpredictable elements in the selection of further audit procedures; and making general changes to the nature, extent, and timing of audit procedures, e.g., performing substantive procedures at period-end instead of at an interim date or modifying the nature of audit procedures to obtain more persuasive audit evidence. Regarding incorrect answer a., an auditor obtains written representations from management and, when appropriate, those charged with governance, regardless of the degree of the assessment of the RMM. Regarding incorrect answer b., when the assessed RMM is high the auditor would respond by performing more substantive procedures at period-end which include tests of details and substantive analytical procedures. Regarding incorrect answer d., the auditor performs tests of controls if the auditor plans to rely on the operating effectiveness of controls in the determination of the nature, extent, and timing of substantive procedures or if substantive procedures alone cannot provide sufficient appropriate audit evidence at the relevant assertion level. And when the assessed risk of RMM is high, the auditor would be more likely to perform more substantive procedures at the end of the period rather than at an interim date.
(Chapter: 2-IX-C; CSO: III.A.1; ID: 90535)

36. (d) Generally accepted government auditing standards (GAGAS) identify professional requirements with specific language (consistent with GAAS) to indicate the degree of responsibility imposed on auditors and audit organizations. The two categories of requirements are: unconditional requirements and presumptively mandatory requirements. Auditors and audit organizations must comply with an unconditional requirement in all cases where such requirement is relevant. Auditors and audit organizations must comply with a presumptively mandatory requirement in all cases where such a requirement is relevant except in rare circumstances. In rare circumstances, auditors and audit organizations may determine it necessary to depart from a relevant presumptively mandatory requirement. If, in rare circumstances, auditors judge it necessary to depart from a relevant presump-

tively mandatory requirement, they must document their justification for the departure and how the alternative procedures performed in the circumstances were sufficient to achieve the intent of that requirement.
(Chapter: 9-II-B; CSO: I.A.0; ID: 90536)

37. (b) An agreed-upon procedures engagement is one in which a practitioner is engaged to issue a report of findings based on specific procedures performed on subject matter; a written assertion is not required. The practitioner's report contains a number of elements, including: a statement that the procedures performed were those agreed to by the specified parties; a statement that the sufficiency of the procedures is solely the specified parties' responsibility and a disclaimer of responsibility on the part of the practitioner for the sufficiency of the procedures; and a statement restricting the report use because it is intended solely for the use of specified parties. No assurance is provided in an agreed-upon procedures engagement, so there would no comment included in a practitioner's report. (Chapter: 13-II-A; CSO: IV.J.6; ID: 90537)

38. (c) Rule 302 states that a member in public practice shall not offer or render services under an agreement whereby the fee is contingent upon the findings or results. Specified services include an audit or review of a financial statement, a compilation of a financial statement when the member reasonably might expect that a third party will use the statement, an examination of prospective financial information; or preparing an original or amended tax return or claim for a tax refund. Contingent fees in certain tax matters are permitted, including: a member representing a client in an examination by a revenue agent of the client's federal or state income tax return; a member representing a client in connection with obtaining a private letter ruling, filing an amended return based on a tax issue that is the subject of a test case involving a different taxpayer or on which the taxing authority is developing a position. (Chapter: 14-III-B; CSO: VI.A.1; ID: 90538)

39. (d) The MD&A section is provided in a company's annual report, along with the financial statements. It provides an overview of the previous year of operations and explains the period's financial results. Management may also comment on the upcoming year, outlining future goals and new projects. After obtaining an understanding of the entity's internal controls over preparation of the MD&A section, the CPA assesses control risk for the MD&A content. Control risk may be assessed at the maximum level (i.e., the greatest probability that a material misstatement would occur in an MD&A assertion and would not be prevented or detected in a timely manner) if the CPA believes controls are ineffective. (Chapter: 13-II-F; CSO: II.H.3; ID: 90539)

40. (d) Each required annual report of an issuer must contain an internal control report stating it is the responsibility of management for establishing and maintaining an adequate internal control structure and procedures for financial reporting. It must also contain an assessment, as of the end of the most recent fiscal year of the issuer, of the effectiveness of the internal control structure and procedures of the issuer for financial reporting. Each public accounting firm that prepares or issues the audit report for the issuer shall attest to, and report on, the assessment made by management of the issuer. (Chapter: 14-IX-B; CSO: VI.B.2; ID: 90540)

41. (b) To ensure that the audit report for the integrated audit an issuer (a public company) is prepared in accordance with Section 404 of the Sarbanes-Oxley Act of 2002, the report must, answer b., attest to [audit] and report on the internal control assessment made by the management of the issuer. Regarding incorrect answers a. and c., there is no requirement to prepare the report within 60 days of the end of the entity's fiscal year. Regarding incorrect answer d., the auditor's objective in an audit of internal control over financial reporting is to express an opinion on the effectiveness (not the efficiency) of the company's internal control over financial reporting. (Chapter: 10-V-A; CSO: IV.J.4; ID: 90541)

42. (b) AT 501, An Examination of an Entity's Internal Control Over Financial Reporting That Is Integrated With an Audit of Its Financial Statements, establishes requirements and provides guidance for the performance of an examination of a nonissuer's internal control over financial reporting that is integrated with an audit of financial statements. If there is a material weakness, the auditor should express an adverse opinion. The auditor is prohibited from expressing an opinion on management's assertion and should report directly on the effectiveness of internal control. The auditor should determine the effect of an adverse opinion on the auditor's opinion on the financial statements and disclose whether the auditor's opinion on the financial statements was affected by the material weakness. None of the other situations require an adverse opinion.
(Chapter: 13-II-D; CSO: IV.J.4; ID: 90542)

43. (d) To obtain an initial understanding of internal control sufficient to [identify and] assess the risk of material misstatement (RMM) of the financial statements, an auditor would most likely perform, answer d., risk assessment procedures to evaluate [obtain an understanding of] the design [and implementation] of relevant controls. The purpose of performing risk assessment procedures is to obtain an understanding of the entity and its environment, *including its internal control*, to identify and assess the RMM, whether due to error or fraud, at the financial statement and relevant assertion levels. Risk assessment procedures to obtain audit evidence about the design and implementation of relevant controls may include inquiring of entity personnel; observing the application of specific controls; inspecting documents and reports; and tracing transactions through the information system relevant to financial reporting. (Inquiry alone, however, is *not* sufficient for such purposes.) Regarding incorrect answer a., tests of controls test the operating effectiveness of controls in preventing, or detecting and correcting, material misstatements at the assertion level; *not* their design and implementation. (However, because the same types of procedures are often used, it may prove efficient to test the operating effectiveness of controls at the same time the auditor is evaluating their design and determining that they have been implemented.) Regarding incorrect answer b., substantive procedures are *not* used to identify relevant controls. They are designed to detect material misstatements at the assertion level and are comprised of tests of details and substantive analytical procedures. Tests of controls and substantive procedures are *not* risk assessment procedures. Regarding incorrect answer c., analytical procedures are *not* used to determine the need for specific controls. (Analytical procedures performed as risk assessment procedures may enhance the auditor's understanding of the client's business and the significant transactions and events that have occurred since the prior audit and also may help to identify the existence of unusual transactions or events and amounts, ratios, and trends that might indicate matters that have audit implications. Unusual or unexpected relationships that are identified may assist the auditor in identifying RMM, especially RMM due to fraud.)
(Chapter: 2-V-D; CSO: II.F.4; ID: 90543)

44. (c) A review provides only limited assurance that there are no material modifications that should be made to the financial statements for them to be in conformity with the applicable financial reporting framework. A review does not involve obtaining an understanding of internal control, assessing fraud risk, testing accounting records, examining source documents, or other procedures ordinarily performed in an audit. A review does consist primarily of analytical procedures (such as comparing ratios to various benchmarks) and inquires of management. (Chapter 12-I-C; CSO: V.B.3; ID: 90544)

45. (a) The auditor should use a "top-down" approach to identify risks, and select and evaluate controls. The auditor should verify his or her understanding of the risks in the company's processes. The auditor's objectives are to (1) understand the flow of transactions (including the effect of information technology) related to the relevant assertions, including how these transactions are initiated, authorized, processed, and recorded; (2) confirm that all the points within the company's processes at which a material (individually or combined with other misstatements) misstatement could arise have been identified; and (3) Identify the preventative and detective controls that management has implemented. An effective method to achieve these objectives is to perform walk-throughs. The auditor follows a transaction from its origin to its reflection in the financial statements.
(Chapter: 10-V-F: CSO: II.H.4; ID: 90545)

46. (b) Title III, Section 303 of the Sarbanes-Oxley Act (SOX) states that It is illegal for any officer or director of an issuer, or any other person acting under the direction thereof, to take any action to fraudulently influence, coerce, manipulate, or mislead any independent public or certified accountant engaged in the performance of an audit of the financial statements of that issuer for the purpose of rendering such financial statements materially misleading. The other situations listed do not meet the criteria for undue influence on the conduct of an audit under SOX Section 303. (Chapter: 14-II-1; CSO: VI.A.2; ID: 90546)

47. (c) The objective of a compilation is limited to assisting management in presenting financial information in the form of financial statements without obtaining or providing any assurance that there are no material modifications that should be made to the financial statements in order for the statements to be in conformity with the applicable financial reporting framework. Substantially all required disclosures can be omitted, as long as the intent is not to mislead. An explanatory paragraph should be added after the accountant's responsibilities paragraph. The financial statements can be: compiled under GAAP; used by a third-party as long as a report accompanies the compiled financial statements; and consistency with prior year statements is not required.
(Chapter: 12-I-B; CSO: V.B.6; ID: 90547)

48. (a) Answer a., including a list of the items or invoices that constitute the account balance, would most likely improve the response rate of the confirmation of accounts receivable. The design of the confirmation request may directly affect the confirmation response rate (and the reliability and nature of the audit evidence obtained from the responses). One of the design factors to consider is the ability of the recipients to confirm or provide the requested information. Providing the individual invoice amounts that comprise the account balance will make it much easier for recipients to research their records and confirm their balances. The other answer alternatives are not as likely to improve the response rate. Regarding incorrect answer b., customers who owe the largest amounts, worst case, may be less inclined to respond; and best case, don't have any more incentive to do so. Regarding incorrect answer c., requests to respond directly to the auditor by fax or e-mail could cause an increase in the response rate due to ease, but it is unlikely to cause as much improvement as providing a breakdown of the account balance. Editor Note: All confirmation requests should be received directly by the auditor regardless of the mode of communication. Regarding incorrect answer d., even such a mild "threat" (notifying recipients that a second request will be mailed if they fail to respond in a timely manner) may cause some recipients to take offense, i.e., backfire and reduce the response rate; or, it could prove to be an incentive for recipients to procrastinate until the second request arrives. (Chapter: 5-II-B; CSO: III.B.8; ID: 90548)

49. (d) Incorrect answers a., b., and c., describe scope limitations that could result in a disclaimer of opinion. A disclaimer of opinion should be expressed when the auditor is unable to obtain sufficient appropriate audit evidence [a scope limitation] that the financial statements as a whole are free from material misstatement and the possible effects of the undetected misstatements, if any, on the financial statements could be both material and pervasive. Regarding the scope limitation described in answer a., when management does not provide written representations, the auditor may either disclaim an opinion or withdraw from the engagement. Withdrawal could also be an alternative for the auditor in the case of the management-imposed scope limitation described in answer c., refusal to provide documentation regarding the ownership of equipment and production facilities, when it is not possible to obtain sufficient appropriate evidence using alternative procedures. Regarding answer b., when fraud is identified, because of the variety of circumstances that may arise, it is not possible to describe definitely when withdrawal is appropriate. Regarding the correct answer d., the omission of the statement of cash flows is *not* a scope limitation; thus, a disclaimer of opinion would *not* be appropriate. The omission of the statement of cash flows is a material misstatement of the presentation of the financial statements; thus, a qualified or an adverse opinion should be expressed. Public company auditing guidance explicitly states that such an omission normally requires qualification of the opinion. The auditing guidance for nonpublic companies explicitly states that the omission of the statement of cash flows is material enough to warrant a modified opinion, but does not provide a similar indication as to whether it should normally be qualified or adverse; thus, the auditor would need to determine which type of opinion was appropriate depending on the facts and circumstances. (Chapter: 8-IV-F; CSO: IV.J.1; ID: 90549)

50. (d) *Statements of Standards for Accounting and Review Services* (SSARS) are issued by the AICPA and provide performance and reporting guidance for compilations and reviews of unaudited financial statements or other unaudited financial information of nonissuers. SSARS also applies to engagements to issue a compilation report on specified elements, accounts, or items of a nonissuer's financial statements, or on a nonissuer's pro forma financial information. SSARS do not apply to other accounting services, such as preparing adjusting entries, consulting on financial matters, processing financial data for clients of other accounting firms, or preparing tax returns. Therefore, neither of the above situations would require compliance with SSARS.
(Chapter: 12-I-A; CSO: V.A.1; ID: 90550)

Solution E-3 SIMULATION ANSWER: Inherent Risk

For each independent situation below, select from the lists provided the appropriate inherent risk factor and the effect of the inherent risk, if any, on the company's net income. A response may be used once, more than once, or not at all.

		Column I		Column II
Situation		**Inherent risk factor**		**The effect of inherent risk on the company's net income**
Sales orders for an internet text-book distributor increased 100% over the last year. Additionally, the company's asset turnover has doubled since the previous year.	1.	F. Volume	2.	A. Overstatement
JRM Co. recorded its first hedging transaction for mortgage-backed securities in year 1. At the end of year 1, the fair value of mortgage-backed securities had decreased significantly.	3.	A. Complexity	4.	A. Overstatement
Metal, Inc. supplies copper pipes to home builders. During year 1, copper prices doubled. At any given time, a significant amount of inventory is in transit or located at job sites.	5.	E. Susceptibility of asset to theft	6.	A. Overstatement
Joe's Computers provides three-year money back warranties on all laptops. During year 1, warranty claims decreased significantly and the company has not reduced the warranty reserve.	7.	B. Estimates	8.	B. Understatement
Global Co. imports most of its products from a foreign supplier. During year 1, a new technology made part of the Global Co. inventory obsolete.	9.	C. Industry circumstances	10.	A. Overstatement

(ID: 90443)

1. F. Volume

Increases in amounts [volume] of sales orders and asset turnover were described.

2. A. Overstatement

The increase in sales could cause revenue to be more susceptible to overstatement.

3. A. Complexity

A hedging transaction was described; such a transaction involves complex calculations.

4. A. Overstatement

As the fair value of the mortgage-backed securities has decreased significantly, net income is more susceptible to overstatement if losses are understated.

5. E. Susceptibility of asset to theft

The copper pipes are more susceptible to theft because they have increased in value and are more difficult to protect because many of them are in transit or located at job sites vs. a secure warehouse.

6. A. Overstatement

If inventory is stolen, the insurance recovery most likely would be less than the sales revenue; thus, net income is more susceptible to overstatement.

7. B. Estimates

Warranty liabilities are estimated and thus, subject to uncertainty.

8. B. Understatement

Net income is more susceptible to understatement if warranty claims have decreased and the related reserve has not been reduced.

9. C. Industry circumstances

Technological developments, i.e., an external circumstance which gave rise to a business risk, have made part of the entity's inventory obsolete.

10. A. Overstatement

Obsolete inventory causes inventory to be more susceptible to overstatement which in turn makes net income more susceptible to overstatement (the ending inventory overstatement reduces the cost of goods sold which results in net income being overstated).

Solution E-4 SIMULATION ANSWER: Review Draft Report Wording

Question	Phrase or word
1	applying analytical procedures to
2	preparation and fair presentation
3	designing, implementing, and maintaining
4	conduct the review
5	Statements on Standards for Accounting and Review Services
6	limited assurance
7	accounting principles

(ID: 90444)

1. applying analytical procedures to

In a review engagement, the CPA should apply professional judgment in determining the specific nature, extent, and timing of review procedures (i.e., analytical procedures and inquiries) to provide the CPA with a reasonable basis for obtaining limited assurance. A review does NOT involve obtaining an understanding of internal control, assessing fraud risk, testing accounting records, examining source documents, or other procedures ordinarily performed in an audit.

2. preparation and fair presentation

Management is responsible for the selection of the entity's applicable financial reporting framework, as well as individual accounting policies when the reporting framework contains acceptable alternatives. Management is responsible for the preparation and fair presentation of the financial statements in accordance with the applicable financial reporting framework.

3. designing, implementing, and maintaining

Management is responsible for the design, implementation, and maintenance of internal control. Rearranging the order would not make any sense (i.e., you can't maintain before you implement, etc.) A CPA is precluded from issuing an unmodified review report unless management accepts these responsibilities.

4. conduct the review

A review does NOT involve obtaining an understanding of internal control, assessing fraud risk, testing accounting records, examining source documents, or other procedures ordinarily performed in an audit. The design and performance of review procedures should be based on the CPA's understanding of the industry and the client as well as awareness of the risk that the financial statements may be materially misstated.

5. Statements on Standards for Accounting and Review Services

The AICPA issues *Statements on Standards for Accounting and Review Services* (SSARS), providing performance and reporting guidance for reviews of unaudited financial statements or other unaudited financial information of nonissuers. SSARS also applies to engagements to issue a compilation report on specified elements, accounts, or items of a nonissuer's financial statements, or on a nonissuer's pro forma financial information. SSARS does not apply to other accounting services, such as preparing adjusting entries, consulting on financial matters, or preparing tax returns. The other standards listed as choices do not apply to reviews.

6. limited assurance

The term used in reports prepared by CPAs is "assurance". An audit provides reasonable assurance; a review provides limited assurance; and a compilation provides no assurance. The accountant's responsibility is to conduct the review in accordance with SSARS; those standards require the accountant to perform procedures to obtain limited assurance that no material modifications should be made to the financial statements; and the accountant believes that the results of the engagement procedures provide a reasonable basis for the report

7. accounting principles

Management is responsible for the selection of the entity's applicable financial reporting framework, as well as individual accounting policies when the reporting framework contains acceptable alternatives. The applicable financial reporting framework determines what constitutes a complete set of financial statements. US GAAP, as promulgated by the FASB, GASB, or FASAB; IFRS issued by the IASB; and OCBOA are examples of financial reporting frameworks.

Solution E-5 SIMULATION ANSWER: Research

AR	§	60	50	(ID: 90445)

.50 The accountant's determination of materiality is a matter of professional judgment and is affected by the accountant's perception of the financial information needs of users of the financial statements. In this context, it is reasonable for the accountant to assume that users

a. Have a reasonable knowledge of business and economic activities and accounting and a willingness to study the information in the financial statements with reasonable diligence
b. Understand that financial statements are prepared, presented, and reviewed to levels of materiality
c. Recognize the uncertainties inherent in the measurement of amounts based on the use of estimates, judgment, and the consideration of future events
d. Make reasonable economic decisions on the basis on the information in the financial statements

---

INDEX

A

B

C

F

G

H

I

J

K

L

M

N

O

S

T

U

V

W

GOOD LUCK
ON YOUR
EXAM!